Emma 0033 233 518 331
Stuart 07851 796 544

Dunkerque
alais
oulogne-
ur-Mer
6
Lille-Lomme
10 Lens
Arras
12 Valenciennes
beville
18 Amiens
St-Quentin
20
24
Laon
22 Charleville-Mézières
26
38 Beauvais
Soissons
40
42
44 Thionville
Reims
Verdun
Metz
68 Sarreguemines
25 Haguenau
58 PARIS
sailles
60 Château-Thierry
62 Châlons-en-Champagne
64 Bar-le-Duc
66 Nancy
70 Saverne
Strasbourg 71
86 Fontainebleau
88
90 Troyes
92 Neufchâteau
94 Épinal
96
97 Colmar
110 Montargis
Orléans
112 Sens
Auxerre
114 Chaumont
Châtillon--sur-Seine
116
118 Belfort
Mulhouse
130 Salbris
132 Avallon
134 Montbard
136 Dijon
138 Besançon
Montbéliard
148 Bourges
roux
150 Nevers
152 Autun
154 Dole
156 Pontarlier
Mouthe
166 St-Amand--Montrond
168 Moulins
170 Charolles
Mâcon
172 Lons-le--Saunier
174
184 Guéret
Vichy
186 Roanne
188 Bourg-en--Bresse
190
192 Chamonix-Mont-Blanc
Annecy
200
202 Clermont--Ferrand
Ussel
204 St-Étienne
206 Lyon
208 Chambéry
Bourg-St-Maurice
193
16 lle
218 St-Flour
220 le Puy-en-Velay
222 Valence
224 Grenoble
Briançon
226
34 Aurillac
236
238
240 Privas
242 Gap
Guillestre
227
252 Villefranche--de-Rouergue
Millau
254 Mende
Alès
256 Carpentras
258 Digne-les-Bains
260 Barcelonnette
311 Tende
270 Albi
272 Lodève
274 Montpellier
Nîmes
Arles
276 Avignon
Aix-en-Provence
278 Draguignan
280 Nice
Monaco
Cannes
290 Béziers
Carcassonne
292
294
296 Marseille
Toulon
298 St-Tropez
300
308 Limoux
310
314 Mont-Louis
Perpignan
Céret

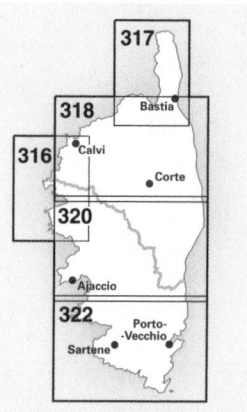

317
318 Bastia
316 Calvi
Corte
320
322 Porto--Vecchio
Sartène
Ajaccio

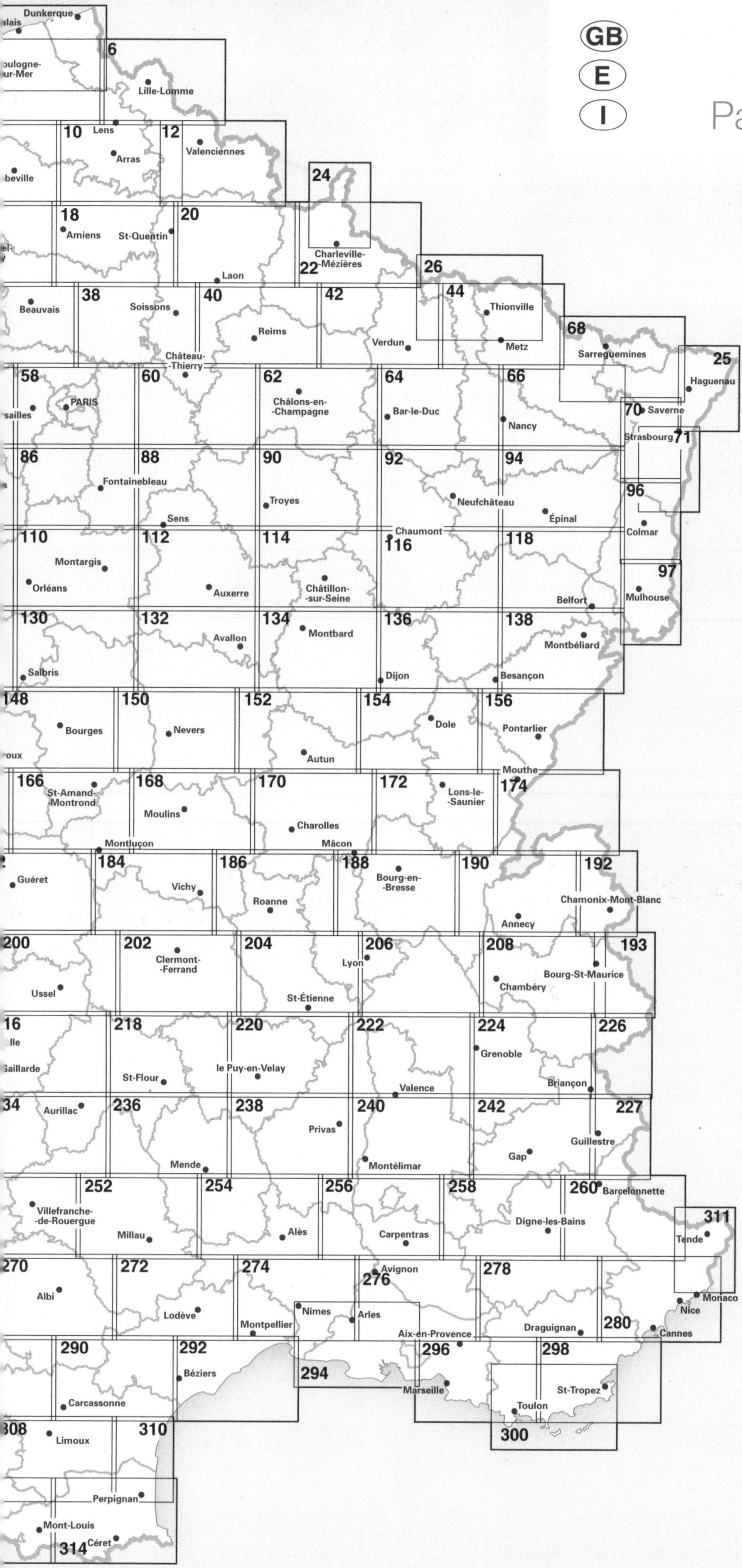

EASY READ
FRANCE

Scale 1:180 000
or 2.84 miles to 1 inch
(1.8km to 1cm)

2nd edition November 2006

© Automobile Association Developments Limited 2006
Original edition printed 2004.

Maps © Institut Géographique National (France)

Published by AA Publishing (a trading name of Automobile Association Developments Limited, whose registered office is Fanum House, Basing View, Basingstoke, Hampshire RG21 4EA, UK. Registered number 1878835).

ISBN-10: 0 7495 4991 2
ISBN-13: 978 0 7495 4991 6

A CIP catalogue record for this book is available from The British Library.

Printed in Italy by Pizzi, Milan.

Contents

Key to map pages	inside front cover
Route planner	II–V
Map legend	VI–1
Road maps	**2–323**
Town plans	324–345
Paris routes	324–325
Paris	326–327
Key to town plans	328
Index to place names	346–410
Département map	346
Distances and journey times	inside back cover

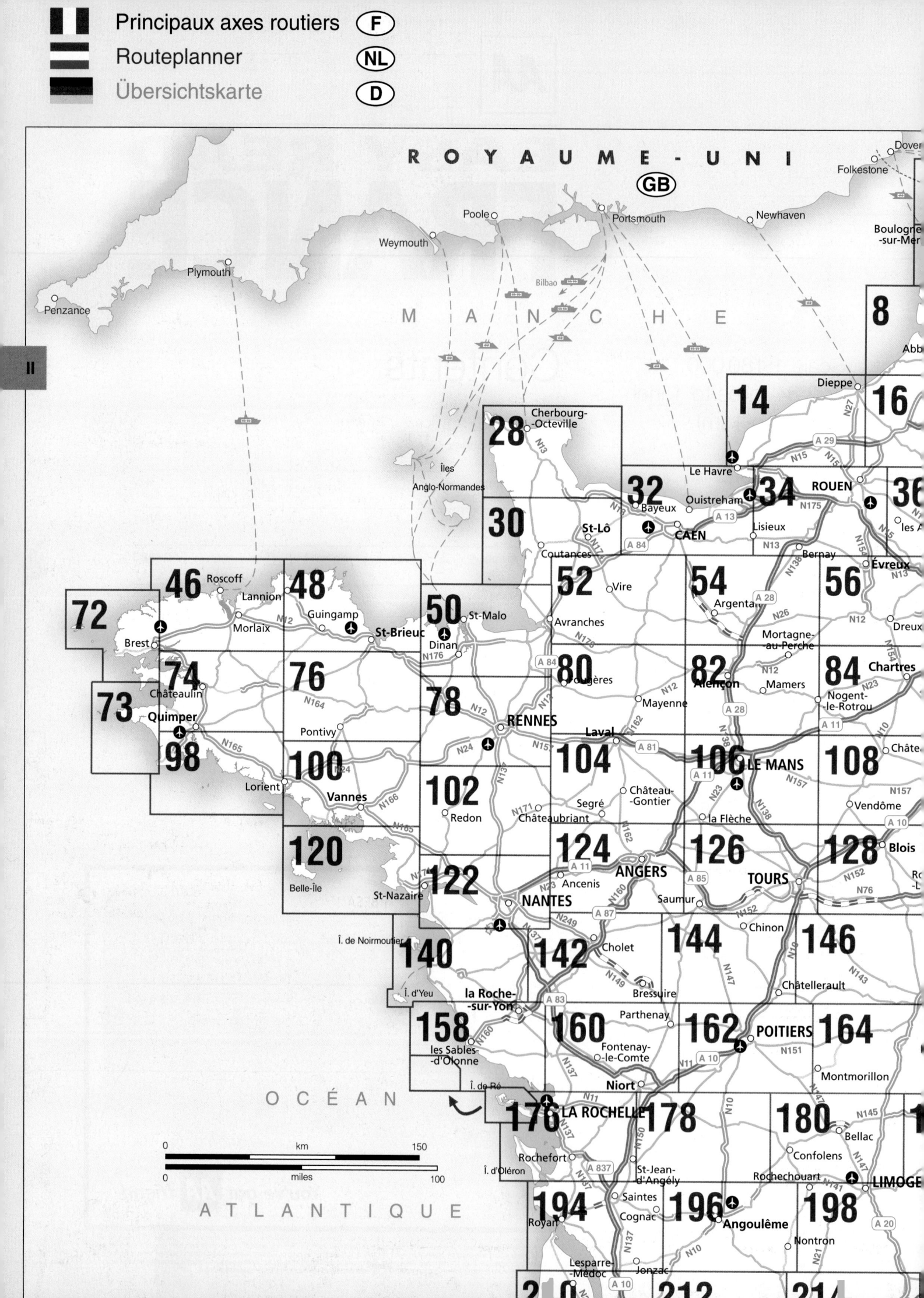

II

ROYAUME-UNI
GB

Dover
Folkestone
Poole
Portsmouth
Newhaven
Weymouth
Boulogne
-sur-Mer
Plymouth
Bilbao
MANCHE
8
Penzance
Abb
Dieppe
14   16
Îles
Anglo-Normandes
Cherbourg
-Octeville
28
N13
Le Havre
32   34 ROUEN 36
30   Bayeux Ouistreham les A
St-Lô   A 13 CAEN Lisieux
Coutances   N13 Bernay Évreux
52   Vire 54   56 N13
46 Roscoff   48   Argentan   A 28
72   Lannion Guingamp   Avranches   Mortagne Dreux
Morlaix   50 St-Malo   N176 -au-Perche N12
Brest   St-Brieuc Dinan   80   82   84 Chartres
74   76   N176   Fougères Alençon Mamers   N23
73   Châteaulin   78   Mayenne   N12 Nogent- N10
Quimper   Pontivy   N12 RENNES N157 Laval   A 28 le-Rotrou A 11
98   N165   N24   N155 104   A 81 106 LE MANS 108 Châte
100   Château-   A 11   Vendôme
Lorient   Vannes   102   -Gontier   la Flèche N157
120   Redon Châteaubriant Segré   N152   128 Blois
Belle-Île   122   124   126   N76
St-Nazaire   ANGERS A 85 TOURS   Rc
Î. de Noirmoutier   NANTES Ancenis Saumur N152 Chinon
140   142 Cholet   144   146   N143
Î. d'Yeu la Roche   N149 Bressuire Châtellerault
-sur-Yon   A 83
158   160 Parthenay 162 POITIERS 164
les Sables-   Fontenay A 10 N151 Montmorillon
d'Olonne   -le-Comte N11
Î. de Ré   Niort   N145
OCÉAN   176 LA ROCHELLE 178 180 Bellac
Rochefort   A 837 Confolens N147
Î. d'Oléron St-Jean-   Rochechouart LIMOGE
d'Angély   N141
ATLANTIQUE   194 Saintes 196 198 A 20
Royan Cognac Angoulême Nontron N21
Lesparre-   Jonzac
Médoc   A 10   212   214

0   km   150
0   miles   100

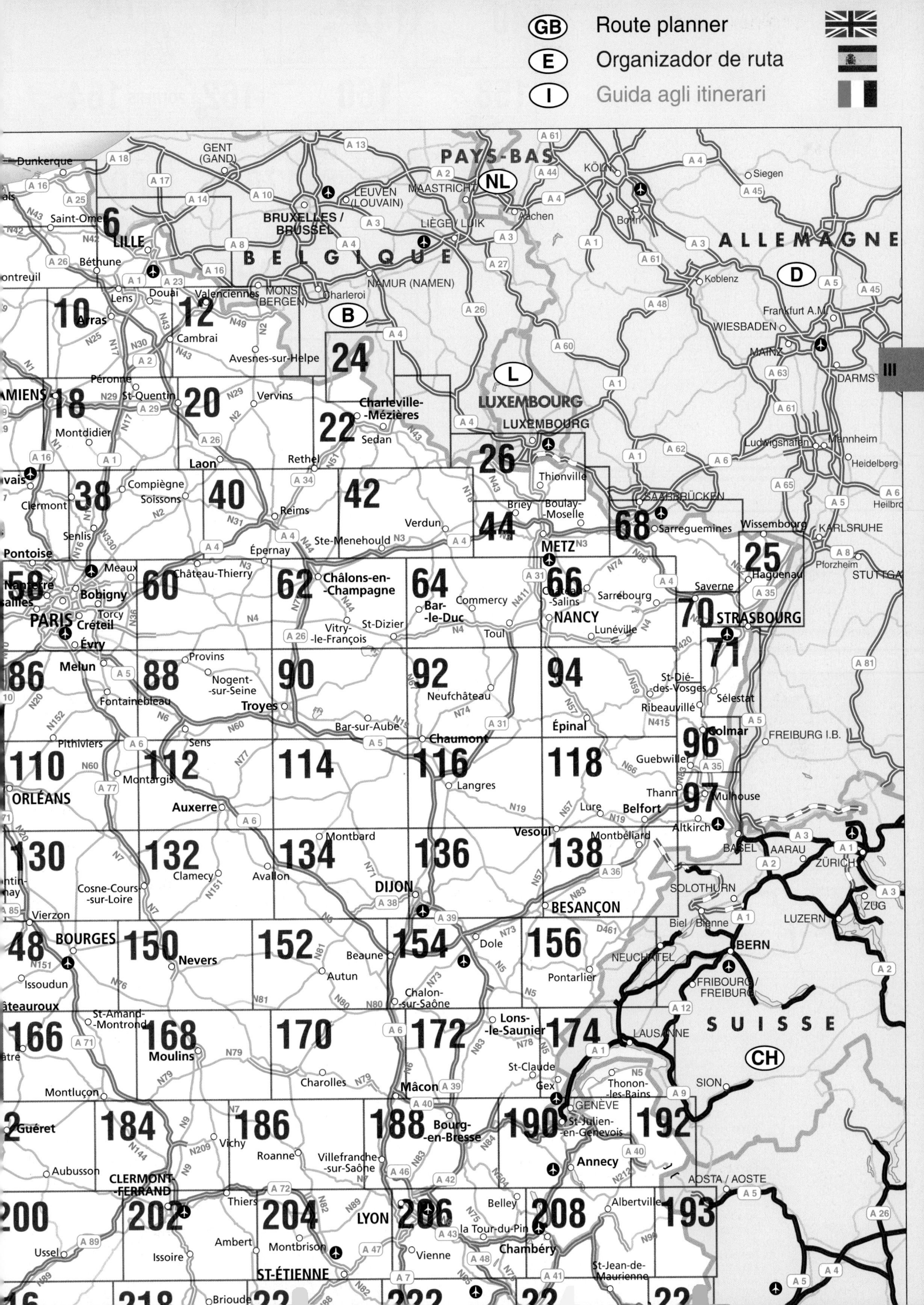

GB Route planner
E Organizador de ruta
I Guida agli itinerari

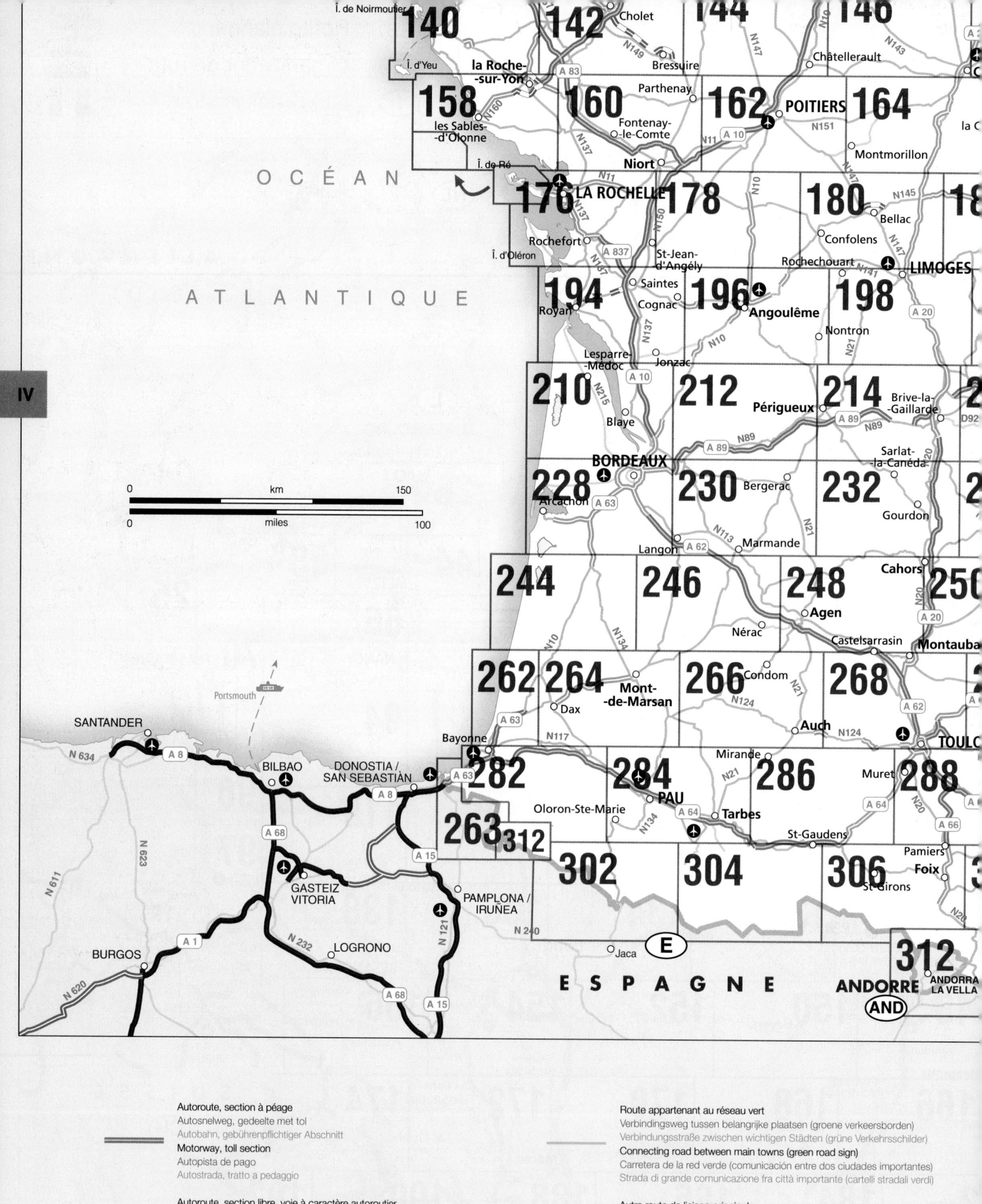

IV

140 Î. de Noirmoutier Cholet
142 **144** **146**
Î. d'Yeu   la Roche--sur-Yon   N149 Bressuire   N147 Châtellerault   N143

158 **160** Parthenay **162** POITIERS **164**
les Sables--d'Olonne   Fontenay--le-Comte   N151   la C
Î. de Ré   Niort   N11 A 10   Montmorillon

OCÉAN

176 LA ROCHELLE **178** **180** **18**
Rochefort   N750   St-Jean--d'Angély   N145   Bellac
Î. d'Oléron   A 837   Confolens   N147
Rochechouart   N141   LIMOGES

ATLANTIQUE

Saintes
194 **196** **198**
Royan   Cognac   Angoulême   Nontron   A 20

Lesparre--Médoc   Jonzac
210 **212** Périgueux **214** Brive-la--Gaillarde **2**
N215   Blaye   A 89   N89   A 89   D92
Sarlat--la-Canéda
BORDEAUX
228 **230** Bergerac **232** **2**
Arcachon   A 63   Gourdon
Langon   N113 Marmande   N21

244 **246** **248** Cahors **250**
Agen   A 20
Nérac   Castelsarrasin   Montauba
N134

262 **264** **266** Condom **268** **2**
Mont--de-Marsan   N124   A 62
A 63   Dax   N124   Auch
N117

Bayonne
282 **284** PAU **286** Mirande **288**
SANTANDER   N634   A 8   BILBAO   DONOSTIA / SAN SEBASTIÀN   A 63   Oloron-Ste-Marie   N21   Muret   A 64   TOULO
Portsmouth   A 8   N134   A 64   Tarbes   A 64   N20
A 68   **263** **312**   St-Gaudens   A 66
A 15   Pamiers
GASTEIZ VITORIA   **302** **304** **306** Foix **3**
BURGOS   A 1   N232   LOGRONO   PAMPLONA / IRUÑEA   St-Girons
N611   N623   N240   Jaca   E
N620   A 68   A 15   **312** ANDORRA LA VELLA
ESPAGNE   ANDORRE   AND

km 0 — 150
miles 0 — 100

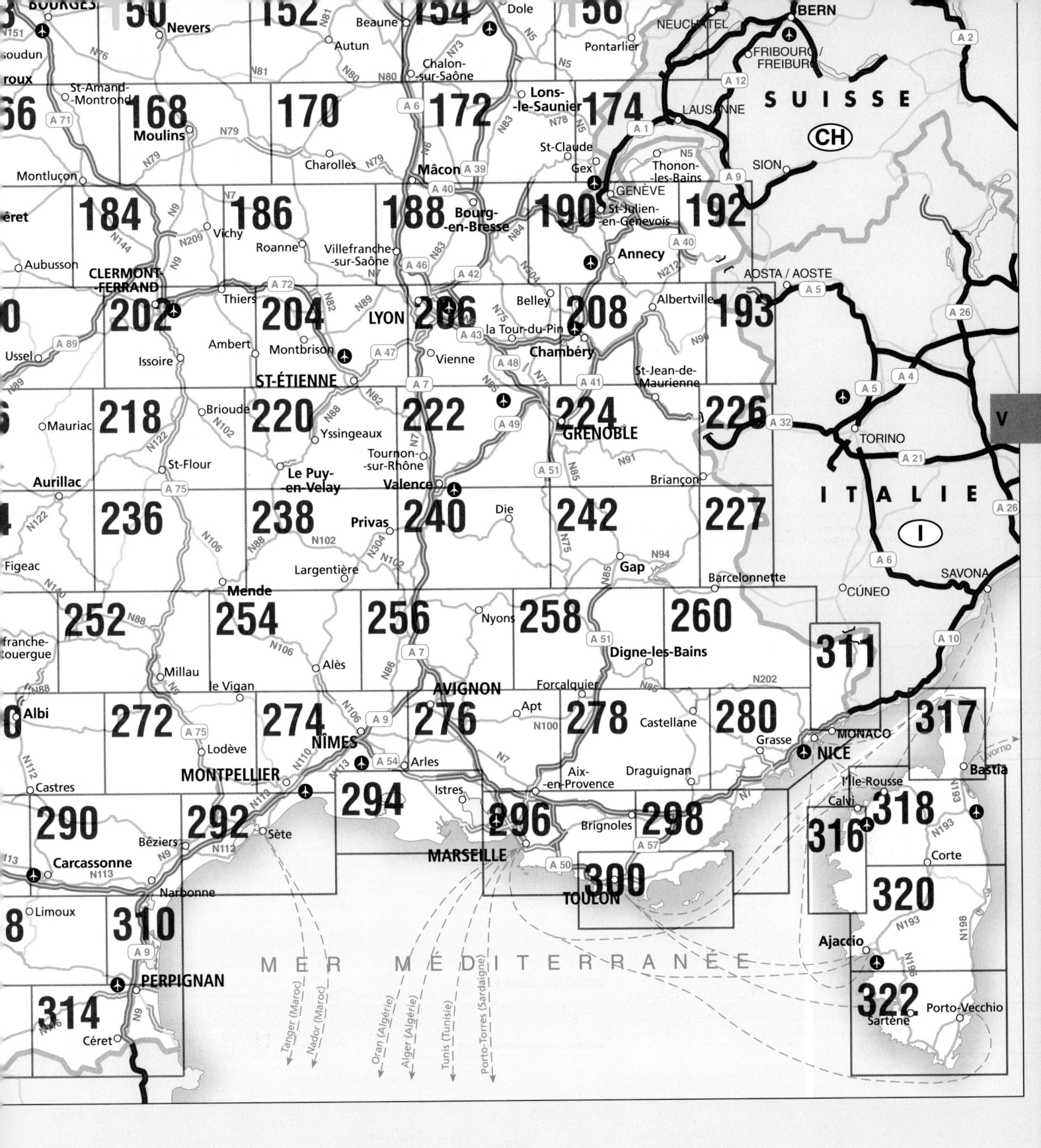

(F) Légende
(NL) Legenda
(D) Legende
Legend (GB)
Leyenda (E)
Legenda (I)

Autoroute, section à péage
Autosnelweg, gedeelte met tol
Autobahn, gebührenpflichtiger Abschnitt

Motorway, toll section
Autopista de peaje
Autostrada, tratto a pedaggio

Autoroute, section libre
Autosnelweg, tolvrij gedeelte
Autobahn, gebührenfreier Abschnitt

Motorway, toll-free section
Autopista gratuita
Autostrada, tratto libero

Voie à caractère autoroutier
Weg van het type autosnelweg
Schnellstraße

Dual carriageway with motorway characteristics
Autovía
Strada con caratteristiche autostradale

Échangeur: complet (1), partiel (2), numéro
Knooppunt: volledig (1), gedeeltelijk (2), nummer
Vollanschlußstelle (1), beschränkte Anschlußstelle (2), Nummer

Junction: complete (1), restricted (2), number
Acceso: completo (1), parcial (2), número
Svincolo: completo (1), parziale (2), numero

Barrière de péage (1), Aire de service (2), Aire de repos (3)
Tolversperring (1), Tankstation (2), Rustplaats (3)
Mautstelle (1), Tankstelle (2), Rastplatz (3)

Tollgate (1), Service area (2), Rest area (3)
Barrera de peaje (1), Área de servicio (2), Área de descanso (3)
Barriera di pedaggio (1), Area di servizio (2), Area di riposo (3)

Autoroute en construction (1), Radar fixe (2)
Autosnelweg in aanleg (1), Verkeersradar (2)
Autobahn im Bau (1), Radarkontrolle (2)

Motorway under construction (1), Speed camera (fixed radar) (2)
Autopista en construcción (1), Radar (2)
Autostrada in costruzione (1), Radar (2)

Route appartenant au réseau vert
Verbindingsweg tussen belangrijke plaatsen (groene verkeersborden)
Verbindungsstraße zwischen wichtigen Städten (grüne Verkehrsschilder)

Connecting road between main towns (green road sign)
Carretera de la red verde (comunicación entre dos ciudades importantes)
Strada di grande comunicazione fra città importante (cartelli stradali verdi)

Autre route de liaison principale
Hoofdweg
Hauptstraße

Other main road
Otra carretera principal
Strada di grande comunicazione

Route de liaison régionale
Streekverbindingsweg
Regionale Verbindungsstraße

Regional connecting road
Carretera regional
Strada di collegamento regionale

Autre route
Andere weg
Sonstige Straße

Other road
Carretera local
Altra strada

Route en construction
Weg in aanleg
Straße im Bau

Road under construction
Carretera en construcción
Strada in construzione

Route irrégulièrement entretenue (1), Chemin (2)
Onregelmatig onderhoude weg (1), Pad (2)
Nicht regelmäßig instandgehaltene Straße (1), Fußweg (2)

Not regularly maintained road (1), Footpath (2)
Carretera sin revestir (1), Camino (2)
Strada di irregolare manutenzione (1), Sentiero (2)

Tunnel (1), Route interdite (2)
Tunnel (1), Verboden weg (2)
Tunnel (1), Gesperrte Straße (2)

Tunnel (1), Prohibited road (2)
Túnel (1), Carretera prohibida (2)
Galleria (1), Strada vietata (2)

Distances kilométriques (km), Numérotation: Autoroute, type autoroutier
Afstanden in kilometers (km), Wegnummers: Autosnelweg
Entfernungen in Kilometern (km), Straßennumerierung: Autobahn

Distances in kilometres (km), Road numbering: Motorway
Distancia en kilómetros (km), Numeración de las carreteras: Autopista
Distanze in chilometri (km), Numero di strada: Autostrada

Distances kilométriques sur route, Numérotation: Autre route
Wegafstanden in kilometers, Wegnummers: Andere weg
Straßenentfernungen in Kilometern, Straßennumerierung: Sonstige Straße

Distances in kilometres on road, Road numbering: Other road
Distancia en kilómetros por carretera, Numeración de las carreteras: Otra carretera
Distanze in chilometri su strada, Numero di strada: Altra strada

Chemin de fer, gare, arrêt, tunnel
Spoorweg, station, halte, tunnel
Eisenbahn, Bahnhof, Haltepunkt, Tunnel

Railway, station, halt, tunnel
Ferrocarril, estación, parada, túnel
Ferrovia, stazione, fermata, galleria

Liaison maritime
Bootdienst met autovervoer
Autofähre

Bastia

Ferry route
Linea maritima (ferry)
Collegamento maritimo (ferry)

Aéroport (1), Aérodrome (2)
Luchthaven (1), Vliegveld (2)
Flughafen (1), Flugplatz (2)

Airport (1), Airfield (2)
Aeropuerto (1), Aeródromo (2)
Aeroporto (1), Aerodromo (2)

Zone bâtie
Bebouwde kom
Geschlossene Bebauung

Built-up area
Zona edificada
Zona urbanistica

Zone industrielle
Industriegebied
Industriegebeit

Industrial park
Zona industrial
Zona industriale

Bois
Bos
Wald

Woods
Bosque
Bosco

1

French / Nederlands / Deutsch	Symbol	English / Español / Italiano
Limite de département / Departementsgrens / Departementsgrenze		Département boundary / Límite de departamento / Confine di dipartimento
Limite de région / Gewestgrens / Regionsgrenze		Region boundary / Límite de región / Confine di regione
Limite d'État / Staatsgrens / Staatsgrenze	+ + + + + + + + + + + +	International boundary / Límite de Nación / Confine di Stato
Limite de camp militaire (1), Limite de Parc / Grens van militair kamp (1), Parkgrens (2) / Truppenübungsplatzgrenze (1), Naturparkgrenze (2)	1 2	Military camp boundary (1), Park boundary (2) / Límite de campo militar (1), Límite de Parque (2) / Limite di campo militare (1), Limite di parco (2)
Marais (1), Marais salants (2), Glacier (3) / Moeras (1), Zoutpan (2), Gletsjer (3) / Sumpf (1), Salzteiche (2), Gletscher (3)	1 2 3	Marsh (1), Salt pan (2), Glacier (3) / Marisma (1), Salinas (2), Glaciar (3) / Palude (1), Saline (2), Ghiacciaio (3)
Région sableuse (1), Sable humide (2) / Zandig gebied (1), Getijdengebied (2) / Sandgebiet (1), Gezeiten (2)	1 2	Dry sand (1), Wet sand (2) / Zona arenosa (1), Arena húmida (2) / Area sabbiosa (1), Sabbia bagnata (2)
Cathédrale (1), Abbaye (2) / Kathedraal (1), Abdij (2) / Dom (1), Abtei (2)	1 2	Cathedral (1), Abbey (2) / Catedral (1), Abadía (2) / Cattedrale (1), Abbazia (2)
Église (1), Chapelle (2) / Kerkgebouw (1), Kapel (2) / Kirche (1), Kapelle (2)	1 2	Church (1), Chapel (2) / Iglesia (1), Capilla (2) / Chiesa (1), Cappella (2)
Château (1), Château ouvert au public (2), Musée (3) / Kasteel (1), Kasteel open voor publiek (2), Museum (3) / Schloß (1), Schloßbesichtigung (2), Museum (3)	1 2 3 [M]	Castle (1), Castle open to the public (2), Museum (3) / Castillo (1), Castillo abierto al público (2), Museo (3) / Castello (1), Castello aperto al pubblico (2), Museo (3)
Localité d'intérêt touristique / Bezienswaardige plaats / Sehenswerter Ort	**LA ROCHELLE** *Baou-des-Blanc*	Place of tourist interest / Localidad de interés turístico / Località di interesse turistico
Phare (1), Moulin (2) / Vuurtoren (1), Molen (2) / Leuchtturm (1), Mühle (2)	1 2	Lighthouse (1), Mill (2) / Faro (1), Molino (2) / Faro (1), Mulino (2)
Curiosité (1), Cimetière militaire (2) / Bezienswaardigheid (1), Militaire begraafplaats (2) / Sehenswürdigkeit (1), Soldatenfriedhof (2)	1 ★★★ 2	Place of interest (1), Military cemetery (2) / Curiosidad (1), Cementerio militar (2) / Curiosità (1), Cimitero militare (2)
Grotte (1), Mégalithe (2) / Grot (1), Megaliet (2) / Höhle (1), Megalith (2)	1 2	Cave (1), Megalith (2) / Cueva (1), Megalito (2) / Grotta (1), Megalite (2)
Vestiges antiques (1), Ruines (2) / Historische overblijfselen (1), Ruïnes (2) / Altertümliche Ruinen (1), Ruinen (2)	1 2	Antiquities (1), Ruins (2) / Vestigios antiguos (1), Ruinas (2) / Vestigia antiche (1), Rovine (2)
Pointe de vue (1), Panorama (2), Cascade ou source (3) / Uitzichtspunt (1), Panorama (2), Waterval of bron (3) / Aussichtspunkt (1), Rundblick (2), Wasserfall oder Quelle (3)	1 2 3 ★	Viewpoint (1), Panorama (2), Waterfall or spring (3) / Punto de vista (1), Panorama (2), Cascada o fuente (3) / Punto di vista (1), Panorama (2), Cascata o sorgente (3)
Station thermale (1), Sports d'hiver (2) / Kuuroord (1), Wintersport (2) / Kurort mit Thermalbad (1), Wintersportort (2)	1 2	Spa (1), Winter sports resort (2) / Estación termal (1), Estación de deportes de invierno (2) / Stazione termale (1), Stazione di sport invernali (2)
Refuge (1), Activités de loisirs (2) / Schuilhut (1), Recreatieactiviteiten (2) / Berghütte (1), Freizeittätigkeiten (2)	1 2	Refuge hut (1), Leisure activities (2) / Refugio (1), Actividades de ocios (2) / Rifugio (1), Attività di divertimenti (2)
Maison du Parc (1), Réserve naturelle (2), Parc ou jardin (3) / Informatiebureau van natuurreservaat (1), Natuurreservaat (2), Park of tuin (3) / Informationsbüro des Parks (1), Naturschutzgebiet (2), Park oder Garten (3)	1 2 3	Park visitor centre (1), Nature reserve (2), Park or garden (3) / Casa del parque (1), Reserva natural (2), Parque o jardín (3) / Casa del parco (1), Riserva naturale (2), Parco o giardino (3)
Chemin de fer touristique (1), Téléphérique (2) / Toeristische trein (1), Kabelspoor (2) / Touristische Kleinbahn (1), Seilbahn (2)	1 2	Tourist railway (1), Aerial cableway (2) / Tren turístico (1), Teleférico (2) / Ferrovia di interesse turistico (1), Teleferica (2)

0   5   kilometres   10   15

0   miles   5   10

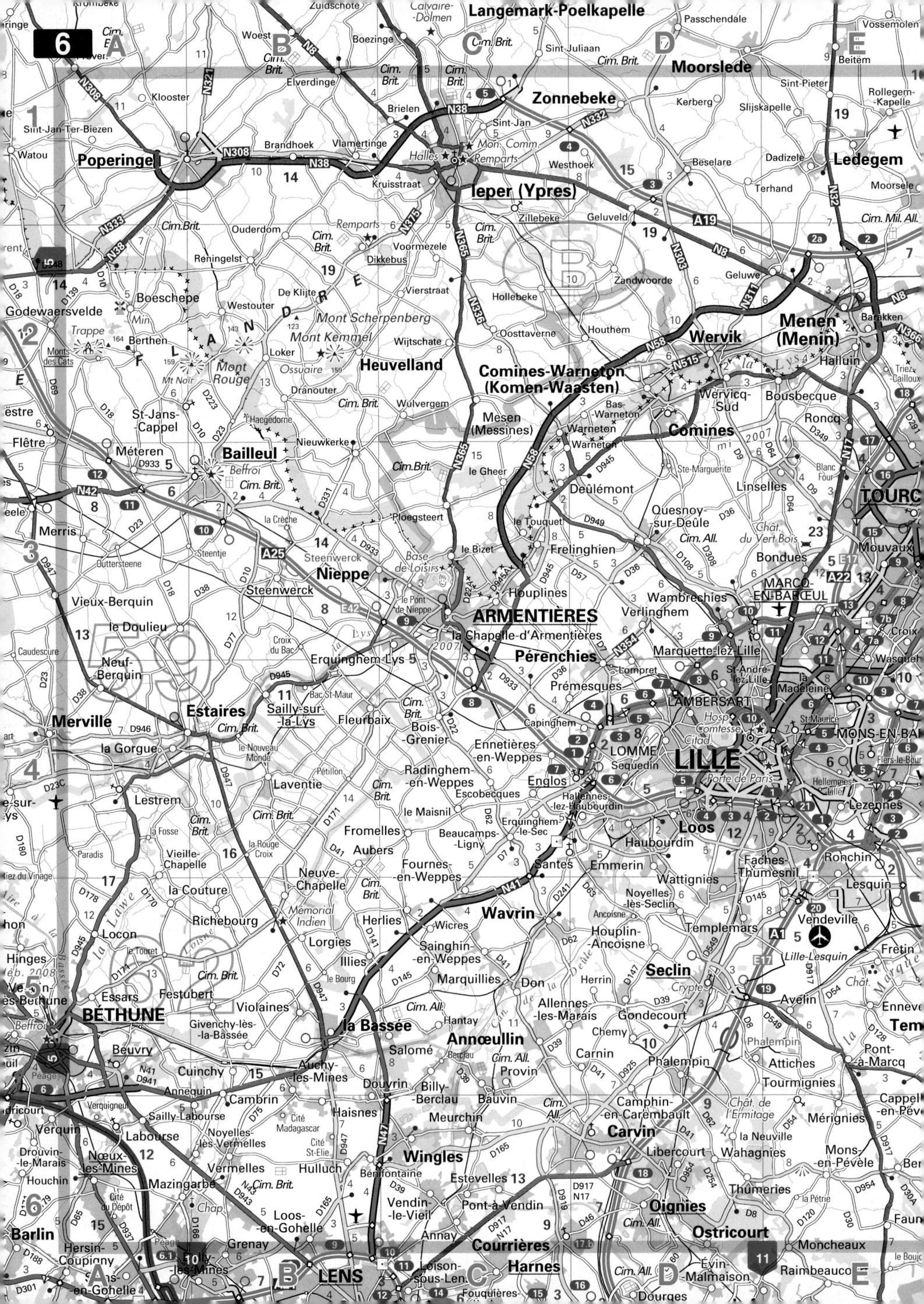

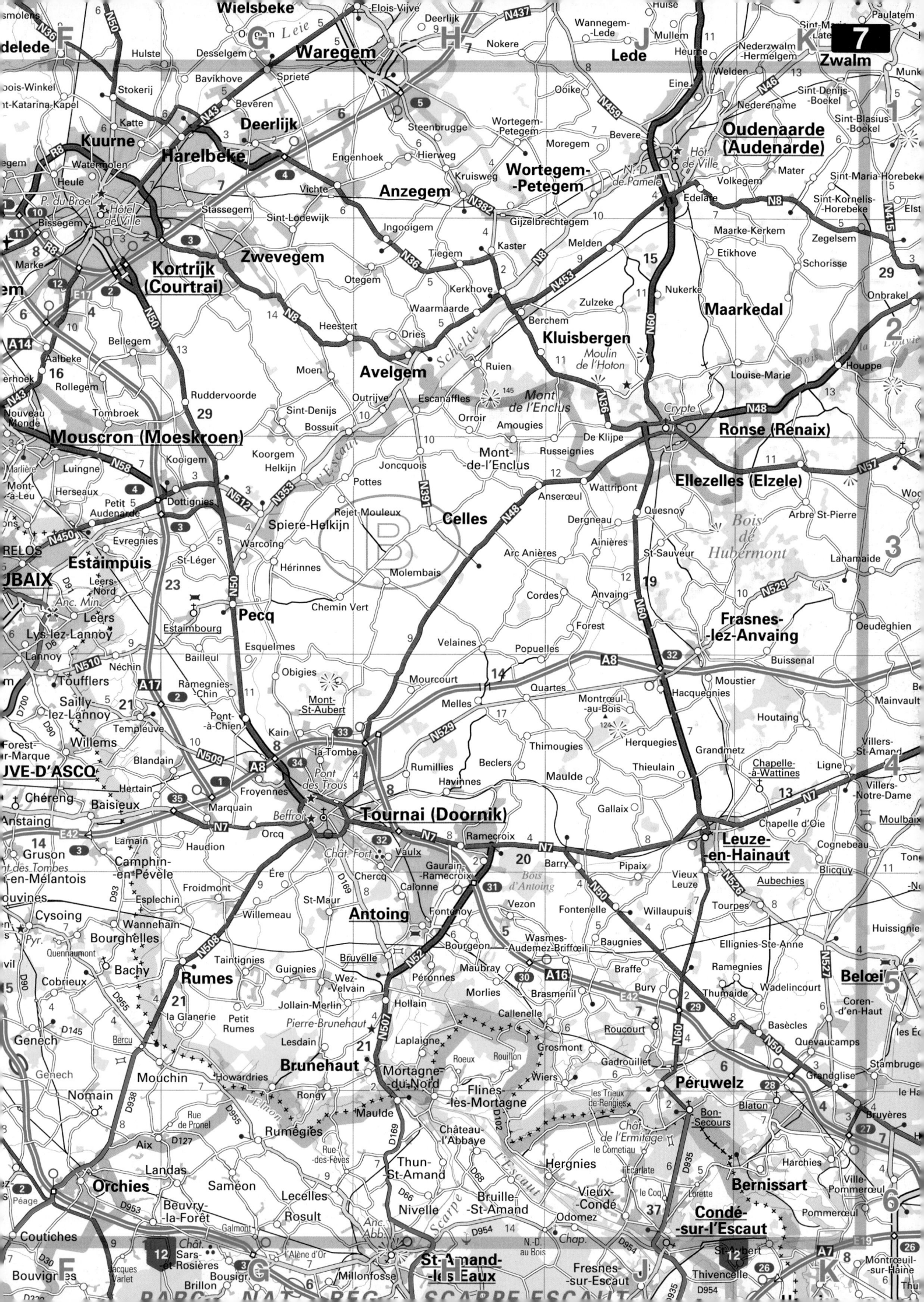

1

2

3

4

5

6

Mérlimont

Bagatelle
Parc d'Attractions   D940   D143   St

Airon

Hal   Airon
-St-Va

Rang
-du-Fliers   D317   D317

Berck   D317E1

Berck-
Plage   D303   Verton   D142E

D940

Grofflieres   Waben   Fond
Comma

Baie de l'Authie   21

Conc
-le-Ter

Fort-Mahon-
Plage   D532   Col
Beau

Aquaclub de Belle-Dune   D32   D940   3

Quend-
Plage   D32D   Monchaux   13   Quend

MARQUENTERRE   Froise   7

Flandre

Dunes   St-Quentin
-en-Tourmont   Chap.
du St-Esprit

le Bout
des Crocs   St-Firmin   D4

Parc Ornithologique
du Marquenterre   Madagascar   7

CÔTE   Rés. Nat. de la Baie
de Somme   D4   D940   Fav

PICARDE   le Hamele

le Hourdel   Baie   le Crotoy   8

D102   de   Mollières
Somme   St-Valery
-sur-Somme

Brighton   6   Cap Hornu

Maison
de l'Oiseau   Chap.
des Marins   9

Cayeux-
-sur-Mer   D3   Anc. Abb.   fer   3

D102   Chemin   Sallenelle   de   7

le Marais   11   Pendé   D2   D940

D102   6   Drancourt   Pinch

Lanchères   Estréboeuf

Chât.   D940   10

24   Brutelles   D63   Tilloy   16   Mons-
Boubert

D102   V   I   M   E

Hautebut   D106   Arrest

Vaudricourt   St-Blimont   Boubert   D80

Onival   D463   7   Woignarue   la Râperie   Quesno
-le-Mont

Ault   D19   Bourseville   D2A

la Belle Vue   D63   Belloy-
sur-Mer   7   Nibas   Ochancourt

le Bois de Cise   6   Friaucourt   Allenay   Tully   Franleu   Frireulle

St-Quentin-la-Motte-
Croix-au-Bailly   Friville-
Escarbotin   Saucourt   31   10

Mers-les-Bains   Béthencourt-
sur-Mer   Fressenneville   Valines   St-Marc

le Tréport   3   D925   Yzengremer   Woincourt   Chépy

Calvaire
des Terrasses   St-Laurent   Ménéslies   Feuquières
-en-Vimeu

Mesnil-Val-Plage   Cim. Brit.   Eu   Ponts-
et-Marais   Oust-Marest   D2   Dargnies   D67   D65   D29   D80

Criel-Plage   D126E   Flocques   D925C   Bouvaincourt-
sur-Bresle   14   Embreville   Aigneville   Corroy   To

D940   D126   Étalondes   St-Pierre-
en-Val   D49   Beauchamps   Buigny-
lès-Gamaches   11   Maisnières

Manoir
de Briançon   les Quesnets   6   Inchevile   14   Chaussée Brunehaut   Frettemeule   Visn

Criel-sur-Mer   D925   Boscrocourt   le Fresne   D1015   la Vimeuse   D22

Mesnil-à-Caux   Heudelimont   St-Rémy-
Boscrocourt   Hélicourt   Floriville   Tilloy
Florivi

Central
Nucléaire
Penly   Penly   Biville-sur-Mer   Assigny   Litteville   St-Sulpice
-sur-Yères   Étocquigny   Baromesnil   D58   Monchy-
sur-Eu   Leroy   Gamaches   10   12

35   7   22   14   2E   16

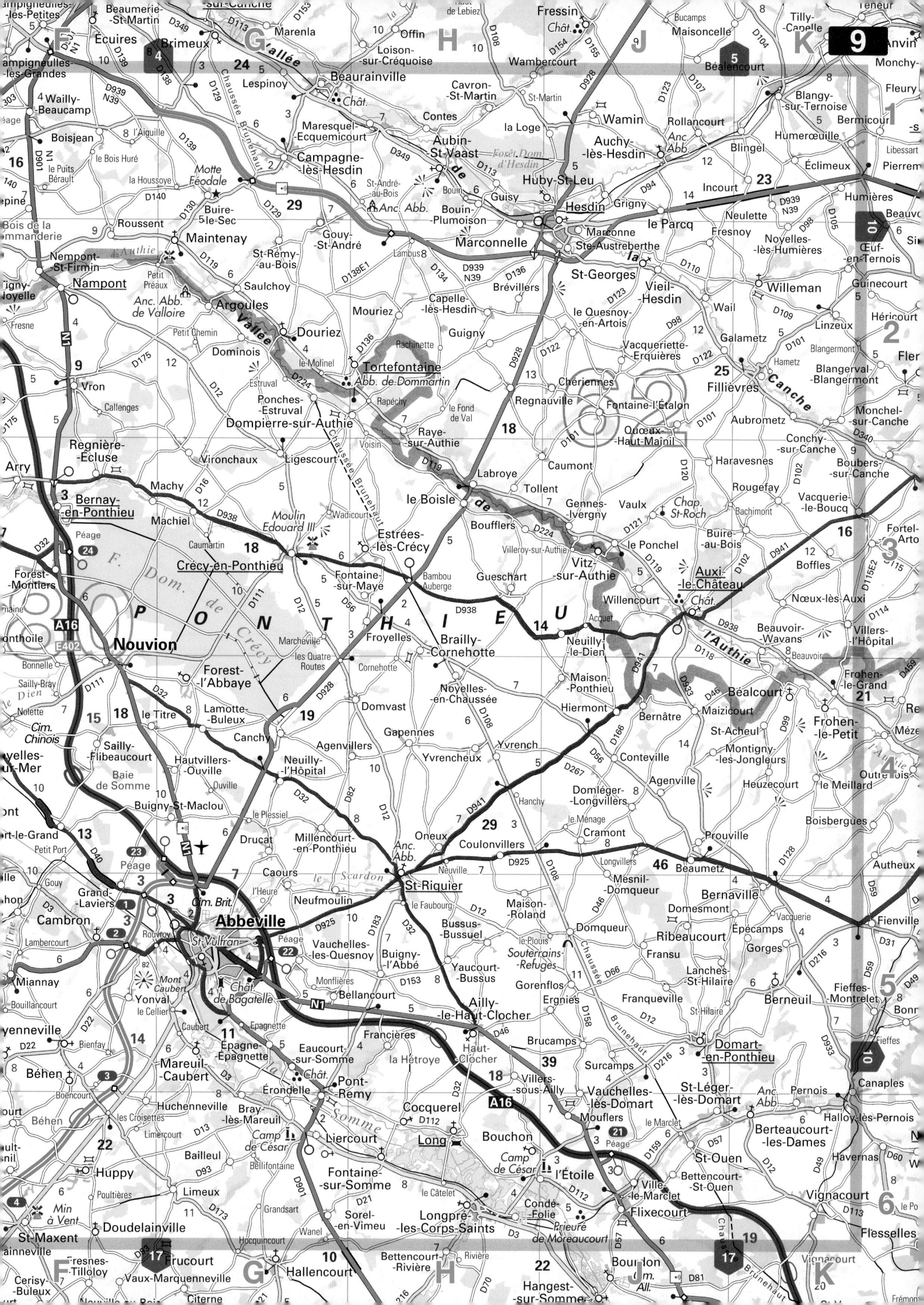

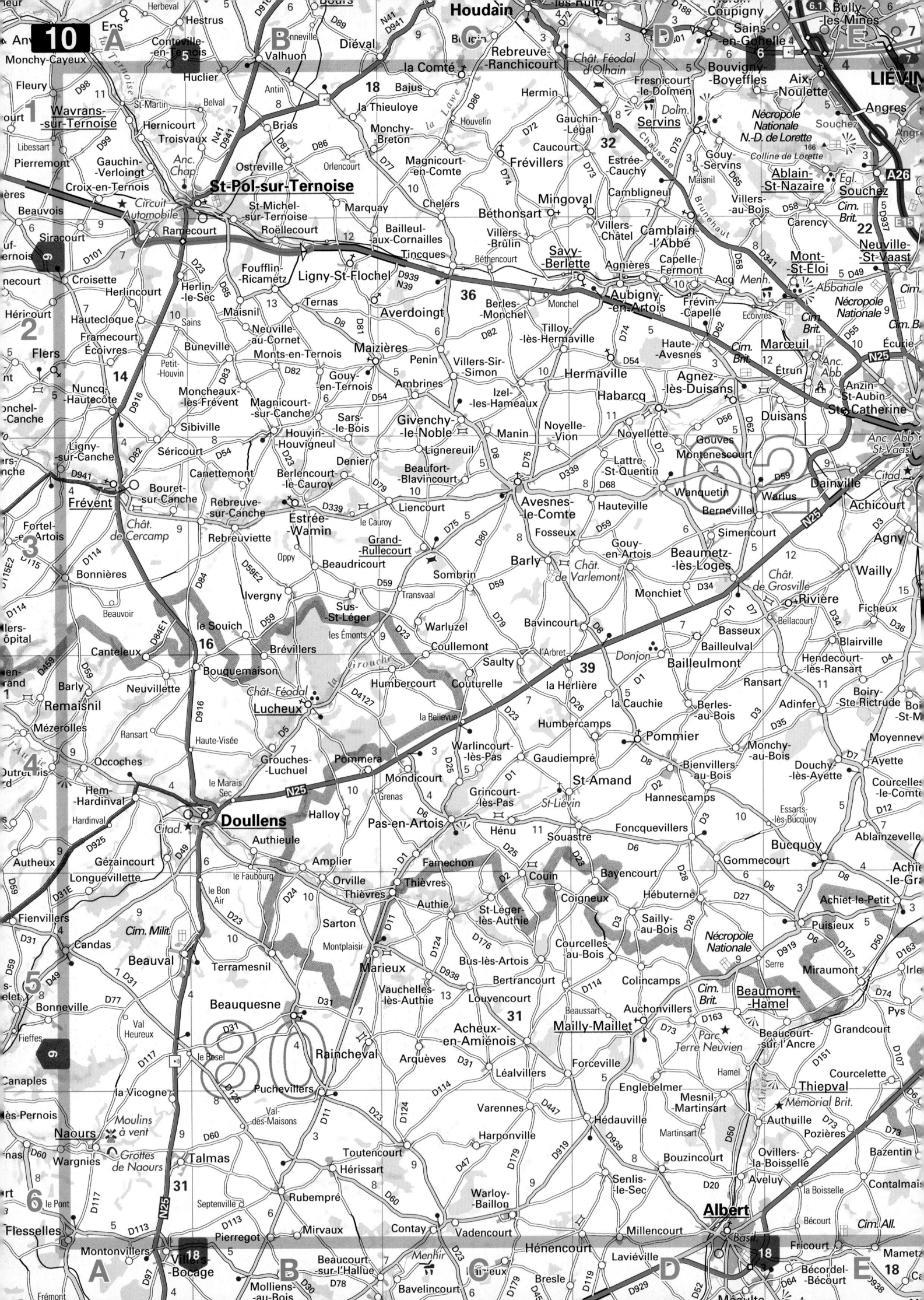

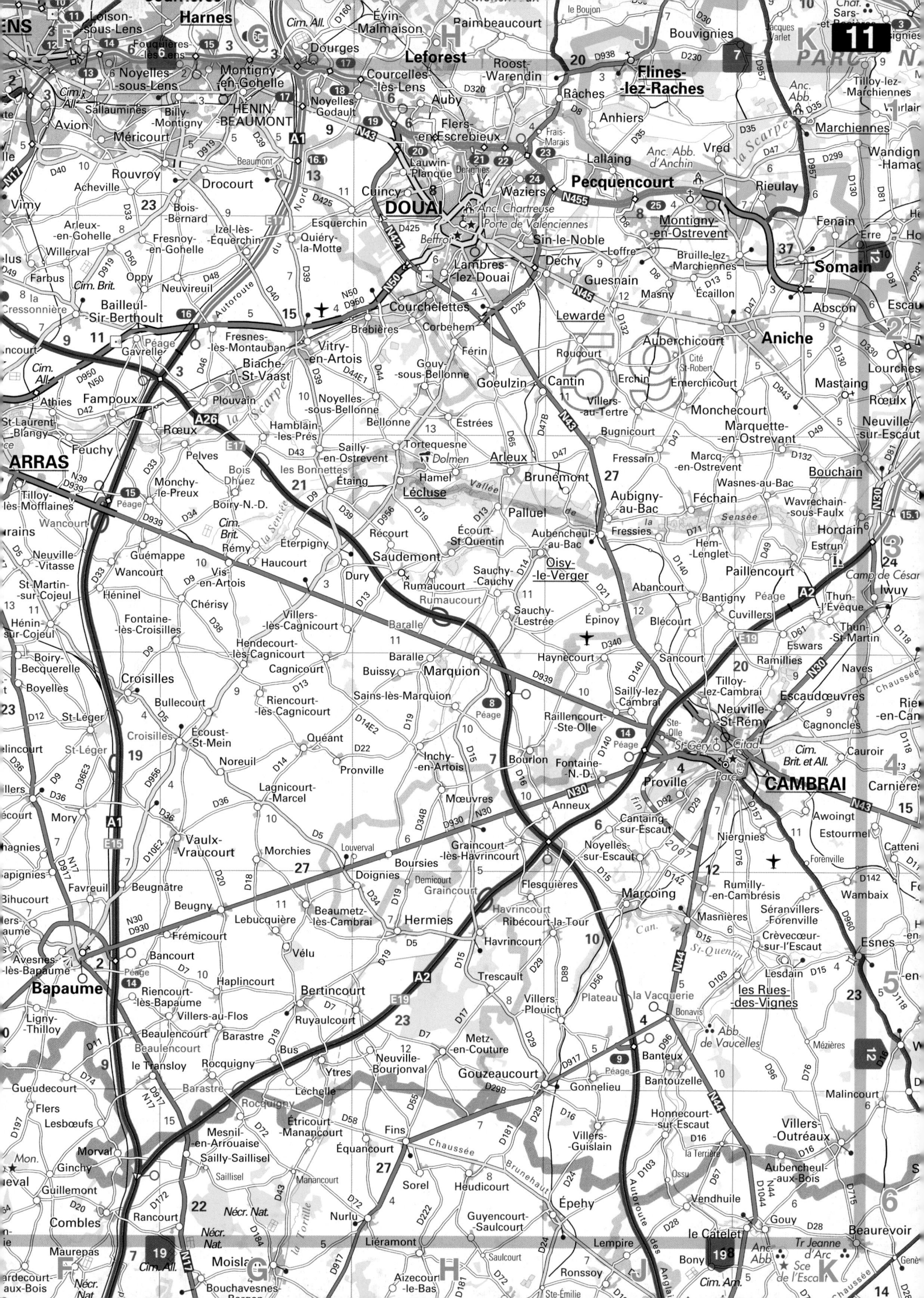

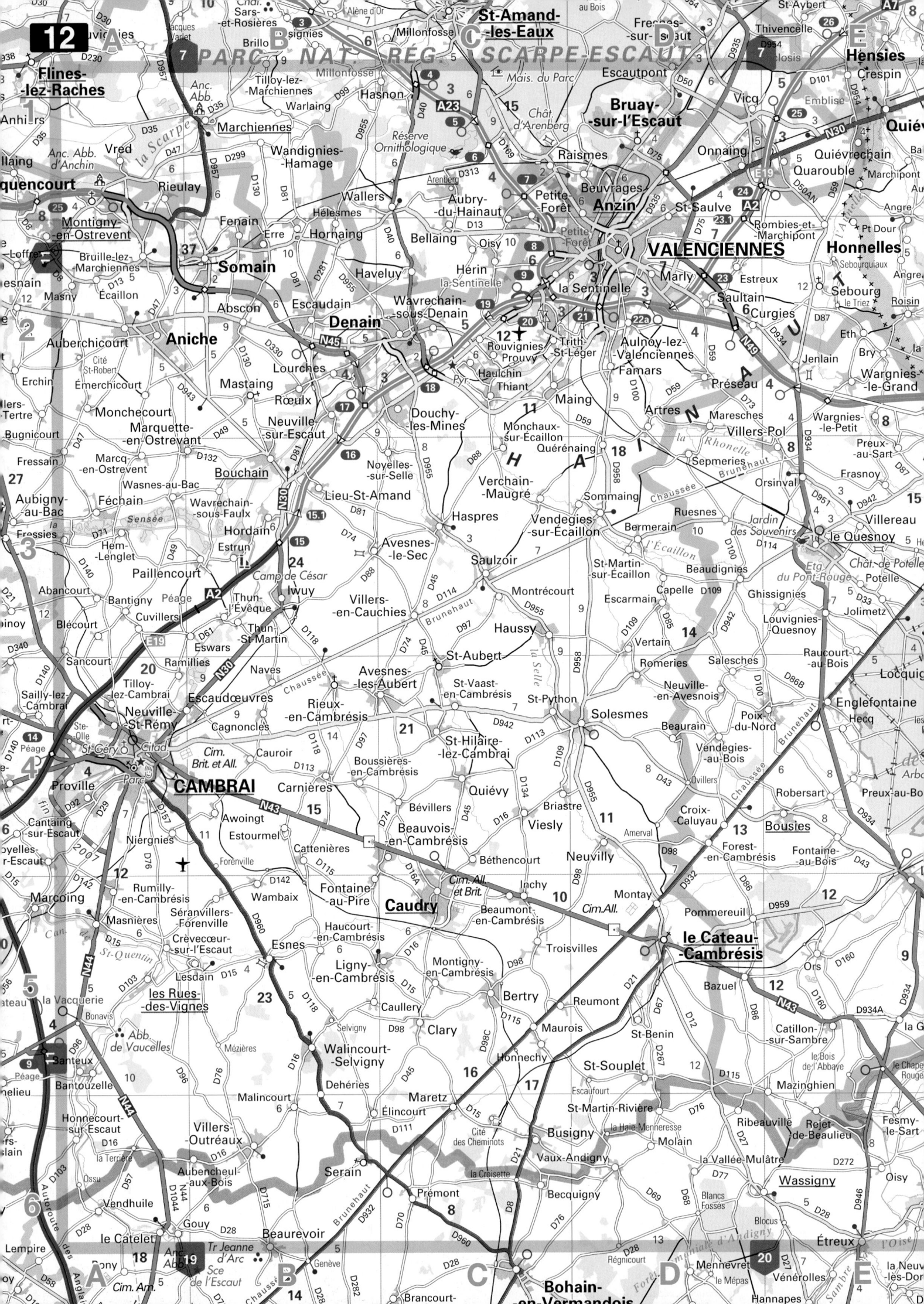

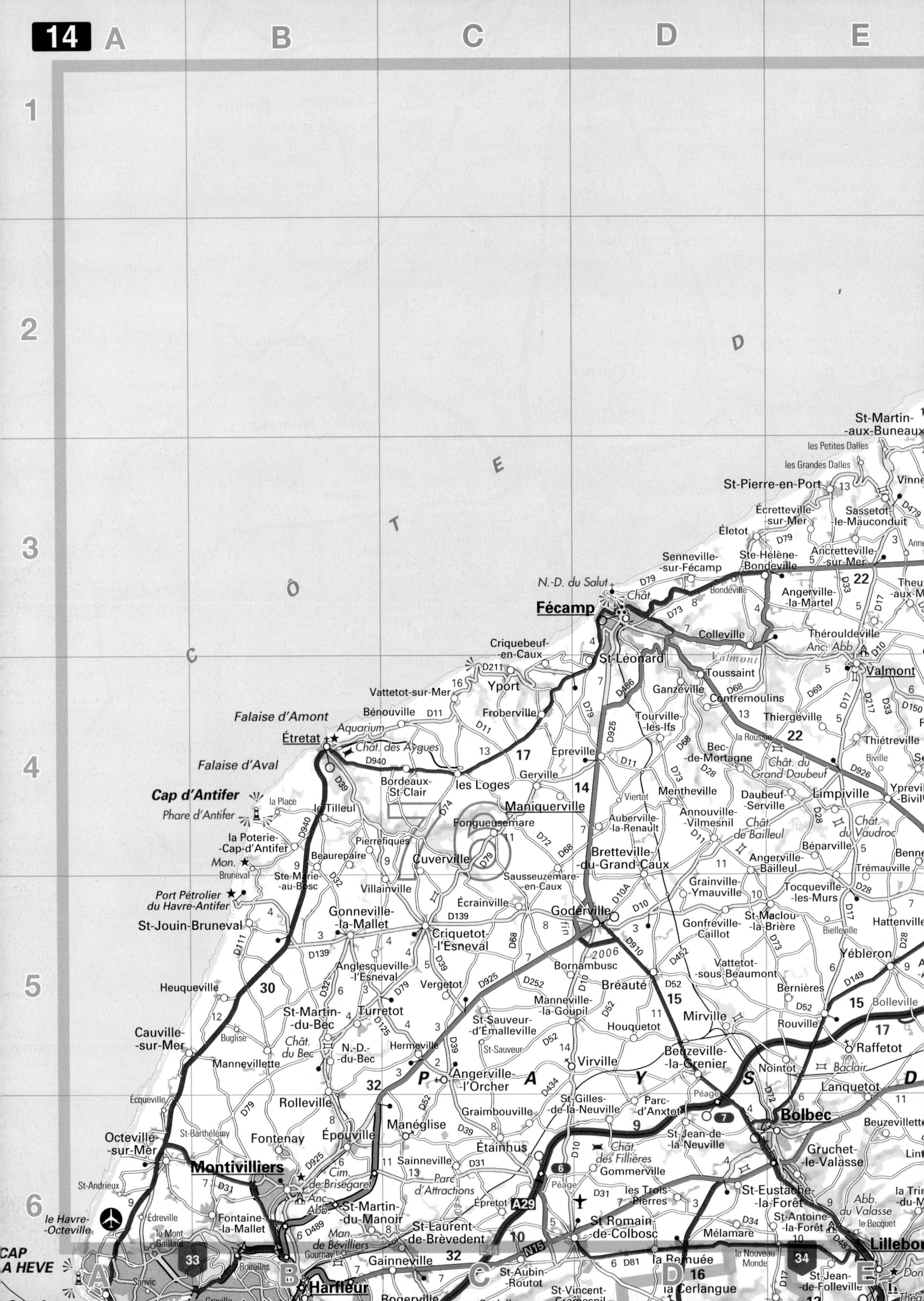

1

2

3

4

5

6

St-Martin
-aux-Buneaux
les Petites Dalles
les Grandes Dalles
St-Pierre-en-Port   13   Vinne
D479
Écretteville-   Sassetot-
sur-Mer   le-Mauconduit
Életot   D79
Senneville-   Ste-Hélène-   Ancretteville-
N.-D. du Salut   sur-Fécamp   Bondeville   sur-Mer   Anne
Chât.   D79   Bondeville   22
Fécamp   D73   8   Angerville-   Theu
  4   -la-Martel   -aux-M
Criquebeuf-   7   Colleville   5   D17   D33
-en-Caux   St-Léonard   Thérouldeville   Anc. Abb. D10
D211   4   Toussaint   Valmont   Valmont
Yport   7   Ganzeville   D68   5   D150
16   D486   Contremoulins   D69   D17   D33   6
Vattetot-sur-Mer   Froberville   Tourville-   13   Thiergeville   Thiétreville
Bénouville   D11   D925   les-Ifs   la Roussie   Biville
Falaise d'Amont   D11   D79   Bec-   Chât. du   22   D926   Se
Aquarium   13   Épreville   de-Mortagne   Grand-Daubeuf
Étretat   D11   **17**   Gerville   D11   D28   Daubeuf-   Limpiville   Yprevi
Chât. des Aygues   les Loges   **14**   Viertot   Mentheville   Serville   -Bivil
Falaise d'Aval   D940   Maniquerville   Auberville-   Annouville-   Chât.
Bordeaux-   Fonqueusemare   D72   D68   -la-Renault   -Vilmesnil   du Vaudroc
Cap d'Antifer   St-Clair   11   7   Chât.   Bénarville
la Place   le Tilleul   D74   Bretteville-   de Bailleul   Benne
Phare d'Antifer   Pierrefiques   Cuverville   D79   -du-Grand-Caux   Angerville-   Trémauville
la Poterie-   Beaurepaire   9   Sausseuzemare-   11   -Bailleul   D28
-Cap-d'Antifer   D940   Villainville   en-Caux   Grainville-   Tocqueville-
Mon.   Ste-Marie-   D32   Écrainville   -Ymauville   10   -les-Murs   D17
Bruneval   -au-Bosc   Goderville   St-Maclou-   Hattenville
Port Pétrolier   Gonneville-   D139   D10A   D10   Gonfreville-   -la-Brière   Bielleville
du Havre-Antifer   -la-Mallet   8   Caillot   D73
St-Jouin-Bruneval   3   Criquetot-   D68   3   2006   Yébleron
D11   D139   -l'Esneval   fin   D910   Vattetot-   D28   A
4   4   Anglesqueville-   D39   2   Bornambusc   D452   -sous-Beaumont   D149
30   -l'Esneval   D79   Vergetot   D925   D252   Bréauté   Bernières   D52   **15**   Bolleville
Heuqueville   D32   St-Sauveur-   Manneville-   D52   **15**   Mirville   Rouville   **17**
12   St-Martin-   Turretot   4   d'Émalleville   la-Goupil   D52   11   Raffetot
Cauville-   -du-Bec   D125   3   Houquetot   Beuzeville-   Nointot   Baclair   D
sur-Mer   Buglise   Hermeville   St-Sauveur   14   -la-Grenier   Lanquetot
Chât.   N.-D.-   2   D52   Péage   D52
Mannevillette   du Bec   -du-Bec   3   Virville   Parc-   7   **Bolbec**
32   P   Angerville-   A   St-Gilles-   d'Anxtot   4   Beuzevillett
Écqueville   Rolleville   -l'Orcher   D434   -de-la-Neuville   **9**   St-Jean-   Gruchet-   Lin
D79   D52   Graimbouville   D39   -la-Neuville   -le-Valasse
Octeville-   St-Barthélemy   Fontenay   Maneglise   8   Chât.   D10   St-Eustache-   la Tri
-sur-Mer   D925   Épouville   11   Étainhus   des Fillières   6   les Trois-   -la-Forêt   Abb.   -du-M
St-Andrieux   **Montivilliers**   Cim.   Sainneville   D31   Péage   Pierres   3   St-Antoine-   du Valasse
9   de-Brisegaret   13   Parc   Gommerville   D31   7   D34   -la-Forêt   le Becquet
le Havre   7   D31   d'Attractions   Épretot   A29   5   St-Romain-   Mélamare   10
-Octeville   Fontaine-   Anc.   **32**   -de-Colbosc   **34**   **Lillebo**
le Mont   la-Mallet   Abb.   St-Martin-   N15   10   D17   St-Jean-
CAP   Gaillard   D489   -du-Manoir   E4   le Nouveau   -de-Folleville   12
A HEVE   **33**   Man.   St-Laurent-   **6**   Monde   Théo
Sanvic   de Bévilliers   -de-Brèvedent   D81   6   D81   la Remuée   **16**   Don
Rouelles   Gournay   **32**   la Cerlangue
Harfleur   Gainneville   St-Aubin-   St-Vincent-   St-Jean-
Graville   Rogerville   -Routot   -Cramesnil

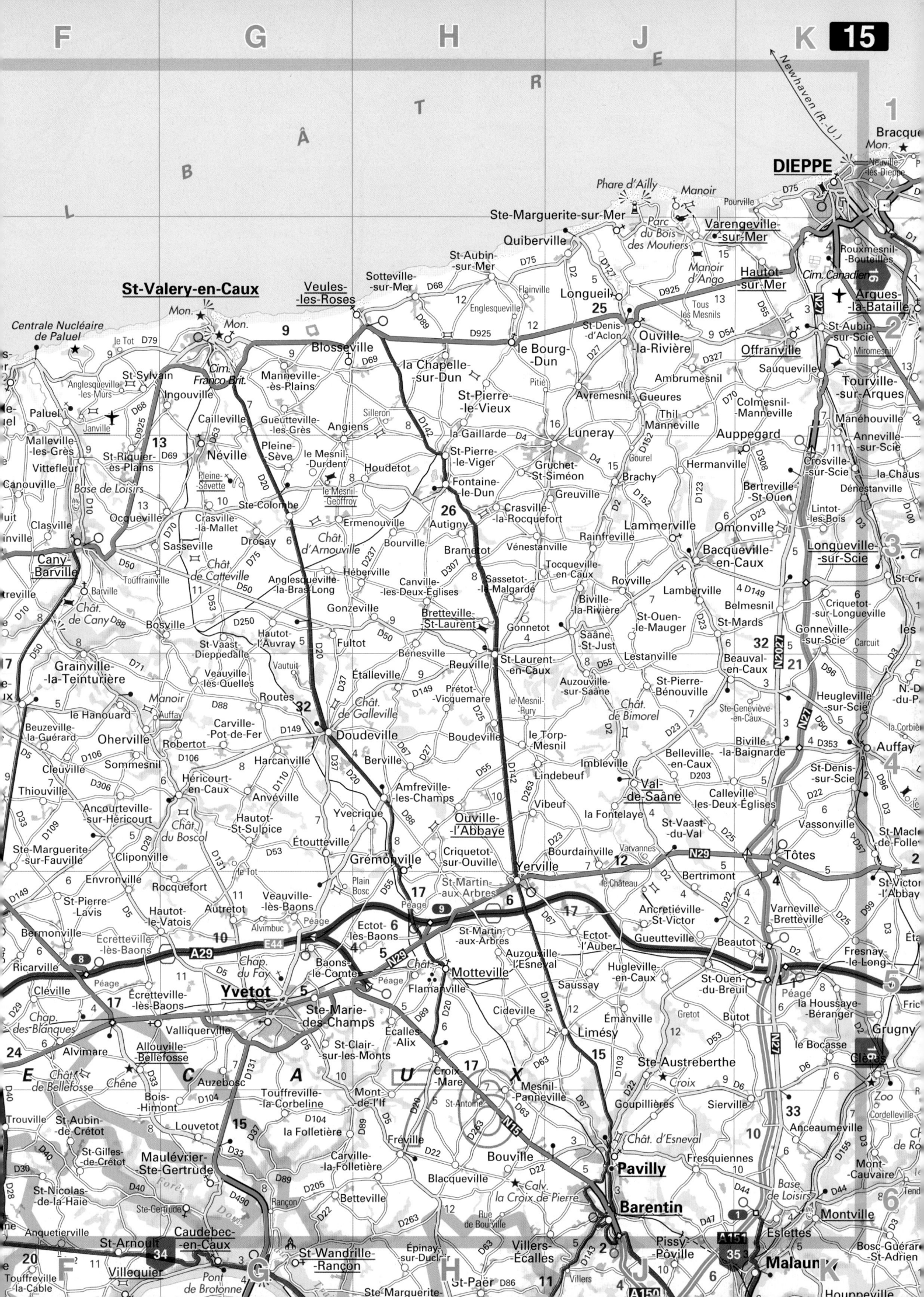

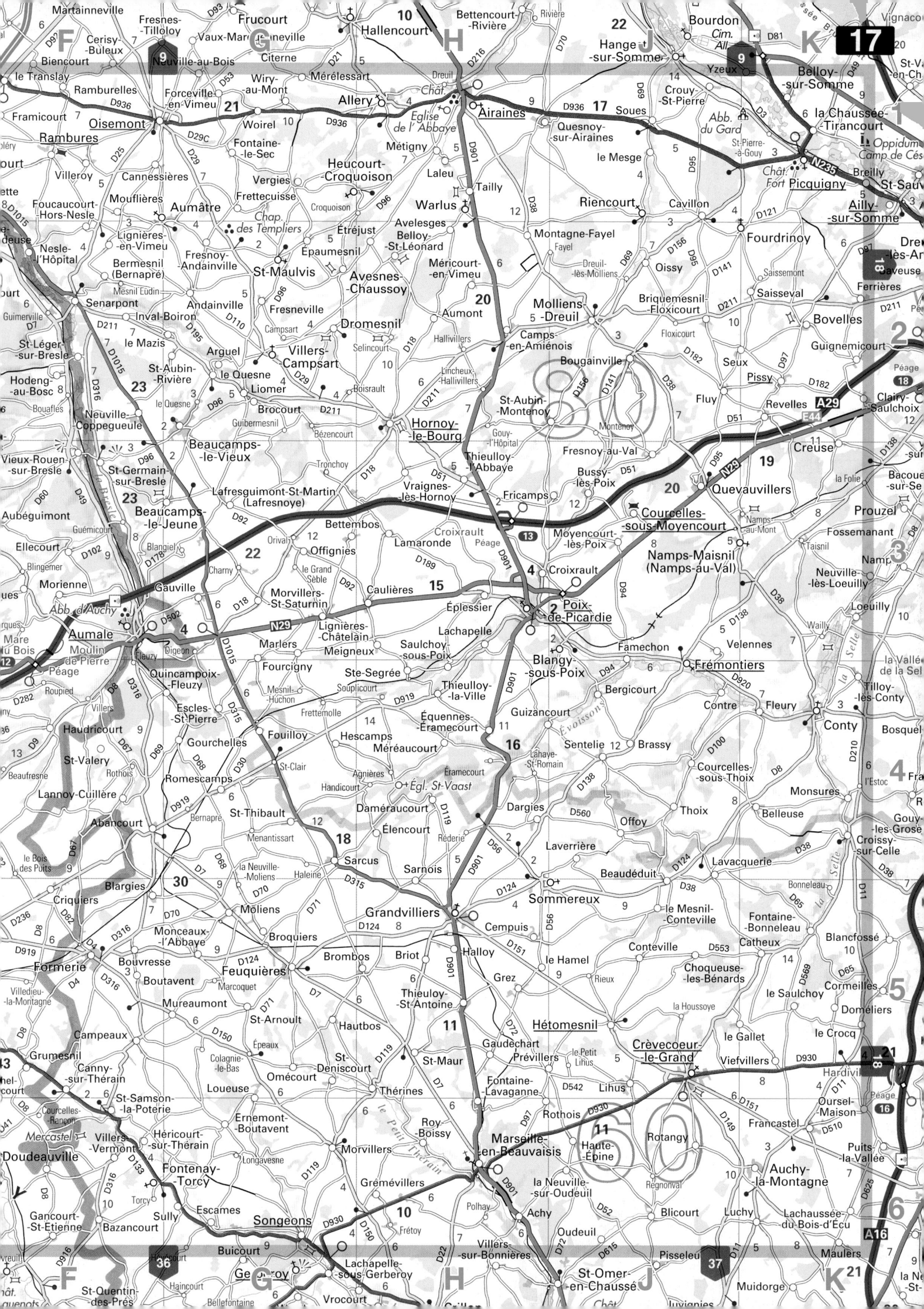

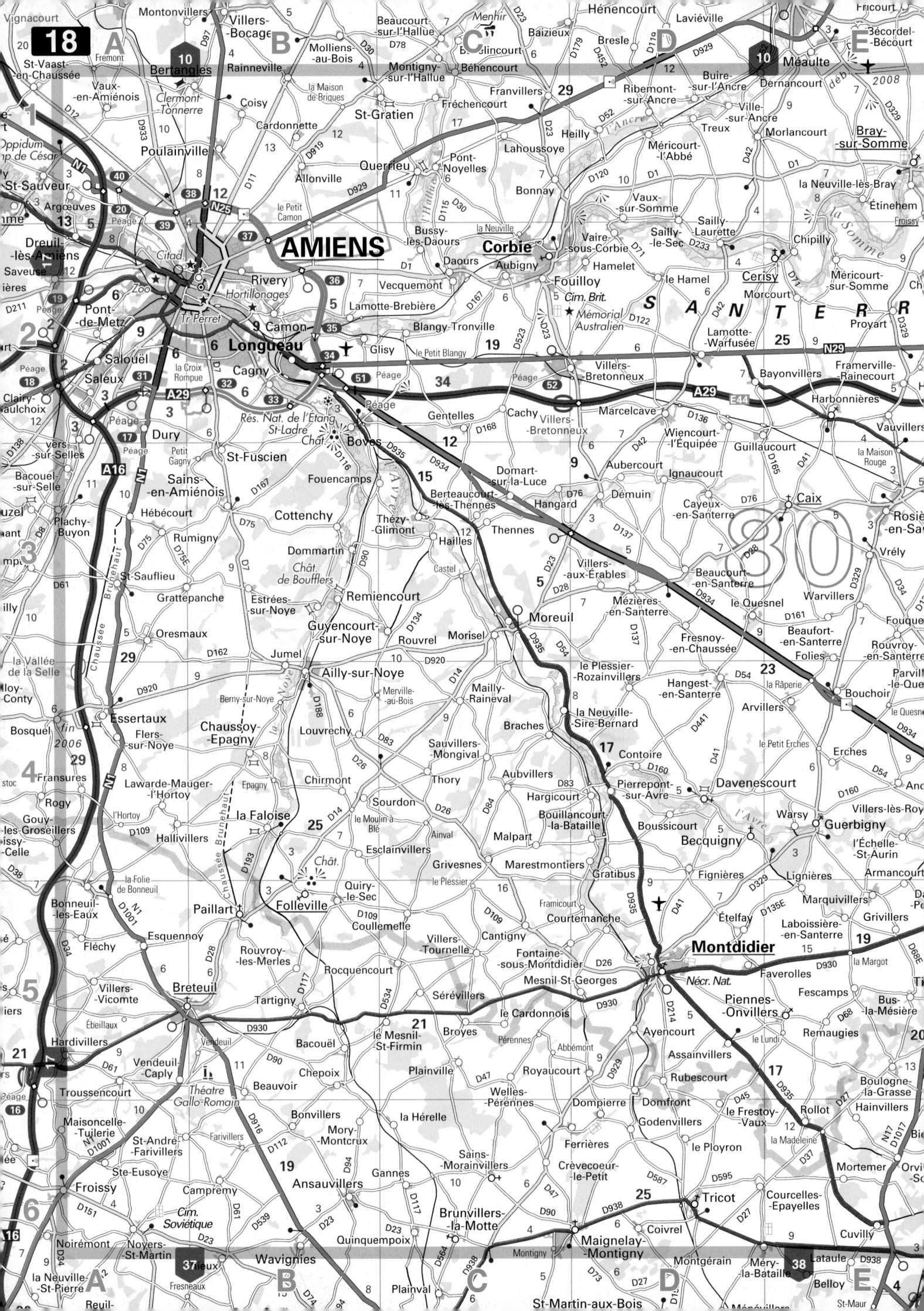

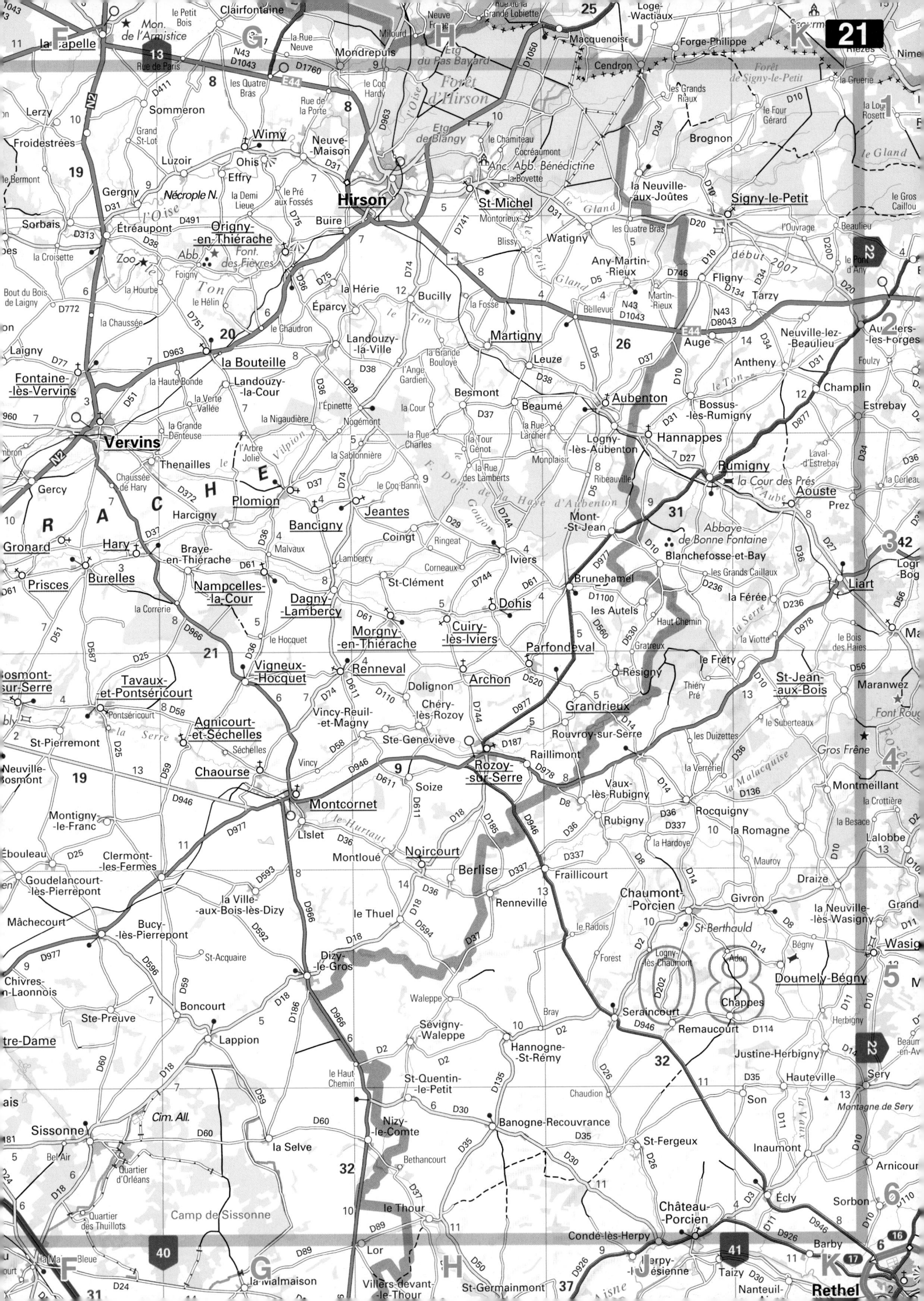

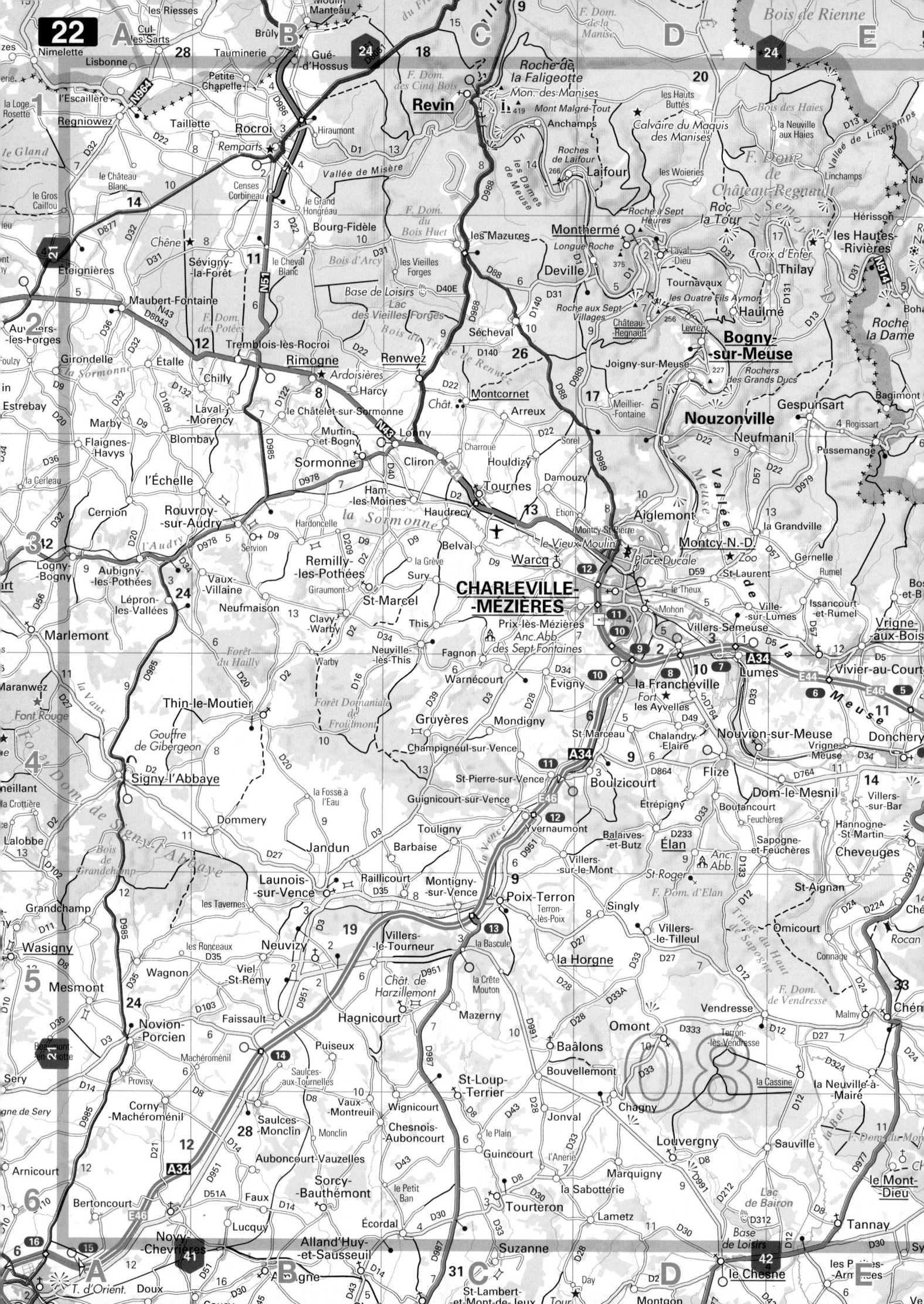

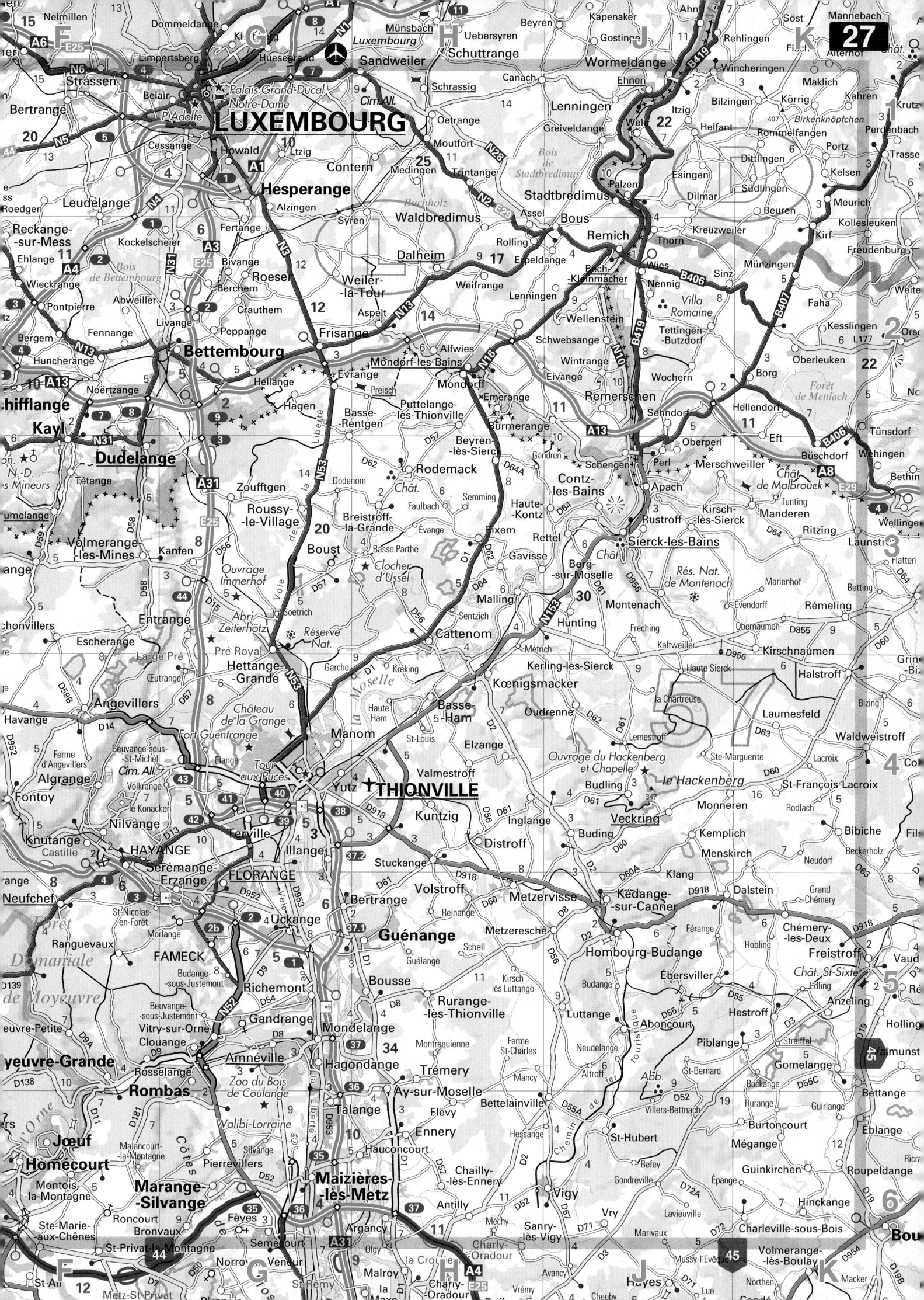

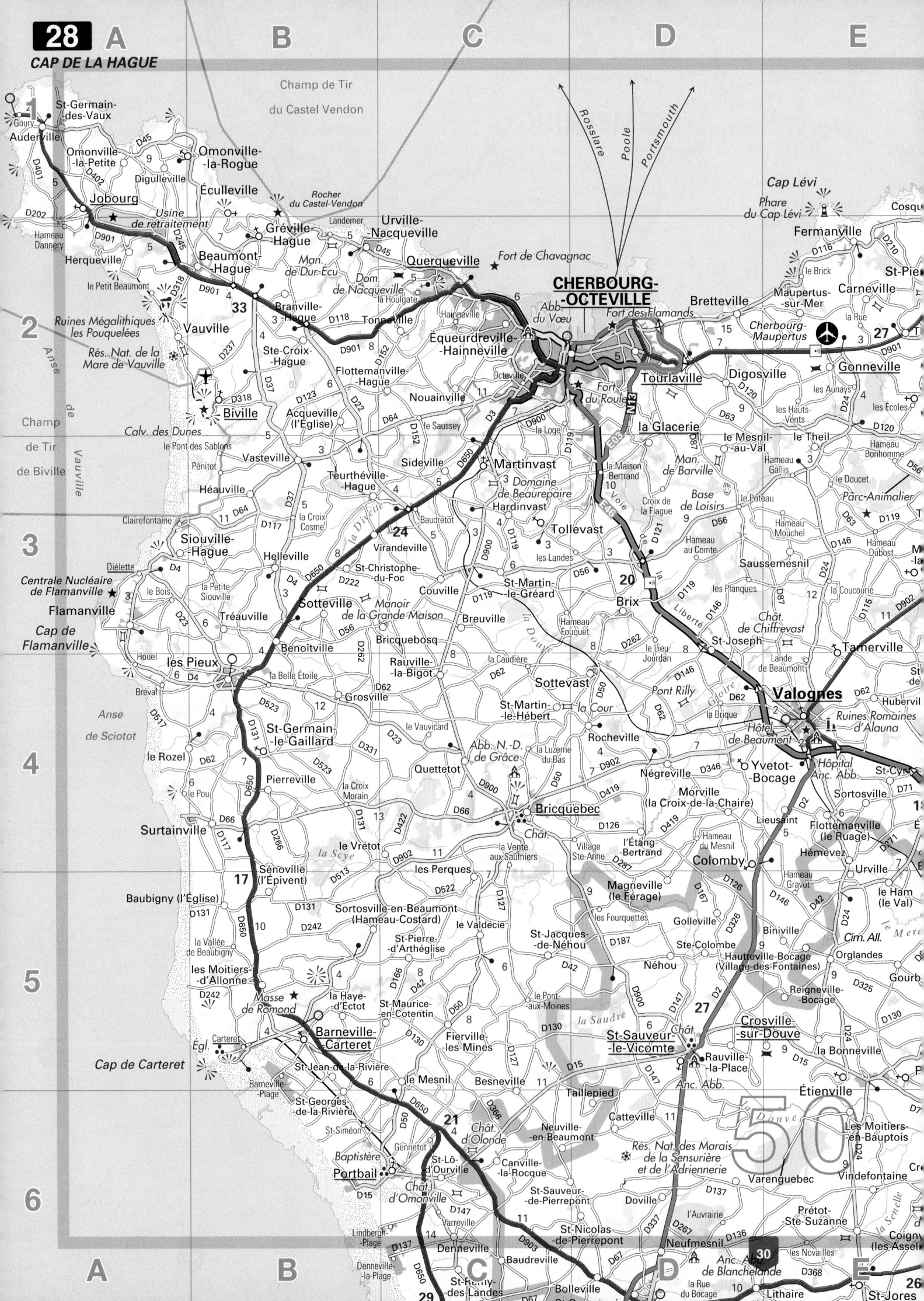

POINTE DE BARFLEUR

Phare de Gatteville

Réthoville
Néville-sur-Mer
arouville
D116
Gouberville
Gatteville-le-Phare
Tocqueville
urps
D210
D125
D901
Barfleur
Ste-Geneviève
D1
Canteloup
D25
Montfarville
D902
Landemer
Valcanville
le Vicel
Anneville-en-Saire
Crasville
Manoir de la Crasvillerie
le Vast
D125
D10
T. d'Orient
la Pernelle
Réville
Hameau Néel
D26
Pointe de Saire
le Tronquet
la Buhotterie
D56
Quettehou
27
Forts
Île de Tatihou
Piédechou
D902
St-Vaast-la-Hougue
D25
D1
Videcosville
Morsalines
Fort de la Hougue
D216
teville
Crasville
Avenel
D62
Aumeville-Lestre
t-Martin-Audouville
D14
Lestre
Chap.
audreville
D42
Quinéville
Ozeville
D421
St-Floxel
Fontenay-sur-Mer
les Gougins
Châti de Courcy
tebourg
Vaudville
Dangueville
Ravenoville-Plage
D69
Fort de St-Marcouf
Joganville
D269
Grand Hameau des Dunes
Émondeville
St-Marcouf
NT3
D115
D14
D15
Azeville
Ravenoville
la Selleraie
D269
D17
Cibrantot
Foucarville
Monument
Neuville-au-Plain
St-Germain-de-Varréville
D421
Utah Beach
Beuzeville-au-Plain
D7
St-Martin-de-Varreville
Ste-Mère-Église
D115
D14
Audouville-la-Hubert
Monument
Turqueville
la Madeleine
M
Écoqueneauville
le Grand Chemin
Réserve Naturelle de Beau Guillot
Chef-du-Pont
Boutteville
D913
Pointe du Hoc
Sébeville (les Fontaines)
Ste-Marie-du-Mont
Pouppeville
Grandcamp-Maisy
Mon.
St-Pierre-du-Mont
Carquebut
Blosville
Hiesville
le Grand Vey
Maisy
D514
Liesville-sur-Douve
la Rue
la Dune
l'Hermerel
Cricqueville-en-Bessin
D194
Englesqueville-la-Percée
Vierville-sur-Mer
Houesville
D913
Vierville
Géfosse-Fontenay (le Bas-de-Géfosse)
D199
D113
Châti de Beaumont
Châti de Vaumicel
Omaha Beach
St-Côme-du-Mont
Angoville-au-Plain
D89
les Vignets
Asnières-en-Bessin
Louvières
Cim. Am.
Mémorial
Appeville
le Moulin
Brévands
St-Clément
Osmanville
D200
Cardonville
la Cambe
Deux-Jumeaux
St-Laurent-sur-Mer
Colleville-sur-Mer
PARC
NATUR
31
3 RÉGIONAL
Les Veys (l'Église)
Isigny-sur-Mer
St-Germain-du-Pert
Cim. All.
St-Louis
Longueville
9
31
Formigny
St-Hilaire-Petit (le Mont)
Catz
Canchy
arville (Normanville)
Surrain
D124
Écrammeville
D123

32

33

6

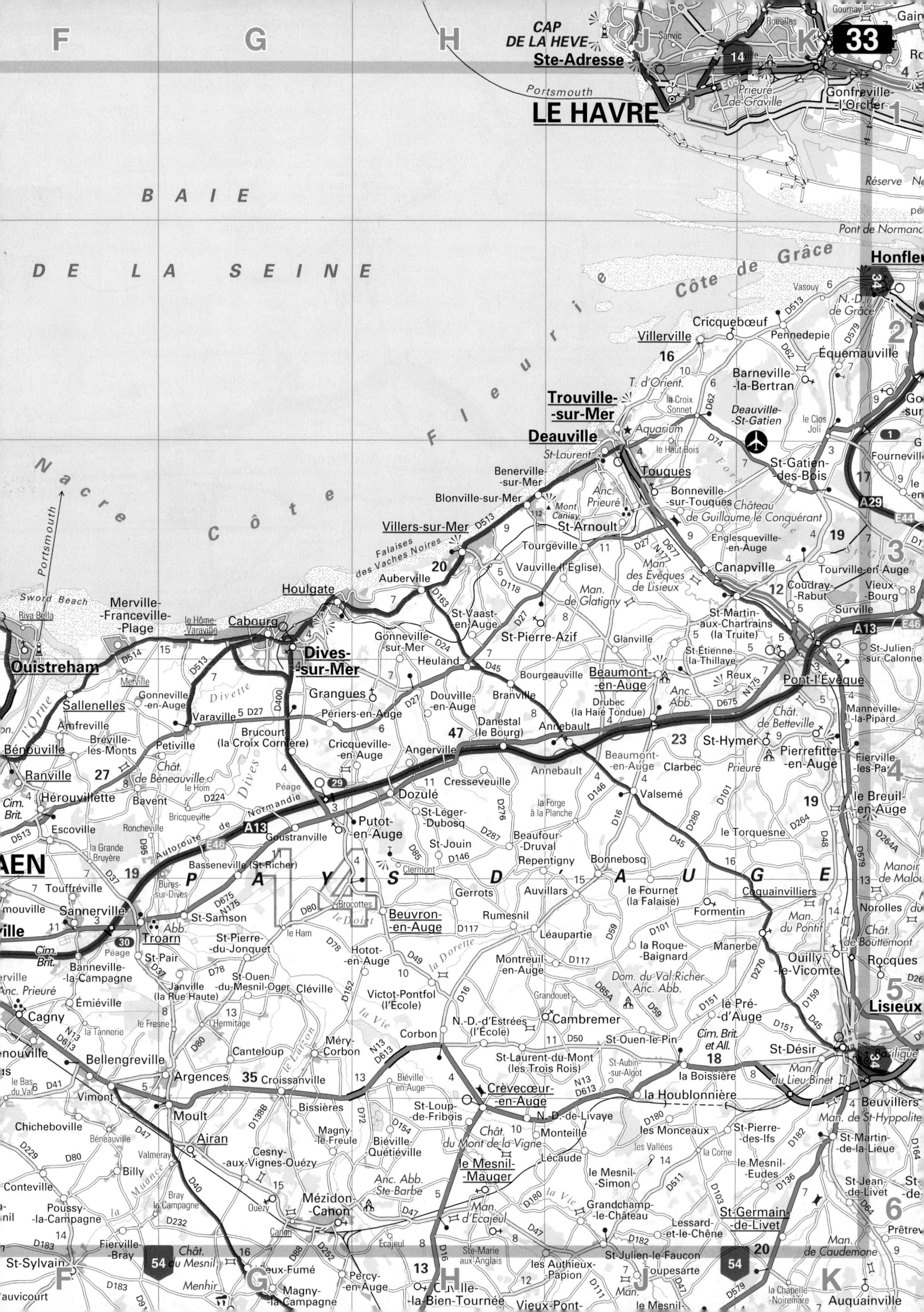

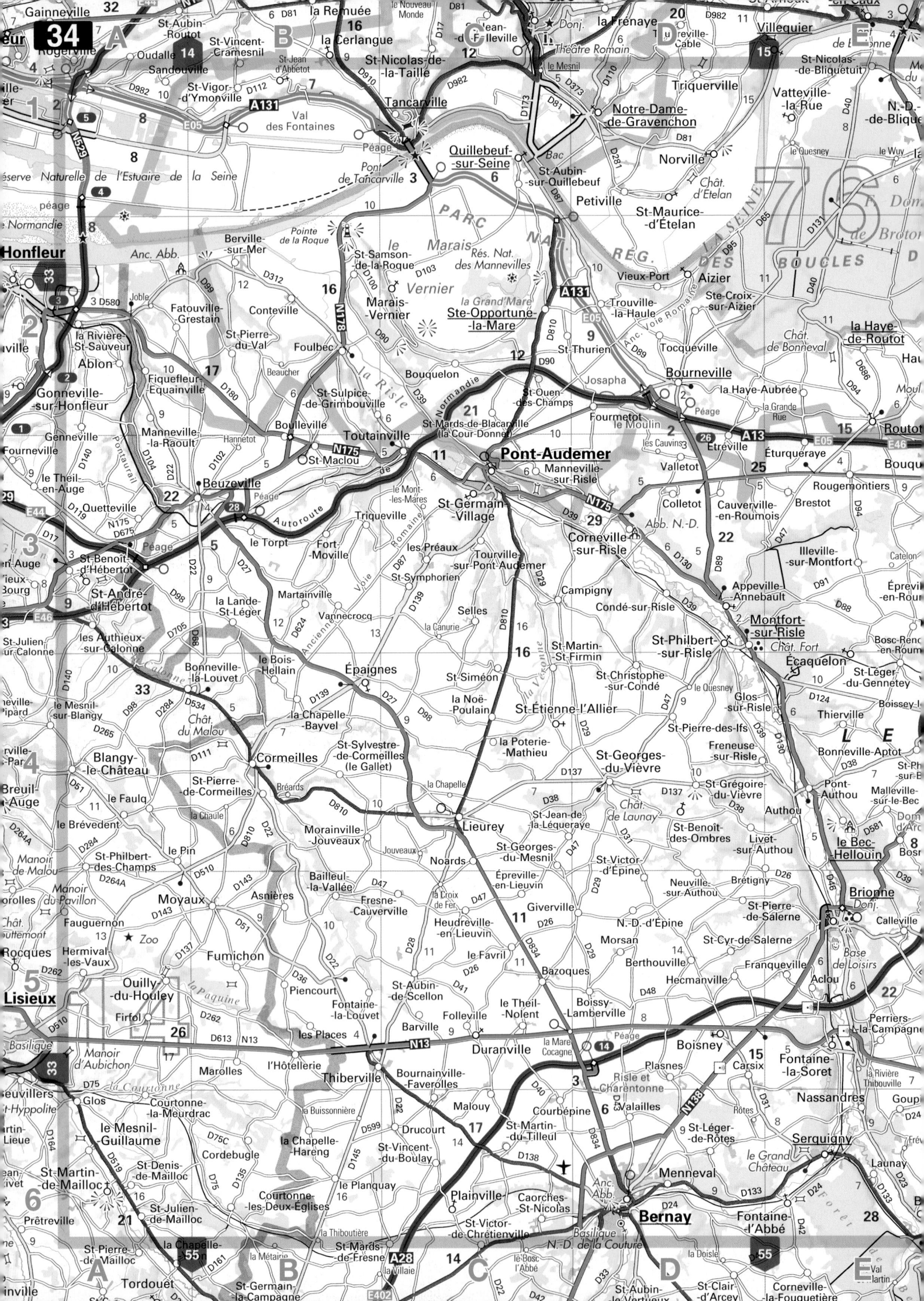

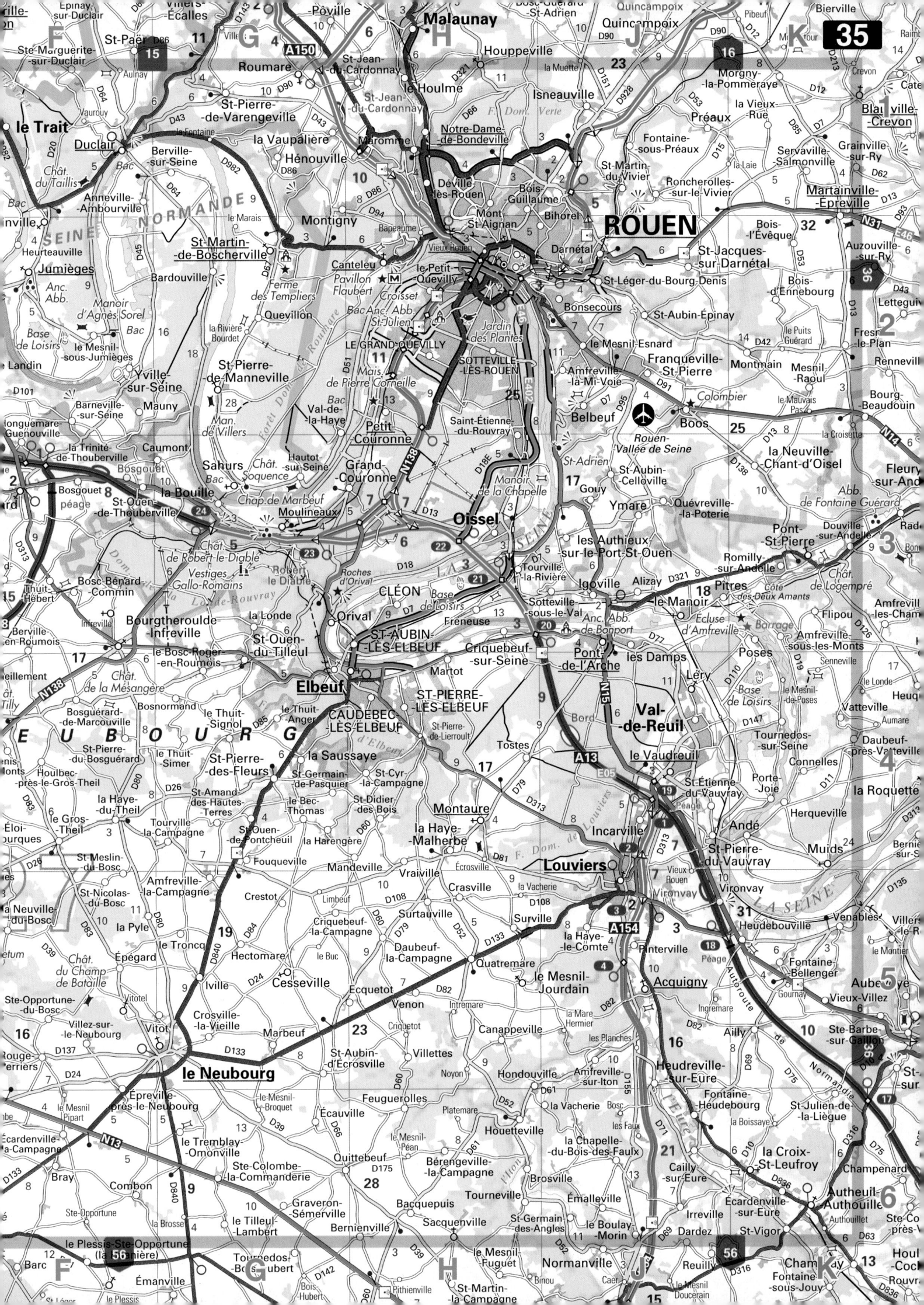

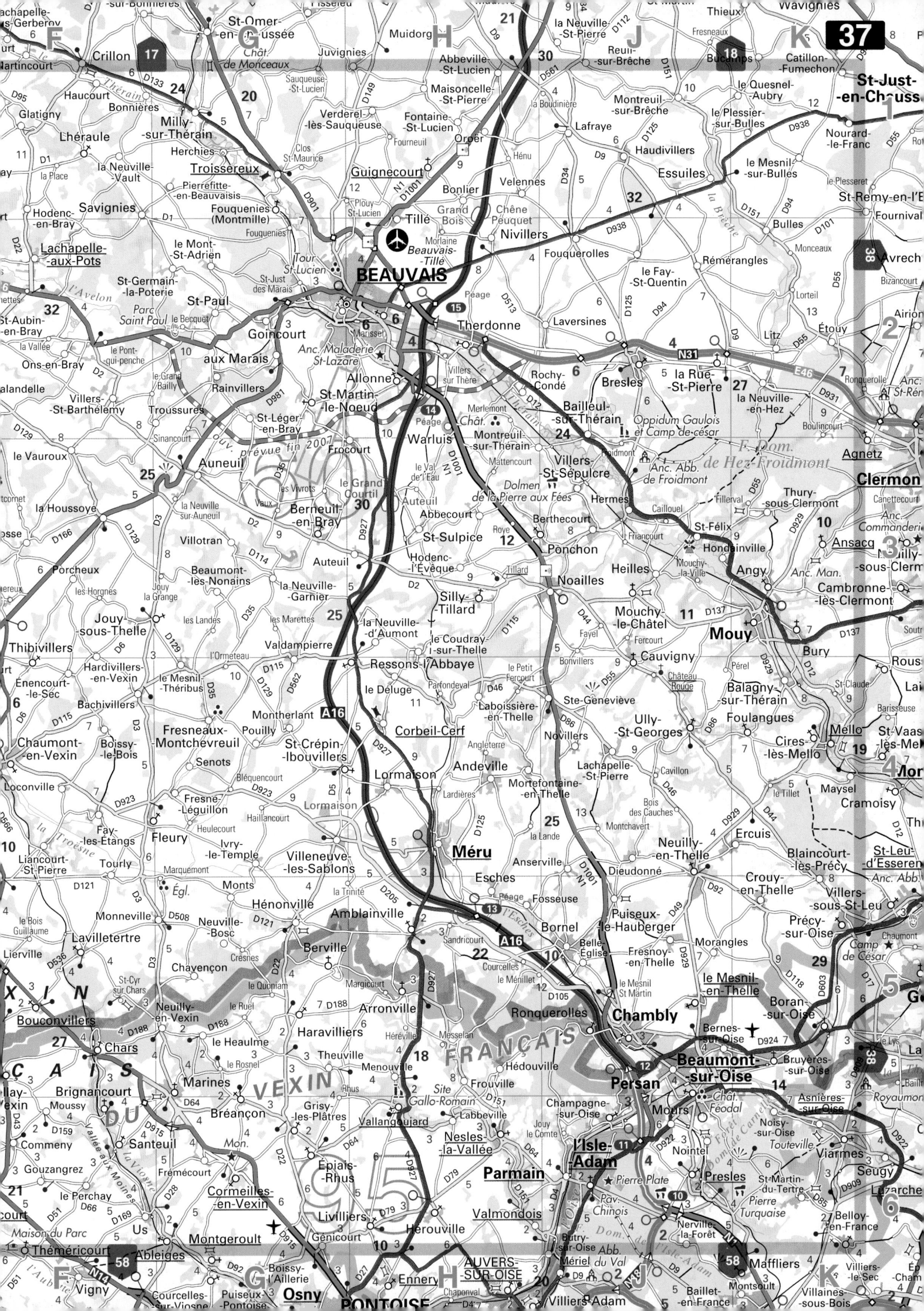

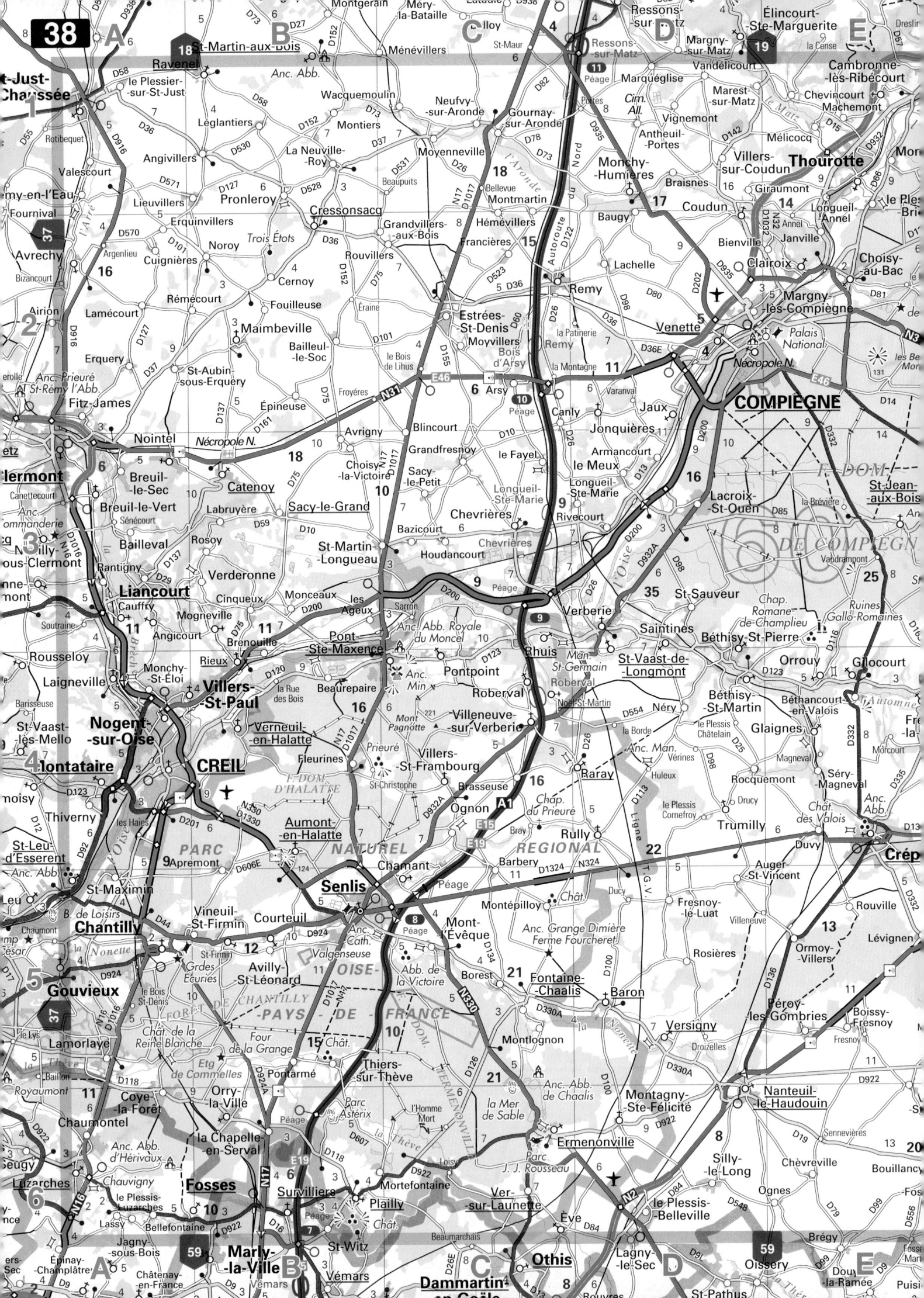

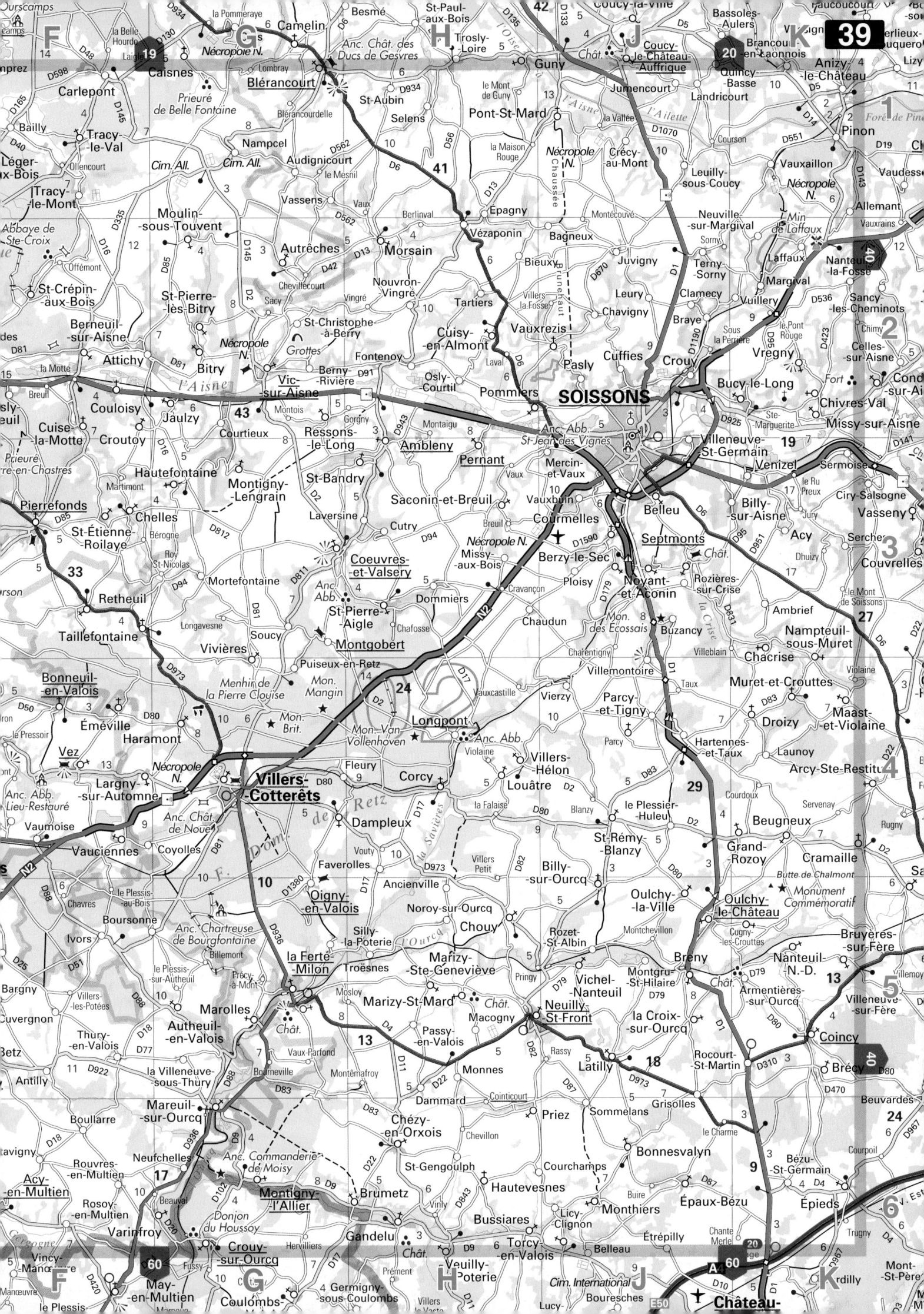

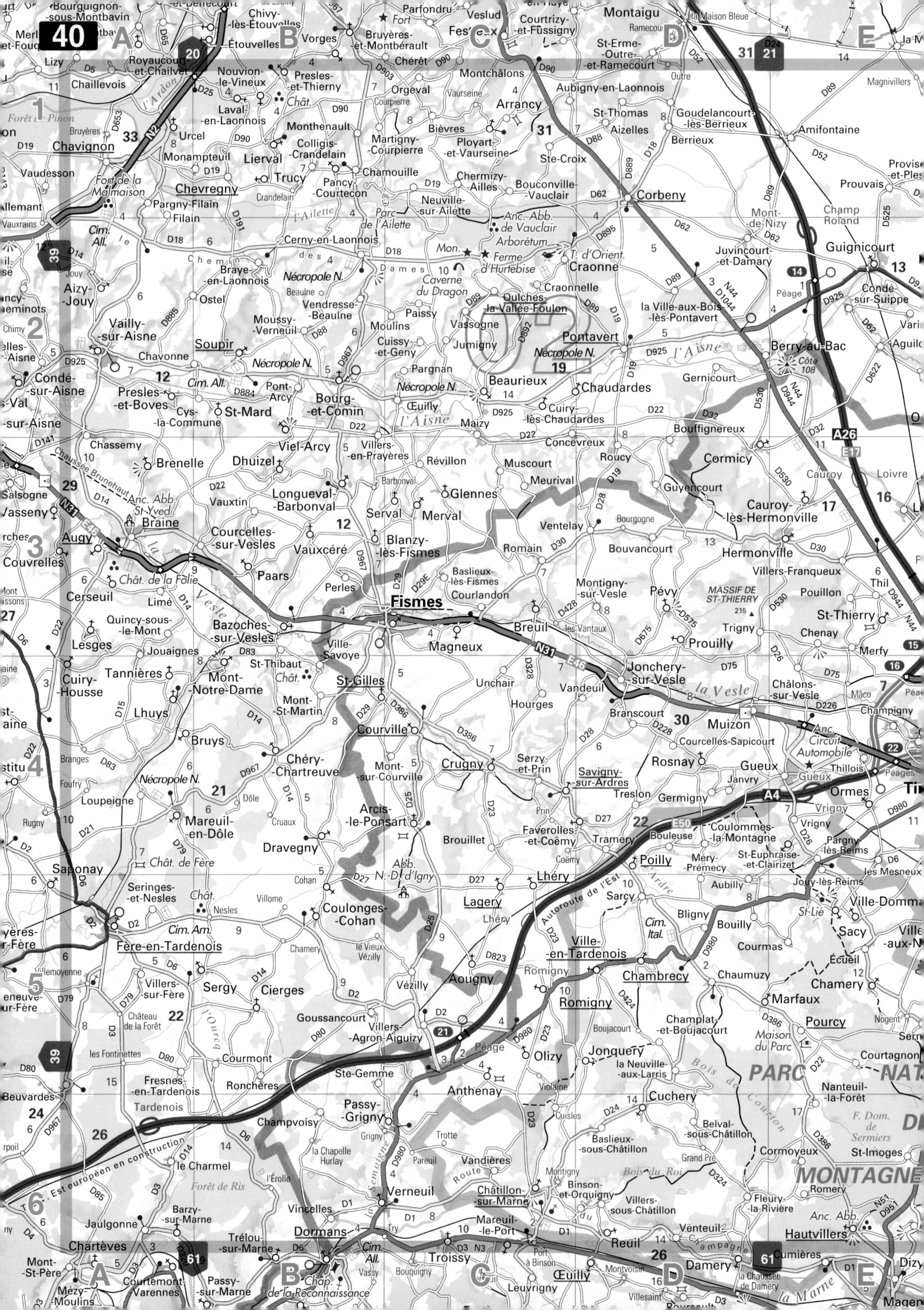

1

2

GOLFE DE SAINT-MALO

3

Côte de Goëlo

BAIE DE ST-BRIEUC

Côte de Penthièvre

4

Port-Moguer
Kerouziel
le Palus
Tréveneuc
St-Quay
poëns
D786
St-Barnabé
D9
St-Quay-Portrieux
Plourhan
Étables-sur-Mer
D51 D21
St-Roch
tic
D47 D4
Binic
le Bourgneuf
Dame-Cour
Zoo D47
la Ville Rouault
le Vaudic
22
Grève des Rosaires
Trégomeur
Pordic
Tréméloir
St-Éloy
les Rosaires
13
D786 D1
Martin
Pointe du Roselier
le Roselier
D36
St-Laurent
Réserve Naturelle
Plérin
D36
les Mines
la Cotentin
Trémuson
D712
ST-BRIEUC
Plerneuf
St-Hervé
la Méaugon
D45
Colombier
Maison de la Baie
la Grandville
Hillion
Croix
Colombier
Morieux
Licantois
Langueux
D80
Yffiniac
St-René
Ploufragan
D45
Tréqueux
le Créac'h
la Croix Bertrand
D10 D700
Château de la Ville Daniel

Cap d'Erquy
Tu-Es-Roc
Sables-d'Or-les-Pins
D34
Erquy
les Hôpitaux
D786
D34
Plurien
D786
19
le Dréneuf
la Ville Berneuf
D34
les Tertres Charbonnet
D89
Pointe de Pléneuf
l'Islet
D52
Pléneuf-Val-André
la Couture
le Val-André
St-Laurent
Château Bien-Assis
Dahouët
D17
la Bouillie
D786
D68
D17A
9
6
le Poirier
St-Jacques
St-Alban
D34
D14
D52
St-Jean
D14
50
Hér
Hénansal
D13
D89
les Rigaudais
9
D791
Planguenoual
D786
12
la Ville Gontier
10
St-Aaron
Quintenic
D68
St-Gueltas
St-Denoual
27
Coëtmieux
D59A
Andel
Boudehen
D14
la Doberie
D768
D52
Lar
D59
Haras National
la Poterie
77
D28
Aubin
Château
Manc de Vau-M

5

6

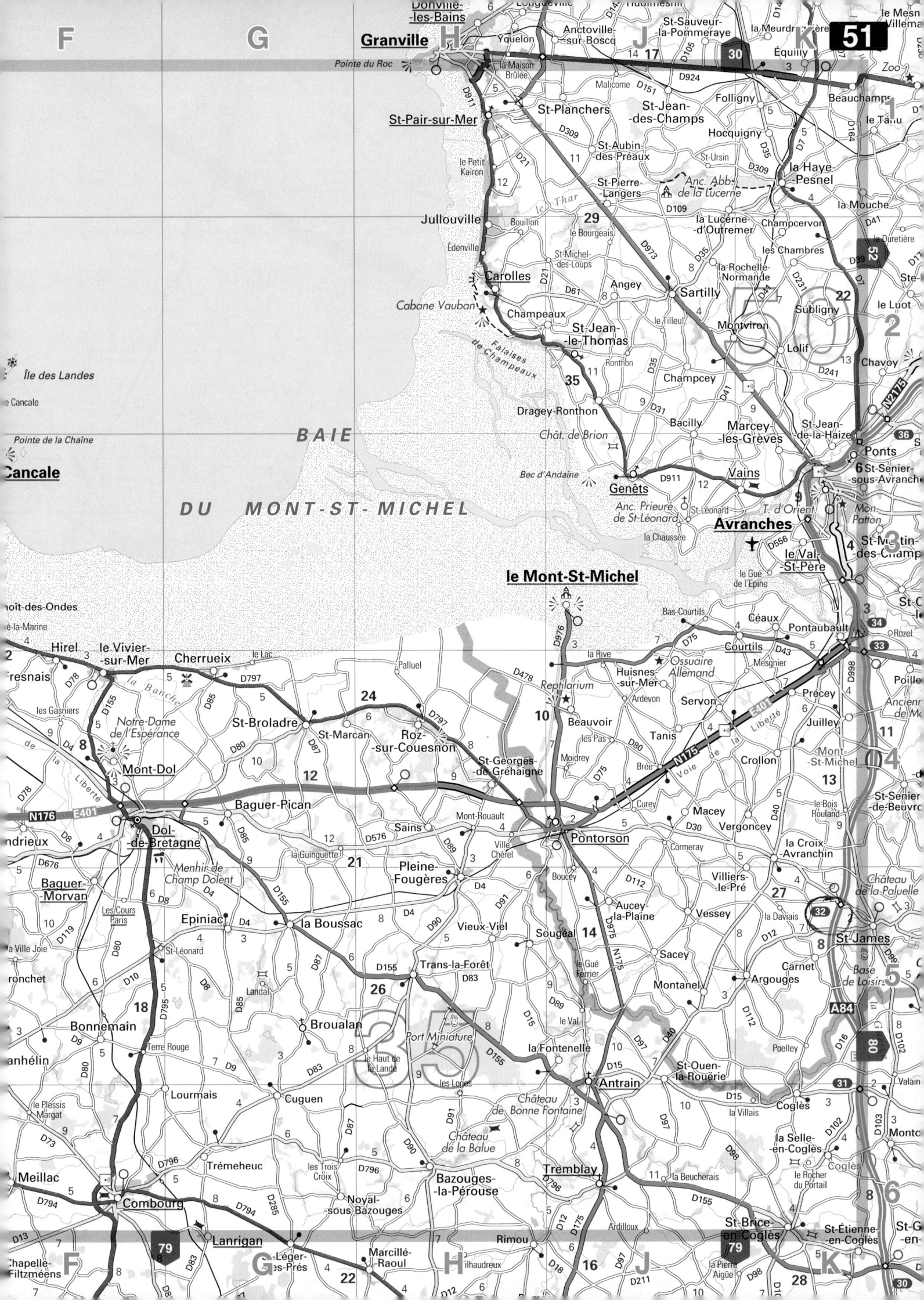

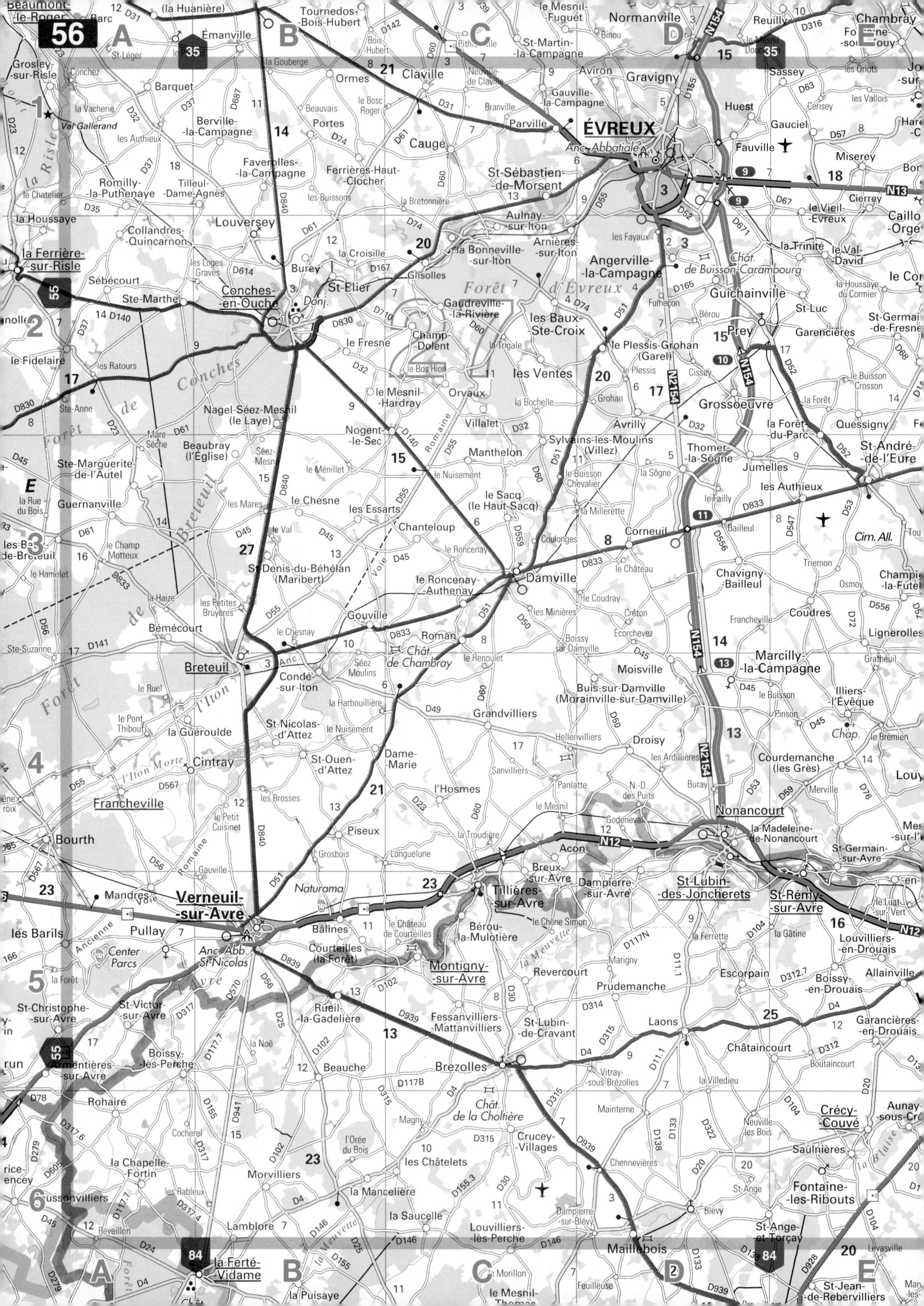

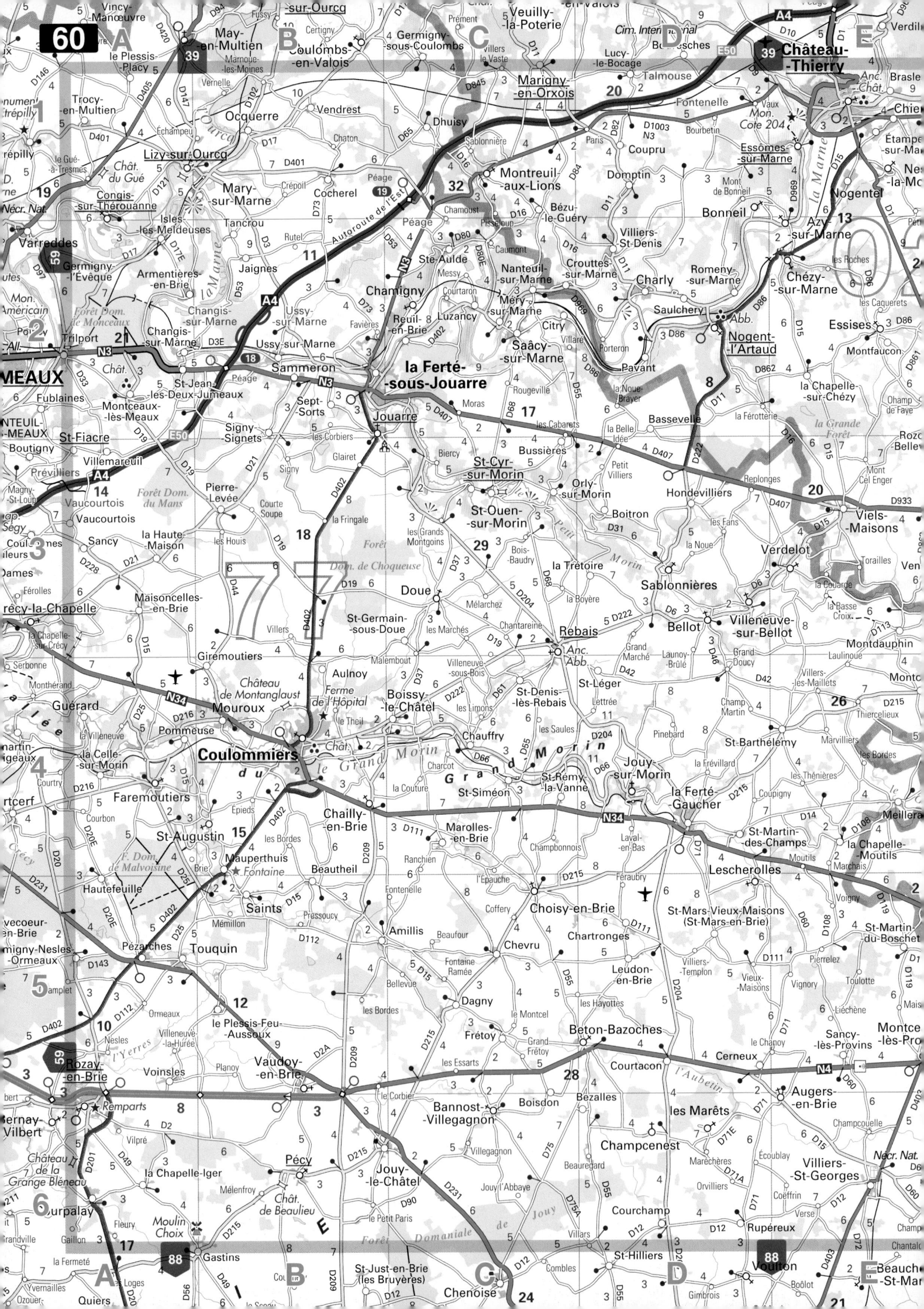

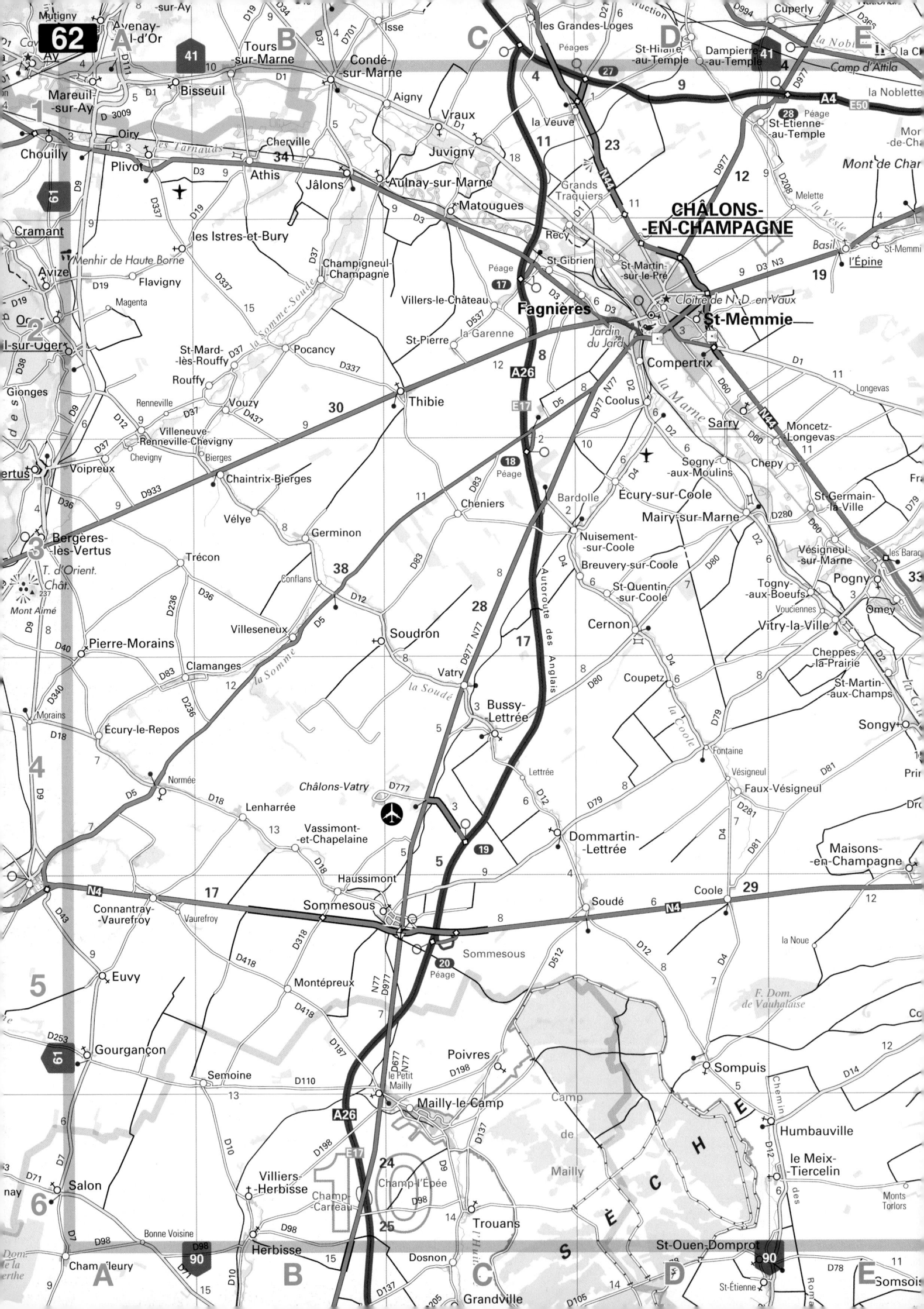

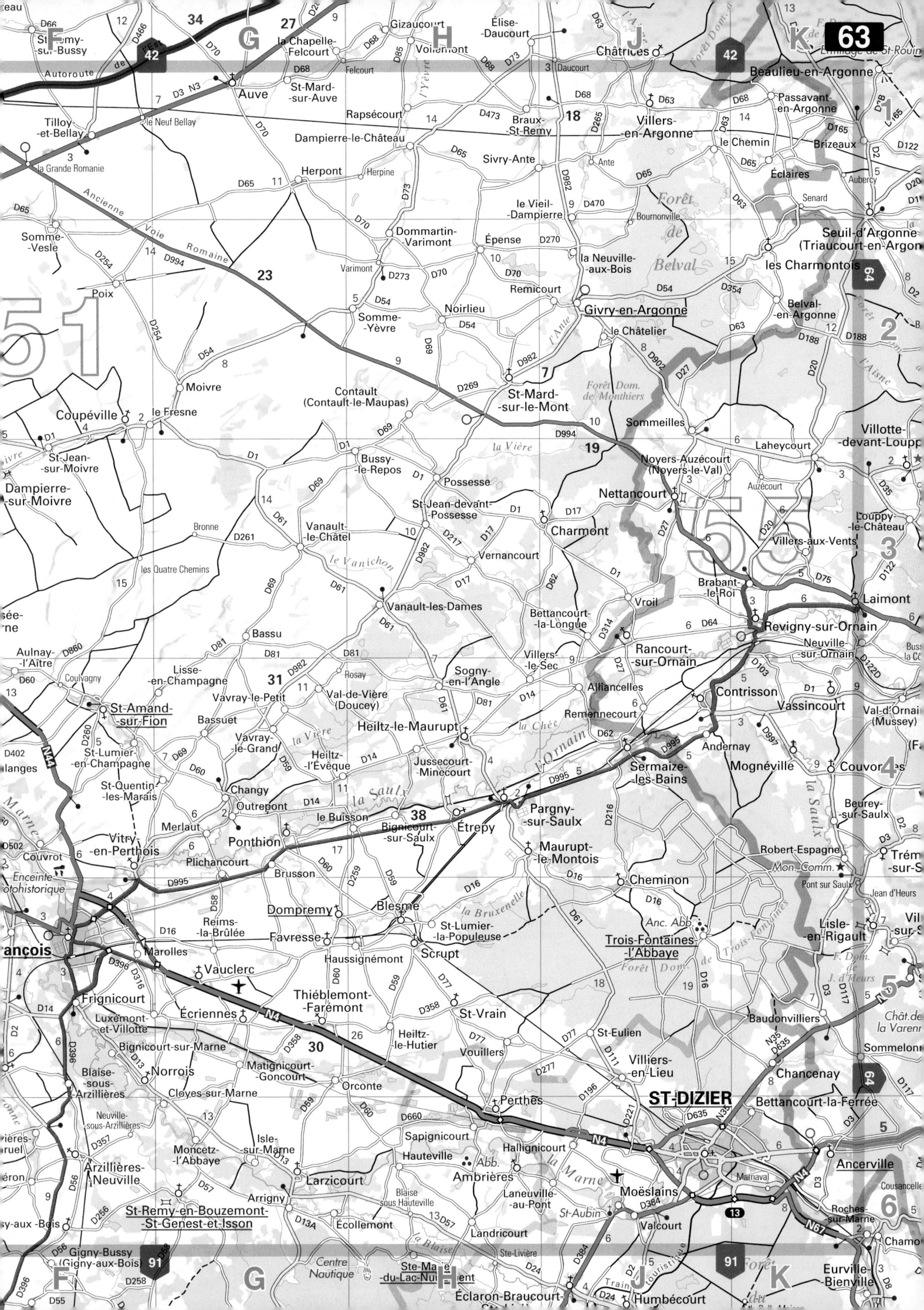

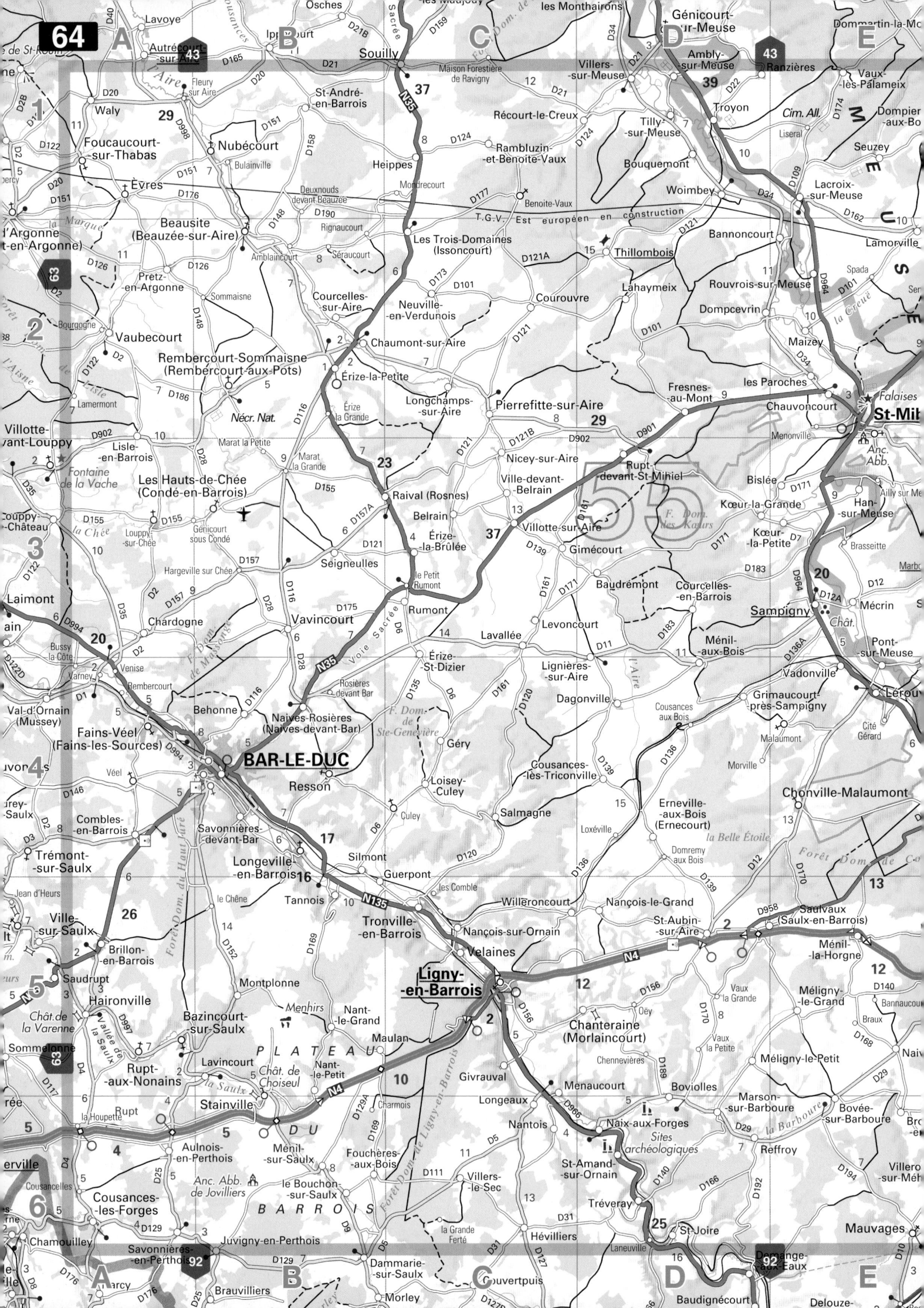

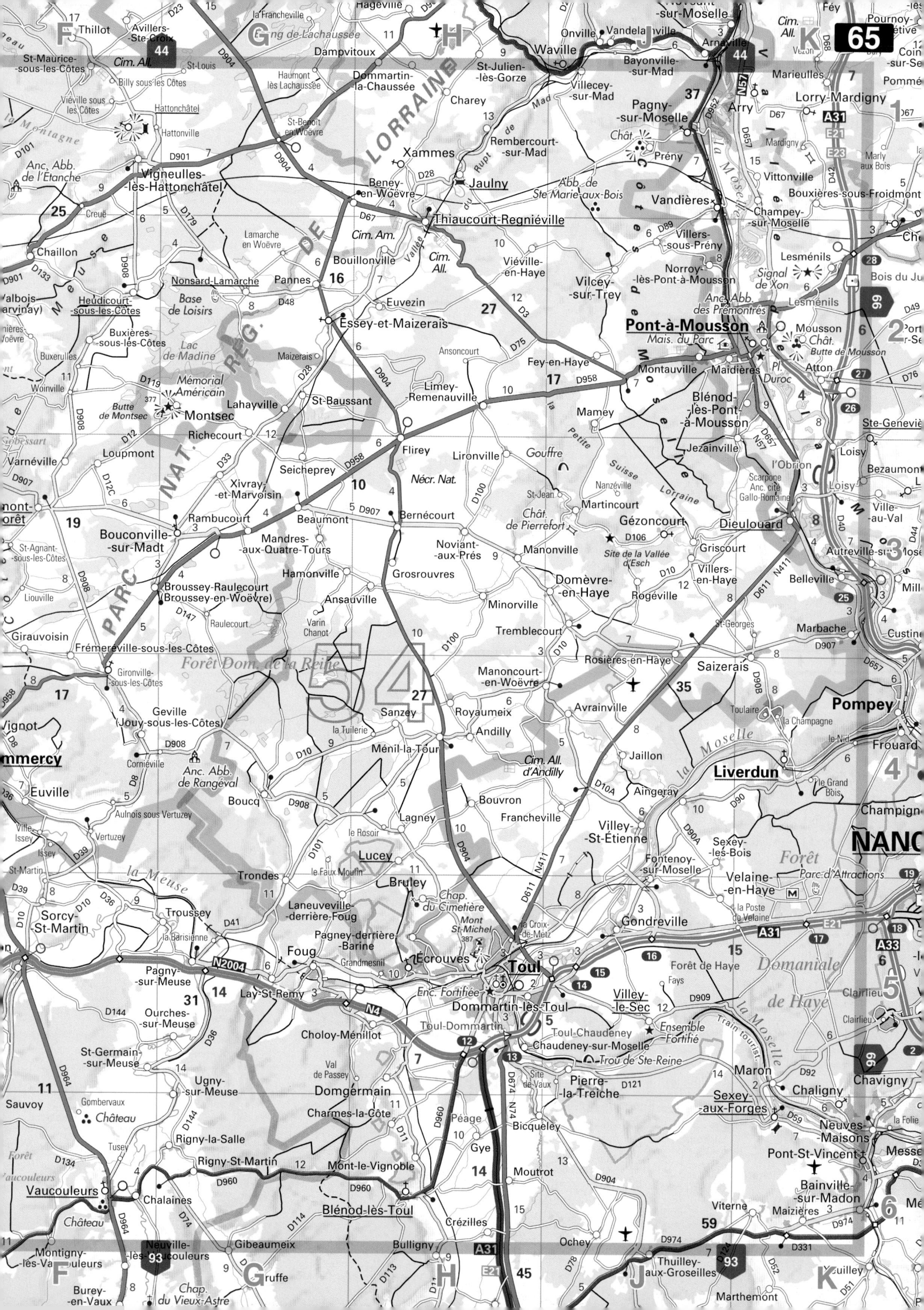

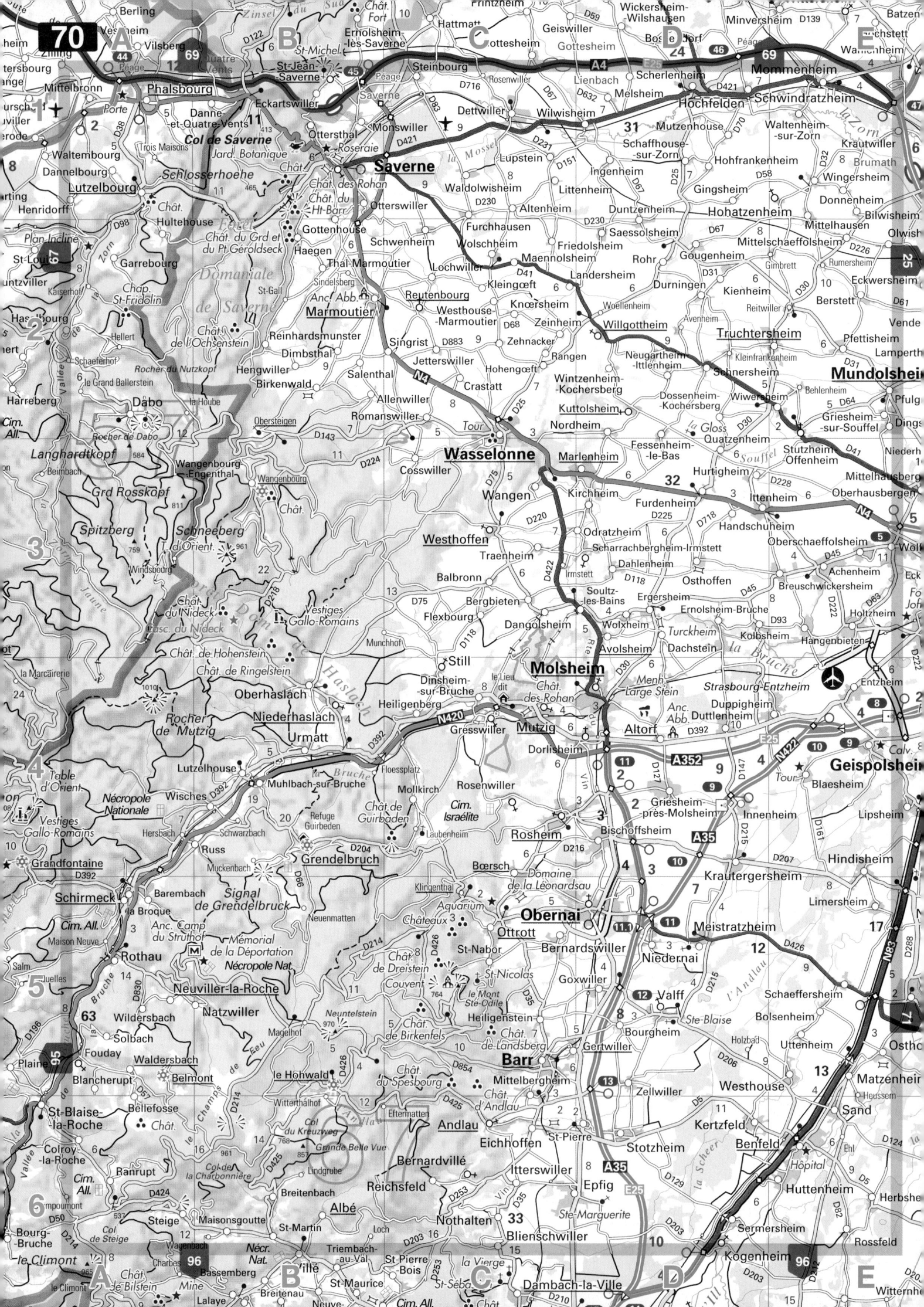

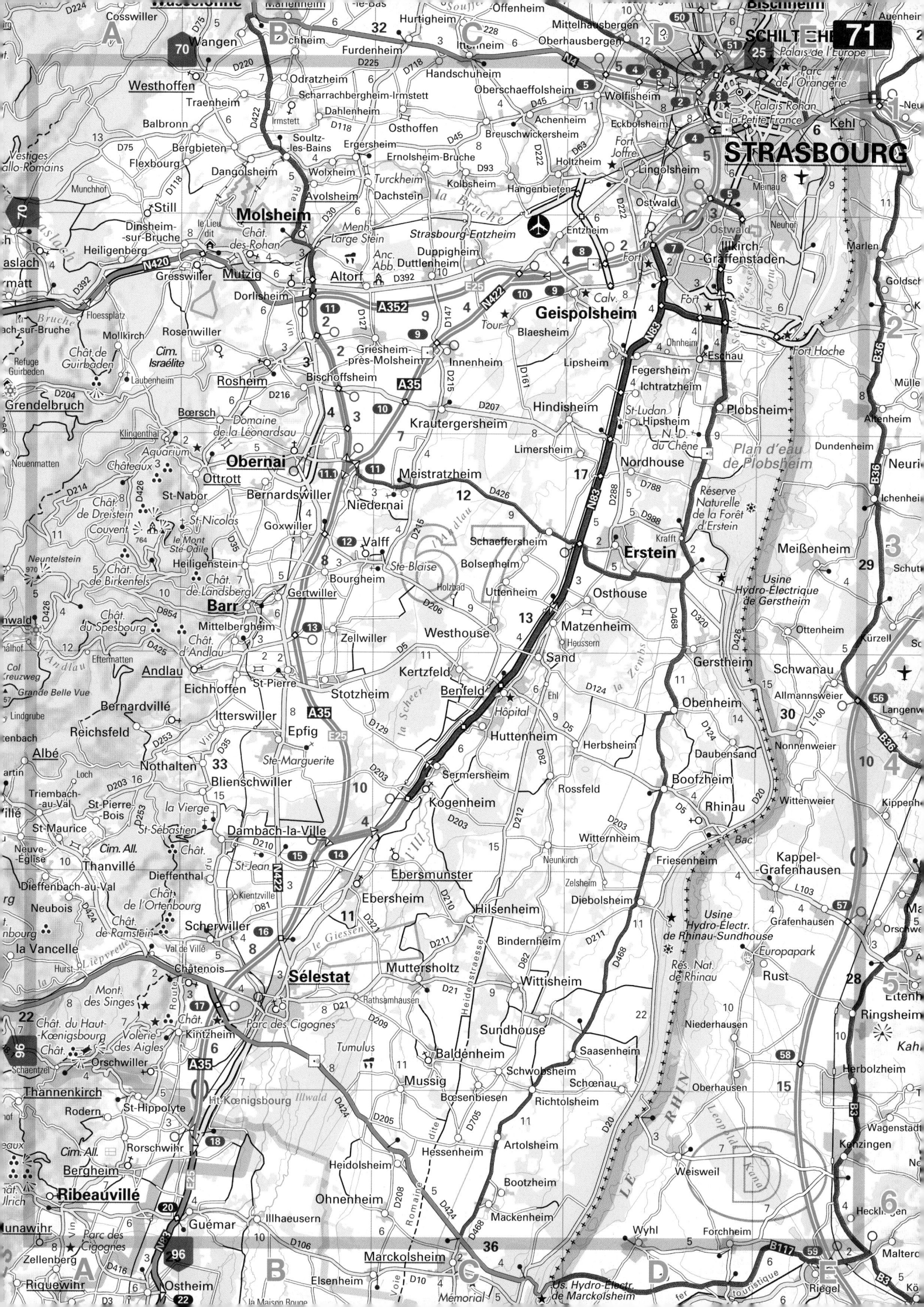

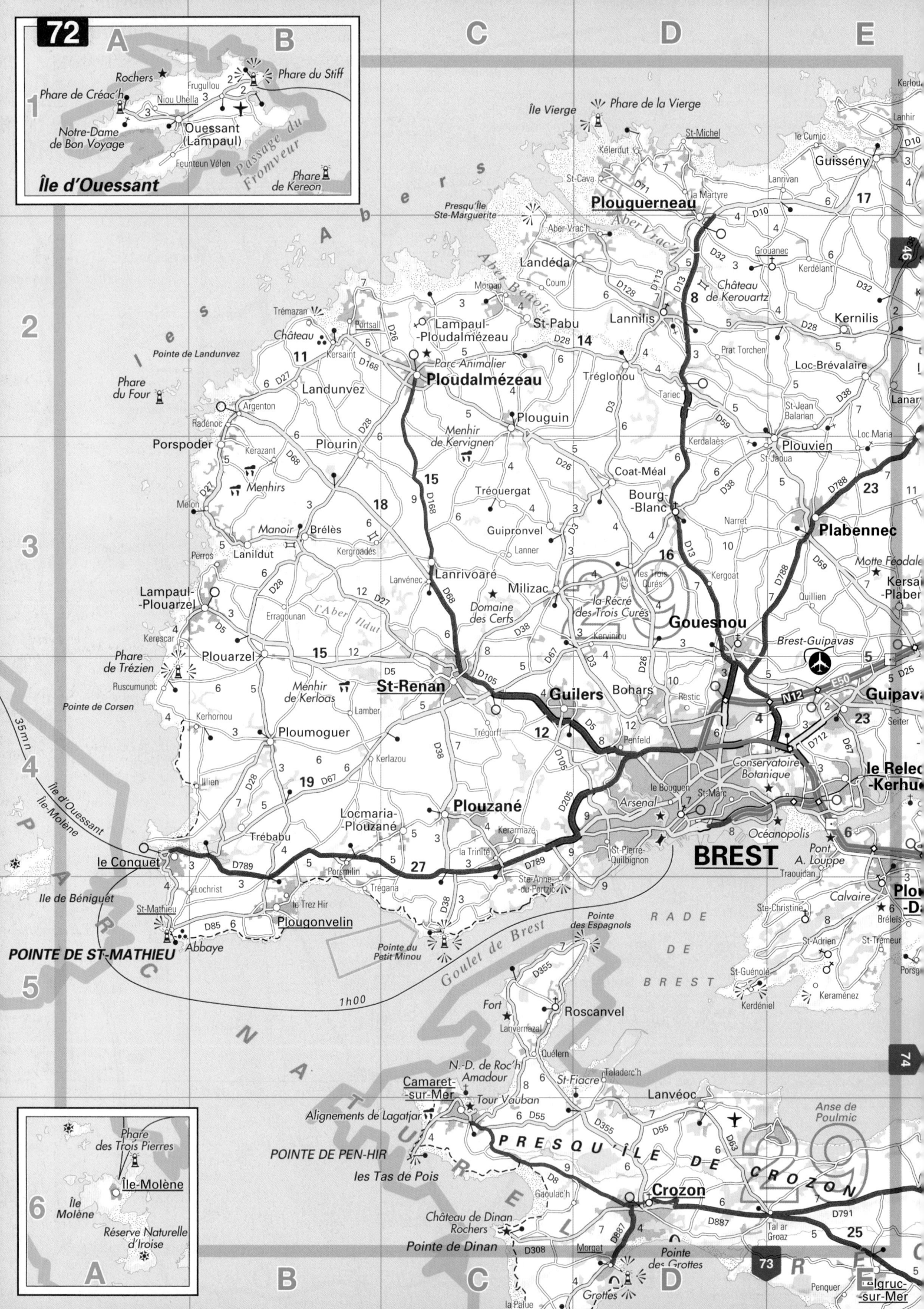

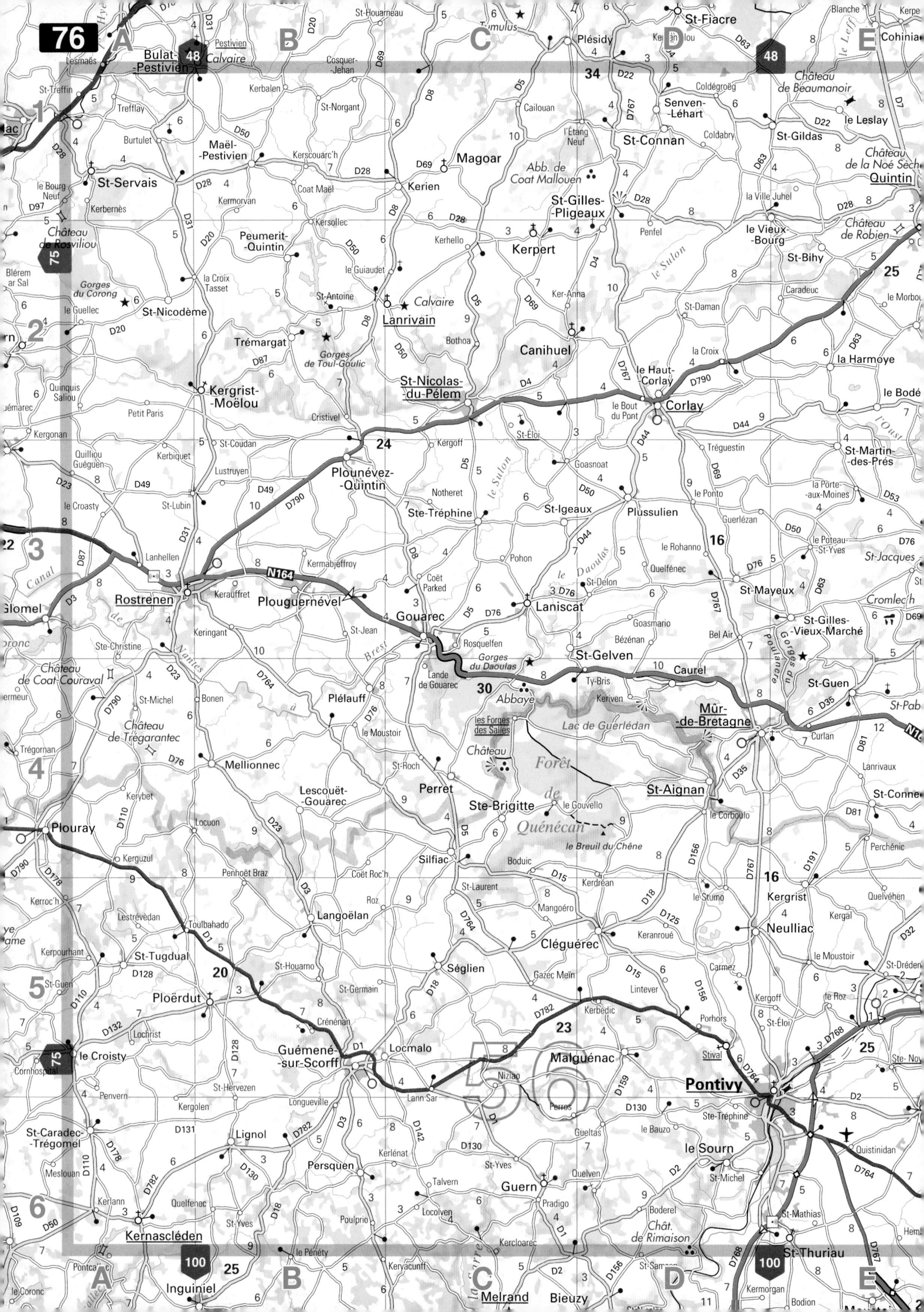

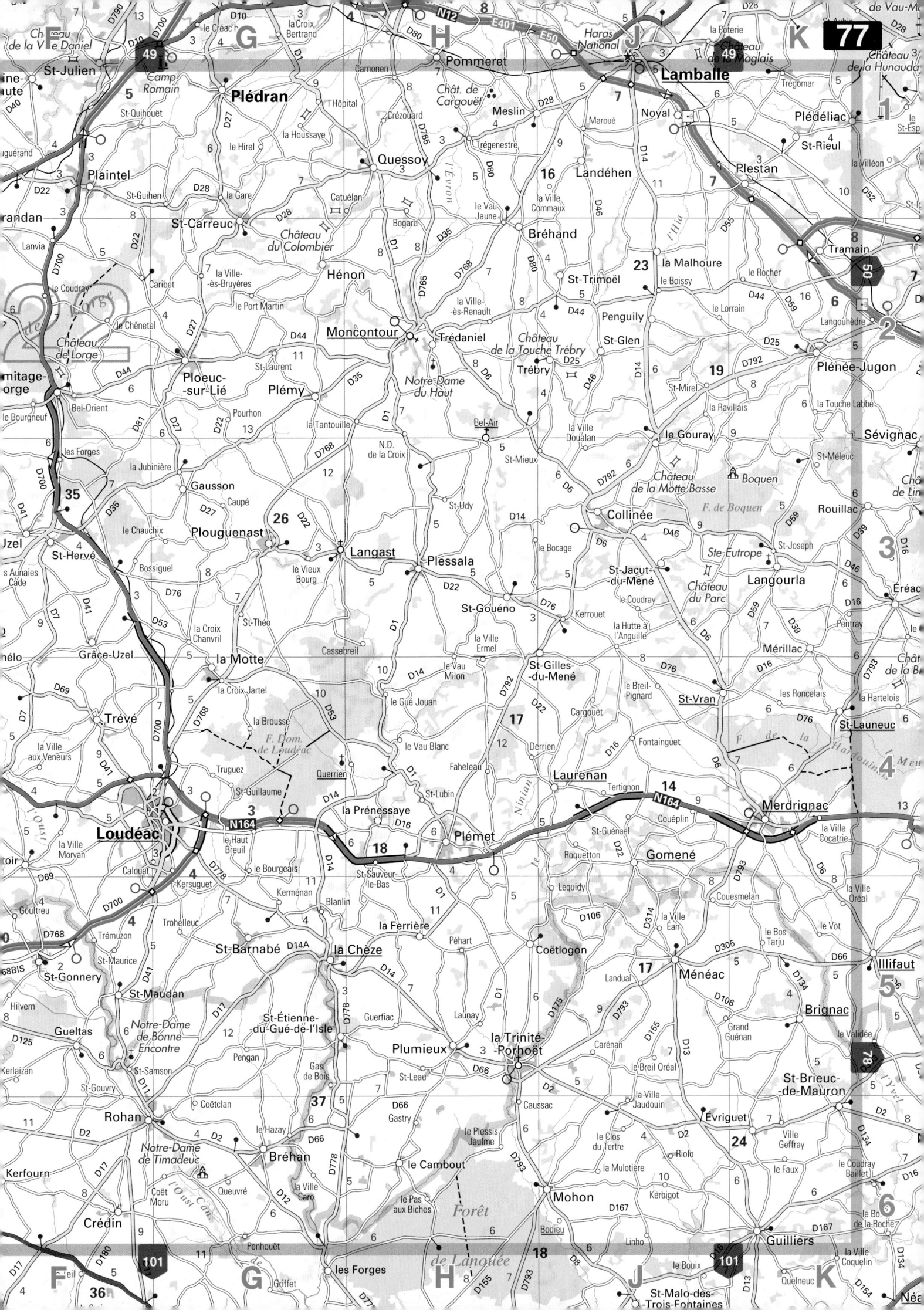

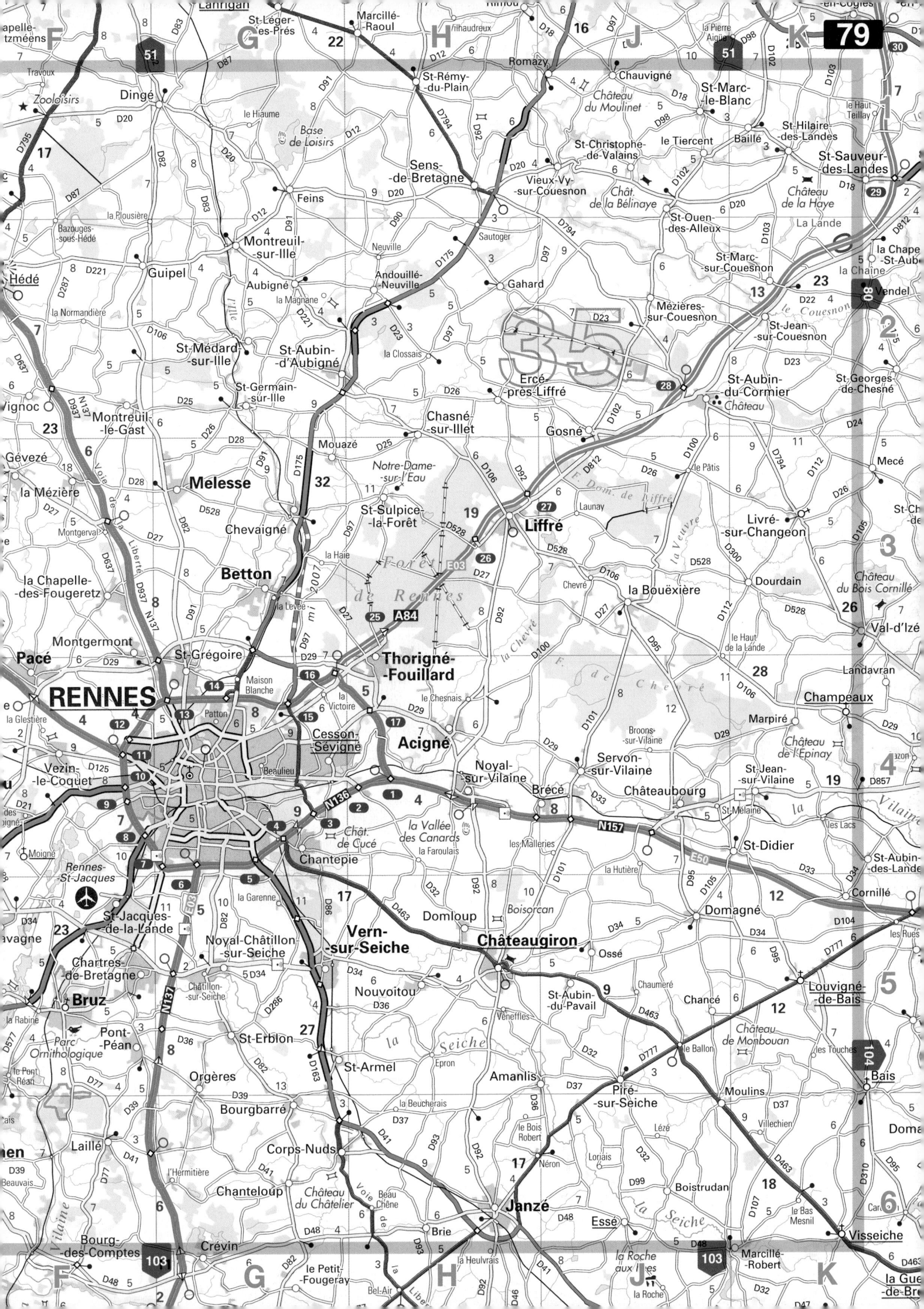

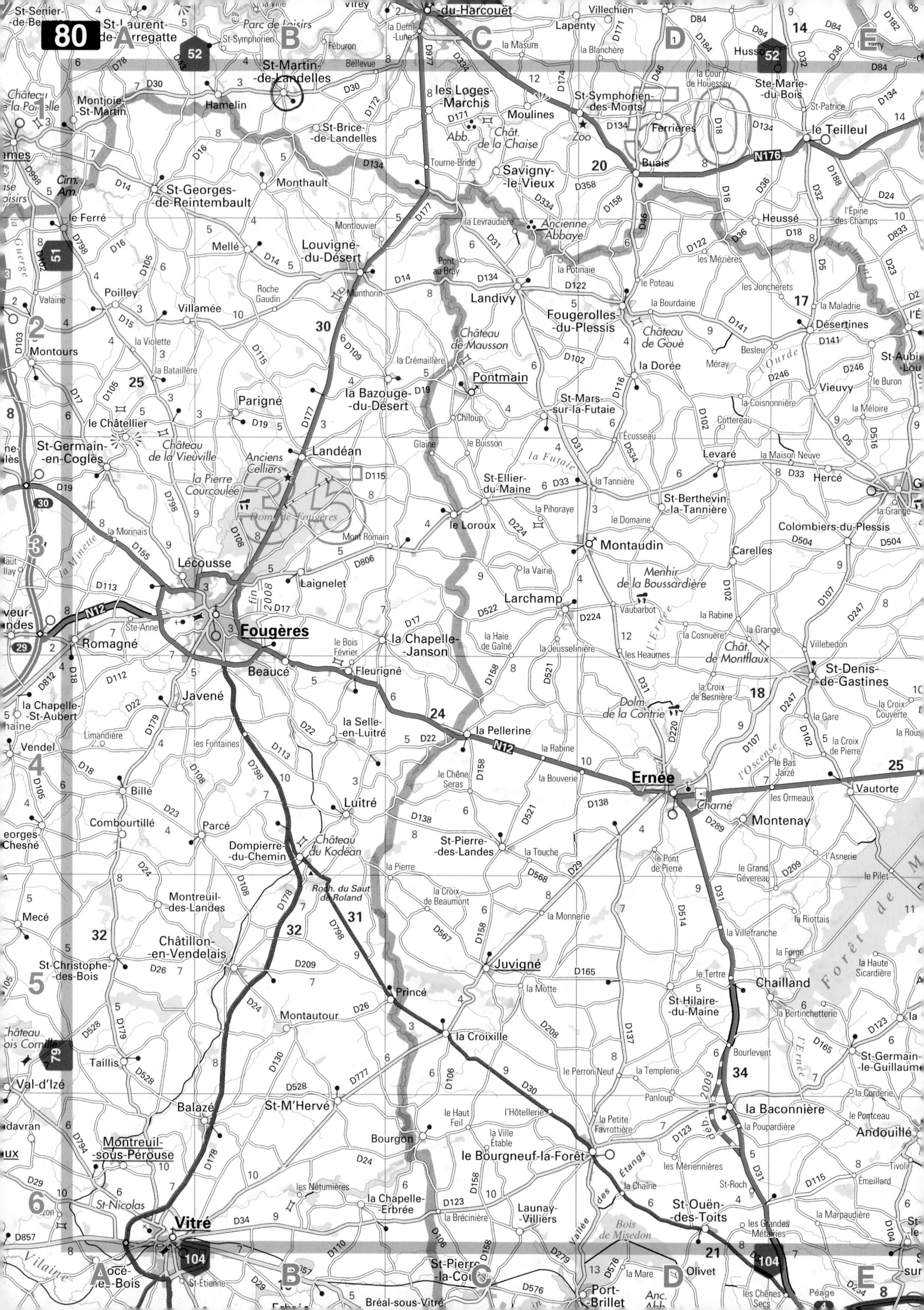

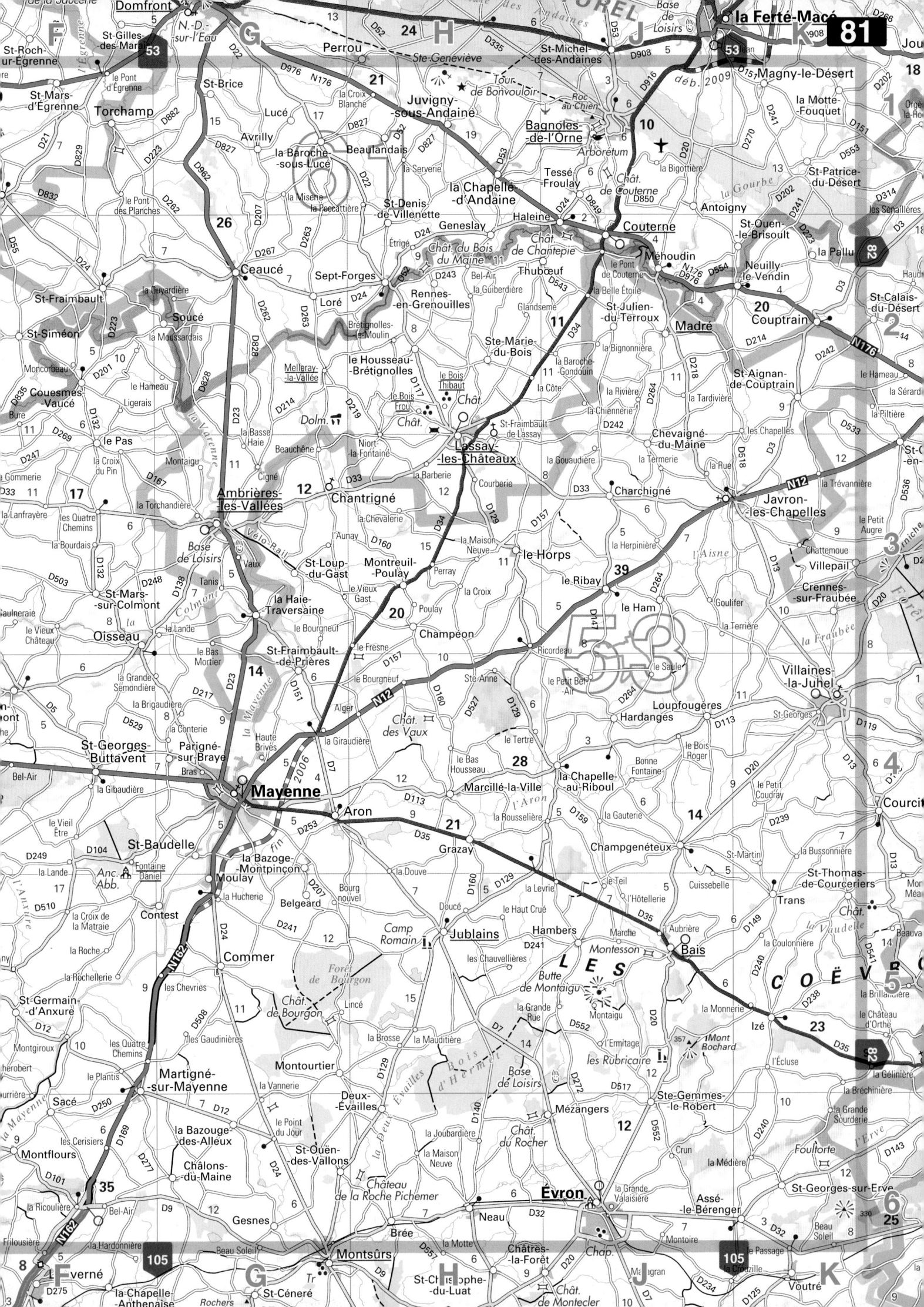

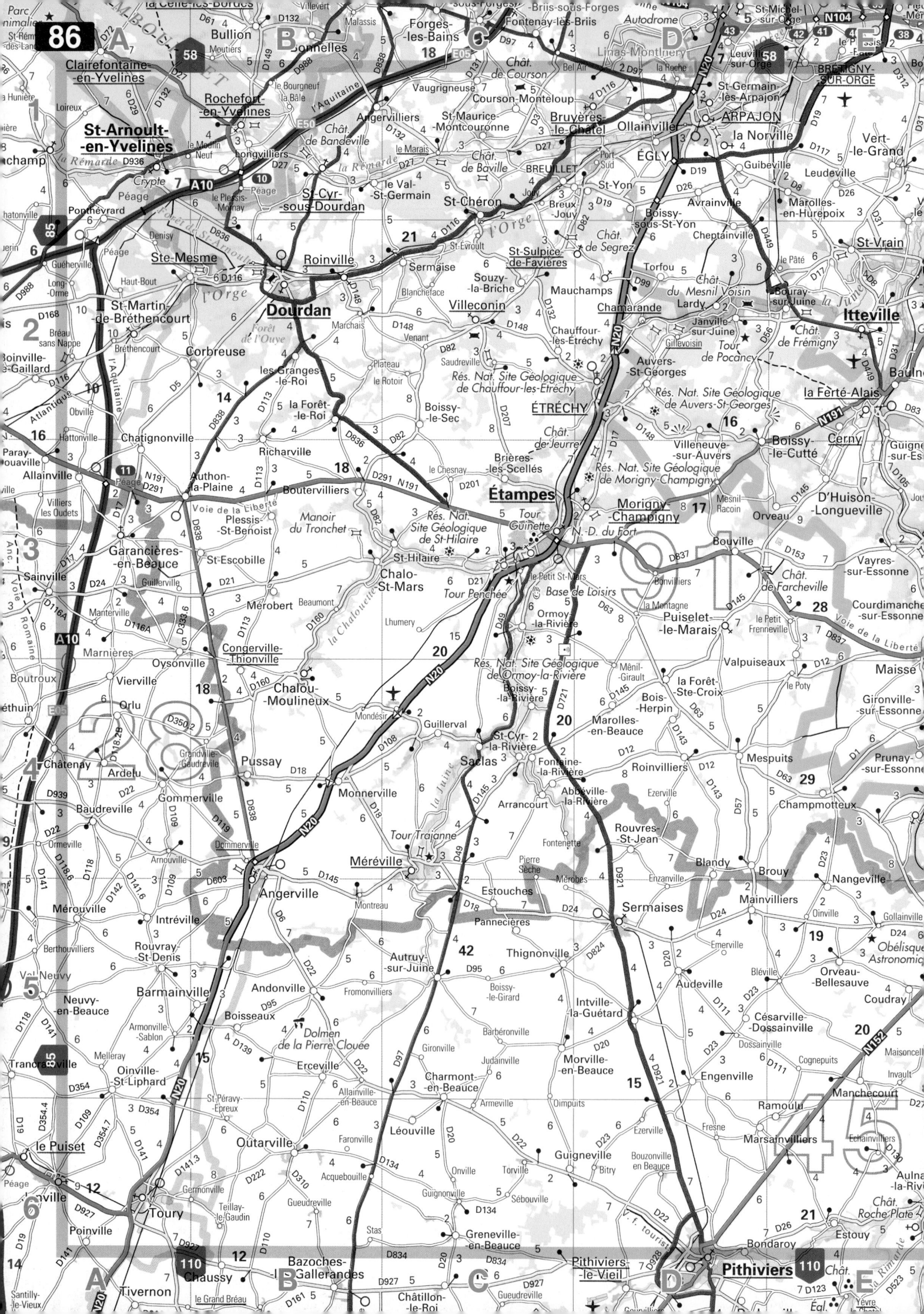

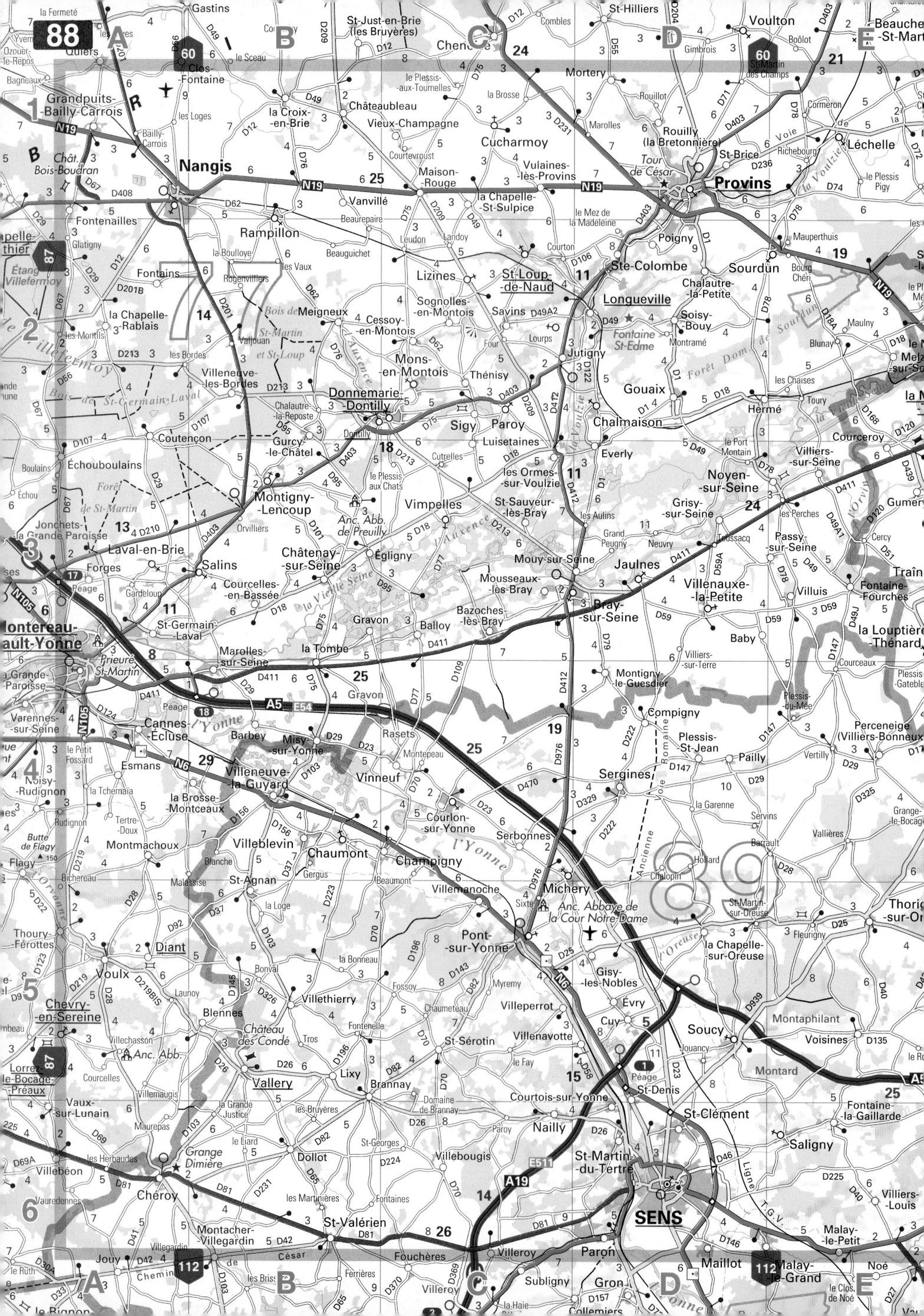

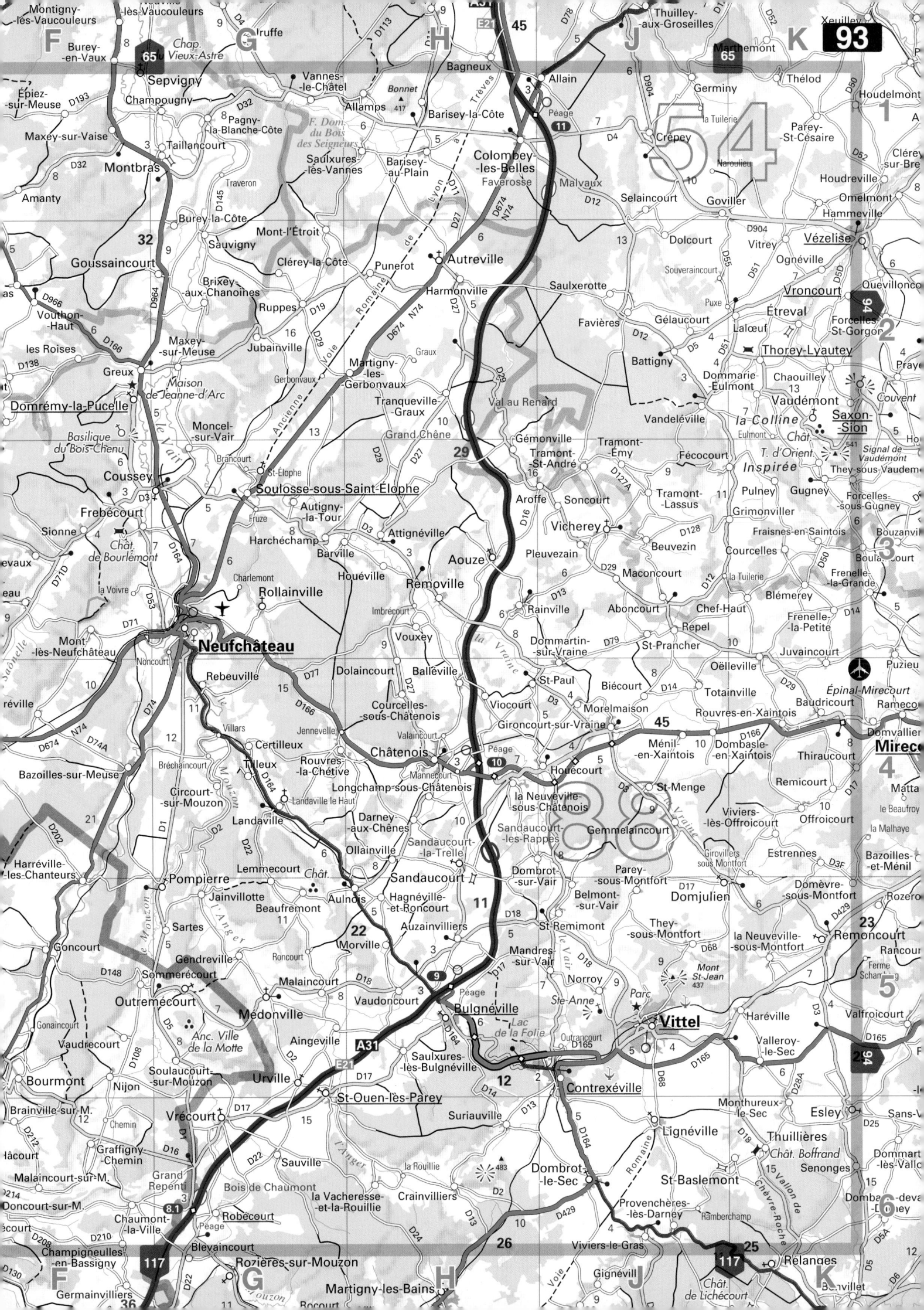

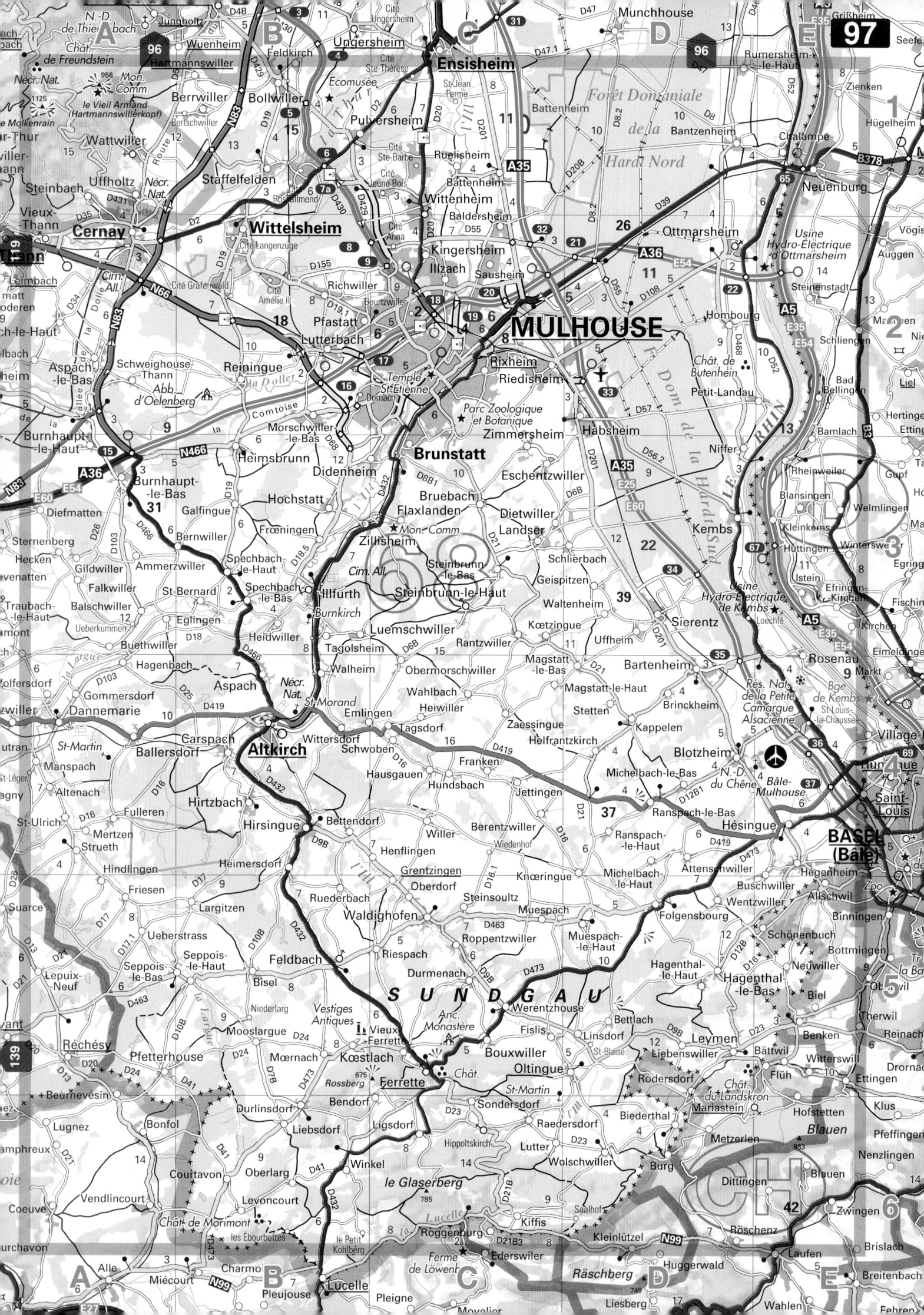

A-ler-sur-Goyen
74
D243
le Fort
D43
23
D56
12
le Stangala
Odet-Lois
E l'Odet

D57
Gourlizon
D765
QUIMPER
2008
74
St-André
D51
5
Quémenec
Lestonan
Château
Erqué-Gabéric
Kerdévot
25

la Trinité
8
Landudec
D784
Hent-Meur
5
Plonéis
D765
Kerfeunteun
Penhars
début
ouv.
Locmaria
3
D15
6
Chât.
D115
St-Yvi

zévet
1
Kerlaéron
D143
Kerstridic
31
3
Pluguffan
D40
Quimper-Pluguffan
8
D365
N365
9
5
D765
Kerdévot

Menhir
D2
Plogastel-St-Germain
D40
Kervéyen
St-Germain
7
Château Lanniron
Aquarive
D783
l'Arbre du Chapon
26
Lanvéron
11
N165
E60

Lababan
Pouldreuzic
D40
Zoo de la Pommeraie
24
St-Joseph
Plomelin
Baie de Kérogan
18
D34
11
St-Évarzec
Parc de Kersimomou

2
Plovan
D2
Peumérit
Tréogat
Ploneour-Lanvern
Languivoa
Tréméoc
Plomelin
Site des Vire-Court
Boutiguéry
Ty Glaz
Château du Pérennou
Gouesnach
D45
Pleuven
Prajou
la Forêt-Fouesnant
Ste-Anne
13
D44

Rés. Nat.
D156
D240
Barrage du Moulin Neuf
D785
Ménez Kerdréanton
Combrit
Clohars-Fouesnant
Chât. de Cheffontaines
Fouesnant
les Balnéides
D44

Étang de Trunvel
Tréguennec
D57
Kerbascol
Manoir de Trévilit
Kéréon
6
12
Pont-l'Abbé
D144
Ste-Marine
Bénodet
Perguet
le Potea Vert

3
St-Guénolé
Notre-Dame de Tronoën
Calvaire
Beuzec
N.-D. de Tréminou
Plomeur
12
Château de Kernuz
Chât. de Kérazan
D2
le Sillon
le Letty
Pont Henvez
Concarneau
Ville Close
Marinarium
Beg Meil
Pointe du Cabello

Notre-Dame de la Joie
Phare d'Eckmühl
St-Pierre
Menhir
Dolmen
Penmarch
D53
D57
Treffiagat
Plobannalec-Lesconil
Île-Tudy
Loctudy
Lodonnec
Anse de Bénodet
Pointe de Mousterlin

POINTE DE PENMARC'H
Kerity
Guilvinec
Léchiagat
Lesconil

4
Île aux Moutons

5
Réserve Naturelle de St-Nicolas-des-Glénans
Îles de Glénan

6

A B C D E

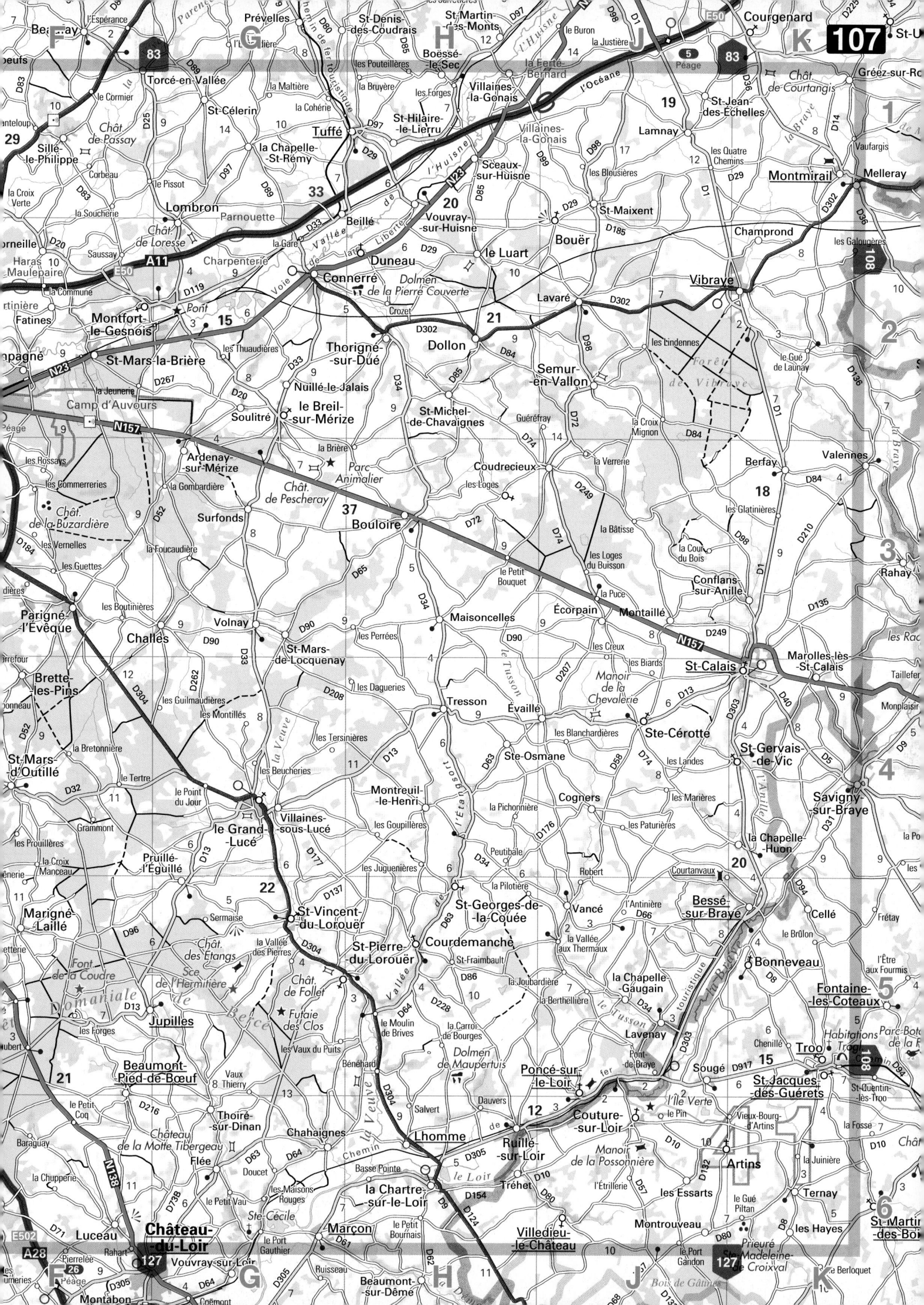

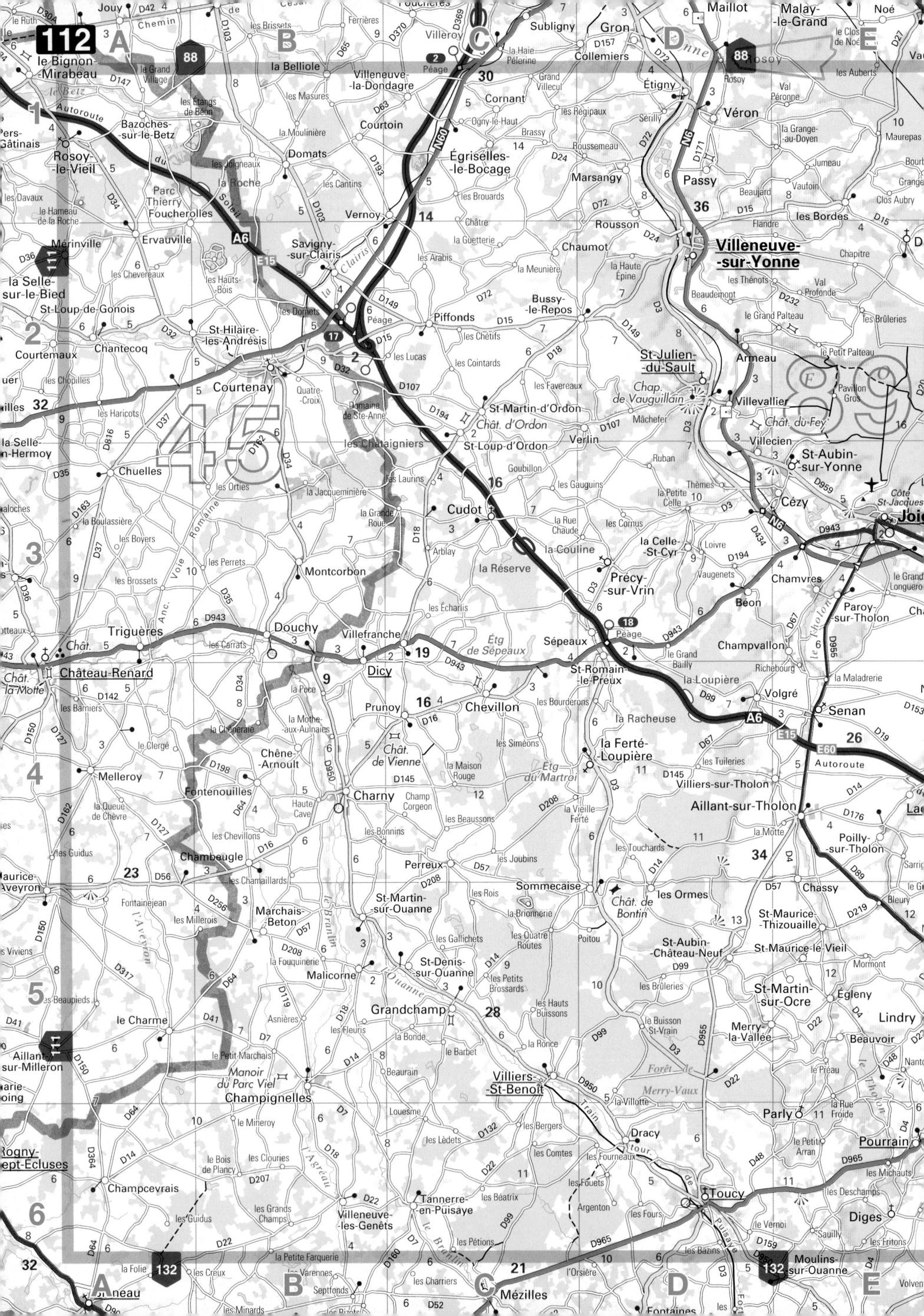

A   B   C   D   E

1

le Ménec   St-Michel   St-Philibert   Port Blanc   aux
St-Colomban   Carnac   12   la Trinité   Kerouarc'h   Larmor-Baden   Kergo
D186   8   Carnac-   -sur-Mer   Locmariaguer   Ile aux M
10   Plage   100   Penhap

Penthièvre   Côte des Mégalithes   Dolmen des   Kerners
15   Marchands   Tumulus
Kerhostin   Pointe de   de César
Portivy   Kerpenhir   Port-   Kerners   Arzon   7
Navalo
Pointe du Percho   St-Pierre-Quiberon   le Net
PRESQU'ÎLE   Port
DE QUIBERON   Beg Rohu   B a i e   du Crouesty   D7

Côte Sauvage   Kerniscob   4
5   d e   St-Gildas-
15   Port-Haliguen   Q u i b e r o n   de-Rhuys

2   Pointe du Conguel
Quiberon   Îlot de Toul Braz
Phare de la Teignouse

Passage de la Teignouse

Pointe des Poulains
3   Fort   Île-d'Houat
Sarah-Bernardt   Sauzon   Site Archéologique
Grotte   Île d'Houat
de l'Apothicairerie   Grotte de
Port Fouquet
3   Pointe   Île d'Hœdic
Tum.   de Taillefer   île aux Chevaux
BELLE-ÎLE   Menh.   Citadelle
Kerlédan   D30   9   le Palais   Hœdic
8   D190
Port de Donnant   D25   4
Donnant   Bangor
Port Coton   7   Samzun
Aiguilles   D190   Grand Phare   Pointe
4   Port Goulphar   de Kerdonis
Domois   le Grand   9   D25
Cosquet   Locmaria

Pointe du Skeul

5

6

A   B   C   D   E

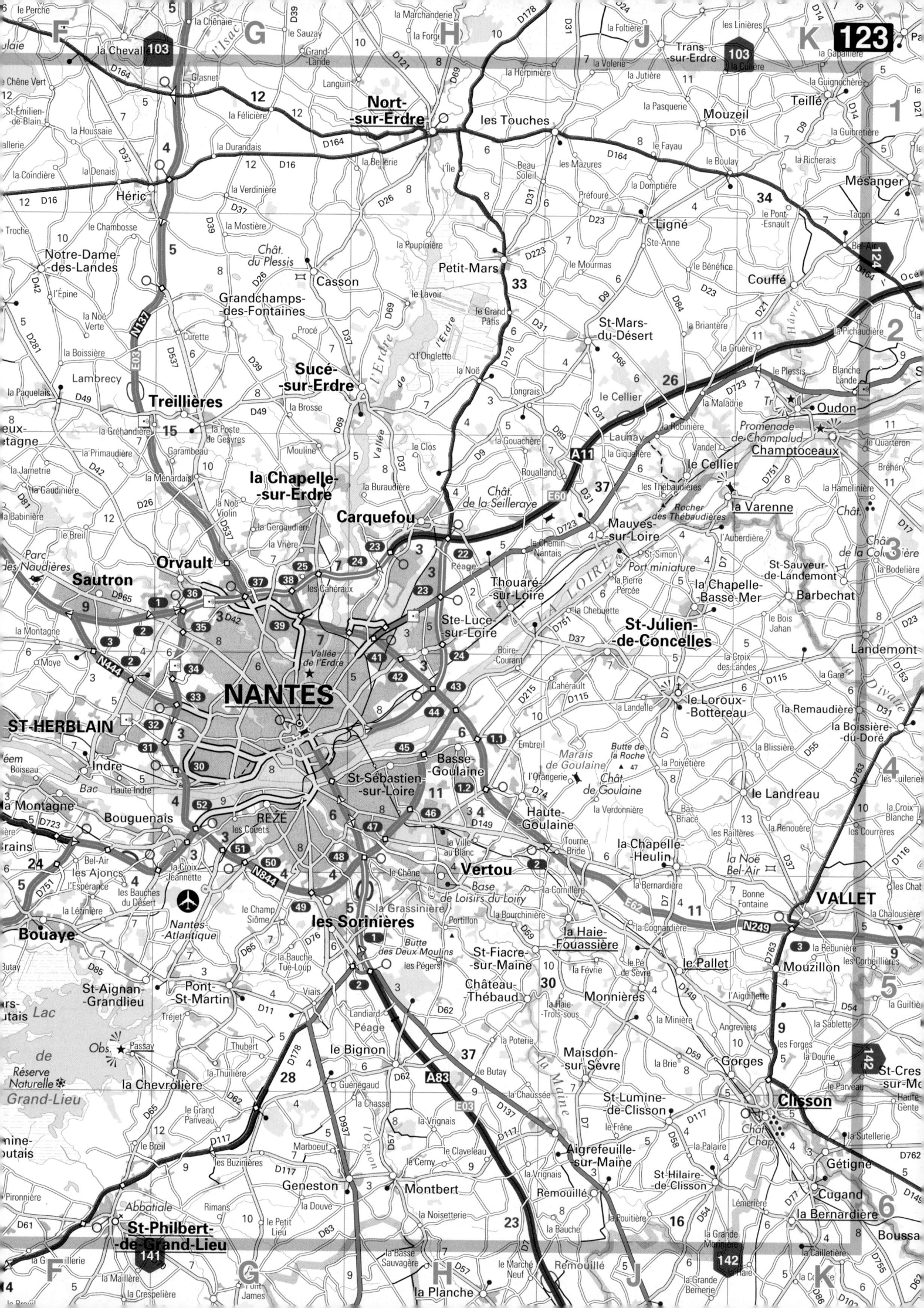

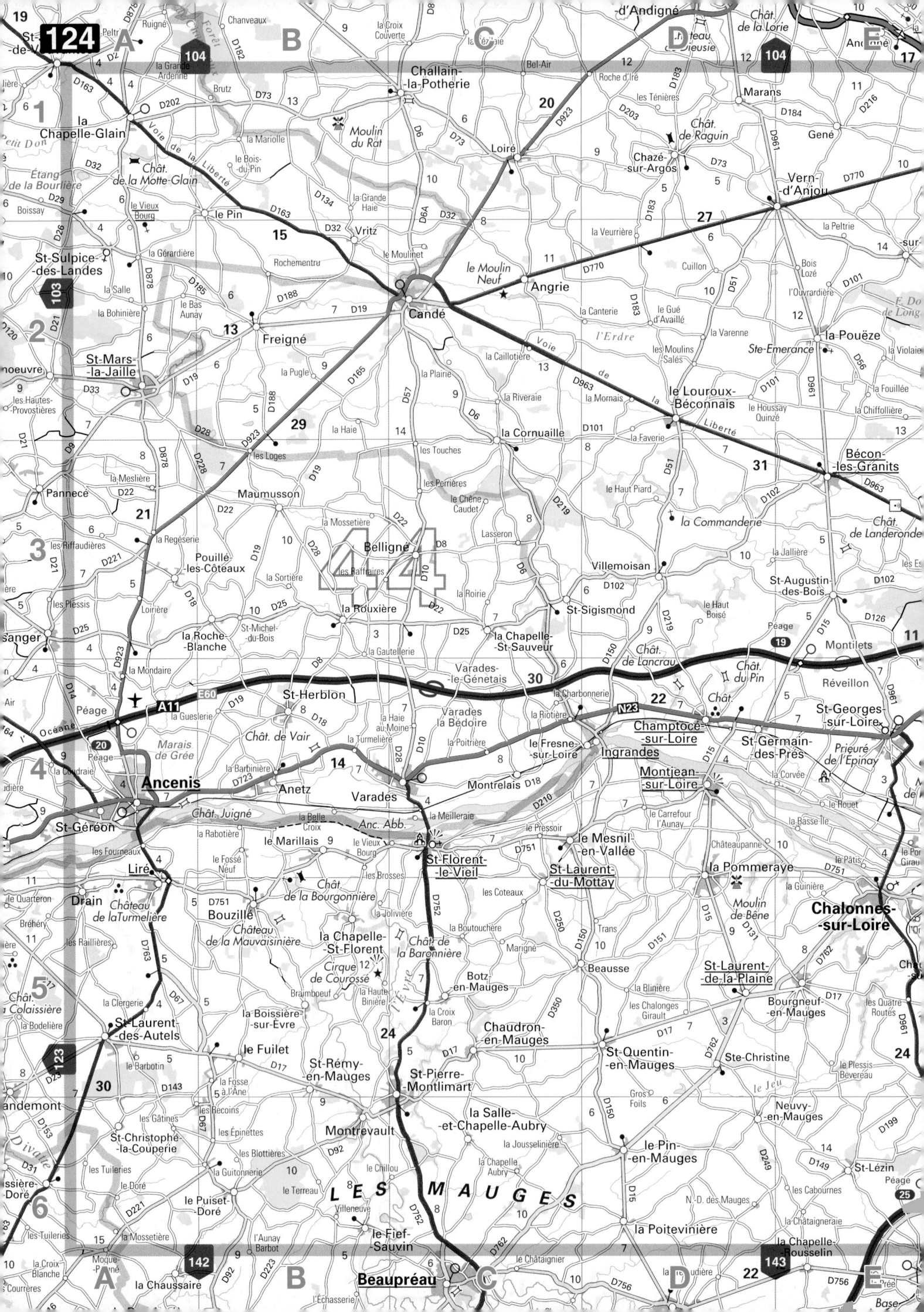

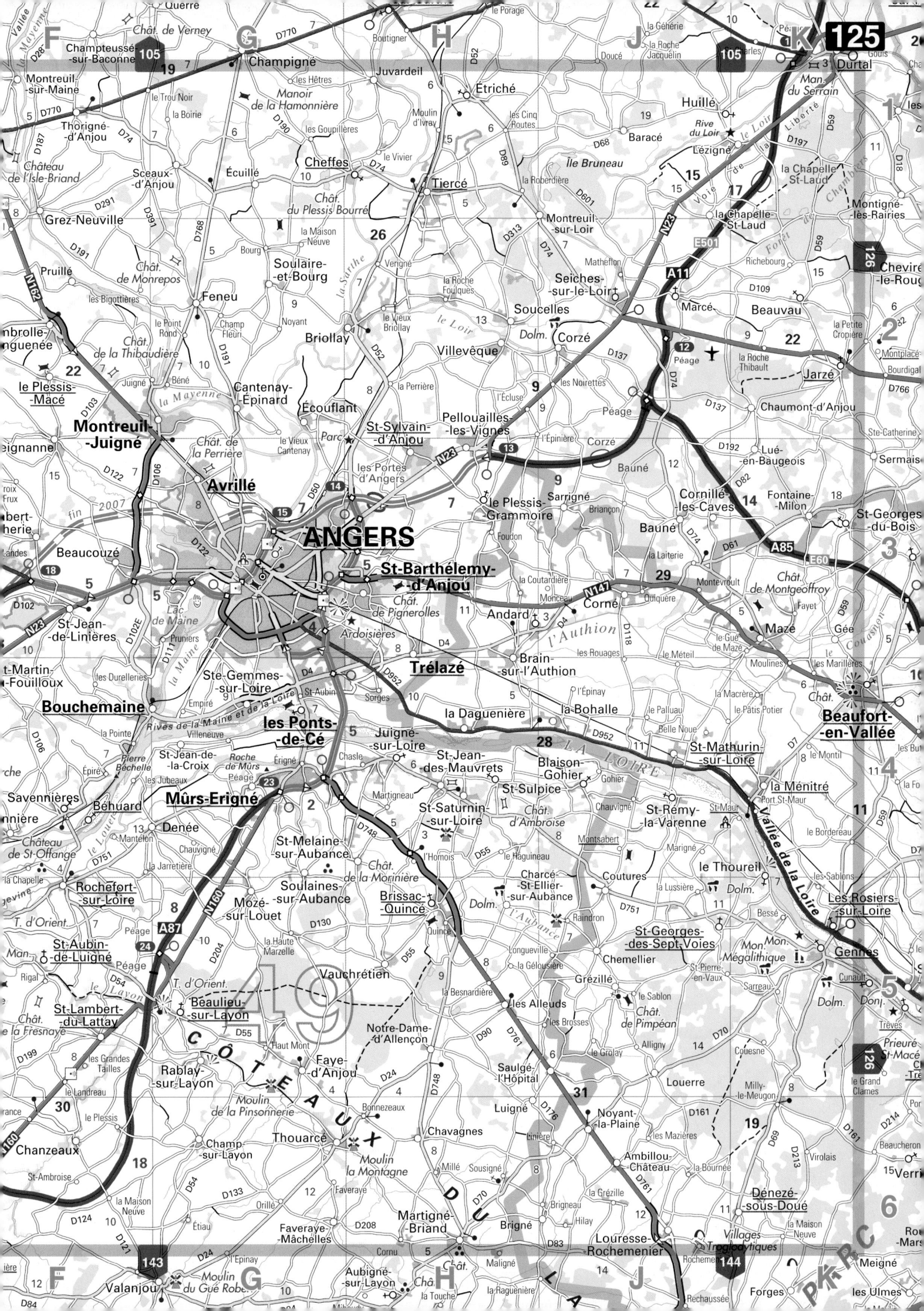

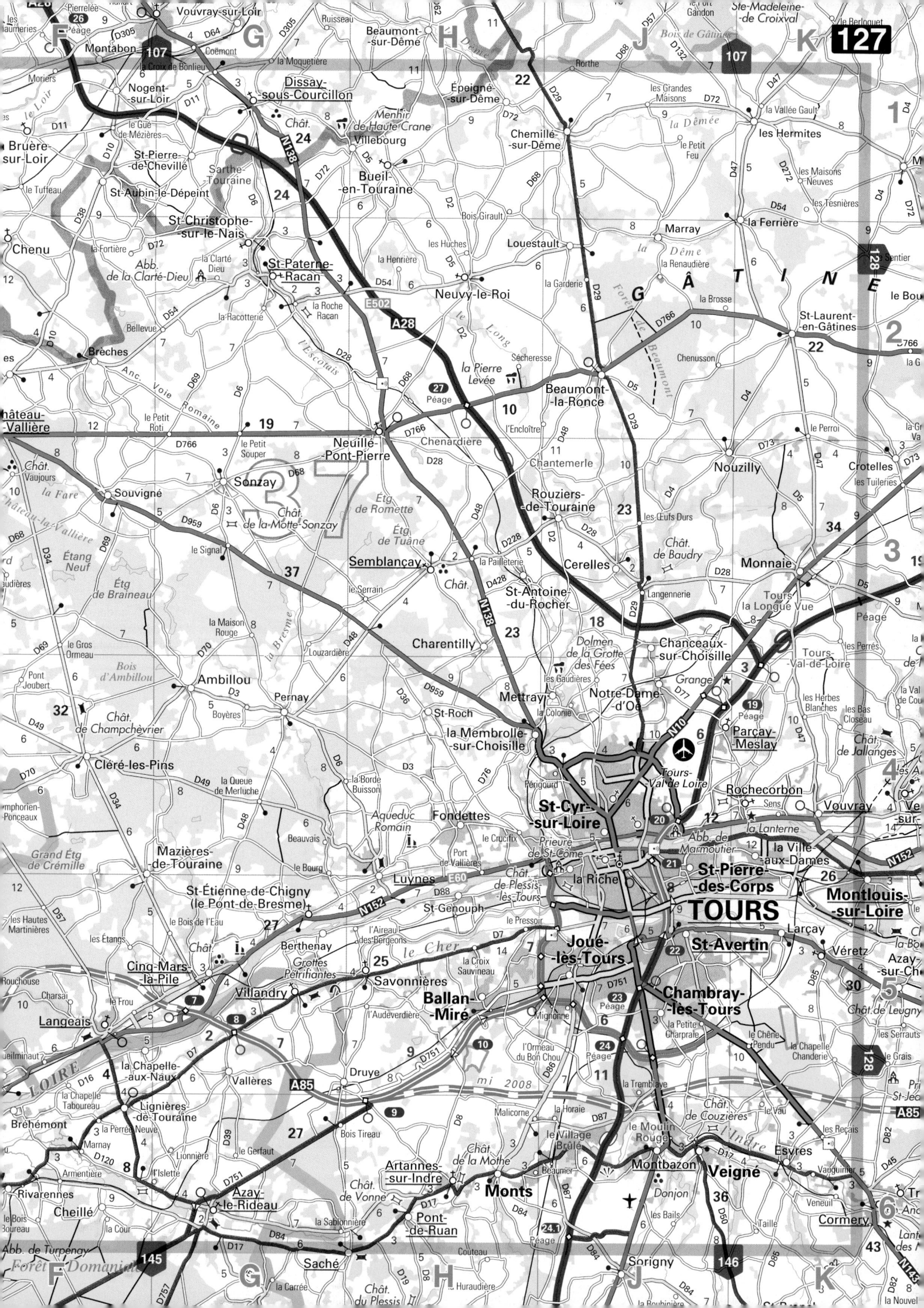

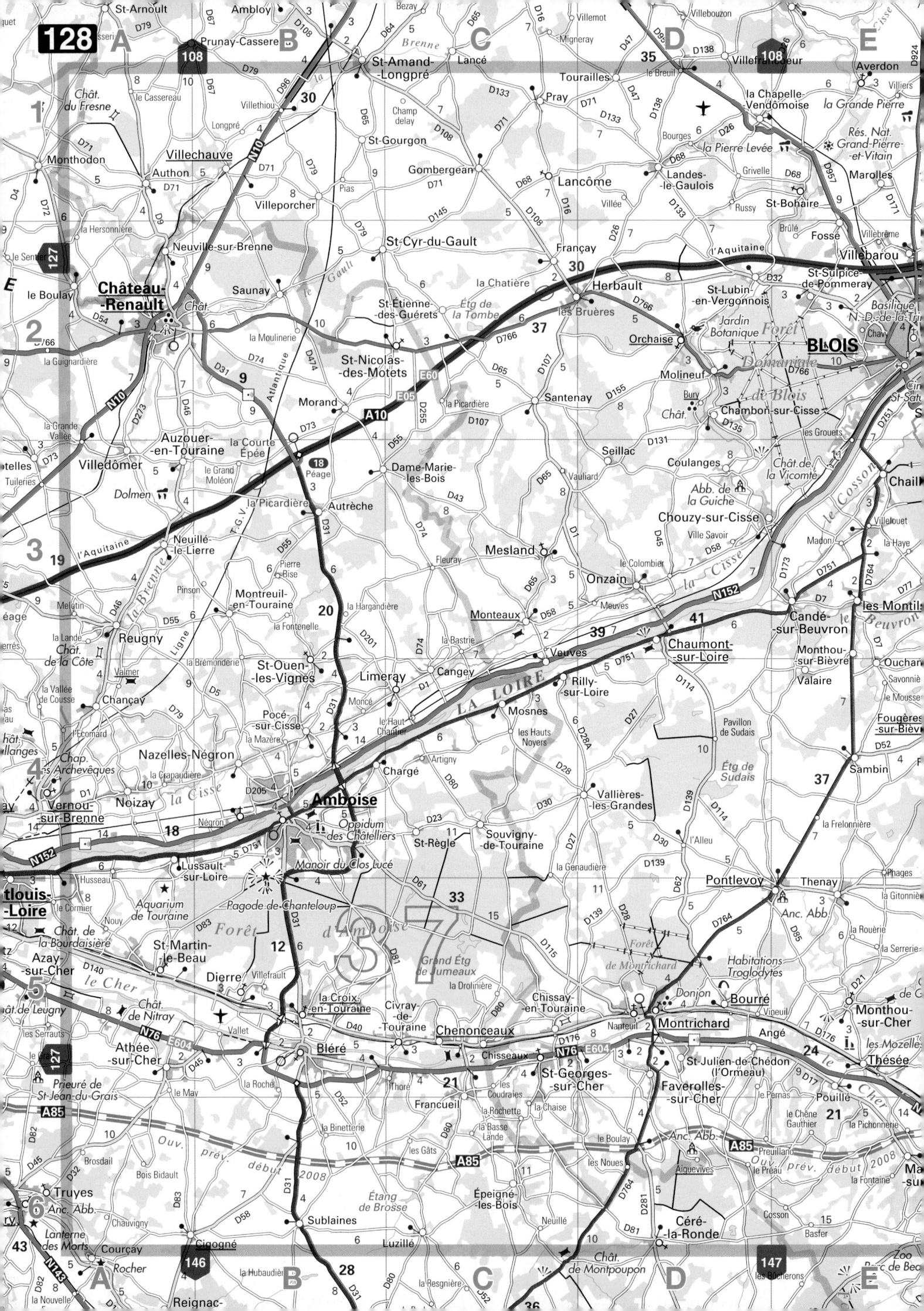

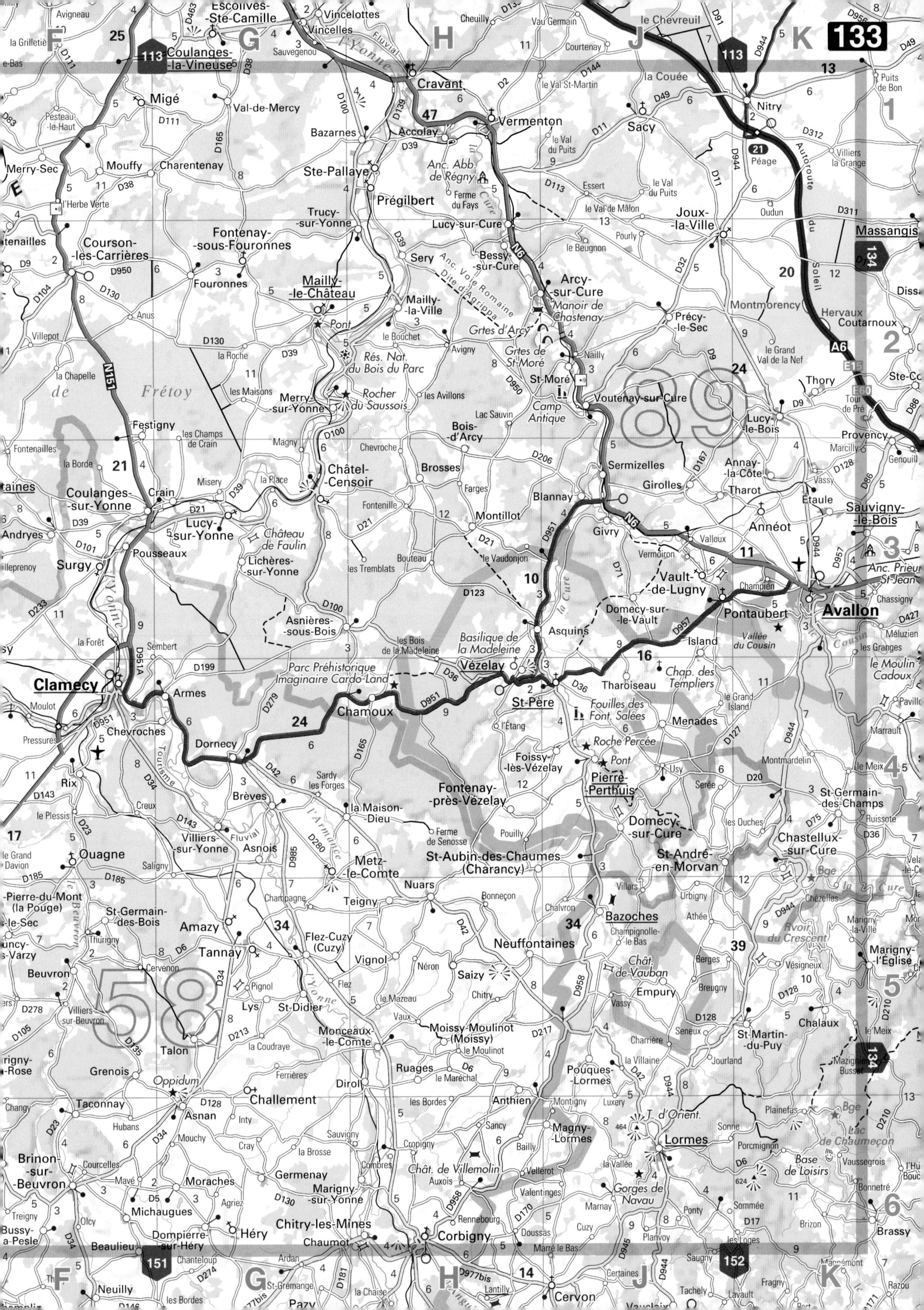

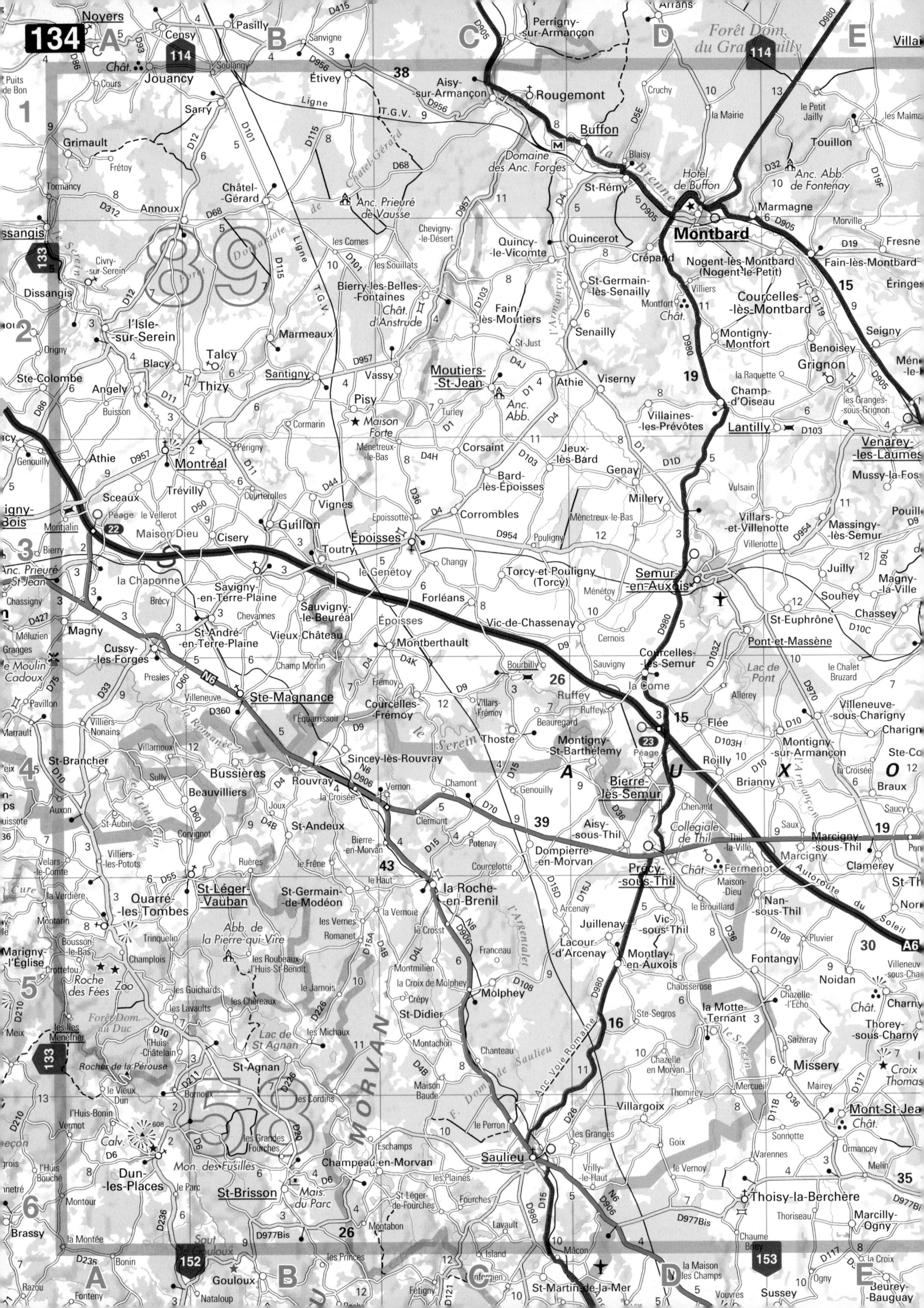

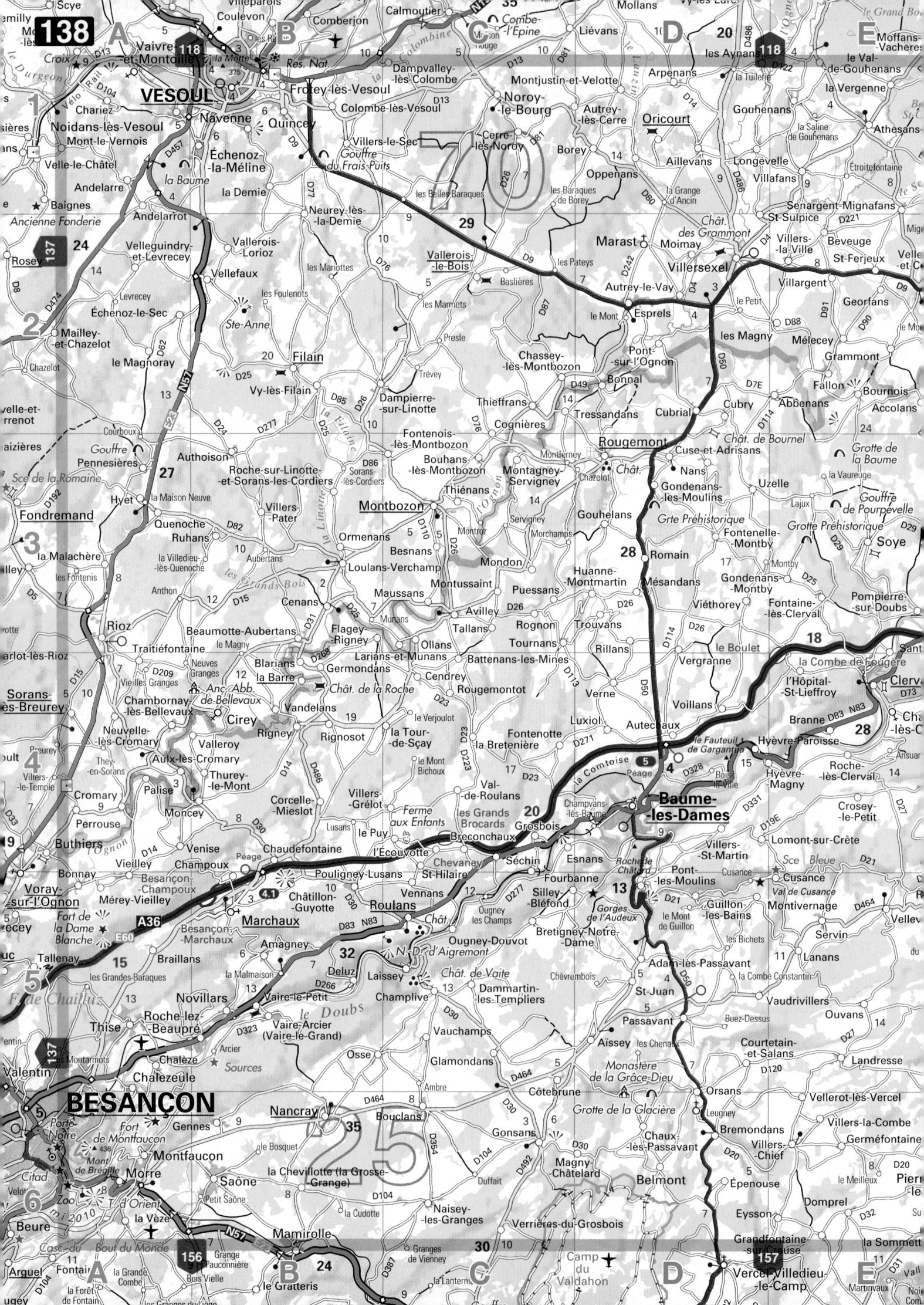

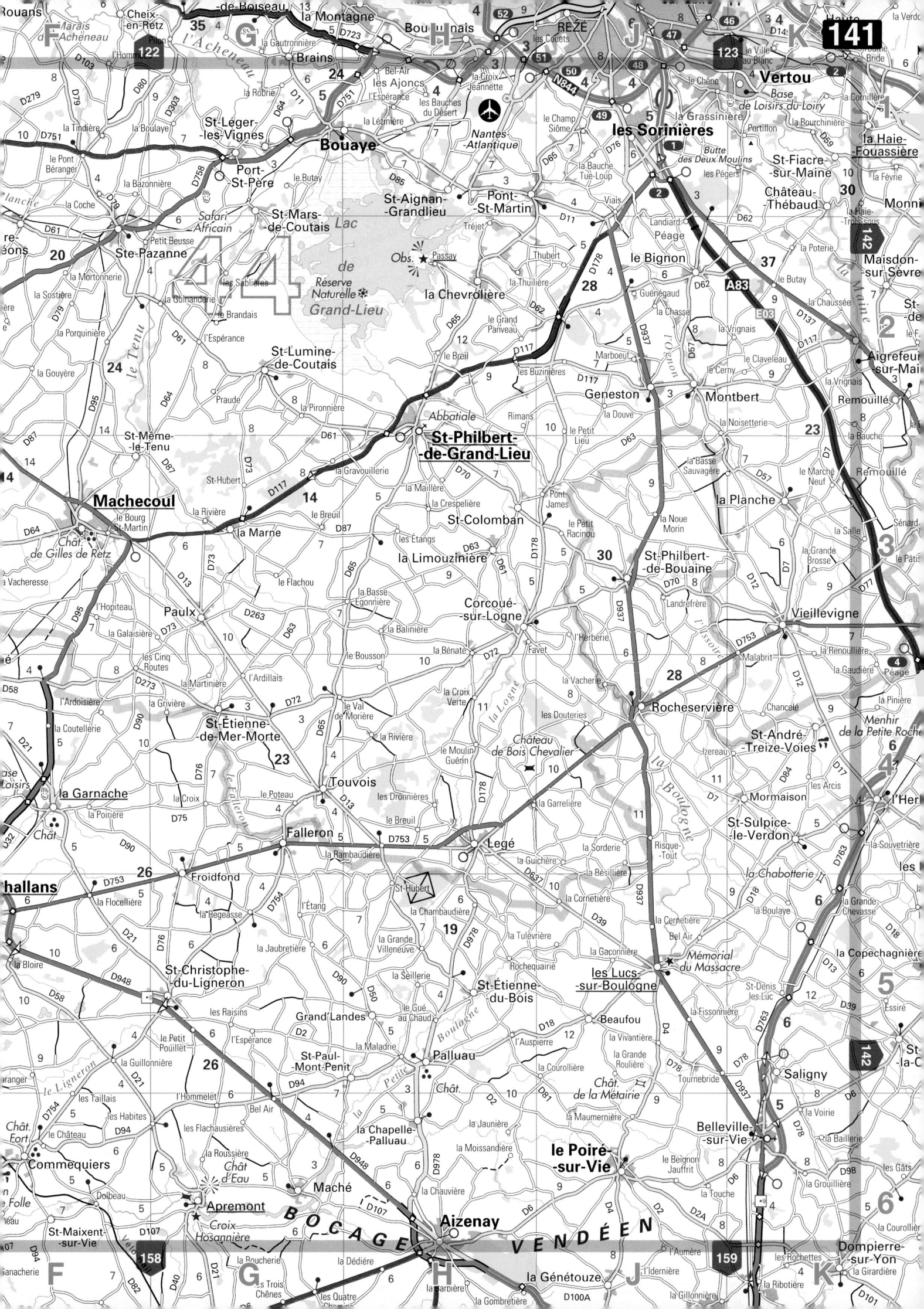

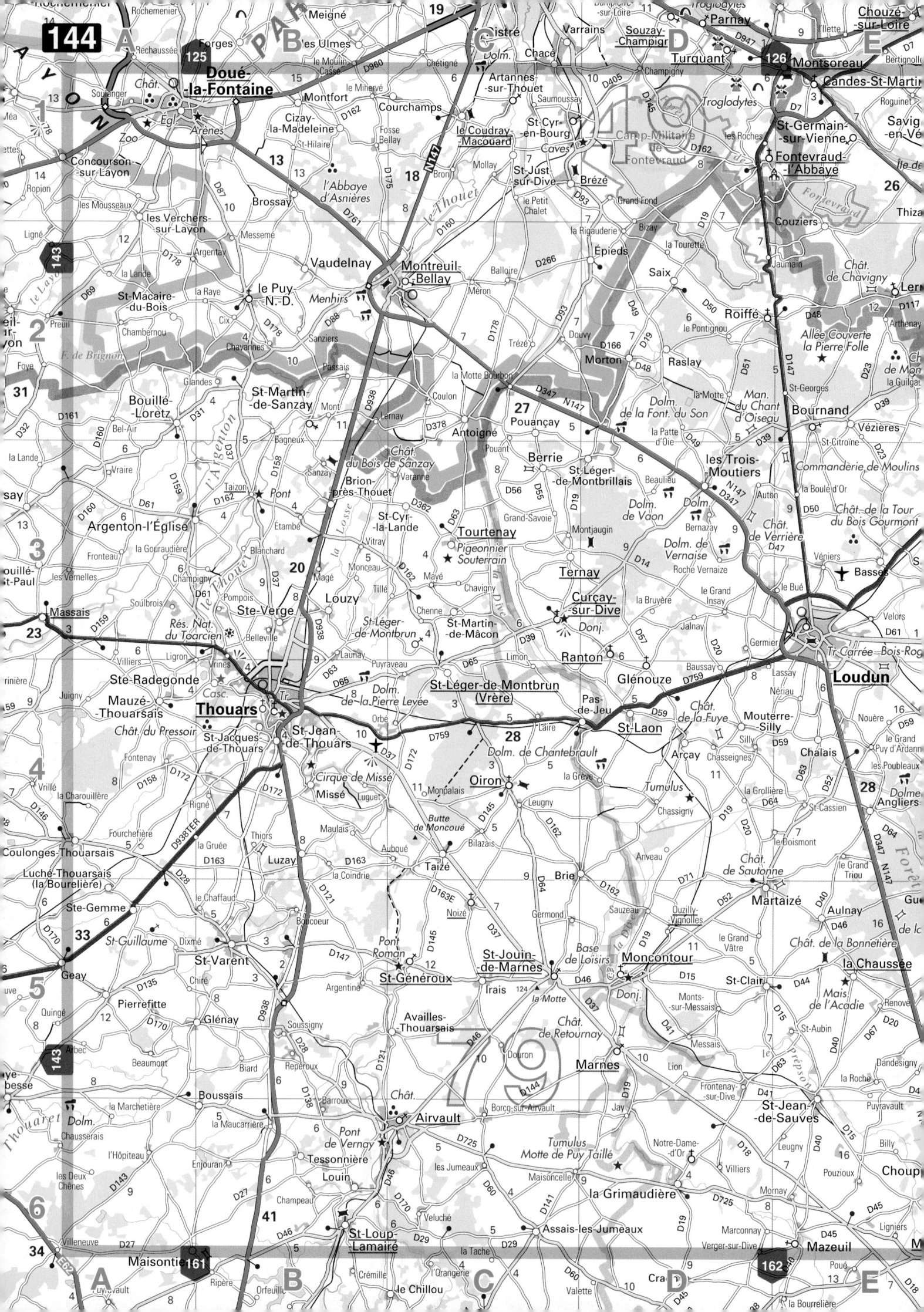

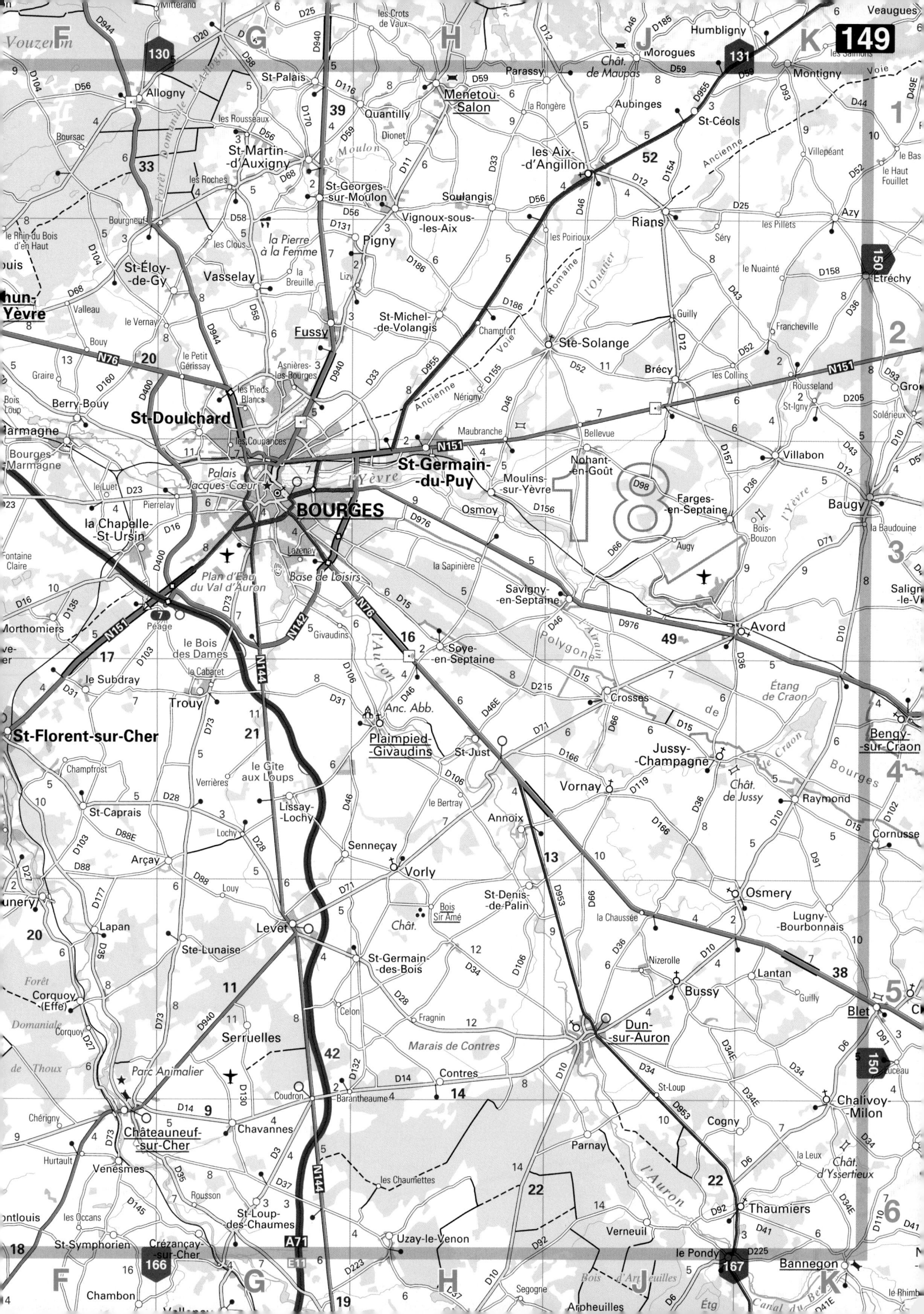

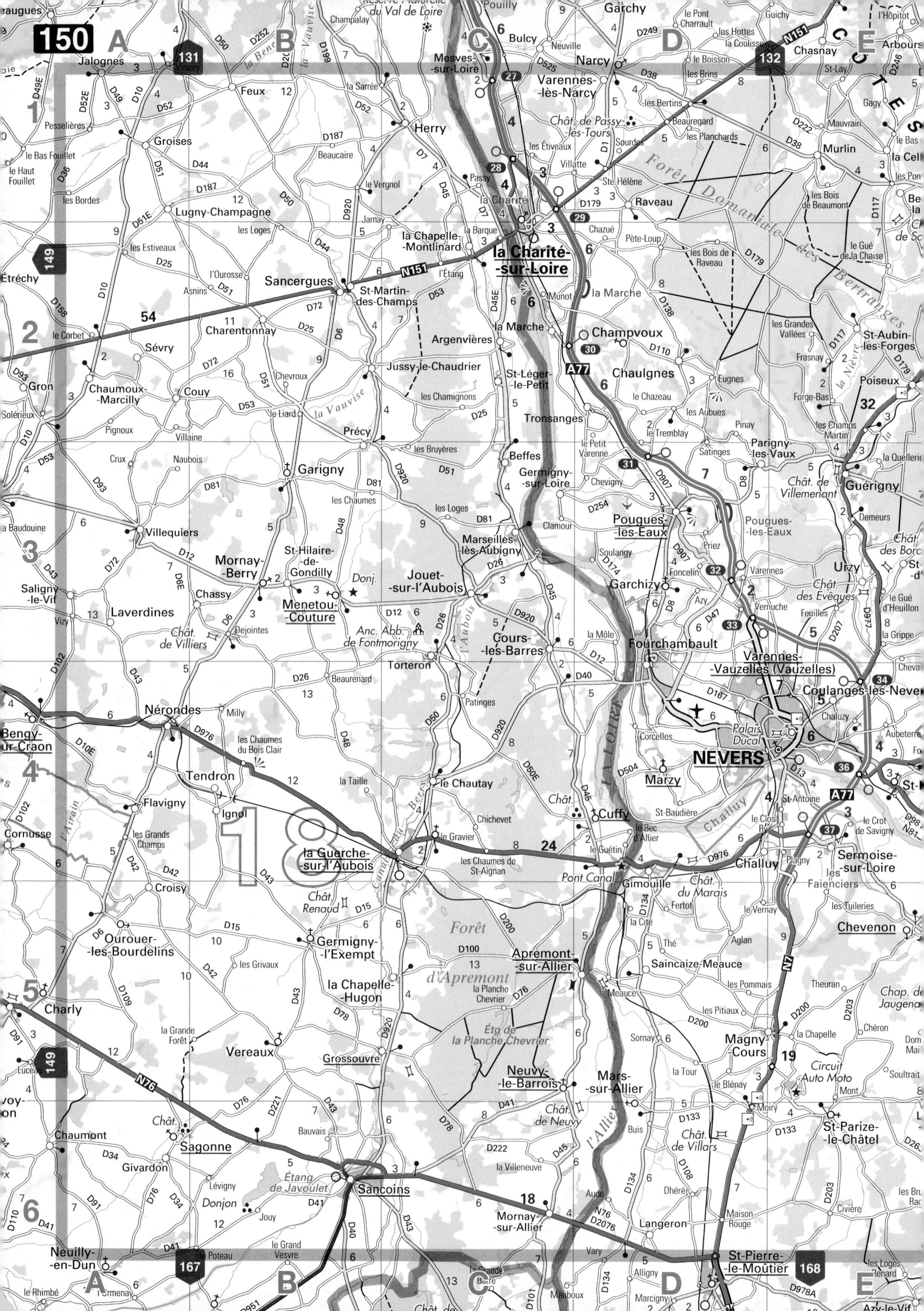

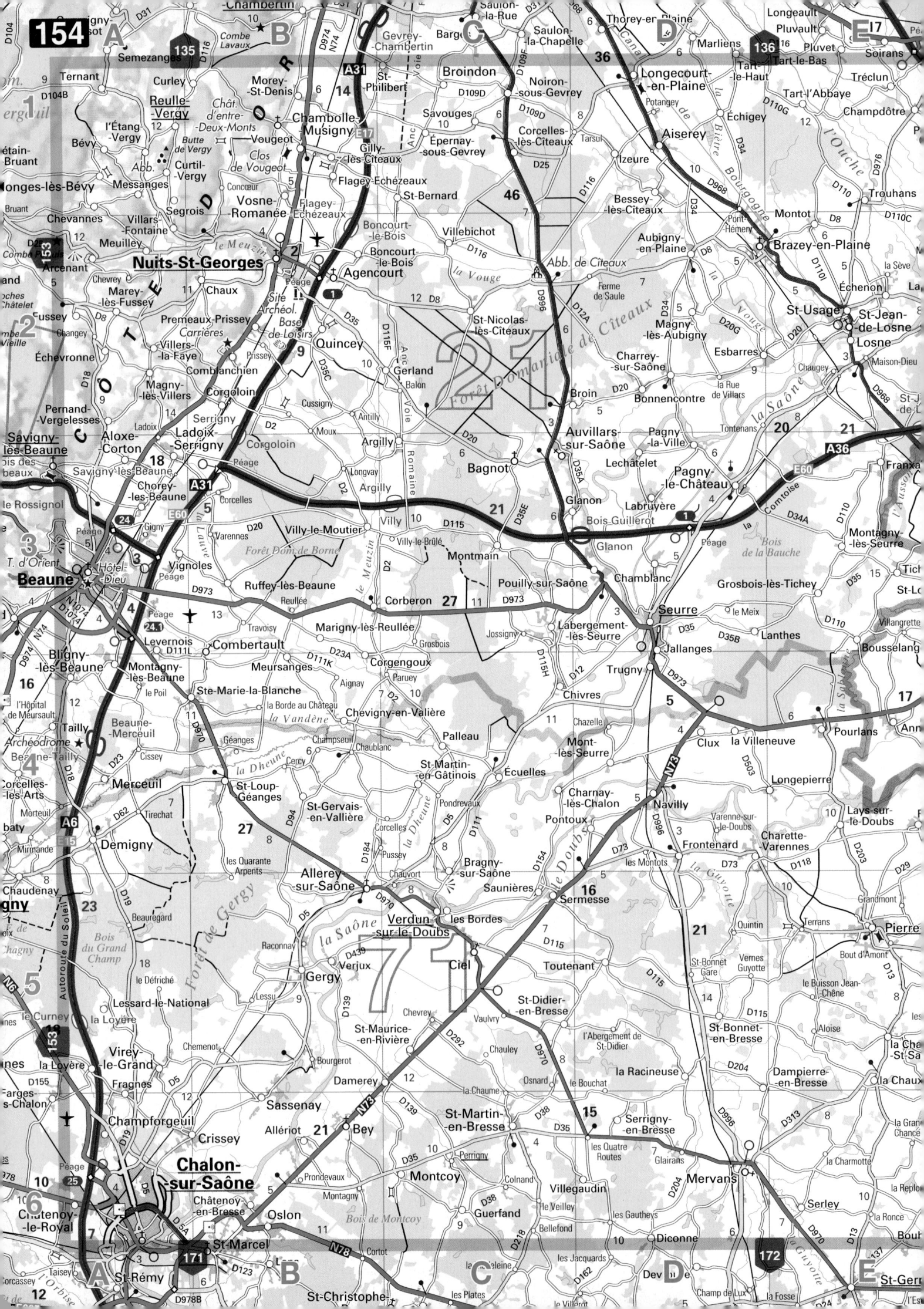

St-Hilaire-de-Riez

le Plessis
le Fenouiller
la Ganacherie
Sion sur l'Océan
D754
141
la Largerie
D82
St-Gilles-
-Croix-de-Vie
Corniche Vendéenne
D6A
D6
St-Révérend
l'Aiguillon-
-sur-Vie
28
Jardi
Givrand
D42
la Faver
D38
Chât.
de Beaumarchais
Lac
du Jaunay
D32
D40
le Pré
la Sauzaie
D12
la Chaize-
-Giraud
le Noyer
Landevieille
la Parée
D32
Bretignolles-
-sur-Mer
la Fremière
le Pl
le Marais Girard
St-Nicolas
de Brem
Parc
de Loisirs
D54
Vairé
Brem-sur-Mer
31
D38
les Granges
Menhir
la Conche Verte
D80
F Dom. d'Olonne
la Salaire
la Burelière
l'Île-
-d'Olonne
D87
Champclou
la Bauduère
Olonne-
-sur-Mer
la Girvière
Gahou
la Chaume
Fort St-Nicolas
Phare de l'Armandèche
les Sables-
-d'Olonne
Zoo
la Pironnière
Puits d'Enfer
Baie de

Pertuis
Breton
Phare
des Baleines
les Portes-en-Ré
D101
le Gillieux
Rés. Nat.
de Lileau
des Niges
B. de
Trousse-Chemise
St-Clément-des-Baleines
(le Chabot)
D735
Loix
Ars-en-Ré
la Passe
D735
St-Martin-de-Ré
D103
la Flotte
Anc. Abb.
des Châteliers
la Couarde-sur-Mer
D201
le Morinant
le Bois-Plage-en-Ré
les Gros Joncs
Fort de
la Prée
Ph.
de Chanchardon
Ensembles Littoraux et Marais
de l'Île de Ré
D201E1
Rivedoux-
-Plage
D735
ÎLE DE RÉ
D201
la Noue
Sablanceaux
Ste-Marie-
-de-Ré
Ph.
de Chauveau

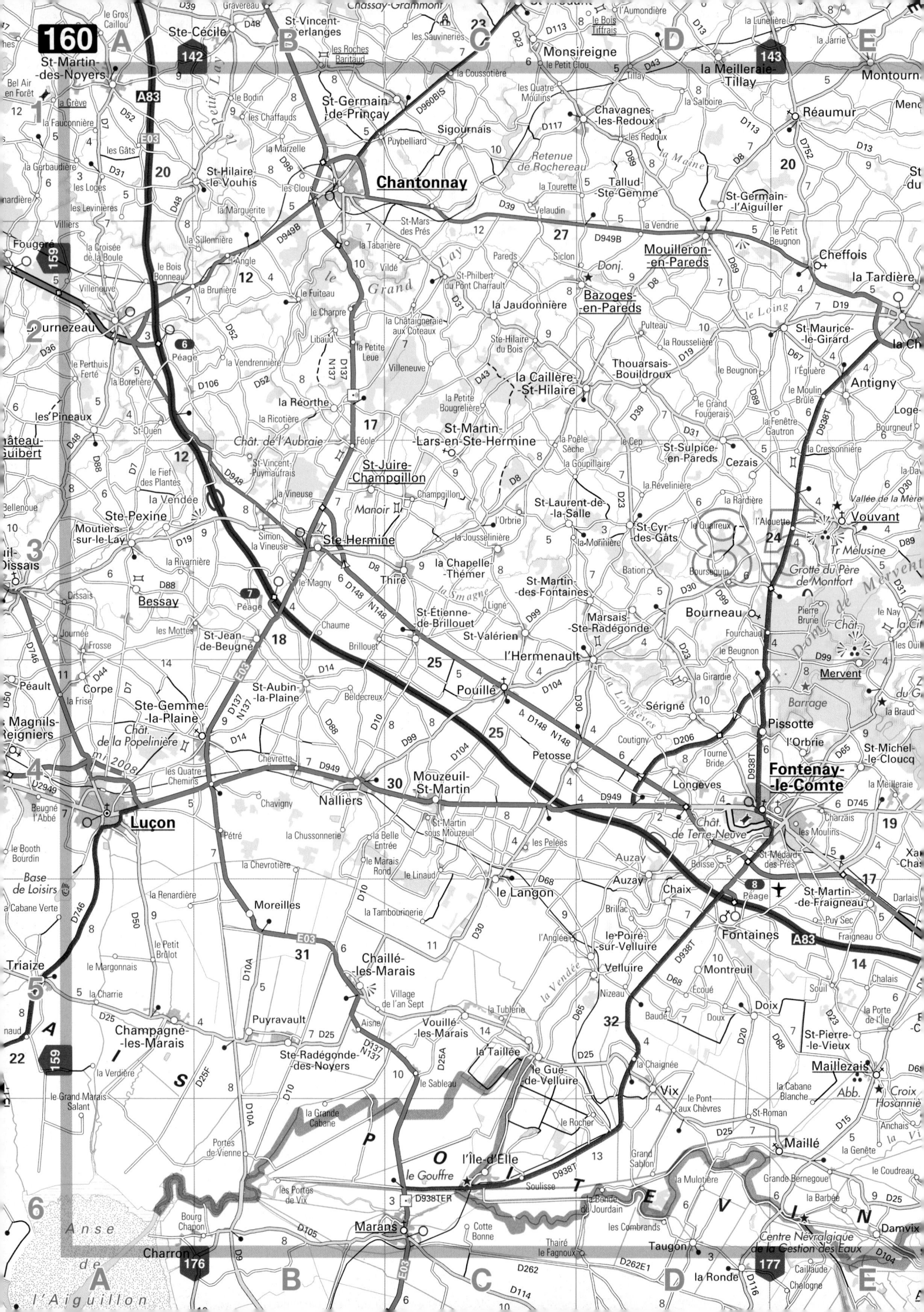

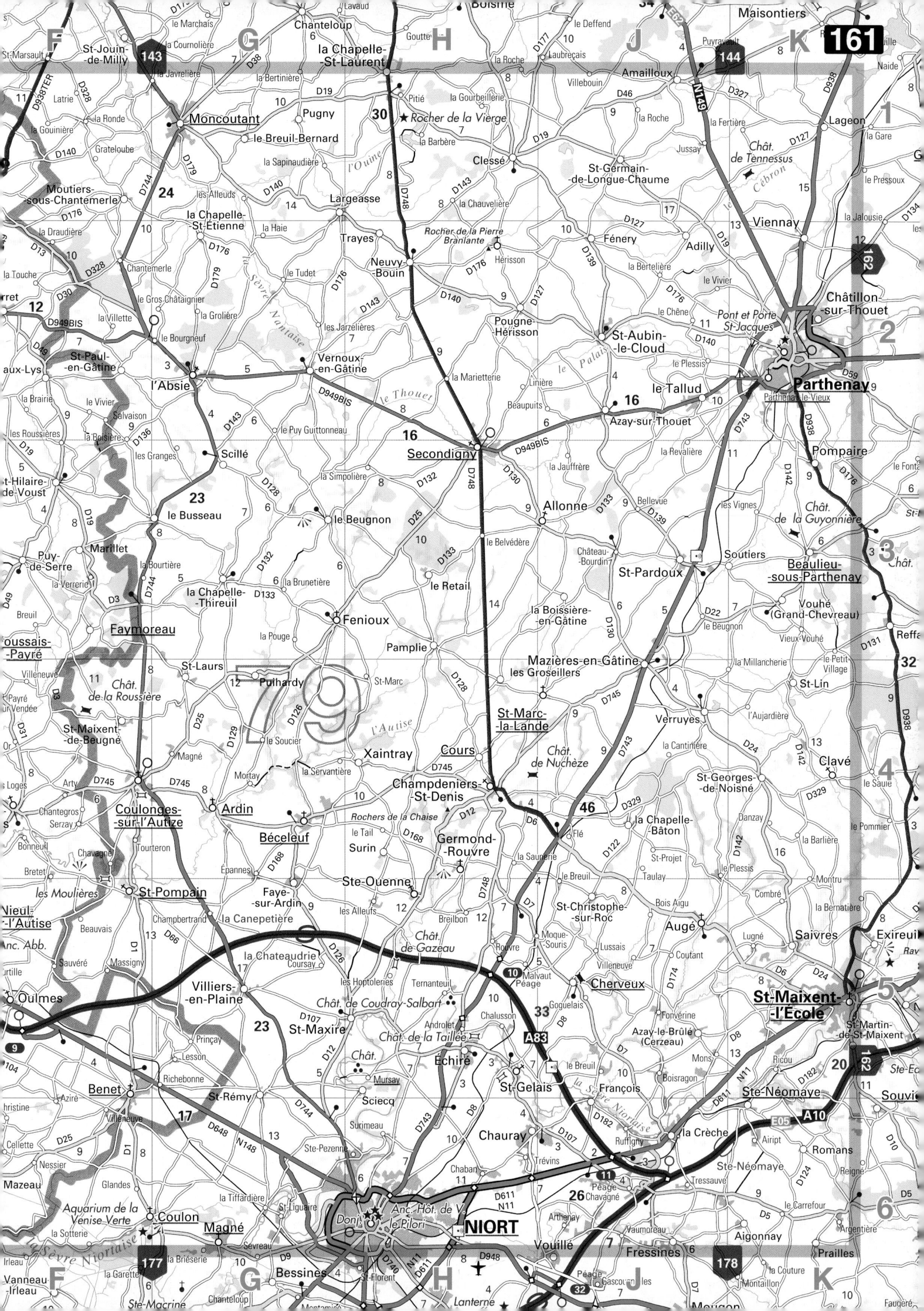

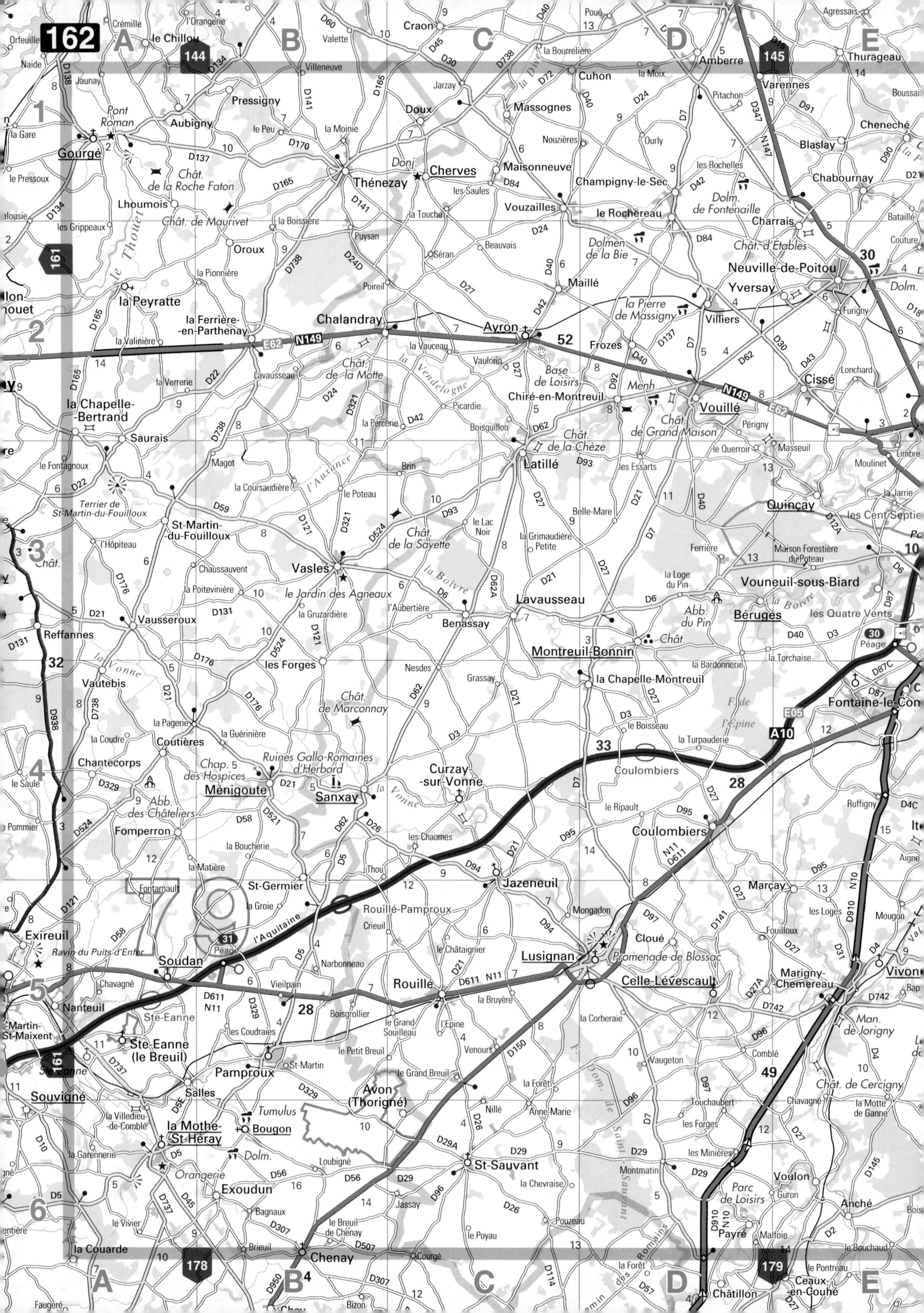

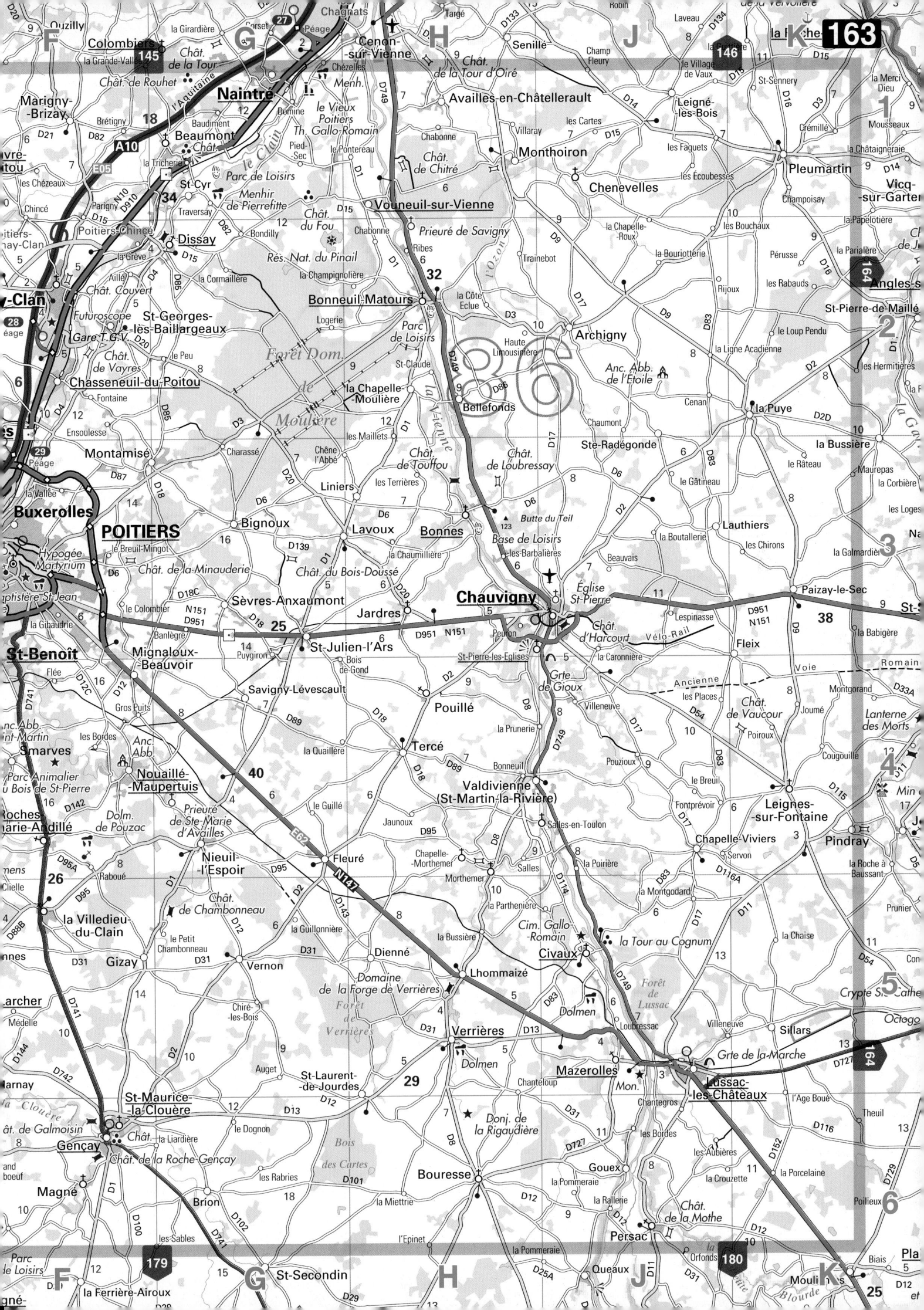

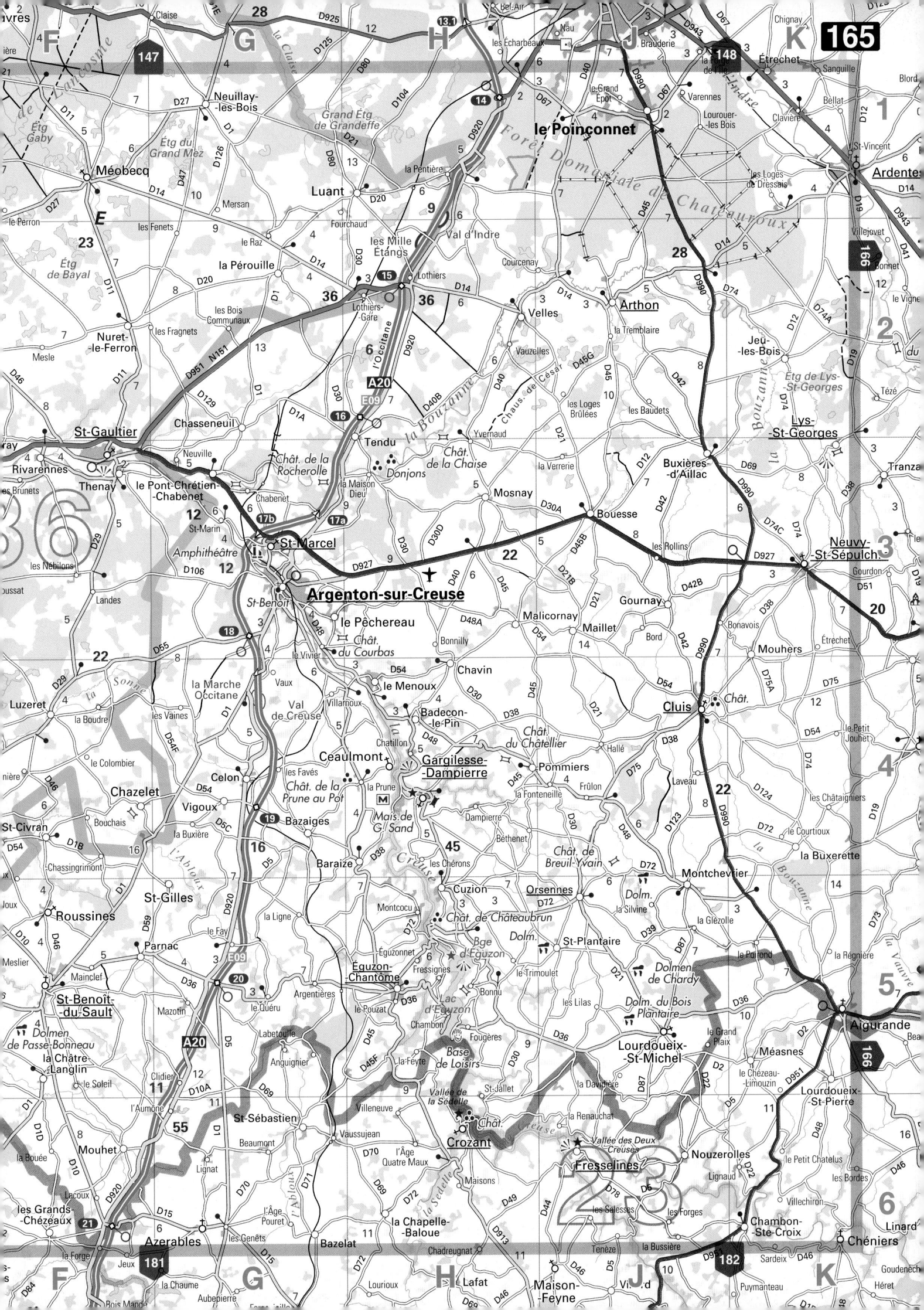

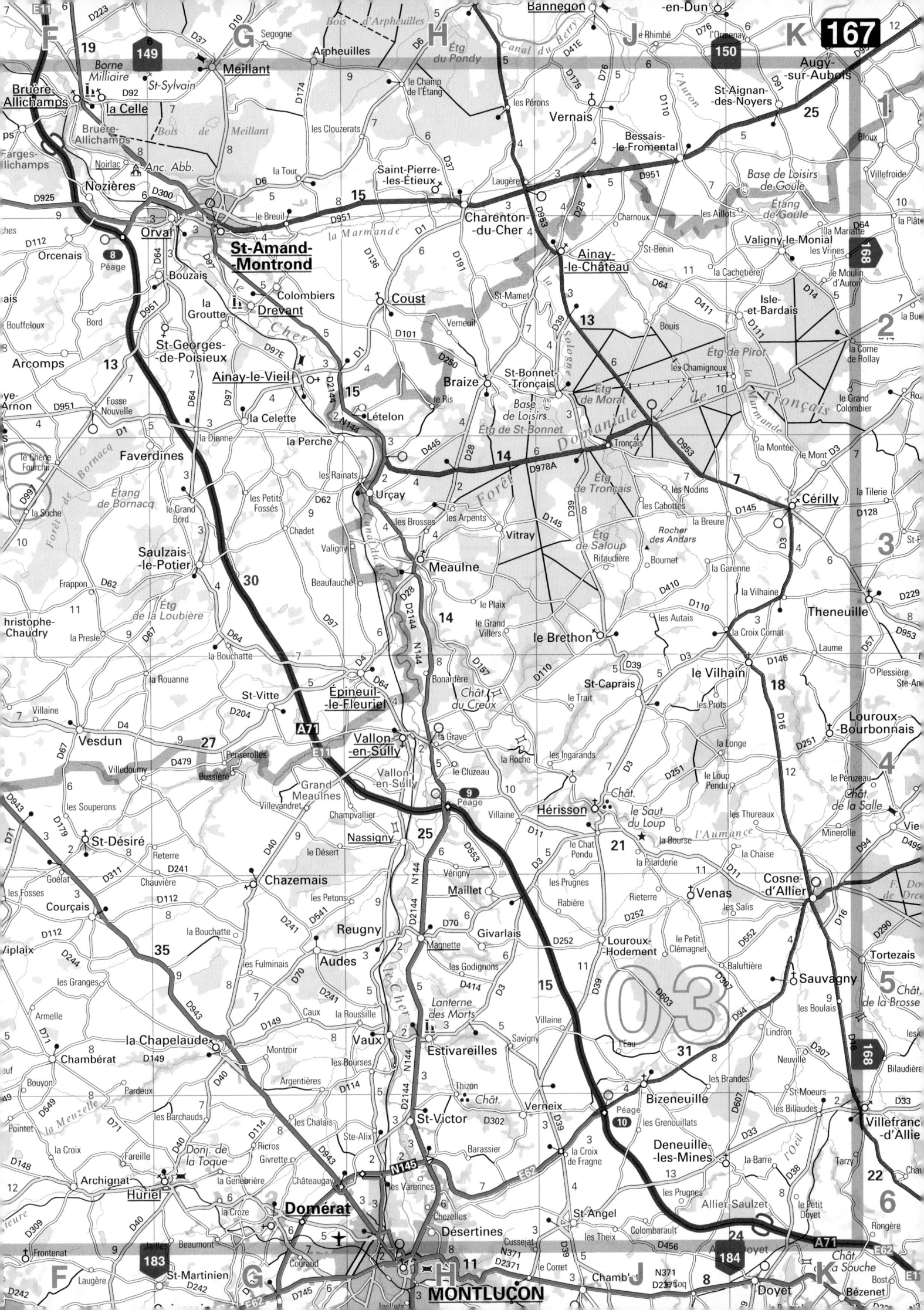

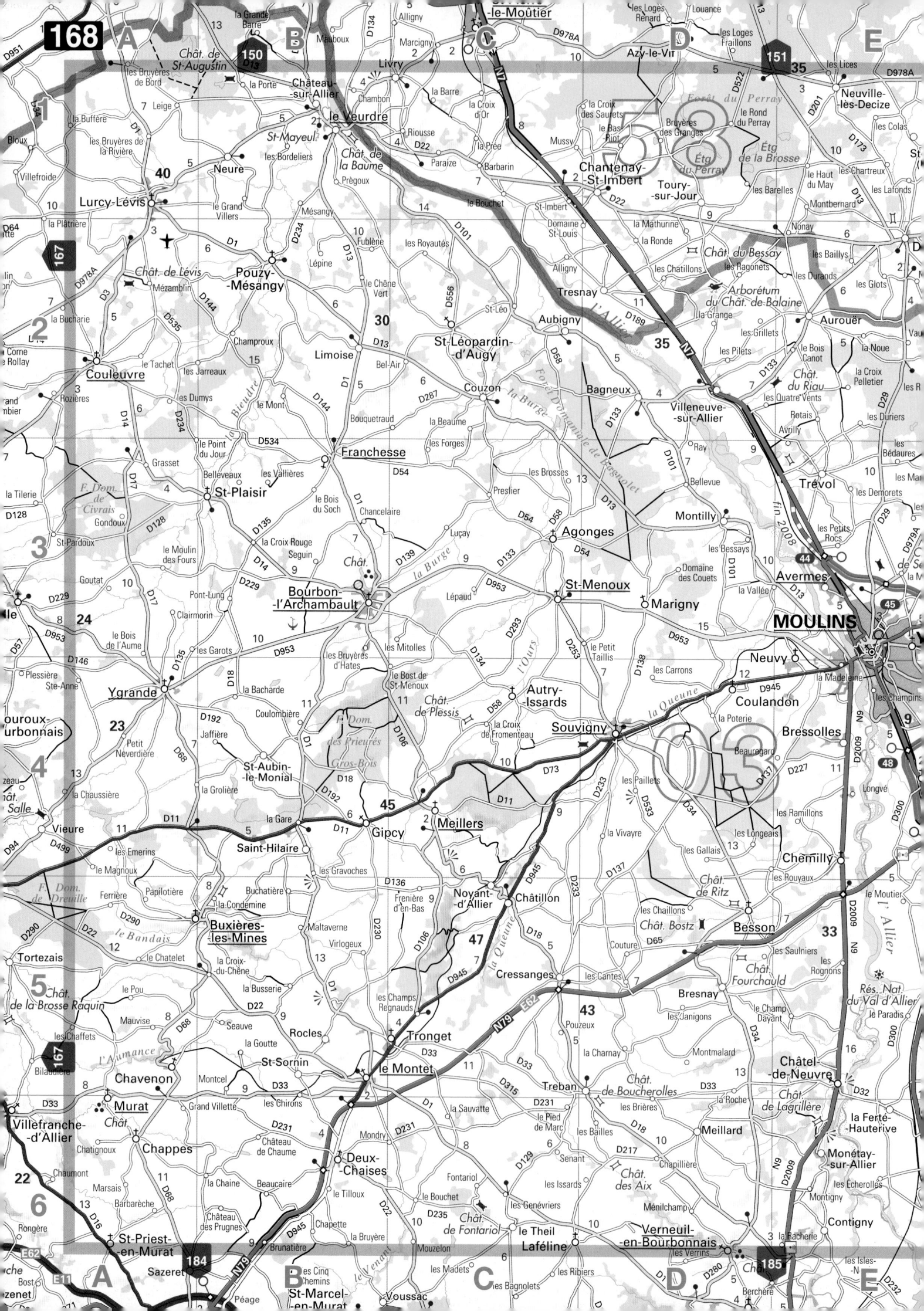

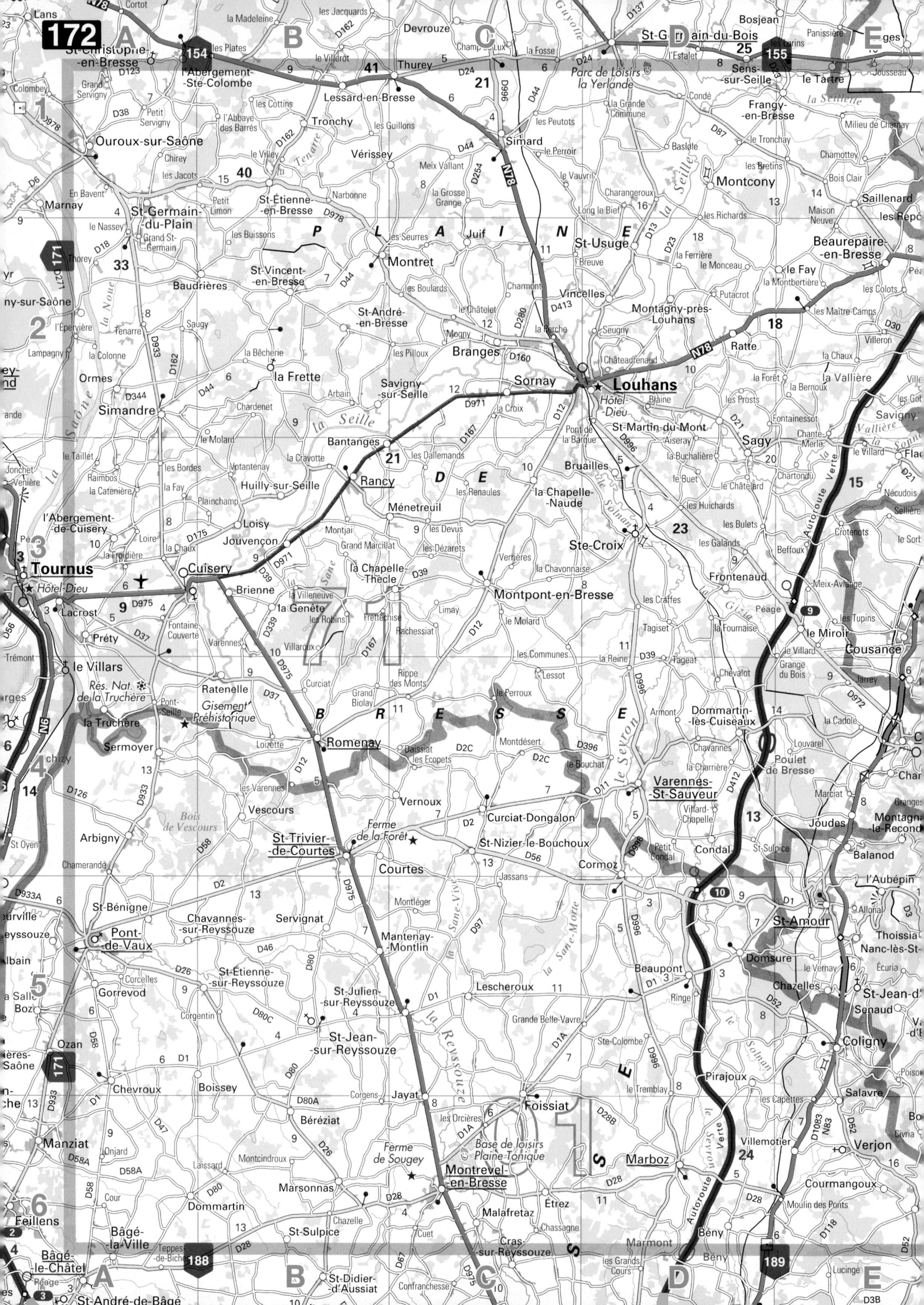

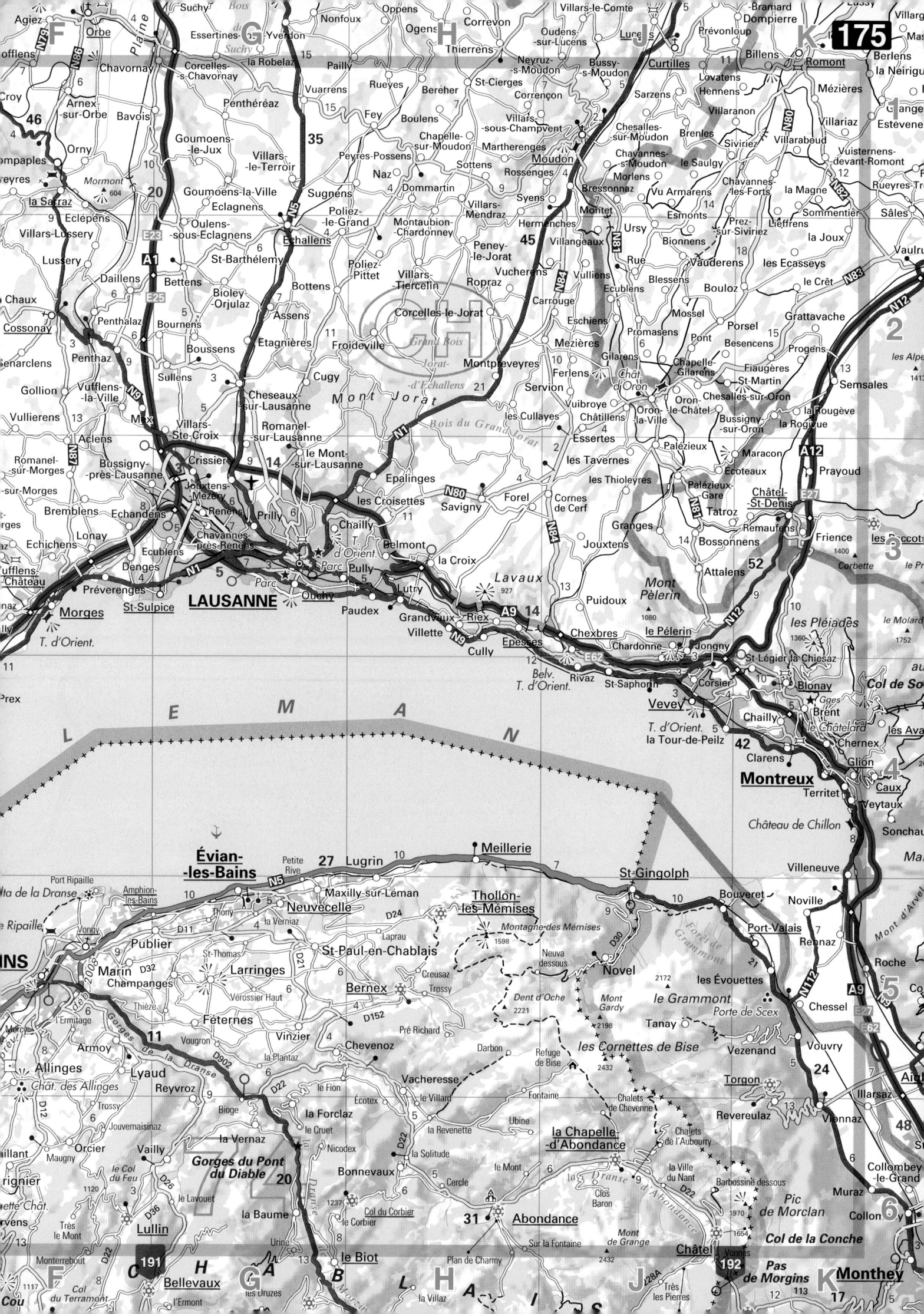

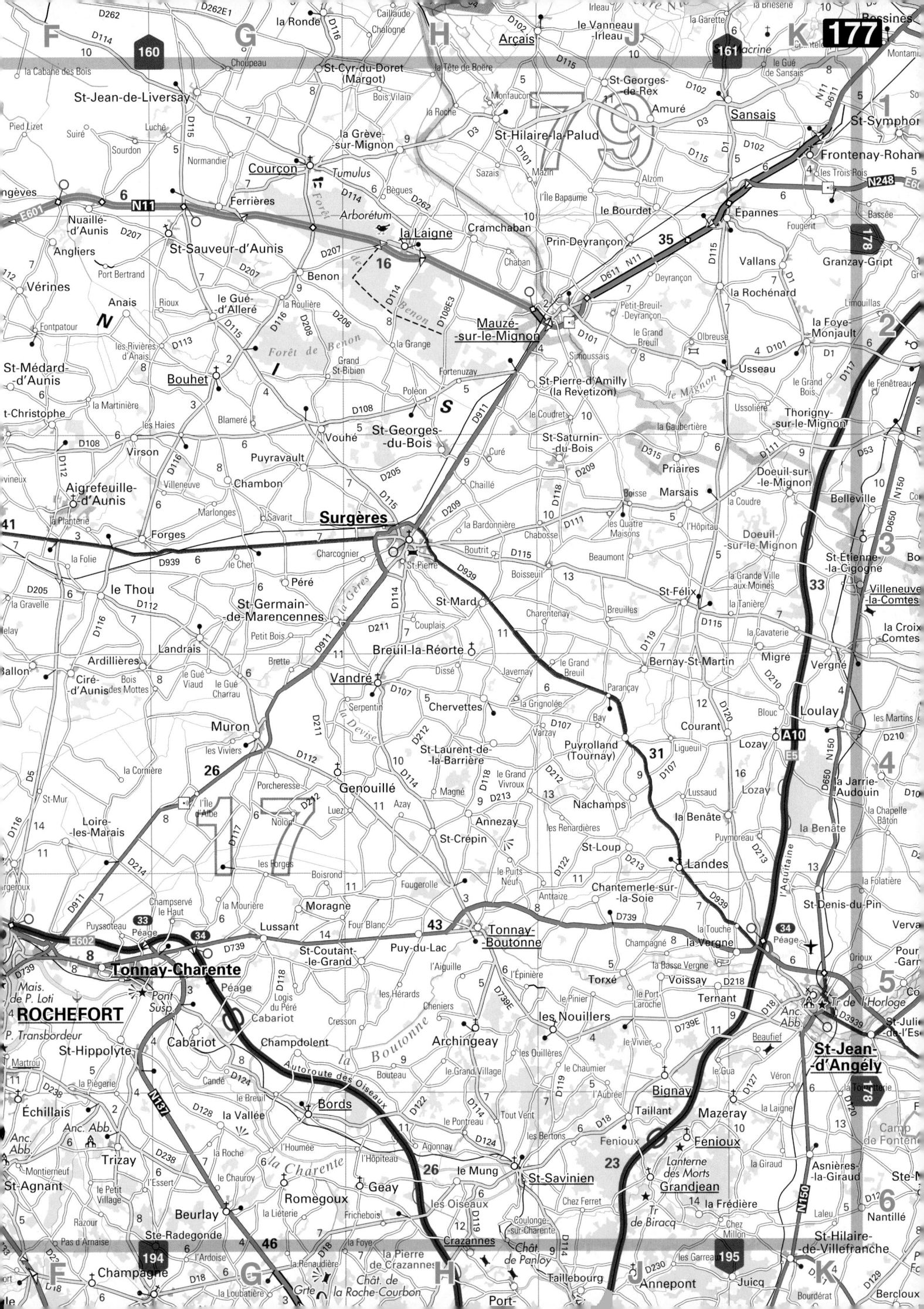

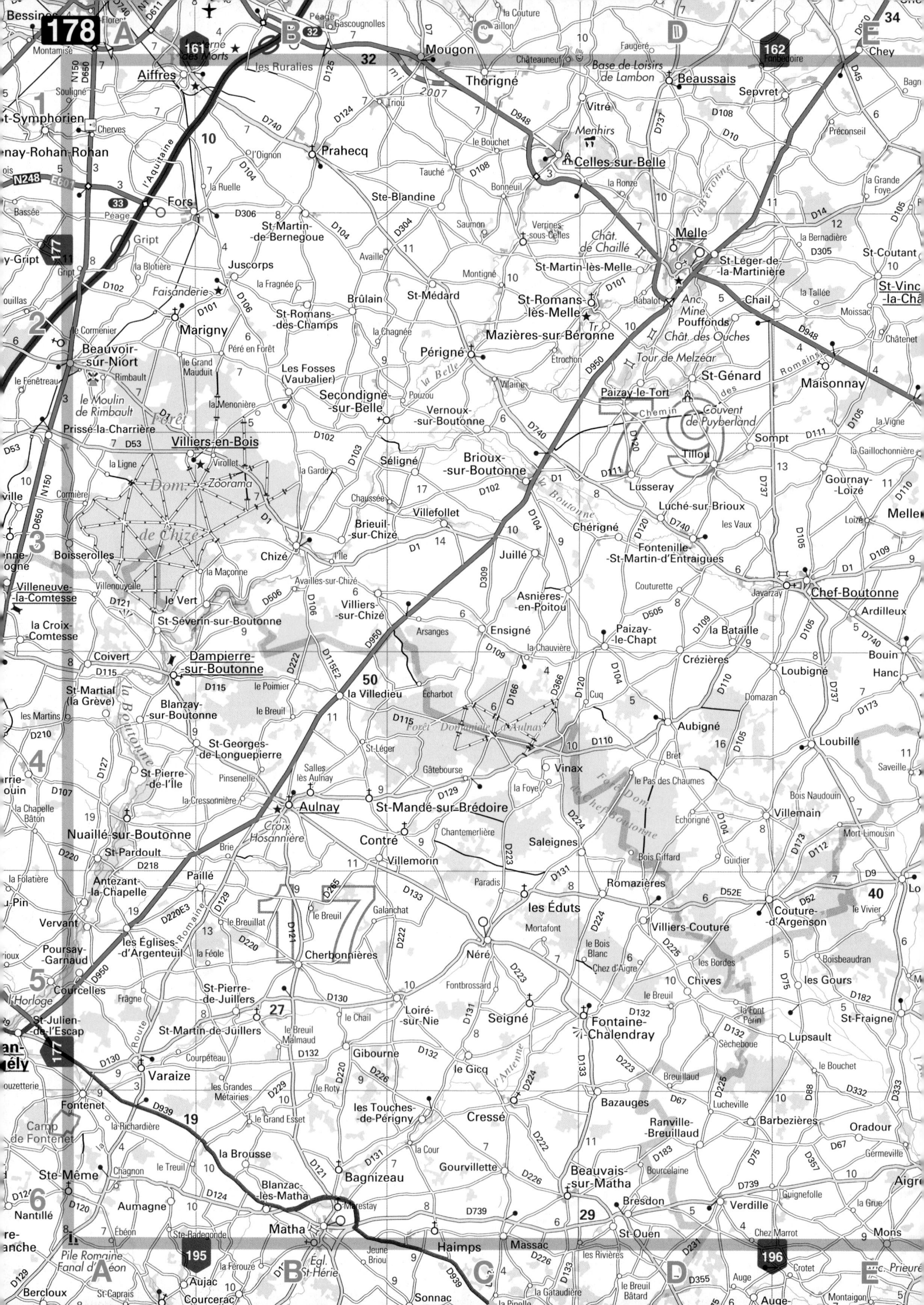

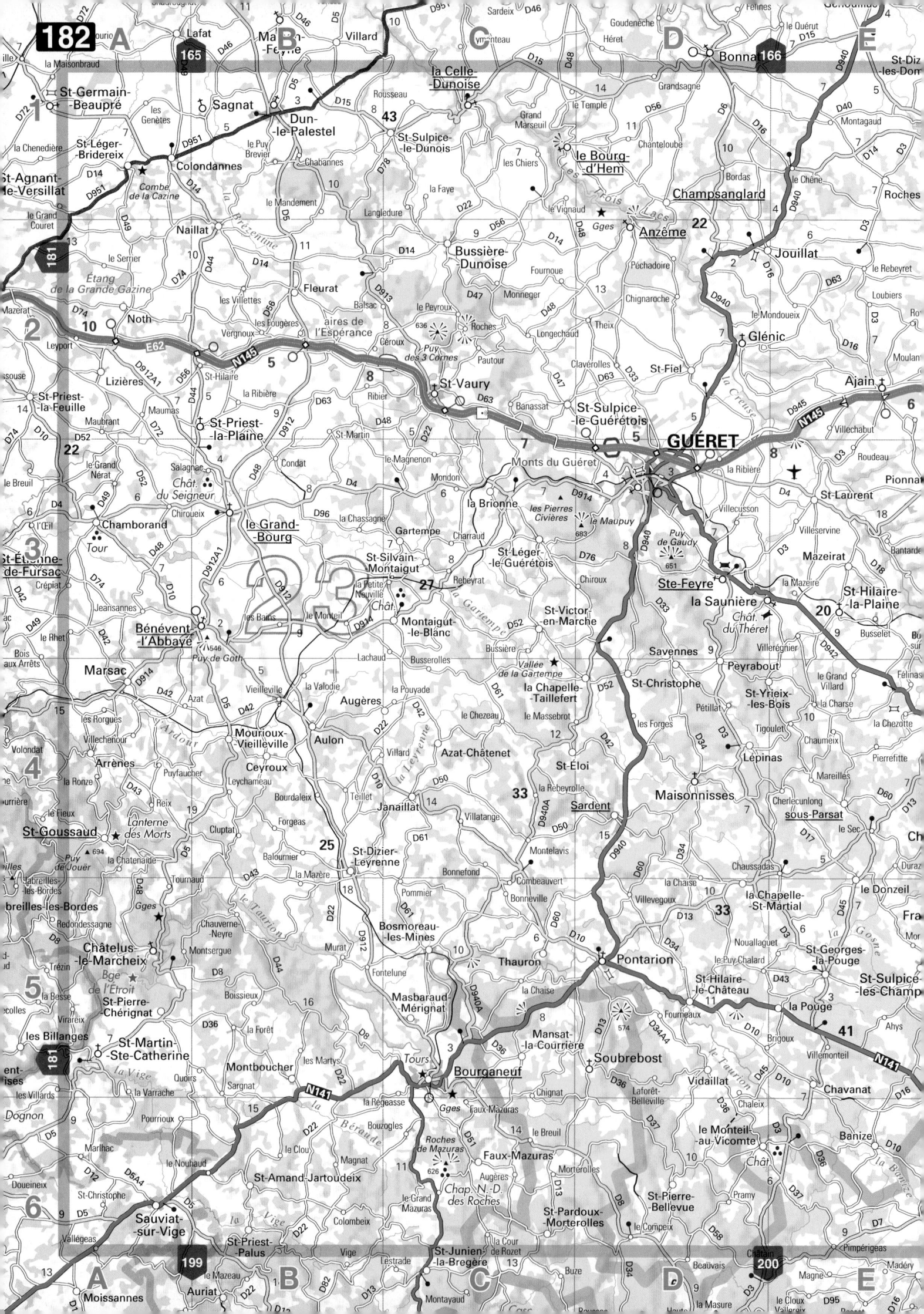

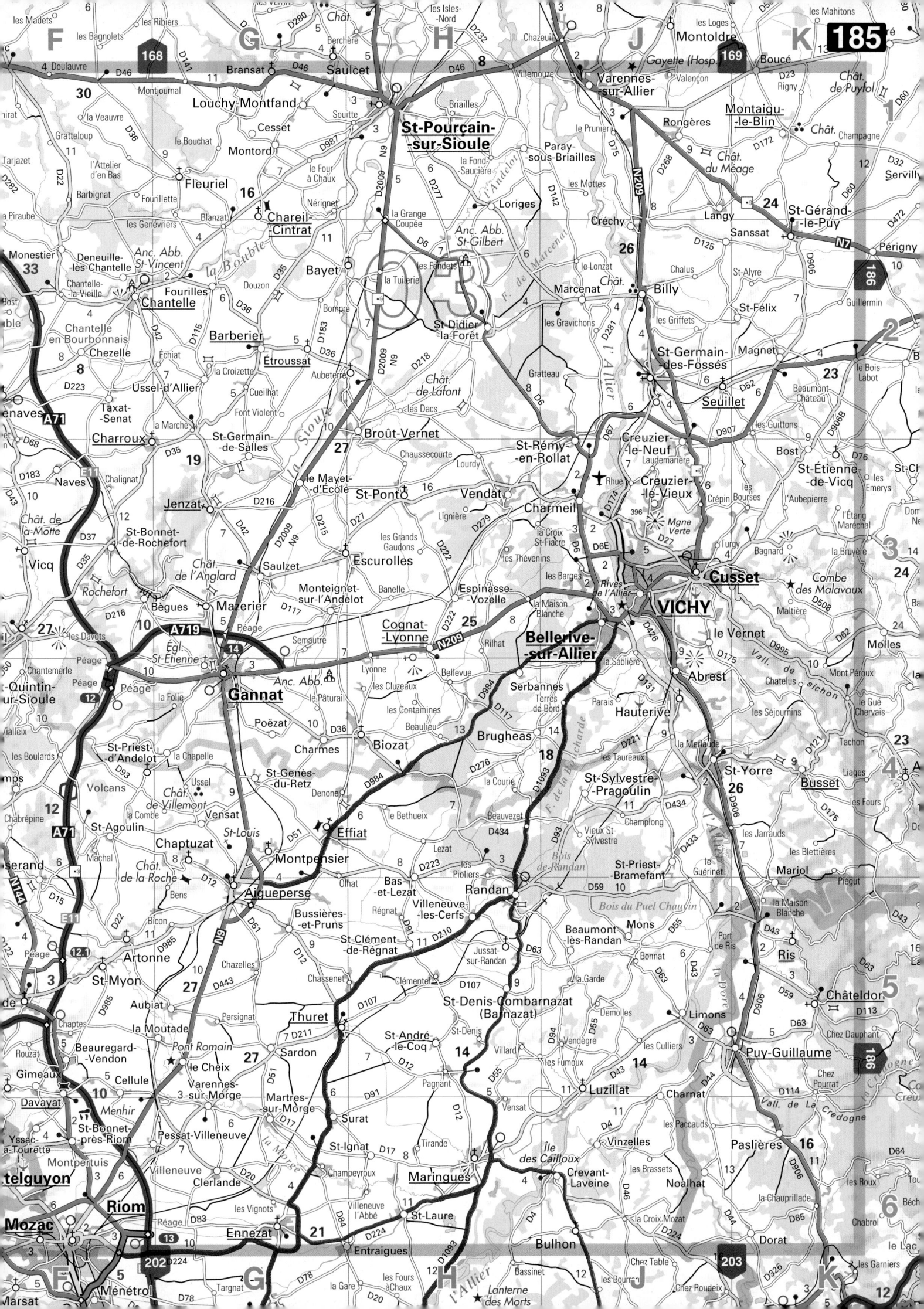

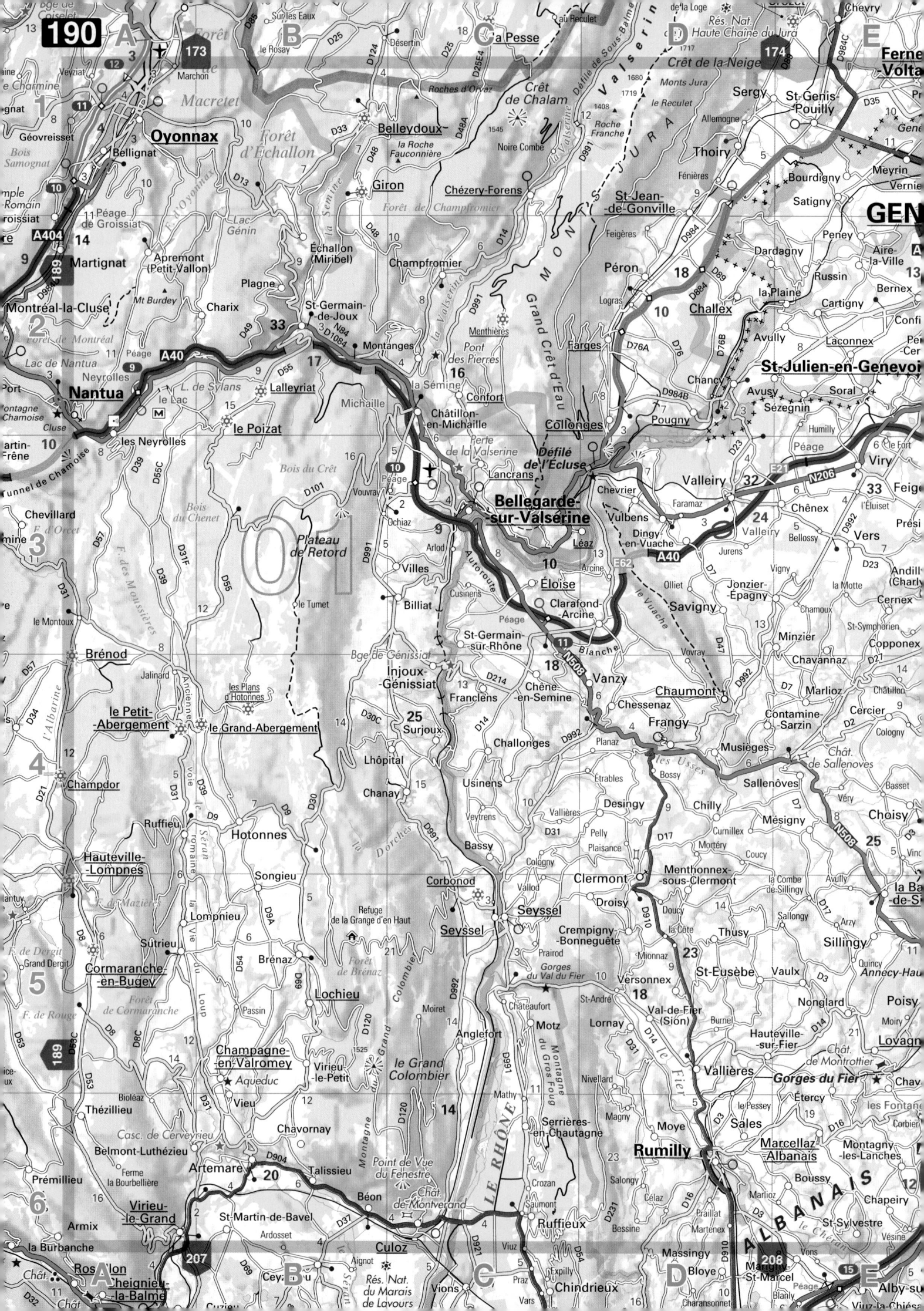

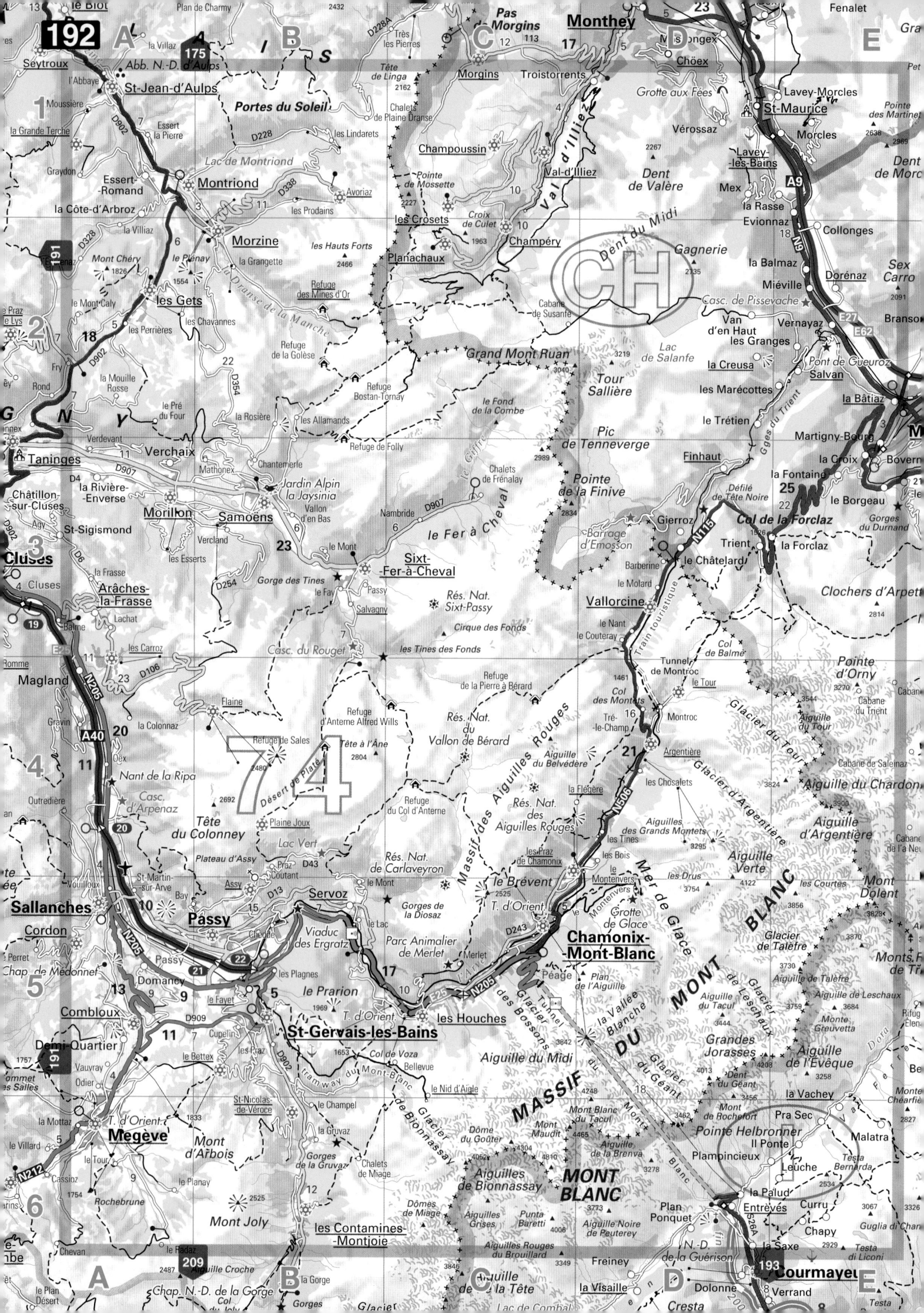

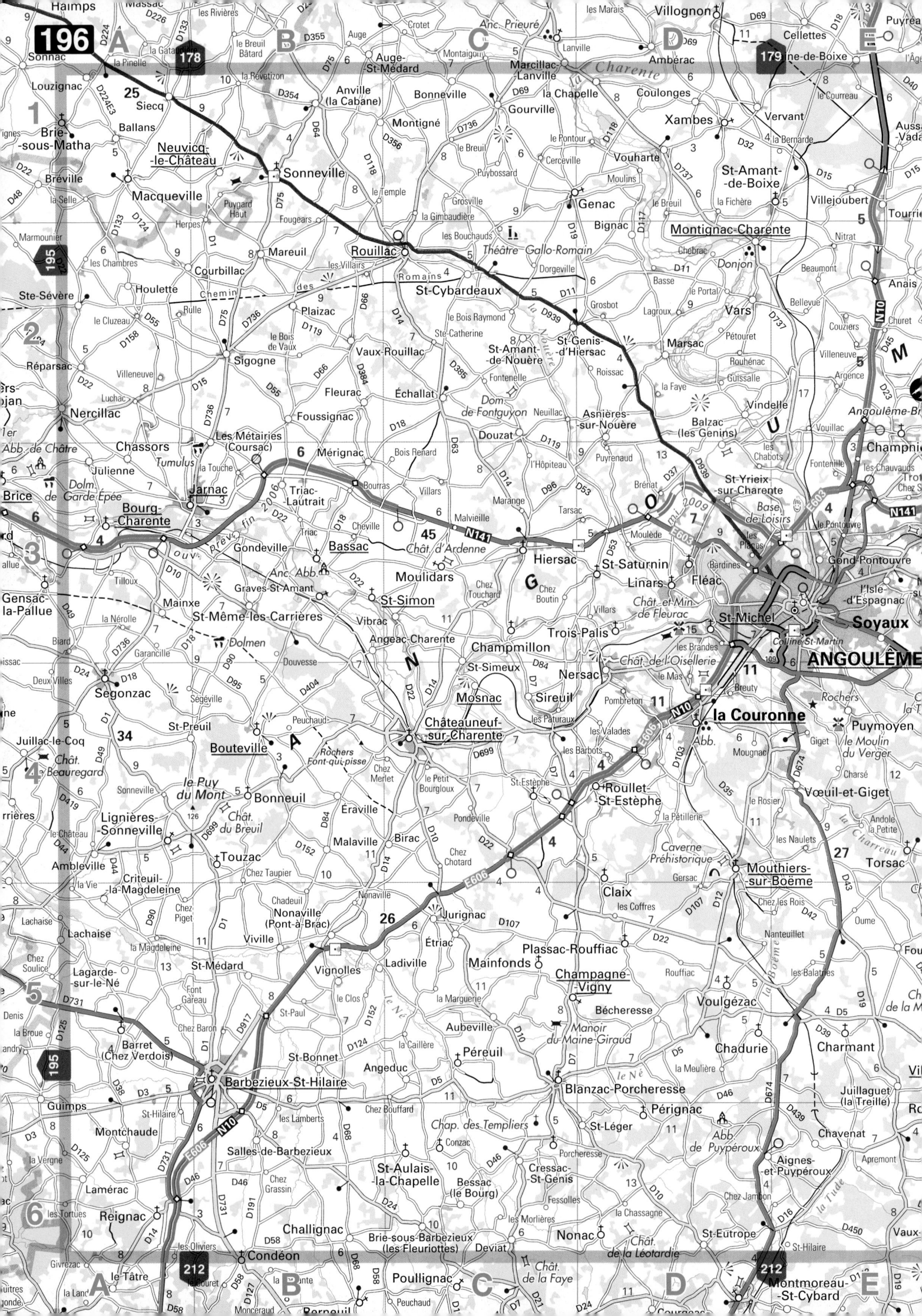

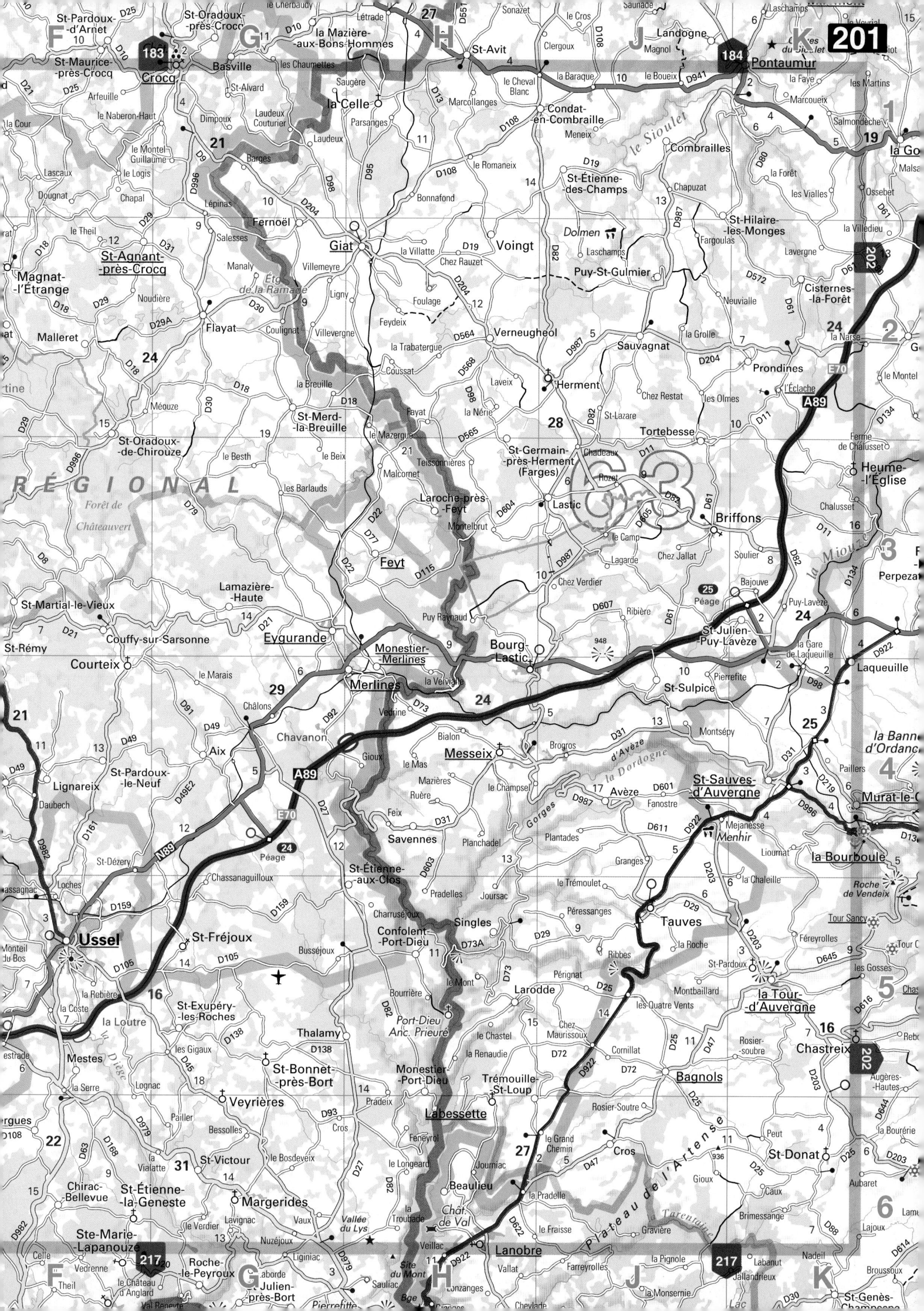

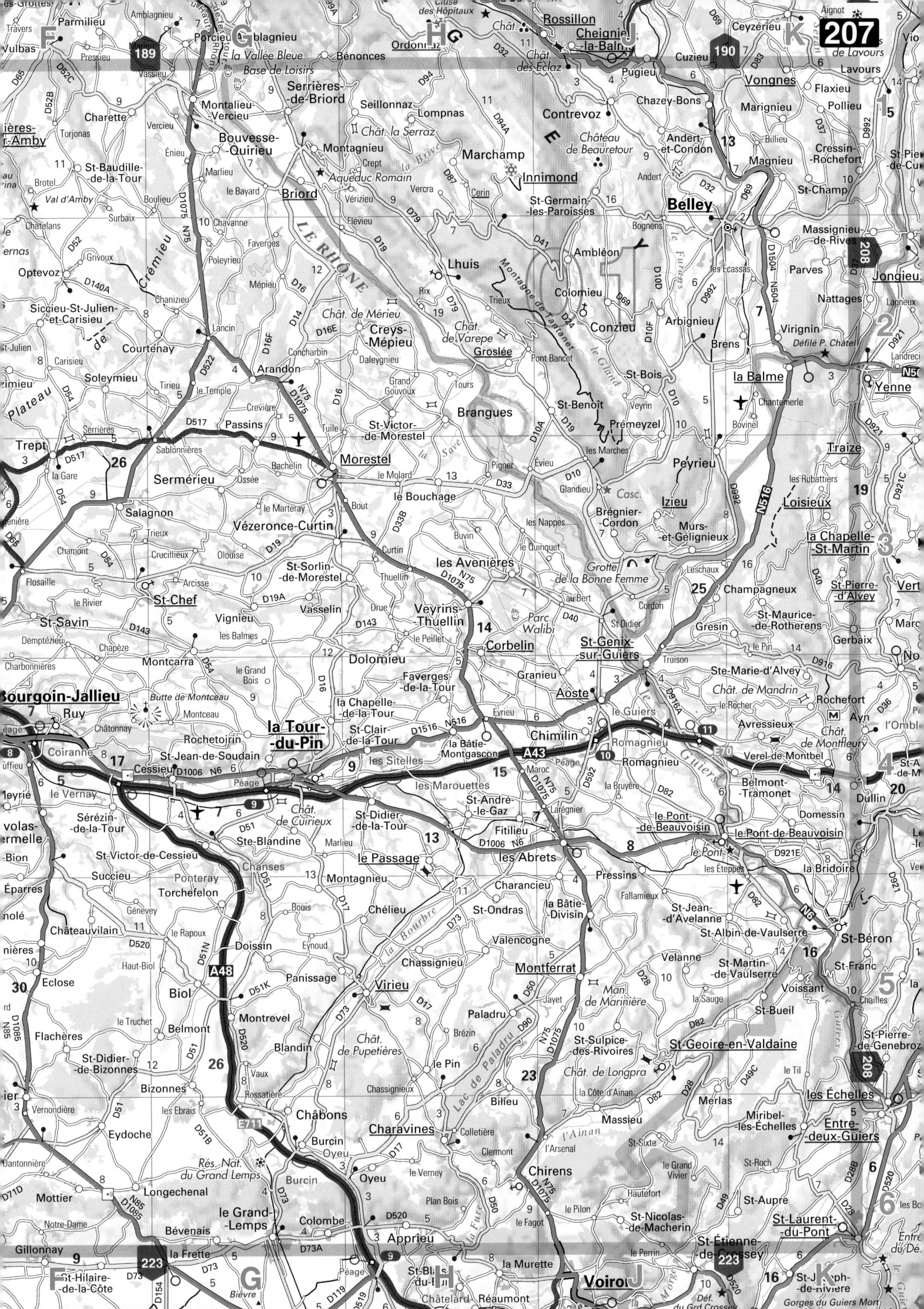

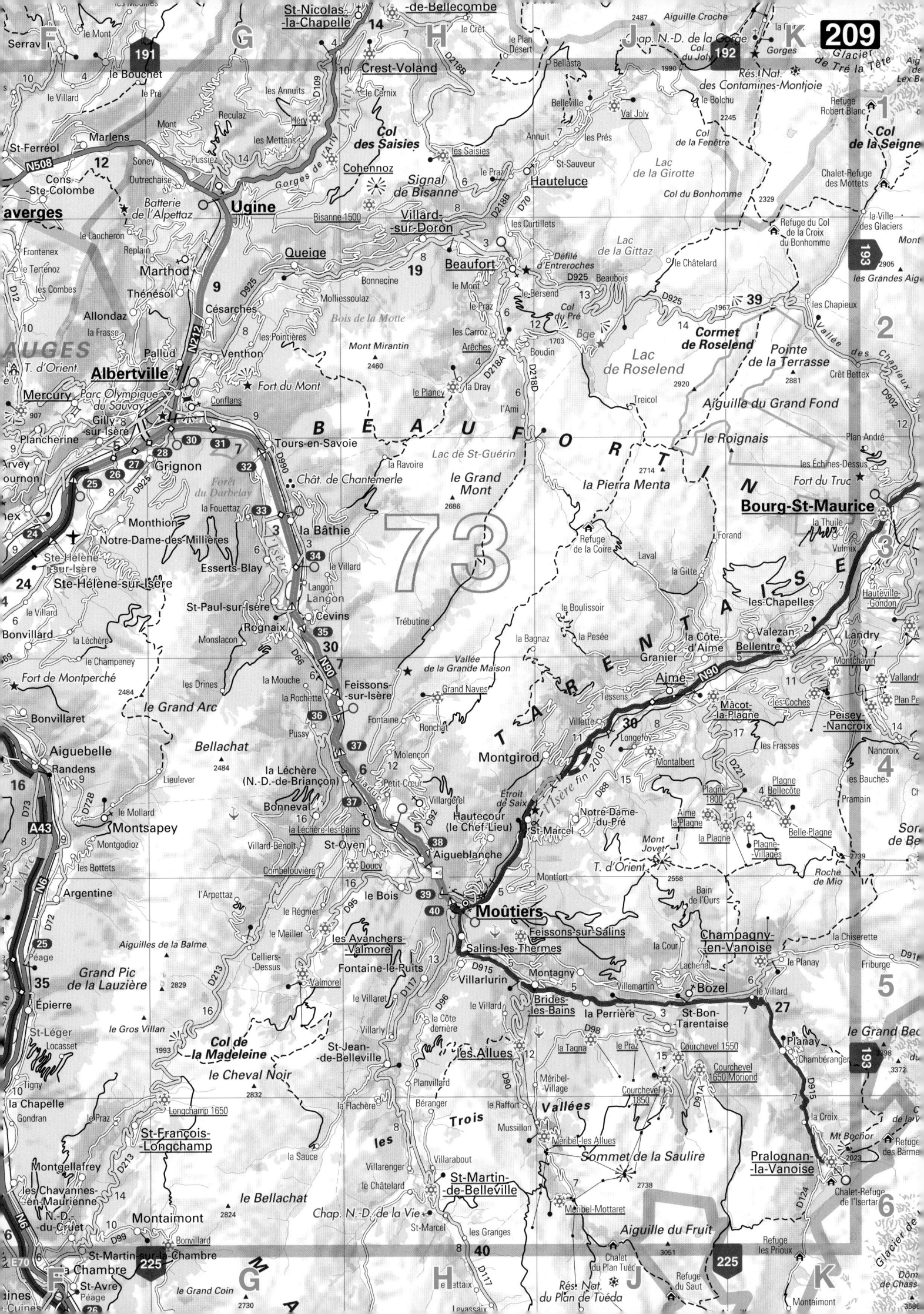

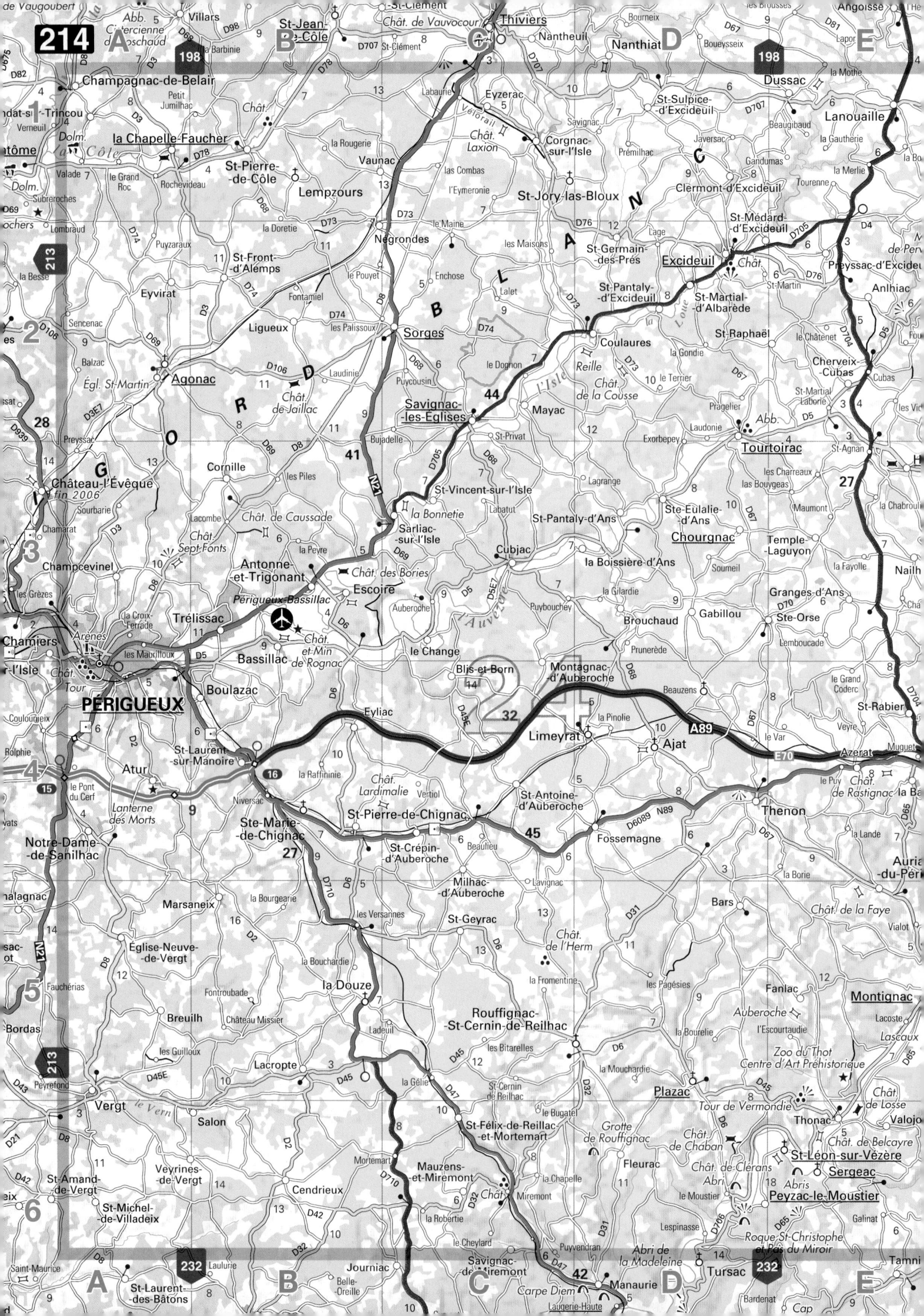

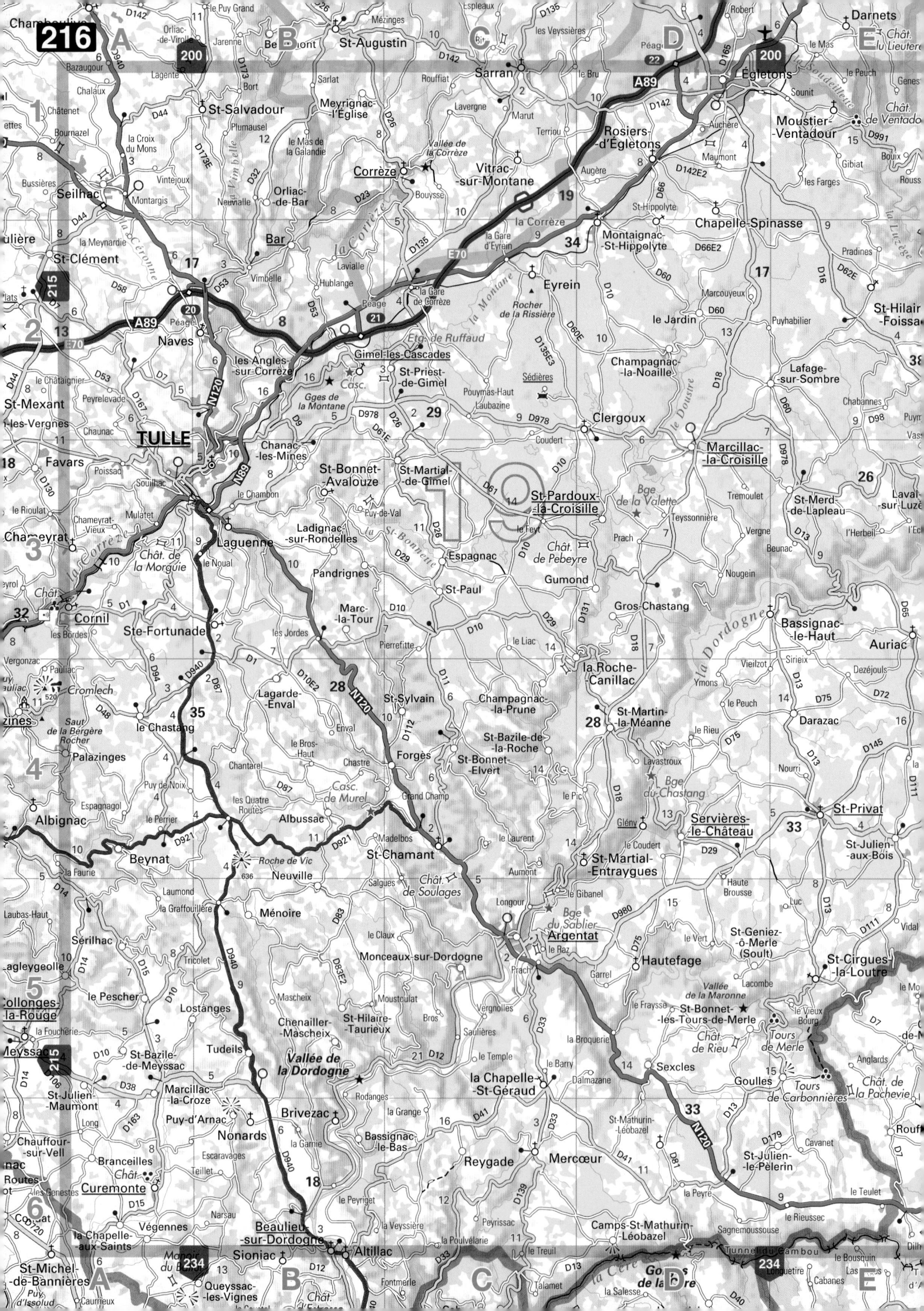

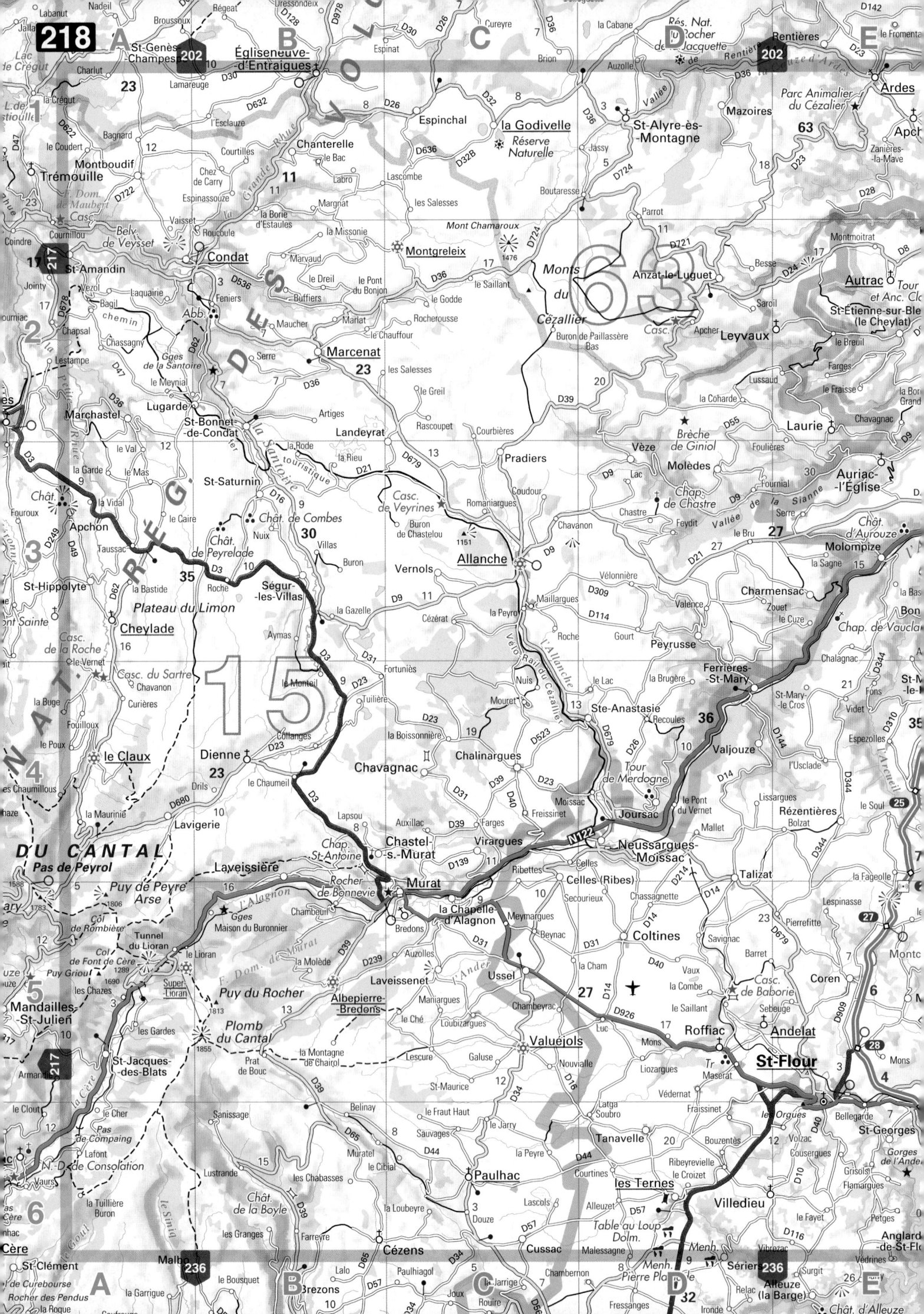

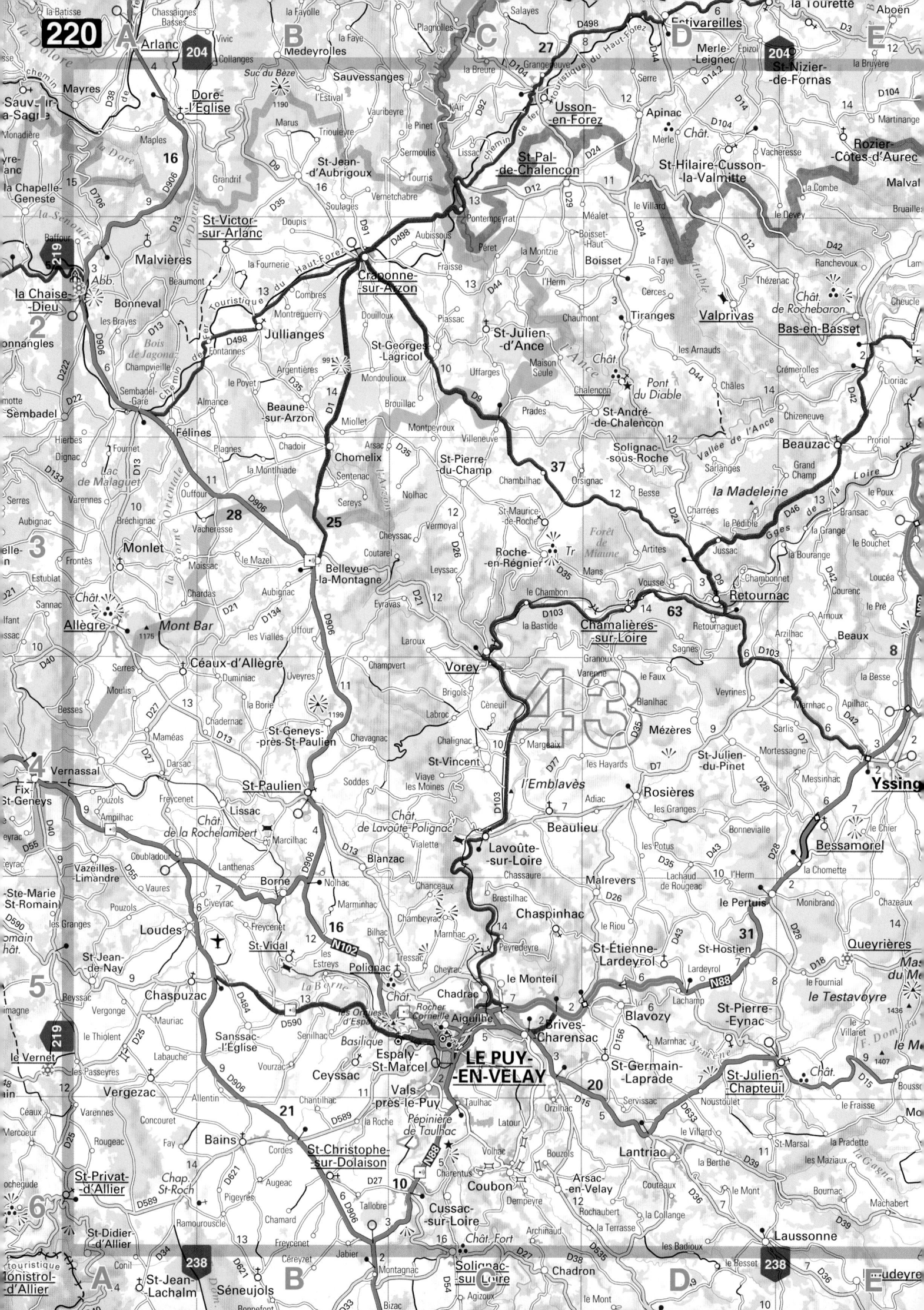

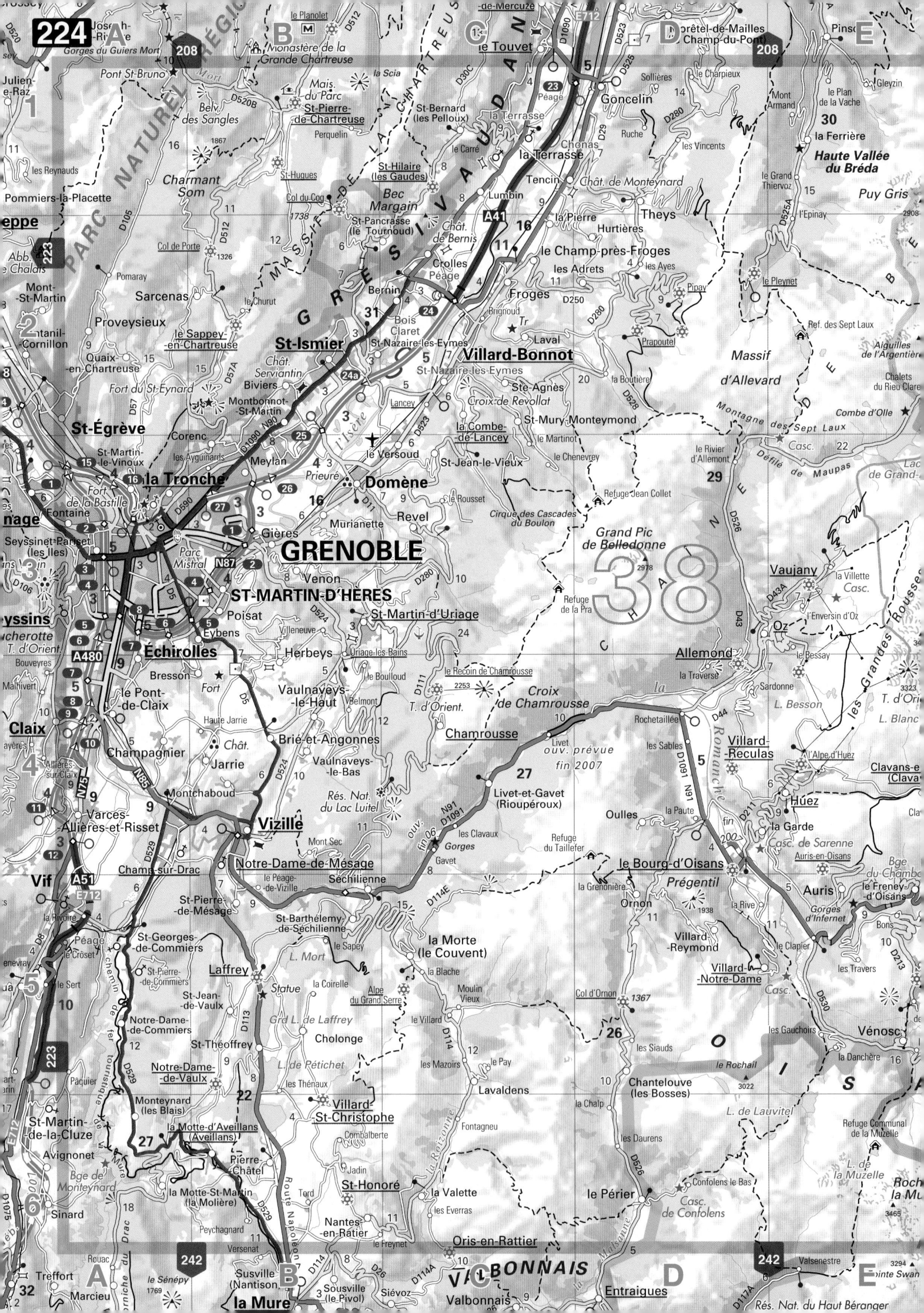

228 A B C D E

1

le Porge-Océan
le Grand Bos
Saumos
le Petit Bos
210
le Vignas
D5E4
le Temple
D107
25
le Porge
D107
9
Laruau
D3
Sautuges
Lauros
Camp de Souge
la Saussouze
33
12
12
D5

2
le Grand-Crohot
Dunes Boisées
D106E3
8
Lège-Cap-Ferret
Blagon
les Chalets
D106
10
le las
60
D213
15
Martigr
D213
D213
D10
22

Rés. Nat.
des prés Salés
d'Arès Lège-Cap Ferret
Arès
D3
D215E1
D215
D3E9
Andernos-
-les-Bains
D3E10
14
5
6
D5
12
la Pointe

3
le Truc Vert
24
Claouey
D106
Pointe
des Quinconce
Parcs à Huîtres
le Petit Piquey
les Jacquets
le Piquey
20
Taussat
D3
Cassy
Lubec
D5E5
PARC
le Grand
Piquey
BASSIN
7
Lanton
Pisciculture
4
Marcheprime
le Canon
l'Herbe
Île
aux Oiseaux
Parcs à Huîtres
Certes
Audenge
la Courbe
les Trucails
11
les Argentières
Lacanau de Mios
3
23
les Arbousiers
D'ARCACHON
Vigneau
D3
les Douils
22

4
Phare du
Cap-Ferret
Bélisaire
le Moulleau
3
D650
Arcachon
6
9
Parc
Ornithologique
Château
Ruat
Biganos
N250
Facture
N250
D650
2
les Douils
5
22
5
le Cap-
Ferret
2
4
Pyla
sur Mer
D217
la Hume
22
8
le Teich
D650
5
2
5
Lamothe
A660
2
1
5
CAP FERRET
la Pointe
5
la Teste-
de-Buch
3
Gujan-
Mestras
8
3
A660
Mios
la Carreyre
4
A63
le Pilat
Notre-Dame
des Monts
D260
Base
de Loisirs
Chante-
Cigale
7
3
D3
Peyot
Arnauton
E05
5
le Pilat
Plage
D259
7
Truc de la Truque
76
Lillet
9
D3
Argilas
11
E70
Rés. Nat. du Banc
d'Arguin
103
Castandet
24
Salles
Perrin
D108

5
Dune du Pilat
Maison Forestière
de Gaillouneys
D218
14
D256
14
D112
D652
D108
Caudos
10
D108
D108
le Caplanne
Bilos
Lanot
le Béguey
21

6
F. Dom.
de
la Teste
20
D218
Cazaux
Étang de Cazaux
et de Sanguinet
Langeot
D46
l'Aiguille
3
8
Lugos
D108E3
13
le Vieux
Lugos
Mais.
du Parc
les Hautes Rives
Sanguinet
Lombard
Méoule
244
D652
le Clercq
12
Corneilley
D147
15
Lugos
245
D110
D110E1
10

Biscarrosse
Plage
D83

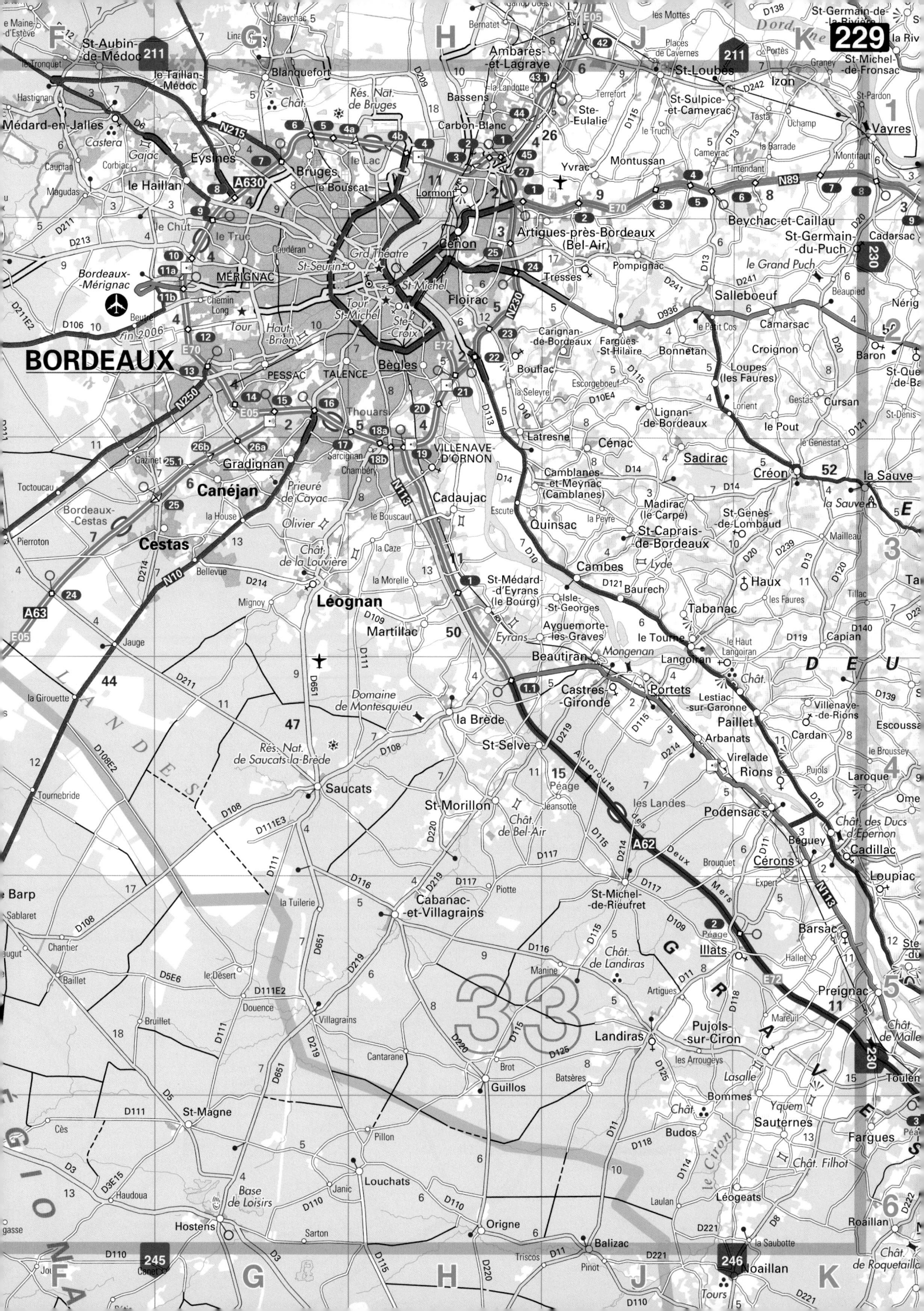

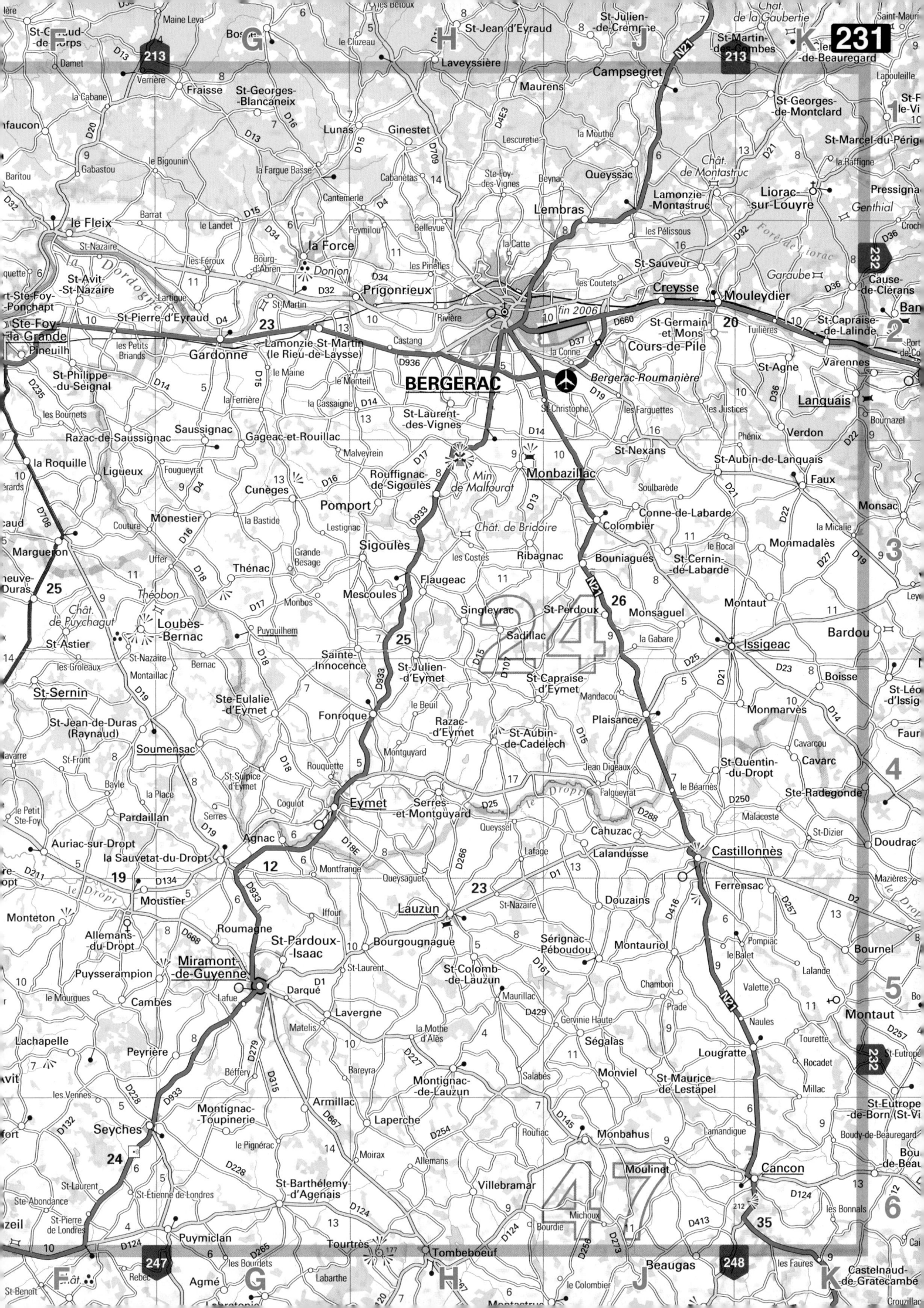

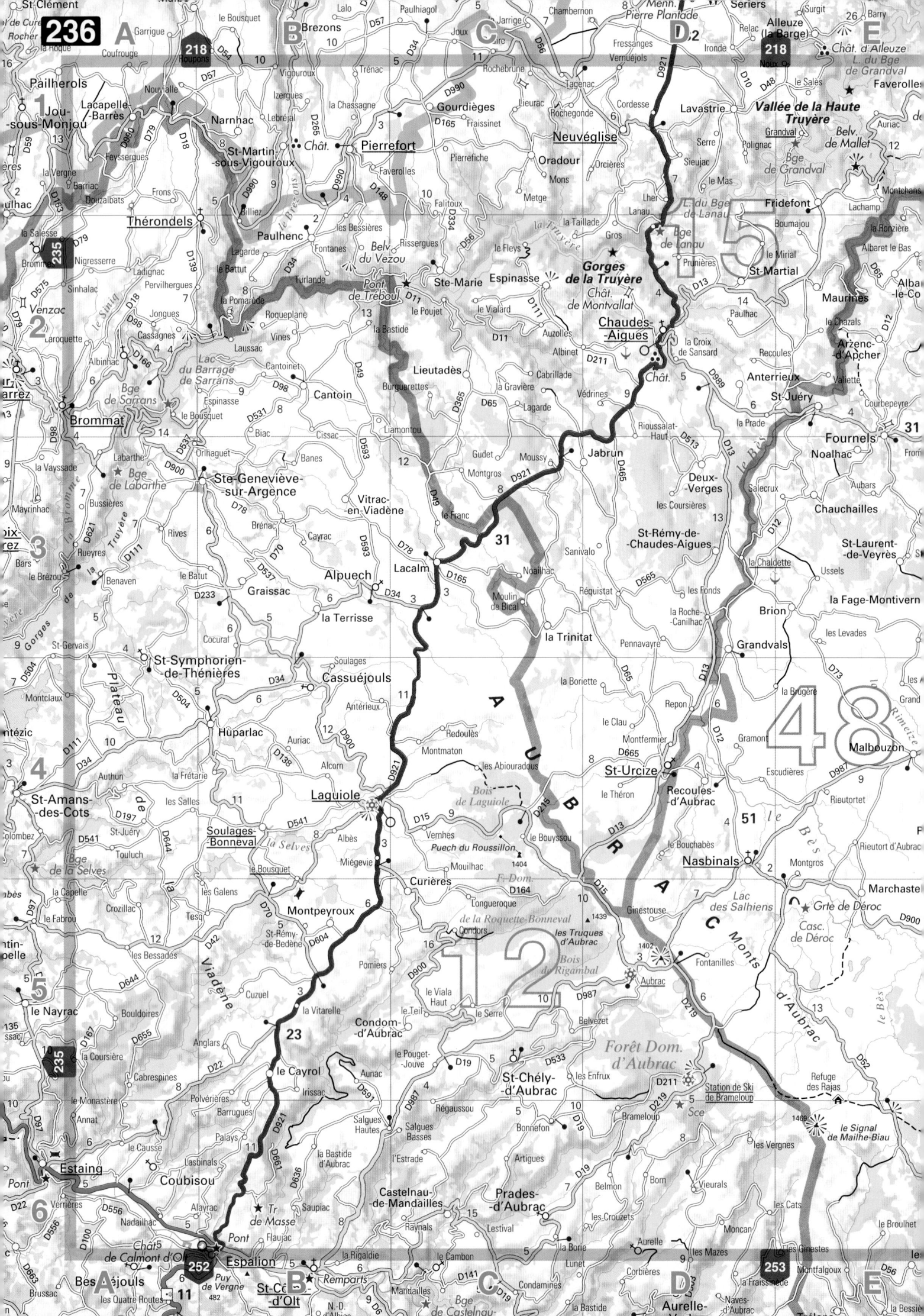

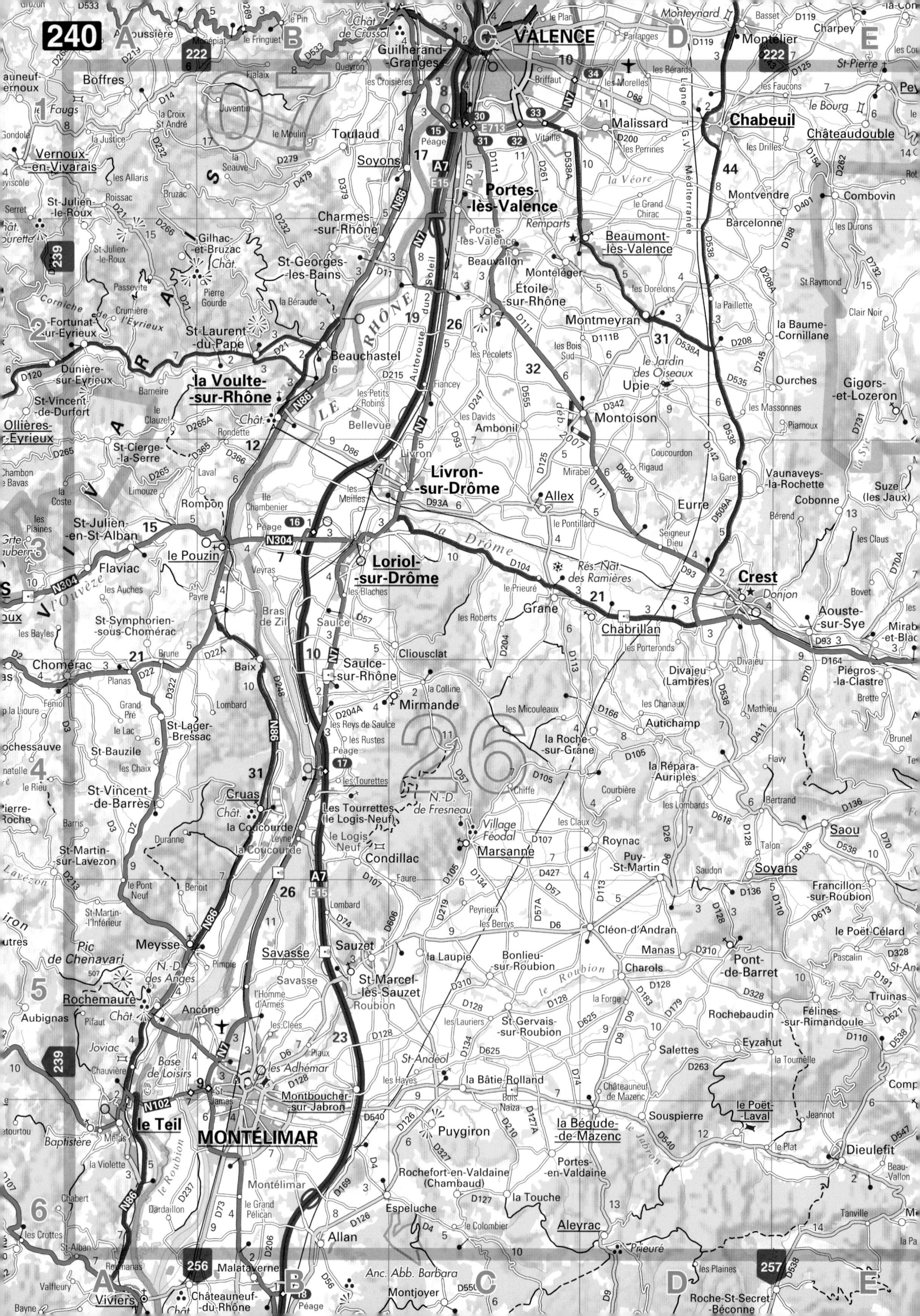

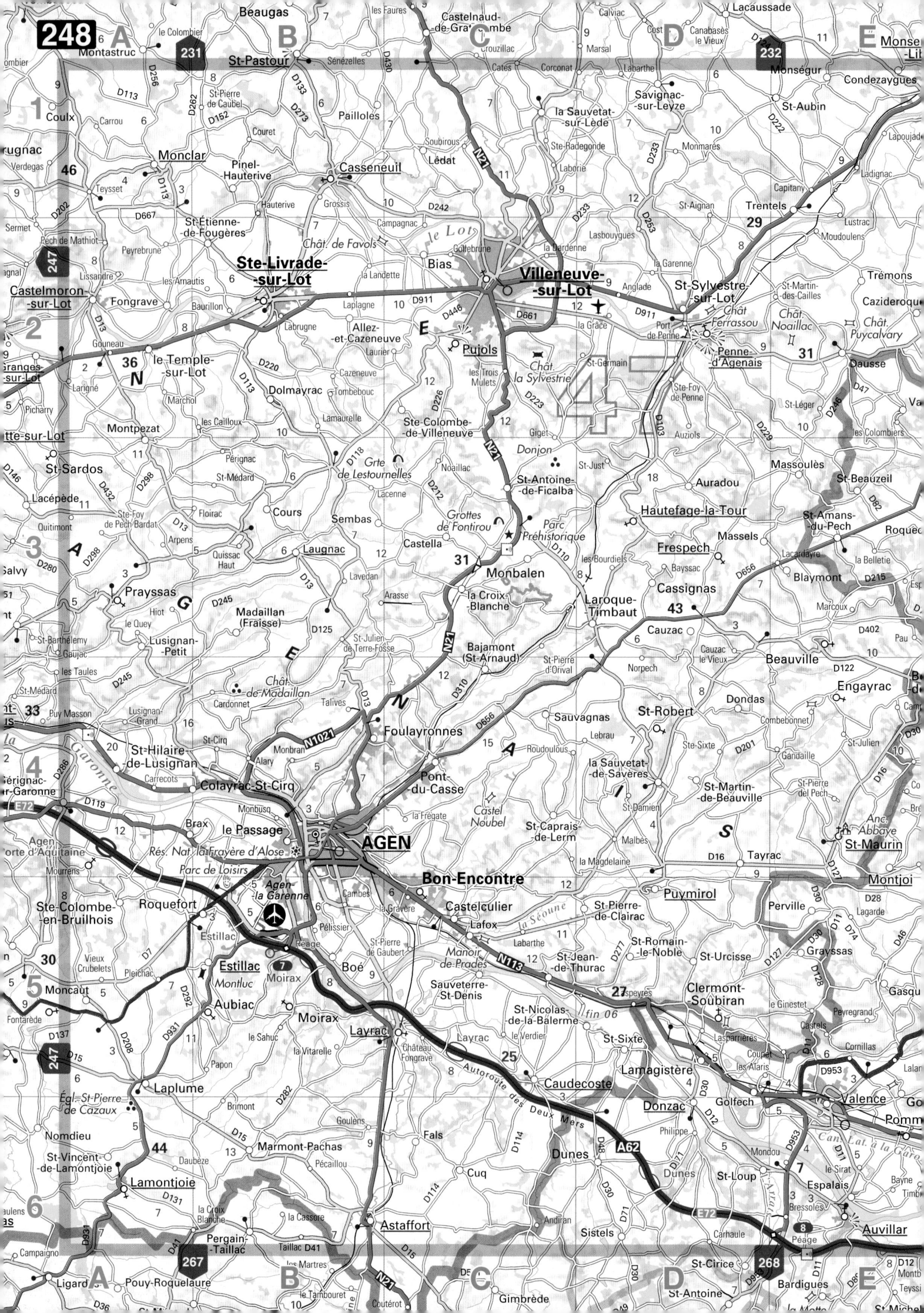

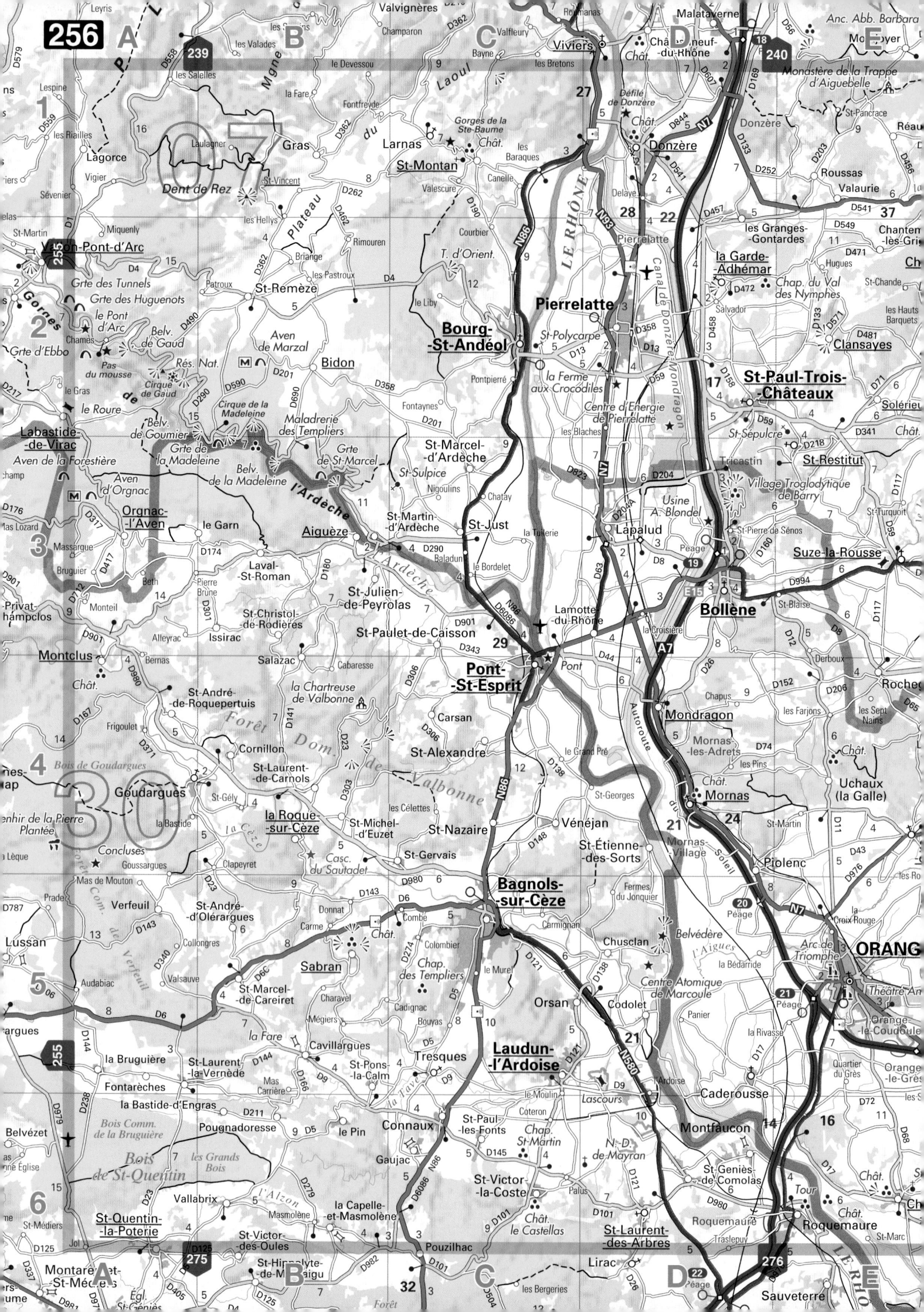

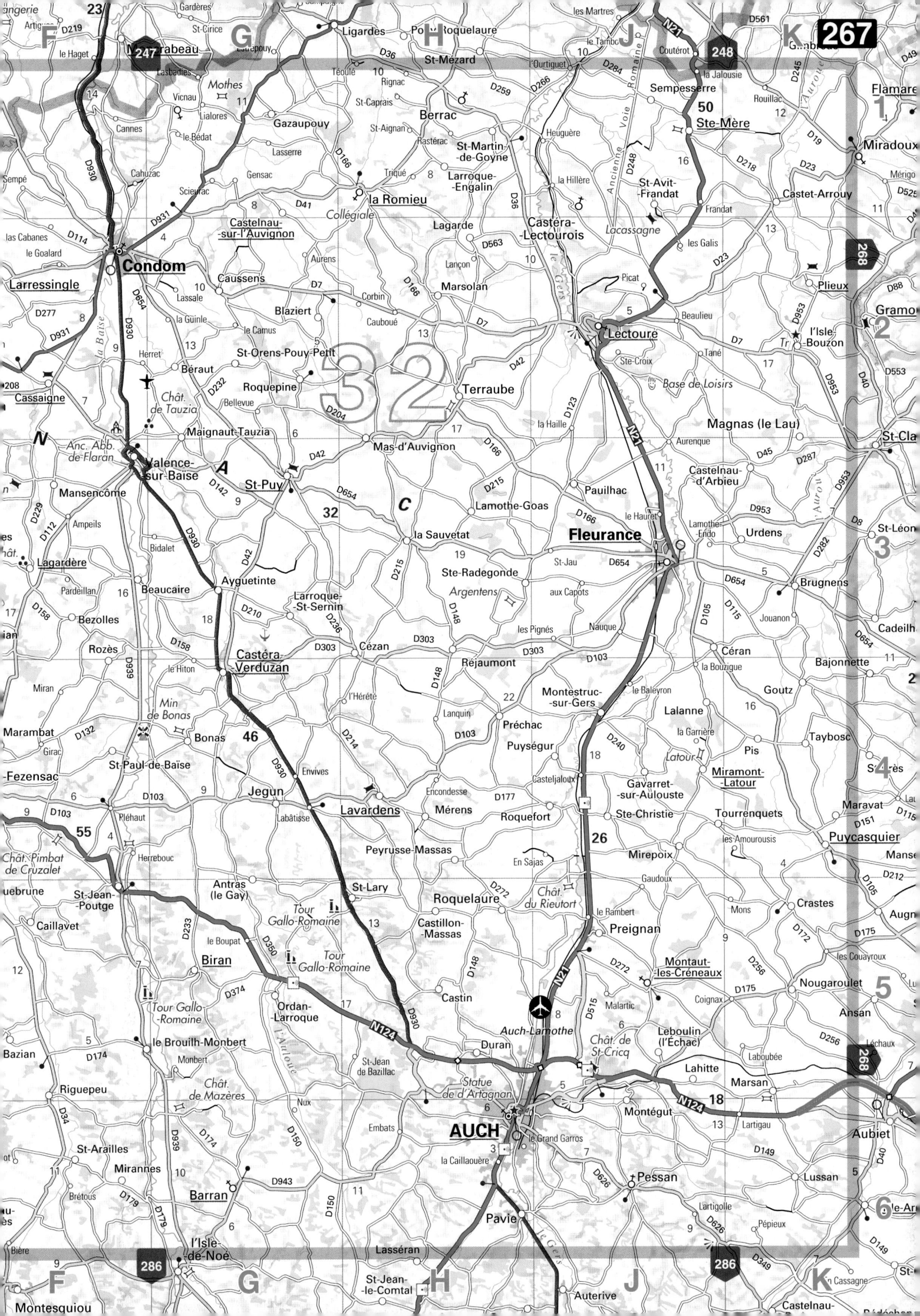

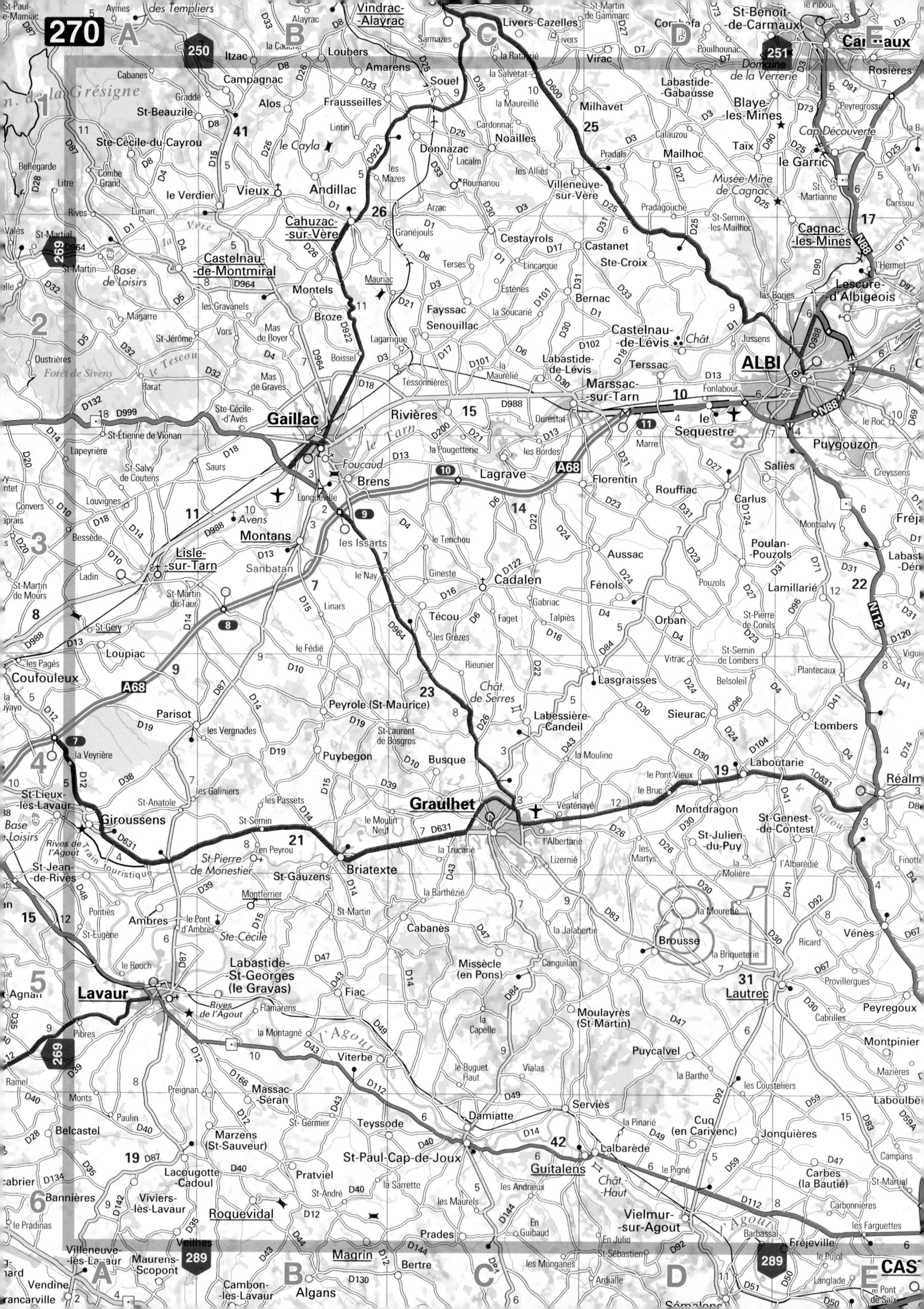

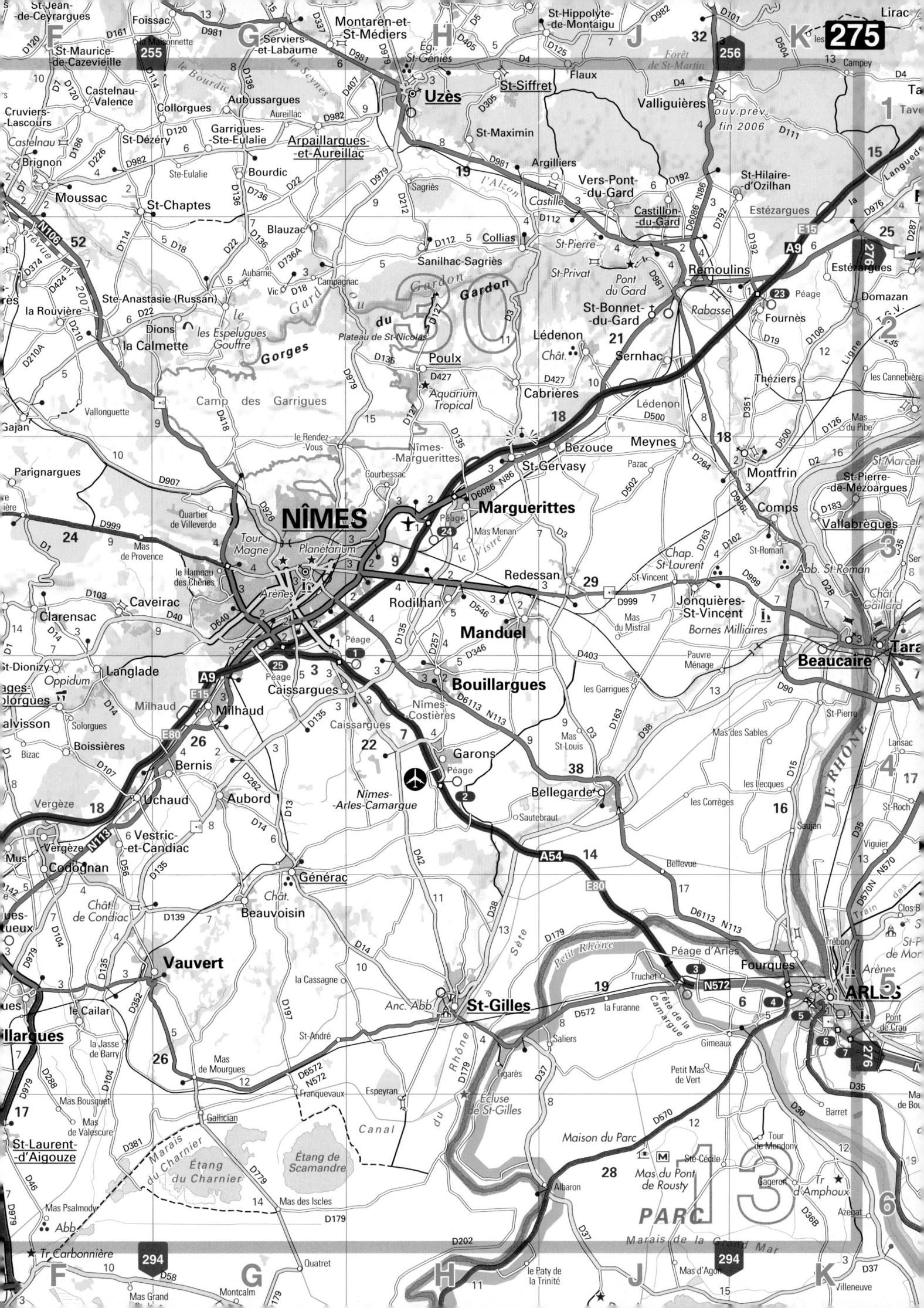

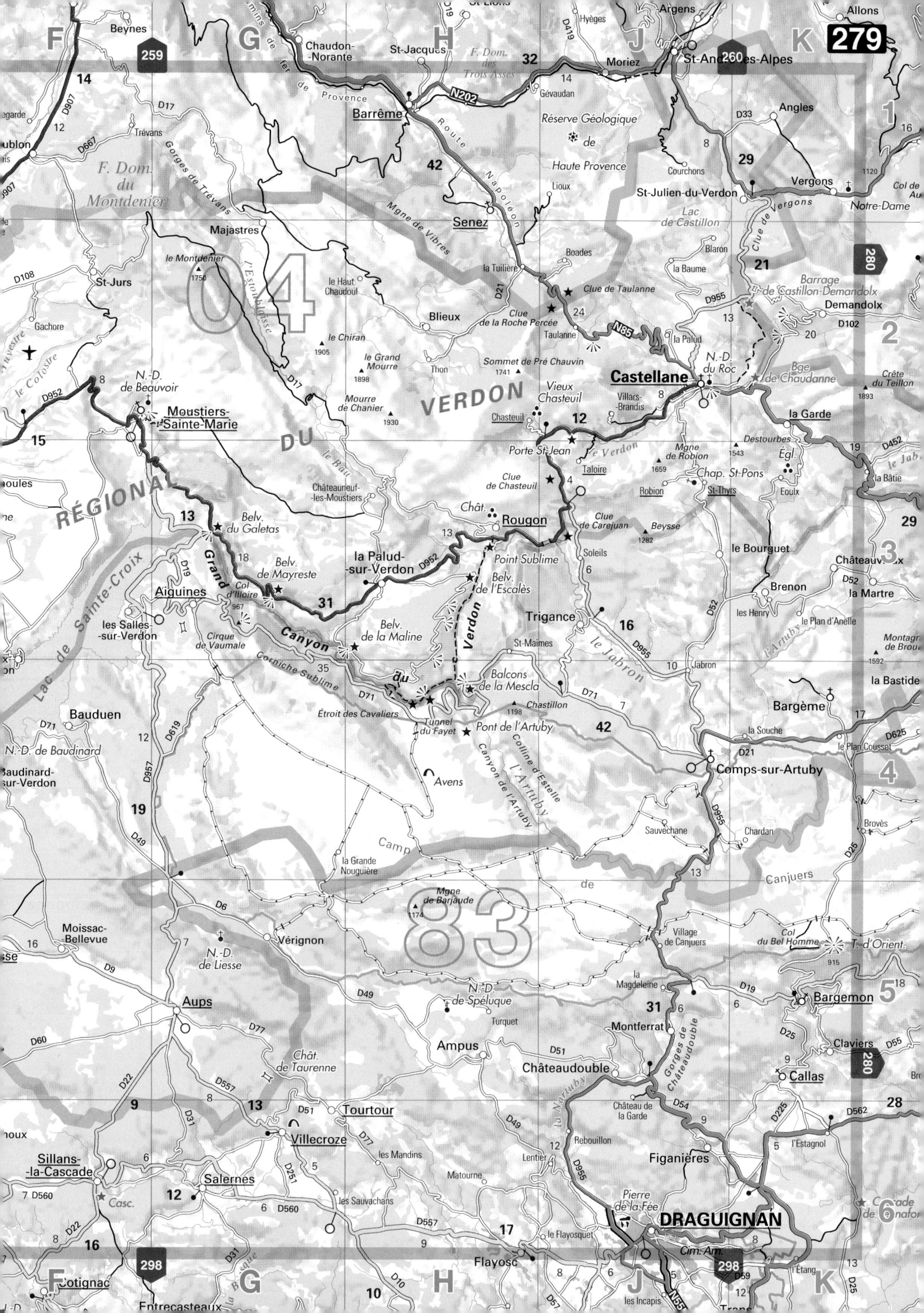

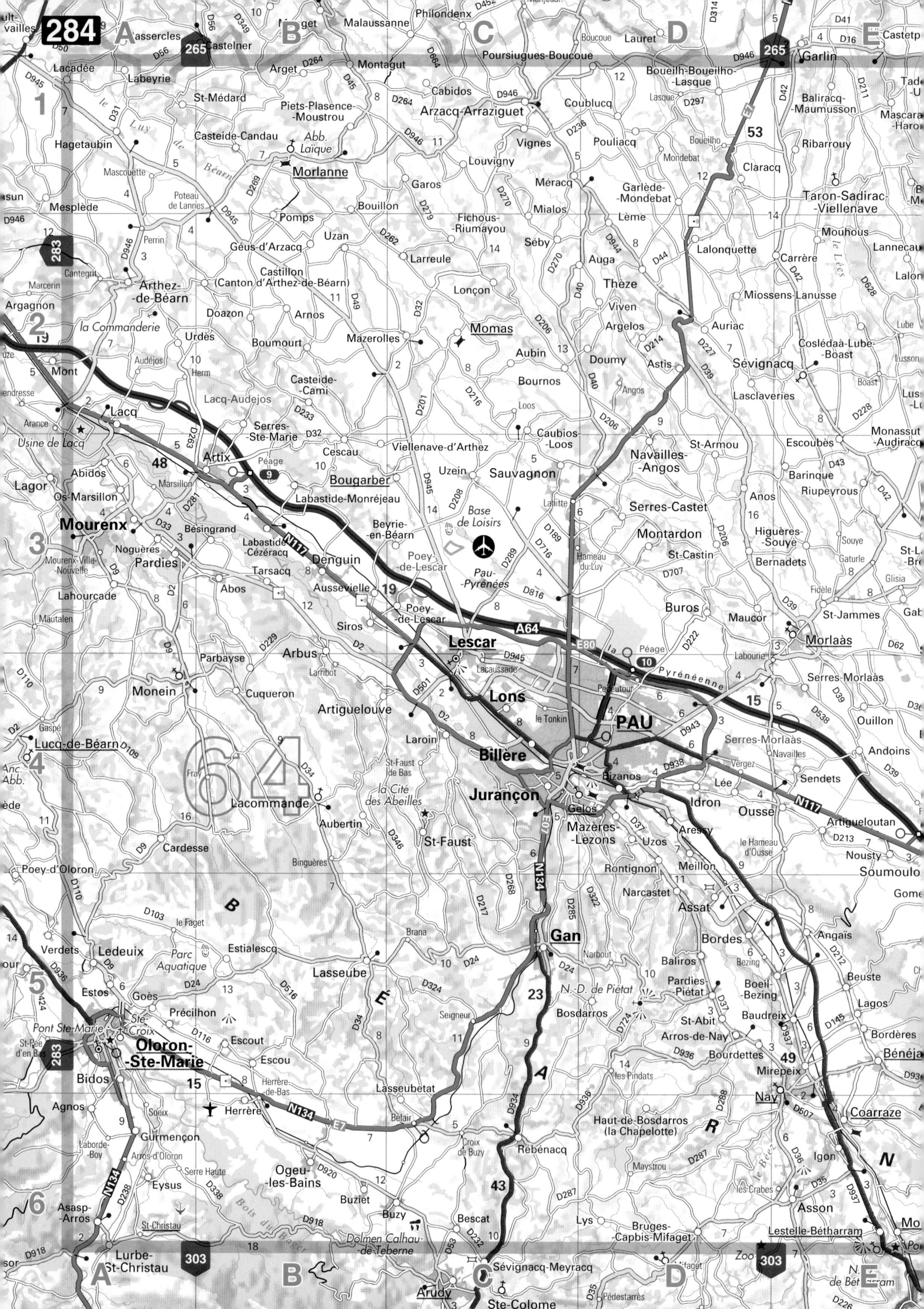

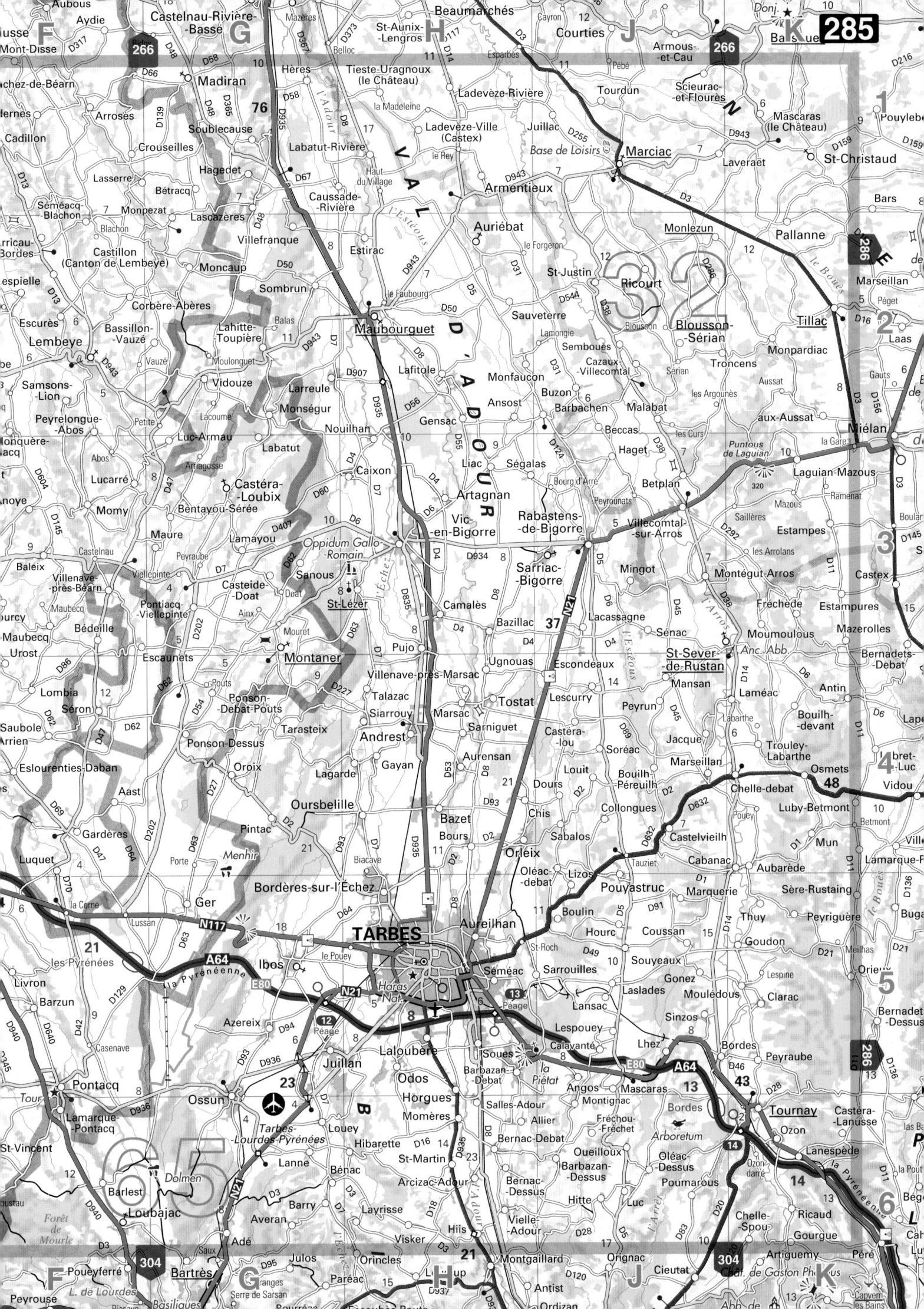

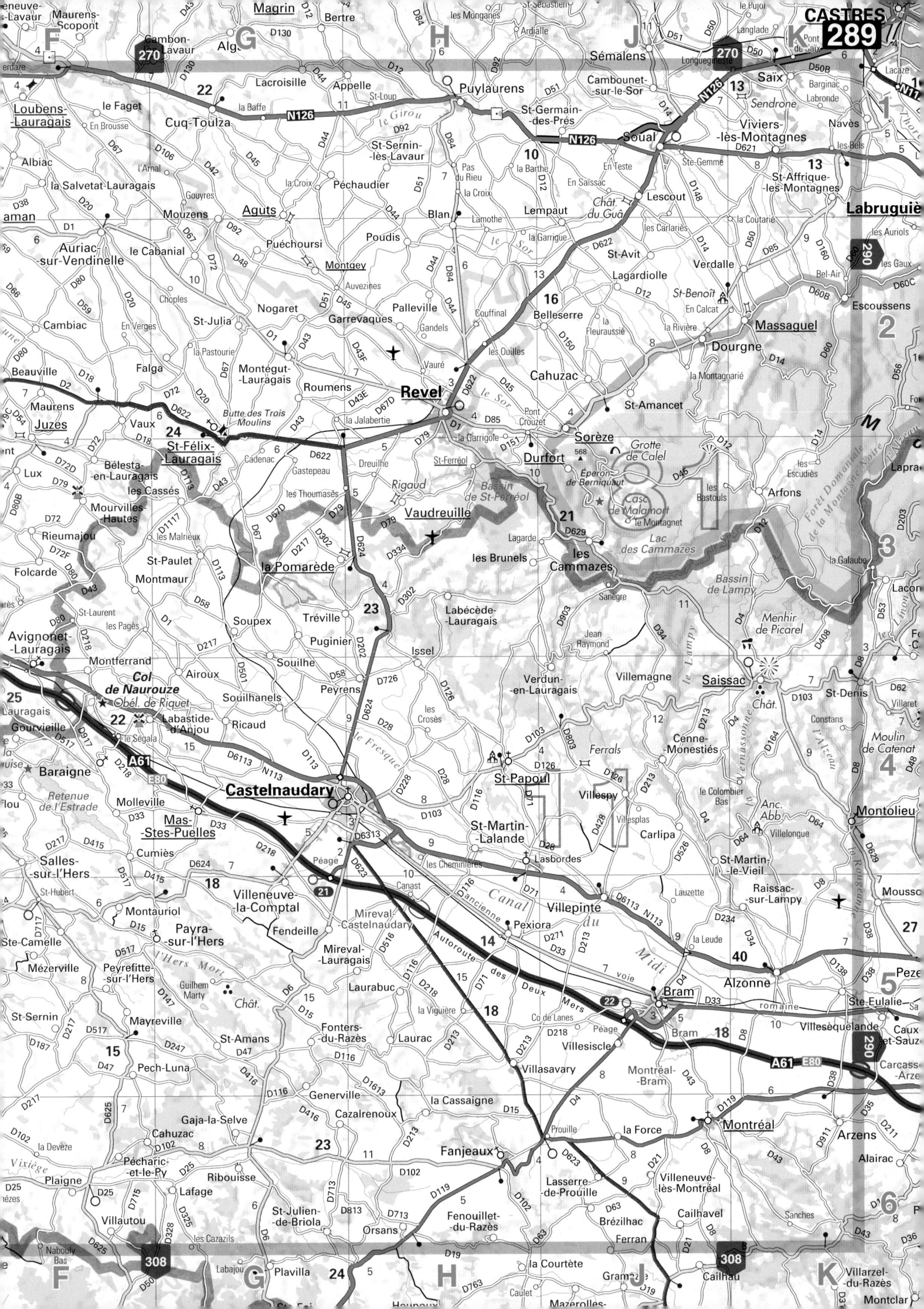

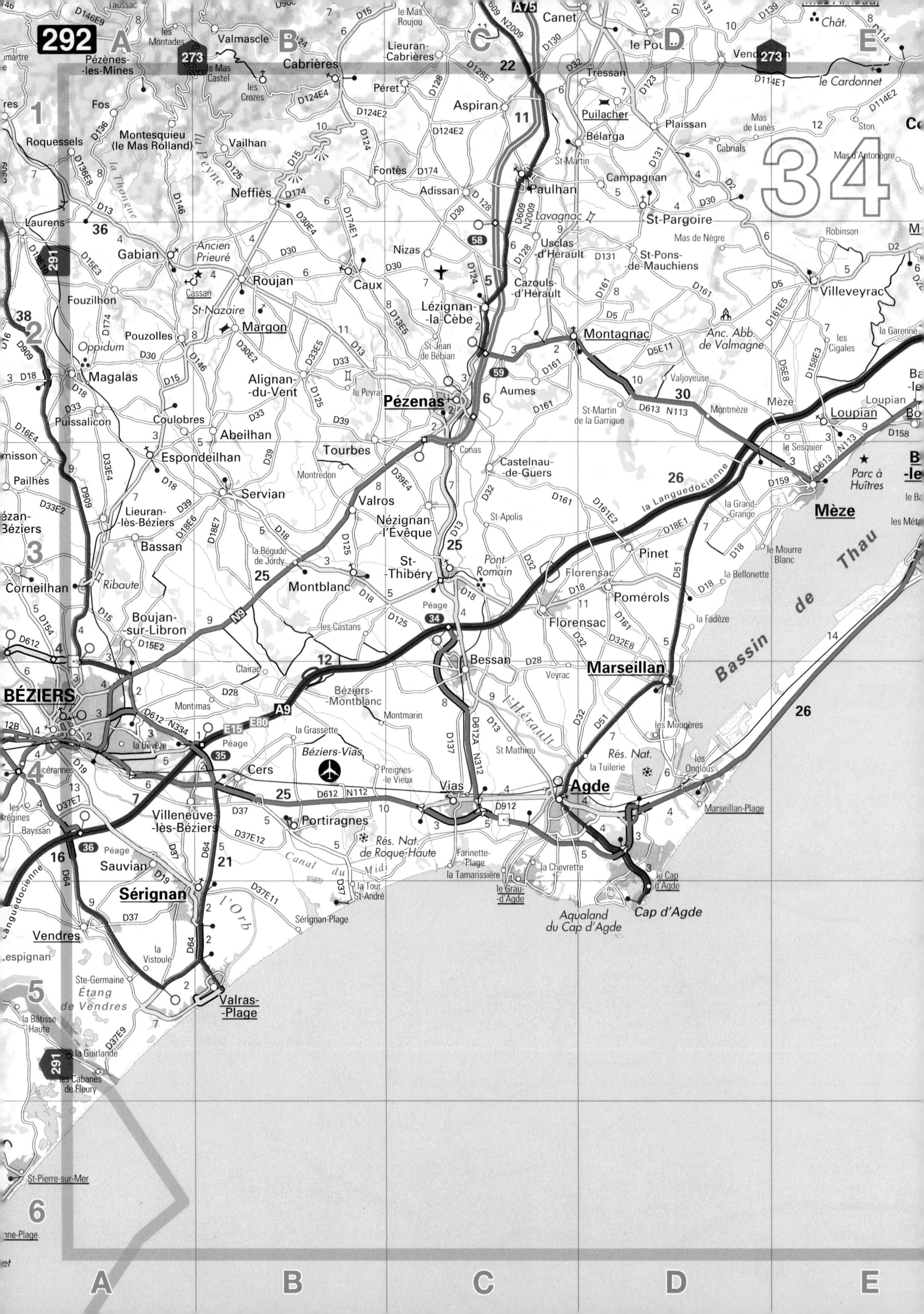

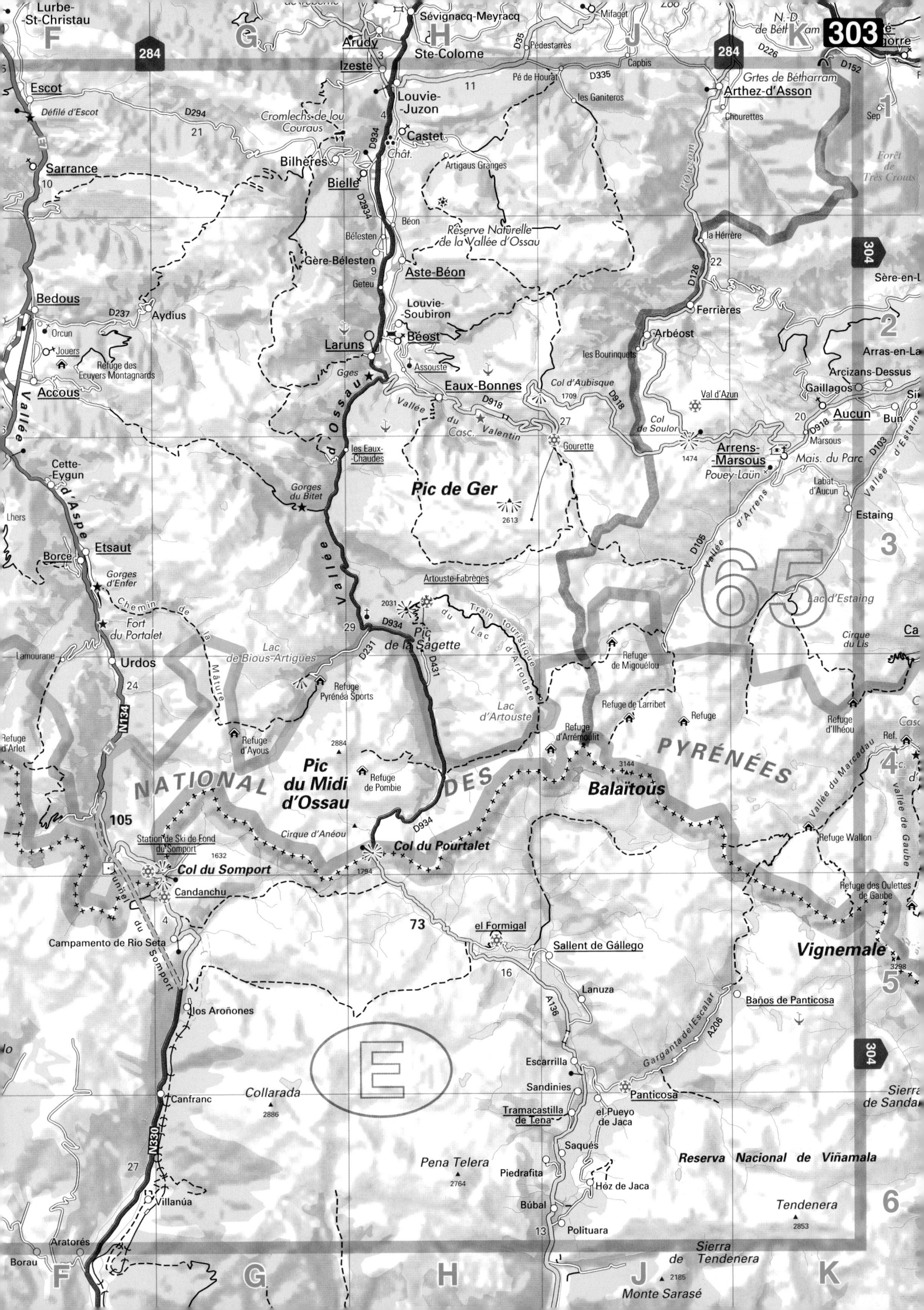

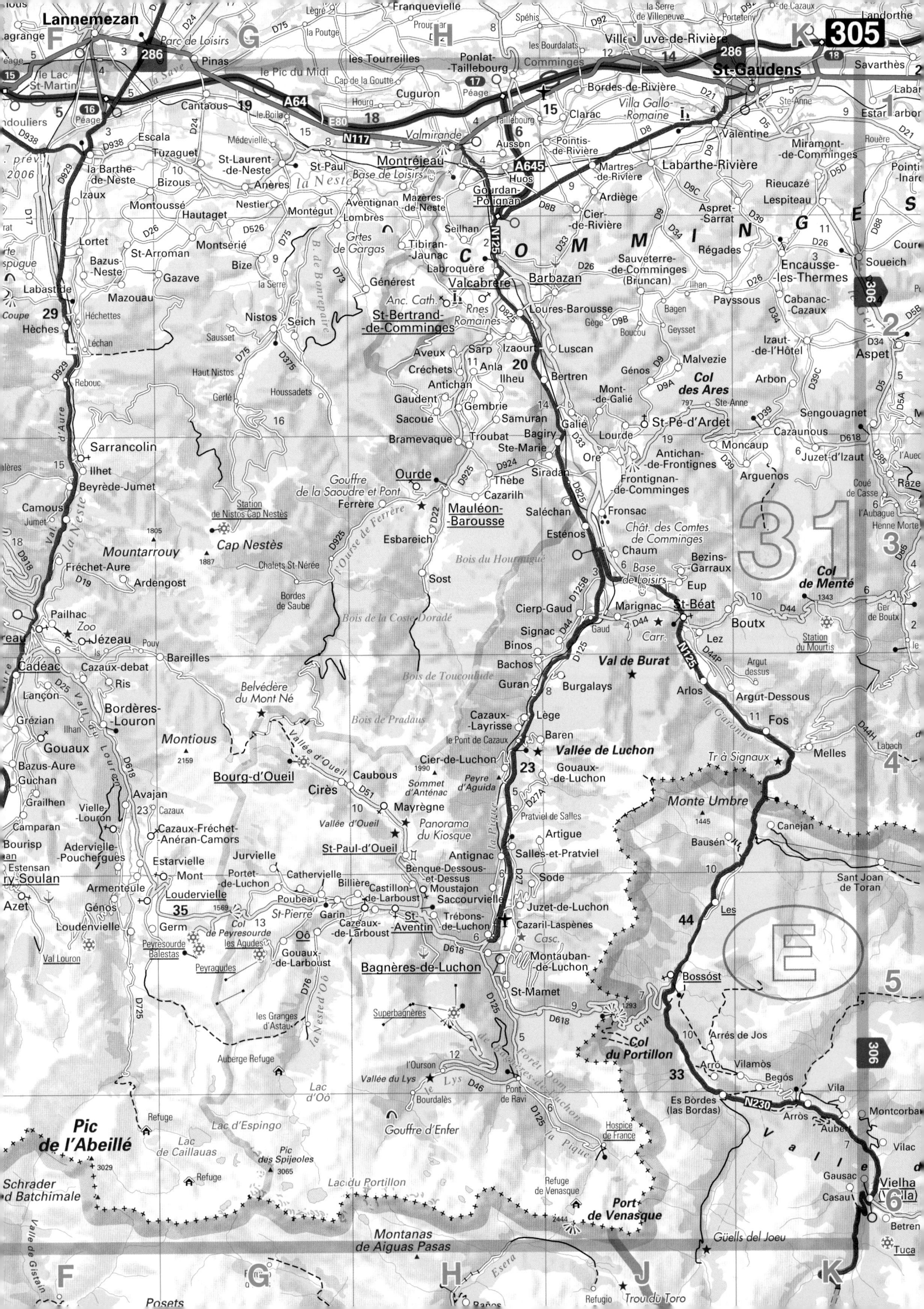

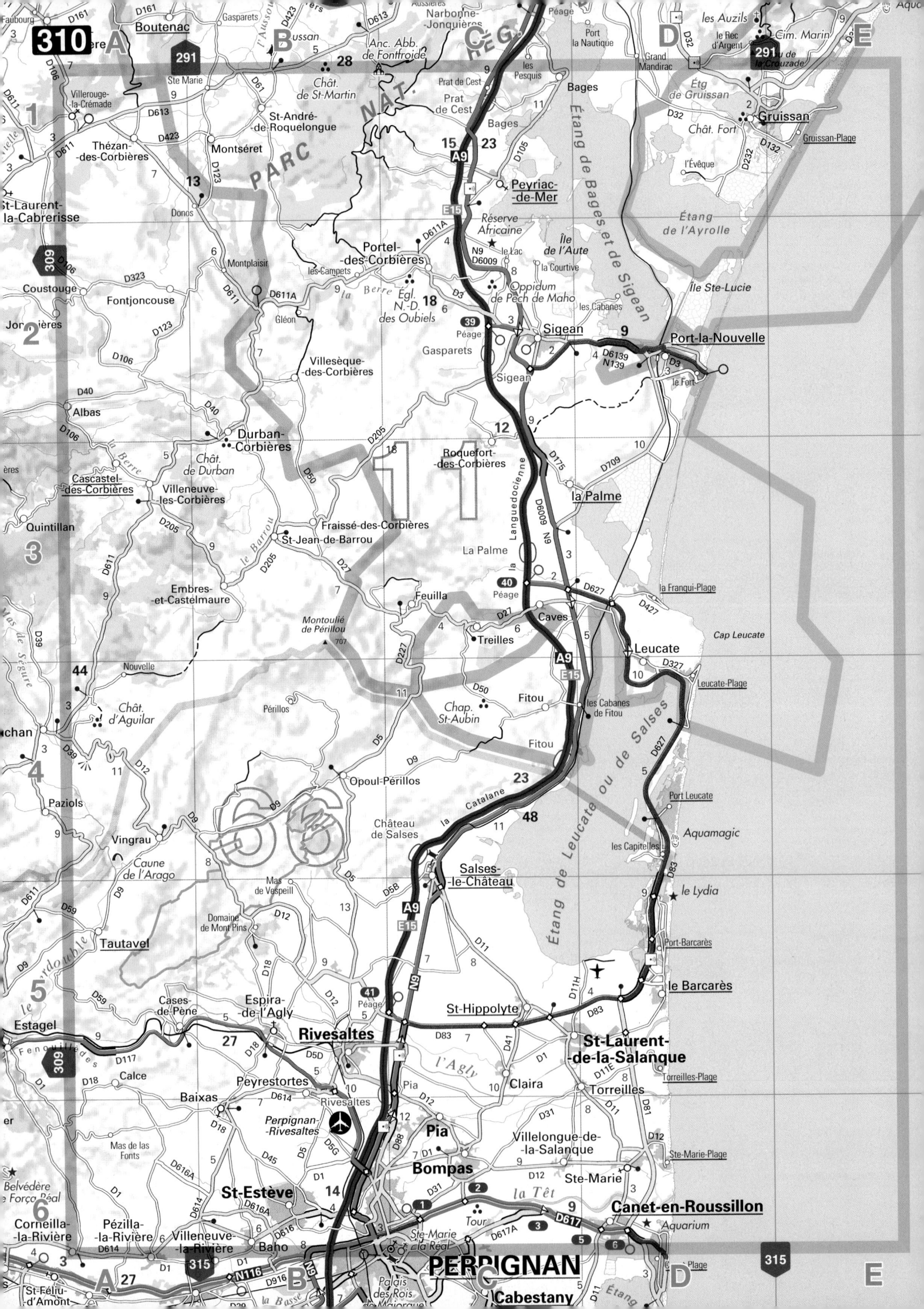

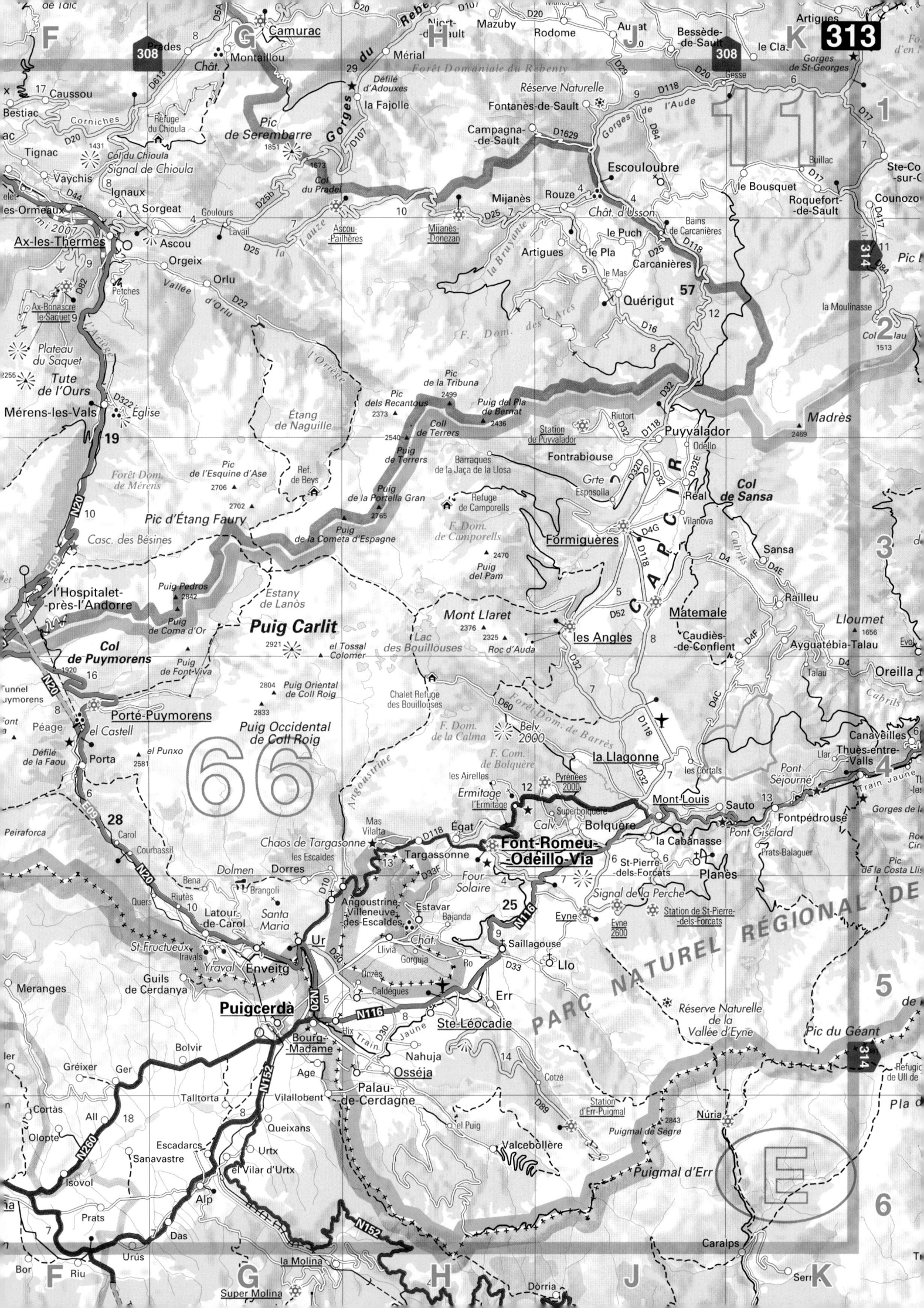

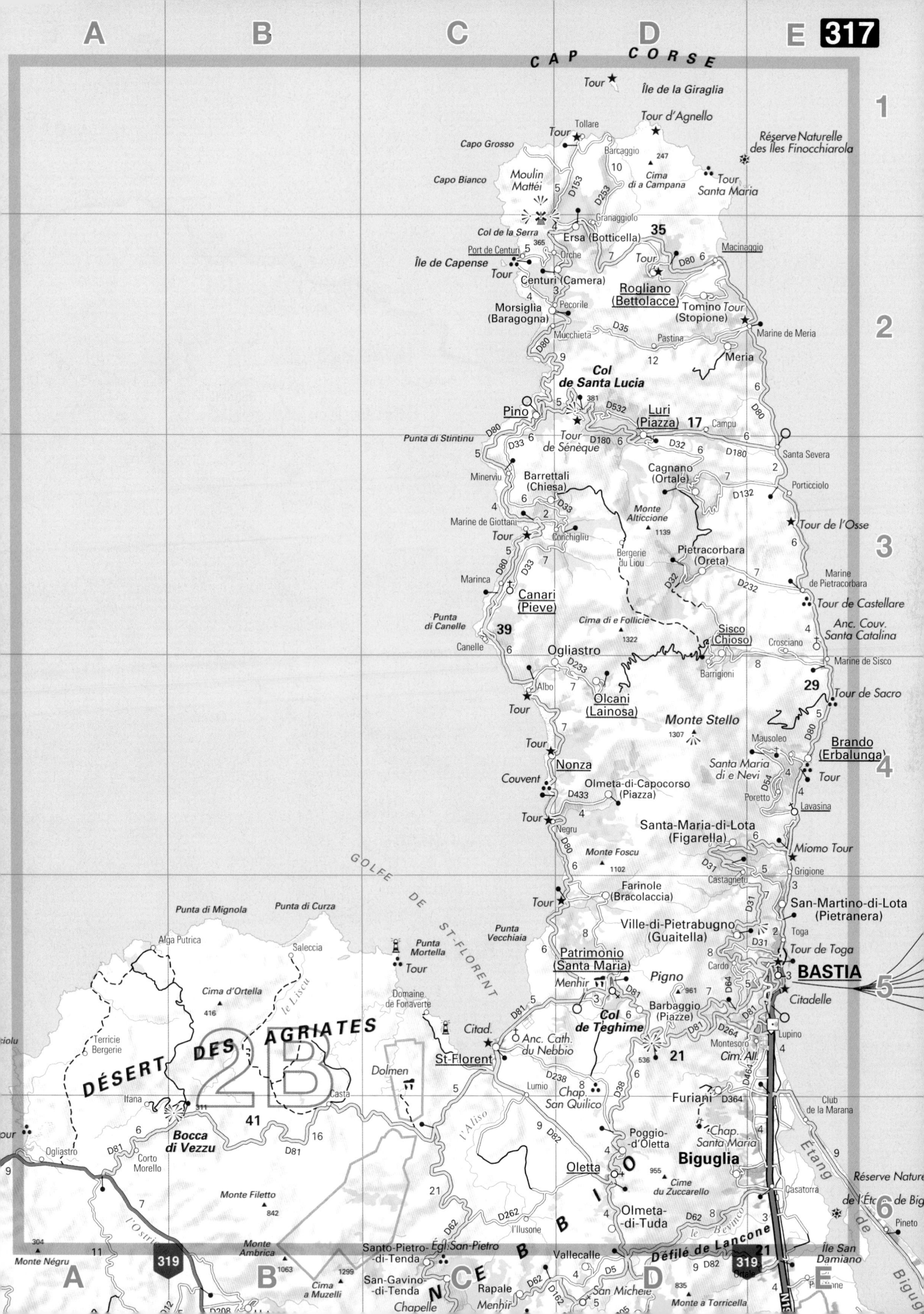

CAP CORSE

A   B   C   D   E

Tour ★
Île de la Giraglia
Tour d'Agnello ★
Réserve Naturelle
des Îles Finocchiarola

Tollare
Tour ★
Capo Grosso
Barcaggio
Cima
di a Campana ▲ 247
10
Tour ★
Santa Maria

Capo Bianco
Moulin
Mattéi
5 D153
D253
Granaggiolo
35

Col de la Serra
4
Ersa (Botticella)
Macinaggio

Orche
365
5
7
Tour ★
D80 6

Port de Centuri
Île de Capense
Tour
Centuri (Camera)
3
Rogliano
(Bettolacce)
Tomino Tour
(Stopione) ★
Marine de Meria

Morsiglia
(Baragogna)
Pecorile
D35
Pastina
Meria

D80
Mucchieta
12
6
9

Col
de Santa Lucia

Pino ★
381
5
D532
Luri
(Piazza) **17**
Campu

Punta di Stintinu
D80
Tour de Sénèque
D180 6
D32
6
D180
Santa Severa

5
D33 6
2
Barrettali
(Chiesa)
Cagnano
(Ortale)
7
D132
Porticciolo

4
6
D33
Monte
Alticcione
▲ 1139
Tour de l'Osse ★

Marine de Giottani
2
Conchigliu
6

Tour ★
Bergerie
du Liou
Pietracorbara
(Oreta)
Marine
de Pietracorbara

5
D33 7
D32
D232
Tour de Castellare

Marinca
Canari
(Pieve)
Cima di e Follicie
▲ 1322
Sisco
(Chioso)
Crosciano
Anc. Couv.
Santa Catalina

Punta
di Canelle
39
8
Marine de Sisco

Canelle
6
Ogliastro
D233
Barrigioni
29
Tour de Sacro ★

Albo
7
Olcani
(Lainosa)
Monte Stello
▲ 1307
5
D80

Tour ★
7
Tour ★
Mausoleo
Brando
(Erbalunga)

Nonza
Santa Maria
di e Nevi
Tour ★

Couvent
Olmeta-di-Capocorso
(Piazza)
Poretto
4
Lavasina

D433
4
Santa-Maria-di-Lota
(Figarella)
Miomo Tour ★

Tour ★
Negru
4
D31
5
Grigione

D80
Monte Foscu
▲ 1102
6
Castagneti
3

Farinole
(Bracolaccia)
D31
San-Martino-di-Lota
(Pietranera)

Tour ★
Punta
Vecchiaia
Ville-di-Pietrabugno
(Guaitella)
2
Toga

Punta
Mortella
8
D31
Tour de Toga

Tour
Patrimonio
(Santa Maria)
8
Cardo
Pigno
BASTIA

Domaine
de Fonaverte
Menhir
5
D81
Barbaggio
(Piazze)
D64
7
Citadelle

Citad.
Anc. Cath.
du Nebbio
3
Col
de Teghime
6
▲ 961
D81
Lupino

St-Florent
D238
536
21
Montesoro
Cim. All.
4

Dolmen
Lumio
Chap.
San Quilico
8
D38
Furiani
D364
Club
de la Marana

DÉSERT DES AGRIATES
5
9
D82
Poggio-
d'Oletta
Chap.
Santa Maria
Biguglia
4

2B
Oletta
955
Cime
du Zuccarello

Punta di Mignola
Punta di Curza
41
16
D81
B I O
Casatorra
Réserve Nature
de l'Éta de Bigu

Alga Putrica
Salecca
le Liscu

Cima d'Ortella
▲ 416
B
Olmeta-
di-Tuda
D62
8
3
Pineto

Terricie
Bergerie
Ifana
311
Bocca
di Vezzu
21
Santo-Pietro-
di-Tenda
Égl. San-Pietro
Vallecalle
D5
319
21
Île San
Damiano

Ogliastro
D81
6
Corto
Morello
D262
l'Ilusone
San-Gavino-
di-Tenda
San Michele
Montee a Torricella
Étang de
Biguglia

9
7
Monte Filetto
▲ 842
NCE
Rapale
Menhir
D62
D162
835
▲

Monte Négru
304
11
319
Monte
Ambrica
▲ 1063
Cima
a Muzelli
▲ 1299
Chapelle
D
Défilé de Lancone
D82
Ortale
E

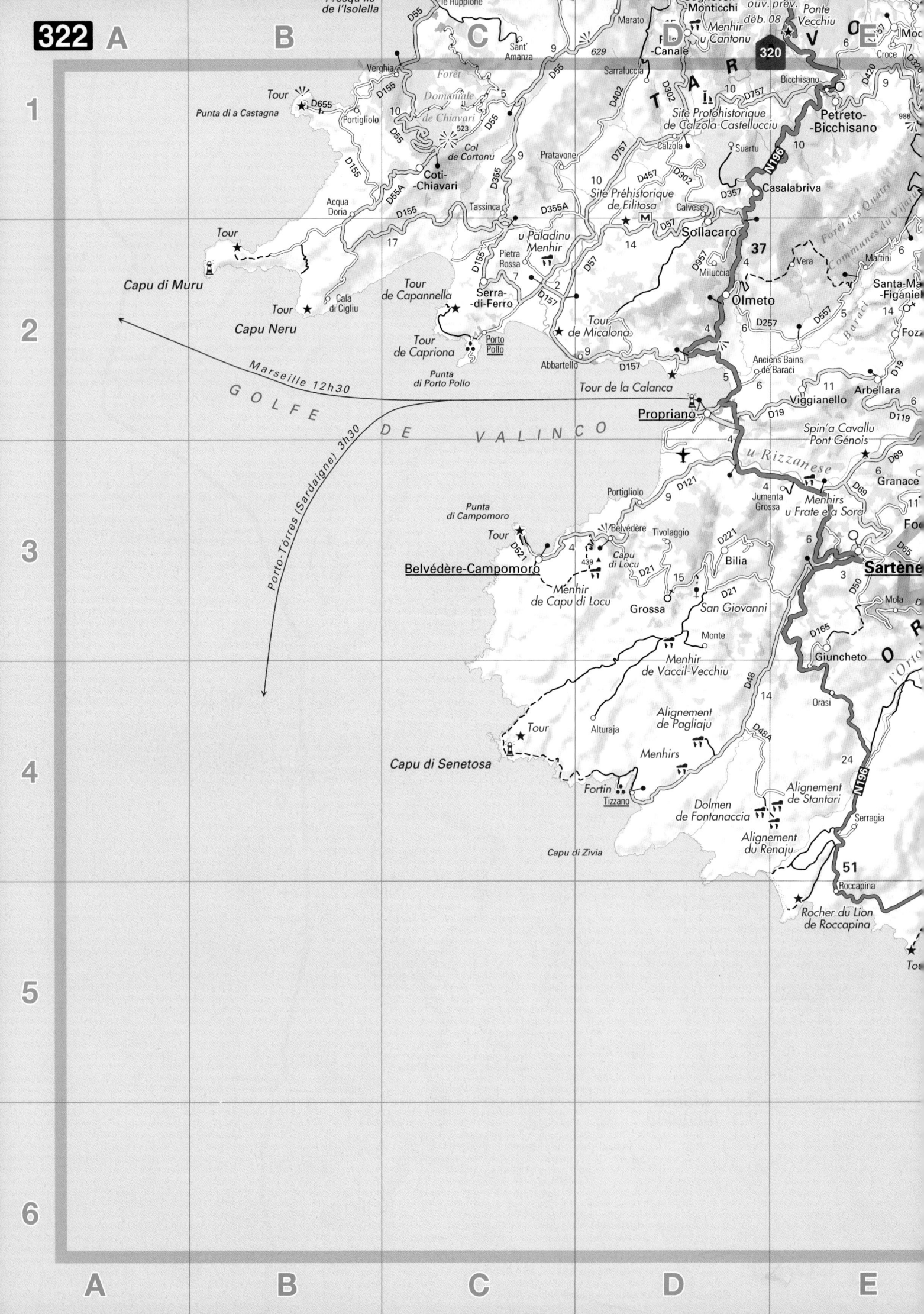

A B C D E

1

2

3

4

5

6

Presqu'île
de l'Isolella
le Ruppione
Monticchi
ouv. prév.
déb. 08
Ponte
Vecchiu

D55
Marato
Menhir
u Cantonu
320

Verghia
Sant'
Amanza
9
629
-Canale
T A R V E
Croce

Forêt
Sarraluccia
Bicchisano
NT96

Tour
D655
D155
D155
10
D55
5
D402
10
D757
Site Protohistorique
de Calzola-Castellucciu
Petreto-
Bicchisano

Punta di a Castagna
Portigliolo
10
D55
D55
Domaniale
de Chiavari
523
5
9
D302
Suartu
10
986

D155
Col
de Cortonu
9
Pratavone
D757
Calzola
Calvese
10

Acqua
Doria
D55A
Coti-
Chiavari
D355
Tassinca
9
D302
Casalabriva

D155
D155
D355A
Site Préhistorique
de Filitosa
M
D457
D357
37

Tour
17
u Paladinu
Menhir
D57
14
Sollacaro
D957
Vera

Capu di Muru
D155
Pietra
Rossa
7
D57
2
Miluccia
4
Martini

Tour
Capu Neru
Tour
de Capannella
Serra-
di-Ferro
D157
Olmeto
D557
Santa-Ma
-Figaniel

Cala
di Cigliu
Tour
de Capriona
Porto
Pollo
Tour
de Micalona
4
D257
6
14
Fozz

Marseille 12h30
Punta
di Porto Pollo
9
Abbartello
D157
Ancien Bains
de Baraci
11
Arbellara
D19

G O L F E
Tour de la Calanca
5
6
Viggianello
D119

D E
Propriano
D19
Spin'a Cavallu
Pont Génois
D69

V A L I N C O
4
u Rizzanese
D69
Granace
6

Porto-Tóres (Sardaigne) 3h30
Portigliolo
D21
4
Jumenta
Grossa
Menhirs
u Frate e a Sora
11
Foc

Punta
di Campomoro
9
Belvédère
Tivolaggio
D221
6
D65

Tour
D521
4
Capu
di Locu
D21
15
Bilia
6
Sartène

Belvédère-Campomoro
439
D21
San Giovanni
3
D50
Mola

Menhir
de Capu di Locu
Grossa
Monte
D165
Giuncheto

Menhir
de Vaccil-Vecchiu
D48
14
Orasi
O R

Tour
Alignement
de Pagliaju
D48A
24
Alignement
de Stantari
NT96

Capu di Senetosa
Alturaja
Menhirs
Serragia

Fortin
Tizzano
Dolmen
de Fontanaccia
Alignement
du Renaju
51

Capu di Zivia
Roccapina

Rocher du Lion
de Roccapina
Tou

A B C D E

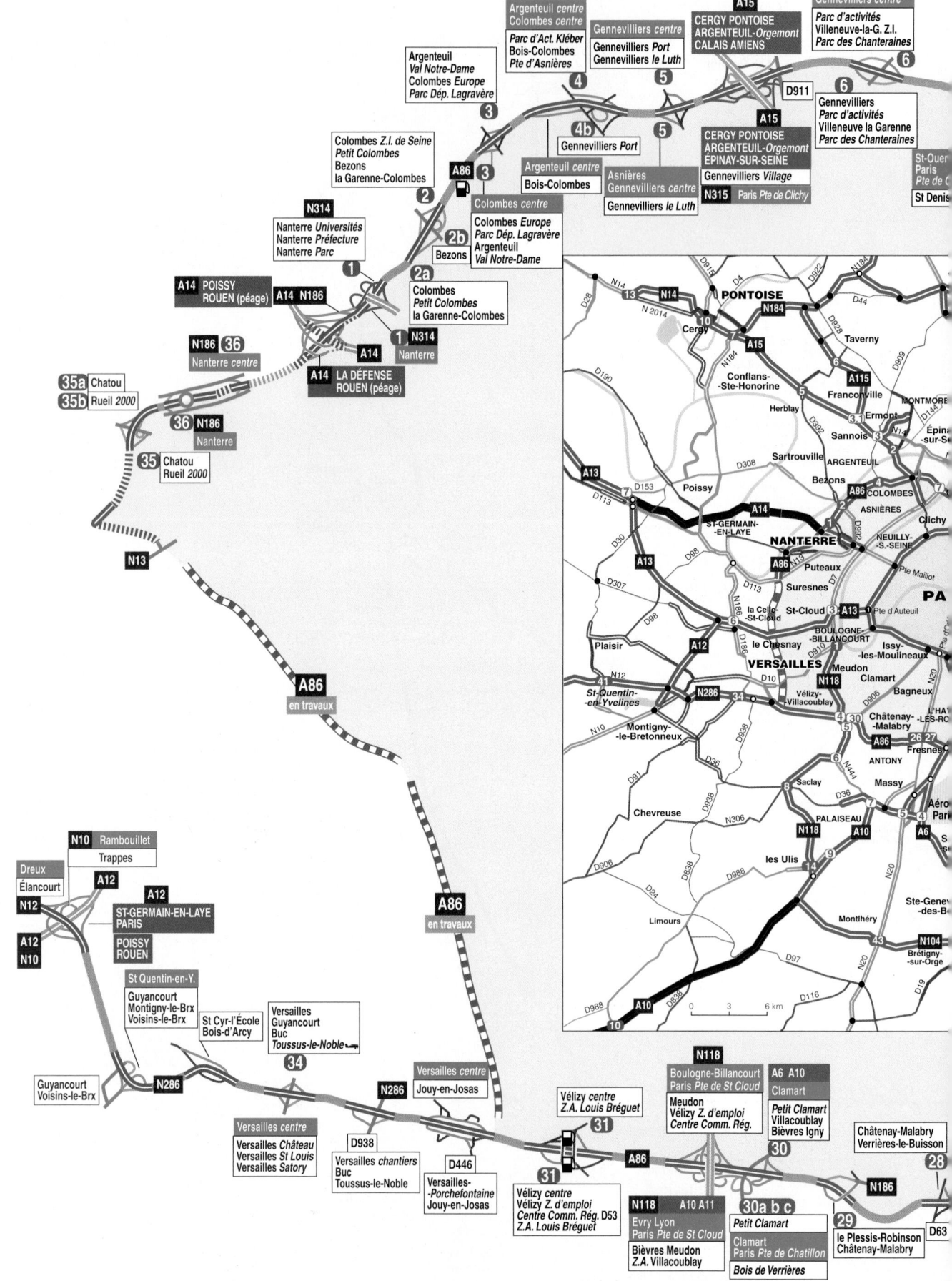

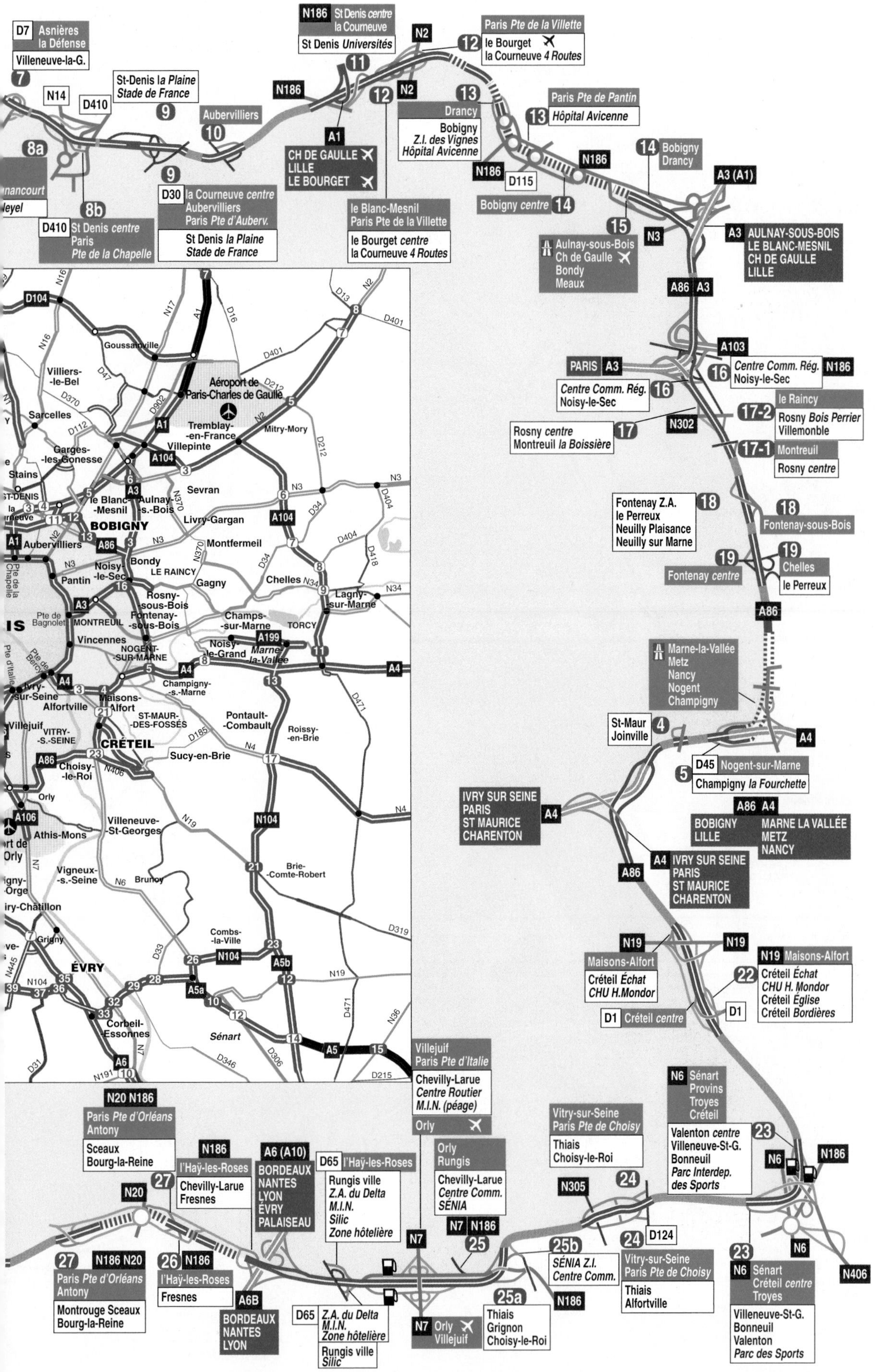

D7 Asnières la Défense
Villeneuve-la-G.
N186 St Denis centre la Courneuve
St Denis Universités
Paris Pte de la Villette
le Bourget
la Courneuve 4 Routes
St-Denis la Plaine Stade de France
Aubervilliers
CH DE GAULLE LILLE LE BOURGET
Drancy
Bobigny Z.I. des Vignes Hôpital Avicenne
Paris Pte de Pantin
Hôpital Avicenne
Bobigny Drancy
D30 la Courneuve centre Aubervilliers Paris Pte d'Auberv.
St Denis la Plaine Stade de France
D410 St Denis centre Paris Pte de la Chapelle
le Blanc-Mesnil Paris Pte de la Villette
le Bourget centre la Courneuve 4 Routes
Bobigny centre
Aulnay-sous-Bois Ch de Gaulle Bondy Meaux
A3 AULNAY-SOUS-BOIS LE BLANC-MESNIL CH DE GAULLE LILLE
PARIS A3
Centre Comm. Rég. Noisy-le-Sec
le Raincy
Rosny Bois Perrier Villemonble
Rosny centre Montreuil la Boissière
Montreuil
Rosny centre
Fontenay Z.A. le Perreux Neuilly Plaisance Neuilly sur Marne
Fontenay-sous-Bois
Fontenay centre
Chelles
le Perreux
Marne-la-Vallée Metz Nancy Nogent Champigny
St-Maur Joinville
D45 Nogent-sur-Marne
Champigny la Fourchette
IVRY SUR SEINE PARIS ST MAURICE CHARENTON
BOBIGNY LILLE
MARNE LA VALLÉE METZ NANCY
A4 IVRY SUR SEINE PARIS ST MAURICE CHARENTON
Maisons-Alfort
Créteil Échat CHU H.Mondor
D1 Créteil centre
N19 Maisons-Alfort
Créteil Échat CHU H. Mondor Créteil Église Créteil Bordières
Aéroport de Paris-Charles de Gaulle
Villejuif Paris Pte d'Italie
Chevilly-Larue Centre Routier M.I.N. (péage)
Orly
N6 Sénart Provins Troyes Créteil
Valenton centre Villeneuve-St-G. Bonneuil Parc Interdep. des Sports
Vitry-sur-Seine Paris Pte de Choisy
Thiais Choisy-le-Roi
N20 N186 Paris Pte d'Orléans Antony
Sceaux Bourg-la-Reine
l'Haÿ-les-Roses
Chevilly-Larue Fresnes
A6 (A10) BORDEAUX NANTES LYON ÉVRY PALAISEAU
D65 l'Haÿ-les-Roses
Rungis ville Z.A. du Delta M.I.N. Silic Zone hôtelière
Orly Rungis
Chevilly-Larue Centre Comm. SÉNIA
SÉNIA Z.I. Centre Comm.
Vitry-sur-Seine Paris Pte de Choisy
Thiais Alfortville
N6 Sénart Créteil centre Troyes
Villeneuve-St-G. Bonneuil Valenton Parc des Sports
N186 N20 Paris Pte d'Orléans Antony
Montrouge Sceaux Bourg-la-Reine
N186 l'Haÿ-les-Roses
Fresnes
A6B BORDEAUX NANTES LYON
D65 Z.A. du Delta M.I.N. Zone hôtelière
Rungis ville Silic
N7 Orly Villejuif
Thiais Grignon Choisy-le-Roi

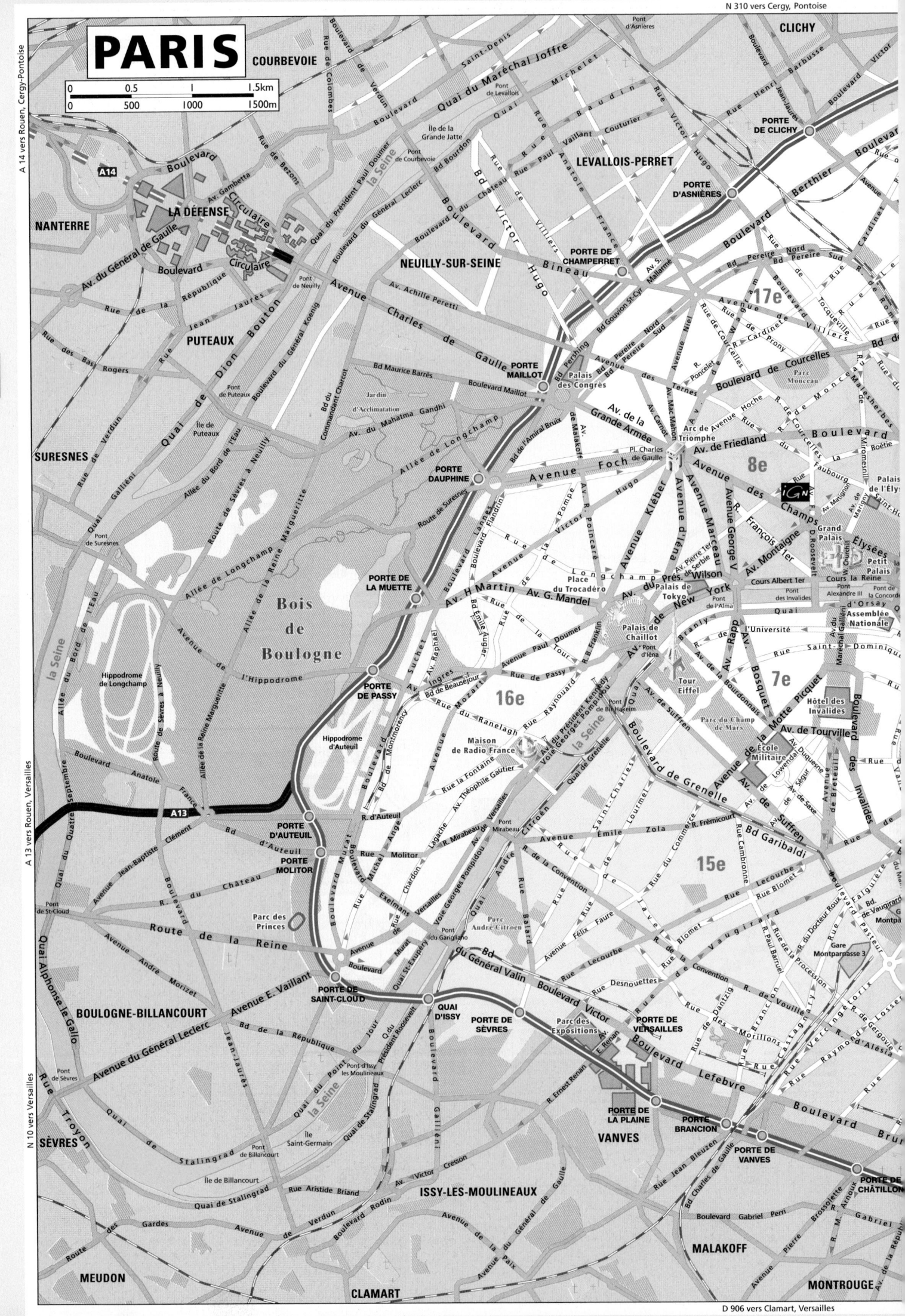

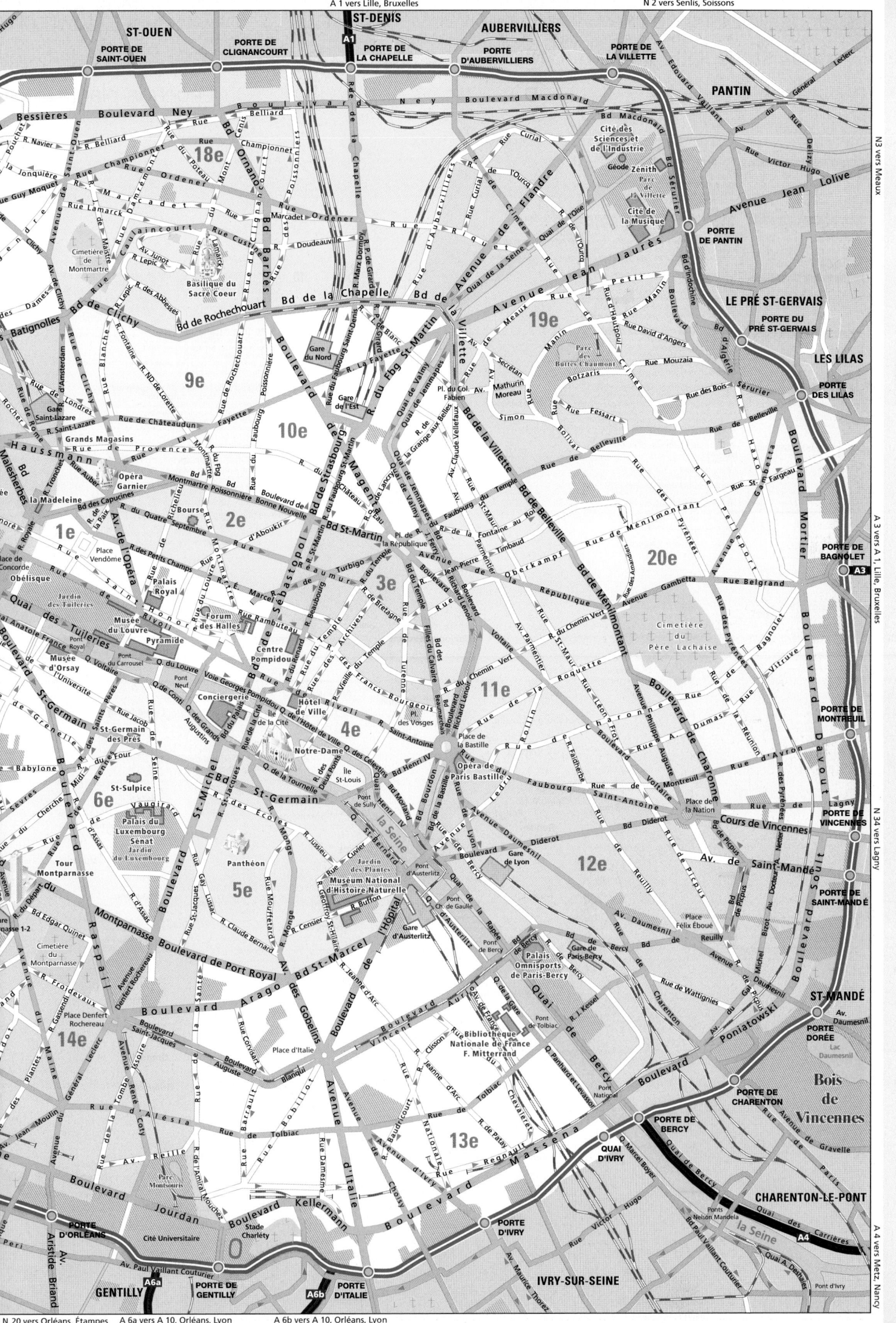

Légende de plans de ville (F)

Legenda stadsplattegronden (NL)

Legende: Stadtpläne (D)

Key to town plan (GB)

Leyenda plano de ciuda (E)

Legenda pianta di citt (I)

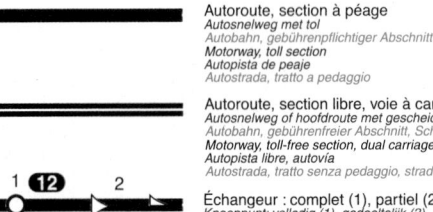

Autoroute, section à péage
Autosnelweg met tol
Autobahn, gebührenpflichtiger Abschnitt
Motorway, toll section
Autopista de peaje
Autostrada, tratto a pedaggio

Autoroute, section libre, voie à caractère autoroutier
Autosnelweg of hoofdroute met gescheiden rijbanen
Autobahn, gebührenfreier Abschnitt, Schnellverkehrsstraße
Motorway, toll-free section, dual carriageway with motorway characteristics
Autopista libre, autovía
Autostrada, tratto senza pedaggio, strada con carretterische autostradali

Échangeur : complet (1), partiel (2), numéro
Knooppunt: volledig (1), gedeeltelijk (2), nummer
Vollanschlußstelle (1), beschränkte Anschlußstelle (2), Nummer
Junction : complete (1), restricted (2), number
Acceso: completo (1), parcial (2), número
Svincolo: completo (1) parziale (2), numero

Barrière de péage (1), aire de service (2)
Tolstation (1), tankstation (2)
Mautstelle (1), Tankstelle (2)
Toll gate (1), service area (2)
Punto de peaje (1), área de servicio (2)
Barriera di pedaggio (1), area di servizio (2)

Route appartenant au réseau vert
Verbindingsweg tussen grote steden (groene borden)
Verbindungsstraße zwischen wichtigen Städten (grüne Verkehrsschilder)
Connecting road between main towns (green road sign)
Carretera verde (comunicación entre dos ciudades importantes)
Collegamento stradale tra città principali (cartelli stradali verdi)

Autre route de liaison principale
Hoofdweg
Fernverkehrsstraße
Other main road
Otra carretera principal
Strada di grande comunicazione

Route de liaison régionale
Regionale verbindingsweg
Regionale Verbindungsstraße
Regional connecting road
Carretera regional
Strada di collegamento regionale

Autre route
Andere weg
Sonstige Straße
Other road
Otra carretera
Altra strada

Tunnel routier
Wegtunnel
Straßentunnel
Road tunnel
Túnel
Galleria stradale

Bâtiment administratif (1), église, chapelle (2), hôpital (3)
Administratief gebouw (1), kerk, kapel (2), ziekenhuis (3)
Verwaltungsgebäude (1), Kirche, Kapelle (2), Krankenhaus (3)
Administrative building (1), church, chapel (2), hospital (3)
Edificio administrative (1), iglesia, capilla (2), hospital (3)
Edificio pubblico (1), chiesa, cappella (2), ospedale (3)

Limite de commune, de canton
Gemeente-, provinciegrens
Gemeindegrenze, Kreisgrenze
Commune, canton boundary
Límite de municipio, límite de cantón
Confine di comune, confine di cantone

Limite d'arrondissement, de département
Arrondissements-, departementsgrens
Bezirksgrenze, Departementsgrenze
Arrondissement, département boundary
Límite de arrondissement, límite de departamento
Confine di arrondissement, confine di dipartimento

Limite de région, d'État
Gewest-, staatsgrens
Regionsgrenze, Staatsgrenze
Region, international boundary
Límite de región, límite de nación
Confine di regione, confine di stato

Zone bâtie, superficie > 8 ha (1), < 8 ha (2), zone industrielle (3)
Bebouwde kom, groter dan 8 ha (1), kleiner dan 8 ha (2), industriegebied (3)
Geschlossene Bebauung, über 8 ha (1), unter 8 ha (2), industriegebiet (3)
Built-up area, more than 8 ha (1), less than 8 ha (2), industrial park (3)
Zona edificada: más de 8 ha (1), menos de 8 ha (2), polígono industrial (3)
Area edificata, più di 8 ha (1), meno di 8 ha (2), zona industriale (3)

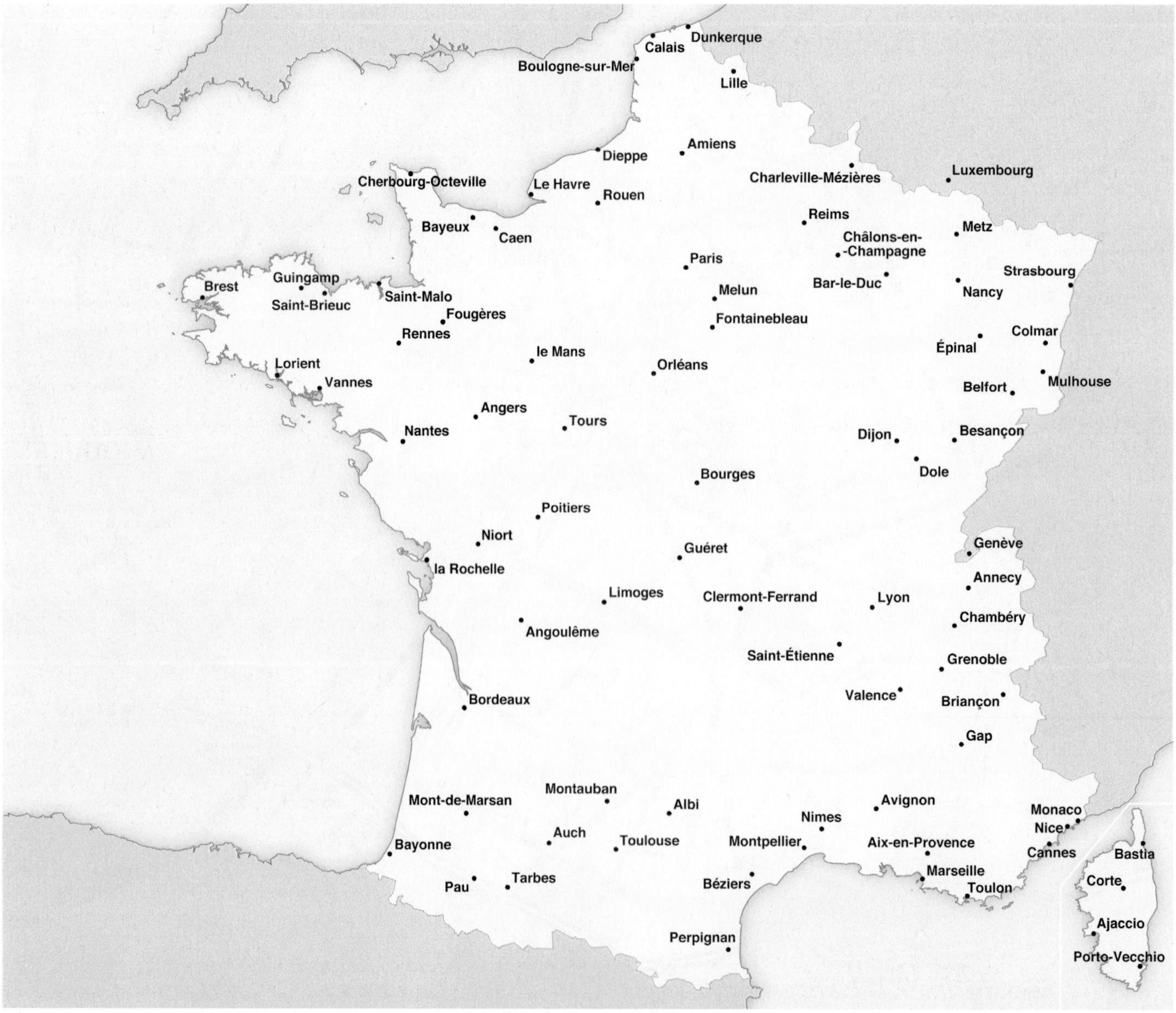

328

Dunkerque
Calais
Boulogne-sur-Mer
Lille
Amiens
Dieppe
Charleville-Mézières
Luxembourg
Cherbourg-Octeville
Le Havre
Rouen
Reims
Metz
Bayeux
Caen
Châlons-en-
-Champagne
Strasbourg
Paris
Bar-le-Duc
Nancy
Brest
Guingamp
Melun
Saint-Malo
Saint-Brieuc
Fougères
Fontainebleau
Colmar
Rennes
Épinal
le Mans
Belfort
Mulhouse
Lorient
Orléans
Vannes
Angers
Tours
Dijon
Besançon
Nantes
Dole
Bourges
Poitiers
Niort
Guéret
Genève
la Rochelle
Annecy
Limoges
Clermont-Ferrand
Lyon
Angoulême
Chambéry
Saint-Étienne
Grenoble
Bordeaux
Valence
Briançon
Gap
Montauban
Mont-de-Marsan
Albi
Avignon
Monaco
Nice
Bayonne
Auch
Toulouse
Nîmes
Aix-en-Provence
Cannes
Bastia
Montpellier
Pau
Tarbes
Béziers
Marseille
Toulon
Corte
Perpignan
Ajaccio
Porto-Vecchio

AIX-EN-PROVENCE

la Violette
l'Hôpital
Av. Ph. Solari
D14
Av. de Lattre de Tassigny
N296
Av. J. Dalmas
Route de Galice
Rocade Ouest
7
Encagnane
D 65
Av. du Pigonnet
le Pigonnet
les Fenouillères
Av. G. Berger
A8
A51
6
30
Brassiette
Cuques
Rocade Sud
Bd F. et E. Zola
Av. J. et M. Fontenaille
D10
Av. Ste Victoire
Hôt. de V.
S.-préf.
Palais de Justice
Bd de la République
Crs Mirabeau
Bd des Poilus
Av. J. Perry
Bd du Roi Renée
Av. P. Puget
Avenue de l'Europe
Av. J.-P. Coste
D17
Cours Gambetta
R. P. de Coubertin
N7
31
A8
0   500   1000 m
l'Arc

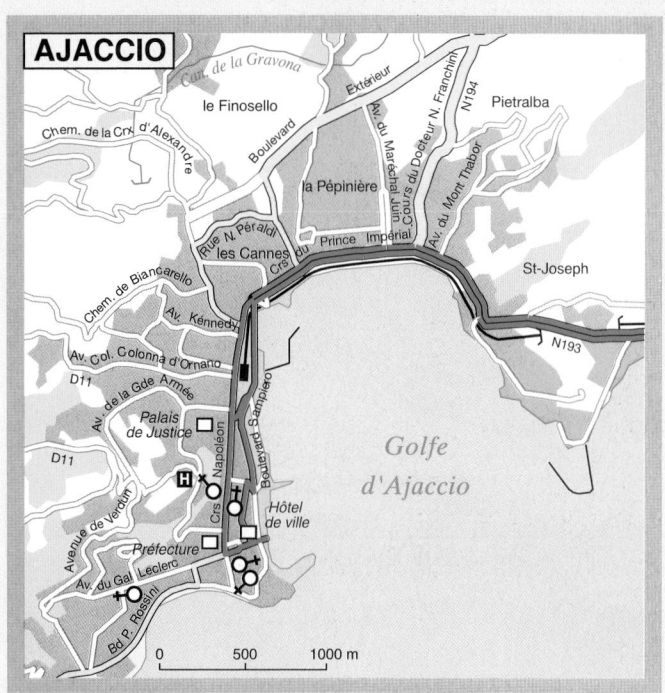

AJACCIO

Can de la Gravona
le Finosello
Pietralba
Chem. de la Crx d'Alexandre
Boulevard
Extérieur
Av. du Maréchal Juin
Av. du Docteur N. Franchini
N194
la Pépinière
Rue N. Péraldi
les Cannes
Prince Impérial
Crs
Av. du Mont Thabor
St-Joseph
Chem. de Biancarello
Av. Kennedy
Crs du
N193
Av. Col. Colonna d'Ornano
D11
Av. de la Gde Armée
D11
Palais de Justice
Crs Napoléon
Bastion Sampiero
Hôtel de ville
Avenue de Verdun
Préfecture
Av. du Gal Leclerc
Bd P. Rossini
Golfe d'Ajaccio
0   500   1000 m

329

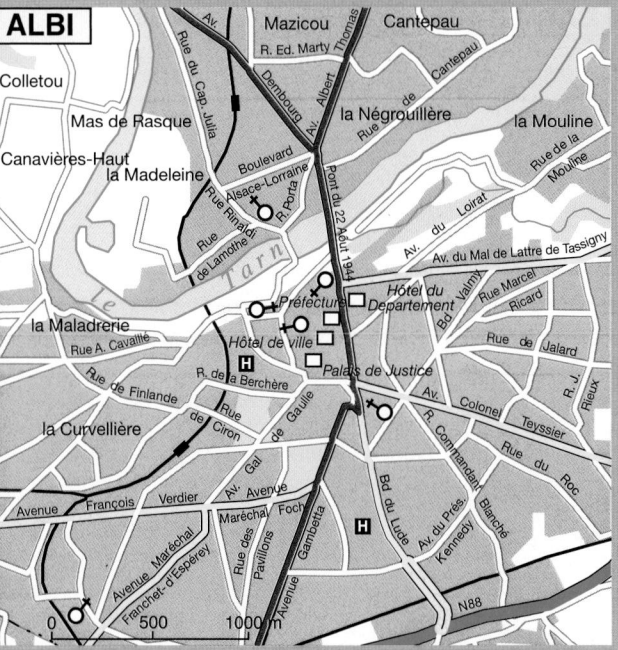

ALBI

Colletou
Mazicou
Cantepau
R. Ed. Marty
de Cantepau
Mas de Rasque
Av. du Cap. Julia
la Négrouillère
la Mouline
Canavières-Haut
la Madeleine
Boulevard
Alsace-Lorraine
Rue Rinaldi
R. Porta
Dembourg
Albert Thomas
Pont du 22 Août 1944
Rue de la Mouline
Av. du Loirat
Av. du Mal de Lattre de Tassigny
Rue de Lamothe
Préfecture
Hôtel du Département
Rue Marcel Ricard
la Maladrerie
Rue A. Cavaillé
Hôtel de ville
R. de la Berchère
Palais de Justice
Rue de Jalard
R. J. Rieux
la Curvellière
Rue de Finlande
R. de Ciron
R. Commandant Blanche
Av. Colonel Teyssier
Rue du Roc
Avenue François
Verdier
Av. Gal de Gaulle
Av. du Prés. Kennedy
Maréchal Foch
Bd du Lude
Avenue Maréchal
Franchet-d'Espérey
Rue des Pavillons
Avenue Gambetta
N88
0   500   1000 m
Le Tarn

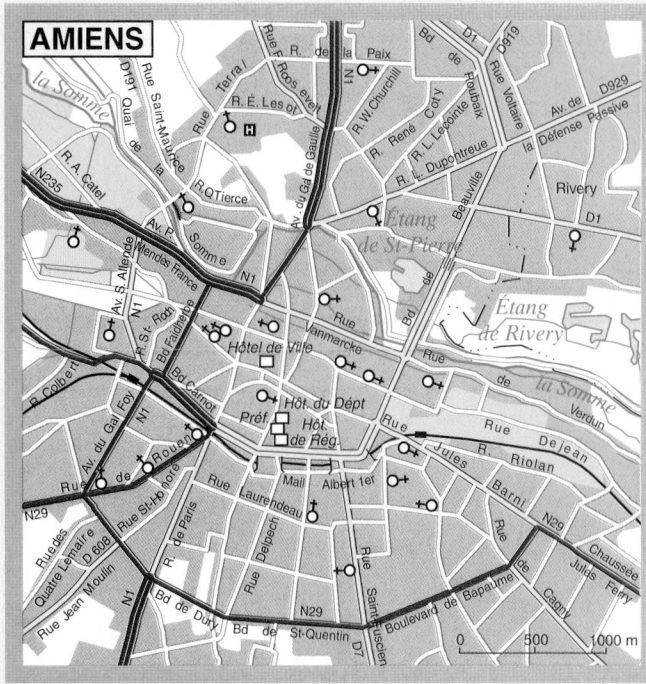

AMIENS

Rue de la Paix
Bd
D1
la Somme
Rue Saint-Maurice
D91
Quai
R. F. Roosevelt
N1
Rue Terral
R. W. Churchill
Av. de
D929
Rue Voltaire
R. A. Catel
N35
R. René Coty
la Défense Passive
R. Q Tierce
R. L'Espingle
Roubaix
Beauvillé
H
Av. P. Somme
Wenvès France
N1
Rivery
Étang de St-Pierre
D1
Av. S. Allende
R. St-Roch
Rue
Vanmarcke
Hôtel de Ville
Étang de Rivery
Rue Colbert
Bd Faidherbe
Bd Carnot
Rue
Verdun
la Somme
Av. du Gal Foy
N1
Rouen
Hôt. du Dépt
Préf.
Hôt. de Rég.
Rue Jules Barni
N29
Av. de
Mail
Albert 1er
R. Riolan
N29
Rue des Quatre Lemaire
D608
Rue St-Honoré
Rue Laurendeau
Rue Delpech
Chaussée
Jules Ferry
Rue Jean Moulin
N1
Bd de Dury
Rue de Paris
N29
Bd St-Quentin
Boulevard de Bapaume
D7
Cathy
0   500   1000 m

ANGERS

Bd G. Raimon
Monplaisir
Chatenay
N23
Rue des Capucins
Bd Henri Dunant
Bd de la
Av. Gasnier
Av. Victor
Romanerie
Rue Barra
H
la Maine
Bd Daviers
Rue du Maine
Rue de la Chalotière
Av.
la Croix Blanche
Rue de la Meignanne
R. V. Hugo
Pasteur
Rue Gaston
Rue des Portières
St-Jacques
les Banchais
Larevellière
Hôtel de Ville
Avenue
N23
Préfecture
Palais de Justice
R. Franklin
Montaigne
d'Angers
Bd du Mal Foch
Rue
Av. E. d'Orves
Léonard
N160
Lafayette
Rue Volney
Bd
Rue Eblé
R.P.
Rue
Beauval
Bédier
la Roseraie
Bd J. Portet
Bd A.
Rte de
Rue
D952
Bd Robert d'Arbrissel
N260
0   500   1000 m

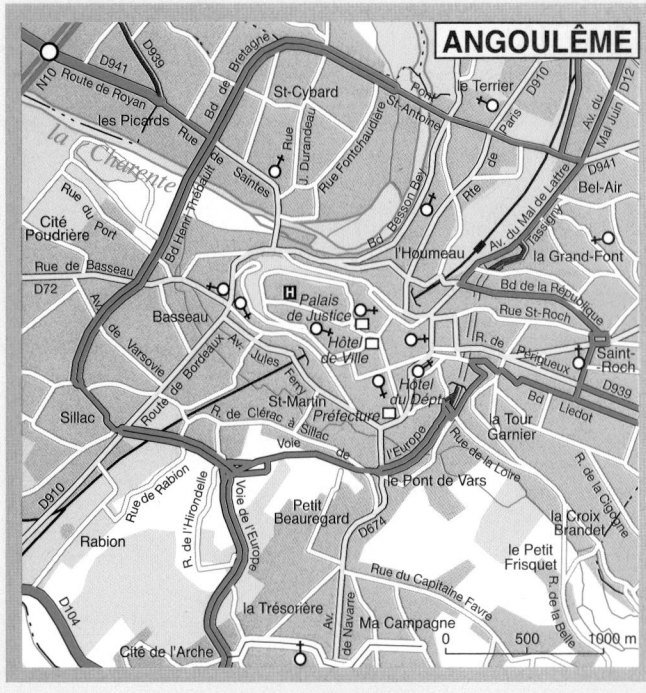

ANGOULÊME

N10 Route de Royan
D941
D939
Bd de Bretagne
St-Cybard
le Terrier
D310
D12
les Picards
Rue
Rte
de Paris
la Charente
J. Durandeau
Rue Fontchaudière
St-Antoine
D941
Bd
Av. du Mal de Lattre de Tassigny
Bel-Air
Cité Poudrière
Rue du Port
Bd Henri Thébault
de Saintes
l'Houmeau
la Grand-Font
Rue de Basseau
D72
H
Palais de Justice
Basseau
Hôtel de Ville
Av. de Varsovie
Av. Jules Ferry
St-Martin
Préfecture
Bd Besson Bey
Bd de la République
Rue St-Roch
R. de
Périgueux
Saint-Roch
D939
Hôtel du Dépt
Sillac
R. de Clérac à Sillac
Voie
l'Europe
la Tour Garnier
Liedot
Route de Bordeaux
D910
R. de l'Hirondelle
Petit Beauregard
D674
Voie de l'Europe
le Pont de Vars
la Croix Brandet
Rabion
Rue du Capitaine Favré
le Petit Frisquet
la Trésorière
D104
Ma Campagne
Cité de l'Arche
0   500   1000 m

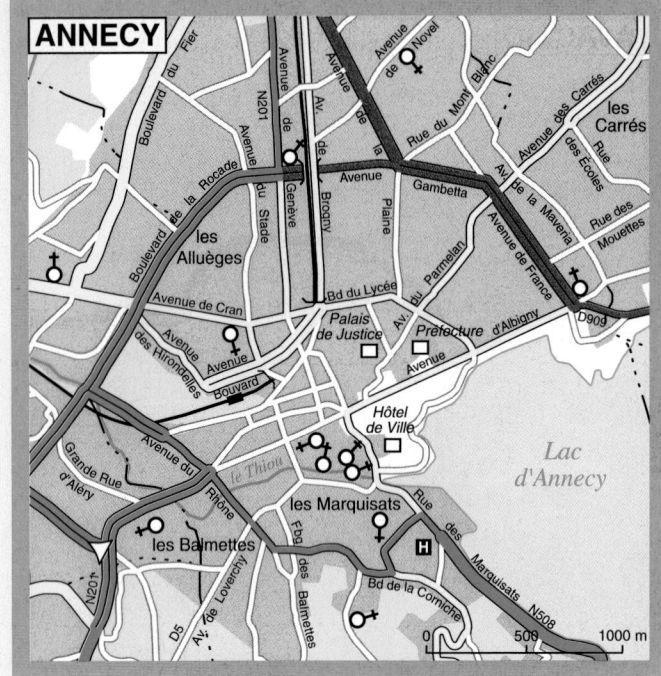

ANNECY

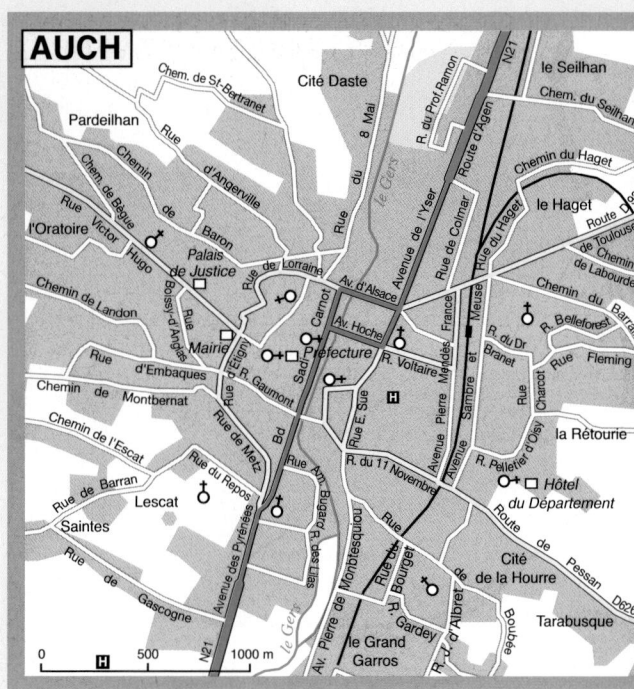

AUCH

AVIGNON

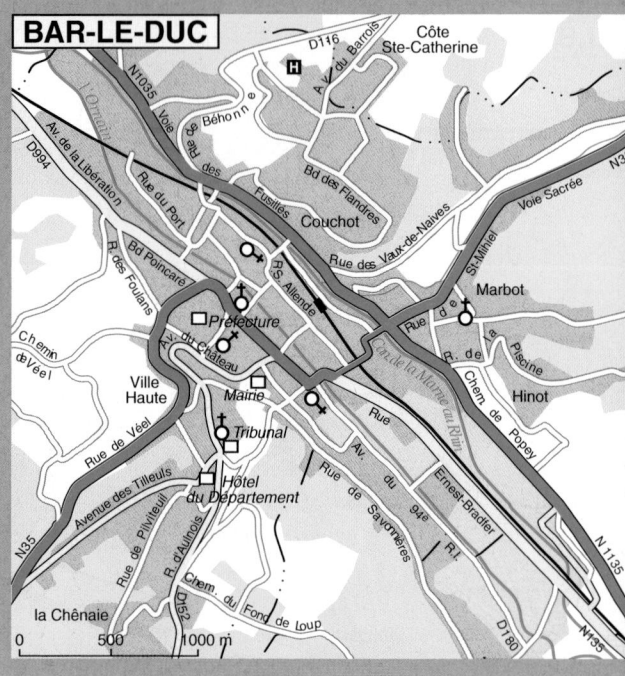

BAR-LE-DUC

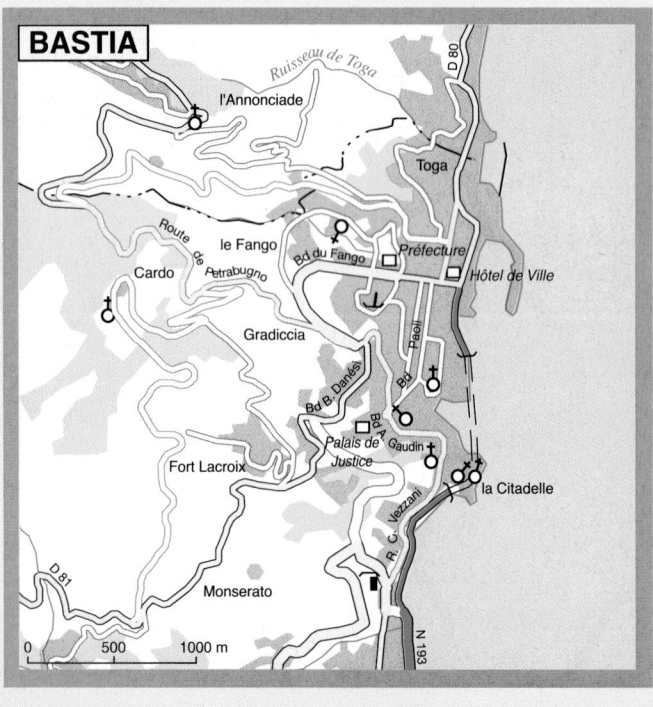

BASTIA

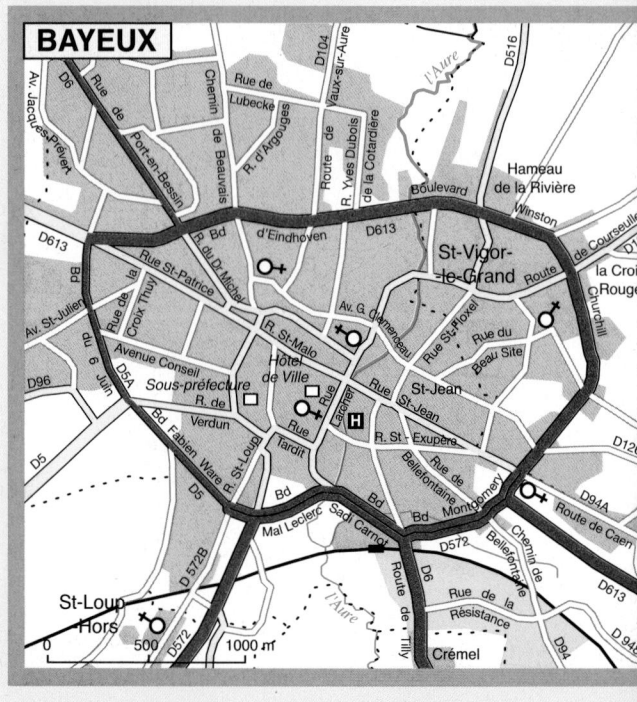

BAYEUX

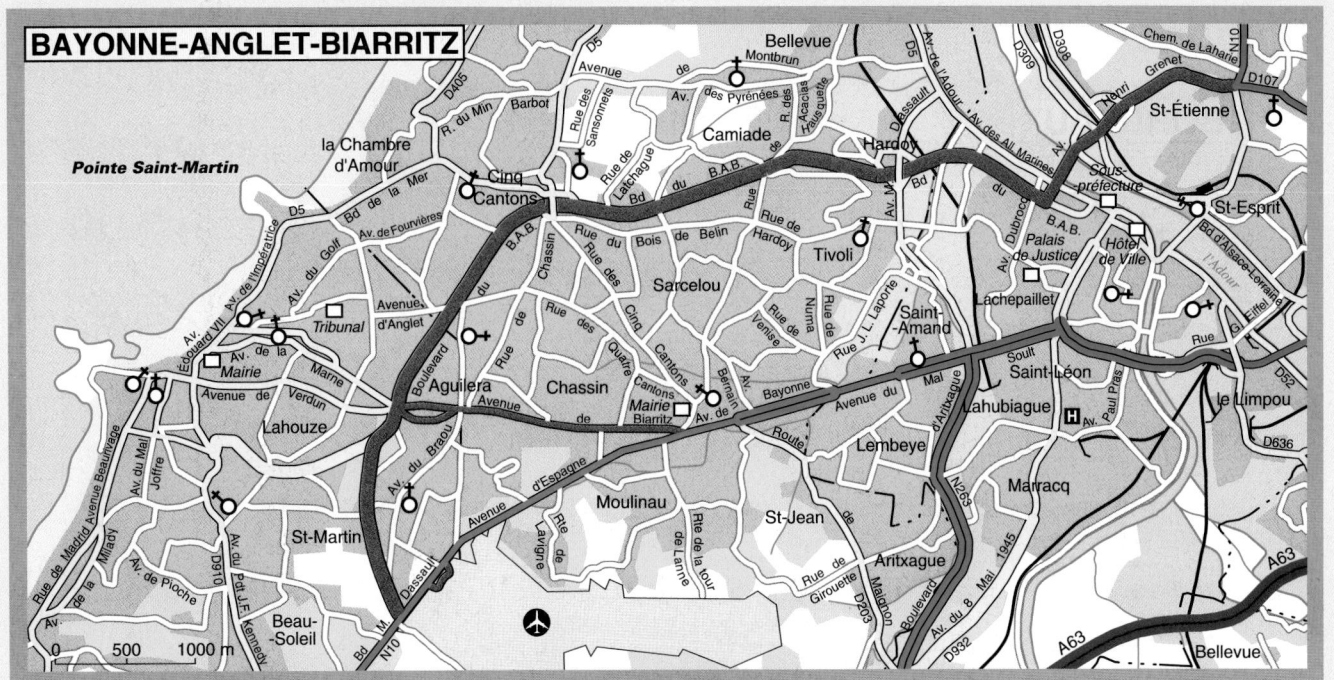

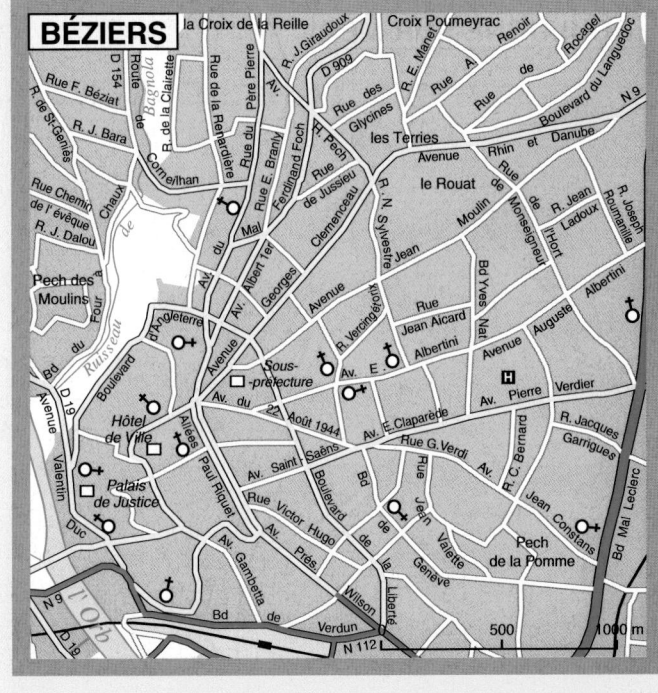

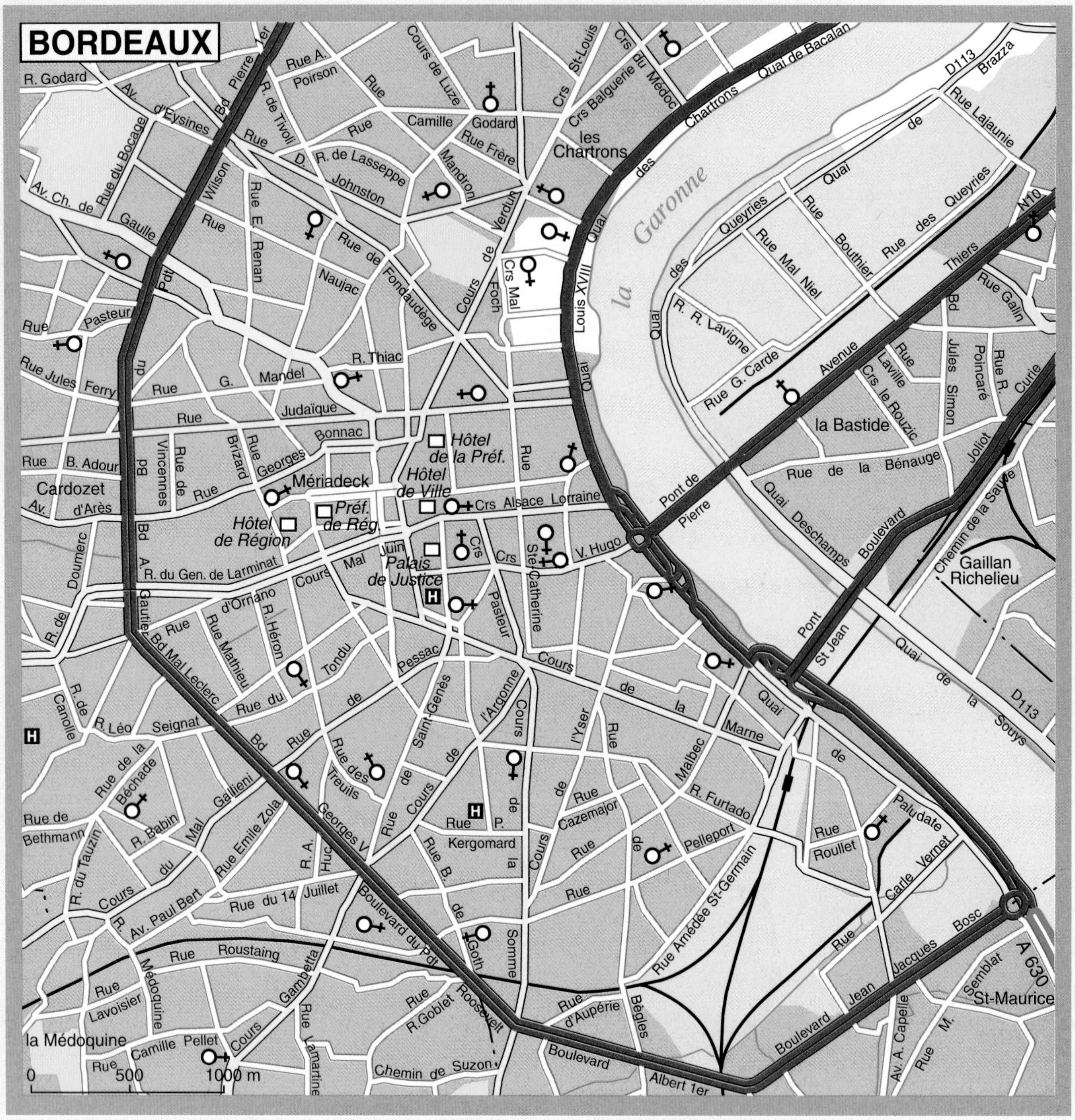

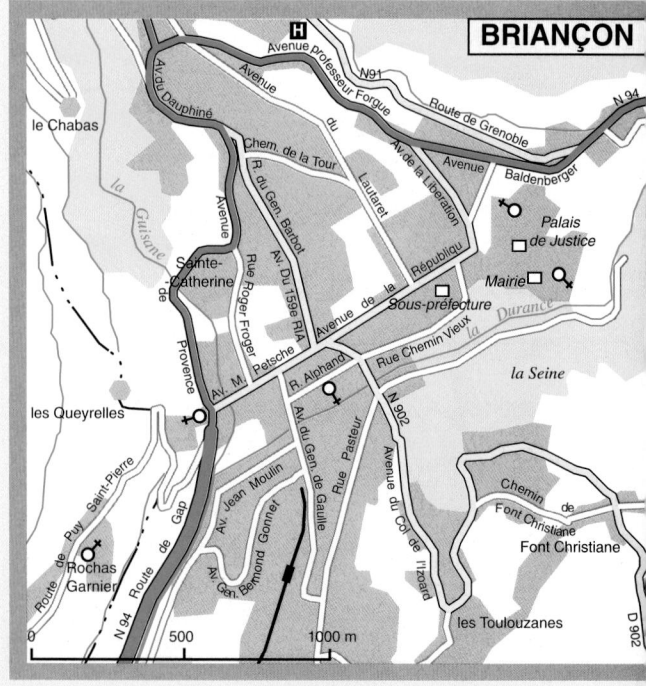

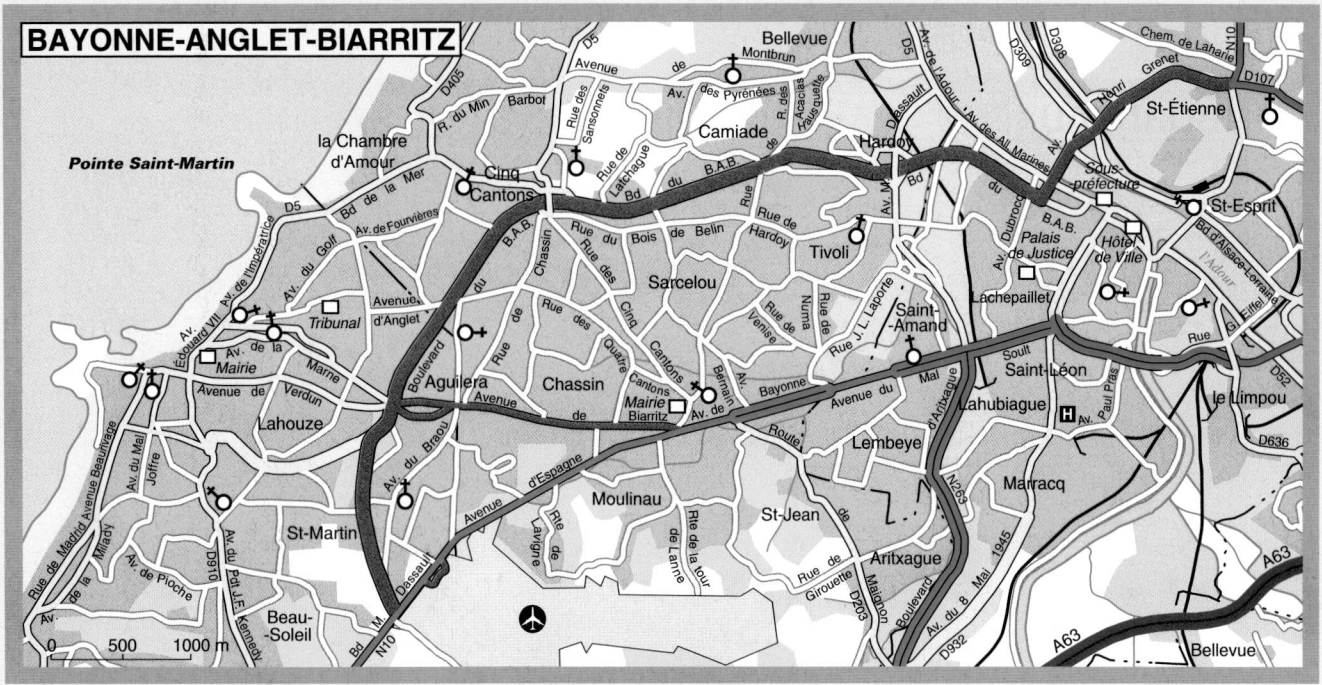

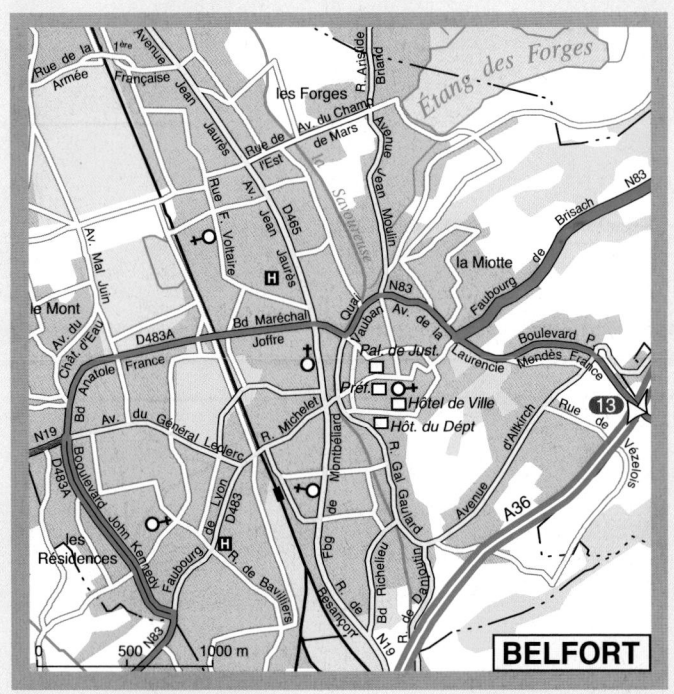

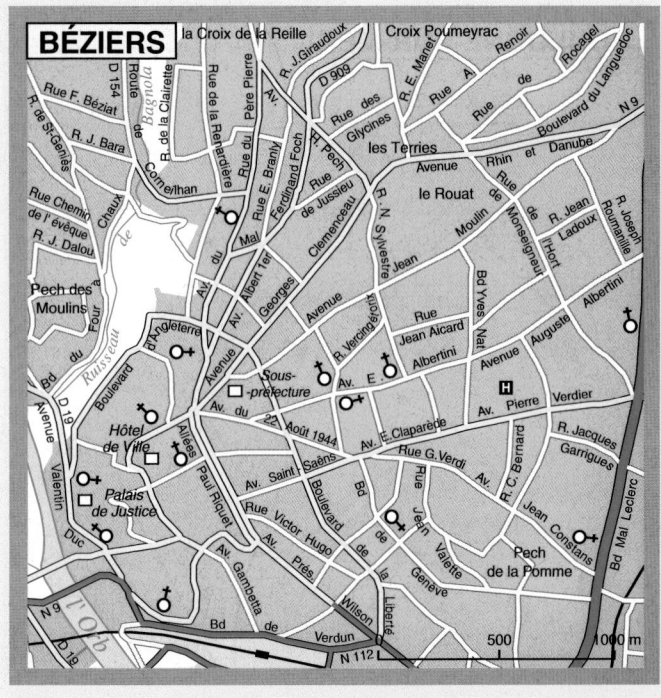

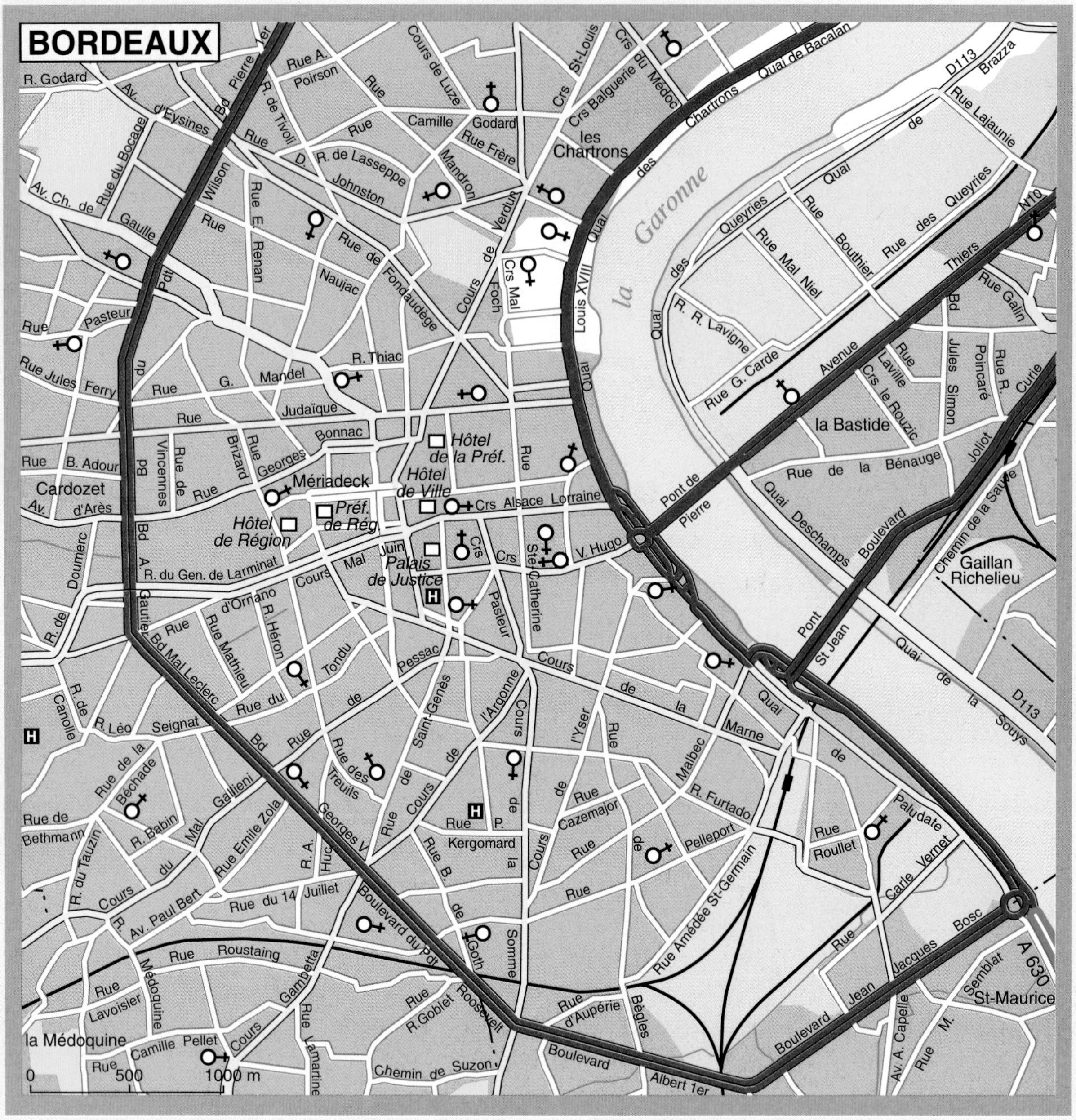

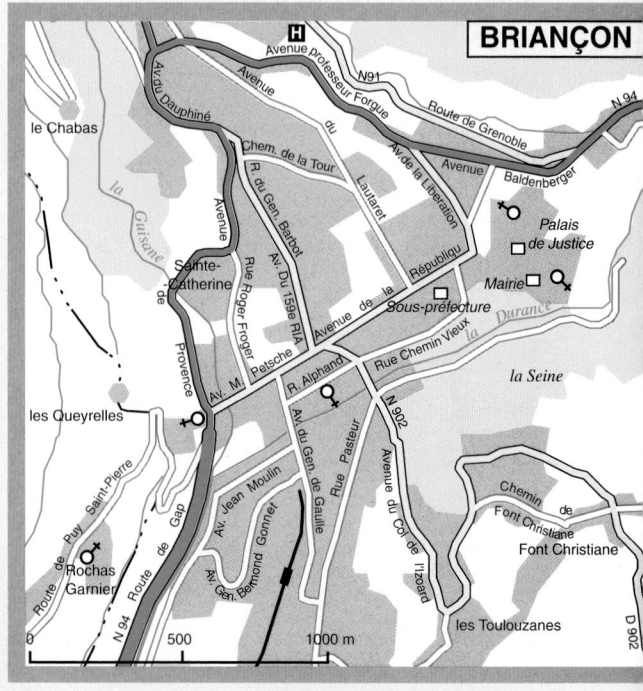

BREST

Lambezellec
Boulevard de l'Europe
Boulevard de l'Europe
Tourbihan D712
Kergonan
Av. de Provence
Kervirit
Kerhallet
Bellevue
Vendée
Kergoat
de Normandie
Lanrédec
Kernou
la Cavale Blanche
Kervallon
le Bouguen
St-Martin
Saint-Marc
le Polygone
Marne
Rue St-Marc
St-Martin
Rue Yves Collet
le Polygone
les Quatre Moulins
Recouvrance
Boulevard Gambetta
St-Pierre-Quilbignon
le Stiff
0   500   1000 m
Kerastel
RADE DE BREST

333

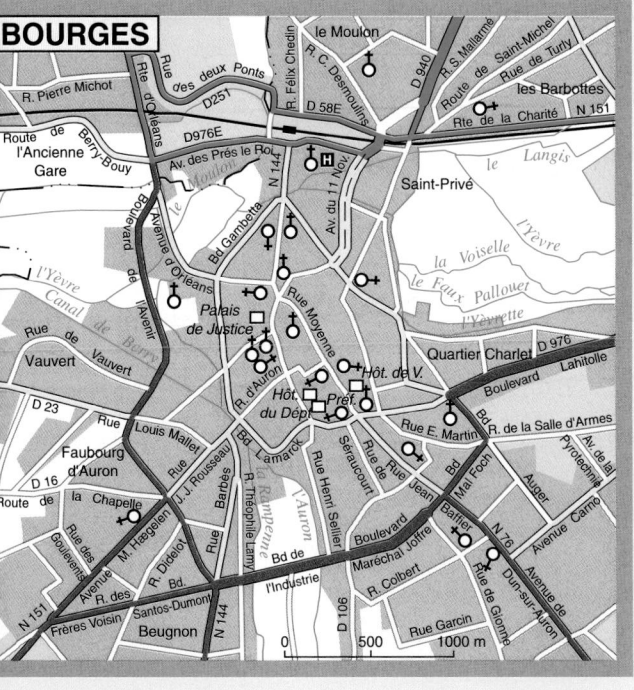

BOURGES

le Moulon
R. Pierre Michot
Rte de Saint-Michel
les Barbottes
les Barbottes
la Charité
N 151
Route de Berry-Bouy
l'Ancienne Gare
Saint-Privé
le Langis
l'Yèvre
l'Yèvre Canal
la Voiselle
le Faux Pallouet
Bd Gambetta
Rue Moyenne
Quartier Charlet D 976
Lahitolle
Vauvert
Palais de Justice
Hôt. de V.
Boulevard
Rue de Vauvert
D 23
Rue Louis Mallet
Faubourg d'Auron
Hôt. du Dépt. Préf.
Rue E. Martin
R. de la Salle d'Armes
D 16
Route de la Chapelle
Maréchal Joffre
Rue Colbert
Rue de Glomne
N 151
Frères Voisin
Santos-Dumont
N 144
l'Industrie
Rue Garcin
Beugnon
0   500   1000 m

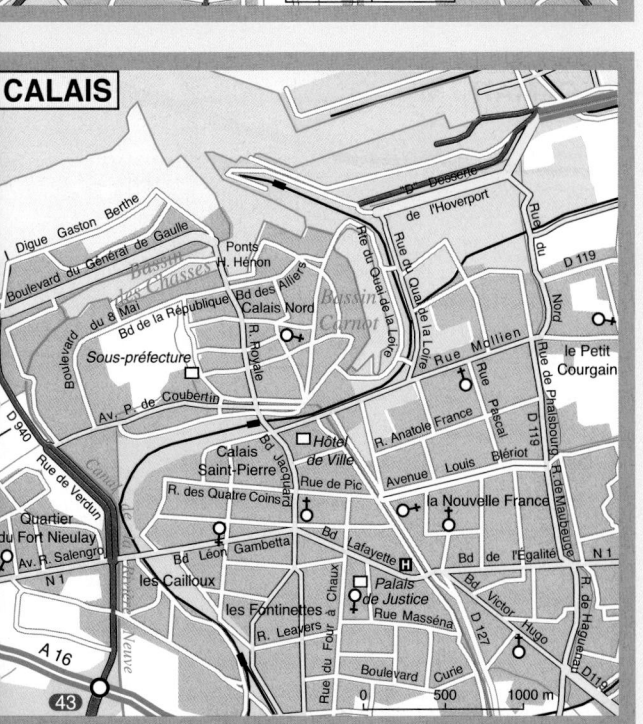

CALAIS

de l'Hoverport
D 119
Digue Gaston Berthe
Boulevard du Général de Gaulle
Ponts H. Hénon
Bd des Alliés
Bd de la République
Calais Nord
Bassin Carnot
Rue Royale
Rue Mollien
le Petit Courgain
Sous-préfecture
Av. P. de Coubertin
R. Anatole France
D 940
Rue de Verdun
Hôtel de Ville
Calais Saint-Pierre
Rue de Pic
Avenue Louis Blériot
R. des Quatre Coins
la Nouvelle France
Quartier du Fort Nieulay
Av. R. Salengro
Léon Gambetta
Bd de l'Egalité
N 1
N 1
les Cailloux
Bd Lafayette
les Fontinettes
Palais de Justice
Rue Masséna
A 16
Boulevard
43
0   500   1000 m

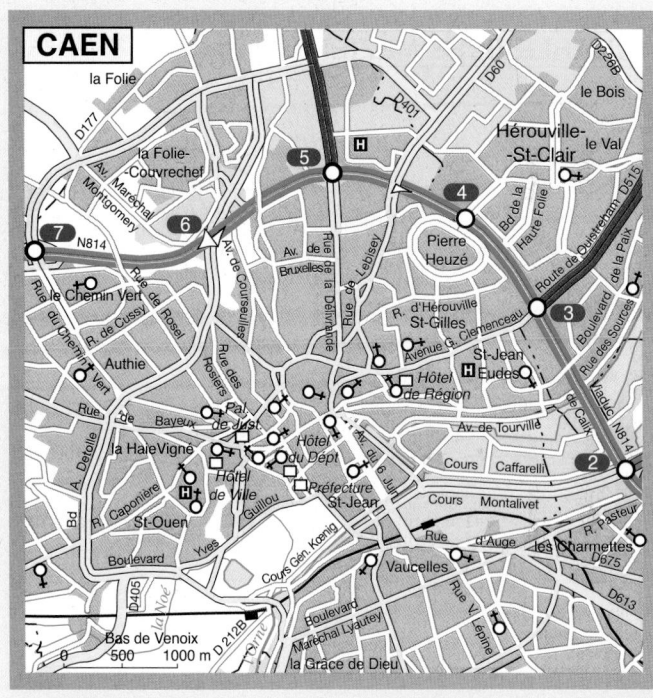

CAEN

la Folie
le Bois
Hérouville-St-Clair
le Val
la Folie-Couvrechef
Av. Maréchal Montgomery
5
H
4
7   N814
6
Haute Folie
Route de Ouistreham D515
Rue le Chemin Vert
R. de Cussy
R. d'Hérouville St-Gilles
3
Authie
Avenue G. Clemenceau
St-Jean Eudes
Pal. de Just.
2
la Haie Vignée
Hôtel du Dépt
Hôtel de Ville
Préfecture St-Jean
Cours Caffarelli
St-Ouen
Cours Montalivet
Vaucelles
les Charmettes
D 975
Bas de Venoix
500   1000 m
la Grâce de Dieu
D 613

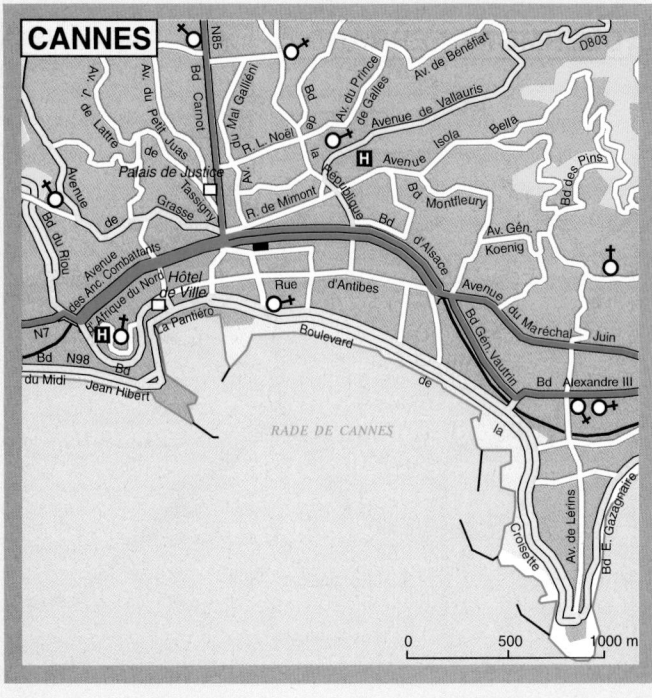

CANNES

N85
Av. de Bénéfiat
D803
Av. du Petit Juas
Av. du Prince de Galles
Avenue de Vallauris
Bd Carnot
R. L. Noël
Isola
Bella
Palais de Justice
Av. de Lattre de Tassigny
Avenue
H
Montfleury
Bd des Pins
Rue de Mimont
Av. Gén. Koenig
Avenue de Grasse
N7
Hôtel de Ville
Rue d'Antibes
Avenue du Maréchal Juin
Bd du Riou
Africa du Nord
la Panthéro
Bd Alexandre III
Bd N98
Jean Hibert
du Midi
Boulevard
RADE DE CANNES
Bd E. Gazagnaire
Av. de Lérins
Croisette
0   500   1000 m

CHÂLONS-EN-CHAMPAGNE

Av. Ampère · Av. du 106ème R.I. · Chem. de Bouy · Fbg St-Jacques · Avenue de la Voie · Rue La Voi · Av. du Général Sarrail · N 44 · Faubourg St Antoine · R. C. Jacquiert · Rue du Camp d'Attila · Av. du Gal Patton · Av. de Valmy · Avenue de Ste - Menehould · N 3 · Cité St-Pierre · Palais de Justice · Av. de Metz · St-Mémmie · Bd L. Blum · Hôtel de Ville · Rue Jaurès · Préfecture · Allées · Av. P. Doumet · Avenue · R. du Gd Mbll · Hôtel du Département · Hôtel de Région · Jacques · D 3 · Allées · Voltaire · Cté de Gaulle · Allées · Allées de Forêts · A. Karr · R. d'Alsace · Avenue du Président Roosevelt · Simon · D 1 · N 77 · N 44

0 500 1000 m

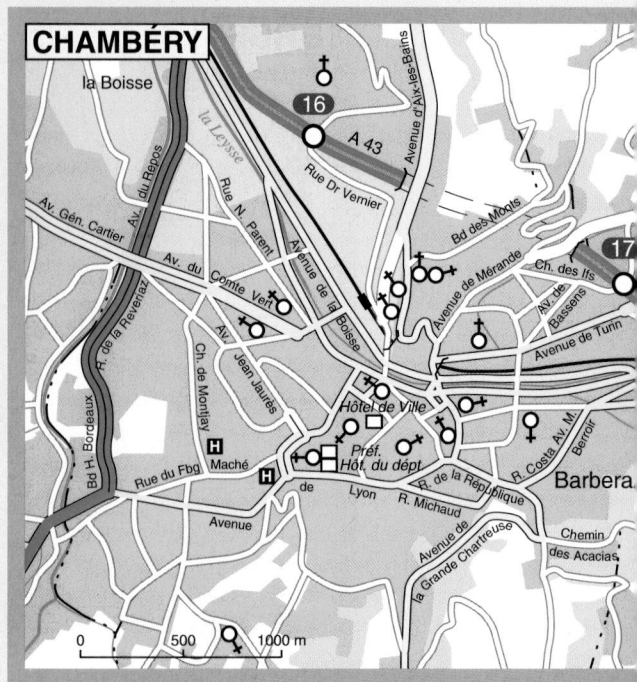

CHAMBÉRY

la Boisse · la Leysse · 16 · A 43 · Avenue d'Aix-les-Bains · Rue Dr Vernier · Av. Gén. Cartier · Av. de la Repos · Bd des Monts · Rue N. Parent · Avenue de la Boisse · 17 · Av. du Comte Vert · Avenue de Mérande · Ch. des Îls · Av. de la Revériaz · Avenue de Turin · Ch. de Monlay · Rue Jean Jaurès · Hôtel de Ville · Av. Costa Av. M. · Berroir · Préf. · Hôt. du dépt · Barbera · Bd H. Bordeaux · Maché · de · Rue du Fbg · R. de la République · Lyon · R. Michaud · Chemin des Acacias · Avenue · Avenue de la Grande Chartreuse

0 500 1000 m

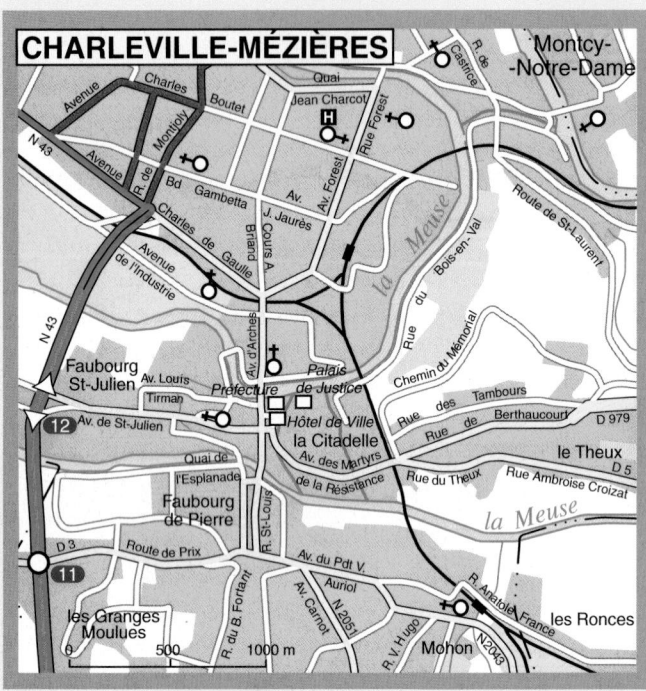

CHARLEVILLE-MÉZIÈRES

R. de Castrice · Montcy--Notre-Dame · Quai · Charles Boutet · Jean Charcot · Avenue · Rue Forest · N 43 · Av. de Montjoly · Bd Gambetta · Av. Forest · Rue du Bois-en-Val · Charles de Gaulle · J. Jaurès · Route de St-Laurent · la Meuse · Avenue de l'Industrie · J. Cours A. · Rue du Mémorial · Chemin du Mémorial · Faubourg St-Julien · Av. Louis Tirman · Av. d'Arches · Palais de Justice · Rue des Tambours · Préfecture · Rue de Berthaucourt · D 979 · 12 · Av. de St-Julien · Hôtel de Ville · la Citadelle · le Theux · Quai de l'Esplanade · Av. des Martyrs · Rue Ambroise Croizat · D 5 · Faubourg de Pierre · de la Résistance · Rue du Theux · la Meuse · D 3 · Route de Prix · 11 · Av. du Pdt V. · R. St-Louis · Auriol · R. du B. Fortant · N 2051 · R. Anatole France · N 2043 · les Granges Moulues · Av. Carnot · R. V. Hugo · Mohon · les Ronces

0 500 1000 m

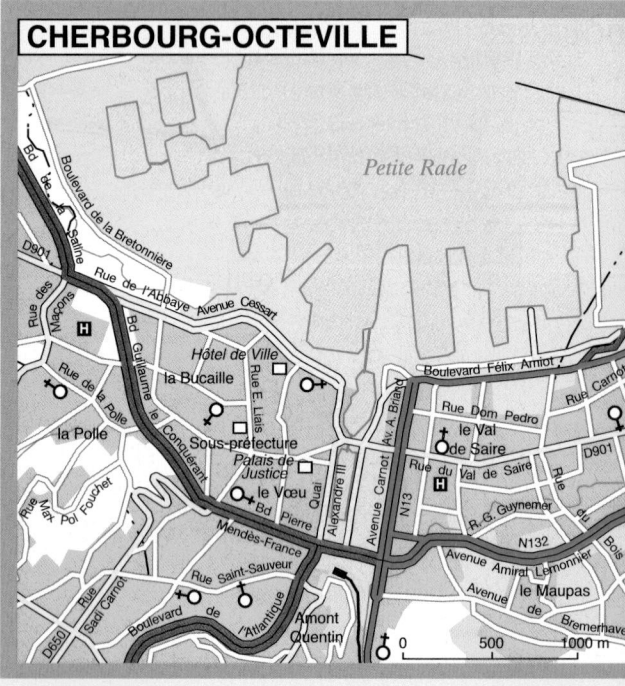

CHERBOURG-OCTEVILLE

Quai · Bd de la Saline · Boulevard de la Bretonnière · Petite Rade · D901 · Rue de l'Abbaye · Avenue Cessart · Rue des Maçons · Boulevard Félix Amiot · Hôtel de Ville · Rue E. Liais · Rue Carnot · Rue de la Polle · la Bucaille · Rue Dom Pedro · Bd Guillaume · Av. A. Briand · le Val · N 901 · la Polle · Sous-préfecture · de Saire · Rue Max Pol Fouchet · Palais de Justice · Rue du Val de Saire · R. G. Guynemer · Alexandre III · Avenue Carnot · N 13 · N 132 · le Vœu · Bd Pierre · Avenue Amiral Lemonnier · Rue Saint-Sauveur · Mendès-France · le Maupas · Boulevard · de · Bremerhave · Amont Quentin · l'Atlantique · Av. · de · D 650 · Bd Sad Carnot · Bois

0 500 1000 m

CLERMONT-FERRAND

Catarou · D 69 · Champfleuri · Rue du Clos Four · Bd Gordon Bennett · Rue · Av. Barbier Daubrée · les Carmes · N 9 · Fontgiève · Bd Lavoisier · R. St-Alyre · Bd de Blanzat · H. Barbusse · Avenue de la République · Rue du Ressort · R. Fontgiève · R. Menier R. Montlosier · Avenue · R. Niel Rue Auger · N 89 · Tribunal · Hôtel de Ville · Av. d'Italie · E. · Michelin · Bd Berthelot · R. Menat · Avenue de l'Union Soviétique · R. Guynemer · France Herbet · D 5 · R. Blatin · Hôt. du Dépt · Av. Carnot · Anatole · Rue la Pradelle · Bd Lafayette · Préfecture · Côte Blatin · Rue · de · la Cartouchère · R. Gilbert · Rue de la Pradelle · Av. Julien · Av. Pasteur · Bd Pasteur · Bd Mitterrand Crs · Avenue · Rue Clovis Hugues · l'Oradou · les Ormeaux · A. Briand · Bd · Jean Jaurès · de Gaulle · Neuf Soleil · Bd P. Pochet Lagaye · Rue de l'Oradou · D 69 · R. de Bellevue · R. André Theuriet · la Liberation · Cote Blatin · Léon Blum · Rue des Chambrettes · la Raye Dieu · N 89 · R. des Liondards · R. Berteaud · D 771 · St-Jacques · N 9

0 500 1000 m

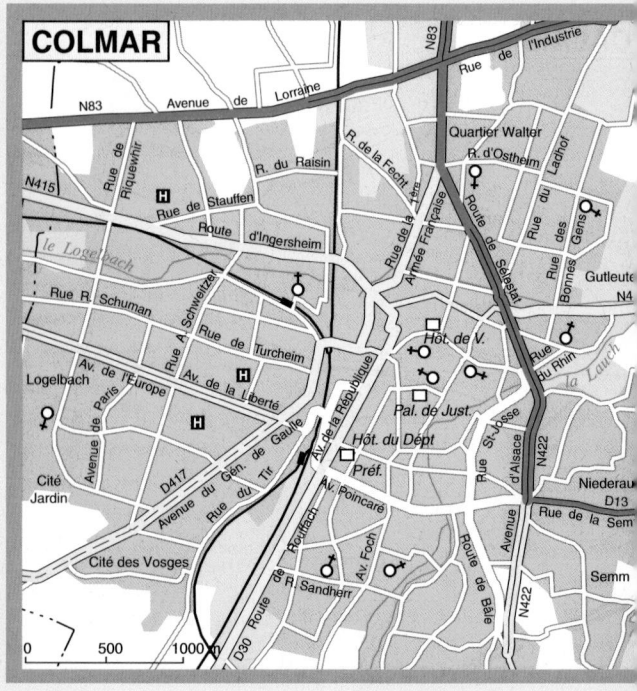

COLMAR

N83 · Rue de l'Industrie · N83 · Avenue de Lorraine · Quartier Walter · R. d'Ostheim · R. de Riquewihr · R. du Raisin · R. de la Feofit · N415 · Rue de Stauffen · Rue de la 1ère · Route du Ladhof · le Logelbach · Route d'Ingersheim · Rue de l'Armée Française · Rue des Bonnes Gens · Gutleute · Rue R. Schuman · Av. A. Schweitzer · Rue de Turcheim · N4 · Logelbach · Av. de l'Europe · Av. de la Liberté · Hôt. de V. · Rue du Rhin · la Lauch · Cité Jardin · Avenue de Paris · D417 · Avenue du Gén. de Gaulle · Pal. de Just. · Rue St-Josse · N422 · Niederau · Cité des Vosges · R. du Tir · Hôt. du Dépt · D13 · R. Sandherr · Av. Poincaré · Préf. · Av. de la République · Rue de la Sem · Route de Sélestat · D30 · Route de Bâle · Av. Foch · D417 · Semm · Avenue d'Alsace

0 500 1000 m

334

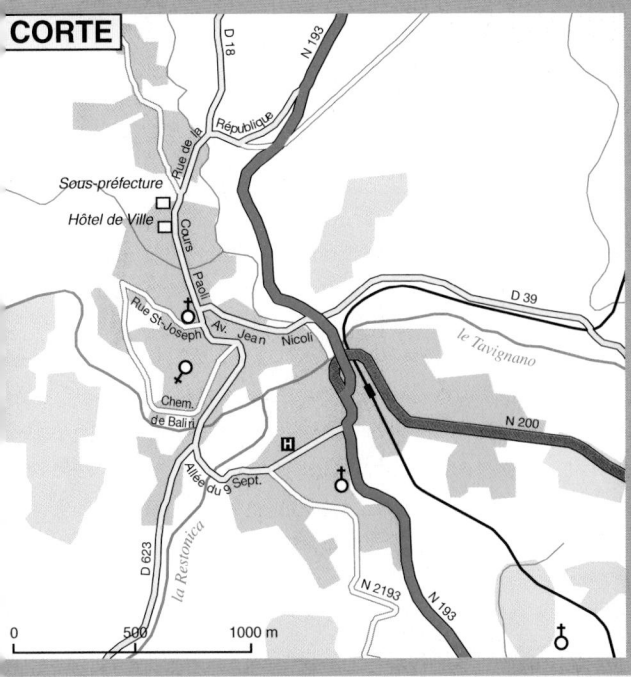

CORTE

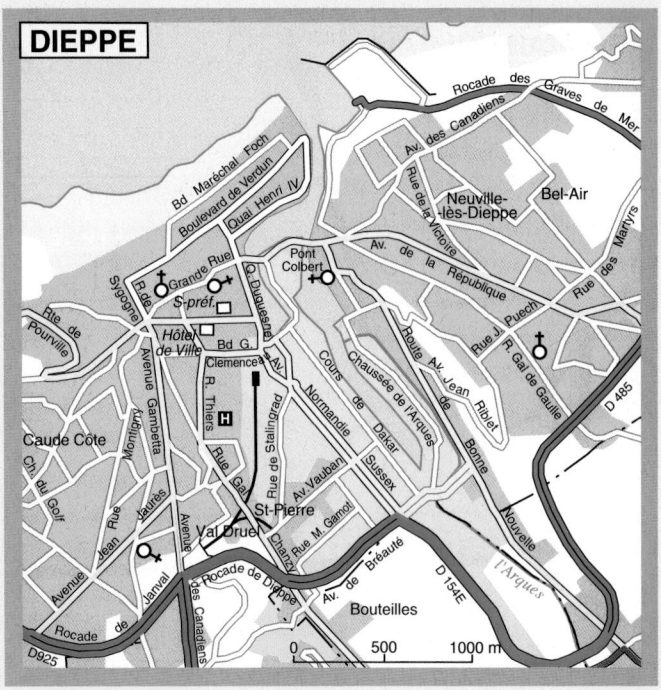

DIEPPE

DIJON

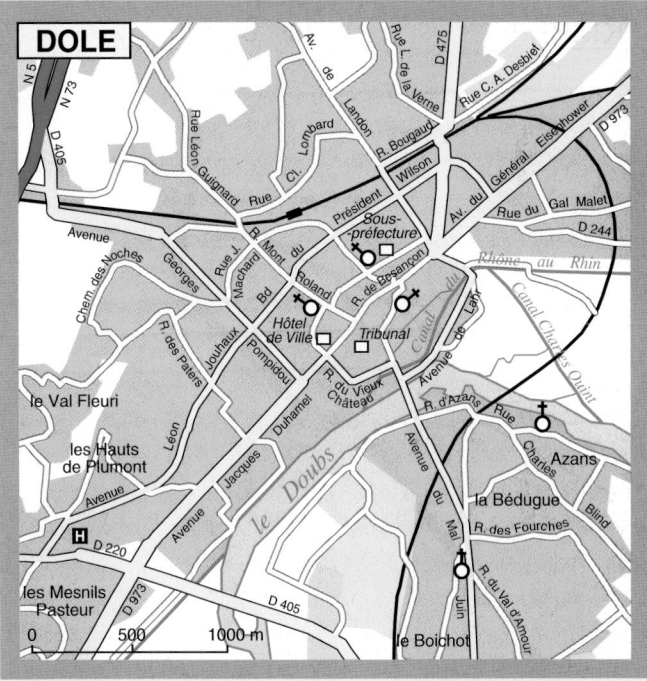

DOLE

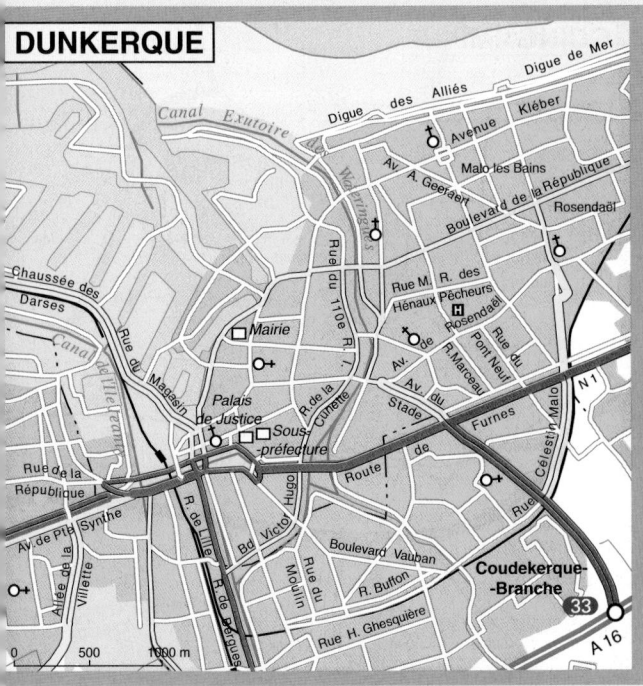

DUNKERQUE

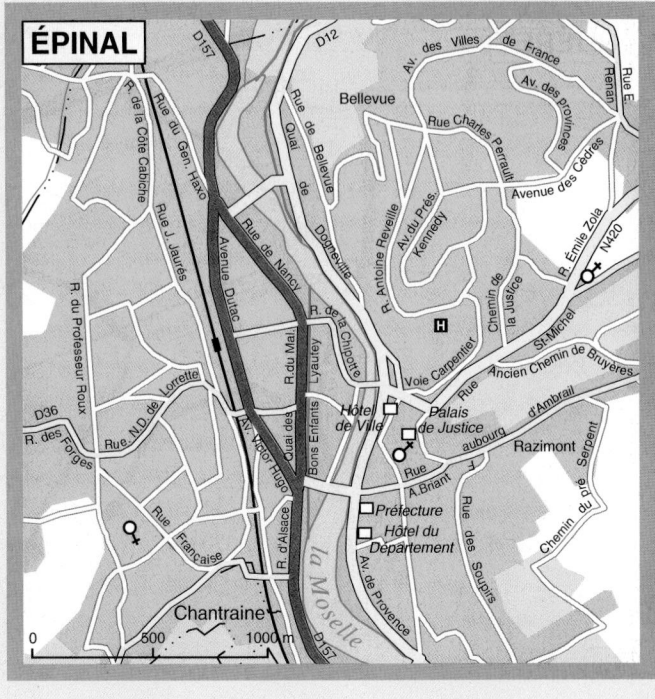

ÉPINAL

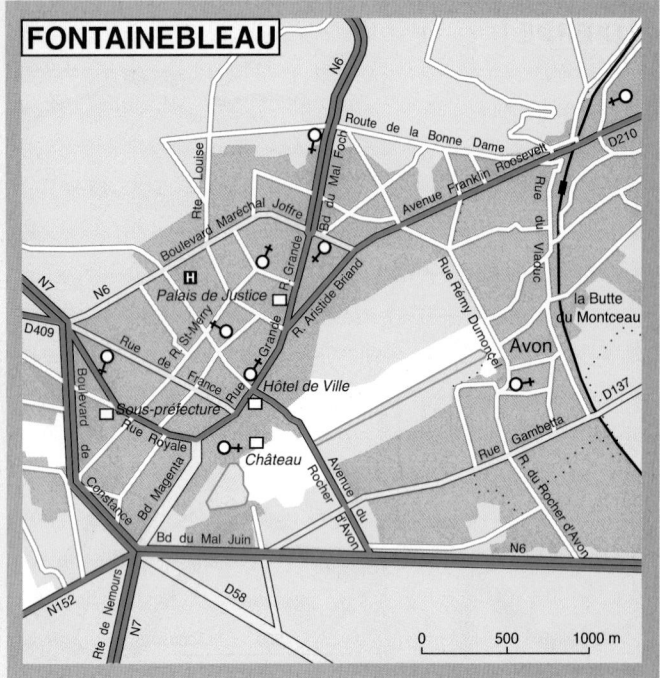

FONTAINEBLEAU

- N6
- Route de la Bonne Dame
- Avenue Franklin Roosevelt
- D210
- Rue du Mal Foch
- Boulevard Maréchal Joffre
- Rue Grande
- Rue Aristide Briand
- Rue du Viaduc
- Rue Rémy Dumoncel
- la Butte du Montceau
- N7
- N6
- Palais de Justice
- H
- R. St-Merry
- D409
- Rue de France
- Rue Royale
- Sous-préfecture
- Hôtel de Ville
- Avon
- Rue Gambetta
- D137
- Bd Magenta
- Château
- Avenue du Rocher d'Avon
- Boulevard de Constance
- Bd du Mal Juin
- N6
- N152
- Rte de Nemours
- N7
- D58

0 — 500 — 1000 m

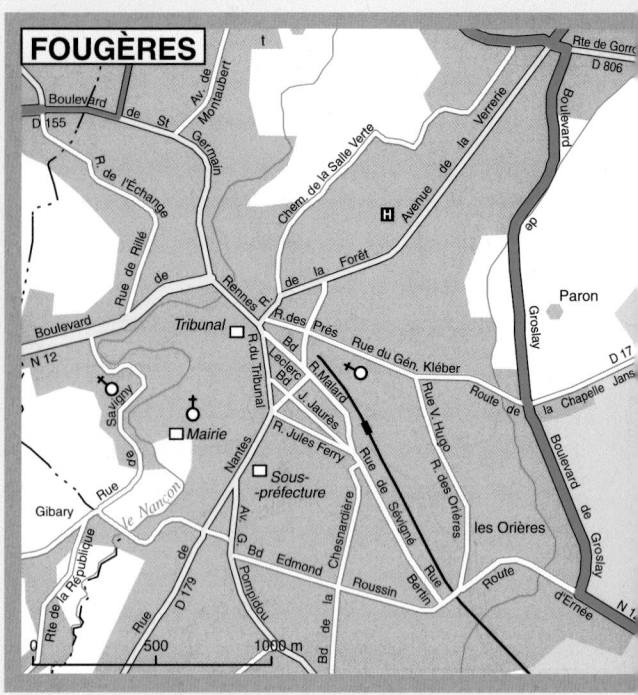

FOUGÈRES

- Rte de Gorro
- D 806
- Boulevard de St Germain
- Av. de Montaubert
- Avenue de la Verrerie
- Boulevard
- D 155
- R. de l'Échange
- Chem. de la Salle Verte
- H
- Paron
- Rue de Rillé
- de
- Rue de la Forêt
- Groslay
- D 17
- Boulevard
- N 12
- Rennes
- R. des Prés
- Rue du Gén. Kléber
- Tribunal
- R. du Tribunal
- R. Malard
- Rue V. Hugo
- R. des Orières
- Route de
- la Chapelle Jans
- Savigny
- Leclerc Bd
- R. J. Jaurès
- les Orières
- Mairie
- R. Jules Ferry
- Rue de Sévigné
- Boulevard de Groslay
- de
- Nantes
- Sous-préfecture
- Av. G. Bd Edmond
- Rue de la République
- Gibary
- le Nançon
- Rue de
- D 179
- Pompidou
- Chesnardière
- Roussin
- Bertin
- Rue
- Route d'Ernée
- N 1

0 — 500 — 1000 m

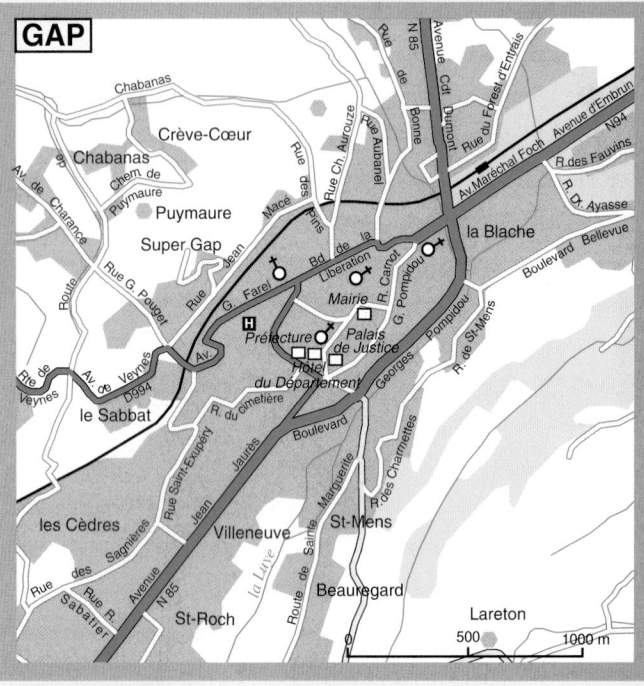

GAP

- Chabanas
- N 85
- Avenue Cdt Dumont
- Rue du Forest d'Entrais
- Crève-Cœur
- Rue de Bonne
- Avenue d'Embrun
- N94
- Chabanas
- Chem. de Puymaure
- Rue Ch. Aubanel
- Av. Maréchal Foch
- R. des Fauvins
- Av. de Charance
- Puymaure
- Rue Macé
- R. D. Ayasse
- Super Gap
- Rue G. Pouget
- Rue Jean
- Rue de la
- la Blache
- Boulevard Bellevue
- Route de Veynes
- Liberation
- Bd de
- R. Carnot
- G. Pompidou
- Pompidou
- Av. de Veynes
- G. Farel
- Mairie
- R. de St-Mens
- D994
- H
- Préfecture
- Palais de Justice
- Rue Saint-Exupéry
- Jaurès
- Hôtel du Département
- R. du cimetière
- Georges
- R. des Charmettes
- le Sabbat
- Rue Sainte Marguerite
- Boulevard
- les Cèdres
- Rue des Sagnières
- Villeneuve
- St-Mens
- la Luye
- Rue R.
- Avenue
- Sabarrel
- N 85
- Route de Sainte
- Beauregard
- Lareton
- St-Roch

0 — 500 — 1000 m

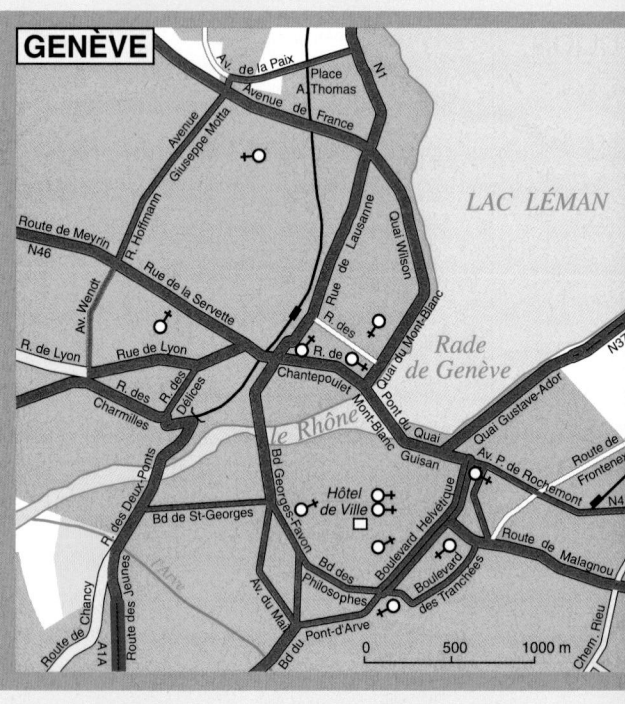

GENÈVE

- Av. de la Paix
- Place A. Thomas
- N1
- Avenue de France
- Avenue
- R. Hoffmann
- Rue Giuseppe Motta
- LAC LÉMAN
- Route de Meyrin
- N46
- Rue de la Servette
- Quai Wilson
- Rade de Genève
- N37
- Av. Wendt
- Rue de Lyon
- Rue de
- R. de
- R. des
- Quai du Mont-Blanc
- R. de Lyon
- Chantepoulet
- Mont-Blanc
- R. de Lyon
- Charmilles
- R. des
- Délices
- Pont du Quai
- le Rhône
- Quai Gustave-Ador
- Bd des Deux-Ponts
- Bd Georges-Favon
- Hôtel de Ville
- Boulevard Helvétique
- Av. P. de Rochemont
- Route de Frontenex
- N4
- Bd de St-Georges
- Bd des Philosophes
- Boulevard des Tranchées
- Route de Malagnou
- Route de Chancy
- A1A
- Route des Jeunes
- Av. du Mail
- l'Arve
- Bd du Pont-d'Arve
- Chem. Rieu

0 — 500 — 1000 m

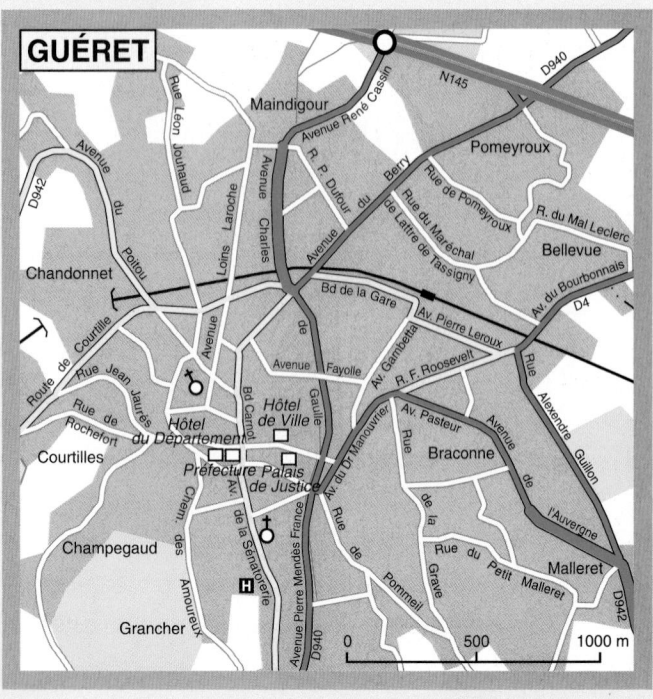

GUÉRET

- D940
- N145
- Maindigour
- Avenue René Cassin
- Pomeyroux
- Avenue du Poitou
- Avenue
- Rue Léon Jouhaud
- R. P. Dufour
- Rue du Berry
- Rue de Pomeyroux
- Avenue Charles
- R. du Mal Leclerc
- D942
- Avenue de Courtille
- Larcoche
- de Lattre de Tassigny
- Bellevue
- Chandonnet
- Loins
- Bd de la Gare
- Av. du Bourbonnais
- D4
- Route de Courtille
- Rue Jean Jaurès
- Avenue Pierre Leroux
- Avenue Fayolle
- Avenue Gambetta
- R. F. Roosevelt
- Rue de Rochefort
- Hôtel du Département
- Bd Carnot
- Hôtel de Ville
- Av. Pasteur
- Braconne
- Avenue Guillon
- Courtilles
- Préfecture Palais de Justice
- Rue du Dr Marcouyeau
- Avenue
- l'Auvergne
- Champegaud
- Chem. des Amouroux
- Avenue Pierre Mendès France
- Av. de la Sénatorerie
- Rue de Pommeil
- Rue du Petit Malleret
- Malleret
- H
- Grancher
- D940
- D442

0 — 500 — 1000 m

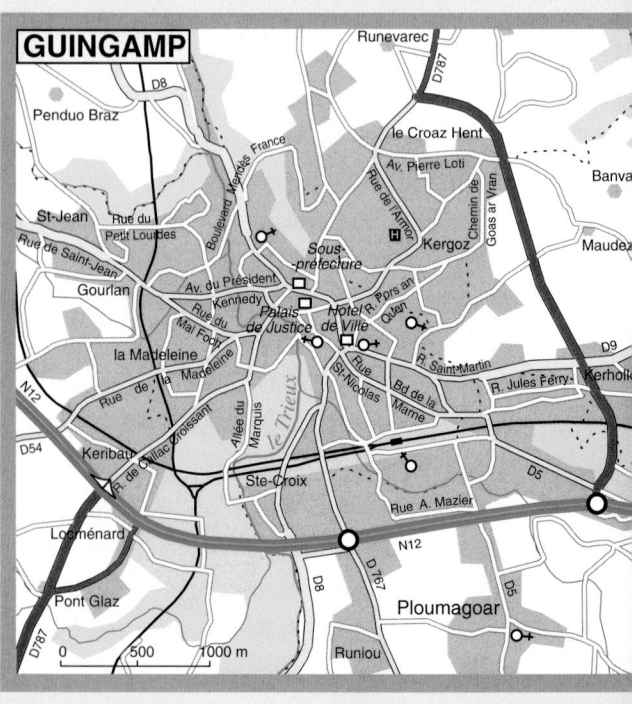

GUINGAMP

- Runevarec
- D787
- D8
- Penduo Braz
- le Croaz Hent
- Boulevard Maréchal France
- Av. Pierre Loti
- Banva
- St-Jean
- Rue du Petit Louédec
- Rue de l'Arm
- Goas ar Vran
- Kergoz
- Maudez
- Rue de Saint-Jean
- H
- Chemin de
- Gourlan
- Av. du Président Kennedy
- Sous-préfecture
- R. Pors an
- Palais de Justice
- Hôtel de Ville
- Olen
- D9
- Rue du Mal Foch
- la Madeleine
- R. Saint-Martin
- Kerholic
- Rue de la Madeleine
- St-Nicolas
- Bd de la Marne
- R. Jules Ferry
- N12
- le Trieux
- Allée du Marquis
- Croissant
- D54
- Keribau
- Rue de Village
- Ste-Croix
- D5
- Rue A. Mazier
- Locménard
- N12
- D767
- Pont Glaz
- D8
- Ploumagoar
- D787
- Runiou

0 — 500 — 1000 m

GRENOBLE
St-Laurent
A480
A48
Rue Félix Esclangon
Palais de Justice
Bd Mal Leclerc
Préfecture
N2087
Cours Berriat
Hôt. du Dépt
Mairie
Av. Gabriel Péri
Av. A. Croizat
Jean Jaurès
Bd Gambetta
Bd Clémenceau
Rue Ampère
Bd Joseph Vallier
Bd Maréchal Foch
la Croix Rouge
la Bajatière
Jules Vallès
le Drac
les Eaux Claires
la Capuche
Rue de Stalingrad
Rue Marcellin Berthelot
Avenue Jean Perrot
Avenue des Jeux Olympiques
Av. Rhin et Danube
Cours de la Libération
Rue des Alliés
Cité Paul Mistral
Avenue Léon Blum
Grenoble-Sud
Av. Cachin
Cité Teisseire
les Maisons Neuves
Av. Marie Reynoard
Ville Neuve
Av. E. Esmonin
Av. du Général de Gaulle
Jean Jaurès
N87
les Granges
0 500 1000 m
2
3
4
5
8

LE HAVRE
Bléville
la Mare Rouge
Forêt de Montgeon
Rte d'Octeville
R. F. Chatel
Av. du Bois au Coq
R. Th. Gautier
Samain
R. Maurice Genevois
R. Curie
R. Weber
R. F. Léger
R. de la Sous Bretonne
Sanvic
la Mare au Clerc
Av. J. Anquetil
Rue P. Mendès France
R. Barbusse
R. Gal de Gaulle
R.A. Copieux
Salengro
R. Roger
Rue de la Cavée Verte
Rue L. Blanc
Rue du 329 ème
Rue Félix Faure
R. G. Lafaurie
R. Mal Joffre
Rue A. Briand
Bd Albert 1er
R. d'Etretat
R. des Gobelins
R. Coty
R. A. France
Hôtel de Ville
S. préf.
Pal. de just.
Bd W. Churchill
N 15
Av. Foch
Bd de Strasbourg
Quai Georges V
Quai Colbert
Bd Clemenceau
R. François 1er
Rue Marceau
l'Eure
Rue Brindeau
D481
R. de la Vallée
Bd Amiral Mouchez
Graville
Avenue Lucien Corbeaux
Avenue C. Colomb
R. Cuvier
0 500 1000 m

LILLE
Av. Becquart
R. de Lille
Boulevard Robert Shuman
Lambersart
Av. Mal Leclerc
Rue du Bois
Rue St-Sébastien
Av. de la République
Rue du Ballon
Rue H. Delecaux
Avenue de l'Hippodrome
Canal de la Deûle
R. Négrier
R. du Pont Neuf
Palais de Justice
Rue Royale
Rue de Gand
Faubourg Saint-Maurice
Avenue Ste Cécile
Av. M. Delobel
R. de la Barre
Boulevard Carnot
Av. Soubise
Avenue M. Dormoy
Avenue V. Jouhaux
Boulevard R. Nationale
Hôtel du Département
Rue de la Rue du Molinel
les Bois Blancs
Bd de Lorraine
R. Colbert
Boulevard Vauban
Rue Solférino
Préfecture
Av. du Prés. Kennedy
Hôtel de Ville
Liberté
Rue Nationale
Rue Gambetta
Boulevard Louis XIV
Bd de la Moselle
Rue de Turenne
Rue Léon
Rue des Postes
Solférino
Rue de la Bassée
Rue d'Isly
Montebello
Boulevard
R. J. Guesde
R. Paul Lafargue
R. Brule Maison
R. de Cambrai
Rue Victor Hugo
R. d'Arras
Rue de Trévise
Bd de la Moselle
Boulevard de Metz
Bd de Belfort
R. de Douai
Rue de Condé
le Petit Maroc
Bd de Strasbourg
Boulevard d'Alsace
A 25
A 1
R. de Marquillies
0 500 1000 m
1
2
3
4
5

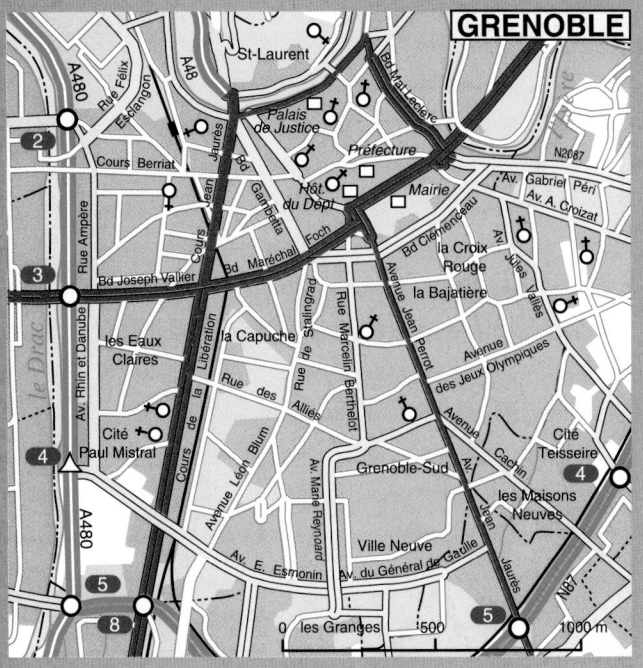

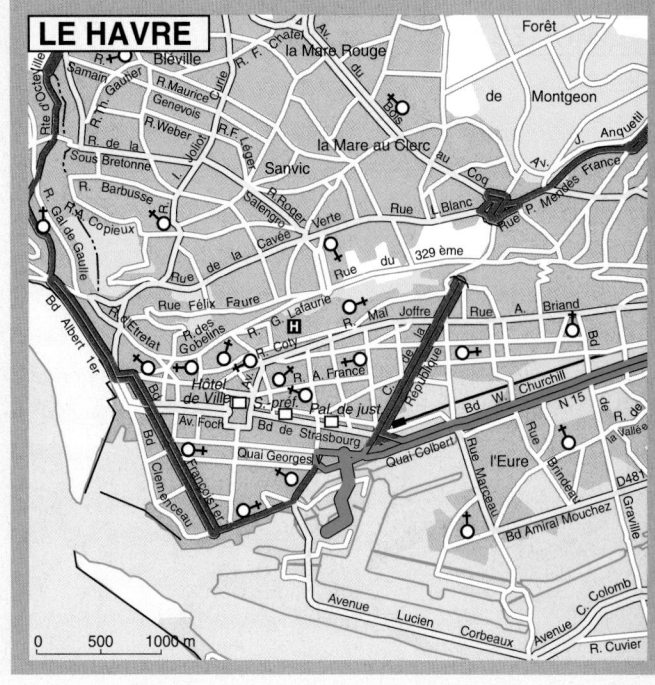

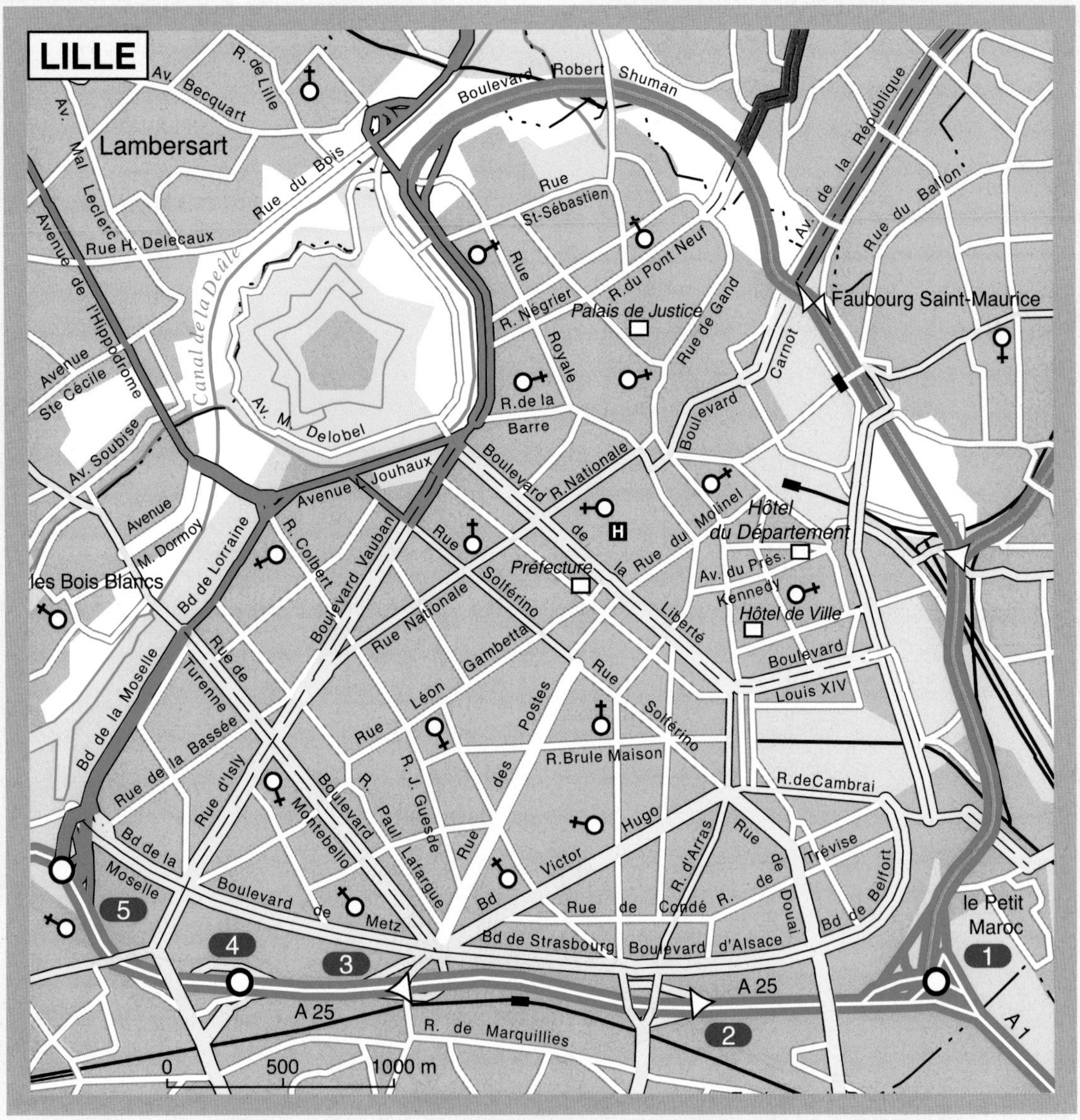

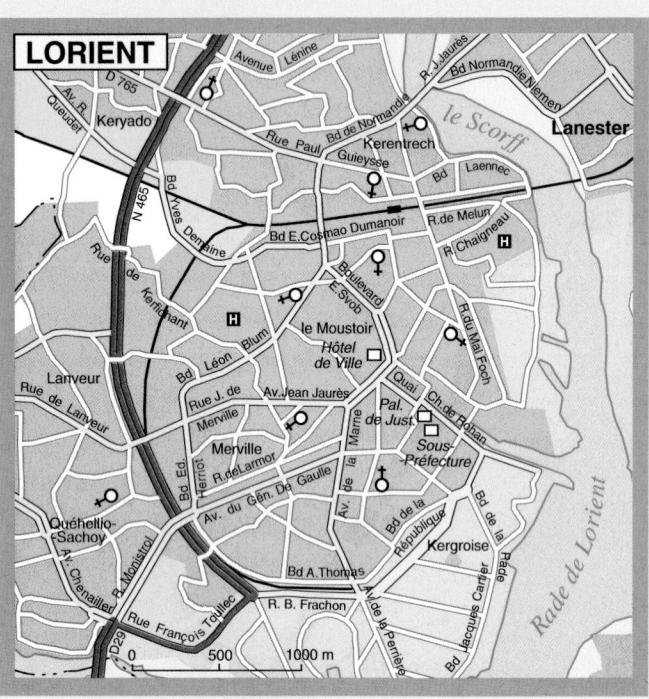

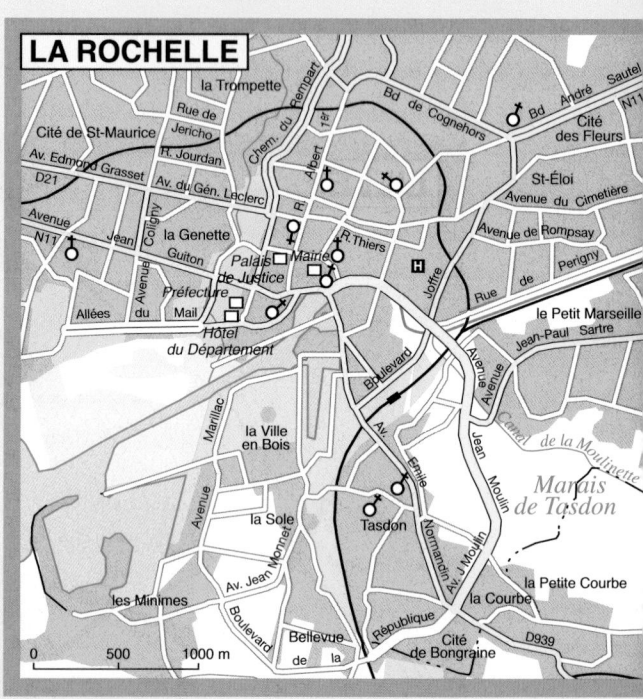

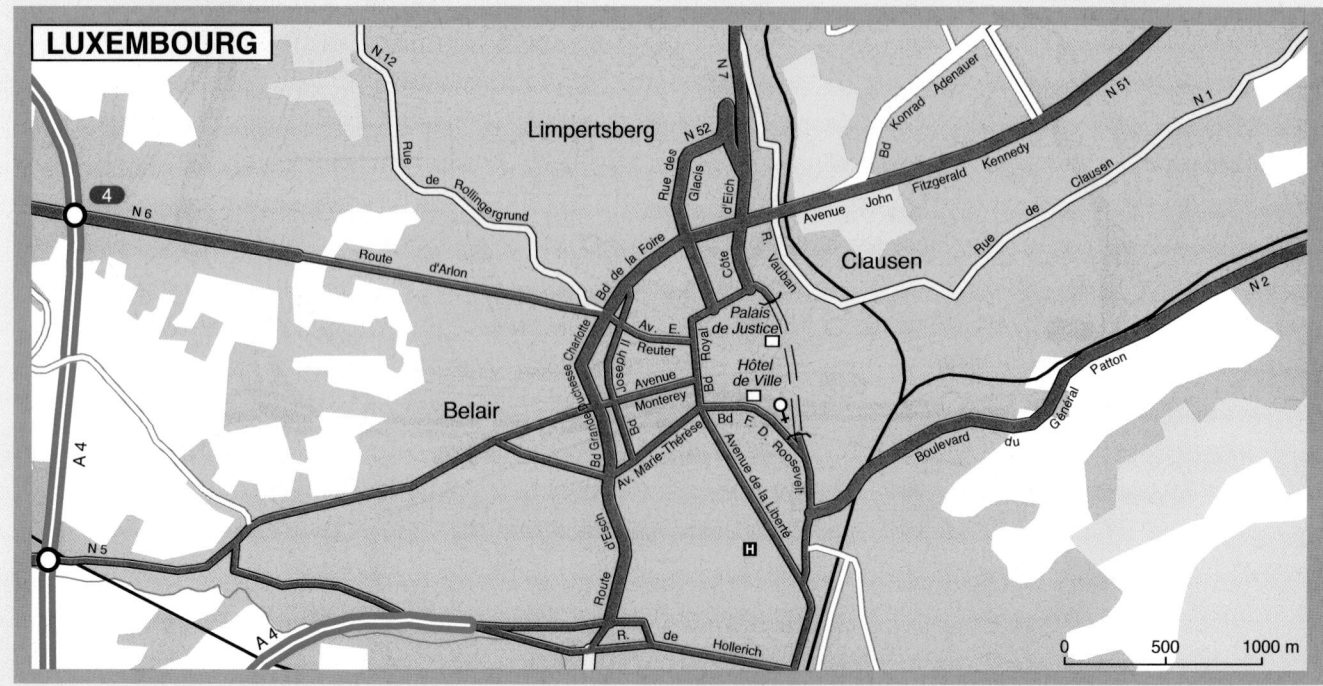

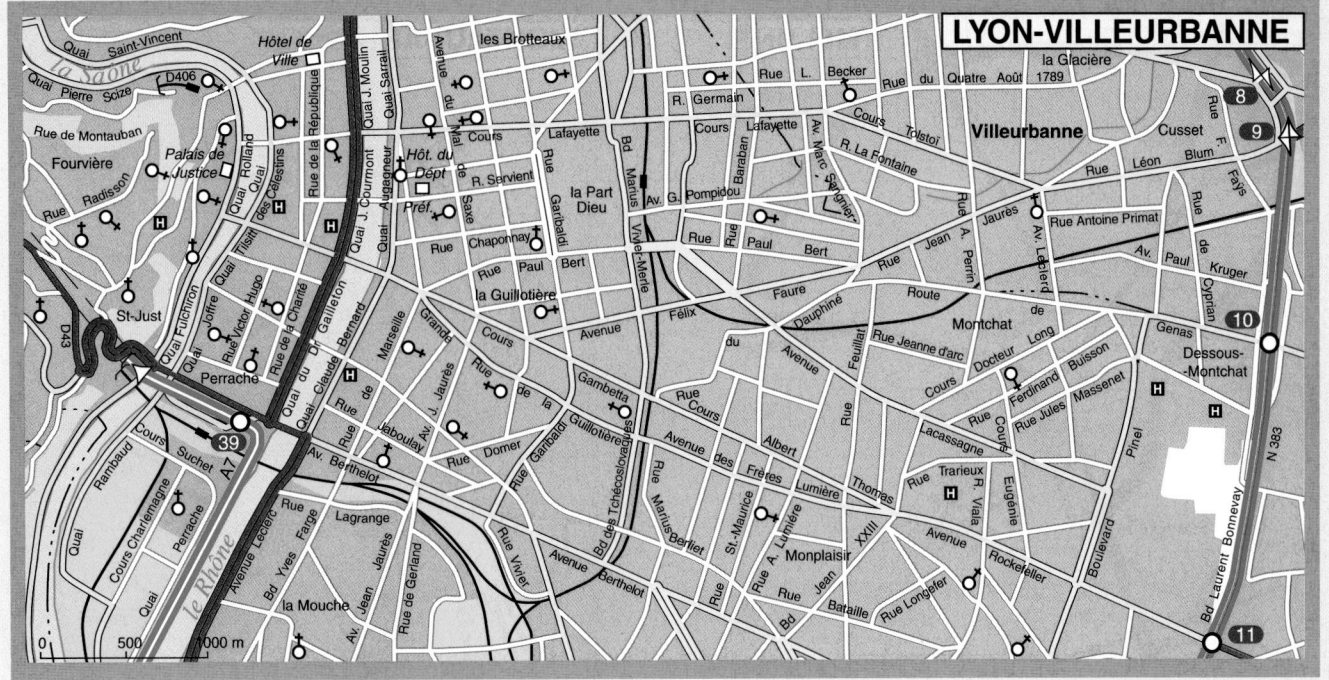

LYON-VILLEURBANNE

Quai Saint-Vincent
la Saône
Quai Pierre Scize
D406
Hôtel de Ville
les Brotteaux
Rue L. Becker
Rue du Quatre Août 1789
la Glacière
8
9
Rue de Montauban
Fourvière
Quai J. Moulin
Quai Sarrail
Avenue du Mal de Mal
Cours
Rue
R. Germain
Villeurbanne
Cusset
Rue F. Fays
Palais de Justice
Quai Rolland
Rue de la République
Lafayette
Cours
Lafayette
Rue Tolstoï
Rue Léon Blum
Rue de Kruger
Rue de Montauban
Rue Radisson
Hôt. du Dépt
Préf.
R. Servient
R. de Saxe
la Part Dieu
Bd Marius Vivier-Merle
Cours
Baraban
Av. Marc Sangnier
R. La Fontaine
Av. Lacassagne
Rue Antoine Primat
Av. Paul
de
Av. de Cyprian
St-Just
D43
Quai Tilsitt Quai Victor Hugo
Quai Célestins
Quai
Rue de la Charité
R. Chaponnay
la Guillotière
Rue Paul
Bert
Rue Paul
Bert
Jean A. Perrin
Montchat
Genas
Dessous-Montchat
10
Perrache
Rue Claude Bernard
Rue du Dr Gailleton
Grande Rue de Marseille
Cours
Faure
Dauphiné
Rue Jeanne d'arc
Docteur
Ferdinand Buisson
Rue Jules Massenet
Pinel
N 383
39
A7
Av. J. Jaurès
Rue Domer
Jaboulay
Gambetta
Avenue
du
Cours
Lacassagne
Eugénie
Rue Trarieux
R. Viala
Cours Suchet
Cours Rambaud
Quai
Cours Charlemagne
Perrache
Rue Farge
Lagrange
Rue de la Guillotière
Rue Garibaldi
Albert
St-Maurice
Frères
Lumière
Thomas
XXIII
Avenue
Eugénie
Rockefeller
Boulevard
Bd Laurent Bonnevay
la Mouche
Av. Jean Jaurès
Avenue Berthelot
Bd des Tchécoslovaques
Avenue
Berthelot
Rue Vivier
Rue Marius Berliet
St-Maurice
Rue A. Lumière
Monplaisir
Rue Jean
Bataille
Rue Longfier
11
0   500   1000 m

MARSEILLE

les Crottes
A 557
36
A 55
Bd. F. de Lesseps
St-Mauront
D 4c
Bon Secours
Bd. Alexandre Fleming
D 908
D 4c
Av. J.-P. Sartre
2
Av. R. Salengro
A 7
Bd. de Plombières
Chutes Lavie
Rade
de
Marseille
A 55
Belle de Mai
les Chartreux
Av. de St-Barnbé
St-Lazare
37
la Blancarde
A 55
Bd. des Dames
Hôt. rég.
Bd. de la Libération
Pharo
Bd. Ch. Livon
Hôt. de V.
la Canebière
Cours Lieutaud
Rue Saint Pierre
St-Pierre
D 2
Pal. de Just.
Préf.
Rue de Rome
Boulevard Baille
H
la Timone
St-Lambert
2
A 50
N 8
Endoume
Rue du Prado
la Capelette
Bompard
Rue Paradis
Périer
Bd. Schloesing
Bd. R. Rolland
Corniche
le Roucas Blanc
Président
John Kennedy
la Plage
Av. du Prado
St-Giniez
D 559
Bd. Michelet
Ste-Marguerite
l'Huveaune
0   500   1000 m

339

MELUN

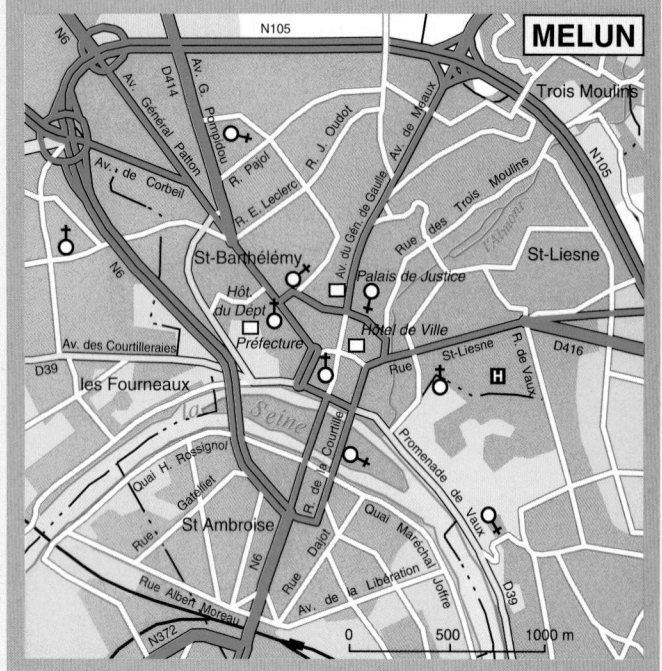

METZ

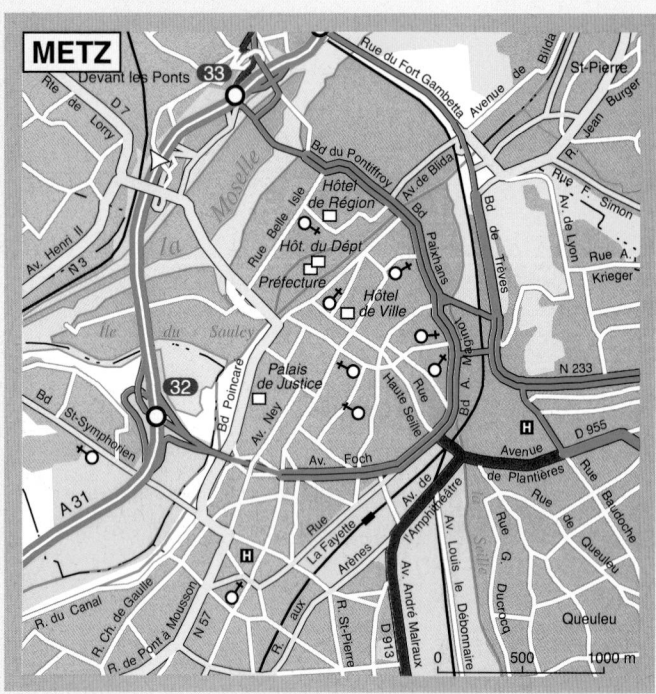

MONACO

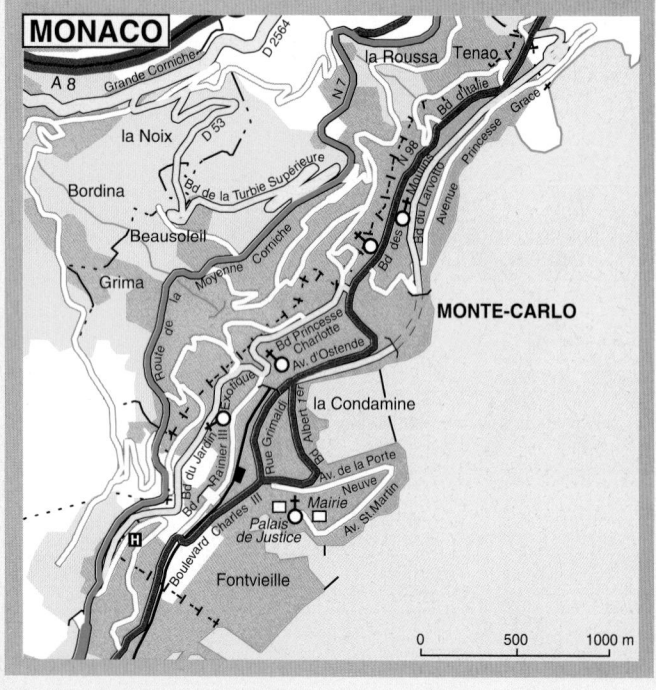

MONTAUBAN

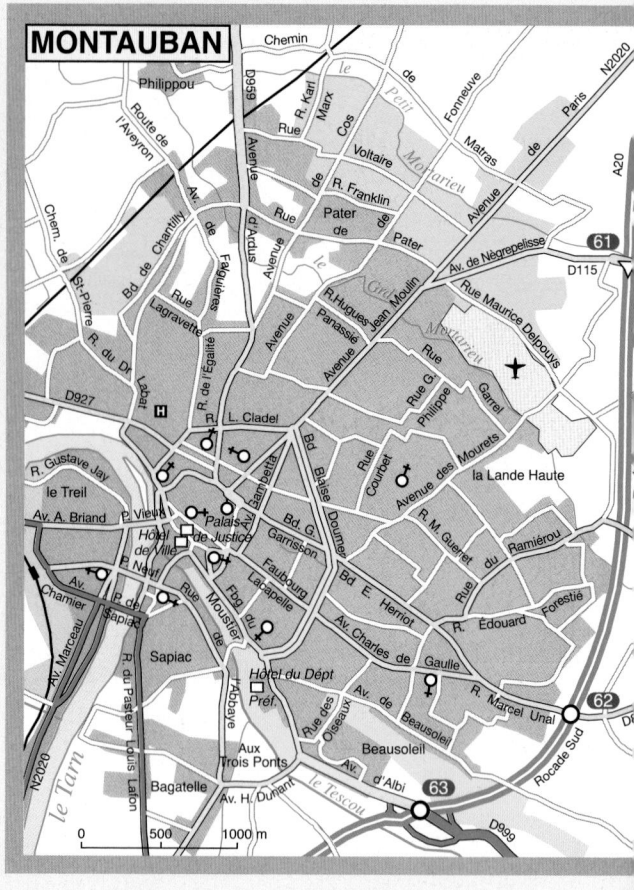

MONTPELLIER

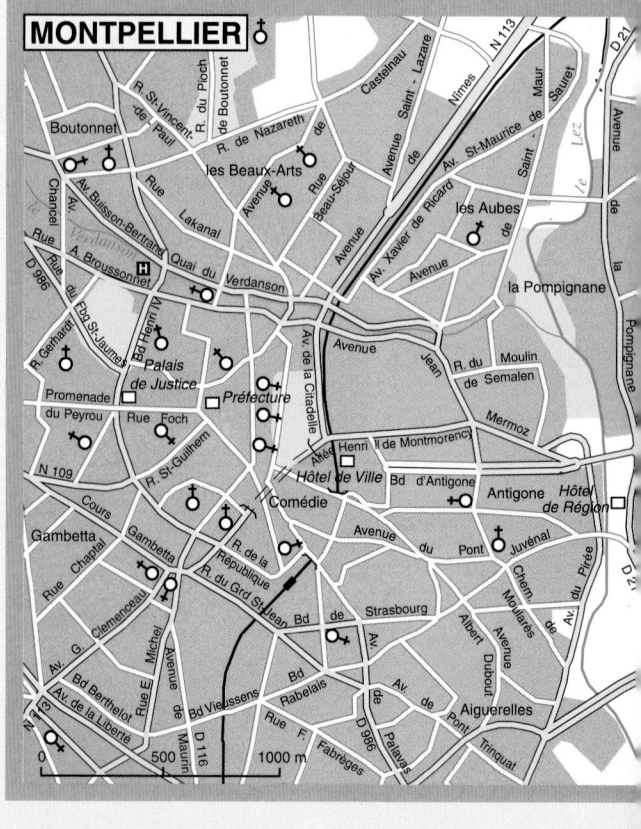

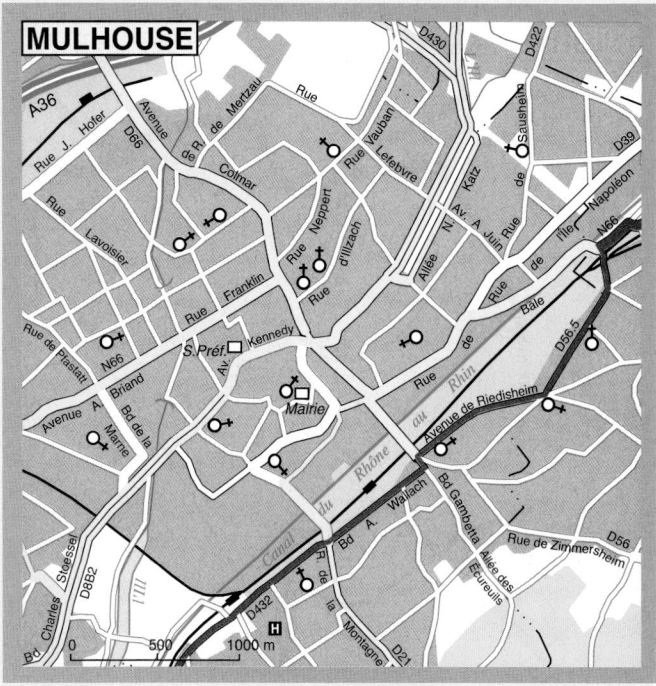

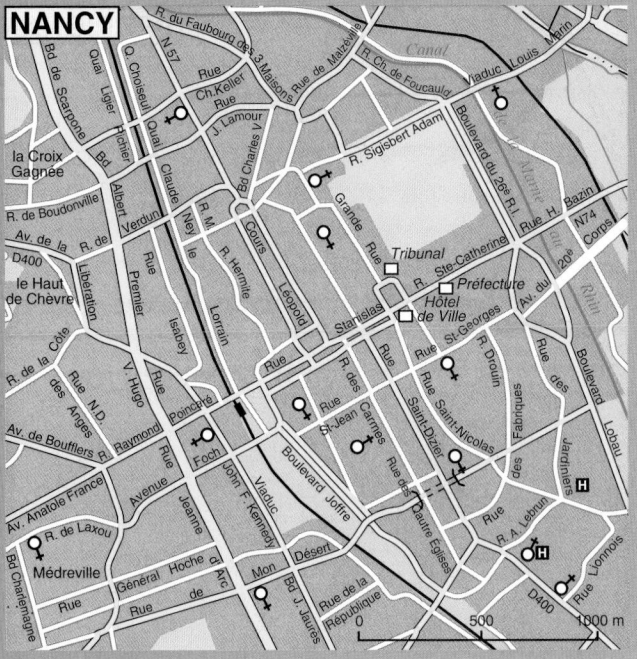

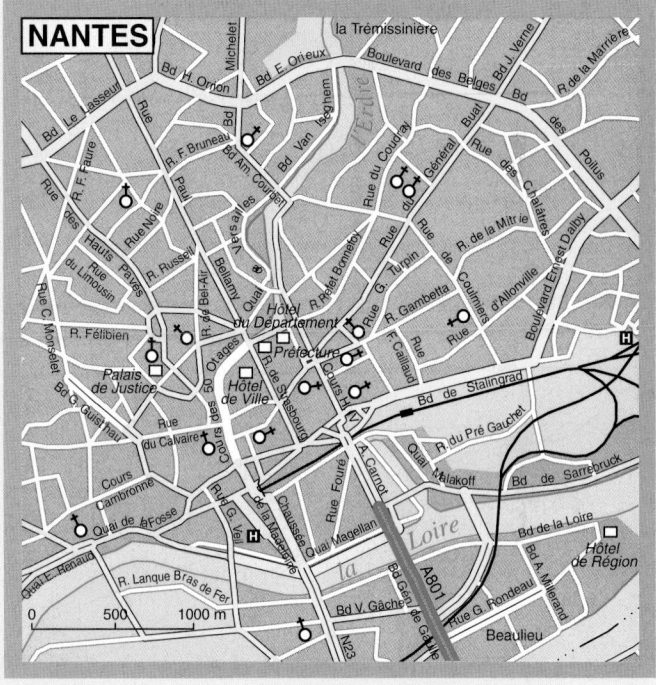

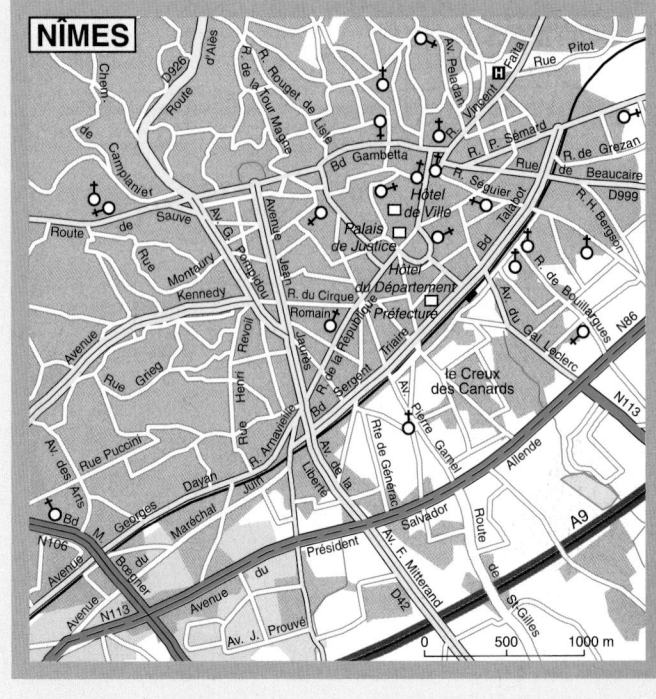

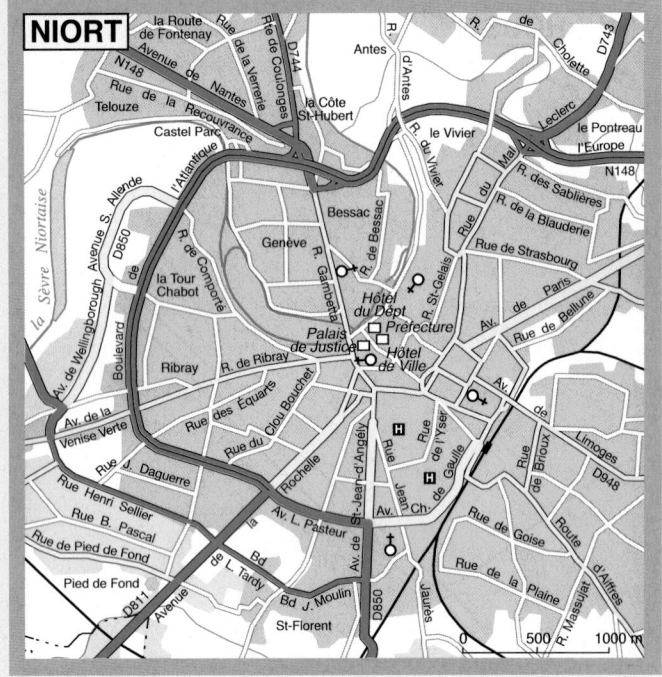

NIORT

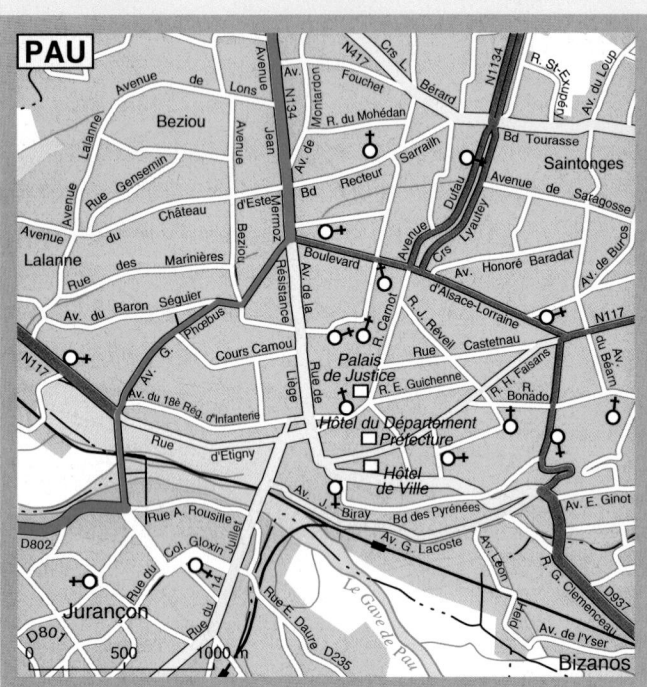

PAU

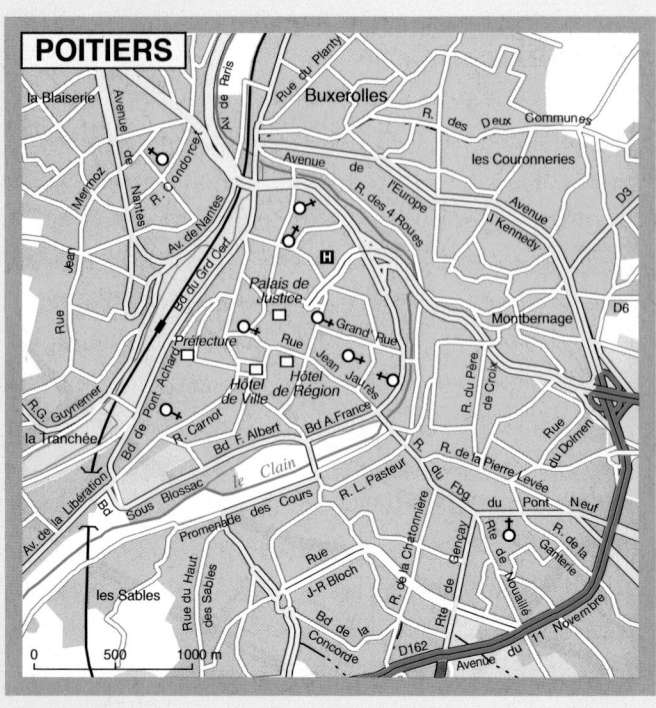

POITIERS

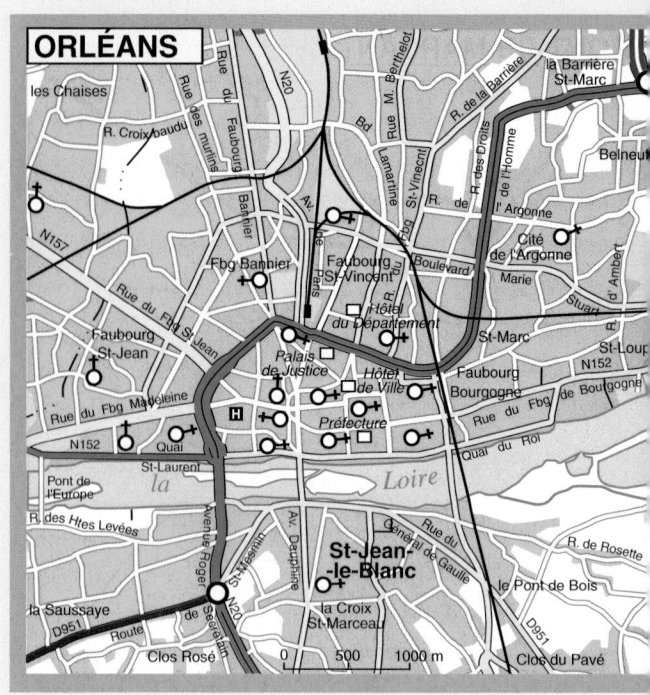

ORLÉANS

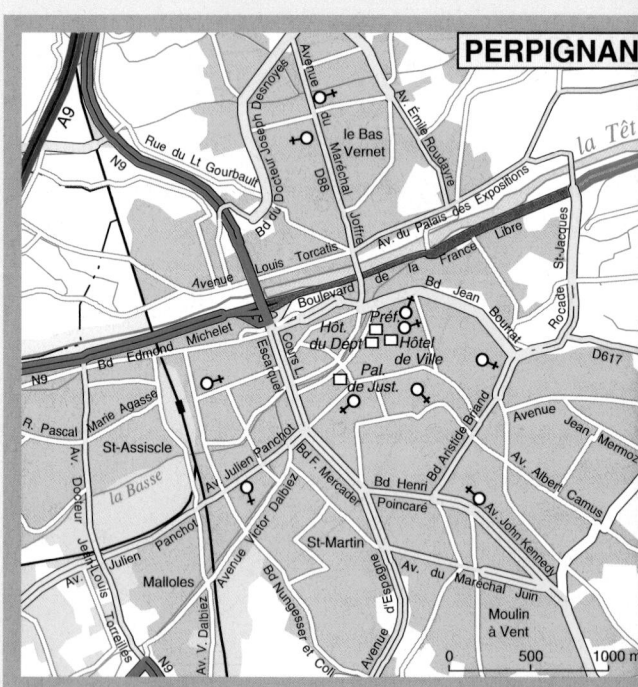

PERPIGNAN

PORTO-VECCHIO

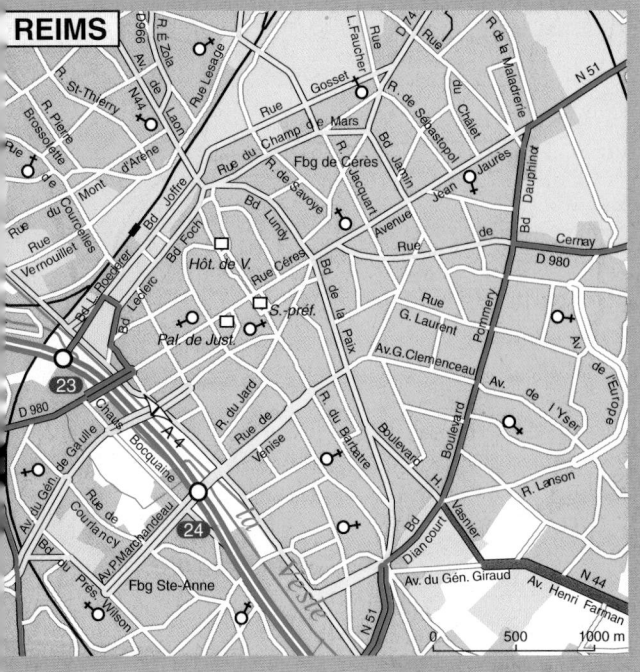

REIMS

RENNES

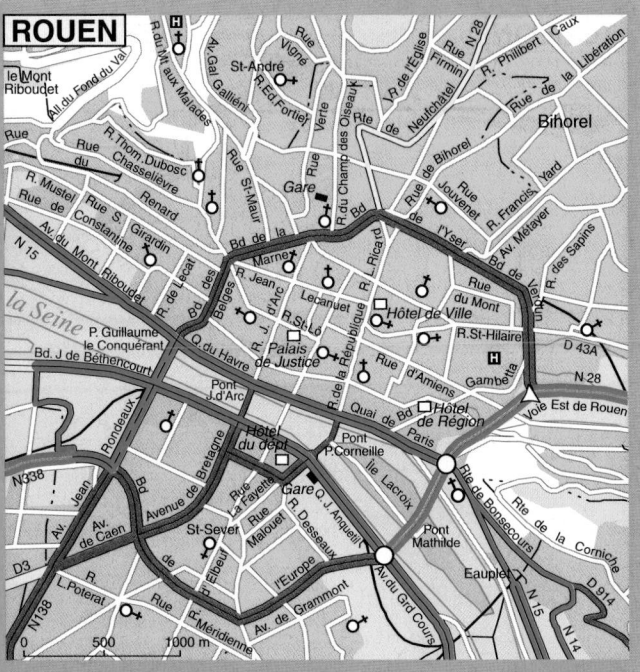

ROUEN

SAINT-ÉTIENNE

SAINT-BRIEUC

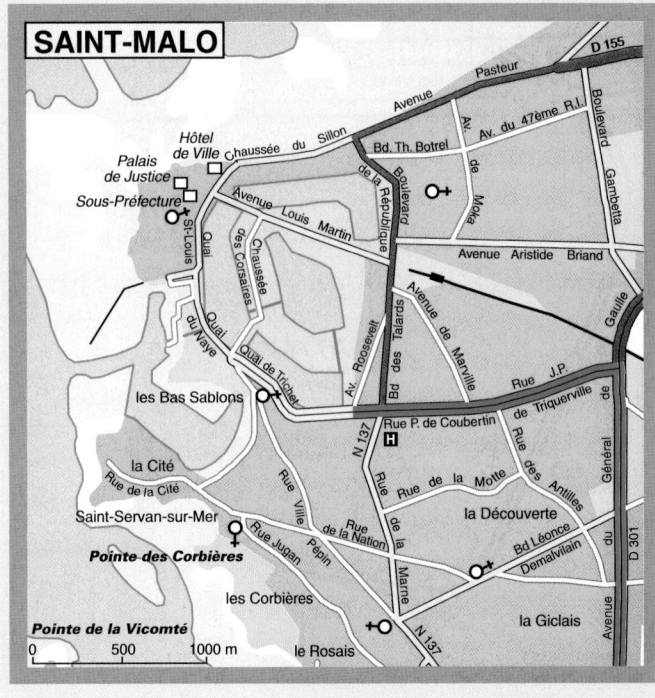

SAINT-MALO

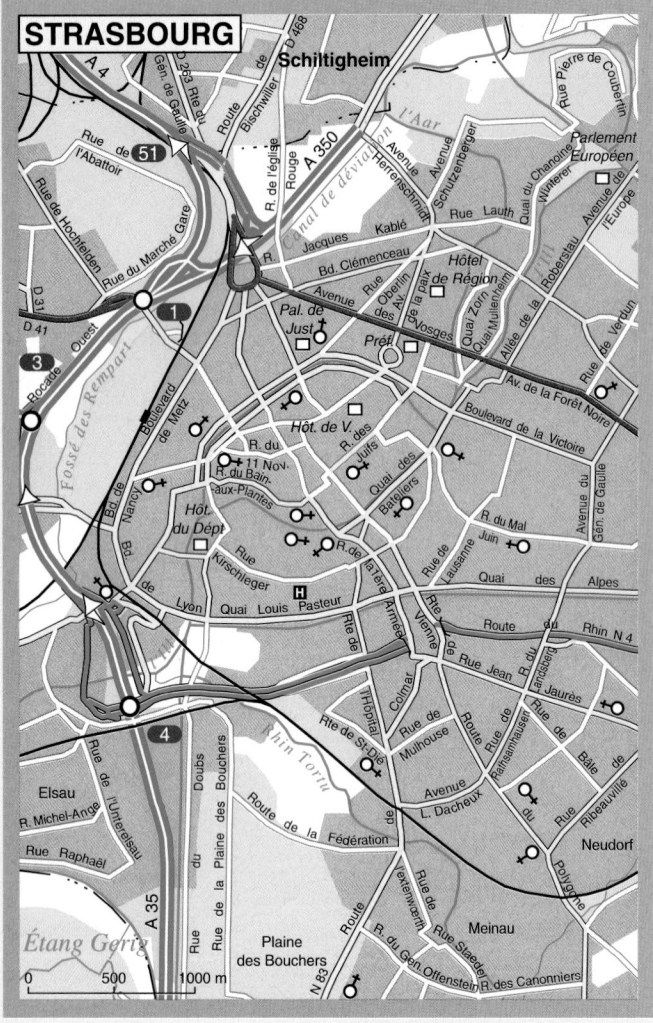

STRASBOURG

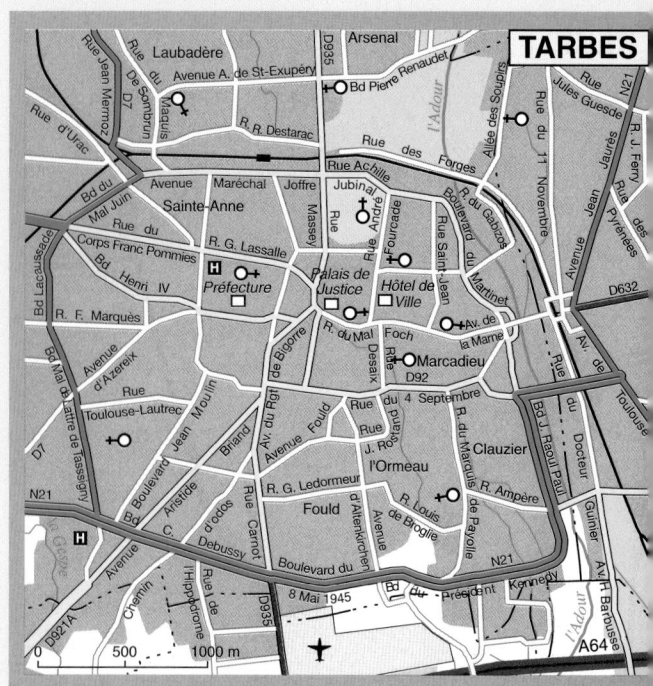

TARBES

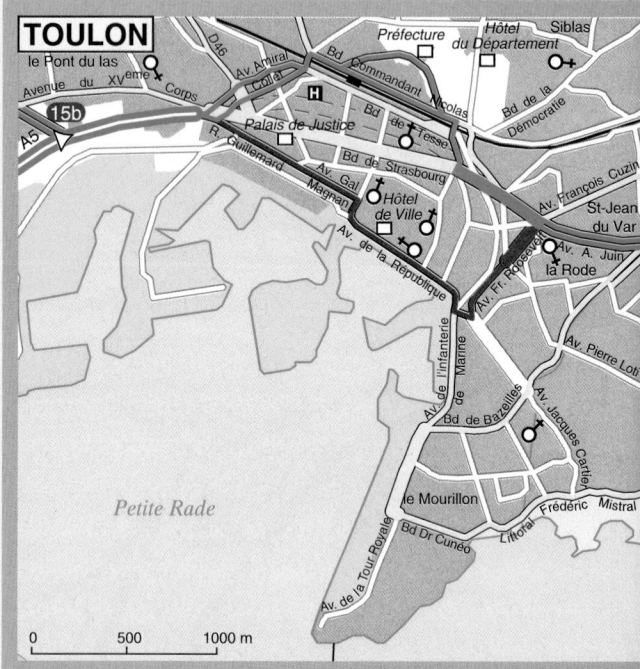

TOULON

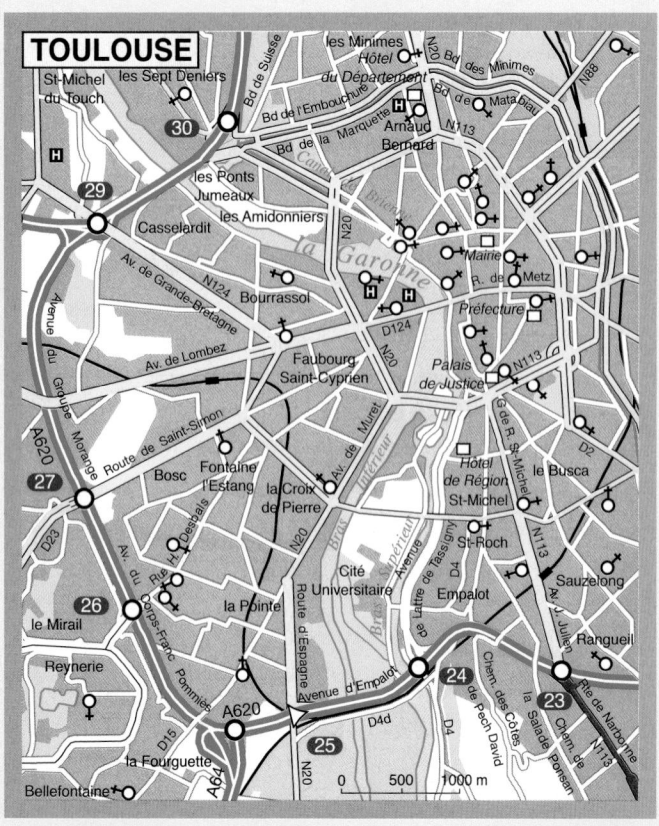

TOULOUSE

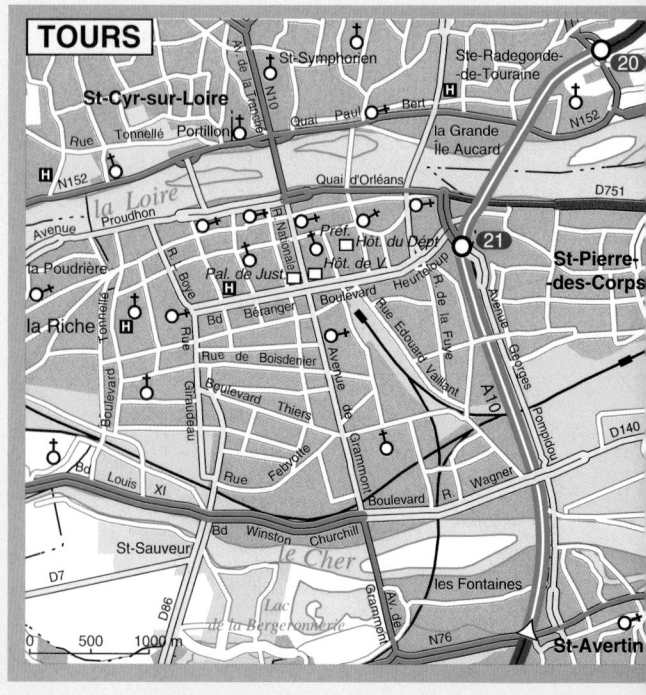

TOURS

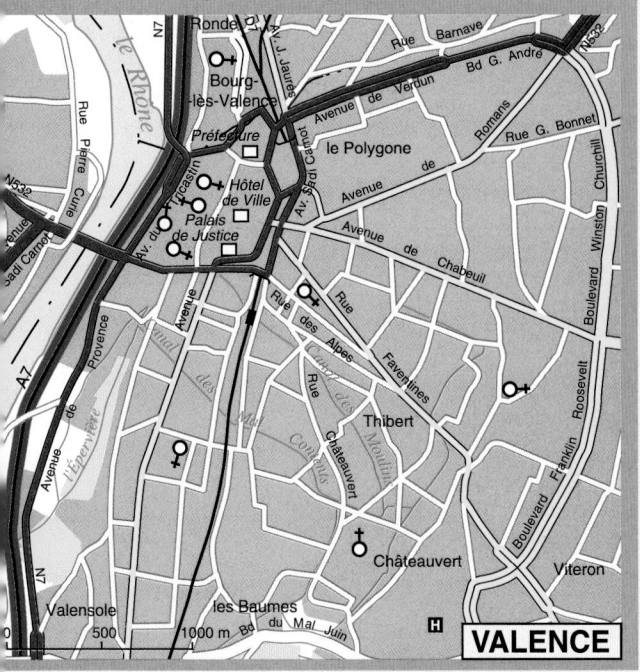

VALENCE

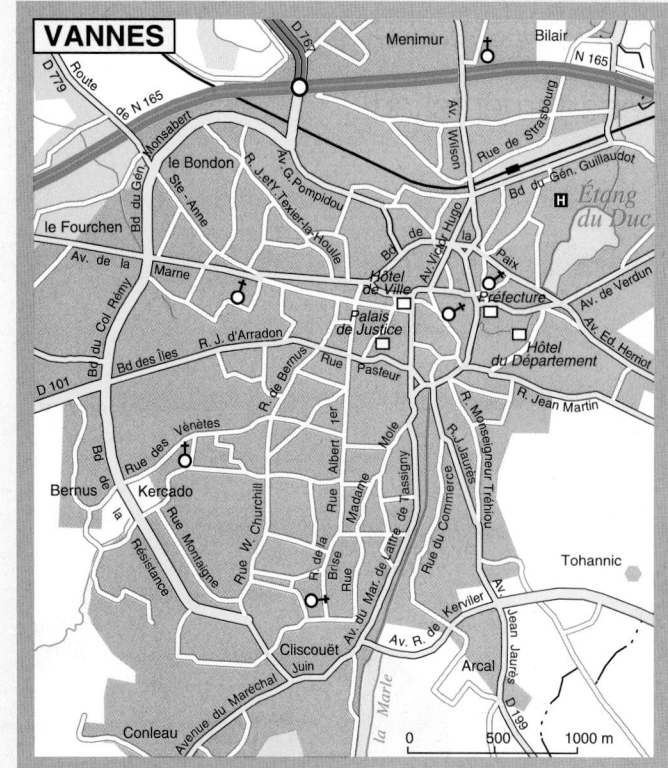

VANNES

345

France administrative   Département map

Overzicht departementen
Departementskarte

Mapa departamental
Carta dipartimentale

ILE DE FRANCE
95 VAL D'OISE
78 YVELINES
92
75
93
94
91 ESSONNE
77 SEINE-ET-MARNE

NORD PAS-DE-CALAIS
62 PAS-DE-CALAIS
59 NORD
80 SOMME

HAUTE NORMANDIE
76 SEINE-MARITIME
02 AISNE
08 ARDENNES
PICARDIE
60 OISE
95 VAL D'OISE
27 EURE

CHAMPAGNE-ARDENNE
55 MEUSE
57 MOSELLE
LORRAINE
67 BAS-RHIN
50 MANCHE
14 CALVADOS
BASSE NORMANDIE
77 SEINE-ET-MARNE
78 YVELINES
ILE DE FRANCE
51 MARNE
54 MEURTHE-ET-MOSELLE
ALSACE
61 ORNE
91 ESSONNE
10 AUBE
88 VOSGES
68 HAUT-RHIN

22 CÔTES-D'ARMOR
BRETAGNE
35 ILLE-ET-VILAINE
53 MAYENNE
28 EURE-ET-LOIR
52 HAUTE-MARNE
90 TERRITOIRE DE BELFORT
29 FINISTÈRE
56 MORBIHAN
72 SARTHE
45 LOIRET
89 YONNE
70 HAUTE-SAÔNE
FRANCHE-COMTÉ

PAYS DE LA LOIRE
CENTRE
BOURGOGNE
44 LOIRE-ATLANTIQUE
41 LOIR-ET-CHER
21 CÔTE-D'OR
25 DOUBS
49 MAINE-ET-LOIRE
37 INDRE-ET-LOIRE
18 CHER
58 NIÈVRE
39 JURA

85 VENDÉE
36 INDRE
71 SAÔNE-ET-LOIRE
79 DEUX-SÈVRES
86 VIENNE
03 ALLIER
01 AIN
74 HAUTE-SAVOIE

POITOU-CHARENTES
23 CREUSE
17 CHARENTE-MARITIME
87 HAUTE-VIENNE
63 PUY-DE-DÔME
42 LOIRE
69 RHÔNE
16 CHARENTE
LIMOUSIN
AUVERGNE
RHÔNE-ALPES
73 SAVOIE
19 CORRÈZE
38 ISÈRE

24 DORDOGNE
15 CANTAL
43 HAUTE-LOIRE
33 GIRONDE
07 ARDÈCHE
26 DRÔME
05 HAUTES-ALPES
46 LOT
48 LOZÈRE
47 LOT-ET-GARONNE
12 AVEYRON
PROVENCE-ALPES-CÔTE D'AZUR
82 TARN-ET-GARONNE
04 ALPES-DE-HAUTE-PROVENCE
06 ALPES-MARITIMES
AQUITAINE
81 TARN
30 GARD
84 VAUCLUSE
40 LANDES
32 GERS
MIDI-PYRÉNÉES
34 HÉRAULT
13 BOUCHES-DU-RHÔNE
83 VAR
64 PYRÉNÉES-ATLANTIQUES
31 HAUTE-GARONNE
2B HAUTE-CORSE
65 HAUTES-PYRÉNÉES
11 AUDE
LANGUEDOC-ROUSSILLON
CORSE
09 ARIÈGE
66 PYRÉNÉES-ORIENTALES
2A CORSE-DU-SUD

01 Ain		
02 Aisne		
03 Allier		
04 Alpes-de-Haute-Provence		
05 Hautes-Alpes	28 Eure-et-Loir	52 Haute-Marne
06 Alpes-Maritimes	29 Finistère	53 Mayenne
07 Ardèche	30 Gard	54 Meurthe-et-Moselle
08 Ardennes	31 Haute-Garonne	55 Meuse
09 Ariège	32 Gers	56 Morbihan
10 Aube	33 Gironde	57 Moselle
11 Aude	34 Hérault	58 Nièvre
12 Aveyron	35 Ille-et-Vilaine	59 Nord
13 Bouches-du-Rhône	36 Indre	60 Oise
14 Calvados	37 Indre-et-Loire	61 Orne
15 Cantal	38 Isère	62 Pas-de-Calais
16 Charente	39 Jura	63 Puy-de-Dôme
17 Charente-Maritime	40 Landes	64 Pyrénées-Atlantiques
18 Cher	41 Loir-et-Cher	65 Hautes-Pyrénées
19 Corrèze	42 Loire	66 Pyrénées-Orientales
2A Corse-du-Sud	43 Haute-Loire	67 Bas-Rhin
2B Haute-Corse	44 Loire-Atlantique	68 Haut-Rhin
21 Côte-d'Or	45 Loiret	69 Rhône
22 Côtes d'Armor	46 Lot	70 Haute-Saône
23 Creuse	47 Lot-et-Garonne	71 Saône-et-Loire
24 Dordogne	48 Lozère	72 Sarthe
25 Doubs	49 Maine-et-Loire	73 Savoie
26 Drôme	50 Manche	74 Haute-Savoie
27 Eure	51 Marne	75 Paris

76 Seine-Maritime
77 Seine-et-Marne
78 Yvelines
79 Deux-Sèvres
80 Somme
81 Tarn
82 Tarn-et-Garonne
83 Var
84 Vaucluse
85 Vendée
86 Vienne
87 Haute-Vienne
88 Vosges
89 Yonne
90 Territoire de Belfort
91 Essonne
92 Hauts-de-Seine
93 Seine-Saint-Denis
94 Val-de-Marne
95 Val-d'Oise

A

Aast (64) 285 F4
Abainville (55) 92 E1
Abancourt (59) 11 J3
Abancourt (60) 17 F4
Abaucourt (54) 66 B2
Abaucourt-Hautecourt (55) 43 K4
Abbans-Dessous (25) 156 A1
Abbans-Dessus (25) 156 A2
Abbaretz (44) 103 H5
Abbécourt (02) 19 J6
Abbecourt (60) 37 H3
Abbenans (25) 138 E2
Abbéville (80) 9 G5
Abbéville-la-Rivière (91) 86 C4
Abbéville-lès-Conflans (54) 44 C4
Abbeville-Saint-Lucien (60) 37 H1
Abbévillers (25) 139 J3
Abeilhan (34) 292 B2
Abelcourt (70) 118 C5
Abère (64) 285 F3
l'Abergement-Clémenciat (01) 188 D3
l'Abergement-de-Cuisery (71) 172 A3
l'Abergement-de-Varey (01) 189 J4
Abergement-la-Ronce (39) 155 F2
Abergement-le-Grand (39) 155 H4
Abergement-le-Petit (39) 155 J4
Abergement-lès-Thésy (39) 156 A4
l'Abergement-
    -Sainte-Colombe (71) 172 A1
Abidos (64) 284 A3
Abilly (37) 146 A4
Abitain (64) 283 G2
Abjat-sur-Bandiat (24) 198 A4
Ablain-Saint-Nazaire (62) 10 E1
Ablaincourt-Pressoir (80) 19 F2
Ablainzevelle (62) 10 E4
Ablancourt (51) 62 E4
Ableiges (95) 37 G6
les Ableuvenettes (88) 94 B5
Ablis (78) 85 K2
Ablon (14) 34 A2
Ablon-sur-Seine (94) 59 F5
Aboën (42) 204 D6
Aboncourt (54) 93 J3
Aboncourt (57) 45 G3
Aboncourt-Gesincourt (70) 117 K5
Aboncourt-sur-Seille (57) 66 C3
Abondance (74) 175 H6
Abondant (28) 57 F4
Abos (64) 284 B3
Abreschviller (57) 67 K5
Abrest (03) 185 J4
les Abrets (38) 207 J4
Abriès (05) 227 D2
Abscon (59) 12 B2
l'Absie (79) 161 G2
Abzac (16) 180 B3
Abzac (33) 212 B5
Accolans (25) 138 E2
Accolay (89) 133 H1
Accons (07) 239 H1
Accous (64) 303 F2
Achain (57) 66 E2
Achen (57) 68 E3
Achenheim (67) 70 E3
Achères (18) 131 F6
Achères (78) 58 C2
Achères-la-Forêt (77) 87 G4
Achery (02) 20 B4
Acheux-en-Amiénois (80) 10 C5
Acheux-en-Vimeu (80) 8 E5
Acheville (62) 11 F1
Achey (70) 137 F2
Achicourt (62) 10 E3
Achiet-le-Grand (62) 10 E5
Achiet-le-Petit (62) 10 E5
Achun (58) 151 J2
Achy (60) 17 H6
Aclou (27) 34 E5
Acon (27) 56 C4
Acq (62) 10 D2
Acqueville (14) 53 J2
Acqueville (50) 28 B2
Acquigny (27) 35 J5
Acquin-Westbécourt (62) 5 F3
Acy (02) 39 K3
Acy-en-Multien (60) 39 F6
Acy-Romance (08) 41 H1
Adaincourt (57) 66 C1
Adainville (78) 57 H5
Adam-lès-Passavant (25) 138 D5
Adam-lès-Vercel (25) 157 F1
Adamswiller (67) 68 E5
Adast (65) 304 A4
Adé (65) 285 G6
Adelange (57) 45 K6
Adelans-et-le-
    -Val-de-Bithaine (70) 118 D5
Adervielle-Pouchergues (65) 305 G4
Adilly (79) 161 J2
Adinfer (62) 10 E4
Adissan (34) 292 C1
les Adjots (16) 179 G4
Adon (45) 111 J6
les Adrets (38) 224 D2
les Adrets-de-l'Estérel (83) 280 C6
Adriers (86) 180 C2
Afa (2A) 320 C4
Affieux (19) 200 A5
Afféville (54) 44 B3
Affoux (69) 205 G1
Affracourt (54) 94 A2

Affringues (62) 4 E3
Agassac (31) 287 F3
Agde (34) 292 C4
Agel (34) 291 G4
Agen (47) 248 B4
Agen-d'Aveyron (12) 252 C3
Agencourt (21) 154 B2
Agenville (80) 9 J4
Agenvillers (80) 9 H4
les Ageux (60) 38 B3
Ageville (52) 116 D1
Agey (21) 135 H6
Aghione (2B) 321 J2
Agincourt (54) 66 B4
Agmé (47) 247 J1
Agnac (47) 231 G4
Agnat (43) 219 H2
Agneaux (50) 31 H3
Agnetz (60) 37 K3
Agnez-lès-Duisans (62) 10 D2
Agnicourt-et-Séchelles (02) 21 G4
Agnières (62) 10 D2
Agnières-en-Dévoluy (05) 242 C3
Agnin (38) 222 B1
Agnos (64) 284 A6
Agon-Coutainville (50) 30 C4
Agonac (24) 214 A2
Agonès (34) 274 A2
Agonges (03) 168 C3
Agos-Vidalos (65) 304 B2
Agris (16) 197 F2
Agudelle (17) 211 J1
Aguessac (12) 253 G5
Aguilcourt (02) 40 E2
Aguts (81) 289 G1
Agy (14) 32 A4
Ahaxe-Alciette-Bascassan (64) 282 E6
Ahetze (64) 282 A2
Ahéville (88) 94 B4
Ahuillé (53) 104 D2
Ahun (23) 183 F4
Ahuy (21) 136 A4
Aibes (59) 13 J3
Aibre (25) 139 G2
Aïcirits-Camou-Suhast (64) 283 G3
Aiffres (79) 178 A1
Aigaliers (30) 255 K6
l'Aigle (61) 55 J4
Aiglemont (08) 22 D3
Aiglepierre (39) 155 K4
Aigleville (27) 57 F1
Aiglun (04) 259 H6
Aiglun (06) 280 D2
Aignan (32) 266 C5
Aignay-le-Duc (21) 135 H1
Aigne (34) 291 F4
Aigné (72) 106 D2
Aignerville (14) 29 K6
Aignes (31) 288 D4
Aignes-et-Puypéroux (16) 196 D6
Aigneville (80) 8 E6
Aigny (51) 62 C1
Aigonnay (79) 161 K6
Aigre (16) 178 E6
Aigrefeuille (31) 288 D1
Aigrefeuille-d'Aunis (17) 177 F3
Aigrefeuille-sur-Maine (44) 141 K2
Aigremont (30) 274 E2
Aigremont (52) 117 G2
Aigremont (78) 58 B3
Aigremont (89) 113 K6
Aiguebelette-le-Lac (73) 208 A4
Aiguebelle (73) 209 F4
Aigueblanche (73) 209 H4
Aiguefonde (81) 290 A2
Aigueperse (63) 185 G5
Aigueperse (69) 187 J1
Aigues-Juntes (09) 307 G2
Aigues-Mortes (30) 294 A3
Aigues-Vives (09) 308 B2
Aigues-Vives (11) 290 D5
Aigues-Vives (30) 275 F4
Aigues-Vives (34) 291 G4
Aiguèze (30) 256 B3
Aiguilhe (43) 220 C5
Aiguilles (05) 227 C2
l'Aiguillon (09) 308 B3
Aiguillon (47) 247 J3
l'Aiguillon-sur-Mer (85) 159 J6
l'Aiguillon-sur-Vie (85) 158 E1
Aiguines (83) 279 G3
Aigurande (36) 165 K5
Ailhon (07) 239 G5
Aillant-sur-Milleron (45) 112 A5
Aillant-sur-Tholon (89) 112 E4
Aillas (33) 246 E1
Ailleux (42) 204 B1
Aillevans (70) 138 D1
Ailleville (10) 91 G5
Aillevillers-et-Lyaumont (70) 118 C3
Aillianville (52) 92 C2
Aillières-Beauvoir (72) 83 F3
Aillon-le-Jeune (73) 208 D3
Aillon-le-Vieux (73) 208 D3
Ailloncourt (70) 118 D5
Ailly (27) 35 K5
Ailly-le-Haut-Clocher (80) 9 H5
Ailly-sur-Noye (80) 18 B4
Ailly-sur-Somme (80) 17 K1
Aimargues (30) 275 F5
Aime (73) 209 J4
Ainay-le-Château (03) 167 J2
Ainay-le-Vieil (18) 167 J2
Aincille (64) 282 E6
Aincourt (95) 57 K1

Aincreville (55) 43 F2
Aingeray (54) 65 J4
Aingeville (88) 93 G5
Aingoulaincourt (52) 92 C2
Ainharp (64) 283 H4
Ainhice-Mongelos (64) 282 E5
Ainhoa (64) 282 B3
Ainvelle (70) 118 B4
Ainvelle (88) 117 J2
Airaines (80) 17 H1
Airan (14) 33 G6
Aire (08) 41 G1
Aire-sur-la-Lys (62) 5 H4
Aire-sur-l'Adour (40) 265 K5
Airel (50) 31 H2
les Aires (34) 291 J1
Airion (60) 38 A2
Airon-Notre-Dame (62) 8 E1
Airon-Saint-Vaast (62) 8 E1
Airoux (11) 289 G4
Airvault (79) 144 C6
Aiserey (21) 154 D1
Aisey-et-Richecourt (70) 117 J3
Aisey-sur-Seine (21) 115 F6
Aisonville-et-Bernoville (02) 20 C1
Aïssey (25) 138 D5
Aisy-sous-Thil (21) 134 D4
Aisy-sur-Armançon (89) 134 C1
Aiti (2B) 319 G4
Aiton (73) 208 E4
Aix (19) 201 G4
Aix (59) 7 F6
les Aix-d'Angillon (18) 149 J1
Aix-en-Diois (26) 241 H3
Aix-en-Ergny (62) 4 E5
Aix-en-Issart (62) 4 D6
Aix-en-Othe (10) 89 H5
Aix-en-Provence (13) 296 D1
Aix-la-Fayette (63) 203 H5
Aix-les-Bains (73) 208 B2
Aix-Noulette (62) 10 E1
Aixe-sur-Vienne (87) 198 D2
Aizac (07) 239 G4
Aizanville (52) 115 J1
Aize (36) 147 K2
Aizecourt-le-Bas (80) 19 H1
Aizecourt-le-Haut (80) 19 H1
Aizelles (02) 40 D1
Aizenay (85) 141 H6
Aizier (27) 34 D2
Aizy-Jouy (02) 40 A2
Ajac (11) 308 E2
Ajaccio (2A) 320 B5
Ajain (23) 182 E2
Ajat (24) 214 D4
Ajoncourt (57) 66 B3
Ajou (27) 55 K2
Ajoux (07) 239 J3
Alaigne (11) 308 D1
Alaincourt (02) 20 A3
Alaincourt (70) 118 A3
Alaincourt-la-Côte (57) 66 C2
Alairac (11) 290 A1
Alan (31) 287 G5
Alando (2B) 319 G6
Alata (2A) 320 B4
Alba-la-Romaine (07) 239 K6
Alban (81) 271 H3
Albaret-le-Comtal (48) 236 E2
Albaret-Sainte-Marie (48) 237 F2
Albas (11) 310 A2
Albas (46) 249 H1
Albé (67) 70 B6
Albefeuille-Lagarde (82) 249 J6
l'Albenc (38) 223 H3
Albens (73) 208 B1
Albepierre-Bredons (15) 218 B5
l'Albère (66) 315 G5
Albert (80) 10 D6
Albertacce (2B) 318 D6
Albertville (73) 209 G2
Albestroff (57) 68 B5
Albi (81) 270 E2
Albiac (31) 289 F1
Albiac (46) 234 B3
Albias (82) 250 A6
Albières (11) 309 H3
Albiès (09) 307 K5
Albiez-le-Jeune (73) 225 G2
Albiez-Montrond (73) 225 G2
Albignac (19) 216 A4
Albigny-sur-Saône (69) 188 C6
Albine (81) 290 D2
Albitreccia (2A) 320 D6
Albon (26) 222 B3
Albon-d'Ardèche (07) 239 H2
Alboussière (07) 222 A6
les Albres (12) 234 E6
Albussac (19) 216 B4
Alby-sur-Chéran (74) 208 C1
Alçay-Alçabéhéty-
    -Sunharette (64) 283 H6
Aldudes (64) 282 B6
Alembon (62) 2 D4
Alençon (61) 82 D3
Alénya (66) 315 H3
Aléria (2B) 321 K2
Alès (30) 255 G5
Alet-les-Bains (11) 309 F2
Alette (62) 4 C5
Aleu (09) 306 E4
Alex (74) 191 G5
Alexain (53) 80 E5
Aleyrac (26) 240 D6
Alfortville (94) 59 F4
Algajola (2B) 318 C2

Algans (81) 270 B6
Algolsheim (68) 96 E5
Algrange (57) 27 F4
Alièze (39) 173 G3
Alignan-du-Vent (34) 292 B2
Alincourt (08) 41 H2
Alincthun (62) 4 C3
Alise-Sainte-Reine (21) 135 F3
Alissas (07) 239 K4
Alix (69) 188 A6
Alixan (26) 222 D6
Alizay (27) 35 J3
Allain (54) 93 J1
Allaines (80) 19 G1
Allaines-Mervilliers (28) 85 K6
Allainville (28) 56 E5
Allainville (78) 86 A3
Allaire (56) 102 B4
Allamont (54) 44 B5
Allamps (54) 93 H1
Allan (26) 240 B6
Allanche (15) 218 C3
Alland'Huy-et-Sausseuil (08) 22 B6
Allarmont (88) 95 J1
Allas-Bocage (17) 211 J1
Allas-Champagne (17) 195 K5
Allas-les-Mines (24) 232 D2
Allassac (19) 215 H3
Allauch (13) 296 D3
Allègre (43) 220 A3
Allègre-les-Fumades (30) 255 J4
Alleins (13) 277 F5
Allemagne-en-Provence (04) 278 D3
Allemanche-Launay-et-
    -Soyer (51) 89 H1
Allemans (24) 213 G4
Allemans-du-Dropt (47) 231 F5
Allemant (02) 39 K1
Allemant (51) 61 J4
Allemond (38) 224 D4
Allenay (80) 8 D5
Allenc (48) 238 A6
Allenjoie (25) 139 J2
Allennes-les-Marais (59) 6 C5
Allenwiller (67) 70 B2
Allerey (21) 153 G1
Allerey-sur-Saône (71) 154 B5
Alleriot (71) 154 B6
Allery (80) 17 H1
Alles-sur-Dordogne (24) 232 B2
Allerie (42) 186 D3
les Alleuds (49) 125 H5
les Alleuds (79) 178 E3
les Alleux (08) 42 B1
Alleuze (15) 236 E1
Allevard (38) 208 D6
Allèves (74) 208 D1
Allex (26) 240 C3
Alleyrac (43) 238 D1
Alleyras (43) 238 A1
Alleyrat (19) 200 E4
Alleyrat (23) 183 F5
Allez-et-Cazeneuve (47) 248 B2
Alliancelles (51) 63 J4
Alliat (09) 307 J5
Allibaudières (10) 90 B1
Allichamps (52) 91 J1
Allier (65) 285 H6
Allières (09) 307 F2
les Alliés (25) 157 F4
Alligny-Cosne (58) 132 B4
Alligny-en-Morvan (58) 152 D1
Allineuc (22) 77 F3
Allinges (74) 175 F5
Allogny (18) 149 F1
Allondans (25) 139 G2
Allondaz (73) 209 F2
Allondrelle-la-Malmaison (54) 26 D1
Allonne (60) 37 H2
Allonne (79) 161 J3
Allonnes (28) 85 H4
Allonnes (49) 126 C6
Allonnes (72) 106 D3
Allons (04) 260 C6
Allons (47) 246 E4
Allonville (80) 18 B1
Allonzier-la-Caille (74) 191 F4
Allos (04) 260 C4
Allouagne (62) 5 J5
Alloue (16) 179 K4
Allouis (18) 149 G2
Allouville-Bellefosse (76) 15 F5
les Allues (73) 209 H5
les Alluets-le-Roi (78) 58 A3
Alluy (58) 151 J3
Alluyes (28) 85 F5
Almayrac (81) 251 H6
Almenêches (61) 54 D5
Almont-les-Junies (12) 235 G2
Alos (09) 306 D3
Alos (81) 270 B1
Alos-Sibas-Abense (64) 283 H6
Aloxe-Corton (21) 154 A3
Alpuech (12) 236 B3
Alquines (62) 4 E3
Alrance (12) 252 C5
Alsting (57) 68 C2
Altagène (2A) 323 F2
Alteckendorf (67) 69 H2
Altenach (68) 97 A4
Altenheim (67) 70 C1
Althen-des-Paluds (84) 276 D1
Altiani (2B) 321 G1
Altier (48) 254 C1
Altillac (19) 216 B6

Altkirch (68) 97 B4
Altorf (67) 70 D4
Altrippe (57) 68 B4
Altviller (57) 68 A3
Altwiller (67) 68 C5
Aluze (71) 153 J5
Alvignac (46) 234 A2
Alvimare (76) 15 F5
Alzen (09) 307 G3
Alzi (2B) 319 G6
Alzing (57) 45 J3
Alzon (30) 273 H2
Alzonne (11) 289 K5
Amage (70) 118 E4
Amagne (08) 22 B6
Amagney (25) 138 B5
Amailloux (79) 161 J1
Amance (10) 91 F4
Amance (54) 66 B4
Amance (70) 118 A4
Amancey (25) 156 C3
Amancy (74) 191 H3
Amange (39) 155 H1
Amanlis (35) 79 H5
Amanty (55) 93 F1
Amanvillers (57) 44 D4
Amanzé (71) 170 D6
Amarens (81) 270 B1
Amathay-Vésigneux (25) 156 D3
Amayé-sur-Orne (14) 32 D6
Amayé-sur-Seulles (14) 32 B6
Amazy (58) 133 G5
Ambacourt (88) 94 A3
Ambarès-et-Lagrave (33) 229 J1
Ambax (31) 287 G3
Ambazac (87) 181 J5
Ambel (38) 242 D2
Ambenay (27) 55 K3
Ambérac (16) 196 D1
Ambérieu-en-Bugey (01) 189 H5
Ambérieux (69) 188 B5
Ambérieux-en-Dombes (01) 188 D5
Ambernac (16) 180 A5
Amberre (86) 162 D1
Ambert (63) 203 K5
Ambès (33) 211 H5
Ambeyrac (12) 251 F1
Ambialet (81) 271 G2
Ambiegna (2A) 320 C3
Ambierle (42) 186 D3
Ambiévillers (70) 118 B2
Ambillou (37) 127 G4
Ambillou-Château (49) 125 J6
Ambilly (74) 191 G2
Amblaincourt (55) 64 B2
Amblainville (60) 37 H5
Amblans-et-Velotte (70) 118 D6
Ambleny (02) 39 H3
Ambléon (01) 207 J2
Ambleteuse (62) 2 A4
Ambleville (16) 196 A4
Ambleville (95) 36 D5
Amblie (14) 32 D3
Amblimont (08) 23 G5
Ambloy (41) 108 B6
Ambly-Fleury (08) 41 K1
Ambly-sur-Meuse (55) 64 D1
Amboise (37) 128 B4
Ambon (56) 121 H1
Ambonil (26) 240 C2
Ambonnay (51) 41 G6
Ambonville (52) 91 K4
Ambrault (36) 166 B1
Ambres (81) 270 A5
Ambricourt (62) 5 F6
Ambrief (02) 39 K3
Ambrières (51) 63 H6
Ambrières-les-Vallées (53) 81 G3
Ambrines (62) 10 C2
Ambronay (01) 189 H4
Ambrugeat (19) 200 D5
Ambrumesnil (76) 15 J2
Ambrus (47) 247 H4
Ambutrix (01) 189 H5
Amécourt (27) 36 D3
Amel-sur-l'Étang (55) 44 A3
Amelécourt (57) 66 D3
Amélie-les-Bains-Palalda (66) 314 E5
Amendeuix-Oneix (64) 283 F3
Amenoncourt (54) 67 G5
Amenucourt (95) 36 D6
Ames (62) 5 H5
Amettes (62) 5 H5
Ameugny (71) 171 H4
Ameuvelle (88) 117 J3
Amfreville (14) 33 F4
Amfreville (50) 28 E5
Amfreville-la-Campagne (27) 35 G5
Amfreville-la-Mi-Voie (76) 35 J2
Amfreville-les-Champs (27) 35 K3
Amfreville-les-Champs (76) 15 H4
Amfreville-sous-les-Monts (27) . . . 35 K3
Amfroipret (59) 13 F3
Amiens (80) 18 B2
Amifontaine (02) 40 E1
Amigny (50) 31 G3
Amigny-Rouy (02) 20 A5
Amillis (77) 60 B5
Amilly (28) 85 F3
Amilly (45) 111 J3
Amions (42) 186 E6
Amné (72) 106 C2
Amnéville (57) 44 E3

Amoncourt (70) . . . 118 A5
Amondans (25) . . . 156 C2
Amont-et-Effreney (70) . . . 118 E3
Amorots-Succos (64) . . . 283 F3
Amou (40) . . . 264 E6
Ampilly-le-Sec (21) . . . 115 F5
Ampilly-les-Bordes (21) . . . 135 G1
Amplepuis (69) . . . 187 H5
Amplier (62) . . . 10 B4
Ampoigné (53) . . . 104 E5
Amponville (77) . . . 87 G5
Ampriani (2B) . . . 319 H6
Ampuis (69) . . . 206 A5
Ampus (83) . . . 279 H5
Amuré (79) . . . 177 J1
Amy (60) . . . 19 F5
Anais (16) . . . 196 E3
Anais (17) . . . 177 F2
Anan (31) . . . 287 F4
Anceaumeville (76) . . . 15 K6
Anceins (61) . . . 55 H3
Ancelle (05) . . . 243 F4
Ancemont (55) . . . 43 H6
Ancenis (44) . . . 124 A4
Ancerville (55) . . . 63 K6
Ancerville (57) . . . 45 H6
Ancerviller (54) . . . 95 G1
Ancey (21) . . . 135 J5
Anchamps (08) . . . 22 C1
Anché (37) . . . 145 G2
Anché (86) . . . 162 E6
Anchenoncourt-et-Chazel (70) . . . 118 A4
Ancienville (02) . . . 39 H5
Ancier (70) . . . 137 G3
Ancinnes (72) . . . 82 E4
Ancizan (65) . . . 305 F4
les Ancizes-Comps (63) . . . 184 C6
Ancône (26) . . . 240 B5
Ancourt (76) . . . 16 A2
Ancourteville-sur-Héricourt (76) . . . 15 H4
Ancretiéville-Saint-Victor (76) . . . 15 J5
Ancretteville-sur-Mer (76) . . . 14 E4
Ancteville (50) . . . 30 D3
Anctoville (14) . . . 32 B6
Anctoville-sur-Boscq (50) . . . 51 J1
Ancy (69) . . . 205 H1
Ancy-le-Franc (89) . . . 114 C5
Ancy-le-Libre (89) . . . 114 B5
Ancy-sur-Moselle (57) . . . 44 G6
Andainville (80) . . . 17 G2
Andance (07) . . . 222 B3
Andancette (26) . . . 222 B3
Andard (49) . . . 125 H3
Andé (27) . . . 35 K4
Andechy (80) . . . 18 E4
Andel (22) . . . 49 J6
Andelain (02) . . . 20 A5
Andelaroche (03) . . . 186 B2
Andelarre (70) . . . 138 A1
Andelarrot (70) . . . 138 A1
Andelat (15) . . . 218 D5
Andelnans (90) . . . 139 H1
Andelot-Blancheville (52) . . . 92 C5
Andelot-en-Montagne (39) . . . 156 B5
Andelot-Morval (39) . . . 172 E5
Andelu (78) . . . 57 K3
les Andelys (27) . . . 36 B4
Andernay (55) . . . 63 J4
Andernos-les-Bains (33) . . . 228 C3
Anderny (54) . . . 26 E4
Andert-et-Condon (01) . . . 207 J1
Andeville (60) . . . 37 H4
Andigné (49) . . . 104 E6
Andillac (81) . . . 270 B1
Andilly (17) . . . 176 E1
Andilly (54) . . . 65 H4
Andilly (74) . . . 190 E3
Andilly (95) . . . 58 E2
Andilly-en-Bassigny (52) . . . 116 E3
Andiran (47) . . . 247 H6
Andlau (67) . . . 70 C6
Andoins (64) . . . 284 E4
Andolsheim (68) . . . 96 C4
Andon (06) . . . 280 B3
Andonville (45) . . . 86 B5
Andornay (70) . . . 119 F6
Andouillé (53) . . . 80 E6
Andouillé-Neuville (35) . . . 79 H2
Andouque (81) . . . 271 F1
Andrein (64) . . . 283 H3
Andres (62) . . . 2 D3
Andrest (65) . . . 285 H4
Andrésy (78) . . . 58 B2
Andrezé (49) . . . 142 E1
Andrezel (77) . . . 87 J1
Andrézieux-Bouthéon (42) . . . 205 F5
Andryes (89) . . . 133 F3
Anduze (30) . . . 255 F6
Anères (65) . . . 305 G1
Anet (28) . . . 57 F3
Anetz (44) . . . 124 B4
Angaïs (64) . . . 284 E4
Angé (41) . . . 128 D5
Angeac-Champagne (16) . . . 195 K4
Angeac-Charente (16) . . . 196 B3
Angecourt (08) . . . 23 F5
Angeduc (16) . . . 196 C5
Angely (89) . . . 134 A2
Angeot (90) . . . 119 K5
Angers (49) . . . 125 G3
Angerville (14) . . . 33 H4
Angerville (91) . . . 86 B5
Angerville-Bailleul (76) . . . 14 D4
Angerville-la-Campagne (27) . . . 56 D2
Angerville-la-Martel (76) . . . 14 E3

Angerville-l'Orcher (76) . . . 14 C5
Angervilliers (91) . . . 86 B1
Angeville (82) . . . 268 C1
Angevillers (57) . . . 27 F4
Angey (50) . . . 51 J2
Angicourt (60) . . . 38 B3
Angiens (76) . . . 15 G3
Angirey (70) . . . 137 H3
Angivillers (60) . . . 38 B1
Anglade (33) . . . 211 G3
Anglards-de-Saint-Flour (15) . . . 218 E6
Anglards-de-Salers (15) . . . 217 H3
Anglars (46) . . . 234 C3
Anglars-Juillac (46) . . . 249 H1
Anglars-Nozac (46) . . . 233 H3
Anglars-Saint-Félix (12) . . . 251 H2
Anglefort (01) . . . 190 C5
Anglemont (88) . . . 95 F3
Angles (04) . . . 279 K1
les Angles (30) . . . 276 B2
les Angles (65) . . . 304 B1
les Angles (66) . . . 313 J6
Anglès (81) . . . 290 D1
Angles (85) . . . 159 H5
les Angles-sur-Corrèze (19) . . . 216 B2
Angles-sur-l'Anglin (86) . . . 164 A2
Anglesqueville-la-Bras-Long (76) . . . 15 G3
Anglesqueville-l'Esneval (76) . . . 14 B5
Anglet (64) . . . 282 B1
Angliers (17) . . . 177 F2
Angliers (86) . . . 144 E4
Anglure (51) . . . 89 J1
Anglure-sous-Dun (71) . . . 187 H2
Angluzelles-et-Courcelles (51) . . . 61 J6
Angoisse (24) . . . 198 D6
Angomont (54) . . . 95 H1
Angos (65) . . . 285 J5
Angoulême (16) . . . 196 E3
Angoulins (17) . . . 176 D3
Angoumé (40) . . . 264 A5
Angous (64) . . . 283 J4
Angoustrine-Villeneuve-
    -des-Escaldes (66) . . . 313 G5
Angoville (14) . . . 53 J2
Angoville-au-Plain (50) . . . 29 G6
Angoville-sur-Ay (50) . . . 30 D1
Angres (62) . . . 10 E1
Angresse (40) . . . 262 C5
Angrie (49) . . . 124 C2
Anguerny (14) . . . 32 E4
Anguilcourt-le-Sart (02) . . . 20 B4
Angy (60) . . . 37 K3
Anhaux (64) . . . 282 D5
Anhiers (59) . . . 11 J1
Aniane (34) . . . 273 J4
Aniche (59) . . . 11 K2
Anisy (14) . . . 32 E4
Anizy-le-Château (02) . . . 39 K1
Anjeux (70) . . . 118 B3
Anjou (38) . . . 222 C1
Anjoutey (90) . . . 119 J5
Anla (65) . . . 305 H2
Anlezy (58) . . . 151 H4
Anlhiac (24) . . . 214 E2
Annay (58) . . . 132 A3
Annay (62) . . . 6 C6
Annay-la-Côte (89) . . . 133 K3
Annay-sur-Serein (89) . . . 113 K6
Annebault (14) . . . 33 J4
Annecy (74) . . . 191 F5
Annecy-le-Vieux (74) . . . 191 F5
Annelles (08) . . . 41 J2
Annemasse (74) . . . 191 G2
Annéot (89) . . . 133 K3
Annepont (17) . . . 177 J6
Annequin (62) . . . 6 B6
Annesse-et-Beaulieu (24) . . . 213 J4
Annet-sur-Marne (77) . . . 59 H3
Anneux (59) . . . 11 J4
Anneville-Ambourville (76) . . . 35 F1
Anneville-en-Saire (50) . . . 29 F2
Annéville-la-Prairie (52) . . . 92 A6
Anneville-sur-Mer (50) . . . 30 C3
Anneville-sur-Scie (76) . . . 15 K3
Anneyron (26) . . . 222 C4
Annezay (17) . . . 177 H4
Annezin (62) . . . 5 K5
Annœullin (59) . . . 6 C5
Annoire (39) . . . 154 E4
Annois (02) . . . 19 J4
Annoisin-Chatelans (38) . . . 207 F2
Annoix (18) . . . 149 H4
Annonay (07) . . . 222 A4
Annonville (52) . . . 92 C3
Annot (04) . . . 280 A1
Annouville-Vilmesnil (76) . . . 14 D4
Annoux (89) . . . 134 B2
Annoville (50) . . . 30 D5
Anor (59) . . . 13 J6
Anos (64) . . . 284 D3
Anost (71) . . . 152 D3
Anould (88) . . . 95 J5
Anoux (54) . . . 44 C3
Anoye (64) . . . 285 F3
Anquetierville (76) . . . 15 F6
Anrosey (52) . . . 117 G4
Ansac-sur-Vienne (16) . . . 180 B5
Ansacq (60) . . . 37 K3
Ansan (32) . . . 267 K5
Ansauville (54) . . . 65 H3
Ansauvillers (60) . . . 18 B6
Anse (69) . . . 188 B5
Anserville (60) . . . 37 J4
Ansignan (66) . . . 309 H5
Ansost (65) . . . 285 H2

Ansouis (84) . . . 277 J4
Anstaing (59) . . . 7 F4
Antagnac (47) . . . 247 F2
Anterrieux (15) . . . 236 D2
Anteuil (25) . . . 139 F4
Antezant-la-Chapelle (17) . . . 178 A5
Anthé (47) . . . 249 F2
Anthelupt (54) . . . 66 C6
Anthenay (51) . . . 40 C5
Antheny (08) . . . 21 K2
Antheuil (21) . . . 153 K1
Antheuil-Portes (60) . . . 38 D1
Anthien (58) . . . 133 H5
Anthon (38) . . . 206 E1
Anthy-sur-Léman (74) . . . 174 E5
Antibes (06) . . . 281 F5
Antichan (65) . . . 305 H2
Antichan-de-Frontignes (31) . . . 305 J3
Antignac (15) . . . 217 J2
Antignac (31) . . . 305 H4
Antigny (85) . . . 160 E2
Antigny (86) . . . 164 A4
Antigny-la-Ville (21) . . . 153 H2
Antilly (57) . . . 45 F4
Antilly (60) . . . 39 F5
Antin (65) . . . 285 K4
Antisanti (2B) . . . 321 H2
Antist (65) . . . 304 D1
Antogny-le-Tillac (37) . . . 145 J4
Antoigné (49) . . . 144 C2
Antoigny (61) . . . 81 J1
Antoingt (63) . . . 202 E5
Antonaves (05) . . . 258 E3
Antonne-et-Trigonant (24) . . . 214 B3
Antony (92) . . . 58 E5
Antraigues-sur-Volane (07) . . . 239 H4
Antrain (35) . . . 51 J5
Antran (86) . . . 145 J5
Antras (09) . . . 306 B4
Antras (32) . . . 267 G5
Antrenas (48) . . . 237 G5
Antugnac (11) . . . 308 E3
Antully (71) . . . 153 G2
Anvéville (76) . . . 15 G4
Anville (16) . . . 196 B1
Any-Martin-Rieux (02) . . . 21 J2
Anzat-le-Luguet (63) . . . 218 D2
Anzeling (57) . . . 45 H3
Anzême (23) . . . 182 D2
Anzex (47) . . . 247 G3
Anzin (59) . . . 12 D1
Anzin-Saint-Aubin (62) . . . 10 E2
Anzy-le-Duc (71) . . . 186 E1
Aoste (38) . . . 207 J4
Aougny (51) . . . 40 C5
Aouste (08) . . . 21 K3
Aouste-sur-Sye (26) . . . 240 E3
Aouze (88) . . . 93 H3
Apach (57) . . . 27 J3
Apchat (63) . . . 218 E1
Apchon (15) . . . 218 A3
Apinac (42) . . . 220 D1
Appelle (81) . . . 289 H1
Appenai-sous-Bellême (61) . . . 83 H4
Appenans (25) . . . 139 F3
Appenwihr (68) . . . 96 D4
Appeville (50) . . . 29 F6
Appeville-Annebault (27) . . . 34 D3
Appietto (2A) . . . 320 B4
Appilly (60) . . . 19 J6
Appoigny (89) . . . 113 F4
Apprieu (38) . . . 207 H6
Appy (09) . . . 307 K5
Apremont (01) . . . 190 A2
Apremont (08) . . . 42 E4
Apremont (60) . . . 38 B5
Apremont (70) . . . 137 F4
Apremont (73) . . . 208 C5
Apremont (85) . . . 141 G6
Apremont-la-Forêt (55) . . . 65 F3
Apremont-sur-Allier (18) . . . 150 D5
Aprey (52) . . . 116 C5
Apt (84) . . . 277 H2
Arabaux (09) . . . 307 J3
Arâches-la-Frasse (74) . . . 192 A3
Aragnouet (65) . . . 304 D5
Aragon (11) . . . 290 A4
Aramits (64) . . . 283 K6
Aramon (30) . . . 276 A2
Aranc (01) . . . 189 K4
Arancou (64) . . . 283 F2
Arandas (01) . . . 189 J6
Arandon (38) . . . 207 G2
Araujuzon (64) . . . 283 J3
Araules (43) . . . 221 F5
Araux (64) . . . 283 J3
Arbanats (33) . . . 229 J4
Arbas (31) . . . 306 B2
Arbecey (70) . . . 117 J5
Arbellara (2A) . . . 322 E2
Arbent (01) . . . 173 H6
Arbéost (65) . . . 303 J2
Arbérats-Sillègue (64) . . . 283 G3
Arbignieu (01) . . . 207 J2
Arbigny (01) . . . 172 A4
Arbigny-sous-Varennes (52) . . . 117 F4
Arbin (73) . . . 208 D5
Arbis (33) . . . 230 A4
Arblade-le-Bas (32) . . . 266 A5
Arblade-le-Haut (32) . . . 266 B4
Arbois (39) . . . 155 K4
Arbon (31) . . . 305 K2
Arbonne (64) . . . 282 A2
Arbonne-la-Forêt (77) . . . 87 G3
Arboras (34) . . . 273 H5

Arbori (2A) . . . 320 C2
Arbot (52) . . . 115 K4
Arbouans (25) . . . 139 H2
Arboucave (40) . . . 265 H6
Arbourse (58) . . . 132 D6
Arboussols (66) . . . 314 C2
l'Arbresle (69) . . . 205 J1
Arbrissel (35) . . . 103 K1
Arbus (64) . . . 284 B3
Arbusigny (74) . . . 191 G3
Arc-en-Barrois (52) . . . 115 K3
Arc-et-Senans (25) . . . 155 K3
Arc-lès-Gray (70) . . . 137 F3
Arc-sous-Cicon (25) . . . 157 F2
Arc-sous-Montenot (25) . . . 156 B4
Arc-sur-Tille (21) . . . 136 C5
Arcachon (33) . . . 228 B4
Arcambal (46) . . . 250 A1
Arcangues (64) . . . 282 B2
Arçay (18) . . . 149 G4
Arçay (86) . . . 144 D4
Arceau (21) . . . 136 C2
Arcenant (21) . . . 154 A2
Arcens (07) . . . 239 G1
Arces (17) . . . 194 E4
Arces-Dilo (89) . . . 113 G1
Arcey (21) . . . 135 J6
Arcey (25) . . . 139 F2
Archail (04) . . . 259 K5
Archamps (74) . . . 191 F2
Archelange (39) . . . 155 G1
Arches (15) . . . 217 G2
Arches (88) . . . 94 E6
Archettes (88) . . . 94 E6
Archiac (17) . . . 195 K5
Archignac (24) . . . 215 G6
Archignat (03) . . . 167 F6
Archigny (86) . . . 163 J2
Archingeay (17) . . . 177 H5
Archon (02) . . . 21 H4
Arcinges (42) . . . 187 H3
Arcins (33) . . . 211 F5
Arcis-le-Ponsart (51) . . . 40 C4
Arcis-sur-Aube (10) . . . 90 D2
Arcizac-Adour (65) . . . 285 H6
Arcizac-ez-Angles (65) . . . 304 B1
Arcizans-Avant (65) . . . 304 B2
Arcizans-Dessus (65) . . . 303 K2
Arcomps (18) . . . 167 G5
Arçon (25) . . . 157 F4
Arcon (42) . . . 186 D5
Arconcey (21) . . . 153 G1
Arçonnay (72) . . . 82 D3
Arconsat (63) . . . 186 B6
Arconville (10) . . . 91 H6
les Arcs (83) . . . 298 D1
Arcueil (94) . . . 58 E4
Arcy-Sainte-Restitue (02) . . . 39 K4
Arcy-sur-Cure (89) . . . 133 H2
Ardelles (28) . . . 84 D2
Ardenais (18) . . . 167 G4
Ardenay-sur-Mérize (72) . . . 107 G3
Ardengost (65) . . . 305 F3
Ardentes (36) . . . 165 K1
Ardes (63) . . . 218 E1
Ardeuil-et-Montfauxelles (08) . . . 42 B4
Ardiège (31) . . . 305 J1
les Ardillats (69) . . . 187 K2
Ardilleux (79) . . . 178 E3
Ardillières (17) . . . 177 F4
Ardin (79) . . . 161 G4
Ardizas (32) . . . 268 C5
Ardoix (07) . . . 222 A3
Ardon (39) . . . 156 A6
Ardon (45) . . . 109 K5
Ardouval (76) . . . 16 B4
Ardres (62) . . . 2 D4
Aregno (2B) . . . 318 D4
Areines (41) . . . 108 C3
Aren (64) . . . 283 K4
Arengosse (40) . . . 264 E1
Arenthon (74) . . . 191 G3
Arès (33) . . . 228 B2
Aresches (39) . . . 156 A4
Aressy (64) . . . 284 D4
Arette (64) . . . 302 E1
Arfeuille-Châtain (23) . . . 183 J4
Arfeuilles (03) . . . 186 B3
Arfons (81) . . . 289 K3
Argagnon (64) . . . 283 K3
Arganchy (14) . . . 32 A4
Argançon (10) . . . 91 F5
Argancy (57) . . . 45 F4
Argein (09) . . . 306 C3
Argelès-Bagnères (65) . . . 304 D1
Argelès-Gazost (65) . . . 304 A2
Argelès-sur-Mer (66) . . . 315 J4
Argeliers (11) . . . 291 G4
Argelliers (34) . . . 273 K5
Argelos (40) . . . 265 H5
Argelos (64) . . . 284 D2
Argelouse (40) . . . 245 J2
Argences (14) . . . 33 G5
Argens-Minervois (11) . . . 291 F5
Argent-sur-Sauldre (18) . . . 131 F2
Argentan (61) . . . 54 C4
Argentat (19) . . . 216 C5
Argentenay (89) . . . 114 B3
Argenteuil (95) . . . 58 D2
Argenteuil-sur-Armançon (89) . . . 114 B6
l'Argentière-la-Bessée (05) . . . 243 G4
Argentières (77) . . . 59 K6
Argentine (73) . . . 209 F5

Argenton (47) . . . 247 G2
Argenton-Château (79) . . . 143 J4
Argenton-l'Église (79) . . . 144 A3
Argenton-Notre-Dame (53) . . . 105 G5
Argenton-sur-Creuse (36) . . . 165 G3
Argentré (53) . . . 105 G1
Argentré-du-Plessis (35) . . . 104 B1
Argenvières (18) . . . 150 C2
Argenvilliers (28) . . . 84 B5
Argers (51) . . . 42 D6
Arget (64) . . . 284 B1
Argiésans (90) . . . 139 H1
Argillières (70) . . . 117 G6
Argilliers (30) . . . 275 J1
Argilly (21) . . . 154 C3
Argis (01) . . . 189 J5
Argiusta-Moriccio (2A) . . . 320 E6
Argœuves (80) . . . 18 A1
Argol (29) . . . 74 B2
Argonay (74) . . . 191 F5
Argouges (50) . . . 51 K5
Argoules (80) . . . 9 G2
Arguel (25) . . . 137 K6
Arguel (80) . . . 17 G2
Arguenos (31) . . . 305 K3
Argut-Dessous (31) . . . 305 J4
Argy (36) . . . 147 H4
Arhansus (64) . . . 283 F5
Aries-Espénan (65) . . . 286 C4
Arifat (81) . . . 271 F4
Arignac (09) . . . 307 J4
Arinthod (39) . . . 173 G5
Arith (73) . . . 208 D2
Arjuzanx (40) . . . 245 G6
Arlanc (63) . . . 220 A1
Arlay (39) . . . 155 H6
Arlebosc (07) . . . 221 K5
Arlempdes (43) . . . 238 C2
Arles (13) . . . 275 J4
Arles-sur-Tech (66) . . . 314 E5
Arlet (43) . . . 219 H4
Arleuf (58) . . . 152 C3
Arleux (59) . . . 11 H3
Arleux-en-Gohelle (62) . . . 11 F2
Arlos (31) . . . 305 J4
Armaillé (49) . . . 104 B6
Armancourt (60) . . . 38 D1
Armancourt (80) . . . 18 E5
Armaucourt (54) . . . 66 B3
Armbouts-Cappel (59) . . . 3 H2
Armeau (89) . . . 112 D2
Armendarits (64) . . . 282 E4
Armenteule (65) . . . 305 F5
Armentières (59) . . . 6 C3
Armentières-en-Brie (77) . . . 60 A2
Armentières-sur-Avre (27) . . . 56 A5
Armentières-sur-Ourcq (02) . . . 39 K5
Armentieux (32) . . . 285 H1
Armes (58) . . . 133 G4
Armillac (47) . . . 231 G6
Armissan (11) . . . 291 J6
Armix (01) . . . 190 A6
Armous-et-Cau (32) . . . 285 J1
Armoy (74) . . . 175 F3
Arnac (19) . . . 217 F5
Arnac-la-Poste (87) . . . 181 J2
Arnac-Pompadour (19) . . . 215 G1
Arnac-sur-Dourdou (12) . . . 272 C5
Arnage (72) . . . 106 D3
Arnancourt (52) . . . 91 J4
Arnas (69) . . . 188 B4
Arnaud-Guilhem (31) . . . 287 G5
Arnave (09) . . . 307 J4
Arnaville (54) . . . 65 J1
Arnay-le-Duc (21) . . . 153 G2
Arnay-sous-Vitteaux (21) . . . 135 F4
Arnayon (26) . . . 241 G4
Arné (65) . . . 286 C6
Arnéguy (64) . . . 282 D6
Arnèke (59) . . . 3 H4
Arnicourt (08) . . . 21 K4
Arnières-sur-Iton (27) . . . 56 C2
Arnos (64) . . . 284 B2
Arnouville-lès-Gonesse (95) . . . 59 F2
Arnouville-lès-Mantes (78) . . . 57 J3
Aroffe (88) . . . 93 J3
Aromas (39) . . . 189 J1
Aron (53) . . . 81 G4
Aroue-Ithorots-Olhaïby (64) . . . 283 H4
Aroz (70) . . . 137 K1
Arpaillargues-et-Aureillac (30) . . . 275 G1
Arpajon (91) . . . 86 D1
Arpajon-sur-Cère (15) . . . 235 H1
Arpavon (26) . . . 257 J2
Arpenans (70) . . . 138 D1
Arpheuilles (18) . . . 167 G1
Arpheuilles (36) . . . 147 F5
Arpheuilles-Saint-Priest (03) . . . 184 B2
Arphy (30) . . . 273 J1
Arquenay (53) . . . 105 G2
Arques (11) . . . 309 G3
Arques (12) . . . 252 D3
les Arques (46) . . . 233 G4
Arques (62) . . . 5 G3
Arques-la-Bataille (76) . . . 16 A2
Arquettes-en-Val (11) . . . 309 H1
Arquèves (80) . . . 10 C5
Arquian (58) . . . 132 A3
Arracourt (54) . . . 66 D4
Arradon (56) . . . 100 E5
Arraincourt (57) . . . 66 D1
Arrancourt (91) . . . 86 C4
Arrancy (02) . . . 40 C1
Arrancy-sur-Crusne (55) . . . 26 C4
Arrans (21) . . . 114 D6

Arras (62) 10   E2
Arras-en-Lavedan (65) 304   A2
Arras-sur-Rhône (07) 222   B4
Arrast-Larrebieu (64) 283   H4
Arraute-Charritte (64) 283   F2
Arraye-et-Han (54) 66   B3
Arrayou-Lahitte (65) 304   C1
Arre (30) 273   J2
Arreau (65) 305   F3
Arrelles (10) 114   C2
Arrembécourt (10) 91   F1
Arrènes (23) 182   A4
Arrens-Marsous (65) 303   K3
Arrentès-de-Corcieux (88) 95   H5
Arrentières (10) 91   H5
Arrest (80) 8   E5
Arreux (08) 22   C2
Arriance (57) 45   J6
Arricau-Bordes (64) 285   F2
Arrien (64) 285   F4
Arrien-en-Bethmale (09) 306   C4
Arrigas (30) 273   H1
Arrigny (51) 63   G6
Arro (2A) 320   C3
Arrodets (65) 304   E2
Arrodets-ez-Angles (65) 304   C1
Arromanches-les-Bains (14) 32   C3
Arronnes (03) 186   A4
Arronville (95) 37   H5
Arros-de-Nay (64) 284   D5
Arrosès (64) 285   F1
Arrou (28) 108   C1
Arrouède (32) 286   D5
Arrout (09) 306   C3
Arry (57) 65   K1
Arry (80) 9   F3
Ars (16) 195   J3
Ars (23) 183   F5
Ars-en-Ré (17) 158   B5
Ars-Laquenexy (57) 45   G5
Ars-les-Favets (63) 184   C2
Ars-sur-Formans (01) 188   C5
Ars-sur-Moselle (57) 44   E6
Arsac (33) 211   G5
Arsac-en-Velay (43) 220   C6
Arsague (40) 264   D6
Arsans (70) 137   G4
Arsonval (10) 91   G5
Arsure-Arsurette (39) 174   B1
les Arsures (39) 155   K4
Arsy (60) 38   C2
Art-sur-Meurthe (54) 66   B5
Artagnan (65) 285   H3
Artaise-le-Vivier (08) 22   E6
Artaix (71) 186   E2
Artalens-Souin (65) 304   B2
Artannes-sur-Indre (37) 127   H6
Artannes-sur-Thouet (49) 144   C1
Artas (38) 206   E5
Artassenx (40) 265   H3
Artemare (01) 190   B6
Artemps (02) 19   J3
Artenay (45) 110   A2
Arthaz-Pont-Notre-Dame (74) . . . 191   G2
Arthel (58) 151   G1
Arthémonay (26) 222   D4
Arthenac (17) 195   K5
Arthenas (39) 173   F3
Arthès (81) 270   E2
Arthez-d'Armagnac (40) 265   K2
Arthez-d'Asson (64) 303   H1
Arthez-de-Béarn (64) 284   A2
Arthezé (72) 106   B5
Arthies (95) 36   M6
Arthon (36) 165   J2
Arthon-en-Retz (44) 122   D5
Arthonnay (89) 114   C3
Arthun (42) 204   C2
Artigat (09) 307   G1
Artignosc-sur-Verdon (83) 278   E4
Artigue (31) 305   H4
Artigueloutan (64) 284   E4
Artiguelouve (64) 284   B4
Artiguemy (65) 285   K6
Artigues (09) 313   J2
Artigues (11) 308   E5
Artigues (65) 304   E1
Artigues (83) 278   C6
les Artigues-de-Lussac (33) 212   B6
Artigues-près-Bordeaux (33) 229   J2
Artins (41) 107   J6
Artix (09) 307   H2
Artix (64) 284   B3
Artolsheim (67) 96   E2
Artonges (02) 61   F2
Artonne (63) 185   F5
Artres (59) 12   D2
Artzenheim (68) 96   D3
Arudy (64) 284   C6
Arue (40) 246   B6
Arvert (17) 194   B2
Arveyres (33) 230   A1
Arvieu (12) 252   C5
Arvieux (05) 227   B2
Arvigna (09) 307   K2
Arville (41) 108   B2
Arville (77) 87   G6
Arvillers (80) 18   E4
Arx (40) 247   F5
Arzacq-Arraziguet (64) 284   C1
Arzal (56) 121   J2
Arzano (29) 99   K3
Arzay (38) 206   E6
Arzembouy (58) 151   F1
Arzenc-d'Apcher (48) 236   E2

Arzenc-de-Randon (48) 237   K4
Arzens (11) 289   K6
Arzillières-Neuville (51) 63   F6
Arzon (56) 120   E1
Arzviller (57) 67   K4
Asasp-Arros (64) 284   A6
Ascain (64) 282   A3
Ascarat (64) 282   D5
Aschbach (67) 25   C2
Aschères-le-Marché (45) 110   B1
Asco (2B) 318   E4
Ascou (09) 313   G2
Ascoux (45) 110   D1
Ascros (06) 280   E1
Asfeld (08) 41   F1
Aslonnes (86) 163   F5
Asnan (58) 133   G6
Asnans-Beauvoisin (39) 155   F4
Asnelles (14) 32   C3
Asnières (27) 34   B5
Asnières-en-Bessin (14) 29   J6
Asnières-en-Montagne (21) 114   D6
Asnières-en-Poitou (79) 178   C3
Asnières-la-Giraud (17) 177   K6
Asnières-lès-Dijon (21) 136   A4
Asnières-sous-Bois (89) 133   G3
Asnières-sur-Blour (86) 180   C3
Asnières-sur-Nouère (16) 196   D2
Asnières-sur-Oise (95) 37   K6
Asnières-sur-Saône (01) 171   K5
Asnières-sur-Seine (92) 58   D3
Asnières-sur-Vègre (72) 105   K4
Asnois (58) 133   G4
Asnois (86) 179   J3
Aspach (57) 67   H5
Aspach (68) 97   B4
Aspach-le-Bas (68) 97   A2
Aspach-le-Haut (68) 97   A2
Aspères (30) 274   D4
Asperjoc (07) 239   H4
Aspet (31) 306   C3
Aspin-Aure (65) 305   F3
Aspin-en-Lavedan (65) 304   B1
Aspiran (34) 292   C1
Aspremont (05) 242   B6
Aspremont (06) 281   G3
les Aspres (61) 55   H5
Aspres-lès-Corps (05) 242   D2
Aspres-sur-Buëch (05) 242   B6
Aspret-Sarrat (31) 305   K1
Asprières (12) 234   E6
Asque (65) 304   E2
Asques (33) 211   J6
Asques (82) 268   B1
Asquins (89) 133   H3
Assac (81) 271   H2
Assainvillers (80) 18   D5
Assais-les-Jumeaux (79) 144   C1
Assas (34) 274   C5
Assat (64) 284   D5
Assay (37) 145   G3
Assé-le-Bérenger (53) 81   K6
Assé-le-Boisne (72) 82   C4
Assé-le-Riboul (72) 82   D6
Assenay (10) 90   A6
Assencières (10) 90   C4
Assenoncourt (57) 67   G3
Assérac (44) 121   J3
Assevent (59) 13   H2
Assevillers (80) 19   F2
Assier (46) 234   C4
Assieu (38) 206   B6
Assignan (34) 291   G3
Assigny (18) 131   J4
Assigny (76) 8   B6
les Assions (07) 255   H2
Assis-sur-Serre (02) 20   C4
Asson (64) 284   E6
Asswiller (67) 69   F5
Astaffort (47) 248   B6
Astaillac (19) 234   B1
Asté (65) 304   D2
Aste-Béon (64) 303   H2
Astet (07) 238   E4
Astillé (53) 104   E3
Astis (64) 284   D2
Aston (09) 307   J5
Astugue (65) 304   C1
Athée (21) 136   D6
Athée (53) 104   D4
Athée-sur-Cher (37) 128   A5
Athesans-Étroitefontaine (70) . . . 138   E1
Athie (21) 134   C2
Athie (89) 134   A3
Athienville (54) 66   D4
Athies (62) 11   F2
Athies (80) 19   H2
Athies-sous-Laon (02) 20   D6
Athis (51) 62   B1
Athis-de-l'Orne (61) 53   H4
Athis-Mons (91) 58   E5
Athos-Aspis (64) 283   G2
Athose (25) 156   E2
Attainville (95) 58   E1
Attancourt (52) 91   J1
les Attaques (62) 2   D3
Attenschwiller (68) 97   D4
Attiches (59) 6   D5
Attichy (60) 39   F2
Attignat (01) 189   F1
Attignat-Oncin (73) 208   A5
Attignéville (88) 93   H3
Attigny (08) 42   A1
Attigny (88) 117   K1
Attilloncourt (57) 66   C3
Attilly (02) 19   J2

Attin (62) 4   C6
Atton (54) 65   K2
Attray (45) 110   C1
Attricourt (70) 136   D3
Atur (24) 214   A4
Aubagnan (40) 265   G5
Aubagne (13) 296   E4
Aubaine (21) 153   J2
Aubais (34) 215   F5
Aubarède (65) 285   K4
Aubas (24) 215   F5
Aubazat (43) 219   H4
Aubazines (19) 215   K4
Aube (57) 45   J6
Aube (61) 55   H5
Aubéguimont (76) 17   F3
Aubenas (07) 239   H5
Aubenas-les-Alpes (04) 278   A2
Aubenasson (26) 241   F4
Aubencheul-au-Bac (59) 11   J3
Aubencheul-aux-Bois (02) 12   B6
Aubenton (02) 21   J2
Aubepierre-Ozouer-le-Repos (77) . 59   K6
Aubepierre-sur-Aube (52) 115   K3
l'Aubépin (39) 172   E5
Auberchicourt (59) 11   J2
Aubercourt (80) 18   D3
Aubergenville (78) 57   K2
Aubérive (51) 41   J5
Auberive (52) 116   A5
Auberives-en-Royans (38) 223   G5
Auberives-sur-Varèze (38) 206   A6
Aubermesnil-aux-Érables (76) . . . 16   E3
Aubermesnil-Beaumais (76) 16   A3
Aubers (59) 6   B4
Aubertin (64) 284   B4
Auberville (14) 33   H1
Auberville-la-Campagne (76) 15   F6
Auberville-la-Manuel (76) 15   F2
Auberville-la-Renault (76) 14   D4
Aubervilliers (93) 58   E3
Aubeterre (16) 90   B3
Aubeterre-sur-Dronne (16) 212   E2
Aubeville (16) 196   C5
Aubevoye (27) 36   A5
Aubiac (33) 246   C1
Aubiac (47) 248   B5
Aubiat (63) 185   G5
Aubie-et-Espessas (33) 211   J5
Aubière (63) 202   D2
Aubiet (32) 268   A6
Aubignan (84) 257   G5
Aubignas (07) 239   K5
Aubigné (35) 79   G2
Aubigné (79) 178   D4
Aubigné-Racan (72) 106   E6
Aubigné-sur-Layon (49) 143   J1
Aubignosc (04) 259   G5
Aubigny (14) 54   A2
Aubigny (79) 162   A1
Aubigny (80) 18   C2
Aubigny (85) 159   H2
Aubigny-au-Bac (59) 11   J3
Aubigny-aux-Kaisnes (02) 19   J3
Aubigny-en-Artois (62) 10   D2
Aubigny-en-Laonnois (02) 40   C1
Aubigny-en-Plaine (21) 154   D2
Aubigny-la-Ronce (21) 153   J4
Aubigny-les-Pothées (08) 22   A3
Aubigny-lès-Sombernon (21) . . . 135   G5
Aubigny-sur-Nère (18) 131   F3
Aubilly (51) 40   D5
Aubin (12) 235   F6
Aubin (64) 284   C2
Aubin-Saint-Vaast (62) 9   H1
Aubinges (18) 149   J1
Auboncourt-Vauzelles (08) 22   B6
Aubonne (25) 156   E2
Aubord (30) 275   G4
Auboué (54) 44   D4
Aubous (64) 266   A6
Aubres (26) 257   H2
Aubréville (55) 43   F5
Aubrives (08) 24   C2
Aubrometz (62) 9   K2
Aubry-du-Hainaut (59) 12   C2
Aubry-en-Exmes (61) 54   D4
Aubry-le-Panthou (61) 54   E3
Aubure (68) 96   A2
Aubussargues (30) 275   G1
Aubusson (23) 183   G5
Aubusson (61) 53   H4
Aubusson-d'Auvergne (63) 203   J2
Aubvillers (80) 18   C4
Auby (59) 11   H1
Aucaleuc (22) 50   C5
Aucamville (31) 269   G5
Aucamville (82) 268   E4
Aucazein (09) 306   B3
Aucelon (26) 241   H4
Aucey-la-Plaine (50) 51   J5
Auch (32) 267   H6
Auchel (62) 5   J6
Auchonvillers (80) 10   D5
Auchy-au-Bois (62) 5   H5
Auchy-la-Montagne (60) 17   K6
Auchy-lès-Hesdin (62) 9   J1
Auchy-les-Mines (62) 6   B5
Auchy-lès-Orchies (59) 7   F6
Aucun (65) 303   K2
Audaux (64) 283   J3
Audelange (39) 155   H2
Audeloncourt (52) 116   E1
Audembert (62) 2   B3
Audenge (33) 228   C4

Auderville (50) 28   A1
Audes (03) 167   G5
Audeux (25) 137   J6
Audeville (45) 86   D5
Audierne (29) 73   C3
Audignicourt (02) 39   G1
Audignies (59) 13   F3
Audignon (40) 265   F4
Audigny (02) 20   D2
Audincourt (25) 139   H2
Audincthun (62) 5   F5
Audinghen (62) 2   A4
Audon (40) 264   D3
Audouville-la-Hubert (50) 29   G5
Audrehem (62) 2   E4
Audressein (09) 306   C3
Audresselles (62) 2   A4
Audrieu (14) 32   C4
Audrix (24) 232   C2
Audruicq (62) 2   E3
Audun-le-Roman (54) 26   E4
Audun-le-Tiche (57) 26   E3
Auenheim (67) 25   C4
Auffargis (78) 58   A5
Auffay (76) 15   K4
Aufferville (77) 87   G6
Auffreville-Brasseuil (78) 57   J2
Auflance (08) 23   J5
Auga (64) 284   C2
Augan (56) 78   A6
Auge (08) 21   J2
Auge (23) 183   H2
Augé (79) 161   J5
Auge-Saint-Médard (16) 196   B1
Augea (39) 172   E3
Auger-Saint-Vincent (60) 38   D5
Augerans (39) 155   H3
Augères (23) 182   C1
Augerolles (63) 203   J3
Augers-en-Brie (77) 60   E6
Augerville-la-Rivière (45) 87   F5
Augicourt (70) 117   J5
Augignac (24) 197   K4
Augirein (09) 306   B3
Auginsey (39) 173   F3
Augnat (63) 219   F1
Augnax (32) 267   K5
Augne (87) 199   K2
Augny (57) 44   E6
Auguaise (61) 55   H5
Augy (02) 40   A3
Augy (89) 113   G6
Augy-sur-Aubois (18) 167   K1
Aujac (17) 195   J1
Aujac (30) 255   G2
Aujan-Mournède (32) 286   C3
Aujargues (30) 274   E4
Aujeurres (52) 116   B5
Aujols (46) 250   B2
Aulan (26) 258   A4
Aulas (30) 273   J1
Aulhat-Saint-Privat (63) 203   F4
Aullène (2A) 323   F1
Aulnat (63) 202   E2
Aulnay (10) 90   E2
Aulnay (17) 178   B4
Aulnay (86) 144   E5
Aulnay-la-Rivière (45) 86   E6
Aulnay-l'Aître (51) 63   F4
Aulnay-sous-Bois (93) 59   F2
Aulnay-sur-Iton (27) 56   C2
Aulnay-sur-Marne (51) 62   B1
Aulnay-sur-Mauldre (78) 57   K2
les Aulneaux (72) 83   F3
Aulnois (88) 93   H5
Aulnois-en-Perthois (55) 64   A6
Aulnois-sous-Laon (02) 20   D5
Aulnois-sur-Seille (57) 66   B2
Aulnoy (77) 60   B4
Aulnoy-lez-Valenciennes (59) . . . 12   D2
Aulnoy-sur-Aube (52) 116   A4
Aulnoye-Aymeries (59) 13   G4
Aulon (23) 182   B4
Aulon (31) 287   F6
Aulon (65) 304   E4
Aulos (09) 307   J5
Ault (80) 8   C5
Aulus-les-Bains (09) 307   F5
Aulx-lès-Cromary (70) 138   A4
Aumagne (17) 178   A6
Aumale (76) 17   F3
Aumâtre (80) 17   F1
Aumelas (34) 273   J6
Aménancourt (51) 41   F2
Aumerval (62) 5   H6
Aumes (34) 292   C2
Aumessas (30) 273   H1
Aumetz (57) 26   E3
Aumeville-Lestre (50) 29   F3
Aumont (39) 155   J4
Aumont (80) 17   H2
Aumont-Aubrac (48) 237   G2
Aumont-en-Halatte (60) 38   B4
Aumontzey (88) 95   G5
Aumur (39) 155   F3
Aunac (16) 179   H6
Aunat (11) 308   D5
Aunay-en-Bazois (58) 151   K2
Aunay-les-Bois (61) 83   F1
Aunay-sous-Auneau (28) 85   K3
Aunay-sous-Crécy (28) 56   E6
Aunay-sur-Odon (14) 53   G1
Auneau (28) 85   J3
Auneuil (60) 37   G3
Aunou-le-Faucon (61) 54   C5
Aunou-sur-Orne (61) 54   E6

Auppegard (76) 15   K3
Aups (83) 279   G5
Auquainville (14) 54   E1
Auquemesnil (76) 16   C1
Auradé (32) 287   H1
Auradou (47) 248   B3
Auragne (31) 288   C3
Auray (56) 100   D5
Aure (08) 42   A4
Aurec-sur-Loire (43) 221   F1
Aureil (87) 199   G2
Aureilhan (40) 244   C4
Aureilhan (65) 285   H5
Aureille (13) 276   D5
Aurel (26) 241   G4
Aurel (84) 258   A5
Aurelle-Verlac (12) 253   F1
Aurensan (32) 265   K6
Aurensan (65) 285   H4
Aureville (31) 288   C2
Auriac (11) 309   H3
Auriac (19) 216   E3
Auriac (64) 284   D2
Auriac-du-Périgord (24) 214   E5
Auriac-Lagast (12) 252   B5
Auriac-l'Église (15) 218   E3
Auriac-sur-Dropt (47) 231   F4
Auriac-sur-Vendinelle (31) 289   F2
Auriat (23) 199   J1
Auribail (31) 288   B4
Auribeau (84) 277   J3
Auribeau-sur-Siagne (06) 280   D5
Aurice (40) 265   F3
Auriébat (65) 285   H2
Aurières (63) 202   B3
Aurignac (31) 287   F5
Aurillac (15) 235   H1
Aurimont (32) 287   F1
Aurin (31) 288   E1
Auriol (13) 297   F3
Auriolles (33) 230   D3
Aurions-Idernes (64) 285   F1
Auris (38) 224   E5
Aurons (13) 277   F5
Auros (33) 230   B6
Aurouër (03) 168   E2
Auroux (48) 238   A3
Aussac (81) 270   D3
Aussac-Vadalle (16) 196   E1
Ausseing (31) 287   H6
Aussevielle (64) 284   B3
Aussillon (81) 290   B2
Aussois (73) 226   A2
Ausson (31) 305   H1
Aussonce (08) 41   H3
Aussonne (31) 269   F5
Aussos (32) 286   D3
Aussurucq (64) 283   G6
Autainville (41) 109   F4
Autechaux (25) 138   D4
Autechaux-Roide (25) 139   H4
les Autels (02) 21   J3
les Autels-Saint-Bazile (14) 54   D2
les Autels-Villevillon (28) 84   B6
Auterive (31) 288   C4
Auterive (32) 286   D1
Auterive (82) 268   C3
Auterrive (64) 283   G2
Autet (70) 137   G2
Auteuil (60) 37   H3
Auteuil (78) 57   K4
Autevielle-Saint-Martin-
    -Bideren (64) 283   G3
Authe (08) 42   D1
Autheuil (28) 108   E3
Autheuil (61) 83   J1
Autheuil-Authouillet (27) 35   K6
Autheuil-en-Valois (60) 39   G5
Autheux (80) 9   K4
Authevernes (27) 36   D5
Authezat (63) 202   E4
Authie (14) 32   D4
Authie (80) 10   C5
Authieule (80) 10   B4
les Authieux (27) 56   E3
les Authieux-du-Puits (61) 55   F5
les Authieux-Papion (14) 33   J6
Authieux-Ratiéville (76) 16   A5
les Authieux-sur-Calonne (14) . . . 34   A3
les Authieux-sur-le-Port-
    -Saint-Ouen (76) 35   J2
Authiou (58) 132   E6
Authoison (70) 138   B3
Authon (04) 259   H3
Authon (41) 128   A1
Authon-du-Perche (28) 84   A6
Authon-Ébéon (17) 195   J1
Authon-la-Plaine (91) 86   A3
Authou (27) 34   E4
Authuille (80) 10   D6
Authume (39) 155   G2
Authumes (71) 154   E5
Autichamp (26) 240   D4
Autignac (34) 291   K2
Autigny (76) 15   H3
Autigny-la-Tour (88) 93   G3
Autigny-le-Grand (52) 92   A2
Autigny-le-Petit (52) 92   A2
Autingues (62) 2   D4
Autoire (46) 234   B2
Autoreille (70) 137   H4
Autouillet (78) 57   K3
Autrac (43) 218   E2
Autrans (38) 223   J3
Autrèche (37) 128   B3
Autrechêne (90) 139   J1

Autrêches (60) 39 G2
Autrecourt-et-Pourron (08) 23 G5
Autrécourt-sur-Aire (55) 64 A1
Autremencourt (02) 20 E4
Autrepierre (54) 67 G5
Autreppes (02) 21 F2
Autretot (76) 15 G3
Autreville (02) 19 K6
Autreville (88) 93 H2
Autréville-Saint-Lambert (55) 23 G6
Autreville-sur-la-Renne (52) 115 K1
Autreville-sur-Moselle (54) 65 K3
Autrey (54) 94 A1
Autrey (88) 95 F4
Autrey-le-Vay (70) 138 D2
Autrey-lès-Cerre (70) 138 C1
Autrey-lès-Gray (70) 136 E3
Autricourt (21) 115 G2
Autruche (08) 42 D1
Autruy-sur-Juine (45) 86 C5
Autry (08) 42 C4
Autry-Issards (03) 168 C4
Autry-le-Châtel (45) 131 G2
Autun (71) 153 F4
Auty (82) 250 A5
Auvare (06) 261 F6
Auve (51) 63 G1
Auvernaux (91) 87 F2
Auvers (43) 219 H6
Auvers (50) 31 F1
Auvers-le-Hamon (72) 105 J3
Auvers-Saint-Georges (91) 86 D2
Auvers-sous-Montfaucon (72) 106 B2
Auvers-sur-Oise (95) 58 C1
Auverse (49) 126 C3
Auvet-et-la-Chapelotte (70) 137 F3
Auvillar (82) 248 E6
Auvillars (14) 33 J5
Auvillars-sur-Saône (21) 154 C3
Auvillers-les-Forges (08) 21 K2
Auvilliers (76) 16 E3
Auvilliers-en-Gâtinais (45) 111 H3
Aux-Aussat (32) 285 K2
Aux Marais (60) 37 G2
Auxais (50) 31 F2
Auxange (39) 155 J1
Auxant (21) 153 J2
Auxelles-Bas (90) 119 G5
Auxelles-Haut (90) 119 G5
Auxerre (89) 113 G5
Auxey-Duresses (21) 153 K4
Auxi-le-Château (62) 9 J3
Auxon (10) 113 K1
Auxon (70) 118 B6
Auxon-Dessous (25) 137 K5
Auxon-Dessus (25) 137 K5
Auxonne (21) 155 F1
Auxy (45) 111 F1
Auxy (71) 153 G4
Auzainvilliers (88) 93 H5
Auzances (23) 183 K5
Auzas (31) 287 F6
Auzat (09) 307 H5
Auzat-la-Combelle (63) 203 F6
Auzay (85) 160 D4
Auzebosc (76) 15 G5
Auzelles (63) 203 H4
Auzers (15) 217 H3
Auzet (04) 259 K2
Auzeville-Tolosane (31) 288 C1
Auzielle (31) 288 D1
Auzits (12) 251 J1
Auzon (43) 219 G1
Auzouer-en-Touraine (37) 128 A3
Auzouville-Auberbosc (76) 14 E5
Auzouville-l'Esneval (76) 15 H5
Auzouville-sur-Ry (76) 35 K2
Auzouville-sur-Saâne (76) 15 J4
Availles-en-Châtellerault (86) . . . 163 H1
Availles-Limouzine (86) 180 B3
Availles-sur-Seiche (35) 104 A3
Availles-Thouarsais (79) 144 C5
Avajan (65) 305 F4
Avallon (89) 133 K3
les Avanchers-Valmorel (73) 209 G5
Avançon (05) 243 F5
Avançon (08) 41 H1
Avanne-Aveney (25) 137 K6
Avant-lès-Marcilly (10) 89 G3
Avant-lès-Ramerupt (10) 90 C3
Avanton (86) 162 E2
Avapessa (2B) 318 C3
Avaray (41) 109 G6
Avaux (08) 41 F1
Aveize (69) 205 H3
Aveizieux (42) 205 G4
Avelanges (21) 136 A2
Avelesges (80) 17 H2
Avelin (59) 6 E5
Aveluy (80) 10 D6
Avenas (69) 188 A2
Avenay (14) 32 D6
Avenay-Val-d'Or (51) 41 F6
Avène (34) 272 D4
les Avenières (38) 207 H3
Avensac (32) 268 B3
Avensan (33) 211 F5
Aventignan (65) 305 H1
Averan (65) 285 G6
Averdoingt (62) 10 B2
Averdon (41) 128 E1
Avermes (03) 168 E3
Avernes (95) 37 H6
Avernes-Saint-Gourgon (61) 55 F2
Avernes-sous-Exmes (61) 54 E4
Avéron-Bergelle (32) 266 C4

Averton (53) 82 A4
Avesnelles (59) 13 H5
Avesnes (62) 4 E5
Avesnes-Chaussoy (80) 17 G2
Avesnes-en-Bray (76) 36 D1
Avesnes-en-Saosnois (72) 83 F5
Avesnes-en-Val (76) 16 C1
Avesnes-le-Comte (62) 10 C3
Avesnes-le-Sec (59) 12 B3
Avesnes-les-Aubert (59) 12 C4
Avesnes-lès-Bapaume (62) 11 F5
Avesnes-sur-Helpe (59) 13 G5
Avessac (44) 102 D4
Avessé (72) 105 K3
Aveux (65) 305 H2
Avezac-Prat-Lahitte (65) 305 F1
Avezan (32) 268 A3
Avèze (30) 273 J2
Avèze (63) 201 J4
Avezé (72) 83 J5
Aviernoz (74) 191 G4
Avignon (84) 276 B2
Avignon-lès-Saint-Claude (39) . . . 173 K5
Avignonet (38) 224 A6
Avignonet-Lauragais (31) 289 F4
Avillers (54) 44 B3
Avillers (88) 94 B4
Avillers-Sainte-Croix (55) 44 A6
Avilley (25) 138 C3
Avilly-Saint-Léonard (60) 38 B5
Avion (62) 11 F1
Avioth (55) 23 K5
Aviré (49) 104 E4
Avirey-Lingey (10) 114 D2
Aviron (27) 56 D1
Avize (51) 62 A2
Avocourt (55) 43 F4
Avoine (37) 145 F1
Avoine (61) 54 B5
Avoise (72) 106 A4
Avolsheim (67) 70 D3
Avon (77) 87 H3
Avon (79) 162 C6
Avon-la-Pèze (10) 89 G3
Avon-les-Roches (37) 145 H2
Avondance (62) 5 F6
Avord (18) 149 K3
Avosnes (21) 135 G5
Avot (21) 136 A1
Avoudrey (25) 157 F1
Avrainville (54) 65 J4
Avrainville (88) 94 B3
Avrainville (91) 86 D1
Avranches (50) 51 K3
Avranville (88) 92 E3
Avrechy (60) 38 A2
Avrée (58) 152 B6
Avremesnil (76) 15 J2
Avressieux (73) 207 K4
Avreuil (10) 114 A2
Avricourt (54) 67 G5
Avricourt (57) 67 G5
Avricourt (60) 19 G5
Avrieux (73) 226 A2
Avrigney-Virey (70) 137 H5
Avrigny (60) 38 B3
Avril (54) 44 D3
Avril-sur-Loire (58) 151 F6
Avrillé (49) 125 G3
Avrillé (85) 159 H4
Avrillé-les-Ponceaux (37) 126 E4
Avrilly (03) 170 B6
Avrilly (27) 56 D2
Avrilly (61) 81 G1
Avroult (62) 5 F4
Avy (73) 195 H4
Awoingt (59) 12 B4
Ax-les-Thermes (09) 313 F2
Axat (11) 308 E5
Axiat (09) 307 K5
Ay (51) 62 A1
Ay-sur-Moselle (57) 45 F3
Ayat-sur-Sioule (63) 184 D4
Aydat (63) 202 C3
Aydie (64) 285 F1
Aydius (64) 303 F2
Aydoilles (88) 94 E5
Ayen (19) 215 G3
Ayencourt (80) 18 D5
Ayette (62) 10 E4
Ayguatébia-Talau (66) 313 K3
Ayguemorte-les-Graves (33) 229 H3
Ayguesvives (31) 288 D3
Ayguetinte (32) 267 G3
Ayherre (64) 282 D2
Ayn (73) 207 K4
Aynac (46) 234 B3
les Aynans (70) 138 D1
Ayron (86) 162 C2
Ayros-Arbouix (65) 304 B2
Ayse (74) 191 J3
Ayssènes (12) 252 D6
Aytré (17) 176 D3
les Ayvelles (08) 22 D4
Ayzac-Ost (65) 304 A2
Ayzieu (32) 266 B3
Azannes-et-Soumazannes (55) 43 J3
Azas (31) 269 K5
Azat-Châtenet (23) 182 C4
Azat-le-Ris (87) 181 F1
Azay-le-Brûlé (79) 161 J5
Azay-le-Ferron (36) 146 D6
Azay-le-Rideau (37) 127 G6
Azay-sur-Cher (37) 128 A5
Azay-sur-Indre (37) 146 C1

Azay-sur-Thouet (79) 161 J2
Azé (41) 108 B4
Azé (53) 105 H4
Azé (71) 171 J5
Azelot (54) 66 B6
Azerables (23) 165 G6
Azerailles (54) 95 F1
Azerat (24) 214 E4
Azérat (43) 219 H1
Azereix (65) 285 G5
Azet (65) 305 F5
Azeville (50) 29 F4
Azillanet (34) 291 F4
Azille (11) 290 E5
Azilone-Ampaza (2A) 320 E6
Azincourt (62) 5 F6
Azolette (69) 187 J2
Azoudange (57) 67 G4
Azur (40) 262 C3
Azy (18) 149 K1
Azy-le-Vif (58) 168 D1
Azy-sur-Marne (02) 60 E2
Azzana (2A) 320 D3

B

Baâlon (55) 43 G1
Baâlons (08) 22 C5
Babeau-Bouldoux (34) 291 G3
Babœuf (60) 19 J6
Baby (77) 88 D3
Baccarat (54) 95 F2
Baccon (45) 109 H4
Bach (46) 250 C3
Bachant (59) 13 G3
Bachas (31) 287 G5
la Bachellerie (24) 214 E4
Bachivillers (60) 37 F4
Bachos (31) 305 H4
Bachy (59) 7 F5
Bacilly (50) 51 J3
Baconnes (51) 41 H5
la Baconnière (53) 80 D6
Bacouël (60) 18 B5
Bacouel-sur-Selle (80) 18 A3
Bacourt (57) 66 C2
Bacquepuis (27) 35 H6
Bacqueville (27) 36 A3
Bacqueville-en-Caux (76) 15 J3
Badailhac (15) 235 K1
Badaroux (48) 237 J6
Badecon-le-Pin (36) 165 H4
Badefols-d'Ans (24) 215 F3
Badefols-sur-Dordogne (24) 232 B2
Baden (56) 100 E5
Badens (11) 290 C5
Badevel (25) 139 J2
Badinières (38) 207 F5
Badménil-aux-Bois (88) 94 E4
Badonviller (54) 95 H1
Badonvilliers-Gérauvilliers (55) . . 93 F1
Baerendorf (67) 67 J2
Baerenthal (57) 69 H4
la Baffe (88) 94 E5
Baffie (63) 204 A6
Bagard (30) 255 G6
Bagas (33) 230 C5
Bagat-en-Quercy (46) 249 H2
Bâgé-la-Ville (01) 172 A6
Bâgé-le-Châtel (01) 172 A6
Bagert (09) 306 D1
Bages (11) 310 C1
Bages (66) 315 G3
Bagiry (31) 305 J3
Bagnac-sur-Célé (46) 234 E4
Bagneaux (89) 89 G5
Bagneaux-sur-Loing (77) 87 H5
Bagnères-de-Bigorre (65) 304 D1
Bagnères-de-Luchon (31) 305 H5
Bagneux (02) 39 J2
Bagneux (03) 168 D2
Bagneux (36) 148 A1
Bagneux (51) 89 J1
Bagneux (54) 93 H1
Bagneux (92) 58 E4
Bagneux-la-Fosse (10) 114 D3
Bagnizeau (17) 178 B6
Bagnoles (11) 290 C5
Bagnoles-de-l'Orne (61) 81 J1
Bagnolet (93) 59 F3
Bagnols (63) 201 J6
Bagnols (69) 188 A6
Bagnols-en-Forêt (83) 280 B6
Bagnols-les-Bains (48) 238 A6
Bagnols-sur-Cèze (30) 256 C5
Bagnot (21) 154 C3
Baguer-Morvan (35) 51 F5
Baguer-Pican (35) 51 G4
Baho (66) 315 G2
Bahus-Soubiran (40) 265 J5
Baigneaux (28) 109 K1
Baigneaux (33) 230 B3
Baigneaux (41) 108 E5
Baignes (70) 138 A1
Baignes-Sainte-Radegonde (16) . . . 212 B1
Baigneux-les-Juifs (21) 135 G2
Baigts (28) 85 H6
Baigts (40) 264 D5
Baigts-de-Béarn (64) 283 J1
Baillargues (34) 274 D5
Baillé (35) 79 K1
Bailleau-Armenonville (28) 85 H2
Bailleau-le-Pin (28) 84 E4

Bailleau-l'Évêque (28) 85 F2
Baillestavy (66) 314 D4
Baillet-en-France (95) 58 C1
Bailleul (59) 6 B3
Bailleul (61) 54 C4
le Bailleul (72) 106 A5
Bailleul (80) 9 G6
Bailleul-aux-Cornailles (62) 10 B2
Bailleul-la-Vallée (27) 34 B5
Bailleul-le-Soc (60) 38 B2
Bailleul-lès-Pernes (62) 5 H6
Bailleul-Neuville (76) 16 C3
Bailleul-Sir-Berthoult (62) 11 F2
Bailleul-sur-Thérain (60) 37 J2
Bailleulmont (62) 10 D4
Bailleulval (62) 10 D3
Bailleval (60) 38 A3
Baillolet (76) 16 D3
Baillou (41) 108 A3
Bailly (60) 39 F1
Bailly (78) 58 C4
Bailly-aux-Forges (52) 91 J2
Bailly-en-Rivière (76) 16 C2
Bailly-le-Franc (10) 91 G2
Bailly-Romainvilliers (77) 59 J4
Bain-de-Bretagne (35) 103 F2
Bainctun (62) 4 B3
Bainghen (62) 4 D2
Bains (43) 220 B6
Bains-les-Bains (88) 118 B2
Bains-sur-Oust (35) 102 C3
Bainville-aux-Miroirs (54) 94 B2
Bainville-aux-Saules (88) 94 A5
Bainville-sur-Madon (54) 65 K6
Bairols (06) 261 J6
Bais (35) 79 K5
Bais (53) 81 J5
Baisieux (59) 7 F4
Baissey (52) 116 C5
Baives (59) 13 K5
Baix (07) 240 B3
Baixas (66) 310 B6
Baizieux (80) 10 C6
le Baizil (51) 61 H2
Bajamont (47) 248 C4
Bajonnette (32) 267 K4
Bajus (62) 10 C1
Balacet (09) 306 B4
Baladou (46) 233 J1
Balagny-sur-Thérain (60) 37 K4
Balaguères (09) 306 C4
Balaguier-d'Olt (12) 234 C6
Balaguier-sur-Rance (12) 271 J3
Balaiseaux (39) 155 G4
Balaives-et-Butz (08) 22 D4
Balan (01) 206 D1
Balan (08) 23 F4
Balanod (39) 172 E4
Balansun (64) 283 K1
Balanzac (17) 194 E2
Balaruc-le-Vieux (34) 293 F2
Balaruc-les-Bains (34) 292 E3
Balâtre (80) 19 G4
Balazé (35) 80 B6
Balazuc (07) 239 H6
Balbigny (42) 204 E1
Balbins (38) 206 E6
Balbronn (67) 70 C3
Baldenheim (67) 96 D2
Baldersheim (68) 97 C2
la Baleine (50) 52 A2
Baleix (64) 285 F3
Balesmes-sur-Marne (52) 116 D4
Balesta (31) 286 C5
Baleyssagues (47) 230 E4
Balgau (68) 96 E6
Balham (08) 41 G1
Balignac (82) 268 B2
Balignicourt (10) 90 E2
Bâlines (27) 56 B5
Balinghem (62) 2 D1
Baliracq-Maumusson (64) 284 E1
Baliros (64) 284 D5
Balizac (33) 229 J6
Ballainvilliers (91) 58 E6
Ballaison (74) 174 E6
Ballan-Miré (37) 127 H5
Ballancourt-sur-Essonne (91) . . . 86 E2
Ballans (17) 196 A1
Ballay (08) 42 B2
Balledent (87) 181 G3
Ballée (53) 105 J3
Balleray (58) 151 F2
Balleroy (14) 31 K2
Ballersdorf (68) 97 A4
Balléville (88) 93 H4
Ballon (17) 177 F4
Ballon (72) 82 E6
Ballons (26) 258 C3
Ballore (71) 170 E4
Ballots (53) 104 C3
Balloy (77) 88 C3
Balma (31) 269 H6
la Balme (73) 207 K2
la Balme-de-Sillingy (74) 190 E5
la Balme-de-Thuy (74) 191 G5
la Balme-d'Épy (39) 172 E5
la Balme-les-Grottes (38) 189 H6
Balnot-la-Grange (10) 114 C3
Balnot-sur-Laignes (10) 114 D2
Balogna (2A) 320 D2
Balot (21) 114 E5
Balsac (12) 252 A3
Balschwiller (68) 97 A3
Balsièges (48) 254 A1
Baltzenheim (68) 96 E3

Balzac (16) 196 D3
Bambecque (59) 3 J3
Bambiderstroff (57) 45 J5
Ban-de-Laveline (88) 95 K4
Ban-de-Sapt (88) 95 J3
le Ban-Saint-Martin (57) 44 E5
Banassac (48) 253 H2
Banca (64) 282 C6
Bancigny (02) 21 G3
Bancourt (62) 11 F5
Bandol (83) 300 A4
Baneins (01) 188 D3
Baneuil (24) 231 K2
Bangor (56) 120 B4
Banios (65) 304 E2
Banize (23) 182 E6
Bannalec (29) 99 G2
Bannans (25) 156 E4
Bannay (18) 131 K5
Bannay (51) 61 H3
Bannay (57) 45 H5
Banne (07) 255 H2
Bannegon (18) 149 K6
Bannes (46) 234 C3
Bannes (51) 61 K4
Bannes (52) 116 D3
Bannes (53) 105 J3
Banneville-la-Campagne (14) 33 F5
Banneville-sur-Ajon (14) 32 C6
Bannières (81) 270 A6
Bannoncourt (55) 64 C2
Bannost-Villegagnon (77) 60 C6
Banogne-Recouvrance (08) 21 H6
Banon (04) 258 C6
Banos (40) 265 F4
Bans (39) 155 H3
Bansat (63) 203 F6
Bantanges (71) 172 B3
Banteux (59) 11 J5
Banthelu (95) 36 E6
Bantheville (55) 42 E2
Bantigny (59) 11 J3
Bantouzelle (59) 11 J5
Bantzenheim (68) 97 D1
Banvillars (90) 139 H1
Banville (14) 32 C3
Banvou (61) 53 H5
Banyuls-dels-Aspres (66) 315 G4
Banyuls-sur-Mer (66) 315 K5
Baon (89) 114 B4
Baons-le-Comte (76) 15 G5
Bapaume (62) 11 F5
Bar (19) 216 B2
Bar-le-Duc (55) 64 B4
Bar-lès-Buzancy (08) 42 D2
Bar-sur-Aube (10) 91 G5
le Bar-sur-Loup (06) 280 E4
Bar-sur-Seine (10) 114 D1
Baracé (49) 125 J1
Baraigne (11) 289 F4
Baraize (36) 165 H4
Baralle (62) 11 H4
Baraqueville (12) 252 A4
Barastre (62) 11 G5
Baratier (05) 243 J5
Barbachen (65) 285 J2
Barbaggio (2B) 319 H1
Barbaira (11) 290 C6
Barbaise (08) 22 C4
Barbas (54) 67 G6
Barbaste (47) 247 J5
Barbâtre (85) 140 C3
Barbazan (31) 305 J2
Barbazan-Debat (65) 285 H5
Barbazan-Dessus (65) 285 H6
Barbechat (44) 123 K3
la Barben (13) 277 F5
Barbentane (13) 276 A2
Barberaz (73) 208 B4
Barberey-Saint-Sulpice (10) 90 A4
Barberier (03) 185 G2
Barbery (14) 53 K1
Barbery (60) 38 C5
Barbeville (14) 32 A3
Barbey (77) 88 B4
Barbey-Seroux (88) 95 H6
Barbezières (16) 178 D6
Barbezieux-Saint-Hilaire (16) . . . 196 B5
Barbières (26) 222 E6
Barbirey-sur-Ouche (21) 135 H6
Barbizon (77) 87 G3
Barbonne-Fayel (51) 61 H6
Barbonville (54) 66 C6
le Barboux (25) 157 J1
Barbuise (10) 89 G1
Barby (08) 21 K6
Barby (73) 208 C4
Barc (27) 35 H6
le Barcarès (66) 310 D5
Barcelonne (26) 240 E1
Barcelonne-du-Gers (32) 265 K5
Barcelonnette (04) 260 D1
Barchain (57) 67 H4
Barcillonnette (05) 259 F1
Barcugnan (32) 286 B3
Barcus (64) 283 J5
Barcy (77) 59 K1
Bard (42) 204 E4
Bard-le-Régulier (21) 153 F2
Bard-lès-Époisses (21) 134 C3
Bard-lès-Pesmes (70) 137 G5
la Barde (17) 212 C4
Bardenac (16) 212 D2
Bardigues (82) 268 B1
le Bardon (45) 109 H5

Bardos (64) 282 E1
Bardou (24) 231 K3
Bardouville (76) 35 G2
Barèges (65) 304 C5
Bareilles (65) 305 F1
Barembach (67) 70 A5
Baren (31) 305 H4
Barentin (76) 15 A6
Barenton (50) 52 E6
Barenton-Bugny (02) 20 D5
Barenton-Cel (02) 20 D5
Barenton-sur-Serre (02) 20 D5
Barésia-sur-l'Ain (39) 173 H3
Barfleur (50) 29 G2
Bargème (83) 279 K4
Bargemon (83) 279 K5
Barges (21) 154 C1
Barges (43) 238 C2
Barges (70) 117 H4
Bargny (60) 39 F5
Barie (33) 230 B5
les Barils (27) 56 A5
Barinque (64) 284 E3
Barisey-au-Plain (54) 93 H1
Barisey-la-Côte (54) 93 H1
Barisis (02) 20 A6
Barizey (71) 153 J6
Barjac (09) 306 D2
Barjac (30) 255 K3
Barjac (48) 253 H4
Barjols (83) 278 E6
Barjon (21) 135 K1
Barjouville (28) 85 G3
Barles (04) 259 K3
Barlest (65) 285 F6
Barleux (80) 19 G2
Barlieu (18) 131 H3
Barlin (62) 5 K6
Barly (62) 10 C3
Barly (80) 10 A4
Barmainville (28) 86 B5
Barnas (07) 239 F4
Barnave (26) 241 H4
Barnay (71) 153 F2
Barneville-Carteret (50) 28 B5
Barneville-la-Bertran (14) 33 K2
Barneville-sur-Seine (27) 35 F2
la Baroche-sous-Lucé (61) 81 G1
les Baroches (54) 44 C4
Baromesnil (76) 8 C6
Baron (30) 255 J6
Baron (33) 229 K2
Baron (60) 38 D5
Baron (71) 170 D4
Baron-sur-Odon (14) 32 D5
Baronville (57) 66 E1
Barou-en-Auge (14) 54 C2
Baroville (10) 91 G6
le Barp (33) 229 F5
Barquet (27) 56 A1
Barr (67) 70 C5
Barrais-Bussolles (03) 186 B1
Barran (32) 267 G6
Barrancoueu (65) 305 F3
Barras (04) 259 H5
Barraute-Camu (64) 283 H1
Barraux (38) 208 C5
la Barre (39) 155 J1
la Barre (70) 138 B4
Barre (81) 272 B4
la Barre-de-Monts (85) 140 C4
la Barre-de-Semilly (50) 31 H3
Barre-des-Cévennes (48) 254 C4
la Barre-en-Ouche (27) 55 J2
Barrême (04) 279 H1
Barret (16) 196 A5
Barret-de-Lioure (26) 258 B4
Barret-sur-Méouge (05) 258 D3
Barretaine (39) 155 J1
Barrettali (2B) 317 C3
Barriac-les-Bosquets (15) 217 F4
Barro (16) 179 G5
Barrou (37) 146 A5
le Barroux (84) 257 H5
Barry (65) 285 G6
Barry-d'Islemade (82) 249 H6
Bars (24) 214 C3
Bars (32) 285 K1
Barsac (26) 241 G4
Barsac (33) 229 K5
Barst (57) 68 B3
Bart (25) 139 F2
Bartenheim (68) 97 D4
Barthe (65) 286 B4
la Barthe-de-Neste (65) 305 F1
Bartherans (25) 156 B3
les Barthes (82) 249 H6
Bartrès (65) 285 G6
Barville (27) 34 C5
Barville (61) 83 F2
Barville (88) 93 G3
Barville-en-Gâtinais (45) 111 F1
Barzan (17) 194 E5
Barzun (64) 285 F5
Barzy-en-Thiérache (02) 13 F6
Barzy-sur-Marne (02) 40 A6
Bas-en-Basset (43) 220 E2
Bas-et-Lezat (63) 185 H4
Bas-Lieu (59) 13 G4
Bas-Mauco (40) 265 G3
Bascons (40) 265 H3
Bascous (32) 266 D4
Baslieux (54) 26 C4
Baslieux-lès-Fismes (51) 40 C3
Baslieux-sous-Châtillon (51) 40 D6
Basly (14) 32 D3

Bassac (16) 196 B3
Bassan (34) 292 A3
Bassanne (33) 230 C5
Basse-Goulaine (44) 123 H4
Basse-Ham (57) 27 H4
Basse-Rentgen (57) 27 G3
Basse-sur-le-Rupt (88) 119 G2
la Basse-Vaivre (70) 117 K3
la Bassée (59) 6 B5
Bassemberg (67) 70 B6
Basseneville (14) 33 G4
Bassens (33) 229 H1
Bassens (73) 208 B4
Bassercles (40) 284 A1
Basses (86) 144 E3
Basseux (62) 10 D3
Bassevelle (77) 60 D2
Bassignac (15) 217 H2
Bassignac-le-Bas (19) 216 B6
Bassignac-le-Haut (19) 216 E3
Bassigney (70) 118 B4
Bassillac (24) 214 B3
Bassillon-Vauzé (64) 285 G2
Bassing (57) 67 G2
Bassoles-Aulers (02) 39 J1
Bassoncourt (52) 117 F1
Bassou (89) 113 F4
Bassoues (32) 266 E6
Bassu (51) 63 G3
Bassuet (51) 63 G4
Bassurels (48) 254 C5
Bassussarry (64) 282 B2
Bassy (74) 190 C4
Bastanès (64) 283 J1
Bastelica (2A) 320 E4
Bastelicaccia (2A) 320 C5
Bastennes (40) 264 D5
Bastia (2B) 317 E5
la Bastide (66) 314 D4
la Bastide (83) 280 A4
la Bastide-Clairence (64) 282 D2
la Bastide-de-Besplas (09) 288 A6
la Bastide-de-Bousignac (09) . . . 308 B2
la Bastide-de-Lordat (09) 288 E6
la Bastide-de-Sérou (09) 307 G2
la Bastide-d'Engras (30) 256 B6
la Bastide-des-Jourdans (84) . . . 277 K3
la Bastide-du-Salat (09) 306 C2
la Bastide-l'Évêque (12) 251 J3
la Bastide-Pradines (12) 272 D1
la Bastide-Puylaurent (48) 238 C5
la Bastide-Solages (12) 271 H2
la Bastide-sur-l'Hers (09) 308 B3
la Bastidonne (84) 277 K4
le Bastit (46) 233 K4
Basville (23) 201 G1
la Bataille (79) 178 D3
Bathelémont-lès-Bauzemont (54) . . 66 D5
Bathernay (26) 222 D3
la Bâthie (73) 209 G3
la Bâtie-des-Fonds (26) 242 A6
la Bâtie-Divisin (38) 207 J5
la Bâtie-Montgascon (38) 207 H4
la Bâtie-Montsaléon (05) 258 D1
la Bâtie-Neuve (05) 243 F5
la Bâtie-Rolland (26) 240 C5
la Bâtie-Vieille (05) 243 F5
les Bâties (70) 137 J2
Batilly (54) 44 D4
Batilly (61) 54 A5
Batilly-en-Gâtinais (45) 110 E2
Batilly-en-Puisaye (45) 131 K2
Bats (40) 265 H5
Batsère (65) 304 E1
Battenans-les-Mines (25) 138 C4
Battenans-Varin (25) 139 G5
Battenheim (68) 97 C1
Battexey (88) 94 A3
Battigny (54) 93 J2
Battrans (70) 137 G4
Batz-sur-Mer (44) 121 H5
Batzendorf (67) 69 K6
la Bauche (73) 208 A5
Baud (56) 100 D2
Baudement (51) 89 H1
Baudemont (71) 187 H1
Baudignan (40) 247 F6
Baudignécourt (55) 92 D1
Baudinard-sur-Verdon (83) 279 F4
Baudoncourt (70) 118 C5
Baudonvilliers (55) 63 K5
Baudre (50) 31 H3
Baudrecourt (52) 91 K3
Baudrecourt (57) 66 C1
Baudreix (64) 284 E5
Baudrémont (55) 64 D3
Baudres (36) 147 J3
Baudreville (28) 86 A4
Baudreville (50) 28 C6
Baudricourt (88) 93 K4
Baudrières (71) 172 B2
Bauduen (83) 279 F4
Baugé (49) 126 B2
Baugy (18) 149 K3
Baugy (60) 38 D2
Baugy (71) 186 E1
Baulay (70) 117 K5
Baule (45) 109 H5
la Baule-Escoublac (44) 121 J5
Baulme-la-Roche (21) 135 J5
Baulne (91) 86 E2
Baulne-en-Brie (02) 61 G2
Baulny (55) 42 E4
Baulon (35) 78 D6

Baulou (09) 307 H2
la Baume (74) 175 G6
la Baume-Cornillane (26) 240 C2
la Baume-de-Transit (26) 256 E2
la Baume-d'Hostun (26) 223 F5
Baume-les-Dames (25) 138 D4
Baume-les-Messieurs (39) 173 H1
Bauné (49) 125 J3
Baupte (50) 31 F1
Bauquay (14) 53 G1
Baurech (33) 229 J3
la Baussaine (35) 78 E1
les Baux-de-Breteuil (27) 56 A3
les Baux-de-Provence (13) 276 B4
les Baux-Sainte-Croix (27) 56 C2
Bauzemont (54) 66 D5
Bauzy (41) 129 H3
Bavans (25) 139 G2
Bavay (59) 13 F2
Bavelincourt (80) 18 C1
Bavent (14) 33 F4
Baverans (39) 155 H2
Bavilliers (90) 139 H1
Bavinchove (59) 3 J4
Bavincourt (62) 10 D3
Bax (31) 288 A5
Bay (70) 137 H5
Bay-sur-Aube (52) 116 A5
Bayac (24) 232 A3
Bayard-sur-Marne (52) 92 A1
Bayas (33) 212 B5
Baye (29) 99 H3
Baye (51) 61 H1
Bayecourt (88) 94 D4
Bayel (10) 91 H6
Bayencourt (80) 10 D5
Bayenghem-lès-Éperlecques (62) . . 3 F4
Bayenghem-lès-Seninghem (62) . . . 5 F3
Bayers (16) 179 G6
Bayet (03) 185 H2
Bayeux (14) 32 B3
Bayon (54) 94 C2
Bayon-sur-Gironde (33) 211 H5
Bayonne (64) 282 B1
Bayons (04) 259 H2
Bayonville (08) 42 C2
Bayonville-sur-Mad (54) 65 J1
Bayonvillers (80) 18 D2
Bazac (16) 212 D3
Bazaiges (36) 165 G4
Bazailles (54) 26 D4
Bazainville (78) 57 J4
Bazancourt (51) 41 G3
Bazancourt (60) 17 F6
Bazarnes (89) 133 H1
Bazas (33) 230 C5
Bazauges (17) 178 D6
Bazegney (88) 94 B4
Bazeilles (08) 23 F4
Bazeilles-sur-Othain (55) 23 K6
Bazelat (23) 165 G6
Bazemont (78) 58 A2
Bazens (47) 247 K4
Bazentin (80) 10 E6
Bazenville (14) 32 C3
la Bazeuge (87) 181 F2
Bazian (32) 267 F5
Bazicourt (60) 38 C3
Baziège (31) 288 D2
Bazien (88) 95 F2
Bazillac (65) 285 H3
Bazincourt-sur-Epte (27) 36 E3
Bazincourt-sur-Saulx (55) 64 A5
Bazinghen (62) 2 B4
Bazinval (76) 16 E1
la Bazoche-Gouet (28) 108 B1
Bazoches (58) 133 J5
Bazoches-au-Houlme (61) 54 A4
Bazoches-en-Dunois (28) 109 H1
Bazoches-lès-Bray (77) 88 C3
Bazoches-les-Gallerandes (45) . . 110 B1
Bazoches-les-Hautes (28) 109 K1
Bazoches-sur-Guyonne (78) 57 K4
Bazoches-sur-Hoëne (61) 83 G1
Bazoches-sur-le-Betz (45) 112 A1
Bazoches-sur-Vesles (02) 40 B3
la Bazoge (50) 52 C5
la Bazoge (72) 106 D1
la Bazoge-Montpinçon (53) 81 G2
Bazoges-en-Paillers (85) 142 C4
Bazoges-en-Pareds (85) 160 D2
Bazoilles-et-Ménil (88) 94 A4
Bazoilles-sur-Meuse (88) 93 F4
Bazolles (58) 151 J2
Bazoncourt (57) 45 G6
la Bazoque (14) 31 K3
la Bazoque (61) 53 G4
Bazoques (27) 34 C5
Bazordan (65) 286 C5
la Bazouge-de-Chemeré (53) . . . 105 H2
la Bazouge-des-Alleux (53) 81 G6
la Bazouge-du-Désert (35) 80 C2
Bazougers (53) 105 G2
Bazouges-la-Pérouse (35) 51 H4
Bazouges-sur-le-Loir (72) 106 A6
Bazuel (59) 12 D5
Bazugues (32) 286 A2
Bazus (31) 269 H5
Bazus-Aure (65) 305 F4
Bazus-Neste (65) 305 F2
le Béage (07) 238 E2
Béalcourt (80) 9 K4
Béalencourt (62) 9 J1
Béard (58) 151 F5

Beaubec-la-Rosière (76) 16 D5
Beaubery (71) 170 E5
Beaubray (27) 56 B3
Beaucaire (30) 275 K3
Beaucaire (32) 267 F3
Beaucamps-le-Jeune (80) 17 G3
Beaucamps-le-Vieux (80) 17 G2
Beaucamps-Ligny (59) 6 C4
Beaucé (35) 80 B4
Beaucens (65) 304 B2
le Beaucet (84) 276 E1
Beauchalot (31) 306 A1
Beauchamp (95) 58 D1
Beauchamps (50) 51 K1
Beauchamps (80) 8 D6
Beauchamps-sur-Huillard (45) . . . 111 F3
Beauchastel (07) 240 B2
Beauche (28) 56 B5
Beauchemin (52) 116 C3
Beauchêne (41) 108 B3
Beauchêne (61) 53 F5
Beauchery-Saint-Martin (77) 88 E1
Beauclair (55) 43 F1
Beaucoudray (50) 31 G5
Beaucourt (90) 139 J2
Beaucourt-en-Santerre (80) 18 D3
Beaucourt-sur-l'Ancre (80) 10 E5
Beaucourt-sur-l'Hallue (80) 18 C1
Beaucouzé (49) 125 F3
Beaucroissant (38) 223 H1
Beaudéan (65) 304 D2
Beaudéduit (60) 17 J5
Beaudignies (59) 12 D3
Beaudricourt (62) 10 B3
Beaufai (61) 55 H5
Beaufay (72) 83 F6
Beauficel (50) 52 D4
Beauficel-en-Lyons (27) 36 B2
Beaufin (38) 242 D2
Beaufort (31) 287 J2
Beaufort (34) 291 F4
Beaufort (38) 222 E1
Beaufort (39) 173 F3
Beaufort (59) 13 H3
Beaufort (73) 209 H2
Beaufort-Blavincourt (62) 10 C3
Beaufort-en-Argonne (55) 43 F1
Beaufort-en-Santerre (80) 18 E3
Beaufort-en-Vallée (49) 125 K4
Beaufort-sur-Gervanne (26) 240 E3
Beaufou (85) 141 J5
Beaufour-Druval (14) 33 H4
Beaufremont (88) 93 G5
Beaugas (47) 231 J6
Beaugeay (17) 176 E6
Beaugency (45) 109 H5
Beaugies-sous-Bois (60) 19 J5
Beaujeu (04) 260 A4
Beaujeu (69) 188 A3
Beaujeu-Saint-Vallier-
 -Pierrejux-et-Quitteur (70) . . 137 G3
Beaulandais (61) 81 H1
Beaulencourt (62) 11 F5
Beaulieu (07) 255 J2
Beaulieu (14) 52 E2
Beaulieu (15) 201 H6
Beaulieu (21) 115 H6
Beaulieu (34) 274 D5
Beaulieu (36) 164 E6
Beaulieu (38) 223 H3
Beaulieu (43) 220 C4
Beaulieu (58) 133 F6
Beaulieu (61) 55 K5
Beaulieu (63) 203 F6
Beaulieu-en-Argonne (55) 63 K1
Beaulieu-les-Fontaines (60) 19 G5
Beaulieu-lès-Loches (37) 146 D2
Beaulieu-sous-la-Roche (85) 159 G1
Beaulieu-sous-Parthenay (79) . . . 161 K3
Beaulieu-sur-Dordogne (19) 216 B6
Beaulieu-sur-Layon (49) 125 G5
Beaulieu-sur-Loire (45) 131 J3
Beaulieu-sur-Mer (06) 281 H4
Beaulieu-sur-Oudon (53) 104 C2
Beaulieu-sur-Sonnette (16) 179 J6
Beaulon (03) 169 H3
Beaumais (14) 54 B3
Beaumarchés (32) 266 C6
Beaumat (46) 233 J4
Beaumé (02) 21 H2
la Beaume (05) 242 A5
Beauménil (88) 95 G3
Beaumerie-Saint-Martin (62) 4 C6
Beaumes-de-Venise (84) 257 G5
Beaumesnil (14) 52 D2
Beaumesnil (27) 55 K1
Beaumettes (84) 277 F3
Beaumetz (80) 9 J4
Beaumetz-lès-Aire (62) 5 G5
Beaumetz-lès-Cambrai (62) 11 G5
Beaumetz-lès-Loges (62) 10 D3
Beaumont (07) 239 F6
Beaumont (19) 216 B1
Beaumont (32) 266 E2
Beaumont (43) 219 G2
Beaumont (54) 65 G3
Beaumont (63) 202 D2
Beaumont (74) 191 F3
Beaumont (86) 163 G1
Beaumont (89) 113 G4
Beaumont-de-Lomagne (82) 268 C3
Beaumont-de-Pertuis (84) 277 K4
Beaumont-du-Gâtinais (77) 111 F1
Beaumont-du-Lac (87) 200 B2
Beaumont-du-Périgord (24) 232 A3
Beaumont-du-Ventoux (84) 257 H4

Beaumont-en-Argonne (08) 23 G6
Beaumont-en-Auge (14) 33 J4
Beaumont-en-Beine (02) 19 J4
Beaumont-en-Cambrésis (59) . . . 12 C5
Beaumont-en-Diois (26) 241 J5
Beaumont-en-Verdunois (55) 43 H4
Beaumont-en-Véron (37) 145 F1
Beaumont-Hague (50) 28 B2
Beaumont-Hamel (80) 10 D5
Beaumont-la-Ferrière (58) 150 E1
Beaumont-la-Ronce (37) 127 J2
Beaumont-le-Hareng (76) 16 B5
Beaumont-le-Roger (27) 34 E6
Beaumont-les-Autels (28) 84 B5
Beaumont-les-Nonains (60) 37 G3
Beaumont-lès-Randan (63) 185 J5
Beaumont-lès-Valence (26) 240 D2
Beaumont-Monteux (26) 222 C5
Beaumont-Pied-de-Bœuf (53) . . . 105 H3
Beaumont-Pied-de-Bœuf (72) . . . 107 F5
Beaumont-Sardolles (58) 151 G5
Beaumont-sur-Dême (72) 107 H6
Beaumont-sur-Grosne (71) 171 K2
Beaumont-sur-Lèze (31) 288 B3
Beaumont-sur-Oise (95) 37 J5
Beaumont-sur-Sarthe (72) 82 D5
Beaumont-sur-Vesle (51) 41 G5
Beaumont-sur-Vingeanne (21) . . . 136 D3
Beaumont-Village (37) 147 F1
Beaumontel (27) 34 E6
Beaumotte-Aubertans (70) 138 B3
Beaumotte-lès-Pin (70) 137 J5
Beaunay (51) 61 J3
Beaune (21) 154 A3
Beaune-d'Allier (03) 184 D1
Beaune-la-Rolande (45) 111 F2
Beaune-sur-Arzon (43) 220 B2
Beaunotte (21) 135 H1
Beaupont (01) 172 D5
Beaupouyet (24) 213 F6
Beaupréau (49) 142 D1
Beaupuy (31) 269 H6
Beaupuy (32) 268 C6
Beaupuy (47) 230 E6
Beaupuy (82) 268 D3
Beauquesne (80) 10 B5
Beaurain (59) 12 D4
Beaurains (62) 11 F3
Beaurains-lès-Noyon (60) 19 H5
Beaurainville (62) 9 G1
Beaurecueil (13) 296 E1
Beauregard (01) 188 B5
Beauregard (46) 250 D3
Beauregard-Baret (26) 222 E5
Beauregard-de-Terrasson (24) . . 215 F4
Beauregard-et-Bassac (24) 213 K6
Beauregard-l'Évêque (63) 203 F1
Beauregard-Vendon (63) 185 F5
Beaurepaire (38) 222 D1
Beaurepaire (60) 38 B4
Beaurepaire (76) 14 B4
Beaurepaire (85) 142 C4
Beaurepaire-en-Bresse (71) 172 E2
Beaurepaire-sur-Sambre (59) . . . 13 F5
Beaurevoir (02) 12 B6
Beaurières (26) 241 K5
Beaurieux (02) 40 C2
Beaurieux (59) 13 J4
Beauronne (24) 213 G5
Beausemblant (26) 222 B3
Beausite (55) 64 B2
Beausoleil (06) 281 J3
Beaussac (24) 197 H5
Beaussais (79) 178 D1
Beaussault (76) 16 E4
Beausse (49) 124 C5
le Beausset (83) 300 A3
Beauteville (31) 288 E4
Beautheil (77) 60 B5
Beautiran (33) 229 J3
Beautor (02) 20 A5
Beautot (76) 15 K5
Beauvain (61) 53 K6
Beauvais (60) 37 G2
Beauvais-sur-Matha (17) 178 C6
Beauvais-sur-Tescou (81) 269 J2
Beauval (80) 10 A5
Beauval-en-Caux (76) 15 J4
Beauvallon (26) 240 C2
Beauvau (49) 125 K2
Beauvène (07) 239 J2
Beauvernois (71) 155 G5
Beauvezer (04) 260 C4
Beauville (31) 289 F2
Beauville (47) 248 E3
Beauvilliers (28) 85 H5
Beauvilliers (41) 108 E5
Beauvilliers (89) 134 A4
Beauvoir (50) 51 J4
Beauvoir (60) 18 B5
Beauvoir (77) 59 K6
Beauvoir (89) 112 E3
Beauvoir-de-Marc (38) 206 D5
Beauvoir-en-Lyons (76) 36 C1
Beauvoir-en-Royans (38) 223 G4
Beauvoir-sur-Mer (85) 140 C4
Beauvoir-sur-Niort (79) 178 A2
Beauvoir-Wavans (62) 9 K3
Beauvois (62) 9 J2
Beauvois-en-Cambrésis (59) 12 C4
Beauvois-en-Vermandois (02) . . . 19 J2
Beauvoisin (26) 257 J3
Beauvoisin (30) 275 G5
Beaux (43) 220 E3
Beauzac (43) 220 E1
Beauzelle (31) 269 G5

Beauziac (47) 247 F3
Bébing (57) 67 J4
Beblenheim (68) 96 B3
Bec-de-Mortagne (76) 14 D4
le Bec-Hellouin (27) 34 E4
le Bec-Thomas (27) 35 G4
Beccas (32) 285 J2
Béceleuf (79) 161 G4
Béchamps (54) 44 B4
Bécherel (35) 78 D2
Bécheresse (16) 196 D5
Béchy (57) 66 C1
Bécon-les-Granits (49) 124 E3
Bécordel-Bécourt (80) 10 E6
Bécourt (62) 4 D4
Becquigny (02) 12 C6
Becquigny (80) 18 D4
Bédarieux (34) 272 E6
Bédarrides (84) 257 F6
Beddes (18) 166 D3
Bédéchan (32) 287 F1
Bédée (35) 78 D3
Bédeilhac-et-Aynat (09) 307 H4
Bédeille (09) 306 D1
Bédeille (64) 285 F3
Bedenac (17) 212 A3
Bédoin (84) 257 J5
Bédouès (48) 254 C3
Bedous (64) 303 F2
Béduer (46) 234 C5
Beffes (18) 150 C3
Beffia (39) 173 G3
Beffu-et-le-Morthomme (08) . . 42 D2
Bégaar (40) 264 D3
Bégadan (33) 210 E1
Béganne (56) 102 A5
Bégard (22) 48 B4
Bègles (33) 229 H2
Begnécourt (88) 94 A5
Bégole (65) 286 A6
Bégrolles-en-Mauges (49) . . . 142 E1
la Bégude-de-Mazenc (26) . . . 240 D6
Bègues (03) 185 F3
Béguey (33) 229 K4
Béguios (64) 283 F3
Béhagnies (62) 11 F4
Béhasque-Lapiste (64) 283 G3
Béhen (80) 9 F5
Béhencourt (80) 18 C1
Béhéricourt (60) 19 H6
Behonne (55) 64 B4
Béhorléguy (64) 283 F6
Béhoust (78) 57 J4
Behren-lès-Forbach (57) 68 C2
Béhuard (49) 125 F4
Beignon (56) 78 B6
Beillé (72) 107 G1
Beine (89) 113 H5
Beine-Nauroy (51) 41 G4
Beinheim (67) 25 D3
Beire-le-Châtel (21) 136 C4
Beire-le-Fort (21) 136 C6
Beissat (23) 201 F2
Bélâbre (36) 164 D4
Belan-sur-Ource (21) 115 G3
Bélarga (34) 292 D1
Bélaye (46) 249 H1
Belberaud (31) 288 D2
Belbèse (82) 268 C2
Belbeuf (76) 35 J2
Belbèze-de-Lauragais (31) . . . 288 D3
Belbèze-en-Comminges (31) . . 306 C1
Belcaire (11) 308 C5
Belcastel (12) 251 J4
Belcastel (81) 270 A6
Belcastel-et-Buc (11) 309 G2
Belcodène (13) 296 E2
Bélesta (09) 308 B4
Bélesta (66) 314 C1
Bélesta-en-Lauragais (31) . . . 289 F3
Beleymas (24) 213 J6
Belfahy (70) 119 G4
Belfays (25) 139 J5
Belflou (11) 289 F4
Belfonds (61) 54 D6
Belfort (90) 119 H6
Belfort-du-Quercy (46) 250 B4
Belfort-sur-Rebenty (11) 308 D5
Belgeard (53) 81 G5
Belgentier (83) 297 J4
Belgodère (2B) 318 D2
Belhade (40) 245 J2
Belhomert-Guéhouville (28) . . . 84 C2
le Bélieu (25) 157 H1
Béligneux (01) 189 F6
Belin-Béliet (33) 228 E6
Bélis (40) 246 A6
Bellac (87) 181 F3
Bellaffaire (04) 259 J1
Bellaing (59) 12 C5
Bellancourt (80) 9 G5
Bellange (57) 66 G2
Bellavilliers (61) 83 G3
le Bellay-en-Vexin (95) 37 H4
Belle-Église (60) 37 J5
Belle-et-Houllefort (62) 4 C3
Belle-Isle-en-Terre (22) 48 A5
Belleau (02) 39 J6
Belleau (54) 66 A3
Bellebat (33) 230 A3
Bellebrune (62) 4 C3
Bellechassagne (19) 200 E4
Bellechaume (89) 113 G6
Bellecombe (39) 173 K6
Bellecombe-en-Bauges (73) . . 208 D2
Bellecombe-Tarendol (26) 257 K2

Bellefond (21) 136 A4
Bellefond (33) 230 B3
Bellefonds (86) 163 H2
Bellefontaine (39) 174 B3
Bellefontaine (50) 52 D5
Bellefontaine (88) 118 D2
Bellefontaine (95) 38 A6
Bellefosse (67) 70 A6
Bellegarde (30) 275 J4
Bellegarde (32) 286 D3
Bellegarde (45) 111 F3
Bellegarde (81) 271 F2
Bellegarde-du-Razès (11) 308 D1
Bellegarde-en-Diois (26) 241 H5
Bellegarde-en-Forez (42) 205 H3
Bellegarde-en-Marche (23) . . . 183 H5
Bellegarde-Poussieu (38) 222 C1
Bellegarde-Sainte-Marie (31) . . 268 D5
Bellegarde-sur-Valserine (01) . . 190 C3
Belleherbe (25) 139 G5
Bellemagny (68) 119 K5
Bellême (61) 83 H4
Bellenaves (03) 185 F2
Bellencombre (76) 16 B4
Belleneuve (21) 136 C5
Bellenglise (02) 19 K1
Bellengreville (14) 33 F5
Bellengreville (76) 16 B2
Bellenod-sur-Seine (21) 115 G6
Bellenot-sous-Pouilly (21) 135 F6
Bellentre (73) 209 K3
Belleray (55) 43 H5
Bellerive-sur-Allier (03) 185 J3
Belleroche (42) 187 J3
Belles-Forêts (57) 67 H3
Belleserre (81) 289 J2
Bellesserre (31) 268 D4
Belleu (02) 39 J3
Belleuse (80) 17 K4
Bellevaux (74) 191 K1
Bellevesvre (71) 155 F5
Belleville (54) 65 K3
Belleville (69) 188 B3
Belleville (79) 177 K3
Belleville-en-Caux (76) 15 J4
Belleville-et-Châtillon-
  -sur-Bar (08) 42 C1
Belleville-sur-Loire (18) 131 K3
Belleville-sur-Mer (76) 16 A1
Belleville-sur-Meuse (55) 43 H5
Belleville-sur-Vie (85) 141 K6
Bellevue-la-Montagne (43) . . . 220 B3
Belley (01) 207 K2
Belleydoux (01) 190 B1
Bellicourt (02) 19 K1
la Bellière (61) 54 E4
la Bellière (76) 16 E5
Bellignat (01) 190 A1
Belligné (44) 124 C3
Bellignies (59) 13 F2
la Belliole (89) 112 B1
Belloc (09) 308 B2
Belloc-Saint-Clamens (32) . . . 286 B2
Bellocq (64) 283 H1
Bellon (16) 212 C2
Bellonne (62) 11 H2
Bellot (77) 60 D3
Bellou (14) 54 E2
Bellou-en-Houlme (61) 53 J5
Bellou-le-Trichard (61) 83 H5
Bellou-sur-Huisne (61) 83 K3
Belloy (60) 18 E6
Belloy-en-France (95) 37 K6
Belloy-en-Santerre (80) 19 F2
Belloy-Saint-Léonard (80) 17 H2
Belloy-sur-Somme (80) 17 K1
Belluire (17) 195 G4
Belmesnil (76) 15 K3
Belmont (25) 138 D6
Belmont (32) 266 E5
Belmont (38) 207 G5
Belmont (39) 155 H3
Belmont (52) 117 F6
Belmont (67) 70 A5
Belmont (70) 118 E4
Belmont-Bretenoux (46) 234 C2
Belmont-d'Azergues (69) 188 B6
Belmont-de-la-Loire (42) 187 H3
Belmont-lès-Darney (88) 117 K1
Belmont-Luthézieu (01) 190 A6
Belmont-Sainte-Foi (46) 250 C3
Belmont-sur-Buttant (88) 95 G5
Belmont-sur-Rance (12) 272 A4
Belmont-sur-Vair (88) 93 J5
Belmont-Tramonet (73) 207 K4
Belonchamp (70) 119 F5
Belpech (11) 288 E6
Belrain (55) 64 C3
Belrupt (88) 118 A1
Belrupt-en-Verdunois (55) 43 J5
Bélus (40) 264 A6
Belval (08) 22 C3
Belval (50) 30 E4
Belval (88) 95 J2
Belval-Bois-des-Dames (08) . . 42 E1
Belval-en-Argonne (51) 63 K2
Belval-sous-Châtillon (51) 40 D6
Belvédère (06) 311 A3
Belvédère-Campomoro (2A) . . 322 C3
Belverne (70) 119 F6
Belvès (24) 232 D3
Belvès-de-Castillon (33) 230 C1
Belvèze (82) 249 G3
Belvèze-du-Razès (11) 308 D1
Belvézet (30) 255 K6

Belvezet (48) 238 B6
Belvianes-et-Cavirac (11) 308 E4
Belvis (11) 308 D4
Belvoir (25) 139 F5
Belz (56) 100 B5
Bémécourt (27) 56 A3
Bénac (09) 307 H3
Bénac (65) 285 G6
Benagues (09) 307 J1
Benais (37) 126 D6
Bénaix (09) 308 B4
Bénaménil (54) 67 F6
Bénarville (76) 14 E4
Benassay (86) 162 C3
la Benâte (17) 177 J4
Benay (02) 20 A3
Benayes (19) 199 H5
Bendejun (06) 281 G2
Bendorf (68) 97 C6
Bénéjacq (64) 284 E5
Benerville-sur-Mer (14) 33 H4
Bénesse-lès-Dax (40) 264 B5
Bénesse-Maremne (40) 262 C5
Benest (16) 179 K4
Bénestroff (57) 68 A5
Bénesville (76) 15 H3
Benet (85) 161 F5
Beneuvre (21) 115 K6
Bénévent-et-Charbillac (05) . . . 242 E3
Bénévent-l'Abbaye (23) 182 B3
Beney-en-Woëvre (55) 65 G1
Benfeld (67) 70 E6
Bengy-sur-Craon (18) 150 A4
Bénifontaine (62) 6 B6
Béning-lès-Saint-Avold (57) . . . 68 B2
la Bénisson-Dieu (42) 186 E3
Bénivay-Ollon (26) 257 J3
Bennecourt (78) 57 H1
Bennetot (76) 14 E4
Benney (54) 94 B1
Bennwihr (68) 96 B3
Bénodet (29) 98 C3
Benoisey (21) 134 E2
Benoîtville (50) 28 B3
Benon (17) 177 G2
Bénonces (01) 207 G1
Bénouville (14) 33 F4
Bénouville (76) 14 C4
Benque (31) 287 G5
Benqué (65) 304 E1
Benque-Dessous-et-Dessus (31) . . 305 H5
Benquet (40) 265 G3
Bentayou-Sérée (64) 285 G3
Bény (01) 172 D6
le Bény-Bocage (14) 52 E2
Bény-sur-Mer (14) 32 D3
Béon (01) 190 B6
Béon (89) 112 D3
Béost (64) 303 H2
Bérat (31) 287 J3
Béraut (32) 267 G2
Berbérust-Lias (65) 304 E2
Berbezit (43) 219 K2
Berbiguières (24) 232 D2
Bercenay-en-Othe (10) 89 K6
Bercenay-le-Hayer (10) 89 G4
Berche (25) 139 G3
Berchères-les-Pierres (28) 85 G4
Berchères-Saint-Germain (28) . . 85 G2
Berchères-sur-Vesgre (28) . . . 57 G4
Berck (62) 8 E1
Bercloux (17) 195 H1
Berd'Huis (61) 83 K4
Berdoues (32) 286 B2
Bérelles (59) 13 J3
Bérengeville-la-Campagne (27) . . 35 H6
Berentzwiller (68) 97 C4
Béréziat (01) 172 B6
Berfay (72) 107 K3
Berg (67) 68 C5
Berg-sur-Moselle (57) 27 H3
Bergbieten (67) 70 C5
Bergerac (24) 231 H2
Bergères (10) 91 G6
Bergères-lès-Vertus (51) 62 A3
Bergères-sous-Montmirail (51) . . 61 G3
Bergesserin (71) 171 G5
Bergheim (68) 96 C2
Bergholtz (68) 96 B6
Bergholtzzell (68) 96 B6
Bergicourt (80) 17 J4
Bergnicourt (08) 41 H2
Bergonne (63) 202 E5
Bergouey (40) 264 E5
Bergouey-Viellenave (64) 283 F2
Bergueneuse (62) 5 G6
Bergues (59) 3 H2
Bergues-sur-Sambre (02) 12 E6
Berhet (22) 48 B3
Bérig-Vintrange (57) 68 A4
Bérigny (50) 31 J3
Berjou (61) 53 H3
Berlaimont (59) 13 F4
Berlancourt (02) 20 B3
Berlancourt (60) 19 H5
Berlats (81) 271 J5
Berles-le-Cauroy (62) 10 B3
Berles-au-Bois (62) 10 D4
Berles-Monchel (62) 10 C2
la Berlière (08) 23 F6
Berling (57) 69 F6
Berlise (02) 21 H5
Berlou (34) 291 H2
Bermerain (59) 12 D3

Berméricourt (51) 40 E3
Bermeries (59) 13 F3
Bermering (57) 68 A5
Bermesnil (80) 17 F2
Bermicourt (62) 9 K1
Bermont (90) 139 H1
Bermonville (76) 15 F5
Bernac (16) 179 G4
Bernac (81) 270 C2
Bernac-Debat (65) 285 H6
Bernac-Dessus (65) 285 H6
Bernadets (64) 284 D5
Bernadets-Debat (65) 286 A3
Bernadets-Dessus (65) 285 H6
le Bernard (85) 159 H4
la Bernardière (85) 142 B2
Bernardswiller (67) 70 C5
Bernardvillé (67) 70 B6
Bernâtre (80) 9 J4
Bernaville (80) 9 K5
Bernay (27) 34 D6
Bernay (72) 106 B1
Bernay-en-Ponthieu (80) 9 F3
Bernay-Saint-Martin (17) 177 J4
Bernay-Vilbert (77) 60 A6
Berné (56) 99 K2
Bernécourt (54) 65 H3
Bernède (32) 265 K5
la Bernerie-en-Retz (44) 140 D2
Bernes (80) 19 J2
Bernes-sur-Oise (95) 37 J5
Bernesq (14) 31 J1
Berneuil (16) 212 C1
Berneuil (17) 195 G3
Berneuil (80) 9 K5
Berneuil (87) 181 F4
Berneuil-en-Bray (60) 37 G3
Berneuil-sur-Aisne (60) 39 F4
Berneval-le-Grand (76) 16 A1
Berneville (62) 10 D3
Bernex (74) 175 H5
Bernienville (27) 35 H6
Bernières (76) 14 E5
Bernières-d'Ailly (14) 54 B2
Bernières-le-Patry (14) 53 F3
Bernières-sur-Mer (14) 32 D3
Bernières-sur-Seine (27) 36 A4
Bernieulles (62) 4 C5
Bernin (38) 224 C2
Bernis (30) 275 G4
Bernolsheim (67) 25 A4
Bernon (10) 114 A3
Bernos-Beaulac (33) 246 D2
Bernot (02) 20 C2
Bernouil (89) 113 K4
Bernouville (27) 36 D4
Bernwiller (68) 97 B3
Berny-en-Santerre (80) 19 F2
Berny-Rivière (02) 39 G2
Bérou-la-Mulotière (28) 56 C5
Berrac (32) 267 H1
Berre-les-Alpes (06) 281 H2
Berre-l'Étang (13) 296 A2
Berriac (11) 290 B5
Berrias-et-Casteljau (07) 255 H2
Berric (56) 101 H5
Berrie (86) 144 C3
Berrien (29) 75 G1
Berrieux (02) 40 C3
Berrogain-Laruns (64) 283 H4
Berru (51) 41 G4
Berrwiller (68) 97 B1
Berry-au-Bac (02) 40 D2
Berry-Bouy (18) 149 F2
le Bersac (05) 258 D1
Bersac-sur-Rivalier (87) 181 J4
Bersaillin (39) 155 H5
Berson (33) 211 H4
Berstett (67) 70 E2
Berstheim (67) 69 K6
Bert (03) 186 B1
Bertangles (80) 18 B1
Bertaucourt-Epourdon (02) . . . 20 B5
Berteaucourt-les-Dames (80) . . 9 K6
Berteaucourt-lès-Thennes (80) . . 18 C3
Bertheauville (76) 15 F3
Berthecourt (60) 37 J3
Berthegon (86) 145 F5
Berthelange (25) 155 K1
Berthelming (57) 67 J3
Berthen (59) 6 A2
Berthenay (37) 127 G5
Berthenicourt (02) 20 B3
Berthenonville (27) 36 D5
la Berthenoux (36) 166 C4
Berthez (33) 230 B6
Bertholène (12) 252 D2
Berthouville (27) 34 D5
Bertignat (63) 203 K4
Bertignolles (10) 115 F1
Bertincourt (62) 11 G5
Bertoncourt (08) 22 A6
Bertrambois (54) 67 J6
Bertrancourt (80) 10 C5
Bertrange (57) 45 F3
Bertre (81) 270 C6
Bertren (65) 305 J2
Bertreville (76) 15 F3
Bertreville-Saint-Ouen (76) . . . 15 K3
Bertric-Burée (24) 213 G3
Bertrichamps (54) 95 G2
Bertricourt (02) 40 E2
Bertrimont (76) 15 J5
Bertrimoutier (88) 95 J3

Bertry (59) 12 C5
Béru (89) 113 K5
Béruges (86) 162 D3
Bérulle (10) 89 G6
Bérus (72) 82 C3
Berville (76) 15 H4
Berville (95) 37 G5
Berville-en-Roumois (27) 35 F3
Berville-la-Campagne (27) 56 B1
Berville-sur-Mer (27) 34 B2
Berville-sur-Seine (76) 35 G1
Berviller-en-Moselle (57) 45 K3
Berzé-la-Ville (71) 171 H6
Berzieux (51) 42 C5
Berzy-le-Sec (02) 39 J3
la Besace (08) 23 F6
Besain (39) 155 K6
Besançon (25) 138 A6
Bésayes (26) 222 E6
Bescat (64) 284 C6
Bésignan (26) 257 K3
Bésingrand (64) 284 B3
Beslon (50) 52 B3
Besmé (02) 19 J6
Besmont (02) 21 H2
Besnans (70) 138 C3
Besné (44) 122 B1
Besneville (50) 28 C6
Besny-et-Loizy (02) 20 C5
Bessac (16) 196 C6
Bessais-le-Fromental (18) 167 J1
Bessamorel (43) 220 E4
Bessan (34) 292 C4
Bessancourt (95) 58 D1
Bessans (73) 226 D1
Bessay (85) 160 A3
Bessay-sur-Allier (03) 168 A4
Besse (15) 217 G5
Bessé (16) 179 F5
Besse (24) 232 E4
Besse (38) 225 F4
Besse-et-Saint-Anastaise (63) . . 202 B5
Bessé-sur-Braye (72) 107 K5
Besse-sur-Issole (83) 298 A5
Bessède-de-Sault (11) 308 D5
Bessèges (30) 255 H3
Bessenay (69) 205 H2
Bessens (82) 268 E3
Besset (09) 308 A1
Bessey (42) 222 A4
Bessey-en-Chaume (21) 153 K2
Bessey-la-Cour (21) 153 J2
Bessey-lès-Cîteaux (21) 154 D1
la Besseyre-Saint-Mary (43) . . 219 H6
Bessières (31) 269 J4
Bessines (79) 161 G6
Bessines-sur-Gartempe (87) . . 181 J3
Bessins (38) 223 F3
Besson (03) 168 D5
Bessoncourt (90) 119 J6
Bessonies (46) 234 B3
les Bessons (48) 237 F3
Bessuéjouls (12) 236 A6
Bessy (10) 90 A1
Bessy-sur-Cure (89) 133 H2
Bestiac (09) 308 A5
Bétaille (46) 234 A1
Betaucourt (70) 117 J3
Betbèze (65) 286 A4
Betbezer-d'Armagnac (40) . . . 266 A1
Betcave-Aguin (32) 286 E2
Betchat (09) 306 C1
Bétête (23) 166 C6
Béthancourt-en-Valois (60) . . . 38 E4
Béthancourt-en-Vaux (02) 19 J5
Béthelainville (55) 43 G5
Béthemont-la-Forêt (95) 58 D1
Béthencourt (59) 12 C4
Béthencourt-sur-Mer (80) 8 D5
Béthencourt-sur-Somme (80) . . 19 G3
Bétheniville (51) 41 J3
Bétheny (51) 41 F4
Béthincourt (55) 43 G4
Béthines (86) 164 B4
Béthisy-Saint-Martin (60) 38 D4
Béthisy-Saint-Pierre (60) 38 D4
Bethmale (09) 306 C4
Bethon (51) 61 G6
Béthon (72) 82 D4
Bethoncourt (25) 139 H2
Béthonsart (62) 10 C1
Béthonvilliers (28) 84 B6
Bethonvilliers (90) 119 J6
Béthune (62) 6 A5
Bétignicourt (10) 90 E3
Beton-Bazoches (77) 60 D5
Betoncourt-lès-Brotte (70) 118 C5
Betoncourt-Saint-Pancras (70) . . 118 B3
Betoncourt-sur-Mance (70) . . . 117 H4
Bétous (32) 266 C5
Betplan (32) 285 J3
Betpouey (65) 304 C4
Betpouy (65) 286 B4
Bétracq (64) 285 G1
Betschdorf (67) 25 B3
Bettainvillers (54) 44 C3
Bettancourt-la-Ferrée (52) 63 K6
Bettancourt-la-Longue (51) . . . 63 J3
Bettange (57) 45 H3
Bettant (01) 189 H5
Bettborn (57) 67 J3
Bettegney-Saint-Brice (88) . . . 94 C4

Bettelainville (57) 45 G4
Bettembos (80) 17 G3
Bettencourt-Rivière (80) 9 H6
Bettencourt-Saint-Ouen (80) 9 J6
Bettendorf (68) 97 B4
Bettes (65) 304 D1
Betteville (76) 15 G6
Bettignies (59) 13 H2
Betting (57) 68 B2
Bettlach (68) 97 D5
Betton (35) 79 G3
Betton-Bettonet (73) 208 E4
Bettoncourt (88) 94 A3
Bettrechies (59) 13 F2
Bettviller (57) 69 F3
Bettwiller (67) 67 K2
Betz (60) 39 F5
Betz-le-Château (37) 146 C4
Beugin (62) 10 C1
Beugnâtre (62) 11 F5
Beugneux (02) 39 K4
Beugnies (59) 13 H4
le Beugnon (79) 161 G3
Beugnon (89) 113 J2
Beugny (62) 11 G5
Beuil (06) 261 G5
le Beulay (88) 95 K3
Beulotte-Saint-Laurent (70) 119 F3
Beure (25) 137 K6
Beurey (10) 90 E6
Beurey-Bauguay (21) 134 E6
Beurey-sur-Saulx (55) 63 K4
Beurières (63) 204 A6
Beurizot (21) 135 F5
Beurlay (17) 177 G6
Beurville (52) 91 H4
Beussent (62) 4 C5
Beuste (64) 284 E5
Beutal (25) 139 F3
Beutin (62) 4 B6
Beuvardes (02) 40 A5
Beuveille (54) 26 C3
Beuvezin (54) 93 J3
Beuvillers (14) 33 K5
Beuvillers (54) 26 E4
Beuvrages (59) 12 D1
Beuvraignes (80) 19 F5
Beuvrequen (62) 2 B4
Beuvrigny (50) 31 J5
Beuvron (58) 133 F6
Beuvron-en-Auge (14) 33 H5
Beuvry (62) 6 A4
Beuvry-la-Forêt (59) 7 F6
Beux (57) 66 B1
Beuxes (86) 145 F2
Beuzec-Cap-Sizun (29) 73 C2
Beuzeville (27) 34 B3
Beuzeville-au-Plain (50) 29 F5
Beuzeville-la-Bastille (50) 29 F6
Beuzeville-la-Grenier (76) 14 D5
Beuzeville-la-Guérard (76) 15 F4
Beuzevillette (76) 14 E6
Bévenais (38) 207 G6
Beveuge (70) 138 E2
Béville-le-Comte (28) 85 J3
Bévillers (59) 12 C4
Bevons (04) 259 F4
Bévy (21) 154 A1
Bey (01) 188 C2
Bey (71) 154 B6
Bey-sur-Seille (54) 66 C3
Beychac-et-Caillau (33) 229 K1
Beylongue (40) 264 D2
Beynac (87) 198 E2
Beynac-et-Cazenac (24) 232 E2
Beynat (19) 216 A4
Beynes (04) 259 J6
Beynes (78) 58 A3
Beynost (01) 206 D1
Beyrède-Jumet (65) 305 F3
Beyren-lès-Sierck (57) 27 H3
Beyrie-en-Béarn (64) 284 C3
Beyrie-sur-Joyeuse (64) 283 F4
Beyries (40) 265 F6
Beyssac (19) 215 H1
Beyssenac (19) 215 G1
le Bez (81) 271 H6
Bez-et-Esparon (30) 273 J2
Bézac (09) 288 D6
Bezalles (77) 60 D6
Bézancourt (76) 36 C2
Bezange-la-Grande (54) 66 C4
Bezange-la-Petite (57) 66 E4
Bezannes (51) 40 E4
Bézaudun-les-Alpes (06) 280 E2
Bézaudun-sur-Bîne (26) 241 F5
Bezaumont (54) 65 K3
Bèze (21) 136 C3
Bézenac (24) 232 E2
Bézenet (03) 184 C1
Bézéril (32) 287 F1
Béziers (34) 292 A4
Bezinghem (62) 4 C4
Bezins-Garraux (31) 305 J3
la Bezole (11) 308 D3
Bezolles (32) 267 F3
Bezons (95) 58 D3
Bezonvaux (55) 43 J4
Bezouce (30) 275 J3
Bézouotte (21) 136 D4
Bézu-la-Forêt (27) 36 C2
Bézu-le-Guéry (02) 60 C1
Bézu-Saint-Éloi (27) 36 C2
Bézu-Saint-Germain (02) 39 K6
Bézues-Bajon (32) 286 D3
Biache-Saint-Vaast (62) 11 G2

Biaches (80) 19 G1
Bians-les-Usiers (25) 156 E3
Biard (86) 162 E3
Biarne (39) 155 G1
Biarre (39) 19 G4
Biarritz (64) 282 A1
Biarrotte (40) 262 D6
Biars-sur-Cère (46) 234 B1
Bias (40) 244 C4
Bias (47) 248 C2
Biaudos (40) 262 C6
Bibiche (57) 27 K4
Biblisheim (67) 25 A3
Bibost (69) 205 H1
Bichancourt (02) 19 K6
Biches (58) 151 J4
Bickenholtz (57) 67 K3
Bicqueley (54) 65 H6
Bidache (64) 283 F1
Bidarray (64) 282 C4
Bidart (64) 282 A2
Bidestroff (57) 67 G2
Biding (57) 68 B3
Bidon (07) 256 B2
Bidos (64) 284 A5
Biécourt (88) 93 J4
Biederthal (68) 97 D6
Bief (25) 139 H4
Bief-des-Maisons (39) 174 B1
Bief-du-Fourg (39) 156 C5
Biefmorin (39) 155 H4
Biefvillers-lès-Bapaume (62) 11 F5
Bielle (64) 303 H1
Biencourt (80) 17 F1
Biencourt-sur-Orge (55) 92 C1
Bienville (60) 38 C2
Bienville-la-Petite (54) 66 D5
Bienvillers-au-Bois (62) 10 D4
Biermes (08) 41 J1
Biermont (60) 18 E6
Bierné (53) 105 G5
Bierne (59) 3 H2
Bierre-lès-Semur (21) 134 D4
Bierry-les-Belles-Fontaines (89) 134 C2
Biert (09) 307 H1
Bierville (76) 16 B6
Biesheim (68) 96 E4
Biesles (52) 116 C1
Bietlenheim (67) 25 A5
Bieujac (33) 230 B6
Bieuxy (02) 39 H2
Bieuzy (56) 100 D1
Biéville (50) 31 K4
Biéville-Beuville (14) 32 E4
Biéville-Quétiéville (14) 33 H6
Bièvres (02) 40 C1
Bièvres (08) 23 J4
Bièvres (91) 58 D5
Biffontaine (88) 95 G5
Biganos (33) 228 D4
Bignac (16) 196 D2
Bignan (56) 101 F2
Bignay (17) 177 J5
la Bigne (14) 53 F1
Bignicourt (08) 41 J2
Bignicourt-sur-Marne (51) 63 F5
Bignicourt-sur-Saulx (51) 63 H4
le Bignon (44) 141 J2
le Bignon-du-Maine (53) 105 G3
le Bignon-Mirabeau (45) 111 K1
Bignoux (86) 163 G3
Bigorno (2B) 319 G3
la Bigottière (53) 80 E5
Bihorel (76) 35 J2
Bihucourt (62) 11 F5
Bilhères (64) 303 G1
Bilia (2A) 322 D3
Bilieu (38) 207 H5
Billac (19) 234 B1
Billancelles (28) 84 D2
Billancourt (80) 19 G4
les Billanges (87) 181 K5
les Billaux (33) 212 A6
Billé (35) 80 A4
Billecul (39) 156 C6
Billère (64) 284 C4
Billey (21) 155 F1
Billezois (03) 186 A2
Billiat (01) 190 C3
Billième (73) 208 A2
Billière (31) 305 H5
Billiers (56) 121 H2
Billio (56) 101 G2
Billom (63) 203 F3
Billy (03) 185 J2
Billy (14) 33 F6
Billy (41) 129 G6
Billy-Berclau (62) 6 C5
Billy-Chevannes (58) 151 G4
Billy-le-Grand (51) 41 H6
Billy-lès-Chanceaux (21) 135 H2
Billy-Montigny (62) 11 G1
Billy-sur-Aisne (02) 39 K3
Billy-sur-Oisy (58) 132 E3
Billy-sur-Ourcq (02) 39 J5
Biltzheim (68) 96 C5
Bilwisheim (67) 70 E1
Bimont (62) 4 D5
Binarville (51) 42 D4
Binas (41) 109 G4
Bindernheim (67) 96 E1
Binges (21) 136 C5
Binic (22) 49 F5
Bining (57) 69 F3

Biniville (50) 28 E5
Binos (31) 305 H3
Binson-et-Orquigny (51) 40 D3
Bio (46) 234 B3
Biol (38) 207 G5
la Biolle (73) 208 B1
Biollet (63) 184 B5
Bion (50) 52 D6
Bioncourt (57) 66 C3
Bionville (54) 95 J1
Bionville-sur-Nied (57) 45 H5
Biot (06) 281 F5
le Biot (74) 175 G6
Bioule (82) 250 B6
Bioussac (16) 179 H4
Biozat (03) 185 H4
Birac (16) 196 C4
Birac (33) 246 D1
Birac-sur-Trec (47) 247 H1
Biran (32) 267 G5
Biras (24) 213 K2
Biriatou (64) 263 A2
Birieux (01) 188 E5
Birkenwald (67) 70 B2
Biron (17) 195 H4
Biron (24) 232 B5
Biron (64) 283 K2
Biscarrosse (40) 244 D1
Bischheim (67) 25 A6
Bischholtz (67) 69 J5
Bischoffsheim (67) 70 D4
Bischwihr (68) 96 C4
Bischwiller (67) 25 B4
Bisel (68) 97 B5
Bisinchi (2B) 319 H3
Bislée (55) 64 E3
Bissert (67) 68 D5
Bisseuil (51) 62 A1
Bissey-la-Côte (21) 115 H3
Bissey-la-Pierre (21) 114 E4
Bissey-sous-Cruchaud (71) 171 H1
Bissezeele (59) 3 H3
Bissières (14) 33 G6
Bissy-la-Mâconnaise (71) 171 J4
Bissy-sous-Uxelles (71) 171 H3
Bissy-sur-Fley (71) 171 G2
Bisten-en-Lorraine (57) 45 J4
Bistroff (57) 68 A4
Bitche (57) 69 G3
Bitry (58) 132 B3
Bitry (60) 39 G2
Bitschhoffen (67) 69 J5
Bitschwiller-lès-Thann (68) 119 K4
Bivès (32) 268 A3
Biviers (38) 224 B2
Biville (50) 28 B2
Biville-la-Baignarde (76) 15 K4
Biville-la-Rivière (76) 15 J3
Biville-sur-Mer (76) 16 B1
Bivilliers (61) 83 J1
Bizanet (11) 291 G6
Bizanos (64) 284 D4
Bize (52) 117 F4
Bize (65) 305 G2
Bize-Minervois (11) 291 G4
Bizeneuille (03) 167 J5
Biziat (01) 188 D2
Bizonnes (38) 207 G5
le Bizot (25) 157 H1
les Bizots (71) 170 E1
Bizou (61) 83 K2
Bizous (65) 305 G1
Blacé (69) 188 A4
Blacourt (60) 36 E2
Blacqueville (76) 15 H6
Blacy (51) 63 F5
Blacy (89) 134 A2
Blaesheim (67) 70 E4
Blagnac (31) 269 G6
Blagny (08) 23 H5
Blagny-sur-Vingeanne (21) 136 D4
Blaignac (33) 230 C6
Blaignan (33) 210 E1
Blain (44) 102 E6
Blaincourt-lès-Précy (60) 37 K5
Blaincourt-sur-Aube (10) 90 E3
Blainville-Crevon (76) 35 K1
Blainville-sur-l'Eau (54) 66 C4
Blainville-sur-Mer (50) 30 C4
Blainville-sur-Orne (14) 32 E4
Blaise-sous-Arzillières (51) 63 F5
Blaison-Gohier (49) 125 J4
Blaisy (52) 91 K6
Blaisy-Bas (21) 135 H5
Blaisy-Haut (21) 135 H5
Blajan (31) 286 D5
Blamont (25) 139 H4
Blâmont (54) 67 G6
Blan (81) 289 H2
le Blanc (36) 164 C3
le Blanc-Mesnil (93) 59 F2
Blancafort (18) 131 G3
Blancey (21) 134 E5
Blancfossé (60) 17 K5
Blanche-Église (57) 67 F3
Blanchefosse-et-Bay (08) 21 J3
Blancherupt (67) 70 A5
Blandainville (28) 84 E4
Blandas (30) 273 J2
Blandin (38) 207 G5
Blandouet (53) 105 J2
Blandy (77) 87 J1
Blandy (91) 86 D4
Blangerval-Blangermont (62) 9 K2
Blangy-le-Château (14) 34 A4

Blangy-sous-Poix (80) 17 J3
Blangy-sur-Bresle (76) 16 E1
Blangy-sur-Ternoise (62) 9 K1
Blangy-Tronville (80) 18 C2
Blannay (89) 133 J3
Blanot (21) 152 E1
Blanot (71) 171 J4
Blanquefort (32) 268 A5
Blanquefort (33) 229 G1
Blanquefort-sur-Briolance (47) 232 C5
Blanzac (43) 220 B4
Blanzac (87) 181 F3
Blanzac-lès-Matha (17) 178 B6
Blanzac-Porcheresse (16) 196 C5
Blanzaguet-Saint-Cybard (16) 197 F6
Blanzat (63) 202 D1
Blanzay (86) 179 H2
Blanzay-sur-Boutonne (17) 178 A4
Blanzée (55) 43 K5
Blanzy (71) 170 E2
Blanzy-la-Salonnaise (08) 41 G1
Blanzy-lès-Fismes (02) 40 B3
Blargies (60) 17 F5
Blarians (25) 138 B4
Blaringhem (59) 5 H3
Blars (46) 234 A6
Blaru (78) 57 G1
Blasimon (33) 230 C3
Blaslay (86) 162 E1
Blassac (43) 219 H4
Blaudeix (23) 183 F2
Blausasc (06) 281 F4
Blauvac (84) 257 J6
Blauzac (30) 275 G2
Blavignac (48) 237 G2
Blavozy (43) 220 D5
Blay (14) 31 K1
Blaye (33) 211 G4
Blaye-les-Mines (81) 270 D1
Blaymont (47) 248 E3
Blaziert (32) 267 G2
Blécourt (52) 92 A3
Blécourt (59) 11 J3
Bleigny-le-Carreau (89) 113 H5
Blémerey (54) 67 F6
Blémerey (88) 93 K3
Blendecques (62) 5 G3
Bléneau (89) 132 A1
Blennes (77) 88 B5
Blénod-lès-Pont-à-Mousson (54) 65 J2
Blénod-lès-Toul (54) 65 H6
Bléquin (62) 4 E4
Blérancourt (02) 39 G1
Bléré (37) 128 B5
Bléruais (35) 78 C4
Blésignac (33) 230 A3
Blesle (43) 218 E2
Blesme (51) 63 H5
Blesmes (02) 60 E1
Blessac (23) 183 F5
Blessey (21) 135 G3
Blessonville (52) 115 K2
Blessy (62) 5 H4
Blet (18) 149 K5
Bletterans (39) 173 F1
Bleurville (88) 117 J1
Bleury (28) 85 J2
Blevaincourt (88) 93 G6
Blèves (72) 83 F2
le Bleymard (48) 254 D1
Blicourt (60) 17 J6
Blienschwiller (67) 70 C6
Blies-Ebersing (57) 68 E2
Blies-Guersviller (57) 68 D2
Bliesbruck (57) 68 E2
Blieux (04) 279 H2
Blignicourt (10) 91 F2
Bligny (10) 91 G6
Bligny (51) 40 D5
Bligny-le-Sec (21) 135 H4
Bligny-lès-Beaune (21) 154 A4
Bligny-sur-Ouche (21) 153 J2
Blincourt (60) 38 C3
Blingel (62) 9 K1
Blis-et-Born (24) 214 C4
Blismes (58) 152 A2
Blodelsheim (68) 96 E6
Blois (41) 128 E2
Blois-sur-Seille (39) 155 J6
Blomac (11) 290 D6
Blomard (03) 184 E1
Blombay (08) 22 A4
Blond (87) 180 E4
Blondefontaine (70) 117 J4
Blonville-sur-Mer (14) 33 H3
Blosseville (76) 15 G2
Blosville (50) 29 F6
Blot-l'Église (63) 184 E4
Blotzheim (68) 97 D5
Blou (49) 126 B5
Blousson-Sérian (32) 285 J2
la Bloutière (50) 52 B2
Bloye (74) 190 D6
Bluffy (74) 191 G6
Blumeray (52) 91 J3
Blussangeaux (25) 139 F3
Blussans (25) 139 F3
Blye (39) 173 H2
Blyes (01) 189 G6
le Bô (14) 53 J1
Bobigny (93) 59 F3
Bobital (22) 50 C6
Bocé (49) 126 B3
le Bocasse (76) 15 K5
Bocognano (2A) 320 E3
Bocquegney (88) 94 C5

Bocquencé (61) 55 G3
le Bodéo (22) 76 E2
Bodilis (29) 46 D5
Boé (47) 248 B5
Boëcé (61) 83 G2
Boëge (74) 191 H1
Boeil-Bezing (64) 284 E5
Boën (42) 204 C2
Bœrsch (67) 70 C4
Boeschepe (59) 6 A2
Bœseghem (59) 5 J4
Bœsenbiesen (67) 96 E2
Boëssé-le-Sec (72) 107 H1
Boësses (45) 111 F1
Bœurs-en-Othe (89) 113 H1
Boffles (62) 9 K3
Boffres (07) 240 A1
Bogève (74) 191 J2
Bogny-sur-Meuse (08) 22 D2
Bogy (07) 222 B2
Bohain-en-Vermandois (02) 12 C6
Bohal (56) 101 J4
la Bohalle (49) 125 J4
Bohars (29) 72 D4
Bohas-Meyriat-Rignat (01) 189 H3
Boigneville (91) 86 E4
Boigny-sur-Bionne (45) 110 B4
Boinville-en-Mantois (78) 57 J2
Boinville-en-Woëvre (55) 44 A4
Boinville-le-Gaillard (78) 86 A2
Boinvilliers (78) 57 H3
Boiry-Becquerelle (62) 11 F4
Boiry-Notre-Dame (62) 11 G3
Boiry-Saint-Martin (62) 10 E4
Boiry-Sainte-Rictrude (62) 10 E4
Bois (17) 195 G5
le Bois (73) 209 H5
Bois-Anzeray (27) 55 J2
Bois-Arnault (27) 55 K4
Bois-Bernard (62) 11 G1
Bois-Colombes (92) 58 D3
Bois-d'Amont (39) 174 C3
Bois-d'Arcy (78) 58 B4
Bois-d'Arcy (89) 133 H3
Bois-de-Céné (85) 141 F4
Bois-de-Champ (88) 95 G4
Bois-de-Gand (39) 155 G5
Bois-de-la-Pierre (31) 287 J4
Bois-d'Ennebourg (76) 35 K2
le Bois-d'Oingt (69) 188 A6
Bois-Grenier (59) 6 C4
Bois-Guilbert (76) 16 C6
Bois-Guillaume (76) 35 H1
le Bois-Hellain (27) 34 B4
Bois-Héroult (76) 16 C6
Bois-Herpin (91) 86 D4
Bois-Himont (76) 15 G6
Bois-Jérôme-Saint-Ouen (27) 36 C6
Bois-le-Roi (27) 57 F3
Bois-le-Roi (77) 87 H2
Bois-lès-Pargny (02) 20 D4
Bois-l'Évêque (76) 35 K2
Bois-Normand-près-Lyre (27) 55 J3
le Bois-Plage-en-Ré (17) 158 C5
le Bois-Robert (76) 16 A2
Bois-Sainte-Marie (71) 170 E6
Boisbergues (80) 9 K4
Boisbreteau (16) 212 B2
Boiscommun (45) 110 E2
Boisdinghem (62) 5 F3
Boisdon (77) 60 C5
Boisemont (27) 36 B4
Boisemont (95) 58 B1
Boisgasson (28) 108 D2
Boisgervilly (35) 78 C3
Boisjean (62) 9 F1
le Boisle (80) 9 H3
Boisleux-au-Mont (62) 10 E4
Boisleux-Saint-Marc (62) 11 F4
Boismé (79) 143 J6
Boismont (54) 26 C4
Boismont (80) 8 E4
Boismorand (45) 111 H5
Boisney (27) 34 D5
Boisredon (17) 211 H3
Boisroger (50) 30 D3
Boissay (76) 36 A1
la Boisse (01) 206 C1
Boisse (24) 231 K4
Boisse-Penchot (12) 235 F5
Boisseau (41) 108 E5
Boisseaux (45) 86 B5
Boissède (31) 287 F3
Boissei-la-Lande (61) 54 D5
Boisserolles (79) 178 A3
Boisseron (34) 274 E4
Boisset (15) 235 F3
Boisset (34) 290 E3
Boisset (43) 220 D2
Boisset-et-Gaujac (30) 255 G6
Boisset-lès-Montrond (42) 204 E4
Boisset-les-Prévanches (27) 56 E2
Boisset-Saint-Priest (42) 204 D5
Boissets (78) 57 H3
Boissettes (77) 87 G2
Boisseuil (87) 199 F2
Boisseuilh (24) 215 F3
Boissey (01) 172 A5
Boissey (14) 54 D1
Boissey-le-Châtel (27) 34 E4
Boissezon (81) 290 B1
Boissia (39) 173 H3
la Boissière (14) 33 J4
la Boissière (27) 57 F2
la Boissière (34) 273 K5

354

la Boissière (39) . . . 173 G5
la Boissière (53) . . . 104 C5
la Boissière-d'Ans (24) . . . 214 D3
la Boissière-de-Montaigu (85) . . . 142 B4
la Boissière-des-Landes (85) . . . 159 H3
la Boissière-du-Doré (44) . . . 124 A6
la Boissière-École (78) . . . 57 H6
la Boissière-en-Gâtine (79) . . . 161 J3
la Boissière-sur-Èvre (49) . . . 124 B5
Boissières (30) . . . 275 F4
Boissières (46) . . . 233 H6
Boissise-la-Bertrand (77) . . . 87 G2
Boissise-le-Roi (77) . . . 87 G2
Boissy-aux-Cailles (77) . . . 87 F4
Boissy-en-Drouais (28) . . . 56 E5
Boissy-Fresnoy (60) . . . 38 E5
Boissy-la-Rivière (91) . . . 86 C4
Boissy-l'Aillerie (95) . . . 37 G6
Boissy-Lamberville (27) . . . 34 D5
Boissy-le-Bois (60) . . . 37 H4
Boissy-le-Châtel (77) . . . 60 C4
Boissy-le-Cutté (91) . . . 86 D3
Boissy-le-Repos (51) . . . 61 G3
Boissy-le-Sec (91) . . . 86 C2
Boissy-lès-Perche (28) . . . 56 A5
Boissy-Maugis (61) . . . 83 J3
Boissy-Mauvoisin (78) . . . 57 H2
Boissy-Saint-Léger (94) . . . 59 G5
Boissy-sans-Avoir (78) . . . 57 K4
Boissy-sous-Saint-Yon (91) . . . 86 D1
Boistrudan (35) . . . 79 J6
Boisville-la-Saint-Père (28) . . . 85 J4
Boisyvon (50) . . . 52 C3
Boitron (61) . . . 82 K1
Boitron (77) . . . 60 D3
Bolandoz (25) . . . 156 C3
Bolazec (29) . . . 47 J6
Bolbec (76) . . . 14 E6
Bollène (84) . . . 256 D3
la Bollène-Vésubie (06) . . . 311 A3
Bolleville (50) . . . 30 D1
Bolleville (76) . . . 14 E5
Bollezeele (59) . . . 3 H3
Bollwiller (68) . . . 97 B1
Bologne (52) . . . 92 B5
Bolozon (01) . . . 189 J2
Bolquère (66) . . . 313 J4
Bolsenheim (67) . . . 70 E5
Bombon (77) . . . 87 K1
Bommes (33) . . . 229 K5
Bommiers (36) . . . 148 C6
Bompas (09) . . . 307 J4
Bompas (66) . . . 315 H1
Bomy (62) . . . 5 G5
Bon-Encontre (47) . . . 248 C5
Bona (58) . . . 151 G3
Bonac-Irazein (09) . . . 306 B4
Bonas (32) . . . 267 G4
Bonboillon (70) . . . 137 G5
Boncé (28) . . . 85 G5
Bonchamp-lès-Laval (53) . . . 105 F1
Boncourt (02) . . . 21 G5
Boncourt (27) . . . 56 E1
Boncourt (28) . . . 57 G3
Boncourt (54) . . . 44 C5
Boncourt-le-Bois (21) . . . 154 B2
Boncourt-sur-Meuse (55) . . . 64 E4
Bondaroy (45) . . . 86 D6
Bondeval (25) . . . 139 H3
Bondigoux (31) . . . 269 H3
les Bondons (48) . . . 254 C2
Bondoufle (91) . . . 86 E1
Bondues (59) . . . 6 E3
Bondy (93) . . . 59 F3
Bongheat (63) . . . 203 G3
le Bonhomme (68) . . . 95 K5
Bonifacio (2A) . . . 323 G6
Bonlier (60) . . . 37 H1
Bonlieu (39) . . . 173 K2
Bonlieu-sur-Roubion (26) . . . 240 C5
Bonloc (64) . . . 282 D3
Bonnac (09) . . . 288 D6
Bonnac (15) . . . 218 E3
Bonnac-la-Côte (87) . . . 181 H6
Bonnal (25) . . . 138 D2
Bonnard (89) . . . 113 F4
Bonnat (23) . . . 182 D1
Bonnaud (39) . . . 172 E2
Bonnay (25) . . . 138 A5
Bonnay (71) . . . 171 H3
Bonnay (80) . . . 18 C1
Bonne (74) . . . 191 H2
Bonnebosq (14) . . . 33 J4
Bonnecourt (52) . . . 116 E3
Bonnée (45) . . . 110 E5
Bonnefamille (38) . . . 206 D4
Bonnefoi (61) . . . 55 H6
Bonnefond (19) . . . 200 C5
Bonnefont (65) . . . 286 A5
Bonnefontaine (39) . . . 173 H1
Bonnegarde (40) . . . 264 E6
Bonneil (02) . . . 60 D1
Bonnelles (78) . . . 86 B1
Bonnemain (35) . . . 51 F5
Bonnemaison (14) . . . 53 H1
Bonnemazon (65) . . . 304 E1
Bonnencontre (21) . . . 154 D2
Bonnes (16) . . . 212 E3
Bonnes (86) . . . 163 H3
Bonnesvalyn (02) . . . 39 J6
Bonnet (55) . . . 92 D1
Bonnétable (72) . . . 83 G6
Bonnétage (25) . . . 139 G6
Bonnetan (33) . . . 229 J2
Bonneuil (16) . . . 196 B4
Bonneuil (36) . . . 164 D6

Bonneuil-en-France (95) . . . 59 F2
Bonneuil-en-Valois (60) . . . 39 F4
Bonneuil-les-Eaux (60) . . . 18 A5
Bonneuil-Matours (86) . . . 163 H2
Bonneuil-sur-Marne (94) . . . 59 F4
Bonneval (28) . . . 85 F6
Bonneval (43) . . . 220 A2
Bonneval (73) . . . 209 G4
Bonneval-sur-Arc (73) . . . 193 D6
Bonnevaux (25) . . . 156 D5
Bonnevaux (30) . . . 255 G2
Bonnevaux (74) . . . 175 H6
Bonnevaux-le-Prieuré (25) . . . 156 D1
Bonneveau (41) . . . 107 K5
Bonnevent-Velloreille (70) . . . 137 J4
Bonneville (16) . . . 196 C1
la Bonneville (50) . . . 28 E5
Bonneville (74) . . . 191 H3
Bonneville (80) . . . 10 A5
Bonneville-Aptot (27) . . . 34 E4
Bonneville-et-Saint-Avit-
    -de-Fumadières (24) . . . 230 D1
Bonneville-la-Louvet (14) . . . 34 A4
la Bonneville-sur-Iton (27) . . . 56 C2
Bonneville-sur-Touques (14) . . . 33 J3
Bonnières (60) . . . 37 F1
Bonnières (62) . . . 10 A3
Bonnières-sur-Seine (78) . . . 57 H1
Bonnieux (84) . . . 277 G3
Bonningues-lès-Ardres (62) . . . 2 E4
Bonningues-lès-Calais (62) . . . 2 C3
Bonnœil (14) . . . 53 J2
Bonnœuvre (44) . . . 124 A2
Bonnut (64) . . . 283 J1
Bonny-sur-Loire (45) . . . 131 K2
Bono (56) . . . 100 D5
Bonrepos (65) . . . 286 A5
Bonrepos-Riquet (31) . . . 269 J5
Bonrepos-sur-Aussonnelle (31) . . . 287 J1
Bons-en-Chablais (74) . . . 191 H1
Bons-Tassilly (14) . . . 54 A2
Bonsecours (76) . . . 35 J2
Bonsmoulins (61) . . . 55 H6
Bonson (06) . . . 281 F2
Bonson (42) . . . 204 E5
Bonvillard (73) . . . 209 F3
Bonvillaret (73) . . . 209 F4
Bonviller (54) . . . 66 D1
Bonvillers (60) . . . 18 B6
Bonvillet (88) . . . 117 K1
Bony (02) . . . 11 J6
Bonzac (33) . . . 212 A5
Bonzée (55) . . . 43 K6
Boô-Silhen (65) . . . 304 B2
Boofzheim (67) . . . 71 D4
Boos (40) . . . 264 B2
Boos (76) . . . 35 J2
Bootzheim (67) . . . 96 E2
Boqueho (22) . . . 48 E6
Bor-et-Bar (12) . . . 251 G5
Boran-sur-Oise (60) . . . 37 K5
Borce (64) . . . 303 F3
Bord-Saint-Georges (23) . . . 183 H2
Bordeaux (33) . . . 229 H2
Bordeaux-en-Gâtinais (45) . . . 111 G1
Bordeaux-Saint-Clair (76) . . . 14 C4
Bordères (64) . . . 284 E5
Bordères-et-Lamensans (40) . . . 265 J4
Bordères-Louron (65) . . . 305 G2
Bordères-sur-l'Échez (65) . . . 285 H5
les Bordes (36) . . . 148 C4
les Bordes (45) . . . 111 F5
les Bordes (64) . . . 284 D5
les Bordes (65) . . . 285 J5
les Bordes (71) . . . 154 C5
les Bordes (89) . . . 112 E1
les Bordes-Aumont (10) . . . 90 B6
Bordes-de-Rivière (31) . . . 305 J1
les Bordes-sur-Arize (09) . . . 307 F1
les Bordes-sur-Lez (09) . . . 306 C4
Bordezac (30) . . . 255 G3
Bords (17) . . . 177 G6
Borée (07) . . . 239 F1
Boresse-et-Martron (17) . . . 212 C2
Borest (60) . . . 38 C5
Borey (70) . . . 138 D3
Borgo (2B) . . . 319 H2
Bormes-les-Mimosas (83) . . . 301 G3
le Born (31) . . . 269 H3
le Born (48) . . . 237 J6
Bornambusc (76) . . . 14 C5
Bornay (39) . . . 173 G2
Borne (07) . . . 238 D5
Borne (43) . . . 220 B5
Bornel (60) . . . 37 J5
Boron (90) . . . 139 K1
Borre (59) . . . 5 K3
Borrèze (24) . . . 233 G1
Bors (Canton de Baignes-
   -Sainte-Radegonde) (16) . . . 212 B2
Bors (Canton de Montmoreau-
   -Saint-Cybard) (16) . . . 212 E1
Bort-les-Orgues (19) . . . 217 J1
Bort-l'Étang (63) . . . 203 G2
Borville (54) . . . 94 C2
le Bosc (09) . . . 307 G3
le Bosc (34) . . . 273 G5
Bosc-Bénard-Commin (27) . . . 35 F3
Bosc-Bénard-Crescy (27) . . . 35 F3
Bosc-Bérenger (76) . . . 16 A5
Bosc-Bordel (76) . . . 16 C6
Bosc-Edeline (76) . . . 16 C6
Bosc-Guérard-Saint-Adrien (76) . . . 15 K6
Bosc-Hyons (76) . . . 36 D2
Bosc-le-Hard (76) . . . 16 A5
Bosc-Mesnil (76) . . . 16 C5

le Bosc-Renoult (61) . . . 55 F2
Bosc-Renoult-en-Ouche (27) . . . 55 K2
Bosc-Renoult-en-Roumois (27) . . . 34 E3
le Bosc-Roger-en-Roumois (27) . . . 35 G4
Bosc-Roger-sur-Buchy (76) . . . 16 C6
Boscamnant (17) . . . 212 C3
Bosdarros (64) . . . 284 D5
Bosgouet (27) . . . 35 F3
Bosguérard-de-Marcouville (27) . . . 35 F4
Bosjean (71) . . . 155 F6
Bosmie-l'Aiguille (87) . . . 198 E2
Bosmont-sur-Serre (02) . . . 21 F4
Bosmoreau-les-Mines (23) . . . 182 C5
Bosnormand (27) . . . 35 G4
Bosquel (80) . . . 18 A4
Bosquentin (27) . . . 36 C2
Bosrobert (27) . . . 34 E4
Bosroger (23) . . . 183 G5
Bossancourt (10) . . . 91 F5
Bossay-sur-Claise (37) . . . 146 C6
la Bosse (25) . . . 157 H1
la Bosse (72) . . . 83 H6
la Bosse-de-Bretagne (35) . . . 103 G1
Bossée (37) . . . 146 A2
Bossendorf (67) . . . 69 J6
Bosset (24) . . . 213 G6
Bosseval-et-Briancourt (08) . . . 22 E3
Bossey (74) . . . 191 F2
Bossieu (38) . . . 206 D6
Bossugan (33) . . . 230 C3
Bossus-lès-Rumigny (08) . . . 21 J2
Bost (03) . . . 185 K3
Bostens (40) . . . 265 J1
Bosville (76) . . . 15 G3
Botans (90) . . . 139 H1
Botmeur (29) . . . 75 F1
Botsorhel (29) . . . 47 H5
les Bottereaux (27) . . . 55 J3
Botz-en-Mauges (49) . . . 124 C5
Bou (45) . . . 110 B4
Bouafle (78) . . . 58 A2
Bouafles (27) . . . 36 A5
Bouan (09) . . . 307 J5
Bouaye (44) . . . 123 F5
Boubers-lès-Hesmond (62) . . . 4 D6
Boubers-sur-Canche (62) . . . 9 K3
Boubiers (60) . . . 37 F5
Bouc-Bel-Air (13) . . . 296 C2
Boucagnères (32) . . . 286 D1
Boucau (64) . . . 282 B1
Boucé (03) . . . 185 K1
Boucé (61) . . . 54 B6
le Bouchage (16) . . . 179 J4
le Bouchage (38) . . . 207 H3
Bouchain (59) . . . 12 B3
Bouchamps-lès-Craon (53) . . . 104 C4
le Bouchaud (03) . . . 186 D1
Bouchavesnes-Bergen (80) . . . 19 G1
Bouchemaine (49) . . . 125 G4
Boucheporn (57) . . . 45 K5
Bouchet (26) . . . 256 E3
le Bouchet (74) . . . 209 F1
le Bouchet-Saint-Nicolas (43) . . . 238 B1
Bouchevilliers (27) . . . 36 D2
Bouchoir (80) . . . 18 E4
Bouchon (80) . . . 9 H6
le Bouchon-sur-Saulx (55) . . . 64 B6
les Bouchoux (39) . . . 173 J6
Bouchy-Saint-Genest (51) . . . 61 F6
Boucieu-le-Roi (07) . . . 222 A5
Bouclans (25) . . . 138 C4
Boucoiran-et-Nozières (30) . . . 275 F1
Bouconville (08) . . . 42 C4
Bouconville-sur-Madt (55) . . . 65 G3
Bouconville-Vauclair (02) . . . 40 C1
Bouconvillers (60) . . . 37 F5
Boucq (54) . . . 65 G4
Boudes (63) . . . 202 E6
Boudeville (76) . . . 15 H4
Boudou (82) . . . 249 F6
Boudrac (31) . . . 286 C6
Boudreville (21) . . . 115 J3
Boudy-de-Beauregard (47) . . . 231 K6
Boué (02) . . . 12 E1
Bouée (44) . . . 122 D2
Boueilh-Boueilho-Lasque (64) . . . 284 D1
Bouelles (76) . . . 16 D4
Bouër (72) . . . 107 J2
Bouère (53) . . . 105 H4
Bouessay (53) . . . 105 J4
Bouesse (36) . . . 165 J3
Bouëx (16) . . . 197 F4
la Bouëxière (35) . . . 79 J3
Bouffémont (95) . . . 58 E1
Boufféré (85) . . . 142 A4
Bouffignereux (02) . . . 40 D3
Boufflers (80) . . . 9 H3
Bouffry (41) . . . 108 C3
Bougainville (80) . . . 17 J2
Bougarber (64) . . . 284 C3
Bougé-Chambalud (38) . . . 222 A2
Bouges-le-Château (36) . . . 147 K3
Bougey (70) . . . 117 J5
Bougival (78) . . . 58 C4
Bouglainval (28) . . . 85 G1
Bougligny (77) . . . 87 H6
Bougneau (17) . . . 195 H4
Bougnon (70) . . . 118 A6
Bougon (79) . . . 162 B6
Bougue (40) . . . 265 H2
Bouguenais (44) . . . 123 G4
Bougy (14) . . . 32 C5
Bougy-lez-Neuville (45) . . . 110 D3
Bouhans (71) . . . 154 E6
Bouhans-et-Feurg (70) . . . 136 E3

Bouhans-lès-Lure (70) . . . 118 D6
Bouhans-lès-Montbozon (70) . . . 138 C3
Bouhet (17) . . . 177 G2
Bouhey (21) . . . 153 J1
Bouhy (58) . . . 132 C3
Bouilh-Devant (65) . . . 285 K4
Bouilh-Péreuilh (65) . . . 285 J4
Bouilhonnac (11) . . . 290 C5
Bouillac (12) . . . 234 E6
Bouillac (24) . . . 232 C3
Bouillac (82) . . . 268 D3
la Bouilladisse (13) . . . 296 E3
Bouillancourt-en-Séry (80) . . . 16 E1
Bouillancourt-la-Bataille (80) . . . 18 D4
Bouillancy (60) . . . 38 E6
Bouilland (21) . . . 153 K2
Bouillargues (30) . . . 275 H4
la Bouille (76) . . . 35 G3
Bouillé-Courdault (85) . . . 161 F5
Bouillé-Loretz (79) . . . 144 A2
Bouillé-Ménard (49) . . . 104 C5
Bouillé-Saint-Paul (79) . . . 144 A3
la Bouillie (22) . . . 49 K5
le Bouillon (61) . . . 82 D1
Bouillon (64) . . . 284 B1
Bouillonville (54) . . . 65 H2
Bouilly (10) . . . 90 A6
Bouilly (51) . . . 40 D5
Bouilly-en-Gâtinais (45) . . . 110 D2
Bouin (79) . . . 178 E3
Bouin (85) . . . 140 D3
Bouin-Plumoison (62) . . . 9 H1
Bouisse (11) . . . 309 H3
Bouix (21) . . . 114 E4
Boujailles (25) . . . 156 C4
Boujan-sur-Libron (34) . . . 292 A3
Boulages (10) . . . 89 K1
Boulaincourt (88) . . . 93 K3
Boulancourt (77) . . . 87 F5
Boulange (57) . . . 26 E4
Boulaur (32) . . . 286 E1
le Boulay (37) . . . 128 A2
Boulay-les-Barres (45) . . . 109 K3
Boulay-les-Ifs (53) . . . 82 B3
le Boulay-Morin (27) . . . 35 J6
Boulay-Moselle (57) . . . 45 J4
la Boulaye (71) . . . 170 C1
Boulazac (24) . . . 214 B4
Boulbon (13) . . . 276 A3
Boulc (26) . . . 241 K4
Boule-d'Amont (66) . . . 314 C3
Bouleternère (66) . . . 314 D2
Bouleurs (77) . . . 59 K3
Bouleuse (51) . . . 40 D4
Bouliac (33) . . . 229 H2
Boulieu-lès-Annonay (07) . . . 221 K2
Bouligneux (01) . . . 188 E4
Bouligney (70) . . . 118 B3
Bouligny (55) . . . 44 B3
Boulin (65) . . . 285 J5
Boullarre (60) . . . 39 F6
le Boullay-les-Deux-Églises (28) . . . 56 E6
Boullay-les-Troux (91) . . . 58 B6
le Boullay-Mivoye (28) . . . 57 F6
le Boullay-Thierry (28) . . . 57 F6
Boulleret (18) . . . 131 K4
Boulleville (27) . . . 34 B3
Bouloc (31) . . . 269 G4
Bouloc (82) . . . 249 G3
Boulogne (85) . . . 142 A6
Boulogne-Billancourt (92) . . . 58 D4
Boulogne-la-Grasse (60) . . . 18 E5
Boulogne-sur-Gesse (31) . . . 286 D4
Boulogne-sur-Helpe (59) . . . 13 G5
Boulogne-sur-Mer (62) . . . 4 A3
Bouloire (72) . . . 107 H3
Boulon (14) . . . 32 D6
Boulot (21) . . . 137 K4
le Boulou (66) . . . 315 G4
Boult (70) . . . 137 K4
Boult-aux-Bois (08) . . . 42 C2
Boult-sur-Suippe (51) . . . 41 G2
le Boulvé (46) . . . 249 G2
Boulzicourt (08) . . . 22 D4
Boumourt (64) . . . 284 B2
Bouniagues (24) . . . 231 J3
le Boupère (85) . . . 142 E6
Bouquehault (62) . . . 2 D4
Bouquelon (27) . . . 34 C2
Bouquemaison (80) . . . 10 B4
Bouquemont (55) . . . 64 D1
Bouquet (30) . . . 255 J5
Bouquetot (27) . . . 35 F3
Bouqueval (95) . . . 59 F1
Bouranton (10) . . . 90 B4
Bouray-sur-Juine (91) . . . 86 E2
Bourbach-le-Bas (68) . . . 119 K4
Bourbach-le-Haut (68) . . . 119 K4
Bourberain (21) . . . 136 C3
Bourbévelle (70) . . . 117 J3
Bourbon-Lancy (71) . . . 169 J3
Bourbon-l'Archambault (03) . . . 168 B3
Bourbonne-les-Bains (52) . . . 117 G3
la Bourboule (63) . . . 201 K4
Bourbourg (59) . . . 3 F2
Bourbriac (22) . . . 48 C6
Bourcefranc-le-Chapus (17) . . . 176 D6
Bourcia (39) . . . 172 E6
Bourcq (08) . . . 42 A2
Bourdainville (76) . . . 15 J4
Bourdalat (40) . . . 265 K3
Bourdeau (73) . . . 208 A2
Bourdeaux (26) . . . 241 F5
Bourdeilles (24) . . . 213 J2
le Bourdeix (24) . . . 197 J3
Bourdelles (33) . . . 230 C6

Bourdenay (10) . . . 89 G4
le Bourdet (79) . . . 177 J1
Bourdettes (64) . . . 284 C5
Bourdic (30) . . . 275 G1
la Bourdinière-Saint-Loup (28) . . . 85 F4
Bourdon (80) . . . 9 J6
Bourdonnay (57) . . . 67 F4
Bourdonné (78) . . . 57 H5
Bourdons-sur-Rognon (52) . . . 92 D3
Bourecq (62) . . . 5 J5
Bouresches (02) . . . 60 D1
Bouresse (86) . . . 163 H6
Bouret-sur-Canche (62) . . . 10 A3
Boureuilles (55) . . . 42 E4
Bourg (33) . . . 211 H5
le Bourg (46) . . . 234 C4
Bourg (52) . . . 116 C3
Bourg-Achard (27) . . . 35 F3
Bourg-Archambault (86) . . . 164 B6
Bourg-Argental (42) . . . 221 J2
Bourg-Beaudouin (27) . . . 35 K2
Bourg-Blanc (29) . . . 72 D3
Bourg-Bruche (67) . . . 95 K3
Bourg-Charente (16) . . . 196 A3
Bourg-de-Bigorre (65) . . . 304 E1
Bourg-de-Péage (26) . . . 222 D5
Bourg-de-Sirod (39) . . . 174 A1
Bourg-de-Thizy (69) . . . 187 H4
Bourg-de-Visa (82) . . . 249 F4
Bourg-des-Comptes (35) . . . 79 F6
Bourg-des-Maisons (24) . . . 213 H2
le Bourg-d'Hem (23) . . . 182 C1
le Bourg-d'Iré (49) . . . 104 C6
le Bourg-d'Oisans (38) . . . 224 D4
Bourg-d'Oueil (31) . . . 305 G4
Bourg-du-Bost (24) . . . 213 F2
le Bourg-Dun (76) . . . 15 H2
Bourg-en-Bresse (01) . . . 189 G2
Bourg-et-Comin (02) . . . 40 B2
Bourg-Fidèle (08) . . . 22 B2
Bourg-la-Reine (92) . . . 58 E4
Bourg-Lastic (63) . . . 201 H4
Bourg-le-Comte (71) . . . 186 E1
Bourg-le-Roi (72) . . . 82 D4
Bourg-lès-Valence (26) . . . 222 C6
Bourg-l'Évêque (49) . . . 104 C5
Bourg-Madame (66) . . . 313 G6
Bourg-Saint-Andéol (07) . . . 256 C2
Bourg-Saint-Bernard (31) . . . 269 K6
Bourg-Saint-Christophe (01) . . . 189 F6
le Bourg-Saint-Léonard (61) . . . 54 D4
Bourg-Saint-Maurice (73) . . . 209 K3
Bourg-Sainte-Marie (52) . . . 93 F6
Bourg-sous-Châtelet (90) . . . 119 J5
Bourgaltroff (57) . . . 67 F2
Bourganeuf (23) . . . 182 C5
Bourgbarré (35) . . . 79 G6
Bourgeauville (14) . . . 33 J4
Bourges (18) . . . 149 G3
le Bourget (93) . . . 59 F2
le Bourget-du-Lac (73) . . . 208 B3
Bourget-en-Huile (73) . . . 208 E5
Bourgheim (67) . . . 70 D5
Bourghelles (59) . . . 7 F3
Bourgnac (24) . . . 213 H6
Bourgneuf (17) . . . 176 E2
Bourgneuf (73) . . . 208 E4
Bourgneuf-en-Mauges (49) . . . 124 D5
Bourgneuf-en-Retz (44) . . . 140 E2
le Bourgneuf-la-Forêt (53) . . . 80 D6
Bourgogne (51) . . . 41 F3
Bourgoin-Jallieu (38) . . . 207 F4
Bourgon (53) . . . 80 C6
la Bourgonce (88) . . . 95 H4
Bourgougnague (47) . . . 231 H5
Bourgtheroulde-Infreville (27) . . . 35 F3
Bourguébus (14) . . . 32 E5
Bourgueil (37) . . . 126 D6
Bourguenolles (50) . . . 52 A3
le Bourguet (83) . . . 279 H3
Bourguignon (25) . . . 139 H3
Bourguignon-lès-Conflans (70) . . . 118 C3
Bourguignon-lès-la-Charité (70) . . . 137 K2
Bourguignon-lès-Morey (70) . . . 117 G6
Bourguignon-sous-Coucy (02) . . . 19 J6
Bourguignon-
   -sous-Montbavin (02) . . . 20 C3
Bourguignons (10) . . . 114 D1
Bourgvilain (71) . . . 171 H6
Bourideys (33) . . . 246 A2
Bouriège (11) . . . 308 E3
Bourigeole (11) . . . 308 D3
Bourisp (65) . . . 305 F4
Bourlens (47) . . . 249 F2
Bourlon (62) . . . 11 H4
Bourmont (52) . . . 93 F3
Bournainville-Faverolles (27) . . . 34 C6
Bournan (37) . . . 146 A3
Bournand (86) . . . 144 E2
Bournazel (12) . . . 251 J4
Bournazel (81) . . . 251 F6
Bourneau (85) . . . 160 D3
Bournel (47) . . . 231 K5
Bourneville (27) . . . 34 D2
Bournezeau (85) . . . 160 A2
Bournoncle-Saint-Pierre (43) . . . 219 G6
Bournonville (62) . . . 4 D3
Bourogne (90) . . . 139 J1
Bourran (47) . . . 247 K3
Bourré (41) . . . 128 C3
Bourréac (65) . . . 304 B1
Bourret (82) . . . 268 E2
Bourriot-Bergonce (40) . . . 246 C5

Bourron-Marlotte (77) 87 H4
Bourrou (24) 213 J5
Bourrouillan (32) 266 B3
Bours (62) 5 H6
Bours (65) 285 H4
Boursault (51) 61 J1
Boursay (41) 108 B2
Bourscheid (57) 67 K3
Bourseul (22) 50 B5
Bourseville (80) 8 D5
Boursières (70) 137 K1
Boursies (59) 11 H4
Boursin (62) 2 C5
Boursonne (60) 39 F5
Bourth (27) 56 A4
Bourthes (62) 4 D4
Bourville (76) 15 H3
Boury-en-Vexin (60) 36 D4
Bousbach (57) 68 C2
Bousbecque (59) 6 E2
le Bouscat (33) 229 G1
Bousies (59) 12 E4
Bousignies (59) 12 B1
Bousignies-sur-Roc (59) 13 K3
le Bousquet (11) 308 E6
le Bousquet-d'Orb (34) 272 E5
Boussac (12) 251 K4
Boussac (23) 166 D6
la Boussac (35) 51 G5
Boussac (46) 234 C5
Boussac-Bourg (23) 166 D6
Boussais (79) 144 B6
Boussan (31) 287 F5
Boussay (37) 146 C6
Boussay (44) 142 B3
Bousse (57) 45 F3
Bousse (72) 106 B5
Bousselange (21) 154 E3
Boussenac (09) 307 F4
Boussenois (21) 136 C1
Boussens (31) 287 G6
Bousseraucourt (70) 117 J2
Boussès (47) 247 G5
Bousseviller (57) 69 H2
Boussey (21) 135 F5
Boussicourt (80) 18 D4
Boussières (25) 156 A1
Boussières-en-Cambrésis (59) . . . 12 B4
Boussières-sur-Sambre (59) 13 G3
Boussois (59) 13 H2
Boussy (74) 190 E6
Boussy-Saint-Antoine (91) 59 G5
Boust (57) 27 G3
Boustroff (57) 45 K6
Bout-du-Pont-de-Larn (81) 290 D6
Boutancourt (08) 22 D4
Boutavent (60) 17 F5
la Bouteille (02) 21 G2
Bouteilles-Saint-Sébastien (24) . . 213 G1
Boutenac (11) 291 F6
Boutenac-Touvent (17) 194 E5
Boutencourt (60) 36 E3
Boutervilliers (91) 86 B3
Bouteville (16) 196 B4
Boutiers-Saint-Trojan (16) 195 K2
Boutigny (77) 59 K3
Boutigny-Prouais (28) 57 H5
Boutigny-sur-Essonne (91) 86 E3
Bouttencourt (80) 16 E1
Boutteville (50) 29 G5
Boutx (31) 305 J3
Bouvaincourt-sur-Bresle (80) 8 D6
Bouvancourt (51) 40 D3
Bouvante (26) 223 G6
Bouvelinghem (62) 4 E3
Bouvellemont (08) 22 C5
Bouverans (25) 156 D5
Bouvesse-Quirieu (38) 207 G1
Bouvières (26) 241 F6
Bouvignies (59) 11 K1
Bouvigny-Boyeffles (62) 10 D1
Bouville (28) 85 F1
Bouville (76) 15 H6
Bouville (91) 86 D3
Bouvincourt-en-Vermandois (80) . . 19 H2
Bouvines (59) 7 F5
Bouvresse (60) 17 F5
Bouvron (44) 122 E1
Bouvron (54) 65 H4
Boux-sous-Salmaise (21) 135 G3
Bouxières-aux-Bois (88) 94 C4
Bouxières-aux-Chênes (54) 66 B4
Bouxières-aux-Dames (54) 66 A4
Bouxières-sous-Froidmont (54) . . 65 K1
Bouxurulles (88) 94 B3
Bouxwiller (67) 69 H6
Bouxwiller (68) 97 C5
Bouy (51) 41 J6
Bouy-Luxembourg (10) 90 C3
Bouy-sur-Orvin (10) 89 J3
Bouyon (06) 281 F2
le Bouyssou (46) 234 C4
Bouzais (18) 167 G2
Bouzancourt (52) 91 K4
Bouzanville (54) 94 A3
Bouze-lès-Beaune (21) 153 K3
Bouzel (63) 203 F2
Bouzemont (88) 94 B4
Bouzeron (71) 153 K5
Bouzic (24) 233 F4
Bouziès (46) 250 C1
Bouzigues (34) 292 E2
Bouzillé (49) 124 B5
Bouzin (31) 287 F6
Bouzincourt (80) 10 D6
Bouzon-Gellenave (32) 266 C5

Bouzonville (57) 45 J3
Bouzonville-aux-Bois (45) 110 D1
Bouzy (51) 41 G6
Bouzy-la-Forêt (45) 110 E5
Bovée-sur-Barboure (55) 64 E6
Bovel (35) 78 D6
Bovelles (80) 17 K2
Boves (80) 18 B2
Boviolles (55) 64 D6
Boyaval (62) 5 G6
Boyelles (62) 11 F4
Boyer (42) 187 G3
Boyer (71) 171 K3
Boyeux-Saint-Jérôme (01) 189 J4
Boynes (45) 110 E1
Boz (01) 171 K5
Bozas (07) 221 K5
Bozel (73) 209 J5
Bozouls (12) 252 D1
Brabant-en-Argonne (55) 43 F5
Brabant-le-Roi (55) 63 K3
Brabant-sur-Meuse (55) 43 H3
Brach (33) 210 D5
Brachay (52) 91 K3
Braches (80) 18 C4
Brachy (76) 15 J3
Bracieux (41) 129 G3
Bracon (39) 156 A4
Bracquemont (76) 16 A1
Bracquetuit (76) 16 A5
Bradiancourt (76) 16 C5
Braffais (50) 52 A4
Bragassargues (30) 274 D2
Bragayrac (31) 287 H2
Brageac (15) 217 G3
Bragelogne-Beauvoir (10) 114 C3
Bragny-sur-Saône (71) 154 C4
Braillans (25) 138 A5
Brailly-Cornehotte (80) 9 H3
Brain (21) 135 F3
Brain-sur-Allonnes (49) 126 C5
Brain-sur-l'Authion (49) 125 H4
Brain-sur-Longuenée (49) 124 E2
Brainans (39) 155 H5
Braine (02) 40 A3
Brains (44) 123 F4
Brains-sur-Gée (72) 106 C2
Brains-sur-les-Marches (53) 104 A3
Brainville (50) 30 D3
Brainville (54) 44 B5
Brainville-sur-Meuse (52) 93 F6
Braisnes (60) 38 D1
Braize (03) 167 H2
Bralleville (54) 94 B3
Bram (11) 289 J5
Bramans (73) 226 B2
Brametot (76) 15 H3
Bramevaque (65) 305 H3
Bran (17) 212 A1
Branceilles (19) 216 A6
Branches (89) 113 F4
Brancourt-en-Laonnois (02) 39 K1
Brancourt-le-Grand (02) 20 A1
Brandérion (56) 100 B3
Brandeville (55) 43 G2
Brandivy (56) 100 D3
Brando (2B) 317 E4
Brandon (71) 171 G6
Brandonnet (12) 251 G2
Brandonvillers (51) 91 F1
Branges (71) 172 C2
Brangues (38) 207 H2
Brannay (89) 88 B5
Branne (25) 138 E4
Branne (33) 230 B3
Brannens (33) 230 B6
Branoux-les-Taillades (30) 255 F6
Brans (39) 137 F6
Bransat (03) 185 G1
Branscourt (51) 40 D4
Bransles (77) 111 K1
Brantes (84) 257 K4
Brantigny (88) 94 B3
Brantôme (24) 213 K1
Branville (14) 33 H4
Branville-Hague (50) 28 B2
Braquis (55) 44 A5
Bras (83) 297 J1
Bras-d'Asse (04) 278 C1
Bras-sur-Meuse (55) 43 H4
Brasc (12) 271 J2
Brasles (02) 60 E1
Braslou (37) 145 H4
Brasparts (29) 74 E2
Brassac (09) 307 H3
Brassac (81) 271 H6
Brassac (82) 249 F4
Brassac-les-Mines (63) 219 G1
Brassempouy (40) 264 E5
Brasseuse (60) 38 C4
Brassy (58) 133 K6
Brassy (80) 17 J4
Bratte (54) 66 A3
Braud-et-Saint-Louis (33) 211 G2
Brauvilliers (55) 92 B1
Braux (04) 260 D6
Braux (10) 90 E2
Braux (21) 134 C2
Braux-le-Châtel (52) 115 K1
Braux-Saint-Remy (51) 63 H1
Brax (31) 288 C2
Brax (47) 248 A4
Bray (27) 35 F6
Bray (71) 171 J4
Bray-Dunes (59) 3 J1

Bray-en-Val (45) 110 E5
Bray-et-Lû (95) 36 D6
Bray-lès-Mareuil (80) 9 G6
Bray-Saint-Christophe (02) 19 J3
Bray-sur-Seine (77) 88 C3
Bray-sur-Somme (80) 18 E1
Braye (02) 39 J2
Braye-en-Laonnois (02) 40 B2
Braye-en-Thiérache (02) 21 G3
Braye-sous-Faye (37) 145 G4
Braye-sur-Maulne (37) 126 A2
Brazey-en-Morvan (21) 152 E1
Brazey-en-Plaine (21) 154 D2
Bréal-sous-Montfort (35) 78 A3
Bréal-sous-Vitré (35) 104 C1
Bréançon (95) 37 G6
Bréau (77) 87 K1
Bréau-et-Salagosse (30) 273 J1
Bréauté (76) 14 D5
Bréban (51) 90 D1
Brebières (62) 11 J2
Brebotte (90) 139 J1
Brécé (35) 79 J4
Brécé (53) 80 E3
Brécey (50) 52 B4
Brech (56) 100 D4
Brechainville (88) 92 E3
Bréchamps (28) 57 G6
Bréchaumont (68) 119 K6
Brèches (37) 127 F2
Breconchaux (25) 138 C4
Brectouville (50) 31 H4
Brécy (02) 39 K5
Brécy (18) 149 J2
Brécy-Brières (08) 42 C3
la Brède (33) 229 H4
Brée (53) 81 H6
la Brée-les-Bains (17) 176 B4
Bréel (61) 53 J4
Brégnier-Cordon (01) 207 J3
Brégy (60) 38 E6
Bréhain (57) 66 D2
Bréhain-la-Ville (54) 26 E3
Bréhal (50) 30 D6
Bréhan (56) 77 G6
Bréhand (22) 77 H2
Bréhémont (37) 127 F6
Bréhéville (55) 43 H2
Breidenbach (57) 69 G2
Breil (49) 126 D3
le Breil-sur-Mérize (72) 107 G2
Breil-sur-Roya (06) 311 C4
la Breille-les-Pins (49) 126 C5
Breilly (80) 17 K1
Breistroff-la-Grande (57) 27 H3
Breitenau (67) 96 B1
Breitenbach (67) 70 B6
Breitenbach-Haut-Rhin (68) 119 K1
Brélès (29) 72 B3
Brélidy (22) 48 C1
Brem-sur-Mer (85) 158 E2
Bréménil (54) 95 H1
Brêmes (62) 2 D1
Brémoncourt (54) 94 C1
Bremondans (25) 138 D6
Brémontier-Merval (76) 36 C1
Brémoy (14) 53 F1
Brémur-et-Vaurois (21) 115 G6
Bren (26) 222 E4
Brenac (11) 308 E4
Brenas (34) 273 F6
Brenat (63) 203 F5
Brénaz (01) 190 B5
Brenelle (02) 40 A3
Brengues (46) 234 B5
Brennes (52) 116 C5
Brennilis (29) 75 F1
Brénod (01) 190 A4
Brenon (83) 279 K3
Brenouille (60) 38 B4
Brenoux (48) 254 B1
Brens (01) 207 K2
Brens (81) 270 B3
Brenthonne (74) 174 E4
Breny (02) 39 J5
la Bréole (04) 243 G6
Brères (25) 156 A2
Bréry (39) 155 H6
Bresdon (17) 178 D6
les Bréseux (25) 139 H5
Bresilley (70) 137 G6
Bresle (80) 18 D1
Bresles (60) 37 J2
Bresnay (03) 168 D5
Bresolettes (61) 55 J6
la Bresse (88) 119 H2
Bresse-sur-Grosne (71) 171 J3
Bressey-sur-Tille (21) 136 C5
Bressieux (38) 223 G1
Bressolles (01) 189 F6
Bressolles (03) 168 E4
Bressols (82) 269 F2
Bresson (38) 224 B4
Bressuire (79) 143 J5
Brest (29) 72 D4
Brestot (27) 34 E3
Bretagne (36) 147 K4
Bretagne (90) 139 K1
Bretagne-d'Armagnac (32) 266 D2
Bretagne-de-Marsan (40) 265 H3
Bretagnolles (27) 57 F2
Breteau (45) 131 K1
Breteil (35) 78 A4
la Bretenière (21) 136 B6
la Bretenière (25) 138 C4
la Bretenière (39) 155 J2

Bretenières (39) 155 H4
Bretenoux (46) 234 B1
Breteuil (27) 56 B4
Breteuil (60) 18 A5
Brethel (61) 55 H5
Brethenay (52) 92 B6
le Brethon (03) 167 J1
Bretigney (25) 139 F2
Bretigney-Notre-Dame (25) 138 C5
Bretignolles (79) 143 H5
Bretignolles-sur-Mer (85) 158 D2
Bretigny (21) 136 B4
Brétigny (27) 34 E4
Brétigny (60) 19 J6
Brétigny-sur-Orge (91) 86 E1
Bretoncelles (61) 84 A3
la Bretonnière-la-Claye (85) . . . 159 K4
Bretonvillers (25) 139 F6
Brette (21) 241 G5
Brette-les-Pins (72) 107 F4
Bretten (68) 119 K5
Brettes (16) 179 F5
Bretteville (50) 28 D2
Bretteville-du-Grand-Caux (76) . . 14 D4
Bretteville-le-Rabet (14) 54 A1
Bretteville-l'Orgueilleuse (14) . . . 32 C4
Bretteville-Saint-Laurent (76) . . . 15 H3
Bretteville-sur-Ay (50) 30 C1
Bretteville-sur-Dives (14) 54 C1
Bretteville-sur-Laize (14) 53 K1
Bretteville-sur-Odon (14) 32 D5
Brettnach (57) 45 J3
Bretx (31) 268 E5
Breuches (70) 118 D4
Breuchotte (70) 118 D4
Breugnon (58) 133 F4
le Breuil (03) 186 B2
le Breuil (51) 61 G2
le Breuil (69) 188 A6
le Breuil (71) 153 G6
Breuil (80) 19 G4
Breuil-Barret (85) 161 F2
le Breuil-Bernard (79) 161 G1
Breuil-Bois-Robert (78) 57 J2
le Breuil-en-Auge (14) 33 K4
le Breuil-en-Bessin (14) 31 K2
Breuil-la-Réorte (17) 177 H1
Breuil-le-Sec (60) 38 A3
Breuil-le-Vert (60) 38 A3
Breuil-Magné (17) 177 F1
le Breuil-sous-Argenton (79) . . . 143 K3
le Breuil-sur-Couze (63) 203 F6
Breuilaufa (87) 181 F4
Breuilh (24) 214 A5
Breuillet (17) 194 C2
Breuillet (91) 86 C1
Breuilpont (27) 57 F2
Breurey-lès-Faverney (70) 118 A3
Breuschwickersheim (67) 70 E3
Breuvannes-en-Bassigny (52) . . . 117 F1
Breuvery-sur-Coole (51) 62 D3
Breuville (50) 28 C3
Breux (55) 23 K1
Breux-Jouy (91) 86 C1
Breux-sur-Avre (27) 56 C4
Brévainville (41) 108 E3
Bréval (78) 57 G2
Brévands (50) 29 G6
Brevans (39) 155 G2
le Brévedent (14) 34 A4
Brèves (58) 133 G4
les Bréviaires (78) 57 K5
Bréviandes (10) 90 B3
la Brévière (14) 54 E2
Bréville (16) 196 A1
Bréville-les-Monts (14) 33 H4
Bréville-sur-Mer (50) 30 D6
Brévillers (62) 9 H2
Brévillers (80) 10 B1
Brévilliers (70) 139 H1
Brévilly (08) 23 G1
Brévonnes (10) 90 D4
Bréxent-Enocq (62) 4 B5
Brey-et-Maison-du-Bois (25) . . . 156 E6
Brézé (49) 144 C1
Bréziers (05) 259 J1
Brézilhac (11) 289 J6
Brézins (38) 223 G1
Brezolles (28) 56 C5
Brezons (15) 218 B6
Briançon (05) 225 K6
Briançonnet (06) 280 B2
Brianny (21) 134 E4
Briant (71) 187 F1
Briantes (36) 166 B4
Briare (45) 131 G2
Briarres-sur-Essonne (45) 87 F6
Brias (62) 10 B1
Briastre (59) 12 C4
Briatexte (81) 270 B4
Briaucourt (52) 92 B5
Briaucourt (70) 118 B4
Bricon (52) 115 K1
Briconville (28) 85 F2
Bricquebec (50) 28 C4
Bricquebosq (50) 28 C3
Bricqueville (14) 31 J1
Bricqueville-la-Blouette (50) 30 D4
Bricqueville-sur-Mer (50) 30 D6
Bricy (45) 109 J3
Brides-les-Bains (73) 209 H5
la Bridoire (73) 207 K4
Bridoré (37) 146 D3
Brie (02) 20 B5
Brie (09) 288 C6

Brie (16) 197 F2
Brie (35) 79 H6
Brie (79) 144 C4
Brie (80) 19 G2
Brie-Comte-Robert (77) 59 G6
Brié-et-Angonnes (38) 224 B4
Brie-sous-Archiac (17) 195 K5
Brie-sous-Barbezieux (16) 196 C6
Brie-sous-Chalais (16) 212 D2
Brie-sous-Matha (17) 196 A1
Brie-sous-Mortagne (17) 195 F5
Briec (29) 74 E4
Briel-sur-Barse (10) 90 D6
Brielles (35) 104 B3
Brienne (71) 172 B3
Brienne-la-Vieille (10) 91 F3
Brienne-le-Château (10) 91 F3
Brienne-sur-Aisne (08) 41 F2
Briennon (42) 187 F3
Brienon-sur-Armançon (89) 113 G3
Brières-les-Scellés (91) 86 C3
Brieuil-sur-Chizé (79) 178 B3
Brieulles-sur-Bar (08) 42 C1
Brieulles-sur-Meuse (55) 43 F3
Brieux (61) 54 B3
Briey (54) 44 C4
Briffons (63) 201 J3
Brignac (34) 273 H6
Brignac (56) 77 K5
Brignac-la-Plaine (19) 215 G4
Brignais (69) 205 K3
Brignancourt (95) 37 F6
Brigné (49) 125 J6
Brignemont (31) 268 C4
Brignogan-Plage (29) 46 B3
Brignoles (83) 297 K2
Brignon (30) 275 F1
le Brignon (43) 238 C1
la Brigue (06) 311 D2
Briguemesnil-le-Chantre (86) . . . 164 C6
Brigueuil (16) 180 D5
Briis-sous-Forges (91) 58 C6
Brillac (16) 180 C4
la Brillanne (04) 278 C2
Brillecourt (10) 90 D2
Brillevast (50) 28 E2
Brillon (59) 12 B1
Brillon-en-Barrois (55) 64 A5
Brimeux (62) 9 G1
Brimont (51) 41 F3
Brin-sur-Seille (54) 66 C4
Brinay (18) 148 E2
Brinay (58) 151 K4
Brinckheim (68) 97 D4
Brindas (69) 205 K2
Bringolo (22) 48 E5
Brinon-sur-Beuvron (58) 133 F6
Brinon-sur-Sauldre (18) 130 D2
Briod (39) 173 G2
Briollay (49) 125 H2
Brion (01) 189 K2
Brion (36) 148 A4
Brion (38) 223 G2
Brion (48) 236 E3
Brion (49) 126 A4
Brion (71) 152 E5
Brion (86) 163 G6
Brion (89) 113 F3
Brion-près-Thouet (79) 144 B3
Brion-sur-Ource (21) 115 G3
la Brionne (23) 182 C3
Brionne (27) 34 E5
Briord (01) 207 G1
Briosne-lès-Sables (72) 83 F6
Briot (60) 17 H5
Briou (41) 109 G5
Brioude (43) 219 H2
Brioux-sur-Boutonne (79) 178 C3
Briouze (61) 53 J5
Briquemesnil-Floxicourt (80) 17 J2
Briquenay (08) 42 D2
Briscous (64) 282 D2
Brison-Saint-Innocent (73) 208 B2
Brissac (34) 274 A3
Brissac-Quincé (49) 125 H5
Brissarthe (49) 105 H6
Brissay-Choigny (02) 20 A4
Brissy-Hamégicourt (02) 20 B4
Brive-la-Gaillarde (19) 215 J4
Brives (36) 148 C6
Brives-Charensac (43) 220 C5
Brives-sur-Charente (17) 195 H3
Brivezac (19) 216 B6
Brix (50) 28 D3
Brixey-aux-Chanoines (55) 93 G2
Brizambourg (17) 195 H1
Brizay (37) 145 H2
Brizeaux (55) 63 K1
Brizon (74) 191 J3
le Broc (06) 281 F2
Broc (49) 126 D2
le Broc (63) 202 E5
Brocas (40) 245 K6
Brochon (21) 154 A1
Brocourt (80) 17 G2
Brocourt-en-Argonne (55) 43 F5
Broglie (27) 55 H1
Brognard (25) 139 H2
Brognon (08) 21 K1
Brognon (21) 136 B4
Broin (21) 154 D2
Broindon (21) 154 C1
Broissia (39) 173 F6
Brombos (60) 17 H5
Bromeilles (45) 87 F6
Brommat (12) 236 A2

356

Bromont-Lamothe (63) 202 A1
Bron (69) 206 B2
Bronvaux (57) 44 A4
Broons (22) 78 B1
la Broque (67) 70 A5
Broquiers (60) 17 G5
Broquiès (12) 271 K1
Brossac (16) 212 C1
Brossainc (07) 222 A2
Brossay (49) 144 B1
la Brosse-Montceaux (77) 88 B4
Brosses (89) 133 H3
Brosville (27) 35 H6
Brotte-lès-Luxeuil (70) 118 C5
Brotte-lès-Ray (70) 137 G1
Brou (28) 84 D6
Brou-sur-Chantereine (77) 59 H4
Brouains (50) 52 D5
Broualan (35) 51 G5
Brouay (14) 32 C4
Brouchaud (24) 214 D3
Brouchy (80) 19 J4
Brouck (57) 45 J5
Brouckerque (59) 3 G2
Brouderdorff (57) 67 K4
Broué (28) 57 G5
Brouennes (55) 23 J4
le Brouilh-Monbert (32) 267 F5
Brouilla (66) 315 G3
Brouillet (51) 40 C4
Brouqueyran (33) 230 B6
la Brousse (17) 178 B6
Brousse (23) 183 J5
Brousse (63) 203 G4
Brousse (81) 270 D5
Brousse-le-Château (12) 271 J1
Brousses-et-Villaret (11) 290 A4
Brousseval (52) 91 K2
Broussey-en-Blois (55) 64 E6
Broussey-Raulecourt (55) 65 F3
Broussy-le-Grand (51) 61 J4
Broussy-le-Petit (51) 61 J4
Broût-Vernet (03) 185 H2
Brouvelieures (88) 95 G4
Brouville (54) 95 G1
Brouviller (57) 67 K3
Brouy (91) 86 D4
Brouzet-lès-Alès (30) 255 J5
Brouzet-lès-Quissac (30) 274 D3
les Brouzils (85) 142 A4
Broxeele (59) 3 G4
Broye (71) 153 F5
Broye-Aubigney-Montseugny (70) . 137 F5
Broye-les-Loups-et-
    -Verfontaine (70) 136 E3
Broyes (51) 61 H5
Broyes (60) 18 C5
Broze (81) 270 B2
Brû (88) 95 F3
Bruailles (71) 172 D3
Bruay-la-Buissière (62) 5 K6
Bruay-sur-l'Escaut (59) 12 D1
Bruc-sur-Aff (35) 102 C2
Brucamps (80) 9 J5
Bruch (47) 247 K4
Brucheville (50) 29 G6
Brucourt (14) 33 G4
Brue-Auriac (83) 297 J1
Bruebach (68) 97 C3
Brueil-en-Vexin (78) 57 K1
Bruère-Allichamps (18) 167 F1
la Bruère-sur-Loir (72) 127 F1
la Bruffière (85) 142 B3
Brugairolles (11) 308 E1
le Brugeron (63) 203 K3
Bruges (33) 229 G1
Bruges-Capbis-Mifaget (64) 284 D6
Brugheas (03) 185 H4
Brugnac (47) 247 K1
Brugnens (32) 267 K3
Brugny-Vaudancourt (51) 61 J1
la Bruguière (30) 256 A5
Bruguières (31) 269 G5
Bruille-lez-Marchiennes (59) 11 K2
Bruille-Saint-Amand (59) 7 H6
Bruis (05) 241 J6
Brûlain (79) 178 B2
les Brulais (35) 102 C1
Brulange (57) 66 D1
la Brûlatte (53) 104 D1
Bruley (54) 65 H5
Brullemail (61) 55 F6
Brullioles (69) 205 H2
Brûlon (72) 105 K3
Brumath (67) 25 A5
Brumetz (02) 39 H6
Brunehamel (02) 21 J3
Brunelles (28) 84 A4
les Brunels (11) 289 H3
Brunembert (62) 4 D3
Brunémont (59) 11 J3
Brunet (04) 278 E2
Bruniquel (82) 250 C6
Brunoy (91) 59 F5
Brunstatt (68) 97 C3
Brunville (76) 16 B1
Brunvillers-la-Motte (60) 18 C6
Brusque (12) 272 C4
le Brusquet (04) 259 K4
Brussey (70) 137 H5
Brussieu (69) 205 H2
Brusson (51) 63 G4
Brusvily (22) 50 C6
Brutelles (80) 8 D4
Bruville (54) 44 C5
Brux (86) 179 G2

la Bruyère (70) 118 E4
Bruyères (88) 95 F5
Bruyères-et-Montbérault (02) 40 B1
Bruyères-le-Châtel (91) 86 D1
Bruyères-sur-Fère (02) 39 K5
Bruyères-sur-Oise (95) 37 K5
Bruys (02) 40 A4
Bruz (35) 79 F5
Bry (59) 12 E2
Bry-sur-Marne (94) 59 G4
Bû (28) 57 G4
le Bû-sur-Rouvres (14) 54 B1
Buais (50) 80 D1
Buanes (40) 265 H4
Bubertré (61) 83 H1
Bubry (56) 100 C1
Buc (78) 58 C4
Buc (90) 139 H1
Bucamps (60) 37 K1
Bucéels (14) 32 B4
Bucey-en-Othe (10) 89 J5
Bucey-lès-Gy (70) 137 J4
Bucey-lès-Traves (70) 137 K1
Buchelay (78) 57 J2
Buchères (10) 90 B5
Buchy (57) 66 B1
Buchy (76) 16 C6
Bucilly (02) 21 H2
Bucquoy (62) 10 E4
Bucy-le-Long (02) 39 K2
Bucy-le-Roi (45) 110 A2
Bucy-lès-Cerny (02) 20 C6
Bucy-lès-Pierrepont (02) 21 F5
Bucy-Saint-Liphard (45) 109 J3
Budelière (23) 183 K2
Buding (57) 27 J4
Budling (57) 27 J4
Budos (33) 229 J6
Bué (18) 131 J6
Bueil (27) 57 G2
Bueil-en-Touraine (37) 127 H1
Buellas (01) 189 F2
Buethwiller (68) 97 A3
Buffard (25) 155 K3
Buffières (71) 171 G5
Buffignécourt (70) 117 K4
Buffon (21) 134 D1
Bugarach (11) 309 G4
Bugard (65) 286 A5
Bugeat (19) 200 B4
Bugnein (64) 283 J3
Bugnicourt (59) 11 J3
Bugnières (52) 116 A3
Bugny (25) 157 F3
le Bugue (24) 232 C1
Buhl (67) 25 C2
Buhl (68) 96 A6
Buhl-Lorraine (57) 67 J4
Buhy (95) 36 D5
Buicourt (60) 17 G6
Buigny-l'Abbé (80) 9 H5
Buigny-lès-Gamaches (80) 8 D6
Buigny-Saint-Maclou (80) 9 G4
Buire (02) 21 G2
Buire-au-Bois (62) 9 K3
Buire-Courcelles (80) 19 H1
Buire-le-Sec (62) 9 G1
Buire-sur-l'Ancre (80) 18 D1
Buironfosse (02) 20 E1
le Buis (87) 181 G4
Buis-les-Baronnies (26) 257 J3
Buis-sur-Damville (27) 56 D4
Buissard (05) 243 F4
la Buisse (38) 223 K1
la Buissière (38) 208 C6
le Buisson (48) 237 F5
le Buisson (51) 63 H4
Buisson (84) 257 G3
le Buisson-de-Cadouin (24) 232 C2
Buissoncourt (54) 66 C5
Buissy (62) 11 H4
Bujaleuf (87) 199 J2
Bulan (65) 304 E2
Bulat-Pestivien (22) 76 B1
Bulcy (58) 150 C1
Buléon (56) 101 G2
Bulgnéville (88) 93 H5
Bulhon (63) 185 J6
Bullainville (28) 85 G6
Bulle (25) 156 D4
Bullecourt (62) 11 G4
Bulles (60) 37 K2
Bulligny (54) 65 H6
Bullion (78) 58 B6
Bullou (28) 84 E5
Bully (42) 186 E6
Bully (69) 205 J1
Bully (76) 16 C4
Bully-les-Mines (62) 10 E1
Bulson (08) 23 F5
Bult (88) 94 E4
Bun (65) 304 A2
Buncey (21) 115 F5
Buneville (62) 10 B2
Buno-Bonnevaux (91) 86 E4
Bunzac (16) 197 G3
Buoux (84) 277 H3
Burbach (67) 68 C5
la Burbanche (01) 189 K6
Burbure (62) 5 J5
Burcin (38) 207 G6
Burcy (14) 53 F3
Burcy (77) 87 G3
Burdignes (42) 221 J2
Burdignin (74) 191 J1

Bure (55) 92 C2
Buré (61) 83 G2
Bure-les-Templiers (21) 115 J3
Burelles (02) 21 F3
Bures (54) 66 E4
Bures (61) 83 G1
Bures-en-Bray (76) 16 C3
Bures-les-Monts (14) 52 D2
Bures-sur-Yvette (91) 58 C5
le Buret (53) 105 H3
Burey (27) 56 B2
Burey-en-Vaux (55) 93 F1
Burey-la-Côte (55) 93 G2
Burg (65) 286 A6
Burgalays (31) 305 J4
Burgaronne (64) 283 H2
le Burgaud (31) 268 D4
Burgille (25) 137 H5
Burgnac (87) 198 E2
Burgy (71) 171 K4
Burie (17) 195 J2
Buriville (54) 95 F1
Burlats (81) 271 F6
Burlioncourt (57) 66 E2
Burnand (71) 171 H3
Burnevillers (25) 139 K4
Burnhaupt-le-Bas (68) 97 A3
Burnhaupt-le-Haut (68) 97 A3
Buros (64) 284 D3
Burosse-Mendousse (64) 284 E1
Burret (09) 307 H3
Bursard (61) 82 E1
Burthecourt-aux-Chênes (54) 66 B6
Burtoncourt (57) 45 H4
Bury (60) 37 K3
Burzet (07) 239 F3
Burzy (71) 171 G3
Bus (62) 11 G5
Bus-la-Mésière (80) 18 E5
Bus-lès-Artois (80) 10 C5
Bus-Saint-Rémy (27) 36 C5
Buschwiller (68) 97 E4
Busigny (59) 12 C6
Busloup (41) 108 C4
Busnes (62) 5 J5
Busque (81) 270 C4
Bussac (24) 213 K2
Bussac-Forêt (17) 211 K3
Bussac-sur-Charente (17) 195 G1
Bussang (88) 119 H3
le Busseau (79) 161 G3
Busseaut (21) 115 G6
Busséol (63) 202 E3
Busserolles (24) 197 J3
Busserotte-et-Montenaille (21) . . . 135 K1
Bussiares (02) 39 H6
la Bussière (45) 111 J6
la Bussière (86) 163 K3
Bussière-Badil (24) 197 J3
Bussière-Boffy (87) 180 D4
Bussière-Dunoise (23) 182 C2
Bussière-Galant (87) 198 C4
Bussière-Nouvelle (23) 183 J5
Bussière-Poitevine (87) 180 D2
Bussière-Saint-Georges (23) 166 C6
la Bussière-sur-Ouche (21) 153 J1
Bussières (21) 135 K1
Bussières (42) 205 F1
Bussières (63) 184 A4
Bussières (70) 137 K5
Bussières (71) 171 H6
Bussières (77) 60 C3
Bussières (89) 134 B4
Bussières-et-Pruns (63) 185 G5
Busson (52) 92 D4
Bussu (80) 19 H1
Bussunarits-Sarrasquette (64) . . . 282 E5
Bussus-Bussuel (80) 9 H5
Bussy (18) 149 J5
Bussy (60) 19 H5
Bussy-Albieux (42) 204 C2
Bussy-en-Othe (89) 113 F2
Bussy-la-Pesle (21) 135 H5
Bussy-la-Pesle (58) 133 F6
Bussy-le-Château (51) 42 A6
Bussy-le-Grand (21) 135 F2
Bussy-le-Repos (51) 63 H3
Bussy-le-Repos (89) 112 D2
Bussy-lès-Daours (80) 18 C2
Bussy-lès-Poix (80) 17 J3
Bussy-Lettrée (51) 62 C4
Bussy-Saint-Georges (77) 59 H4
Bussy-Saint-Martin (77) 59 H3
Bust (67) 69 F6
Bustanico (2B) 319 G6
Bustince-Iriberry (64) 282 E5
Buswiller (67) 69 J6
Busy (25) 156 B1
Buthiers (70) 138 A4
Buthiers (77) 87 F5
Butot (76) 15 K5
Butot-Vénesville (76) 15 J3
Butry-sur-Oise (95) 37 J3
Butteaux (89) 113 J3
Butten (67) 69 F4
Buverchy (80) 19 H4
Buvilly (39) 155 J5
la Buxerette (36) 165 K4
Buxerolles (21) 115 K5
Buxerolles (86) 163 F3
Buxeuil (10) 114 E2
Buxeuil (36) 147 K2
Buxeuil (86) 145 K4
Buxières-d'Aillac (36) 165 J3
Buxières-lès-Clefmont (52) 116 E1

Buxières-les-Mines (03) 168 A5
Buxières-lès-Villiers (52) 116 A1
Buxières-sous-les-Côtes (55) 65 F2
Buxières-sous-Montaigut (63) 184 D2
Buxières-sur-Arce (10) 114 E1
Buxy (71) 171 H1
Buysscheure (59) 3 H4
Buzan (09) 306 B3
Buzançais (36) 147 H5
Buzancy (02) 39 J3
Buzancy (08) 42 D2
Buzeins (12) 253 F2
Buzet-sur-Baïse (47) 247 J4
Buzet-sur-Tarn (31) 269 J4
Buziet (64) 284 B6
Buzignargues (34) 274 D4
Buzon (65) 285 J2
Buzy (64) 284 C6
Buzy-Darmont (55) 44 A5
By (25) 156 A3
Byans-sur-Doubs (25) 156 A2

C

Cabanac (65) 285 K4
Cabanac-Cazaux (31) 305 K2
Cabanac-et-Villagrains (33) 229 H5
Cabanac-Séguenville (31) 268 C4
la Cabanasse (66) 313 J4
Cabanès (12) 251 J5
Cabanès (81) 270 C5
le Cabanial (31) 289 G2
les Cabannes (09) 307 K5
Cabannes (13) 276 C3
les Cabannes (81) 251 F6
Cabara (33) 230 B2
Cabariot (17) 177 G5
Cabas-Loumassès (32) 286 D4
Cabasse (83) 298 B2
Cabestany (66) 315 H2
Cabidos (64) 284 C1
Cabourg (14) 33 G3
Cabrerets (46) 250 C1
Cabrerolles (34) 291 K1
Cabrespine (11) 290 C4
Cabrières (30) 275 H2
Cabrières (34) 292 B1
Cabrières-d'Aigues (84) 277 J3
Cabrières-d'Avignon (84) 276 C2
Cabriès (13) 296 C2
Cabris (06) 280 C4
Cachan (94) 58 E4
Cachen (40) 246 A6
Cachy (80) 18 C2
Cadalen (81) 270 C3
Cadarcet (09) 307 H2
Cadarsac (33) 230 A2
Cadaujac (33) 229 H3
Cadéac (65) 305 F4
Cadeilhan (32) 267 K3
Cadeilhan-Trachère (65) 304 E4
Cadeillan (32) 287 F3
Cademène (25) 156 B2
Caden (56) 102 A4
Cadenet (84) 277 H4
Caderousse (84) 256 D5
la Cadière-d'Azur (83) 300 A3
la Cadière-et-Cambo (30) 274 B2
Cadillac (33) 229 K4
Cadillac-en-Fronsadais (33) 211 K6
Cadillon (64) 285 F1
Cadix (81) 271 H2
Cadolive (13) 296 E3
Cadours (31) 268 C5
Cadrieu (46) 250 E1
Caen (14) 32 E5
Caëstre (59) 5 K2
Caffiers (62) 2 C4
Cagnac-les-Mines (81) 270 E4
Cagnano (2B) 317 D3
Cagnes-sur-Mer (06) 281 F4
Cagnicourt (62) 11 G4
Cagnoncles (59) 12 B4
Cagnotte (40) 264 B6
Cagny (14) 33 F5
Cagny (80) 18 B2
Cahagnes (14) 32 A6
Cahagnolles (14) 32 A5
Cahaignes (27) 36 C5
Cahan (61) 53 J3
Caharet (65) 286 A6
Cahon (80) 9 F5
Cahors (46) 249 K1
Cahus (46) 234 C1
Cahuzac (11) 289 F6
Cahuzac (47) 231 J4
Cahuzac (81) 289 J2
Cahuzac-sur-Adour (32) 266 B6
Cahuzac-sur-Vère (81) 270 B2
Caignac (31) 288 C3
le Cailar (30) 275 F5
Cailhau (11) 289 F6
Cailhavel (11) 289 J6
Cailla (11) 308 E5
Caillac (46) 249 J1
Caillavet (32) 267 F5
Caille (06) 280 B3
la Caillère-Saint-Hilaire (85) 160 E3
Cailleville (76) 15 G2
Caillouël-Crépigny (02) 19 J5
Caillouet-Orgeville (27) 56 E1
Cailloux-sur-Fontaines (69) 188 D6
Cailly (76) 16 B6

Cailly-sur-Eure (27) 35 J6
la Caine (14) 53 H1
Cairanne (84) 257 F4
le Caire (04) 259 G2
Cairon (14) 32 D4
Caisnes (60) 39 G1
Caissargues (30) 275 G4
Caix (80) 18 C3
Caixas (66) 314 E3
Caixon (65) 285 H3
Cajarc (46) 250 E1
Calacuccia (2B) 318 E5
Calais (62) 2 C2
Calamane (46) 233 G6
Calan (56) 100 A2
Calanhel (22) 47 K6
Calavanté (65) 285 J5
Calcatoggio (2A) 320 B4
Calce (66) 310 A5
Calenzana (2B) 318 C3
Calès (24) 232 B2
Calès (46) 233 J3
Calignac (47) 247 K5
Caligny (61) 53 G4
Callac (22) 75 K1
Callas (83) 279 K5
Callen (40) 246 A3
Callengeville (76) 16 D3
Calleville (27) 34 E5
Calleville-les-Deux-Églises (76) . . . 15 J4
Callian (32) 266 E6
Callian (83) 280 B5
Calmeilles (66) 314 E4
Calmels-et-le-Viala (12) 272 A2
la Calmette (30) 275 F2
Calmont (12) 252 B4
Calmont (31) 288 D5
Calmoutier (70) 118 C6
Caloire (42) 204 E6
Calonges (47) 247 H2
Calonne-Ricouart (62) 5 J6
Calonne-sur-la-Lys (62) 5 K4
Calorguen (22) 50 D6
la Calotterie (62) 4 B6
Caluire-et-Cuire (69) 206 A1
Calvi (2B) 318 B3
Calviac (46) 234 D1
Calviac-en-Périgord (24) 233 G2
Calvignac (46) 250 D1
Calvinet (15) 235 G4
Calvisson (30) 275 F4
Calzan (09) 307 K2
Camalès (65) 285 H3
Camarade (09) 307 F1
Camarès (12) 272 B4
Camaret-sur-Aigues (84) 257 F5
Camaret-sur-Mer (29) 72 A4
Camarsac (33) 229 K2
Cambayrac (46) 249 J2
la Cambe (14) 29 J4
Cambernard (31) 287 J2
Cambernon (50) 30 E3
Cambes (33) 229 J3
Cambes (46) 234 C5
Cambes (47) 231 F5
Cambes-en-Plaine (14) 32 E4
Cambia (2B) 319 G5
Cambiac (31) 289 F2
Cambieure (11) 308 D1
Camblain-Châtelain (62) 5 J6
Camblain-l'Abbé (62) 10 D1
Camblanes-et-Meynac (33) 229 H3
Cambligneul (62) 10 D1
Cambo-les-Bains (64) 282 C3
Cambon (81) 270 E2
Cambon-et-Salvergues (34) 272 B6
Cambon-lès-Lavaur (81) 289 G1
Camboulazet (12) 252 A4
Camboulit (46) 234 C5
Cambounès (81) 290 C1
Cambounet-sur-le-Sor (81) 289 J1
le Cambout (22) 77 H6
Cambrai (59) 11 J4
Cambremer (14) 33 J5
Cambrin (62) 6 B5
Cambron (80) 9 F5
Cambronne-lès-Clermont (60) 38 A3
Cambronne-lès-Ribécourt (60) 38 E1
Camburat (46) 234 D5
Came (64) 283 F2
Camélas (66) 314 E3
Camelin (02) 39 G1
Camembert (61) 54 E3
Cametours (50) 31 F4
Camiac-et-Saint-Denis (33) 230 A2
Camiers (62) 4 A5
Camiran (33) 230 C5
Camjac (12) 251 K5
les Cammazes (81) 289 J3
Camoël (56) 121 J2
Camon (09) 308 C2
Camon (80) 18 B2
Camors (56) 100 D3
Camou-Cihigue (64) 283 H6
Camous (65) 305 F3
Campagna-de-Sault (11) 308 D5
Campagnac (12) 253 G2
Campagnac (81) 270 B1
Campagnac-lès-Quercy (24) 232 E4
Campagnan (34) 292 D1
Campagne (24) 232 C1
Campagne (34) 274 D4
Campagne (40) 265 F3
Campagne (60) 19 G5
Campagne-d'Armagnac (32) 266 C3

Campagne-lès-Boulonnais (62) . . . 4   E4
Campagne-lès-Guines (62). 2   D4
Campagne-lès-Hesdin (62). 9   G1
Campagne-lès-Wardrecques (62) . . 5   H3
Campagne-sur-Arize (09) 307 F1
Campagne-sur-Aude (11). 308 J3
Campagnolles (14). 52   D2
Campan (65) 304 D2
Campana (2B) 319 H5
Campandré-Valcongrain (14) 53   H1
Camparan (65) 305 F4
Campbon (44) 122 D1
Campeaux (14). 31   J5
Campeaux (60). 17   F5
Campel (35) 78   D6
Campénéac (56) 78   A6
Campestre-et-Luc (30) 273 H2
Campet-et-Lamolère (40) 265 F2
Camphin-en-Carembault (59) 6   D5
Camphin-en-Pévèle (59). 7   F4
Campi (2B) 319 J6
Campigneulles-les-Grandes (62) . . 9   F1
Campigneulles-les-Petites (62) . . . 4   B6
Campigny (14). 32   J4
Campigny (27) 34   C3
Campile (2B) 319 H3
Campistrous (65) 286 A6
Campitello (2B) 319 G3
Camplong (83) 272 E5
Camplong-d'Aude (11) 309 K1
Campneuseville (76) 17   F2
Campo (2A) 320 E5
Campôme (66) 314 B2
Campouriez (12). 235 K4
Campoussy (66) 314 C2
Campremy (60) 18   B6
Camprond (50) 31   J3
Camps-en-Amiénois (80) 17   H2
Camps-la-Source (83) 297 K2
Camps-Saint-Mathurin-
  -Léobazel (19) 216 D6
Camps-sur-l'Agly (11). 309 G4
Camps-sur-l'Isle (33) 212 C5
Campsas (82). 269 F3
Campsegret (24) 231 J1
Campuac (12) 235 K6
Campugnan (33) 211 H3
Campuzan (65) 286 B5
Camurac (11) 308 B5
Canale-di-Verde (2B) 319 J6
Canals (82). 269 F3
Canaples (80). 9   K5
Canappeville (27) 35   H5
Canapville (14). 33   J3
Canapville (61) 55   F2
Canari (2B) 317 C3
Canaules-et-Argentières (30) 274 D1
Canavaggia (2B) 319 G3
Canaveilles (66) 314 A4
Cancale (35) 51   F3
Canchy (14) 29   J6
Canchy (80) 9   G4
Cancon (47) 231 K6
Candas (80) 10   A5
Candé (49) 124 C2
Candé-sur-Beuvron (41) 128 E3
Candes-Saint-Martin (37) 144 E1
Candillargues (34) 274 D6
Candor (60) 19   G5
Candresse (40). 264 B4
Canehan (76) 16   C1
Canéjan (33) 229 G3
Canens (31) 288 A5
Canenx-et-Réaut (40) 265 H1
Canet (11) 291 G5
Canet (34) 273 H6
Canet-de-Salars (12) 252 D4
Canet-en-Roussillon (66) 315 H2
Canettemont (62) 10   B3
Cangey (37) 128 C4
Caniac-du-Causse (46) 233 K5
Canihuel (22) 76   D2
Canilhac (48) 253 H2
Canisy (50) 31   G4
Canlers (62) 5   F6
Canly (60). 38   C2
Cannectancourt (60). 19   G6
Cannelle (2A) 320 C3
Cannes (06) 280 E6
Cannes-Écluse (77) 88   A4
Cannes-et-Clairan (30) 274 E2
Cannessières (80). 17   F1
le Cannet (06). 280 E5
Cannet (32) 266 B6
le Cannet-des-Maures (83). 298 C2
Canny-sur-Matz (60). 19   F5
Canny-sur-Thérain (60). 17   F5
Canohès (66) 315 G2
la Canourgue (48). 253 H2
Canouville (76) 15   H3
Cantaing-sur-Escaut (59) 11   J4
Cantaous (65). 305 G1
Cantaron (06). 281 H3
Canté (09) 288 C5
Canteleu (76) 35   H2
Canteleux (62) 10   A4
Canteloup (14). 33   G5
Canteloup (50). 29   F2
Cantenac (33). 211 G5
Cantenay-Épinard (49) 125 G2
Cantiers (27) 36   C4
Cantigny (80) 18   C5
Cantillac (24) 213 K1
Cantin (59) 11   H2
Cantoin (12) 236 B2
Cantois (33) 230 A4

Canville-la-Rocque (50) 28   C6
Canville-les-Deux-Églises (76) . . . 15   H3
Cany-Barville (76). 15   F3
Caorches-Saint-Nicolas (27) 34   C6
Caouënnec-Lanvézéac (22) 48   A3
Caours (80) 9   G5
Cap-d'Ail (06). 281 J3
Capbreton (40). 262 B5
Capdenac (46) 234 D5
Capdenac-Gare (12). 234 E6
Capdrot (24). 232 C4
la Capelle (02) 21   F1
Capelle (59) 12   D3
la Capelle-Balaguier (12) 251 F2
la Capelle-Bleys (12) 251 H3
la Capelle-Bonance (12) 253 F1
la Capelle-et-Masmolène (30). . . . 256 B6
Capelle-Fermont (62) 10   D2
la Capelle-lès-Boulogne (62) 4   B3
Capelle-les-Grands (27) 55   G1
Capelle-lès-Hesdin (62) 9   H2
Capendu (11) 290 D6
Capens (31) 287 K4
Capestang (34). 291 J4
Capian (33) 229 K3
Capinghem (59) 6   D4
Caplong (33) 230 E3
Cappel (57) 68   B3
Cappelle-Brouck (59) 3   G3
Cappelle-en-Pévèle (59). 6   E5
Cappelle-la-Grande (59) 3   H2
Cappy (80) 19   F1
Captieux (33) 246 C3
Capvern (65) 305 F1
Caragoudes (31). 288 E2
Caraman (31) 289 F1
Caramany (66) 314 D1
Carantec (29) 47   F3
Carantilly (50). 31   F4
Carayac (46). 234 C6
Carbay (49) 104 A5
Carbes (81) 270 E6
Carbini (2A) 323 G2
Carbon-Blanc (33) 229 H1
Carbuccia (2A) 320 D3
Carcagny (14). 32   C4
Carcanières (09). 313 J2
Carcans (33) 210 C4
Carcarès-Sainte-Croix (40) 264 C5
Carcassonne (11) 290 B6
Carcen-Ponson (40) 264 D2
Carcès (83) 298 A1
Carcheto-Brustico (2B). 319 H5
Cardaillac (46) 234 D4
Cardan (33) 229 K4
Cardeilhac (31). 286 D5
Cardesse (64). 284 A4
Cardet (30) 274 D1
Cardo-Torgia (2A). 320 E6
Cardonnette (80) 18   B1
le Cardonnois (80) 18   C5
Cardonville (14) 29   H6
Cardroc (35). 78   E2
Carelles (53). 80   D3
Carency (62). 10   E1
Carennac (46). 234 A1
Carentan (50). 31   G1
Carentoir (56) 102 B2
Cargèse (2A) 316 C6
Cargiaca (2A) 323 F2
Carhaix-Plouguer (29) 75   J2
Carignan (08) 23   H5
Carignan-de-Bordeaux (33) 229 J2
Carisey (89) 113 J4
Carla-Bayle (09) 288 B6
Carla-de-Roquefort (09) 308 A3
le Carlaret (09) 307 K1
Carlat (15) 235 J2
Carlencas-et-Levas (34) 273 F6
Carlepont (60). 39   F1
Carling (57) 68   A2
Carlipa (11) 289 J4
Carlucet (46) 233 K4
Carlus (81) 270 D3
Carlux (24) 233 G2
Carly (62). 4   B7
Carmaux (81) 270 E1
Carnac (56) 100 C6
Carnac-Rouffiac (46) 249 H2
Carnas (30) 274 D3
la Carneille (61) 53   J4
Carnet (50). 51   K5
Carnetin (77) 59   H3
Carneville (50) 28   E2
Carnières (59). 12   B4
Carnin (59) 6   D5
Carnoët (22) 75   J1
Carnoules (83) 298 B3
Carnoux-en-Provence (13) 296 E4
Carnoy (80) 19   F1
Caro (56) 101 K3
Caro (64) 282 B6
Carolles (50). 51   H2
Caromb (84) 257 H6
Carpentras (84) 257 G6
Carpineto (2B) 319 H5
Carpiquet (14) 32   D5
Carquebut (50) 29   F6
Carquefou (44) 123 H3
Carqueiranne (83) 300 D4
Carrépuis (80) 19   F4
Carrère (64) 284 E2
Carresse-Cassaber (64) 283 G2
Carrières-sous-Poissy (78) 58   B2

Carrières-sur-Seine (78) 58   D3
Carros (06) 281 F3
Carrouges (61). 82   B1
Carry-le-Rouet (13). 296 A4
Cars (33) 211 G4
les Cars (87) 198 D3
Carsac-Aillac (24). 233 F2
Carsac-de-Gurson (24). 212 E6
Carsan (30) 256 C4
Carsix (27) 34   D5
Carspach (68) 97   A4
Cartelègue (33). 211 H3
Carticasi (2B) 319 G5
Cartignies (59) 13   G5
Cartigny (80) 19   H2
Cartigny-l'Épinay (14) 31   J2
Carves (24). 232 D3
Carville (14) 52   E2
Carville-la-Folletière (76). 15   H4
Carville-Pot-de-Fer (76). 15   G4
Casabianca (2B). 319 H4
Casaglione (2A) 320 C3
Casalabriva (2A). 322 D1
Casalta (2B) 319 H4
Casamaccioli (2B) 318 D6
Casanova (2B) 319 F6
Cascastel-des-Corbières (11) 310 A3
Casefabre (66) 314 E3
Caseneuve (84) 277 J2
Cases-de-Pène (66) 310 A5
Casevecchie (2B) 321 F1
Cassagnabère-Tournas (31) 286 E5
Cassagnas (48) 254 D4
la Cassagne (24) 215 G5
Cassagne (31) 306 C1
Cassagnes (46) 232 E6
Cassagnes (66) 309 J6
Cassagnes-Bégonhès (12) 252 B5
Cassagnoles (30) 274 E1
Cassagnoles (34) 290 E3
la Cassaigne (11) 289 H6
Cassaigne (32). 267 F2
Cassaignes (11) 309 F3
Cassaniouze (15) 235 H4
Cassel (59). 3   J4
Cassen (40) 264 C4
Casseneuil (47) 248 B1
les Cassés (11) 289 G3
Casseuil (33) 230 B5
Cassignas (47) 248 B3
Cassis (13) 296 E5
Casson (44) 123 G2
Cassuéjouls (12). 236 B4
Cast (29) 74   D4
Castagnac (31). 288 A5
Castagnède (31) 306 B2
Castagnède (64). 283 G2
Castagniers (06). 281 G3
Castaignos-Souslens (40). 265 F6
Castandet (40) 265 J3
Castanet (12) 251 J4
Castanet (81) 270 C2
Castanet (82) 251 F4
Castanet-le-Haut (34). 272 C5
Castanet-Tolosan (31) 288 C2
Castans (11). 290 C3
Casteide-Cami (64) 284 B2
Casteide-Candau (64). 284 B1
Casteide-Doat (64). 285 G3
Casteil (66) 314 B4
Castel-Sarrazin (40) 264 D6
Castelbajac (65) 286 A6
Castelbiague (31) 306 B2
Castelculier (47) 248 C5
Castelferrus (82). 268 D1
Castelfranc (46) 249 H1
Castelgaillard (31). 287 G4
Castelginest (31) 269 G5
Casteljaloux (47). 247 G3
Castella (47) 248 C3
Castellane (04). 279 J2
Castellar (06) 281 J2
le Castellard-Melan (04) 259 H4
Castellare-di-Casinca (2B) 319 J3
Castellare-di-Mercurio (2B). 319 G6
le Castellet (04) 278 D1
le Castellet (83) 300 A3
Castellet (84) 277 J3
Castellet-lès-Sausses (04) 260 E6
Castello-di-Rostino (2B). 319 G4
Castelmary (12) 251 J3
Castelmaurou (31) 269 H5
Castelmayran (82) 268 C1
Castelmoron-d'Albret (33) 230 C4
Castelmoron-sur-Lot (47) 248 A2
Castelnau-Barbarens (32) 286 E1
Castelnau-Chalosse (40) 264 D5
Castelnau-d'Anglès (32) 266 B6
Castelnau-d'Arbieu (32) 267 K3
Castelnau-d'Aude (11) 290 A3
Castelnau-d'Auzan (32) 266 D2
Castelnau-de-Brassac (81) 271 H6
Castelnau-de-Guers (34) 292 C3
Castelnau-de-Lévis (81) 270 D2
Castelnau-de-Mandailles (12) 236 C6
Castelnau-de-Médoc (33). 211 F5
Castelnau-de-Montmiral (81) 270 A2
Castelnau-d'Estrétefonds (31) . . . 269 F4
Castelnau-Durban (09) 307 F2
Castelnau-le-Lez (34) 274 C6
Castelnau-Magnoac (65) 286 C4
Castelnau-Montratier (46) 249 K4
Castelnau-Pégayrols (12) 253 F5
Castelnau-Picampeau (31) 287 H4
Castelnau-Rivière-Basse (65) 266 B6

Castelnau-sur-Gupie (47) 230 E5
Castelnau-sur-l'Auvignon (32). . . . 267 G1
Castelnau-Tursan (40) 265 H5
Castelnau-de-Gratecambe (47) . . . 248 C1
Castelnau-la-Chapelle (24) 232 E2
Castelnaudary (11) 289 H4
Castelnavet (32) 266 D5
Castelner (64) 284 B1
Castelnou (66) 314 E3
Castelreng (11) 308 D2
Castels (24) 232 D2
Castelsagrat (82) 248 E5
Castelsarrasin (82) 268 D1
Castelvieilh (65) 285 J4
Castelviel (33) 230 B4
le Castéra (31) 268 D5
Castéra-Bouzet (82) 268 B1
Castéra-Lanusse (65). 285 K6
Castéra-Lectourois (32) 267 J1
Castéra-Lou (65) 285 J4
Castéra-Loubix (64) 285 G3
Castéra-Verduzan (32) 267 G4
Castéra-Vignoles (31) 286 E5
Castéras (09) 307 G1
Casterets (65). 286 C4
Castéron (32) 268 B3
Castet (64) 303 H1
Castet-Arrouy (32) 267 K1
Castetbon (64) 283 J3
Castétis (64). 283 K2
Castetnau-Camblong (64) 283 J3
Castetner (64) 283 J2
Castetpugon (64) 284 E1
Castets (40) 264 A2
Castets-en-Dorthe (33) 230 B5
Castex (09) 288 A6
Castex (32). 286 A3
Castex-d'Armagnac (32). 266 A3
Casties-Labrande (31) 287 H4
Castifao (2B) 318 E3
Castiglione (2B) 319 F4
Castillon (06) 281 J2
Castillon (14) 32   A4
Castillon (65) 304 D1
Castillon (Canton d'Arthez-
  -de-Béarn) (64). 284 B2
Castillon (Canton
  de Lembeye) (64) 285 F2
Castillon-de-Castets (33) 230 B6
Castillon-de-Larboust (31) 305 H5
Castillon-de-Saint-Martory (31) . . . 287 F6
Castillon-Debats (32) 266 E4
Castillon-du-Gard (30) 275 J1
Castillon-en-Auge (14) 54   D1
Castillon-en-Couserans (09) 306 C3
Castillon-la-Bataille (33) 230 C2
Castillon-Massas (32) 267 H5
Castillon-Savès (32) 287 H1
Castillonnès (47). 231 J4
Castilly (14) 31   J1
Castin (32) 267 H5
Castineta (2B) 319 G6
Castirla (2B) 319 F5
Castres (02) 19   K3
Castres (81) 271 F6
Castres-Gironde (33) 229 J4
Castries (34). 274 D5
le Cateau-Cambrésis (59). 12   D5
le Catelet (02). 11   K6
le Catelier (76) 16   A3
Catenay (76). 36   A1
Catenoy (60) 38   B3
Cateri (2B) 318 C3
Cathervielle (31) 305 G5
Catheux (60) 17   K5
Catigny (60) 19   G5
Catillon-Fumechon (60) 37   K1
Catillon-sur-Sambre (59). 12   E5
Catllar (66) 314 C3
Catonvielle (32) 268 B5
Cattenières (59) 12   B4
Cattenom (57) 27   H3
Catteville (50). 28   D6
Catus (46) 233 G6
Catz (50) 31   J1
Caubeyres (47). 247 H4
Caubiac (31). 268 D5
Caubios-Loos (64). 284 C2
Caubon-Saint-Sauveur (47) 230 E5
Caubous (31) 305 G4
Caubous (65) 286 B5
Caucalières (81). 290 A2
la Cauchie (62) 10   D4
Cauchy-à-la-Tour (62) 5   J6
Caucourt (62) 10   D1
Caudan (56) 100 A3
Caudebec-en-Caux (76). 15   G6
Caudebec-lès-Elbeuf (76). 35   H4
Caudebronde (11) 290 A3
Caudecoste (47). 248 C5
Caudeval (47) 308 C1
Caudiès-de-Conflent (66) 313 K3
Caudiès-de-Fenouillèdes (66). . . . 309 G5
Caudrot (33) 230 B5
Caudry (59) 12   C5
Cauffry (60) 38   A3
Caugé (27) 56   C1
Caujac (31) 288 C4
Caulaincourt (02). 19   J2
le Caule-Sainte-Beuve (76) 16   E3
Caulières (80). 17   H3
Caullery (59). 12   B5
Caulnes (22) 78   B2
Caumont (02). 19   J5
Caumont (09) 306 D2

Caumont (27) 35   G3
Caumont (32) 266 B5
Caumont (33) 230 C4
Caumont (62) 9   H3
Caumont (82) 268 C1
Caumont-l'Éventé (14) 32   C6
Caumont-sur-Durance (84) 276 C2
Caumont-sur-Garonne (47) 247 H1
Caumont-sur-Orne (14) 53   H2
Cauna (40) 265 F4
Caunay (79) 179 F2
Cauneille (40) 264 B6
Caunes-Minervois (11) 290 D4
la Caunette (34) 291 F4
Caunette-sur-Lauquet (11) 309 G2
Caunettes-en-Val (11). 309 J2
Caupenne (40) 264 E5
Caupenne-d'Armagnac (32) 266 B4
la Caure (51) 61   H3
Caurel (22) 76   D4
Caurel (51) 41   G3
Cauro (2A) 320 D5
Cauroir (59) 12   B4
Cauroy (08) 41   K3
Cauroy-lès-Hermonville (51) 40   E3
le Causé (82) 268 C4
Cause-de-Clérans (24) 231 K2
Caussade (82) 250 B5
Caussade-Rivière (65) 285 H1
Causse-Bégon (30) 253 K6
Causse-de-la-Selle (34) 273 K4
Causse-et-Diège (12) 234 D6
Caussens (32) 267 G2
Causses-et-Veyran (34) 291 J2
Caussiniojouls (34) 291 K1
Caussols (06) 280 D3
Caussou (09) 308 A5
Cauterets (65) 304 A3
Cauverville-en-Roumois (27). 34   D3
Cauvicourt (14). 54   A1
Cauvignac (33) 246 E1
Cauvigny (60). 37   J4
Cauville (14) 53   H2
Cauville-sur-Mer (76) 14   A5
Caux (34) 292 B3
Caux-et-Sauzens (11). 290 A5
Cauzac (47) 248 D3
Cavagnac (46) 215 K6
Cavaillon (84) 276 D3
Cavalaire-sur-Mer (83) 301 J3
la Cavalerie (12) 272 E1
Cavan (22) 48   B3
Cavanac (11) 290 B6
Cavarc (47) 231 K4
Caveirac (30) 275 F3
Caves (11) 310 C3
Cavignac (33) 211 K4
Cavigny (50) 31   H2
Cavillargues (30) 256 B5
Cavillon (80). 17   J1
Cavron-Saint-Martin (62) 9   H1
Caychax (09) 307 K5
Cayeux-en-Santerre (80) 18   D3
Cayeux-sur-Mer (80) 8   D4
le Caylar (34) 273 G3
Caylus (82) 250 D4
Cayrac (82) 250 A6
Cayres (43) 238 B1
Cayriech (82) 250 B4
le Cayrol (12) 236 B5
Cayrols (15) 235 F2
Cazac (31) 287 G4
Cazalis (33) 246 B2
Cazalis (40) 265 F5
Cazalrenoux (11) 289 G6
Cazals (46). 233 F5
Cazals (82). 250 C5
Cazals-des-Baylès (09). 308 C1
Cazaril-Laspènes (31). 305 H5
Cazaril-Tambourès (31). 286 C6
Cazarilh (65). 305 H3
Cazats (33). 246 D1
Cazaubon (32) 266 B2
Cazaugitat (33). 230 D3
Cazaunous (31) 305 K2
Cazaux (09) 307 H2
Cazaux-d'Anglès (32) 266 E5
Cazaux-Debat (65) 305 F4
Cazaux-Fréchet-Anéran-
  -Camors (65) 305 F4
Cazaux-Layrisse (31) 305 H4
Cazaux-Savès (32). 287 G1
Cazaux-Villecomtal (32) 285 J2
Cazavet (09) 306 C2
Cazeaux-de-Larboust (31) 305 H5
Cazedarnes (34) 291 J3
Cazeneuve-Serres-et-Allens (09) . . 307 J4
Cazeneuve (32) 266 D2
Cazeneuve-Montaut (31) 287 F6
Cazères (31). 287 H5
Cazères-sur-l'Adour (40). 265 J4
Cazes-Mondenard (82). 249 H4
Cazevieille (34) 274 B4
Cazideroque (47) 248 E2
Cazilhac (11) 290 B6
Cazilhac (34) 274 A2
Cazillac (46). 215 K6
Cazoulès (24) 233 G2
Cazouls-d'Hérault (34) 292 C2
Cazouls-lès-Béziers (34) 291 J3
Ceaucé (61) 81   G2
Ceaulmont (36). 165 H4
Céaux (50) 51   K3
Céaux-d'Allègre (43). 220 A4
Ceaux-en-Couhé (86) 162 E6
Ceaux-en-Loudun (86) 145 F3

Cébazan (34) 291 H3
Cébazat (63) 202 D1
Ceffonds (52) 91 H2
Ceignes (01) 189 J3
Ceilhes-et-Rocozels (34) 272 E4
Ceillac (05) 227 B3
Ceilloux (63) 203 H3
Ceintrey (54) 94 A1
la Celette (18) 167 G2
la Celle (18) 167 F1
Cellé (41) 107 K5
la Celle (63) 201 H1
la Celle (83) 297 K2
la Celle-Condé (18) 148 E6
la Celle-Dunoise (23) 182 C1
la Celle-en-Morvan (71) 152 E3
la Celle-Guenand (37) 146 C4
la Celle-les-Bordes (78) 58 A6
Celle-Lévescault (86) 162 D5
la Celle-Saint-Avant (37) 145 K3
la Celle-Saint-Cloud (78) 58 C3
la Celle-Saint-Cyr (89) 112 D3
la Celle-sous-Chantemerle (51) . . . 61 G6
la Celle-sous-Gouzon (23) 183 G2
la Celle-sous-Montmirail (02) . . . 61 F3
la Celle-sur-Loire (58) 132 A4
la Celle-sur-Morin (77) 60 A4
la Celle-sur-Nièvre (58) 150 E1
Cellefrouin (16) 179 J6
Celles (09) 307 K3
Celles (15) 218 C4
Celles (17) 195 J4
Celles (24) 213 H2
Celles (34) 273 G6
Celles-en-Bassigny (52) 117 F3
Celles-lès-Condé (02) 61 F1
Celles-sur-Aisne (02) 40 A2
Celles-sur-Belle (79) 178 C1
Celles-sur-Durolle (63) 203 J1
Celles-sur-Ource (10) 114 E2
Celles-sur-Plaine (88) 95 H2
la Cellette (23) 166 B6
la Cellette (63) 184 B4
Cellettes (16) 179 G6
Cellettes (41) 129 F3
le Cellier (44) 123 J3
Cellier-du-Luc (07) 238 C4
Cellieu (42) 205 H5
Cellule (63) 185 F5
Celon (36) 165 G4
Celoux (15) 219 F4
Celsoy (52) 116 E4
Cély (77) 87 G3
Cemboing (70) 117 H4
Cempuis (60) 17 H5
Cénac (33) 229 J3
Cénac-et-Saint-Julien (24) 233 F3
Cenans (70) 138 B3
Cendras (30) 255 G5
le Cendre (63) 202 D2
Cendrecourt (70) 117 J4
Cendrey (25) 138 C4
Cendrieux (24) 214 B6
Cénevières (46) 250 D1
Cenne-Monestiés (11) 289 J4
Cenon (33) 229 H2
Cenon-sur-Vienne (86) 163 H1
Censeau (39) 156 C5
Censerey (21) 153 F1
Censy (89) 114 A6
les Cent-Acres (76) 16 A3
Centrès (12) 251 K5
Centuri (2B) 317 D2
Cenves (69) 188 A1
Cépet (31) 269 G4
Cépie (11) 309 F1
Cepoy (45) 111 J2
Céran (32) 267 J3
Cérans-Foulletourte (72) 106 C5
Cerbère (66) 315 K5
Cerbois (18) 148 C2
Cercié (69) 188 B3
Cercier (74) 190 E4
Cercles (24) 213 H1
Cercottes (45) 110 A3
Cercoux (17) 212 B4
le Cercueil (61) 82 C1
Cercy-la-Tour (58) 151 J5
Cerdon (01) 189 J3
Cerdon (45) 130 E2
Cère (40) 265 G1
Céré-la-Ronde (37) 128 D6
Cerelles (37) 127 J3
Cérences (50) 30 E6
Céreste (04) 277 K3
Céret (66) 315 F5
Cerfontaine (59) 13 H3
le Cergne (42) 187 H3
Cergy (95) 58 B1
Cérilly (03) 167 K3
Cérilly (21) 115 F4
Cérilly (89) 89 G6
Cerisé (61) 82 D3
Cerisières (52) 92 A4
Cerisiers (89) 113 F1
Cerisy (80) 18 E2
Cerisy-Belle-Étoile (61) 53 G4
Cerisy-Buleux (80) 17 F1
Cerisy-la-Forêt (50) 31 J2
Cerisy-la-Salle (50) 31 H4
Cerizay (85) 143 G6
Cérizols (09) 306 C1
Cerizy (02) 20 A3
la Cerlangue (76) 34 B1
Cernans (39) 156 B4

Cernay (14) 55 F1
Cernay (28) 84 E4
Cernay (68) 97 A2
Cernay (86) 145 G6
Cernay-en-Dormois (51) 42 C4
Cernay-la-Ville (78) 58 B6
Cernay-l'Église (25) 139 H5
Cernay-lès-Reims (51) 41 F4
Cerneux (77) 60 D5
Cernex (74) 190 E3
Cerniébaud (39) 156 C6
Cernion (08) 22 A3
Cernon (39) 173 H5
Cernon (51) 62 D3
Cernoy (60) 38 B2
Cernoy-en-Berry (45) 131 H3
Cernusson (49) 143 J1
Céron (71) 186 D1
Cérons (33) 229 K4
Cerqueux (14) 55 F1
les Cerqueux (49) 143 H3
les Cerqueux-sous-
   -Passavant (49) 143 J2
Cerre-lès-Noroy (70) 138 C1
Cers (34) 292 B4
Cersay (79) 143 K3
Cerseuil (02) 40 A3
Cersot (71) 171 H1
Certilleux (88) 93 G4
Certines (01) 189 G3
Cervens (74) 175 F6
Cervières (05) 227 B1
Cervières (42) 204 A1
Cerville (54) 66 B5
Cervione (2B) 319 J5
Cervon (58) 151 K1
Cerzat (43) 219 H4
Cesancey (39) 173 F2
Césarches (73) 209 G2
Césarville-Dossainville (45) . . . 86 D5
Cescau (09) 306 C3
Cescau (64) 284 B3
Cesny-aux-Vignes-Ouézy (14) . . . 33 G6
Cesny-Bois-Halbout (14) 53 J1
Cessac (33) 230 B3
Cessales (31) 288 E2
Cesse (55) 23 H6
Cessenon-sur-Orb (34) 291 J2
Cessens (73) 208 B1
Cesseras (34) 290 E4
Cesset (03) 185 G1
Cesseville (27) 35 G5
Cessey (25) 156 A2
Cessey-sur-Tille (21) 136 C6
Cessières (02) 20 C6
Cessieu (38) 207 G4
Cesson (77) 87 G1
Cesson-Sévigné (35) 79 G4
Cessoy-en-Montois (77) 88 C2
Cessy (01) 174 B6
Cessy-les-Bois (58) 132 C5
Cestas (33) 229 G3
Cestayrols (81) 270 C2
Ceton (61) 83 K5
Cette-Eygun (64) 303 F3
Cevins (73) 209 G3
Ceyras (34) 273 H6
Ceyrat (63) 202 D2
Ceyreste (13) 297 F5
Ceyroux (23) 182 B4
Ceyssac (43) 220 B5
Ceyssat (63) 202 B2
Ceyzériat (01) 189 H2
Ceyzérieu (01) 190 B6
Cézac (33) 211 J4
Cézac (46) 249 J3
Cezais (85) 160 D3
Cézan (32) 267 H3
Cezay (42) 204 C1
Cézens (15) 218 B6
Cézia (39) 173 G5
Cézy (89) 112 E3
Chabanais (16) 180 B6
la Chabanne (03) 186 C4
Chabestan (05) 242 B6
Chabeuil (26) 240 D1
Chablis (89) 113 J5
Châbons (38) 207 G6
Chabottes (05) 243 F4
Chabournay (86) 162 E1
Chabrac (16) 180 C6
Chabreloche (63) 186 B6
Chabrignac (19) 215 G2
Chabrillan (26) 240 D3
Chabris (36) 129 H6
Chacé (49) 144 C1
Chacenay (10) 115 F1
Chacrise (02) 39 K3
Chadeleuf (63) 202 D4
Chadenac (17) 195 J4
Chadenet (48) 237 K6
Chadrac (43) 220 C5
Chadron (43) 220 C6
Chadurie (16) 196 D5
le Chaffal (26) 241 F1
le Chaffaut-Saint-Jurson (04) . . . 259 J6
Chaffois (25) 156 E4
Chagey (70) 139 G1
Chagnon (42) 205 H5
Chagny (08) 22 D6
Chagny (71) 153 K5
Chahaignes (72) 107 G6
Chahains (61) 82 B1

Chaignay (21) 136 A3
Chaignes (27) 57 G1
Chail (79) 178 E2
Chaillac (36) 164 E5
Chaillac-sur-Vienne (87) 180 D6
Chailland (53) 80 E5
Chaillé-les-Marais (85) 160 B5
Chaillé-sous-les-Ormeaux (85) . . . 159 J3
Chailles (41) 128 E3
Chaillevette (17) 194 C2
Chaillevois (02) 40 A1
Chailley (89) 113 H2
Chaillon (55) 65 F2
Chailloué (61) 54 E6
Chailly-en-Bière (77) 87 G3
Chailly-en-Brie (77) 60 B4
Chailly-en-Gâtinais (45) 111 G3
Chailly-lès-Ennery (57) 45 F4
Chainaz-les-Frasses (74) 208 C1
Chaînée-des-Coupis (39) 155 G4
Chaingy (45) 109 J4
Chaintré (71) 188 B1
Chaintreaux (77) 87 J6
Chaintrix-Bierges (51) 62 B3
la Chaise (10) 91 G4
la Chaise-Baudouin (50) 52 B4
la Chaise-Dieu (43) 220 A2
Chaise-Dieu-du-Theil (27) 55 K4
Chaix (85) 160 D5
la Chaize-Giraud (85) 158 E2
la Chaize-le-Vicomte (85) 159 K1
Chalabre (11) 308 C3
Chalagnac (24) 213 K5
Chalain-d'Uzore (42) 204 D3
Chalain-le-Comtal (42) 204 E3
Chalaines (55) 65 F6
Chalais (16) 212 D2
Chalais (36) 164 D4
Chalais (86) 144 A4
Chalampé (68) 97 C1
Chalancey (52) 116 B6
Chalancon (26) 241 H6
Chalandray (86) 162 B2
Chalandry (02) 20 D4
Chalandry-Elaire (08) 22 C4
le Chalange (61) 83 F1
le Chalard (87) 198 D5
Chalaux (58) 133 K5
Chaleins (01) 188 C4
Chaleix (24) 198 A5
Chalencon (07) 239 K1
les Chalesmes (39) 174 B1
Châlette-sur-Loing (45) 111 J3
Chalette-sur-Voire (10) 90 E1
Chaley (01) 189 K5
Chalèze (25) 138 A5
Chalezeule (25) 138 A5
Chaliers (15) 237 F1
Chalifert (77) 59 J3
Chaligny (54) 65 K6
Chalinargues (15) 218 C4
Chalindrey (52) 116 E5
Chalivoy-Milon (18) 149 K5
Challain-la-Potherie (49) 124 C1
Challans (85) 141 F6
Challement (58) 133 G5
Challerange (08) 42 B3
Challes (01) 189 J3
Challes (72) 107 G3
Challes-les-Eaux (73) 208 C4
Challet (28) 85 F1
Challex (01) 190 D2
Challignac (16) 196 B6
Challonges (74) 190 C4
Challuy (58) 150 D4
Chalmaison (77) 88 D2
Chalmazel (42) 204 B3
Chalmoux (71) 169 K3
Chalo-Saint-Mars (91) 86 B3
le Chalon (26) 222 E4
Chalon-sur-Saône (71) 154 A6
Chalonnes-sous-le-Lude (49) . . . 126 D2
Chalonnes-sur-Loire (49) 124 E5
Châlons (38) 206 B6
Châlons-du-Maine (53) 81 G6
Châlons-en-Champagne (51) . . . 62 D2
Châlons-sur-Vesle (51) 40 E4
Châlonvillars (70) 119 H6
Chalou-Moulineux (91) 86 B4
Chaltrait (51) 61 J2
Chalus (63) 202 E6
Châlus (87) 198 C3
Chalvignac (15) 217 F3
Chalvraines (52) 92 E5
Chamadelle (33) 212 C4
Chamagne (88) 94 B2
Chamagnieu (38) 206 E3
Chamalières (63) 202 D2
Chamalières-sur-Loire (43) . . . 220 D3
Chamaloc (26) 241 H2
Chamant (60) 38 C5
Chamarande (91) 86 D2
Chamarandes-Choignes (52) . . . 116 B3
Chamaret (26) 257 F2
la Chamba (42) 203 K2
Chambain (21) 115 K5
Chambeire (21) 136 C5
Chambellay (49) 105 F6
Chambéon (42) 204 E3
Chambérat (03) 167 F5
Chamberaud (23) 183 F4
Chambéret (19) 199 K4

Chambéria (39) 173 G4
Chambéry (73) 208 B4
Chambeugle (89) 112 B4
Chambezon (43) 219 F1
Chambilly (71) 186 E1
Chamblac (27) 55 H2
Chamblanc (21) 154 D3
Chamblay (39) 155 J3
Chambles (42) 204 E6
Chamblet (03) 184 B1
Chambley-Bussières (54) 44 C6
Chambly (60) 37 J5
Chambœuf (21) 135 K6
Chambœuf (42) 205 F4
Chambois (61) 54 D4
Chambolle-Musigny (21) 154 B1
le Chambon (07) 239 G2
Chambon (17) 177 G3
Chambon (18) 166 E1
Chambon (30) 255 G5
Chambon (37) 146 B6
le Chambon-Feugerolles (42) . . . 221 G1
Chambon-la-Forêt (45) 110 E2
Chambon-le-Château (48) 237 K2
Chambon-Sainte-Croix (23) . . . 165 K6
Chambon-sur-Cisse (41) 128 D2
Chambon-sur-Dolore (63) 203 J5
Chambon-sur-Lac (63) 202 B4
le Chambon-sur-Lignon (43) . . . 221 G5
Chambon-sur-Voueize (23) . . . 183 J2
Chambonas (07) 255 H2
Chambonchard (23) 184 A3
la Chambonie (42) 203 K2
Chamborand (23) 182 A3
Chambord (27) 55 H3
Chambord (41) 129 G2
Chamboret (87) 181 F5
Chamborigaud (30) 255 F3
Chambornay-lès-Bellevaux (70) . . . 138 A4
Chambornay-lès-Pin (70) 137 J5
Chambors (60) 36 E4
Chambost-Allières (69) 187 K4
Chambost-Longessaigne (69) . . . 205 G2
Chamboulive (19) 199 K6
Chambourcy (78) 58 B3
Chambourg-sur-Indre (37) 146 C1
Chambray (27) 35 K6
Chambray-lès-Tours (37) 127 J5
la Chambre (73) 209 F6
Chambrecy (51) 40 D5
les Chambres (50) 51 K2
Chambretaud (85) 142 D4
Chambrey (57) 66 D3
Chambroncourt (52) 92 D3
Chambry (02) 20 D6
Chambry (77) 59 H2
Chaméane (63) 203 G5
Chamelet (69) 187 K5
Chameyrat (19) 216 A3
Chamigny (77) 60 D2
Chamilly (71) 153 J5
Chammes (53) 105 J1
Chamole (39) 155 J5
Chamonix-Mont-Blanc (74) . . . 192 C5
Chamouillac (17) 211 J2
Chamouille (02) 40 B1
Chamouilley (52) 63 K6
Chamousset (73) 208 E4
Chamoux (89) 133 H4
Chamoux-sur-Gelon (73) 208 E4
Chamoy (10) 113 K1
le Champ-de-la-Pierre (61) . . . 54 A6
Champ-d'Oiseau (21) 134 D2
Champ-Dolent (27) 56 C2
Champ-du-Boult (14) 52 D4
Champ-Haut (61) 55 F5
Champ-Laurent (73) 208 E4
Champ-le-Duc (88) 95 F5
le Champ-près-Froges (38) . . . 224 C2
le Champ-Saint-Père (85) 159 J3
Champ-sur-Barse (10) 90 E3
Champ-sur-Drac (38) 224 A4
Champ-sur-Layon (49) 125 G6
Champagnac (15) 217 H1
Champagnac (17) 195 J6
Champagnac-de-Belair (24) . . . 214 A1
Champagnac-la-Noaille (19) . . . 216 D2
Champagnac-la-Prune (19) . . . 216 C4
Champagnac-la-Rivière (87) . . . 198 B3
Champagnac-le-Vieux (43) . . . 219 J1
Champagnat (23) 183 H5
Champagnat (71) 172 E4
Champagnat-le-Jeune (63) . . . 203 G6
Champagne (07) 222 D4
Champagne (17) 194 D1
Champagne (28) 57 H5
Champagné (72) 107 F2
Champagne-au-Mont-d'Or (69) . . . 206 A1
Champagne-en-Valromey (01) . . . 190 B5
Champagne-et-Fontaine (24) . . . 197 F6
Champagné-le-Sec (86) 179 G6
Champagné-les-Marais (85) . . . 160 A5
Champagne-Mouton (16) 179 J5
Champagné-Saint-Hilaire (86) . . . 162 E6
Champagne-sur-Loue (39) 155 K3
Champagne-sur-Oise (95) 37 J4
Champagne-sur-Seine (77) . . . 87 J3
Champagne-sur-Vingeanne (21) . . . 136 D3
Champagne-Vigny (16) 196 C5
Champagneux (73) 207 J3
Champagney (25) 137 J6
Champagney (39) 137 F6

Champagney (70) 119 G5
Champagnier (38) 224 A4
Champagnole (39) 156 B6
Champagnolles (17) 195 G5
Champagny (21) 135 H3
Champagny-en-Vanoise (73) . . . 209 K5
Champagny-sous-Uxelles (71) . . . 171 J3
Champallement (58) 151 H1
Champanges (74) 175 G5
Champaubert (51) 61 H3
Champcella (05) 243 G3
Champcenest (77) 60 D6
Champcerie (61) 54 A4
Champcervon (50) 51 K2
Champcevinel (24) 214 A3
Champcevrais (89) 112 A6
Champcey (50) 51 J2
Champclause (43) 221 F5
Champcueil (91) 87 F2
Champdeniers-Saint-Denis (79) . . . 161 H4
Champdeuil (77) 59 G3
Champdieu (42) 204 D3
Champdivers (39) 155 F3
Champdolent (17) 177 G5
Champdor (01) 190 A4
Champdôtre (21) 154 E1
Champdray (88) 95 G6
Champeau-en-Morvan (21) . . . 134 B6
Champeaux (35) 79 K4
Champeaux (50) 51 J2
les Champeaux (61) 54 D3
Champeaux (77) 87 J1
Champeaux-et-la-Chapelle-
   -Pommier (24) 197 G6
Champeaux-sur-Sarthe (61) . . . 83 G1
Champeix (63) 202 D4
Champenard (27) 36 A5
la Champenoise (36) 148 A5
Champenoux (54) 66 C4
Champéon (53) 81 H3
Champétières (63) 203 K5
Champey (70) 139 G1
Champey-sur-Moselle (54) 65 K1
Champfleur (72) 82 D3
Champfleury (10) 62 A6
Champfleury (51) 41 F5
Champforgeuil (71) 154 A6
Champfrémont (53) 82 B3
Champfromier (01) 190 C2
Champgenéteux (53) 81 J4
Champguyon (51) 61 F4
Champhol (28) 85 G3
Champien (80) 19 G4
Champier (38) 207 F5
Champigné (49) 125 G1
Champignelles (89) 112 B5
Champigneul-Champagne (51) . . . 62 B2
Champigneul-sur-Vence (08) . . . 22 C4
Champigneulle (08) 42 D3
Champigneulles (54) 66 A4
Champigneulles-
   -en-Bassigny (52) 93 F6
Champignol-lez-Mondeville (10) . . . 115 G1
Champignolles (21) 153 H3
Champignolles (27) 55 K2
Champigny (51) 40 E4
Champigny (89) 88 C4
Champigny-en-Beauce (41) . . . 108 E6
Champigny-la-Futelaye (27) . . . 56 E3
Champigny-le-Sec (86) 162 D1
Champigny-lès-Langres (52) . . . 116 D4
Champigny-sous-Varennes (52) . . . 117 F4
Champigny-sur-Aube (10) 90 A1
Champigny-sur-Marne (94) . . . 59 F4
Champigny-sur-Veude (37) 145 G3
Champillet (36) 166 C4
Champillon (51) 40 E6
Champis (07) 222 B6
Champlan (91) 58 E6
Champlat-et-Boujacourt (51) . . . 40 E5
Champlay (89) 112 E3
Champlecy (71) 170 D4
Champlemy (58) 132 E6
Champlin (08) 21 K2
Champlin (58) 151 G1
Champlitte (70) 136 E1
Champlive (25) 138 C5
Champlost (89) 113 H2
Champmillon (16) 196 C3
Champmotteux (91) 86 E4
Champnétery (87) 199 J1
Champneuville (55) 43 H4
Champniers (16) 196 E2
Champniers (86) 179 J2
Champniers-et-Reilhac (24) . . . 197 K3
Champoléon (05) 243 G4
Champoly (42) 204 A1
Champosoult (61) 54 D3
Champougny (55) 93 G1
Champoulet (45) 132 A2
Champoux (25) 138 B5
Champrenault (21) 135 G4
Champrepus (50) 52 A3
Champrond (72) 107 K2
Champrond-en-Gâtine (28) . . . 84 C3
Champrond-en-Perchet (28) . . . 84 A4
Champrougier (39) 155 G5
Champs (02) 19 K6
Champs (61) 83 H1
Champs (63) 185 F4
les Champs-de-Losque (50) . . . 31 G2
les Champs-Géraux (22) 50 D6
Champs-Romain (24) 198 A5
Champs-sur-Marne (77) 59 G3
Champs-sur-Tarentaine-
   -Marchal (15) 217 J1

Champs-sur-Yonne (89) 113 G6
Champsac (87). 198 C3
Champsanglard (23). 182 D1
Champsecret (61). 53 H6
Champseru (28) 85 H2
Champsevraine (52) 117 F5
Champtercier (04) 259 J5
Champteussé-sur-Baconne (49) . . . 125 F1
Champtocé-sur-Loire (49). 124 D1
Champtoceaux (49) 123 K2
Champtonnay (70) 137 G4
Champvallon (89) 112 E3
Champvans (39). 155 G2
Champvans (70) 137 F4
Champvans-les-Moulins (25) 137 J6
Champvert (58) 151 H6
Champvoisy (51) 40 B6
Champvoux (58). 150 D2
Chamrousse (38) 224 C4
Chamvres (89) 112 E3
Chanac (48) 253 K1
Chanac-les-Mines (19) 216 B3
Chanaleilles (43) 237 J2
Chanas (38) 222 B2
Chanat-la-Mouteyre (63). 202 C1
Chanay (01) 190 C4
Chanaz (73) 208 A1
Chançay (37) 128 A4
Chancé (35) 79 J5
Chanceaux (21) 135 H3
Chanceaux-près-Loches (37) 146 C2
Chanceaux-sur-Choisille (37) 127 J3
Chancelade (24) 213 K3
Chancenay (52) 63 K5
Chancey (70) 137 G5
Chancia (39). 173 H6
Chandai (61) 55 K5
Chandolas (07). 255 J2
Chandon (42) 187 G3
Chanéac (07) 239 G1
Chaneins (01) 188 C3
Chânes (71) 188 B1
le Change (24) 214 C3
Changé (53) 104 E1
Change (71) 153 J4
Changé (72) 106 E3
Changey (52) 116 D3
Changis-sur-Marne (77) 60 A2
Changy (42) 186 D5
Changy (51) 63 G4
Changy (71) 170 D5
Chaniat (43) 219 J2
Chaniers (17) 195 H2
Channay (21) 114 D4
Channay-sur-Lathan (37) 126 E3
Channes (10) 114 C3
Chanonat (63) 202 D3
Chanos-Curson (26) 222 C5
Chanousse (05) 258 C3
Chanoy (52) 116 C3
Chanoz-Châtenay (01) 188 C2
Chanteau (45) 110 B3
Chantecoq (45) 112 A2
Chantecorps (79) 162 A4
Chanteheux (54) 66 D6
Chanteix (19) 215 K2
Chantelle (03) 185 F2
Chanteloup (27) 56 C3
Chanteloup (35) 79 G6
Chanteloup (50) 30 D6
Chanteloup (79) 143 J6
Chanteloup-en-Brie (77) 59 J3
Chanteloup-les-Bois (49) 143 G2
Chanteloup-les-Vignes (78) 58 B2
Chantelouve (38) 224 D5
Chantemerle (51) 89 G1
Chantemerle-les-Blés (26) 222 C4
Chantemerle-lès-Grignan (26). 256 E2
Chantemerle-sur-la-Soie (17) 177 J5
Chantenay-Saint-Imbert (58) 168 D1
Chantenay-Villedieu (72). 106 A3
Chantepie (35) 79 G4
Chantérac (24) 213 H4
Chanteraine (55) 64 D5
Chanterelle (15) 218 B1
Chantes (70) 137 J1
Chantesse (38) 223 H2
Chanteuges (43) 219 J5
Chantillac (16) 212 A1
Chantilly (60) 38 A5
Chantonnay (85) 160 B1
Chantraine (88) 94 D5
Chantraines (52) 92 C5
Chantrans (25) 156 D2
Chantrigné (53) 81 G3
Chanu (61) 53 G5
Chanville (57) 45 H6
Chanzeaux (49) 125 F6
Chaon (41) 130 C2
Chaouilley (54) 93 K2
Chaource (10) 114 B2
Chaourse (02) 21 G4
Chapaize (71) 171 J3
Chapareillan (38) 208 C5
Chapdes-Beaufort (63) 184 D6
Chapdeuil (24) 213 H1
Chapeau (03) 169 G4
Chapeiry (74) 190 E6
Chapelaine (51) 90 E1
la Chapelaude (03) 167 G5
la Chapelle (03) 186 A4
la Chapelle (08) 23 F3
la Chapelle (16) 196 D1
la Chapelle (73) 209 F6
la Chapelle-Achard (85) 159 F2
la Chapelle-Agnon (63). 203 J4

la Chapelle-Anthenaise (53) 105 F1
la Chapelle-au-Mans (71) 170 A3
la Chapelle-au-Moine (61) 53 G5
la Chapelle-au-Riboul (53) 81 J4
la Chapelle-Aubareil (24) 215 F6
la Chapelle-aux-Bois (88) 118 C1
la Chapelle-aux-Brocs (19) 215 K4
la Chapelle-aux-Chasses (03) 169 G2
la Chapelle-aux-Choux (72) 126 E1
la Chapelle-aux-Filtzméens (35) . . . 51 F6
la Chapelle-aux-Lys (85) 161 F2
la Chapelle-aux-Naux (37) 127 F5
la Chapelle-aux-Saints (19) 216 A6
la Chapelle-Baloue (23) 165 H6
la Chapelle-Bâton (79) 161 J4
la Chapelle-Bâton (86) 179 J2
la Chapelle-Bayvel (27) 34 B4
la Chapelle-Bertin (43) 219 K3
la Chapelle-Bertrand (79) 162 A2
la Chapelle-Biche (61) 53 G5
la Chapelle-Blanche (22) 78 C2
la Chapelle-Blanche (73) 208 D5
la Chapelle-Blanche-
    -Saint-Martin (37) 146 B3
la Chapelle-Bouëxic (35) 78 D6
la Chapelle-Caro (56) 101 J3
la Chapelle-Cécelin (50) 52 B3
la Chapelle-Chaussée (35) 78 E2
la Chapelle-Craonnaise (53) 104 D3
la Chapelle-d'Abondance (74) 175 J6
la Chapelle-d'Alagnon (15) 218 C5
la Chapelle-d'Aligné (72) 105 K6
la Chapelle-d'Andaine (61) 81 H1
la Chapelle-d'Angillon (18) 131 F5
la Chapelle-d'Armentières (59) 6 C3
la Chapelle-d'Aunainville (28) 85 K3
la Chapelle-d'Aurec (43) 221 F2
la Chapelle-de-Bragny (71) 171 J2
la Chapelle-de-Brain (35) 102 D3
la Chapelle-de-Guinchay (71) 188 B2
la Chapelle-de-la-Tour (38) 207 G4
la Chapelle-de-Mardore (69) 187 H4
la Chapelle-de-Surieu (38) 222 C1
Chapelle-des-Bois (25) 174 B2
la Chapelle-des-Fougeretz (35) 79 F3
la Chapelle-des-Marais (44) 122 A1
la Chapelle-des-Pots (17) 195 H2
la Chapelle-devant-Bruyères (88) . . . 95 G5
Chapelle-d'Huin (25) 156 D4
la Chapelle-du-Bard (38) 208 D6
la Chapelle-du-Bois (72) 83 H5
la Chapelle-du-Bois-
    -des-Faulx (27) 35 J6
la Chapelle-du-Bourgay (76) 16 A3
la Chapelle-du-Châtelard (01). 188 C4
la Chapelle-du-Genêt (49) 142 D1
la Chapelle-du-Lou (35) 78 D3
la Chapelle-du-Mont-
    -de-France (71) 171 G6
la Chapelle-du-Mont-
    -du-Chat (73) 208 A2
la Chapelle-en-Juger (50) 31 G3
la Chapelle-en-Lafaye (42) 204 C6
la Chapelle-en-Serval (60) 38 B6
la Chapelle-en-Valgaudémar (05) . . 243 F2
la Chapelle-en-Vercors (26) 223 H6
la Chapelle-en-Vexin (95) 36 D5
la Chapelle-Enchérie (41) 108 D5
la Chapelle-Engerbold (14) 53 G3
la Chapelle-Erbrée (35) 80 B6
la Chapelle-Faucher (24) 214 A1
la Chapelle-Felcourt (51) 63 G1
la Chapelle-Forainvilliers (28) 57 G5
la Chapelle-Fortin (28) 56 A4
la Chapelle-Gaceline (56) 102 C2
la Chapelle-Gaudin (79) 143 K4
la Chapelle-Gaugain (72) 107 J5
la Chapelle-Gauthier (27) 55 G2
la Chapelle-Gauthier (77) 87 K2
la Chapelle-Geneste (43) 219 K1
la Chapelle-Glain (44) 124 A1
la Chapelle-Gonaguet (24) 213 K3
la Chapelle-Grésignac (24) 213 G1
Chapelle-Guillaume (28) 108 A1
la Chapelle-Hareng (27) 34 B6
la Chapelle-Haute-Grue (14) 54 D2
la Chapelle-Hermier (85) 159 F1
la Chapelle-Heulin (44) 142 A1
la Chapelle-Hugon (18) 150 C5
la Chapelle-Hullin (49) 104 B5
la Chapelle-Huon (72) 107 K4
la Chapelle-Iger (77) 60 A6
la Chapelle-Janson (35) 80 B3
la Chapelle-la-Reine (77) 87 G4
la Chapelle-Lasson (51) 61 J4
la Chapelle-Launay (44) 122 C2
la Chapelle-Laurent (15) 219 H4
la Chapelle-lès-Luxeuil (70) 118 D5
la Chapelle-Marcousse (63) 202 D6
la Chapelle-Montabourlet (24) 213 H1
la Chapelle-Montbrandeix (87) 198 B3
la Chapelle-Monthodon (02) 61 G1
la Chapelle-Montligeon (61) 83 J2
la Chapelle-Montlinard (18) 150 C2
la Chapelle-Montmartin (41) 129 J4
la Chapelle-Montmoreau (24) 197 J6
la Chapelle-Montreuil (86) 162 D4
la Chapelle-Moulière (86) 163 H2
la Chapelle-Moutils (77) 60 E4
la Chapelle-Naude (71) 172 C1
la Chapelle-Neuve (22) 48 A4
la Chapelle-Neuve (56) 100 E2
la Chapelle-Onzerain (45) 109 H2
la Chapelle-Orthemale (36) 147 H5

la Chapelle-Palluau (85) 141 H6
la Chapelle-Pouilloux (79) 179 F3
la Chapelle-près-Sées (61) 82 D1
la Chapelle-Rablais (77) 88 A2
la Chapelle-Rainsouin (53) 105 H1
la Chapelle-Rambaud (74) 191 G3
la Chapelle-Réanville (27) 36 A6
la Chapelle-Rousselin (49) 124 E6
la Chapelle-Royale (28) 108 C1
la Chapelle-Saint-André (58) 132 E5
la Chapelle-Saint-Aubert (35) 79 K2
la Chapelle-Saint-Aubin (72) 106 D2
la Chapelle-Saint-Étienne (79) 161 G2
la Chapelle-Saint-Florent (49) 124 B5
la Chapelle-Saint-Fray (72) 106 D1
la Chapelle-Saint-Géraud (19) 216 C5
la Chapelle-Saint-Jean (24) 214 E3
la Chapelle-Saint-Laud (49) 125 J1
la Chapelle-Saint-Laurent (79) 161 H1
la Chapelle-Saint-Laurian (36) 148 A3
la Chapelle-Saint-Luc (10) 90 A4
la Chapelle-Saint-Martial (23) 182 D5
la Chapelle-Saint-Martin (73) 207 K3
la Chapelle-Saint-Martin-
    en-Plaine (41) 109 F6
la Chapelle-Saint-Maurice (74) 208 D1
la Chapelle-Saint-Mesmin (45) 109 K4
la Chapelle-Saint-Ouen (76) 16 C6
la Chapelle-Saint-Quillain (70) 137 H3
la Chapelle-Saint-Rémy (72) 107 G1
la Chapelle-Saint-Sauveur (44) 124 C2
la Chapelle-Saint-Sauveur (71) 154 E5
la Chapelle-Saint-Sépulcre (45) . . . 111 K2
la Chapelle-Saint-Sulpice (77) 88 C1
la Chapelle-Saint-Ursin (18) 149 F3
la Chapelle-Souëf (61) 83 H4
la Chapelle-sous-Brancion (71) . . . 171 J3
la Chapelle-sous-Dun (71) 187 H1
la Chapelle-sous-Orbais (51) 61 H3
la Chapelle-sous-Uchon (71) 152 E6
la Chapelle-Spinasse (19) 216 D1
la Chapelle-sur-Aveyron (45). 111 K4
la Chapelle-sur-Chézy (02) 60 C2
la Chapelle-sur-Coise (69) 205 H3
la Chapelle-sur-Dun (76) 15 J2
la Chapelle-sur-Erdre (44) 123 G3
la Chapelle-sur-Furieuse (39) 156 A3
la Chapelle-sur-Loire (37) 126 E6
la Chapelle-sur-Oreuse (89) 88 D5
la Chapelle-sur-Oudon (49) 104 E6
la Chapelle-sur-Usson (63) 203 G6
la Chapelle-Taillefert (23) 182 D4
la Chapelle-Thècle (71) 172 C3
la Chapelle-Thémer (85) 160 C3
la Chapelle-Thireuil (79) 161 G3
la Chapelle-Thouarault (35) 78 E4
la Chapelle-Urée (50) 52 B5
Chapelle-Vallon (07) 90 A3
la Chapelle-Vaupelteigne (89) 113 H5
la Chapelle-Vendômoise (41) 128 D1
la Chapelle-Vicomtesse (41) 108 C3
la Chapelle-Viel (61) 55 J5
la Chapelle-Villars (42) 205 K5
Chapelle-Viviers (86) 163 J4
Chapelle-Voland (39) 155 F6
la Chapelle-Yvon (14) 34 A6
les Chapelles (73) 209 K3
les Chapelles-Bourbon (77) 59 K5
Chapelon (45) 111 G2
la Chapelotte (18) 131 G5
Chapet (78) 58 A2
Chapois (39) 156 B5
Chaponnay (69) 206 B3
Chaponost (69) 205 K2
Chappes (03) 168 A6
Chappes (08) 21 J4
Chappes (10) 90 C6
Chappes (63) 202 E1
Chaptelat (87) 181 H6
Chaptuzat (63) 185 G4
Charancieu (38) 207 J5
Charantonnay (38) 206 D5
Charavines (38) 207 H6
Charbogne (08) 42 A1
Charbonnat (71) 152 D6
Charbonnier-les-Mines (63) 219 G1
Charbonnières (28) 84 B6
Charbonnières (71) 171 K5
Charbonnières-les-Bains (69) 205 K2
Charbonnières-les-Sapins (25) 156 D1
Charbonnières-les-Varennes (63) . . 184 E6
Charbonnières-les-Vieilles (63) 184 E5
Charbuy (89) 113 F5
la Charce (26) 241 J6
Charcé-Saint-Ellier-
    -sur-Aubance (49) 125 H5
Charcenne (70) 137 H4
Charchigné (53) 81 J3
Charchilla (39) 173 H4
Charcier (39) 173 J2
Chard (23) 183 K6
Chardeny (08) 42 A2
Chardogne (55) 64 A3
Chardonnay (71) 171 K4
Chareil-Cintrat (03) 185 G1
Charency (21) 135 G4
Charency (39). 156 B6
Charency-Vezin (54) 43 J1
Charens (26) 241 J5
Charensat (63) 184 A5
Charentay (69) 188 B3
Charentenay (89) 133 F1
Charentilly (37) 127 H3
Charenton-du-Cher (18) 167 H1
Charenton-le-Pont (94) 59 F4
Charentonnay (18) 150 B2

Charette (38) 207 F1
Charette-Varennes (71) 154 D4
Charey (54) 65 H1
Charézier (39) 173 H2
Chargé (37) 128 B4
Chargey-lès-Gray (70) 137 F3
Chargey-lès-Port (70) 117 K5
Chariez (70) 138 A1
Charigny (21) 134 E4
la Charité-sur-Loire (58) 150 C1
Charix (01) 190 B2
Charlas (31) 286 E5
Charleval (13) 277 F4
Charleval (27) 36 A3
Charleville (51) 61 G4
Charleville-Mézières (08) 22 D3
Charleville-sous-Bois (57) 45 H4
Charlieu (42) 187 F3
Charly (02) 60 D2
Charly (18) 150 A5
Charly (69) 206 A3
Charly-Oradour (57) 45 F4
Charmant (16) 196 E5
Charmauvillers (25) 139 J5
Charmé (16) 179 F5
la Charme (39) 155 H5
le Charme (45) 112 A5
la Charmée (71) 171 J1
Charmeil (03) 185 J3
le Charmel (02) 40 A6
Charmensac (15) 218 E3
Charmentray (77) 59 J2
Charmes (02) 20 B5
Charmes (03) 185 G4
Charmes (21) 136 D4
Charmes (52) 116 D3
Charmes (88) 94 B3
Charmes-en-l'Angle (52). 91 K3
Charmes-la-Côte (54) 65 H6
Charmes-la-Grande (52) 91 K3
Charmes-Saint-Valbert (70) 117 G5
Charmes-sur-l'Herbasse (26) 222 D4
Charmes-sur-Rhône (07) 240 B2
Charmoille (25) 139 G5
Charmoille (70) 118 A6
Charmois (54) 94 C1
Charmois (90) 139 J1
Charmois-devant-Bruyères (88) 94 E5
Charmois-l'Orgueilleux (88) 94 B6
Charmont (51) 63 J3
Charmont (95) 36 E6
Charmont-en-Beauce (45) 86 C5
Charmont-sous-Barbuise (10) 90 B3
les Charmontois (51) 63 K2
Charmoy (10) 89 G3
Charmoy (71) 170 E1
Charmoy (89) 113 F3
Charnas (07) 222 A1
Charnat (63) 185 J5
Charnay (25) 156 B1
Charnay (69) 188 B6
Charnay-lès-Chalon (71) 154 C4
Charnay-lès-Mâcon (71) 188 C1
Charnècles (38) 223 J1
Charnizay (37) 146 C3
Charnod (39) 173 F6
Charnois (08) 24 C2
Charnoz-sur-Ain (01) 189 G6
Charny (21) 134 E5
Charny (77) 59 J2
Charny (89) 112 B4
Charny-le-Bachot (10) 89 K1
Charny-sur-Meuse (55) 43 H4
Charolles (71) 170 D5
Charols (26) 240 C5
Charonville (28) 84 E5
Chârost (18) 148 D4
Charpentry (55) 42 E4
Charpey (26) 222 E6
Charpont (28) 57 F5
Charquemont (25) 139 H6
Charrais (86) 162 E2
Charraix (43) 219 J6
Charras (16) 197 G5
Charray (28) 108 E3
Charre (64) 283 H4
Charrecey (71) 153 J5
Charrey-sur-Saône (21) 154 D2
Charrey-sur-Seine (21) 115 F3
Charrin (58) 151 J6
Charritte-de-Bas (64) 283 H4
Charron (17) 160 B6
Charron (23) 184 A4
Charroux (03) 185 F3
Charroux (86) 179 J3
Chars (95) 37 F5
Charsonville (45) 109 H4
Chartainvilliers (28) 85 G2
Chartèves (02) 40 A6
la Chartre-sur-le-Loir (72) 107 H6
Chartrené (49) 126 A3
Chartres (28) 85 G3
Chartres-de-Bretagne (35) 79 F5
Chartrettes (77) 87 H2
Chartrier-Ferrière (19) 215 K5
Chartronges (77) 60 D5
Chartuzac (17) 211 J1
Charvieu-Chavagneux (38) 206 D2
Charvonnex (74) 191 F4
Chas (63) 203 F2
Chasnais (85) 159 K4
Chasnans (25) 156 E2
Chasnay (58) 150 E1
Chasné-sur-Illet (35) 79 H2
Chaspinhac (43) 220 C5

Chaspuzac (43) 220 A5
la Chassagne (39) 155 G5
Chassagne (63) 202 D5
Chassagne-Montrachet (21) 153 K4
Chassagnes (43) 219 J3
Chassagny (69) 205 K4
Chassaignes (24) 213 F3
Chassal (39) 173 J5
Chassant (28) 84 C5
Chassé (72) 82 E3
Chasse-sur-Rhône (38). 206 A4
Chasseguey (50) 52 C5
Chasselas (71) 188 B1
Chasselay (38) 223 G2
Chasselay (69) 188 C6
Chassemy (02) 40 A2
Chassenard (03) 170 B5
Chasseneuil (36) 165 G2
Chasseneuil-du-Poitou (86) 163 F2
Chasseneuil-sur-Bonnieure (16) . . . 197 H1
Chassenon (16) 198 A1
Chasseradès (48) 238 B6
Chassey (21) 134 E3
Chassey-Beaupré (55) 92 D2
Chassey-le-Camp (71) 153 J5
Chassey-lès-Montbozon (70) 138 C2
Chassey-lès-Scey (70) 137 K1
Chassiecq (16) 179 J5
Chassiers (07) 239 G6
Chassieu (69) 206 C2
Chassignelles (89) 114 C5
Chassignieu (38) 207 H5
Chassignolles (36) 166 A4
Chassignolles (43) 219 J1
Chassigny (52) 116 D6
Chassigny-sous-Dun (71) 187 H2
Chassillé (72) 106 B2
Chassors (16). 196 A3
Chassy (18) 150 B3
Chassy (71) 170 C3
Chassy (89) 112 E4
le Chastang (19) 216 A4
Chastanier (48). 238 B4
Chasteaux (19) 215 H5
Chastel (43) 219 G5
Chastel-Arnaud (26) 241 F4
Chastel-Nouvel (48) 237 J6
Chastel-sur-Murat (15) 218 B4
Chastellux-sur-Cure (89). 133 K4
Chastreix (63) 201 K5
la Châtaigneraie (85) 160 E2
Chatain (86) 179 J4
Châtaincourt (28) 56 E5
Châtas (88) 95 J3
Château-Arnoux-
    -Saint-Auban (04) 259 G5
Château-Bernard (38) 223 K6
Château-Bréhain (57) 66 D2
Château-Chalon (39) 155 J6
Château-Chervix (87) 199 G4
Château-Chinon
    (Campagne) (58) 152 B3
Château-Chinon (Ville) (58) 152 B3
le Château-d'Almenêches (61) 54 D3
Château-des-Prés (39) 173 K4
le Château-d'Oléron (17) 176 D6
Château-d'Olonne (85) 158 E3
Château-du-Loir (72) 107 G6
Château-Gaillard (01) 189 H5
Château-Garnier (86) 179 J1
Château-Gontier (53) 105 F4
Château-Guibert (85) 159 K3
Château-la-Vallière (37) 127 F2
Château-l'Abbaye (59) 7 H1
Château-Landon (77) 111 H1
Château-Larcher (86) 162 E5
Château-l'Évêque (24) 214 A3
Château-l'Hermitage (72) 106 D5
Château-Porcien (08) 21 J6
Château-Renard (45) 112 A3
Château-Renault (37) 128 A2
Château-Rouge (57) 45 J3
Château-Salins (57) 66 D3
Château-sur-Allier (03) 168 B1
Château-sur-Cher (63) 184 A3
Château-sur-Epte (27) 36 D5
Château-Thébaud (44) 123 H6
Château-Thierry (02) 60 E1
Château-Verdun (09) 307 K5
Château-Ville-Vieille (05). 227 B2
Château-Voué (57) 66 D3
Châteaubernard (16) 195 K3
Châteaubleau (77) 88 B1
Châteaubourg (07) 222 B6
Châteaubourg (35) 79 J4
Châteaubriant (44) 103 J3
Châteaudouble (26) 240 E1
Châteaudouble (83) 279 J5
Châteaudun (28) 108 E2
Châteaufort (04) 259 G3
Châteaufort (78) 58 C5
Châteaugay (63) 202 D1
Châteaugiron (35) 79 H5
Châteaulin (29) 74 D3
Châteaumeillant (18) 166 C4
Châteauneuf (21) 153 J1
Châteauneuf (42) 205 J5
Châteauneuf (71) 187 G2
Châteauneuf (73) 208 D4
Châteauneuf (85) 140 E4
Châteauneuf-de-Bordette (26) 257 H2
Châteauneuf-de-Chabre (05) 258 E3
Châteauneuf-de-Gadagne (84) 276 C2
Châteauneuf-de-Galaure (26) 222 C3

Châteauneuf-de-Randon (48) 238 A5
Châteauneuf-de-Vernoux (07) 239 K1
Châteauneuf-d'Entraunes (06) 261 F4
Châteauneuf-d'Ille-et-Vilaine (35) . . 50 H4
Châteauneuf-du-Faou (29) 75 G4
Châteauneuf-du-Pape (84) 256 E6
Châteauneuf-du-Rhône (26) 240 A6
Châteauneuf-en-Thymerais (28) . . . 84 E1
Châteauneuf-Grasse (06) 280 D4
Châteauneuf-la-Forêt (87) 199 J3
Châteauneuf-le-Rouge (13) 296 E5
Châteauneuf-les-Bains (63) 184 D4
Châteauneuf-les-Martigues (13) . . . 296 A3
Châteauneuf-Miravail (04) 258 D4
Châteauneuf-sur-Charente (16) . . . 196 C4
Châteauneuf-sur-Cher (18) 149 F6
Châteauneuf-sur-Isère (26) 222 C5
Châteauneuf-sur-Loire (45) 110 D4
Châteauneuf-sur-Sarthe (49) 105 H6
Châteauneuf-Val-de-Bargis (58) . . . 132 D6
Châteauneuf-Val-
    -Saint-Donat (04) 259 G5
Châteauneuf-Villevieille (06) 281 G2
Châteauponsac (87) 181 H3
Châteauredon (04) 259 J6
Châteaurenard (13) 276 C2
Châteauroux (36) 147 K6
Châteauroux-les-Alpes (05) 243 J4
Châteauvert (83) 297 K1
Châteauvieux (05) 242 E6
Châteauvieux (41) 147 G1
Châteauvieux (83) 279 K3
Châteauvieux-les-Fossés (25) 156 D2
Châteauvilain (38) 207 F5
Châteauvillain (52) 115 J2
le Châtel (73) 225 G1
Châtel (74) 175 J6
Châtel-Censoir (89) 133 G3
Chatel-Chéhéry (08) 42 D3
Châtel-de-Joux (39) 173 J3
Châtel-de-Neuvre (03) 168 E5
Châtel-Gérard (89) 134 B1
Châtel-Montagne (03) 186 B3
Châtel-Moron (71) 153 J6
Châtel-Saint-Germain (57) 44 E5
Châtel-sur-Moselle (88) 94 C4
Châtelaillon-Plage (17) 176 E3
Châtelain (53) 105 G5
la Châtelaine (39) 155 K5
Châtelais (49) 104 D5
Châtelard (23) 183 K5
le Châtelard (73) 208 D2
Châtelaudren (22) 48 E5
Chatelay (39) 155 J3
Châtelblanc (25) 174 B1
Châteldon (63) 185 K5
le Châtelet (18) 166 B3
le Châtelet-en-Brie (77) 87 J2
le Châtelet-sur-Meuse (52) 117 F2
le Châtelet-sur-Retourne (08) 41 H2
le Châtelet-sur-Sormonne (08) . . . 22 B2
les Châtelets (28) 56 C6
le Cheley (39) 155 H5
Châtelguyon (63) 185 F6
le Châtelier (35) 63 J2
Châtellenot (21) 135 F6
Châtellerault (86) 145 J6
le Châtellier (35) 80 A3
le Châtellier (61) 53 G5
les Châtelliers-Châteaumur (85) . . 143 F5
les Châtelliers-Notre-Dame (28) . . 84 D4
Châtelneuf (39) 173 K1
Châtelneuf (42) 204 C4
Châtelperron (03) 169 H5
Châtelraould-Saint-Louvent (51) . . 63 F5
Châtelus (03) 186 B2
Châtelus (38) 223 H5
Châtelus (42) 205 G4
Châtelus-le-Marcheix (23) 182 A5
Châtelus-Malvaleix (23) 182 E1
Châtenay (01) 189 G4
Châtenay (28) 86 A4
Châtenay (38) 223 F1
Châtenay (71) 187 H1
Châtenay-en-France (95) 59 F1
Chatenay-Mâcheron (52) 116 D4
Châtenay-Malabry (92) 58 D5
Châtenay-sur-Seine (77) 88 B3
Chatenay-Vaudin (52) 116 E4
Chatenet (17) 212 A2
le Châtenet-en-Dognon (87) 181 K6
Châteney (70) 118 C6
Chatenois (39) 155 H1
Châtenois (67) 96 C1
Châtenois (70) 118 C6
Châtenois (88) 93 H4
Châtenois-les-Forges (90) 139 H1
Châtenoy (45) 110 E4
Châtenoy (77) 87 H5
Châtenoy-en-Bresse (71) 154 B6
Châtenoy-le-Royal (71) 154 A6
Châtignac (16) 212 D1
Chatignonville (91) 86 A3
Châtillon (03) 168 C5
Châtillon (39) 173 H2
Châtillon (69) 188 A6
Châtillon (86) 162 D6
Châtillon (92) 58 E4
Châtillon-Coligny (45) 111 K5
Châtillon-en-Bazois (58) 151 J3
Châtillon-en-Diois (26) 241 J3
Châtillon-en-Dunois (28) 108 D1
Châtillon-en-Michaille (01) 190 C2
Châtillon-en-Vendelais (35) 80 B5
Châtillon-Guyotte (25) 138 B5

Châtillon-la-Borde (77) 87 J2
Châtillon-la-Palud (01) 189 G5
Châtillon-le-Duc (25) 137 K5
Châtillon-le-Roi (45) 86 C6
Châtillon-lès-Sons (02) 20 D3
Châtillon-Saint-Jean (26) 222 E4
Châtillon-sous-les-Côtes (55) 43 K5
Châtillon-sur-Broué (51) 91 G1
Châtillon-sur-Chalaronne (01) 188 D3
Châtillon-sur-Cher (41) 129 G6
Châtillon-sur-Cluses (74) 191 K3
Châtillon-sur-Colmont (53) 81 F4
Châtillon-sur-Indre (36) 146 E4
Châtillon-sur-Lison (25) 156 B2
Châtillon-sur-Loire (45) 131 J2
Châtillon-sur-Marne (51) 40 C6
Châtillon-sur-Morin (51) 61 G5
Châtillon-sur-Oise (02) 20 B3
Châtillon-sur-Saône (88) 117 J3
Châtillon-sur-Seine (21) 115 F4
Châtillon-sur-Thouet (79) 161 K2
Châtin (58) 152 B2
Châtonnay (38) 206 E5
Chatonnay (39) 173 G5
Chatonrupt-Sommermont (52) 92 A2
Chatou (78) 58 C3
la Châtre (36) 166 B3
la Châtre-Langlin (36) 165 F5
Châtres (10) 89 J2
Châtres (24) 215 F4
Châtres (77) 59 J5
Châtres-la-Forêt (53) 81 J6
Châtres-sur-Cher (41) 130 A6
Châtrices (51) 63 J1
Chattancourt (55) 43 G4
Chatte (38) 223 G4
Chatuzange-le-Goubet (26) 222 E5
Chaucenne (25) 137 J5
Chauchailles (48) 236 E3
Chauché (85) 142 B5
le Chauchet (23) 183 H4
Chauchigny (10) 89 K3
Chauconin-Neufmontiers (77) 59 J2
Chaudardes (02) 40 C2
Chaudebonne (26) 241 F6
Chaudefonds-sur-Layon (49) 125 F5
Chaudefontaine (25) 138 B4
Chaudefontaine (51) 42 D6
Chaudenay (52) 116 E4
Chaudenay (71) 153 K5
Chaudenay-la-Ville (21) 153 J1
Chaudenay-le-Château (21) 153 J1
Chaudeney-sur-Moselle (54) 65 H5
Chaudes-Aigues (15) 236 D2
Chaudeyrac (48) 238 B2
Chaudeyrolles (43) 239 F1
la Chaudière (26) 241 F4
Chaudon (28) 57 G6
Chaudon-Norante (04) 279 G1
Chaudrey (10) 90 C2
Chaudron-en-Mauges (49) 124 C5
Chaudun (02) 39 H3
Chauffailles (71) 187 H2
Chauffayer (05) 242 D3
Chauffecourt (88) 94 A3
Chauffour-lès-Bailly (10) 90 D6
Chauffour-lès-Étréchy (91) 86 C2
Chauffour-sur-Vell (19) 215 K6
Chauffours (28) 85 F3
Chauffourt (52) 116 D2
Chauffry (77) 60 C4
Chaufour-lès-Bonnières (78) 57 G1
Chaufour-Notre-Dame (72) 106 C2
Chaugey (21) 115 K5
Chaulgnes (58) 150 D2
Chaulhac (48) 237 F1
Chaulieu (50) 52 E4
la Chaulme (63) 204 C6
Chaulnes (80) 19 F3
Chaum (31) 305 J3
Chaumard (58) 152 B2
la Chaume (21) 115 J4
Chaume-et-Courchamp (21) 136 D2
Chaume-lès-Baigneux (21) 135 F1
Chaumeil (19) 200 B6
Chaumercenne (70) 137 G5
Chaumergy (39) 155 G5
Chaumes-en-Brie (77) 59 K6
Chaumesnil (10) 91 H4
Chaumont (18) 150 A6
Chaumont (52) 116 B1
Chaumont (61) 55 F3
Chaumont (74) 190 D4
Chaumont (89) 88 B4
Chaumont-d'Anjou (49) 125 K2
Chaumont-devant-
    -Damvillers (55) 43 J3
Chaumont-en-Vexin (60) 37 H4
Chaumont-la-Ville (52) 93 F6
Chaumont-le-Bois (21) 115 F3
Chaumont-le-Bourg (63) 204 A6
Chaumont-Porcien (08) 21 J5
Chaumont-sur-Aire (55) 64 B2
Chaumont-sur-Loire (41) 128 D3
Chaumont-sur-Tharonne (41) 130 A2
Chaumontel (95) 38 A6
Chaumot (58) 133 H6
Chaumot (89) 112 C2
Chaumousey (88) 94 C5
Chaumoux-Marcilly (18) 150 A2
Chaumussay (37) 146 B5
la Chaumusse (39) 173 K3
Chaumuzy (51) 40 C6
Chaunac (17) 211 K1
Chaunay (86) 179 G2
Chauny (02) 19 K5

Chauray (79) 161 H6
Chauriat (63) 203 F2
la Chaussade (23) 183 G5
la Chaussaire (49) 124 A6
Chaussan (69) 205 J3
la Chaussée (76) 16 A3
la Chaussée (86) 144 E5
la Chaussée-d'Ivry (28) 57 G3
la Chaussée-Saint-Victor (41) 129 F2
la Chaussée-sur-Marne (51) 62 E3
la Chaussée-Tirancourt (80) 17 K1
Chaussenac (15) 217 G5
Chaussenans (39) 155 J5
Chausseterre (42) 186 C6
Chaussin (39) 155 F4
Chaussoy-Epagny (80) 18 B4
Chaussy (45) 86 B6
Chaussy (95) 36 D6
le Chautay (18) 150 C4
Chauvac-Laux-Montaux (26) 258 B2
Chauvé (44) 122 C4
Chauvency-le-Château (55) 23 J6
Chauvency-Saint-Hubert (55) 23 J6
Chauvigné (35) 79 J1
Chauvigny (86) 163 J3
Chauvigny-du-Perche (41) 108 C3
Chauvincourt-Provemont (27) 36 D4
Chauvirey-le-Châtel (70) 117 H5
Chauvirey-le-Vieil (70) 117 H5
Chauvoncourt (55) 64 C2
Chauvry (95) 58 D1
Chaux (21) 154 B2
la Chaux (25) 157 F3
la Chaux (61) 53 K6
la Chaux (71) 154 E5
Chaux (90) 119 H5
Chaux-Champagny (39) 156 A4
Chaux-des-Crotenay (39) 174 A2
Chaux-des-Prés (39) 173 K4
la Chaux-du-Dombief (39) 173 K2
la Chaux-en-Bresse (39) 155 G5
Chaux-la-Lotière (70) 137 K4
Chaux-lès-Clerval (25) 138 E4
Chaux-lès-Passavant (25) 138 D6
Chaux-lès-Port (70) 117 K6
Chaux-Neuve (25) 174 B1
Chauzon (07) 255 K1
Chavagnac (15) 218 C4
Chavagnac (24) 215 G5
Chavagne (35) 79 F5
Chavagnes (49) 125 H6
Chavagnes-en-Paillers (85) 142 B4
Chavagnes-les-Redoux (85) 160 D1
Chavaignes (49) 126 C2
Chavanac (19) 200 D4
Chavanat (23) 182 E5
Chavanatte (90) 139 K1
Chavanay (42) 205 K6
Chavanges (10) 91 F2
Chavaniac-Lafayette (43) 219 J4
Chavannaz (74) 190 E3
Chavanne (70) 139 F2
la Chavanne (73) 208 D5
Chavannes (18) 149 G6
Chavannes (26) 222 C4
les Chavannes-
    -en-Maurienne (73) 209 F6
Chavannes-les-Grands (90) 139 K1
Chavannes-sur-l'Étang (68) 119 K6
Chavannes-sur-Reyssouze (01) . . . 172 A5
Chavannes-sur-Suran (01) 189 J1
Chavanod (74) 190 E5
Chavanoz (38) 206 E1
Chavaroux (63) 203 F1
la Chavatte (80) 19 F4
Chavelot (88) 94 D5
Chavenat (16) 196 E6
Chavenay (78) 58 B3
Chavençon (60) 37 G5
Chavenon (03) 168 A5
Chavéria (39) 173 G4
Chaveroche (19) 201 F4
Chaveyriat (01) 188 E2
Chavignon (02) 40 A1
Chavigny (02) 39 J2
Chavigny (54) 66 A5
Chavigny-Bailleul (27) 56 D3
Chaville (92) 58 D4
Chavin (36) 165 H4
Chavonne (02) 40 B2
Chavornay (01) 190 B6
Chavot-Courcourt (51) 61 K1
Chavoy (50) 51 K2
Chavroches (03) 169 G6
le Chay (17) 194 D3
Chay (25) 156 A3
Chazay-d'Azergues (69) 188 B6
la Chaze-de-Peyre (48) 237 F4
Chazé-Henry (49) 104 B5
Chazé-sur-Argos (49) 124 D1
Chazeaux (07) 239 G5
Chazelet (36) 165 F4
Chazelles (15) 219 G5
Chazelles (16) 197 G3
Chazelles (43) 219 J6
Chazelles-sur-Albe (54) 67 G6
Chazelles-sur-Lavieu (42) 204 C5
Chazelles-sur-Lyon (42) 205 G3
Chazemais (03) 167 G5
Chazeuil (21) 136 C2
Chazeuil (58) 132 E6
Chazey-Bons (01) 207 J1
Chazey-sur-Ain (01) 189 G6
Chazilly (21) 153 H1

Chazot (25) 139 F4
Chécy (45) 110 B4
Chédigny (37) 146 D1
Chef-Boutonne (79) 178 E3
Chef-du-Pont (50) 29 F5
Chef-Haut (88) 93 K3
Cheffes (49) 125 H1
Cheffois (85) 160 E2
Cheffreville-Tonnencourt (14) 54 E1
le Chefresne (50) 52 B2
Chéhéry (08) 22 E5
Cheignieu-la-Balme (01) 207 J1
Cheillé (37) 127 F6
Cheilly-lès-Maranges (71) 153 J5
Chein-Dessus (31) 306 B2
Cheissoux (87) 199 J1
le Cheix (63) 185 G5
Cheix-en-Retz (44) 122 E4
Chélan (32) 286 C4
Chelers (62) 10 C1
Chelle-Debat (65) 285 K4
Chelle-Spou (65) 285 K6
Chelles (60) 39 F3
Chelles (77) 59 G3
Chelun (35) 104 A4
Chemaudin (25) 137 J6
Chemazé (53) 104 E5
Chemellier (49) 125 J5
Chemenot (39) 155 H5
Chéméré (44) 122 D5
Chéméré-le-Roi (53) 105 H3
Chémery (41) 129 G5
Chémery-les-Deux (57) 45 H3
Chémery-sur-Bar (08) 22 E5
Chemilla (39) 173 G6
Chemillé (49) 124 E6
Chemillé-sur-Dême (37) 127 J1
Chemillé-sur-Indrois (37) 146 E2
Chemilli (61) 83 G4
Chemilly (03) 168 E4
Chemilly (70) 137 K1
Chemilly-sur-Serein (89) 113 J5
Chemilly-sur-Yonne (89) 113 G4
Chemin (39) 154 E4
le Chemin (51) 63 J1
Chemin-d'Aisey (21) 115 F6
Cheminas (07) 222 B4
Cheminon (51) 63 J5
Cheminot (57) 65 K2
Chemiré-en-Charnie (72) 106 A2
Chemiré-le-Gaudin (72) 106 C3
Chemiré-sur-Sarthe (49) 105 H5
Chemy (59) 6 D5
Chenac-Saint-Seurin-d'Uzet (17) . . 194 E5
Chenailler-Mascheix (19) 216 B5
la Chenalotte (25) 157 J1
Chénas (69) 188 B2
Chenaud (24) 212 E3
Chenay (51) 40 E3
Chenay (72) 82 D3
Chenay (79) 162 B6
le Chêne (10) 90 B1
Chêne-Arnoult (89) 112 B4
Chêne-Bernard (39) 155 G4
Chêne-en-Semine (74) 190 C4
Chêne-Sec (39) 155 G5
Chenebier (70) 139 G6
Chenecey-Buillon (25) 156 B1
Cheneché (86) 162 E1
Chênedollé (14) 53 F3
Chênedouit (61) 53 K4
Chêne hutte-Trèves-Cunault (49) . . 126 A5
Chénelette (69) 187 K2
Chénérailles (23) 183 G3
Chenereilles (42) 204 D5
Chenereilles (43) 221 F4
Chenevelles (86) 163 J1
Chenevières (54) 94 E1
Chenevrey-et-Morogne (70) 137 H5
Chênex (74) 190 E3
Cheney (89) 113 K4
Chenicourt (54) 66 B3
Chenières (54) 26 D3
Chéniers (23) 165 K6
Cheniers (51) 62 C3
Chenillé-Changé (49) 105 H2
Cheniménil (88) 94 E6
Chennebrun (27) 55 K5
Chennegy (10) 89 J5
Chennevières-lès-Louvres (95) 59 G1
Chennevières-sur-Marne (94) 59 G4
Chenois (57) 66 D1
Chenoise (77) 88 C1
Chenommet (16) 179 H5
Chenon (16) 179 H5
Chenonceaux (37) 128 C5
Chenou (77) 87 H6
Chenôve (21) 136 A5
Chenôves (71) 171 H2
Chens-sur-Léman (74) 174 D6
Chenu (72) 127 F2
Cheny (89) 113 F3
Chepniers (17) 212 A2
Chepoix (60) 18 B5
la Cheppe (51) 62 E1
Cheppes-la-Prairie (51) 62 E3
Cheppy (55) 42 E4
Cheptainville (91) 86 D2
Chepy (80) 17 F3
Chépy (51) 62 E3
Chépy (80) 8 E5
Chérac (17) 195 J2
Chérancé (53) 104 D5
Chérancé (72) 82 D2
Chéraute (64) 283 H5

Cherbonnières (17) 178 B5
Cherbourg-Octeville (50) 28 D2
Chérence (95) 36 D6
Chérencé-le-Héron (50) 52 B3
Chérencé-le-Roussel (50) 52 C5
Chéreng (59) 7 F4
les Chères (69) 188 B6
Chérêt (02) 40 C1
Chériennes (62) 9 J2
Chérier (42) 186 D5
Chérigné (79) 178 D3
les Chéris (50) 52 A5
Chérisay (72) 82 D4
Chérisey (57) 45 F6
Chérisy (28) 57 F3
Chérisy (62) 11 F3
Chérizet (71) 171 G4
Chermignac (17) 195 F3
Chermisey (88) 92 E3
Chermizy-Ailles (02) 40 C1
Chéronnac (87) 198 A2
Chéronvilliers (27) 55 K4
Chéroy (89) 88 A6
Cherré (49) 105 G6
Cherré (72) 83 J6
Cherreau (72) 83 J6
Cherrueix (35) 51 G4
Cherval (24) 213 G1
Cherveix-Cubas (24) 214 E2
Cherves (86) 162 C1
Cherves-Châtelars (16) 197 H1
Cherves-Richemont (16) 195 J2
Chervettes (17) 177 H4
Cherveux (79) 161 J5
Chervey (10) 114 E1
Cherville (51) 62 B1
Chéry (18) 148 D2
Chéry-Chartreuve (02) 40 B4
Chéry-lès-Pouilly (02) 20 D5
Chéry-lès-Rozoy (02) 21 H4
Chesley (10) 114 B3
le Chesnay (78) 58 C4
le Chesne (08) 22 D6
le Chesne (27) 56 B3
Chesnois-Auboncourt (08) 22 B6
Chesny (57) 45 F6
Chessenaz (74) 190 D4
Chessy (69) 188 A6
Chessy (77) 59 J3
Chessy-les-Prés (10) 113 K2
Chéu (89) 113 H3
Cheuge (21) 136 D4
Cheust (65) 304 B1
Cheux (14) 32 C5
Chevagnes (03) 169 G5
Chevagny-les-Chevrières (71) 171 J6
Chevagny-sur-Guye (71) 171 F4
Chevaigné (35) 79 G3
Chevaigné-du-Maine (53) 81 J3
le Chevain (72) 82 D3
Cheval-Blanc (84) 276 E3
Chevaline (74) 208 E1
la Chevallerais (44) 123 F1
Chevanceaux (17) 212 B2
Chevannay (21) 135 G4
Chevannes (21) 154 A1
Chevannes (45) 111 K1
Chevannes (89) 113 F6
Chevannes (91) 87 F2
Chevannes-Changy (58) 133 F6
Chevennes (02) 20 E3
Chevenon (58) 150 E5
Chevenoz (74) 175 G5
Cheverny (41) 129 F3
Cheveuges (08) 22 E4
Chevières (08) 42 D3
Chevigney (70) 137 F5
Chevigney-lès-Vercel (25) 157 F1
Chevigney-sur-l'Ognon (25) 137 J5
Chevigny (39) 155 G1
Chevigny-en-Valière (21) 154 B4
Chevigny-Saint-Sauveur (21) 136 B5
Chevillard (01) 189 K3
Chevillé (72) 105 K3
Chevillon (52) 92 A1
Chevillon (89) 112 C4
Chevillon-sur-Huillard (45) 111 H3
la Chevillotte (25) 138 B6
Chevilly (45) 110 A2
Chevilly-Larue (94) 58 E5
Chevinay (69) 205 J2
Chevincourt (60) 38 E1
Cheviré-le-Rouge (49) 126 A2
Chevrainvilliers (77) 87 G5
Chevreaux (39) 172 E4
Chevregny (02) 40 B1
Chèvremont (90) 119 J6
la Chèvrerie (16) 179 G4
Chevresis-Monceau (02) 20 C3
Chevreuse (78) 58 B5
Chèvreville (50) 52 C6
Chèvreville (60) 38 E6
Chevrier (74) 190 D3
Chevières (38) 223 G4
Chevrières (42) 205 G4
Chevrières (60) 38 C3
Chevroches (58) 133 G4
la Chevrolière (44) 141 H2
Chevrotaine (39) 173 J2
Chevroux (01) 172 A5
Chevroz (25) 137 K5
Chevru (77) 60 C5
Chevry (01) 190 E1
Chevry (50) 31 H5
Chevry-Cossigny (77) 59 H5
Chevry-en-Sereine (77) 88 A5

Chevry-sous-le-Bignon (45) 111 K1
Chey (79) 178 E1
Cheylade (15) 218 A3
le Cheylard (07) 239 H1
Cheylard-l'Évêque (48) 238 B5
le Cheylas (38) 208 C6
Cheyssieu (38) 206 B6
Chezal-Benoît (18) 148 D6
la Chèze (22) 77 G5
Chèze (65) 304 B3
Chezelle (03) 185 F2
Chezelles (36) 147 J5
Chezelles (37) 145 H3
Chèzeneuve (38) 206 E4
Chézery-Forens (01) 190 C1
Chézy (03) 169 F3
Chézy-en-Orxois (02) 39 H6
Chézy-sur-Marne (02) 60 E2
Chiatra (2B) 319 J4
Chiché (79) 143 K6
Chicheboville (14) 33 F6
Chichée (89) 113 J5
Chichery (89) 113 F4
Chichey (51) 61 H5
Chichilianne (38) 241 K2
Chicourt (57) 66 D2
Chiddes (58) 152 B5
Chiddes (71) 171 G5
Chidrac (63) 202 D5
Chierry (02) 60 E1
Chieulles (57) 45 F5
Chigné (49) 126 C2
Chignin (73) 208 C4
Chigny (02) 20 E1
Chigny-les-Roses (51) 41 F5
Chigy (89) 89 F6
Chilhac (43) 219 H4
Chillac (16) 212 C1
Chille (39) 173 G1
Chilleurs-aux-Bois (45) 110 C2
le Chillou (79) 162 A1
Chilly (08) 22 B2
Chilly (74) 190 D4
Chilly (80) 19 F3
Chilly-le-Vignoble (39) 173 F2
Chilly-Mazarin (91) 58 E5
Chilly-sur-Salins (39) 156 A4
Chimilin (38) 207 J4
Chindrieux (73) 208 A1
Chinon (37) 145 F1
Chipilly (80) 18 E2
Chirac (16) 180 B6
Chirac (48) 237 G6
Chirac-Bellevue (19) 201 F6
Chirassimont (42) 187 H6
Chirat-l'Église (03) 184 E2
Chiré-en-Montreuil (86) 162 D2
Chirens (38) 207 H6
Chirmont (80) 18 B4
Chirols (07) 239 G4
Chiroubles (69) 188 A2
Chiry-Ourscamp (60) 19 G6
Chis (65) 285 H4
Chisa (2B) 321 H5
Chissay-en-Touraine (41) 128 C5
Chisseaux (37) 128 C5
Chisséria (39) 173 G5
Chissey-en-Morvan (71) 152 E2
Chissey-lès-Mâcon (71) 171 J4
Chissey-sur-Loue (39) 155 J3
Chitenay (41) 129 F3
Chitray (36) 165 F3
Chitry (89) 113 H6
Chitry-les-Mines (58) 133 H6
Chives (17) 178 D5
Chivres (21) 154 C4
Chivres-en-Laonnois (02) 21 F5
Chivres-Val (02) 39 K2
Chivy-lès-Étouvelles (02) 20 C6
Chizé (79) 178 B3
Chocques (62) 5 K5
Choilley-Dardenay (52) 136 D1
Choisel (78) 58 B6
Choiseul (52) 117 F1
Choisey (39) 155 G2
Choisies (59) 13 H3
Choisy (74) 190 E4
Choisy-au-Bac (60) 38 E2
Choisy-en-Brie (77) 60 C5
Choisy-la-Victoire (60) 38 B3
Choisy-le-Roi (94) 59 F5
Cholet (49) 142 E2
Cholonge (38) 224 B5
Choloy-Ménillot (54) 65 H5
Chomelix (43) 220 B3
Chomérac (07) 240 A4
la Chomette (43) 219 H3
Chonas-l'Amballan (38) 206 A6
Chonville-Malaumont (55) 64 E4
Chooz (08) 24 C2
Choqueuse-les-Bénards (60) 17 J5
Choranche (38) 223 H5
Chorey-les-Beaune (21) 154 A3
Chorges (05) 243 G5
Chouain (14) 32 B4
Chouday (36) 148 D5
Choue (41) 108 B3
Chougny (58) 151 K3
Chouilly (51) 62 A1
Chouppes (86) 144 E6
Chourgnac (24) 214 D3
Choussy (41) 128 E5
Chouvigny (03) 184 C3
Choux (39) 173 J6
les Choux (45) 111 H5
Chouy (02) 39 H5

Chouzé-sur-Loire (37) 126 D6
Chouzelot (25) 156 A2
Chouzy-sur-Cisse (41) 128 D3
Choye (70) 137 H4
Chozeau (38) 206 E2
Chuelles (45) 112 A3
Chuffilly-Roche (08) 42 A1
Chuignes (80) 19 F2
Chuignolles (80) 18 E2
Chuisnes (28) 84 D3
Chusclan (30) 256 D5
Chuyer (42) 205 K6
Chuzelles (38) 206 B4
Ciadoux (31) 286 E5
Ciamannacce (2A) 321 F4
Ciboure (64) 263 B2
Cideville (76) 15 H5
Ciel (71) 154 C5
Cier-de-Luchon (31) 305 H4
Cier-de-Rivière (31) 305 J1
Cierges (02) 40 B5
Cierges-sous-Montfaucon (55) 43 F3
Cierp-Gaud (31) 305 J3
Cierrey (27) 56 E1
Cierzac (17) 195 K4
Cieurac (46) 250 A2
Cieutat (65) 285 J6
Cieux (87) 181 F5
Ciez (58) 132 C4
Cigogné (37) 128 A6
Cilly (02) 21 F4
Cinais (37) 145 F2
Cindré (03) 185 K1
Cinq-Mars-la-Pile (37) 127 G5
Cinqueux (60) 38 B3
Cintegabelle (31) 288 C4
Cintheaux (14) 32 E6
Cintray (27) 56 A4
Cintray (28) 85 F3
Cintré (35) 78 E4
Cintrey (70) 117 H5
la Ciotat (13) 297 F5
Cipières (06) 280 D3
Ciral (61) 82 B2
Ciran (37) 146 B3
Circourt (88) 94 B4
Circourt-sur-Mouzon (88) 93 G4
Ciré-d'Aunis (17) 177 F4
Cirès (31) 305 G4
Cires-lès-Mello (60) 37 K4
Cirey (21) 154 B1
Cirey (70) 138 B4
Cirey-lès-Mareilles (52) 92 C5
Cirey-lès-Pontailler (21) 136 D5
Cirey-sur-Blaise (52) 91 J4
Cirey-sur-Vezouze (54) 67 H6
Cirfontaines-en-Azois (52) 115 J1
Cirfontaines-en-Ornois (52) 92 D1
Cirières (79) 143 H5
Ciron (36) 164 E3
Ciry-le-Noble (71) 170 D3
Ciry-Salsogne (02) 39 K3
Cisai-Saint-Aubin (61) 55 F4
Cisery (89) 134 B3
Cissac-Médoc (33) 210 E3
Cissé (86) 162 E2
Cisternes-la-Forêt (63) 201 K2
Cistrières (43) 219 K2
Citerne (80) 17 G1
Citers (70) 118 D5
Citey (70) 137 H3
Citou (11) 290 D3
Citry (77) 60 C2
Civaux (86) 163 J5
Civens (42) 204 E2
Civières (27) 36 C5
Civrac-de-Blaye (33) 211 J4
Civrac-en-Médoc (33) 210 E1
Civrac-sur-Dordogne (33) 230 C2
Civray (18) 148 E4
Civray (86) 179 H3
Civray-de-Touraine (37) 128 C5
Civray-sur-Esves (37) 146 A3
Civrieux (01) 188 D3
Civrieux-d'Azergues (69) 188 B6
Civry (28) 109 G2
Civry-en-Montagne (21) 135 G6
Civry-la-Forêt (78) 57 H3
Cizancourt (80) 19 G2
Cizay-la-Madeleine (49) 144 B1
Cize (01) 189 J2
Cize (39) 173 K1
Cizely (58) 151 H4
Cizos (65) 286 B5
Clacy-et-Thierret (02) 20 C6
Cladech (24) 232 D2
Claira (66) 310 C5
Clairac (47) 247 J2
Clairavaux (23) 200 E2
Clairefontaine-en-Yvelines (78) 86 A1
Clairefougère (61) 53 F4
Clairegoutte (70) 119 F6
Clairfayts (59) 13 H1
Clairfontaine (02) 13 H6
Clairmarais (62) 3 G5
Clairoix (60) 38 E2
Clairvaux-d'Aveyron (12) 251 K2
Clairvaux-les-Lacs (39) 173 J3
Clairy-Saulchoix (80) 17 K2
Clais (76) 16 D3
Claix (16) 196 D4
Claix (38) 224 A4
Clam (17) 195 H5
Clamanges (51) 62 A4
Clamart (92) 58 D4
Clamecy (02) 39 J2
Clamecy (58) 133 F4

Clamensane (04) 259 H2
Clamerey (21) 134 E4
Clans (06) 261 J6
Clans (70) 137 K1
Clansayes (26) 256 E5
le Claon (55) 42 E5
le Clapier (12) 272 E3
Clapiers (34) 274 C5
Clara (66) 314 C3
Clarac (31) 305 J1
Clarac (65) 285 K5
Claracq (64) 284 D1
Clarafond-Arcine (74) 190 D3
Clarbec (14) 33 J4
Clarens (65) 286 B6
Clarensac (30) 275 F3
Claret (04) 259 F2
Claret (34) 274 C3
Clarques (62) 5 J2
Clary (59) 12 C5
Classun (40) 265 H5
Clastres (02) 19 K4
Clasville (76) 15 H1
le Clat (11) 308 E5
Claudon (88) 117 K2
le Claux (15) 218 A4
Clavans-en-Haut-Oisans (38) 225 F4
Clavé (79) 161 K4
Claveisolles (69) 187 K3
Clavette (17) 176 E2
Claveyson (26) 222 C3
Clavières (15) 219 G6
Claviers (83) 279 K5
Claville (27) 56 C1
Claville-Motteville (76) 16 A5
Clavy-Warby (08) 22 B3
Claye-Souilly (77) 59 H2
les Clayes-sous-Bois (78) 58 B4
la Clayette (71) 187 H1
Clayeures (54) 94 C2
Clécy (14) 53 H2
Cléden-Cap-Sizun (29) 73 B3
Cléden-Poher (29) 75 H3
Cléder (29) 46 D3
Clèdes (40) 265 H6
Cleebourg (67) 25 B1
Clefmont (52) 116 E1
Clefs (49) 126 B1
les Clefs (74) 191 H6
Cléguer (56) 99 K3
Cléguérec (56) 76 D5
Clelles (38) 241 K2
Clémencey (21) 135 J6
Clémensat (63) 202 D5
Clémery (54) 66 A2
Clémont (18) 130 E2
Clénay (21) 136 B4
Clenleu (62) 4 D5
Cléon (76) 35 H3
Cléon-d'Andran (26) 240 D5
Cleppé (42) 204 E2
Clérac (17) 212 B3
Cléré-du-Bois (36) 146 E5
Cléré-les-Pins (37) 127 F4
Cléré-sur-Layon (49) 143 K2
Clères (76) 15 K5
Clérey (10) 90 C6
Clérey-la-Côte (88) 93 G2
Clérey-sur-Brenon (54) 94 A1
Clergoux (19) 216 D2
Clérieux (26) 222 D5
les Clérimois (89) 88 E5
le Clerjus (88) 118 C2
Clerlande (63) 185 G6
Clermain (71) 171 G6
Clermont (09) 307 F2
Clermont (40) 264 C5
Clermont (60) 38 A3
Clermont (74) 190 D5
Clermont-Créans (72) 106 B6
Clermont-de-Beauregard (24) 231 K1
Clermont-Dessous (47) 247 K4
Clermont-d'Excideuil (24) 214 D1
Clermont-en-Argonne (55) 42 E6
Clermont-Ferrand (63) 202 D2
Clermont-le-Fort (31) 288 B2
Clermont-les-Fermes (02) 21 G5
Clermont-l'Hérault (34) 273 H6
Clermont-Pouyguillès (32) 286 C2
Clermont-Savès (32) 268 C6
Clermont-Soubiran (47) 248 D5
Clermont-sur-Lauquet (11) 309 G2
Cléron (25) 156 C2
Clerques (62) 2 E4
Clerval (25) 138 E4
Cléry (21) 136 E5
Cléry (73) 209 F3
Cléry-en-Vexin (95) 36 E6
Cléry-le-Grand (55) 43 F2
Cléry-le-Petit (55) 43 F2
Cléry-Saint-André (45) 109 J5
Cléry-sur-Somme (80) 19 G1
Clesles (51) 89 J2
Clessé (71) 171 J5
Clessé (79) 161 H1
Clessy (71) 170 B3
Cléty (62) 5 F2
Cleurie (88) 119 F1
Cleuville (76) 15 F4
Cléville (14) 33 G5
Cléville (76) 15 F5
Clévilliers (28) 85 F2
Cleyrac (33) 230 C3
Cleyzieu (01) 189 J5
Clézentaine (88) 94 E2

Clichy (92) 58 E3
Clichy-sous-Bois (93) 59 G3
Climbach (67) 25 B1
Clinchamp (52) 92 E5
Clinchamps-sur-Orne (14) 32 D6
Clion (17) 195 H5
Clion (36) 147 F4
Cliousclat (26) 240 C5
Cliponville (76) 15 F4
Cliron (08) 22 C3
la Clisse (17) 195 F2
Clisson (44) 142 B2
Clitourps (50) 29 F2
Clohars-Carnoët (29) 99 H4
Clohars-Fouesnant (29) 98 D2
le Cloître-Pleyben (29) 75 F3
le Cloître-Saint-Thégonnec (29) 47 G6
Clomot (21) 153 G1
Clonas-sur-Varèze (38) 206 A6
Clos-Fontaine (77) 88 A1
la Clotte (17) 212 B4
Clouange (57) 44 E3
Cloué (86) 162 D5
les Clouzeaux (85) 159 H2
Cloyes-sur-le-Loir (28) 108 D3
Cloyes-sur-Marne (51) 63 G6
Clucy (39) 156 A4
Clugnat (23) 183 F1
Cluis (36) 165 J4
Clumanc (04) 260 A6
Cluny (71) 171 H5
la Clusaz (74) 191 J5
la Cluse (05) 242 C4
la Cluse-et-Mijoux (25) 157 F4
les Cluses (66) 315 G4
Cluses (74) 191 K3
Clussais-la-Pommeraie (79) 179 F2
Clux (71) 154 D4
Coadout (22) 48 C5
Coaraze (06) 281 G2
Coarraze (64) 284 E6
Coat-Méal (29) 72 D3
Coatascorn (22) 48 C3
Coatréven (22) 48 B2
Cobonne (26) 240 E3
Cobrieux (59) 7 F5
la Cochère (61) 54 D5
Cocheren (57) 68 B2
Coclois (10) 90 D2
Cocquerel (80) 9 H6
Cocumont (47) 247 F1
Cocurès (48) 254 C3
Codalet (66) 314 B3
Codognan (30) 275 F4
Codolet (30) 256 D5
Coësmes (35) 103 J1
Coëtlogon (22) 77 H5
Coëtmieux (22) 49 H6
Cœuvres-et-Valsery (02) 39 G3
Coëx (85) 158 E1
Coggia (2A) 320 B3
Coglès (35) 51 K6
Cogna (39) 173 J3
Cognac (16) 195 K3
Cognac-la-Forêt (87) 198 C1
Cognat-Lyonne (03) 185 H3
Cogners (72) 107 J4
Cognet (38) 242 B1
Cognières (70) 138 C3
Cognin (73) 208 B4
Cognin-les-Gorges (38) 223 H3
Cognocoli-Monticchi (2A) 320 D6
Cogny (18) 149 K6
Cogny (69) 188 A5
Cogolin (83) 298 E4
Cohade (43) 219 G2
Cohennoz (73) 209 G1
Cohiniac (22) 48 E6
Cohons (52) 116 D5
Coiffy-le-Bas (52) 117 G3
Coiffy-le-Haut (52) 117 G3
Coigneux (80) 10 C5
Coignières (78) 58 A5
Coigny (50) 28 E6
Coimères (33) 230 A6
Coin-lès-Cuvry (57) 45 F6
Coin-sur-Seille (57) 66 A1
Coinces (45) 109 J3
Coinches (88) 95 J4
Coincourt (54) 66 E4
Coincy (02) 39 K5
Coincy (57) 45 G5
Coings (36) 148 A5
Coingt (02) 21 H3
Coirac (33) 230 B4
Coise (69) 205 H4
Coise-Saint-Jean-Pied-
-Gauthier (73) 208 D4
Coiserette (39) 173 J6
Coisevaux (70) 139 G1
Coisia (39) 173 G6
Coisy (80) 18 B1
Coivert (17) 178 A4
Coivrel (60) 18 D6
Coizard-Joches (51) 61 J4
Colayrac-Saint-Cirq (47) 248 B4
Colembert (62) 4 C3
Coligny (01) 172 E5
Colincamps (80) 10 D5
Collan (89) 113 J4
la Collancelle (58) 151 J2
Collandres (15) 217 K3
Collandres-Quincarnon (27) 56 A2
Collanges (63) 202 E6
Collat (43) 219 K3

la Colle-sur-Loup (06) 281 F4
Collégien (77) 59 H4
Collemiers (89) 112 D1
Colleret (59) 13 J3
le Collet-de-Dèze (48) 255 H1
Colletot (27) 34 D3
Colleville (76) 14 D3
Colleville-Montgomery (14) 32 E4
Colleville-sur-Mer (14) 29 K6
Collias (30) 275 H2
Colligis-Crandelain (02) 40 B1
Colligny (57) 45 G5
Colline-Beaumont (62) 8 E2
Collinée (22) 77 J3
Collioure (66) 315 J4
Collobrières (83) 298 C4
Collonge-en-Charollais (71) 171 G2
Collonge-la-Madeleine (71) 153 H4
Collonges (01) 190 D2
Collonges-au-Mont-d'Or (69) 206 A1
Collonges-la-Rouge (19) 215 K5
Collonges-lès-Bévy (21) 154 A1
Collonges-lès-Premières (21) 136 C6
Collonges-sous-Salève (74) 191 F2
Collongues (06) 280 C2
Collongues (65) 285 J4
Collorec (29) 75 G2
Collorgues (30) 275 G1
Colmar (68) 96 C4
Colmars (04) 260 C4
Colmen (57) 45 J2
Colméry (58) 132 D5
Colmesnil-Manneville (76) 15 K2
Colmey (54) 43 K1
Colmier-le-Bas (52) 115 K5
Colmier-le-Haut (52) 115 K5
Colognac (30) 274 B1
Cologne (32) 268 C5
Colomars (06) 281 G3
Colombe (38) 207 G6
la Colombe (41) 109 F4
la Colombe (50) 52 B3
Colombé-la-Fosse (10) 91 H5
Colombé-le-Sec (10) 91 H5
Colombe-lès-Vesoul (70) 138 B1
Colombelles (14) 32 E4
Colombes (92) 58 D3
Colombey-les-Belles (54) 93 H1
Colombey-les-Deux-Églises (52) 91 J5
Colombier (03) 184 C1
Colombier (21) 153 J1
Colombier (24) 231 J3
Colombier (42) 221 K1
Colombier (70) 118 B6
Colombier-en-Brionnais (71) 170 E6
Colombier-Fontaine (25) 139 G3
Colombier-le-Cardinal (07) 222 A2
Colombier-le-Jeune (07) 222 A5
Colombier-le-Vieux (07) 222 A5
Colombier-Saugnieu (69) 206 D2
Colombières (14) 31 J1
Colombières-sur-Orb (34) 291 H1
Colombiers (17) 195 H3
Colombiers (18) 167 G2
Colombiers (34) 291 K4
Colombiers (61) 82 C2
Colombiers (86) 163 G1
Colombiers-du-Plessis (53) 80 E3
Colombiers-sur-Seulles (14) 32 D3
Colombiès (12) 251 J3
Colombotte (70) 118 C6
Colomby (50) 28 D4
Colomby-sur-Thaon (14) 32 D4
Colomiers (31) 269 F6
Colomieu (01) 207 J2
Colonard-Corubert (61) 83 J3
Colondannes (23) 182 A1
Colonfay (02) 20 D2
Colonne (39) 155 H5
Colonzelle (26) 257 F2
Colpo (56) 101 F3
Colroy-la-Grande (88) 95 K3
Colroy-la-Roche (67) 70 A6
Coltainville (28) 85 H2
Coltines (15) 218 D5
Coly (24) 215 F5
Combaillaux (34) 274 A5
Combas (30) 274 E3
la Combe-de-Lancey (38) 224 C2
Combeaufontaine (70) 117 J6
Combefa (81) 251 G6
Comberanche-et-Épeluche (24) 213 F2
Comberjon (70) 118 B6
Comberouger (82) 268 D3
Combertault (21) 154 B3
les Combes (25) 157 G2
Combes (34) 291 H1
Combiers (16) 197 G3
Comblanchien (21) 154 B2
Combles (80) 11 F6
Combles-en-Barrois (55) 64 A4
Comblessac (35) 102 C1
Combleux (45) 110 B4
Comblot (61) 83 H2
Combloux (74) 192 A5
Combon (27) 35 G4
Combourg (35) 51 F6
Combourtillé (35) 80 A4
Combovin (26) 240 E1
Combrailles (63) 201 J1
Combrand (79) 143 G5
Combray (14) 53 J2
Combre (42) 187 G4
Combrée (49) 104 C6
Combres (28) 84 C4
Combres-sous-les-Côtes (55) 44 A6

Combressol (19). 200 E6
Combret (12) 271 K3
Combreux (45) 110 E3
Combrimont (88) 95 K4
Combrit (29). 98 C2
Combronde (63) 185 F5
Combs-la-Ville (77). 59 G6
la Comelle (71) 152 D5
Comiac (46) 234 D1
Comigne (11) 290 D6
Comines (59) 6 D2
Commana (29) 46 E6
Commarin (21) 135 G6
Commeaux (61) 54 B4
Commelle (38) 206 A6
Commelle-Vernay (42) 187 F5
Commenailles (39) 155 G6
Commensacq (40) 245 G4
Commentry (03) 184 B1
Commeny (95) 37 F6
Commequiers (85) 141 F6
Commer (53) 81 G5
Commercy (55) 65 F4
Commerveil (72) 83 F4
Commes (14) 32 B3
Communailles-en-Montagne (39) . . 156 C6
Communay (69) 206 A4
Compains (63) 202 B6
Compainville (76) 16 E5
Compans (77) 59 H2
le Compas (23) 183 K5
Compertrix (51) 62 D2
Compeyre (12) 253 G5
Compiègne (60) 38 D2
Compigny (89) 88 D4
Compolibat (12) 251 H2
la Compôte (73) 208 D2
Comprégnac (12) 253 F6
Compreignac (87) 181 H5
Comps (26) 240 E5
Comps (30) 275 K3
Comps (33) 211 H5
Comps-la-Grand-Ville (12) 252 B4
Comps-sur-Artuby (83) 279 J4
la Comté (62) 10 C1
Comus (11) 308 B5
Conan (41) 108 E6
Conand (01) 189 J6
Conat (66) 314 B3
Conca (2A) 323 J1
Concarneau (29). 98 E3
Concevreux (02) 40 C2
Concèze (19) 215 G1
Conches-en-Ouche (27) 56 B2
Conches-sur-Gondoire (77) 59 H3
Conchez-de-Béarn (64) 285 F1
Conchil-le-Temple (62) 8 E2
Conchy-les-Pots (60) 18 E5
Conchy-sur-Canche (62) 9 K2
Concorès (46) 233 H4
Concoret (56) 78 B4
Concots (46) 250 C2
Concoules (30) 255 F2
Concourson-sur-Layon (49) 144 A1
Concremiers (36) 164 B3
Concressault (18) 131 G3
Concriers (41) 109 G6
Condac (16) 179 G4
Condal (71) 172 D4
Condamine (01) 189 K3
Condamine (39) 173 F2
la Condamine-Châtelard (04) 227 B6
Condat (15) 218 A2
Condat (46) 215 K6
Condat-en-Combraille (63) 201 H1
Condat-lès-Montboissier (63) 203 H5
Condat-sur-Ganaveix (19) 199 J6
Condat-sur-Trincou (24) 214 A1
Condat-sur-Vézère (24) 215 F4
Condat-sur-Vienne (87) 198 E2
Condé (36) 148 C5
Condé-en-Brie (02). 61 F1
Condé-Folie (80) 9 H6
Condé-lès-Autry (08) 42 C4
Condé-lès-Herpy (08) 21 J6
Condé-Northen (57) 45 H4
Condé-Sainte-Libiaire (77) 59 J3
Condé-sur-Aisne (02) 39 K2
Condé-sur-Huisne (61) 84 A4
Condé-sur-Ifs (14) 54 B1
Condé-sur-Iton (27) 56 B4
Condé-sur-l'Escaut (59) 7 J6
Condé-sur-Marne (51) 62 B1
Condé-sur-Noireau (14) 53 H3
Condé-sur-Risle (27) 34 D3
Condé-sur-Sarthe (61) 82 C3
Condé-sur-Seulles (14). 32 B4
Condé-sur-Suippe (02) 40 E2
Condé-sur-Vesgre (78) 57 H5
Condé-sur-Vire (50) 31 H4
Condeau (61) 84 A3
Condécourt (95) 58 A1
Condéon (16) 196 B6
Condes (39) 173 G6
Condes (52) 92 B6
Condette (62) 4 B4
Condezaygues (47) 248 E1
Condillac (26) 240 B4
Condom (32) 267 F2
Condom-d'Aubrac (12). 236 C5
Condorcet (26) 257 J1
Condren (02) 19 K5
Condrieu (69) 206 A6
Conflandey (70) 117 K5

Conflans-en-Jarnisy (54) 44 C5
Conflans-Sainte-Honorine (78) . . . 58 C2
Conflans-sur-Anille (72) 107 K3
Conflans-sur-Lanterne (70) 118 B4
Conflans-sur-Loing (45) 111 J3
Conflans-sur-Seine (51) 89 H1
Confolens (16) 180 B5
Confolent-Port-Dieu (19) 201 H5
Confort (01) 190 C2
Confort-Meilars (29) 74 A5
Confracourt (70) 117 J6
Confrançon (01) 188 E1
Congé-sur-Orne (72) 82 E6
Congénies (30) 274 E4
Congerville-Thionville (91) 86 B4
Congis-sur-Thérouanne (77) 60 A1
Congrier (53) 104 B4
Congy (51) 61 J3
Conie-Molitard (28) 109 F1
Conilhac-Corbières (11) 290 E6
Conilhac-de-la-Montagne (11) . . . 308 E3
Conjux (73) 208 A1
Conlie (72) 106 C1
Conliège (39) 173 G2
Connac (12) 271 J1
Connangles (43) 219 K2
Connantray-Vaurefroy (51) 62 A5
Connantre (51) 61 K5
Connaux (30) 256 C6
Conne-de-Labarde (24) 231 J3
Connelles (27) 35 K4
Connerré (72) 107 G2
Connezac (24) 197 H5
Connigis (02) 61 F1
Conquereuil (44) 103 F4
Conques (12) 235 H5
Conques-sur-Orbiel (11) 290 B5
le Conquet (29) 72 A4
Conqueyrac (30) 274 C2
Cons-la-Grandville (54) 26 C3
Cons-Sainte-Colombe (74) 209 F1
Consac (17) 195 G6
Conségudes (06) 280 E2
Consenvoye (55) 43 G3
Consigny (52) 92 D5
Consolation-Maisonnettes (25) . . . 157 H1
Contalmaison (80) 10 E6
Contamine-Sarzin (74) 190 D4
Contamine-sur-Arve (74) 191 H2
les Contamines-Montjoie (74). 192 B6
Contault (51) 63 H2
Contay (80) 10 C6
Conte (39) 156 B6
Contes (06) 281 H2
Contes (62) 9 H1
Contescourt (02) 19 K3
Contest (53) 81 G5
Conteville (14) 33 H6
Conteville (27) 34 B2
Conteville (60) 17 J5
Conteville (76) 16 K4
Conteville (80) 9 J4
Conteville-en-Ternois (62) 10 A1
Conteville-lès-Boulogne (62). 4 B3
Conthil (57) 66 E2
Contigné (49) 105 H6
Contigny (03) 168 E6
Contilly (72) 83 F3
Continvoir (37) 126 E4
Contoire (80) 18 D4
Contrazy (09) 306 E2
Contré (17) 178 C4
Contre (80) 17 J4
Contréglise (70) 117 K4
Contremoulins (76) 14 D4
Contres (18) 149 H5
Contres (41) 129 F4
Contreuve (08) 42 A3
Contrevoz (01) 207 J1
Contrexéville (88) 93 J5
Contrières (50) 30 E5
Contrisson (55) 63 J4
Conty (80) 17 K4
Contz-les-Bains (57) 27 J3
Conzieu (01). 207 J2
Coole (51) 62 D5
Coolus (51) 62 D2
la Copechagnière (85) 142 A5
Copponex (74) 190 D3
Coquainvilliers (14) 33 K5
Coquelles (62) 2 C3
la Coquille (24) 198 C5
Corancez (28) 85 G4
Corancy (58) 152 B2
Coray (29) 75 F5
Corbara (2B) 318 C2
Corbarieu (82) 269 G2
Corbas (69) 206 B3
Corbehem (62) 11 H2
Corbeil (51) 90 E1
Corbeil-Cerf (60) 37 H4
Corbeil-Essonnes (91) 87 F1
Corbeilles (45) 111 G2
Corbel (73) 208 A6
Corbelin (38) 207 H3
Corbenay (70) 118 C3
Corbeny (02) 40 D1
Corbère (83) 314 E2
Corbère-Abères (64) 285 F2
Corbère-les-Cabanes (66) 314 E2
Corberon (21) 154 B3
Corbès (30) 255 F6
Corbie (80) 18 C1
la Corbière (70) 118 E4
Corbières (04) 278 B4
Corbières (11) 308 C2

Corbigny (58) 133 H6
Corbon (14) 33 H5
Corbon (61) 83 J3
Corbonod (01) 190 C5
Corbreuse (91) 86 B2
Corcelle-Mieslot (25) 138 B4
Corcelles (01) 189 K4
Corcelles-en-Beaujolais (69) 188 B3
Corcelles-Ferrières (25) 137 H6
Corcelles-les-Arts (21) 153 K4
Corcelles-lès-Cîteaux (21) 154 C1
Corcelles-les-Monts (21) 135 K5
Corcieux (88) 95 H5
Corcondray (25) 137 J6
Corconne (30) 274 C3
Corcoué-sur-Logne (44) 141 H3
Corcy (02) 39 H4
Cordéac (38) 242 C2
Cordebugle (14) 34 B4
Cordelle (42) 186 E5
Cordemais (44) 122 D3
Cordes-sur-Ciel (81) 251 F6
Cordes-Tolosannes (82) 268 D1
Cordesse (71) 153 F3
Cordey (14) 54 A3
Cordon (74) 192 A5
Cordonnet (70) 137 K4
Coren (15) 218 E5
Corenc (38) 224 B3
Corent (63) 202 E3
Corfélix (51) 61 H4
Corgengoux (21) 154 B4
Corgnac-sur-l'Isle (24) 214 C1
Corgoloin (21) 154 B2
Corignac (17) 211 K2
Corlay (22) 76 D2
Corlier (01) 189 K4
Cormainville (28) 109 H1
Cormaranche-en-Bugey (01) 190 A5
Cormatin (71) 171 H3
Corme-Ecluse (17) 194 E3
Corme-Royal (17) 194 E2
Cormeilles (27) 34 B4
Cormeilles (60) 17 K5
Cormeilles-en-Parisis (95) 58 D2
Cormeilles-en-Vexin (95) 37 G6
Cormelles-le-Royal (14) 32 E5
Cormenon (41) 108 A3
Cormeray (41) 129 F3
Cormery (37) 127 K6
Cormes (72) 83 J4
Cormicy (51) 40 D3
le Cormier (27) 56 E2
Cormolain (14) 31 K3
Cormont (62) 4 C5
Cormontreuil (51) 41 F4
Cormoranche-sur-Saône (01) 188 C2
Cormost (10) 90 B6
Cormot-le-Grand (21) 153 J4
Cormoyeux (51) 40 E6
Cormoz (01) 172 D4
Corn (46) 234 C5
Cornac (46) 234 C1
Cornant (89) 112 C1
Cornas (07) 222 C6
Cornay (08) 42 D3
Corné (49) 125 J3
Cornebarrieu (31) 269 F6
Corneilhan (34) 291 K3
Corneilla-de-Conflent (66) 314 B4
Corneilla-del-Vercol (66) 315 H3
Corneilla-la-Rivière (66) 315 F2
Corneillan (32) 266 A5
Corneuil (27) 56 D3
Corneville-la-Fouquetière (27) 34 E6
Corneville-sur-Risle (27) 34 D3
Cornier (74) 191 G3
Cornil (19) 216 A3
Cornillac (26) 258 A1
Cornille (24) 214 B3
Cornillé (35) 79 K5
Cornillé-les-Caves (49) 125 J3
Cornillon (30) 256 B4
Cornillon-Confoux (13) 295 K3
Cornillon-en-Trièves (38) 242 A2
Cornillon-sur-l'Oule (26) 257 K1
Cornimont (88) 119 H2
Cornod (39) 173 G6
Cornot (70) 117 H6
la Cornuaille (49) 124 C3
Cornus (12) 272 E3
Cornusse (18) 149 K4
Corny (27) 36 B4
Corny-Machéroménil (08) 22 A6
Corny-sur-Moselle (57) 44 E6
Coron (49) 143 H2
Corpe (85) 160 A4
Corpeau (21) 153 K4
Corpoyer-la-Chapelle (21) 135 G2
Corps (38) 242 D2
Corps-Nuds (35) 79 G6
Corquilleroy (45) 111 H2
Corquoy (18) 149 F5
Corrano (2A) 321 F5
Corravillers (70) 119 F2
Corre (70) 117 K3
Corrençon-en-Vercors (38) 223 J4
Correns (83) 297 K1
Corrèze (19) 216 C1
Corribert (51) 61 H1
Corrobert (51) 61 G3
Corrombles (21) 134 C3
Corronsac (31) 288 C2
Corroy (51) 61 K5
Corsaint (21) 134 C3
Corsavy (66) 314 D5

Corscia (2B) 318 E5
Corsept (44) 122 C3
Corseul (22) 50 B5
Cortambert (71) 171 H4
Corte (2B) 319 F6
Cortevaix (71). 171 H4
Cortrat (45). 111 J4
les Corvées-les-Yys (28) 84 D4
Corveissiat (01) 189 J1
Corvol-d'Embernard (58) 132 E6
Corvol-l'Orgueilleux (58) 132 E4
Corzé (49) 125 J2
Cos (09) 307 H3
Cosges (30) 172 E1
Coslédaà-Lube-Boast (64) 284 E2
Cosmes (53) 104 D3
Cosnac (19) 215 J4
Cosne-Cours-sur-Loire (58) 132 A4
Cosne-d'Allier (03) 167 K5
Cosnes-et-Romain (54) 26 C2
Cosqueville (50) 28 E2
Cossaye (58) 169 F1
Cossé-d'Anjou (49) 143 G1
Cossé-en-Champagne (53) 105 J3
Cossé-le-Vivien (53) 104 D3
Cossesseville (14) 53 J3
Cosswiller (67) 70 C3
Costa (2B) 318 D2
Costaros (43) 238 C1
les Costes (05) 242 E3
les Costes-Gozon (12) 272 A1
la Côte (70) 119 F6
la Côte-d'Aime (73) 209 J4
la Côte-d'Arbroz (74) 192 A1
la Côte-en-Couzan (42) 204 A2
la Côte-Saint-André (38) 207 F6
le Coteau (42) 187 F4
Côtebrune (25) 138 C5
les Côtes-d'Arey (38) 206 B6
les Côtes-de-Corps (38) 242 C2
Coti-Chiavari (2A) 322 C1
Cotignac (83) 298 A1
Cottance (42) 205 F2
Cottenchy (80) 18 B3
Cottévrard (76) 16 B5
Cottun (14) 32 A3
la Couarde (79) 162 A6
la Couarde-sur-Mer (17) 158 C5
Couargues (18) 132 A6
Coubert (77) 59 H6
Coubeyrac (33) 230 D3
Coubisou (12) 236 A6
Coubjours (24) 215 F3
Coublanc (52) 116 E6
Coublanc (71) 187 G2
Coublevie (38) 223 K1
Coublucq (64) 284 D1
Coubon (43) 220 C6
Coubron (93) 59 G3
Couches (71) 153 H5
Couchey (21) 135 K6
la Coucourde (26) 240 B4
Coucouron (07) 238 D3
Coucy (08) 41 J1
Coucy-la-Ville (02) 20 A6
Coucy-le-Château-Auffrique (02) . . 39 J1
Coucy-lès-Eppes (02) 20 E6
Couddes (41) 129 F5
Coudehard (61) 54 D3
Coudekerque (59) 3 H2
Coudekerque-Branche (59) 3 H1
Coudes (63) 202 E4
Coudeville-sur-Mer (50) 30 D6
Coudons (11) 308 D4
Coudoux (13) 296 B1
Coudray (27) 36 A4
le Coudray (28). 85 G3
Coudray (45) 86 E5
Coudray (53) 105 F5
Coudray-au-Perche (28) 84 A5
le Coudray-Macouard (49) 144 C1
le Coudray-Montceaux (91) 87 F1
Coudray-Rabut (14) 33 K3
le Coudray-Saint-Germer (60) 36 E2
le Coudray-sur-Thelle (60) 37 H3
la Coudre (79) 143 J4
Coudreceau (28) 84 B4
Coudrecieux (72) 107 J3
Coudres (27) 56 E3
Coudroy (45) 111 F4
Coudun (60) 38 D2
Coudures (40) 265 G5
Coueilles (31) 287 F2
Couëron (44) 123 F4
Couesmes (37) 127 F2
Couesmes-Vaucé (53) 81 F2
Couffé (44) 123 H4
Couffoulens (11) 290 A6
Couffy (41) 129 F6
Couffy-sur-Sarsonne (19) 201 F3
Couflens (09) 306 E5
Coufouleux (81) 269 K4
Couhé (86) 179 G1
Couilly-Pont-aux-Dames (77) 59 K2
Couin (62) 10 C5
Couiza (11). 309 D3
Couladère (31) 287 H2
Coulaines (72) 106 D2
Coulandon (03) 168 D4
Coulangeron (89) 133 F1
Coulanges (03) 169 K4
Coulanges (41) 128 D3
Coulanges-la-Vineuse (89) 113 G6
Coulanges-lès-Nevers (58) 150 D4
Coulanges-sur-Yonne (89) 133 F3
Coulans-sur-Gée (72) 106 C2

Coulaures (24) 214 D2
Couleuvre (03) 168 A2
Coulevon (70) 118 B6
Coulgens (16) 197 F3
Coulimer (61) 83 G2
Coullemelle (80) 18 C5
Coullemont (62) 10 C4
Coullons (45) 131 F2
Coulmer (61) 55 F4
Coulmier-le-Sec (21) 115 F6
Coulmiers (45) 109 H4
Coulobres (34) 292 A3
Coulogne (62) 2 D3
Couloisy (60) 39 F2
Coulombiers (72) 82 D4
Coulombiers (86) 162 D4
Coulombs (14) 32 C4
Coulombs (28) 57 G6
Coulombs-en-Valois (77) 60 B1
Coulomby (62) 4 E3
Coulommes (77). 59 K3
Coulommes-et-Marqueny (08) 42 A2
Coulommes-la-Montagne (51) 40 E4
Coulommiers (77). 60 B4
Coulommiers-la-Tour (41) 108 D5
Coulon (79) 161 F6
Coulonces (14) 52 D3
Coulonces (61) 54 C3
la Coulonche (61) 53 J6
Coulongé (72) 106 D6
Coulonges (16) 196 D1
Coulonges (17) 195 J4
Coulonges (86) 164 D5
Coulonges-Cohan (02) 40 B5
Coulonges-les-Sablons (61) 84 A3
Coulonges-sur-l'Autize (79) 161 F4
Coulonges-sur-Sarthe (61) 83 G2
Coulonges-Thouarsais (79). 144 A4
Coulonvillers (80) 9 H4
Couloumé-Mondebat (32) 266 C6
Coulounieix-Chamiers (24) 214 A3
Coulours (89) 89 G6
Couloutre (58) 132 D4
Coulouvray-Boisbenâtre (50) 52 C4
Coulvain (14) 32 A6
Coulx (47) 248 A1
Coume (57) 45 J4
Counozouls (11) 313 K1
Coupelle-Neuve (62) 5 F6
Coupelle-Vieille (62) 5 F5
Coupesarte (14) 33 J6
Coupetz (51) 62 D4
Coupéville (51) 63 F2
Coupiac (12) 271 J2
Coupray (52) 115 K3
Coupru (02) 60 D1
Couptrain (53) 81 K2
Coupvray (77) 59 J3
Couquèques (33) 210 E1
Cour-Cheverny (41) 129 F3
Cour-et-Buis (38) 206 C6
Cour-l'Évêque (52) 115 K3
la Cour-Marigny (45) 111 G4
Cour-Saint-Maurice (25) 139 G5
Cour-sur-Loire (41) 129 F1
Courances (91) 87 F3
Courant (17) 177 J4
Courban (21) 115 H3
la Courbe (61) 54 A4
Courbehaye (28). 109 H1
Courbépine (27) 34 C6
Courbes (02) 20 B4
Courbesseaux (54) 66 C5
Courbette (39) 173 G3
Courbeveille (53) 104 D2
Courbevoie (92) 58 D3
Courbiac (47) 249 F2
Courbillac (16) 196 A2
Courboin (02) 61 F2
Courbouzon (39) 173 F2
Courbouzon (41) 109 G6
Courçais (03) 167 F5
Courçay (37) 128 A6
Courcebœufs (72) 106 E1
Courcelette (80) 10 E5
Courcelles (17) 178 A5
Courcelles (45) 110 E1
Courcelles (45) 111 G2
Courcelles (54) 93 K3
Courcelles (58) 132 E4
Courcelles (90) 97 A5
Courcelles-au-Bois (80) 10 D5
Courcelles-Chaussy (57) 45 H5
Courcelles-de-Touraine (37) 126 E3
Courcelles-en-Barrois (55) 64 D3
Courcelles-en-Bassée (77) 88 B3
Courcelles-en-Montagne (52) 116 C4
Courcelles-Epayelles (60) 18 D6
Courcelles-Frémoy (21) 134 C4
Courcelles-la-Forêt (72) 106 C5
Courcelles-le-Comte (62) 10 E4
Courcelles-lès-Gisors (60) 36 D4
Courcelles-lès-Lens (62). 11 H1
Courcelles-lès-Montbard (21) 134 E2
Courcelles-lès-Montbéliard (25) . . . 139 H2
Courcelles-lès-Semur (21) 134 D4
Courcelles-Sapicourt (51) 40 D4
Courcelles-sous-Châtenois (88) . . . 93 H4
Courcelles-sous-Moyencourt (80). . 17 J3
Courcelles-sous-Thoix (80) 17 J4
Courcelles-sur-Aire (55) 64 B2
Courcelles-sur-Blaise (52) 91 J3
Courcelles-sur-Nied (57) 45 G6
Courcelles-sur-Seine (27) 36 A5
Courcelles-sur-Vesles (02) 40 B3
Courcelles-sur-Viosne (95) 37 G6

Courcelles-sur-Voire (10) . . . 91 F2
Courcemain (51) . . . 61 K6
Courcemont (72) . . . 83 F6
Courcerac (17) . . . 195 J1
Courcerault (61) . . . 83 J3
Courceroy (10) . . . 88 E3
Courchamp (77) . . . 60 D6
Courchamps (02) . . . 39 H6
Courchamps (49) . . . 144 C1
Courchapon (25) . . . 137 H6
Courchaton (70) . . . 138 E2
Courchelettes (59) . . . 11 H2
Courcité (53) . . . 81 K4
Courcival (72) . . . 83 F5
Courcôme (16) . . . 179 G5
Courçon (17) . . . 177 G1
Courcoué (49) . . . 145 H3
Courcouronnes (91) . . . 87 F1
Courcoury (17) . . . 195 G2
Courcuire (70) . . . 137 H5
Courcy (14) . . . 54 C2
Courcy (50) . . . 30 E4
Courcy (51) . . . 40 E3
Courcy-aux-Loges (45) . . . 110 D2
Courdemanche (27) . . . 56 E4
Courdemanche (72) . . . 107 H5
Courdemanges (51) . . . 63 F5
Courdimanche (95) . . . 58 B1
Courdimanche-sur-Essonne (91) . . . 86 E3
Couret (31) . . . 306 A2
Courgains (72) . . . 82 E5
Courgeac (16) . . . 212 E1
Courgenard (72) . . . 83 K6
Courgenay (89) . . . 89 F5
Courgent (78) . . . 57 H3
Courgeon (61) . . . 83 J2
Courgeoût (61) . . . 83 G2
Courgis (89) . . . 113 H5
Courgivaux (51) . . . 61 F5
Courgoul (63) . . . 202 C5
Courjeonnet (51) . . . 61 J4
Courlac (16) . . . 212 E2
Courlandon (51) . . . 40 C3
Courlans (39) . . . 173 F2
Courlaoux (39) . . . 173 F2
Courlay (79) . . . 143 H6
Courléon (49) . . . 126 D4
Courlon (21) . . . 136 A1
Courlon-sur-Yonne (89) . . . 88 C4
Courmangoux (01) . . . 172 E6
Courmas (51) . . . 40 E5
Courmelles (02) . . . 39 J3
Courmemin (41) . . . 129 H4
Courménil (61) . . . 54 E4
Courmes (06) . . . 280 E3
Courmont (02) . . . 40 B5
Courmont (70) . . . 139 F1
Cournanel (11) . . . 308 E2
la Courneuve (93) . . . 58 E2
Courniou (34) . . . 290 E2
Cournols (63) . . . 202 C4
Cournon (56) . . . 102 C3
Cournon-d'Auvergne (63) . . . 202 E2
Cournonsec (34) . . . 293 F1
Cournonterral (34) . . . 293 F1
la Couronne (16) . . . 196 D4
Courouvre (55) . . . 64 C2
Courpalay (77) . . . 60 A6
Courpiac (33) . . . 230 B3
Courpière (63) . . . 203 H2
Courpignac (17) . . . 211 J1
Courquetaine (77) . . . 59 J6
Courrensan (32) . . . 266 E3
Courrières (62) . . . 6 C6
Courris (81) . . . 271 G2
Courry (30) . . . 255 H3
Cours (46) . . . 233 J6
Cours (47) . . . 248 B3
le Cours (56) . . . 101 J4
Cours (79) . . . 161 H4
Cours-de-Monségur (33) . . . 230 E4
Cours-de-Pile (24) . . . 231 J2
Cours-la-Ville (69) . . . 187 H3
Cours-les-Bains (33) . . . 247 F2
Cours-les-Barres (18) . . . 150 C3
Coursac (24) . . . 213 K4
Coursan (11) . . . 291 J5
Coursan-en-Othe (10) . . . 113 J2
Coursegoules (06) . . . 280 E3
Courset (62) . . . 4 C4
Courseulles-sur-Mer (14) . . . 32 D3
Courson (14) . . . 52 C3
Courson-les-Carrières (89) . . . 133 F2
Courson-Monteloup (91) . . . 86 C1
Courtacon (77) . . . 60 D5
Courtagnon (51) . . . 40 E5
Courtalain (28) . . . 108 D2
Courtaoult (10) . . . 113 J2
Courtauly (11) . . . 308 D2
Courtavon (68) . . . 97 B6
Courtefontaine (25) . . . 139 J4
Courtefontaine (39) . . . 155 K1
Courteilles (27) . . . 56 B5
Courteix (19) . . . 201 F4
Courtelevant (90) . . . 97 A5
Courtemanche (80) . . . 18 D5
Courtemaux (45) . . . 112 A2
Courtémont (51) . . . 42 C5
Courtemont-Varennes (02) . . . 40 A6
Courtempierre (45) . . . 111 G1
Courtenay (38) . . . 207 G2
Courtenay (45) . . . 112 B2
Courtenot (10) . . . 90 D6
Courteranges (10) . . . 90 C5
Courteron (10) . . . 114 E2
Courtes (01) . . . 172 B4

Courtesoult-et-Gatey (70) . . . 137 F1
Courtetain-et-Salans (25) . . . 138 D5
la Courtète (11) . . . 289 H6
Courteuil (60) . . . 38 B5
Courthézon (84) . . . 257 F6
Courthiézy (51) . . . 61 G1
Courties (32) . . . 285 J1
Courtieux (60) . . . 39 G2
Courtillers (72) . . . 105 K5
Courtils (50) . . . 51 K3
la Courtine (23) . . . 201 F3
Courtisols (51) . . . 62 E2
Courtivron (21) . . . 135 K2
Courtoin (89) . . . 112 B1
Courtois-sur-Yonne (89) . . . 88 D6
Courtomer (61) . . . 55 F6
Courtomer (77) . . . 59 K6
Courtonne-la-Meurdrac (14) . . . 34 A6
Courtonne-les-Deux-Églises (14) . . . 34 B6
Courtrizy-et-Fussigny (02) . . . 40 C1
Courtry (77) . . . 59 G3
Courvaudon (14) . . . 53 H1
Courvières (25) . . . 156 C5
Courville (51) . . . 40 C4
Courville-sur-Eure (28) . . . 84 E3
Courzieu (69) . . . 205 H2
Cousance (39) . . . 172 E3
Cousances-les-Forges (55) . . . 64 A6
Cousances-lès-Triconville (55) . . . 64 D4
Cousolre (59) . . . 13 J3
Coussa (09) . . . 307 K2
Coussac-Bonneval (87) . . . 199 F5
Coussan (65) . . . 285 J5
Coussay (86) . . . 145 F6
Coussay-les-Bois (86) . . . 146 A6
Coussegrey (10) . . . 114 A3
Coussergues (12) . . . 252 E2
Coussey (88) . . . 93 G3
Coust (18) . . . 167 H2
Coustaussa (11) . . . 309 F3
Coustouge (11) . . . 310 A3
Coustouges (66) . . . 314 E6
Coutances (50) . . . 30 E4
Coutansouze (03) . . . 184 E2
Coutarnoux (89) . . . 134 A2
Coutençon (77) . . . 88 A2
Coutens (09) . . . 308 A1
Couterne (61) . . . 81 J2
Couternon (21) . . . 136 B5
Couteuges (43) . . . 219 J4
Coutevroult (77) . . . 59 K3
Couthenans (70) . . . 139 G1
Couthures-sur-Garonne (47) . . . 230 D6
Coutiches (59) . . . 7 F6
Coutières (79) . . . 162 A4
Coutouvre (42) . . . 187 G4
Coutras (33) . . . 212 B5
Couture (16) . . . 179 H6
la Couture (62) . . . 6 A5
la Couture (85) . . . 159 K3
la Couture-Boussey (27) . . . 57 F3
Couture-d'Argenson (79) . . . 178 D5
Couture-sur-Loir (41) . . . 107 J6
Couturelle (62) . . . 10 C4
Coutures (24) . . . 213 H2
Coutures (33) . . . 230 D4
Coutures (49) . . . 125 J5
Coutures (82) . . . 268 C2
Couvains (50) . . . 31 J3
Couvains (61) . . . 55 H3
la Couvertoirade (12) . . . 273 G2
Couvertpuis (55) . . . 92 C1
Couvignon (10) . . . 91 G6
Couville (50) . . . 28 C3
Couvonges (55) . . . 63 K4
Couvrelles (02) . . . 40 A3
Couvron-et-Aumencourt (02) . . . 20 C5
Couvrot (51) . . . 63 F4
Coux (07) . . . 239 K5
Coux (17) . . . 211 K2
Coux-et-Bigaroque (24) . . . 232 C2
Couy (18) . . . 150 A2
la Couyère (35) . . . 103 H1
Couze-et-Saint-Front (24) . . . 232 A2
Couzeix (87) . . . 181 G6
Couziers (37) . . . 144 E2
Couzon (03) . . . 168 C2
Couzon-au-Mont-d'Or (69) . . . 206 A1
Couzou (46) . . . 233 K3
Cox (31) . . . 268 C4
Coye-la-Forêt (60) . . . 38 A6
Coyecques (62) . . . 5 F4
Coyolles (02) . . . 39 F4
Coyrière (39) . . . 173 K6
Coyron (39) . . . 173 H4
Coyviller (54) . . . 66 B6
Cozes (17) . . . 194 E4
Cozzano (2A) . . . 321 F5
Crach (56) . . . 100 D5
Crachier (38) . . . 206 E4
Crain (89) . . . 133 G3
Craincourt (57) . . . 66 B2
Craintilleux (42) . . . 204 E4
Crainvilliers (88) . . . 93 H4
Cramaille (02) . . . 39 K4
Cramans (39) . . . 155 K3
Cramant (51) . . . 61 K2
Cramchaban (17) . . . 177 H2
Craménil (61) . . . 53 J4
Cramoisy (60) . . . 38 A4
Cramont (80) . . . 9 J4
Crampagna (09) . . . 307 J2
Crancey (10) . . . 89 G2
Crançot (39) . . . 173 H1

Crandelles (15) . . . 235 G1
Crannes-en-Champagne (72) . . . 106 B3
Crans (01) . . . 189 G5
Crans (39) . . . 174 A1
Cransac (12) . . . 235 G6
Crantenoy (54) . . . 94 B2
Cranves-Sales (74) . . . 191 G2
Craon (53) . . . 104 D4
Craon (86) . . . 144 D6
Craonne (02) . . . 40 C2
Craonnelle (02) . . . 40 C2
Crapeaumesnil (60) . . . 19 F5
Craponne (69) . . . 205 K2
Craponne-sur-Arzon (43) . . . 220 B2
Cras (38) . . . 223 H2
Cras (46) . . . 233 J6
Cras-sur-Reyssouze (01) . . . 172 C6
Crastatt (67) . . . 70 C2
Crastes (32) . . . 267 K5
Crasville (27) . . . 35 H5
Crasville (50) . . . 29 F3
Crasville-la-Mallet (76) . . . 15 G3
Crasville-la-Rocquefort (76) . . . 15 H3
la Crau (83) . . . 300 D4
Cravanche (90) . . . 119 H6
Cravans (17) . . . 195 F4
Cravant (45) . . . 109 H5
Cravant (89) . . . 133 H1
Cravant-les-Côteaux (37) . . . 145 G2
Cravencères (32) . . . 266 C4
Cravent (78) . . . 57 G2
Crayssac (46) . . . 233 G6
Craywick (59) . . . 3 G2
Crazannes (17) . . . 177 H6
Cré (72) . . . 126 A1
Créances (50) . . . 30 D2
Créancey (21) . . . 135 G6
Crécey-sur-Tille (21) . . . 136 B2
la Crèche (79) . . . 161 J6
Crèches-sur-Saône (71) . . . 188 C1
Créchets (65) . . . 305 H2
Créchy (03) . . . 185 J2
Crécy-au-Mont (02) . . . 39 J1
Crécy-Couvé (28) . . . 56 E6
Crécy-en-Ponthieu (80) . . . 9 G3
Crécy-la-Chapelle (77) . . . 59 K3
Crécy-sur-Serre (02) . . . 20 D4
Crédin (56) . . . 77 F6
Crégols (46) . . . 250 C1
Crégy-lès-Meaux (77) . . . 59 K2
Créhange (57) . . . 45 J6
Créhen (22) . . . 50 B4
Creil (60) . . . 38 A4
Creissan (34) . . . 291 H3
Creissels (12) . . . 253 G6
Crémarest (62) . . . 4 C3
Cremeaux (42) . . . 186 D6
Crémery (80) . . . 19 F4
Crémieu (38) . . . 206 E2
Crempigny-Bonneguête (74) . . . 190 D5
Cremps (46) . . . 250 B2
Crenans (39) . . . 173 H4
Creney-près-Troyes (10) . . . 90 B4
Crennes-sur-Fraubée (53) . . . 81 K3
Créon (33) . . . 229 K3
Créon-d'Armagnac (40) . . . 266 B1
Créot (71) . . . 153 J5
Crépand (21) . . . 134 D2
Crépey (54) . . . 93 J1
Crépol (26) . . . 222 E3
Crépon (14) . . . 32 C3
Crépy (02) . . . 20 C5
Crépy (62) . . . 5 G2
Crépy-en-Valois (60) . . . 38 E4
Créquy (62) . . . 4 E6
le Crès (34) . . . 274 C6
Cresancey (70) . . . 137 G4
Crésantignes (10) . . . 114 A1
les Cresnays (50) . . . 52 C4
Crespian (30) . . . 274 E3
Crespières (78) . . . 58 A3
Crespin (12) . . . 251 J5
Crespin (59) . . . 12 E1
Crespin (81) . . . 271 F1
Crespinet (81) . . . 271 F2
Crespy-le-Neuf (10) . . . 91 F3
Cressac-Saint-Genis (16) . . . 196 C6
Cressanges (03) . . . 168 C5
Cressat (23) . . . 183 F3
la Cresse (12) . . . 253 H5
Cressé (17) . . . 178 C6
Cresserons (14) . . . 32 E3
Cresseveuille (14) . . . 33 H4
Cressia (39) . . . 173 F3
Cressin-Rochefort (01) . . . 207 K1
Cressonsacq (60) . . . 38 B2
Cressy (76) . . . 16 A4
Cressy-Omencourt (80) . . . 19 G4
Cressy-sur-Somme (71) . . . 169 K2
Crest (26) . . . 240 D3
le Crest (63) . . . 202 D3
Crest-Voland (73) . . . 209 H1
Creste (63) . . . 202 C5
le Crestet (07) . . . 221 K5
Crestet (84) . . . 257 H4
Crestot (27) . . . 35 G5
Créteil (94) . . . 59 F4
Cretteville (50) . . . 28 E6
Creully (14) . . . 32 C3
la Creuse (70) . . . 118 C6
Creuse (80) . . . 17 K3
le Creusot (71) . . . 153 G6
Cronce (43) . . . 219 G5
Creutzwald (57) . . . 68 A1
Creuzier-le-Neuf (03) . . . 185 J3
Creuzier-le-Vieux (03) . . . 185 J3

Crevans-et-la-Chapelle-
-lès-Granges (70) . . . 139 F2
Crevant (36) . . . 166 B4
Crevant-Laveine (63) . . . 185 J6
Crévéchamps (54) . . . 94 B1
Crèvecœur-en-Auge (14) . . . 33 H6
Crèvecœur-en-Brie (77) . . . 59 K5
Crèvecœur-le-Grand (60) . . . 17 J5
Crèvecœur-le-Petit (60) . . . 18 C6
Crèvecœur-sur-l'Escaut (59) . . . 12 A5
Creveney (70) . . . 118 C6
Crévic (54) . . . 66 C5
Crevin (35) . . . 79 G6
Crévoux (05) . . . 243 K5
Creys-Mépieu (38) . . . 207 H2
Creyssac (24) . . . 213 J2
Creysse (24) . . . 231 J2
Creysse (46) . . . 233 K2
Creysseilles (07) . . . 239 J3
Creyssensac-et-Pissot (24) . . . 213 K5
Crézançay-sur-Cher (18) . . . 149 G6
Crézancy (02) . . . 61 F1
Crézancy-en-Sancerre (18) . . . 131 J6
Crézières (79) . . . 178 D3
Crézilles (54) . . . 65 H6
Cricquebœuf (14) . . . 33 J2
Cricqueville-en-Auge (14) . . . 33 H4
Cricqueville-en-Bessin (14) . . . 29 J6
Criel-sur-Mer (76) . . . 8 B6
Crillon (60) . . . 37 F1
Crillon-le-Brave (84) . . . 257 H5
Crimolois (21) . . . 136 B6
Crion (54) . . . 66 D5
la Crique (76) . . . 16 A4
Criquebeuf-en-Caux (76) . . . 14 C4
Criquebeuf-la-Campagne (27) . . . 35 G5
Criquebeuf-sur-Seine (27) . . . 35 H3
Criquetot-l'Esneval (76) . . . 14 C5
Criquetot-le-Mauconduit (76) . . . 14 E3
Criquetot-sur-Longueville (76) . . . 15 K3
Criquetot-sur-Ouville (76) . . . 15 H4
Criquiers (76) . . . 17 F5
Crisenoy (77) . . . 87 J1
Crisolles (60) . . . 19 H5
Crissay-sur-Manse (37) . . . 145 J2
Crissé (72) . . . 82 B6
Crissey (39) . . . 155 G2
Crissey (71) . . . 154 A6
Cristinacce (2A) . . . 320 C1
Cristot (14) . . . 32 C4
Criteuil-la-Magdeleine (16) . . . 196 A5
Critot (76) . . . 16 B5
Croce (2B) . . . 319 H6
Crochte (59) . . . 3 H3
Crocicchia (2B) . . . 319 H4
Crocq (23) . . . 201 G1
le Crocq (60) . . . 17 K5
Crocy (14) . . . 54 C3
Crœttwiller (67) . . . 25 C2
Croignon (33) . . . 229 K2
Croisances (43) . . . 237 K1
Croisette (62) . . . 10 A2
le Croisic (44) . . . 121 H5
la Croisille (27) . . . 56 B2
la Croisille-sur-Briance (87) . . . 199 J4
Croisilles (14) . . . 53 J1
Croisilles (28) . . . 57 G5
Croisilles (61) . . . 54 E4
Croisilles (62) . . . 11 F4
Croismare (54) . . . 66 E6
Croissanville (14) . . . 33 G5
Croissy-Beaubourg (77) . . . 59 H4
Croissy-sur-Celle (60) . . . 17 K4
Croissy-sur-Seine (78) . . . 58 C3
Croix (90) . . . 139 J3
la Croix-aux-Bois (08) . . . 42 C2
la Croix-aux-Mines (88) . . . 95 J4
la Croix-Avranchin (50) . . . 51 K4
la Croix-Blanche (47) . . . 248 C3
Croix-Caluyau (59) . . . 12 D4
Croix-Chapeau (17) . . . 176 E3
la Croix-Comtesse (17) . . . 177 K3
la Croix-de-la-Rochette (73) . . . 208 D5
la Croix-du-Perche (28) . . . 84 C5
la Croix-en-Brie (77) . . . 88 B1
la Croix-en-Champagne (51) . . . 42 B5
Croix-en-Ternois (62) . . . 10 A1
la Croix-en-Touraine (37) . . . 128 D5
Croix-Fonsomme (02) . . . 20 B1
la Croix-Helléan (56) . . . 101 J1
Croix-Mare (76) . . . 15 H5
la Croix-Moligneaux (80) . . . 19 H3
la Croix-Saint-Leufroy (27) . . . 35 K6
la Croix-Saint-Gartempe (87) . . . 180 E3
la Croix-sur-Ourcq (02) . . . 39 J5
la Croix-sur-Roudoule (06) . . . 261 F6
la Croix-Valmer (83) . . . 301 J3
Croixanvec (56) . . . 76 E5
Croixdalle (76) . . . 16 B3
la Croixille (53) . . . 80 C5
Croixrault (80) . . . 17 H3
Croizet-sur-Gand (42) . . . 187 G6
Crolles (38) . . . 224 C2
Crollon (50) . . . 51 K4
Cromac (87) . . . 164 E6
Cromary (70) . . . 138 A4
Cronat (71) . . . 169 H1
Cronce (43) . . . 219 G5
la Cropte (53) . . . 105 H3
Cropus (76) . . . 16 A4
Cros (30) . . . 274 B1

le Cros (34) . . . 273 G3
Cros (63) . . . 201 J6
Cros-de-Géorand (07) . . . 238 E3
Cros-de-Montvert (15) . . . 216 E5
Cros-de-Ronesque (15) . . . 235 K2
Crosey-le-Grand (25) . . . 138 E4
Crosey-le-Petit (25) . . . 138 E4
Crosmières (72) . . . 106 A6
Crosne (91) . . . 59 F5
Crossac (44) . . . 122 B1
Crosses (18) . . . 149 J4
Crosville-la-Vieille (27) . . . 35 G5
Crosville-sur-Douve (50) . . . 28 E5
Crosville-sur-Scie (76) . . . 15 K3
Crotelles (37) . . . 128 A3
Crotenay (39) . . . 155 K6
Croth (27) . . . 57 F3
le Crotoy (80) . . . 8 E3
Crots (05) . . . 243 J5
Crottes-en-Pithiverais (45) . . . 110 B1
Crottet (01) . . . 188 D1
le Crouais (35) . . . 78 C3
Crouay (14) . . . 32 A3
la Croupte (14) . . . 55 F1
Crouseilles (64) . . . 285 F1
Croutelle (86) . . . 162 E4
les Croûtes (10) . . . 113 J3
Croutoy (60) . . . 39 F2
Crouttes (61) . . . 54 D2
Crouttes-sur-Marne (02) . . . 60 C2
Crouy (02) . . . 39 J2
Crouy-en-Thelle (60) . . . 37 K5
Crouy-Saint-Pierre (80) . . . 17 J1
Crouy-sur-Cosson (41) . . . 129 H1
Crouy-sur-Ourcq (77) . . . 39 G6
le Crouzet (25) . . . 174 B1
Crouzet-Migette (25) . . . 156 B4
la Crouzille (63) . . . 184 C3
Crouzilles (37) . . . 145 H2
Crozant (23) . . . 165 H6
Croze (23) . . . 200 E1
Crozes-Hermitage (26) . . . 222 B4
Crozet (01) . . . 174 B6
le Crozet (42) . . . 186 C3
les Crozets (39) . . . 173 J4
Crozon (29) . . . 72 D6
Crozon-sur-Vauvre (36) . . . 166 A4
Cruas (07) . . . 240 B4
Crucey-Villages (28) . . . 56 C6
Crucheray (41) . . . 108 C6
Cruéjouls (12) . . . 252 E1
Cruet (73) . . . 208 D4
Crugey (21) . . . 153 J1
Crugny (51) . . . 40 C4
Cruguel (56) . . . 101 K2
Cruis (04) . . . 258 E6
Crulai (61) . . . 55 J5
Crupies (26) . . . 241 F5
Crupilly (02) . . . 20 E1
Cruscades (11) . . . 291 G6
Cruseilles (74) . . . 191 F4
Crusnes (54) . . . 26 E3
Cruviers-Lascours (30) . . . 275 F1
Crux-la-Ville (58) . . . 151 H2
Cruzille (71) . . . 171 J4
Cruzilles-lès-Mépillat (01) . . . 188 D2
Cruzy (34) . . . 291 H4
Cruzy-le-Châtel (89) . . . 114 C4
Cry (89) . . . 114 C6
Cubelles (43) . . . 219 J6
Cubières (48) . . . 254 D1
Cubières-sur-Cinoble (11) . . . 309 H4
Cubiérettes (48) . . . 254 D1
Cubjac (24) . . . 214 C3
Cublac (19) . . . 215 G4
Cublize (69) . . . 187 H4
Cubnezais (33) . . . 211 J5
Cubrial (25) . . . 138 D2
Cubry (25) . . . 138 D2
Cubry-lès-Faverney (70) . . . 118 A4
Cubzac-les-Ponts (33) . . . 211 J6
Cucharmoy (77) . . . 88 C1
Cuchery (51) . . . 40 D6
Cucq (62) . . . 4 C6
Cucugnan (11) . . . 309 J4
Cucuron (84) . . . 277 H4
Cudos (33) . . . 246 D2
Cudot (89) . . . 112 C3
Cuébris (06) . . . 280 E2
Cuélas (32) . . . 286 B4
Cuers (83) . . . 297 K4
Cuffies (02) . . . 39 J2
Cuffy (18) . . . 150 D4
Cugand (85) . . . 142 B2
Cuges-les-Pins (13) . . . 297 G4
Cugnaux (31) . . . 288 A1
Cugney (70) . . . 137 G4
Cugny (02) . . . 19 J4
Cuguen (35) . . . 51 G6
Cuguron (31) . . . 305 H1
Cuhon (86) . . . 162 C1
Cuignières (60) . . . 38 A2
Cuigy-en-Bray (60) . . . 36 E3
Cuillé (53) . . . 104 B2
Cuinchy (62) . . . 6 B5
Cuincy (59) . . . 11 H1
le Cuing (31) . . . 286 D6
Cuinzier (42) . . . 187 G3
Cuirieux (02) . . . 20 E4
Cuiry-Housse (02) . . . 40 A4
Cuiry-lès-Chaudardes (02) . . . 40 C2
Cuiry-lès-Iviers (02) . . . 21 H3
Cuis (51) . . . 61 K1
Cuise-la-Motte (60) . . . 39 F2
Cuiseaux (71) . . . 172 E4
Cuiserey (21) . . . 136 D4

Cuisery (71) 172 A3
Cuisia (39) 172 E3
Cuisles (51) 40 C6
Cuissai (61) 82 C2
Cuissy-et-Geny (02) 40 C2
Cuisy (55) 43 F4
Cuisy (77) 59 J1
Cuisy-en-Almont (02) 39 H2
Culan (18) 166 E4
Culètre (21) 153 H2
Culey-le-Patry (14) 53 H2
Culhat (63) 203 F1
Culin (38) 206 E5
Culles-les-Roches (71) 171 H2
Cully (14) 32 C4
Culmont (52) 116 E4
Culoz (01) 190 C6
Cult (70) 137 H5
Cultures (48) 253 K1
Cumières (51) 40 E6
Cumières-le-Mort-Homme (55) . . . 43 G4
Cumiès (11) 289 F4
Cumont (82) 268 B3
Cunac (81) 270 E2
Cuncy-lès-Varzy (58) 133 F5
Cunèges (24) 231 G3
Cunel (55) 43 F3
Cunelières (90) 119 J6
Cunfin (10) 115 G2
Cunlhat (63) 203 H4
Cuon (49) 126 B3
Cuperly (51) 41 J6
Cuq (47) 248 C6
Cuq (81) 270 D6
Cuq-Toulza (81) 289 G1
Cuqueron (64) 284 B4
Curac (16) 212 D2
Curan (12) 252 E5
Curbans (04) 259 G1
Curbigny (71) 187 H1
Curçay-sur-Dive (86) 144 C3
Curchy (80) 19 G3
Curciat-Dongalon (01) 172 C4
Curcy-sur-Orne (14) 53 H1
Curdin (71) 170 B3
Curel (04) 258 C4
Curel (52) 92 A2
Curemonte (19) 216 A4
Cures (72) 106 C1
Curgies (59) 12 D2
Curgy (71) 153 F4
Curienne (73) 208 C4
Curières (12) 236 C5
Curis-au-Mont-d'Or (69) 188 C6
Curley (21) 154 B1
Curlu (80) 19 F1
Curmont (52) 91 K5
Curnier (26) 257 J2
Cursan (33) 229 K2
Curtafond (01) 188 E1
Curtil-Saint-Seine (21) 135 K3
Curtil-sous-Buffières (71) 171 G5
Curtil-sous-Burnand (71) 171 H3
Curtil-Vergy (21) 154 A1
Curvalle (81) 271 H2
Curzay-sur-Vonne (86) 162 C4
Curzon (85) 159 J4
Cusance (25) 138 E5
Cuse-et-Adrisans (25) 138 D3
Cusey (52) 136 D1
Cussac (15) 218 C6
Cussac (87) 198 B5
Cussac-Fort-Médoc (33) 211 F4
Cussac-sur-Loire (43) 220 C6
Cussangy (10) 114 B3
Cussay (37) 146 B3
Cusset (03) 185 J3
Cussey-les-Forges (21) 136 A1
Cussey-sur-Lison (25) 156 B2
Cussey-sur-l'Ognon (25) 137 K5
Cussy (14) 32 A3
Cussy-en-Morvan (71) 152 D2
Cussy-la-Colonne (21) 153 J3
Cussy-le-Châtel (21) 153 H1
Cussy-les-Forges (89) 134 A3
Custines (54) 66 A3
Cusy (74) 208 C1
Cutry (02) 39 H3
Cutry (54) 26 C3
Cuts (60) 19 J6
Cutting (57) 67 G2
Cuttoli-Corticchiato (2A) 320 D4
Cuttura (39) 173 J5
Cuvat (74) 191 F4
Cuve (70) 118 B3
Cuvergnon (60) 39 F5
Cuverville (14) 33 F5
Cuverville (27) 36 A4
Cuverville (76) 14 C4
Cuverville-sur-Yères (76) 16 C1
Cuves (50) 52 C4
Cuves (52) 116 D1
Cuvier (39) 156 C5
Cuvillers (59) 11 J3
Cuvilly (60) 18 E6
Cuvry (57) 45 F6
Cuxac-Cabardès (11) 290 A3
Cuxac-d'Aude (11) 291 H5
Cuy (60) 19 G6
Cuy (89) 88 D5
Cuy-Saint-Fiacre (76) 36 D2
Cuzac (46) 234 E5
Cuzance (46) 233 J1
Cuzieu (01) 207 J1
Cuzieu (42) 205 F2
Cuzion (36) 165 H5

Cuzorn (47) 232 C6
Cuzy (71) 170 B1
Cys-la-Commune (02) 40 B2
Cysoing (59) 7 F5

D

Dabo (57) 70 A2
Dachstein (67) 70 D3
Dadonville (45) 110 D1
Daglan (24) 233 F3
Dagneux (01) 188 E6
Dagny (77) 60 C5
Dagny-Lambercy (02) 21 G3
Dagonville (55) 64 D4
la Daguenière (49) 125 H4
Dahlenheim (67) 70 D3
Daignac (33) 230 A2
Daigny (08) 23 F4
Daillancourt (52) 91 K4
Daillecourt (52) 116 E1
Dainville (62) 10 E3
Dainville-Bertheléville (55) 92 E2
Daix (21) 136 A5
Dalem (57) 45 K3
Dalhain (57) 66 E2
Dalhunden (67) 25 C4
Dallet (63) 202 E2
Dallon (02) 19 K3
Dalou (09) 307 J2
Dalstein (57) 45 H3
Daluis (06) 260 E6
Damas-aux-Bois (88) 94 D3
Damas-et-Bettegney (88) 94 B5
Damazan (47) 247 H3
Dambach (67) 69 J4
Dambach-la-Ville (67) 96 C1
Dambelin (25) 139 G4
Dambenois (25) 139 H2
Dambenoît-lès-Colombe (70) . . . 118 D5
Damblain (88) 117 F1
Damblainville (14) 54 B2
Dambron (28) 109 K1
Dame-Marie (27) 56 B4
Dame-Marie (61) 83 J4
Dame-Marie-les-Bois (37) 128 B3
Damelevières (54) 66 C6
Daméraucourt (60) 17 H4
Damerey (71) 154 C5
Damery (51) 40 D6
Damery (80) 18 E4
Damgan (56) 121 H2
Damiatte (81) 270 C6
Damigny (61) 82 D3
Damloup (55) 43 J4
Dammard (02) 39 H5
Dammarie (28) 85 G4
Dammarie-en-Puisaye (45) 131 K2
Dammarie-les-Lys (77) 87 H2
Dammarie-sur-Loing (45) 111 K5
Dammarie-sur-Saulx (55) 64 B6
Dammartin-en-Goële (77) 59 H1
Dammartin-en-Serve (78) 57 H3
Dammartin-les-Templiers (25) . . . 138 C5
Dammartin-Marpain (39) 137 F6
Dammartin-sur-Meuse (52) 117 F2
Dammartin-sur-Tigeaux (77) 59 K4
Damousies (59) 13 H3
Damouzy (08) 22 C3
Damparis (39) 155 F2
Dampierre (10) 90 D1
Dampierre (14) 31 K4
Dampierre (39) 155 J1
Dampierre (52) 116 D3
Dampierre-au-Temple (51) 62 D1
Dampierre-en-Bray (76) 16 E4
Dampierre-en-Bresse (71) 154 D5
Dampierre-en-Burly (45) 111 G6
Dampierre-en-Crot (18) 131 G4
Dampierre-en-Graçay (18) 148 C2
Dampierre-en-Montagne (21) . . . 135 T4
Dampierre-en-Yvelines (78) 58 B5
Dampierre-et-Flée (21) 136 D3
Dampierre-le-Château (51) 63 H1
Dampierre-les-Bois (25) 139 J2
Dampierre-lès-Conflans (70) 118 B4
Dampierre-Saint-Nicolas (76) . . . 16 A2
Dampierre-sous-Bouhy (58) 132 C3
Dampierre-sous-Brou (28) 84 C6
Dampierre-sur-Avre (28) 56 D4
Dampierre-sur-Boutonne (17) . . . 178 A4
Dampierre-sur-le-Doubs (25) . . . 139 G3
Dampierre-sur-Linotte (70) 138 B2
Dampierre-sur-Moivre (51) 63 F3
Dampierre-sur-Salon (70) 137 G2
Dampjoux (25) 139 G4
Dampleux (02) 39 G4
Dampmart (77) 59 J3
Dampniat (19) 215 K4
Damprichard (25) 139 J5
les Damps (27) 35 J3
Dampsmesnil (27) 36 C5
Dampvalley-lès-Colombe (70) . . . 138 C1
Dampvalley-Saint-Pancras (70) . . 118 B3
Dampvitoux (54) 65 H1
Damrémont (52) 117 F3
Damville (27) 56 C3
Damvillers (55) 43 H3
Damvix (85) 160 E6
Dancé (42) 186 E6
Dancé (61) 83 K4
Dancevoir (52) 115 J3
Dancourt (76) 16 E2

Dancourt-Popincourt (80) 18 E5
Dancy (28) 109 G1
Danestal (14) 33 H4
Dangé-Saint-Romain (86) 145 K4
Dangeau (28) 84 E6
Dangers (28) 85 F2
Dangeul (72) 82 E5
Dangolsheim (67) 70 C3
Dangu (27) 36 D3
Dangy (50) 31 G4
Danizy (02) 20 B5
Danjoutin (90) 139 H1
Danne-et-Quatre-Vents (57) 70 B1
Dannelbourg (57) 70 A1
Dannemarie (25) 139 J3
Dannemarie (68) 97 A4
Dannemarie (78) 57 H5
Dannemarie-sur-Crête (25) 137 J6
Dannemoine (89) 113 K4
Dannemois (91) 87 F3
Dannes (62) 4 A4
Dannevoux (55) 43 G3
Danvou-la-Ferrière (14) 53 G2
Danzé (41) 108 C4
Daon (53) 105 F5
Daoulas (29) 74 C1
Daours (80) 18 C2
Darazac (19) 216 E4
Darbonnay (39) 155 H5
Darbres (07) 239 J4
Darcey (21) 135 F2
Darcey (21) 135 F2
Dardenac (33) 230 A3
Dardez (27) 35 J6
Dardilly (69) 205 K1
Dareizé (69) 187 K6
Dargies (60) 17 H4
Dargnies (80) 8 D6
Dargoire (42) 205 J4
Darmannes (52) 92 B6
Darnac (87) 180 E2
Darnétal (76) 35 J2
Darnets (19) 200 D6
Darney (88) 117 K1
Darney-aux-Chênes (88) 93 H4
Darnieulles (88) 94 C5
Darois (21) 135 K4
Darvault (77) 87 J5
Darvoy (45) 110 C4
Dasle (25) 139 J2
Daubensand (67) 71 D4
Daubeuf-la-Campagne (27) 35 H5
Daubeuf-près-Vatteville (27) 35 K4
Daubeuf-Serville (76) 14 E4
Daubèze (33) 230 B3
Dauendorf (67) 69 K6
Daumazan-sur-Arize (09) 288 A6
Daumeray (49) 105 J6
Dauphin (04) 278 B2
Dausse (47) 248 E2
Daux (31) 269 F5
Dauzat-sur-Vodable (63) 202 D6
Davayat (63) 185 F5
Davayé (71) 188 B1
Davejean (11) 309 J3
Davenescourt (80) 18 D4
Davézieux (07) 222 A2
Davignac (19) 200 D6
Davrey (10) 113 K2
Davron (78) 58 A3
Dax (40) 264 B4
Deauville (14) 33 J3
Deaux (30) 255 H6
Débats-Rivière-d'Orpra (42) 204 B2
Decazeville (12) 235 F6
Dechy (59) 11 J2
Décines-Charpieu (69) 206 C2
Decize (58) 151 G6
Dégagnac (46) 233 G4
Degré (72) 106 C2
Dehault (72) 83 H6
Dehéries (59) 12 B5
Dehlingen (67) 68 E4
Deinvillers (88) 94 E2
Delain (70) 137 G2
Delettes (62) 5 G4
Delincourt (60) 36 E4
Delle (90) 139 K2
Delme (57) 66 C2
Delouze-Rosières (55) 92 C1
le Déluge (60) 37 H4
Delut (55) 43 J2
Deluz (25) 138 B5
Demandolx (04) 279 K2
Demange-aux-Eaux (55) 64 D4
Demangevelle (70) 117 K3
Demi-Quartier (74) 192 A5
la Demie (70) 138 B1
Demigny (71) 154 A4
Démouville (14) 33 F5
Dému (32) 266 D4
Démuin (80) 18 D3
Denain (59) 12 C2
Dénat (81) 270 E3
Denazé (53) 104 D4
Dénestanville (76) 15 K3
Deneuille-lès-Chantelle (03) 185 F2
Deneuille-les-Mines (03) 167 J6
Deneuvre (54) 95 F2
Denève (70) 137 G2
Dénezé-sous-Doué (49) 125 K6
Dénezé-sous-le-Lude (49) 126 D3
Denezières (39) 173 J2
Denguin (64) 284 B3
Denicé (69) 188 A5
Denier (62) 10 B3

Denipaire (88) 95 J3
Dennebrœucq (62) 5 F5
Denneville (50) 28 C6
Dennevy (71) 153 J5
Denonville (28) 85 K3
Denting (57) 45 J4
Déols (36) 147 K6
Derbamont (88) 94 B4
Dercé (86) 145 F4
Derchigny (76) 16 B1
Dercy (02) 20 D4
Dernacueillette (11) 309 J3
Dernancourt (80) 18 D1
Derval (44) 103 F4
Désaignes (07) 221 J6
Désandans (25) 139 G2
Descartes (37) 146 A3
le Deschaux (39) 155 G4
le Désert (14) 52 A2
Désertines (03) 167 H6
Désertines (53) 80 E2
les Déserts (73) 208 C3
Déservillers (25) 156 C3
Desges (43) 219 H6
Desingy (74) 190 D4
Desmonts (45) 87 F6
Desnes (39) 155 G6
Dessenheim (68) 96 D5
Dessia (39) 173 F5
Destord (88) 95 F4
la Destrousse (13) 296 C4
Destry (57) 66 E1
Desvres (62) 4 C4
Détain-et-Bruant (21) 153 K1
Détrier (73) 208 D5
le Détroit (14) 53 K3
Dettey (71) 170 C1
Dettwiller (67) 70 C1
Deuil-la-Barre (95) 58 E4
Deuillet (02) 20 A5
Deûlémont (59) 6 C3
Deux-Chaises (03) 168 A4
Deux-Évailles (53) 81 H6
les Deux-Fays (39) 155 G6
Deux-Jumeaux (14) 29 J6
Deux-Verges (15) 236 D3
les Deux-Villes (08) 23 H4
Deuxville (54) 66 D5
Devay (58) 151 H6
Devecey (25) 137 K5
Devesset (07) 221 H5
Devèze (65) 286 C5
Deviat (16) 196 C6
Dévillac (47) 232 B5
Deville (08) 22 D2
Déville-lès-Rouen (76) 35 H1
Devise (80) 19 H2
Devrouze (71) 154 D6
Deycimont (88) 95 F5
Deyme (31) 288 C2
Deyvillers (88) 94 E5
le Dézert (50) 31 G2
Dezize-lès-Maranges (71) 153 J5
D'Huison-Longueville (91) 86 E3
Dhuisy (77) 60 C1
Dhuizel (02) 40 B3
Dhuizon (41) 129 H2
Diancey (21) 153 F1
Diane-Capelle (57) 67 H4
Diant (77) 88 A5
Diarville (54) 94 A3
Diconne (71) 154 D6
Dicy (89) 112 B3
Didenheim (68) 97 C3
Die (26) 241 H3
Diebling (57) 68 C3
Diebolsheim (67) 71 D5
Diedendorf (67) 67 J2
Dieffenbach-au-Val (67) 96 B1
Dieffenbach-lès-Wœrth (67) 25 D3
Dieffenthal (67) 96 C1
Diefmatten (68) 97 A3
Dième (69) 187 J5
Diemeringen (67) 68 E5
Diémoz (38) 206 D4
Diénay (21) 136 A3
Dienne (15) 218 B4
Dienné (86) 163 H5
Diennes-Aubigny (58) 151 J5
Dienville (10) 91 H4
Dieppe (76) 15 K1
Dieppe-sous-Douaumont (55) . . . 43 J4
Dierre (37) 128 B5
Dierrey-Saint-Julien (10) 89 J4
Dierrey-Saint-Pierre (10) 89 J4
Diesen (57) 45 K4
Dietwiller (68) 97 C3
Dieudonné (60) 37 J4
Dieue-sur-Meuse (55) 43 J6
Dieulefit (26) 240 E6
Dieulivol (33) 230 E4
Dieulouard (54) 65 K3
Dieupentale (82) 269 F3
Dieuze (57) 67 F3
Diéval (62) 5 J6
Diffembach-lès-Hellimer (57) . . . 68 B4
Diges (89) 112 E6
Digna (39) 172 E4
Dignac (16) 197 F4
la Digne-d'Amont (11) 308 E2
la Digne-d'Aval (11) 308 E2
Digne-les-Bains (04) 259 J4
Dignonville (88) 94 D5
Digny (28) 84 D2

Digoin (71) 170 A4
Digosville (50) 28 D2
Digulleville (50) 28 A1
Dijon (21) 136 A5
Dimancheville (45) 87 F5
Dimbsthal (67) 70 B2
Dimechaux (59) 13 H4
Dimont (59) 13 H4
Dinan (22) 50 D5
Dinard (35) 50 D3
Dinéault (29) 74 C3
Dingé (35) 79 G1
Dingsheim (67) 70 D3
Dingy-en-Vuache (74) 190 D3
Dingy-Saint-Clair (74) 191 G5
Dinozé (88) 94 D5
Dinsac (87) 181 F2
Dinsheim-sur-Bruche (67) 70 C4
Dinteville (52) 115 H2
Dio-et-Valquières (34) 273 F5
Dionay (38) 223 F3
Dions (30) 275 G2
Diors (36) 148 B6
Diou (03) 169 J4
Diou (36) 148 D3
Dirac (16) 197 F4
Dirinon (29) 46 C6
Dirol (58) 133 H5
Dissangis (89) 134 A2
Dissay (86) 163 G2
Dissay-sous-Courcillon (72) 127 G1
Dissé-sous-Ballon (72) 83 F5
Dissé-sous-le-Lude (72) 126 D2
Distré (49) 144 C1
Distroff (57) 27 H4
Diusse (64) 285 F1
Divajeu (26) 240 D4
Dives (60) 19 G6
Dives-sur-Mer (14) 33 G3
Divion (62) 5 J6
Divonne-les-Bains (01) 174 C5
Dixmont (89) 112 E2
Dizimieu (38) 207 F2
Dizy (51) 40 E6
Dizy-le-Gros (02) 21 G5
Doazit (40) 265 F5
Doazon (64) 284 C2
Docelles (88) 95 F6
Dœuil-sur-le-Mignon (17) 177 K3
Dognen (64) 283 J4
Dogneville (88) 94 D5
Dohem (62) 5 F4
Dohis (02) 21 H3
Doignies (59) 11 H5
Doingt (80) 19 G1
Doissat (24) 232 D4
Doissin (38) 207 H3
Doix (85) 160 D5
Doizieux (42) 205 J6
Dol-de-Bretagne (35) 51 F4
Dolaincourt (88) 93 H4
Dolancourt (10) 91 G5
Dolcourt (54) 93 J2
Dole (39) 155 G2
Dolignon (02) 21 H4
Dolleren (68) 119 J4
Dollon (72) 107 H2
Dollot (89) 88 B6
Dolmayrac (47) 248 B2
Dolo (22) 50 A6
Dolomieu (38) 207 H3
Dolus-d'Oléron (17) 176 C5
Dolus-le-Sec (37) 146 C2
Dolving (57) 67 J3
Dom-le-Mesnil (08) 22 E4
Domagné (35) 79 J5
Domaize (63) 203 H3
Domalain (35) 104 A3
Domancy (74) 192 A5
Domarin (38) 206 E4
Domart-en-Ponthieu (80) 9 J5
Domart-sur-la-Luce (80) 18 C3
Domats (89) 112 B1
Domazan (30) 275 K2
Dombasle-devant-Darney (88) . . 93 K6
Dombasle-en-Argonne (55) 43 G5
Dombasle-en-Xaintois (88) 93 J4
Dombasle-sur-Meurthe (54) 66 C5
Domblain (52) 91 K2
Domblans (39) 155 H6
Dombras (55) 43 J2
Dombrot-le-Sec (88) 93 J6
Dombrot-sur-Vair (88) 93 H4
Domecy-sur-Cure (89) 133 J4
Domecy-sur-le-Vault (89) 133 J3
Doméliers (60) 17 K4
Domène (38) 224 B3
Domérat (03) 167 G6
Domesmont (80) 9 K5
Domessargues (30) 274 E1
Domessin (73) 207 K4
Domèvre-en-Haye (54) 65 J3
Domèvre-sous-Montfort (88) . . . 93 K5
Domèvre-sur-Avière (88) 94 C5
Domèvre-sur-Durbion (88) 94 D4
Domèvre-sur-Vezouze (54) 67 G4
Domeyrat (43) 219 J3
Domeyrot (23) 183 G2
Domezain-Berraute (64) 283 G3
Domfaing (88) 95 G4
Domfessel (67) 68 E4
Domfront (60) 18 D5
Domfront (61) 53 G6
Domfront-en-Champagne (72) . . 106 C1
Domgermain (54) 65 H5
la Dominelais (35) 103 F3

Dominois (80) 9 G2
Domjean (50) 31 H5
Domjevin (54) 67 F6
Domjulien (88) 93 J5
Domléger-Longvillers (80) 9 J4
Domloup (35) 79 H5
Dommarie-Eulmont (54) 93 K2
Dommarien (52) 116 D6
Dommartemont (54) 66 B4
Dommartin (01) 172 A6
Dommartin (25) 156 E4
Dommartin (58) 152 A3
Dommartin (69) 205 K1
Dommartin (80) 18 B3
Dommartin-aux-Bois (88) 94 B6
Dommartin-Dampierre (51) 42 C6
Dommartin-la-Chaussée (54) . . . 65 H1
Dommartin-la-Montagne (55) . . . 43 K6
Dommartin-le-Coq (10) 90 D2
Dommartin-le-Franc (52) 91 K3
Dommartin-le-Saint-Père (52) . . . 91 J3
Dommartin-lès-Cuiseaux (71) . . 172 D4
Dommartin-lès-Remiremont (88) . 119 F2
Dommartin-lès-Toul (54) 65 H5
Dommartin-lès-Vallois (88) 94 A6
Dommartin-Lettrée (51) 62 C4
Dommartin-sous-Amance (54) . . 66 B4
Dommartin-sous-Hans (51) 42 C5
Dommartin-sur-Vraine (88) 93 J4
Dommartin-Varimont (51) 63 H2
Dommary-Baroncourt (55) 44 A3
Domme (24) 233 F3
Dommery (08) 22 B4
Dommiers (02) 39 H3
Domnon-lès-Dieuze (57) 67 G2
Domont (95) 58 E1
Dompaire (88) 94 B5
Dompcevrin (55) 64 D2
Dompierre (60) 18 D6
Dompierre (61) 53 H6
Dompierre (88) 94 E4
Dompierre-aux-Bois (55) 64 E1
Dompierre-Becquincourt (80) . . 19 F2
Dompierre-du-Chemin (35) 80 B4
Dompierre-en-Morvan (21) . . . 134 C4
Dompierre-les-Églises (87) . . . 181 H2
Dompierre-les-Ormes (71) 171 F6
Dompierre-les-Tilleuls (25) 156 D5
Dompierre-sous-Sanvignes (71) . 170 D2
Dompierre-sur-Authie (80) 9 H2
Dompierre-sur-Besbre (03) . . . 169 H4
Dompierre-sur-Chalaronne (01) . 188 D3
Dompierre-sur-Charente (17) . . 195 H2
Dompierre-sur-Helpe (59) 13 G4
Dompierre-sur-Héry (58) 133 G6
Dompierre-sur-Mer (17) 176 E2
Dompierre-sur-Mont (39) 173 G3
Dompierre-sur-Nièvre (58) 150 E1
Dompierre-sur-Veyle (01) 189 G4
Dompierre-sur-Yon (85) 141 K6
Dompnac (07) 238 E6
Domprel (25) 138 E6
Dompremy (51) 63 G5
Domprix (54) 44 B3
Domps (87) 199 K3
Domptail (88) 94 E2
Domptail-en-l'Air (54) 94 C1
Domptin (02) 60 D1
Domqueur (80) 9 J5
Domremy-la-Canne (55) 44 A3
Domrémy-la-Pucelle (88) 93 F2
Domremy-Landéville (52) 92 C3
Domsure (01) 172 D5
Domvallier (88) 93 K4
Domvast (80) 9 H4
Don (59) 6 C5
Donazac (11) 308 D1
Donchery (08) 22 E4
Doncières (88) 95 F2
Doncourt-aux-Templiers (55) . . . 44 B6
Doncourt-lès-Conflans (54) 44 D5
Doncourt-lès-Longuyon (54) . . . 26 C3
Doncourt-sur-Meuse (52) 93 F6
Dondas (47) 248 D4
Donges (44) 122 B2
Donjeux (52) 92 B3
Donjeux (57) 66 C2
le Donjon (03) 169 J6
Donnay (14) 53 J2
Donnazac (81) 270 C1
Donnelay (57) 67 F4
Donnemain-Saint-Mamès (28) . 109 F1
Donnemarie-Dontilly (77) 88 C2
Donnement (10) 90 E2
Donnenheim (67) 70 E1
Donnery (45) 110 C4
Donneville (31) 288 C2
Donnezac (33) 211 J2
Dontreix (23) 184 A5
Dontrien (51) 41 J4
Donville-les-Bains (50) 30 C6
Donzac (33) 230 A4
Donzac (82) 248 D6
Donzacq (40) 264 D5
le Donzeil (23) 182 E5
Donzenac (19) 215 J3
Donzère (26) 256 D1
Donzy (58) 132 C5
Donzy-le-National (71) 171 G5
Donzy-le-Pertuis (71) 171 H5
Doranges (63) 219 K1
Dorans (90) 139 H1
Dorat (63) 185 K6
le Dorat (87) 181 F2
Dorceau (61) 83 K3
Dordives (45) 111 J1

Dore-l'Église (63) 220 A1
la Dorée (53) 80 D2
Dorengt (02) 20 D1
Dorlisheim (67) 70 D4
Dormans (51) 40 B6
Dormelles (77) 87 K4
la Dornac (24) 215 G5
Dornas (07) 239 G2
Dornecy (58) 133 G4
Dornes (58) 168 E2
Dornot (57) 44 E6
Dorres (66) 313 G5
Dortan (01) 173 H6
Dosches (10) 90 C4
Dosnon (10) 62 C6
Dossenheim-Kochersberg (67) . . 70 D2
Dossenheim-sur-Zinsel (67) . . . 69 G2
Douadic (36) 164 C2
Douai (59) 11 H2
Douains (27) 57 F1
Douarnenez (29) 74 B4
Douaumont (55) 43 J4
Doubs (25) 157 F4
Doucelles (72) 82 D5
Douchapt (24) 213 H3
Douchy (02) 19 J3
Douchy (45) 112 B3
Douchy-lès-Ayette (62) 10 E4
Douchy-les-Mines (59) 12 C2
Doucier (39) 173 J2
Doucy-en-Bauges (73) 208 D2
Doudeauville (62) 4 C4
Doudeauville (76) 17 F6
Doudeauville-en-Vexin (27) . . . 36 C3
Doudelainville (80) 9 F6
Doudeville (76) 15 G4
Doudrac (47) 231 K4
Doue (77) 60 C4
Doué-la-Fontaine (49) 144 A1
Douelle (46) 249 K1
le Douhet (17) 195 G1
Douillet (72) 82 B5
Douilly (80) 19 H3
Doulaincourt-Saucourt (52) . . . 92 B4
Doulcon (55) 43 F2
Doulevant-le-Château (52) 91 J3
Doulevant-le-Petit (52) 91 K2
Doulezon (33) 230 D3
le Doulieu (59) 6 A3
Doullens (80) 10 B4
Doumely-Bégny (08) 21 K5
Doumy (64) 284 D2
Dounoux (88) 94 D6
Dourbies (30) 254 A6
Dourdain (35) 79 K3
Dourdan (91) 86 B2
Dourges (62) 11 G1
Dourgne (81) 289 J2
Douriez (62) 9 G2
Dourlers (59) 13 G4
le Dourn (81) 271 H1
Dournazac (87) 198 B4
Dournon (39) 156 B4
Dours (65) 285 J4
Doussard (74) 208 E1
Doussay (86) 145 F5
Douvaine (74) 174 D6
Douville (24) 213 J6
Douville-en-Auge (14) 33 H4
Douville-sur-Andelle (27) 35 K3
Douvrend (76) 16 C2
Douvres (01) 189 H4
Douvres-la-Délivrande (14) 32 E3
Douvrin (62) 6 A6
Doux (08) 41 J1
Doux (79) 162 C1
Douy (28) 108 E2
Douy-la-Ramée (77) 59 K1
Douzains (47) 231 J5
Douzat (16) 196 C2
la Douze (24) 214 B5
Douzens (11) 290 D6
Douzillac (24) 213 H5
Douzy (08) 23 G4
Doville (50) 28 C6
Doye (39) 156 C6
Doyet (03) 184 C1
Dozulé (14) 33 H4
Dracé (69) 188 B3
Draché (37) 145 K3
Drachenbronn-Birlenbach (67) . . 25 B2
Dracy (89) 112 D6
Dracy-le-Fort (71) 153 K6
Dracy-lès-Couches (71) 153 H5
Dracy-Saint-Loup (71) 153 F3
Dragey-Ronthon (50) 51 J2
Draguignan (83) 279 J6
Draillant (74) 175 F6
Drain (49) 124 A5
Draix (04) 260 A4
Draize (08) 21 K5
Drambon (21) 136 D5
Dramelay (39) 173 G6
Drancy (93) 59 F3
Drap (06) 281 H3
Dravegny (02) 40 B4
Draveil (91) 59 F6
Drée (21) 135 H5
Drefféac (44) 102 C6
Drémil-Lafage (31) 269 H6
le Drennec (29) 46 B4
Dreuil-lès-Amiens (80) 18 A2
Dreuilhe (09) 308 B3
Dreux (28) 57 F1
Drevant (18) 167 G2
Dricourt (08) 41 K2

Driencourt (80) 19 H1
Drincham (59) 3 G3
Drocourt (62) 11 G1
Drocourt (78) 57 J1
Droisy (27) 56 D4
Droisy (74) 190 D5
Droiturier (03) 186 B2
Droizy (02) 39 K4
Drom (01) 189 H2
Dromesnil (80) 17 G2
Drosay (76) 15 G3
Drosnay (51) 91 F1
Droué (41) 108 C2
Droue-sur-Drouette (28) 85 J1
Drouges (35) 104 A3
Drouilly (51) 62 E4
Droupt-Saint-Basle (10) 89 K2
Droupt-Sainte-Marie (10) 89 K2
Drouville (54) 66 C5
Drouvin-le-Marais (62) 6 A6
Droux (87) 181 G3
Droyes (52) 91 G2
Drubec (14) 33 J4
Drucat (80) 9 G4
Drucourt (27) 34 C6
Drudas (31) 268 D4
Druelle (12) 252 A3
Drugeac (15) 217 H4
Druillat (01) 189 H4
Drulhe (12) 251 G1
Drulingen (67) 67 K2
Drumettaz-Clarafond (73) 208 B3
Drusenheim (67) 25 C4
Druy-Parigny (58) 151 G5
Druye (37) 127 G5
Druyes-les-Belles-Fontaines (89) . 132 E3
Dry (45) 109 J5
l'Échelle (08) 22 B1
Duault (22) 75 K2
Ducey (50) 52 A6
Duclair (76) 35 F1
Ducy-Sainte-Marguerite (14) . . . 32 C4
Duerne (69) 205 H3
Duesme (21) 135 G1
Duffort (32) 286 B4
Dugny (93) 59 F2
Dugny-sur-Meuse (55) 43 H5
Duhort-Bachen (40) 265 J4
Duilhac-sous-Peyrepertuse (11) . 309 J4
Duingt (74) 191 G6
Duisans (62) 10 E2
Dullin (73) 207 K4
Dumes (40) 265 F5
Dun (09) 308 A2
Dun-le-Palestel (23) 182 B1
Dun-le-Poëlier (36) 148 A1
Dun-les-Places (58) 134 A6
Dun-sur-Auron (18) 149 J5
Dun-sur-Grandry (58) 152 A3
Dun-sur-Meuse (55) 43 F2
Duneau (72) 107 H2
Dunes (82) 248 E6
Dunet (36) 164 E5
Dunière-sur-Eyrieux (07) 240 A2
Dunières (43) 221 G3
Dunkerque (59) 3 H1
Duntzenheim (67) 70 D2
Duppigheim (67) 70 E4
Duran (32) 267 H5
Durance (47) 247 G5
Duranus (06) 281 G1
Duranville (27) 34 C5
Duras (47) 230 E4
Duravel (46) 232 D6
Durban (32) 286 C1
Durban-Corbières (11) 310 B2
Durban-sur-Arize (09) 307 F2
Durbans (46) 234 B4
Durcet (61) 53 J4
Durdat-Larequille (03) 184 B2
Dureil (72) 106 A4
Durenque (12) 252 C6
Durfort (09) 288 C5
Durfort (81) 289 J3
Durfort-et-Saint-Martin-
  -de-Sossenac (30) 274 C1
Durfort-Lacapelette (82) 249 G5
Durlinsdorf (68) 97 B6
Durmenach (68) 97 C5
Durmignat (63) 184 D3
Durnes (25) 156 D2
Durningen (67) 70 D2
Durrenbach (67) 25 A3
Durrenentzen (68) 96 D4
Durstel (67) 68 E5
Durtal (49) 125 K1
Durtol (63) 202 D2
Dury (02) 19 J4
Dury (62) 11 G3
Dury (80) 18 A2
Dussac (24) 214 E1
Duttlenheim (67) 70 D4
Duvy (60) 38 E4
Duzey (55) 26 B4
Dyé (89) 113 J4
Dyo (71) 170 D6

E

Eancé (35) 104 A4
Eaubonne (95) 58 D2
Eaucourt-sur-Somme (80) 9 G5
Eaunes (31) 288 B3

Eaux-Bonnes (64) 303 H2
Eaux-Puiseaux (10) 113 K1
Eauze (32) 266 D3
Ébaty (21) 153 K4
Ebblinghem (59) 5 H3
Eberbach-Seltz (67) 25 D2
Ebersheim (67) 96 D1
Ebersmunster (67) 96 D1
Ébersviller (57) 45 H3
Éblange (57) 45 H4
Ébouleau (02) 21 F4
Ébréon (16) 179 F5
Ébreuil (03) 185 F3
l'Écaille (08) 41 G2
Écaquelon (27) 34 E4
Écalles-Alix (76) 15 H5
Écaquelon (27) 34 E4
Écardenville-la-Campagne (27) . 35 F6
Écardenville-sur-Eure (27) 35 K6
Écausseville (50) 29 F4
Écauville (27) 35 G6
Eccica-Suarella (2A) 320 D5
Eccles (59) 13 J3
Échalas (69) 205 K4
Échallat (16) 196 C2
Échallon (01) 190 B2
Échalot (21) 135 J2
Échalou (61) 53 H5
Échandelys (63) 203 H5
Échannay (21) 135 G6
Écharcon (91) 87 F1
Échassières (03) 184 D3
Échauffour (61) 55 G5
Échavanne (70) 119 G6
Échay (37) 156 B3
Échebrune (17) 195 J4
l'Échelle-Saint-Aurin (80) 18 E4
les Échelles (73) 207 K6
Échemines (10) 89 J3
Échemiré (49) 126 A2
Échenans (25) 139 G2
Échenans-sous-Mont-Vaudois (70) . 139 G1
Échenay (52) 92 C2
Échenevex (01) 174 B6
Échenon (21) 154 E2
Échenoz-la-Méline (70) 138 B1
Échenoz-le-Sec (70) 138 A2
Échevannes (21) 136 B2
Échevannes (25) 156 D2
Échevis (26) 223 H5
Échevronne (21) 154 A2
Échigey (21) 154 D1
Échillais (17) 177 F6
Échilleuses (45) 87 F6
Echinghen (62) 4 B3
Échiré (79) 161 H5
Échirolles (38) 224 A4
Échouboulains (77) 88 A3
Échourgnac (24) 213 F4
Eckartswiller (67) 70 B1
Eckbolsheim (67) 71 D1
Eckwersheim (67) 25 A5
Éclaibes (59) 13 G4
Éclaires (51) 63 K1
Éclance (10) 91 G4
Éclans-Nenon (39) 155 H2
Éclaron-Braucourt-
  -Sainte-Livière (52) 91 J1
Eclassan (07) 222 B4
Écleux (39) 155 J3
Éclimeux (62) 9 K1
Éclose (38) 207 F5
Écluzelles (28) 57 F5
Écluzelles (28) 57 F5
Écly (08) 21 K6
Écoche (42) 187 H3
Écoivres (62) 10 A2
École (73) 208 E3
École-Valentin (25) 137 K5
Écollemont (51) 63 G6
Écommoy (72) 106 E5
Écoquenéauville (50) 29 F5
Écorcei (61) 55 H5
les Écorces (25) 139 H6
Écorches (61) 54 D3
Écordal (08) 22 C6
Écorpain (72) 107 J3
Écos (27) 36 C5
Écot (25) 139 G3
Ecot-la-Combe (52) 92 D5
Écotay-l'Olme (42) 204 C4
Écouché (61) 54 B5
Écouen (95) 59 E1
Écouflant (49) 125 G2
Écouis (27) 36 B3
Écourt-Saint-Quentin (62) 11 H3
Écoust-Saint-Mein (62) 11 G4
Écouviez (55) 26 A2
l'Écouvotte (25) 138 C4
Écoyeux (17) 195 H1
Ecquedecques (62) 5 J5
Ecques (62) 5 G4
Ecquetot (27) 35 H5
Ecquevilly (78) 58 A2
Écrainville (76) 14 C5
les Écrennes (77) 87 K2
Écretteville-lès-Baons (76) 15 F5
Écretteville-sur-Mer (76) 14 E3
Écriennes (51) 63 G5
Écrille (39) 173 G4
Écromagny (70) 118 E4
Écrosnes (28) 85 J2
Écrouves (54) 65 H5
Ectot-l'Auber (76) 15 J5

Ectot-lès-Baons (76) 15 H5
Écueil (51) 40 E5
Écueillé (36) 147 G3
Écuélin (59) 13 G4
Écuelle (70) 137 F2
Écuelles (71) 154 C4
Écuelles (77) 87 J4
Écuillé (49) 125 G1
Écuires (62) 4 C6
Écuisses (71) 171 G1
Éculleville (50) 28 B1
Écully (69) 206 A2
Écuras (16) 197 J3
Écurat (17) 195 F1
Écurcey (25) 139 H3
Écurey-en-Verdunois (55) 43 H2
Écurie (52) 10 E2
Écury-le-Repos (51) 62 A4
Écury-sur-Coole (51) 62 D3
Écutigny (21) 153 J2
Écuvilly (60) 19 G5
Edern (29) 74 E4
Édon (16) 197 G5
les Éduts (17) 178 C5
Eecke (59) 3 K5
Effiat (63) 185 G4
Effincourt (52) 92 C2
Effry (02) 21 G1
Égat (66) 313 H4
Égleny (89) 112 E5
Égletons (19) 216 D1
Égligny (77) 88 B3
Eglingen (68) 97 B4
l'Église-aux-Bois (19) 200 A4
Église-Neuve-de-Vergt (24) . . . 214 A5
Église-Neuve-d'Issac (24) 213 H6
Égliseneuve-d'Entraigues (63) . 218 B1
Égliseneuve-des-Liards (63) . . 203 G4
Égliseneuve-près-Billom (63) . . 203 G3
les Églises-d'Argenteuil (17) . . 178 A5
Églisolles (63) 204 B6
les Églisottes-et-Chalaures (33) . 212 C4
Égly (91) 86 D1
Égreville (77) 87 K6
Égriselles-le-Bocage (89) 112 C1
Égry (45) 111 F1
Éguelshardt (57) 69 H3
Éguenigue (90) 119 H6
l'Éguille (17) 194 C2
Éguilles (13) 277 H6
Éguilly (21) 135 F5
Éguilly-sous-Bois (10) 115 F1
Eguisheim (68) 96 B4
Éguzon-Chantôme (36) 165 H5
Éhuns (70) 118 C5
Eichhoffen (67) 70 C6
Eincheville (57) 66 E1
Einvaux (54) 94 C1
Einville-au-Jard (54) 66 D5
Eix (55) 43 J5
Élan (08) 22 D4
Élancourt (78) 58 B4
Elbach (68) 119 K6
Elbeuf (76) 35 H4
Elbeuf-en-Bray (76) 36 D1
Elbeuf-sur-Andelle (76) 36 A1
Élencourt (60) 17 H4
Élesmes (59) 13 H2
Életot (76) 14 D3
Éleu-dit-Leauwette (62) 11 F1
Élincourt (59) 12 B6
Élincourt-Sainte-Marguerite (60) . 38 C2
Élise-Daucourt (51) 63 H1
Ellecourt (76) 17 F3
Elliant (29) 99 F1
Ellon (14) 32 B4
Elne (66) 315 H3
Elnes (62) 5 F3
Éloie (90) 119 H5
Éloise (74) 190 C3
Éloyes (88) 95 F6
Elsenheim (67) 96 D3
Elvange (57) 45 J6
Elven (56) 101 H4
Elzange (57) 27 H4
Émagny (25) 137 J5
Émalleville (27) 35 J6
Émancé (78) 85 J1
Émanville (27) 56 B1
Émanville (76) 15 J5
Emberménil (54) 67 F5
Embres-et-Castelmaure (11) . . 310 B3
Embreville (80) 8 D6
Embrun (05) 243 J5
Embry (62) 4 E6
Émerainville (77) 59 H4
Émerchicourt (59) 11 K2
Émeringes (69) 188 B2
Éméville (60) 39 F4
Émiéville (14) 33 H5
Emlingen (68) 97 B4
Emmerin (59) 6 D4
Émondeville (50) 29 F4
Empeaux (31) 287 J1
Empurany (07) 221 K5
Empuré (16) 179 F4
Empury (58) 133 J5
Encausse (32) 268 C5
Encausse-les-Thermes (31) . . . 305 K2
Enchastrayes (04) 260 D1
Enchenberg (57) 69 G4
Encourtiech (09) 306 E3
Endoufielle (32) 287 J1
Énencourt-le-Sec (60) 37 F4
Énencourt-Léage (60) 36 E4
Enfonvelle (52) 117 H3

Engayrac (47)	248 E4	Épineu-le-Chevreuil (72)	106 B2
Engente (10)	91 H5	Épineuil (89)	114 A4
Engenville (45)	86 D5	Épineuil-le-Fleuriel (18)	167 H4
Enghien-les-Bains (95)	58 E2	Épineuse (60)	38 B2
Engins (38)	223 K3	Épineux-le-Seguin (53)	105 J3
Englancourt (02)	20 E1	Épiniac (35)	51 G5
Englebelmer (80)	10 D5	Épinonville (55)	42 E3
Englefontaine (59)	12 E4	Épinouze (26)	222 C2
Englesqueville-en-Auge (14)	33 J3	Épiry (58)	151 K1
Englesqueville-la-Percée (14)	29 J6	Épisy (77)	87 J4
Englos (59)	6 D4	Épizon (52)	92 C3
Engomer (09)	306 C3	Éplessier (80)	17 H3
Enguinegatte (62)	5 G4	Éply (54)	66 A2
Engwiller (67)	69 G5	Époisses (21)	134 C3
Ennemain (80)	19 G2	Épône (78)	57 K2
Ennery (57)	45 F4	Épothémont (10)	91 G3
Ennery (95)	58 C1	Épouville (76)	14 B6
Ennetières-en-Weppes (59)	6 C4	Époye (51)	41 H4
Ennevelin (59)	6 E5	Eppe-Sauvage (59)	13 K5
Ennezat (63)	185 G6	Eppes (02)	20 E6
Ennordres (18)	130 E4	Eppeville (80)	19 H4
Enquin-les-Mines (62)	5 G5	Epping (57)	69 F2
Enquin-sur-Baillons (62)	4 C5	Épretot (76)	14 C6
Ens (65)	305 F5	Épreville (76)	14 D4
Ensigné (79)	178 C3	Épreville-en-Lieuvin (27)	34 C5
Ensisheim (68)	97 C1	Épreville-en-Roumois (27)	34 E3
Ensuès-la-Redonne (13)	296 A3	Épreville-près-le-Neubourg (27)	35 F5
Entrages (04)	259 K6	Épron (14)	32 E4
Entraigues (38)	242 D1	Épuisay (41)	108 B4
Entraigues (63)	185 G6	Équancourt (80)	11 H6
Entraigues-sur-la-Sorgue (84)	276 C1	Équemauville (14)	33 K2
Entrains-sur-Nohain (58)	132 D4	Équennes-Éramecourt (80)	17 H4
Entrammes (53)	105 F2	Équeurdreville-Hainneville (50)	28 C2
Entrange (57)	27 G3	Équevilley (70)	118 B5
Entraunes (06)	260 E4	Équevillon (39)	156 B6
Entraygues-sur-Truyère (12)	235 J5	Équihen-Plage (62)	4 A3
Entre-deux-Eaux (88)	95 J4	Équilly (50)	51 K1
Entre-deux-Guiers (38)	207 K6	Équirre (62)	5 G4
Entre-deux-Monts (39)	174 A2	Éragny (95)	58 C1
Entrecasteaux (83)	298 B1	Éragny-sur-Epte (60)	36 E3
Entrechaux (84)	257 H4	Éraines (14)	54 B2
Entremont (74)	191 H4	Éraville (16)	196 B4
Entremont-le-Vieux (73)	208 B5	Erbajolo (2B)	319 G6
Entrepierres (04)	259 G4	Erbéviller-sur-Amezule (54)	66 C4
Entrevaux (04)	280 C1	Erbray (44)	103 K4
Entrevennes (04)	278 D1	Erbrée (35)	104 B1
Entrevernes (74)	208 E1	Ercé (09)	307 F4
Entzheim (67)	70 E4	Ercé-en-Lamée (35)	103 H2
Enval (63)	184 E6	Ercé-près-Liffré (35)	79 H2
Enveitg (66)	313 G5	Erceville (45)	86 B5
Envermeu (76)	16 B2	Erches (80)	18 E4
Envronville (76)	15 F5	Ercheu (80)	19 G4
Éourres (05)	258 D4	Erchin (59)	11 J2
Éoux (31)	287 F5	Erching (57)	69 F2
Épagne (10)	90 E3	Erckartswiller (67)	69 G5
Épagne-Épagnette (80)	9 G5	Ercourt (80)	9 F4
Épagny (02)	39 H1	Ercuis (60)	37 K4
Épagny (21)	136 A3	Erdeven (56)	100 B5
Épagny (74)	191 H5	Éréac (22)	78 A2
Épaignes (27)	34 B4	Ergersheim (67)	70 D3
Épaney (14)	54 B2	Ergnies (80)	9 J5
Épannes (79)	177 J2	Ergny (62)	4 E5
Éparcy (02)	21 H2	Ergué-Gabéric (29)	74 D6
les Éparges (55)	43 K6	Érin (62)	5 G4
Épargnes (17)	194 E4	Éringes (21)	134 E2
les Éparres (38)	207 F4	Eringhem (59)	3 H3
Épaumesnil (80)	17 G2	Érize-la-Brûlée (55)	64 C3
Épaux-Bézu (02)	39 J6	Érize-la-Petite (55)	64 B2
Épeautrolles (28)	84 E4	Érize-Saint-Dizier (55)	64 C3
Épécamps (80)	9 K5	Erlon (02)	20 D4
Épégard (27)	35 F5	Erloy (02)	20 E1
Épehy (80)	11 J6	Ermenonville (60)	38 C6
Épeigné-les-Bois (37)	128 C6	Ermenonville-la-Grande (28)	85 F4
Épeigné-sur-Dême (37)	127 H1	Ermenonville-la-Petite (28)	85 F5
Épénancourt (80)	19 G3	Ermenouville (76)	15 G3
Épenède (16)	180 A4	Ermont (95)	58 D2
Épenouse (25)	138 D6	Ernée (53)	80 D4
Épenoy (25)	157 F1	Ernemont-Boutavent (60)	17 G6
Épense (51)	63 H2	Ernemont-la-Villette (76)	36 D2
Épercieux-Saint-Paul (42)	204 E2	Ernemont-sur-Buchy (76)	16 C6
Éperlecques (62)	3 F4	Ernes (14)	54 B1
Épernay (51)	61 K1	Ernestviller (57)	68 C3
Épernay-sous-Gevrey (21)	154 C1	Erneville-aux-Bois (55)	64 C4
Épernon (28)	85 J1	Ernolsheim-Bruche (67)	70 D3
Éperrais (61)	83 H3	Ernolsheim-lès-Saverne (67)	69 G2
Épersy (73)	208 B2	Erny-Saint-Julien (62)	5 G5
Épertully (71)	153 J4	Érôme (26)	222 B4
Épervans (71)	171 K1	Érondelle (80)	9 G4
les Epesses (85)	142 E5	Érone (2B)	319 G5
Épeugney (25)	156 B2	Éroudeville (50)	28 E4
Epfig (67)	70 C6	Erp (09)	306 E3
Épiais (41)	108 E5	Erquery (60)	38 A2
Épiais-lès-Louvres (95)	59 G1	Erquinghem-le-Sec (59)	6 C4
Épiais-Rhus (95)	37 G6	Erquinghem-Lys (59)	6 C3
Épieds (02)	39 K6	Erquinvillers (60)	38 A2
Épieds (27)	57 F2	Erquy (22)	49 K4
Épieds (49)	144 D2	Err (66)	313 H5
Épieds-en-Beauce (45)	109 H3	Erre (59)	12 B2
Épierre (73)	209 F5	Errevet (70)	119 G6
Épiez-sur-Chiers (54)	26 A4	Errouville (54)	26 E3
Épiez-sur-Meuse (55)	93 F1	Ersa (2B)	317 D2
Épinac (71)	153 H4	Erstein (67)	70 E5
Épinal (88)	94 D5	Erstroff (57)	68 B4
Épinay (27)	55 J2	Ervauville (45)	112 A2
Épinay-Champlâtreux (95)	38 A6	Ervillers (62)	11 F4
l'Épinay-le-Comte (61)	80 E2	Ervy-le-Châtel (10)	113 K2
Épinay-sous-Sénart (91)	59 G5	Esbareich (65)	305 H3
Épinay-sur-Duclair (76)	15 H6	Esbarres (21)	154 D2
Épinay-sur-Odon (14)	32 B6	Esboz-Brest (70)	118 D4
Épinay-sur-Orge (91)	58 E6	Escala (65)	305 F1
Épinay-sur-Seine (93)	58 E2	Escalans (40)	266 C1
l'Épine (05)	258 C4	l'Escale (04)	259 G5
l'Épine (51)	62 E2	Escales (11)	290 E5
l'Épine (85)	140 B3		
l'Épine-aux-Bois (02)	60 E3		
Épineau-les-Voves (89)	113 F3		

Escalles (62)	2 B3	Espiet (33)	230 A2
Escalquens (31)	288 D2	Espinas (82)	250 D5
Escames (60)	17 G6	Espinasse (15)	236 C2
Escamps (46)	250 C2	Espinasse (63)	184 B4
Escamps (89)	113 F6	Espinasse-Vozelle (03)	185 H3
Escandolières (12)	251 J1	Espinasses (05)	243 G6
Escanecrabe (31)	286 E5	Espinchal (63)	218 C1
Escardes (51)	61 F5	Espins (14)	53 J1
l'Escarène (06)	281 H2	Espira-de-Conflent (66)	314 C3
Escarmain (59)	12 D3	Espira-de-l'Agly (66)	310 B5
Escaro (66)	314 A4	Espirat (63)	203 F2
Escassefort (47)	231 F6	Espiute (64)	283 H3
Escatalens (82)	268 E1	Esplantas (43)	237 J1
Escaudain (59)	12 B2	Esplas (09)	288 C6
Escaudes (33)	246 D3	Esplas-de-Sérou (09)	307 F3
Escaudœuvres (59)	12 A4	Espoey (64)	285 F5
Escaunets (65)	285 F3	Espondeilhan (34)	292 A3
Escautpont (59)	12 D1	Esprels (70)	138 D2
Escazeaux (82)	268 C3	Esquay-Notre-Dame (14)	32 D5
Eschau (67)	71 D2	Esquay-sur-Seulles (14)	32 C4
Eschbach (67)	25 A3	Esquéhéries (02)	13 F6
Eschbach-au-Val (68)	96 A4	Esquelbecq (59)	3 H3
Eschbourg (67)	69 F6	Esquennoy (60)	18 A5
Eschentzwiller (68)	97 C3	Esquerchin (59)	11 G1
Escherange (57)	27 F3	Esquerdes (62)	5 F3
Esches (60)	37 H5	Esquibien (29)	73 C3
Eschwiller (67)	67 K2	Esquièze-Sère (65)	304 E4
Esclagne (09)	308 B3	Esquiule (64)	283 K5
Esclainvillers (80)	18 B4	les Essards (16)	212 E3
Esclanèdes (48)	253 K1	les Essards (17)	195 F1
Esclassan-Labastide (32)	286 C3	les Essards (37)	126 E5
Esclauzels (46)	250 B2	les Essards-Taignevaux (39)	155 F4
Esclavelles (76)	16 C4	Essarois (21)	115 H5
Esclavolles-Lurey (51)	89 G1	Essars (62)	6 A5
Escles (88)	94 B6	les Essarts (27)	56 B3
Escles-Saint-Pierre (60)	17 G4	les Essarts (41)	107 J6
Esclottes (47)	230 E4	les Essarts (85)	142 B6
Escobecques (59)	6 C4	les Essarts-le-Roi (78)	58 A4
Escœuilles (62)	4 D3	les Essarts-le-Vicomte (51)	61 F6
Escoire (24)	214 B3	les Essarts-lès-Sézanne (51)	61 G5
Escolives-Sainte-Camille (89)	113 G6	Essay (61)	82 E1
Escombres-et-le-Chesnois (08)	23 J4	Esse (16)	180 C4
Escondeaux (65)	285 J4	Essé (35)	79 J6
Esconnets (65)	304 E1	Essegney (88)	94 C3
Escorailles (15)	217 G4	les Esseintes (33)	230 C5
Escornebœuf (32)	268 B6	Essert (90)	119 H6
Escorpain (28)	56 D5	Essert-Romand (74)	192 A1
Escos (64)	283 G2	Essertaux (80)	18 A4
Escosse (09)	307 H1	Essertenne (71)	153 J2
Escot (64)	303 F1	Essertenne-et-Cecey (70)	136 E4
Escots (65)	304 E1	Essertines-en-Châtelneuf (42)	204 C4
Escou (64)	284 B5	Essertines-en-Donzy (42)	205 F2
Escoubès (64)	284 E3	Esserts-Blay (73)	209 G3
Escoubès-Pouts (65)	304 C1	Esserval-Combe (39)	156 C5
Escoulis (31)	306 C1	Esserval-Tartre (39)	156 C5
Escouloubre (11)	313 J1	Essey (21)	153 H1
Escource (40)	244 E4	Essey-et-Maizerais (54)	65 G2
Escoussans (33)	230 A4	Essey-la-Côte (54)	94 D2
Escoussens (81)	289 K2	Essey-lès-Nancy (54)	66 B4
Escout (64)	284 B5	Essia (39)	173 G3
Escoutoux (63)	203 H1	Essigny-le-Grand (02)	19 K3
Escoville (14)	33 F4	Essigny-le-Petit (02)	20 A2
Escragnolles (06)	280 B4	Essises (02)	60 E2
Escrennes (45)	110 D1	Essômes-sur-Marne (02)	60 E1
Escrignelles (45)	111 J6	Esson (14)	53 J2
Escroux (81)	271 J4	Essoyes (10)	115 F2
Escueillens-et-Saint-Just-de-Bélengard (11)	308 C1	Essuiles (60)	37 J1
Escurès (64)	285 F2	les Estables (43)	238 E1
Escurolles (03)	185 G3	Estables (48)	237 J4
Eslettes (76)	15 K6	Establet (26)	241 J6
Esley (88)	93 K6	Estadens (31)	306 A2
Eslourenties-Daban (64)	285 F4	Estagel (66)	309 K5
Esmans (77)	88 A4	Estaing (12)	236 A6
Esmery-Hallon (80)	19 H4	Estaing (65)	303 K3
Esmoulières (70)	119 F4	Estaires (59)	6 A4
Esmoulins (70)	137 F4	Estal (46)	234 C1
Esnandes (17)	176 D1	Estampes (32)	285 J3
Esnans (25)	138 C4	Estampures (65)	285 K3
Esnes (59)	12 B5	Estancarbon (31)	305 K1
Esnes-en-Argonne (55)	43 G4	Estandeuil (63)	203 H2
Esnon (89)	113 G3	Estang (32)	266 B3
Esnouveaux (52)	92 D6	Estarvielle (65)	305 F4
Espagnac (19)	216 C3	Estavar (66)	313 H5
Espagnac-Sainte-Eulalie (46)	234 B5	Esteil (63)	203 G6
Espalais (82)	248 E6	Esténos (31)	305 K2
Espalem (43)	219 F2	Estensan (65)	305 F4
Espalion (12)	236 B6	Estérençuby (64)	282 E6
Espaly-Saint-Marcel (43)	220 C5	Esternay (51)	61 F5
Espanès (31)	288 C2	Esterre (65)	304 E4
Espaon (32)	287 F3	Estevelles (62)	6 C5
Esparron (05)	242 C6	Esteville (76)	16 B5
Esparron (31)	287 F5	Estézargues (30)	275 K2
Esparron (83)	278 C6	Estialescq (64)	284 B5
Esparron-de-Verdon (04)	278 D4	Estibeaux (40)	264 C6
Esparros (65)	305 F2	Estigarde (40)	246 E6
Esparsac (82)	268 A2	Estillac (47)	248 B5
Espartignac (19)	215 K1	Estipouy (32)	286 A1
Espas (32)	266 C4	Estirac (65)	285 H2
Espaubourg (60)	37 F2	Estissac (10)	89 J5
Espèche (65)	304 E1	Estivals (19)	215 H6
Espéchède (64)	284 E4	Estivareilles (03)	167 H5
Espédaillac (46)	234 B5	Estivareilles (42)	204 C6
Espelette (64)	282 B3	Estivaux (19)	215 H2
Espeluche (26)	240 B6	Estoher (66)	314 C3
Espenel (26)	241 F4	Estos (64)	284 A5
Espérausses (81)	271 H5	Estoublon (04)	279 F3
Espéraza (11)	308 E3	Estourmel (59)	12 B4
Esperce (31)	288 B4	Estouteville-Écalles (76)	16 B6
Espès-Undurein (64)	283 H4	Estouy (45)	86 C5
Espeyrac (12)	235 J3	Estrablin (38)	206 C3
Espeyroux (46)	234 C3	Estramiac (32)	268 A3
Espezel (11)	308 C5	Estrebay (08)	21 K2
Espieilh (65)	304 E1	Estrébœuf (80)	8 E4
Espiens (47)	247 J5	l'Estréchure (30)	254 D6
		Estrée (62)	4 C6

Estrée-Blanche (62)	5 H4
Estrée-Cauchy (62)	10 D1
Estrée-Wamin (62)	10 B3
Estréelles (62)	4 C6
Estrées (02)	19 K1
Estrées (59)	11 H2
Estrées-Deniécourt (80)	19 F2
Estrées-la-Campagne (14)	54 A1
Estrées-lès-Crécy (80)	9 H3
Estrées-Mons (80)	19 H2
Estrées-Saint-Denis (60)	38 C2
Estrées-sur-Noye (80)	18 A3
Estrennes (88)	93 K4
Estreux (59)	12 C2
Estrun (59)	12 B3
Estry (14)	53 F2
Esves-le-Moutier (37)	146 C2
Esvres (37)	127 K6
Eswars (59)	12 B3
Étable (73)	208 D5
Étables (07)	222 A4
Étables-sur-Mer (22)	49 F4
Étagnac (16)	180 C6
Étaimpuis (76)	16 A5
Étain (55)	44 A4
Étaing (62)	11 G3
Étainhus (76)	14 C6
Étais (21)	114 E6
Étais-la-Sauvin (89)	132 E3
Étalans (25)	156 E1
Étalante (21)	135 H1
Étalleville (76)	15 H4
Étalon (80)	19 G3
Étalondes (76)	8 C6
Étampes (91)	86 C3
Étampes-sur-Marne (02)	60 E1
l'Étang-Bertrand (50)	28 D4
l'Étang-la-Ville (78)	58 C3
Étang-sur-Arroux (71)	152 E5
l'Étang-Vergy (21)	154 A1
les Étangs (57)	45 H1
Étaples (62)	4 B5
Étaule (89)	133 K3
Étaules (17)	194 B2
Étaules (21)	135 K4
Étauliers (33)	211 H3
Étaux (74)	191 G3
Étaves-et-Bocquiaux (02)	20 B1
Étavigny (60)	39 F6
Etcharry (64)	283 H3
Etchebar (64)	302 C1
Éteimbes (68)	119 K5
Étel (56)	100 B5
Ételfay (80)	18 D4
Étercy (74)	190 E5
Éternoz (25)	156 C3
Éterpigny (62)	11 G3
Éterpigny (80)	19 G2
Éterville (14)	32 D5
Étevaux (21)	136 D5
Eth (59)	12 E2
Étienville (50)	28 E5
Étigny (89)	112 E1
les Étilleux (28)	84 A5
Étinehem (80)	18 E1
Étiolles (91)	59 F6
Étival (39)	173 J4
Étival-Clairefontaine (88)	95 H3
Étival-lès-le-Mans (72)	106 D3
Étivey (89)	134 B1
Étobon (70)	119 G6
Étoges (51)	61 J3
l'Étoile (39)	173 F1
l'Étoile (80)	9 J6
Étoile-Saint-Cyrice (05)	258 C2
Étoile-sur-Rhône (26)	240 C5
Éton (55)	44 A3
Étormay (21)	135 F2
Étouars (24)	197 J3
Étourvy (10)	114 C3
Étoutteville (76)	15 G4
Étouvans (25)	139 G3
Étouvelles (02)	40 B1
Étouvy (14)	52 E2
Étouy (60)	37 K2
Étrabonne (25)	137 H6
Étrappe (25)	139 F3
l'Étrat (42)	205 G5
Étray (25)	156 E1
Étraye (55)	43 H3
Étréaupont (02)	21 F2
Étrechet (36)	165 K1
Étréchy (18)	149 K2
Étréchy (51)	61 K3
Étréchy (91)	86 D2
Étréham (14)	32 A3
Étreillers (02)	19 J3
Étréjust (80)	17 H2
Étrelles (35)	104 A1
Étrelles-et-la-Montbleuse (70)	137 J3
Étrelles-sur-Aube (10)	89 J1
Étrembières (74)	191 G2
Étrépagny (27)	36 C3
Étrepigney (39)	155 J2
Étrépigny (08)	22 D4
Étrépilly (02)	39 J6
Étrépilly (77)	59 K1
Étrepy (51)	63 H4
Étretat (76)	14 B4
Étreux (02)	12 E6
Étréville (27)	34 D3
Étrez (01)	172 C6
Étriac (16)	196 C5

Étriché (49). 125 H1
Étricourt-Manancourt (80). . . . 11 G6
Étrigny (71). 171 J3
Étrochey (21). 115 F4
Étrœungt (59). 13 G5
Étroussat (03). 185 G2
Étrun (62). 10 E2
Etsaut (64). 303 F3
Ettendorf (67). 69 J6
Etting (57). 68 J3
Étueffont (90). 119 J5
Étupes (25). 139 H2
Éturqueraye (27). 34 E3
Étusson (79). 143 J3
Étuz (70). 137 K4
Etzling (57). 68 C2
Eu (76). 8 C6
Euffigneix (52). 116 A1
Eugénie-les-Bains (40). 265 H5
Euilly-et-Lombut (08). 23 C4
Eulmont (54). 66 B4
Eup (31). 305 J3
Eurre (26). 240 D3
Eurville-Bienville (52). 91 K1
Eus (66). 314 C3
Euvezin (54). 65 H2
Euville (55). 65 F4
Euvy (51). 62 A5
Euzet (30). 255 J6
Évaillé (72). 107 J4
Évans (39). 155 K1
Évaux-et-Ménil (88). 94 C4
Évaux-les-Bains (23). 183 K3
Ève (60). 38 C6
Évecquemont (78). 58 A1
Évenos (83). 300 B3
Évergnicourt (02). 41 F2
Everly (77). 88 D3
Évette-Salbert (90). 119 H6
Éveux (69). 205 J1
Évian-les-Bains (74). 175 G5
Évigny (08). 22 C4
Évillers (25). 156 D3
Évin-Malmaison (62). 11 H1
Évires (74). 191 G4
Évisa (2A). 320 B1
Évosges (01). 189 K5
Évran (22). 50 D6
Évrange (57). 27 G2
Évrecy (14). 32 C6
Èvres (55). 64 A1
Évreux (27). 56 D1
Évricourt (60). 19 G6
Évriguet (56). 77 K6
Évron (53). 81 J6
Évry (89). 88 D5
Évry (91). 59 F6
Évry-Grégy-sur-Yerre (77). . . . 59 H6
Excenevex (74). 174 E5
Excideuil (24). 214 D2
Exermont (08). 42 E3
Exideuil (16). 180 B6
Exincourt (25). 139 H2
Exireuil (79). 161 K5
Exmes (61). 54 E4
Exoudun (79). 162 B6
Expiremont (17). 211 K1
Eybens (38). 224 B3
Eybouleuf (87). 199 H2
Eyburie (19). 199 J6
Eycheil (09). 306 D3
Eydoche (38). 207 F6
Eygalayes (26). 258 C3
Eygalières (13). 276 D4
Eygaliers (26). 257 J4
Eygliers (05). 227 A3
Eygluy-Escoulin (26). 241 F2
Eyguians (05). 258 C2
Eyguières (13). 276 D5
Eygurande (19). 201 G3
Eygurande-et-Gardedeuil (24). . . 212 C5
Eyjeaux (87). 199 G2
Eyliac (24). 214 B4
Eymet (24). 231 G4
Eymeux (26). 223 F5
Eymouthiers (16). 197 H3
Eymoutiers (87). 199 K2
Eyne (66). 313 J5
Eynesse (33). 230 E2
Eyragues (13). 276 B3
Eyrans (33). 211 G3
Eyrein (19). 216 C2
Eyres-Moncube (40). 265 G4
Eyroles (26). 257 J1
Eysines (33). 229 H1
Eysson (25). 138 E6
Eysus (64). 284 A6
Eyvirat (24). 214 A2
Eywiller (67). 67 K2
Eyzahut (26). 240 D5
Eyzerac (24). 214 C1
les Eyzies-de-Tayac-Sireuil (24). . 232 D1
Eyzin-Pinet (38). 206 C5
Ézanville (95). 58 F1
Èze (06). 281 H3
Ézy-sur-Eure (27). 57 F3

Fa (11). 308 E3
Fabas (09). 306 D1
Fabas (31). 287 G4
Fabas (82). 269 F3

Fabras (07). 239 G4
Fabrègues (34). 293 F1
Fabrezan (11). 309 K1
Faches-Thumesnil (59). 6 E4
Fâchin (58). 152 C4
la Fage-Montivernoux (48). . . . 236 E3
la Fage-Saint-Julien (48). 237 F3
le Faget (31). 289 F1
Faget-Abbatial (32). 286 E2
Fagnières (51). 62 D2
Fagnon (08). 22 C4
Fahy-lès-Autrey (70). 136 E3
Failly (57). 45 F5
Faimbe (25). 139 F2
Fain-lès-Montbard (21). 134 E2
Fain-lès-Moutiers (21). 134 C2
Fains (27). 57 F2
Fains-la-Folie (28). 85 H6
Fains-Véel (55). 64 D4
Faissault (08). 22 B5
Fajac-en-Val (11). 309 H1
Fajac-la-Relenque (11). 288 E5
Fajoles (46). 233 H3
la Fajolle (11). 308 C1
Fajolles (82). 268 C2
Falaise (08). 42 B2
Falaise (14). 54 A3
la Falaise (78). 57 K2
Falck (57). 45 K4
Faleyras (33). 230 A3
Falga (31). 289 G2
le Falgoux (15). 217 K4
Falicon (06). 281 G5
Falkwiller (68). 97 A3
Fallencourt (76). 16 E2
Fallerans (25). 156 E1
Falleron (85). 141 G4
Falletans (39). 155 H2
la Faloise (80). 18 B4
Fals (47). 248 C6
Falvy (80). 19 G3
Famars (59). 12 D2
Famechon (62). 10 C4
Famechon (80). 17 J3
Fameck (57). 44 E1
Familly (14). 55 F2
Fampoux (62). 11 F2
Fanjeaux (11). 289 H6
Fanlac (24). 214 E5
le Faou (29). 74 C2
le Faouët (22). 48 D3
le Faouët (56). 75 J6
Faramans (01). 189 F6
Faramans (38). 206 E6
Farbus (62). 11 F2
Farceaux (27). 36 B4
la Fare-en-Champsaur (05). . . 242 E4
la Fare-les-Oliviers (13). 296 A1
Farébersviller (57). 68 B3
Fareins (01). 188 B4
Faremoutiers (77). 60 A4
Farges (01). 190 D2
les Farges (24). 215 F4
Farges-Allichamps (18). 167 F1
Farges-en-Septaine (18). 149 J3
Farges-lès-Chalon (71). 154 A6
Farges-lès-Mâcon (71). 171 K4
Fargues (33). 229 K6
Fargues (40). 265 H4
Fargues (46). 249 H2
Fargues-Saint-Hilaire (33). . . . 229 J2
Fargues-sur-Ourbise (47). . . . 247 G4
Farincourt (52). 117 G6
Farinole (2B). 317 D5
la Farlède (83). 300 D3
Farnay (42). 205 J5
Farschviller (57). 68 C3
Fatines (72). 107 F2
Fatouville-Grestain (27). 34 A2
le Fau (15). 217 J3
Fau-de-Peyre (48). 237 F3
Fauch (81). 271 F3
Faucigny (74). 191 H2
Faucogney-et-la-Mer (70). . . . 118 E4
Faucompierre (88). 95 F6
Faucon (84). 257 H3
Faucon-de-Barcelonnette (04). . 260 D1
Faucon-du-Caire (04). 259 H1
Fauconcourt (88). 94 E3
Faucoucourt (02). 20 B4
Faudoas (82). 268 B3
le Fauga (31). 288 A3
Faugères (34). 291 K1
Fauguernon (14). 34 A5
Fauguerolles (47). 247 H1
Fauillet (47). 247 J1
le Faulq (14). 34 A4
Faulquemont (57). 45 K6
Faulx (54). 66 A4
Faumont (59). 6 E6
Fauquembergues (62). 5 F3
la Faurie (05). 242 B5
Faurilles (24). 231 K4
Fauroux (82). 249 G4
Faussergues (81). 271 H1
la Faute-sur-Mer (85). 159 J6
Fauverney (21). 136 B6
Fauville (27). 56 D1
Fauville-en-Caux (76). 15 F5
Faux (08). 22 B6
Faux (24). 231 K3
Faux-Fresnay (51). 61 K4
Faux-la-Montagne (23). 200 B2
Faux-Mazuras (23). 182 C6

Faux-Vésigneul (51). 62 D4
Faux-Villecerf (10). 89 H4
Favalello (2B). 319 G6
Favars (19). 216 A3
Faveraye-Mâchelles (49). 125 G6
Faverdines (18). 167 G3
Faverelles (45). 132 A2
Faverges (74). 209 F1
Faverges-de-la-Tour (38). 207 H4
Faverney (70). 118 A5
Faverois (90). 139 K2
Faverolles (02). 39 H4
Faverolles (15). 236 E1
Faverolles (28). 57 H5
Faverolles (36). 147 H2
Faverolles (52). 116 B3
Faverolles (61). 53 K5
Faverolles (80). 18 D5
Faverolles-et-Coëmy (51). 40 D4
Faverolles-la-Campagne (27). . . 56 B1
Faverolles-lès-Lucey (21). 115 J3
Faverolles-sur-Cher (41). 128 D5
la Favière (39). 156 C6
Favières (28). 84 D1
Favières (54). 93 J2
Favières (77). 59 J5
Favières (80). 8 E3
Favresse (51). 63 G5
Favreuil (62). 11 F5
Favrieux (78). 57 H2
le Favril (27). 34 C5
le Favril (28). 84 D2
le Favril (59). 13 F5
Fay (61). 55 G6
le Fay (71). 172 E2
Fay (72). 106 C2
Fay (80). 19 F2
Fay-aux-Loges (45). 110 C4
Fay-de-Bretagne (44). 122 E1
Fay-en-Montagne (39). 155 H6
Fay-le-Clos (26). 222 C3
Fay-les-Étangs (60). 37 F4
Fay-lès-Marcilly (10). 89 G3
Fay-lès-Nemours (77). 87 H5
le Fay-Saint-Quentin (60). 37 J2
Fay-sur-Lignon (43). 221 F6
Faycelles (46). 234 B5
la Faye (16). 179 G4
Faye (41). 108 D5
Faye-d'Anjou (49). 125 G5
Faye-la-Vineuse (37). 145 G4
Faye-l'Abbesse (79). 143 K6
Faye-sur-Ardin (79). 161 G5
le Fayel (60). 38 C3
Fayence (83). 280 B5
Fayet (02). 19 K2
Fayet (12). 272 C4
Fayet-le-Château (63). 203 G3
Fayet-Ronaye (63). 203 H6
Fayl-Billot (52). 117 F5
Faymont (70). 139 F1
Faymoreau (85). 161 F3
Fays (52). 91 K2
Fays (88). 95 F5
Fays-la-Chapelle (10). 114 A1
Fayssac (81). 270 C2
Féas (64). 283 K6
Febvin-Palfart (62). 5 H5
Fécamp (76). 14 D3
Féchain (59). 11 J3
Fèche-l'Église (90). 139 J2
Fécocourt (54). 93 K3
Fédry (70). 137 J1
Fegersheim (67). 71 D2
Fégréac (44). 102 C5
Feigères (74). 190 E3
Feigneux (60). 38 E4
Feignies (59). 13 G2
Feillens (01). 171 K6
Feings (41). 128 E4
Feings (61). 83 J1
Feins (35). 79 G1
Feins-en-Gâtinais (45). 111 K6
Feissons-sur-Isère (73). 209 G4
Feissons-sur-Salins (73). 209 H5
le Fel (12). 235 J3
Fel (61). 54 D4
Felce (2B). 319 J5
Feldbach (68). 97 B5
Feldkirch (68). 97 B1
Feliceto (2B). 318 C3
Félines (07). 222 A2
Félines (43). 220 A2
Félines-Minervois (34). 290 D4
Félines-sur-Rimandoule (26). . 240 E5
Félines-Termenès (11). 309 J3
Felleries (59). 13 H4
Fellering (68). 119 J3
Felletin (23). 183 G6
Felluns (66). 309 H5
Felon (90). 119 J5
Felzins (46). 234 E5
Fenain (59). 12 B2
Fénay (21). 136 A6
Fendeille (11). 289 G5
Fénery (79). 161 J2
Fénétrange (57). 67 J2
Feneu (49). 125 G2
Féneyrols (82). 250 D5
Féniers (23). 200 B3
Fenioux (17). 177 J6
Fenioux (79). 161 G3
Fenneviller (54). 95 H1
Fénols (81). 270 D3
le Fenouiller (85). 140 E6
Fenouillet (31). 269 G5

Fenouillet (66). 309 G5
Fenouillet-du-Razès (11). 289 H6
Fépin (08). 24 C3
Fercé (44). 103 J2
Fercé-sur-Sarthe (72). 106 B4
Ferdrupt (88). 119 G3
la Fère (02). 20 A5
Fère-Champenoise (51). 61 K5
Fère-en-Tardenois (02). 40 A5
Fèrebrianges (51). 61 J3
la Férée (08). 21 K3
Férel (56). 121 K2
Ferfay (62). 5 J5
Féricy (77). 87 J3
Férin (59). 11 H2
Fermanville (50). 28 C2
la Fermeté (58). 151 F4
Ferney-Voltaire (01). 191 F1
Fernoël (63). 201 G2
Férolles (45). 110 C5
Férolles-Attilly (77). 59 H5
Féron (59). 13 H5
Ferques (62). 2 C4
Ferrals-les-Corbières (11). . . . 291 F6
Ferrals-les-Montagnes (34). . . 290 E4
Ferran (11). 289 J6
Ferrassières (26). 258 B5
le Ferré (35). 80 A2
Ferrensac (47). 231 K5
Ferrère (65). 305 H3
les Ferres (06). 280 E2
Ferrette (68). 97 C5
Ferreux-Quincey (10). 89 G3
la Ferrière (22). 77 H5
la Ferrière (37). 127 K1
la Ferrière (38). 224 E1
la Ferrière (85). 159 J1
la Ferrière-Airoux (86). 163 F6
la Ferrière-au-Doyen (61). 55 H6
la Ferrière-aux-Étangs (61). . . . 53 H5
la Ferrière-Béchet (61). 82 D1
la Ferrière-Bochard (61). 82 C3
la Ferrière-de-Flée (49). 104 D6
la Ferrière-en-Parthenay (79). . 162 B2
Ferrière-et-Lafolie (52). 92 A3
la Ferrière-Harang (14). 31 K5
Ferrière-la-Grande (59). 13 H3
Ferrière-la-Petite (59). 13 H3
Ferrière-Larçon (37). 146 C4
Ferrière-sur-Beaulieu (37). . . . 146 D2
la Ferrière-sur-Risle (27). 55 K2
Ferrières (17). 177 G1
Ferrières (50). 80 D1
Ferrières (54). 66 B6
Ferrières (60). 18 D6
Ferrières (65). 303 J1
Ferrières (80). 17 K2
Ferrières (81). 271 H6
Ferrières-en-Bray (76). 36 D1
Ferrières-en-Brie (77). 59 H4
Ferrières-en-Gâtinais (45). . . . 111 J2
Ferrières-Haut-Clocher (27). . . 56 B1
Ferrières-la-Verrerie (61). 55 F6
Ferrières-le-Lac (25). 139 J1
Ferrières-les-Bois (25). 137 H6
Ferrières-lès-Ray (70). 137 H2
Ferrières-lès-Scey (70). 117 K6
Ferrières-les-Verreries (34). . . 274 B3
Ferrières-Poussarou (34). 291 G2
Ferrières-Saint-Hilaire (27). . . . 55 H1
Ferrières-Saint-Mary (15). . . . 218 D4
Ferrières-sur-Ariège (09). 307 J3
Ferrières-sur-Sichon (03). . . . 186 B4
Ferrussac (43). 219 H5
Fertans (25). 156 C2
la Ferté (39). 155 J4
la Ferté-Alais (91). 86 E2
la Ferté-Beauharnais (41). . . . 129 K3
la Ferté-Bernard (72). 83 J3
la Ferté-Chevresis (02). 20 C4
la Ferté-Frênel (61). 55 H3
la Ferté-Gaucher (77). 60 D4
la Ferté-Hauterive (03). 168 E6
la Ferté-Imbault (41). 130 A5
la Ferté-Loupière (89). 112 D4
le Ferté-Macé (61). 53 J6
la Ferté-Milon (02). 39 G5
la Ferté-Saint-Aubin (45). 110 A6
la Ferté-Saint-Cyr (41). 129 H1
la Ferté-Saint-Samson (76). . . . 16 D6
la Ferté-sous-Jouarre (77). . . . 60 B2
la Ferté-sur-Chiers (08). 23 J5
la Ferté-Vidame (28). 56 B6
la Ferté-Villeneuil (28). 108 E3
Fertrève (58). 151 F4
Fervaches (50). 31 H5
Fervaques (14). 54 E1
Fescamps (80). 18 E5
Fesches-le-Châtel (25). 139 J2
Fesmy-le-Sart (02). 12 E6
Fesques (76). 16 D3
Fessanvilliers-Mattanvilliers (28). . 56 C5
Fessenheim (68). 96 C3
Fessenheim-le-Bas (67). 70 D2
Fessevillers (25). 139 J1
les Fessey (70). 118 E4
Fessy (74). 174 E6
Festalemps (24). 213 F3
Festes-et-Saint-André (11). . . 308 D5
Festieux (02). 40 C1
Festigny (51). 61 H1
Festigny (89). 133 F2
Festubert (62). 6 B5
le Fête (21). 153 H1
Féternes (74). 175 G5
Fétigny (39). 173 G4

Feucherolles (78). 58 B3
Feuchy (62). 11 F3
Feugarolles (47). 247 G6
Feugères (50). 31 F3
Feuges (10). 90 B3
Feuguerolles (27). 35 H6
Feuguerolles-Bully (14). 32 D5
Feuilla (11). 310 C3
Feuillade (16). 197 H4
la Feuillade (24). 215 H4
la Feuillée (29). 75 F1
Feuillères (80). 19 F1
la Feuillie (50). 30 D2
la Feuillie (76). 36 B1
Feule (25). 139 G4
Feuquières (60). 17 G5
Feuquières-en-Vimeu (80). 8 D3
Feurs (42). 204 E2
Feusines (36). 166 C4
Feux (18). 150 B1
Fèves (57). 44 E4
Féy (57). 44 E6
Fey-en-Haye (54). 65 J2
Feyt (19). 201 H3
Feytiat (87). 199 F1
Feyzin (69). 206 B3
Fiac (81). 270 B5
Ficaja (2B). 319 H4
Ficheux (62). 10 E3
Fichous-Riumayou (64). 284 C2
le Fidelaire (27). 56 A2
le Fied (39). 155 H6
le Fief-Sauvin (49). 124 B6
Fieffes-Montrelet (80). 9 K5
Fiefs (62). 5 H6
Fiennes (62). 2 C4
Fienvillers (80). 9 K5
Fierville-Bray (14). 33 H6
Fierville-les-Mines (50). 28 C4
Fierville-les-Parcs (14). 33 K4
le Fieu (33). 212 C5
Fieulaine (02). 20 B2
Fieux (47). 247 K6
Figanières (83). 279 J6
Figari (2A). 323 G5
Figarol (31). 306 B1
Figeac (46). 234 D5
Fignévelle (88). 117 J2
Fignières (80). 18 D4
Filain (02). 40 A1
Filain (70). 138 B2
Fillé (72). 106 D4
Fillières (54). 26 A4
Fillièvres (62). 9 K2
Fillinges (74). 191 H2
Fillols (66). 314 B4
Filstroff (57). 45 J2
Fiménil (88). 95 F5
Finestret (66). 314 C3
Finhan (82). 268 C2
les Fins (25). 157 H2
Fins (80). 11 H6
Fiquefleur-Equainville (27). 34 K2
Firbeix (24). 198 C4
Firfol (14). 34 A5
Firmi (12). 235 G6
Firminy (42). 221 G1
Fislis (68). 97 C5
Fismes (51). 40 C3
Fitilieu (38). 207 H4
Fitou (11). 310 C4
Fitz-James (60). 38 A2
Fix-Saint-Geneys (43). 219 K4
Fixem (57). 27 H3
Fixin (21). 135 K6
Flacey (21). 136 B4
Flacey (28). 109 F1
Flacey-en-Bresse (71). 172 E3
la Flachère (38). 208 C6
Flachères (38). 207 F5
Flacourt (78). 57 H2
Flacy (89). 89 G5
Flagey (21). 156 C3
Flagey (52). 116 C5
Flagey-Echézeaux (21). 154 B1
Flagey-lès-Auxonne (21). 155 F1
Flagey-Rigney (25). 138 B3
Flagnac (12). 235 F5
Flagy (70). 118 B6
Flagy (71). 171 H4
Flagy (77). 87 K4
Flaignes-Havys (08). 22 A3
Flainval (54). 66 C5
Flamanville (50). 28 A3
Flamanville (76). 15 H5
Flamarens (32). 268 A1
la Flamengrie (02). 13 G6
la Flamengrie (59). 12 E2
Flamets-Frétils (76). 16 E4
Flammerans (21). 136 E6
Flammerécourt (52). 92 A3
Flancourt-Catelon (27). 34 E3
Flangebouche (25). 157 G1
Flassan (84). 257 J5
Flassans-sur-Issole (83). 298 B3
Flassigny (55). 43 J1
Flastroff (57). 45 J2
Flat (63). 203 F4
Flaucourt (80). 19 G2
Flaugeac (24). 231 H3
Flaujac-Gare (46). 234 B4
Flaujac-Poujols (46). 250 A2
Flaujagues (33). 230 D2
Flaumont-Waudrechies (59). . . 13 H4
Flaux (30). 275 J1

Flavacourt (60) 36 E3
Flaviac (07) 240 A3
Flavignac (87) 198 D3
Flavignerot (21) 135 K6
Flavigny (18) 150 A4
Flavigny (51) 62 A2
Flavigny-le-Grand-et-
-Beaurain (02) 20 D2
Flavigny-sur-Moselle (54) 66 A6
Flavigny-sur-Ozerain (21) 135 J5
Flavin (12) 252 B3
Flavy-le-Martel (02) 19 K4
Flavy-le-Meldeux (60) 19 H4
Flaxieu (01) 207 K1
Flaxlanden (68) 97 C3
Flayat (23) 201 G2
Flayosc (83) 279 H6
Fléac (16) 196 D3
Fléac-sur-Seugne (17) 195 H5
la Flèche (72) 106 B6
Fléchin (62) 5 G5
Fléchy (60) 18 A5
Flée (21) 134 D4
Flée (72) 107 G6
Fleigneux (08) 23 F3
Fleisheim (57) 67 K3
le Fleix (24) 231 F2
Fleix (86) 163 K3
Fléré-la-Rivière (36) 146 E3
Flers (61) 53 H4
Flers (62) 10 A2
Flers (80) 11 F6
Flers-en-Escrebieux (59) 11 H1
Flers-sur-Noye (80) 18 A4
Flesquières (59) 11 H5
Flesselles (80) 10 A6
Flétrange (57) 45 J6
Flêtre (59) 6 A2
Fléty (58) 152 B6
Fleurac (16) 196 B2
Fleurac (24) 214 D6
Fleurance (32) 267 J3
Fleurat (23) 182 B2
Fleurbaix (62) 6 B4
Fleuré (61) 54 C5
Fleuré (86) 163 G4
Fleurey (25) 139 H5
Fleurey-lès-Faverney (70) 118 A5
Fleurey-lès-Lavoncourt (70) 117 H6
Fleurey-Saint-Loup (70) 118 C3
Fleurey-sur-Ouche (21) 135 J5
Fleurie (69) 188 B2
Fleuriel (03) 185 G1
Fleurieu-sur-Saône (69) 188 C6
Fleurieux-sur-l'Arbresle (69) 205 J1
Fleurigné (35) 80 B4
Fleurines (60) 38 B4
Fleurville (71) 171 K5
Fleury (02) 39 G4
Fleury (11) 291 K5
Fleury (50) 52 A3
Fleury (57) 45 F6
Fleury (60) 37 F4
Fleury (62) 10 A1
Fleury (80) 17 K4
Fleury-devant-Douaumont (55) 43 J4
Fleury-en-Bière (77) 87 G3
Fleury-la-Forêt (27) 36 C2
Fleury-la-Montagne (71) 187 F2
Fleury-la-Rivière (51) 40 D6
Fleury-la-Vallée (89) 113 F4
Fleury-les-Aubrais (45) 110 A4
Fleury-Mérogis (91) 58 E6
Fleury-sur-Andelle (27) 36 A3
Fleury-sur-Loire (58) 151 F6
Fleury-sur-Orne (14) 32 E5
Fléville (08) 42 D3
Fléville-devant-Nancy (54) 66 A5
Fléville-Lixières (54) 44 B4
Flévy (57) 45 F4
Flexanville (78) 57 J3
Flexbourg (67) 70 C3
Fley (71) 171 H2
Fleys (89) 113 J5
Flez-Cuzy (58) 133 G5
Fligny (08) 21 J2
Flin (54) 95 F1
Flines-lès-Mortagne (59) 7 H5
Flines-lez-Raches (59) 11 J1
Flins-Neuve-Église (78) 57 H3
Flins-sur-Seine (78) 58 A2
Flipou (27) 35 K3
Flirey (54) 65 H3
Flixecourt (80) 9 J6
Flize (08) 22 D4
la Flocellière (85) 142 E5
Flocourt (57) 66 C1
Flocques (76) 8 C6
Flogny-la-Chapelle (89) 113 J3
Floing (08) 23 F4
Floirac (17) 195 F5
Floirac (33) 229 H2
Floirac (46) 233 K1
Florac (48) 254 B3
Florange (57) 44 E3
Florémont (88) 94 B3
Florensac (34) 292 C3
Florent-en-Argonne (51) 42 D5
Florentia (39) 173 F5
Florentin (81) 270 D3
Florentin-la-Capelle (12) 235 K5
Floressas (46) 249 G1
Florimont (90) 139 K2
Florimont-Gaumier (24) 233 F4
Floringhem (62) 5 J6
la Flotte (17) 158 D5

Flottemanville (50) 28 E4
Flottemanville-Hague (50) 28 C2
Floudès (33) 230 C5
Floure (11) 290 C6
Flourens (31) 269 H6
Floursies (59) 13 H4
Floyon (59) 13 G6
Flumet (73) 191 K6
Fluquières (02) 19 J3
Fluy (80) 17 J2
Foameix-Ornel (55) 43 K4
Foce (2A) 322 E3
Focicchia (2B) 319 G6
Foëcy (18) 148 E2
le Fœil (22) 76 E1
Foisches (08) 24 C1
Foissac (12) 234 D6
Foissac (30) 255 K6
Foissiat (01) 172 C5
Foissy (21) 153 H2
Foissy-lès-Vézelay (89) 133 J4
Foissy-sur-Vanne (89) 89 F6
Foix (09) 307 J3
Folcarde (31) 289 F3
Folembray (02) 20 A6
Folgensbourg (68) 97 D5
le Folgoët (29) 46 B4
la Folie (14) 31 J1
Folies (80) 18 E3
Folkling (57) 68 C2
Follainville-Dennemont (78) 57 J1
Folles (87) 181 K3
la Folletière (76) 15 G6
la Folletière-Abenon (14) 55 G2
Folleville (27) 34 C5
Folleville (80) 18 B5
Folligny (50) 51 K1
Folschviller (57) 68 A3
Fomerey (88) 94 C5
Fomperron (79) 162 A4
Fonbeauzard (31) 269 G5
Foncegrive (21) 136 B1
Fonches-Fonchette (80) 19 F3
Foncine-le-Bas (39) 174 A2
Foncine-le-Haut (39) 174 B2
Foncquevillers (62) 10 D4
Fondamente (12) 272 E3
Fondettes (37) 127 H4
Fondremand (70) 137 K3
Fongrave (47) 248 A2
Fongueusemare (76) 14 C4
Fonroque (24) 231 H4
Fons (07) 239 G5
Fons (30) 275 F2
Fons (46) 234 C4
Fons-sur-Lussan (30) 255 K4
Fonsommes (02) 20 B2
Fonsorbes (31) 287 K1
Font-Romeu-Odeillo-Via (66) 313 H6
Fontain (25) 138 A6
Fontaine (10) 91 G5
Fontaine (38) 224 A3
Fontaine (90) 119 J6
Fontaine-au-Bois (59) 12 E4
Fontaine-au-Pire (59) 12 B5
Fontaine-Bellenger (27) 35 K5
Fontaine-Bonneleau (60) 17 K5
Fontaine-Chaalis (60) 38 C5
Fontaine-Chalendray (17) 178 D5
Fontaine-Couverte (53) 104 B3
Fontaine-de-Vaucluse (84) 276 E2
Fontaine-Denis-Nuisy (51) 61 H6
Fontaine-en-Bray (76) 16 C5
Fontaine-en-Dormois (51) 42 B4
Fontaine-Étoupefour (14) 32 D5
Fontaine-Fourches (77) 88 E3
Fontaine-Française (21) 136 D2
Fontaine-Guérin (49) 126 A3
Fontaine-Henry (14) 32 D3
Fontaine-Heudebourg (27) 35 J6
Fontaine-la-Gaillarde (89) 88 E6
Fontaine-la-Guyon (28) 84 E2
Fontaine-la-Louvet (27) 34 B5
Fontaine-la-Mallet (76) 14 B6
Fontaine-la-Rivière (91) 86 C4
Fontaine-la-Soret (27) 34 C5
Fontaine-l'Abbé (27) 34 E6
Fontaine-Lavaganne (60) 17 H6
Fontaine-le-Bourg (76) 16 A6
Fontaine-le-Comte (86) 162 E4
Fontaine-le-Dun (76) 15 H3
Fontaine-le-Pin (14) 53 K2
Fontaine-le-Port (77) 87 J2
Fontaine-le-Puits (73) 209 H5
Fontaine-le-Sec (80) 17 G1
Fontaine-les-Bassets (61) 54 C5
Fontaine-lès-Boulans (62) 5 H5
Fontaine-lès-Cappy (80) 19 F2
Fontaine-lès-Clercs (02) 19 K3
Fontaine-lès-Clerval (25) 138 E3
Fontaine-les-Coteaux (41) 107 K5
Fontaine-lès-Croisilles (62) 11 G3
Fontaine-lès-Dijon (21) 136 A5
Fontaine-lès-Grès (10) 89 K3
Fontaine-lès-Hermans (62) 5 H5
Fontaine-lès-Luxeuil (70) 118 C4
Fontaine-les-Ribouts (28) 56 E6
Fontaine-lès-Vervins (02) 21 F2
Fontaine-l'Étalon (62) 9 J2
Fontaine-Mâcon (10) 89 F3
Fontaine-Milon (49) 125 K3
Fontaine-Notre-Dame (02) 20 B2
Fontaine-Notre-Dame (59) 11 J4
Fontaine-Raoul (41) 108 D3
Fontaine-Saint-Lucien (60) 37 H1
la Fontaine-Saint-Martin (72) 106 C5

Fontaine-Simon (28) 84 C2
Fontaine-sous-Jouy (27) 56 E1
Fontaine-sous-Montdidier (80) 18 D5
Fontaine-sous-Préaux (76) 35 J1
Fontaine-sur-Ay (51) 41 F6
Fontaine-sur-Maye (80) 9 H3
Fontaine-sur-Somme (80) 9 H6
Fontaine-Uterte (02) 20 A1
Fontainebleau (77) 87 H3
Fontainebrux (39) 172 E1
Fontaines (71) 153 K5
Fontaines (85) 160 D5
Fontaines (89) 132 D1
Fontaines-d'Ozillac (17) 211 K1
Fontaines-en-Duesmois (21) 135 F1
Fontaines-en-Sologne (41) 129 G3
Fontaines-les-Sèches (21) 114 D5
Fontaines-Saint-Clair (55) 43 G2
Fontaines-Saint-Martin (69) 206 A1
Fontaines-sur-Marne (52) 92 A1
Fontaines-sur-Saône (69) 206 A1
Fontains (77) 88 A2
Fontan (06) 311 D3
Fontanès (30) 274 E3
Fontanès (34) 274 C4
Fontanès (42) 205 G5
Fontanes (46) 250 A3
Fontanes (48) 238 B3
Fontanès-de-Sault (11) 308 D5
Fontanes-du-Causse (46) 233 K4
Fontanges (15) 217 J5
Fontangy (21) 134 D5
Fontanières (23) 183 K3
Fontanil-Cornillon (38) 223 K2
Fontannes (43) 219 H2
Fontans (48) 237 H3
Fontarèches (30) 256 A5
Fontclaireau (16) 179 G6
Fontcouverte (11) 290 E6
Fontcouverte (17) 195 G2
Fontcouverte-la-Toussuire (73) 225 G2
la Fontelaye (76) 15 J4
Fontenai-les-Louvets (61) 82 C2
Fontenai-sur-Orne (61) 54 B5
Fontenailles (77) 88 A1
Fontenailles (89) 133 F2
Fontenay (27) 36 C5
Fontenay (36) 148 A3
Fontenay (50) 52 C6
Fontenay (71) 170 E4
Fontenay (76) 14 B6
Fontenay (88) 94 E5
Fontenay-aux-Roses (92) 58 E4
Fontenay-de-Bossery (10) 89 F3
Fontenay-en-Parisis (95) 59 F1
Fontenay-le-Comte (85) 160 D4
Fontenay-le-Fleury (78) 58 B4
Fontenay-le-Marmion (14) 32 E6
Fontenay-le-Pesnel (14) 32 C5
Fontenay-le-Vicomte (91) 87 F2
Fontenay-lès-Briis (91) 58 C6
Fontenay-Mauvoisin (78) 57 H2
Fontenay-près-Chablis (89) 113 J4
Fontenay-près-Vézelay (89) 133 H4
Fontenay-Saint-Père (78) 57 J1
Fontenay-sous-Bois (94) 59 F3
Fontenay-sous-Fouronnes (89) 133 G2
Fontenay-sur-Conie (28) 85 H6
Fontenay-sur-Eure (28) 85 F3
Fontenay-sur-Loing (45) 111 J1
Fontenay-sur-Mer (50) 29 F4
Fontenay-sur-Vègre (72) 106 A4
Fontenay-Torcy (60) 17 F4
Fontenay-Trésigny (77) 59 K5
Fontenelle (02) 13 G6
Fontenelle (21) 136 D3
la Fontenelle (35) 51 J5
la Fontenelle (41) 108 C2
Fontenelle (90) 119 J6
Fontenelle-en-Brie (02) 61 F3
Fontenelle-Montby (25) 138 D3
les Fontenelles (25) 139 G6
Fontenermont (14) 52 C3
Fontenet (17) 178 A6
Fontenille (16) 179 G6
Fontenille-Saint-Martin-
-d'Entraigues (79) 178 D3
Fontenilles (31) 287 K1
Fontenois-la-Ville (70) 118 B3
Fontenois-lès-Montbozon (70) 138 C3
Fontenotte (25) 138 C4
Fontenouilles (89) 112 B4
Fontenoy (02) 39 H2
Fontenoy (89) 132 D1
Fontenoy-la-Joûte (54) 95 F2
Fontenoy-le-Château (88) 118 B2
Fontenoy-sur-Moselle (54) 65 J3
Fontenu (39) 173 J2
Fonteny (57) 66 D2
Fonters-du-Razès (11) 289 G5
Fontès (34) 292 B1
Fontet (33) 230 C5
Fontette (10) 115 G1
Fontevraud-l'Abbaye (49) 144 D1
Fontgombault (36) 164 B2
Fontguenand (36) 147 J1
Fontienne (04) 258 C6
Fontiers-Cabardès (11) 290 A4
Fontiès-d'Aude (11) 290 C6
Fontjoncouse (11) 310 A2
Fontoy (57) 27 F4
Fontpédrouse (66) 313 K4
Fontrabiouse (66) 313 J3
Fontrailles (65) 286 A4
Fontvannes (10) 89 J5
Fontvieille (13) 276 A4

Forbach (57) 68 C2
Forcalqueiret (83) 297 K3
Forcalquier (04) 278 B1
la Force (11) 289 J6
la Force (24) 231 G2
Forcé (53) 105 F2
Forcelles-Saint-Gorgon (54) 93 K2
Forcelles-sous-Gugney (54) 93 K3
Forceville (80) 10 C5
Forceville-en-Vimeu (80) 17 G1
Forcey (52) 92 D6
Forciolo (2A) 320 E6
la Forclaz (74) 175 G6
Forest-en-Cambrésis (59) 12 D4
Forest-l'Abbaye (80) 9 G4
la Forest-Landerneau (29) 46 B6
Forest-Montiers (80) 9 F3
Forest-Saint-Julien (05) 243 F4
Forest-sur-Marque (59) 7 F4
Foreste (02) 19 J3
la Forestière (51) 61 G6
la Forêt-de-Tessé (16) 179 F4
la Forêt-du-Parc (27) 56 E3
la Forêt-du-Temple (23) 166 A5
la Forêt-Fouesnant (29) 98 E2
Forêt-la-Folie (27) 36 B4
la Forêt-le-Roi (91) 86 B2
la Forêt-Sainte-Croix (91) 86 D4
la Forêt-sur-Sèvre (79) 143 G6
Forfry (77) 59 K1
la Forge (88) 119 G1
Forges (17) 177 F3
Forgès (19) 216 C4
Forges (49) 144 B1
les Forges (56) 77 G6
Forges (61) 82 D2
les Forges (79) 162 B4
les Forges (88) 94 D5
Forges-la-Forêt (35) 103 K2
Forges-les-Bains (91) 58 C6
Forges-les-Eaux (76) 16 D5
Forges-sur-Meuse (55) 43 G4
Forgues (31) 287 H3
la Forie (63) 204 A4
Forléans (21) 134 C3
Formentin (14) 33 J5
Formerie (60) 17 F5
Formigny (14) 29 K6
Formiguères (66) 313 J3
Fornex (09) 287 K6
Fors (79) 178 A1
Forstfeld (67) 25 D3
Forstheim (67) 69 K5
Fort-du-Plasne (39) 174 A2
Fort-Louis (67) 25 D4
Fort-Mahon-Plage (80) 8 D2
Fort-Mardyck (59) 3 G1
Fort-Moville (27) 34 B3
Fortan (41) 108 A5
Fortel-en-Artois (62) 9 K3
la Forteresse (38) 223 H2
Fortschwihr (68) 96 C3
Fos (31) 305 K4
Fos (34) 292 A1
Fos-sur-Mer (13) 295 H5
le Fossat (09) 288 B6
Fossé (08) 42 E1
Fossé (41) 128 E2
Fosse (66) 309 G5
le Fossé (76) 16 E5
la Fosse-Corduan (10) 89 G3
la Fosse-de-Tigné (49) 143 K1
Fossemagne (24) 214 D4
Fossemanant (80) 17 K3
les Fosses (79) 178 B2
Fosses (95) 38 A6
Fossès-et-Baleyssac (33) 230 D5
Fosseuse (60) 37 H5
Fosseux (62) 10 D3
Fossieux (57) 66 B3
Fossoy (02) 61 F1
Foucarmont (76) 16 E2
Foucart (76) 15 F5
Foucarville (50) 29 G5
Foucaucourt-en-Santerre (80) 19 F2
Foucaucourt-Hors-Nesle (80) 17 F2
Foucaucourt-sur-Thabas (55) 64 A1
Fouchécourt (70) 117 K5
Fouchécourt (88) 117 H2
Foucherans (25) 156 C1
Foucherans (39) 155 G2
Fouchères (10) 90 C6
Fouchères (89) 88 C6
Fouchères-aux-Bois (55) 64 B6
Foucherolles (45) 112 A2
Fouchy (67) 96 B1
Foucrainville (27) 56 E2
Fouday (67) 70 A5
Fouencamps (80) 18 C3
Fouesnant (29) 98 D2
Foufflin-Ricametz (62) 10 C2
Foug (54) 65 G5
Fougaron (31) 306 B2
Fougax-et-Barrineuf (09) 308 B3
Fougeré (49) 125 A1
Fougeré (85) 159 K2
Fougères (35) 80 B3
Fougères-sur-Bièvre (41) 128 E4
les Fougerêts (56) 102 B3
Fougerolles (36) 166 A4
Fougerolles (70) 118 C3
Fougerolles-du-Plessis (53) 80 D2
Fougueyrolles (24) 230 E2
la Fouillade (12) 251 G4

Fouilleuse (60) 38 B2
Fouillouse (05) 242 D6
la Fouillouse (42) 205 F5
le Fouilloux (17) 212 C3
Fouilloy (60) 17 G4
Fouilloy (80) 18 C2
Fouju (77) 87 J1
Foulain (52) 116 B2
Foulangues (60) 37 K4
Foulayronnes (47) 248 B4
Foulbec (27) 34 B2
Foulcrey (57) 67 G5
Fouleix (24) 213 K6
Foulenay (39) 155 G5
Fouligny (57) 45 J5
Foulognes (14) 32 A5
Fouquebrune (16) 196 E5
Fouquenies (60) 37 G1
Fouquereuil (62) 5 K5
Fouquerolles (60) 37 J2
Fouquescourt (80) 19 F3
Fouqueure (16) 179 F6
Fouqueville (27) 35 G4
Fouquières-lès-Béthune (62) 5 K5
Fouquières-lès-Lens (62) 11 G1
Four (38) 206 E4
Fouras (17) 176 E4
Fourbanne (25) 138 C4
Fourcatier-et-
-Maison-Neuve (25) 156 E6
Fourcès (32) 266 E1
Fourchambault (58) 150 D4
Fourches (14) 54 B3
Fourcigny (80) 17 G3
Fourdrain (02) 20 B5
Fourdrinoy (80) 17 J2
Fourg (25) 155 K2
Fourges (27) 36 C6
les Fourgs (25) 157 F5
Fourilles (03) 185 G2
Fourmagnac (46) 234 D4
Fourmetot (27) 34 D2
Fourmies (59) 13 J6
Fournaudin (89) 113 G1
Fourneaux (42) 187 G5
Fourneaux (50) 31 H5
Fourneaux (73) 225 K3
Fourneaux-le-Val (14) 54 A3
Fournels (48) 236 E2
Fournès (30) 275 K2
Fournes-Cabardès (11) 290 B4
Fournes-en-Weppes (59) 6 C5
le Fournet (14) 33 J5
Fournet-Blancheroche (25) 139 H6
Fournets-Luisans (25) 157 G1
Fourneville (14) 33 K3
Fournival (60) 37 K1
Fournols (63) 203 J5
Fouronnes (89) 133 G2
Fourques (30) 275 K5
Fourques (66) 315 F3
Fourques-sur-Garonne (47) 247 G1
Fourqueux (78) 58 B3
Fourquevaux (31) 288 D2
Fours (33) 211 G3
Fours (58) 151 K6
Fours-en-Vexin (27) 36 C5
Fourtou (11) 309 G4
Foussais-Payré (85) 161 F3
Foussemagne (90) 119 K6
le Fousseret (31) 287 H5
Foussignac (16) 196 B2
Fouvent-Saint-Andoche (70) 137 G1
Fouzilhon (34) 292 A2
Foville (57) 66 B2
Fox-Amphoux (83) 278 E6
la Foye-Monjault (79) 177 K2
Fozières (34) 273 G4
Fozzano (2A) 322 E2
Fragnes (71) 154 A6
Frahier-et-Chatebier (70) 119 G6
Fraignot-et-Vesvrotte (21) 135 K1
Fraillicourt (08) 21 J4
Fraimbois (54) 94 E1
Frain (88) 117 J3
Frais (90) 119 J6
Fraisans (39) 155 K1
Fraisnes-en-Saintois (54) 93 K3
Fraisse (24) 231 G1
Fraisse-Cabardès (11) 290 A4
Fraissé-des-Corbières (11) 310 B3
Fraisse-sur-Agout (34) 272 A6
Fraisses (42) 221 F1
Fraissines (81) 271 H2
Fraissinet-de-Fourques (48) 254 B4
Fraissinet-de-Lozère (48) 254 D2
Fraize (88) 95 J5
Fralignes (10) 90 D6
la Framboisière (28) 84 C1
Frambouhans (25) 139 H6
Framecourt (62) 10 A2
Framerville-Rainecourt (80) 18 E2
Framicourt (80) 17 F1
Framont (70) 137 F2
Frampas (52) 91 H2
Francalmont (70) 118 C4
Francaltroff (57) 68 B4
Francarville (31) 288 E1
Francastel (60) 17 K6
Françay (41) 128 C2
Francazal (31) 306 C2
Francescas (47) 247 K6
Francheleins (01) 188 C4
Franchesse (03) 168 B3
Francheval (08) 23 G4

Franchevelle (70) 118 D5
la Francheville (08) 22 D4
Francheville (21) 135 J3
Francheville (27) 56 A4
Francheville (39) 155 G5
Francheville (51) 63 F3
Francheville (54) 65 J4
Francheville (61) 54 B6
Francheville (69) 205 K2
Francières (60) 38 C2
Francières (80) 9 H5
Francillon (36) 147 J4
Francillon-sur-Roubion (26) 240 E5
Francilly-Selency (02) 19 K2
Francin (73) 208 C5
Franclens (74) 190 C4
François (79) 161 J6
Francon (31) 287 G5
Franconville (54) 94 D1
Franconville (95) 58 D2
Francoulès (46) 233 H6
Francourt (70) 137 H1
Francourville (28) 85 H3
Francs (33) 212 D6
Francueil (37) 128 C5
Franey (25) 137 H6
Frangy (74) 190 D4
Frangy-en-Bresse (71) 172 E1
Franken (68) 97 C4
Franleu (80) 8 E5
Franois (25) 137 J6
Franqueville (31) 286 C6
Franqueville (02) 20 E3
Franqueville (27) 34 E5
Franqueville (80) 9 J5
Franqueville-Saint-Pierre (76) 35 J2
Frans (01) 188 C3
Fransart (80) 19 F3
Fransèches (23) 183 F5
Fransu (80) 9 J5
Fransures (80) 18 A4
Franvillers (80) 18 C1
Franxault (21) 154 E3
Frapelle (88) 95 K4
Fraquelfing (57) 67 J3
Fraroz (39) 156 C6
Frasnay-Reugny (58) 151 H4
Frasne (25) 156 D5
Frasne-le-Château (70) 137 J3
Frasne-les-Meulières (39) 155 G1
la Frasnée (39) 173 J3
le Frasnois (39) 173 K2
Frasnoy (59) 12 E3
Frasseto (2A) 320 E5
Frauenberg (57) 68 C2
Frausseilles (81) 270 B1
Fravaux (10) 91 G5
le Fraysse (81) 271 G3
Frayssinet (46) 233 H4
Frayssinet-le-Gélat (46) 232 E5
Frayssinhes (46) 234 C2
Frazé (28) 84 C5
Fréauville (76) 16 C3
Frebécourt (88) 93 F3
Frébuans (39) 173 F2
le Frêche (40) 265 K2
Fréchède (65) 285 K3
Fréchencourt (80) 18 C1
Fréchendets (65) 304 E1
le Fréchet (31) 287 G6
Fréchet-Aure (65) 305 F3
Fréchou (47) 247 J6
Fréchou-Fréchet (65) 285 K4
Frécourt (52) 116 E3
Frédéric-Fontaine (70) 119 F6
la Frédière (17) 177 J6
Frédille (36) 147 H4
Frégimont (47) 247 K3
Frégouville (32) 287 G1
Fréhel (22) 50 A3
Freigné (49) 124 B2
Freissinières (05) 243 J2
la Freissinouse (05) 242 D5
Freistroff (57) 45 H3
Freix-Anglards (15) 217 H6
Fréjairolles (81) 270 E3
Fréjeville (81) 270 E4
Fréjus (83) 299 G2
Fréland (68) 96 A3
Frelinghien (59) 6 B5
Frémainville (95) 58 A1
Frémécourt (95) 37 G6
Fréménil (54) 67 F6
Frémeréville-sous-les-Côtes (55) . . 65 F4
Frémery (57) 66 D2
Frémestroff (57) 68 B4
Frémicourt (62) 11 G5
Fremifontaine (88) 95 F4
Frémontiers (80) 17 J4
Frémonville (54) 67 H6
la Frénaye (76) 14 E6
Frencq (62) 4 B5
Frenelle-la-Grande (88) 93 K3
Frenelle-la-Petite (88) 93 K3
Frênes (61) 53 G4
Freneuse (76) 35 H3
Freneuse (78) 57 H1
Freneuse-sur-Risle (27) 34 D4
Freney (73) 225 K2
le Freney-d'Oisans (38) 224 E5
Fréniches (60) 19 H5
Frénois (21) 135 J3
Frénois (88) 94 A5
Frénouville (14) 33 F5
Frépillon (95) 58 D1
Fresles (76) 16 C4

la Fresnaie-Fayel (61) 54 E4
la Fresnais (35) 51 F4
Fresnay (10) 91 H4
Fresnay-en-Retz (44) 141 F3
Fresnay-le-Comte (28) 85 G5
Fresnay-le-Gilmert (28) 85 F2
Fresnay-le-Long (76) 15 K5
Fresnay-le-Samson (61) 54 D4
Fresnay-l'Évêque (28) 85 K5
Fresnay-sur-Sarthe (72) 82 C5
la Fresnaye-au-Sauvage (61) . . . 54 A5
la Fresnaye-sur-Chédouet (72) . . 82 E3
le Fresne (27) 56 B2
le Fresne (51) 63 F2
le Fresne-Camilly (14) 32 D4
Fresne-Cauverville (27) 34 C5
Fresné-la-Mère (14) 54 B3
Fresne-l'Archevêque (27) 36 A4
Fresne-le-Plan (76) 35 K2
Fresne-Léguillon (60) 37 G4
Fresne-lès-Reims (51) 41 F3
le Fresne-Poret (50) 52 E5
Fresne-Saint-Mamès (70) 137 J2
le Fresne-sur-Loire (44) 124 D4
Fresneaux-Montchevreuil (60) . . . 37 G4
Fresnes (02) 20 A4
Fresnes (21) 134 E2
Fresnes (41) 129 F4
Fresnes (89) 114 A6
Fresnes (94) 58 E5
Fresnes-au-Mont (55) 64 D2
Fresnes-en-Saulnois (57) 66 C3
Fresnes-en-Tardenois (02) 40 A5
Fresnes-en-Woëvre (55) 44 A6
Fresnes-lès-Montauban (62) 11 G2
Fresnes-Mazancourt (80) 19 G2
Fresnes-sur-Apance (52) 117 H3
Fresnes-sur-Escaut (59) 12 D1
Fresnes-sur-Marne (77) 59 J2
Fresnes-Tilloloy (80) 17 F1
Fresneville (80) 17 G2
Fresney (27) 56 E2
Fresney-le-Puceux (14) 32 E6
Fresney-le-Vieux (14) 53 J1
Fresnicourt-le-Dolmen (62) 10 D1
Fresnières (60) 19 F5
Fresnois-la-Montagne (54) 26 C3
Fresnoy (62) 9 J2
Fresnoy-Andainville (80) 17 G2
Fresnoy-au-Val (80) 17 J3
Fresnoy-en-Chaussée (80) 18 D3
Fresnoy-en-Gohelle (62) 11 F2
Fresnoy-en-Thelle (60) 37 J5
Fresnoy-Folny (76) 16 C2
Fresnoy-la-Rivière (60) 38 E4
Fresnoy-le-Château (10) 90 C6
Fresnoy-le-Grand (02) 20 B1
Fresnoy-le-Luat (60) 38 D5
Fresnoy-lès-Roye (80) 19 F4
Frespech (47) 248 D3
Fresquiennes (76) 15 J6
Fressac (30) 274 C1
Fressain (59) 11 J3
Fressancourt (02) 20 B5
Fresse (70) 119 F5
Fresse-sur-Moselle (88) 119 G3
Fresselines (23) 165 J6
Fressenneville (80) 8 D5
Fressies (59) 11 J3
Fressin (62) 4 E6
Fressines (79) 161 J6
le Frestoy-Vaux (60) 18 D6
Fresville (50) 29 F5
Fréterive (73) 208 E4
Fréteval (41) 108 D4
Fréthun (62) 2 C2
Fretigney-et-Velloreille (70) 137 K3
Frétigny (28) 84 B4
Fretin (59) 6 E5
Frétoy (77) 60 C5
Frétoy-le-Château (60) 19 H5
la Frette (38) 207 G6
la Frette (71) 172 B2
la Frette-sur-Seine (95) 58 D2
Frettecuisse (80) 17 G1
Frettemeule (80) 8 E6
Fretterans (71) 154 E4
le Fréty (08) 21 K4
Freulleville (76) 16 B3
Frévent (62) 10 A3
Fréville (76) 15 H6
Fréville (88) 93 H4
Fréville-du-Gâtinais (45) 111 F2
Frévillers (62) 10 C1
Frévin-Capelle (62) 10 D2
Freybouse (57) 68 B4
Freycenet-la-Cuche (43) 238 E1
Freycenet-la-Tour (43) 238 E1
Freychenet (09) 307 K4
Freyming-Merlebach (57) 68 B3
Freyssenet (07) 239 J4
Friaize (28) 84 D3
Friardel (14) 55 G1
Friaucourt (80) 8 D5
Friauville (54) 44 C5
Fribourg (57) 67 G3
Frichemesnil (76) 16 A5
Fricourt (80) 10 E6
Fridefont (15) 236 E1
Friedolsheim (67) 70 C2
Frières-Faillouël (02) 19 K4
Friesen (68) 97 A5
Friesenheim (67) 71 D4
Frignicourt (51) 63 H3
Frise (80) 19 F1

Friville-Escarbotin (80) 8 D5
Frizon (88) 94 C4
Froberville (76) 14 C4
Frocourt (60) 37 H3
Frœningen (68) 97 B3
Frœschwiller (67) 69 K4
Froges (38) 224 C2
Frohen-le-Grand (80) 9 K4
Frohen-le-Petit (80) 9 K4
Frohmuhl (67) 69 F5
Froideconche (70) 118 D4
Froidefontaine (90) 139 J1
Froidestrées (02) 21 F1
Froideterre (70) 118 E5
Froidevaux (25) 139 G5
Froideville (39) 155 G6
Froidfond (85) 141 G4
Froidmont-Cohartille (02) 20 D4
Froidos (55) 43 F6
Froissy (60) 18 A6
Frôlois (21) 135 G3
Frolois (54) 66 A6
Fromelennes (08) 24 D1
Fromelles (59) 6 C4
Fromental (87) 181 J3
Fromentières (51) 61 H1
Fromentières (53) 105 F4
Fromeréville-les-Vallons (55) 43 G5
Fromezey (55) 43 K4
Fromont (77) 87 F5
Fromy (08) 23 J5
Froncles (52) 92 B4
Fronsac (31) 305 J3
Fronsac (33) 230 A1
Frontenac (33) 230 B3
Frontenac (46) 234 C6
Frontenard (71) 154 D4
Frontenas (69) 188 A5
Frontenaud (71) 172 D3
Frontenay (39) 155 H6
Frontenay-Rohan-Rohan (79) 177 K1
Frontenex (73) 209 F3
Frontignan (34) 293 F2
Frontignan-de-Comminges (31) . . 305 J3
Frontignan-Savès (31) 287 G3
Fronton (31) 269 G3
Frontonas (38) 206 E3
Fronville (52) 92 B3
Frossay (44) 122 D3
Frotey-lès-Lure (70) 118 E6
Frotey-lès-Vesoul (70) 138 B1
Frouard (54) 66 A4
Frouville (95) 37 H5
Frouzins (31) 288 A2
Froville (54) 94 C2
Froyelles (80) 9 H3
Frozes (86) 162 D2
Frucourt (80) 9 G6
Frugerès-les-Mines (43) 219 G1
Fruges (62) 5 F5
Frugières-le-Pin (43) 219 J3
Fruncé (28) 84 D3
Fry (76) 16 D6
Fuans (25) 157 G1
Fublaines (77) 60 A2
le Fugeret (04) 260 D6
le Fuilet (49) 124 B5
Fuilla (66) 314 B4
Fuissé (71) 188 B1
Fuligny (10) 91 G4
Fulleren (68) 97 A4
Fultot (76) 15 G3
Fulvy (89) 114 C6
Fumay (08) 24 B3
Fumel (47) 249 F1
Fumichon (14) 34 B6
Furchhausen (67) 70 C1
Furdenheim (67) 70 D3
Furiani (2B) 319 H1
Furmeyer (05) 242 C5
Fussey (21) 154 A2
Fussy (18) 149 G2
Fustérouau (32) 266 C5
Fustignac (31) 287 G4
Futeau (55) 42 E6
Fuveau (13) 296 C2
Fyé (72) 82 D4

G

Gaas (40) 264 B5
Gabarnac (33) 230 A5
Gabarret (40) 266 C1
Gabaston (64) 284 E3
Gabat (64) 283 G3
Gabian (34) 292 A2
Gabillou (24) 214 D3
Gabre (09) 307 G3
Gabriac (12) 252 D1
Gabriac (48) 254 D5
Gabrias (48) 237 H6
Gacé (61) 55 F4
la Gacilly (56) 102 B2
Gâcogne (58) 152 B1
Gadancourt (95) 36 E6
Gadencourt (27) 57 F2
Gaël (35) 78 B4
Gageac-et-Rouillac (24) 231 G3
Gagnac-sur-Cère (46) 234 C1
Gagnac-sur-Garonne (31) 269 G5
Gagnières (30) 255 H3
Gagny (93) 59 G3
Gahard (35) 79 H2

Gailhan (30) 274 D3
Gaillac (81) 270 B3
Gaillac-d'Aveyron (12) 253 F3
Gaillac-Toulza (31) 288 C5
Gaillagos (65) 303 K2
Gaillan-en-Médoc (33) 210 D1
Gaillard (74) 191 F2
Gaillardbois-Cressenville (27) . . . 36 A3
la Gaillarde (76) 15 H2
Gaillefontaine (76) 16 E5
Gaillères (40) 265 J2
Gaillon (27) 36 A5
Gaillon-sur-Montcient (78) 58 A1
Gainneville (76) 14 C6
Gaja-et-Villedieu (11) 308 E1
Gaja-la-Selve (11) 289 G5
Gajac (33) 246 E1
Gajan (09) 306 D2
Gajan (30) 275 F2
Gajoubert (87) 180 D3
Galametz (62) 9 J2
Galan (65) 286 B5
Galapian (47) 247 K3
Galargues (34) 274 D4
Galéria (2B) 318 A5
Galey (09) 306 B3
Galez (65) 286 B6
Galfingue (68) 97 B3
Galgan (12) 251 H1
Galgon (33) 212 A6
Galiax (32) 266 C6
Galié (31) 305 J2
Galinagues (11) 308 D5
Gallardon (28) 85 J2
Gallargues-le-Montueux (30) . . . 274 D5
le Gallet (60) 17 K5
Gallluis (78) 57 K4
Gamaches (80) 8 D6
Gamaches-en-Vexin (27) 36 C4
Gamarde-les-Bains (40) 264 D4
Gamarthe (64) 282 E5
Gambais (78) 57 J4
Gambaiseuil (78) 57 J5
Gambsheim (67) 25 B5
Gan (64) 284 C4
Ganac (09) 307 H3
Ganagobie (04) 259 F6
Gancourt-Saint-Étienne (76) 17 F6
Gandelain (61) 82 B2
Gandelu (02) 39 H6
Gandrange (57) 44 E3
Ganges (34) 274 A2
Gannat (03) 185 G4
Gannay-sur-Loire (03) 169 H1
Gannes (60) 18 C6
Gans (33) 246 D1
Ganties (31) 306 A1
Ganzeville (76) 14 D4
Gap (05) 242 E5
Gapennes (80) 9 H4
Gâprée (61) 55 F6
Garac (31) 268 D5
Garancières (78) 57 J4
Garancières-en-Beauce (28) 86 A3
Garancières-en-Drouais (28) 56 E5
Garanou (09) 307 K5
Garat (16) 197 F4
Garcelles-Secqueville (14) 32 E6
Garches (92) 58 D4
Garchizy (58) 150 D3
Garchy (58) 132 B6
Gardanne (13) 296 D2
la Garde (04) 279 K2
la Garde (38) 224 D4
la Garde (83) 300 D4
la Garde-Adhémar (26) 256 D2
la Garde-Freinet (83) 298 D3
Gardefort (18) 131 K6
Gardegan-et-Tourtirac (33) 230 C1
Gardères (65) 285 F4
Gardes-le-Pontaroux (16) 197 F5
Gardie (11) 309 F1
Gardonne (24) 231 G2
Gardouch (31) 288 E3
Garein (40) 245 J6
Garencières (27) 56 E2
la Garenne-Colombes (92) 58 D3
Garennes-sur-Eure (27) 57 F3
Garentreville (77) 87 G5
Garéoult (83) 297 K3
Garganvillar (82) 268 D2
Gargas (31) 269 H4
Gargas (84) 277 H2
Gargenville (78) 57 K2
Garges-lès-Gonesse (95) 59 F2
Gargilesse-Dampierre (36) 165 H4
Garidech (31) 269 H5
Gariès (82) 268 C4
Garigny (18) 150 B3
Garin (31) 305 K3
Garindein (64) 283 H5
Garlan (29) 47 G4
Garlède-Mondebat (64) 284 D3
Garlin (64) 284 E1
le Garn (30) 256 D2
la Garnache (85) 141 F4
Garnat-sur-Engièvre (03) 169 H3
Garnay (28) 57 F4
Garnerans (01) 188 C3
Garons (30) 275 H4
Garos (64) 284 C1
Garravet (32) 287 G3
Garrebourg (57) 70 A2
Garrevaques (81) 289 H2
Garrey (40) 264 C5
le Garric (81) 270 E1

Garrigues (34) 274 D4
Garrigues (81) 269 K5
Garrigues-Sainte-Eulalie (30) . . . 275 G1
Garris (64) 283 F3
Garrosse (40) 245 F6
Gars (06) 280 C2
Gartempe (23) 182 C3
Gas (28) 85 J1
Gasny (27) 36 C6
Gasques (82) 248 E5
Gassin (83) 299 F4
le Gast (14) 52 C4
Gastes (40) 244 D2
Gastines (53) 104 B3
Gastins (77) 60 A6
Gaubertin (45) 111 F1
la Gaubretière (85) 142 D4
Gauchin-Légal (62) 10 D1
Gauchin-Verloingt (62) 10 A1
Gauchy (02) 19 K3
Gauciel (27) 56 E1
la Gaudaine (28) 84 B5
la Gaude (06) 281 F3
Gaudechart (60) 17 H5
Gaudent (65) 305 H2
Gaudiempré (62) 10 C2
Gaudiès (09) 288 E6
Gaudonville (32) 268 A3
Gaudreville-la-Rivière (27) 56 C2
Gaugeac (24) 232 B4
Gaujac (30) 256 C6
Gaujac (32) 287 F2
Gaujac (47) 230 E6
Gaujacq (40) 264 E5
Gaujan (32) 286 E3
Gault-Perche (41) 108 E1
le Gault-Saint-Denis (28) 85 G5
le Gault-Soigny (51) 61 G4
Gauré (31) 269 J6
Gauriac (33) 211 G5
Gauriaguet (33) 211 K5
Gaussan (32) 286 B5
Gausson (22) 77 G3
Gauville (61) 55 H4
Gauville (80) 17 G3
Gauville-la-Campagne (27) 56 C1
Gavarnie (65) 304 B5
Gavarret-sur-Aulouste (32) 267 J4
Gavaudun (47) 232 C6
Gavignano (2B) 319 G4
Gavisse (57) 27 H3
Gavray (50) 30 E6
le Gâvre (44) 103 F6
Gavrelle (62) 11 F2
Gâvres (56) 99 K5
Gavrus (14) 32 C5
Gayan (65) 285 H4
Gaye (51) 61 J5
Gayon (64) 285 F2
Gazaupouy (32) 267 G1
Gazave (65) 305 G2
Gazax-et-Baccarisse (32) 266 D6
Gazeran (78) 57 J6
Gazost (65) 304 D2
Geaune (40) 265 H5
Geay (17) 177 H6
Geay (79) 144 A5
Gèdre (65) 304 B5
Gée (49) 125 K3
Gée-Rivière (32) 266 A4
Geffosses (50) 30 D3
Géfosse-Fontenay (14) 29 H3
Gehée (36) 147 H3
Geishouse (68) 119 K3
Geispitzen (68) 97 B3
Geispolsheim (67) 70 E4
Geiswasser (68) 96 E5
Geiswiller (67) 69 H6
Gélacourt (54) 95 F1
Gélannes (10) 89 G2
Gélaucourt (54) 93 J2
Gellainville (28) 85 G3
Gellenoncourt (54) 66 C5
Gelles (63) 202 A2
Gellin (25) 156 E6
Gelos (64) 284 C4
Geloux (40) 265 F1
Gelucourt (57) 67 F4
Gelvécourt-et-Adompt (88) 94 A5
Gémages (61) 83 J5
Gemaingoutte (88) 95 K4
Gembrie (65) 305 H2
Gemeaux (21) 136 B3
Gémenos (13) 297 F4
Gémigny (45) 109 J3
Gémil (31) 269 J5
Gemmelaincourt (88) 93 J4
Gémonval (25) 139 F2
Gémonville (54) 93 H3
Gémozac (17) 195 F4
Genac (16) 196 C1
Genainville (95) 36 D6
Génas (69) 206 C2
Génat (09) 307 H5
Genay (21) 134 D3
Genay (69) 188 C6
Gençay (86) 163 F6
Gendreville (88) 93 G5
Gendrey (39) 137 G6
Gené (49) 124 E1

Génébrières (82). 269 H1
Genech (59). 7 F5
Genelard (71). 170 D3
Générac (30). 275 G4
Générac (33). 211 H3
Générargues (30). 255 F6
Générest (65). 305 H2
Generville (11). 289 G5
Geneslay (61). 81 H2
le Genest-Saint-Isle (53). 104 D1
Genestelle (07). 239 H4
Geneston (44). 141 J2
la Genête (71). 172 B3
la Génétouze (17). 212 C3
la Génétouze (85). 159 H1
Genêts (50). 51 J3
les Genettes (61). 55 H6
Geneuille (25). 137 K5
la Genevraie (61). 55 F5
la Genevraye (77). 87 J4
Genevreuille (70). 118 D6
Genevrey (70). 118 C5
Genevrières (52). 117 F6
la Genevroye (52). 92 A5
Geney (25). 139 F2
la Geneytouse (87). 199 H2
Génicourt (95). 37 G6
Génicourt-sur-Meuse (55). 43 J6
Genilac (42). 205 J5
Génissac (33). 230 A2
Génissieux (26). 222 E4
Genlis (21). 136 C6
Gennes (25). 138 B6
Gennes (49). 125 K5
Gennes-Ivergny (62). 9 J3
Gennes-sur-Glaize (53). 105 G4
Gennes-sur-Seiche (35). 104 B2
Genneteil (49). 126 C2
Gennetines (03). 169 F3
Genneton (79). 143 K3
Genneville (14). 34 A2
Gennevilliers (92). 58 E2
Genod (39). 173 G6
Génolhac (30). 255 G6
Génos (31). 305 J2
Génos (65). 305 F5
Genouillac (16). 197 J1
Genouillac (23). 166 B6
Genouillé (17). 177 H4
Genouillé (86). 179 J3
Genouilleux (01). 188 C3
Genouilly (18). 148 B1
Genouilly (71). 171 G2
Gensac (33). 230 A2
Gensac (65). 285 H2
Gensac (82). 268 B2
Gensac-de-Boulogne (31). . . . 286 C5
Gensac-la-Pallue (16). 196 A3
Gensac-sur-Garonne (31). . . . 287 J5
Genté (16). 195 K3
Gentelles (80). 18 C2
Gentilly (94). 58 E4
Gentioux-Pigerolles (23). 200 C2
Genvry (60). 19 H5
Georfans (70). 138 E2
Géovreisset (01). 190 A1
Géovreissiat (01). 189 K2
Ger (50). 53 F5
Ger (64). 285 G5
Ger (65). 304 B1
Geraise (39). 156 B4
Gérardmer (88). 119 H4
Géraudot (10). 90 D4
Gerbaix (73). 207 K3
Gerbamont (88). 119 G6
Gerbécourt (57). 66 D3
Gerbécourt-et-Haplemont (54). . . 94 A2
Gerbépal (88). 95 H5
Gerberoy (60). 17 G6
Gerbéviller (54). 94 D1
Gercourt-et-Drillancourt (55). . . . 43 G3
Gercy (02). 21 F3
Gerde (65). 304 D1
Gerderest (65). 285 F3
Gère-Bélesten (64). 303 H2
Gergny (02). 21 F1
Gergueil (21). 135 J6
Gergy (71). 154 B5
Gerland (21). 154 C2
Germ (65). 305 F5
Germagnat (01). 173 F6
Germagny (71). 171 G2
Germaine (02). 19 J3
Germaine (51). 41 H6
Germaines (52). 116 A5
Germainville (28). 57 G5
Germainvilliers (52). 117 F1
Germay (52). 92 D3
Germéfontaine (25). 138 C6
Germenay (58). 133 G6
Germignac (17). 195 K4
Germigney (39). 155 J3
Germigney (70). 137 F3
Germignonville (28). 85 J6
Germigny (51). 40 D4
Germigny (89). 113 J3
Germigny-des-Prés (45). 110 D5
Germigny-l'Évêque (77). 60 C1
Germigny-l'Exempt (18). 150 B5
Germigny-sous-Coulombs (77). . . 60 C1
Germigny-sur-Loire (58). 150 D4
Germinon (51). 62 B3
Germiny (54). 93 J1
Germisay (52). 92 D3

Germolles-sur-Grosne (71). . . . 188 A1
Germond-Rouvre (79). 161 H4
Germondans (25). 138 B4
Germont (08). 42 D2
Germonville (54). 94 B3
Germs-sur-l'Oussouet (65). . . . 304 C1
Gernelle (08). 22 E3
Gernicourt (02). 40 D2
Géronce (64). 283 K5
Gerponville (76). 14 E3
Gerrots (14). 33 H5
Gerstheim (67). 71 D3
Gertwiller (67). 70 C5
Geruge (39). 173 F2
Gervans (26). 222 B4
Gerville (76). 14 C4
Géry (55). 64 C3
Gerzat (63). 202 D1
Gesnes (53). 81 G6
Gesnes-en-Argonne (55). 42 E3
Gesnes-le-Gandelin (72). 82 C4
Gespunsart (08). 22 E2
Gestas (64). 283 H3
Gesté (49). 142 C1
Gestel (56). 99 K4
Gestiès (09). 307 H5
Gesvres (53). 82 B3
Gesvres-le-Chapitre (77). 59 K1
Gétigné (44). 142 B2
les Gets (74). 192 A2
Geu (65). 304 C1
Geudertheim (67). 25 A5
Géus-d'Arzacq (64). 284 B2
Geüs-d'Oloron (64). 283 K4
Gévezé (35). 79 F3
Gevigney-et-Mercey (70). 117 J5
Geville (55). 65 F4
Gevingey (39). 173 F2
Gevresin (25). 156 C3
Gevrey-Chambertin (21). 135 K6
Gevrolles (21). 115 H3
Gevry (39). 155 G3
Gex (01). 174 B6
Geyssans (26). 222 E4
Gez (65). 304 A2
Gez-ez-Angles (65). 304 C1
Gézaincourt (80). 10 A4
Gézier-et-Fontenelay (70). 137 J4
Gézoncourt (54). 65 J3
Ghisonaccia (2B). 321 J3
Ghisoni (2B). 321 G2
Ghissignies (59). 12 E3
Ghyvelde (59). 3 J1
Giat (63). 201 H2
Gibeaumeix (54). 65 G6
Gibel (31). 288 E4
Gibercourt (02). 19 K4
Giberville (14). 33 F5
Gibles (71). 170 E6
Gibourne (17). 178 B5
Gibret (40). 264 D5
le Gicq (17). 178 C5
Gidy (45). 109 K3
Giel-Courteilles (61). 54 A4
Gien (45). 131 H1
Gien-sur-Cure (58). 152 D2
Gières (38). 224 B3
la Giettaz (73). 191 J6
Giéville (50). 31 J4
Gièvres (41). 129 H6
Giey-sur-Aujon (52). 116 A3
Giez (74). 208 E1
Gif-sur-Yvette (91). 58 C5
Giffaumont-Champaubert (51). . . 91 H1
Gigean (34). 293 F2
Gignac (34). 273 J6
Gignac (46). 215 H6
Gignac (84). 277 J2
Gignac-la-Nerthe (13). 296 B3
Gignat (63). 202 E6
Gignéville (88). 117 J1
Gigney (88). 94 C5
Gigny (39). 173 F4
Gigny (89). 114 D5
Gigny-Bussy (51). 63 F6
Gigny-sur-Saône (71). 172 A2
Gigondas (84). 257 G5
Gigors (04). 259 H1
Gigors-et-Lozeron (26). 240 E2
Gigouzac (46). 233 H5
Gijounet (81). 271 J5
Gildwiller (68). 97 A3
Gilette (06). 281 F2
Gilhac-et-Bruzac (07). 240 A2
Gilhoc-sur-Ormèze (07). 222 A6
Gillancourt (52). 91 K6
Gillaumé (52). 92 C2
Gilles (28). 57 G3
Gilley (25). 157 G2
Gilley (52). 117 G6
Gillois (39). 174 A1
Gillonnay (38). 207 F6
Gilly-lès-Cîteaux (21). 154 B1
Gilly-sur-Isère (73). 209 F3
Gilly-sur-Loire (71). 169 J4
Gilocourt (60). 38 E4
Gimat (82). 268 B3
Gimbrède (32). 267 K1
Gimeaux (63). 185 F5
Gimécourt (55). 64 C3
Gimel-les-Cascades (19). 216 B2
Gimeux (16). 195 J3
la Gimond (42). 205 J6
Gimont (32). 268 B6
Gimouille (58). 150 D4
Ginai (61). 54 E5

Ginals (82). 250 E5
Ginasservis (83). 278 C5
Ginchy (80). 11 F6
Gincla (11). 309 F5
Gincrey (55). 43 K4
Gindou (46). 233 G5
Ginestas (11). 291 G5
Ginestet (24). 231 H1
Gingsheim (67). 70 D1
Ginoles (11). 308 E4
Ginouillac (46). 233 J4
Gintrac (46). 234 A2
Giocatojo (2B). 319 H4
Giou-de-Mamou (15). 235 J1
Gioux (23). 200 D3
Gipcy (03). 168 B4
Girac (46). 234 B1
Girancourt (88). 94 C6
Giraumont (54). 44 C4
Giraumont (60). 38 D1
Girauvoisin (55). 65 F3
Gircourt-lès-Viéville (88). 94 B3
Girecourt-sur-Durbion (88). 94 E4
Girefontaine (70). 118 B3
Giremoutiers (77). 60 B4
Girgols (15). 217 H5
Giriviller (54). 94 D2
Girmont (88). 94 D4
Girmont-Val-d'Ajol (88). 118 E2
Girolles (45). 111 H2
Girolles (89). 133 J3
Giromagny (90). 119 H5
Giron (01). 190 B1
Gironcourt-sur-Vraine (88). 93 J4
Gironde-sur-Dropt (33). 230 C5
Girondelle (08). 22 A2
Gironville (77). 87 G6
Gironville-sur-Essonne (91). . . . 86 E4
le Girouard (85). 159 G3
Giroussens (81). 270 A4
Giroux (36). 148 C3
Giry (58). 151 F1
Gisay-la-Coudre (27). 55 J2
Giscaro (32). 268 B6
Giscos (33). 246 D3
Gisors (27). 36 E4
Gissac (12). 272 C3
Gissey-le-Vieil (21). 135 F5
Gissey-sous-Flavigny (21). . . . 135 G3
Gissey-sur-Ouche (21). 135 H6
Gisy-les-Nobles (89). 88 D5
Giuncaggio (2B). 321 H1
Giuncheto (2A). 322 E3
Givardon (18). 150 A6
Givarlais (03). 167 H5
Givenchy-en-Gohelle (62). 10 E1
Givenchy-le-Noble (62). 10 C2
Givenchy-lès-la-Bassée (62). . . . 6 B5
Giverny (27). 36 B6
Giverville (27). 34 D5
Givet (08). 24 C1
Givonne (08). 23 F4
Givors (69). 206 A4
Givraines (45). 110 E1
Givrand (85). 158 D1
Givrauval (55). 64 C5
le Givre (85). 159 J4
Givrezac (17). 195 G4
Givron (08). 21 K5
Givry (08). 41 K1
Givry (71). 153 K6
Givry (89). 133 J3
Givry-en-Argonne (51). 63 J2
Givry-lès-Loisy (51). 61 K3
Givrycourt (57). 68 C5
Gizaucourt (51). 42 C6
Gizay (86). 163 F5
Gizeux (37). 126 D4
Gizia (39). 172 E3
Gizy (02). 20 E5
la Glacerie (50). 28 D3
Glageon (59). 13 J4
Glaignes (60). 38 E4
Glaine-Montaigut (63). 203 G2
Glaire (08). 23 F4
le Glaizil (05). 242 D3
Glamondans (25). 138 C5
Gland (02). 60 E1
Gland (89). 114 C5
Glandage (26). 241 K4
Glandon (87). 198 E6
Glanes (46). 234 C1
Glanges (87). 199 G3
Glannes (51). 63 F5
Glanon (21). 154 D3
Glanville (14). 33 J3
Glatens (82). 268 B3
Glatigny (50). 30 C1
Glatigny (57). 45 G5
Glatigny (60). 37 F1
Glay (25). 139 J3
Gleizé (69). 188 B5
Glénac (56). 102 B3
Glénat (15). 235 F1
Glénay (79). 144 B5
Glennes (02). 40 C3
Glénouze (86). 144 D4
Glère (25). 139 K4
Glicourt (76). 16 B1
Glisolles (27). 56 C2
Glisy (80). 18 B2
Glomel (22). 76 A3
Glonville (54). 95 F1
Glorianes (66). 314 D3

Glos (14). 34 A6
Glos-la-Ferrière (61). 55 J3
Glos-sur-Risle (27). 34 E4
Gluiras (07). 239 J2
Glun (07). 222 B5
Glux-en-Glenne (58). 152 C4
Goas (82). 268 C4
la Godefroy (50). 52 A5
Godenvillers (60). 18 D6
Goderville (76). 14 D5
Godewaersvelde (59). 6 A2
Godisson (61). 54 E5
la Godivelle (63). 218 C1
Godoncourt (88). 117 J2
Gœrlingen (67). 67 J3
Gœrsdorf (67). 25 A2
Goès (64). 284 A5
Gœulzin (59). 11 H2
Gogney (54). 67 G5
Gognies-Chaussée (59). 13 G2
la Gohannière (50). 52 A5
Gohory (28). 84 D6
Goin (57). 66 A1
Goincourt (60). 37 G2
Golancourt (60). 19 H4
Golbey (88). 94 D5
Goldbach-Altenbach (68). 119 K3
Golfech (82). 248 D5
Golinhac (12). 235 J5
Golleville (50). 28 D5
Gombergean (41). 128 C1
Gomelange (57). 45 H3
Gomené (22). 77 J4
Gomer (64). 284 E5
Gometz-la-Ville (91). 58 C6
Gometz-le-Châtel (91). 58 C6
Gomiécourt (62). 11 F4
Gommecourt (62). 10 D4
Gommecourt (78). 36 C6
Gommegnies (59). 12 E3
Gommenec'h (22). 48 D4
Gommersdorf (68). 97 A4
Gommerville (28). 86 A4
Gommerville (76). 14 D6
Gomméville (21). 115 F3
Gomont (08). 41 G1
Goncelin (38). 224 D1
Goncourt (52). 93 F5
Gond-Pontouvre (16). 196 B3
Gondecourt (59). 6 D5
Gondenans-les-Moulins (25). . . 138 D3
Gondenans-Montby (25). 138 E3
Gondeville (16). 196 B3
Gondrecourt-Aix (54). 44 B4
Gondrecourt-le-Château (55). . . 92 E1
Gondreville (45). 111 H2
Gondreville (54). 65 J5
Gondreville (60). 39 F5
Gondrexange (57). 67 H4
Gondrexon (54). 67 G5
Gondrin (32). 266 E3
les Gonds (17). 195 G2
Gonesse (95). 59 F2
Gonez (65). 285 J5
Gonfaron (83). 298 C3
Gonfreville (50). 30 C2
Gonfreville-Caillot (76). 14 D5
Gonfreville-l'Orcher (76). 33 K1
la Gonfrière (61). 55 G4
Gonnehem (62). 5 K5
Gonnelieu (59). 11 J5
Gonnetot (76). 15 H3
Gonneville (50). 28 E2
Gonneville-en-Auge (14). 33 F4
Gonneville-la-Mallet (76). 14 B5
Gonneville-sur-Honfleur (14). . . 33 K2
Gonneville-sur-Mer (14). 33 H3
Gonneville-sur-Scie (76). 15 K3
Gonsans (25). 138 C6
Gontaud-de-Nogaret (47). 247 J1
la Gonterie-Boulouneix (24). . . 213 K1
Gonzeville (76). 15 H3
Goos (40). 264 C4
Gorbio (06). 281 J2
Gorcy (54). 26 C2
Gordes (84). 277 F2
Gorenflos (80). 9 J5
Gorges (44). 142 A2
Gorges (50). 30 C1
Gorges (80). 9 K5
la Gorgue (59). 6 A4
Gorhey (88). 94 C5
Gornac (33). 230 B4
Gorniès (34). 273 K3
Gorre (87). 198 C2
Gorrevod (01). 172 A5
Gorron (53). 80 E3
Gorses (46). 234 D3
Gorze (57). 44 D6
Gosnay (62). 5 K6
Gosné (35). 79 J2
Gosselming (57). 67 J3
Gotein-Libarrenx (64). 283 H5
Gottenhouse (67). 70 D1
Gottesheim (67). 70 C1
Gouaix (77). 88 D2
Goualade (33). 246 D4
Gouarec (22). 76 C3
Gouaux (65). 305 F5
Gouaux-de-Larboust (31). 305 G5
Gouaux-de-Luchon (31). 305 H4
Gouberville (50). 29 F2
Gouchaupre (76). 16 B1
Goudargues (30). 256 A4
Goudelancourt-lès-Berrieux (02). . . 40 D1

Goudelancourt-
    lès-Pierrepont (02). 21 F5
Goudelin (22). 48 E5
Goudet (43). 238 C1
Goudex (31). 287 G3
Goudon (65). 285 K5
Goudourville (82). 248 E5
Gouesnach (29). 98 C2
la Gouesnière (35). 50 E4
Gouesnou (29). 46 A5
Gouex (86). 163 J6
Gouézec (29). 74 E4
Gougenheim (67). 70 D2
Gouhelans (25). 138 D3
Gouhenans (70). 138 E1
Gouillons (28). 85 K4
Gouise (03). 169 F5
Goujounac (46). 233 F5
la Goulafrière (27). 55 G2
Goulet (61). 54 B5
Goulien (29). 73 C3
Goulier (09). 307 H5
Goulles (19). 216 E5
les Goulles (21). 115 J4
Gouloux (58). 134 B6
Goult (84). 277 F3
Goulven (29). 46 C3
Goumois (25). 139 J5
Goupillières (14). 53 J1
Goupillières (27). 34 E6
Goupillières (76). 15 J6
Goupillières (78). 57 J3
Gouraincourt (55). 44 A3
le Gouray (22). 77 J3
Gourbera (40). 264 B3
Gourbesville (50). 28 E5
Gourbit (09). 307 H4
Gourchelles (60). 17 G4
Gourdan-Polignan (31). 305 H1
Gourdièges (15). 236 C1
Gourdon (06). 280 D4
Gourdon (07). 239 H3
Gourdon (46). 233 G3
Gourdon (71). 171 F2
Gourdon-Murat (19). 200 B3
Gourfaleur (50). 31 H4
Gourgançon (51). 62 A5
Gourgé (79). 162 A1
Gourgeon (70). 117 H6
Gourgue (65). 285 K6
Gourhel (56). 101 K2
Gourin (56). 75 H4
Gourlizon (29). 74 B5
Gournay (36). 165 J3
Gournay-en-Bray (76). 36 D1
Gournay-le-Guérin (27). 55 K5
Gournay-Loizé (79). 178 B3
Gournay-sur-Aronde (60). 38 C1
Gournay-sur-Marne (93). 59 G3
les Gours (16). 178 E5
Gours (33). 212 D6
Gourvieille (11). 289 F4
Gourville (16). 196 C1
Gourvillette (17). 178 C6
Goussaincourt (55). 93 G2
Goussainville (28). 57 H4
Goussainville (95). 59 F1
Goussancourt (02). 40 B5
Gousse (40). 264 C4
Goussonville (78). 57 J3
Goustranville (14). 33 G4
Gout-Rossignol (24). 197 G6
la Goutelle (63). 202 A1
Goutevernisse (31). 287 J5
Goutrens (12). 251 K1
Gouts (40). 264 D3
Gouttières (27). 55 K1
Gouttières (63). 184 C4
Goutz (32). 267 K4
Gouvernes (77). 59 H3
Gouves (62). 10 D2
Gouvets (50). 52 C2
Gouvieux (60). 38 A5
Gouville (27). 56 B3
Gouville-sur-Mer (50). 30 C3
Gouvix (14). 53 K1
Goux (32). 266 B6
Goux-lès-Dambelin (25). 139 G4
Goux-les-Usiers (25). 156 E3
Goux-sous-Landet (25). 156 B2
Gouy (02). 12 A6
Gouy (76). 35 J3
Gouy-en-Artois (62). 10 D3
Gouy-en-Ternois (62). 10 B2
Gouy-les-Groseillers (60). 18 A4
Gouy-Saint-André (62). 9 G2
Gouy-Servins (62). 10 D1
Gouy-sous-Bellonne (62). 11 H2
Gouzangrez (95). 37 G6
Gouzeaucourt (59). 11 J5
Gouzens (31). 287 J6
Gouzon (23). 183 G2
Goven (35). 78 E5
Goviller (54). 93 J1
Goxwiller (67). 70 D5
Goyencourt (80). 19 F4
Goyrans (31). 288 B2
Grabels (34). 274 A6
Graçay (18). 148 B2
Grâce-Uzel (22). 77 H3
Grâces (22). 48 C5
Gradignan (33). 229 G3
Graffigny-Chemin (52). 93 F4
Gragnague (31). 269 G6
Graignes (50). 31 G2
Grailhen (65). 305 F4

Graimbouville (76) . . . . 14　C6
Graincourt-lès-Havrincourt (62) . . . 11　H4
Grainville (27) . . . . 36　A3
Grainville-la-Teinturière (76) . . . . . 15　F4
Grainville-Langannerie (14) . . . . . . 54　A1
Grainville-sur-Odon (14) . . . . 32　C5
Grainville-sur-Ry (76) . . . . 35　K1
Grainville-Ymauville (76) . . . . 14　D5
le Grais (61) . . . . 53　K6
Graissac (12) . . . . 236　B3
Graissessac (34) . . . . 272　D5
Graix (42) . . . . 221　J1
Gramat (46) . . . . 234　A3
Gramazie (11) . . . . 308　D1
Grambois (84) . . . . 277　K4
Grammond (42) . . . . 205　G4
Grammont (70) . . . . 138　E2
Gramond (12) . . . . 251　K4
Gramont (82) . . . . 267　K2
Granace (2A) . . . . 322　E3
Grancey-le-
　-Château-Neuvelle (21) . . . . . . 136　A1
Grancey-sur-Ource (21) . . . . 115　F2
Grand (88) . . . . 92　E3
le Grand-Abergement (01) . . . . . 190　B4
Grand-Auverné (44) . . . . 103　K5
le Grand-Bornand (74) . . . . 191　J5
le Grand-Bourg (23) . . . . 182　B3
Grand-Brassac (24) . . . . 213　H2
Grand-Camp (27) . . . . 55　H1
Grand-Camp (76) . . . . 15　F6
le Grand-Celland (50) . . . . 52　B5
Grand-Champ (56) . . . . 100　E4
Grand-Charmont (25) . . . . 139　H2
la Grand-Combe (30) . . . . 255　G4
Grand-Corent (01) . . . . 189　J2
Grand-Couronne (76) . . . . 35　H3
la Grand-Croix (42) . . . . 205　J5
Grand-Failly (54) . . . . 43　J2
Grand-Fayt (59) . . . . 13　F5
Grand-Fort-Philippe (59) . . . . 3　F2
Grand-Fougeray (35) . . . . 103　F3
Grand-Laviers (80) . . . . 9　F5
le Grand-Lemps (38) . . . . 207　G6
le Grand-Lucé (72) . . . . 107　G4
le Grand-Madieu (16) . . . . 179　K5
le Grand-Pressigny (37) . . . . 146　B5
le Grand-Quevilly (76) . . . . 35　H2
Grand-Rozoy (02) . . . . 39　K4
Grand-Rullecourt (62) . . . . 10　C3
le Grand-Serre (26) . . . . 222　E2
Grand-Vabre (12) . . . . 235　G5
Grand-Verly (02) . . . . 20　C1
le Grand-Village-Plage (17) . . . . . 176　C6
Grandcamp-Maisy (14) . . . . 29　H5
Grandchain (27) . . . . 55　J1
Grandchamp (08) . . . . 22　A5
Grandchamp (52) . . . . 116　E6
Grandchamp (72) . . . . 82　E4
Grandchamp (78) . . . . 57　H5
Grandchamp (89) . . . . 112　C5
Grandchamp-le-Château (14) . . . . 33　J6
Grandchamps-
　-des-Fontaines (44) . . . . 123　G2
Grand'Combe-Châteleu (25) . . . . 157　H2
Grand'Combe-des-Bois (25) . . . . 157　K1
Grandcourt (76) . . . . 16　D2
Grandcourt (80) . . . . 10　E5
la Grande-Fosse (88) . . . . 95　K3
la Grande-Motte (34) . . . . 293　J1
Grande-Paroisse (77) . . . . 87　K4
la Grande-Résie (70) . . . . 137　F5
Grande-Rivière (39) . . . . 173　K3
Grande-Synthe (59) . . . . 3　G2
la Grande-Verrière (71) . . . . 152　D4
Grandecourt (70) . . . . 137　J1
les Grandes-Armoises (08) . . . . . 22　E6
les Grandes-Chapelles (10) . . . . . 90　A2
les Grandes-Loges (51) . . . . 41　H6
les Grandes-Ventes (76) . . . . 16　B3
Grandeyrolles (63) . . . . 202　D4
Grandfontaine (25) . . . . 137　J6
Grandfontaine (67) . . . . 95　K1
Grandfontaine-sur-Creuse (25) . . . 138　E6
Grandfresnoy (60) . . . . 38　C3
Grandham (08) . . . . 42　C3
Grandjean (17) . . . . 177　J6
Grand'Landes (85) . . . . 141　H5
Grandlup-et-Fay (02) . . . . 20　E5
Grandpré (08) . . . . 42　D3
Grandpuits-Bailly-Carrois (77) . . . . 88　A1
Grandrieu (48) . . . . 237　K3
Grandrieux (02) . . . . 21　J4
Grandrif (63) . . . . 204　A5
Grandris (69) . . . . 187　J4
Grandrû (60) . . . . 19　J5
Grandrupt (88) . . . . 95　J3
Grandrupt-de-Bains (88) . . . . . . 118　B1
les Grands-Chézeaux (87) . . . . . 165　F6
Grandsaigne (19) . . . . 200　B6
Grandval (63) . . . . 203　J4
Grandvals (48) . . . . 236　D3
Grandvaux (71) . . . . 170　D4
Grandvelle-et-le-Perrenot (70) . . . 137　K2
Grandvillars (90) . . . . 139　J2
la Grandville (08) . . . . 22　D3
Grandville (10) . . . . 90　C1
Grandvillers (88) . . . . 95　F4
Grandvillers-aux-Bois (60) . . . . . . 38　C2
Grandvillers (27) . . . . 56　C4
Grandvilliers (60) . . . . 17　H5
Grane (26) . . . . 240　C3
Granès (11) . . . . 309　H1
la Grange (25) . . . . 139　G5
Grange-de-Vaivre (39) . . . . 156　A3
Grangermont (45) . . . . 87　F6

les Granges (10) . . . . 114　A2
Granges (71) . . . . 171　H1
Granges-d'Ans (24) . . . . 214　E3
les Granges-Gontardes (26) . . . . 256　D1
Granges-la-Ville (70) . . . . 139　F1
Granges-le-Bourg (70) . . . . 139　F1
les Granges-le-Roi (91) . . . . 86　B2
Granges-les-Beaumont (26) . . . . 222　D5
Granges-Narboz (25) . . . . 156　E4
Granges-sur-Aube (51) . . . . 89　J1
Granges-sur-Baume (39) . . . . . . 173　G1
Granges-sur-Lot (47) . . . . 248　A2
Granges-sur-Vologne (88) . . . . . . 95　G6
les Grangettes (25) . . . . 156　E5
Grangues (14) . . . . 33　H4
Granier (73) . . . . 209　J3
Granieu (38) . . . . 207　J4
Grans (13) . . . . 276　E6
Granville (50) . . . . 51　H1
Granzay-Gript (79) . . . . 178　A2
Gras (07) . . . . 256　B1
les Gras (25) . . . . 157　G3
Grassac (16) . . . . 197　G4
Grasse (06) . . . . 280　D4
Grassendorf (67) . . . . 69　J6
Grateloup-Saint-Gayrand (47) . . . 247　K2
Gratens (31) . . . . 287　J4
Gratentour (31) . . . . 269　G5
Gratibus (80) . . . . 18　D4
Gratot (50) . . . . 30　D4
Gratreuil (51) . . . . 42　B4
Grattepanche (80) . . . . 18　A3
le Gratteris (25) . . . . 156　C1
Grattery (70) . . . . 118　A6
le Grau-du-Roi (30) . . . . 293　K1
les Graulges (24) . . . . 197　G5
Graulhet (81) . . . . 270　C4
Grauves (51) . . . . 61　K2
Graval (76) . . . . 16　D4
la Grave (05) . . . . 225　G4
Gravelines (59) . . . . 3　F2
la Gravelle (53) . . . . 104　C1
Gravelotte (57) . . . . 44　D5
la Graverie (14) . . . . 52　E2
Graveron-Sémerville (27) . . . . 35　G6
Graves-Saint-Amant (16) . . . . . . 196　B3
Graveson (13) . . . . 276　B3
Gravières (07) . . . . 255　G2
Gravigny (27) . . . . 56　D1
Gravon (77) . . . . 88　B3
Gray (70) . . . . 137　F3
Gray-la-Ville (70) . . . . 137　F3
Grayan-et-l'Hôpital (33) . . . . 194　B5
Graye-et-Charnay (39) . . . . 173　F4
Graye-sur-Mer (14) . . . . 32　D3
Grayssas (47) . . . . 248　E5
Grazac (31) . . . . 288　C4
Grazac (43) . . . . 221　F3
Grazac (81) . . . . 269　J3
Grazay (53) . . . . 81　H4
Gréalou (46) . . . . 234　C6
Gréasque (13) . . . . 296　E2
Grébault-Mesnil (80) . . . . 9　F6
Grécourt (80) . . . . 19　H4
Gredisans (39) . . . . 155　G1
la Grée-Saint-Laurent (56) . . . . . 101　J1
Gréez-sur-Roc (72) . . . . 107　K1
Greffeil (11) . . . . 309　G1
Grèges (76) . . . . 16　A1
Grémecey (57) . . . . 66　C3
Grémévillers (60) . . . . 17　H6
Gremilly (55) . . . . 43　J3
Grémonville (76) . . . . 15　H4
Grenade (31) . . . . 269　F4
Grenade-sur-l'Adour (40) . . . . . . 265　H4
Grenant (52) . . . . 116　E6
Grenant-lès-Sombernon (21) . . . 135　H6
Grenay (38) . . . . 206　D3
Grenay (62) . . . . 6　B6
Grendelbruch (67) . . . . 70　B4
Greneville-en-Beauce (45) . . . . . . 86　C6
Grenier-Montgon (43) . . . . 219　G2
Gréning (57) . . . . 68　B4
Grenoble (38) . . . . 224　A3
Grenois (58) . . . . 133　F5
Grentheville (14) . . . . 32　E5
Grentzingen (68) . . . . 97　C5
Greny (76) . . . . 16　B1
Gréolières (06) . . . . 280　D3
Gréoux-les-Bains (04) . . . . 278　A4
Grépiac (31) . . . . 288　B3
le Grès (31) . . . . 268　D5
Grésigny-Sainte-Reine (21) . . . . 135　F2
Gresin (73) . . . . 207　K3
la Gresle (42) . . . . 187　H4
Gresse-en-Vercors (38) . . . . 241　K1
Gressey (78) . . . . 57　H4
Gresswiller (67) . . . . 70　C4
Gressy (77) . . . . 59　H2
Grésy-sur-Aix (73) . . . . 208　B2
Grésy-sur-Isère (73) . . . . 208　A3
Gretz-Armainvilliers (77) . . . . 59　J5
Greucourt (70) . . . . 137　J2
Greuville (76) . . . . 15　J3
Greux (88) . . . . 93　F2
la Grève-sur-Mignon (17) . . . . . . 177　H1
Gréville-Hague (50) . . . . 28　B2
Grévillers (62) . . . . 11　F5
Grevilly (71) . . . . 171　J3
le Grez (72) . . . . 82　A6
Grez (60) . . . . 17　H5
Grez-en-Bouère (53) . . . . 105　H4
Grez-Neuville (49) . . . . 125　F1
Grez-sur-Loing (77) . . . . 87　H4
Grézac (17) . . . . 194　D4
Grézels (46) . . . . 249　G1

Grèzes (24) . . . . 215　G5
Grèzes (43) . . . . 237　J1
Grèzes (46) . . . . 234　B5
Grèzes (48) . . . . 237　G6
Grézet-Cavagnan (47) . . . . 247　G2
Grézian (65) . . . . 305　F4
Grézieu-la-Varenne (69) . . . . 205　K2
Grézieu-le-Marché (69) . . . . 205　G3
Grézillac (33) . . . . 230　A2
Grézillé (49) . . . . 125　J3
Grézolles (42) . . . . 204　B1
Gricourt (02) . . . . 19　K2
Grièges (01) . . . . 188　C1
Gries (67) . . . . 25　B4
Griesbach-au-Val (68) . . . . 96　A4
Griesheim-près-Molsheim (67) . . . 70　D4
Griesheim-sur-Souffel (67) . . . . . 70　E2
Grignan (26) . . . . 257　F1
Grigneuseville (76) . . . . 16　A5
Grignols (24) . . . . 213　J5
Grignols (33) . . . . 246　E2
Grignon (21) . . . . 134　E2
Grignon (73) . . . . 209　G3
Grignoncourt (88) . . . . 117　J3
Grigny (62) . . . . 9　J1
Grigny (69) . . . . 206　A4
Grigny (91) . . . . 58　E6
la Grigonnais (44) . . . . 103　F6
Grillon (84) . . . . 257　F2
Grilly (01) . . . . 174　B6
Grimaucourt-en-Woëvre (55) . . . . 43　K5
Grimaucourt-près-Sampigny (55) . . 64　D4
Grimaud (83) . . . . 298　C4
la Grimaudière (86) . . . . 144　D6
Grimault (89) . . . . 134　A1
Grimbosq (14) . . . . 32　D6
Grimesnil (50) . . . . 30　E5
Grimonviller (54) . . . . 93　K3
Grincourt-lès-Pas (62) . . . . 10　C4
Grindorff-Bizing (57) . . . . 45　J2
la Gripperie-Saint-
　-Symphorien (17) . . . . 194　D1
Gripport (54) . . . . 94　B2
Griscourt (54) . . . . 65　J3
Griselles (21) . . . . 114　C3
Griselles (45) . . . . 111　J2
Grisolles (02) . . . . 39　J5
Grisolles (82) . . . . 269　F3
Grisy-les-Plâtres (95) . . . . 37　G5
Grisy-Suisnes (77) . . . . 59　H6
Grisy-sur-Seine (77) . . . . 88　D3
Grives (24) . . . . 232　D3
Grivesnes (80) . . . . 18　C4
Grivillers (80) . . . . 18　E5
Grivy-Loisy (08) . . . . 42　A2
Groffliers (62) . . . . 8　E1
la Groise (59) . . . . 12　E5
Groises (18) . . . . 150　A1
Groissiat (01) . . . . 190　A2
Groisy (74) . . . . 191　F4
Groix (56) . . . . 99　J6
Groléjac (24) . . . . 233　G2
Gron (18) . . . . 149　K2
Gron (89) . . . . 112　D1
Gronard (02) . . . . 21　F3
Gros-Chastang (19) . . . . 216　D3
Gros-Réderching (57) . . . . 68　E3
le Gros-Theil (27) . . . . 35　F4
Grosbliederstroff (57) . . . . 68　D2
Grosbois (25) . . . . 138　C4
Grosbois-en-Montagne (21) . . . . 135　G5
Grosbois-lès-Tichey (21) . . . . . . 154　E3
Grosbreuil (85) . . . . 159　F3
les Groseillers (79) . . . . 161　H4
Groslay (95) . . . . 58　E2
Groslée (01) . . . . 207　H2
Grosley-sur-Risle (27) . . . . 56　A1
Grosmagny (90) . . . . 119　H5
Grosne (90) . . . . 139　K1
Grospierres (07) . . . . 255　J2
Grosrouvre (78) . . . . 57　J4
Grosrouvres (54) . . . . 65　H3
Grossa (2A) . . . . 322　D3
Grosseto-Prugna (2A) . . . . 320　E6
Grossœuvre (27) . . . . 56　D2
Grossouvre (18) . . . . 150　C5
Grostenquin (57) . . . . 68　A4
Grosville (50) . . . . 28　B3
Grouches-Luchuel (80) . . . . 10　B4
Grougis (02) . . . . 20　C1
la Groutte (18) . . . . 167　G2
Grozon (39) . . . . 155　J5
Gruchet-le-Valasse (76) . . . . 14　E6
Gruchet-Saint-Siméon (76) . . . . . 15　H3
Grues (85) . . . . 159　J5
Gruey-lès-Surance (88) . . . . 118　B1
Gruffy (74) . . . . 208　C1
Grugé-l'Hôpital (49) . . . . 104　C5
Grugies (02) . . . . 19　K3
Grugny (76) . . . . 15　K5
Gruissan (11) . . . . 310　D1
Grumesnil (76) . . . . 17　F5
Grun-Bordas (24) . . . . 213　K5
Grundviller (57) . . . . 68　C3
Gruny (80) . . . . 19　F4
Grury (71) . . . . 170　A2
Gruson (59) . . . . 7　F4
Grusse (39) . . . . 173　F3
Grussenheim (68) . . . . 96　D3
Grust (65) . . . . 304　B3
Gruyères (08) . . . . 22　C4
le Gua (17) . . . . 194　D2
le Gua (38) . . . . 223　K5
Guagno (2A) . . . . 320　D5
Guainville (28) . . . . 57　G3

Guarbecque (62) . . . . 5　J4
Guargualé (2A) . . . . 320　D6
Guchan (65) . . . . 305　F4
Guchen (65) . . . . 305　F4
Gudas (09) . . . . 307　K2
Gudmont-Villiers (52) . . . . 92　B4
le Gué-d'Alléré (17) . . . . 177　D2
le Gué-de-la-Chaîne (61) . . . . . . 83　H1
le Gué-de-Longroi (28) . . . . 85　J2
le Gué-de-Velluire (85) . . . . 160　C5
Gué-d'Hossus (08) . . . . 22　B1
Guebenhouse (57) . . . . 68　C3
Gueberschwihr (68) . . . . 96　B5
Guébestroff (57) . . . . 67　F3
Guéblange-lès-Dieuze (57) . . . . . 67　F3
Guébling (57) . . . . 67　F2
Guebwiller (68) . . . . 96　B6
Guécélard (72) . . . . 106　D4
le Guédéniau (49) . . . . 126　B3
Guégon (56) . . . . 101　H2
Guéhébert (50) . . . . 30　E5
Guéhenno (56) . . . . 101　G2
Gueltas (56) . . . . 77　F5
Guémappe (62) . . . . 11　F3
Guémar (68) . . . . 96　C2
Guémené-Penfao (44) . . . . 102　E4
Guémené-sur-Scorff (56) . . . . . . 76　B5
Guemps (62) . . . . 2　E3
Guénange (57) . . . . 45　F3
Guengat (29) . . . . 74　C5
Guénin (56) . . . . 100　D2
Guenroc (22) . . . . 78　C1
Guenrouet (44) . . . . 102　D6
Guenviller (57) . . . . 68　B3
Guêprei (61) . . . . 54　C3
Guer (56) . . . . 102　B1
Guérande (44) . . . . 121　J4
Guérard (77) . . . . 60　A4
Guerbigny (80) . . . . 18　E4
la Guerche (37) . . . . 146　A5
la Guerche-de-Bretagne (35) . . . . 104　A3
la Guerche-sur-l'Aubois (18) . . . . 150　C4
Guercheville (77) . . . . 87　G5
Guerchy (89) . . . . 112　E4
Guéreins (01) . . . . 188　C3
Guéret (23) . . . . 182　D3
Guerfand (71) . . . . 154　C6
Guérigny (58) . . . . 150　D3
Guérin (47) . . . . 247　F2
la Guérinière (85) . . . . 140　B3
Guerlesquin (29) . . . . 47　J5
Guermange (57) . . . . 67　G3
Guermantes (77) . . . . 59　H3
Guern (56) . . . . 76　C6
Guernanville (27) . . . . 56　A3
Guernes (78) . . . . 57　H1
le Guerno (56) . . . . 121　J1
Guerny (27) . . . . 36　D5
Guéron (14) . . . . 32　B4
la Guéroulde (27) . . . . 56　A4
Guerpont (55) . . . . 64　B5
Guerquesalles (61) . . . . 54　E3
les Guerreaux (71) . . . . 170　A4
Guerstling (57) . . . . 45　J2
Guerting (57) . . . . 45　K4
Guerville (76) . . . . 16　D1
Guerville (78) . . . . 57　J2
Gueschart (80) . . . . 9　H3
Guesnain (59) . . . . 11　J2
Guesnes (86) . . . . 144　E5
Guessling-Hémering (57) . . . . . . 45　K6
Guéthary (64) . . . . 282　A2
Gueudecourt (80) . . . . 11　F5
Gueugnon (71) . . . . 170　B3
Gueures (76) . . . . 15　J2
Gueutteville (76) . . . . 15　J5
Gueutteville-les-Grès (76) . . . . . . 15　G2
Gueux (51) . . . . 40　E4
Guevenatten (68) . . . . 119　K5
Guewenheim (68) . . . . 119　K5
Gueytes-et-Labastide (11) . . . . . 308　C2
Gugnécourt (88) . . . . 95　F4
Gugney (54) . . . . 93　K3
Gugney-aux-Aulx (88) . . . . 94　D3
Guibeville (91) . . . . 86　D1
Guichainville (27) . . . . 56　D2
Guiche (64) . . . . 282　C1
la Guiche (71) . . . . 171　F4
Guichen (35) . . . . 79　F6
Guiclan (29) . . . . 47　H5
Guidel (56) . . . . 99　J4
la Guierche (72) . . . . 106　D2
Guignecourt (60) . . . . 37　H1
Guignemicourt (80) . . . . 17　K2
Guignen (35) . . . . 102　E1
Guignes (77) . . . . 59　J6
Guigneville (45) . . . . 86　C6
Guigneville-sur-Essonne (91) . . . . 86　E2
Guignicourt (02) . . . . 40　E2
Guignicourt-sur-Vence (08) . . . . . 22　C4
Guigny (62) . . . . 9　H2
Guilberville (50) . . . . 31　J5
Guiler-sur-Goyen (29) . . . . 74　A5
Guilers (29) . . . . 72　C5
Guilherand-Granges (07) . . . . . . 240　C1
Guillac (33) . . . . 230　A2
Guillac (56) . . . . 101　J2
Guillaucourt (80) . . . . 18　D2
Guillaumes (06) . . . . 261　F5
Guillemont (80) . . . . 11　F6
la Guillermie (03) . . . . 186　A5
Guillerval (91) . . . . 86　C4
Guillestre (05) . . . . 227　A3
Guilleville (28) . . . . 85　K6
Guilliers (56) . . . . 77　K6
Guilligomarc'h (29) . . . . 99　K2

Guillon (89) . . . . 134　B3
Guillon-les-Bains (25) . . . . 138　D5
Guillonville (28) . . . . 109　H2
Guillos (33) . . . . 229　H5
Guilly (36) . . . . 148　A3
Guilly (45) . . . . 110　C5
Guilmécourt (76) . . . . 16　B1
Guilvinec (29) . . . . 98　B3
Guimaëc (29) . . . . 47　H3
Guimiliau (29) . . . . 46　E5
Guimps (16) . . . . 196　A5
Guinarthe-Parenties (64) . . . . . . 283　G3
Guincourt (08) . . . . 22　C6
Guindrecourt-aux-Ormes (52) . . . . 91　K4
Guindrecourt-sur-Blaise (52) . . . . 91　K4
Guinecourt (62) . . . . 9　K2
Guînes (62) . . . . 2　D3
Guingamp (22) . . . . 48　C5
Guinglange (57) . . . . 45　J5
Guinkirchen (57) . . . . 45　H4
Guinzeling (57) . . . . 67　G2
Guipavas (29) . . . . 46　A6
Guipel (35) . . . . 79　F2
Guipronvel (29) . . . . 72　C3
Guipry (35) . . . . 102　E2
Guipy (58) . . . . 151　H1
Guiry-en-Vexin (95) . . . . 36　E6
Guiscard (60) . . . . 19　H5
Guiscriff (56) . . . . 75　H5
Guise (02) . . . . 20　D2
Guiseniers (27) . . . . 36　B5
le Guislain (50) . . . . 31　G5
Guissény (29) . . . . 46　B3
Guisy (62) . . . . 9　H1
Guitalens (81) . . . . 270　D6
Guitera-les-Bains (2A) . . . . 321　F5
Guitinières (17) . . . . 195　H6
Guitrancourt (78) . . . . 57　K1
Guîtres (33) . . . . 212　B5
Guitry (27) . . . . 36　C5
Guitté (22) . . . . 78　C2
Guivry (02) . . . . 19　J5
Guizancourt (80) . . . . 17　H4
Guizengeard (16) . . . . 212　C2
Guizerix (65) . . . . 286　B4
Gujan-Mestras (33) . . . . 228　C4
Gumbrechtshoffen (67) . . . . 69　J5
Gumery (10) . . . . 88　E3
Gumiane (26) . . . . 241　G6
Gumières (42) . . . . 204　C5
Gumond (19) . . . . 216　D3
Gundershoffen (67) . . . . 69　K5
Gundolsheim (68) . . . . 96　B6
Gungwiller (67) . . . . 67　K2
Gunsbach (68) . . . . 96　A4
Gunstett (67) . . . . 25　A2
Guntzviller (57) . . . . 67　K4
Guny (02) . . . . 39　H1
Guran (31) . . . . 305　H4
Gurat (16) . . . . 197　F6
Gurcy-le-Châtel (77) . . . . 88　B2
Gurgy (89) . . . . 113　G4
Gurgy-la-Ville (21) . . . . 115　H4
Gurgy-le-Château (21) . . . . 115　K4
Gurmençon (64) . . . . 284　A6
Gurs (64) . . . . 283　J4
Gurunhuel (22) . . . . 48　B5
Gury (60) . . . . 19　F6
Gussainville (55) . . . . 44　A5
Gussignies (59) . . . . 13　F2
Guyancourt (78) . . . . 58　C4
Guyans-Durnes (25) . . . . 156　D1
Guyans-Vennes (25) . . . . 157　G1
Guyencourt (02) . . . . 40　D3
Guyencourt-Saulcourt (80) . . . . . 11　H6
Guyencourt-sur-Noye (80) . . . . . . 18　B3
la Guyonnière (85) . . . . 142　B4
Guyonvelle (52) . . . . 117　G4
Guzargues (34) . . . . 274　C5
Gy (70) . . . . 137　H4
Gy-en-Sologne (41) . . . . 129　H5
Gy-les-Nonains (45) . . . . 111　K3
Gy-l'Évêque (89) . . . . 113　G6
Gye (54) . . . . 65　H6
Gyé-sur-Seine (10) . . . . 114　E2

H

Habarcq (62) . . . . 10　D2
Habas (40) . . . . 264　C6
Habère-Lullin (74) . . . . 191　J1
Habère-Poche (74) . . . . 191　J1
l'Habit (27) . . . . 57　F3
Hablainville (54) . . . . 95　F1
Habloville (61) . . . . 54　A4
Haboudange (57) . . . . 66　E2
Habsheim (68) . . . . 97　D2
Hachan (65) . . . . 286　A4
Hâcourt (52) . . . . 93　F6
Hacqueville (27) . . . . 36　C4
Hadancourt-le-Haut-Clocher (60) . . 36　E5
Hadigny-les-Verrières (88) . . . . . . 94　D3
Hadol (88) . . . . 94　D6
Haegen (67) . . . . 70　B2
Hagécourt (88) . . . . 94　A5
Hagedet (65) . . . . 285　G1
Hagen (57) . . . . 27　C2
Hagenbach (68) . . . . 97　A4
Hagenthal-le-Bas (68) . . . . 97　D5
Hagenthal-le-Haut (68) . . . . 97　D5
Haget (65) . . . . 285　J3
Hagetaubin (64) . . . . 284　A1
Hagetmau (40) . . . . 265　F5

Hagéville (54) . . . 44 C6
Hagnéville-et-Roncourt (88) . . . 93 H5
Hagnicourt (08) . . . 22 C5
Hagondange (57) . . . 45 F3
Haguenau (67) . . . 25 A4
la Haie-Fouassière (44) . . . 123 J5
la Haie-Traversaine (53) . . . 81 G3
les Haies (69) . . . 205 K5
Haigneville (54) . . . 94 C1
Haillainville (88) . . . 94 D3
le Haillan (33) . . . 229 G1
Hailles (80) . . . 18 C3
Haillicourt (62) . . . 5 K6
Haimps (17) . . . 178 C6
Haims (86) . . . 164 A4
Hainvillers (60) . . . 18 E6
Haironville (55) . . . 64 C3
Haisnes (62) . . . 6 B6
Haleine (61) . . . 81 J2
Halinghen (62) . . . 4 B4
Hallencourt (80) . . . 18 D5
Hallennes-lez-Haubourdin (59) . . . 6 D4
Hallering (57) . . . 45 J5
les Halles (69) . . . 205 G2
Halles-sous-les-Côtes (55) . . . 43 F1
Hallignicourt (52) . . . 63 J6
Hallines (62) . . . 5 G4
Hallivillers (80) . . . 18 A4
la Hallotière (76) . . . 36 B1
Halloville (54) . . . 67 H6
Halloy (60) . . . 17 H5
Halloy (62) . . . 10 B4
Halloy-lès-Pernois (80) . . . 9 K6
Hallu (80) . . . 19 F3
Halluin (59) . . . 6 E2
Halsou (64) . . . 282 C3
Halstroff (57) . . . 27 K4
le Ham (50) . . . 28 E5
le Ham (53) . . . 81 J3
Ham (80) . . . 19 H4
Ham-en-Artois (62) . . . 5 J5
Ham-les-Moines (08) . . . 22 C3
Ham-sous-Varsberg (57) . . . 45 K4
Ham-sur-Meuse (08) . . . 24 C2
Hamars (14) . . . 53 H1
Hambach (57) . . . 68 D3
Hambers (53) . . . 81 J5
Hamblain-les-Prés (62) . . . 11 H5
Hambye (50) . . . 31 F5
Hamel (59) . . . 11 H3
le Hamel (60) . . . 17 H5
le Hamel (80) . . . 18 D2
Hamelet (80) . . . 18 D2
Hamelin (50) . . . 80 B1
Hamelincourt (62) . . . 11 H4
Hames-Boucres (62) . . . 2 C3
Hammeville (54) . . . 93 K1
Hamonville (54) . . . 65 G3
Hampigny (10) . . . 91 F2
Hampont (57) . . . 66 E3
Han-devant-Pierrepont (54) . . . 26 C4
Han-lès-Juvigny (55) . . . 43 H1
Han-sur-Meuse (55) . . . 64 B3
Han-sur-Nied (57) . . . 66 C1
Hanc (79) . . . 178 E4
Hanches (28) . . . 85 H1
Hancourt (80) . . . 19 H2
Handschuheim (67) . . . 70 D3
Hangard (80) . . . 18 C3
Hangenbieten (67) . . . 70 E3
Hangest-en-Santerre (80) . . . 18 D4
Hangest-sur-Somme (80) . . . 17 J1
Hangviller (57) . . . 69 F6
Hannaches (60) . . . 36 E1
Hannapes (02) . . . 20 D1
Hannappes (08) . . . 21 J3
Hannescamps (62) . . . 10 E4
Hannocourt (57) . . . 66 C2
Hannogne-Saint-Martin (08) . . . 22 E4
Hannogne-Saint-Rémy (08) . . . 21 H5
Hannonville-sous-les-Côtes (55) . . . 44 A6
Hannonville-Suzémont (54) . . . 44 C5
le Hanouard (76) . . . 15 F4
Hans (51) . . . 42 C6
Hantay (59) . . . 6 C5
Hanvec (29) . . . 74 D2
Hanviller (57) . . . 69 H2
Hanvoile (60) . . . 37 F1
Haplincourt (62) . . . 11 G5
Happencourt (02) . . . 19 J2
Happonvilliers (28) . . . 84 C4
Haramont (02) . . . 39 G4
Haraucourt (08) . . . 23 F5
Haraucourt (54) . . . 66 C5
Haraucourt-sur-Seille (57) . . . 66 C1
Haravesnes (62) . . . 9 J3
Haravilliers (95) . . . 37 G5
Harbonnières (80) . . . 18 E2
Harbouey (54) . . . 67 H6
Harcanville (76) . . . 15 G4
Harchéchamp (88) . . . 93 G3
Harcigny (02) . . . 21 G3
Harcourt (27) . . . 34 E5
Harcy (08) . . . 22 C2
Hardancourt (88) . . . 94 E3
Hardanges (53) . . . 81 J4
Hardecourt-aux-Bois (80) . . . 11 F6
Hardencourt-Cocherel (27) . . . 56 E3
Hardifort (59) . . . 3 J4
Hardinghen (62) . . . 2 C4
Hardinvast (50) . . . 28 C3
Hardivillers (60) . . . 18 A5
Hardivillers-en-Vexin (60) . . . 37 G3
Hardricourt (78) . . . 58 A1
la Harengère (27) . . . 35 G4
Haréville (88) . . . 93 K5

Harfleur (76) . . . 33 K1
Hargarten-aux-Mines (57) . . . 45 K4
Hargeville (78) . . . 57 J3
Hargicourt (02) . . . 19 J1
Hargicourt (80) . . . 18 D4
Hargnies (08) . . . 24 C3
Hargnies (59) . . . 13 G3
Harly (02) . . . 20 A2
Harmonville (88) . . . 93 H2
la Harmoye (22) . . . 76 E2
Harnes (62) . . . 6 C6
Harol (88) . . . 94 B6
Haroué (54) . . . 94 A2
Harponville (80) . . . 10 C6
Harprich (57) . . . 66 E1
Harquency (27) . . . 36 B4
Harreberg (57) . . . 67 K5
Harréville-les-Chanteurs (52) . . . 93 F5
Harricourt (08) . . . 42 D2
Harsault (88) . . . 118 B1
Harskirchen (67) . . . 68 D5
Hartennes-et-Taux (02) . . . 39 J4
Hartmannswiller (68) . . . 97 B1
Hartzviller (57) . . . 67 J5
Harville (55) . . . 44 B5
Hary (02) . . . 21 H3
Haselbourg (57) . . . 70 A2
Hasnon (59) . . . 12 C1
Hasparren (64) . . . 282 D3
Haspelschiedt (57) . . . 69 H3
Haspres (59) . . . 12 C3
Hastingues (40) . . . 283 F1
Hatten (67) . . . 25 C3
Hattencourt (80) . . . 19 F3
Hattenville (76) . . . 14 E5
Hattigny (57) . . . 67 H6
Hattmatt (67) . . . 69 H6
Hattstatt (68) . . . 96 B5
Hauban (65) . . . 304 D1
Haubourdin (59) . . . 6 D4
Hauconcourt (57) . . . 45 F4
Haucourt (60) . . . 37 F1
Haucourt (62) . . . 11 G3
Haucourt (76) . . . 17 F5
Haucourt-en-Cambrésis (59) . . . 12 B5
Haucourt-Moulaine (54) . . . 26 D3
Haudainville (55) . . . 43 J5
Haudiomont (55) . . . 43 K5
Haudivillers (60) . . . 37 J1
Haudonville (54) . . . 94 D1
Haudrecy (08) . . . 22 C3
Haudricourt (76) . . . 17 F4
Haulchin (59) . . . 12 C2
Haulies (32) . . . 286 D1
Haulmé (08) . . . 22 D2
Haumont-près-Samogneux (55) . . . 43 H3
Hauriet (40) . . . 264 E4
Hausgauen (68) . . . 97 C4
Haussez (76) . . . 17 F6
Haussignémont (51) . . . 63 H5
Haussimont (51) . . . 62 B5
Haussonville (54) . . . 94 C1
Haussy (59) . . . 12 C3
Haut-Clocher (57) . . . 67 J3
le Haut-Corlay (22) . . . 76 D2
Haut-de-Bosdarros (64) . . . 284 D6
Haut-du-Them-
    -Château-Lambert (70) . . . 119 G4
Haut-Lieu (59) . . . 13 G5
Haut-Loquin (62) . . . 4 E3
Haut-Mauco (40) . . . 265 G3
Hautaget (65) . . . 305 G2
Hautbos (60) . . . 17 G5
Haute-Amance (52) . . . 117 F4
Haute-Avesnes (62) . . . 10 D2
la Haute-Beaume (05) . . . 242 A5
la Haute-Chapelle (61) . . . 53 G6
Haute-Épine (60) . . . 17 J6
Haute-Goulaine (44) . . . 123 H4
Haute-Isle (95) . . . 36 D6
Haute-Kontz (57) . . . 27 J3
la Haute-Maison (77) . . . 60 A3
Haute-Rivoire (69) . . . 205 G2
Haute-Vigneulles (57) . . . 45 J5
Hautecloque (62) . . . 10 A2
Hautecour (39) . . . 173 J3
Hautecour (73) . . . 209 H4
Hautecourt-Romanèche (01) . . . 189 J2
Hautefage (19) . . . 216 D5
Hautefage-la-Tour (47) . . . 248 D3
Hautefaye (24) . . . 197 H5
Hautefeuille (77) . . . 60 A5
Hautefond (71) . . . 170 D5
Hautefontaine (60) . . . 39 G3
Hautefort (24) . . . 214 E3
Hauteluce (73) . . . 209 H1
Hautepierre-le-Châtelet (25) . . . 156 E2
Hauterive (03) . . . 185 J4
Hauterive (61) . . . 82 E2
Hauterive (89) . . . 113 G4
Hauterive-la-Fresse (25) . . . 157 F3
Hauterives (26) . . . 222 D2
Hauteroche (21) . . . 135 F3
Hautes-Duyes (04) . . . 259 J4
les Hautes-Rivières (08) . . . 22 E2
Hautesvignes (47) . . . 247 J3
Hautevelle (70) . . . 118 C4
Hautevesnes (02) . . . 39 H6
Hauteville (08) . . . 20 C2
Hauteville (08) . . . 21 K6
Hauteville (51) . . . 63 H6
Hauteville (62) . . . 10 D3
Hauteville (73) . . . 208 E4
la Hauteville (78) . . . 57 H1
Hauteville-la-Guichard (50) . . . 31 F3

Hauteville-lès-Dijon (21) . . . 136 A5
Hauteville-Lompnes (01) . . . 190 A5
Hauteville-sur-Fier (74) . . . 190 D5
Hauteville-sur-Mer (50) . . . 30 D5
Haution (02) . . . 21 F2
Hautmont (59) . . . 13 G3
Hautmougey (88) . . . 118 B2
Hautot-l'Auvray (76) . . . 15 G3
Hautot-le-Vatois (76) . . . 15 G5
Hautot-Saint-Sulpice (76) . . . 15 G4
Hautot-sur-Mer (76) . . . 15 K2
Hautot-sur-Seine (76) . . . 35 G3
les Hauts-de-Chée (55) . . . 64 B3
Hauttecôte-Bocage (50) . . . 28 C5
Hautvillers (51) . . . 40 E6
Hautvillers-Ouville (80) . . . 9 G4
Hauville (27) . . . 34 E2
Hauviné (08) . . . 41 J3
Haux (33) . . . 229 K4
Haux (64) . . . 302 C1
Havange (57) . . . 27 F4
Havelu (28) . . . 57 G4
Haveluy (59) . . . 12 C2
Havernas (80) . . . 9 K6
Haverskerque (59) . . . 5 K4
le Havre (76) . . . 33 J1
Havrincourt (62) . . . 11 H5
l'Hay-les-Roses (94) . . . 58 E4
Hayange (57) . . . 27 F4
Haybes (08) . . . 24 B3
la Haye (76) . . . 36 B1
la Haye (88) . . . 118 A1
la Haye-Aubrée (27) . . . 34 E2
la Haye-Bellefond (50) . . . 31 G5
la Haye-de-Calleville (27) . . . 34 E5
la Haye-de-Routot (27) . . . 34 E2
la Haye-d'Ectot (50) . . . 28 B5
la Haye-du-Puits (50) . . . 30 D1
la Haye-du-Theil (27) . . . 35 F4
la Haye-le-Comte (27) . . . 35 J5
la Haye-Malherbe (27) . . . 35 H4
la Haye-Pesnel (50) . . . 51 K1
la Haye-Saint-Sylvestre (27) . . . 55 J3
les Hayes (41) . . . 107 K6
Hayes (77) . . . 45 G4
Haynecourt (59) . . . 11 J4
les Hays (39) . . . 155 F4
Hazebrouck (59) . . . 5 K3
Hazembourg (57) . . . 68 C4
le Heaulme (95) . . . 37 G5
Héauville (50) . . . 28 B3
Hébécourt (27) . . . 36 D3
Hébécourt (80) . . . 18 A3
Hébécrevon (50) . . . 31 G3
Héberville (76) . . . 15 H3
Hébuterne (62) . . . 10 D5
Hèches (65) . . . 305 F2
Hecken (68) . . . 97 A3
Hecmanville (27) . . . 34 D5
Hécourt (27) . . . 57 F2
Hécourt (60) . . . 36 E1
Hecq (59) . . . 12 E4
Hectomare (27) . . . 35 G5
Hédauville (80) . . . 10 D6
Hédé (35) . . . 79 F2
Hédouville (95) . . . 37 H5
Hegeney (67) . . . 25 A3
Hégenheim (68) . . . 97 E4
Heidolsheim (67) . . . 96 D2
Heidwiller (68) . . . 97 B3
Heiligenberg (67) . . . 70 C4
Heiligenstein (67) . . . 70 C5
Heillecourt (54) . . . 66 A5
Heilles (60) . . . 37 J3
Heilly (80) . . . 18 D1
Heiltz-le-Hutier (51) . . . 63 H5
Heiltz-le-Maurupt (51) . . . 63 H4
Heiltz-l'Évêque (51) . . . 63 G4
Heimersdorf (68) . . . 97 B4
Heimsbrunn (68) . . . 97 B3
Heining-lès-Bouzonville (57) . . . 45 J2
Heippes (55) . . . 64 C1
Heiteren (68) . . . 96 E5
Heiwiller (68) . . . 97 C4
Hélesmes (59) . . . 12 B2
Hélette (64) . . . 282 D4
Helfaut (62) . . . 5 G3
Helfrantzkirch (68) . . . 97 D4
Helléan (56) . . . 101 J4
Hellering-lès-Fénétrange (57) . . . 67 J3
Helleville (50) . . . 28 B3
Hellimer (57) . . . 68 B4
Héloup (61) . . . 82 C3
Helstroff (57) . . . 45 H4
Hem (59) . . . 7 F4
Hem-Hardinval (80) . . . 10 A4
Hem-Lenglet (59) . . . 11 J3
Hem-Monacu (80) . . . 19 F1
Hémevez (50) . . . 28 E4
Hémévillers (60) . . . 38 C2
Hémilly (57) . . . 45 J6
Hémonstoir (22) . . . 77 F4
Hénaménil (54) . . . 66 D6
Hénanbihen (22) . . . 50 A4
Hénansal (22) . . . 49 K6
Hendecourt-lès-Cagnicourt (62) . . . 11 G4
Hendecourt-lès-Ransart (62) . . . 10 E4
Hénencourt (80) . . . 10 D6
Henflingen (68) . . . 97 C4
Hengoat (22) . . . 48 C3
Hengwiller (67) . . . 70 B2
Hénin-Beaumont (62) . . . 11 G1
Hénin-sur-Cojeul (62) . . . 11 F3
Héninel (62) . . . 11 F3

Hennebont (56) . . . 100 A3
Hennecourt (88) . . . 94 C5
Hennemont (55) . . . 44 A5
Henneveux (62) . . . 4 D3
Hennezel (88) . . . 118 A1
Hennezis (27) . . . 36 B5
Hénon (22) . . . 77 G2
Hénonville (60) . . . 37 G5
Hénouville (76) . . . 35 G1
Henrichemont (18) . . . 131 G6
Henridorff (57) . . . 70 A1
Henriville (57) . . . 68 B3
Hénu (62) . . . 10 C4
Henvic (29) . . . 47 F4
Hérange (57) . . . 67 K3
Herbault (41) . . . 128 C2
Herbécourt (80) . . . 19 F1
Herbelles (62) . . . 5 G4
l'Herbergement (85) . . . 141 K4
Herbeuval (08) . . . 23 J5
Herbeuville (55) . . . 44 A6
Herbéviller (54) . . . 67 G6
Herbeys (38) . . . 224 B4
les Herbiers (85) . . . 142 D5
Herbignac (44) . . . 121 K3
Herbinghen (62) . . . 2 D5
Herbisse (10) . . . 62 B6
Herbitzheim (67) . . . 68 D4
Herblay (95) . . . 58 C2
Herbsheim (67) . . . 70 E6
Hercé (53) . . . 80 E3
Herchies (60) . . . 37 G1
la Hérelle (60) . . . 18 C6
Hérenguerville (50) . . . 30 D5
Hérépian (34) . . . 291 J1
Hères (65) . . . 285 G1
Hergnies (59) . . . 7 J6
Hergugney (88) . . . 94 B3
Héric (44) . . . 123 F1
Héricourt (62) . . . 10 A2
Héricourt (70) . . . 139 G1
Héricourt-en-Caux (76) . . . 15 G3
Héricourt-sur-Thérain (60) . . . 17 F6
Héricy (77) . . . 87 J3
la Hérie (02) . . . 21 G2
le Hérie-la-Viéville (02) . . . 20 D3
Hériménil (54) . . . 66 D6
Hérimoncourt (25) . . . 139 J3
Hérin (59) . . . 12 C2
Hérissart (80) . . . 10 B6
Hérisson (03) . . . 167 J4
Herleville (80) . . . 19 F2
la Herlière (62) . . . 10 C4
Herlies (59) . . . 6 C5
Herlin-le-Sec (62) . . . 10 A2
Herlincourt (62) . . . 10 A2
Herly (62) . . . 4 E5
Herly (80) . . . 19 G4
l'Herm (09) . . . 307 K3
Herm (40) . . . 264 A3
Hermanville (76) . . . 15 J3
Hermanville-sur-Mer (14) . . . 32 E3
les Hermaux (48) . . . 236 G6
Hermaville (62) . . . 10 D2
Hermé (77) . . . 88 D2
Hermelange (57) . . . 67 J4
Hermelinghen (62) . . . 2 C4
l'Hermenault (85) . . . 160 D3
Herment (63) . . . 201 J2
Hermeray (78) . . . 57 J6
Hermes (60) . . . 37 J3
Hermeville (76) . . . 14 C5
Herméville-en-Woëvre (55) . . . 43 K5
Hermies (62) . . . 11 H5
Hermillon (73) . . . 225 G1
Hermin (62) . . . 10 C1
l'Hermitage (35) . . . 78 E4
l'Hermitage-Lorge (22) . . . 77 F2
les Hermites (37) . . . 127 K1
l'Hermitière (61) . . . 83 J5
Hermival-les-Vaux (14) . . . 34 A5
Hermonville (51) . . . 40 E3
Hernicourt (62) . . . 10 A1
Herny (57) . . . 66 D1
le Héron (76) . . . 36 A1
Héronchelles (76) . . . 16 C6
Hérouville (95) . . . 37 H6
Hérouville-Saint-Clair (14) . . . 32 E4
Hérouvillette (14) . . . 33 F4
Herpelmont (88) . . . 95 G5
Herpont (51) . . . 63 G1
Herpy-l'Arlésienne (08) . . . 21 J6
Herqueville (27) . . . 35 K4
Herqueville (50) . . . 28 A2
Herran (31) . . . 306 B3
Herré (40) . . . 266 B1
Herrère (64) . . . 284 B6
Herrin (59) . . . 6 D5
Herrlisheim (67) . . . 25 C5
Herrlisheim-près-Colmar (68) . . . 96 C5
Herry (18) . . . 150 C1
Herserange (54) . . . 26 D2
Hersin-Coupigny (62) . . . 6 A6
Hertzing (57) . . . 67 H4
Hervelinghen (62) . . . 2 B3
Hervilly (80) . . . 19 J1
Héry (58) . . . 133 G6
Héry (89) . . . 113 G4
Héry-sur-Alby (74) . . . 208 C1
Herzeele (59) . . . 3 J3
Hesbécourt (80) . . . 19 J1
Hescamps (80) . . . 17 G4
Hesdigneul-lès-Béthune (62) . . . 5 K6
Hesdigneul-lès-Boulogne (62) . . . 4 B4
Hesdin (62) . . . 9 J1

Hesdin-l'Abbé (62) . . . 4 B4
Hésingue (68) . . . 97 E4
Hesmond (62) . . . 4 D6
Hesse (57) . . . 67 J4
Hessenheim (67) . . . 96 D2
Hestroff (57) . . . 45 H3
Hestrud (59) . . . 13 J4
Hestrus (62) . . . 5 H6
Hétomesnil (60) . . . 17 J5
Hettange-Grande (57) . . . 27 G3
Hettenschlag (68) . . . 96 D5
Heubécourt-Haricourt (27) . . . 36 C6
Heuchin (62) . . . 5 G6
Heucourt-Croquoison (80) . . . 17 G1
Heudebouville (27) . . . 35 K5
Heudicourt (27) . . . 36 D3
Heudicourt (80) . . . 11 H6
Heudicourt-sous-les-Côtes (55) . . . 65 F2
Heudreville-en-Lieuvin (27) . . . 34 C5
Heudreville-sur-Eure (27) . . . 35 J5
Heugas (40) . . . 264 A5
Heugleville-sur-Scie (76) . . . 15 K4
Heugnes (36) . . . 147 G4
Heugon (61) . . . 55 G3
Heugueville-sur-Sienne (50) . . . 30 D4
Heuilley-Cotton (52) . . . 116 D5
Heuilley-le-Grand (52) . . . 116 D5
Heuilley-sur-Saône (21) . . . 136 E5
Heuland (14) . . . 33 H4
Heume-l'Église (63) . . . 201 K3
la Heunière (27) . . . 57 F3
Heuqueville (27) . . . 36 A4
Heuqueville (76) . . . 14 B5
Heuringhem (62) . . . 5 G3
Heurteauville (76) . . . 35 F2
Heurtevent (14) . . . 54 D2
Heussé (50) . . . 80 D2
Heutrégiville (51) . . . 41 H3
Heuzecourt (80) . . . 9 K4
Hévilliers (55) . . . 64 C6
Heyrieux (38) . . . 206 D3
Hézecques (62) . . . 5 F5
le Hézo (56) . . . 101 G6
Hibarette (65) . . . 285 H6
Hières-sur-Amby (38) . . . 207 F1
Hierges (08) . . . 24 C2
Hiermont (80) . . . 9 J4
Hiers-Brouage (17) . . . 176 E6
Hiersac (16) . . . 196 C3
Hiesse (16) . . . 180 A4
Hiesville (50) . . . 29 F6
Hiéville (14) . . . 54 C1
Higuères-Souye (64) . . . 284 E3
Hiis (65) . . . 285 H6
Hilbesheim (57) . . . 67 J3
Hillion (22) . . . 49 H6
Hilsenheim (67) . . . 96 D1
Hilsprich (57) . . . 68 C4
Hinacourt (02) . . . 20 A4
Hinckange (57) . . . 45 H4
Hindisheim (67) . . . 70 E4
Hindlingen (68) . . . 97 A5
Hinges (62) . . . 5 K5
le Hinglé (22) . . . 50 C6
Hinsbourg (67) . . . 69 F3
Hinsingen (67) . . . 68 D4
Hinx (40) . . . 264 C4
Hipsheim (67) . . . 71 D2
Hirel (35) . . . 51 F4
Hirschland (67) . . . 67 K2
Hirsingue (68) . . . 97 B4
Hirson (02) . . . 21 H1
Hirtzbach (68) . . . 97 B4
Hirtzfelden (68) . . . 96 D6
His (31) . . . 306 B1
Hitte (65) . . . 285 H6
Hochfelden (67) . . . 70 D1
Hochstatt (68) . . . 97 B3
Hochstett (67) . . . 69 K6
Hocquigny (50) . . . 51 K1
Hodenc-en-Bray (60) . . . 37 F1
Hodenc-l'Évêque (60) . . . 37 H3
Hodeng-au-Bosc (76) . . . 17 F2
Hodeng-Hodenger (76) . . . 36 C1
Hodent (95) . . . 36 E5
Hœdic (56) . . . 120 E4
Hœnheim (67) . . . 25 A6
Hœrdt (67) . . . 25 A5
Hœville (54) . . . 66 D4
Hoffen (67) . . . 25 C2
les Hogues (27) . . . 36 A2
la Hoguette (14) . . . 54 B3
Hohatzenheim (67) . . . 70 E1
Hohengœft (67) . . . 70 C2
Hohfrankenheim (67) . . . 70 D1
Hohrod (68) . . . 119 K1
le Hohwald (67) . . . 70 B5
Holacourt (57) . . . 66 D1
Holling (57) . . . 45 J3
Holnon (02) . . . 19 K2
Holque (59) . . . 3 F4
Holtzheim (67) . . . 70 D4
Holtzwihr (68) . . . 96 C3
Holving (57) . . . 68 C4
Hombleux (80) . . . 19 H4
Homblières (02) . . . 20 A2
Hombourg (68) . . . 97 D2
Hombourg-Budange (57) . . . 45 G3
Hombourg-Haut (57) . . . 68 A2
l'Hôme-Chamondot (61) . . . 83 K1
Homécourt (54) . . . 44 D4
Hommarting (57) . . . 67 K4
Hommert (57) . . . 67 K4
Hommes (37) . . . 126 E4
le Hommet-d'Arthenay (50) . . . 31 G2

Homps (11) 291 F5
Homps (32) 268 A4
Hon-Hergies (59) 13 F2
Hondainville (60) 37 J3
Hondeghem (59) 5 J2
Hondevilliers (77) 60 D3
Hondouville (27) 35 H5
Hondschoote (59) 3 K2
Honfleur (14) 33 K2
Honguemare-Guenouville (27) . . 35 F3
Honnechy (59) 12 C5
Honnecourt-sur-Escaut (59) . . . 11 J6
l'Honor-de-Cos (82) 249 J5
Honskirch (57) 68 C5
Hontanx (40) 265 K3
l'Hôpital (57) 68 A2
l'Hôpital-Camfrout (29) 74 C1
l'Hôpital-d'Orion (64) 283 H2
l'Hôpital-du-Grosbois (25) . . . 156 D1
l'Hôpital-le-Grand (42) 204 E4
l'Hôpital-le-Mercier (71) 170 B6
l'Hôpital-Saint-Blaise (64) . . . 283 J4
l'Hôpital-Saint-Lieffroy (25) . . 138 E4
l'Hôpital-sous-Rochefort (42) . . 204 B2
les Hôpitaux-Neufs (25) 157 F6
les Hôpitaux-Vieux (25) 157 F6
Horbourg-Wihr (68) 96 C4
Hordain (59) 12 B3
la Horgne (08) 22 C5
Horgues (65) 285 H5
l'Horme (42) 205 H5
Hornaing (59) 12 B2
Hornoy-le-Bourg (80) 17 H2
le Horps (53) 81 H3
Horsarrieu (40) 265 F5
Horville-en-Ornois (55) 92 E2
l'Hosmes (27) 56 C4
l'Hospitalet (04) 258 D5
l'Hospitalet-du-Larzac (12) . . . 272 E2
l'Hospitalet-près-l'Andorre (09) . 313 F3
Hosta (64) 283 F5
Hoste (57) 68 B3
Hostens (33) 229 G6
Hostias (01) 189 K6
Hostun (26) 223 F5
l'Hôtellerie (14) 34 B5
l'Hôtellerie-de-Flée (49) 104 D5
Hotonnes (01) 190 B4
Hotot-en-Auge (14) 33 H5
Hottot-les-Bagues (14) 32 B5
Hottviller (57) 69 G3
la Houblonnière (14) 33 J5
les Houches (74) 192 C5
Houchin (62) 5 K6
Houdain (62) 5 K6
Houdain-lez-Bavay (59) 13 F2
Houdan (78) 57 H4
Houdancourt (60) 38 C3
Houdelaincourt (55) 92 E1
Houdelmont (54) 93 K1
Houdemont (54) 66 A5
Houdetot (76) 15 H3
Houdilcourt (08) 41 F2
Houdreville (54) 93 K1
Houécourt (88) 93 J4
Houeillès (47) 247 F4
Houesville (50) 29 F6
Houetteville (27) 35 H6
Houéville (88) 93 H3
Houeydets (65) 286 A6
le Houga (32) 266 A4
Houilles (78) 58 D3
Houlbec-Cocherel (27) 36 A6
Houlbec-près-le-Gros-Theil (27) . 35 F4
Houldizy (08) 22 C3
Houlette (16) 196 A2
Houlgate (14) 33 G3
Houlle (62) 3 F4
le Houlme (76) 35 H1
l'Houmeau (17) 176 D2
Hounoux (11) 308 C1
Houplin-Ancoisne (59) 6 D5
Houplines (59) 6 C3
Houppeville (76) 35 H1
Houquetot (76) 14 D5
Hourc (65) 285 J5
Hourges (51) 40 C4
Hours (64) 285 F5
Hourtin (33) 210 C3
Houry (02) 21 F4
Houssay (41) 108 B6
Houssay (53) 105 F3
la Houssaye (27) 56 A2
la Houssaye-Béranger (76) 15 K5
la Houssaye-en-Brie (77) 59 K6
le Housseau-Brétignolles (53) . . 81 H1
Houssen (68) 96 C3
Housseras (88) 95 F3
Housset (02) 20 D3
Housséville (54) 94 A3
la Houssière (88) 95 H5
la Houssoye (60) 37 F3
Houtaud (25) 156 E4
Houtkerque (59) 3 K3
Houtteville (50) 29 F6
Houville-en-Vexin (27) 36 A4
Houville-la-Branche (28) 85 H3
Houvin-Houvigneul (62) 10 B2
Houx (28) 85 H1
Hoymille (59) 3 J2
Huanne-Montmartin (25) 138 D3
Hubersent (62) 4 B5
Hubert-Folie (14) 32 E5
Huberville (50) 28 E4
Huby-Saint-Leu (62) 9 J1
Huchenneville (80) 9 F6

Huclier (62) 10 B1
Hucqueliers (62) 4 D5
Hudimesnil (50) 30 D6
Hudiviller (54) 66 C6
Huelgoat (29) 75 G1
Huest (27) 56 D1
Huêtre (45) 109 K2
Huez (38) 224 E4
Hugier (70) 137 G5
Hugleville-en-Caux (76) 15 J5
Huillé (49) 125 J1
Huilliécourt (52) 92 E6
Huilly-sur-Seille (71) 172 B3
Huiron (51) 63 F5
Huismes (37) 145 F1
Huisnes-sur-Mer (50) 51 J4
Huisseau-en-Beauce (41) 108 B6
Huisseau-sur-Cosson (41) 129 F2
Huisseau-sur-Mauves (45) 109 J4
l'Huisserie (53) 104 E2
Hulluch (62) 6 B6
Hultehouse (57) 70 A2
Humbauville (51) 62 E6
Humbécourt (52) 91 J1
Humbercamps (62) 10 D4
Humbercourt (80) 10 C4
Humbert (62) 4 D6
Humberville (52) 92 D4
Humbligny (18) 131 H6
Humerœuille (62) 9 K1
Humes-Jorquenay (52) 116 C3
Humières (62) 9 K1
Hunawihr (68) 96 B3
Hundling (57) 68 C3
Hundsbach (68) 97 C4
Huningue (68) 97 E4
Hunspach (67) 25 C2
Hunting (57) 27 J3
Huos (31) 305 H1
Huparlac (12) 236 B4
Huppy (80) 9 F6
Hurbache (88) 95 H3
Hure (33) 230 C6
Hurecourt (70) 118 A3
Hures-la-Parade (48) 253 K4
Huriel (03) 167 G6
Hurigny (71) 171 J6
Hurtières (38) 224 D2
Hurtigheim (67) 70 D3
Husseren-les-Châteaux (68) . . . 96 B4
Husseren-Wesserling (68) 119 J3
Hussigny-Godbrange (54) 26 E3
Husson (50) 80 E1
Huttendorf (67) 69 K6
Huttenheim (67) 70 E6
Hyds (03) 184 C1
Hyémondans (25) 139 F4
Hyencourt-le-Grand (80) 19 F3
Hyenville (50) 30 D5
Hyères (83) 300 E4
Hyet (70) 138 A3
Hyèvre-Magny (25) 138 D4
Hyèvre-Paroisse (25) 138 D4
Hymont (88) 94 A4

I

Ibarrolle (64) 283 F5
Ibigny (57) 67 H5
Ibos (65) 285 G5
Ichtratzheim (67) 71 D2
Ichy (77) 87 G6
Idaux-Mendy (64) 283 H5
Idrac-Respaillès (32) 286 B1
Idron (64) 284 D4
Ids-Saint-Roch (18) 166 D2
Iffendic (35) 78 C4
les Iffs (35) 78 E2
Ifs (14) 32 E5
les Ifs (76) 16 C2
Igé (61) 83 H4
Igé (71) 171 J5
Ignaucourt (80) 18 D3
Ignaux (09) 313 F1
Igney (54) 67 G5
Igney (88) 94 C4
Ignol (18) 150 B4
Igny (70) 137 H3
Igny (91) 58 D5
Igny-Comblizy (51) 61 H1
Igon (64) 284 D4
Igornay (71) 153 F3
Igoville (27) 35 J3
Iguerande (71) 187 F2
Iholdy (64) 282 E4
Île-aux-Moines (56) 100 E6
l'Île-Bouchard (37) 145 H2
Île-d'Aix (17) 176 D4
Île-d'Arz (56) 101 F6
Île-de-Batz (29) 46 E2
Île-de-Bréhat (22) 48 E1
Île-de-Sein (29) 73 A6
l'Île-d'Elle (85) 160 C4
l'Île-d'Houat (56) 120 D3
l'Île-d'Olonne (85) 158 E3
l'Île-d'Yeu (85) 140 B6
Île-Molène (29) 72 A6
l'Île-Rousse (2B) 318 C2
l'Île-Saint-Denis (93) 58 E2
Île-Tudy (29) 98 C3
Ilharre (64) 283 G3
Ilhat (64) 308 H3
les Ilhes (11) 290 B4

Ilhet (65) 305 F3
Ilheu (65) 305 H2
Illange (57) 27 G4
Illartein (09) 306 B3
Illats (33) 229 K5
Ille-sur-Têt (66) 314 E2
Illeville-sur-Montfort (27) . . . 34 E3
Illfurth (68) 97 B3
Illhaeusern (68) 96 C2
Illiat (01) 188 D2
Illier-et-Laramade (09) 307 H1
Illiers-Combray (28) 84 E5
Illiers-l'Évêque (27) 56 E4
Illies (59) 6 B5
Illifaut (22) 77 K5
Illkirch-Graffenstaden (67) . . . 71 D2
Illois (76) 16 E4
Illoud (52) 93 F5
Illy (08) 23 F3
Illzach (68) 97 C2
Ilonse (06) 261 H5
Imbleville (76) 15 J4
Imécourt (08) 42 D2
Imling (57) 67 J4
Imphy (58) 151 F5
Inaumont (08) 21 K6
Incarville (27) 35 J4
Incheville (76) 8 D6
Inchy (59) 12 C5
Inchy-en-Artois (62) 11 H4
Incourt (62) 9 K1
Indevillers (25) 139 J4
Indre (44) 123 F4
Ineuil (18) 166 E1
les Infournas (05) 242 E3
Ingenheim (67) 70 D1
Ingersheim (68) 96 B4
Inghem (62) 5 G4
Inglange (57) 27 H4
Ingolsheim (67) 25 C2
Ingouville (76) 15 G2
Ingrandes (36) 164 B3
Ingrandes (49) 124 D4
Ingrandes (86) 145 J5
Ingrandes-de-Touraine (37) . . . 126 E6
Ingrannes (45) 110 D3
Ingré (45) 109 K4
Inguiniel (56) 100 B1
Ingwiller (67) 69 H5
Injoux-Génissiat (01) 190 C4
Innenheim (67) 70 D4
Innimond (01) 207 H1
Inor (55) 23 H6
Insming (57) 68 B4
Insviller (57) 67 H2
Intraville (76) 16 B1
Intres (07) 221 G6
Intréville (28) 86 A5
Intville-la-Guétard (45) 86 D5
Inval-Boiron (80) 17 F2
Inxent (62) 4 C5
Inzinzac-Lochrist (56) 100 B2
Ippécourt (55) 64 B1
Ippling (57) 68 D3
Irai (61) 55 J6
Irais (79) 144 C5
Irancy (89) 113 H6
Iré-le-Sec (55) 43 H1
Irigny (69) 206 A3
Irissarry (64) 282 E4
Irles (80) 10 E5
Irodouër (35) 78 D2
Iron (02) 20 D1
Irouléguy (64) 282 D5
Irreville (27) 35 J6
Irvillac (29) 74 C1
Is-en-Bassigny (52) 116 E2
Is-sur-Tille (21) 136 B3
Isbergues (62) 5 J4
Isches (88) 117 H2
Isdes (45) 130 D1
Isenay (58) 151 K5
Isigny-le-Buat (50) 52 B6
Isigny-sur-Mer (14) 29 H6
Island (89) 133 J3
Isle (87) 198 E2
l'Isle-Adam (95) 37 J6
l'Isle-Arné (32) 267 K6
Isle-Aubigny (10) 90 C2
Isle-Aumont (10) 90 B6
l'Isle-Bouzon (32) 267 K2
l'Isle-d'Abeau (38) 206 E3
l'Isle-de-Noé (32) 267 G6
l'Isle-d'Espagnac (16) 196 E3
l'Isle-en-Dodon (31) 287 F3
Isle-et-Bardais (03) 167 K2
l'Isle-Jourdain (32) 268 D6
l'Isle-Jourdain (86) 180 B2
Isle-Saint-Georges (33) 229 J3
l'Isle-sur-la-Sorgue (84) 276 D2
l'Isle-sur-le-Doubs (25) 139 F3
Isle-sur-Marne (51) 63 G6
l'Isle-sur-Serein (89) 134 A2
les Isles-Bardel (14) 53 K3
Isles-les-Meldeuses (77) 60 A2
Isles-lès-Villenoy (77) 59 J3
les Islettes (55) 42 E6
Isneauville (76) 35 J1
Isola (06) 261 H3
Isolaccio-di-Fiumorbo (2B) . . . 321 H4
Isômes (52) 136 C1
Ispagnac (48) 254 B2
Ispoure (64) 282 D5
Isques (62) 4 B3
Issac (24) 213 H6

Issamoulenc (07) 239 J3
Issancourt-et-Rumel (08) 22 E3
Issanlas (07) 238 D3
Issans (25) 139 G3
les Issards (09) 307 K1
Issarlès (07) 238 C3
Issé (44) 103 H3
Isse (51) 41 G6
Issel (11) 289 H4
Issendolus (46) 234 B3
Issenhausen (67) 69 J6
Issenheim (68) 96 B6
Issepts (46) 234 C4
Isserpent (03) 186 A3
Isserteaux (63) 203 G3
Issigeac (24) 231 J3
Issirac (30) 256 C5
Issoire (63) 202 E5
Issor (64) 283 K6
Issou (78) 57 K2
Issoudun (36) 148 C4
Issoudun-Létrieix (23) 183 F4
Issus (31) 288 C3
Issy-les-Moulineaux (92) 58 D4
Issy-l'Évêque (71) 170 A2
Istres (13) 295 J4
les Istres-et-Bury (51) 62 A2
Isturits (64) 282 E3
Itancourt (02) 20 A3
Iteuil (86) 162 E4
Ittenheim (67) 70 D3
Itterswiller (67) 70 C6
Itteville (91) 86 E2
Itxassou (64) 282 C3
Itzac (81) 270 B1
Ivergny (62) 10 B3
Iverny (77) 59 J2
Iviers (02) 21 H3
Iville (27) 35 G5
Ivors (60) 39 F5
Ivory (39) 156 A4
Ivoy-le-Pré (18) 131 F5
Ivrey (39) 156 A3
Ivry-en-Montagne (21) 153 J3
Ivry-la-Bataille (27) 57 G3
Ivry-le-Temple (60) 37 G4
Ivry-sur-Seine (94) 58 E4
Iwuy (59) 12 B3
Izaourt (65) 305 H2
Izaut-de-l'Hôtel (31) 305 K2
Izaux (65) 305 F1
Izé (53) 81 K5
Izeaux (38) 223 H4
Izel-lès-Équerchin (62) 11 G2
Izel-lès-Hameaux (62) 10 C2
Izenave (01) 189 K4
Izernore (01) 189 K2
Izeron (38) 223 H4
Izeste (64) 303 H1
Izeure (21) 154 D1
Izier (21) 136 C5
Izieu (01) 207 J3
Izon (33) 229 K1
Izon-la-Bruisse (26) 258 C2
Izotges (32) 266 B5

J

Jablines (77) 59 J3
Jabreilles-les-Bordes (87) . . . 181 K5
Jabrun (15) 236 D3
Jacob-Bellecombette (73) 208 B4
Jacou (34) 274 C5
Jacque (65) 285 J4
Jagny-sous-Bois (95) 38 A6
Jaignes (77) 60 B2
Jaillans (26) 223 F5
la Jaille-Yvon (49) 105 F6
Jaillon (54) 65 J4
Jailly (58) 151 H2
Jailly-les-Moulins (21) 135 G3
Jainvillotte (88) 93 G5
Jalesches (23) 183 F1
Jaleyrac (15) 217 G3
Jaligny-sur-Besbre (03) 169 H6
Jallais (49) 143 F1
Jallanges (21) 154 D3
Jallans (28) 109 F2
Jallaucourt (57) 66 C3
Jallerange (25) 137 H6
Jalognes (18) 150 A1
Jalogny (71) 171 H5
Jâlons (51) 62 B1
Jambles (71) 153 J6
Jambville (78) 57 K1
Jaméricourt (60) 37 F3
Jametz (55) 43 H1
Janailhac (87) 198 E4
Janaillat (23) 182 C4
Jancigny (21) 136 E4
Jandun (08) 22 B3
Janneyrias (38) 206 D2
Jans (44) 103 G5
Janville (28) 86 A4
Janville (60) 38 E2
Janville-sur-Juine (91) 86 D2
Janvilliers (51) 61 G3
Janvry (51) 40 D4
Janvry (91) 58 C5
Janzé (35) 79 H6
Jarcieu (38) 222 C1
la Jard (17) 195 G3

Jard-sur-Mer (85) 159 G4
le Jardin (19) 216 D2
Jardin (38) 206 D5
Jardres (86) 163 H3
Jargeau (45) 110 C4
Jarjayes (05) 242 E6
Jarménil (88) 94 E6
Jarnac (16) 196 A3
Jarnac-Champagne (17) 195 J4
Jarnages (23) 183 F3
la Jarne (17) 176 E3
Jarnioux (69) 188 A5
Jarnosse (42) 187 G3
Jarny (54) 44 C5
la Jarrie (17) 176 E3
Jarrie (38) 224 D4
la Jarrie-Audouin (17) 177 K4
Jarrier (73) 225 G2
Jars (18) 131 H5
Jarsy (73) 208 E3
Jarville-la-Malgrange (54) . . . 66 A5
Jarzé (49) 125 K2
Jas (42) 205 F2
Jasney (70) 118 B4
Jassans-Riottier (01) 188 B5
Jasseines (10) 90 D2
Jasseron (01) 189 H2
Jasses (64) 283 J4
Jatxou (64) 282 C2
Jau-Dignac-et-Loirac (33) 194 C6
Jaucourt (10) 91 G5
la Jaudonnière (85) 160 C2
Jaudrais (28) 84 D1
Jaujac (07) 239 G5
Jauldes (16) 197 F2
Jaulges (89) 113 J3
Jaulgonne (02) 40 A6
Jaulnay (37) 145 H4
Jaulnes (77) 88 D3
Jaulny (54) 65 H1
Jaulzy (60) 39 G2
Jaunac (07) 239 H1
Jaunay-Clan (86) 163 F2
Jaure (24) 213 J5
Jausiers (04) 260 D1
Jaux (60) 38 D2
Jauzé (72) 83 F6
Javaugues (43) 219 H2
Javené (35) 80 A4
Javerdat (87) 180 E5
Javerlhac-et-la-Chapelle-
  -Saint-Robert (24) 197 J4
Javernant (10) 90 A6
la Javie (04) 260 A4
Javols (48) 237 G4
Javrezac (16) 195 J2
Javron-les-Chapelles (53) 81 J3
Jax (43) 219 K4
Jaxu (64) 282 E5
Jayac (24) 215 G5
Jayat (01) 172 C6
Jazeneuil (86) 162 C4
Jazennes (17) 195 G4
Jeancourt (02) 19 J1
Jeandelaincourt (54) 66 B3
Jeandelize (54) 44 B5
Jeanménil (88) 95 F3
Jeansagnière (42) 204 A2
Jeantes (02) 21 H3
Jebsheim (68) 96 D3
Jegun (32) 267 G4
la Jemaye (24) 213 F4
Jenlain (59) 12 E2
Jenzat (03) 185 G3
Jésonville (88) 94 A6
Jessains (10) 91 F4
Jetterswiller (67) 70 C2
Jettingen (68) 97 C4
Jeu-les-Bois (36) 165 K2
Jeu-Maloches (36) 147 H3
Jeufosse (78) 57 G1
Jeugny (10) 114 A1
Jeumont (59) 13 J2
Jeurre (39) 173 H5
Jeux-lès-Bard (21) 134 C3
Jeuxey (88) 94 D5
Jevoncourt (54) 94 A2
Jezainville (54) 65 K2
Jézeau (65) 305 F3
Joannas (07) 239 G5
Job (63) 203 K4
Jobourg (50) 28 A1
Joch (66) 314 D3
Jœuf (54) 44 D4
Joganville (50) 29 F4
Joigny (89) 112 E2
Joigny-sur-Meuse (08) 22 D2
Joinville (52) 92 B2
Joinville-le-Pont (94) 59 F4
Joiselle (51) 61 F4
Jolimetz (59) 12 E3
Jolivet (54) 66 D6
Jonage (69) 206 C2
Joncels (34) 272 E5
la Jonchère (85) 159 J4
la Jonchère-Saint-Maurice (87) . 181 K5
Jonchères (26) 241 H5
Joncherey (90) 139 K2
Jonchery (52) 92 A6
Jonchery-sur-Suippe (51) 41 K5
Jonchery-sur-Vesle (51) 40 D4
Joncourt (02) 20 A1
Joncreuil (10) 91 F2
Joncy (71) 171 J3
Jongieux (73) 208 A2

Jonquerets-de-Livet (27) 55   J1
Jonquerettes (84) 276   C2
Jonquery (51) 40   D5
Jonquières (11) 310   B3
Jonquières (34) 273   H5
Jonquières (60) 38   D2
Jonquières (81) 270   D6
Jonquières (84) 257   F5
Jonquières-Saint-Vincent (30) . . . 275   J3
Jons (69) 206   D1
Jonval (08) 22   C6
Jonvelle (70) 117   J3
Jonville-en-Woëvre (55) 44   B6
Jonzac (17) 195   J6
Jonzier-Épagny (74) 190   E3
Jonzieux (42) 221   G2
Joppécourt (54) 26   D4
Jort (14) 54   B2
Jorxey (88) 94   B4
Josat (43) 219   K3
Joserand (63) 185   F5
Josnes (41) 109   G5
Josse (40) 262   D5
Josselin (56) 101   H1
Jossigny (77) 59   J4
Jou-sous-Monjou (15) 235   K1
Jouac (87) 164   E6
Jouaignes (02) 40   A3
Jouancy (89) 134   A1
Jouarre (77) 60   B2
Jouars-Pontchartrain (78) 58   A4
Jouaville (54) 44   D5
Joucas (84) 277   H4
Joucou (11) 308   D1
Joudes (71) 172   E4
Joudreville (54) 44   B3
Joué-du-Bois (61) 82   A1
Joué-du-Plain (61) 54   H4
Joué-en-Charnie (72) 106   A2
Joué-l'Abbé (72) 106   E1
Joué-lès-Tours (37) 127   J5
Joué-sur-Erdre (44) 103   J6
Jouet-sur-l'Aubois (18) 150   C3
Jouey (21) 153   G2
Jougne (25) 157   F6
Jouhe (39) 155   J1
Jouhet (86) 164   A4
Jouillat (23) 182   D2
Jouques (13) 278   A5
Jouqueviel (81) 251   G5
Jourgnac (87) 198   D3
Journans (01) 189   H3
Journet (86) 164   B5
Journiac (24) 214   A5
Journy (62) 4   E2
Jours-en-Vaux (21) 153   H4
Jours-lès-Baigneux (21) 135   G1
Joursac (15) 218   D4
Joussé (86) 179   K2
Jouvençon (71) 172   B3
Joux (69) 187   H6
Joux-la-Ville (89) 133   J2
Jouy (28) 85   G2
Jouy (89) 88   A6
Jouy-aux-Arches (57) 44   E6
Jouy-en-Argonne (55) 43   G5
Jouy-en-Josas (78) 58   C5
Jouy-en-Pithiverais (45) 110   C1
Jouy-le-Châtel (77) 60   B6
Jouy-le-Moutier (95) 58   B1
Jouy-le-Potier (45) 109   K6
Jouy-lès-Reims (51) 40   E4
Jouy-Mauvoisin (78) 57   H2
Jouy-sous-Thelle (60) 37   G3
Jouy-sur-Eure (27) 56   E1
Jouy-sur-Morin (77) 60   D4
Joyeuse (07) 255   J1
Joyeux (01) 189   F5
Joze (63) 203   F1
Jû-Belloc (32) 266   C6
Juaye-Mondaye (14) 32   B4
Jubainville (88) 93   G2
la Jubaudière (49) 142   E1
Jublains (53) 81   H5
le Juch (29) 74   B4
Jugazan (33) 230   B3
Jugeals-Nazareth (19) 215   G5
Jugon-les-Lacs (22) 50   A6
Jugy (71) 171   K3
Juicq (17) 177   K6
Juif (71) 172   C2
Juignac (16) 212   F1
Juigné-des-Moutiers (44) 104   A6
Juigné-sur-Loire (49) 125   H4
Juigné-sur-Sarthe (72) 105   H4
Juignettes (27) 55   J3
Juillac (19) 215   G2
Juillac (32) 285   J1
Juillac (33) 230   D2
Juillac-le-Coq (16) 195   K4
Juillaguet (16) 196   E5
Juillan (65) 285   G5
Juillé (16) 179   G5
Juillé (72) 82   D5
Juillé (79) 178   D4
Juillenay (21) 134   D5
Juilles (32) 268   A6
Juilley (50) 51   K4
Juilly (21) 134   E3
Juilly (77) 59   H1
Jujols (66) 314   A3
Jujurieux (01) 189   J4
Julianges (48) 237   G1
Juliénas (69) 188   B2
Julienne (16) 196   A3
Jullianges (43) 220   B2

Jullié (69) 188   B2
Jullouville (50) 51   H2
Jully (89) 114   D6
Jully-lès-Buxy (71) 171   F3
Jully-sur-Sarce (10) 114   D1
Julos (65) 285   G6
Julvécourt (55) 43   G6
Jumeauville (78) 57   K3
Jumeaux (63) 203   F6
Jumel (80) 18   B4
Jumelles (27) 56   D3
la Jumellière (49) 124   E5
Jumencourt (02) 39   J1
Jumièges (76) 35   F2
Jumigny (02) 40   C2
Jumilhac-le-Grand (24) 198   D5
Junas (30) 274   E4
Junay (89) 113   K4
Juncalas (65) 304   G1
Jungholtz (68) 96   A6
Junhac (15) 235   H4
les Junies (46) 233   F3
Juniville (08) 41   J2
Jupilles (72) 107   F5
Jurançon (64) 284   C3
Juranville (45) 111   F2
Juré (42) 186   D6
Jurignac (16) 196   C5
Jurques (14) 53   F1
Jurvielle (31) 305   G4
Jury (57) 45   F6
Juscorps (79) 178   B2
Jusix (47) 230   E2
Jussac (15) 217   H6
Jussarupt (88) 95   G3
Jussas (17) 211   K2
Jussecourt-Minecourt (51) 63   H4
Jussey (70) 117   J4
Jussy (02) 19   K4
Jussy (57) 44   E5
Jussy (89) 113   G6
Jussy-Champagne (18) 149   J4
Jussy-le-Chaudrier (18) 150   B2
Justian (32) 267   F2
Justine-Herbigny (08) 21   K5
Justiniac (09) 288   C5
Jutigny (77) 88   C2
Juvaincourt (88) 93   K4
Juvancourt (10) 115   H1
Juvanzé (10) 91   H4
Juvardeil (49) 125   H3
Juvelize (57) 66   E4
Juvignac (34) 274   B6
Juvigné (53) 80   C5
Juvignies (60) 37   H1
Juvigny (02) 39   J2
Juvigny (51) 62   C1
Juvigny (74) 191   G1
Juvigny-en-Perthois (55) 64   B6
Juvigny-le-Tertre (50) 52   C5
Juvigny-sous-Andaine (61) 81   H1
Juvigny-sur-Loison (55) 43   H1
Juvigny-sur-Orne (61) 54   C5
Juvigny-sur-Seulles (14) 32   C5
Juville (57) 66   C2
Juvinas (07) 239   G4
Juvincourt-et-Damary (02) 40   D2
Juvisy-sur-Orge (91) 58   E5
Juvrecourt (54) 66   E4
Juxue (64) 283   F5
Juzanvigny (10) 91   F3
Juzennecourt (52) 91   K6
Juzes (31) 289   F4
Juzet-de-Luchon (31) 305   H5
Juzet-d'Izaut (31) 305   K3
Juziers (78) 57   K2

K

Kalhausen (57) 68   C4
Kaltenhouse (67) 25   B4
Kanfen (57) 27   G3
Kappelen (68) 97   D4
Kappelkinger (57) 68   C4
Katzenthal (68) 96   B3
Kauffenheim (67) 25   C3
Kaysersberg (68) 96   B3
Kédange-sur-Canner (57) 45   G3
Keffenach (67) 25   B3
Kembs (68) 97   D3
Kemplich (57) 27   J4
Kerbach (57) 68   C2
Kerbors (22) 48   C2
Kerfot (22) 48   E3
Kerfourn (56) 77   F6
Kergloff (29) 75   H3
Kergrist (56) 76   E5
Kergrist-Moëlou (22) 76   B2
Kerien (22) 76   C1
Kerlaz (29) 74   B4
Kerling-lès-Sierck (57) 27   J3
Kerlouan (29) 46   B3
Kermaria-Sulard (22) 48   B2
Kermoroc'h (22) 48   B2
Kernascléden (56) 76   A6
Kernilis (29) 46   A4
Kernouës (29) 46   A4
Kerpert (22) 76   C2
Kerprich-aux-Bois (57) 67   H4
Kersaint-Plabennec (29) 46   B5
Kertzfeld (67) 70   D6
Kervignac (56) 100   B3
Keskastel (67) 68   D4

Kesseldorf (67) 25   D3
Kienheim (67) 70   D4
Kientzheim (68) 96   B3
Kiffis (68) 97   C6
Killem (59) 3   K2
Kilstett (67) 25   B5
Kindwiller (67) 69   J5
Kingersheim (68) 97   C2
Kintzheim (67) 96   C2
Kirchberg (68) 119   J4
Kirchheim (67) 70   D4
Kirrberg (67) 67   J3
Kirrwiller-Bosselshausen (67) . . . 69   J4
Kirsch-lès-Sierck (57) 27   J3
Kirschnaumen (57) 27   K3
Kirviller (57) 68   C4
Klang (57) 27   J4
Kleingœft (67) 70   C2
Knœringue (68) 97   C4
Knœrsheim (67) 70   C2
Knutange (57) 27   F4
Kœnigsmacker (57) 27   H4
Kœstlach (68) 97   B5
Kœtzingue (68) 97   C3
Kœur-la-Grande (55) 64   D3
Kœur-la-Petite (55) 64   F3
Kogenheim (67) 70   D6
Kolbsheim (67) 70   D3
Krautergersheim (67) 70   D4
Krautwiller (67) 70   E1
le Kremlin-Bicêtre (94) 58   E4
Kriegsheim (67) 25   A4
Kruth (68) 119   J2
Kunheim (68) 96   C4
Kuntzig (57) 27   H1
Kurtzenhouse (67) 25   B5
Kuttolsheim (67) 70   D3
Kutzenhausen (67) 25   B2

L

Laà-Mondrans (64) 283   J2
Laas (32) 286   A2
Laas (45) 110   D1
Laàs (64) 283   H3
Labalme (01) 189   J3
Labarde (33) 211   G4
Labaroche (68) 96   A3
Labarrère (32) 266   D2
Labarthe (32) 286   C2
Labarthe (82) 249   J4
Labarthe-Bleys (81) 250   F6
Labarthe-Inard (31) 306   A1
Labarthe-Rivière (31) 305   J1
Labarthe-sur-Lèze (31) 288   D2
Labarthète (32) 266   A6
Labassère (65) 304   C1
Labastide (65) 305   F2
Labastide-Beauvoir (31) 288   E2
Labastide-Castel-Amouroux (47) . 247   G1
Labastide-Cézéracq (64) 284   B3
Labastide-Chalosse (40) 265   F6
Labastide-Clermont (31) 287   J1
Labastide-d'Anjou (11) 289   F4
Labastide-d'Armagnac (40) 266   A1
Labastide-de-Lévis (81) 270   C1
Labastide-de-Penne (82) 250   B3
Labastide-de-Virac (07) 256   A2
Labastide-Dénat (81) 270   E1
Labastide-du-Haut-Mont (46) . . . 234   C2
Labastide-du-Temple (82) 249   H6
Labastide-du-Vert (46) 233   F6
Labastide-en-Val (11) 309   H1
Labastide-Esparbairenque (11) . . 290   B3
Labastide-Gabausse (81) 270   D1
Labastide-Marnhac (46) 249   K2
Labastide-Monréjeau (64) 284   B3
Labastide-Murat (46) 233   J5
Labastide-Paumès (31) 287   G4
Labastide-Rouairoux (81) 290   C4
Labastide-Saint-Georges (81) . . . 270   B5
Labastide-Saint-Pierre (82) 269   G2
Labastide-Saint-Sernin (31) 269   H5
Labastide-Savès (32) 287   H1
Labastide-sur-Bésorgues (07) . . . 239   G3
Labastide-Villefranche (64) 283   G2
Labastidette (31) 287   K2
Labathude (46) 234   D3
Labatie-d'Andaure (07) 221   J5
Labatmale (64) 285   F5
Labatut (09) 288   C5
Labatut (40) 264   B6
Labatut (64) 285   G3
Labatut-Rivière (65) 285   H1
Labbeville (95) 37   H6
Labeaume (07) 255   J1
Labécède-Lauragais (11) 289   H3
Labège (31) 288   C1
Labégude (07) 239   H4
Labéjan (32) 286   C1
Labenne (40) 262   C3
Labergement-du-Navois (25) . . . 156   C3
Labergement-Foigney (21) 136   C6
Labergement-lès-Auxonne (21) . . 155   F1
Labergement-lès-Seurre (21) . . . 154   C2
Labergement-Sainte-Marie (25) . . 156   F6
Laberlière (60) 19   F6
Labescau (33) 246   E1
Labesserette (15) 235   H4
Labessette (63) 201   H6
Labessière-Candeil (81) 270   C4
Labets-Biscay (64) 283   F3
Labeuville (55) 44   B5

Labeuvrière (62) 5   K5
Labeyrie (64) 284   A1
Lablachère (07) 255   J1
Laboissière-en-Santerre (80) . . . 18   E4
Laboissière-en-Thelle (60) 37   H4
Laborde (65) 304   G2
Laborel (26) 258   C5
Labosse (60) 37   F3
Labouheyre (40) 245   F1
Laboulbène (81) 270   E4
Laboule (07) 239   F5
Labouquerie (24) 232   A3
Labourgade (82) 268   D2
Labourse (62) 6   A6
Laboutarie (81) 270   C4
Labretonie (47) 247   H1
Labrihe (32) 268   A5
Labrit (40) 245   K5
Labroquère (31) 305   H2
Labrosse (45) 86   E5
Labrousse (15) 235   J2
Labroye (62) 9   G2
Labruguière (81) 290   A1
Labruyère (21) 154   C2
Labruyère (60) 38   B5
Labruyère-Dorsa (31) 288   C3
Labry (54) 44   C4
Laburgade (46) 250   A1
Lac-des-Rouges-Truites (39) . . . 174   A2
le Lac-d'Issarlès (07) 238   C3
Lacabarède (81) 290   D4
Lacadée (64) 284   A1
Lacajunte (40) 265   H6
Lacalm (12) 236   C3
Lacam-d'Ourcet (46) 234   D2
Lacanau (33) 210   A5
Lacanche (21) 153   H3
Lacapelle-Barrès (15) 236   A1
Lacapelle-Biron (47) 232   C5
Lacapelle-Cabanac (46) 249   G1
Lacapelle-del-Fraisse (15) 235   H3
Lacapelle-Livron (82) 250   D4
Lacapelle-Marival (46) 234   C4
Lacapelle-Pinet (81) 251   J6
Lacapelle-Ségalar (81) 251   F6
Lacapelle-Viescamp (15) 235   F1
Lacarre (64) 282   E5
Lacarry-Arhan-Charritte-
  -de-Haut (64) 302   C1
Lacassagne (65) 285   J3
Lacaugne (31) 287   J3
Lacaune (81) 271   K5
Lacaussade (47) 232   B6
Lacave (09) 306   C2
Lacave (46) 233   J2
Lacaze (81) 271   H5
Lacelle (19) 200   A4
Lacenas (69) 188   A4
Lacépède (47) 247   K3
Lachaise (16) 196   A5
Lachalade (55) 42   D5
Lachambre (57) 68   A3
Lachamp (48) 237   H5
Lachamp-Raphaël (07) 239   G2
Lachapelle (47) 231   F5
Lachapelle (54) 95   J2
Lachapelle (80) 17   H3
Lachapelle (82) 268   C1
Lachapelle-aux-Pots (60) 37   F2
Lachapelle-Auzac (46) 233   H1
Lachapelle-en-Blaisy (52) 91   K6
Lachapelle-Graillouse (07) 238   C2
Lachapelle-Saint-Pierre (60) 37   J4
Lachapelle-sous-Aubenas (07) . . 239   H4
Lachapelle-sous-Chanéac (07) . . 239   G1
Lachapelle-sous-Chaux (90) 119   H5
Lachapelle-sous-Gerberoy (60) . . 17   F3
Lachapelle-sous-Rougemont (90) . 119   J5
Lachassagne (69) 188   B5
Lachau (26) 258   C4
Lachaussée (55) 44   C6
Lachaussée-du-Bois-d'Écu (60) . . 17   J4
Lachaux (63) 186   A5
Lachelle (60) 38   C2
Lachy (51) 61   H4
Lacollonge (90) 119   J6
Lacombe (11) 289   K3
Lacommande (64) 284   B4
Lacoste (34) 273   H6
Lacoste (84) 277   H4
Lacougotte-Cadoul (81) 270   A6
Lacour (82) 248   E1
Lacour-d'Arcenay (21) 134   C3
Lacourt (09) 306   D3
Lacourt-Saint-Pierre (82) 269   F2
Lacq (64) 284   A2
Lacquy (40) 265   K2
Lacrabe (40) 265   F6
Lacres (62) 4   C4
Lacroisille (81) 289   F1
Lacroix-Barrez (12) 235   K4
Lacroix-Falgarde (31) 288   B2
Lacroix-Saint-Ouen (60) 38   D3
Lacroix-sur-Meuse (55) 64   E1
Lacropte (24) 214   C4
Lacrost (71) 172   A3
Lacrouzette (81) 271   G6
Lacs (36) 166   D3
Ladapeyre (23) 183   J1
Ladaux (33) 230   A1
Ladern-sur-Lauquet (11) 309   G1
Ladevèze-Rivière (32) 285   J1
Ladevèze-Ville (32) 285   H1
Ladignac-le-Long (87) 198   D4
Ladignac-sur-Rondelles (19) . . . 216   B3
Ladinhac (15) 235   J3

Ladirat (46) 234   C3
Ladiville (16) 196   B5
Ladoix-Serrigny (21) 154   A3
Ladon (45) 111   G3
Lados (33) 246   D1
Ladoye-sur-Seille (39) 155   G3
Laduz (89) 112   E4
Lafage (11) 289   G6
Lafage-sur-Sombre (19) 216   C2
Lafare (84) 257   G5
Lafarre (07) 221   J5
Lafarre (43) 238   C2
Lafat (23) 182   A1
Lafauche (52) 92   C4
Laféline (03) 168   C4
Laferté-sur-Amance (52) 117   G4
Laferté-sur-Aube (52) 115   H1
Lafeuillade-en-Vézie (15) 235   H3
Laffaux (02) 39   K2
Laffite-Toupière (31) 287   G6
Laffrey (38) 224   B5
Lafitole (65) 285   H2
Lafitte (82) 268   D2
Lafitte-sur-Lot (47) 247   K2
Lafitte-Vigordane (31) 287   J4
Lafox (47) 248   C5
Lafrançaise (82) 249   H5
Lafraye (60) 37   J1
Lafresguimont-Saint-Martin (80) . . 17   G3
Lafrimbolle (57) 67   J6
Lagamas (34) 273   J5
Lagarde (09) 308   D2
Lagarde (31) 288   E4
Lagarde (32) 267   F2
Lagarde (57) 67   F4
Lagarde (65) 285   H4
Lagarde-d'Apt (84) 277   J1
Lagarde-Enval (19) 216   B4
Lagarde-Hachan (32) 286   C2
Lagarde-Paréol (84) 256   E4
Lagarde-sur-le-Né (16) 196   A5
Lagardelle (31) 288   B3
Lagardelle-sur-Lèze (31) 288   B3
Lagardère (32) 267   F3
Lagardiolle (81) 289   J2
Lagarrigue (47) 247   J3
Lagarrigue (81) 290   A1
Lageon (79) 161   K1
Lagery (51) 40   C5
Lagesse (10) 114   B2
Lagleygeolle (19) 216   A5
Laglorieuse (40) 265   H2
Lagnes (84) 276   E2
Lagney (54) 65   H4
Lagnicourt-Marcel (62) 11   G4
Lagnieu (01) 189   H1
Lagny (60) 19   G5
Lagny-le-Sec (60) 38   D6
Lagny-sur-Marne (77) 59   H3
Lagor (64) 284   A3
Lagorce (07) 256   A1
Lagorce (33) 212   B5
Lagord (17) 176   D2
Lagos (64) 284   E5
Lagrâce-Dieu (31) 288   B4
Lagrand (05) 258   C2
Lagrange (40) 266   B1
Lagrange (65) 286   A6
Lagrange (90) 119   J6
Lagrasse (11) 309   H1
Lagraulet-du-Gers (32) 266   E2
Lagraulet-Saint-Nicolas (31) 268   D4
Lagraulière (19) 215   K2
Lagrave (81) 270   C2
Lagruère (47) 247   H2
Laguenne (19) 216   A3
Laguépie (82) 251   F5
Laguian-Mazous (32) 285   K3
Laguinge-Restoue (64) 302   C1
Laguiole (12) 236   C3
Lagupie (47) 230   E5
Lahage (31) 287   H2
Lahas (32) 287   G1
Lahaymeix (55) 64   C2
Lahayville (55) 65   G2
Laheycourt (55) 63   K3
Lahitère (31) 287   K6
Lahitte (32) 267   J5
Lahitte-Toupière (65) 285   G2
Lahonce (64) 282   C1
Lahontan (64) 283   G1
Lahosse (40) 264   D4
Lahourcade (64) 284   A3
Lahoussoye (80) 18   C1
Laifour (08) 22   C1
la Laigne (17) 177   H2
Laigné (53) 104   E4
Laigné-en-Belin (72) 106   E4
Laignelet (35) 80   B3
Laignes (21) 114   C4
Laigneville (60) 38   B4
Laigny (02) 21   F2
Laillé (35) 79   F6
Lailly (89) 89   F5
Lailly-en-Val (45) 109   J4
Laimont (55) 63   K3
Lain (89) 132   E2
Laines-aux-Bois (10) 90   A5
Lains (39) 173   H5
Lainsecq (89) 132   D3
Lainville-en-Vexin (78) 57   K1
Laire (25) 139   G2
Laires (62) 5   F5
Lairière (11) 309   H1
Lairoux (85) 159   H4
Laissac (12) 252   E2

Laissaud (73) . . . 208 C5
Laissey (25) . . . 138 C5
Laître-sous-Amance (54) . . . 66 B4
Laives (71) . . . 171 K4
Laix (54) . . . 26 D3
Laiz (01) . . . 188 D1
Laizé (71) . . . 171 J5
Laize-la-Ville (14) . . . 32 E6
Laizy (71) . . . 152 E5
Lajo (48) . . . 237 H2
Lajoux (39) . . . 174 A5
Lalacelle (61) . . . 82 B2
Lalande (89) . . . 132 D1
Lalande-de-Pomerol (33) . . . 212 D5
Lalande-en-Son (60) . . . 36 E2
Lalandelle (60) . . . 37 E2
Lalandusse (47) . . . 231 J4
Lalanne (32) . . . 267 J4
Lalanne (65) . . . 286 C5
Lalanne-Arqué (32) . . . 286 D4
Lalanne-Trie (65) . . . 286 A4
Lalaye (67) . . . 96 B1
Lalbarède (81) . . . 270 D6
Lalbenque (46) . . . 250 B3
Laleu (61) . . . 83 F1
Laleu (80) . . . 17 H1
Lalevade-d'Ardèche (07) . . . 239 G4
Lalheue (71) . . . 171 J4
Lalinde (24) . . . 232 D4
Lalizolle (03) . . . 184 E3
Lallaing (59) . . . 11 J1
Lalleu (35) . . . 103 J4
Lalley (38) . . . 242 A3
Lalleyriat (01) . . . 190 B2
Lalobbe (08) . . . 22 A4
Lalœuf (54) . . . 93 K2
Lalongue (64) . . . 284 E4
Lalonquette (64) . . . 284 D3
Laloubère (65) . . . 285 H5
Lalouret-Laffiteau (31) . . . 286 E6
Lalouvesc (07) . . . 221 J4
Laluque (40) . . . 264 B3
Lama (2B) . . . 319 F2
Lamadeleine-Val-des-Anges (90) . . . 119 G6
Lamagdelaine (46) . . . 250 A1
Lamagistère (82) . . . 248 E6
Lamaguère (32) . . . 286 D2
Lamaids (03) . . . 183 J1
Lamalou-les-Bains (34) . . . 272 D6
Lamancine (52) . . . 92 A5
Lamanère (66) . . . 314 E6
Lamanon (13) . . . 276 E5
Lamarche (88) . . . 117 H1
Lamarche-sur-Saône (21) . . . 136 D6
Lamargelle (21) . . . 135 J2
Lamaronde (80) . . . 17 H3
Lamarque (33) . . . 211 F4
Lamarque-Pontacq (65) . . . 285 F6
Lamarque-Rustaing (65) . . . 285 J6
Lamasquère (31) . . . 287 J2
Lamastre (07) . . . 221 K6
Lamath (54) . . . 94 D1
Lamativie (46) . . . 234 C1
Lamayou (64) . . . 285 G3
Lamazère (32) . . . 286 E1
Lamazière-Basse (19) . . . 216 E1
Lamazière-Haute (19) . . . 201 H5
Lambach (57) . . . 69 G3
Lamballe (22) . . . 77 H3
Lambersart (59) . . . 6 D4
Lamberville (50) . . . 31 K4
Lamberville (76) . . . 15 J4
Lambesc (13) . . . 277 F5
Lamblore (28) . . . 56 B6
Lambres (62) . . . 5 H4
Lambres-lez-Douai (59) . . . 11 H2
Lambrey (70) . . . 117 J5
Lambruisse (04) . . . 260 B5
Laméac (65) . . . 285 K4
Lamécourt (60) . . . 38 A2
Lamelouze (30) . . . 255 F4
Lamenay-sur-Loire (58) . . . 169 G1
Lamérac (16) . . . 196 A6
Lametz (08) . . . 22 D6
Lamillarié (81) . . . 270 C4
Lammerville (76) . . . 15 J4
Lamnay (72) . . . 107 J3
Lamongerie (19) . . . 199 J5
Lamontélarié (81) . . . 271 J4
Lamontgie (63) . . . 203 F6
Lamontjoie (47) . . . 248 D5
Lamonzie-Montastruc (24) . . . 231 J2
Lamonzie-Saint-Martin (24) . . . 231 G2
Lamorlaye (60) . . . 38 A5
Lamorville (55) . . . 64 D1
Lamothe (40) . . . 265 F3
Lamothe (43) . . . 219 H2
Lamothe-Capdeville (82) . . . 249 H6
Lamothe-Cassel (46) . . . 233 J6
Lamothe-Cumont (82) . . . 268 D2
Lamothe-en-Blaisy (52) . . . 91 K5
Lamothe-Fénelon (46) . . . 233 H4
Lamothe-Goas (32) . . . 267 H3
Lamothe-Landerron (33) . . . 230 D4
Lamothe-Montravel (24) . . . 230 D2
Lamotte-Beuvron (41) . . . 130 B2
Lamotte-Brebière (80) . . . 18 B2
Lamotte-Buleux (80) . . . 9 G4
Lamotte-du-Rhône (84) . . . 256 D3
Lamotte-Warfusée (80) . . . 18 C2
Lamouilly (55) . . . 23 H5
Lamoura (39) . . . 174 A5
Lampaul-Guimiliau (29) . . . 46 D5
Lampaul-Plouarzel (29) . . . 72 B3
Lampaul-Ploudalmézeau (29) . . . 72 C2
Lampertheim (67) . . . 25 A6

Lampertsloch (67) . . . 25 A2
Lamure-sur-Azergues (69) . . . 187 K4
Lanans (25) . . . 138 E5
Lanarce (07) . . . 238 C1
Lanarvily (29) . . . 46 C4
Lanas (07) . . . 239 H5
Lancé (41) . . . 128 C3
Lanchères (80) . . . 8 D4
Lanches-Saint-Hilaire (80) . . . 9 J5
Lanchy (02) . . . 19 K4
Lancié (69) . . . 188 B3
Lancieux (22) . . . 50 D4
Lancôme (41) . . . 128 C3
Lançon (08) . . . 42 C4
Lançon (65) . . . 305 F2
Lançon-Provence (13) . . . 276 E5
Lancrans (01) . . . 190 C1
Landange (57) . . . 67 H5
Landas (59) . . . 7 G6
Landaul (56) . . . 100 C4
Landaville (88) . . . 93 G4
Landavran (35) . . . 79 K4
la Lande-Chasles (49) . . . 126 B1
la Lande-d'Airou (50) . . . 52 A3
la Lande-de-Fronsac (33) . . . 211 K6
la Lande-de-Goult (61) . . . 82 C1
la Lande-de-Lougé (61) . . . 54 A5
la Lande-Patry (61) . . . 53 H3
la Lande-Saint-Léger (27) . . . 34 C3
la Lande-Saint-Siméon (61) . . . 53 J4
la Lande-sur-Drôme (14) . . . 31 K4
la Lande-sur-Eure (61) . . . 84 A1
Landéan (35) . . . 80 A2
Landebaëron (22) . . . 48 C3
Landébia (22) . . . 50 A4
la Landec (22) . . . 50 B5
Landécourt (54) . . . 94 C1
Landéda (29) . . . 72 C2
Landéhen (22) . . . 77 K3
Landeleau (29) . . . 75 J3
Landelles (28) . . . 84 E1
Landelles-et-Coupigny (14) . . . 52 D2
Landemont (49) . . . 123 K3
Landepéreuse (27) . . . 55 J1
Landerneau (29) . . . 46 D5
Landeronde (85) . . . 159 J3
Landerrouat (33) . . . 230 E3
Landerrouet-sur-Ségur (33) . . . 230 E4
Landersheim (67) . . . 70 C2
Landes (17) . . . 177 J4
les Landes-Genusson (85) . . . 142 C4
Landes-le-Gaulois (41) . . . 128 C3
Landes-sur-Ajon (14) . . . 32 C6
Landes-Vieilles-et-Neuves (76) . . . 16 E4
Landévant (56) . . . 100 C4
Landévennec (29) . . . 74 D4
Landevieille (85) . . . 158 E3
Landeyrat (15) . . . 218 C3
Landifay-et-Bertaignemont (02) . . . 20 C3
Landigou (61) . . . 53 H4
le Landin (27) . . . 35 F2
Landiras (33) . . . 229 J4
Landisacq (61) . . . 53 G4
Landivisiau (29) . . . 46 E4
Landivy (53) . . . 80 C2
Landogne (63) . . . 201 H3
Landorthe (31) . . . 286 C5
Landos (43) . . . 238 C2
Landouzy-la-Cour (02) . . . 21 G3
Landouzy-la-Ville (02) . . . 21 G3
Landrais (17) . . . 177 G2
le Landreau (44) . . . 123 K4
Landrecies (59) . . . 12 E5
Landrecourt-Lempire (55) . . . 43 H6
Landremont (54) . . . 66 A3
Landres (54) . . . 44 B4
Landres-et-Saint-Georges (08) . . . 42 E2
Landresse (25) . . . 138 D5
Landrethun-le-Nord (62) . . . 2 C4
Landrethun-lès-Ardres (62) . . . 2 D4
Landrévarzec (29) . . . 74 D5
Landreville (10) . . . 114 E5
Landrichamps (08) . . . 24 D1
Landricourt (02) . . . 39 J1
Landricourt (51) . . . 63 F6
Landroff (57) . . . 66 E1
Landry (73) . . . 209 H2
Landser (68) . . . 97 C3
Landudal (29) . . . 74 E5
Landudec (29) . . . 74 B5
Landujan (35) . . . 78 D2
Landunvez (29) . . . 72 B2
Lanespède (65) . . . 285 J5
Lanester (56) . . . 100 B4
Lanet (11) . . . 309 F2
Laneuvelle (52) . . . 117 G3
Laneuvelotte (54) . . . 66 B4
Laneuveville-aux-Bois (54) . . . 67 F4
Laneuveville-derrière-Foug (54) . . . 65 J4
Laneuveville-devant-Bayon (54) . . . 94 B2
Laneuveville-devant-Nancy (54) . . . 66 B4
Laneuveville-en-Saulnois (57) . . . 66 D2
Laneuveville-lès-Lorquin (57) . . . 67 G4
Laneuville-au-Pont (52) . . . 63 G3
Laneuville-au-Rupt (55) . . . 64 E4
Laneuville-sur-Meuse (55) . . . 43 H2
Lanfains (22) . . . 76 E4
Lanfroicourt (54) . . . 66 C3
Langan (35) . . . 78 E2
Langast (22) . . . 77 G4
Langatte (57) . . . 67 G3
Langé (36) . . . 147 H3
Langeac (43) . . . 219 G4
Langeais (37) . . . 127 F4
Langensoultzbach (67) . . . 69 G1
Langeron (58) . . . 150 D6

Langesse (45) . . . 111 H5
Langey (28) . . . 108 D2
Langlade (30) . . . 275 G4
Langley (88) . . . 94 C3
Langoat (22) . . . 48 B3
Langoëlan (56) . . . 76 B3
Langogne (48) . . . 238 C4
Langoiran (33) . . . 229 J3
Langolen (29) . . . 74 E5
Langon (33) . . . 230 A5
Langon (35) . . . 102 E4
Langon (41) . . . 129 K6
le Langon (85) . . . 160 C5
Langonnet (56) . . . 75 J3
Langouet (35) . . . 78 E2
Langourla (22) . . . 77 K3
Langres (52) . . . 116 D4
Langrolay-sur-Rance (22) . . . 50 D4
Langrune-sur-Mer (14) . . . 32 E3
Languédias (22) . . . 50 B6
Languenan (22) . . . 50 C5
Langueux (22) . . . 49 G6
Languevoisin-Quiquery (80) . . . 19 G4
Languidic (56) . . . 100 C3
Languimberg (57) . . . 67 G4
Langy (03) . . . 185 J1
Lanhélin (35) . . . 51 F5
Lanhères (55) . . . 44 B4
Lanhouarneau (29) . . . 46 C4
Lanildut (29) . . . 72 B3
Laning (57) . . . 68 B4
Laniscat (22) . . . 76 C3
Laniscourt (02) . . . 20 C6
Lanleff (22) . . . 48 D3
Lanloup (22) . . . 48 E3
Lanmérin (22) . . . 48 B3
Lanmeur (29) . . . 47 H4
Lanmodez (22) . . . 48 D1
Lanne (65) . . . 285 G6
Lanne-en-Barétous (64) . . . 283 G4
Lanne-Soubiran (32) . . . 266 A4
Lannéanou (29) . . . 47 H6
Lannebert (22) . . . 48 E4
Lannecaube (64) . . . 284 E2
Lannédern (29) . . . 75 F2
Lannemaignan (32) . . . 265 K2
Lannemezan (65) . . . 305 J1
Lannepax (32) . . . 266 E4
Lanneplaà (64) . . . 283 J2
Lanneray (28) . . . 108 E2
Lannes (47) . . . 267 F1
Lanneuffret (29) . . . 46 C5
Lannilis (29) . . . 72 D2
Lannion (22) . . . 48 A3
Lannoy (59) . . . 7 F4
Lannoy-Cuillère (60) . . . 17 F4
Lannux (32) . . . 265 K5
Lano (2B) . . . 319 G5
Lanobre (15) . . . 201 H6
Lanouaille (24) . . . 214 E1
Lanouée (56) . . . 101 H1
Lanoux (09) . . . 307 G1
Lanquais (24) . . . 231 K2
Lanques-sur-Rognon (52) . . . 116 D1
Lanquetot (76) . . . 14 E5
Lanrelas (22) . . . 78 A2
Lanrigan (35) . . . 51 G6
Lanrivain (22) . . . 76 C2
Lanrivoaré (29) . . . 72 C3
Lanrodec (22) . . . 48 D6
Lans (71) . . . 154 B4
Lans-en-Vercors (38) . . . 223 K4
Lansac (33) . . . 211 H5
Lansac (65) . . . 285 J5
Lansac (66) . . . 309 J5
Lansargues (34) . . . 274 D6
Lanslebourg-Mont-Cenis (73) . . . 226 C1
Lanslevillard (73) . . . 226 C1
Lanta (31) . . . 288 E1
Lantabat (64) . . . 283 F4
Lantages (10) . . . 114 C2
Lantan (18) . . . 149 K5
Lantéfontaine (54) . . . 44 C4
Lantenay (01) . . . 189 K4
Lantenay (21) . . . 135 J5
Lantenne-Vertière (25) . . . 137 J5
Lantenot (70) . . . 118 E5
la Lanterne-et-les-Armonts (70) . . . 118 E4
Lanteuil (19) . . . 216 A3
Lanthenans (25) . . . 139 F4
Lanthes (21) . . . 154 D1
Lantheuil (14) . . . 32 D4
Lantic (22) . . . 49 F5
Lantignié (69) . . . 188 B3
Lantillac (56) . . . 101 G1
Lantilly (21) . . . 134 E2
Lanton (33) . . . 228 C3
Lantosque (06) . . . 311 A4
Lantriac (43) . . . 220 D6
Lanty (58) . . . 152 A6
Lanty-sur-Aube (52) . . . 115 H2
Lanuéjols (30) . . . 253 K5
Lanuéjols (48) . . . 254 B1
Lanuéjouls (12) . . . 251 J2
Lanvallay (22) . . . 50 D5
Lanvaudan (56) . . . 100 B2
Lanvellec (22) . . . 47 K4
Lanvénégen (56) . . . 99 J1
Lanvéoc (29) . . . 74 A2
Lanvollon (22) . . . 48 E4
Lanzac (46) . . . 233 H2
Laon (02) . . . 20 D4
Laons (28) . . . 56 D5
Lapalisse (03) . . . 186 A2
Lapalud (84) . . . 256 D3
Lapan (18) . . . 149 F5

Lapanouse (12) . . . 253 G3
Lapanouse-de-Cernon (12) . . . 272 D1
Laparade (47) . . . 247 K2
Laparrouquial (81) . . . 251 F6
Lapège (09) . . . 307 H5
Lapenche (82) . . . 250 B4
Lapenne (09) . . . 288 E6
Lapenty (50) . . . 52 C6
Laperche (47) . . . 231 H1
Laperrière-sur-Saône (21) . . . 155 F2
Lapeyre (65) . . . 286 A5
Lapeyrère (31) . . . 288 A5
Lapeyrouse (01) . . . 188 E5
Lapeyrouse (63) . . . 184 D2
Lapeyrouse-Fossat (31) . . . 269 H5
Lapeyrouse-Mornay (26) . . . 222 D3
Lapeyrugue (15) . . . 235 J4
Lapleau (19) . . . 216 E2
Laplume (47) . . . 248 A5
Lapoutroie (68) . . . 96 A3
Lapouyade (33) . . . 212 A4
Lappion (02) . . . 21 G5
Laprade (11) . . . 290 A3
Laprade (16) . . . 213 F2
Laprugne (03) . . . 186 B5
Laps (63) . . . 203 F3
Lapte (43) . . . 221 F3
Lapugnoy (62) . . . 5 K5
Laquenexy (57) . . . 45 G6
Laqueuille (63) . . . 201 K4
Laragne-Montéglin (05) . . . 258 E6
Larajasse (69) . . . 205 H4
Laramière (46) . . . 250 E3
Laran (65) . . . 286 B5
Larbey (40) . . . 264 E4
Larbont (09) . . . 307 G2
Larbroye (60) . . . 19 G6
Larcan (31) . . . 286 E6
Larcat (09) . . . 307 J5
Larçay (37) . . . 127 K5
Larceveau-Arros-Cibits (64) . . . 283 F5
Larchamp (53) . . . 80 C3
Larchamp (61) . . . 53 F5
Larchant (77) . . . 87 G5
Larche (04) . . . 227 C6
Larche (19) . . . 215 H4
le Larderet (39) . . . 156 B5
Lardier-et-Valença (05) . . . 259 G1
Lardiers (04) . . . 258 D6
le Lardin-Saint-Lazare (24) . . . 215 F4
Lardy (91) . . . 86 D2
Larée (32) . . . 266 B2
Laréole (31) . . . 268 C5
Largeasse (79) . . . 161 G3
Largentière (07) . . . 239 G6
Largillay-Marsonnay (39) . . . 173 H3
Largitzen (68) . . . 97 B5
Largny-sur-Automne (02) . . . 39 F4
Larians-et-Munans (70) . . . 138 C3
Larivière (90) . . . 119 J6
Larivière-Arnoncourt (52) . . . 117 G2
Larmor-Baden (56) . . . 100 E6
Larmor-Plage (56) . . . 99 K5
Larnage (26) . . . 222 C4
Larnagol (46) . . . 250 D1
Larnas (07) . . . 256 C1
Larnat (09) . . . 307 J5
Larnaud (39) . . . 173 F1
Larnod (25) . . . 156 B1
Laroche-près-Feyt (19) . . . 201 H3
Laroche-Saint-Cydroine (89) . . . 113 F4
Larochemillay (58) . . . 152 C5
Larodde (63) . . . 201 H5
Laroin (64) . . . 284 C4
Laronxe (54) . . . 94 E1
Laroque (33) . . . 229 K4
Laroque (34) . . . 274 C4
Laroque-de-Fa (11) . . . 309 J3
Laroque-des-Albères (66) . . . 315 H4
Laroque-des-Arcs (46) . . . 250 A1
Laroque-d'Olmes (09) . . . 308 D3
Laroque-Timbaut (47) . . . 248 D3
Laroquebrou (15) . . . 217 F6
Laroquevieille (15) . . . 217 J6
Larouillies (59) . . . 13 G6
Larra (31) . . . 268 E5
Larrau (64) . . . 302 E1
Larrazet (82) . . . 268 D2
Larré (56) . . . 101 H4
Larré (61) . . . 82 D2
Larressingle (32) . . . 267 F2
Larressore (64) . . . 282 C3
Larret (70) . . . 137 F1
Larreule (64) . . . 284 C2
Larreule (65) . . . 285 G5
Larrey (21) . . . 114 E4
Larribar-Sorhapuru (64) . . . 283 G4
Larringes (74) . . . 175 G5
Larrivière (40) . . . 265 H4
Larrivoire (39) . . . 173 J6
Larroque (31) . . . 286 D6
Larroque (65) . . . 286 B4
Larroque (81) . . . 269 K1
Larroque-Engalin (32) . . . 267 H1
Larroque-Saint-Sernin (32) . . . 267 G3
Larroque-sur-l'Osse (32) . . . 266 E2
Larroque-Toirac (46) . . . 234 C6
Lartigue (32) . . . 286 E1
Lartigue (33) . . . 246 E4
Laruns (64) . . . 303 H2
Laruscade (33) . . . 211 K4
Larzac (24) . . . 232 D3
Larzicourt (51) . . . 63 D3
Lasalle (30) . . . 254 E6
Lasbordes (11) . . . 289 H4
Lascabanes (46) . . . 249 J3

Lascaux (19) . . . 215 G2
Lascazères (65) . . . 285 G1
Lascelle (15) . . . 217 J6
Lasclaveries (64) . . . 284 D2
Lasfaillades (81) . . . 290 C1
Lasgraisses (81) . . . 270 C4
Laslades (65) . . . 285 J5
Lassales (65) . . . 286 B5
Lassay-les-Châteaux (53) . . . 81 H3
Lassay-sur-Croisne (41) . . . 129 H5
Lasse (49) . . . 126 C2
Lasse (64) . . . 282 D5
Lasserade (32) . . . 266 C6
Lasséran (32) . . . 267 H6
Lasserre (09) . . . 306 D1
Lasserre (31) . . . 268 E6
Lasserre (47) . . . 247 K5
Lasserre (64) . . . 285 F1
Lasserre-de-Prouille (11) . . . 289 J6
Lasseube (64) . . . 284 B5
Lasseube-Propre (32) . . . 286 D1
Lasseubetat (64) . . . 284 C6
Lassicourt (10) . . . 90 E3
Lassigny (60) . . . 19 F6
Lasson (14) . . . 32 D4
Lasson (89) . . . 113 J2
Lassouts (12) . . . 252 E1
Lassur (09) . . . 307 K5
Lassy (14) . . . 53 G2
Lassy (35) . . . 78 E6
Lassy (95) . . . 38 A6
Lastic (15) . . . 219 F4
Lastic (63) . . . 201 J3
Lastours (11) . . . 290 B4
Lataule (60) . . . 18 E6
le Latet (39) . . . 156 B6
la Latette (39) . . . 156 C6
Lathuile (74) . . . 208 E1
Lathus-Saint-Rémy (86) . . . 164 B6
Latillé (86) . . . 162 C3
Latilly (02) . . . 39 J5
Latoue (31) . . . 286 E6
Latouille-Lentillac (46) . . . 234 C2
Latour (31) . . . 288 A6
Latour-Bas-Elne (66) . . . 315 H3
Latour-de-Carol (66) . . . 313 G5
Latour-de-France (66) . . . 309 K5
Latour-en-Woëvre (55) . . . 44 B6
Latrape (31) . . . 288 A5
Latrecey-Ormoy-sur-Aube (52) . . . 115 J3
Latresne (33) . . . 229 H2
Latrille (40) . . . 265 J6
Latronche (19) . . . 217 F2
Latronquière (46) . . . 234 E3
Lattainville (60) . . . 36 E4
Lattes (34) . . . 293 H1
Lattre-Saint-Quentin (62) . . . 10 D3
Lau-Balagnas (65) . . . 304 A2
Laubach (67) . . . 69 K5
Laubert (48) . . . 237 K5
les Laubies (48) . . . 237 H4
Laubressel (10) . . . 90 C4
Laubrières (53) . . . 104 B3
Laucourt (80) . . . 19 F5
Laudrefang (57) . . . 45 K5
Laudun-l'Ardoise (30) . . . 256 C5
Laugnac (47) . . . 248 B3
Laujuzan (32) . . . 266 A3
Laulne (50) . . . 30 E1
Laumesfeld (57) . . . 27 K4
Launac (31) . . . 268 E4
Launaguet (31) . . . 269 G5
Launay (27) . . . 34 E6
Launay-Villiers (53) . . . 80 C6
Launois-sur-Vence (08) . . . 22 B5
Launstroff (57) . . . 27 K3
la Laupie (26) . . . 240 C5
Laurabuc (11) . . . 289 H5
Laurac (11) . . . 289 H5
Laurac-en-Vivarais (07) . . . 239 G6
Lauraët (32) . . . 266 E2
Lauraguel (11) . . . 308 E1
Laurède (40) . . . 264 C4
Laurenan (22) . . . 77 J4
Laurens (34) . . . 291 K2
Lauresses (46) . . . 234 E3
Lauret (34) . . . 274 C3
Lauret (40) . . . 284 D1
Laurie (15) . . . 218 E2
Laurière (87) . . . 181 K4
Lauris (84) . . . 277 G4
Lauroux (34) . . . 273 F4
Laussonne (43) . . . 220 D6
Laussou (47) . . . 232 B5
Lautenbach (68) . . . 96 A6
Lautenbachzell (68) . . . 96 A6
Lauterbourg (67) . . . 25 E2
Lauthiers (86) . . . 163 J3
Lautignac (31) . . . 287 H3
Lautrec (81) . . . 270 C5
Lauw (68) . . . 119 K5
Lauwin-Planque (59) . . . 11 H1
Lauzach (56) . . . 101 H6
Lauzerte (82) . . . 249 G4
Lauzerville (31) . . . 288 D1
Lauzès (46) . . . 233 J6
le Lauzet-Ubaye (04) . . . 260 A1
Lauzun (47) . . . 231 H3
Lavacquerie (60) . . . 17 J4
Laval (38) . . . 224 C2
Laval (53) . . . 104 E1
Laval-Atger (48) . . . 238 A3
Laval-d'Aix (26) . . . 241 H3
Laval-d'Aurelle (07) . . . 238 D6

Laval-de-Cère (46) . . . 234 C1
Laval-du-Tarn (48) . . . 253 K3
Laval-en-Brie (77) . . . 88 A3
Laval-en-Laonnois (02) . . . 40 B1
Laval-le-Prieuré (25) . . . 139 F6
Laval-Morency (08) . . . 22 B2
Laval-Pradel (30) . . . 255 G4
Laval-Roquecézière (12) . . . 271 K4
Laval-Saint-Roman (30) . . . 256 H3
Laval-sur-Doulon (43) . . . 219 J1
Laval-sur-Luzège (19) . . . 216 E3
Laval-sur-Tourbe (51) . . . 42 B5
Laval-sur-Vologne (88) . . . 95 F5
Lavalade (24) . . . 232 B4
Lavaldens (38) . . . 224 C5
Lavalette (11) . . . 290 A6
Lavalette (31) . . . 269 J6
Lavalette (34) . . . 273 F5
Lavallée (55) . . . 64 C3
Lavancia-Epercy (39) . . . 173 H6
le Lavandou (83) . . . 301 G4
Lavangeot (39) . . . 155 H1
Lavannes (51) . . . 41 G3
Lavans-lès-Dole (39) . . . 155 H1
Lavans-lès-Saint-Claude (39) . . . 173 J5
Lavans-Quingey (25) . . . 156 A2
Lavans-sur-Valouse (39) . . . 173 G6
Lavans-Vuillafans (25) . . . 156 D2
Lavaqueresse (02) . . . 20 D1
Lavardac (47) . . . 247 J5
Lavardens (32) . . . 267 H4
Lavardin (41) . . . 108 A6
Lavardin (72) . . . 106 C1
Lavaré (72) . . . 107 J2
Lavars (39) . . . 242 A1
Lavastrie (15) . . . 236 D1
Lavatoggio (2B) . . . 318 C3
Lavau (10) . . . 90 B4
Lavau (89) . . . 132 A2
Lavau-sur-Loire (44) . . . 122 C3
Lavaudieu (43) . . . 219 H3
Lavaufranche (23) . . . 183 H1
Lavault-de-Frétoy (58) . . . 152 C2
Lavault-Sainte-Anne (03) . . . 184 A1
Lavaur (24) . . . 232 D5
Lavaur (81) . . . 270 A5
Lavaurette (82) . . . 250 C4
Lavausseau (86) . . . 162 C3
Lavaveix-les-Mines (23) . . . 183 F4
Lavazan (33) . . . 246 C2
Laveissenet (15) . . . 218 C5
Laveissière (15) . . . 218 B4
Lavelanet (09) . . . 308 H3
Lavelanet-de-Comminges (31) . . . 287 J5
Laveline-devant-Bruyères (88) . . . 95 G5
Laveline-du-Houx (88) . . . 95 H6
Lavenay (72) . . . 107 J5
Laventie (62) . . . 6 B4
Laveraët (32) . . . 285 J1
Lavercantière (46) . . . 233 G5
Laverdines (18) . . . 150 A3
Lavergne (46) . . . 234 A3
Lavergne (47) . . . 231 G5
Lavernat (72) . . . 107 F6
Lavernay (25) . . . 137 H6
Lavernhe (12) . . . 253 F3
Lavernose-Lacasse (31) . . . 287 K3
Lavernoy (52) . . . 117 F3
Laverrière (60) . . . 17 J4
Laversine (02) . . . 39 H3
Laversines (60) . . . 37 J2
Lavérune (34) . . . 293 G1
Laveyron (26) . . . 222 B3
Laveyrune (07) . . . 238 C5
Laveyssière (24) . . . 231 H1
Lavieu (42) . . . 204 C5
Laviéville (80) . . . 10 D6
Lavigerie (15) . . . 218 A4
Lavignac (87) . . . 198 D3
Lavigney (70) . . . 117 H6
Lavigny (39) . . . 173 G1
Lavillatte (07) . . . 238 C5
Laville-aux-Bois (52) . . . 116 C1
Lavilledieu (07) . . . 239 J3
Lavilleneuve (52) . . . 116 E2
Lavilletertre (60) . . . 37 F5
Lavincourt (55) . . . 64 B5
Laviolle (07) . . . 239 G3
Laviron (25) . . . 139 F5
Lavit (82) . . . 268 B2
Lavoine (03) . . . 186 B5
Lavoncourt (70) . . . 137 H1
Lavours (01) . . . 207 K1
Lavoûte-Chilhac (43) . . . 219 H4
Lavoûte-sur-Loire (43) . . . 220 C4
Lavoux (86) . . . 163 G3
Lavoye (55) . . . 43 F6
Lawarde-Mauger-l'Hortoy (80) . . . 18 A4
Laxou (54) . . . 66 A5
Lay (42) . . . 187 G5
Lay-Lamidou (64) . . . 283 K4
Lay-Saint-Christophe (54) . . . 66 A4
Lay-Saint-Remy (54) . . . 65 G5
Laye (05) . . . 242 E4
Laymont (32) . . . 287 G3
Layrac (47) . . . 248 C5
Layrac-sur-Tarn (31) . . . 269 H3
Layrisse (65) . . . 285 H6
Lays-sur-le-Doubs (71) . . . 154 E4
Laz (29) . . . 75 F4
Lazenay (18) . . . 148 D3
Lazer (05) . . . 258 E2
Léalvillers (80) . . . 10 C5
Léaupartie (14) . . . 33 H5
Léaz (01) . . . 190 D3
Lebetain (90) . . . 139 J2

Lebeuville (54) . . . 94 B2
Lebiez (62) . . . 4 E6
Leboulin (32) . . . 267 J5
Lebreil (46) . . . 249 H3
Lebucquière (62) . . . 11 G5
Lécaude (14) . . . 33 J6
Lecci (2A) . . . 323 H2
Lecelles (59) . . . 7 G6
Lecey (52) . . . 116 E4
Lechâtelet (21) . . . 154 D3
Léchelle (62) . . . 11 G5
Léchelle (77) . . . 88 E1
la Léchère (73) . . . 209 H4
les Lèches (24) . . . 213 G6
Lécluse (59) . . . 11 H3
Lécousse (35) . . . 80 A3
Lecques (30) . . . 274 D3
Lect (39) . . . 173 H5
Lectoure (32) . . . 267 J2
Lecumberry (64) . . . 282 E6
Lécussan (31) . . . 286 C6
Lédas-et-Penthiès (81) . . . 251 K6
Lédat (47) . . . 248 C1
Lédenon (30) . . . 275 J2
Lédergues (12) . . . 252 K6
Lederzeele (59) . . . 3 G4
Ledeuix (64) . . . 284 A5
Lédignan (30) . . . 274 E1
Ledinghem (62) . . . 4 E4
Ledringhem (59) . . . 3 J4
Lée (64) . . . 284 D4
Leers (59) . . . 7 F3
Lées-Athas (64) . . . 303 F2
Lefaux (62) . . . 4 B5
Leffard (14) . . . 53 K2
Leffincourt (08) . . . 41 K2
Leffonds (52) . . . 116 B3
Leffrinckoucke (59) . . . 3 H1
Leforest (62) . . . 11 H1
Lège (31) . . . 305 H4
Legé (44) . . . 141 H4
Lège-Cap-Ferret (33) . . . 228 B2
Légéville-et-Bonfays (88) . . . 94 A5
Léglantiers (60) . . . 38 B1
Légna (39) . . . 173 G5
Légny (69) . . . 188 A6
Léguevin (31) . . . 268 E6
Léguillac-de-Cercles (24) . . . 213 J1
Léguillac-de-l'Auche (24) . . . 213 J3
Lehaucourt (02) . . . 19 K1
Léhon (22) . . . 50 D5
Leigné-les-Bois (86) . . . 163 J1
Leigné-sur-Usseau (86) . . . 145 H5
Leignes-sur-Fontaine (86) . . . 163 K4
Leigneux (42) . . . 204 C2
Leimbach (68) . . . 119 K4
Leintrey (54) . . . 67 F5
Lélex (01) . . . 174 A6
Lelin-Lapujolle (32) . . . 266 A5
Lelling (57) . . . 68 A4
Lemainville (54) . . . 94 B1
Lembach (67) . . . 25 A1
Lemberg (57) . . . 69 G4
Lembeye (64) . . . 285 F2
Lembras (24) . . . 231 J1
Lemé (02) . . . 20 E2
Lème (64) . . . 284 D2
Leménil-Mitry (54) . . . 94 B2
Lémeré (37) . . . 145 G2
Lemmecourt (88) . . . 93 G5
Lemmes (55) . . . 43 G6
Lemoncourt (57) . . . 66 C2
Lempaut (81) . . . 289 J2
Lempdes (63) . . . 202 E2
Lempdes-sur-Allagnon (43) . . . 219 F1
Lempire (02) . . . 11 J6
Lemps (07) . . . 222 B4
Lemps (26) . . . 258 A2
Lempty (63) . . . 203 F1
Lempzours (24) . . . 214 B1
Lemud (57) . . . 45 G6
Lemuy (39) . . . 156 B4
Lénault (14) . . . 53 G2
Lenax (03) . . . 186 C1
Lencloître (86) . . . 145 G6
Lencouacq (40) . . . 246 B5
Lengelsheim (57) . . . 69 G2
Lengronne (50) . . . 30 D6
Lenharrée (51) . . . 62 B4
Léning (57) . . . 68 B5
Lennon (29) . . . 75 F3
Lenoncourt (54) . . . 66 B5
Lens (62) . . . 11 F1
Lens-Lestang (26) . . . 222 D2
Lent (01) . . . 189 G3
Lent (39) . . . 156 B6
Lentigny (42) . . . 186 E5
Lentillac-du-Causse (46) . . . 233 K6
Lentillac-Saint-Blaise (46) . . . 234 E5
Lentillères (07) . . . 239 G5
Lentilles (10) . . . 91 F2
Lentilly (69) . . . 205 J1
Lentiol (38) . . . 222 E2
Lento (2B) . . . 319 G3
Léobard (46) . . . 233 G4
Léogeats (33) . . . 229 K6
Léognan (33) . . . 229 G3
Léojac (82) . . . 269 G1
Léon (40) . . . 262 D2
Léoncel (26) . . . 241 F1
Léotoing (43) . . . 219 F1
Léouville (45) . . . 86 C6
Léoville (17) . . . 211 K1
Lépanges-sur-Vologne (88) . . . 95 F5
Lépaud (23) . . . 183 J2
Lépin-le-Lac (73) . . . 208 A4

Lépinas (23) . . . 182 D4
Lépine (62) . . . 9 F1
Lépron-les-Vallées (08) . . . 22 A3
Lepuix (90) . . . 119 H5
Lepuix-Neuf (90) . . . 97 A5
Léran (09) . . . 308 B3
Lercoul (09) . . . 307 H5
Léré (18) . . . 131 K4
Lérigneux (42) . . . 204 C4
Lerm-et-Musset (33) . . . 246 D3
Lerné (37) . . . 144 E2
Lérouville (55) . . . 64 E4
Lerrain (88) . . . 94 A6
Léry (21) . . . 135 J2
Léry (27) . . . 35 J4
Lesbœufs (80) . . . 11 F6
Lesbois (53) . . . 80 E2
Lescar (64) . . . 284 C4
Leschaux (74) . . . 208 D1
Leschelles (02) . . . 20 E1
Lescheraines (73) . . . 208 D2
Leschères (39) . . . 173 J4
Leschères-sur-le-Blaiseron (52) . . . 92 A4
Lescherolles (77) . . . 60 D5
Lescheroux (01) . . . 172 C5
Lesches (77) . . . 59 J3
Lesches-en-Diois (26) . . . 241 J5
Lescouët-Gouarec (22) . . . 76 B4
Lescousse (09) . . . 288 C6
Lescout (81) . . . 289 J1
Lescun (64) . . . 303 F3
Lescuns (31) . . . 287 H5
Lescure (09) . . . 306 E2
Lescure-d'Albigeois (81) . . . 270 E2
Lescure-Jaoul (12) . . . 251 H4
Lescurry (65) . . . 285 J4
Lesdain (59) . . . 12 B5
Lesdins (02) . . . 20 A2
Lesges (02) . . . 40 A3
Lesgor (40) . . . 264 C3
Lesme (71) . . . 169 J2
Lesménils (54) . . . 65 K2
Lesmont (10) . . . 90 E3
Lesneven (29) . . . 46 B4
Lesparre-Médoc (33) . . . 210 D2
Lesparrou (09) . . . 308 B3
Lespéron (07) . . . 238 C3
Lesperon (40) . . . 264 B1
Lespesses (62) . . . 5 J5
Lespielle (64) . . . 285 F2
Lespignan (34) . . . 291 K5
Lespinasse (31) . . . 269 G5
Lespinassière (11) . . . 290 D3
Lespinoy (62) . . . 9 G1
Lespiteau (31) . . . 305 K1
Lespouey (65) . . . 285 J5
Lespourcy (64) . . . 285 F3
Lespugue (31) . . . 286 D5
Lesquerde (66) . . . 309 H5
Lesquielles-Saint-Germain (02) . . . 20 D1
Lesquin (59) . . . 6 E4
Lessac (16) . . . 180 B4
Lessard-en-Bresse (71) . . . 172 B1
Lessard-et-le-Chêne (14) . . . 33 J6
Lessard-le-National (71) . . . 154 A5
Lessay (50) . . . 30 D2
Lesse (57) . . . 66 D1
Lesseux (88) . . . 95 K4
Lessy (57) . . . 44 E5
Lestanville (76) . . . 15 J4
Lestards (19) . . . 200 B5
Lestelle-Bétharram (64) . . . 284 E6
Lestelle-de-Saint-Martory (31) . . . 306 B1
Lesterps (16) . . . 180 C5
Lestiac-sur-Garonne (33) . . . 229 K4
Lestiou (41) . . . 109 H5
Lestrade-et-Thouels (12) . . . 252 C6
Lestre (50) . . . 29 F4
Lestrem (62) . . . 6 A4
Létanne (08) . . . 23 G6
Léteton (03) . . . 167 H2
Léthuin (28) . . . 85 K4
Letia (2A) . . . 320 C2
Létra (69) . . . 187 K5
Létricourt (54) . . . 66 B2
Letteguives (27) . . . 36 A2
Lettret (05) . . . 242 E6
Leubringhen (62) . . . 2 B4
Leuc (11) . . . 290 B6
Leucamp (15) . . . 235 J3
Leucate (11) . . . 310 D4
Leuchey (52) . . . 116 C6
Leudeville (91) . . . 86 E1
Leudon-en-Brie (77) . . . 60 D5
Leuglay (21) . . . 115 H5
Leugny (86) . . . 146 A5
Leugny (89) . . . 132 E1
Leuhan (29) . . . 75 G5
Leuilly-sous-Coucy (02) . . . 39 J1
Leulinghem (62) . . . 5 F3
Leulinghen-Bernes (62) . . . 2 B4
Leurville (52) . . . 92 D4
Leury (02) . . . 39 J2
Leuville-sur-Orge (91) . . . 86 D1
Leuvrigny (51) . . . 40 C6
le Leuy (40) . . . 265 F3
Leuze (02) . . . 21 H2
Levainville (28) . . . 85 J2
Leval (59) . . . 13 F4

Leval (90) . . . 119 J5
Levallois-Perret (92) . . . 58 E3
Levaré (53) . . . 80 D3
Levécourt (52) . . . 93 F6
Levens (06) . . . 281 G5
Levergies (02) . . . 20 A1
Levernois (21) . . . 154 A3
Lèves (28) . . . 85 G2
les Lèves-et-
-Thoumeyragues (33) . . . 230 E3
Levesville-la-Chenard (28) . . . 85 K5
Levet (18) . . . 149 G5
Levie (2A) . . . 323 G2
Levier (25) . . . 156 C4
Lévignac (31) . . . 268 E5
Lévignac-de-Guyenne (47) . . . 230 E5
Lévignacq (40) . . . 244 D6
Lévignen (60) . . . 38 E5
Lévigny (10) . . . 91 G4
Levis (89) . . . 132 D1
Lévis-Saint-Nom (78) . . . 58 A5
Levoncourt (55) . . . 64 C3
Levoncourt (68) . . . 97 B6
Levroux (36) . . . 147 J4
Lewarde (59) . . . 11 J2
Lexy (54) . . . 26 C2
Ley (57) . . . 67 F4
Leychert (09) . . . 307 K3
Leyme (46) . . . 234 C3
Leymen (68) . . . 97 D5
Leyment (01) . . . 189 K5
Leynes (71) . . . 188 B1
Leynhac (15) . . . 235 G3
Leyr (54) . . . 66 B3
Leyrat (23) . . . 166 E6
Leyrieu (38) . . . 206 E4
Leyritz-Moncassin (47) . . . 247 G3
Leyssard (01) . . . 189 J2
Leyvaux (15) . . . 218 E2
Leyviller (57) . . . 68 B4
Lez (31) . . . 305 J3
Lez-Fontaine (59) . . . 13 J4
Lézan (30) . . . 274 D1
Lézardrieux (22) . . . 48 D3
Lézat (39) . . . 174 A4
Lézat-sur-Lèze (09) . . . 288 A5
Lezay (79) . . . 178 E1
Lezennes (59) . . . 6 E4
Lézéville (52) . . . 92 D3
Lezey (57) . . . 66 E4
Lézignan (65) . . . 304 B1
Lézignan-Corbières (11) . . . 291 F6
Lézignan-la-Cèbe (34) . . . 292 C2
Lézigné (49) . . . 125 K1
Lézigneux (42) . . . 204 D4
Lézinnes (89) . . . 114 B5
Lezoux (63) . . . 203 G1
Lhéraule (60) . . . 37 F1
Lherm (31) . . . 287 K3
Lherm (46) . . . 233 F6
Lhéry (51) . . . 40 C5
Lhez (65) . . . 285 J5
Lhommaizé (86) . . . 163 H5
Lhomme (72) . . . 107 H6
Lhôpital (01) . . . 190 C4
Lhor (57) . . . 67 G2
Lhospitalet (46) . . . 249 K2
Lhoumois (79) . . . 162 A1
Lhuis (01) . . . 207 H2
Lhuître (10) . . . 90 C1
Lhuys (02) . . . 40 A4
Liac (65) . . . 285 H3
Liancourt (60) . . . 38 A3
Liancourt-Fosse (80) . . . 19 F4
Liancourt-Saint-Pierre (60) . . . 37 F4
Liart (08) . . . 21 K3
Lias (32) . . . 287 J1
Lias-d'Armagnac (32) . . . 266 B3
Liausson (34) . . . 273 G6
Libaros (65) . . . 286 A5
Libercourt (62) . . . 6 D6
Libermont (60) . . . 19 H4
Libourne (33) . . . 230 A1
Licey-sur-Vingeanne (21) . . . 136 D3
Lichans-Sunhar (64) . . . 302 C1
Lichères (16) . . . 179 G6
Lichères-près-Aigremont (89) . . . 113 J6
Lichères-sur-Yonne (89) . . . 133 G3
Lichos (64) . . . 283 H4
Lichtenberg (67) . . . 69 H5
Licourt (80) . . . 19 G3
Licq-Athérey (64) . . . 302 C1
Licques (62) . . . 2 D4
Licy-Clignon (02) . . . 39 J6
Lidrezing (57) . . . 67 F2
Liebenswiller (68) . . . 97 D5
Liebsdorf (68) . . . 97 B6
Liebvillers (25) . . . 139 H4
Liederschiedt (57) . . . 69 H2
Lieffrans (70) . . . 137 K2
le Liège (37) . . . 146 E1
Liéhon (57) . . . 66 E1
Liencourt (62) . . . 10 C3
Lièpvre (68) . . . 96 B1
Liéramont (80) . . . 11 H6
Liercourt (80) . . . 9 G6
Lières (62) . . . 5 H5
Liergues (69) . . . 188 B5
Liernais (21) . . . 152 E1
Liernolles (03) . . . 169 A6
Lierval (02) . . . 40 B1
Lierville (60) . . . 37 F5
Lies (65) . . . 304 D1
Liesle (25) . . . 155 K2
Liesse-Notre-Dame (02) . . . 20 E5
Liessies (59) . . . 13 J5

Liesville-sur-Douve (50) . . . 29 H6
Liettres (62) . . . 5 H4
Lieu-Saint-Amand (59) . . . 12 B3
Lieuche (06) . . . 261 G6
Lieucourt (70) . . . 137 G5
Lieudieu (38) . . . 206 E5
Lieurac (09) . . . 308 A3
Lieuran-Cabrières (34) . . . 292 C1
Lieuran-lès-Béziers (34) . . . 292 A3
Lieurey (27) . . . 34 C4
Lieuron (35) . . . 102 D1
Lieusaint (50) . . . 28 E4
Lieusaint (77) . . . 59 G6
Lieutadès (15) . . . 236 C2
Lieuvillers (60) . . . 38 B1
Liévans (70) . . . 138 C1
Liévin (62) . . . 10 E1
Liez (02) . . . 20 A4
Liez (85) . . . 160 E5
Liézey (88) . . . 95 G6
Liffol-le-Grand (88) . . . 93 F4
Liffol-le-Petit (52) . . . 92 F4
Liffré (35) . . . 79 H3
Ligardes (32) . . . 248 A6
Ligescourt (80) . . . 9 G3
Liginiac (19) . . . 217 G1
Liglet (86) . . . 164 C4
Lignac (36) . . . 164 D5
Lignairolles (11) . . . 308 C1
Lignan-de-Bazas (33) . . . 246 C1
Lignan-de-Bordeaux (33) . . . 229 J2
Lignan-sur-Orb (34) . . . 291 K3
Lignareix (19) . . . 201 F4
Ligné (16) . . . 179 F6
Ligné (44) . . . 123 J2
Lignères (61) . . . 55 F5
Lignereuil (62) . . . 10 C3
Lignerolles (03) . . . 184 A1
Lignerolles (21) . . . 115 J4
Lignerolles (27) . . . 56 E3
Lignerolles (36) . . . 166 C4
Lignerolles (61) . . . 83 H1
Ligneville (88) . . . 93 J6
Ligneyrac (19) . . . 215 K5
Lignières (10) . . . 113 K3
Lignières (18) . . . 166 D1
Lignières (41) . . . 108 D4
Lignières (80) . . . 18 E5
Lignières-Châtelain (80) . . . 17 G3
Lignières-de-Touraine (37) . . . 127 F6
Lignières-en-Vimeu (80) . . . 17 F2
Lignières-la-Carelle (72) . . . 82 E3
Lignières-Orgères (53) . . . 82 A1
Lignières-Sonneville (16) . . . 196 A4
Lignières-sur-Aire (55) . . . 64 D4
Lignol (56) . . . 76 B6
Lignol-le-Château (10) . . . 91 H4
Lignon (51) . . . 91 F1
Lignorelles (89) . . . 113 H4
Lignou (61) . . . 53 K5
Ligny-en-Barrois (55) . . . 64 C5
Ligny-en-Brionnais (71) . . . 187 G2
Ligny-en-Cambrésis (59) . . . 12 C5
Ligny-le-Châtel (89) . . . 113 H4
Ligny-le-Ribault (45) . . . 129 J1
Ligny-lès-Aire (62) . . . 5 H5
Ligny-Saint-Flochel (62) . . . 10 B2
Ligny-sur-Canche (62) . . . 10 A3
Ligny-Thilloy (62) . . . 11 F5
Ligré (37) . . . 145 G2
Ligron (72) . . . 106 C5
Ligsdorf (68) . . . 97 C6
Ligueil (37) . . . 146 B3
Ligueux (24) . . . 214 B2
Ligueux (33) . . . 231 F3
Lihons (80) . . . 19 F3
Lihus (60) . . . 17 J5
les Lilas (93) . . . 59 F3
Lilhac (31) . . . 287 F4
Lille (59) . . . 6 D4
Lillebonne (76) . . . 14 E6
Lillemer (35) . . . 50 E4
Lillers (62) . . . 5 J5
Lilly (27) . . . 36 C2
Limalonges (79) . . . 179 G3
Limans (04) . . . 278 A1
Limanton (58) . . . 151 K4
Limas (69) . . . 188 B5
Limay (78) . . . 57 J2
Limbrassac (09) . . . 308 B2
Limé (02) . . . 40 A3
Limeil-Brévannes (94) . . . 59 F5
Limendous (64) . . . 284 E4
Limeray (37) . . . 128 C4
Limersheim (67) . . . 70 E5
Limerzel (56) . . . 101 K6
Limésy (76) . . . 15 J5
Limeuil (24) . . . 232 C2
Limeux (18) . . . 148 D3
Limeux (80) . . . 9 G6
Limey-Remenauville (54) . . . 65 H2
Limeyrat (24) . . . 214 D4
Limoges (87) . . . 199 F1
Limoges-Fourches (77) . . . 59 H6
Limogne-en-Quercy (46) . . . 250 D2
Limoise (58) . . . 168 B2
Limon (58) . . . 151 G4
Limonest (69) . . . 206 A1
Limons (63) . . . 185 J5
Limont-Fontaine (59) . . . 13 G3
Limony (07) . . . 222 A1
Limours (91) . . . 58 C6
Limousis (11) . . . 290 B4
Limoux (11) . . . 308 E2

la Limouzinière – Luchapt

377

la Limouzinière (44) 141 H3
Limpiville (76) 14 E4
Linac (46) 234 E4
Linard (23) 166 A6
Linards (87) 199 H3
Linars (16) 196 D3
Linas (91) 58 D6
Linay (08) 23 H5
Linazay (86) 179 G3
Lindebeuf (76) 15 H4
le Lindois (16) 197 J2
Lindre-Basse (57) 67 F3
Lindre-Haute (57) 67 F3
Lindry (89) 112 E5
Linexert (70) 118 E5
Lingé (36) 164 C1
Lingeard (50) 52 C4
Lingèvres (14) 32 B5
Linghem (62) 5 H4
Lingolsheim (67) 71 D1
Lingreville (50) 30 D5
Linguizzetta (2B) 319 J6
Linières-Bouton (49) 126 C3
Liniers (86) 163 H3
Liniez (36) 148 A3
Linsdorf (68) 97 D5
Linselles (59) 6 E3
Linthal (68) 96 A6
Linthelles (51) 61 J5
Linthes (51) 61 J5
Lintot (76) 14 E6
Lintot-les-Bois (76) 15 K3
Linxe (40) 262 D2
Liny-devant-Dun (55) 43 F2
Linzeux (62) 9 K2
Liocourt (57) 66 C2
Liomer (80) 17 G2
le Lion-d'Angers (49) 125 F1
Lion-devant-Dun (55) 43 G2
Lion-en-Beauce (45) 110 A1
Lion-en-Sullias (45) 111 F6
Lion-sur-Mer (14) 32 E3
Liorac-sur-Louyre (24) 231 K1
Liouc (30) 274 D2
Liourdres (19) 234 B1
Lioux (84) 277 G1
Lioux-les-Monges (23) 183 J5
Liposthey (40) 245 G2
Lipsheim (67) 70 E4
Lirac (30) 256 D6
Liré (49) 124 A5
Lirey (10) 90 A6
Lironcourt (88) 117 J2
Lironville (54) 65 H3
Liry (08) 42 B3
Lisbourg (62) 5 G6
Lisieux (14) 33 K5
Lisle (24) 213 J2
Lisle (41) 108 C4
Lisle-en-Barrois (55) 64 A2
Lisle-en-Rigault (55) 63 K5
Lisle-sur-Tarn (81) 270 A3
Lislet (02) 21 G4
Lison (14) 31 H2
Lisores (14) 54 E2
Lisors (27) 36 B3
Lissac (09) 288 C5
Lissac (43) 220 B4
Lissac-et-Mouret (46) 234 D5
Lissac-sur-Couze (19) 215 H5
Lissay-Lochy (18) 149 G4
Lisse-en-Champagne (51) 63 G4
Lisses (91) 87 F1
Lisseuil (63) 184 D4
Lissey (55) 43 H2
Lissieu (69) 188 B6
Lissy (77) 59 H6
Listrac-de-Durèze (33) 230 D3
Listrac-Médoc (33) 211 F4
Lit-et-Mixe (40) 244 C6
Lithaire (50) 30 D1
Litteau (14) 31 K3
Littenheim (67) 70 C1
Litz (60) 37 K2
Livaie (61) 82 C2
Livarot (14) 54 E1
Liverdun (54) 65 K4
Liverdy-en-Brie (77) 59 J5
Livernon (46) 234 B5
Livers-Cazelles (81) 270 C1
Livet (53) 105 H1
Livet-en-Saosnois (72) 82 E4
Livet-et-Gavet (38) 224 C4
Livet-sur-Authou (27) 34 D4
Livilliers (95) 37 H6
Livinhac-le-Haut (12) 235 F5
la Livinière (34) 290 E4
Livré (53) 104 C4
Livré-sur-Changeon (35) 79 K3
Livron (64) 285 F5
Livron-sur-Drôme (26) 240 C3
Livry (14) 32 A5
Livry (58) 168 C1
Livry-Gargan (93) 59 G3
Livry-Louvercy (51) 41 H6
Livry-sur-Seine (77) 87 H2
Lixhausen (67) 69 J6
Lixheim (57) 67 K3
Lixing-lès-Rouhling (57) 68 C2
Lixing-lès-Saint-Avold (57) 68 A4
Lixy (89) 88 B5
Lizac (82) 249 H6
Lizant (86) 179 H4
Lizeray (36) 148 B4
Lizières (23) 182 A2
Lizine (25) 156 B2
Lizines (77) 88 C2
Lizio (56) 101 H3
Lizos (65) 285 J5
Lizy (02) 40 A1
Lizy-sur-Ourcq (77) 60 A1
la Llagonne (66) 313 J4
Llauro (66) 315 F4
Llo (66) 313 J5
Llupia (66) 315 F3
Lobsann (67) 25 B2
Loc-Brévalaire (29) 46 B4
Loc-Eguiner (29) 46 D5
Loc-Eguiner-
-Saint-Thégonnec (29) 46 E6
Loc-Envel (22) 48 A5
Locarn (22) 75 K2
Loché-sur-Indrois (37) 147 F3
Loches (37) 146 D2
Loches-sur-Ource (10) 115 F2
le Locheur (14) 32 C6
Lochieu (01) 190 B5
Lochwiller (67) 70 C2
Locmalo (56) 76 B5
Locmaria (56) 120 C4
Locmaria-Berrien (29) 75 H2
Locmaria-Grand-Champ (56) 101 F4
Locmaria-Plouzané (29) 72 C4
Locmariaquer (56) 100 D6
Locmélar (29) 46 E6
Locminé (56) 101 F2
Locmiquélic (56) 100 A4
Locoal-Mendon (56) 100 C4
Locon (62) 6 A5
Loconville (60) 37 F4
Locqueltas (56) 101 F4
Locquénolé (29) 47 G4
Locquignol (59) 12 E4
Locquirec (29) 47 J3
Locronan (29) 74 C4
Loctudy (29) 98 C3
Locunolé (29) 99 J2
Loddes (03) 186 C1
Lodes (31) 286 D6
Lodève (34) 273 G5
Lods (25) 156 E2
Lœuilley (70) 136 D3
Lœuilly (80) 17 K3
Loffre (59) 11 J2
la Loge (62) 9 J1
la Loge-aux-Chèvres (10) 90 E5
Loge-Fougereuse (85) 161 F2
la Loge-Pomblin (10) 114 A2
Logelheim (68) 96 C4
les Loges (14) 32 A6
les Loges (52) 116 E5
les Loges (76) 14 C4
les Loges-en-Josas (78) 58 C5
les Loges-Marchis (50) 80 C1
les Loges-Margueron (10) 114 B1
les Loges-Saulces (14) 53 K3
les Loges-sur-Brécey (50) 52 B4
Lognes (77) 59 H4
Logny-Bogny (08) 22 A3
Logny-lès-Aubenton (02) 21 J2
Logonna-Daoulas (29) 74 B2
Logrian-Florian (30) 274 D2
Logron (28) 108 E1
Loguivy-Plougras (22) 47 K5
Lohéac (35) 102 E1
Lohitzun-Oyhercq (64) 283 G4
Lohr (67) 69 F6
Lohuec (22) 47 J6
Loigné-sur-Mayenne (53) 104 E4
Loigny-la-Bataille (28) 109 J1
Loiré (49) 124 C1
Loire-les-Marais (17) 177 F4
Loiré-sur-Nie (17) 178 C5
Loire-sur-Rhône (69) 206 A4
Loiron (53) 104 D1
Loisail (61) 83 H2
Loisey-Culey (55) 64 C4
Loisia (39) 173 F4
Loisieux (73) 207 K3
Loisin (74) 174 D6
Loison (55) 43 K3
Loison-sous-Lens (62) 11 F1
Loison-sur-Créquoise (62) 9 H1
Loisy (54) 65 K3
Loisy (71) 172 B3
Loisy-en-Brie (51) 61 J3
Loisy-sur-Marne (51) 63 F4
Loivre (51) 40 E3
Loix (17) 158 C5
Lolif (50) 51 K2
Lolme (24) 232 B4
Lombard (25) 156 A2
Lombard (39) 155 G6
Lombers (81) 270 E4
Lombez (32) 287 G2
Lombia (64) 285 F4
Lombrès (65) 305 G2
Lombreuil (45) 111 H3
Lombron (72) 107 G2
Lommerange (57) 44 D3
Lommoye (78) 57 G2
Lomné (65) 304 E2
Lomont (70) 139 F1
Lomont-sur-Crête (25) 138 D4
Lompnas (01) 207 H1
Lompnieu (01) 190 A5
Lompret (59) 6 D4
Lonçon (64) 284 C2
la Londe (76) 35 G3
la Londe-les-Maures (83) 301 F4
Londigny (16) 179 G4
Londinières (76) 16 C3
Long (80) 9 H6
Longages (31) 287 K4
Longaulnay (35) 78 D1
Longavesnes (80) 19 H1
Longchamp (21) 136 D6
Longchamp (52) 92 D6
Longchamp (88) 94 E5
Longchamp-sous-Châtenois (88) 93 H4
Longchamp-sur-Aujon (10) 91 J6
Longchamps (27) 36 C3
Longchamps-sur-Aire (55) 64 C2
Longchaumois (39) 174 A4
Longcochon (39) 156 C6
Longeau-Percey (52) 116 C5
Longeault (21) 136 C6
Longeaux (55) 64 C6
Longechaux (25) 157 F1
Longechenal (38) 207 F6
Longecourt-en-Plaine (21) 154 D1
Longecourt-lès-Culêtre (21) 153 H2
Longemaison (25) 157 F2
Longepierre (71) 154 E4
le Longeron (49) 142 D3
Longes (69) 205 K5
Longessaigne (69) 205 G2
Longevelle (70) 138 D1
Longevelle-lès-Russey (25) 139 G6
Longevelle-sur-Doubs (25) 139 F3
Longèves (17) 177 F1
Longèves (85) 160 D4
Longeville (25) 156 D3
la Longeville (25) 157 G3
Longeville-en-Barrois (55) 64 B4
Longeville-lès-Metz (57) 44 E5
Longeville-lès-Saint-Avold (57) 45 K5
Longeville-sur-la-Laines (52) 91 G2
Longeville-sur-Mer (85) 159 H4
Longeville-sur-Mogne (10) 114 A1
Longevilles-Mont-d'Or (25) 156 E6
Longfossé (62) 4 C4
la Longine (70) 119 F3
Longjumeau (91) 58 E5
Longlaville (54) 26 D2
Longmesnil (76) 16 E5
Longnes (72) 106 B2
Longnes (78) 57 H3
Longny-au-Perche (61) 83 K2
Longperrier (77) 59 H1
Longpont (02) 39 H4
Longpont-sur-Orge (91) 58 E6
Longpré-le-Sec (10) 91 F6
Longpré-les-Corps-Saints (80) 9 H6
Longraye (14) 32 B5
Longré (16) 178 E5
Longroy (76) 8 D6
Longsols (10) 90 C3
Longué-Jumelles (49) 126 A4
Longueau (80) 18 B2
Longuefuye (53) 105 G4
Longueil (76) 15 J2
Longueil-Annel (60) 38 E1
Longueil-Sainte-Marie (60) 38 D3
Longuenesse (62) 5 G3
Longuenoë (61) 82 B2
Longuerue (76) 16 B6
Longues-sur-Mer (14) 32 B3
Longuesse (95) 58 A1
Longueval (80) 11 F6
Longueval-Barbonval (02) 40 B3
Longueville (14) 29 J6
Longueville (47) 247 H1
Longueville (50) 30 D6
la Longueville (59) 13 G2
Longueville (62) 4 D3
Longueville (77) 88 D2
Longueville-sur-Aube (10) 89 K1
Longueville-sur-Scie (76) 15 K3
Longuevillette (80) 10 A5
Longuyon (54) 43 K1
Longvic (21) 136 A5
Longvillers (14) 32 B6
Longvilliers (62) 4 B5
Longvilliers (78) 86 B1
Longwé (08) 42 C2
Longwy (54) 26 C2
Longwy-sur-le-Doubs (39) 155 F4
Lonlay-l'Abbaye (61) 53 F6
Lonlay-le-Tesson (61) 53 J6
Lonnes (16) 179 G5
Lonny (08) 22 C3
Lonrai (61) 82 C2
Lons (64) 284 C4
Lons-le-Saunier (39) 173 G2
Lonzac (17) 195 J4
le Lonzac (19) 199 K6
Looberghe (59) 3 G3
Loon-Plage (59) 3 G2
Loos (59) 6 D4
Loos-en-Gohelle (62) 6 B6
Looze (89) 112 E3
Lopérec (29) 74 D2
Loperhet (29) 74 B1
Lopigna (2A) 320 C3
Loqueffret (29) 75 F2
Lor (02) 21 H6
Loray (25) 157 G1
Lorcières (15) 237 G1
Lorcy (45) 111 G2
Lordat (09) 307 K5
Loré (61) 81 G2
Lorentzen (67) 68 E4
Loreto-di-Casinca (2B) 319 J3
Loreto-di-Tallano (2A) 322 E2
Lorette (42) 205 J5
le Loreur (50) 30 E6
Loreux (41) 129 K4
le Lorey (50) 31 F3
Lorey (54) 94 B1
Lorges (41) 109 G5
Lorgies (62) 6 B5
Lorgues (83) 298 C1
Lorient (56) 99 K5
Loriges (03) 185 H1
Lorignac (17) 195 F5
Lorigné (79) 179 F3
Loriol-du-Comtat (84) 257 G6
Loriol-sur-Drôme (26) 240 B3
Lorlanges (43) 219 F2
Lorleau (27) 36 B2
Lormaison (60) 37 H4
Lormaye (28) 57 G6
Lormes (58) 133 J6
Lormont (33) 229 H1
Lornay (74) 190 D5
Loromontzey (54) 94 C2
le Loroux (35) 80 C3
le Loroux-Bottereau (44) 123 J4
Lorp-Sentaraille (09) 306 D2
Lorquin (57) 67 J5
Lorrez-le-Bocage-Préaux (77) 87 K5
Lorris (45) 111 G4
Lorry-lès-Metz (57) 44 E5
Lorry-Mardigny (57) 65 K1
Lortet (65) 305 F2
Los Masos (66) 314 C3
Loscouët-sur-Meu (22) 78 B3
Losne (21) 154 E2
Losse (40) 246 E5
Lostanges (19) 216 A5
Lostroff (57) 67 G2
Lothey (29) 74 E3
Lottinghen (62) 4 D3
le Lou-du-Lac (35) 78 D3
Louailles (72) 105 K5
Louan-Villegruis-Fontaine (77) 61 F6
Louannec (22) 48 A2
Louans (37) 146 A1
Louargat (22) 48 B5
Louâtre (02) 39 H4
Loubajac (65) 285 F6
Loubaresse (07) 238 E5
Loubaresse (15) 237 F1
Loubaut (09) 288 A6
Loubédat (32) 266 C4
Loubejac (24) 232 D5
Loubens (09) 307 H2
Loubens (33) 230 C5
Loubens-Lauragais (31) 289 F1
Loubers (81) 270 B1
Loubersan (32) 286 C2
Loubès-Bernac (47) 231 F3
Loubeyrat (63) 184 E6
Loubieng (64) 283 J2
la Loubière (12) 252 C2
Loubières (09) 307 J2
Loubigné (79) 178 D4
Loubillé (79) 178 E4
Loubressac (46) 234 B2
Loucé (61) 54 B5
Loucelles (14) 32 C4
Louchats (33) 229 H6
Louches (62) 2 E4
Louchy-Montfand (03) 185 G1
Loucrup (65) 285 H6
Loudéac (22) 77 G4
Loudenvielle (65) 305 F5
Loudervielle (65) 305 F5
Loudes (43) 220 A5
Loudet (31) 286 C6
Loudrefing (57) 67 G2
Loudun (86) 144 E3
Loué (72) 106 A2
Louer (40) 264 C4
Louerre (49) 125 J5
Louesme (21) 115 H4
Louestault (37) 127 J2
Loueuse (60) 17 G5
Louey (65) 285 G6
Lougé-sur-Maire (61) 54 A5
Lougratte (47) 231 K5
Lougres (25) 139 G3
Louhans (71) 172 D2
Louhossoa (64) 282 C3
Louignac (19) 215 F3
Louin (79) 144 B6
Louisfert (44) 103 J4
Louit (65) 285 J4
Loulans-Verchamp (70) 138 B3
Loulay (17) 177 K4
Loulle (39) 173 K1
la Loupe (28) 84 C2
Loupeigne (02) 40 A4
Loupershouse (57) 68 C3
Loupes (33) 229 J2
Loupfougères (53) 81 J4
Loupia (11) 308 D2
Loupiac (33) 229 K5
Loupiac (46) 233 H2
Loupiac (81) 270 A3
Loupiac-de-la-Réole (33) 230 C6
Loupian (34) 292 E2
Louplande (72) 106 C3
Loupmont (55) 65 F3
Louppy-le-Château (55) 64 A3
Louppy-sur-Loison (55) 43 H1
la Louptière-Thénard (10) 88 E3
Lourches (59) 12 B2
Lourde (31) 305 J2
Lourdes (65) 304 B1
Lourdios-Ichère (64) 302 E1
Lourdoueix-Saint-Michel (36) 165 J5
Lourdoueix-Saint-Pierre (23) 165 K5
Lourenties (64) 285 F4
Loures-Barousse (65) 305 H2
Louresse-Rochemenier (49) 125 J6
Lourmais (35) 51 G6
Lourmarin (84) 277 H4
Lournand (71) 171 H5
Lourouer-Saint-Laurent (36) 166 B3
le Louroux (37) 146 B2
le Louroux-Béconnais (49) 124 D2
Louroux-Bourbonnais (03) 167 K4
Louroux-de-Beaune (03) 184 D1
Louroux-de-Bouble (03) 184 E2
Louroux-Hodement (03) 167 J5
Lourquen (40) 264 D4
Lourties-Monbrun (32) 286 C2
Loury (45) 110 C3
Louslitges (32) 266 D6
Loussous-Débat (32) 266 C5
Loutehel (35) 78 C6
Loutzviller (57) 69 G2
Louvagny (14) 54 C2
Louvaines (49) 104 E6
Louvatange (39) 155 J1
Louveciennes (78) 58 C3
Louvemont (52) 91 J1
Louvemont-Côte-du-Poivre (55) 43 H4
Louvencourt (80) 10 C5
Louvenne (39) 173 F5
Louvergny (08) 22 D6
Louverné (53) 105 F1
le Louverot (39) 173 G1
Louversey (27) 56 B2
Louvetot (76) 15 G6
Louvie-Juzon (64) 303 H1
Louvie-Soubiron (64) 303 H2
la Louvière-Lauragais (11) 288 E5
Louvières (14) 29 K6
Louvières (52) 116 C2
Louvières-en-Auge (61) 54 C3
Louviers (27) 35 J5
Louvigné (53) 105 G2
Louvigné-de-Bais (35) 79 K5
Louvigné-du-Désert (35) 80 B2
Louvignies-Quesnoy (59) 12 E3
Louvigny (14) 32 E5
Louvigny (57) 66 A1
Louvigny (64) 284 C1
Louvigny (72) 82 E4
Louvil (59) 7 F5
Louville-la-Chenard (28) 85 K4
Louvilliers-en-Drouais (28) 56 E5
Louvilliers-lès-Perche (28) 56 C6
Louvois (51) 41 G6
Louvrechy (80) 18 B4
Louvres (95) 59 F1
Louvroil (59) 13 H3
Louye (27) 56 E4
Louzac-Saint-André (16) 195 J2
Louze (52) 91 G3
Louzes (72) 83 F3
Louzignac (17) 196 A1
Louzouer (45) 111 K2
Louzy (79) 144 B3
Lovagny (74) 190 E5
Loyat (56) 101 K1
la Loye (39) 155 H3
Loye-sur-Arnon (18) 167 F2
la Loyère (71) 154 A5
Loyettes (01) 206 E2
Lozanne (69) 188 B6
Lozay (17) 177 K4
Loze (82) 250 D3
Lozinghem (62) 5 J5
Lozon (50) 31 F3
Lozzi (2B) 318 D5
Luant (36) 165 H1
le Luart (72) 107 H2
Lubbon (40) 246 E5
Lubécourt (57) 66 D3
Lubersac (19) 199 G6
Lubey (54) 44 C4
Lubilhac (43) 219 F3
Lubine (88) 96 A1
Lublé (37) 126 E3
Lubret-Saint-Luc (65) 285 K4
Luby-Betmont (65) 285 K4
Luc (48) 238 C4
Luc (65) 285 J6
le Luc (83) 298 C2
Luc-Armau (64) 285 G3
Luc-en-Diois (26) 241 J4
Luc-la-Primaube (12) 252 B3
Luc-sur-Aude (11) 309 F3
Luc-sur-Mer (14) 32 E3
Luc-sur-Orbieu (11) 291 F6
Lucarré (64) 285 F3
Luçay-le-Libre (36) 148 B3
Luçay-le-Mâle (36) 147 H2
Lucbardez-et-Bargues (40) 265 H1
Lucciana (2B) 319 H3
Lucé (28) 85 G3
Lucé (61) 81 G1
Lucé-sous-Ballon (72) 82 E6
Luceau (72) 107 F6
Lucelle (68) 97 B6
Lucenay (69) 188 B6
Lucenay-le-Duc (21) 135 F2
Lucenay-lès-Aix (58) 169 F2
Lucenay-l'Évêque (71) 152 E3
Lucéram (06) 281 H1
la Lucerne-d'Outremer (50) 51 J1
Lucey (21) 115 J4
Lucey (54) 65 H4
Lucey (73) 208 A2
Lucgarier (64) 284 E5
Luchapt (86) 180 C3

Luchat (17). 195 F2
Luché-Pringé (72). 106 C6
Luché-sur-Brioux (79). 178 D3
Luché-Thouarsais (79). 144 A5
Lucheux (80). 10 B4
Luchy (60). 17 K6
Lucinges (74). 191 H2
Lucmau (33). 246 C2
Luçon (85). 160 A4
Lucq-de-Béarn (64). 283 K4
Lucquy (08). 22 B6
les Lucs-sur-Boulogne (85). 141 J5
Lucy (57). 66 D1
Lucy (76). 16 D3
Lucy-le-Bocage (02). 60 D1
Lucy-le-Bois (89). 133 K2
Lucy-sur-Cure (89). 133 H2
Lucy-sur-Yonne (89). 133 H2
le Lude (72). 126 D1
Ludes (51). 41 F5
Ludesse (63). 202 D4
Ludiès (09). 307 K1
Ludon-Médoc (33). 211 G6
Ludres (54). 66 A6
Lüe (40). 245 F4
Lué-en-Baugeois (49). 125 K3
Luemschwiller (68). 97 B3
Lugagnac (46). 250 D2
Lugagnan (65). 304 B1
Lugaignac (33). 230 B2
Lugan (12). 251 J1
Lugan (81). 269 K5
Lugarde (15). 218 A2
Lugasson (33). 230 B3
Luglon (40). 245 H5
Lugny (71). 171 J4
Lugny (02). 20 E3
Lugny-Bourbonnais (18). 149 K5
Lugny-Champagne (18). 150 A1
Lugny-lès-Charolles (71). 170 D5
Lugo-di-Nazza (2B). 321 K6
Lugon-et-l'Île-du-Carnay (33). . 211 K6
Lugos (33). 228 D6
Lugrin (74). 175 H5
Lugy (62). 5 F5
le Luhier (25). 157 H1
Luigné (49). 125 H6
Luigny (28). 84 C5
Luisant (28). 85 G3
Luisetaines (77). 88 C3
Luitré (35). 80 B4
Lullin (74). 175 F6
Lully (74). 174 E6
Lumbin (38). 224 C1
Lumbres (62). 5 F3
Lumeau (28). 109 K1
Lumes (08). 22 D4
Lumigny-Nesles-Ormeaux (77). . 60 A5
Lumio (2B). 318 B3
Lunac (12). 251 G4
Lunan (46). 234 E5
Lunas (24). 231 H1
Lunas (34). 272 E5
Lunax (31). 286 D4
Lunay (41). 108 A5
Luneau (03). 170 A6
Lunegarde (46). 234 A4
Lunel (34). 274 E5
Lunel-Viel (34). 274 E6
Luneray (76). 15 J3
Lunery (18). 149 F5
Lunéville (54). 66 D6
le Luot (50). 52 A4
Lupcourt (54). 66 B6
Lupé (42). 222 A1
Lupersat (23). 183 H5
Lupiac (32). 266 D5
Luplanté (28). 85 F5
Luppé-Violles (32). 266 A4
Luppy (57). 66 C1
Lupsault (16). 178 E5
Lupstein (67). 70 C1
Luquet (65). 285 F4
Lurais (36). 164 B2
Luray (28). 57 F5
Lurbe-Saint-Christau (64). 284 A6
Lurcy (01). 188 C4
Lurcy-le-Bourg (58). 151 G2
Lurcy-Lévis (03). 168 A1
Luré (42). 186 D6
Lure (70). 118 E6
Lureuil (36). 164 C1
Luri (2B). 317 D2
Luriecq (42). 204 D6
Lurs (04). 278 C1
Lury-sur-Arnon (18). 148 D2
Lus-la-Croix-Haute (26). 242 A4
Lusanger (44). 103 G4
Luscan (31). 305 J2
Lusignac (24). 213 G2
Lusignan (86). 162 D5
Lusignan-Petit (47). 248 A3
Lusigny (03). 169 G3
Lusigny-sur-Barse (10). 90 C5
Lusigny-sur-Ouche (21). 153 G2
Lussac (16). 197 H1
Lussac (17). 195 H5
Lussac (33). 212 C6
Lussac-les-Châteaux (86). 163 J5
Lussac-les-Églises (87). 164 D6
Lussagnet (40). 265 K4
Lussagnet-Lusson (64). 284 E2
Lussan (30). 255 K5
Lussan (32). 267 K6
Lussan-Adeilhac (31). 287 G4
Lussant (17). 177 G5

Lussas (07). 239 J5
Lussas-et-Nontronneau (24). . . 197 J5
Lussat (23). 183 H3
Lussat (63). 202 E1
Lussault-sur-Loire (37). 128 A4
Lusse (88). 95 K4
Lusseray (79). 178 D3
Lustar (65). 286 A5
Lutilhous (65). 286 A6
Luttange (57). 45 G3
Luttenbach-près-Munster (68). . 119 K1
Lutter (68). 97 C6
Lutterbach (68). 97 B3
Lutz-en-Dunois (28). 109 F2
Lutzelbourg (57). 70 A1
Lutzelhouse (67). 70 B4
Luvigny (88). 95 J1
Lux (21). 136 C3
Lux (31). 289 F3
Lux (71). 171 K1
Luxé (16). 179 F6
Luxe-Sumberraute (64). 283 F3
Luxémont-et-Villotte (51). 63 F5
Luxeuil-les-Bains (70). 118 D4
Luxey (40). 245 K3
Luxiol (25). 138 D4
Luyères (10). 90 C3
Luynes (37). 127 H5
Luz-Saint-Sauveur (65). 304 B4
Luzancy (77). 60 C2
Luzarches (95). 38 A3
Luzay (79). 144 B4
Luzé (37). 145 H3
Luze (70). 139 G1
Luzech (46). 249 J1
Luzenac (09). 308 A5
Luzeret (36). 165 F4
la Luzerne (50). 31 H3
Luzillat (63). 185 J5
Luzillé (37). 128 C6
Luzinay (38). 206 C4
Luzoir (02). 21 G1
Luzy (58). 152 C6
Luzy-Saint-Martin (55). 23 H6
Luzy-sur-Marne (52). 116 B2
Ly-Fontaine (02). 20 A4
Lyas (07). 239 K3
Lyaud (74). 175 F5
Lye (36). 147 H1
Lynde (59). 5 H3
Lyoffans (70). 119 F6
Lyon (69). 206 A2
Lyons-la-Forêt (27). 36 B2
Lys (58). 133 G5
Lys (64). 284 D6
Lys-lez-Lannoy (59). 7 F3
Lys-Saint-Georges (36). 165 K3

M

Maast-et-Violaine (02). 39 K4
Maâtz (52). 116 E6
Mably (42). 186 E4
Macau (33). 211 G5
Macaye (64). 282 D3
Macé (61). 54 D6
Macey (10). 89 K5
Macey (50). 51 J4
Machault (08). 41 K3
Machault (77). 87 J3
Maché (85). 141 G6
Machecoul (44). 141 F3
Mâchecourt (02). 21 F5
Machemont (60). 38 E1
Macheren (57). 68 B3
Machézal (42). 187 H6
Machiel (80). 9 G3
Machilly (74). 191 H1
la Machine (58). 151 G5
Machy (10). 114 A1
Machy (80). 9 F3
Mackenheim (67). 96 E2
Mackwiller (67). 68 E5
Maclas (42). 222 A1
Macogny (02). 39 H5
Mâcon (71). 188 C1
Maconcourt (88). 93 J3
Maconge (21). 153 H1
Macornay (39). 173 G2
Mâcot-la-Plagne (73). 209 J4
Macqueville (17). 196 A1
Macquigny (02). 20 C3
Madaillan (47). 248 B3
Madecourt (88). 94 A5
Madegney (88). 94 B4
la Madelaine-sous-Montreuil (62). . 4 C6
la Madeleine (59). 6 E4
la Madeleine-Bouvet (61). 84 B2
la Madeleine-de-Nonancourt (27). . 56 D4
la Madeleine-sur-Loing (77). 87 H6
la Madeleine-Villefrouin (41). . . . 109 F5
Madic (15). 217 H1
Madière (09). 307 H1
Madirac (33). 229 J3
Madiran (65). 285 G1
Madonne-et-Lamerey (88). 94 B5
Madranges (19). 200 A6
Madré (53). 81 J2
Madriat (63). 202 E6
Maël-Carhaix (22). 75 K3
Maël-Pestivien (22). 76 B1
Maennolsheim (67). 70 C2

Maffliers (95). 37 K6
Maffrécourt (51). 42 C6
Magalas (34). 292 A2
la Magdelaine-sur-Tarn (31). 269 H4
la Magdeleine (16). 179 F4
le Mage (61). 83 K2
Magenta (51). 61 K1
les Mages (30). 255 H4
Magescq (40). 262 D3
Magland (74). 192 A4
Magnac-Bourg (87). 199 G4
Magnac-Laval (87). 181 G2
Magnac-Lavalette-Villars (16). . 197 F5
Magnac-sur-Touvre (16). 196 E3
Magnan (32). 266 A4
Magnant (10). 90 E6
Magnanville (78). 57 J2
Magnas (32). 267 K2
Magnat-l'Étrange (23). 201 F2
Magné (79). 161 G6
Magné (86). 163 F6
Magnet (03). 185 K2
Magneux (51). 40 C3
Magneux (52). 91 K2
Magneux-Haute-Rive (42). 204 E3
Magneville (50). 28 D5
Magnicourt (10). 90 D3
Magnicourt-en-Comte (62). 10 C1
Magnicourt-sur-Canche (62). 10 B2
Magnien (21). 153 G2
Magnières (54). 94 E2
Magnieu (01). 207 K1
les Magnils-Reigniers (85). 159 K4
Magnivray (70). 118 E5
Magnoncourt (70). 118 C3
le Magnoray (70). 138 A2
Magny (28). 84 E4
le Magny (36). 166 B3
Magny (68). 139 K1
les Magny (70). 138 E2
le Magny (88). 118 B2
Magny (89). 134 A3
Magny-Châtelard (25). 138 D6
Magny-Cours (58). 150 E5
Magny-Danigon (70). 119 F6
Magny-en-Bessin (14). 32 B3
Magny-en-Vexin (95). 36 E5
Magny-Fouchard (10). 91 F5
Magny-Jobert (70). 119 F6
Magny-la-Campagne (14). 54 B1
Magny-la-Fosse (02). 19 K1
Magny-la-Ville (21). 134 E3
Magny-Lambert (21). 135 F1
Magny-le-Désert (61). 81 K1
Magny-le-Freule (14). 33 G6
Magny-le-Hongre (77). 59 J3
Magny-lès-Aubigny (21). 154 D2
Magny-les-Hameaux (78). 58 B5
Magny-lès-Jussey (70). 117 K4
Magny-lès-Villers (21). 154 A2
Magny-Lormes (58). 133 J6
Magny-Montarlot (21). 136 D6
Magny-Saint-Médard (21). 136 C4
Magny-sur-Tille (21). 136 B6
Magny-Vernois (70). 118 E6
Magoar (22). 76 C1
Magrie (11). 308 E2
Magrin (81). 270 B6
Magstatt-le-Bas (68). 97 D4
Magstatt-le-Haut (68). 97 C4
Mahalon (29). 73 D3
Mahéru (61). 55 G6
Maîche (25). 139 H5
Maidières (54). 65 J2
Maignaut-Tauzia (32). 267 G2
Maigné (72). 106 B3
Maignelay-Montigny (60). 18 D6
Mailhac (11). 291 G4
Mailhac-sur-Benaize (87). 181 H1
Mailhoc (81). 270 D1
Mailholas (31). 287 K5
Maillane (13). 276 B3
Maillas (40). 246 D4
Maillat (01). 189 K3
Maillé (37). 145 J3
Maillé (85). 160 E6
Maillé (86). 162 C2
Maillebois (28). 56 D6
la Mailleraye-sur-Seine (76). 34 E1
Maillères (40). 246 A6
Mailleroncourt-Charette (70). . . . 118 C5
Mailleroncourt-Saint-Pancras (70). . 118 A3
Maillet (03). 167 H5
Maillet (36). 165 J3
Mailley-et-Chazelot (70). 138 A2
Maillezais (85). 160 E5
Maillot (89). 88 D6
Mailly (71). 187 F2
Mailly-Champagne (51). 41 F5
Mailly-la-Ville (89). 133 H2
Mailly-le-Camp (10). 62 C6
Mailly-le-Château (89). 133 G2
Mailly-Maillet (80). 10 D5
Mailly-Raineval (80). 18 C4
Mailly-sur-Seille (54). 66 B2
les Maillys (21). 155 F2
Maimbeville (60). 38 B2
Maincy (77). 87 H2
Maine-de-Boixe (16). 196 E1
Mainfonds (16). 196 C5
Maing (59). 12 C2
Mainneville (27). 36 D3
Mainsat (23). 183 J4
Maintenay (62). 9 G2
Maintenon (28). 85 H1
Mainvillers (57). 45 J6

Mainvilliers (28). 85 G3
Mainvilliers (45). 86 D5
Mainxe (16). 196 A3
Mainzac (16). 197 H5
Mairé (86). 146 A5
Mairé-Levescault (79). 179 F3
Mairieux (59). 13 H2
Mairy (08). 23 G5
Mairy-Mainville (54). 44 C3
Mairy-sur-Marne (51). 62 D3
Maisdon-sur-Sèvre (44). 141 K2
Maisey-le-Duc (21). 115 G4
Maisnières (80). 8 E6
le Maisnil (59). 6 C4
Maisnil (62). 10 B2
Maisnil-lès-Ruitz (62). 5 K6
Maisod (39). 173 H4
Maison-des-Champs (10). 91 F5
la Maison-Dieu (58). 133 G4
Maison-Feyne (23). 165 J6
Maison-Maugis (61). 83 J3
Maison-Ponthieu (80). 9 J4
Maison-Roland (80). 9 H5
Maison-Rouge (77). 88 C1
Maisoncelle (62). 5 F6
Maisoncelle-et-Villers (08). 23 F5
Maisoncelle-Saint-Pierre (60). . . . 37 H1
Maisoncelle-Tuilerie (60). 18 A6
Maisoncelles (52). 92 E6
Maisoncelles (72). 107 H3
Maisoncelles-du-Maine (53). 105 F3
Maisoncelles-en-Brie (77). 60 A3
Maisoncelles-en-Gâtinais (77). . 87 H6
Maisoncelles-la-Jourdan (14). . . . 52 E4
Maisoncelles-Pelvey (14). 32 B6
Maisoncelles-sur-Ajon (14). 32 C6
Maisonnais (18). 166 D3
Maisonnais-sur-Tardoire (87). . . 197 K3
Maisonnay (79). 178 E2
Maisonneuve (86). 162 C1
Maisonnisses (23). 182 D4
Maisons (11). 309 K3
Maisons (14). 32 A3
Maisons (28). 85 K3
Maisons-Alfort (94). 59 F4
Maisons-du-Bois-Lièvremont (25). . 157 F3
Maisons-en-Champagne (51). 62 E4
Maisons-Laffitte (78). 58 C2
Maisons-lès-Chaource (10). 114 B2
Maisons-lès-Soulaines (10). 91 H4
Maisonsgoutte (67). 70 B6
Maisontiers (79). 144 A6
Maisse (91). 86 E3
Maissemy (02). 19 J2
Maixe (54). 66 D5
Maizeray (55). 44 A5
Maizeroy (57). 45 H5
Maizery (57). 45 G5
Maizet (14). 32 D6
Maizey (55). 64 E2
Maizicourt (80). 9 J4
Maizières (14). 54 B1
Maizières (52). 92 A2
Maizières (54). 65 K6
Maizières (62). 10 B2
Maizières (70). 137 K3
Maizières-la-Grande-
-Paroisse (10). 89 J2
Maizières-lès-Brienne (10). 91 F3
Maizières-lès-Metz (57). 45 F4
Maizières-lès-Vic (57). 67 G4
Maizières-sur-Amance (52). 117 F4
Maizilly (42). 187 G2
Maizy (02). 40 C2
Majastres (04). 279 G2
Malabat (32). 285 J2
la Malachère (70). 138 A3
Malafretaz (01). 172 C6
Malain (21). 135 J5
Malaincourt (88). 93 G5
Malaincourt-sur-Meuse (52). 93 F6
Malakoff (92). 58 E4
Malancourt (55). 43 F4
Malandry (08). 23 H5
Malange (39). 155 H1
Malans (25). 156 B2
Malans (70). 137 F6
Malansac (56). 102 A3
Malarce-sur-la-Thines (07). 255 G1
Malataverne (26). 240 B6
Malaucène (84). 257 H4
Malaucourt-sur-Seille (57). 66 C3
Malaunay (76). 15 K6
Malause (82). 249 F6
Malaussanne (64). 284 C1
Malaussène (06). 281 F1
Malauzat (63). 202 D1
Malaville (16). 196 B4
Malavillers (54). 26 A5
Malay (71). 171 H3
Malay-le-Grand (89). 88 E6
Malay-le-Petit (89). 88 E6
Malbo (15). 218 A6
Malbosc (07). 255 G3
Malbouhans (70). 119 F5
Malbouzon (48). 236 E4
Malbrans (25). 156 C2
Malbuisson (25). 156 E5
Mâle (61). 83 K5
Malegoude (09). 308 C1
Malemort-du-Comtat (84). 257 H6
Malemort-sur-Corrèze (19). 215 J4
la Malène (48). 253 J1
Malesherbes (45). 87 F5
Malestroit (56). 101 K3
Malétable (61). 83 J1

Maleville (12). 251 G2
Malguénac (56). 76 D5
la Malhoure (22). 77 J2
Malicornay (36). 165 H3
Malicorne (03). 184 C1
Malicorne (89). 112 B5
Malicorne-sur-Sarthe (72). 106 B5
Maligny (21). 153 H2
Maligny (89). 113 H4
Malijai (04). 259 G6
Malincourt (59). 12 B6
Malintrat (63). 202 E1
Malissard (26). 240 D1
Mallefougasse-Augès (04). 259 F5
Malleloy (54). 66 A3
Mallemoisson (04). 259 H6
Mallemort (13). 277 F4
Malléon (09). 307 K2
Malleret (23). 201 F2
Malleret-Boussac (23). 166 C6
Mallerey (39). 173 F2
Malleval (42). 222 A1
Malleval-en-Vercors (38). 223 H4
Malleville-les-Grès (76). 15 F2
Malleville-sur-le-Bec (27). 34 E4
Mallièvre (85). 142 E4
Malling (57). 27 H5
Malloué (14). 31 J5
la Malmaison (02). 40 E1
Malmerspach (68). 119 K3
Malmy (51). 42 C5
Malons-en-Elze (30). 255 G2
Malouy (27). 34 C6
Malpart (80). 18 C4
Malpas (25). 156 E5
Malras (11). 308 E2
Malrevers (43). 220 D5
Malroy (57). 45 F4
Maltat (71). 169 K2
Maltot (14). 32 D5
Malval (23). 166 A6
Malvalette (43). 220 E1
Malves-en-Minervois (11). 290 C5
Malvezie (31). 305 J2
Malvières (43). 220 A2
Malviès (11). 308 E1
Malville (44). 122 D2
Malzéville (54). 66 A4
le Malzieu-Forain (48). 237 H2
le Malzieu-Ville (48). 237 G2
Malzy (02). 20 E2
Mamers (72). 83 F4
Mametz (62). 5 H4
Mametz (80). 10 E6
Mamey (54). 65 J2
Mamirolle (25). 138 B6
Manas (26). 240 D5
Manas-Bastanous (32). 286 A3
Manaurie (24). 214 D6
Mance (54). 44 C3
la Mancelière (28). 56 B6
la Mancellière-sur-Vire (50). 31 H4
Mancenans (25). 138 E3
Mancenans-Lizerne (25). 139 F3
Mancey (71). 171 K3
Manchecourt (45). 86 E5
Manciet (32). 266 C4
Mancieulles (54). 44 C3
Mancioux (31). 287 G6
Mancy (51). 61 K2
Mandagout (30). 273 K1
Mandailles-Saint-Julien (15). . . . 217 K5
Mandelieu-la-Napoule (06). 280 D6
Manderen (57). 27 K3
Mandeure (25). 139 H3
Mandeville (27). 35 H4
Mandeville-en-Bessin (14). 31 H4
Mandray (88). 95 J3
Mandres (27). 56 A5
Mandres-aux-Quatre-Tours (54). . 65 G3
Mandres-en-Barrois (55). 92 D2
Mandres-la-Côte (52). 116 D1
Mandres-les-Roses (94). 59 G5
Mandres-sur-Vair (88). 93 J5
Mandrevillars (70). 139 G1
Manduel (30). 275 H3
Mane (04). 278 B1
Mane (31). 306 B1
Manéglise (76). 14 C6
Manéhouville (76). 15 K2
Manent-Montané (32). 286 D4
Manerbe (14). 33 K5
Mangiennes (55). 43 J2
Manglieu (63). 203 F4
Mangonville (54). 94 B2
Manhac (12). 252 A4
Manheulles (55). 43 K5
Manhoué (57). 66 C3
Manicamp (02). 19 J6
Manigod (74). 191 H6
Manin (62). 10 C2
Maningham (62). 4 D5
Maninghen-Henne (62). 2 B5
Manlay (21). 153 H6
Manneville-ès-Plains (76). 15 G2
Manneville-la-Goupil (76). 14 C5
Manneville-la-Pipard (14). 33 K4
Manneville-la-Raoult (27). 34 A2
Manneville-sur-Risle (27). 34 C3
Mannevillette (76). 14 B5
Mano (40). 245 G4
le Manoir (14). 32 C3
le Manoir (27). 35 J3
Manois (52). 92 D4

Manom (57) . . . 27 G4
Manoncourt-en-Vermois (54) . . . 66 B6
Manoncourt-en-Woëvre (54) . . . 65 J4
Manonville (54) . . . 65 H3
Manonviller (54) . . . 67 F6
Manosque (04) . . . 278 B3
Manot (16) . . . 180 B5
Manou (28) . . . 84 B2
Manre (08) . . . 42 B4
le Mans (72) . . . 106 E2
Mansac (19) . . . 215 G4
Mansan (65) . . . 285 J4
Mansat-la-Courrière (23) . . . 182 C5
Mansempuy (32) . . . 268 A4
Mansencôme (32) . . . 267 F3
Manses (09) . . . 308 A1
Mansigné (72) . . . 106 D6
Mansle (16) . . . 179 G6
Manso (2B) . . . 318 B5
Mansonville (82) . . . 268 A1
Manspach (68) . . . 97 A4
Mant (40) . . . 265 G6
Mantallot (22) . . . 48 B3
Mantenay-Montlin (01) . . . 172 B5
Mantes-la-Jolie (78) . . . 57 J2
Mantes-la-Ville (78) . . . 57 J2
Mantet (66) . . . 314 A5
Manteyer (05) . . . 242 D5
Manthelan (37) . . . 146 B2
Manthelon (27) . . . 56 C3
Manthes (26) . . . 222 D2
Mantilly (61) . . . 80 E1
Mantoche (70) . . . 137 F4
Mantry (39) . . . 155 H6
Manvieux (14) . . . 32 B3
Many (57) . . . 66 D1
Manzac-sur-Vern (24) . . . 213 J5
Manzat (63) . . . 184 D5
Manziat (01) . . . 172 A6
Marac (52) . . . 116 B3
Marainville-sur-Madon (88) . . . 94 A3
Marainviller (54) . . . 66 E6
le Marais-la-Chapelle (14) . . . 54 C3
Marais-Vernier (27) . . . 34 C2
Marambat (32) . . . 267 F4
Marandeuil (21) . . . 136 D5
Marange-Silvange (57) . . . 44 E4
Marange-Zondrange (57) . . . 45 J5
Marans (17) . . . 160 C6
Marans (49) . . . 124 D1
Maransin (33) . . . 212 A5
Marant (62) . . . 4 C6
Maranville (52) . . . 115 J1
Maranwez (08) . . . 21 K4
Marast (70) . . . 138 D2
Maraussan (34) . . . 291 K4
Maravat (32) . . . 267 K4
Maray (41) . . . 148 B1
Maraye-en-Othe (10) . . . 89 J6
Marbache (54) . . . 65 K3
Marbaix (59) . . . 13 G4
Marbeuf (27) . . . 35 G5
Marbéville (52) . . . 91 K5
Marboué (28) . . . 108 E1
Marboz (01) . . . 172 D6
Marby (08) . . . 22 A2
Marc-la-Tour (19) . . . 216 B3
Marçais (18) . . . 167 F2
Marçay (37) . . . 145 F2
Marçay (86) . . . 162 E5
Marcé (49) . . . 125 J2
Marcé-sur-Esves (37) . . . 145 K3
Marcei (61) . . . 54 C6
Marcelcave (80) . . . 18 D2
Marcellaz (74) . . . 191 F4
Marcellaz-Albanais (74) . . . 190 E6
Marcellois (21) . . . 135 G5
Marcellus (47) . . . 247 G1
Marcenais (33) . . . 211 K5
Marcenat (03) . . . 185 J2
Marcenat (15) . . . 218 B2
Marcenay (21) . . . 114 E4
Marcenod (42) . . . 205 H4
Marcey-les-Grèves (50) . . . 51 K3
Marchainville (61) . . . 84 A1
Marchais (02) . . . 20 E6
Marchais-Beton (89) . . . 112 B5
Marchais-en-Brie (02) . . . 61 F1
Marchamp (01) . . . 207 H1
Marchampt (69) . . . 187 K3
Marchastel (15) . . . 218 A2
Marchastel (48) . . . 236 E5
Marchaux (25) . . . 138 B5
la Marche (58) . . . 150 C2
Marché-Allouarde (80) . . . 19 J1
Marchélepot (80) . . . 19 G3
Marchemaisons (61) . . . 83 F2
Marchémoret (77) . . . 59 J1
Marchenoir (41) . . . 109 F5
Marcheprime (33) . . . 228 E4
Marches (26) . . . 222 E6
les Marches (73) . . . 208 C5
Marcheseuil (21) . . . 153 F2
Marchésieux (50) . . . 31 F2
Marchéville (28) . . . 84 E4
Marchéville-en-Woëvre (55) . . . 44 A4
Marchezais (28) . . . 57 G4
Marchiennes (59) . . . 12 B1
Marciac (32) . . . 285 J1
Marcieu (38) . . . 242 A1
Marcieux (38) . . . 208 A3
Marcigny (71) . . . 186 E1
Marcigny-sous-Thil (21) . . . 134 E4
Marcilhac-sur-Célé (46) . . . 234 B6
Marcillac (33) . . . 211 H2

Marcillac-la-Croisille (19) . . . 216 D3
Marcillac-la-Croze (19) . . . 216 A5
Marcillac-Lanville (16) . . . 196 C1
Marcillac-Saint-Quentin (24) . . . 233 F1
Marcillac-Vallon (12) . . . 252 A1
Marcillat (63) . . . 184 E4
Marcillat-en-Combraille (03) . . . 184 A3
Marcillé-la-Ville (53) . . . 81 H4
Marcillé-Raoul (35) . . . 79 H1
Marcillé-Robert (35) . . . 79 K6
Marcilloles (38) . . . 223 F1
Marcilly (50) . . . 52 A5
Marcilly (77) . . . 59 K1
Marcilly-d'Azergues (69) . . . 188 B5
Marcilly-en-Bassigny (52) . . . 116 E3
Marcilly-en-Beauce (41) . . . 108 B5
Marcilly-en-Gault (41) . . . 129 K4
Marcilly-en-Villette (45) . . . 110 B6
Marcilly-et-Dracy (21) . . . 135 F4
Marcilly-la-Campagne (27) . . . 56 D4
Marcilly-la-Gueurce (71) . . . 170 E5
Marcilly-le-Châtel (42) . . . 204 C3
Marcilly-le-Hayer (10) . . . 89 G4
Marcilly-lès-Buxy (71) . . . 171 G1
Marcilly-Ogny (21) . . . 134 E6
Marcilly-sur-Eure (27) . . . 57 F4
Marcilly-sur-Maulne (37) . . . 126 E2
Marcilly-sur-Seine (51) . . . 89 H1
Marcilly-sur-Tille (21) . . . 136 B3
Marcilly-sur-Vienne (37) . . . 145 J3
Marck (62) . . . 2 D2
Marckolsheim (67) . . . 96 D3
Marclopt (42) . . . 204 E3
Marcoing (59) . . . 11 J5
Marcolès (15) . . . 235 G3
Marcollin (38) . . . 222 E2
Marcols-les-Eaux (07) . . . 239 H2
Marçon (72) . . . 107 G6
Marconne (62) . . . 9 J2
Marconnelle (62) . . . 9 H2
Marcorignan (11) . . . 291 H5
Marcoussis (91) . . . 58 D6
Marcoux (04) . . . 259 K5
Marcoux (42) . . . 204 C3
Marcq (08) . . . 42 D3
Marcq (78) . . . 57 H5
Marcq-en-Barœul (59) . . . 6 E3
Marcq-en-Ostrevent (59) . . . 11 K3
Marcy (02) . . . 20 B2
Marcy (58) . . . 132 E5
Marcy (69) . . . 188 B6
Marcy-l'Étoile (69) . . . 205 K2
Marcy-sous-Marle (02) . . . 20 E4
Mardeuil (51) . . . 61 K1
Mardié (45) . . . 110 B4
Mardilly (61) . . . 55 F5
Mardor (52) . . . 116 B4
Mardore (69) . . . 187 H4
Mareau-aux-Bois (45) . . . 110 D1
Mareau-aux-Prés (45) . . . 109 K5
Mareil-en-Champagne (72) . . . 106 A3
Mareil-en-France (95) . . . 59 F1
Mareil-le-Guyon (78) . . . 57 K4
Mareil-Marly (78) . . . 58 C3
Mareil-sur-Loir (72) . . . 106 C6
Mareil-sur-Mauldre (78) . . . 58 A3
Mareilles (52) . . . 92 C6
Marenla (62) . . . 4 D6
Marennes (17) . . . 194 B1
Marennes (69) . . . 206 B4
Maresché (72) . . . 82 D5
Maresches (59) . . . 12 D2
Maresquel-Ecquemicourt (62) . . . 9 H1
Marest (62) . . . 5 H6
Marest-Dampcourt (02) . . . 19 J5
Marest-sur-Matz (60) . . . 38 D1
Marestaing (32) . . . 287 H1
Marestmontiers (80) . . . 18 D4
Maresville (62) . . . 4 B5
les Marêts (77) . . . 60 D6
Maretz (59) . . . 12 C6
Mareugheol (63) . . . 202 E6
Mareuil (16) . . . 196 B2
Mareuil (24) . . . 197 G6
Mareuil-Caubert (80) . . . 9 G5
Mareuil-en-Brie (51) . . . 61 H2
Mareuil-en-Dôle (02) . . . 40 A4
Mareuil-la-Motte (60) . . . 19 F6
Mareuil-le-Port (51) . . . 40 C6
Mareuil-lès-Meaux (77) . . . 59 K2
Mareuil-sur-Arnon (18) . . . 148 K3
Mareuil-sur-Ay (51) . . . 62 A1
Mareuil-sur-Cher (41) . . . 128 E6
Mareuil-sur-Lay-Dissais (85) . . . 159 K3
Mareuil-sur-Ourcq (60) . . . 39 G6
Marey (88) . . . 117 J1
Marey-lès-Fussey (21) . . . 154 A2
Marey-sur-Tille (21) . . . 136 A2
Marfaux (51) . . . 40 D5
Marfontaine (02) . . . 20 E4
Margaux (33) . . . 211 G5
Margencel (74) . . . 174 E5
Margerides (19) . . . 201 G6
Margerie-Chantagret (42) . . . 204 D5
Margerie-Hancourt (51) . . . 91 F1
Margès (26) . . . 222 D4
Margival (02) . . . 39 K2
le Margnès (81) . . . 271 J6
Margny (08) . . . 23 J5
Margny (51) . . . 61 G2
Margny-aux-Cerises (60) . . . 19 G5
Margny-lès-Compiègne (60) . . . 38 D2
Margny-sur-Matz (60) . . . 38 D1
Margon (28) . . . 84 A4
Margon (34) . . . 292 B2

Margouët-Meymes (32) . . . 266 D4
Margueray (50) . . . 52 B2
Marguerittes (30) . . . 275 H5
Margueron (33) . . . 231 F3
Marguestau (32) . . . 266 B2
Margut (08) . . . 23 J4
Mariac (07) . . . 239 H1
Maricourt (80) . . . 19 H1
Marie (06) . . . 261 J5
Marieulles (57) . . . 65 K1
Marieux (80) . . . 10 B5
Marigna-sur-Valouse (39) . . . 173 G4
Marignac (17) . . . 195 H5
Marignac (31) . . . 305 J3
Marignac (82) . . . 268 C3
Marignac-en-Diois (26) . . . 241 G2
Marignac-Lasclares (31) . . . 287 J4
Marignac-Laspeyres (31) . . . 287 G5
Marignana (2A) . . . 320 B1
Marignane (13) . . . 296 A2
Marigné (49) . . . 105 G6
Marigné-Laillé (72) . . . 107 F5
Marigné-Peuton (53) . . . 104 E4
Marignier (74) . . . 191 J5
Marignieu (01) . . . 207 K1
Marigny (03) . . . 168 D3
Marigny (39) . . . 173 J1
Marigny (50) . . . 31 G3
Marigny (51) . . . 61 J6
Marigny (71) . . . 171 F2
Marigny (79) . . . 178 A2
Marigny-Brizay (86) . . . 163 F1
Marigny-Chemereau (86) . . . 162 D5
Marigny-en-Orxois (02) . . . 60 C1
Marigny-le-Cahouët (21) . . . 134 E3
Marigny-l'Église (58) . . . 133 K5
Marigny-lès-Reullée (21) . . . 154 B3
Marigny-les-Usages (45) . . . 110 B3
Marigny-Marmande (37) . . . 145 J4
Marigny-Saint-Marcel (74) . . . 190 E6
Marigny-sur-Yonne (58) . . . 133 H6
Marillac-le-Franc (16) . . . 197 G2
le Marillais (49) . . . 124 B4
Marillet (85) . . . 161 F3
Marimbault (33) . . . 246 C1
Marimont-lès-Bénestroff (57) . . . 67 G2
Marin (74) . . . 175 F5
Marines (95) . . . 37 G5
Maringes (42) . . . 205 F3
Maringues (63) . . . 185 H6
Mariol (03) . . . 185 K5
Marions (33) . . . 246 C2
Marizy (71) . . . 171 F3
Marizy-Saint-Mard (02) . . . 39 H5
Marizy-Sainte-Geneviève (02) . . . 39 H5
Marle (02) . . . 20 E4
Marlemont (08) . . . 22 A3
Marlenheim (67) . . . 70 D3
Marlens (74) . . . 209 F1
Marlers (80) . . . 17 G3
Marles-en-Brie (77) . . . 59 K5
Marles-les-Mines (62) . . . 5 K6
Marles-sur-Canche (62) . . . 4 C6
Marlhes (42) . . . 221 H4
Marliac (31) . . . 288 C5
Marliens (21) . . . 154 D1
Marlieux (01) . . . 188 C4
Marlioz (74) . . . 190 E4
Marly (57) . . . 45 F6
Marly (59) . . . 12 D2
Marly-Gomont (02) . . . 20 E2
Marly-la-Ville (95) . . . 38 D5
Marly-le-Roi (78) . . . 58 C3
Marly-sous-Issy (71) . . . 170 A1
Marly-sur-Arroux (71) . . . 170 C3
Marmagne (18) . . . 149 F3
Marmagne (21) . . . 134 D1
Marmagne (71) . . . 153 F6
Marmande (47) . . . 230 E6
Marmanhac (15) . . . 217 H6
Marmeaux (89) . . . 134 B2
Marminiac (46) . . . 233 F4
Marmont-Pachas (47) . . . 248 B6
Marmouillé (61) . . . 54 E5
Marmoutier (67) . . . 70 B2
Marnac (24) . . . 232 D2
Marnand (69) . . . 187 H4
Marnans (38) . . . 223 F2
Marnaves (81) . . . 250 E6
Marnay (71) . . . 172 A1
Marnay (86) . . . 163 F5
Marnay-sur-Marne (52) . . . 116 C2
Marnay-sur-Seine (10) . . . 89 F2
Marnaz (74) . . . 191 K3
la Marne (44) . . . 141 J3
Marnes (79) . . . 144 D5
Marnes-la-Coquette (92) . . . 58 C4
Marnézia (39) . . . 173 H3
Marnhagues-et-Latour (12) . . . 272 D3
Marnoz (39) . . . 156 A4
Maroeuil (62) . . . 10 E2
Marolles (14) . . . 34 B5
Marolles (41) . . . 128 C1
Marolles (51) . . . 63 F5
Marolles (60) . . . 39 G5
Marolles-en-Beauce (91) . . . 86 D4
Marolles-en-Brie (77) . . . 60 C4
Marolles-en-Brie (94) . . . 59 G5
Marolles-en-Hurepoix (91) . . . 86 E1
Marolles-lès-Bailly (10) . . . 90 D6
Marolles-les-Braults (72) . . . 83 F5
Marolles-les-Buis (28) . . . 84 B4

Marolles-lès-Saint-Calais (72) . . . 107 K4
Marolles-sous-Lignières (10) . . . 113 K3
Marolles-sur-Seine (77) . . . 88 B4
Marollette (72) . . . 83 F4
Marols (42) . . . 204 C6
Maromme (76) . . . 35 H1
Mâron (36) . . . 148 B6
Maron (54) . . . 65 K5
Maroncourt (88) . . . 94 A5
Marpaps (40) . . . 264 E6
Marpent (59) . . . 13 J2
Marpiré (35) . . . 79 K4
Marquaix (80) . . . 19 H1
Marquay (24) . . . 232 E1
Marquay (62) . . . 10 B1
Marquefave (31) . . . 287 K4
Marquéglise (60) . . . 38 D1
Marquein (11) . . . 288 E4
Marquerie (65) . . . 285 J5
Marques (76) . . . 17 F1
Marquette-en-Ostrevant (59) . . . 12 B3
Marquette-lez-Lille (59) . . . 6 E3
Marquigny (08) . . . 22 D6
Marquillies (59) . . . 6 C5
Marquion (62) . . . 11 H4
Marquise (62) . . . 2 B4
Marquivillers (80) . . . 18 E5
Marquixanes (66) . . . 314 C3
Marray (37) . . . 127 J2
la Marre (39) . . . 173 H1
Marre (55) . . . 43 G4
Mars (07) . . . 221 G5
les Mars (23) . . . 183 K5
Mars (30) . . . 273 J1
Mars (42) . . . 187 G3
Mars-la-Tour (54) . . . 44 C5
Mars-sous-Bourcq (08) . . . 42 A2
Mars-sur-Allier (58) . . . 150 D6
Marsa (11) . . . 308 E5
Marsac (16) . . . 196 D2
Marsac (23) . . . 182 A4
Marsac (65) . . . 285 H4
Marsac (82) . . . 268 A2
Marsac-en-Livradois (63) . . . 203 K6
Marsac-sur-Don (44) . . . 103 F5
Marsac-sur-l'Isle (24) . . . 213 K3
Marsainvilliers (45) . . . 86 D6
Marsais (17) . . . 177 J3
Marsais-Sainte-Radégonde (85) . . . 160 D3
Marsal (57) . . . 66 E3
Marsal (81) . . . 271 F2
Marsalès (24) . . . 232 C4
Marsan (32) . . . 267 K5
Marsaneix (24) . . . 214 B5
Marsangis (51) . . . 89 J1
Marsangy (89) . . . 112 D1
Marsannay-la-Côte (21) . . . 136 A6
Marsannay-le-Bois (21) . . . 136 B4
Marsanne (26) . . . 240 C4
Marsas (33) . . . 211 K5
Marsas (65) . . . 304 E2
Marsat (63) . . . 202 D1
Marsaz (26) . . . 222 C4
Marseillan (32) . . . 286 A2
Marseillan (34) . . . 292 D4
Marseillan (65) . . . 285 J4
Marseille (13) . . . 296 C4
Marseille-en-Beauvaisis (60) . . . 17 H6
Marseilles-lès-Aubigny (18) . . . 150 C3
Marseillette (11) . . . 290 D6
Marsillargues (34) . . . 275 F5
Marsilly (17) . . . 176 D1
Marsilly (57) . . . 45 G5
Marsolan (32) . . . 267 H2
Marson (51) . . . 62 E2
Marson-sur-Barboure (55) . . . 64 D6
Marsonnas (01) . . . 172 B6
Marsoulas (31) . . . 306 C1
Marssac-sur-Tarn (81) . . . 270 C2
Martagny (27) . . . 36 D2
Martailly-lès-Brancion (71) . . . 171 J4
Martainneville (80) . . . 9 F6
Martainville (14) . . . 53 K2
Martainville (27) . . . 34 B3
Martainville-Épreville (76) . . . 35 K1
Martaizé (86) . . . 144 D5
Martel (46) . . . 233 H1
Marthemont (54) . . . 93 K1
Marthille (57) . . . 66 D2
Marthod (73) . . . 209 G2
Marthon (16) . . . 197 G4
Martiel (12) . . . 250 E2
Martigna (39) . . . 173 H5
Martignargues (30) . . . 255 H6
Martignas-sur-Jalle (33) . . . 229 F2
Martignat (01) . . . 190 A2
Martigné-Briand (49) . . . 125 H6
Martigné-Ferchaud (35) . . . 103 K2
Martigné-sur-Mayenne (53) . . . 81 H5
Martigny (02) . . . 21 H2
Martigny (50) . . . 52 C6
Martigny (76) . . . 16 A2
Martigny-Courpierre (02) . . . 40 B1
Martigny-le-Comte (71) . . . 170 E4
Martigny-les-Bains (88) . . . 117 H1
Martigny-les-Gerbonvaux (88) . . . 93 H2
Martigny-sur-l'Ante (14) . . . 53 K3
Martigues (13) . . . 295 J5
Martillac (33) . . . 229 H3
Martin-Église (76) . . . 16 A2
Martincourt (54) . . . 65 J3
Martincourt (60) . . . 37 F1
Martincourt-sur-Meuse (55) . . . 23 H6
le Martinet (30) . . . 255 G4
Martinet (85) . . . 159 F1
Martinpuich (62) . . . 10 E6

Martinvast (50) . . . 28 C3
Martinvelle (88) . . . 117 K2
Martisserre (31) . . . 287 F3
Martizay (36) . . . 146 D6
Martot (27) . . . 35 H4
Martragny (14) . . . 32 C4
la Martre (83) . . . 279 K3
Martres (33) . . . 230 B3
les Martres-d'Artière (63) . . . 203 F1
Martres-de-Rivière (31) . . . 305 J1
les Martres-de-Veyre (63) . . . 202 E3
Martres-sur-Morge (63) . . . 185 G6
Martres-Tolosane (31) . . . 287 H6
Martrin (12) . . . 271 J2
Martrois (21) . . . 135 F5
la Martyre (29) . . . 46 D4
les Martys (11) . . . 290 A3
Maruéjols-lès-Gardon (30) . . . 274 E1
Marval (87) . . . 198 A4
Marvaux-Vieux (08) . . . 42 B3
Marvejols (48) . . . 237 G6
Marvelise (25) . . . 139 F2
Marville (55) . . . 43 J1
Marville-Moutiers-Brûlé (28) . . . 57 F6
Mary (71) . . . 171 G3
Mary-sur-Marne (77) . . . 60 B1
Marzan (56) . . . 121 K2
Marzens (81) . . . 270 B6
Marzy (58) . . . 150 D4
le Mas (06) . . . 280 C2
Mas-Blanc-des-Alpilles (13) . . . 276 B4
Mas-Cabardès (11) . . . 290 B3
le Mas-d'Agenais (47) . . . 247 H2
le Mas-d'Artige (23) . . . 200 E3
Mas-d'Auvignon (32) . . . 267 H2
le Mas-d'Azil (09) . . . 307 F1
Mas-de-Londres (34) . . . 274 A4
le Mas-de-Tence (43) . . . 221 G4
Mas-des-Cours (11) . . . 309 G1
Mas-d'Orcières (48) . . . 254 D1
Mas-Grenier (82) . . . 268 E3
Mas-Saint-Chély (48) . . . 253 K3
Mas-Saintes-Puelles (11) . . . 289 G4
Masbaraud-Mérignat (23) . . . 182 C5
Mascaraàs-Haron (64) . . . 284 E1
Mascaras (32) . . . 285 K1
Mascaras (65) . . . 285 J5
Mascarville (31) . . . 289 F1
Masclat (46) . . . 233 H2
Masevaux (68) . . . 119 J4
Maslacq (64) . . . 283 K2
Masléon (87) . . . 199 J2
Maslives (41) . . . 129 G2
le Masnau-Massuguiès (81) . . . 271 H4
Masnières (59) . . . 11 J5
Masny (59) . . . 11 J2
Masparraute (64) . . . 283 F3
Maspie-Lalonquère-Juillacq (64) . . . 285 F2
Masquières (47) . . . 249 F2
Massabrac (31) . . . 288 B5
Massac (11) . . . 309 G1
Massac (17) . . . 178 C6
Massac-Séran (81) . . . 270 B6
Massaguel (81) . . . 289 K2
Massais (79) . . . 144 A3
Massals (81) . . . 271 H3
Massanes (30) . . . 274 E1
Massangis (89) . . . 134 A2
Massat (09) . . . 307 F4
Massay (18) . . . 148 C2
le Massegros (48) . . . 253 H3
Masseilles (33) . . . 246 E2
Massels (47) . . . 248 D3
Massérac (44) . . . 102 D4
Masseret (19) . . . 199 H5
Masseube (32) . . . 286 C3
Massiac (15) . . . 219 F3
Massieu (38) . . . 207 J6
Massieux (01) . . . 188 C5
Massiges (51) . . . 42 C5
Massignac (16) . . . 197 K2
Massignieu-de-Rives (01) . . . 207 K2
Massillargues-Attuech (30) . . . 274 D1
Massilly (71) . . . 171 H4
Massingy (21) . . . 115 F4
Massingy (74) . . . 190 D6
Massingy-lès-Semur (21) . . . 134 E3
Massingy-lès-Vitteaux (21) . . . 135 G4
Massognes (86) . . . 162 C1
Massoins (06) . . . 281 F1
Massongy (74) . . . 174 E5
Massoulès (47) . . . 248 E3
Massugas (33) . . . 230 D3
Massy (71) . . . 171 G4
Massy (76) . . . 16 C4
Massy (91) . . . 58 D5
Mastaing (59) . . . 12 B2
Matafelon-Granges (01) . . . 189 K1
les Matelles (34) . . . 274 B5
Matemale (66) . . . 313 J3
Matha (17) . . . 178 B6
Mathaux (10) . . . 90 E4
Mathenay (39) . . . 155 H3
Mathieu (14) . . . 32 E4
Mathons (52) . . . 92 A3
Mathonville (76) . . . 16 C5
Matignicourt-Goncourt (51) . . . 63 G5
Matignon (22) . . . 50 A3
Matigny (80) . . . 19 H3
Matougues (51) . . . 62 C1
Matour (71) . . . 187 J1
Matra (2B) . . . 319 H6
Matringhem (62) . . . 5 F5
Mattaincourt (88) . . . 94 A4

Mattexey (54) . . . 94 D2
Matton-et-Clémency (08) . . . 23 H4
Matzenheim (67) . . . 70 E5
Maubec (38) . . . 207 F4
Maubec (82) . . . 268 B4
Maubec (84) . . . 276 E5
Maubert-Fontaine (08) . . . 22 A2
Maubeuge (59) . . . 13 H3
Maubourguet (65) . . . 285 H2
Mauchamps (91) . . . 86 D2
Maucomble (76) . . . 16 C4
Maucor (64) . . . 284 D3
Maucourt (60) . . . 19 H5
Maucourt (80) . . . 19 F3
Maucourt-sur-Orne (55) . . . 43 J4
Maudétour-en-Vexin (95) . . . 36 E6
Mauguio (34) . . . 274 D6
Maulan (55) . . . 64 B5
Maulay (86) . . . 145 F4
Maulde (59) . . . 7 H6
Maule (78) . . . 57 K3
Mauléon (79) . . . 143 G4
Mauléon-Barousse (65) . . . 305 H3
Mauléon-d'Armagnac (32) . . . 266 A2
Mauléon-Licharre (64) . . . 283 H5
Maulers (60) . . . 17 K6
Maulette (78) . . . 57 H4
Maulévrier (49) . . . 143 G3
Maulévrier-Sainte-Gertrude (76) . . . 15 G6
Maulichères (32) . . . 266 B5
Maumusson (44) . . . 124 B3
Maumusson (82) . . . 268 B2
Maumusson-Laguian (32) . . . 266 B6
Mauny (76) . . . 35 F2
Maupas (10) . . . 114 B1
Maupas (32) . . . 266 A3
Mauperthuis (77) . . . 60 B4
Maupertuis (50) . . . 31 G5
Maupertus-sur-Mer (50) . . . 28 E2
Mauprévoir (86) . . . 179 K3
Mauquenchy (76) . . . 16 D5
Mauran (31) . . . 287 H6
Maure (64) . . . 285 G3
Maure-de-Bretagne (35) . . . 102 D1
Maurecourt (78) . . . 58 B2
Mauregard (77) . . . 59 G1
Mauregny-en-Haye (02) . . . 20 E6
Maureilhan (34) . . . 291 K4
Maureillas-las-Illas (66) . . . 315 G4
Mauremont (31) . . . 288 E2
Maurens (24) . . . 231 H1
Maurens (31) . . . 289 F2
Maurens (32) . . . 268 B6
Maurens-Scopont (81) . . . 289 F1
Maurepas (78) . . . 58 A5
Maurepas (80) . . . 11 F6
Mauressac (31) . . . 288 B4
Mauressargues (30) . . . 274 D2
Maureville (31) . . . 288 E2
Mauriac (15) . . . 217 G3
Mauriac (33) . . . 230 C3
Mauries (40) . . . 265 J6
Maurines (15) . . . 236 E2
Maurois (59) . . . 12 C5
Mauron (56) . . . 78 A4
Mauroux (32) . . . 268 A2
Mauroux (46) . . . 249 F1
Maurrin (40) . . . 265 J3
Maurs (15) . . . 235 F4
Maurupt-le-Montois (51) . . . 63 H4
Maury (66) . . . 309 J5
Mausoléo (2B) . . . 318 D3
Maussac (19) . . . 200 D6
Maussane-les-Alpilles (13) . . . 276 B4
Maussans (70) . . . 138 C3
Mautes (23) . . . 183 J6
Mauvages (55) . . . 64 E6
Mauvaisin (31) . . . 288 C4
Mauves (07) . . . 222 B5
Mauves-sur-Huisne (61) . . . 83 J3
Mauves-sur-Loire (44) . . . 123 J3
Mauvezin (31) . . . 287 G3
Mauvezin (32) . . . 268 B5
Mauvezin (65) . . . 304 E1
Mauvezin-d'Armagnac (40) . . . 266 A2
Mauvezin-de-Prat (09) . . . 306 C2
Mauvezin-de-Sainte-Croix (09) . . . 306 E1
Mauvezin-sur-Gupie (47) . . . 230 E6
Mauvières (36) . . . 164 C3
Mauvilly (21) . . . 115 G6
Maux (58) . . . 152 A3
Mauzac (31) . . . 288 A4
Mauzac-et-Grand-Castang (24) . . . 232 B2
Mauzé-sur-le-Mignon (79) . . . 177 J2
Mauzé-Thouarsais (79) . . . 144 A4
Mauzens-et-Miremont (24) . . . 214 C6
Mauzun (63) . . . 203 G3
Maves (41) . . . 109 F6
Mavilly-Mandelot (21) . . . 153 K3
la Maxe (57) . . . 45 F4
Maxent (35) . . . 78 C6
Maxéville (54) . . . 66 A4
Maxey-sur-Meuse (88) . . . 93 G2
Maxey-sur-Vaise (55) . . . 93 F1
Maxilly-sur-Léman (74) . . . 175 G5
Maxilly-sur-Saône (21) . . . 136 E5
Maxou (46) . . . 233 H6
Maxstadt (57) . . . 68 B3
May-en-Multien (77) . . . 60 A1
le May-sur-Èvre (49) . . . 142 E2
May-sur-Orne (14) . . . 32 E6
Mayac (24) . . . 214 C2
Mayenne (53) . . . 81 G4
Mayet (72) . . . 106 E5
le Mayet-de-Montagne (03) . . . 186 B4
le Mayet-d'École (03) . . . 185 G3

Maylis (40) . . . 264 E5
Maynal (39) . . . 172 E3
les Mayons (83) . . . 298 C3
Mayot (02) . . . 20 B4
Mayrac (46) . . . 233 J1
Mayran (12) . . . 251 K2
Mayrègne (31) . . . 305 H4
Mayres (07) . . . 238 E4
Mayres (63) . . . 220 A1
Mayres-Savel (38) . . . 242 A1
Mayreville (11) . . . 289 F5
Mayrinhac-Lentour (46) . . . 234 B3
Maysel (60) . . . 37 K4
Mazamet (81) . . . 290 B2
Mazan (84) . . . 257 H6
Mazan-l'Abbaye (07) . . . 238 E3
Mazangé (41) . . . 108 B5
Mazaugues (83) . . . 297 J3
Mazaye (63) . . . 202 B2
Mazé (49) . . . 125 K3
le Mazeau (79) . . . 161 F6
Mazeirat (23) . . . 182 E3
Mazeley (88) . . . 94 C5
Mazerat-Aurouze (43) . . . 219 J4
Mazeray (17) . . . 177 K6
Mazères (09) . . . 288 E5
Mazères (33) . . . 230 A6
Mazères-de-Neste (65) . . . 305 H1
Mazères-Lezons (64) . . . 284 D4
Mazères-sur-Salat (31) . . . 287 G6
Mazerier (03) . . . 185 G3
Mazerny (08) . . . 22 C5
Mazerolles (16) . . . 197 H2
Mazerolles (17) . . . 195 G4
Mazerolles (40) . . . 265 H2
Mazerolles (64) . . . 284 C2
Mazerolles (65) . . . 285 K3
Mazerolles (86) . . . 163 J5
Mazerolles-du-Razès (11) . . . 308 D1
Mazerolles-le-Salin (25) . . . 137 J6
Mazerulles (54) . . . 66 C4
Mazet-Saint-Voy (43) . . . 221 F5
Mazeuil (86) . . . 144 E6
Mazeyrat-d'Allier (43) . . . 219 J4
Mazeyrolles (24) . . . 232 D4
la Mazière-aux-Bons-
   Hommes (23) . . . 183 J6
Mazières (16) . . . 197 J1
Mazières-de-Touraine (37) . . . 127 F4
Mazières-en-Gâtine (79) . . . 161 J4
Mazières-en-Mauges (49) . . . 143 F3
Mazières-Naresse (47) . . . 232 A4
Mazières-sur-Béronne (79) . . . 178 D2
Mazille (71) . . . 171 G5
Mazingarbe (62) . . . 6 A6
Mazinghem (62) . . . 5 H4
Mazinghien (59) . . . 12 E5
Mazion (33) . . . 211 G3
Mazirat (03) . . . 183 K2
Mazirot (88) . . . 94 A4
le Mazis (80) . . . 17 G2
Mazoires (63) . . . 218 D1
Mazouau (65) . . . 305 F2
Mazuby (11) . . . 308 C5
les Mazures (08) . . . 22 C2
Mazzola (2B) . . . 319 H6
Méailles (04) . . . 260 D6
Méallet (15) . . . 217 H3
Méasnes (23) . . . 165 K5
Meaucé (28) . . . 84 B2
Méaudre (38) . . . 223 J4
la Meauffe (50) . . . 31 H2
la Méaugon (22) . . . 49 F6
Meaulne (03) . . . 167 H3
Méaulte (80) . . . 18 E1
Méautis (50) . . . 31 F1
Meaux (77) . . . 59 K2
Meaux-la-Montagne (69) . . . 187 J4
Meauzac (82) . . . 249 H6
Mecé (35) . . . 79 K3
Mechmont (46) . . . 233 H5
Mécleuves (57) . . . 45 G6
Mecquignies (59) . . . 13 F3
Mécrin (55) . . . 64 E3
Mécringes (51) . . . 61 F3
Médan (78) . . . 58 B2
Médavy (61) . . . 54 D5
Medeyrolles (63) . . . 220 B1
Médière (25) . . . 139 F3
Médillac (16) . . . 212 D3
Médis (17) . . . 194 D3
Médonville (88) . . . 93 G5
Médréac (35) . . . 78 C2
le Mée (28) . . . 109 F3
Mée (53) . . . 104 D5
le Mée-sur-Seine (77) . . . 87 H2
les Mées (04) . . . 259 G6
Mées (40) . . . 264 A4
les Mées (72) . . . 82 E4
Mégange (57) . . . 45 H4
Megève (74) . . . 192 A6
Mégevette (74) . . . 191 J1
Mégrit (22) . . . 50 B6
Méharicourt (80) . . . 18 E3
Méharin (64) . . . 282 E3
Méhers (41) . . . 129 F5
Méhoncourt (54) . . . 94 C1
Méhoudin (61) . . . 81 J2
Mehun-sur-Yèvre (18) . . . 148 E2
la Meignanne (49) . . . 125 F3
Meigné (49) . . . 125 K6
Meigné-le-Vicomte (49) . . . 126 D3
Meigneux (77) . . . 88 B2
Meigneux (80) . . . 17 H3
Meilhac (87) . . . 198 E3

Meilhan (32) . . . 286 D3
Meilhan (40) . . . 264 E2
Meilhan-sur-Garonne (47) . . . 230 D6
Meilhards (19) . . . 199 J5
Meilhaud (63) . . . 202 E5
Meillac (35) . . . 51 F1
Meillant (18) . . . 167 G1
Meillard (03) . . . 168 D6
le Meillard (80) . . . 9 K4
la Meilleraie-Tillay (85) . . . 160 D1
Meilleray (77) . . . 60 E4
la Meilleraye-de-Bretagne (44) . . . 103 J5
Meillerie (74) . . . 175 H4
Meillers (03) . . . 168 C4
Meillon (64) . . . 284 D4
Meillonnas (01) . . . 189 H1
Meilly-sur-Rouvres (21) . . . 153 H1
Meisenthal (57) . . . 69 G4
Meistratzheim (67) . . . 70 D5
le Meix (21) . . . 135 K2
le Meix-Saint-Epoing (51) . . . 61 G5
le Meix-Tiercelin (51) . . . 62 E6
Méjannes-le-Clap (30) . . . 255 K4
Méjannes-lès-Alès (30) . . . 255 H6
Mela (2A) . . . 323 F2
Mélagues (12) . . . 272 D5
Mélamare (76) . . . 14 D6
Melay (49) . . . 143 G1
Melay (52) . . . 117 H3
Melay (71) . . . 186 E2
le Mêle-sur-Sarthe (61) . . . 83 F2
Mélecey (70) . . . 138 E2
Melesse (35) . . . 79 G3
Melgven (29) . . . 99 F2
Mélicocq (60) . . . 38 E1
Mélicourt (27) . . . 55 H2
Méligny-le-Grand (55) . . . 64 E5
Méligny-le-Petit (55) . . . 64 D5
Melin (70) . . . 117 H5
Melincourt (70) . . . 118 A3
Mélisey (70) . . . 119 F5
Mélisey (89) . . . 114 B4
Meljac (12) . . . 252 A5
Mellac (29) . . . 99 H3
Mellé (35) . . . 80 B2
Melle (79) . . . 178 D2
Mellecey (71) . . . 153 K6
Melleran (79) . . . 178 E3
Melleray (72) . . . 107 K1
Melleroy (45) . . . 112 A4
Melles (31) . . . 305 K4
Melleville (76) . . . 16 D1
Mellionnec (22) . . . 76 B4
Mello (60) . . . 37 K4
Meloisey (21) . . . 153 K3
Melrand (56) . . . 100 C1
Melsheim (67) . . . 70 D1
Melun (77) . . . 87 H2
Melve (04) . . . 259 G2
Melz-sur-Seine (77) . . . 88 C2
Membrey (70) . . . 137 H1
la Membrolle-sur-Choisille (37) . . . 127 H4
la Membrolle-sur-Longuenée (49) . . . 125 F2
Membrolles (41) . . . 109 G3
Méménil (88) . . . 94 E5
Memmelshoffen (67) . . . 25 B2
le Mémont (25) . . . 157 J1
Menades (89) . . . 133 J4
Ménarmont (88) . . . 95 F2
Menars (41) . . . 129 F1
Menat (63) . . . 184 D4
Menaucourt (55) . . . 64 C5
Mencas (62) . . . 5 F5
Menchhoffen (67) . . . 69 H5
Mende (48) . . . 237 J6
Mendionde (64) . . . 282 D3
Menditte (64) . . . 283 H5
Mendive (64) . . . 282 E6
Ménéac (56) . . . 77 J5
Menerbes (84) . . . 277 F3
Ménerval (76) . . . 16 E6
Ménerville (78) . . . 57 H2
Menesble (21) . . . 115 J5
Méneslies (80) . . . 8 D5
Menesplet (24) . . . 212 E5
Ménesqueville (27) . . . 36 A3
Ménessaire (21) . . . 152 D2
Menestreau (58) . . . 132 D4
Ménestreau-en-Villette (45) . . . 130 B1
Menet (15) . . . 217 J2
Menetou-Couture (18) . . . 150 B3
Menetou-Râtel (18) . . . 131 J5
Menetou-Salon (18) . . . 149 H1
Menetou-sur-Nahon (36) . . . 147 K1
Ménétréol-sous-Sancerre (18) . . . 131 K5
Ménétréol-sur-Sauldre (18) . . . 130 E4
Ménétréols-sous-Vatan (36) . . . 148 B4
Ménétreuil (71) . . . 172 C3
Ménétreux-le-Pitois (21) . . . 134 D3
Ménétrol (63) . . . 202 D1
Menétru-le-Vignoble (39) . . . 155 H6
Menétrux-en-Joux (39) . . . 173 J2
Ménévillers (60) . . . 38 C1
Menglon (26) . . . 241 J4
Ménigoute (79) . . . 162 B4
Ménil (53) . . . 105 F5
le Ménil (88) . . . 119 G3
Ménil-Annelles (08) . . . 41 J4
Ménil-aux-Bois (55) . . . 64 D4
le Ménil-Bérard (61) . . . 55 H5
le Ménil-Broût (61) . . . 82 E2
le Ménil-Ciboult (61) . . . 53 F4
le Ménil-de-Briouze (61) . . . 53 J5
Ménil-de-Senones (88) . . . 95 J3
Ménil-en-Xaintois (88) . . . 93 J4
Ménil-Erreux (61) . . . 82 E2

Ménil-Froger (61) . . . 55 F5
Ménil-Gondouin (61) . . . 53 K4
le Ménil-Guyon (61) . . . 83 F1
Ménil-Hermei (61) . . . 53 K3
Ménil-Hubert-en-Exmes (61) . . . 54 E4
Ménil-Hubert-sur-Orne (61) . . . 53 J3
Ménil-Jean (61) . . . 54 A5
Ménil-la-Horgne (55) . . . 64 E5
Ménil-la-Tour (54) . . . 65 H4
Ménil-Lépinois (08) . . . 41 H3
le Ménil-Scelleur (61) . . . 54 B6
Ménil-sur-Belvitte (88) . . . 95 F3
Ménil-sur-Saulx (55) . . . 64 B6
le Ménil-Vicomte (61) . . . 55 F5
Ménil-Vin (61) . . . 53 K3
Ménilles (27) . . . 57 F1
la Ménitré (49) . . . 125 K4
Mennecy (91) . . . 87 F1
Mennessis (02) . . . 19 K4
Mennetou-sur-Cher (41) . . . 129 K6
Menneval (27) . . . 34 D6
Menneville (02) . . . 40 E2
Menneville (62) . . . 4 D3
Mennevret (02) . . . 20 C2
Mennouveaux (52) . . . 116 D1
Ménoire (19) . . . 216 B5
Menomblet (85) . . . 160 E1
Menoncourt (90) . . . 119 J6
Ménonval (76) . . . 16 D3
Menotey (39) . . . 155 G1
Menou (58) . . . 132 D5
Menouville (95) . . . 37 H5
le Menoux (36) . . . 165 H4
Menoux (70) . . . 118 A4
Mens (38) . . . 242 B2
Mensignac (24) . . . 213 J3
Menskirch (57) . . . 27 K4
Mentheville (76) . . . 14 D4
Menthon-Saint-Bernard (74) . . . 191 G6
Menthonnex-en-Bornes (74) . . . 191 F3
Menthonnex-sous-Clermont (74) . . . 190 D5
Mentières (15) . . . 218 C2
Menton (06) . . . 281 K3
Mentque-Nortbécourt (62) . . . 2 E4
Menucourt (95) . . . 58 B1
les Menus (61) . . . 84 B2
Menville (31) . . . 268 E5
Méobecq (36) . . . 165 F1
Méolans-Revel (04) . . . 260 B1
Méon (49) . . . 126 D3
Méounes-lès-Montrieux (83) . . . 297 J4
Mer (41) . . . 129 G1
Méracq (64) . . . 284 C1
Méral (53) . . . 104 C3
Méras (09) . . . 288 A6
Mercatel (62) . . . 11 F3
Mercenac (09) . . . 306 C2
Merceuil (21) . . . 154 A4
Mercey (27) . . . 36 A6
Mercey-le-Grand (25) . . . 137 H6
Mercey-sur-Saône (70) . . . 137 G2
Mercin-et-Vaux (02) . . . 39 J3
Merck-Saint-Liévin (62) . . . 5 F4
Merckeghem (59) . . . 3 G3
Mercœur (19) . . . 216 C6
Mercœur (43) . . . 219 G3
Mercuer (07) . . . 239 H5
Mercuès (46) . . . 249 K1
Mercurey (71) . . . 153 K5
Mercurol (26) . . . 222 C5
Mercury (73) . . . 209 F2
Mercus-Garrabet (09) . . . 307 J4
Mercy (03) . . . 169 G5
Mercy (89) . . . 113 G2
Mercy-le-Bas (54) . . . 26 D4
Mercy-le-Haut (54) . . . 26 D4
Merdrignac (22) . . . 77 K4
Méré (78) . . . 57 K4
Méré (89) . . . 113 J4
Méreau (18) . . . 148 D2
Méréaucourt (80) . . . 17 H4
Méréglise (28) . . . 84 D5
Mérélessart (80) . . . 17 G1
Mérens (32) . . . 267 H4
Mérens-les-Vals (09) . . . 313 G6
Mérenville (31) . . . 268 C6
Méreuil (05) . . . 258 D2
Méréville (54) . . . 66 A6
Méréville (91) . . . 86 C4
Merey (27) . . . 57 F2
Mérey-sous-Montrond (25) . . . 156 C1
Mérey-Vieilley (25) . . . 138 A5
Merfy (51) . . . 40 E3
Mergey (10) . . . 90 A3
Meria (2B) . . . 317 D2
Mérial (11) . . . 308 C5
Méricourt (62) . . . 11 F1
Méricourt (78) . . . 57 H1
Méricourt-en-Vimeu (80) . . . 17 H2
Méricourt-l'Abbé (80) . . . 18 D2
Méricourt-sur-Somme (80) . . . 18 E2
Mériel (95) . . . 37 A6
Mérifons (34) . . . 273 F6
Mérignac (16) . . . 196 B3
Mérignac (17) . . . 212 A2
Mérignac (33) . . . 229 G2
Mérignas (33) . . . 230 C3
Mérignat (01) . . . 189 J3
Mérignies (59) . . . 6 E6
Mérigny (36) . . . 164 B3
Mérigon (09) . . . 306 E1
Mérilheu (65) . . . 304 D1
Mérillac (22) . . . 77 K3
Mérinchal (23) . . . 183 K6
Mérindol (84) . . . 277 F4
Mérindol-les-Oliviers (26) . . . 257 H3

Mérinville (45) . . . 112 A2
le Mériot (10) . . . 88 E2
Méritein (64) . . . 283 J3
Merkwiller-Pechelbronn (67) . . . 25 B2
Merlas (38) . . . 207 J5
la Merlatière (85) . . . 142 A6
Merlaut (51) . . . 63 G4
Merle-Leignec (42) . . . 220 D1
Merléac (22) . . . 76 E3
le Merlerault (61) . . . 55 F5
Merles (82) . . . 249 F6
Merles-sur-Loison (55) . . . 43 J3
Merlevenez (56) . . . 100 B4
Merlieux-et-Fouquerolles (02) . . . 40 A1
Merlimont (62) . . . 4 A6
Merlines (19) . . . 201 H4
Mernel (35) . . . 102 D1
Mérobert (91) . . . 86 B3
Mérona (39) . . . 173 G3
Mérouville (28) . . . 86 A5
Meroux (90) . . . 139 J1
Merpins (16) . . . 195 J3
Merrey (52) . . . 117 F1
Merrey-sur-Arce (10) . . . 114 E1
Merri (61) . . . 54 C3
Merris (59) . . . 6 A3
Merry-la-Vallée (89) . . . 112 D5
Merry-Sec (89) . . . 133 F1
Merry-sur-Yonne (89) . . . 133 G2
Mers-les-Bains (80) . . . 8 C5
Mers-sur-Indre (36) . . . 166 A2
Merschweiller (57) . . . 27 J3
Mersuay (70) . . . 118 A5
Merten (57) . . . 45 K3
Mertrud (52) . . . 91 J3
Mertzen (68) . . . 97 A4
Mertzwiller (67) . . . 69 K5
Méru (60) . . . 37 H4
Merval (02) . . . 40 C3
Mervans (71) . . . 154 D6
Mervent (85) . . . 160 E4
Mervilla (31) . . . 288 C2
Merville (31) . . . 269 F5
Merville (59) . . . 6 A4
Merville-Franceville-Plage (14) . . . 33 F3
Merviller (54) . . . 95 G1
Merxheim (68) . . . 96 B6
Méry (73) . . . 208 B3
Méry-Corbon (14) . . . 33 G5
Méry-ès-Bois (18) . . . 130 E6
Méry-la-Bataille (60) . . . 18 D6
Méry-Prémecy (51) . . . 40 D4
Méry-sur-Cher (18) . . . 148 C1
Méry-sur-Marne (77) . . . 60 C2
Méry-sur-Oise (95) . . . 58 D1
Méry-sur-Seine (10) . . . 89 J2
le Merzer (22) . . . 48 C3
Mésandans (25) . . . 138 D3
Mésanger (44) . . . 124 A3
Mésangueville (76) . . . 16 E6
Mesbrecourt-Richecourt (02) . . . 20 C4
Meschers-sur-Gironde (17) . . . 194 D4
Mescoules (24) . . . 231 H3
le Mesge (80) . . . 17 J1
Mesgrigny (10) . . . 89 J2
Mésigny (74) . . . 190 E4
Meslan (56) . . . 99 K2
Mesland (41) . . . 128 C3
Meslay (14) . . . 53 J2
Meslay (41) . . . 108 C3
Meslay-du-Maine (53) . . . 105 G3
Meslay-le-Grenet (28) . . . 85 F4
Meslay-le-Vidame (28) . . . 85 G5
Meslières (25) . . . 139 J3
Meslin (22) . . . 77 H1
Mesmay (25) . . . 156 A2
Mesmont (08) . . . 22 A5
Mesmont (21) . . . 135 H5
Mesnac (16) . . . 195 J2
Mesnard-la-Barotière (85) . . . 142 C5
Mesnay (39) . . . 155 K4
les Mesneux (51) . . . 40 E4
la Mesnière (61) . . . 83 G2
Mesnières-en-Bray (76) . . . 16 C3
le Mesnil (50) . . . 28 C5
le Mesnil-Adelée (50) . . . 52 C5
le Mesnil-Amand (50) . . . 30 E6
le Mesnil-Amelot (77) . . . 59 G1
le Mesnil-Amey (50) . . . 31 G3
le Mesnil-Angot (50) . . . 31 G2
le Mesnil-au-Grain (14) . . . 32 C6
le Mesnil-au-Val (50) . . . 28 D3
le Mesnil-Aubert (50) . . . 30 E5
le Mesnil-Aubry (95) . . . 59 F1
le Mesnil-Auzouf (14) . . . 53 F1
le Mesnil-Bacley (14) . . . 54 D1
le Mesnil-Benoist (14) . . . 52 D2
Mesnil-Bruntel (80) . . . 19 G2
le Mesnil-Caussois (14) . . . 52 D3
le Mesnil-Clinchamps (14) . . . 52 D3
le Mesnil-Conteville (60) . . . 17 J5
le Mesnil-Domqueur (80) . . . 9 J4
le Mesnil-Durand (14) . . . 54 D1
le Mesnil-Durdent (76) . . . 15 G3
Mesnil-en-Arrouaise (80) . . . 11 G6
le Mesnil-en-Thelle (60) . . . 37 J5
le Mesnil-en-Vallée (49) . . . 124 C2
le Mesnil-Esnard (76) . . . 35 J2
le Mesnil-Eudes (14) . . . 33 K6
le Mesnil-Eury (50) . . . 31 G3
Mesnil-Follemprise (76) . . . 16 B3
le Mesnil-Fuguet (27) . . . 35 H6
le Mesnil-Garnier (50) . . . 52 A3
le Mesnil-Germain (14) . . . 54 E1
le Mesnil-Gilbert (50) . . . 52 C5
le Mesnil-Guillaume (14) . . . 34 A6

le Mesnil-Hardray (27) 56 B2
le Mesnil-Herman (50) 31 G4
le Mesnil-Jourdain (27) 35 H5
Mesnil-la-Comtesse (10) 90 C2
le Mesnil-le-Roi (78) 58 C2
Mesnil-Lettre (10) 90 C3
le Mesnil-Lieubray (76) 36 B1
Mesnil-Martinsart (80) 10 D6
le Mesnil-Mauger (14) 33 H6
Mesnil-Mauger (76) 16 D5
le Mesnil-Opac (50) 31 H4
le Mesnil-Ozenne (50) 52 B5
Mesnil-Panneville (76) 15 H6
le Mesnil-Patry (14) 32 C4
Mesnil-Rainfray (50) 52 C5
Mesnil-Raoul (76) 35 K2
le Mesnil-Raoult (50) 31 H4
le Mesnil-Réaume (76) 16 D1
le Mesnil-Robert (14) 52 D3
le Mesnil-Rogues (50) 30 E6
Mesnil-Rousset (27) 55 H3
le Mesnil-Rouxelin (50) 31 H3
le Mesnil-Saint-Denis (78) 58 B5
le Mesnil-Saint-Firmin (60) 18 C5
le Mesnil-Saint-Georges (80) 18 D5
Mesnil-Saint-Laurent (02) 20 A3
Mesnil-Saint-Loup (10) 89 H5
Mesnil-Saint-Nicaise (80) 19 G3
Mesnil-Saint-Père (10) 90 D5
Mesnil-Sellières (10) 90 C4
le Mesnil-Simon (14) 33 J6
le Mesnil-Simon (28) 57 G3
le Mesnil-sous-Jumièges (76) 35 F2
Mesnil-sous-Vienne (27) 36 D2
le Mesnil-sur-Blangy (14) 34 A4
le Mesnil-sur-Bulles (60) 37 K1
Mesnil-sur-l'Estrée (27) 56 E4
le Mesnil-sur-Oger (51) 62 A2
le Mesnil-Théribus (60) 37 G4
le Mesnil-Thomas (28) 84 C1
le Mesnil-Tôve (50) 52 C5
le Mesnil-Véneron (50) 31 G2
Mesnil-Verclives (27) 36 B3
le Mesnil-Vigot (50) 31 F3
le Mesnil-Villeman (50) 52 A3
le Mesnil-Villement (14) 53 J3
le Mesnilbus (50) 31 F3
le Mesnillard (50) 52 C6
Mesnois (39) 173 H2
les Mesnuls (78) 57 H5
Mespaul (29) 46 E4
Mesplède (64) 284 A1
Mesples (03) 166 E5
Mespuits (91) 86 D4
Mesquer (44) 121 J3
Messac (17) 212 A1
Messac (35) 102 E2
Messanges (21) 154 A1
Messanges (40) 262 C3
Messas (45) 109 H5
Messé (79) 179 F1
Messei (61) 53 H5
Messein (54) 66 A6
Messeix (63) 201 H4
Messemé (86) 145 F3
Messery (74) 174 D5
Messey-sur-Grosne (71) 171 J2
Messia-sur-Sorne (39) 173 F2
Messigny-et-Vantoux (21) 136 A4
Messimy (69) 205 J3
Messimy-sur-Saône (01) 188 B4
Messincourt (08) 23 H4
Messon (10) 89 K5
Messy (77) 59 H2
Mesterrieux (33) 230 C4
Mestes (19) 201 F5
Mesves-sur-Loire (58) 150 C1
Mesvres (71) 152 E5
Métabief (25) 157 F6
les Métairies (16) 196 B2
Métairies-Saint-Quirin (57) 67 J3
Méteren (59) 6 A3
Méthamis (84) 277 F1
Métigny (80) 17 H1
Metting (57) 69 F6
Mettray (37) 127 J4
Metz (57) 45 F5
Metz-en-Couture (62) 11 H5
Metz-le-Comte (58) 133 G4
Metz-Robert (10) 114 B2
Metz-Tessy (74) 191 F5
Metzeral (68) 119 K1
Metzeresche (57) 45 G3
Metzervisse (57) 45 G3
Metzing (57) 68 C3
Meucon (56) 101 F4
Meudon (92) 58 D4
Meuilley (21) 154 A2
Meulan (78) 58 A1
Meulers (76) 16 B2
Meulles (14) 55 F2
Meulson (21) 115 G6
Meunet-Planches (36) 148 C6
Meunet-sur-Vatan (36) 148 B3
Meung-sur-Loire (45) 109 J5
Meurcé (72) 82 E5
Meurchin (62) 6 C6
Meurcourt (70) 118 B5
la Meurdraquière (50) 51 K1
Meures (52) 92 A6
Meurival (02) 40 C3
Meursac (17) 194 E3
Meursanges (21) 154 B4
Meursault (21) 153 K4
Meurville (10) 91 G6
Meusnes (41) 129 G6

Meussia (39) 173 H4
Meuvaines (14) 32 C3
Meux (87) 195 J6
le Meux (60) 38 D3
Meuzac (87) 199 G5
Mévoisins (28) 85 H1
Mévouillon (26) 258 B3
Meximieux (01) 189 G6
Mexy (54) 26 D2
Mey (57) 45 F5
Meyenheim (68) 96 C6
Meylan (38) 224 B3
Meymac (19) 200 D5
Meynes (30) 275 J3
Meyrals (24) 232 D1
Meyrannes (30) 255 H3
Meyrargues (13) 277 J5
Meyras (07) 239 G4
Meyreuil (13) 296 D1
Meyrié (38) 207 F4
Meyrieu-les-Étangs (38) 206 E5
Meyrieux-Trouet (73) 208 A3
Meyrignac-l'Église (19) 216 B1
Meyronne (46) 233 J2
Meyronnes (04) 227 C6
Meyrueis (48) 254 A5
Meys (69) 205 G3
Meyssac (19) 215 K5
Meysse (07) 240 A5
Meyssiès (38) 206 D5
Meythet (74) 191 F5
la Meyze (87) 198 E4
Meyzieu (69) 206 C2
Mézangers (53) 81 J6
Mèze (34) 292 E3
Mézel (04) 259 J6
Mezel (63) 202 E2
Mézens (81) 269 K4
Mézeray (72) 106 C5
Mézères (43) 220 D4
Mézériat (01) 188 E2
Mézerolles (80) 9 K4
Mézerville (11) 289 F5
Mézidon-Canon (14) 33 G6
la Mézière (35) 79 F3
Mézières-au-Perche (28) 84 E5
Mézières-en-Brenne (36) 147 F6
Mézières-en-Drouais (28) 57 F5
Mézières-en-Gâtinais (45) 111 F2
Mézières-en-Santerre (80) 18 D3
Mézières-en-Vexin (27) 36 B5
Mézières-lez-Cléry (45) 109 K5
Mézières-sous-Lavardin (72) 82 C6
Mézières-sur-Couesnon (35) 79 J2
Mézières-sur-Issoire (87) 180 D3
Mézières-sur-Oise (02) 20 B3
Mézières-sur-Ponthouin (72) 83 F6
Mézières-sur-Seine (78) 57 K2
Mézilhac (07) 239 G2
Mézilles (89) 132 C1
Mézin (47) 247 H6
Méziré (90) 139 J2
Mézos (40) 244 D5
Mézy-Moulins (02) 61 F1
Mézy-sur-Seine (78) 58 A2
Mhère (58) 152 A1
Mialet (24) 198 B5
Mialet (30) 255 F5
Mialos (64) 284 C2
Miannay (80) 9 F5
Michaugues (58) 133 F6
Michelbach (68) 97 A2
Michelbach-le-Bas (68) 97 D4
Michelbach-le-Haut (68) 97 D4
Michery (89) 88 C3
Midrevaux (88) 93 F3
Mièges (39) 156 C6
Miélan (32) 286 A3
Miellin (70) 119 G4
Miermaigne (28) 84 B5
Miers (46) 234 A2
Miéry (39) 155 J6
Mietesheim (67) 69 J5
Mieussy (74) 191 K2
Mieuxcé (61) 82 C3
Migé (89) 133 F1
Migennes (89) 113 F3
Miglos (09) 307 J5
Mignaloux-Beauvoir (86) 163 F4
Mignavillers (70) 138 E1
Migné (36) 164 E2
Migné-Auxances (86) 162 E3
Mignères (45) 111 H2
Mignerette (45) 111 G2
Mignéville (54) 95 G1
Mignières (28) 85 F4
Mignovillard (39) 156 D6
Migny (36) 148 D3
Migré (17) 177 K3
Migron (17) 195 J1
Mijanès (09) 313 J1
Mijoux (01) 174 A5
la Milesse (72) 106 D2
Milhac (46) 233 G3
Milhac-d'Auberoche (24) 214 C4
Milhac-de-Nontron (24) 198 A6
Milhars (81) 250 E5
Milhas (31) 306 A2
Milhaud (30) 275 G4
Milhavet (81) 270 C1
Milizac (29) 72 C3
Millac (86) 180 B2
Millam (59) 3 G4
Millançay (41) 129 J4
Millas (66) 314 E2
Millau (12) 253 G6

Millay (58) 152 C6
Millebosc (76) 16 D1
Millemont (78) 57 J4
Millencourt (80) 10 D6
Millencourt-en-Ponthieu (80) 9 G4
Millery (21) 134 D3
Millery (54) 66 A3
Millery (69) 206 A3
Millevaches (19) 200 D4
Millières (50) 30 E2
Millières (52) 92 D6
Millonfosse (59) 12 C1
Milly (50) 52 C6
Milly-la-Forêt (91) 87 F3
Milly-Lamartine (71) 171 H6
Milly-sur-Bradon (55) 43 G2
Milly-sur-Thérain (60) 37 G1
Milon-la-Chapelle (78) 58 B5
Mimbaste (40) 264 C5
Mimet (13) 296 D2
Mimeure (21) 153 G2
Mimizan (40) 244 C4
Minaucourt-le-Mesnil-
 -lès-Hurlus (51) 42 B5
Minerve (34) 291 F4
Mingot (65) 285 J3
Mingoval (62) 10 D1
Miniac-Morvan (35) 50 E5
Miniac-sous-Bécherel (35) 78 E2
le Minihic-sur-Rance (35) 50 D4
Minihy-Tréguier (22) 48 C2
Minorville (54) 65 H3
Minot (21) 135 J1
Minversheim (67) 69 J6
Minzac (24) 212 D6
Minzier (74) 190 E3
Miolles (81) 271 J3
Mionnay (01) 188 D6
Mions (69) 206 B3
Mios (33) 228 D5
Miossens-Lanusse (64) 284 D2
Mirabeau (04) 259 H5
Mirabeau (84) 278 A4
Mirabel (07) 239 J5
Mirabel (82) 249 K5
Mirabel-aux-Baronnies (26) 257 H3
Mirabel-et-Blacons (26) 240 E3
Miradoux (32) 267 K1
Miramas (13) 276 D6
Mirambeau (17) 211 H1
Mirambeau (31) 287 F3
Miramont-d'Astarac (32) 286 B1
Miramont-de-Comminges (31) 305 K1
Miramont-de-Guyenne (47) 231 G5
Miramont-de-Quercy (82) 249 G4
Miramont-Latour (32) 267 J4
Miramont-Sensacq (40) 265 J6
Mirande (32) 286 B1
Mirandol-Bourgnounac (81) 251 H5
Mirannes (32) 267 F6
Miraumont (80) 10 E5
Miraval-Cabardès (11) 290 B3
Mirbel (52) 92 A4
Miré (49) 105 H5
Mirebeau (86) 145 F6
Mirebeau-sur-Bèze (21) 136 D4
Mirebel (39) 173 H1
Mirecourt (88) 94 A4
Mirefleurs (63) 202 E3
Miremont (31) 288 B3
Miremont (63) 184 B6
Mirepeisset (11) 291 G5
Mirepeix (64) 284 E5
Mirepoix (09) 308 B1
Mirepoix (32) 267 J4
Mirepoix-sur-Tarn (31) 269 J4
Mireval (34) 293 G2
Mireval-Lauragais (11) 289 H5
Miribel (01) 206 B1
Miribel (26) 222 E3
Miribel-Lanchâtre (38) 223 K6
Miribel-les-Échelles (38) 207 K6
Mirmande (26) 240 C4
le Miroir (71) 172 K3
Mirvaux (80) 10 B6
Mirville (76) 14 D5
Miscon (26) 241 J4
Miserey (27) 56 E1
Miserey-Salines (25) 137 K5
Misérieux (01) 188 C3
Misery (80) 19 G2
Mison (04) 258 E3
Missé (79) 144 B4
Missècle (81) 270 C5
Missègre (11) 309 G2
Missery (21) 134 E5
Missillac (44) 102 B6
Missiriac (56) 101 K3
Misson (40) 264 C6
Missy (14) 32 C5
Missy-aux-Bois (02) 39 H3
Missy-lès-Pierrepont (02) 20 E5
Missy-sur-Aisne (02) 39 K2
Misy-sur-Yonne (77) 88 B4
Mitry-Mory (77) 59 H2
Mittainville (78) 57 H6
Mittainvillers (28) 84 E2
Mittelbergheim (67) 70 C5
Mittelbronn (57) 70 A1
Mittelhausbergen (67) 25 A6
Mittelhausen (67) 70 E1
Mittelschaeffolsheim (67) 70 E1
Mittelwihr (68) 96 B3
Mittersheim (57) 67 H2
Mittlach (68) 119 J1
Mittois (14) 54 C1

Mitzach (68) 119 J3
Mizérieux (42) 204 E2
Mizoën (38) 224 E4
Mobecq (50) 30 D1
Moca-Croce (2A) 320 E6
Modane (73) 226 A2
Modène (84) 257 H5
Moëlan-sur-Mer (29) 99 H4
les Moëres (59) 3 J2
Mœrnach (68) 97 B5
Mœslains (52) 63 J6
Mœurs-Verdey (51) 61 G5
Mœuvres (59) 11 H4
Mœze (17) 176 E5
Moffans-et-Vacheresse (70) 138 E1
Mogeville (55) 43 K4
Mognard (73) 208 B2
Mogneneins (01) 188 C3
Mognéville (55) 63 K4
Mogneville (60) 38 A3
Mogues (08) 23 J4
Mohon (56) 77 J6
Moidieu-Détourbe (38) 206 C5
Moigny-sur-École (91) 87 F3
Moimay (70) 138 D2
Moineville (54) 44 D4
Moings (17) 195 J5
Moinville-la-Jeulin (28) 85 J4
Moirans (38) 223 J1
Moirans-en-Montagne (39) 173 H5
Moirax (47) 248 B5
Moiré (69) 188 A5
Moiremont (51) 42 D5
Moirey-Flabas-Crépion (55) 43 H3
Moiron (39) 173 G2
Moiry (08) 23 J5
Moisdon-la-Rivière (44) 103 J5
Moisenay (77) 87 J1
Moislains (80) 11 G6
Moissac (82) 249 G6
Moissac-Bellevue (83) 279 F5
Moissac-Vallée-Française (48) 254 D5
Moissannes (87) 199 J1
Moissat (63) 203 F2
Moisselles (95) 58 E1
Moissey (39) 155 G1
Moissieu-sur-Dolon (38) 222 D1
Moisson (78) 57 J1
Moissy-Cramayel (77) 59 G6
Moissy-Moulinot (58) 133 H5
Moisville (27) 56 D4
Moisy (41) 108 E4
Moïta (2B) 319 J6
les Moitiers-d'Allonne (50) 28 B5
les Moitiers-en-Bauptois (50) 28 E6
Moitron (21) 135 J1
Moitron-sur-Sarthe (72) 82 C5
Moivre (51) 63 G2
Moivrons (54) 66 B3
Molac (56) 101 J4
Molagnies (76) 36 D1
Molain (02) 12 D6
Molain (39) 155 K5
Molamboz (39) 155 J4
Molandier (11) 288 E5
Molas (31) 286 E3
Molay (39) 155 F3
Molay (70) 117 G5
Môlay (89) 113 K6
le Molay-Littry (14) 31 K2
la Môle (83) 301 H3
Moléans (28) 109 F1
Molèdes (15) 218 D3
Molère (65) 304 E1
Molesme (21) 114 D3
Molesmes (89) 133 F2
Molezon (48) 254 C4
Moliens (60) 17 G5
Molières (24) 232 B2
Molières (46) 234 C3
Molières (82) 249 J5
les Molières (91) 58 C6
Molières-Cavaillac (30) 273 J2
Molières-Glandaz (26) 241 H3
Molières-sur-Cèze (30) 255 H4
Moliets-et-Maa (40) 262 C2
Molinchart (02) 20 C6
Molines-en-Queyras (05) 227 C2
Molinet (03) 170 A5
Molineuf (41) 128 D2
Molinges (39) 173 J5
Molinons (89) 89 F5
Molinot (21) 153 H3
Molins-sur-Aube (10) 90 D3
Molitg-les-Bains (66) 314 B2
Mollans (70) 118 D6
Mollans-sur-Ouvèze (26) 257 J4
Mollau (68) 119 J3
Mollégès (13) 276 C3
Molles (03) 185 K3
les Mollettes (73) 208 D5
Molleville (11) 289 F4
Molliens-au-Bois (80) 10 B6
Molliens-Dreuil (80) 17 J2
Mollkirch (67) 70 C4
Molompize (15) 218 E3
Molosmes (89) 114 A4
Moloy (21) 135 K2
Molphey (21) 134 C5
Molpré (39) 156 C6
Molring (57) 67 G2
Molsheim (67) 70 D4
Moltifao (2B) 318 E3
les Molunes (39) 173 K6
Momas (64) 284 C2
Mombrier (33) 211 H4

Momères (65) 285 H6
Momerstroff (57) 45 J4
Mommenheim (67) 70 E1
Momuy (40) 265 F6
Momy (64) 285 F3
Monacia-d'Aullène (2A) 322 E4
Monacia-d'Orezza (2B) 319 H5
Monampteuil (02) 40 B1
Monassut-Audiracq (64) 284 E3
le Monastère (12) 252 B3
le Monastier-Pin-Moriès (48) 237 F6
le Monastier-sur-Gazeille (43) 238 D1
Monay (39) 155 H5
Monbahus (47) 231 H5
Monbalen (47) 248 C3
Monbardon (32) 286 E3
Monbazillac (24) 231 H3
Monbéqui (82) 268 E3
Monblanc (32) 287 H2
Monbrun (32) 268 C5
Moncale (2B) 318 C3
Moncassin (32) 286 B2
Moncaup (31) 305 J3
Moncaup (64) 285 G2
Moncaut (47) 248 A5
Moncayolle-Larrory-
 -Mendibieu (64) 283 H4
Moncé-en-Belin (72) 106 E4
Moncé-en-Saosnois (72) 83 F5
Monceau-le-Neuf-et-
 -Faucouzy (02) 20 D3
Monceau-le-Waast (02) 20 E5
Monceau-lès-Leups (02) 20 C5
Monceau-Saint-Waast (59) 13 G4
Monceau-sur-Oise (02) 20 D2
les Monceaux (14) 33 J6
Monceaux (60) 38 B3
Monceaux-au-Perche (61) 83 J2
Monceaux-en-Bessin (14) 32 B4
Monceaux-l'Abbaye (60) 17 G5
Monceaux-le-Comte (58) 133 H5
Monceaux-sur-Dordogne (19) 216 C5
Moncel-lès-Lunéville (54) 66 D6
Moncel-sur-Seille (54) 66 C4
Moncel-sur-Vair (88) 93 G3
la Moncelle (08) 23 F4
Moncetz-l'Abbaye (51) 63 G6
Moncetz-Longevas (51) 62 E3
Moncey (25) 138 B4
Monchaux-Soreng (76) 16 E1
Monchaux-sur-Écaillon (59) 12 C3
Moncheaux (59) 6 E6
Moncheaux-lès-Frévent (62) 10 B2
Monchecourt (59) 11 J2
Monchel-sur-Canche (62) 9 K2
Moncheux (57) 66 B2
Monchiet (62) 10 D3
Monchy-au-Bois (62) 10 D4
Monchy-Breton (62) 10 B1
Monchy-Cayeux (62) 10 A1
Monchy-Humières (60) 38 D1
Monchy-Lagache (80) 19 H2
Monchy-le-Preux (62) 11 F3
Monchy-Saint-Éloi (60) 38 A4
Monchy-sur-Eu (76) 8 C2
Moncla (64) 265 K6
Monclar (32) 266 B2
Monclar (47) 248 A1
Monclar-de-Quercy (82) 269 J2
Monclar-sur-Losse (32) 286 A1
Moncley (25) 137 J5
Moncontour (22) 77 H2
Moncontour (86) 144 D5
Moncorneil-Grazan (32) 286 D2
Moncourt (57) 66 E4
Moncoutant (79) 161 G1
Moncrabeau (47) 267 F1
Moncy (61) 53 G3
Mondavezan (31) 287 H5
Mondelange (57) 45 F3
Mondement-Montgivroux (51) 61 H4
Mondescourt (60) 19 J5
Mondevert (35) 104 B1
Mondeville (14) 32 E5
Mondeville (91) 87 F2
Mondicourt (62) 10 C4
Mondigny (08) 22 C4
Mondilhan (31) 286 E4
Mondion (86) 145 H4
Mondon (25) 138 C3
Mondonville (31) 269 F5
Mondonville-Saint-Jean (28) 85 K4
Mondorff (57) 27 H2
Mondoubleau (41) 108 A3
Mondouzil (31) 269 H6
Mondragon (84) 256 D4
Mondrainville (14) 32 C5
Mondrepuis (02) 21 G1
Mondreville (77) 111 G1
Mondreville (78) 57 H3
Monein (64) 284 A4
Monès (31) 287 H3
Monesple (09) 307 G1
Monestier (03) 185 H2
Monestier (07) 221 J3
Monestier (24) 231 G3
Monestier (48) 203 J5
Monestier-d'Ambel (38) 242 C2
Monestier-de-Clermont (38) 241 K1
le Monestier-du-Percy (38) 242 A2
Monestier-Merlines (19) 201 H4
Monestier-Port-Dieu (19) 201 H5
Monestiés (81) 251 G6
Monestrol (31) 288 E4
Monétay-sur-Allier (03) 168 E6
Monétay-sur-Loire (03) 169 K5

381

Monéteau (89) 113 G4
Monêtier-Allemont (05) 259 F1
le Monêtier-les-Bains (05) 225 J5
Monfaucon (24) 231 F1
Monfaucon (65) 285 H2
Monferran-Plavès (32) 286 D2
Monferran-Savès (32) 268 C6
Monflanquin (47) 232 A6
Monfort (32) 268 A4
Monfréville (14) 31 H1
Mongaillard (47) 247 J4
Mongausy (32) 287 F2
Mongauzy (33) 230 D5
Monget (40) 265 G6
Monguilhem (32) 266 A3
Monheurt (47) 247 J3
Monhoudou (72) 83 F5
Monieux (84) 258 A6
Monistrol-d'Allier (43) 219 K6
Monistrol-sur-Loire (43) 221 F2
Monlaur-Bernet (32) 286 C4
Monléon-Magnoac (65) 286 C5
Monlet (43) 220 A3
Monlezun (32) 285 J2
Monlezun-d'Armagnac (32) 266 A3
Monlong (65) 286 B5
Monmadalès (24) 231 K3
Monmarvès (24) 231 K4
Monnai (61) 55 G3
Monnaie (37) 127 K3
Monneren (57) 27 J4
la Monnerie-le-Montel (63) 203 J1
Monnerville (91) 86 B4
Monnes (02) 39 H5
Monnet-la-Ville (39) 173 J1
Monnetay (39) 173 F4
Monnetier-Mornex (74) 191 G4
Monneville (60) 37 G5
Monnières (39) 155 G2
Monnières (44) 142 A1
Monoblet (30) 274 C1
Monpardiac (32) 285 K2
Monpazier (24) 232 C4
Monpezat (64) 285 G2
Monplaisant (24) 232 D3
Monprimblanc (33) 230 A4
Mons (16) 178 E6
Mons (17) 195 K1
Mons (30) 255 H5
Mons (31) 269 J6
Mons (34) 291 H1
Mons (63) 185 J5
Mons (83) 280 B4
Mons-Boubert (80) 8 E5
Mons-en-Barœul (59) 6 E4
Mons-en-Laonnois (02) 20 C6
Mons-en-Montois (77) 88 C2
Mons-en-Pévèle (59) 6 E6
Monsac (24) 232 A4
Monsaguel (24) 231 J3
Monsec (24) 197 H6
Monségur (33) 230 D4
Monségur (40) 265 G6
Monségur (47) 248 E1
Monségur (64) 285 G2
la Monselie (15) 217 J2
Monsempron-Libos (47) 248 E1
Monsireigne (85) 160 C1
Monsols (69) 187 K2
Monsteroux-Milieu (38) 206 C6
Monsures (80) 17 K4
Monswiller (67) 70 B1
Mont (64) 284 A2
Mont (65) 305 G5
Mont (71) 169 K3
le Mont (88) 95 J2
Mont-Bernanchon (62) 5 K5
Mont-Bertrand (14) 31 J5
Mont-Bonvillers (54) 44 C3
Mont-Cauvaire (76) 15 K6
Mont-d'Astarac (32) 286 C4
Mont-Dauphin (05) 227 A3
Mont-de-Galié (31) 305 J2
Mont-de-Lans (38) 224 E6
Mont-de-Laval (25) 157 H1
Mont-de-l'If (76) 15 H6
Mont-de-Marrast (32) 286 A3
Mont-de-Marsan (40) 265 G4
Mont-de-Vougney (25) 139 G5
Mont-devant-Sassey (55) 43 F2
le Mont-Dieu (08) 22 E6
Mont-Disse (64) 285 F1
Mont-Dol (35) 51 F4
Mont-Dore (63) 202 A4
Mont-d'Origny (02) 20 C2
Mont-et-Marré (58) 151 J3
Mont-Laurent (08) 41 K1
Mont-le-Vernois (70) 138 A1
Mont-le-Vignoble (54) 65 H6
Mont-lès-Lamarche (88) 117 H2
Mont-lès-Neufchâteau (88) 93 F3
Mont-lès-Seurre (71) 154 D4
Mont-l'Étroit (54) 93 H2
Mont-l'Évêque (60) 38 C5
Mont-Louis (66) 313 J4
Mont-Notre-Dame (02) 40 B4
Mont-Ormel (61) 54 E3
Mont-près-Chambord (41) 129 F2
Mont-Roc (81) 271 G4
le Mont-Saint-Adrien (60) 37 G2
Mont-Saint-Aignan (76) 35 H1
Mont-Saint-Éloi (62) 10 E2
Mont-Saint-Jean (02) 21 J3
Mont-Saint-Jean (21) 134 E6
Mont-Saint-Jean (72) 82 B5
Mont-Saint-Léger (70) 137 H1

Mont-Saint-Martin (02) 40 B4
Mont-Saint-Martin (08) 42 B3
Mont-Saint-Martin (38) 224 A2
Mont-Saint-Martin (54) 26 D2
le Mont-Saint-Michel (50) 51 J3
Mont-Saint-Père (02) 40 A6
Mont-Saint-Remy (08) 41 K2
Mont-Saint-Sulpice (89) 113 G3
Mont-Saint-Vincent (71) 171 F2
Mont-Saxonnex (74) 191 J3
Mont-sous-Vaudrey (39) 155 H3
Mont-sur-Courville (51) 40 C4
Mont-sur-Meurthe (54) 66 D6
Mont-sur-Monnet (39) 173 J1
Montabard (61) 54 B4
Montabon (72) 127 F1
Montabot (50) 52 C2
Montacher-Villegardin (89) 88 B6
Montadet (32) 287 G3
Montady (34) 291 K4
Montagagne (09) 307 G3
Montagna-le-Reconduit (39) 172 E4
Montagna-le-Templier (39) 173 F6
Montagnac (30) 274 D2
Montagnac (34) 292 C2
Montagnac-d'Auberoche (24) 214 C4
Montagnac-la-Crempse (24) 213 J6
Montagnac-Montpezat (04) 278 E3
Montagnac-sur-Auvignon (47) 247 K5
Montagnac-sur-Lède (47) 232 B6
Montagnat (01) 189 G2
Montagne (33) 230 B1
Montagne (38) 223 F4
la Montagne (44) 123 F4
la Montagne (70) 119 F3
Montagne-Fayel (80) 17 H2
Montagney (70) 137 G5
Montagney-Servigney (25) 138 C3
Montagnieu (01) 207 G1
Montagnieu (38) 207 G5
Montagnol (12) 272 D3
Montagnole (73) 208 B4
Montagny (42) 187 G4
Montagny (69) 205 K3
Montagny (73) 209 J5
Montagny-en-Vexin (60) 36 E5
Montagny-lès-Beaune (21) 154 A4
Montagny-lès-Buxy (71) 171 H1
Montagny-les-Lanches (74) 190 E6
Montagny-les-Seurre (21) 154 E3
Montagny-près-Louhans (71) 172 D2
Montagny-Sainte-Félicité (60) 38 D6
Montagny-sur-Grosne (71) 171 G6
Montagoudin (33) 230 C5
Montagrier (24) 213 H4
Montagudet (82) 249 G4
Montagut (64) 284 B1
Montaignac-Saint-Hippolyte (19) . . 216 D2
Montaigu (02) 21 F6
Montaigu (39) 173 G2
Montaigu (85) 142 A3
Montaigu-de-Quercy (82) 249 F3
Montaigu-la-Brisette (50) 28 E3
Montaigu-le-Blin (03) 185 K1
Montaigu-les-Bois (50) 52 A2
Montaiguët-en-Forez (03) 186 C1
Montaigut (63) 184 C3
Montaigut-le-Blanc (23) 182 C3
Montaigut-le-Blanc (63) 202 D4
Montaigut-sur-Save (31) 268 E5
Montaillé (72) 107 J3
Montailleur (73) 209 F3
Montaillou (09) 308 B6
Montaimont (73) 209 F6
Montain (39) 173 G1
Montain (82) 268 D2
Montainville (28) 85 G5
Montainville (78) 57 K3
Montalba-le-Château (66) 314 D2
Montalembert (79) 179 G3
Montalet-le-Bois (78) 57 K1
Montalieu-Vercieu (38) 207 G3
Montalzat (82) 250 A4
Montamat (32) 287 F2
Montambert (58) 169 H1
Montamel (46) 233 H5
Montamisé (86) 163 F3
Montamy (14) 53 F1
Montanay (69) 188 D6
Montancy (25) 139 K4
Montandon (25) 139 H5
Montanel (50) 51 J5
Montaner (64) 285 G3
Montanges (01) 190 C2
Montans (81) 270 B3
Montapas (58) 151 J3
Montarcher (42) 204 C6
Montardit (09) 306 E1
Montardon (64) 284 D3
Montaren-et-Saint-Médiers (30) . . 275 G1
Montargis (45) 111 J4
Montarlot (77) 87 K4
Montarlot-lès-Rioz (70) 137 K4
Montarnaud (34) 274 A6
Montaron (58) 151 K5
Montastruc (47) 248 A1
Montastruc (65) 286 A5
Montastruc (82) 249 J6
Montastruc-de-Salies (31) 306 B2
Montastruc-la-Conseillère (31) . . . 269 J3
Montastruc-Savès (31) 287 H4
le Montat (46) 250 A2
Montataire (60) 38 A4
Montauban (82) 269 F1
Montauban-de-Bretagne (35) 78 C3
Montauban-de-Luchon (31) 305 H5

Montauban-de-Picardie (80) 10 E6
Montauban-sur-l'Ouvèze (26) 258 B3
Montaud (34) 274 C4
Montaud (38) 223 J2
Montaudin (53) 80 D3
Montaulieu (26) 257 J2
Montaulin (10) 90 C5
Montaure (27) 35 H4
Montauriol (11) 289 F5
Montauriol (47) 231 J5
Montauriol (66) 315 F3
Montauriol (81) 251 J6
Montauroux (83) 280 B5
Montaut (09) 288 D6
Montaut (24) 231 K3
Montaut (31) 288 A4
Montaut (32) 286 B3
Montaut (40) 265 F4
Montaut (47) 231 K5
Montaut (64) 284 E6
Montaut-les-Créneaux (32) 267 H5
Montautour (35) 80 B5
Montay (59) 12 C5
Montayral (47) 249 F1
Montazeau (24) 230 D4
Montazels (11) 309 F3
Montbard (21) 134 D1
Montbarla (82) 249 G4
Montbarrey (39) 155 J3
Montbarrois (45) 111 F2
Montbartier (82) 269 F2
Montbavin (02) 40 A1
Montbazens (12) 251 K1
Montbazin (34) 293 F2
Montbazon (37) 127 J6
Montbel (09) 308 C3
Montbel (48) 238 A5
Montbéliard (25) 139 F1
Montbéliardot (25) 139 G6
Montbellet (71) 171 K4
Montbenoît (25) 157 G3
Montberaud (31) 287 J6
Montbernard (31) 286 E4
Montberon (31) 269 H5
Montbert (44) 141 J2
Montberthault (21) 134 C3
Montbeton (82) 269 F1
Montbeugny (03) 169 F4
Montbizot (72) 82 D6
Montblainville (55) 42 E4
Montblanc (34) 292 B3
Montboillon (70) 137 J4
Montboissier (28) 85 F6
Montbolo (66) 314 E5
Montbonnot-Saint-Martin (38) . . . 224 B2
Montboucher (23) 182 B5
Montboucher-sur-Jabron (26) 240 B5
Montboudif (15) 218 A1
Montbouton (90) 139 J2
Montbouy (45) 111 J4
Montboyer (16) 212 E2
Montbozon (70) 138 C3
Montbrand (05) 242 A5
Montbras (55) 93 G1
Montbray (50) 52 C2
Montbré (51) 41 F5
Montbrehain (02) 20 A1
Montbrison (42) 204 D4
Montbrison-sur-Lez (26) 257 G1
Montbron (16) 197 H3
Montbronn (57) 69 F4
Montbrun (46) 250 E1
Montbrun (48) 254 B3
Montbrun-Bocage (31) 306 E1
Montbrun-des-Corbières (11) 290 E6
Montbrun-Lauragais (31) 288 C2
Montbrun-les-Bains (26) 258 A4
Montcabrier (46) 232 D6
Montcabrier (81) 269 K6
Montcaret (24) 230 D2
Montcarra (38) 207 G3
Montcavrel (62) 4 C5
Montceau-et-Écharnant (21) 153 J3
Montceau-les-Mines (71) 170 E2
Montceaux (01) 188 C3
Montceaux-lès-Meaux (77) 60 A2
Montceaux-lès-Provins (77) 60 B6
Montceaux-lès-Vaudes (10) 90 B6
Montceaux-l'Étoile (71) 170 B6
Montceaux-Ragny (71) 171 K2
Montcel (63) 185 F5
Montcel (73) 208 C2
Montcenis (71) 153 G6
Montcet (01) 189 F2
Montcey (70) 118 B6
Montchaboud (38) 224 B4
Montchal (42) 205 F1
Montchâlons (02) 40 C1
Montchamp (14) 53 F2
Montchamp (15) 219 F5
Montchanin (71) 171 F1
Montcharvot (52) 117 G3
Montchaton (50) 30 D4
Montchaude (16) 196 A6
Montchauvet (14) 53 F2
Montchauvet (78) 57 H3
Montchenu (26) 222 D3
Montcheutin (08) 42 C1
Montchevrel (61) 83 F1
Montchevrier (36) 165 J5
Montclar (04) 259 K1
Montclar (11) 309 F1
Montclar (12) 271 K2
Montclar-de-Comminges (31) 287 H6
Montclar-Lauragais (31) 288 E4

Montclar-sur-Gervanne (26) 241 F3
Montclard (43) 219 J3
Montcléra (46) 233 F5
Montclus (05) 258 D1
Montclus (30) 256 A4
Montcombroux-les-Mines (03) . . . 169 H6
Montcony (71) 172 D1
Montcorbon (45) 112 B3
Montcornet (02) 21 G4
Montcornet (08) 22 C2
Montcourt (70) 117 J3
Montcourt-Fromonville (77) 87 H5
Montcoy (71) 154 C6
Montcresson (45) 111 J4
Montcuit (50) 31 F3
Montcuq (46) 249 H3
Montcusel (39) 173 H6
Montcy-Notre-Dame (08) 22 D3
Montdardier (30) 273 J2
Montdauphin (77) 60 E3
Montdidier (57) 68 B5
Montdidier (80) 18 D5
Montdoré (70) 118 A3
Montdoumerc (46) 250 A3
Montdragon (81) 270 D4
Montdurausse (81) 269 J2
Monte (2B) 319 H3
Monteaux (41) 128 C3
Montebourg (50) 29 F4
Montech (82) 268 E2
Montécheroux (25) 139 H4
Montegrosso (2B) 318 C3
Montégut (32) 267 J6
Montégut (40) 265 K3
Montégut (65) 305 G1
Montégut-Arros (32) 285 J3
Montégut-Bourjac (31) 287 G4
Montégut-en-Couserans (09) 306 D3
Montégut-Lauragais (31) 289 G2
Montégut-Plantaurel (09) 307 H2
Montégut-Savès (32) 287 G2
Monteignet-sur-l'Andelot (03) 185 G3
le Monteil (15) 217 J2
le Monteil (43) 220 C5
le Monteil-au-Vicomte (23) 182 D6
Monteille (14) 33 H6
Monteils (12) 251 F4
Monteils (30) 255 H6
Monteils (82) 250 B5
Montel-de-Gelat (63) 184 A6
Montéléger (26) 240 C2
Montélier (26) 222 D6
Montélimar (26) 240 B5
le Montellier (01) 188 E5
Montels (09) 307 G2
Montels (34) 291 J4
Montels (81) 270 B2
Montembœuf (16) 197 J2
Montenach (57) 27 J3
Montenay (53) 80 D4
Montendre (17) 211 J2
Montendry (73) 208 E4
Montenescourt (62) 10 D3
Monteneuf (56) 102 B1
Montenils (77) 61 F4
Montenois (25) 139 G2
Montenoison (58) 151 G1
Montenoy (54) 66 B3
Montépilloy (60) 38 C5
Monteplain (39) 155 J1
Montépreux (51) 62 B5
Monterblanc (56) 101 G4
Montereau (45) 111 G4
Montereau-Fault-Yonne (77) 88 A4
Montereau-sur-le-Jard (77) 87 H1
Monterfil (35) 78 D4
Montérolier (76) 16 C5
Monterrein (56) 101 K2
Montertelot (56) 101 J2
Montescot (66) 315 H3
Montescourt-Lizerolles (02) 19 K4
Montespan (31) 306 A1
Montesquieu (34) 292 A1
Montesquieu (47) 247 K4
Montesquieu (82) 249 F4
Montesquieu-Avantès (09) 306 E2
Montesquieu-des-Albères (66) . . . 315 G4
Montesquieu-Lauragais (31) 288 D3
Montesquieu-Volvestre (31) 287 K5
Montesquiou (32) 286 A1
Montessaux (70) 118 E5
Montesson (78) 58 C3
Montestruc-sur-Gers (32) 267 J4
le Montet (03) 168 B5
Montet-et-Bouxal (46) 234 D3
Monteton (47) 231 F5
Monteux (84) 257 G6
Montévrain (77) 59 J3
Monteynard (38) 224 A6
Montézic (12) 235 K4
Montfa (09) 307 F1
Montfa (81) 271 F5
Montfalcon (38) 222 E2
Montfarville (50) 29 F2
Montfaucon (02) 60 E2
Montfaucon (24) 231 A6
Montfaucon (30) 256 D6
Montfaucon (46) 233 J4
Montfaucon-d'Argonne (55) 43 F3
Montfaucon-en-Velay (43) 221 G3
Montfaucon-Montigné (49) 142 C2
Montfermeil (93) 59 G3
Montfermier (82) 249 K4
Montfermy (63) 184 C6
Montferrand (11) 289 F4

Montferrand-du-Périgord (24) 232 B5
Montferrand-la-Fare (26) 258 A2
Montferrand-le-Château (25) 156 A1
Montferrat (38) 207 J5
Montferrat (83) 279 J5
Montferrer (66) 314 D5
Montferrier (09) 308 A4
Montferrier-sur-Lez (34) 274 B5
Montfey (10) 113 J2
Montfiquet (14) 31 K3
Montfleur (39) 173 F6
Montflours (53) 81 F3
Montflovin (25) 157 J3
Montfort (04) 259 G4
Montfort (25) 156 A2
Montfort (49) 144 B3
Montfort (64) 283 J5
Montfort-en-Chalosse (40) 264 D4
Montfort-l'Amaury (78) 57 K4
Montfort-le-Gesnois (72) 107 F2
Montfort-sur-Argens (83) 298 A1
Montfort-sur-Boulzane (11) 309 F6
Montfort-sur-Meu (35) 78 D4
Montfort-sur-Risle (27) 34 D2
Montfranc (12) 271 J3
Montfrin (30) 275 K3
Montfroc (26) 258 C4
Montfuron (04) 278 A3
Montgaillard (09) 307 J3
Montgaillard (11) 309 J4
Montgaillard (40) 265 J2
Montgaillard (65) 285 H6
Montgaillard (81) 269 J2
Montgaillard (82) 268 E2
Montgaillard-de-Salies (31) 306 B2
Montgaillard-Lauragais (31) 288 E3
Montgaillard-sur-Save (31) 286 E5
Montgardin (05) 243 G5
Montgardon (50) 30 D1
Montgaroult (61) 54 B4
Montgauch (09) 306 D2
Montgaudry (61) 83 G3
Montgazin (31) 288 A4
Montgé-en-Goële (77) 59 J1
Montgeard (31) 288 D4
Montgellafrey (73) 209 F6
Montgenèvre (05) 226 A6
Montgenost (51) 89 G1
Montgérain (60) 18 D4
Montgermont (35) 79 F3
Montgeron (91) 59 F5
Montgeroult (95) 37 G6
Montgesoye (25) 156 D2
Montgesty (46) 233 G3
Montgey (81) 289 G2
Montgibaud (19) 199 G5
Montgilbert (73) 209 F4
Montgirod (73) 209 J4
Montgiscard (31) 288 D2
Montgivray (36) 166 B3
Montgobert (02) 39 G3
Montgon (08) 42 B1
Montgradail (11) 308 C1
Montgras (31) 287 J2
Montgreleix (15) 218 C2
Montgru-Saint-Hilaire (02) 39 J5
Montguers (26) 258 B3
Montguillon (49) 104 E6
Montguyon (17) 212 B3
les Monthairons (55) 43 J6
Montharville (28) 84 E6
Monthault (35) 80 B1
Monthaut (11) 308 D1
Monthelie (21) 153 K4
Monthelon (51) 61 K2
Monthelon (71) 152 E4
Monthenault (02) 40 B1
Montheries (52) 91 J6
Montherlant (60) 37 G4
Monthermé (08) 22 D2
Monthiers (02) 39 J6
Monthieux (01) 188 D5
Monthion (73) 209 F3
Monthodon (37) 128 A1
Monthoiron (86) 163 H1
Monthois (08) 42 B3
Montholier (39) 155 J4
Monthou-sur-Bièvre (41) 128 E3
Monthou-sur-Cher (41) 128 E3
Monthuchon (50) 30 E3
Monthurel (02) 61 F1
Monthureux-le-Sec (88) 93 K6
Monthureux-sur-Saône (88) 117 J2
Monthyon (77) 59 J1
Monticello (2B) 318 D2
Montier-en-Der (52) 91 H2
Montier-en-l'Isle (10) 91 G5
Montiéramey (10) 90 D5
Montierchaume (36) 148 A5
Montiers (60) 38 B1
Montiers-sur-Saulx (55) 92 C1
Monties (32) 286 D6
Montignac (24) 214 C5
Montignac (33) 230 A3
Montignac (65) 285 J6
Montignac-Charente (16) 196 D5
Montignac-de-Lauzun (47) 231 H5
Montignac-le-Coq (16) 213 F1
Montignac-Toupinerie (47) 231 G6
Montignargues (30) 275 G2
Montigné (16) 196 B1
Montigné-le-Brillant (53) 104 E2
Montigné-lès-Rairies (49) 126 A1
Montigny (14) 32 C6
Montigny (18) 149 K1

Montigny (45). 110 C1
Montigny (54). 95 G1
Montigny (72). 82 E2
Montigny (76) 35 G1
Montigny-aux-Amognes (58) . . . 151 F3
Montigny-devant-Sassey (55). . . 43 F1
Montigny-en-Arrouaise (02) 20 B2
Montigny-en-Cambrésis (59) . . . 12 C5
Montigny-en-Gohelle (62). 11 G1
Montigny-en-Morvan (58). 152 A2
Montigny-en-Ostrevent (59) . . . 11 J2
Montigny-la-Resle (89) 113 H4
Montigny-l'Allier (02) 39 G6
Montigny-le-Bretonneux (78) . . . 58 B4
Montigny-le-Chartif (28) 84 D5
Montigny-le-Franc (02). 21 F4
Montigny-le-Gannelon (28). . . . 108 D2
Montigny-le-Guesdier (77) 88 D4
Montigny-Lencoup (77) 88 B3
Montigny-Lengrain (02) 39 G3
Montigny-lès-Arsures (39) 155 K4
Montigny-lès-Cherlieu (70) 117 H5
Montigny-lès-Condé (02) 61 F2
Montigny-lès-Cormeilles (95) . . . 58 D2
Montigny-les-Jongleurs (80) . . . 9 J4
Montigny-lès-Metz (57) 45 F5
Montigny-les-Monts (10) 113 K1
Montigny-lès-Vaucouleurs (55) . . 65 F6
Montigny-lès-Vesoul (70) 138 A1
Montigny-Montfort (21) 134 D2
Montigny-Mornay-Villeneuve-
  -sur-Vingeanne (21) 136 E2
Montigny-Saint-Barthélemy (21) . . 134 D4
Montigny-sous-Marle (02) 20 E4
Montigny-sur-Armançon (21) . . . 134 E4
Montigny-sur-Aube (21) 115 H3
Montigny-sur-Avre (28) 56 C5
Montigny-sur-Canne (58) 151 J5
Montigny-sur-Chiers (54) 26 C3
Montigny-sur-Crécy (02). 20 C4
Montigny-sur-l'Ain (39) 173 J1
Montigny-sur-l'Hallue (80) 18 C1
Montigny-sur-Loing (77) 87 J4
Montigny-sur-Meuse (08) 24 C2
Montigny-sur-Vence (08) 22 C5
Montigny-sur-Vesle (51) 40 D3
Montilliers (49) 143 J1
Montillot (89) 133 H3
Montilly (03) 168 D3
Montilly-sur-Noireau (61) 53 H3
Montils (17) 195 H3
les Montils (41) 128 E3
Montipouret (36). 166 A2
Montirat (11) 290 C6
Montirat (81) 251 G5
Montireau (28) 84 C3
Montiron (32) 287 F1
Montivernage (25) 138 D5
Montivilliers (76) 14 B6
Montjardin (11) 308 C3
Montjaux (12) 252 E6
Montjavoult (60) 36 E5
Montjay (05) 258 C2
Montjay (71) 155 F6
Montjean (16) 179 F3
Montjean (53) 104 D2
Montjean-sur-Loire (49) 124 D4
Montjoi (11) 309 H3
Montjoi (82) 248 E1
Montjoie-en-Couserans (09) . . . 306 D2
Montjoie-le-Château (25) 139 J4
Montjoie-Saint-Martin (50) 80 A1
Montjoire (31) 269 H4
Montjoux (26) 240 E2
Montjoyer (26) 256 E1
Montjustin (04) 277 K3
Montjustin-et-Velotte (70) 138 D1
Montlandon (28) 84 C3
Montlaur (11) 309 H1
Montlaur (12) 272 B3
Montlaur (31) 288 D2
Montlaur-en-Diois (26) 241 H4
Montlaux (04) 259 F6
Montlauzun (46) 249 H3
Montlay-en-Auxois (21) 134 D5
Montlebon (25) 157 H2
Montlevicq (36) 166 C3
Montlevon (02) 61 F2
Montlhéry (91) 58 D6
Montliard (45) 111 F2
Montlieu-la-Garde (17) 212 A3
Montlignon (95) 58 D1
Montliot-et-Courcelles (21) 115 F2
Montlivault (41) 129 F1
Montlognon (60) 38 C5
Montloué (02) 21 H4
Montlouis (18) 149 F6
Montlouis-sur-Loire (37) 127 K5
Montluçon (03) 167 H6
Montluel (01) 188 E6
Montmachoux (77) 88 A4
Montmacq (60) 38 E1
Montmagny (95) 58 E2
Montmahoux (25) 156 D3
Montmain (21) 154 C3
Montmain (76) 35 K2
Montmançon (21) 136 D5
Montmarault (03) 184 C1
Montmarlon (39) 156 B5
Montmartin (60) 38 C1
Montmartin-en-Graignes (50) . . 31 G1
Montmartin-le-Haut (10) 91 F6
Montmartin-sur-Mer (50) 30 D3
Montmaur (05) 242 C5
Montmaur (11) 289 F3
Montmaur-en-Diois (26) 241 H4

Montmaurin (31). 286 D5
Montmédy (55). 23 K6
Montmeillant (08) 21 K4
Montmelard (71). 171 F6
Montmelas-Saint-Sorlin (69). . . 188 A4
Montmélian (73). 208 D5
Montmerle-sur-Saône (01) 188 B4
Montmerrei (61) 54 C6
Montmeyan (83). 278 E6
Montmeyran (26) 240 D2
Montmin (74) 208 E1
Montmirail (51) 61 F3
Montmirail (72) 107 K1
Montmiral (26) 222 E4
Montmirat (30) 274 D2
Montmirey-la-Ville (39) 137 F6
Montmirey-le-Château (39) 137 F6
Montmoreau-Saint-Cybard (16) . . 212 E1
Montmorency (95) 58 E2
Montmorency-Beaufort (10) . . . 91 F2
Montmorillon (86). 164 A5
Montmorin (05). 258 B1
Montmorin (63). 203 F3
Montmorot (39) 173 F2
Montmort (71) 170 B1
Montmort-Lucy (51) 61 J2
Montmotier (88) 118 B2
Montmoyen (21) 115 H6
Montmurat (15) 235 F5
Montner (66) 309 K6
Montoillot (21) 135 G6
Montoir-de-Bretagne (44) 122 B2
Montoire-sur-le-Loir (41) 108 A6
Montois-la-Montagne (57) 44 D4
Montoison (26) 240 D2
Montoldre (03) 169 H6
Montolieu (11) 289 K4
Montolivet (77) 60 E4
Montonvillers (80) 10 A6
Montord (03) 185 G1
Montory (64) 283 J6
Montot (21) 154 E2
Montot (70) 137 F2
Montot-sur-Rognon (52) 92 C4
Montouliers (34) 291 G4
Montoulieu (09) 307 J4
Montoulieu (34) 274 B2
Montoulieu-Saint-Bernard (31) . . 287 G5
Montournais (85) 160 E1
Montours (35). 51 K6
Montourtier (53) 81 G5
Montoussé (65) 305 F1
Montoussin (31) 287 H5
Montoy-Flanville (57) 45 G5
Montpellier (34) 274 C6
Montpellier-de-Médillan (17) . . . 195 F3
Montpensier (63) 185 G4
Montperreux (25) 157 F5
Montpeyroux (12) 236 B5
Montpeyroux (24) 230 D1
Montpeyroux (34) 273 J5
Montpeyroux (63) 202 E4
Montpezat (30) 274 E3
Montpézat (32) 287 G3
Montpezat (47) 248 A3
Montpezat-de-Quercy (82) 250 A4
Montpezat-sous-Bauzon (07) . . 239 F4
Montpinchon (50) 31 F4
Montpinier (81) 270 E5
Montpitol (31) 269 J5
Montplonne (55) 64 B5
Montpollin (49) 126 B2
Montpon-Ménestérol (24) 212 B6
Montpont-en-Bresse (71) 172 C3
Montpothier (10). 89 F1
Montpouillan (47) 247 G1
Montrabé (31) 269 H6
Montrabot (50) 31 K3
Montracol (01) 189 F2
Montravers (79) 143 G5
Montréal (07) 239 G6
Montréal (11) 289 J6
Montréal (32) 266 E2
Montréal (89) 134 A3
Montréal-la-Cluse (01) 189 K2
Montréal-les-Sources (26) 257 K2
Montrécourt (59) 12 C3
Montredon (46) 235 F5
Montredon-des-Corbières (11) . . 291 H6
Montredon-Labessonnié (81) . . 271 F5
Montregard (43) 221 G4
Montréjeau (31) 305 H1
Montrelais (44) 124 C4
Montrem (24) 213 J4
Montrésor (37) 147 F2
Montret (71) 172 B2
Montreuil (28) 57 F4
Montreuil (62) 4 C6
Montreuil (85). 160 D5
Montreuil (93) 59 F3
Montreuil-au-Houlme (61) 53 K5
Montreuil-aux-Lions (02). 60 C1
Montreuil-Bellay (49) 144 C2
Montreuil-Bonnin (86). 162 D3
Montreuil-des-Landes (35) 80 A5
Montreuil-en-Auge (14). 33 J5
Montreuil-en-Caux (76). 16 A4
Montreuil-en-Touraine (37) 128 B3
Montreuil-Juigné (49) 125 G2
Montreuil-la-Cambe (61). 54 D3
Montreuil-l'Argillé (27). 55 F2
Montreuil-le-Chétif (72). 82 C5
Montreuil-le-Gast (35) 79 F2
Montreuil-le-Henri (72) 107 H4
Montreuil-Poulay (53) 81 H3
Montreuil-sous-Pérouse (35) . . . 80 A6

Montreuil-sur-Barse (10). 90 D5
Montreuil-sur-Blaise (52) 91 K2
Montreuil-sur-Brêche (60) 37 J1
Montreuil-sur-Epte (95). 36 D5
Montreuil-sur-Ille (35) 79 G2
Montreuil-sur-Loir (49) 125 J1
Montreuil-sur-Lozon (50) 31 G3
Montreuil-sur-Maine (49) 125 F1
Montreuil-sur-Thérain (60) 37 H3
Montreuil-sur-Thonnance (52). . . 92 B2
Montreuillon (58) 152 A1
Montreux (54) 67 H6
Montreux-Château (90) 139 K1
Montreux-Jeune (68) 139 K1
Montreux-Vieux (68) 119 K6
Montrevault (49) 124 B6
Montrevel (38) 207 G5
Montrevel (39) 173 F5
Montrevel-en-Bresse (01) 172 C6
Montricher-Albanne (73). 225 H2
Montrichard (41) 128 D5
Montricoux (82) 250 B6
Montrieux-en-Sologne (41) 129 J3
Montrigaud (26) 222 E3
Montriond (74) 192 A1
Montrodat (48) 237 G6
Montrol-Sénard (87) 180 E4
Montrollet (16) 180 D5
Montromant (69) 205 H3
Montrond (05) 258 D2
Montrond (39) 156 A6
Montrond-le-Château (25) 156 C1
Montrond-les-Bains (42) 204 E3
Montrosier (81) 250 E5
Montrottier (69) 205 G2
Montroty (76) 36 D2
Montrouge (92) 58 E4
Montrouveau (41) 107 J6
Montroy (17) 176 E2
Montrozier (12) 252 D2
Montry (77) 59 J3
Monts (37) 127 H6
Monts (60) 37 G5
Monts-en-Bessin (14) 32 C5
Monts-en-Ternois (62) 10 B2
Monts-sur-Guesnes (86) 145 F5
les Monts-Verts (48) 237 F2
Montsalès (12) 251 F1
Montsalier (04) 258 C6
Montsalvy (15) 235 J4
Montsapey (73) 209 F4
Montsauche-les-Settons (58) . . . 152 C1
Montsaugeon (52) 136 D1
Montsaunès (31) 306 B1
Montsec (55) 65 G2
Montsecret (61) 53 G4
Montségur (09) 308 A4
Montségur-sur-Lauzon (26) 256 E2
Montselgues (07) 238 D6
Montséret (11) 310 B1
Montsérié (65) 305 G2
Montseron (09) 307 F2
Montseveroux (38) 206 C6
Montsoreau (49) 144 E1
Montsoué (40) 265 G4
Montsoult (95) 58 E1
Montsûrs (53) 81 G6
Montsurvent (50) 30 D3
Montsuzain (10) 90 B3
Montureux-et-Prantigny (70). . . 137 G3
Montureux-lès-Baulay (70) 117 K4
Montusclat (43) 220 E6
Montussaint (25) 138 C3
Montussan (33) 229 J1
Montvalen (81) 269 J3
Montvalent (46) 233 K2
Montvalezan (73) 193 B3
Montvendre (26) 240 D1
Montverdun (42) 204 D3
Montvernier (73). 225 G1
Montvert (15) 216 B6
Montvicq (03) 184 C1
Montviette (14) 54 D1
Montville (76) 15 K6
Montviron (50) 51 J2
Montzéville (55) 43 G4
Monviel (47) 231 J5
Monze (11) 290 C6
Moon-sur-Elle (50) 31 H2
Moosch (68) 119 K3
Mooslargue (68) 97 B5
Moraches (58) 133 G6
Moragne (17) 177 G5
Morainville (28) 85 K4
Morainville-Jouveaux (27). 34 B4
Morainvilliers (78) 58 A2
Morancé (69) 188 B6
Morancez (28) 85 G3
Morancourt (52) 91 K3
Morand (37) 128 B2
Morangis (51) 61 K2
Morangis (91) 58 E5
Morangles (60) 37 J5
Morannes (49) 105 H5
Moranville (55) 43 K5
Moras (38) 206 E3
Moras-en-Valloire (26) 222 D2
Morbecque (59) 5 J3
Morbier (39) 174 A3
Morcenx (40) 245 F6
Morchain (80) 19 G3
Morchies (62) 11 G4
Morcourt (02) 20 A2
Morcourt (80) 18 E2
Mordelles (35) 78 E4
Moréac (56) 101 F2

Morée (41) 108 D4
Moreilles (85) 160 B5
Morelmaison (88) 93 J4
Morembert (10) 90 D2
Morestel (38) 207 G3
Moret-sur-Loing (77). 87 J4
Morêtel-de-Mailles (38) 208 D2
Morette (38) 223 H2
Moreuil (80) 18 C3
Morey (71) 153 J6
Morey-Saint-Denis (21). 154 B1
Morez (39) 174 A3
Morfontaine (54) 26 D3
Morganx (40) 265 G6
Morgemoulin (55) 43 K4
Morgny (27) 36 C2
Morgny-en-Thiérache (02) 21 H3
Morgny-la-Pommeraye (76) . . . 35 K1
Morhange (57) 66 E2
Moriat (63) 219 F1
Morienne (76) 17 F3
Morienval (60) 38 E4
Morières-lès-Avignon (84). 276 C3
Moriers (28) 85 F6
Morieux (22) 49 H6
Moriez (04) 279 J1
Morigny (50) 52 C2
Morigny-Champigny (91) 86 D3
Morillon (74) 192 A3
Moringhem (62) 5 F2
Morionvilliers (52) 92 D3
Morisel (80) 18 C3
Moriville (88) 94 D3
Moriviller (54) 94 D2
Morizécourt (88) 117 H1
Morizès (33) 230 C5
Morlaàs (64) 284 E3
Morlac (18) 166 E3
Morlaix (29) 47 G4
Morlancourt (80) 18 D1
Morlanne (64) 284 B1
Morlet (71) 153 H4
Morley (55) 92 B3
Morlhon-le-Haut (12) 251 G3
Morlincourt (60) 19 H6
Mormaison (85) 141 K4
Mormant (77) 87 K1
Mormant-sur-Vernisson (45) . . . 111 J3
Mormès (32). 266 A3
Mormoiron (84). 257 J6
Mornac (16) 197 F3
Mornac-sur-Seudre (17) 194 C2
Mornand-en-Forez (42). 204 D3
Mornans (26) 240 E5
Mornant (69) 205 K4
Mornas (84) 256 D4
Mornay (71) 170 E4
Mornay-Berry (18) 150 B3
Mornay-sur-Allier (18) 150 C6
Moroges (71) 171 H1
Morogues (18) 149 J1
Morosaglia (2B) 319 G4
Morre (25) 138 A6
Morsain (02) 39 H2
Morsains (51) 61 F4
Morsalines (50) 29 F3
Morsan (27) 34 D5
Morsang-sur-Orge (91) 58 E6
Morsang-sur-Seine (91) 87 F1
Morsbach (57) 68 B2
Morsbronn-les-Bains (67) 25 A3
Morschwiller (67) 69 A3
Morschwiller-le-Bas (68) 97 B2
Morsiglia (2B) 317 C2
Mortagne (88) 95 G4
Mortagne-au-Perche (61) 83 H2
Mortagne-du-Nord (59) 7 H6
Mortagne-sur-Gironde (17) 194 E5
Mortagne-sur-Sèvre (85) 142 E3
Mortain (50) 52 D5
Mortcerf (77) 59 K4
Morteau (25) 157 H2
Morteaux-Coulibœuf (14) 54 B2
Mortefontaine (02) 39 G3
Mortefontaine (60) 38 B6
Mortefontaine-en-Thelle (60) . . 37 H4
Mortemart (87) 180 E4
Mortemer (60) 18 E6
Mortemer (76) 16 E4
Mortery (77) 88 D1
Morthomiers (18) 149 F3
Mortiers (02). 20 A4
Mortiers (17). 195 K6
Morton (86) 144 D2
Mortrée (61) 54 D6
Mortroux (23) 166 A6
Mortzwiller (68). 119 K5
Morval (62) 11 F6
Morvillars (90) 139 J2
Morville (50) 28 D4
Morville (88) 93 H5
Morville-en-Beauce (45) 86 C5
Morville-lès-Vic (57) 66 D3
Morville-sur-Andelle (76) 36 B1
Morville-sur-Nied (57) 66 C1
Morville-sur-Seille (54) 66 A1
Morvillers (60) 17 G6
Morvillers-Saint-Saturnin (80) . . 17 G3
Morvilliers (10) 91 F3
Morvilliers (28) 56 B6
Mory (62) 11 F4
Mory-Montcrux (60) 18 B6
Morzine (74) 192 B2
Mosles (14) 32 A3
Moslins (51) 61 K2

Mosnac (16) 196 C4
Mosnac (17) 195 H5
Mosnay (36) 165 H3
Mosnes (37) 128 C4
Mosset (66) 314 B2
Mosson (21) 115 G3
Mostuéjouls (12). 253 H4
Motey-Besuche (70) 137 G5
Motey-sur-Saône (70). 137 H2
la Mothe-Achard (85) 159 F2
la Mothe-Saint-Héray (79) 162 A6
Mothern (67) 25 E2
la Motte (22) 77 G4
la Motte (83). 298 E1
la Motte-Chalancon (26) 241 H6
la Motte-d'Aigues (84) 277 J4
la Motte-d'Aveillans (38) 224 B6
la Motte-de-Galaure (26) 222 C3
la Motte-du-Caire (04) 259 G2
la Motte-en-Bauges (73). 208 D2
la Motte-en-Champsaur (05) . . . 242 E3
la Motte-Fanjas (26) 223 G5
la Motte-Feuilly (36) 166 C4
la Motte-Fouquet (61) 81 K1
la Motte-Saint-Jean (71) 170 A4
la Motte-Saint-Martin (38) 224 A6
la Motte-Servolex (73) 208 B3
la Motte-Ternant (21) 134 C2
la Motte-Tilly (10) 88 E2
Mottereau (28) 84 D5
Motteville (76) 15 H5
Mottier (38) 207 H4
Motz (73) 190 C5
Mouacourt (54) 66 E5
Mouais (44) 103 G4
Mouans-Sartoux (06) 280 D5
Mouaville (54) 44 B4
Mouchamps (85) 142 C6
Mouchan (32) 267 F2
Mouchard (39) 155 K3
la Mouche (50) 51 K1
Mouchès (32) 286 B1
Mouchin (59) 7 F5
Mouchy-le-Châtel (60) 37 J3
Moudeyres (43) 220 E6
Mouen (14) 32 D5
Mouettes (27) 57 F3
Mouffy (89) 133 F1
Mouflaines (27) 36 C4
Mouflers (80) 9 J6
Mouflières (80) 17 F1
Mougins (06) 280 E5
Mougon (79) 178 C1
Mouguerre (64) 282 C1
Mouhers (36) 165 K3
Mouhet (36) 165 F6
Mouhous (64) 284 E2
Mouillac (33) 211 K5
Mouillac (82) 250 C4
la Mouille (39) 174 A4
Mouilleron (52) 116 B6
Mouilleron-en-Pareds (85) 160 D2
Mouilleron-le-Captif (85) 159 H1
Mouilly (55) 43 K6
Moulares (81) 270 D3
Moulay (53) 81 G5
Moulayrès (81) 270 C5
Moulédous (65) 285 K5
Moulès-et-Baucels (34) 274 A2
Mouleydier (24) 231 J2
Moulézan (30) 274 E2
Moulhard (28) 84 C6
Moulicent (61) 83 K1
Moulidars (16) 196 C3
Mouliets-et-Villemartin (33) . . . 230 C2
Mouliherne (49) 126 C3
Moulin-Mage (81) 272 B5
Moulin-Neuf (09) 308 C1
Moulin-Neuf (24) 212 D6
Moulin-sous-Touvent (60) 39 G2
Moulineaux (76) 35 G3
Moulines (14) 53 K1
Moulines (50) 80 C1
Moulinet (06) 311 B4
Moulinet (47) 231 J6
le Moulinet-sur-Solin (45) 111 H5
Moulins (02) 40 C2
Moulins (03) 168 E3
Moulins (35) 79 J6
Moulins-en-Tonnerrois (89) 114 A6
Moulins-Engilbert (58) 152 A4
Moulins-la-Marche (61) 55 G6
Moulins-le-Carbonnel (72) 82 C3
Moulins-lès-Metz (57) 44 E5
Moulins-Saint-Hubert (55) 23 G5
Moulins-sur-Céphons (36) 147 J4
Moulins-sur-Orne (61) 54 B4
Moulins-sur-Ouanne (89) 112 E6
Moulins-sur-Yèvre (18) 149 H3
Moulis (09) 306 D3
Moulis-en-Médoc (33) 211 F5
Moulismes (86) 163 K6
Moulle (62) 3 F4
Moulon (33) 230 A2
Moulon (45) 111 G2
Moulotte (55) 44 B5
Moult (14) 33 G6
Moumoulous (65) 285 K3
Moumour (64) 283 K5
Mounes-Prohencoux (12) 272 B4
Mourède (32) 267 F4
Mourens (33) 230 A4
Mourenx (64) 284 A3

Mouret (12) 235 J6
Moureuille (63) 184 D3
Mourèze (34) 273 G6
Mouriès (13) 276 C5
Mouriez (62) 9 H2
Mourioux-Vieilleville (23) 182 B4
Mourjou (15) 235 G4
Mourmelon-le-Grand (51) 41 J5
Mourmelon-le-Petit (51) 41 H5
Mournans-Charbonny (39) . . . 156 B6
Mouron (08) 42 C3
Mouron-sur-Yonne (58) 151 K1
Mouroux (77) 60 B4
Mours (95) 37 J6
Mours-Saint-Eusèbe (26) 222 D5
Mourvilles-Basses (31) 288 E2
Mourvilles-Hautes (31) 289 F3
Mouscardès (40) 264 C6
Moussac (30) 275 F1
Moussac (86) 180 B1
Moussages (15) 217 H3
Moussan (11) 291 H5
Moussé (35) 104 A3
Mousseaux-lès-Bray (77) 88 C3
Mousseaux-Neuville (27) 57 F3
Mousseaux-sur-Seine (78) 57 H1
Moussey (10) 90 B6
Moussey (57) 67 G5
Moussey (88) 95 J2
les Moussières (39) 173 K6
Mousson (54) 65 K2
Moussonvilliers (61) 55 K6
Moussoulens (11) 289 K5
Moussy (51) 61 K1
Moussy (58) 151 G1
Moussy (95) 37 F6
Moussy-le-Neuf (77) 59 G1
Moussy-le-Vieux (77) 59 H1
Moussy-Verneuil (02) 40 B2
Moustajon (31) 305 H5
Moustéru (22) 48 B3
Moustey (40) 245 H2
Moustier (47) 231 F5
Moustier-en-Fagne (59) 13 K5
Moustier-Ventadour (19) 216 E1
Moustiers-Sainte-Marie (04) . . . 279 F2
le Moustoir (22) 75 J3
Moustoir-Ac (56) 101 F3
Moustoir-Remungol (56) 100 E1
la Moutade (63) 185 G5
le Moutaret (38) 208 D5
Mouterhouse (57) 69 H4
Mouterre-Silly (86) 144 D4
Mouterre-sur-Blourde (86) 180 C2
Mouthe (25) 174 C1
le Moutherot (25) 137 H6
Mouthier-en-Bresse (71) 155 F5
Mouthier-Haute-Pierre (25) 156 E2
Mouthiers-sur-Boëme (16) 196 D4
Mouthoumet (11) 309 H3
Moutier-d'Ahun (23) 183 F4
Moutier-Malcard (23) 166 B6
Moutier-Rozeille (23) 183 G6
Moutiers (28) 85 J5
Moutiers (35) 104 A2
Moutiers (54) 44 D4
Moûtiers (73) 209 H5
Moutiers-au-Perche (61) 84 A2
les Moutiers-en-Auge (14) 54 C3
les Moutiers-en-Cinglais (14) . . . 53 J1
Moutiers-en-Puisaye (89) 132 C2
les Moutiers-en-Retz (44) 140 E2
les Moutiers-Hubert (14) 55 F2
Moutiers-les-Mauxfaits (85) . . . 159 H4
Moutiers-Saint-Jean (21) 134 C2
Moutiers-sous-Argenton (79) . . . 143 K4
Moutiers-sous-Chantemerle (79) . . 161 F1
Moutiers-sur-le-Lay (85) 160 A3
Mouton (16) 179 H6
Moutonne (39) 173 G3
Moutonneau (16) 179 H6
Moutoux (39) 156 B6
Moutrot (54) 65 H6
Mouvaux (59) 6 E3
Moux (11) 290 E6
Moux-en-Morvan (58) 152 D1
Mouxy (73) 208 B2
Mouy (60) 37 K3
Mouy-sur-Seine (77) 88 D3
Mouzay (37) 146 C3
Mouzay (55) 43 G1
Mouzeil (44) 123 J1
Mouzens (24) 232 D2
Mouzens (81) 289 G1
Mouzeuil-Saint-Martin (85) 160 C4
Mouzieys-Panens (81) 250 E6
Mouzieys-Teulet (81) 271 F3
Mouzillon (44) 142 B1
Mouzon (08) 23 G5
Mouzon (16) 197 J1
Moval (90) 139 H1
Moy-de-l'Aisne (02) 20 A4
Moyaux (14) 34 B5
Moydans (05) 258 B1
Moye (74) 190 D6
Moyemont (88) 94 E3
Moyen (54) 94 E1
Moyencourt (80) 19 G4
Moyencourt-lès-Poix (80) 17 J3
Moyenmoutier (88) 95 H3
Moyenneville (60) 38 C1
Moyenneville (62) 10 E4
Moyenneville (80) 9 F5
Moyenvic (57) 66 E3
Moyeuvre-Grande (57) 44 D3
Moyeuvre-Petite (57) 44 D3

Moyon (50) 31 H5
Moyrazès (12) 252 A3
Moyvillers (60) 38 C2
Mozac (63) 185 F6
Mozé-sur-Louet (49) 125 G5
Muchedent (76) 16 A3
Mudaison (34) 274 D6
Muel (35) 78 B4
Muespach (68) 97 C5
Muespach-le-Haut (68) 97 D5
Mugron (40) 264 E4
Muhlbach-sur-Bruche (67) 70 B4
Muhlbach-sur-Munster (68) . . . 119 K1
Muides-sur-Loire (41) 129 G1
Muidorge (60) 37 H1
Muids (27) 35 K4
Muille-Villette (80) 19 H5
Muirancourt (60) 19 H5
Muizon (51) 40 D4
les Mujouls (06) 280 C2
la Mulatière (69) 206 A2
Mulcent (78) 57 H3
Mulcey (57) 67 F3
Mulhausen (67) 69 J5
Mulhouse (68) 97 C2
Mulsanne (72) 106 E4
Mulsans (41) 129 F1
Mun (65) 285 K4
Munchhausen (67) 25 D2
Munchhouse (68) 97 D1
Muncq-Nieurlet (62) 3 F1
Mundolsheim (67) 25 A6
Muneville-le-Bingard (50) 30 D3
Muneville-sur-Mer (50) 30 D5
le Mung (17) 177 H6
Munster (57) 68 C5
Munster (68) 96 A4
Muntzenheim (68) 96 D3
Munwiller (68) 96 C6
Mur-de-Barrez (12) 235 K2
Mûr-de-Bretagne (22) 76 D4
Mur-de-Sologne (41) 129 H4
Muracciole (2B) 321 F2
Murasson (12) 272 A4
Murat (03) 168 A6
Murat (15) 218 C5
Murat-le-Quaire (63) 201 K4
Murat-sur-Vèbre (81) 272 B5
Murato (2B) 319 G2
Muraz (74) 191 G2
Murbach (68) 96 A6
la Mure (38) 242 B1
la Mure-Argens (04) 260 C6
Mureaumont (60) 17 G5
les Mureaux (78) 58 A2
Mureils (26) 222 C3
Mûres (74) 208 C1
Muret (31) 288 A2
Muret-et-Crouttes (02) 39 K4
Muret-le-Château (12) 252 B1
la Murette (38) 207 H6
Murianette (38) 224 B3
Murinais (38) 223 G3
Murles (34) 274 A5
Murlin (58) 150 E1
Muro (2B) 318 C3
Murol (63) 202 C4
Murols (12) 235 J3
Muron (17) 177 G4
Murs (36) 146 E5
Murs (84) 277 F1
Mûrs-Erigné (49) 125 G4
Murs-et-Gélignieux (01) 207 J3
Murtin-et-Bogny (08) 22 B3
Murvaux (55) 43 G2
Murviel-lès-Béziers (34) 291 K3
Murviel-lès-Montpellier (34) . . . 274 A6
Murville (54) 26 D4
Murzo (2A) 320 C2
Mus (30) 275 F4
Muscourt (02) 40 C3
Musculdy (64) 283 G5
Musièges (74) 190 D4
Musigny (21) 153 H1
Mussey-sur-Marne (52) 92 B3
Mussidan (24) 213 G5
Mussig (67) 96 D2
Mussy-la-Fosse (21) 134 E3
Mussy-sous-Dun (71) 187 H2
Mussy-sur-Seine (10) 115 F3
Mutigney (39) 137 F5
Mutigny (51) 41 F6
Mutrécy (14) 32 D6
Muttersholtz (67) 96 D1
Mutzenhouse (67) 70 D1
Mutzig (67) 70 C4
le Muy (83) 298 E1
Muzeray (55) 43 K3
Muzillac (56) 121 J1
Muzy (27) 57 F2
Myans (73) 208 C4
Myennes (58) 132 A4
Myon (25) 156 B3

N

Nabas (64) 283 H3
Nabinaud (16) 213 F2
Nabirat (24) 233 G3
Nabringhen (62) 4 D3
Nachamps (17) 177 J4
Nadaillac (24) 215 H5
Nadaillac-de-Rouge (46) 233 H2

Nades (03) 184 E3
Nadillac (46) 233 J6
Nagel-Séez-Mesnil (27) 56 B2
Nages (81) 272 A5
Nages-et-Solorgues (30) 275 F4
Nahuja (66) 313 H5
Nailhac (19) 214 E3
Naillat (23) 182 B2
Nailloux (31) 288 D4
Nailly (89) 88 C6
Naintré (86) 163 G1
Nainville-les-Roches (91) 87 F2
Naisey-les-Granges (25) 138 C6
Naives-en-Blois (55) 64 E5
Naives-Rosières (55) 64 B4
Naix-aux-Forges (55) 64 D6
Naizin (56) 101 F1
Najac (12) 251 F4
Nalliers (85) 160 B4
Nalliers (86) 164 A3
Nalzen (09) 308 A3
Nambsheim (68) 96 E5
Nampcel (60) 39 G1
Nampcelles-la-Cour (02) 21 G3
Nampont (80) 9 F2
Namps-Maisnil (80) 17 J3
Nampteuil-sous-Muret (02) 39 K3
Nampty (80) 18 A3
Nan-sous-Thil (21) 134 D5
Nanc-lès-Saint-Amour (39) 172 E5
Nançay (18) 130 D5
Nance (39) 172 E1
Nances (73) 208 A4
Nanclars (16) 196 E1
Nançois-le-Grand (55) 64 D5
Nançois-sur-Ornain (55) 64 C5
Nancras (17) 194 D2
Nancray (25) 138 B6
Nancray-sur-Rimarde (45) 110 E2
Nancuise (39) 173 G4
Nancy (54) 66 A5
Nancy-sur-Cluses (74) 191 K3
Nandax (42) 187 F3
Nandy (77) 87 G1
Nangeville (45) 86 E5
Nangis (77) 88 A1
Nangy (74) 191 G2
Nannay (58) 132 C6
Nans (25) 138 D3
les Nans (39) 156 B6
Nans-les-Pins (83) 297 G3
Nans-sous-Sainte-Anne (25) . . . 156 B3
Nant (12) 273 F1
Nant-le-Grand (55) 64 B5
Nant-le-Petit (55) 64 B5
Nanteau-sur-Essonne (77) 87 F4
Nanteau-sur-Lunain (77) 87 J5
Nanterre (92) 58 D3
Nantes (44) 123 G4
Nantes-en-Ratier (38) 224 B6
Nanteuil (79) 162 A5
Nanteuil-Auriac-de-Bourzac (24) . . 213 G1
Nanteuil-en-Vallée (16) 179 H5
Nanteuil-la-Forêt (51) 40 E6
Nanteuil-la-Fosse (02) 39 K2
Nanteuil-le-Haudouin (60) 38 D6
Nanteuil-lès-Meaux (77) 59 K2
Nanteuil-Notre-Dame (02) 39 K5
Nanteuil-sur-Aisne (08) 41 H1
Nanteuil-sur-Marne (77) 60 C2
Nantey (39) 172 E5
Nanthiat (24) 214 C1
Nantiat (87) 181 G5
Nantillé (17) 177 K6
Nantillois (55) 43 F3
Nantilly (70) 137 F3
Nantoin (38) 207 F6
Nantois (55) 64 C6
Nanton (71) 171 J2
Nantouillet (77) 59 H2
Nantoux (21) 153 K3
Nantua (01) 190 A2
Naours (80) 10 A6
Narbéfontaine (57) 45 J5
Narbief (25) 157 J1
Narbonne (11) 291 H6
Narcastet (64) 284 D5
Narcy (52) 92 A1
Narcy (58) 150 D1
Nargis (45) 111 J1
Narnhac (15) 236 B1
Narp (64) 283 J3
Narrosse (40) 264 B4
Nasbinals (48) 236 D4
Nassandres (27) 34 E6
Nassiet (40) 264 E6
Nassigny (03) 167 H4
Nastringues (24) 230 E2
Nattages (01) 207 K2
Natzwiller (67) 70 B5
Naucelle (12) 251 K5
Naucelles (15) 235 H1
Naujac-sur-Mer (33) 210 C2
Naujan-et-Postiac (33) 230 B3
Nauroy (02) 19 K1
Naussac (12) 234 E6
Naussac (48) 238 B4
Naussannes (24) 232 A3
Nauvay (72) 83 F5
Nauviale (12) 235 H6
Navacelles (30) 255 J5
Navailles-Angos (64) 284 D3
Navarrenx (64) 283 J4
Naveil (41) 108 C5
Navenne (70) 138 B1

Naves (03) 185 F3
Naves (19) 216 B2
Naves (59) 12 B4
Navès (81) 289 K1
Nâves-Parmelan (74) 191 G5
Navilly (71) 154 D4
Nay (50) 30 C5
Nay (64) 284 E5
Nayemont-les-Fosses (88) 95 J4
le Nayrac (12) 235 K5
Nazelles-Négron (37) 128 B4
Néac (33) 230 B1
Néant-sur-Yvel (56) 101 K1
Neau (53) 81 H6
Neaufles-Auvergny (27) 55 K3
Neaufles-Saint-Martin (27) 36 D3
Neauphe-sous-Essai (61) 82 E1
Neauphe-sur-Dive (61) 54 D3
Neauphle-le-Château (78) 58 A4
Neauphle-le-Vieux (78) 57 K4
Neauphlette (78) 57 G2
Neaux (42) 187 G5
Nébian (34) 273 H6
Nébias (11) 308 D4
Nébing (57) 68 B5
Nébouzat (63) 202 B3
Nécy (61) 54 B3
Nedde (87) 200 A3
Nédon (62) 5 H5
Nédonchel (62) 5 H5
Neewiller-près-Lauterbourg (67) . . 25 D2
Neffes (05) 242 E6
Neffiès (34) 292 B1
Néfiach (66) 314 E2
Nègrepelisse (82) 250 A6
Nègreville (50) 28 D4
Négrondes (24) 214 B2
Néhou (50) 28 D5
Nelling (57) 68 B4
Nemours (77) 87 H5
Nempont-Saint-Firmin (62) 9 F2
Nénigan (31) 286 E3
Néons-sur-Creuse (36) 164 B1
Néoules (83) 297 K3
Néoux (23) 183 H6
Nepvant (55) 23 H6
Nérac (47) 247 J5
Nerbis (40) 264 E4
Nercillac (16) 196 A2
Néré (17) 178 C5
Néret (36) 166 C3
Nérigean (33) 230 A2
Nérignac (86) 180 C1
Néris-les-Bains (03) 184 B1
Nernier (74) 174 D5
Néron (28) 85 G1
Néronde (42) 204 E1
Néronde-sur-Dore (63) 203 H2
Nérondes (18) 150 A4
Ners (30) 274 E1
Nersac (16) 196 D4
Nervieux (42) 204 D1
Nerville-la-Forêt (95) 37 J6
Néry (60) 38 D4
Neschers (63) 202 E4
Nescus (09) 307 G2
Nesle (80) 19 G4
Nesle-et-Massoult (21) 114 E5
Nesle-Hodeng (76) 16 D4
Nesle-la-Reposte (51) 61 F6
Nesle-le-Repons (51) 61 H1
Nesle-l'Hôpital (80) 17 F2
Nesle-Normandeuse (76) 17 F2
Nesles (62) 4 B4
Nesles-la-Montagne (02) 60 E1
Nesles-la-Vallée (95) 37 H6
Neslette (80) 17 F1
Nesmy (85) 159 J2
Nesploy (45) 110 E3
Nespouls (19) 215 J5
Nessa (2B) 318 D3
Nestier (65) 305 G1
Nettancourt (55) 63 J3
Neublans-Abergement (39) 155 F4
Neubois (67) 96 B1
le Neubourg (27) 35 G5
Neuchâtel-Urtière (25) 139 G4
Neuf-Berquin (59) 6 A4
Neuf-Brisach (68) 96 D4
Neuf-Église (63) 184 D4
Neuf-Marché (76) 36 D2
Neuf-Mesnil (59) 13 G3
Neufbosc (76) 16 C5
le Neufbourg (50) 52 D5
Neufchâteau (88) 93 G3
Neufchâtel-en-Bray (76) 16 D4
Neufchâtel-en-Saosnois (72) . . . 82 E3
Neufchâtel-Hardelot (62) 4 B4
Neufchâtel-sur-Aisne (02) 41 F2
Neufchef (57) 44 D2
Neufchelles (60) 39 G6
Neuffons (33) 230 D4
Neuffontaines (58) 133 H5
Neufgrange (57) 68 D3
Neuflieux (02) 19 J5
Neuflize (08) 41 H2
Neufmaison (08) 22 B3
Neufmaisons (54) 95 G2
Neufmanil (08) 22 D3
Neufmesnil (50) 28 D6
Neufmoulin (80) 9 G5
Neufmoulins (57) 67 H4
Neufmoutiers-en-Brie (77) 59 J4
le Neufour (55) 42 E5
Neufvillage (57) 68 B5
Neufvy-sur-Aronde (60) 38 C1

Neugartheim-Ittlenheim (67) 70 D2
Neuhaeusel (67) 25 D3
Neuil (37) 145 J1
Neuilh (65) 304 C1
Neuillac (17) 195 J5
Neuillay-les-Bois (36) 165 G1
Neuillé (49) 126 B5
Neuillé-le-Lierre (37) 128 A3
Neuillé-Pont-Pierre (37) 127 H2
Neuilly (27) 57 F2
Neuilly (58) 151 H1
Neuilly (89) 112 E4
Neuilly-en-Donjon (03) 169 K6
Neuilly-en-Dun (18) 150 A6
Neuilly-en-Sancerre (18) 131 H5
Neuilly-en-Thelle (60) 37 J4
Neuilly-en-Vexin (95) 37 G5
Neuilly-la-Forêt (14) 31 H1
Neuilly-le-Bisson (61) 82 E2
Neuilly-le-Brignon (37) 146 B4
Neuilly-le-Dien (80) 9 J3
Neuilly-le-Réal (03) 169 F5
Neuilly-le-Vendin (53) 81 K2
Neuilly-l'Évêque (52) 116 E3
Neuilly-l'Hôpital (80) 9 G4
Neuilly-Plaisance (93) 59 G3
Neuilly-Saint-Front (02) 39 H5
Neuilly-sous-Clermont (60) 38 A3
Neuilly-sur-Eure (61) 84 B2
Neuilly-sur-Marne (93) 59 G3
Neuilly-sur-Seine (92) 58 D3
Neuilly-sur-Suize (52) 116 B2
Neulette (62) 9 K1
Neulise (42) 187 G6
Neulles (17) 195 J5
Neulliac (56) 76 D5
Neung-sur-Beuvron (41) 129 K3
Neunkirchen-lès-Bouzonville (57) . . 45 J2
Neure (03) 168 B1
Neurey-en-Vaux (70) 118 B5
Neurey-lès-la-Demie (70) 138 B2
Neussargues-Moissac (15) 218 D4
Neuve-Chapelle (62) 6 B5
Neuve-Église (67) 96 B1
la Neuve-Grange (27) 36 C3
la Neuve-Lyre (27) 55 K3
Neuve-Maison (02) 21 G1
Neuvecelle (74) 175 G5
Neuvéglise (15) 236 D1
Neuvelle-lès-Cromary (70) 138 A4
Neuvelle-lès-la-Charité (70) . . . 137 K2
la Neuvelle-lès-Lure (70) 118 E5
la Neuvelle-lès-Scey (70) 117 J6
Neuvelle-lès-Voisey (52) 117 H4
Neuves-Maisons (54) 65 K6
la Neuveville-devant-
 -Lépanges (88) 95 F3
la Neuveville-sous-
 -Châtenois (88) 93 H4
la Neuveville-sous-Montfort (88) . . 93 K5
Neuvic (19) 217 F1
Neuvic (24) 213 H4
Neuvic-Entier (87) 199 J3
Neuvicq (17) 212 B3
Neuvicq-le-Château (17) 196 B1
Neuvillalais (72) 82 C6
la Neuville (19) 216 B5
la Neuville (59) 6 D6
Neuville (63) 203 G2
la Neuville-à-Maire (08) 22 C5
Neuville-au-Bois (80) 17 G1
la Neuville-au-Cornet (62) 10 B2
la Neuville-au-Plain (50) 29 F5
la Neuville-au-Pont (51) 42 C5
la Neuville-aux-Bois (45) 110 B2
la Neuville-aux-Bois (51) 63 J2
la Neuville-aux-Joûtes (08) 21 J1
la Neuville-aux-Larris (51) 40 D5
la Neuville-Bosc (60) 37 G5
la Neuville-Bosmont (02) 21 F4
la Neuville-Bourjonval (62) 11 H5
la Neuville-Chant-d'Oisel (76) . . . 35 K3
la Neuville-Coppegueule (80) . . . 17 F2
la Neuville-d'Aumont (60) 37 H3
la Neuville-Day (08) 42 B1
la Neuville-de-Poitou (86) 162 E2
la Neuville-du-Bosc (27) 35 F5
la Neuville-en-Avesnois (59) 12 D4
la Neuville-en-Beaumont (50) . . . 28 C6
la Neuville-en-Beine (02) 19 J5
la Neuville-en-Ferrain (59) 6 E2
la Neuville-en-Hez (60) 37 K2
la Neuville-en-Tourne-à-Fuy (08) . . 41 J3
la Neuville-en-Verdunois (55) . . . 64 C2
Neuville-Ferrières (76) 16 D4
la Neuville-Garnier (60) 37 G3
la Neuville-Housset (02) 20 E3
la Neuville-lès-Bray (80) 18 E1
Neuville-les-Dames (01) 188 E2
Neuville-lès-Decize (58) 168 E1
la Neuville-lès-Dorengt (02) 20 D1
Neuville-lès-Lœuilly (80) 17 K3
la Neuville-lès-This (02) 22 C3
Neuville-lès-Vaucouleurs (55) . . . 65 F6
la Neuville-lès-Wasigny (08) . . . 21 K5
Neuville-lez-Beaulieu (08) 21 K2
Neuville-près-Sées (61) 54 E6
Neuville-Saint-Amand (02) 20 A3
la Neuville-Saint-Pierre (60) 37 J1
Neuville-Saint-Rémy (59) 11 J4
Neuville-Saint-Vaast (62) 10 E2
la Neuville-Sire-Bernard (80) . . . 18 C2
Neuville-sous-Montreuil (62) 4 C6
Neuville-sur-Ailette (02) 40 C2
Neuville-sur-Ain (01) 189 H3

Neuville-sur-Authou (27). 34 D5
Neuville-sur-Brenne (37). 128 A2
Neuville-sur-Escaut (59) 12 B2
la Neuville-sur-Essonne (45). 86 E6
Neuville-sur-Margival (02). 39 K2
Neuville-sur-Oise (95). 58 B1
Neuville-sur-Ornain (55) 63 K3
la Neuville-sur-Oudeuil (60) 17 J6
la Neuville-sur-Ressons (60) 19 F6
la Neuville-Roy (60) 38 B1
Neuville-sur-Saône (69) 188 C6
Neuville-sur-Sarthe (72) 106 E1
Neuville-sur-Seine (10) 114 E2
Neuville-sur-Touques (61) 55 F3
Neuville-sur-Vannes (10) 89 J5
la Neuville-Vault (60). 37 F1
Neuville-Vitasse (62) 11 F3
Neuviller-la-Roche (67). 70 A5
Neuviller-lès-Badonviller (54) 95 H1
Neuviller-sur-Moselle (54). 94 B1
Neuvillers-sur-Fave (88) 95 J4
Neuvillette (02). 20 B2
Neuvillette (80) 10 A4
Neuvillette-en-Charnie (72) 106 A1
Neuvilley (39) 155 H4
Neuvilly (59) 12 D4
Neuvilly-en-Argonne (55) 42 E5
Neuvireuil (62) 11 G2
Neuvizy (08). 22 B5
Neuvy (03) 168 E3
Neuvy (41) 129 H2
Neuvy (51) 61 F5
Neuvy-au-Houlme (61) 54 A4
Neuvy-Bouin (79) 161 H2
Neuvy-Deux-Clochers (18) 131 H6
Neuvy-en-Beauce (28) 86 A5
Neuvy-en-Champagne (72) 106 B1
Neuvy-en-Dunois (28). 85 G6
Neuvy-en-Mauges (49). 124 D6
Neuvy-en-Sullias (45). 110 D5
Neuvy-Grandchamp (71) 170 A3
Neuvy-le-Barrois (18) 150 C5
Neuvy-le-Roi (37). 127 H2
Neuvy-Pailloux (36) 148 B5
Neuvy-Saint-Sépulchre (36) 165 K3
Neuvy-Sautour (89) 113 J2
Neuvy-sur-Barangeon (18) 130 D6
Neuvy-sur-Loire (58) 131 H4
Neuwiller (68) 97 E5
Neuwiller-lès-Saverne (67) 69 G6
Névache (05) 225 K5
Nevers (58). 150 E4
Névez (29) 99 F4
Névian (11). 291 G5
Néville (76) 15 G3
Néville-sur-Mer (50). 29 F2
Nevoy (45) 111 G6
Nevy-lès-Dole (39) 155 G3
Nevy-sur-Seille (39) 173 G1
Nexon (87) 198 E3
Ney (39) 173 K1
Neydens (74) 191 F3
les Neyrolles (01) 190 A2
Neyron (01) 206 B1
Nézel (78). 57 K2
Nézignan-l'Évêque (34) 292 C3
Niafles (53) 104 C4
Niaux (09) 307 J5
Nibas (80) 8 E5
Nibelle (45) 110 E2
Nibles (04) 259 G3
Nice (06) 281 G4
Nicey (21) 114 D4
Nicey-sur-Aire (55) 64 C3
Nicole (47) 247 J3
Nicorps (50) 30 E4
Niderhoff (57) 67 J5
Niderviller (57) 67 K4
Niederbronn-les-Bains (67). 69 J4
Niederbruck (68) 119 J4
Niederentzen (68) 96 C5
Niederhaslach (67) 70 B4
Niederhausbergen (67) 25 D4
Niederhergheim (68) 96 C5
Niederlauterbach (67) 25 D2
Niedermodern (67) 69 J5
Niedermorschwihr (68) 96 B4
Niedernai (67). 70 D5
Niederrœdern (67) 25 D2
Niederschaeffolsheim (67) 25 A4
Niedersoultzbach (67) 69 H6
Niedersteinbach (67) 69 K3
Niederstinzel (57) 67 J2
Niedervisse (57) 45 J4
Nielles-lès-Ardres (62) 2 E4
Nielles-lès-Bléquin (62). 4 D3
Nielles-lès-Calais (62). 2 C3
Nieppe (59) 6 B3
Niergnies (59). 12 A4
Nieudan (15) 217 F6
Nieuil (16). 179 K6
Nieuil-l'Espoir (86) 163 G4
Nieul (87) 181 G6
Nieul-le-Dolent (85) 159 H3
Nieul-le-Virouil (17). 195 H6
Nieul-lès-Saintes (17) 195 F2
Nieul-sur-l'Autise (85) 161 F5
Nieul-sur-Mer (17) 176 D2
Nieulle-sur-Seudre (17). 194 C2
Nieurlet (59) 3 G4
Niévroz (01) 206 C1
Niffer (68) 97 D3
Niherne (36). 147 J6
Nijon (52) 93 F5
Nilvange (57) 27 F4
Nîmes (30) 275 G3

Ninville (52) 116 D1
Niort (79) 161 H6
Niort-de-Sault (11) 308 C1
Niozelles (04) 278 C1
Nissan-lez-Enserune (34) 291 K4
Nistos (65) 305 G2
Nitry (89) 133 K1
Nitting (57) 67 J5
Nivelle (59) 7 H6
Nivillac (56) 102 A5
Nivillers (60). 37 H2
Nivolas-Vermelle (38) 207 F4
Nivollet-Montgriffon (01). 189 J4
Nixéville-Blercourt (55). 43 G5
le Nizan (33). 246 C1
Nizan-Gesse (31) 286 D5
Nizas (32). 287 H2
Nizas (34). 292 C2
Nizerolles (03) 186 A4
Nizy-le-Comte (02) 21 H6
Noailhac (12) 235 G6
Noailhac (19) 215 K5
Noailhac (81) 290 B1
Noaillac (33). 230 C6
Noaillan (33). 229 K6
Noailles (19) 215 J5
Noailles (60) 37 J3
Noailles (81) 270 C1
Noailly (42) 186 E3
Noalhac (48). 236 E3
Noalhat (63). 185 J6
Noards (27) 34 C4
Nocario (2B). 319 H4
Nocé (61) 83 J4
Noceta (2B) 321 G1
Nochize (71) 170 C5
la Nocle-Maulaix (58) 169 J1
Nod-sur-Seine (21). 115 F5
Nods (25) 156 E2
Noé (31). 288 A4
Noé (89). 88 E6
la Noë-Blanche (35) 103 F2
Noë-les-Mallets (10) 115 F1
la Noë-Poulain (27). 34 C4
Noël-Cerneux (25) 157 H1
Noëllet (49). 104 B6
les Noës (42) 186 C4
les Noës-près-Troyes (10). 90 A4
Nœux-lès-Auxi (62) 9 K3
Nœux-les-Mines (62) 6 A6
Nogaret (31). 289 G2
Nogaro (32). 266 B4
Nogent (52) 116 D2
Nogent-en-Othe (10) 113 J1
Nogent-l'Abbesse (51) 41 G4
Nogent-l'Artaud (02). 60 D2
Nogent-le-Bernard (72). 83 G5
Nogent-le-Phaye (28) 85 H3
Nogent-le-Roi (28) 57 G6
Nogent-le-Rotrou (28) 84 A4
Nogent-le-Sec (27) 56 C2
Nogent-lès-Montbard (21) 134 E2
Nogent-sur-Aube (10). 90 D2
Nogent-sur-Eure (28) 85 F3
Nogent-sur-Loir (72). 127 F1
Nogent-sur-Marne (94) 59 F4
Nogent-sur-Oise (60) 38 A4
Nogent-sur-Seine (10) 89 F2
Nogent-sur-Vernisson (45) 111 J5
Nogentel (02) 60 E1
Nogna (39) 173 H2
Noguères (64) 284 A3
Nohanent (63) 202 D2
Nohant-en-Goût (18) 149 J3
Nohant-en-Graçay (18). 148 B2
Nohant-Vic (36) 166 B3
Nohèdes (66) 314 A3
Nohic (82) 269 G3
Noidan (21) 134 E5
Noidans-le-Ferroux (70) 137 K2
Noidans-lès-Vesoul (70) 138 A1
Noidant-Chatenoy (52) 116 D5
Noidant-le-Rocheux (52) 116 C4
Noilhan (32) 287 G1
Nointel (60) 38 A3
Nointel (95) 37 J6
Nointot (76) 14 E5
Noircourt (02) 21 H4
Noirefontaine (25). 139 H4
Noirémont (60) 18 A6
Noirétable (42) 204 A1
Noirlieu (51) 63 H2
Noirmoutier-en-l'Île (85) 140 B3
Noiron (70) 137 G4
la Nouaille (19) 200 D1
Noiron-sous-Gevrey (21) 154 C1
Noiron-sur-Bèze (21) 136 D4
Noiron-sur-Seine (21). 114 E3
Noironte (25) 137 J5
Noirval (08). 42 C1
Noiseau (94) 59 G4
Noisiel (77) 59 H3
Noisseville (57). 45 G5
Noisy-le-Grand (93) 59 G4
Noisy-le-Roi (78) 58 B4
Noisy-le-Sec (93) 59 F3
Noisy-Rudignon (77) 88 A4
Noisy-sur-École (77) 87 G4
Noisy-sur-Oise (95) 37 K6
Noizay (37). 128 A4
Nojals-et-Clotte (24). 232 A4
Nojeon-en-Vexin (27) 36 C3
Nolay (21) 153 J4
Nolay (58) 151 F2
Nolléval (76) 36 B1
Nollieux (42). 204 C1
Nomain (59) 7 H5

Nomdieu (47) 248 A6
Nomécourt (52) 92 A3
Nomeny (54) 66 A2
Nomexy (88). 94 C4
Nommay (25) 139 H2
Nompatelize (88) 95 H3
Nonac (16) 196 D6
Nonancourt (27) 56 D4
Nonant (14) 32 B4
Nonant-le-Pin (61) 54 E5
Nonards (19) 216 B6
Nonaville (16). 196 B5
Noncourt-sur-le-Rongeant (52) . . 92 C3
Nonette (63). 203 F6
Nonglard (74) 190 E5
Nonhigny (54) 67 H6
Nonières (07) 239 J1
Nonsard-Lamarche (55) 65 G2
Nontron (24) 197 K5
Nonville (77) 87 J4
Nonville (88). 117 K1
Nonvilliers-Grandhoux (28) 84 D4
Nonza (2B) 317 C4
Nonzeville (88) 95 F4
Noordpeene (59) 3 H4
Nordausques (62) 2 E4
Nordheim (67) 70 D2
Nordhouse (67) 71 D3
Noreuil (62) 11 G4
Norges-la-Ville (21) 136 A4
Normandel (61) 55 K6
Normanville (27) 35 J6
Normanville (76) 15 F4
Normier (21) 134 E5
Norolles (14). 33 K5
Noron-la-Poterie (14) 32 A4
Noron-l'Abbaye (14) 54 A3
Noroy (60) 38 B2
Noroy-le-Bourg (70) 138 C1
Noroy-sur-Ourcq (02) 39 H5
Norrent-Fontes (62) 5 H5
Norrey-en-Auge (14). 54 C2
Norrois (51) 63 F5
Norroy (88). 93 J5
Norroy-le-Sec (54) 44 B3
Norroy-le-Veneur (57) 44 E4
Norroy-lès-Pont-à-Mousson (54) . 65 J2
Nort-Leulinghem (62) 2 E4
Nort-sur-Erdre (44) 123 H1
Nortkerque (62) 2 E3
Norville (76) 34 D1
la Norville (91) 86 D1
Nossage-et-Bénévent (05) 258 D2
Nossoncourt (88) 95 F2
Nostang (56) 100 B4
Noth (23) 182 A2
Nothalten (67) 70 C6
Notre-Dame-d'Aliermont (76) . . . 16 B2
Notre-Dame-d'Allençon (49). . . . 125 H5
Notre-Dame-de-Bellecombe (73) . 191 K6
Notre-Dame-de-Bliquetuit (76). . . 34 E1
Notre-Dame-de-Boisset (42) 187 F5
Notre-Dame-de-Cenilly (50) 31 F5
Notre-Dame-de-Commiers (38) . . 224 A5
Notre-Dame-de-Courson (14). . . . 55 F1
Notre-Dame-de-Gravenchon (76) . . 34 D1
Notre-Dame-de-la-Rouvière (30). . 254 D6
Notre-Dame-de-l'Isle (27). 36 B5
Notre-Dame-de-Livaye (14) 33 H6
Notre-Dame-de-Livoye (50) 52 B4
Notre-Dame-de-Londres (34) . . . 274 B3
Notre-Dame-de-l'Osier (38) 223 H2
Notre-Dame-de-Mésage (38). . . . 224 B4
Notre-Dame-de-Monts (85) 140 C5
Notre-Dame-de-Riez (85) 140 E6
Notre-Dame-de-Sanilhac (24) . . . 214 A4
Notre-Dame-de-Vaulx (38) 224 B5
Notre-Dame-d'Elle (50). 31 J3
Notre-Dame-d'Épine (27) 34 D5
Notre-Dame-des-Landes (44). . . 123 F2
Notre-Dame-des-Millières (73) . . 209 F3
Notre-Dame-des-Étrées (14). . . . 33 H5
Notre-Dame-d'Oé (37) 127 J4
Notre-Dame-du-Bec (76) 14 B5
Notre-Dame-du-Cruet (73) 209 F6
Notre-Dame-du-Hamel (27) 55 H3
Notre-Dame-du-Parc (76). 16 A4
Notre-Dame-du-Pé (72) 105 J6
Notre-Dame-du-Pré (73). 209 J4
Notre-Dame-du-Rocher (61). 53 J4
Notre-Dame-du-Touchet (50) 52 D6
Nottonville (28). 109 G1
la Nouaille (19) 200 D1
Nouaillé-Maupertuis (86) 163 F4
Nouainville (50) 28 C2
Nouan-le-Fuzelier (41) 130 B3
Nouans (72) 82 E5
Nouans-les-Fontaines (37) 147 F2
Nouart (08). 42 E1
Nouâtre (37) 145 J3
la Nouaye (35) 78 D3
la Noue (51) 61 G5
Noueilles (31) 288 C3
Nougaroulet (32) 267 K5
Nouhant (23) 183 J1
Nouic (87) 180 D4
Nouilhan (65) 285 H3
les Nouillers (17). 177 J5
Nouillonpont (55) 26 C4
Nouilly (57). 45 F5
Noulens (32) 266 D3
Nourard-le-Franc (60). 37 K1
Nourray (41) 108 C6
Nousse (40). 264 D4
Nousseviller-lès-Bitche (57) 69 G2

Nousseviller-Saint-Nabor (57). . . . 68 C2
Nousty (64) 284 E4
Nouvelle-Église (62) 2 E3
Nouvion (80). 9 F4
le Nouvion-en-Thiérache (02) . . . 13 F6
Nouvion-et-Catillon (02) 20 B4
Nouvion-le-Comte (02) 20 B4
Nouvion-le-Vineux (02) 40 B1
Nouvion-sur-Meuse (08) 22 D4
Nouvoitou (35) 79 H5
Nouvron-Vingré (02) 39 H2
Nouzerines (23) 166 C6
Nouzerolles (23) 165 J6
Nouziers (23) 166 B5
Nouzilly (37) 127 J3
Nouzonville (08) 22 D3
Novacelles (63). 203 J6
Novalaise (73) 208 A4
Novale (2B). 319 G5
Novéant-sur-Moselle (57) 44 E6
Novel (74) 175 J5
Novella (2B) 318 E2
Noves (13) 276 C2
Noviant-aux-Prés (54) 65 H3
Novillard (90) 139 J1
Novillars (25) 138 B5
Novillers (60) 37 J4
Novion-Porcien (08) 22 A5
Novy-Chevrières (08) 22 A6
Noyal (22) 77 J1
Noyal-Châtillon-sur-Seiche (35) . . 79 G5
Noyal-Muzillac (56). 101 J6
Noyal-Pontivy (56) 76 E6
Noyal-sous-Bazouges (35) 51 G6
Noyal-sur-Brutz (44) 103 K3
Noyal-sur-Vilaine (35) 79 H4
Noyales (02) 20 C2
Noyalo (56). 101 G6
Noyant (49) 126 D3
Noyant-d'Allier (03) 168 C5
Noyant-de-Touraine (37). 145 J2
Noyant-et-Aconin (02) 39 J3
Noyant-la-Gravoyère (49) 104 C6
Noyant-la-Plaine (49) 125 J6
Noyarey (38). 223 K2
Noyelle-Vion (62) 10 C3
Noyelles-en-Chaussée (80). 9 F4
Noyelles-Godault (62). 11 G1
Noyelles-lès-Humières (62). 9 K2
Noyelles-lès-Seclin (59) 6 D5
Noyelles-lès-Vermelles (62) 6 B6
Noyelles-sous-Bellonne (62) 11 H2
Noyelles-sous-Lens (62). 11 F1
Noyelles-sur-Escaut (59) 11 J4
Noyelles-sur-Mer (80) 9 F4
Noyelles-sur-Sambre (59) 13 H4
Noyelles-sur-Selle (59) 12 C3
Noyellette (62) 10 D2
Noyen-sur-Sarthe (72) 106 B4
Noyen-sur-Seine (77) 88 E3
le Noyer (05) 242 D3
le Noyer (18) 131 H5
le Noyer (73) 208 C2
le Noyer-en-Ouche (27) 55 K1
Noyers (27) 36 D4
Noyers (45) 111 G4
Noyers (52) 116 E1
Noyers (89) 114 A6
Noyers-Auzécourt (55) 63 J3
Noyers-Bocage (14) 32 C5
Noyers-Pont-Maugis (08) 23 F4
Noyers-Saint-Martin (60) 18 A6
Noyers-sur-Cher (41) 129 F6
Noyers-sur-Jabron (04) 258 E4
Noyon (60) 19 H6
Nozay (10) 90 B2
Nozay (44) 103 G3
Nozay (91) 58 D6
Nozeroy (39). 156 C6
Nozières (07) 221 J5
Nozières (18) 167 F1
Nuaillé (49) 143 F2
Nuaillé-d'Aunis (17) 177 F1
Nuaillé-sur-Boutonne (17). 178 A4
Nuars (58) 133 H5
Nubécourt (55) 64 B1
Nucourt (95). 36 E5
Nueil-les-Aubiers (79) 143 H4
Nueil-sous-Faye (86). 145 G4
Nueil-sur-Layon (49) 143 G6
Nuelles (69) 205 J1
Nuillé-le-Jalais (72) 107 G2
Nuillé-sur-Vicoin (53) 104 E2
Nuisement-sur-Coole (51) 62 C3
Nuits (89) 114 C6
Nuits-Saint-Georges (21) 154 B2
Nullemont (76) 16 E3
Nully (52) 91 H3
Nuncq-Hautecôte (62) 10 A2
Nuret-le-Ferron (36) 165 F2
Nurieux-Volognat (01). 189 K2
Nurlu (80) 11 H6
Nuzéjouls (46) 233 G6
Nyer (66) 314 A4
Nyoiseau (49). 104 C6
Nyons (26) 257 H2

Obenheim (67) 71 D4
Oberbronn (67). 69 J4
Oberbruck (68). 119 J4
Oberdorf (68) 97 C5

Oberdorf-Spachbach (67). 25 A2
Oberdorff (57). 45 J3
Oberentzen (68) 96 C5
Obergailbach (57). 68 C2
Oberhaslach (67) 70 B4
Oberhausbergen (67) 71 D4
Oberhergheim (68) 96 C5
Oberhoffen-lès-
  -Wissembourg (67) 25 B1
Oberhoffen-sur-Moder (67) 25 B1
Oberlarg (68) 97 B6
Oberlauterbach (67) 25 D2
Obermodern-Zutzendorf (67) . . . 69 J6
Obermorschwihr (68) 96 B5
Obermorschwiller (68) 97 C4
Obernai (67). 70 D5
Oberrœdern (67) 25 C2
Obersaasheim (68) 96 E5
Oberschaeffolsheim (67). 70 E3
Obersoultzbach (67) 69 H6
Obersteinbach (67) 69 K3
Oberstinzel (57) 67 J3
Obervisse (57) 45 J4
Obies (59) 13 F3
Objat (19). 215 H3
Oblinghem (62). 5 K5
Obrechies (59) 13 H3
Obreck (57) 66 E3
Obsonville (77) 87 G6
Obterre (36) 146 D5
Obtrée (21). 115 F3
Ocana (2A). 320 D5
Occagnes (61) 54 B4
Occey (52) 136 C1
Occhiatana (2B) 318 D2
Occoches (80) 10 A4
Ochancourt (80) 8 E5
Oches (08) 42 D1
Ochey (54) 65 J6
Ochtezeele (59) 3 H4
Ocquerre (77) 60 B1
Ocqueville (76) 15 G3
Octeville-l'Avenel (50). 29 F3
Octeville-sur-Mer (76). 14 A6
Octon (34) 273 F6
Odars (31) 288 D2
Odenas (69) 188 A3
Oderen (68) 119 J3
Odomez (59) 7 J6
Odos (65). 285 H5
Odratzheim (67) 70 D3
Oëlleville (88) 93 K3
Oermingen (67) 68 E4
Œting (57) 68 C2
Œuf-en-Ternois (62) 9 K2
Œuilly (02) 40 C2
Œuilly (51) 40 D6
Oeyregave (40). 283 F1
Oeyreluy (40) 264 A5
Offekerque (62) 2 E2
Offemont (90) 119 H6
Offendorf (67) 25 C5
Offignies (80) 17 G3
Offin (62) 4 D6
Offlanges (39) 137 F6
Offoy (62) 17 J4
Offoy (80) 19 H3
Offranville (76) 15 K2
Offrethun (62) 2 B4
Offroicourt (88). 93 K4
Offwiller (67). 69 J5
Ogenne-Camptort (64) 283 K4
Oger (51) 62 A2
Ogeu-les-Bains (64) 284 B6
Ogéviller (54) 67 F6
Ogliastro (2B) 317 C4
Ognes (02) 19 K5
Ognes (51) 61 K5
Ognes (60) 38 E6
Ognéville (54) 93 K2
Ognolles (60) 19 G4
Ognon (60) 38 C4
Ogy (57) 45 G5
Ohain (59) 13 J6
Oherville (76) 15 F4
Ohis (02) 21 G1
Ohlungen (67) 69 K6
Ohnenheim (67) 96 D2
l'Oie (85) 142 C6
Oigney (70) 117 H5
Oignies (62) 6 D6
Oigny (21) 135 H2
Oigny (41) 108 B2
Oigny-en-Valois (02) 39 G5
Oingt (69). 188 A5
Oinville-Saint-Liphard (28) 86 A5
Oinville-sous-Auneau (28). 85 J3
Oinville-sur-Montcient (78) 57 K1
Oiron (79) 144 C2
Oiry (51) 62 A1
Oiselay-et-Grachaux (70) 137 J4
Oisemont (80) 17 F1
Oisilly (21) 136 D4
Oisly (41) 129 F5
Oison (45) 110 B1
Oisseau (53) 81 F3
Oisseau-le-Petit (72) 82 D4
Oissel (76) 35 H3
Oissery (77) 59 J1
Oissy (80) 17 J2
Oisy (02) 12 E6
Oisy (58) 133 F3
Oisy (59) 12 C2
Oisy-le-Verger (62) 11 H3
Oizé (72) 106 D5
Oizon (18) 131 G4

385

Olargues (34) 291 G1	Orbigny-au-Val (52) 116 E4	Oroux (79) 162 B2	Ouge (70) 117 G5
Olby (63) 202 B2	l'Orbrie (85) 160 E4	Orphin (78) 85 K1	Ouges (21) 136 B6
Olcani (2B) 317 D4	Orçay (41) 130 C6	Orpierre (05) 258 D2	Ougney (39) 137 G6
Oléac-Debat (65) 285 J4	Orcemont (78) 85 K1	Orquevaux (52) 92 D4	Ougney-Douvot (25) 138 C5
Oléac-Dessus (65) 285 J6	Orcenais (18) 167 F2	les Orres (05) 243 K5	Ougny (58) 151 K3
Olemps (12) 252 B3	Orcet (63) 202 E3	Orret (21) 135 G2	Ouhans (25) 156 E3
Olendon (14) 54 B2	Orcevaux (52) 116 C5	Orriule (64) 283 H2	Ouides (43) 238 A1
Oletta (2B) 319 H2	Orchaise (41) 128 D2	Orrouer (28) 84 E3	Ouillon (64) 284 E4
Olette (66) 314 A4	Orchamps (39) 155 J1	Orrouy (60) 38 E4	Ouilly-du-Houley (14) 34 A5
Olivese (2A) 321 F6	Orchamps-Vennes (25) 157 G1	Orry-la-Ville (60) 38 B6	Ouilly-le-Tesson (14) 54 A4
Olivet (45) 110 A4	Orches (86) 145 G5	Ors (59) 12 E5	Ouilly-le-Vicomte (14) 33 K5
Olivet (53) 80 D6	Orchies (59) 7 F4	Orsan (30) 256 C5	Ouistreham (14) 33 F3
Olizy (51) 40 C5	Orcier (74) 175 F6	Orsanco (64) 283 F4	Oulches (36) 164 E3
Olizy-Primat (08) 42 C3	Orcières (05) 243 G3	Orsans (11) 289 H6	Oulches-la-Vallée-Foulon (02) 40 C2
Olizy-sur-Chiers (55) 23 H6	Orcinas (26) 241 F5	Orsans (25) 138 D5	Oulchy-la-Ville (02) 39 J5
Ollainville (88) 93 H4	Orcines (63) 202 C2	Orsay (91) 58 D5	Oulchy-le-Château (02) 39 J5
Ollainville (91) 86 D1	Orcival (63) 202 B3	Orschwihr (68) 96 B6	Oulins (28) 57 G3
Ollans (25) 138 C3	Orconte (51) 63 G5	Orschwiller (67) 96 C2	Oulles (38) 224 D4
Ollé (28) 84 E3	Ordan-Larroque (32) 267 G5	Orsennes (36) 165 J5	Oullins (69) 206 A2
Olley (54) 44 B5	Ordiarp (64) 283 G5	Orsinval (59) 12 E3	Oulmes (85) 161 F5
Ollezy (02) 19 J4	Ordizan (65) 304 D1	Orsonnette (63) 203 F6	Oulon (58) 151 G1
les Ollières (74) 191 F4	Ordonnac (33) 210 E2	Orsonville (78) 85 K2	Ounans (39) 155 J3
Ollières (83) 297 H1	Ordonnaz (01) 189 K6	Ortaffa (66) 315 H3	Oupia (34) 291 F4
les Ollières-sur-Eyrieux (07) 239 K2	Ore (31) 305 J3	Ortale (2B) 319 J5	Our (39) 155 J2
Olliergues (63) 203 J3	Oreilla (66) 314 A4	Orthevielle (40) 264 A6	Ourches (26) 240 D2
Ollioules (83) 300 B4	Orelle (73) 225 J2	Orthez (64) 283 J1	Ourches-sur-Meuse (55) 65 G5
Olloix (63) 202 D4	Oresmaux (80) 18 A3	Orthoux-Sérignac-Quilhan (30) 274 D3	Ourde (65) 305 H3
les Olmes (69) 187 K6	Organ (65) 286 B4	Ortillon (10) 90 C2	Ourdis-Cotdoussan (65) 304 C2
Olmet (63) 203 J3	Orgeans-Blanchefontaine (25) 139 G5	Ortiporio (2B) 319 H4	Ourdon (65) 304 B2
Olmet-et-Villecun (34) 273 F5	Orgedeuil (16) 197 H3	Orto (2A) 320 D2	Ourouër (65) 151 F3
Olmeta-di-Capocorso (2B) 317 D4	Orgeix (09) 313 G2	Ortoncourt (88) 94 D3	Ourouer-les-Bourdelins (18) 150 A5
Olmeta-di-Tuda (2B) 319 H2	Orgelet (39) 173 G3	Orus (09) 307 H5	Ouroux (69) 188 A2
Olmeto (2A) 322 D2	Orgères (35) 79 G5	Orval (18) 167 G2	Ouroux-en-Morvan (58) 152 B1
Olmi-Cappella (2B) 318 D3	Orgères (61) 55 F4	Orval (50) 30 D4	Ouroux-sous-le-Bois-
Olmiccia (2A) 323 F2	Orgères-en-Beauce (28) 109 J1	Orvault (44) 123 G3	-Sainte-Marie (71) 170 E6
Olmo (2B) 319 H4	Orgerus (78) 57 J4	Orvaux (27) 56 C2	Ouroux-sur-Saône (71) 172 A1
Olonne-sur-Mer (85) 158 A3	Orges (52) 115 J1	Orve (25) 139 F4	Oursbelille (65) 285 H4
Olonzac (34) 291 F5	Orgeux (21) 136 B5	Orveau (91) 86 E3	Oursel-Maison (60) 17 K6
Oloron-Sainte-Marie (64) 284 A5	Orgeval (02) 40 C1	Orveau-Bellesauve (45) 86 E5	Ourton (62) 5 J6
Ols-et-Rinhodes (12) 251 F1	Orgeval (78) 58 B3	Orville (21) 136 C2	Ourville-en-Caux (76) 15 F4
Oltingue (68) 97 D5	Orgibet (09) 306 B3	Orville (36) 148 A2	Ousse (64) 284 E4
Olwisheim (67) 70 E2	Orglandes (50) 28 E5	Orville (45) 87 F5	Ousse-Suzan (40) 264 E1
Omblèze (26) 241 F1	Orgnac-l'Aven (07) 256 A3	Orville (61) 55 F3	Oussières (39) 155 H4
Omécourt (60) 17 G5	Orgnac-sur-Vézère (19) 215 H2	Orville (62) 10 B5	Ousson-sur-Loire (45) 131 J2
Omelmont (54) 94 A1	Orgon (13) 276 D4	Orvillers-Sorel (60) 18 E6	Oussoy-en-Gâtinais (45) 111 H4
les Omergues (04) 258 C4	Orgueil (82) 269 G2	Orvilliers (78) 57 H3	Oust (09) 306 E4
Omerville (95) 36 D6	Oricourt (70) 138 D1	Orvilliers-Saint-Julien (10) 89 J3	Oust-Marest (80) 8 C6
Omessa (2B) 319 F5	Orieux (65) 285 K5	Orx (40) 262 C5	Ousté (65) 304 B1
Omet (33) 230 A4	Orignac (65) 285 J6	Os-Marsillon (64) 284 A3	Outarville (45) 86 B6
Omex (65) 304 B1	Origne (33) 229 H6	Osani (2A) 316 C4	Outines (51) 91 G1
Omey (51) 62 E3	Origné (53) 105 F3	Osches (55) 43 G6	Outreau (62) 4 A3
Omicourt (08) 22 E5	Orignolles (17) 212 A3	Osenbach (68) 96 B5	Outrebois (80) 10 A4
Omiécourt (80) 19 F3	Origny (21) 115 G6	Osly-Courtil (02) 39 H2	Outremécourt (52) 93 G5
Omissy (02) 20 A2	Origny-en-Thiérache (02) 21 G2	Osmanville (14) 29 H6	Outrepont (51) 63 G4
Omméel (61) 54 D4	Origny-le-Butin (61) 83 G4	Osmery (18) 149 J5	Outriaz (01) 189 K3
Ommeray (57) 67 F4	Origny-le-Roux (61) 83 G4	Osmets (65) 285 K4	Ouvans (25) 138 E5
Ommoy (61) 54 C3	Origny-le-Sec (10) 89 H2	Osmoy (18) 149 H3	Ouve-Wirquin (62) 5 F4
Omont (08) 22 D5	Origny-Sainte-Benoite (02) 20 B2	Osmoy (78) 57 J3	Ouveillan (11) 291 H4
Omonville (76) 15 K3	Orin (64) 283 K5	Osmoy-Saint-Valery (76) 16 C3	Ouville (50) 30 E4
Omonville-la-Petite (50) 28 A1	Orincles (65) 285 H6	Osne-le-Val (52) 92 B2	Ouville-la-Bien-Tournée (14) 54 C1
Omonville-la-Rogue (50) 28 B1	Oriocourt (57) 66 C2	Osnes (08) 23 H4	Ouville-la-Rivière (76) 15 J2
Omps (15) 235 F2	Oriol-en-Royans (26) 223 G5	Osny (95) 58 B1	Ouville-l'Abbaye (76) 15 H4
Oms (66) 314 E4	Oriolles (16) 212 C1	Ossages (40) 264 C6	Ouvrouer-les-Champs (45) 110 C5
Onans (25) 139 F2	Orion (64) 283 H2	Ossas-Suhare (64) 283 H6	Ouzilly (86) 163 F1
Onard (40) 264 D3	Oris-en-Rattier (38) 224 C6	Osse (25) 138 B5	Ouzouer-des-Champs (45) 111 H4
Onay (70) 137 G4	Orist (40) 262 E5	Ossé (35) 79 J5	Ouzouer-le-Doyen (41) 108 E3
Oncieu (01) 189 J5	Orival (16) 212 D2	Osse-en-Aspe (64) 303 F2	Ouzouer-le-Marché (41) 109 G4
Oncourt (88) 94 C4	Orival (76) 35 G3	Osséja (66) 313 H5	Ouzouer-sous-Bellegarde (45) 111 F3
Oncy-sur-École (91) 87 F4	Orléans (45) 110 A4	Osselle (25) 156 A1	Ouzouer-sur-Loire (45) 111 F6
Ondefontaine (14) 53 G1	Orléat (63) 203 G1	Ossen (64) 304 B1	Ouzouer-sur-Trézée (45) 131 J1
Ondes (31) 269 F4	Orleix (65) 285 H4	Ossenx (64) 283 J3	Ouzous (65) 304 A2
Ondres (40) 262 B6	Orliac (24) 232 D4	Osserain-Rivareyte (64) 283 G3	Ovanches (70) 137 J3
Ondreville-sur-Essonne (45) 87 F6	Orliac-de-Bar (19) 216 B1	Ossès (64) 282 D4	Ovillers-la-Boisselle (80) 10 E6
Onesse-et-Laharie (40) 244 E6	Orliaguet (24) 233 G1	Ossey-les-Trois-Maisons (10) 89 H3	Oxelaëre (59) 3 J4
Onet-le-Château (12) 252 B3	Orliénas (69) 205 K3	Ossun (65) 285 G5	Oyé (71) 170 D6
Oneux (80) 9 H4	Orlu (09) 313 G2	Ossun-ez-Angles (65) 304 C1	Oye-et-Pallet (25) 156 E5
Ongles (04) 258 D6	Orlu (28) 86 A4	Ostabat-Asme (64) 283 F4	Oye-Plage (62) 2 E2
Onglières (39) 156 B6	Orly (94) 58 E5	Ostel (02) 40 A2	Oyes (51) 61 H4
Onjon (10) 90 C3	Orly-sur-Morin (77) 60 C3	Ostheim (68) 96 C3	Oyeu (38) 207 H6
Onlay (58) 152 B4	Ormancey (52) 116 B3	Osthoffen (67) 70 D3	Oyonnax (01) 190 A1
Onnaing (59) 12 D1	Ormenans (70) 138 B3	Osthouse (67) 70 E5	Oyré (86) 145 K5
Onnion (74) 191 J2	Ormersviller (57) 69 F2	Ostreville (62) 10 B1	Oyrières (70) 137 F2
Onoz (39) 173 H4	Ormes (10) 90 B1	Ostricourt (59) 6 D6	Oysonville (28) 86 A3
Ons-en-Bray (60) 37 F2	Ormes (27) 56 B1	Ostwald (67) 71 D1	Oytier-Saint-Oblas (38) 206 C4
Ontex (73) 208 A2	Ormes (45) 109 K3	Ota (2A) 320 B1	Oz (38) 224 D3
Onville (54) 65 J1	Ormes (51) 40 E4	Othe (54) 26 A3	Ozan (01) 172 A5
Onzain (41) 128 D3	Ormes (71) 172 A2	Othis (77) 38 C6	Oze (05) 242 B6
Oô (31) 305 G5	les Ormes (86) 145 K4	Ottange (57) 27 F3	Ozenay (71) 171 K3
Oost-Cappel (59) 3 K3	les Ormes (89) 112 D5	Ottersthal (67) 70 B1	Ozenx-Montestrucq (64) 283 J2
Opio (06) 280 D4	Ormes-et-Ville (54) 94 B2	Otterswiller (67) 70 B1	Ozerailles (54) 44 C4
Opoul-Périllos (66) 310 B4	les Ormes-sur-Voulzie (77) 88 C3	Ottmarsheim (68) 97 D2	Ozeville (50) 29 F4
Oppède (84) 277 F3	Ormesson (77) 87 H5	Ottonville (57) 45 J4	Ozières (52) 92 E6
Oppedette (04) 277 K2	Ormesson-sur-Marne (94) 59 G4	Ottrott (67) 70 C5	Ozillac (17) 195 J6
Oppenans (70) 138 D1	Ormoiche (70) 118 C4	Ottwiller (67) 69 F5	Ozoir-la-Ferrière (77) 59 H4
Oppy (62) 11 F2	Ormoy (28) 57 G6	Ouagne (58) 133 F4	Ozoir-le-Breuil (28) 109 G2
Optevoz (38) 207 F2	Ormoy (70) 117 K3	Ouainville (76) 15 F3	Ozolles (71) 170 E6
Oraàs (64) 283 G2	Ormoy (89) 113 G3	Ouanne (89) 132 E1	Ozon (07) 222 B4
Oradour (15) 236 C1	Ormoy (91) 87 F1	Ouarville (28) 85 J4	Ozon (65) 285 K6
Oradour (16) 178 E6	Ormoy-la-Rivière (91) 86 C3	les Oubeaux (14) 31 H1	Ozouer-le-Voulgis (77) 59 J6
Oradour-Fanais (16) 180 C3	Ormoy-le-Davien (60) 39 F5	Ouchamps (41) 128 E4	Ozourt (40) 264 C5
Oradour-Saint-Genest (87) 181 F2	Ormoy-lès-Sexfontaines (52) 92 A5	Ouches (42) 186 E5	
Oradour-sur-Glane (87) 180 E6	Ormoy-Villers (60) 38 E5	Oucques (41) 108 E5	
Oradour-sur-Vayres (87) 198 B2	Ornacieux (38) 206 E6	Oudalle (76) 34 A1	
Orain (21) 136 E1	Ornaisons (11) 291 G6	Oudan (58) 132 E5	
Orainville (02) 41 F2	Ornans (25) 156 D2	Oudezeele (59) 3 J4	
Oraison (04) 278 C2	Ornex (01) 190 E1	Oudincourt (52) 92 A5	
Orange (84) 256 E5	Ornézan (32) 286 D2	l'Oudon (14) 54 C2	
Orbagna (39) 173 F3	Orniac (46) 233 K6	Oudon (44) 123 K2	
Orbais-l'Abbaye (51) 61 H2	Ornolac-Ussat-les-Bains (09) 307 J5	Oudrenne (57) 27 J4	
Orban (81) 270 D3	Ornon (38) 224 D5	Oudry (71) 170 C3	
Orbec (14) 55 G1	Orny (57) 45 F6	Oueilloux (65) 285 J6	
Orbeil (63) 203 F5	Oroër (60) 37 H1	Ouerre (28) 57 G5	
Orbessan (32) 286 D1	Oroix (65) 285 G4	Ouessant (29) 72 A1	
Orbey (68) 96 A3	Oron (57) 66 D2	Ouffières (14) 53 H1	
Orbigny (37) 147 F1			
Orbigny-au-Mont (52) 116 E4			

P

Paars (02) 40 B3	Padirac (46) 234 A2
Pabu (22) 48 C5	Padoux (88) 94 E4
la Pacaudière (42) 186 D3	Pageas (87) 198 C3
Pacé (35) 79 F4	Pagney (39) 137 G6
Pacé (61) 82 D3	Pagney-derrière-Barine (54) 65 H5
Pact (38) 222 D1	Pagnoz (39) 155 K4
Pacy-sur-Armançon (89) 114 B5	Pagny-la-Blanche-Côte (55) 93 G1
Pacy-sur-Eure (27) 57 F1	Pagny-la-Ville (21) 154 D3
Padern (11) 309 K4	Pagny-le-Château (21) 154 D3
Padiès (81) 271 G1	Pagny-lès-Goin (57) 66 A1
	Pagny-sur-Meuse (55) 65 G5
	Pagny-sur-Moselle (54) 65 J1
	Pagolle (64) 283 G5
	Pailhac (65) 305 F3
	Pailharès (07) 221 K5
	Pailherols (15) 236 A1
	Pailhès (09) 307 G1
	Pailhès (34) 291 K3
	Paillart (60) 18 B5
	Paillé (17) 178 B5
	Paillencourt (59) 12 B3
	Paillet (33) 229 K4
	Pailloles (47) 248 B1
	le Pailly (52) 116 D5
	Pailly (89) 88 D4
	Paimbœuf (44) 122 C3
	Paimpol (22) 48 D2
	Paimpont (35) 78 B5
	Painblanc (21) 153 J2
	Pair-et-Grandrupt (88) 95 J4
	Paissy (02) 40 C2
	Paisy-Cosdon (10) 89 H5
	Paizay-le-Chapt (79) 178 A4
	Paizay-le-Sec (86) 163 K3
	Paizay-le-Tort (79) 178 D2
	Paizay-Naudouin-Embourie (16) 178 E4
	Pajay (38) 222 F1
	Paladru (38) 207 H5
	Palairac (11) 309 K3
	le Palais (56) 120 B4
	le Palais-sur-Vienne (87) 199 F1
	Palaiseau (91) 58 D5
	Palaiseul (52) 116 D5
	Palaja (11) 290 B6
	Palaminy (31) 287 H5
	Palante (70) 119 F6
	Palantine (25) 156 B2
	Palasca (2B) 318 E2
	Palau-de-Cerdagne (66) 313 H5
	Palau-del-Vidre (66) 315 H3
	Palavas-les-Flots (34) 293 H1
	Palazinges (19) 216 A4
	Paley (77) 87 K5
	Palhers (48) 237 G6
	Palinges (71) 170 D3
	Palis (10) 89 H5
	Palise (25) 138 A4
	Palisse (19) 217 F1
	Palladuc (63) 186 A6
	Pallanne (32) 285 K2
	Palleau (71) 154 C4
	Pallegney (88) 94 D4
	le Pallet (44) 142 A1
	Palleville (81) 289 H2
	la Pallu (53) 81 K2
	Palluau (85) 141 H5
	Palluau-sur-Indre (36) 147 G4
	Palluaud (16) 213 F1
	Pallud (73) 209 G2
	Palluel (62) 11 H3
	Palmas (12) 252 C2
	la Palme (11) 310 C3
	Palneca (2A) 321 G4
	Palogneux (42) 204 B2
	la Palud-sur-Verdon (04) 279 H3
	Paluel (76) 15 F2
	Pamfou (77) 87 K3
	Pamiers (09) 307 J1
	Pampelonne (81) 251 J5
	Pamplie (79) 161 H3
	Pamproux (79) 162 B5
	Panassac (32) 286 C5
	Panazol (87) 199 F1
	Pancé (35) 103 G1
	Pancey (52) 92 C2
	Pancheraccia (2B) 321 H1
	Pancy-Courtecon (02) 40 B1
	Pandrignes (19) 216 B3
	Pange (57) 45 G5
	Panges (21) 135 J5
	Panilleuse (27) 36 B5
	Panissage (38) 207 G5
	Panissières (42) 205 F2
	Panjas (32) 266 B3
	Pannecé (44) 124 A3
	Pannecières (45) 86 C5
	Pannes (45) 111 H2
	Pannes (54) 65 G2
	Pannessières (39) 173 G1
	Panon (72) 83 F4
	Panossas (38) 206 E3
	la Panouse (48) 237 K4
	Pantin (93) 59 F3
	Panzoult (37) 145 H2
	Papleux (02) 13 G6
	Paradou (13) 276 B4
	Parassy (18) 149 H1
	Parata (2B) 319 J5
	Paray-Douaville (78) 86 A3
	Paray-le-Frésil (03) 169 H2
	Paray-le-Monial (71) 170 C5
	Paray-sous-Briailles (03) 185 H1
	Paray-Vieille-Poste (91) 58 E5
	Paraza (11) 291 G5
	Parbayse (64) 284 B1
	Parc-d'Anxtot (76) 14 D6

Parçay-les-Pins (49) 126 D4
Parçay-Meslay (37) 127 J4
Parçay-sur-Vienne (37) 145 H2
Parcé (35) 80 B4
Parcé-sur-Sarthe (72) 106 A4
Parcey (39) 155 G3
Parcieux (01) 188 C6
Parcoul (24) 212 D3
le Parcq (62) 9 J1
Parcy-et-Tigny (02) 39 J4
Pardailhan (34) 291 G4
Pardaillan (47) 231 F4
Pardies (64) 284 A3
Pardies-Piétat (64) 284 D5
Pardines (63) 202 E5
Paréac (65) 304 C1
Pareid (55) 44 B5
Parempuyre (33) 211 G6
Parennes (72) 106 A1
Parent (63) 202 E4
Parentignat (63) 203 F5
Parentis-en-Born (40) 244 E2
Parenty (62) 4 C5
Parey-Saint-Césaire (54) 93 K1
Parey-sous-Montfort (88) 93 J5
Parfondeval (02) 21 H4
Parfondeval (61) 83 H2
Parfondru (02) 20 E6
Parfondrupt (55) 44 B5
Parfouru-sur-Odon (14) 32 C6
Pargnan (02) 40 C2
Pargny (80) 19 G3
Pargny-Filain (02) 40 A1
Pargny-la-Dhuys (02) 61 F2
Pargny-les-Bois (02) 20 D2
Pargny-lès-Reims (51) 40 E4
Pargny-sous-Mureau (88) 93 F3
Pargny-sur-Saulx (51) 63 H4
Paris (75) 58 E3
Paris-l'Hôpital (71) 153 J5
Parisot (81) 270 A4
Parisot (82) 250 E4
Parlan (15) 234 E2
Parleboscq (40) 266 C2
Parly (89) 112 E6
Parmain (95) 37 J6
Parmilieu (38) 189 H6
Parnac (36) 165 F5
Parnac (46) 249 J1
Parnans (26) 222 E4
Parnay (18) 149 J6
Parnay (49) 126 C6
Parné-sur-Roc (53) 105 F2
Parnes (60) 36 D5
Parnoy-en-Bassigny (52) 117 F2
les Paroches (55) 64 E2
Paron (89) 88 D6
Paroy (25) 156 A3
Paroy (77) 88 C2
Paroy-en-Othe (89) 113 G2
Paroy-sur-Saulx (52) 92 C2
Paroy-sur-Tholon (89) 112 E3
Parpeçay (36) 147 K1
Parpeville (02) 20 C3
Parranquet (47) 232 B4
Parroy (54) 66 E5
Pars-lès-Chavanges (10) 90 C2
Pars-lès-Romilly (10) 89 H2
Parsac (23) 183 G2
Parthenay (79) 161 K2
Parthenay-de-Bretagne (35) 78 B3
Partinello (2A) 318 A6
Parux (54) 67 H6
Parves (01) 207 K2
Parville (27) 56 C1
Parvillers-le-Quesnoy (80) 18 E4
Parzac (16) 179 J5
le Pas (53) 81 F3
Pas-de-Jeu (79) 144 D4
Pas-en-Artois (62) 10 C4
le Pas-Saint-l'Homer (61) 84 B2
Pasilly (89) 114 B6
Paslières (63) 185 K6
Pasly (02) 39 J2
Pasques (21) 135 J5
le Pasquier (39) 156 A6
Passa (66) 315 G3
le Passage (38) 207 H4
le Passage (47) 248 B4
Passais (61) 81 F1
Passavant (25) 138 D5
Passavant-en-Argonne (51) 63 K1
Passavant-la-Rochère (70) 117 K2
Passavant-sur-Layon (49) 143 K2
Passel (60) 19 G6
Passenans (39) 155 H6
Passins (38) 207 G3
Passirac (16) 212 C1
Passonfontaine (25) 157 F2
Passy (71) 171 G4
Passy (74) 192 B5
Passy (89) 112 D1
Passy-en-Valois (02) 39 H5
Passy-Grigny (51) 40 C6
Passy-sur-Marne (02) 61 F1
Passy-sur-Seine (77) 88 E3

Pastricciola (2A) 320 D2
Patay (45) 109 J2
Patornay (39) 173 H3
Patrimonio (2B) 319 H1
Pau (64) 284 D4
Paucourt (45) 111 J3
Paudy (36) 148 C3
Pauilhac (32) 267 J3
Pauillac (33) 211 F3
Paule (22) 75 K3
Paulhac (15) 218 C5
Paulhac (31) 269 H4
Paulhac (43) 219 G2
Paulhac-en-Margeride (48) 237 H1
Paulhaguet (43) 219 J3
Paulhan (34) 292 C1
Paulhe (12) 253 G5
Paulhenc (15) 236 B2
Paulhiac (47) 232 B6
Pauligne (11) 308 E2
Paulin (24) 215 G6
Paulinet (81) 271 G3
Paulmy (37) 146 B4
Paulnay (36) 146 E6
Paulx (44) 141 G3
Paunat (24) 232 B1
Paussac-et-Saint-Vivien (24) . . . 213 J1
Pautaines-Augeville (52) 92 C4
Pauvres (08) 41 K2
Pavant (02) 60 D2
Pavezin (42) 205 K6
Pavie (32) 267 H6
le Pavillon-Sainte-Julie (10) 89 K4
les Pavillons-sous-Bois (93) 59 G3
Pavilly (76) 15 J6
Payns (10) 89 K3
Payra-sur-l'Hers (11) 289 G5
Payrac (46) 233 H3
Payré (86) 162 D6
Payrignac (46) 233 G3
Payrin-Augmontel (81) 290 B2
Payros-Cazautets (40) 265 H6
Payroux (86) 179 K2
Payssous (31) 305 J2
Payzac (07) 255 H1
Payzac (24) 215 F1
Pazayac (24) 215 G4
Paziols (11) 310 A4
Pazy (58) 151 J1
le Péage-de-Roussillon (38) 222 B1
Péas (51) 61 H5
Peaugres (07) 222 A2
Péaule (56) 121 K1
Péault (85) 159 K4
Pébées (32) 287 H2
Pébrac (43) 219 J5
Pech (09) 307 K5
Pech-Luna (11) 289 F5
Péchabou (31) 288 C2
Pécharic-et-le-Py (11) 289 F6
Péchaudier (81) 289 G1
Pechbonnieu (31) 269 H5
Pechbusque (31) 288 C1
le Pêchereau (36) 165 G3
Pécorade (40) 265 J5
le Pecq (78) 58 C3
Pecquencourt (59) 11 J1
Pecqueuse (91) 58 B6
Pécy (77) 60 B6
Pédernec (22) 48 B4
Pégairolles-de-Buèges (34) 273 J4
Pégairolles-de-l'Escalette (34) . . 273 G4
Pégomas (06) 280 D5
le Pègue (26) 257 G1
Péguilhan (31) 286 E4
Peigney (52) 116 D4
Peillac (56) 102 A3
Peille (06) 281 J2
Peillon (06) 281 H3
Peillonnex (74) 191 H2
Peintre (39) 155 G1
les Peintures (33) 212 C5
Peipin (04) 259 G5
Peisey-Nancroix (73) 209 K4
Pel-et-Der (10) 90 E3
Pélissanne (13) 277 F5
Pellafol (38) 242 C2
Pelleautier (05) 242 E6
Pellefigue (32) 287 F2
Pellegrue (33) 230 D3
Pelleport (31) 268 D5
Pellerey (21) 135 H3
le Pellerin (44) 122 E4
la Pellerine (49) 126 D3
la Pellerine (53) 80 C4
Pellevoisin (36) 147 H4
Pellouailles-les-Vignes (49) 125 H3
Pelonne (26) 258 A2
Pelouse (48) 237 K6
Pelousey (25) 137 J5
Peltre (57) 45 F6
Pélussin (42) 205 K6
Pelves (62) 11 G3
Pelvoux (05) 243 J1
Penchard (77) 59 K2
Pencran (29) 46 C6
Pendé (80) 8 E4
Pénestin (56) 121 J2
Penguily (22) 77 J2
Penin (62) 10 C2
Penly (76) 16 B1
Penmarch (29) 98 A3
la Penne (06) 280 D1
Penne (81) 250 C6
Penne-d'Agenais (47) 248 D2

la Penne-sur-Huveaune (13) 296 E4
la Penne-sur-l'Ouvèze (26) 257 J3
Pennedepie (14) 33 K2
Pennes-le-Sec (26) 241 G4
les Pennes-Mirabeau (13) 296 B2
Pennesières (70) 138 A3
Penol (38) 206 E6
Pensol (87) 198 A4
Penta-Acquatella (2B) 319 H4
Penta-di-Casinca (2B) 319 J3
Penvénan (22) 48 B3
Péone (06) 261 F4
Pépieux (11) 290 E4
Pérassay (36) 166 C5
Peray (72) 83 F5
Perceneige (89) 88 E4
Percey (89) 113 J3
Percey-le-Grand (70) 136 D1
le Perchay (95) 37 H5
la Perche (18) 167 G3
Perchède (32) 266 A4
Percy (38) 242 A2
Percy (50) 52 B2
Percy-en-Auge (14) 33 G6
Perdreauville (78) 57 H2
Péré (17) 177 G3
Péré (65) 285 K6
Péreille (09) 308 A3
Perelli (2B) 319 H5
Pérenchies (59) 6 D4
Péret (34) 292 C1
Péret-Bel-Air (19) 200 C6
Péreuil (16) 196 C5
Péreyres (07) 239 F3
Pergain-Taillac (32) 248 B6
Peri (2A) 320 D4
le Périer (38) 224 D6
Périers (50) 30 E2
Périers-en-Auge (14) 33 G4
Périers-sur-le-Dan (14) 32 E4
Pérignac (16) 196 D6
Pérignac (17) 195 H3
Pérignat-lès-Sarliève (63) 202 D2
Pérignat-sur-Allier (63) 202 E3
Périgné (79) 178 C2
Périgneux (42) 204 E6
Périgny (03) 185 K2
Périgny (14) 53 G2
Périgny (17) 176 E2
Périgny (41) 108 D6
Périgny (94) 59 G5
Périgny-la-Rose (10) 89 G1
Périgueux (24) 214 A3
Périssac (33) 211 K5
Perles (02) 40 B3
Perles-et-Castelet (09) 308 A6
Pern (46) 249 K3
Pernand-Vergelesses (21) 154 A2
Pernant (02) 39 H3
Pernay (37) 127 G4
la Pernelle (50) 29 F2
Pernes (62) 5 H6
Pernes-les-Boulogne (62) 4 B2
Pernes-les-Fontaines (84) 276 D1
Pernois (80) 9 K6
Pero-Casevecchie (2B) 319 J4
Pérols (34) 293 H1
Pérols-sur-Vézère (19) 200 C4
Péron (01) 190 D2
Péronnas (01) 189 G2
Péronne (71) 171 J5
Péronne (80) 19 G1
Péronne-en-Mélantois (59) 6 E4
Péronville (28) 109 H2
Pérouges (01) 189 G6
la Pérouille (36) 165 G2
Pérouse (90) 119 J6
Péroy-les-Gombries (60) 38 C5
Perpezac-le-Blanc (19) 215 G3
Perpezac-le-Noir (19) 215 J2
Perpezat (63) 202 A3
Perpignan (66) 315 G2
les Perques (50) 28 C5
Perquie (40) 265 J2
Perrancey-les-Vieux-Moulins (52) . 116 C4
le Perray-en-Yvelines (78) 57 K5
Perrecy-les-Forges (71) 170 D3
le Perréon (69) 188 A4
Perret (22) 76 C4
Perreuil (71) 153 H6
Perreux (42) 187 F4
Perreux (89) 112 C4
le Perreux-sur-Marne (94) 59 F4
Perrex (01) 188 D1
Perrier (63) 202 E5
le Perrier (85) 140 D5
la Perrière (61) 83 G3
la Perrière (73) 209 J5
Perrières (14) 54 B2
Perriers-en-Beauficel (50) 52 D4
Perriers-la-Campagne (27) 34 E5
Perriers-sur-Andelle (27) 36 A2
Perrignier (74) 175 F6
Perrigny (39) 173 G2
Perrigny (89) 113 F5
Perrigny-lès-Dijon (21) 136 A6
Perrigny-sur-Armançon (89) 134 C1
Perrigny-sur-l'Ognon (21) 136 E5
Perrigny-sur-Loire (71) 169 K3
Perrogney-les-Fontaines (52) . . . 116 B5
le Perron (50) 31 K4
Perros-Guirec (22) 48 A2
Perrou (61) 81 H1
Perrouse (70) 138 A4
Perroy (58) 132 C4
Perruel (27) 36 A2

Perrusse (52) 116 E1
Perrusson (37) 146 D2
Pers (15) 235 F2
Pers (79) 179 G2
Pers-en-Gâtinais (45) 111 K1
Pers-Jussy (74) 191 G3
Persac (86) 163 J6
Persan (95) 37 J5
Persquen (56) 76 B6
Pertain (80) 19 G3
Perthes (08) 41 H1
Perthes (52) 63 H6
Perthes (77) 87 G2
Perthes-lès-Brienne (10) 91 F3
Pertheville-Ners (14) 54 B3
le Perthus (66) 315 G5
le Pertre (35) 104 C3
le Pertuis (43) 220 D5
Pertuis (84) 277 J5
la Péruse (16) 180 A6
Pervenchères (61) 83 G3
Perville (82) 248 E5
Pescadoires (46) 232 E6
Peschadoires (63) 203 H1
le Pescher (19) 216 A5
Péseux (25) 139 G5
Peseux (39) 155 F3
Peslières (63) 203 H6
Pesmes (70) 137 F5
Pessac (33) 229 G2
Pessac-sur-Dordogne (33) 230 D2
Pessan (32) 267 J6
Pessans (25) 156 A2
Pessat-Villeneuve (63) 185 F6
la Pesse (39) 173 K6
Pessines (17) 195 F2
Pessoulens (32) 268 B3
Petersbach (67) 69 F5
le Petit-Abergement (01) 190 A4
Petit-Auverné (44) 103 K5
le Petit-Bersac (24) 213 F2
le Petit-Bornand-les-Glières (74) . . 191 H4
le Petit-Celland (50) 52 B5
Petit-Couronne (76) 35 H2
Petit-Croix (90) 139 J1
Petit-Failly (54) 43 J1
Petit-Fayt (59) 13 F5
le Petit-Fougeray (35) 103 H1
Petit-Landau (68) 97 E2
Petit-Mars (44) 123 H2
le Petit-Mercey (39) 155 J1
Petit-Mesnil (10) 91 F4
Petit-Noir (39) 155 F4
le Petit-Palais-et-Cornemps (33) . . 212 C6
le Petit-Pressigny (37) 146 C5
le Petit-Quevilly (76) 35 H2
Petit-Réderching (57) 69 F3
Petit-Tenquin (57) 68 B4
Petit-Verly (02) 20 C1
la Petite-Boissière (79) 143 G5
Petite-Chaux (25) 174 C1
Petite-Forêt (59) 12 C1
la Petite-Fosse (88) 95 J3
la Petite-Marche (03) 184 C1
la Petite-Pierre (67) 69 G5
la Petite-Raon (88) 95 J2
Petite-Rosselle (57) 68 B1
la Petite-Verrière (71) 152 D3
Petitefontaine (90) 119 K5
les Petites-Armoises (08) 42 C1
les Petites-Loges (51) 41 G5
Petitmagny (90) 119 J5
Petitmont (54) 67 H6
Petiville (14) 33 G4
Petiville (76) 34 D1
Petosse (85) 160 C4
Petreto-Bicchisano (2A) 322 E1
Pettoncourt (57) 66 C3
Pettonville (54) 95 F1
Peujard (33) 211 J5
Peumérit (29) 98 B2
Peumerit-Quintin (22) 76 B2
Peuplingues (62) 2 C3
Peuton (53) 104 E4
Peuvillers (55) 43 H2
Peux-et-Couffouleux (12) 272 B4
Pévange (57) 66 E2
Pévy (51) 40 D3
Pexiora (11) 289 H5
Pexonne (54) 95 H1
Pey (40) 262 D5
Peymeinade (06) 280 C5
Peynier (13) 297 F2
Peypin (13) 296 E3
Peypin-d'Aigues (84) 277 K3
Peyrabout (23) 182 D4
le Peyrat (09) 308 B3
Peyrat-de-Bellac (87) 181 F3
Peyrat-la-Nonière (23) 183 H4
Peyrat-le-Château (87) 200 A1
la Peyratte (79) 162 A2
Peyraube (65) 285 K5
Peyraud (07) 222 B2
Peyre (40) 265 H6
Peyrecave (32) 268 A3
Peyrefitte-du-Razès (11) 308 C2
Peyrefitte-sur-l'Hers (11) 289 F5
Peyregoux (81) 270 D6
Peyrehorade (40) 264 A6
Peyreleau (12) 253 H5
Peyrelevade (19) 200 D4
Peyrelongue-Abos (64) 285 F2
Peyremale (30) 255 G3
Peyrens (11) 289 H4
Peyrestortes (66) 315 G2
Peyret-Saint-André (65) 286 C4

Peyriac-de-Mer (11) 310 C1
Peyriac-Minervois (11) 290 D4
Peyriat (01) 189 K2
Peyrière (47) 231 G5
Peyrieu (01) 207 J3
Peyrignac (24) 215 F4
Peyriguère (65) 285 K5
Peyrilhac (87) 181 F5
Peyrillac-et-Millac (24) 233 H2
Peyrilles (46) 233 H5
Peyrins (26) 222 D4
Peyrissac (19) 199 K5
Peyrissas (31) 287 G4
Peyrole (81) 270 B4
Peyroles (30) 254 E6
Peyrolles (11) 309 G3
Peyrolles-en-Provence (13) 277 K5
Peyroules (04) 280 A3
Peyrouse (65) 304 A1
Peyrouzet (31) 287 F5
Peyruis (04) 259 F6
Peyrun (65) 285 J4
Peyrus (26) 240 E1
Peyrusse (15) 218 C3
Peyrusse-Grande (32) 266 E6
Peyrusse-le-Roc (12) 251 H1
Peyrusse-Massas (32) 267 H4
Peyrusse-Vieille (32) 266 D6
Peyssies (31) 287 J4
Peyzac-le-Moustier (24) 214 D6
Peyzieux-sur-Saône (01) 188 C3
Pézarches (77) 60 A5
Pezé-le-Robert (72) 82 B6
Pézenas (34) 292 C2
Pézènes-les-Mines (34) 292 A1
Pezens (11) 290 A5
Pézilla-de-Conflent (66) 314 C1
Pézilla-la-Rivière (66) 315 F2
Pezou (41) 108 D4
Pezuls (24) 232 B1
Pézy (28) 85 H4
Pfaffenheim (68) 96 B5
Pfaffenhoffen (67) 69 J6
Pfalzweyer (67) 69 F6
Pfastatt (68) 97 B2
Pfetterhouse (68) 97 A5
Pfettisheim (67) 70 E2
Pfulgriesheim (67) 70 E2
Phaffans (90) 119 J6
Phalempin (59) 6 D5
Phalsbourg (57) 70 A1
Philippsbourg (57) 69 J4
Philondenx (40) 265 H6
Phlin (54) 66 B2
Pia (66) 310 C6
Piacé (72) 82 D5
le Pian-Médoc (33) 211 G6
le Pian-sur-Garonne (33) 230 A5
Piana (2A) 320 A1
Pianello (2B) 319 H6
Piano (2B) 319 H4
Pianottoli-Caldarello (2A) 323 F5
les Piards (39) 173 J4
la Piarre (05) 242 A6
Piazzali (2B) 319 J5
Piazzole (2B) 319 H4
Piblange (57) 45 H3
Pibrac (31) 269 F6
Picarreau (39) 155 K6
Picauville (50) 28 E5
Pichanges (21) 136 B3
Picherande (63) 202 A6
Picquigny (80) 17 K1
Pie-d'Orezza (2B) 319 H5
Pied-de-Borne (48) 255 F1
Piedicorte-di-Gaggio (2B) 321 H1
Piedicroce (2B) 319 H4
Piedigriggio (2B) 319 F4
Piedipartino (2B) 319 H5
Piégon (26) 257 H3
Piégros-la-Clastre (26) 240 E4
Piégut (04) 243 F6
Piégut-Pluviers (24) 197 K4
Piencourt (27) 34 B5
Piennes (54) 44 B3
Piennes-Onvillers (80) 18 E5
Pierlas (06) 261 H5
la Pierre (38) 224 C2
Pierre-Bénite (69) 206 A3
Pierre-Buffière (87) 199 G3
Pierre-Châtel (38) 224 B6
Pierre-de-Bresse (71) 154 E5
Pierre-la-Treiche (54) 65 J5
Pierre-Levée (77) 60 B3
Pierre-Morains (51) 62 A3
Pierre-Percée (54) 95 H1
Pierre-Perthuis (89) 133 J4
Pierreclos (71) 171 H6
Pierrecourt (70) 137 F1
Pierrecourt (76) 17 F2
Pierrefeu (06) 280 E2
Pierrefeu-du-Var (83) 300 E3
Pierrefiche (12) 253 F1
Pierrefiche (48) 238 A4
Pierrefiques (76) 14 B4
Pierrefitte (19) 199 J6
Pierrefitte (23) 183 G3
Pierrefitte (79) 144 A5
Pierrefitte (88) 94 B6
Pierrefitte-en-Auge (14) 33 K4
Pierrefitte-en-Beauvaisis (60) . . . 37 G1
Pierrefitte-en-Cinglais (14) 53 K2
Pierrefitte-ès-Bois (45) 131 H3
Pierrefitte-Nestalas (65) 304 B3
Pierrefitte-sur-Aire (55) 64 C2
Pierrefitte-sur-Loire (03) 169 K4

Pierrefitte-sur-Sauldre (41) 130 C3
Pierrefitte-sur-Seine (93) 58 E2
Pierrefonds (60) 39 F3
Pierrefontaine-lès-Blamont (25) . . 139 H4
Pierrefontaine-les-Varans (25) . . . 139 F6
Pierrefort (15) 236 B1
Pierregot (80) 10 B6
Pierrelatte (26) 256 D2
Pierrelaye (95) 58 C1
Pierrelongue (26) 257 J3
Pierremande (02) 19 K6
Pierremont (62) 10 A1
Pierremont-sur-Amance (52) 117 G5
Pierrepont (02) 20 E5
Pierrepont (14) 53 K3
Pierrepont (54) 26 C4
Pierrepont-sur-Avre (80) 18 D4
Pierrepont-sur-l'Arentèle (88) . . 95 F4
Pierrerue (04) 278 C1
Pierrerue (34) 291 H3
Pierres (14) 53 F3
Pierres (28) 85 H1
Pierreval (76) 16 B6
Pierrevert (04) 278 B3
Pierreville (50) 28 B4
Pierreville (54) 94 A1
Pierrevillers (57) 44 E4
Pierric (44) 103 F4
Pierry (51) 61 K1
Pietra-di-Verde (2B) 319 J6
Pietracorbara (2B) 317 D3
Pietralba (2B) 319 F3
Pietraserena (2B) 321 H1
Pietricaggio (2B) 319 H5
Pietrosella (2A) 320 C6
Pietroso (2B) 321 G2
Piets-Plasence-Moustrou (64) . . 284 B1
Pieusse (11) 308 E1
les Pieux (50) 28 B4
Piève (2B) 319 J6
Piffonds (89) 112 C2
Pigna (2B) 318 C2
Pignan (34) 293 H1
Pignans (83) 298 B3
Pignicourt (02) 41 F2
Pignols (63) 203 H4
Pigny (18) 149 H2
Pihem (62) 5 G3
Pihen-lès-Guînes (62) 2 C3
Pila-Canale (2A) 322 D1
Pillac (16) 213 F2
Pillemoine (39) 173 K1
les Pilles (26) 257 J2
Pillon (55) 43 K2
Pimbo (40) 265 H6
Pimelles (89) 114 C5
Pimorin (39) 173 F4
Pimprez (60) 39 F1
le Pin (03) 170 A5
le Pin (14) 34 A4
le Pin (17) 212 A2
le Pin (30) 256 B6
le Pin (38) 207 H5
le Pin (39) 173 G1
le Pin (44) 124 B1
Pin (70) 137 J5
le Pin (77) 59 H3
le Pin (79) 143 G5
le Pin (82) 268 C1
le Pin-au-Haras (61) 54 D5
Pin-Balma (31) 269 H6
le Pin-en-Mauges (49) 124 D6
le Pin-la-Garenne (61) 83 H3
le Pin-Murelet (31) 287 H3
Pinas (65) 305 G1
Pinay (42) 187 F6
Pincé (72) 105 F3
Pindères (47) 247 F3
Pindray (86) 163 K4
les Pineaux (85) 160 A4
Pinel-Hauterive (47) 248 B1
Pinet (34) 292 D3
Pineuilh (33) 231 F2
Piney (10) 90 D4
Pino (2B) 317 C3
Pinols (43) 219 H5
Pinon (02) 39 K1
les Pins (16) 197 G1
Pins-Justaret (31) 288 B2
Pinsac (46) 233 J2
Pinsaguel (31) 288 B2
Pinsot (38) 224 E1
Pintac (65) 285 G4
Pinterville (27) 35 J5
Pintheville (55) 44 A5
les Pinthières (28) 57 H5
Piobetta (2B) 319 H5
Pioggiola (2B) 318 C3
Piolenc (84) 256 D4
Pionnat (23) 182 E3
Pionsat (63) 184 B3
Pioussay (79) 179 F4
Pipriac (35) 102 D2
Piquecos (82) 249 G1
Pirajoux (01) 172 D5
Piré-sur-Seiche (35) 79 J5
Pirey (25) 137 K5
Piriac-sur-Mer (44) 121 F4
Pirmil (72) 106 B3
Pirou (50) 30 D2
Pis (32) 267 K4
Pisany (17) 194 E2
Piscop (95) 58 E1
Piseux (27) 56 B4
Pisieu (38) 222 D1
Pisseleu (60) 17 J6

Pisseloup (52) 117 G4
la Pisseure (70) 118 B4
Pissos (40) 245 H3
Pissotte (85) 160 D4
Pissy (80) 17 K2
Pissy-Pôville (76) 15 J6
Pisy (89) 134 B2
Pitgam (59) 3 H3
Pithiviers (45) 86 D6
Pithiviers-le-Vieil (45) 110 D1
Pithon (02) 19 J4
Pîtres (27) 35 J3
Pittefaux (62) 4 B2
Pizay (01) 189 F6
Pizieux (72) 83 F4
le Pizou (24) 212 D5
le Pla (09) 313 J2
Plabennec (29) 46 A5
Placé (53) 80 E5
les Places (27) 34 B5
Placey (25) 137 J6
Plachy-Buyon (80) 18 A3
Placy (14) 53 J2
Placy-Montaigu (50) 31 J4
le Plagnal (07) 238 C4
Plagne (01) 190 B2
Plagne (31) 287 H6
Plagnole (31) 287 H3
Plaigne (11) 289 F6
Plailly (60) 38 B6
Plaimbois-du-Miroir (25) . . . 139 G6
Plaimbois-Vennes (25) 139 F6
Plaimpied-Givaudins (18) . . . 149 H4
la Plaine (49) 143 H2
Plaine (67) 95 K2
Plaine-de-Walsch (57) 67 K4
Plaine-Haute (22) 77 F1
la Plaine-sur-Mer (44) 122 A5
Plainemont (70) 118 B4
Plaines-Saint-Lange (10) . . . 114 E3
Plainfaing (88) 95 J5
Plainoiseau (39) 173 G1
les Plains-et-Grands-Essarts (25) . 139 J5
Plaintel (22) 77 F1
Plainval (60) 38 A1
Plainville (27) 34 C6
Plainville (60) 18 C5
Plaisance (12) 271 J2
Plaisance (24) 231 J4
Plaisance (32) 266 C6
Plaisance (86) 164 A6
Plaisance-du-Touch (31) . . . 288 A1
Plaisia (39) 173 G3
Plaisians (26) 257 K4
Plaisir (78) 58 A4
Plaissan (34) 292 D1
Plaizac (16) 196 B2
le Plan (31) 287 J6
Plan (38) 223 H2
Plan-d'Aups-Sainte-Baume (83) . 297 G3
Plan-de-Baix (26) 241 F2
Plan-de-Cuques (13) 296 D3
Plan-de-la-Tour (83) 298 E3
Plan-d'Orgon (13) 276 D3
Planaise (73) 208 D5
Planay (21) 114 E6
Planay (73) 209 K5
la Planche (44) 141 K3
Plancher-Bas (70) 119 G5
Plancher-les-Mines (70) . . . 119 G5
Plancherine (73) 209 F2
Planches (61) 55 F5
les Planches-en-Montagne (39) . . 174 A2
les Planches-près-Arbois (39) . . 155 K5
Planchez (58) 152 C2
Plancoët (22) 50 B4
Plancy-l'Abbaye (10) 89 K1
la Planée (25) 156 E5
Planès (66) 313 J4
Planèzes (66) 309 J5
Planfoy (42) 221 H1
Planguenoual (22) 49 H6
Planioles (46) 234 D5
le Planois (71) 155 F6
le Planquay (27) 34 B6
Planquery (14) 31 K3
Planques (62) 5 F6
Planrupt (52) 91 H2
les Plans (30) 255 J5
les Plans (34) 273 F4
le Plantay (01) 189 F4
les Plantiers (30) 254 D5
le Plantis (61) 83 F1
Planty (10) 89 G5
Planzolles (07) 255 H1
Plappeville (57) 44 E5
Plasne (39) 155 J6
Plasnes (27) 34 D5
Plassac (17) 195 G5
Plassac (33) 211 G4
Plassac-Rouffiac (16) 196 D5
Plassay (17) 195 F1
Plats (07) 222 B5
Plaudren (56) 101 G4
Plauzat (63) 202 D4
Plavilla (11) 289 G6
Plazac (24) 214 D5
Pleaux (15) 217 F4
Pléboulle (22) 50 A3
Pléchâtel (35) 103 F1
Plédéliac (22) 77 K1
Plédran (22) 77 G1
Pléguien (22) 48 E4
Pléhédel (22) 48 E3
Pleine-Fougères (35) 51 H5
Pleine-Selve (02) 20 C3

Pleine-Selve (33) 211 H1
Pleine-Sève (76) 15 G3
Plélan-le-Grand (35) 78 C5
Plélan-le-Petit (22) 50 B5
Plélauff (22) 76 B4
Plélo (22) 48 E5
Plémet (22) 77 H4
Plémy (22) 77 G2
Pléneuf-Val-André (22) 49 J5
Plénée-Jugon (22) 77 K2
Plénise (39) 156 C5
Plénisette (39) 156 C6
Plerguer (35) 50 E5
Plérin (22) 49 G5
Plerneuf (22) 49 F6
Plescop (56) 101 F4
Plesder (35) 50 E6
Plésidy (22) 76 C1
Pleslin-Trigavou (22) 50 D4
Plesnois (57) 44 E4
Plesnoy (52) 116 E4
Plessala (22) 77 H3
Plessé (44) 102 D5
le Plessier-Huleu (02) 39 J4
le Plessier-Rozainvillers (80) . . 18 D4
le Plessier-sur-Bulles (60) . . . 37 K1
le Plessier-sur-Saint-Just (60) . . 38 A1
Plessis-Barbuise (10) 89 G1
le Plessis-Belleville (60) . . . 38 D6
le Plessis-Bouchard (95) . . . 58 D2
le Plessis-Brion (60) 38 E1
le Plessis-Dorin (41) 108 A1
le Plessis-Feu-Aussoux (77) . . 60 B5
le Plessis-Gassot (95) 59 F1
le Plessis-Grammoire (49) . . . 125 H3
le Plessis-Grimoult (14) . . . 53 G2
le Plessis-Grohan (27) 56 D2
le Plessis-Hébert (27) 57 F2
le Plessis-Lastelle (50) 30 E1
le Plessis-l'Échelle (41) . . . 109 F5
le Plessis-l'Evêque (77) . . . 59 J1
le Plessis-Luzarches (95) . . . 38 A6
le Plessis-Macé (49) 125 F2
le Plessis-Pâté (91) 86 E1
le Plessis-Patte-d'Oie (60) . . . 19 H4
le Plessis-Placy (77) 60 A1
le Plessis-Robinson (92) . . . 58 D4
Plessis-Saint-Benoist (91) . . . 86 B3
le Plessis-Saint-Jean (89) . . . 88 D4
le Plessis-Sainte-Opportune (27) . 35 F6
le Plessis-Trévise (94) 59 G4
Plessix-Balisson (22) 50 C4
Plestan (22) 77 K1
Plestin-les-Grèves (22) 47 J3
Pleubian (22) 48 D1
Pleucadeuc (56) 101 K4
Pleudaniel (22) 48 D2
Pleudihen-sur-Rance (22) . . . 50 D5
Pleugriffet (56) 101 G1
Pleugueneuc (35) 50 E6
Pleumartin (86) 163 K1
Pleumeleuc (35) 78 E3
Pleumeur-Bodou (22) 47 K2
Pleumeur-Gautier (22) 48 C2
Pleure (39) 155 G4
Pleurs (51) 61 J3
Pleurtuit (35) 50 D4
Pleuven (29) 98 D2
Pleuvezain (88) 93 J3
Pleuville (16) 179 K4
Pléven (22) 50 A5
Plévenon (22) 50 A3
Plévin (22) 75 J3
Pleyben (29) 74 E2
Pleyber-Christ (29) 47 F5
Pliboux (79) 179 G2
Plichancourt (51) 63 G4
Plieux (32) 267 K2
Plivot (51) 62 A1
Plobannalec-Lesconil (29) . . . 98 B3
Plobsheim (67) 71 D2
Ploemel (56) 100 C5
Ploemeur (56) 99 K5
Ploërdut (56) 76 B5
Ploeren (56) 100 E5
Ploërmel (56) 101 K2
Plœuc-sur-Lié (22) 77 G2
Ploéven (29) 74 C4
Ploëzal (22) 48 C3
Plogastel-Saint-Germain (29) . . 74 B6
Plogoff (29) 73 B3
Plogonnec (29) 74 C5
Ploisy (02) 39 J3
Plomb (50) 52 A4
Plombières-les-Bains (88) . . . 118 D2
Plombières-lès-Dijon (21) . . . 135 K5
Plomelin (29) 98 C2
Plomeur (29) 98 B3
Plomion (02) 21 G3
Plomodiern (29) 74 C3
Plonéis (29) 74 C5
Plonéour-Lanvern (29) 98 B2
Plonévez-du-Faou (29) 75 G3
Plonévez-Porzay (29) 74 C4
Plorec-sur-Arguenon (22) . . . 50 A5
Plottes (71) 171 K4
Plou (18) 148 E3
Plouagat (22) 48 E5
Plouaret (22) 47 K4
Plouarzel (29) 72 B3
Plouasne (22) 78 D2
Plouay (56) 100 A1
Ploubalay (22) 50 C4
Ploubazlanec (22) 48 E2

Ploubezre (22) 48 A3
Ploudalmézeau (29) 72 C2
Ploudaniel (29) 46 B5
Ploudiry (29) 46 D6
Plouëc-du-Trieux (22) 48 C4
Plouédern (29) 46 C5
Plouégat-Guérand (29) 47 H4
Plouégat-Moysan (29) 47 J5
Plouénan (29) 46 E4
Plouër-sur-Rance (22) 50 D4
Plouescat (29) 46 D3
Plouézec (22) 48 E3
Plouézoc'h (29) 47 G4
Ploufragan (22) 49 F6
Plougar (29) 46 D4
Plougasnou (29) 47 G3
Plougastel-Daoulas (29) . . . 74 B1
Plougonvelin (29) 72 B5
Plougonven (29) 47 H5
Plougonver (22) 48 A6
Plougoulm (29) 46 E3
Plougoumelen (56) 100 E5
Plougourvest (29) 46 D4
Plougras (22) 47 J5
Plougrescant (22) 48 C1
Plouguenast (22) 77 G3
Plouguerneau (29) 46 A4
Plouguernével (22) 76 B3
Plouguiel (22) 48 C2
Plouguin (29) 72 C2
Plouha (22) 48 E4
Plouharnel (56) 100 C6
Plouhinec (29) 73 B4
Plouhinec (56) 100 B4
Plouider (29) 46 C4
Plouigneau (29) 47 H5
Plouisy (22) 48 C5
Ploulec'h (22) 47 K3
Ploumagoar (22) 48 C5
Ploumilliau (22) 47 K3
Ploumoguer (29) 72 B4
Plounéour-Ménez (29) 47 F6
Plounéour-Trez (29) 46 B3
Plounérin (22) 47 J5
Plounéventer (29) 46 C5
Plounévez-Lochrist (29) 46 C4
Plounévez-Moëdec (22) 47 K5
Plounévez-Quintin (22) 76 B3
Plounévézel (29) 75 J2
Plourac'h (22) 75 J1
Plouray (56) 76 A4
Plourhan (22) 49 F4
Plourin (29) 72 B3
Plourin-lès-Morlaix (29) 47 G5
Plourivo (22) 48 D3
Plouvain (62) 11 G2
Plouvara (22) 48 E6
Plouvien (29) 46 A5
Plouvorn (29) 46 E4
Plouyé (29) 75 G2
Plouzané (29) 72 C4
Plouzélambre (22) 47 J4
Plouzévédé (29) 46 D4
Plovan (29) 98 A2
Ployart-et-Vaurseine (02) . . . 40 C1
le Ployron (60) 18 D6
Plozévet (29) 74 A4
Pludual (22) 48 E4
Pluduno (22) 50 B4
Plufur (22) 47 J4
Pluguffan (29) 98 C1
Pluherlin (56) 101 K5
Plumaudan (22) 50 C6
Plumaugat (22) 78 B2
Plumelec (56) 101 G3
Pluméliau (56) 100 D1
Plumelin (56) 100 E2
Plumergat (56) 100 E4
Plumetot (14) 32 E3
Plumieux (56) 77 H5
Plumont (39) 155 J2
Pluneret (56) 100 D5
Plurien (22) 49 K5
Plusquellec (22) 75 K1
Plussulien (22) 76 D2
Pluvault (21) 154 E1
Pluvet (21) 154 E1
Pluvigner (56) 100 D3
Pluzunet (22) 48 A4
Pocancy (51) 62 B2
Pocé-les-Bois (35) 80 A6
Pocé-sur-Cisse (37) 128 B4
Podensac (33) 229 K4
le Poët (05) 259 F3
le Poët-Célard (26) 240 E5
le Poët-en-Percip (26) 258 A3
le Poët-Laval (26) 240 D6
le Poët-Sigillat (26) 257 K2
Pœuilly (80) 19 J2
Poey-de-Lescar (64) 284 C3
Poey-d'Oloron (64) 283 K5
Poëzat (03) 185 G4
Poggio-di-Nazza (2B) 321 H3
Poggio-di-Venaco (2B) 319 F6
Poggio-d'Oletta (2B) 319 H1
Poggio-Marinaccio (2B) 319 H5
Poggio-Mezzana (2B) 319 J4
Poggiolo (2A) 320 D2
Pogny (51) 62 E3
Poids-de-Fiole (39) 173 G3
Poigny (77) 88 D2
Poigny-la-Forêt (78) 57 J6
Poil (58) 152 D1
Poilcourt-Sydney (08) 41 F2
Poilhes (34) 291 J4
Poillé-sur-Vègre (72) 105 K3

Poilley (35) 80 A1
Poilley (50) 52 A6
Poilly (51) 40 D4
Poilly-lez-Gien (45) 131 G1
Poilly-sur-Serein (89) 113 K5
Poilly-sur-Tholon (89) 112 E4
Poinçon-lès-Larrey (21) 114 E4
le Poinçonnet (36) 165 J1
Poincy (77) 60 A2
Poinsenot (52) 115 K6
Poinson-lès-Fayl (52) 117 F5
Poinson-lès-Grancey (52) . . . 115 K6
Poinson-lès-Nogent (52) . . . 116 D2
Pointel (61) 53 K5
Pointis-de-Rivière (31) 305 J1
Pointis-Inard (31) 306 A1
Pointre (39) 137 F6
Pointvillers (25) 156 A2
Poinville (28) 86 A6
le Poiré-sur-Velluire (85) . . . 160 D5
le Poiré-sur-Vie (85) 141 J6
Poiroux (85) 159 G3
Poisat (38) 224 B3
Poiseul (52) 116 E3
Poiseul-la-Grange (21) 135 J2
Poiseul-la-Ville-et-Laperrière (21) . 135 G2
Poiseul-lès-Saulx (21) 135 K2
Poiseux (58) 150 E2
Poisieux (18) 148 D3
le Poislay (41) 108 C2
Poisson (71) 170 C6
Poissons (52) 92 B3
Poissy (78) 58 B2
Poisvilliers (28) 85 G3
Poisy (74) 190 E5
la Poitevinière (49) 124 D6
Poitiers (86) 163 F3
Poivres (10) 62 C5
Poix (51) 63 F2
Poix-de-Picardie (80) 17 H3
Poix-du-Nord (59) 12 E4
Poix-Terron (08) 22 C5
le Poizat (01) 190 B2
Polaincourt-et-Clairefontaine (70) . 118 A3
Polastron (31) 287 G4
Polastron (32) 287 F1
Poleymieux-au-Mont-d'Or (69) . . 188 C6
Poliénas (38) 223 H2
Polignac (17) 212 A2
Polignac (43) 220 C5
Poligné (35) 103 F1
Poligny (05) 242 E3
Poligny (10) 90 D6
Poligny (39) 155 J5
Poligny (77) 87 J6
Polincove (62) 2 E4
Polisot (10) 114 D2
Polisy (10) 114 D2
Pollestres (66) 315 G3
Polliat (01) 189 F1
Pollieu (01) 207 K1
Pollionnay (69) 205 J2
Polminhac (15) 235 J1
Polveroso (2B) 319 H4
Pomacle (51) 41 G3
la Pomarède (11) 289 G3
Pomarède (46) 232 E6
Pomarez (40) 264 D5
Pomas (11) 309 F1
Pomayrols (12) 253 G1
Pomerol (33) 230 B1
Pomérols (34) 292 D3
Pomeys (69) 205 G3
Pommard (21) 153 K3
Pommera (62) 10 B4
la Pommeraie-sur-Sèvre (85) . . 143 F5
la Pommeraye (14) 53 J2
la Pommeraye (49) 124 D4
Pommeret (22) 77 H1
Pommereuil (59) 12 D5
Pommereux (76) 16 E5
Pommeréval (76) 16 B4
Pommerieux (53) 104 D3
Pommérieux (57) 66 A1
Pommerit-Jaudy (22) 48 C3
Pommerit-le-Vicomte (22) . . . 48 C3
Pommerol (26) 258 A1
Pommeuse (77) 60 A4
Pommevic (82) 248 E6
Pommier (62) 10 E3
Pommier-de-Beaurepaire (38) . . 206 D4
Pommiers (02) 39 H2
Pommiers (30) 273 J2
Pommiers (36) 165 H4
Pommiers (42) 204 D1
Pommiers (69) 188 B5
Pommiers-la-Placette (38) . . . 223 K1
Pommiers-Moulons (17) 211 K1
Pomoy (70) 118 D6
Pompaire (79) 161 K3
Pompéjac (33) 246 C2
Pompertuzat (31) 288 C2
Pompey (54) 66 A4
Pompiac (32) 287 F2
le Pompidou (48) 254 C4
Pompierre (88) 93 G5
Pompierre-sur-Doubs (25) . . . 138 E3
Pompiey (47) 247 H4
Pompignac (33) 229 J2
Pompignan (30) 274 B3
Pompignan (82) 269 F4
Pompogne (47) 247 F4
Pomponne (77) 59 H3
Pomport (24) 231 H3
Pomps (64) 284 B2
Pomy (11) 308 D2

Poncé-sur-le-Loir (72). 107 J5
Poncey-lès-Athée (21) 136 D6
Poncey-sur-l'Ignon (21) 135 H3
le Ponchel (62) 9 J3
Ponches-Estruval (80) 9 G2
Ponchon (60) 37 J3
Poncin (01). 189 J3
Poncins (42) 204 E2
Pondaurat (33) 230 C6
le Pondy (18) 149 J6
Ponet-et-Saint-Auban (26) 241 G2
Ponlat-Taillebourg (31) 305 H1
Pons (17) 195 H4
Ponsampère (32) 286 A2
Ponsan-Soubiran (32) 286 B4
Ponsas (26) 222 B4
Ponson-Debat-Pouts (64) 285 G4
Ponson-Dessus (64) 285 G4
Ponsonnas (38) 242 B1
Pont (21) 154 E1
Pont-à-Marcq (59) 6 E5
Pont-à-Mousson (54) 65 K2
Pont-à-Vendin (62) 6 C6
Pont-Arcy (02) 40 B2
Pont-Audemer (27) 34 C3
Pont-Authou (27) 34 E4
Pont-Aven (29) 99 G3
Pont-Bellanger (14) 52 D2
le Pont-Chrétien-Chabenet (36) . 165 G3
Pont-Croix (29) 73 D3
Pont-d'Ain (01) 189 H4
Pont-de-Barret (26) 240 D5
le Pont-de-Beauvoisin (38) 207 J4
le Pont-de-Beauvoisin (73) 207 J4
Pont-de-Buis-lès-Quimerch (29) . 74 D2
Pont-de-Chéruy (38) 206 E2
le Pont-de-Claix (38) 224 A4
Pont-de-Labeaume (07) 239 G4
Pont-de-l'Arche (27) 35 J3
Pont-de-Larn (81) 290 B2
Pont-de-l'Isère (26) 222 C6
Pont-de-Metz (80) 18 A2
le Pont-de-Montvert (48) 254 D2
le Pont-de-Planches (70) 137 J2
Pont-de-Poitte (39) 173 H3
Pont-de-Roide (25) 139 H4
Pont-de-Ruan (37) 127 H6
Pont-de-Salars (12) 252 D4
Pont-de-Vaux (01) 172 A5
Pont-de-Veyle (01) 188 D1
Pont-d'Héry (39) 156 A5
Pont-d'Ouilly (14) 53 J3
Pont-du-Bois (70) 118 A2
Pont-du-Casse (47) 248 C4
Pont-du-Château (63) 202 E2
Pont-du-Navoy (39) 173 J1
Pont-en-Royans (38) 223 G5
Pont-et-Massène (21) 134 D3
Pont-Évêque (38) 206 B5
Pont-Farcy (14) 52 C2
Pont-Hébert (50) 31 H3
Pont-la-Ville (52) 115 J1
Pont-l'Abbé (29) 98 B3
Pont-l'Abbé-d'Arnoult (17) 194 E1
Pont-lès-Bonfays (88) 94 A6
Pont-les-Moulins (25) 138 D5
Pont-l'Évêque (14) 33 K3
Pont-l'Évêque (60) 19 H6
Pont-Melvez (22) 48 B6
Pont-Noyelles (80) 18 C1
Pont-Péan (35) 79 F5
Pont-Remy (80) 9 G6
Pont-Saint-Esprit (30) 256 C4
Pont-Saint-Mard (02) 39 J1
Pont-Saint-Martin (44) 123 G5
Pont-Saint-Pierre (27) 35 K3
Pont-Saint-Vincent (54) 65 K6
Pont-Sainte-Marie (10) 90 B4
Pont-Sainte-Maxence (60) 38 C4
Pont-Salomon (43) 221 F2
Pont-Scorff (56) 99 K4
Pont-sur-l'Ognon (70) 138 D2
Pont-sur-Madon (88) 94 A3
Pont-sur-Meuse (55) 64 E4
Pont-sur-Sambre (59) 13 G3
Pont-sur-Seine (10) 89 G2
Pont-sur-Vanne (89) 88 E6
Pont-sur-Yonne (89) 88 C5
Pont-Trambouze (69) 187 H4
Pontacq (64) 285 F5
Pontailler-sur-Saône (21) 136 E5
Pontaix (26) 241 G4
Pontamafrey-Montpascal (73) . . 225 G1
Pontarion (23) 182 D5
Pontarlier (25) 157 F4
Pontarmé (60) 38 B5
Pontaubault (50) 51 K3
Pontaubert (89) 133 J3
Pontault-Combault (77) 59 G4
Pontaumur (63) 201 K1
Pontavert (02) 40 D2
Pontcarré (77) 59 H4
Pontcey (70) 137 K1
Pontchardon (61) 55 F2
Pontcharra (38) 208 C5
Pontcharra-sur-Turdine (69) . . . 187 K6
Pontcharraud (23) 201 F1
Pontchâteau (44) 122 B1
Pontcirq (46) 233 F6
Pontécoulant (14) 53 G3
Ponteilla (66) 315 G3
Ponteils-et-Brésis (30) 255 F2
Pontenx-les-Forges (40) 244 D3
le Pontet (73) 208 E5
le Pontet (84) 276 C1
les Pontets (25) 174 C1

Pontevès (83) 278 E6
Ponteyraud (24) 213 F3
Pontfaverger-Moronvilliers (51) . . 41 H3
Pontgibaud (63) 202 B1
Pontgouin (28) 84 D2
Ponthévrard (78) 86 A1
Ponthion (51) 63 G4
Ponthoile (80) 9 F3
le Ponthou (29) 47 J5
Ponthoux (39) 173 J5
Pontiacq-Viellepinte (64) 285 G3
Pontigné (49) 126 B2
Pontigny (89) 113 H4
Pontis (04) 243 H6
Pontivy (56) 76 E5
Pontlevoy (41) 128 E5
Pontmain (53) 80 C2
Pontoise (95) 58 C1
Pontoise-lès-Noyon (60) 19 H6
Pontonx-sur-l'Adour (40) 264 C3
Pontorson (50) 51 J4
Pontours (24) 232 A2
Pontoux (71) 154 D4
Pontoy (57) 45 G6
Pontpierre (57) 45 K6
Pontpoint (60) 38 C4
Pontrieux (22) 48 C3
Pontru (02) 19 K2
Pontruet (02) 19 K2
Ponts (50) 51 K3
les Ponts-de-Cé (49) 125 G4
Ponts-et-Marais (76) 8 C6
Pontvallain (72) 106 D6
Popian (34) 273 J6
Popolasca (2B) 319 F4
Porcaro (56) 78 B6
Porcelette (57) 45 K4
Porchères (33) 212 D5
la Porcherie (87) 199 H4
Porcheux (60) 37 F3
Porcheville (78) 57 K2
Porcieu-Amblagnieu (38) 207 G1
Pordic (22) 49 F5
le Porge (33) 228 C1
Pornic (44) 122 B5
Pornichet (44) 121 K5
Porquéricourt (60) 19 G6
Porri (2B) 319 J4
Porspoder (29) 72 B3
le Port (09) 307 F4
Port-Brillet (53) 104 D1
Port-de-Bouc (13) 295 J5
Port-de-Lanne (40) 262 E6
Port-de-Piles (86) 145 K4
Port-d'Envaux (17) 195 F1
Port-des-Barques (17) 176 E5
Port-en-Bessin-Huppain (14) . . . 32 A3
Port-la-Nouvelle (11) 310 D2
Port-Launay (29) 74 D3
Port-le-Grand (80) 9 F4
Port-Lesney (39) 155 K3
Port-Louis (56) 99 K5
le Port-Marly (78) 58 C3
Port-Mort (27) 36 A5
Port-Saint-Louis-du-Rhône (13) . 295 G5
Port-Saint-Père (44) 122 E5
Port-Sainte-Foy-et-Ponchapt (24) . 231 F2
Port-Sainte-Marie (47) 247 K4
Port-sur-Saône (70) 117 K6
Port-sur-Seille (54) 66 A2
Port-Vendres (66) 315 J4
Port-Villez (78) 57 G1
la Porta (2B) 319 H4
Porta (66) 313 F4
Portbail (50) 28 C6
Porte-Joie (27) 35 K4
Porté-Puymorens (66) 313 F4
le Portel (62) 4 A3
Portel-des-Corbières (11) 310 C2
Portes (27) 56 B1
Portes (30) 255 G5
les Portes-en-Ré (17) 158 B5
Portes-en-Valdaine (26) 240 C6
Portes-lès-Valence (26) 240 C1
Portet (64) 265 K6
Portet-d'Aspet (31) 306 A3
Portet-de-Luchon (31) 305 G5
Portet-sur-Garonne (31) 288 B2
Portets (33) 229 J4
Portieux (88) 94 C3
Portiragnes (34) 292 B4
Porto-Vecchio (2A) 323 H3
Ports (37) 145 J3
Posanges (21) 135 F4
Poses (27) 35 K3
Possesse (51) 63 H3
la Possonnière (49) 125 F4
la Postolle (89) 88 E5
Postroff (57) 67 J2
Potangis (51) 89 G1
Potelières (30) 255 H2
Potelle (59) 12 E3
la Poterie-au-Perche (61) 55 K6
la Poterie-Cap-d'Antifer (76) . . . 14 B4
la Poterie-Mathieu (27) 34 C4
Pothières (21) 115 F3
Potigny (14) 54 A2
Potte (80) 19 G3
Pouan-les-Vallées (10) 90 A1
Pouançay (86) 144 C2
Pouancé (49) 104 A5
Pouant (86) 145 F3
Poubeau (31) 305 G5
Poucharramet (31) 287 J3
Poudenas (47) 247 H6

Poudenx (40) 265 F6
Poudis (81) 289 H2
Poueyferré (65) 285 F6
la Pouëze (49) 124 E2
Pouffonds (79) 178 D2
la Pouge (23) 182 A5
le Pouget (34) 273 J6
Pougnadoresse (30) 256 B6
Pougne-Hérisson (79) 161 H2
Pougny (01) 190 D2
Pougny (58) 132 A5
Pougues-les-Eaux (58) 150 D3
Pougy (10) 90 D3
Pouillac (17) 212 A2
Pouillat (01) 173 F6
Pouillé (41) 128 E5
Pouillé (85) 160 C4
Pouillé (86) 163 H4
Pouillé-les-Côteaux (44) 124 A3
Pouillenay (21) 134 E3
Pouilley-Français (25) 137 J4
Pouilley-les-Vignes (25) 137 K6
Pouillon (40) 264 B6
Pouillon (51) 40 E3
Pouilloux (71) 170 E3
Pouilly (57) 45 F6
Pouilly (60) 37 G4
Pouilly-en-Auxois (21) 135 F6
Pouilly-le-Monial (69) 188 A5
Pouilly-lès-Feurs (42) 204 E1
Pouilly-les-Nonains (42) 186 E4
Pouilly-sous-Charlieu (42) 187 F3
Pouilly-sur-Loire (58) 132 A6
Pouilly-sur-Meuse (55) 23 G6
Pouilly-sur-Saône (21) 154 D3
Pouilly-sur-Serre (02) 20 C4
Pouilly-sur-Vingeanne (21) 136 E2
le Poujol-sur-Orb (34) 291 J1
Poujols (34) 273 G4
Poulaines (36) 147 K2
Poulainville (80) 18 B1
Poulan-Pouzols (81) 270 D3
Poulangy (52) 116 C2
Pouldergat (29) 74 B5
Pouldouran (22) 48 C2
Pouldreuzic (29) 98 A1
Poule-les-Écharmeaux (69) 187 J3
Pouliacq (64) 284 D1
les Poulières (88) 95 G5
Pouligney-Lusans (25) 138 B5
Pouligny-Notre-Dame (36) 166 B5
Pouligny-Saint-Martin (36) 166 B4
Pouligny-Saint-Pierre (36) 164 C2
le Pouliguen (44) 121 J5
Poullan-sur-Mer (29) 74 A4
Poullaouen (29) 75 H2
Poullignac (16) 196 C6
Poulx (30) 275 H2
Poumarous (65) 285 J6
Poupas (82) 268 A2
Poupry (28) 109 K1
Pouques-Lormes (58) 133 J5
Pourcharesses (48) 255 F1
Pourchères (07) 239 J3
Pourcieux (83) 297 G2
Pourcy (51) 40 E5
Pourlans (71) 154 E4
Pournoy-la-Chétive (57) 45 F6
Pournoy-la-Grasse (57) 45 F6
Pourrain (89) 112 E6
Pourrières (83) 297 G1
Poursac (16) 179 H5
Poursay-Garnaud (17) 178 A5
Poursiugues-Boucoue (64) 284 D1
Pouru-aux-Bois (08) 23 G4
Pouru-Saint-Remy (08) 23 G4
Poussan (34) 292 E2
Poussanges (23) 200 E1
Poussay (88) 94 A4
Pousseaux (58) 133 F3
Poussignac (47) 247 F2
Poussy-la-Campagne (14) 33 F6
Pousthomy (12) 271 J3
le Pout (33) 229 K2
Pouvrai (61) 83 H5
Pouxeux (88) 94 K6
Pouy (65) 286 C5
Pouy-de-Touges (31) 287 H4
Pouy-Loubrin (32) 286 D2
Pouy-Roquelaure (32) 267 H1
Pouy-sur-Vannes (10) 89 G4
Pouyastruc (65) 285 J5
Pouydesseaux (40) 265 J1
Pouydraguin (32) 266 C5
Pouylebon (32) 285 K1
Pouzac (65) 304 D1
Pouzauges (85) 143 F6
Pouzay (37) 145 J3
Pouze (31) 288 C3
Pouzilhac (30) 256 C6
le Pouzin (07) 240 B3
Pouzol (63) 184 E4
Pouzols (34) 292 A2
Pouzols-Minervois (11) 291 G5
Pouzy-Mésangy (03) 168 B2
Poyanne (40) 264 D4
Poyans (70) 136 E3
Poyartin (40) 264 D5
Poyols (26) 241 H5
Pozières (80) 10 E6
le Pradal (34) 272 E6
les Pradeaux (63) 203 F5
Pradelle (26) 241 G5
Pradelles (43) 238 C3
Pradelles (59) 5 K3

Pradelles-Cabardès (11) 290 C3
Pradelles-en-Val (11) 290 C6
Pradère-les-Bourguets (31) 268 E6
Prades (07) 239 G5
Prades (09) 308 B5
Prades (43) 219 K6
Prades (66) 314 C3
Prades (81) 270 C6
Prades-d'Aubrac (12) 236 C6
Prades-le-Lez (34) 274 D5
Prades-Salars (12) 252 D4
Prades-sur-Vernazobre (34) 291 H3
le Pradet (83) 300 D4
Pradettes (09) 308 A3
Pradières (09) 307 J3
Pradiers (15) 218 C3
Pradinas (12) 251 J4
Pradines (19) 200 B5
Pradines (42) 187 G5
Pradines (46) 249 K1
Pradons (07) 255 K1
Prads-Haute-Bléone (04) 260 B3
Prahecq (79) 178 B1
Prailles (79) 161 K6
Pralognan-la-Vanoise (73) 209 K1
Prâlon (21) 135 H5
Pralong (42) 204 C3
Pranles (07) 239 K3
Pranzac (16) 197 G3
Praslay (52) 116 B6
Praslin (10) 114 C2
Prasville (28) 85 J5
Prat (22) 48 B3
Prat-Bonrepaux (09) 306 C2
Prato-di-Giovellina (2B) 319 F4
Prats-de-Carlux (24) 233 G1
Prats-de-Mollo-la-Preste (66) . . . 314 C6
Prats-de-Sournia (66) 309 H6
Prats-du-Périgord (24) 232 D4
Pratviel (81) 270 B6
Pratz (39) 173 J5
Prauthoy (52) 116 C6
Pray (41) 128 C1
Praye (54) 94 A2
Prayols (09) 307 J3
Prayssac (46) 249 H1
Prayssas (47) 248 A3
Praz-sur-Arly (74) 191 K6
le Pré-d'Auge (14) 33 J5
Pré-en-Pail (53) 82 A2
Pré-Saint-Évroult (28) 85 G6
le Pré-Saint-Gervais (93) 59 F3
le Pré-Saint-Martin (28) 85 G6
Préaux (07) 222 A4
les Préaux (27) 34 C3
Préaux (36) 147 J3
Préaux (53) 105 H3
Préaux (76) 35 J1
Préaux-Bocage (14) 32 C6
Préaux-du-Perche (61) 83 J4
Préaux-Saint-Sébastien (14) . . . 55 F2
Prébois (38) 242 A2
Précey (50) 51 K4
Préchac (32) 267 H4
Préchac (33) 246 B2
Préchac (65) 304 D2
Préchac-sur-Adour (32) 266 B6
Préchacq-Josbaig (64) 283 K4
Préchacq-les-Bains (40) 264 C4
Préchacq-Navarrenx (64) 283 K4
Précieux (42) 204 D4
Précigné (72) 105 J5
Précilhon (64) 284 A5
Précorbin (50) 31 J4
Précy (18) 150 B3
Précy-le-Sec (89) 133 J2
Précy-Notre-Dame (10) 90 E3
Précy-Saint-Martin (10) 90 E3
Précy-sous-Thil (21) 134 D4
Précy-sur-Marne (77) 59 J2
Précy-sur-Oise (60) 37 K5
Précy-sur-Vrin (89) 112 D3
Prédefin (62) 5 G6
Préfailles (44) 122 A5
Préfontaines (45) 111 H1
Prégilbert (89) 133 H1
Préguillac (17) 195 G3
Préhy (89) 113 H6
Preignac (33) 229 K5
Preignan (32) 267 J5
Preigney (70) 117 H5
Preixan (11) 290 A6
Prémanon (39) 174 B4
Premeaux-Prissey (21) 154 B2
Prémery (58) 151 F2
Prémesques (59) 6 C4
Prémeyzel (01) 207 J2
Prémian (34) 291 G2
Premières (21) 136 C6
Prémierfait (10) 90 A2
Prémilhat (03) 183 K1
Prémillieu (01) 189 K6
Prémont (02) 12 C6
Prémontré (02) 20 C6
Prendeignes (46) 234 C4
Préneron (32) 266 E4
la Prénessaye (22) 77 H4
Prenois (21) 135 J4
Prénouvellon (41) 109 G3
Prénovel (39) 173 J3
Prény (54) 65 J1
Préporché (58) 152 A5
Prépotin (61) 55 H6
les Prés (26) 241 K6
Présailles (43) 238 D1
Préseau (59) 12 D2

Présentevillers (25) 139 G2
Préserville (31) 288 D2
Présilly (39) 173 G3
Présilly (74) 190 E3
Presle (73) 208 D5
Presles (14) 53 F3
Presles (38) 223 H4
Presles (95) 37 J6
Presles-en-Brie (77) 59 J5
Presles-et-Boves (02) 40 A2
Presles-et-Thierny (02) 40 B1
Presly (18) 130 E5
Presnoy (45) 111 G3
Pressac (86) 180 A3
Pressagny-l'Orgueilleux (27) . . . 36 B6
Pressiat (01) 172 E6
Pressignac (16) 198 A1
Pressignac-Vicq (24) 232 A1
Pressigny (52) 117 G5
Pressigny (79) 162 B1
Pressigny-les-Pins (45) 111 J4
Pressins (38) 207 J4
Pressy (62) 5 H6
Pressy-sous-Dondin (71) 171 G4
la Prétière (25) 139 F3
Pretin (39) 156 A4
Prétot-Sainte-Suzanne (50) 28 E6
Prétot-Vicquemare (76) 15 H4
Prêtreville (14) 33 K6
Préty (71) 172 A3
Pretz-en-Argonne (55) 64 A2
Preuilly (18) 148 E3
Preuilly-la-Ville (36) 164 B2
Preuilly-sur-Claise (37) 146 C5
Preures (62) 4 D5
Preuschdorf (67) 25 A2
Preuseville (76) 16 D2
Preutin-Higny (54) 26 D4
Preux-au-Bois (59) 12 E4
Preux-au-Sart (59) 12 E3
Préval (72) 83 J5
Prévelles (72) 83 G6
Prévenchères (48) 238 C6
Préveranges (18) 166 D5
Prévessin-Moëns (01) 190 E1
la Prévière (49) 104 A6
Prévillers (60) 17 J5
Prévinquières (12) 251 H2
Prévocourt (57) 66 C2
Prey (27) 56 D2
Prey (88) 95 F5
Preyssac-d'Excideuil (24) 214 E2
Prez (08) 21 K3
Prez-sous-Lafauche (52) 92 E4
Priaires (79) 177 J3
Priay (01) 189 H4
Priez (02) 39 H6
Prignac (17) 195 J1
Prignac-en-Médoc (33) 210 E1
Prignac-et-Marcamps (33) 211 J5
Prigonrieux (24) 231 H2
Primarette (38) 206 C6
Primelin (29) 73 B3
Primelles (18) 148 E5
Prin-Deyrançon (79) 177 J2
Prinçay (79) 145 F4
Princé (35) 80 C5
Pringy (51) 62 E4
Pringy (74) 191 F5
Pringy (77) 87 G2
Prinquiau (44) 122 C2
Prinsuéjols (48) 237 F4
Printzheim (67) 69 H6
Prisces (02) 21 F3
Prisches (59) 13 F5
Prissac (36) 164 E4
Prissé (71) 171 J6
Prissé-la-Charrière (79) 178 A3
Privas (07) 239 K3
Privezac (12) 251 H2
Prix-lès-Mézières (08) 22 D3
Priziac (56) 75 K5
Prizy (71) 170 D6
la Proiselière-et-Langle (70) . . . 118 E2
Proissans (24) 233 F1
Proisy (02) 20 E2
Proix (02) 20 C2
Projan (32) 265 K6
Promilhanes (46) 250 D2
Prompsat (63) 185 F5
Prondines (63) 201 K2
Pronleroy (60) 38 B1
Pronville (62) 11 G4
Propiac (26) 257 J3
Propières (69) 187 J2
Propriano (2A) 322 D2
Prosnes (51) 41 H5
Prouilly (51) 40 D3
Proupiary (31) 287 F6
Proussy (14) 53 H3
Prouvais (02) 40 E1
Prouville (80) 9 J4
Prouvy (59) 12 C2
Prouzel (80) 18 A3
Provenchère (25) 139 F5
Provenchère (70) 118 A5
Provenchères-lès-Darney (88) . . 93 J6
Provenchères-sur-Fave (88) 95 K3
Provency (89) 133 K3
Proverville (10) 91 G5
Proveysieux (38) 224 A2
Proville (59) 11 J4
Provin (59) 6 C5
Provins (77) 88 D1
Proviseux-et-Plesnoy (02) 40 E1
Proyart (80) 18 E2

Prudemanche (28) 56 D5
Prudhomat (46) 234 B1
Prugnanes (66) 309 G5
Prugny (10) 89 K5
Pruillé (49) 125 F2
Pruillé-le-Chétif (72) 106 D3
Pruillé-l'Éguillé (72) 107 G5
Pruines (12) 235 J6
Prunay (51) 41 G5
Prunay-Belleville (10) 89 H4
Prunay-Cassereau (41) 128 A1
Prunay-en-Yvelines (78) 85 K2
Prunay-le-Gillon (28) 85 H4
Prunay-le-Temple (78) 57 J3
Prunay-sur-Essonne (91) 86 E4
Prunelli-di-Casacconi (2B) 319 K3
Prunelli-di-Fiumorbo (2B) 321 H4
Prunet (07) 239 G5
Prunet (15) 235 H2
Prunet (31) 288 E1
Prunet-et-Belpuig (66) 314 E4
Prunières (05) 243 H5
Prunières (38) 242 B1
Prunières (48) 237 G2
Pruniers (36) 166 C1
Pruniers-en-Sologne (41) 129 H5
Pruno (2B) 319 J4
Prunoy (89) 112 C4
Prusly-sur-Ource (21) 115 G4
Prusy (10) 114 A3
Pruzilly (71) 188 B1
Puberg (67) 69 F5
Publier (74) 175 G5
Publy (39) 173 G2
Puceul (44) 103 G6
le Puch (09) 313 J2
Puch-d'Agenais (47) 247 H3
Puchay (27) 36 C3
Puchevillers (80) 10 B6
le Puech (34) 273 G5
Puéchabon (34) 273 K5
Puéchoursi (81) 289 G2
Puechredon (30) 274 D2
Puellemontier (52) 91 G2
Puessans (25) 138 C3
Puget (84) 277 K4
Puget-Rostang (06) 261 G6
Puget-sur-Argens (83) 299 G1
Puget-Théniers (06) 280 C1
Puget-Ville (83) 298 A4
Pugey (25) 156 D1
Pugieu (01) 207 J1
Puginier (11) 289 G3
Pugnac (33) 211 J4
Pugny (79) 161 G1
Pugny-Chatenod (73) 208 B2
Puichéric (11) 290 E5
le Puid (88) 95 J2
Puihardy (79) 161 G4
Puilacher (34) 292 D1
Puilaurens (11) 309 F5
Puilboreau (17) 176 D2
Puilly-et-Charbeaux (08) 23 J5
Puimichel (04) 278 D1
Puimisson (34) 292 A3
Puimoisson (04) 278 E2
la Puisaye (28) 84 B1
Puiseaux (45) 87 F6
Puiselet-le-Marais (91) 86 D3
Puisenval (76) 16 D2
le Puiset (28) 85 K6
le Puiset-Doré (49) 124 B6
Puiseux (08) 22 B5
Puiseux (28) 57 F6
Puiseux-en-Bray (60) 36 E2
Puiseux-en-France (95) 59 F1
Puiseux-en-Retz (02) 39 J5
Puiseux-le-Hauberger (60) 37 J5
Puiseux-Pontoise (95) 58 D1
Puisieulx (51) 41 F5
Puisieux (62) 10 E5
Puisieux (77) 59 K1
Puisieux-et-Clanlieu (02) 20 D2
Puissalicon (34) 292 A2
Puisseguin (33) 230 C1
Puisserguier (34) 291 J3
Puits (21) 114 E6
Puits-et-Nuisement (10) 90 E5
Puits-la-Vallée (60) 17 K6
Puivert (11) 308 D3
Pujaudran (32) 287 J2
Pujaut (30) 276 B1
Pujo (65) 285 H3
Pujo-le-Plan (40) 265 J3
les Pujols (09) 307 K5
Pujols (33) 230 C2
Pujols (47) 248 C2
Pujols-sur-Ciron (33) 229 K5
le Puley (71) 171 G2
Puligny-Montrachet (21) 153 K4
Pullay (27) 56 A5
Pulligny (54) 94 A1
Pulney (54) 93 K3
Pulnoy (54) 66 B5
Pulvérières (63) 184 D6
Pulversheim (68) 97 B1
Punchy (80) 19 F3
Punerot (88) 93 H2
Puntous (65) 286 B4
Pupillin (39) 155 K5
Pure (08) 23 H4
Purgerot (70) 117 K5
Pusey (70) 118 A6
Pusignan (69) 206 D2
Pussay (91) 86 B4
Pussigny (37) 145 J4

Pusy-et-Épenoux (70) 118 B6
Putanges-Pont-Écrepin (61) . . . 54 A4
Puteaux (92) 58 D3
Putot-en-Auge (14) 33 G4
Putot-en-Bessin (14) 32 C4
Puttelange-aux-Lacs (57) 68 C3
Puttelange-lès-Thionville (57) . . 27 H2
Puttigny (57) 66 D3
Puxe (54) 44 B5
Puxieux (54) 44 C6
le Puy (25) 138 C4
le Puy (33) 230 D4
Puy-d'Arnac (19) 216 B6
Puy-de-Serre (85) 161 F3
Puy-du-Lac (17) 177 H5
le Puy-en-Velay (43) 220 C5
Puy-Guillaume (63) 185 K5
Puy-l'Évêque (46) 232 E6
Puy-Malsignat (23) 183 G4
le Puy-Notre-Dame (49) 144 B2
Puy-Saint-André (05) 243 K1
Puy-Saint-Eusèbe (05) 243 H5
Puy-Saint-Gulmier (63) 201 J2
Puy-Saint-Martin (26) 240 D4
Puy-Saint-Pierre (05) 225 K6
Puy-Saint-Vincent (05) 243 J1
le Puy-Sainte-Réparade (13) . . . 277 H5
Puy-Sanières (05) 243 J5
Puybarban (33) 230 C5
Puybegon (81) 270 B4
Puybrun (46) 234 B1
Puycalvel (81) 270 D5
Puycasquier (32) 267 K4
Puycelci (81) 269 K1
Puycornet (82) 249 J5
Puydaniel (31) 288 B4
Puydarrieux (65) 286 A4
la Puye (86) 163 K2
Puygaillard-de-Lomagne (82) . . 268 B2
Puygaillard-de-Quercy (82) . . . 269 J1
Puygiron (26) 240 C6
Puygouzon (81) 270 E3
Puygros (73) 208 C4
Puyjourdes (46) 250 E2
Puylagarde (82) 250 E3
Puylaroque (82) 250 A3
Puylaurens (81) 289 H1
Puylausic (32) 287 G2
Puyloubier (13) 297 F1
Puymangou (24) 212 D3
Puymaurin (31) 286 E3
Puyméras (84) 257 H3
Puymiclan (47) 231 G6
Puymirol (47) 248 D5
Puymoyen (16) 196 E4
Puynormand (33) 212 D6
Puyol-Cazalet (40) 265 H6
Puyoô (64) 283 H1
Puyravault (17) 177 G3
Puyravault (85) 160 B5
Puyréaux (16) 179 G6
Puyrenier (24) 197 H5
Puyrolland (17) 177 J4
Puységur (32) 267 J4
Puysségur (31) 268 C1
Puysserampion (47) 231 G5
Puyvalador (66) 313 J3
Puyvert (84) 277 G4
Puzeaux (80) 19 F3
Puzieux (57) 66 C2
Puzieux (88) 94 A3
Py (66) 314 B4
la Pyle (27) 35 F5
Pys (80) 10 E5

Q

Quaëdypre (59) 3 J3
Quaix-en-Chartreuse (38) 224 A2
Quantilly (18) 149 H1
Quarante (34) 291 H4
Quarouble (59) 12 E1
Quarré-les-Tombes (89) 134 A5
la Quarte (70) 117 G5
le Quartier (63) 184 C3
Quasquara (2A) 320 E6
Quatre-Champs (08) 42 C1
les Quatre-Routes-du-Lot (46) . . 215 K6
Quatremare (27) 35 H5
Quatzenheim (67) 70 D3
Quéant (62) 11 G4
Queaux (86) 163 J6
Québriac (35) 79 F1
Quédillac (35) 78 C2
Queige (73) 209 G2
Quelaines-Saint-Gault (53) 104 E3
Quelmes (62) 5 F3
Quelneuc (56) 102 C2
Quéménéven (29) 74 D4
Quemigny-Poisot (21) 135 J6
Quemigny-sur-Seine (21) 135 G1
Quemper-Guézennec (22) 48 D3
Quemperven (22) 48 B3
Quend (80) 8 E2
Quenne (89) 113 G5
Quenoche (70) 138 A3
Quenza (2A) 323 F1
Quercamps (62) 4 C4
Quercitello (2B) 319 H4
Quérénaing (59) 12 C4
Quérigut (09) 313 J2
Quernes (62) 5 H4
Querqueville (50) 28 C2

Querré (49) 105 G6
Querrien (29) 99 J2
Querrieu (80) 18 C1
Quers (70) 118 D5
Quesmy (60) 19 H5
le Quesne (80) 17 G2
le Quesnel (80) 18 D3
le Quesnel-Aubry (60) 37 K1
le Quesnoy (59) 12 E3
le Quesnoy-en-Artois (62) 9 J2
Quesnoy-le-Montant (80) 8 E5
Quesnoy-sur-Airaines (80) 17 H1
Quesnoy-sur-Deûle (59) 6 D3
Quesques (62) 4 D3
Quessigny (27) 56 E2
Quessoy (22) 77 H1
Questembert (56) 101 J5
Questrecques (62) 4 C4
Quet-en-Beaumont (38) 242 C2
Quetigny (21) 136 B5
Quettehou (50) 29 F3
Quettetot (50) 28 C4
Quetteville (14) 34 A3
Quettreville-sur-Sienne (50) . . . 30 D5
Queudes (51) 61 H6
la Queue-en-Brie (94) 59 G4
la Queue-les-Yvelines (78) 57 J4
Rai (61) 55 H5
Raillencourt-Sainte-Olle (59) . . . 11 J3
Railleu (66) 313 K3
Raillicourt (08) 22 C5
Raillimont (02) 21 H4
Raimbeaucourt (59) 11 H1
Rainans (39) 155 G1
Raincheval (80) 10 B5
Raincourt (70) 117 J4
le Raincy (93) 59 G3
Rainfreville (76) 15 H3
Rainneville (80) 18 B1
Rainsars (59) 13 H5
Rainville (88) 93 H3
Rainvillers (60) 37 G2
les Rairies (49) 126 A1
Raismes (59) 12 C1
Raissac (09) 308 A3
Raissac-d'Aude (11) 291 G6
Raissac-sur-Lampy (11) 289 K5
Raival (55) 64 C3
Raix (16) 179 F5
Raizeux (78) 57 J6
Ramasse (01) 189 H2
Ramatuelle (83) 299 F4
Rambaud (05) 243 F5
Rambervillers (88) 95 F3
Rambluzin-et-Benoite-Vaux (55) . . 64 C1
Rambouillet (78) 57 K6
Rambucourt (55) 65 G3
Ramburelles (80) 17 F1
Rambures (80) 17 F1
Ramecourt (62) 10 A2
Ramecourt (88) 94 A4
Ramerupt (10) 90 C2
Ramicourt (02) 20 A1
Ramillies (59) 12 A4
Rammersmatt (68) 119 K4
Ramonchamp (88) 119 G3
Ramonville-Saint-Agne (31) . . . 288 C1
Ramoulu (45) 86 E6
Ramous (64) 283 H1
Ramousies (59) 13 H5
Ramouzens (32) 266 D3
Rampan (50) 31 G3
Rampieux (24) 232 B4
Rampillon (77) 88 B1
Rampoux (46) 233 G5
Rancé (01) 188 D5
Rancennes (08) 24 C1
Rances (10) 91 F2
Ranchal (69) 187 J3
Ranchot (39) 155 J1
Ranchy (14) 32 A4
Rancogne (16) 197 G3
Rancon (87) 181 G3
Rançonnières (52) 117 F3
Rancourt (80) 11 G6
Rancourt (88) 94 A4
Rancourt-sur-Ornain (55) 63 J3
Rancy (71) 172 B3
Randan (63) 185 H5
Randens (73) 208 E4
Randevillers (25) 138 E5
Randonnai (61) 55 J6
Rânes (61) 54 A6
Rang (25) 139 F3
Rang-du-Fliers (62) 8 E1
Rangecourt (52) 116 E2
Rangen (67) 70 C2
Ranguevaux (57) 44 E3
Rannée (35) 104 A3
Ranrupt (67) 70 A6
Rans (39) 155 J1
Ransart (62) 10 E4
Ranspach (68) 119 J3
Ranspach-le-Bas (68) 97 D4
Ranspach-le-Haut (68) 97 D4
Rantechaux (25) 157 F1
Rantigny (60) 38 A3
Ranton (86) 144 D3
Rantzwiller (68) 97 C3
Ranville (14) 33 F4
Ranville-Breuillaud (16) 178 D6
Ranzevelle (70) 117 K3
Ranzières (55) 64 D1
Raon-aux-Bois (88) 118 E1
Raon-lès-Leau (54) 95 K1

Rabou (05) 242 D5
Rabouillet (66) 314 B1
Racécourt (88) 94 B4
Rachecourt-sur-Marne (52) 92 A1
Rachecourt-Suzémont (52) 91 K2
Râches (59) 11 J1
Racines (10) 113 J2
la Racineuse (71) 154 D5
Racquinghem (62) 5 H3
Racrange (57) 68 C3
Raddon-et-Chapendu (70) 118 D4
Radenac (56) 101 G1
Radepont (27) 36 A3
Radinghem (62) 5 F5
Radinghem-en-Weppes (59) . . . 6 C4
Radon (61) 82 D2
Radonvilliers (10) 90 E4
Raedersdorf (68) 97 C6
Raedersheim (68) 96 B6
Raffetot (76) 14 E5
Rageade (15) 219 G5
Rahart (41) 108 C4
Rahay (72) 108 A3
Rahling (57) 69 F4
Rahon (25) 139 F4
Rahon (39) 155 G3
Rai (61) 55 H5
Raids (50) 31 F2
Raillencourt-Sainte-Olle (59) . . . 11 J3
Railleu (66) 313 K3
Raillicourt (08) 22 C5
Raillimont (02) 21 H4
Raimbeaucourt (59) 11 H1
Rainans (39) 155 G1
Raincheval (80) 10 B5
Raincourt (70) 117 J4
le Raincy (93) 59 G3
Rainfreville (76) 15 H3
Rainneville (80) 18 B1
Rainsars (59) 13 H5
Rainville (88) 93 H3
Rainvillers (60) 37 G2
les Rairies (49) 126 A1
Raismes (59) 12 C1
Raissac (09) 308 A3
Raissac-d'Aude (11) 291 G6
Raissac-sur-Lampy (11) 289 K5
Raival (55) 64 C3
Raix (16) 179 F5
Raizeux (78) 57 J6
Ramasse (01) 189 H2
Ramatuelle (83) 299 F4
Rambaud (05) 243 F5
Rambervillers (88) 95 F3
Rambluzin-et-Benoite-Vaux (55) . . 64 C1
Rambouillet (78) 57 K6
Rambucourt (55) 65 G3
Ramburelles (80) 17 F1
Rambures (80) 17 F1
Ramecourt (62) 10 A2
Ramecourt (88) 94 A4
Ramerupt (10) 90 C2
Ramicourt (02) 20 A1
Ramillies (59) 12 A4
Rammersmatt (68) 119 K4
Ramonchamp (88) 119 G3
Ramonville-Saint-Agne (31) . . . 288 C1
Ramoulu (45) 86 E6
Ramous (64) 283 H1
Ramousies (59) 13 H5
Ramouzens (32) 266 D3
Rampan (50) 31 G3
Rampieux (24) 232 B4
Rampillon (77) 88 B1
Rampoux (46) 233 G5
Rancé (01) 188 D5
Rancennes (08) 24 C1
Rances (10) 91 F2
Ranchal (69) 187 J3
Ranchot (39) 155 J1
Ranchy (14) 32 A4
Rancogne (16) 197 G3
Rancon (87) 181 G3
Rançonnières (52) 117 F3
Rancourt (80) 11 G6
Rancourt (88) 94 A4
Rancourt-sur-Ornain (55) 63 J3
Rancy (71) 172 B3
Randan (63) 185 H5
Randens (73) 208 E4
Randevillers (25) 138 E5
Randonnai (61) 55 J6
Rânes (61) 54 A6
Rang (25) 139 F3
Rang-du-Fliers (62) 8 E1
Rangecourt (52) 116 E2
Rangen (67) 70 C2
Ranguevaux (57) 44 E3
Rannée (35) 104 A3
Ranrupt (67) 70 A6
Rans (39) 155 J1
Ransart (62) 10 E4
Ranspach (68) 119 J3
Ranspach-le-Bas (68) 97 D4
Ranspach-le-Haut (68) 97 D4
Rantechaux (25) 157 F1
Rantigny (60) 38 A3
Ranton (86) 144 D3
Rantzwiller (68) 97 C3
Ranville (14) 33 F4
Ranville-Breuillaud (16) 178 D6
Ranzevelle (70) 117 K3
Ranzières (55) 64 D1
Raon-aux-Bois (88) 118 E1
Raon-lès-Leau (54) 95 K1

Raon-l'Étape (88) 95 G2
Raon-sur-Plaine (88) 95 K1
Rapaggio (2B) 319 H5
Rapale (2B) 319 G2
Rapey (88) 94 B4
Rapilly (14) 53 K3
Rapsécourt (51) 63 H1
Raray (60) 38 D4
Rarécourt (55) 43 F6
Rasiguères (66) 309 J5
Raslay (86) 144 D2
Rasteau (84) 257 G4
Ratenelle (71) 172 B3
Ratières (26) 222 D3
Ratte (71) 172 C2
Ratzwiller (67) 69 F4
Raucoules (43) 221 G3
Raucourt (54) 66 A2
Raucourt-au-Bois (59) 12 E3
Raucourt-et-Flaba (08) 23 F5
Raulhac (15) 235 K1
Rauret (43) 238 B2
Rauville-la-Bigot (50) 28 C4
Rauville-la-Place (50) 28 C5
Rauwiller (67) 67 K3
Rauzan (33) 230 B3
Raveau (58) 150 D1
Ravel (63) 203 G2
Ravenel (60) 38 B1
Ravenoville (50) 29 F5
Raves (88) 95 J4
Ravières (89) 114 C6
Ravigny (53) 82 B3
Raville (57) 45 J5
Raville-sur-Sânon (54) 66 C3
Ravilloles (39) 173 J5
la Ravoire (73) 208 C4
Ray-sur-Saône (70) 137 H2
Raye-sur-Authie (62) 9 H2
Rayet (47) 232 B4
Raymond (18) 149 K4
Rayol-Canadel-sur-Mer (83) . . . 301 H3
Rayssac (81) 271 G4
Razac-de-Saussignac (24) 231 F2
Razac-d'Eymet (24) 231 H4
Razac-sur-l'Isle (24) 213 K4
Raze (70) 137 K1
Razecueillé (31) 305 K3
Razengues (32) 268 C6
Razès (87) 181 H4
Razimet (47) 247 H1
Razines (37) 145 G4
Réal (66) 313 J3
Réalcamp (76) 16 E2
Réallon (05) 243 H4
Réalmont (81) 270 E4
Réalville (82) 250 A6
Réans (32) 266 C3
Réau (77) 87 H1
Réaumur (85) 160 E1
Réaup-Lisse (47) 247 H6
Réauville (26) 256 E1
Réaux (17) 195 J5
Rebais (77) 60 C3
Rebecques (62) 5 H4
Rébénacq (64) 284 C6
Rebergues (62) 4 D2
Rebets (76) 36 A1
Rebeuville (88) 93 G4
Rebigue (31) 288 C2
Rebourguil (12) 272 A3
Reboursin (36) 148 B2
Rebréchien (45) 110 B3
Rebreuve-Ranchicourt (62) 10 C1
Rebreuve-sur-Canche (62) 10 B3
Rebreuviette (62) 10 B3
Recanoz (39) 155 G6
Recey-sur-Ource (21) 115 G3
Réchésy (90) 97 A5
Réchicourt-la-Petite (54) 66 C4
Réchicourt-le-Château (57) . . . 67 G5
Récicourt (55) 43 F5
Réclainville (28) 85 J4
Reclesne (71) 152 E3
Reclinghem (62) 5 F5
Réclonville (54) 67 F6
Recloses (77) 87 H4
Recologne (25) 137 J5
Recologne (70) 137 H2
Recologne-lès-Rioz (70) 137 K3
Recoubeau-Jansac (26) 241 H4
Recoules-d'Aubrac (48) 236 D4
Recoules-de-Fumas (48) 237 G5
Recoules-Prévinquières (12) . . . 253 F3
Récourt (62) 11 H3
Récourt (52) 116 D2
Récourt-le-Creux (55) 64 C1
Recouvrance (90) 139 J1
le Recoux (48) 253 H3
Recques-sur-Course (62) 4 C5
Recques-sur-Hem (62) 2 E2
Recquignies (59) 13 H3
le Reculey (14) 52 E2
Reculfoz (25) 174 C1
Recurt (65) 286 B4
Recy (51) 62 C2
Rédange (57) 26 A3
Rédené (29) 99 J3
Redessan (30) 275 J3
Réding (57) 67 K4
Redon (35) 102 C4
la Redorte (11) 290 E5
Redortiers (04) 258 C5
Réez-Fosse-Martin (60) 38 E6
Reffannes (79) 162 A3

Reffroy (55) 64 D6
Reffuveille (50) 52 C5
Régades (31) 305 K2
Régat (09) 308 B3
Regnauville (62) 9 H2
Regnéville (88) 117 J2
Regnéville-sur-Mer (50) 30 D4
Regnéville-sur-Meuse (55) 43 H4
Regney (88) 94 C4
Régnié-Durette (69) 188 A3
Regnière-Écluse (80) 9 F3
Regniowez (08) 22 A1
Regny (02) 20 B3
Régny (42) 187 G5
la Regrippière (44) 142 C1
Réguiny (56) 101 F1
Réguisheim (68) 96 C6
Régusse (83) 279 F5
Rehaincourt (88) 94 D3
Rehainviller (54) 66 D6
Rehaupal (88) 95 G6
Reherrey (54) 95 G1
Réhon (54) 26 C2
Reichsfeld (67) 70 C6
Reichshoffen (67) 69 K4
Reichstett (67) 25 C4
Reignac (16) 196 A6
Reignac (33) 211 H3
Reignac-sur-Indre (37) 146 C1
Reignat (63) 203 F2
Reigneville-Bocage (50) 28 E5
Reignier (74) 191 G2
Reigny (18) 166 E3
Reilhac (15) 217 H6
Reilhac (46) 234 A4
Reilhaguet (46) 233 J3
Reilhanette (26) 258 A4
Reillanne (04) 278 A2
Reillon (54) 67 F6
Reilly (60) 36 E4
Reims (51) 41 F4
Reims-la-Brûlée (51) 63 G5
Reinhardsmunster (67) 70 B2
Reiningue (68) 97 B2
Reipertswiller (67) 69 H4
Reithouse (39) 173 G3
Réjaumont (32) 267 H3
Réjaumont (65) 286 B6
Rejet-de-Beaulieu (59) 12 E6
Relanges (88) 93 K6
Relans (39) 155 G6
le Relecq-Kerhuon (29) 46 A4
Relevant (01) 188 D3
Rely (62) 5 H5
Remaisnil (80) 10 A4
Rémalard (61) 83 K3
Remaucourt (02) 20 A2
Remaucourt (08) 21 J5
la Remaudière (44) 123 K4
Remaugies (80) 18 E5
Remauville (77) 87 J6
Rembercourt-Sommaisne (55) 64 B2
Rembercourt-sur-Mad (54) 65 H1
Rémécourt (60) 38 B2
Rémelfing (57) 45 J3
Rémeling (57) 68 D3
Rémeling (57) 27 K3
Remennecourt (55) 63 J4
Remenoville (54) 94 D2
Rémérangles (60) 37 J2
Réméréville (54) 66 C4
Rémering (57) 45 K3
Rémering-lès-Puttelange (57) 68 C3
Remicourt (51) 63 J2
Remicourt (88) 93 K4
Remiencourt (80) 18 B3
Remies (02) 20 C4
Remigny (02) 20 A4
Remigny (71) 153 K5
Rémilly (57) 45 H6
Rémilly (58) 152 A4
Remilly-Aillicourt (08) 23 F4
Remilly-en-Montagne (21) 135 H6
Remilly-les-Pothées (08) 22 B3
Remilly-sur-Lozon (50) 31 F2
Remilly-sur-Tille (21) 136 C5
Remilly-Wirquin (62) 5 F4
Réminiac (56) 102 A1
Remiremont (88) 118 E2
Remoiville (55) 43 H1
Remollon (05) 243 F6
Remomeix (88) 95 J4
Remoncourt (54) 67 F5
Remoncourt (88) 93 K5
Rémondans-Vaivre (25) 139 G4
Remoray-Boujeons (25) 156 E6
Remouillé (44) 142 A2
Remoulins (30) 275 J2
Removille (88) 93 H3
Rempnat (87) 200 B3
la Remuée (76) 14 D6
Remungol (56) 100 E2
Rémuzat (26) 257 K1
Remy (60) 38 C2
Rémy (62) 11 G3
Renac (35) 102 D3
Renage (38) 223 J1
Renaison (42) 186 D4
Renansart (02) 20 B4
Renaucourt (70) 137 H1
la Renaudie (63) 203 K2
la Renaudière (49) 142 D2
Renauvoid (88) 94 C6
Renay (41) 108 D5
Renazé (53) 104 C5
Rencurel (38) 223 J4

René (72) 82 E5
Renédale (25) 156 E3
Renescure (59) 5 H3
Renève (21) 136 E4
Réning (57) 68 B5
Rennemoulin (78) 58 B4
Rennepont (52) 91 J6
Rennes (35) 79 G4
Rennes-en-Grenouilles (53) 81 H2
Rennes-le-Château (11) 309 F3
Rennes-les-Bains (11) 309 F3
Rennes-sur-Loue (25) 156 A3
Renneval (02) 21 G4
Renneville (08) 21 H5
Renneville (27) 36 A2
Renneville (31) 288 E2
Renno (2A) 320 C1
le Renouard (61) 54 D2
Rentières (63) 218 E1
Renty (62) 4 E5
Renung (40) 265 J4
Renwez (08) 22 C2
la Réole (33) 230 C5
la Réorthe (85) 160 B2
Réotier (05) 243 K3
Repaix (54) 67 G5
la Répara-Auriples (26) 240 D4
Réparsac (16) 196 A2
Repel (88) 93 J3
Repentigny (14) 33 H4
Replonges (01) 188 D4
le Reposoir (74) 191 K4
les Repôts (39) 172 E2
Reppe (90) 119 K6
Requeil (72) 106 D5
Réquista (12) 271 H1
Résenlieu (61) 55 F4
la Résie-Saint-Martin (70) 137 F5
Résigny (02) 21 J4
Resson (55) 64 B4
Ressons-l'Abbaye (60) 37 H4
Ressons-le-Long (02) 39 G2
Ressons-sur-Matz (60) 19 F6
les Ressuintes (28) 84 B1
Restigné (37) 126 E6
Restinclières (34) 274 D5
le Retail (79) 161 H3
Rétaud (17) 195 F3
Reterre (23) 183 K4
Rethel (08) 41 J1
Retheuil (02) 39 F3
Rethondes (60) 39 F2
Rethonvillers (80) 19 G4
Réthoville (50) 29 F2
Retiers (35) 103 J1
Retjons (40) 246 C5
Retonfey (57) 45 G5
Rétonval (76) 16 E3
Retournac (43) 220 D3
Retschwiller (67) 25 B2
Rettel (57) 27 J3
Rety (62) 2 C4
Retzwiller (68) 97 A4
Reugney (25) 156 D3
Reugny (03) 167 H5
Reugny (37) 128 A3
Reuil (51) 40 D6
Reuil-en-Brie (77) 60 C2
Reuil-sur-Brêche (60) 37 J1
Reuilly (27) 35 J5
Reuilly (36) 148 D3
Reuilly-Sauvigny (02) 61 F1
Reulle-Vergy (21) 154 A1
Reumont (59) 12 C5
la Réunion (47) 247 G3
Reutenbourg (67) 70 C2
Reuves (51) 61 J4
Reuville (76) 15 H4
Reux (14) 33 J4
Réveillon (51) 60 E5
Réveillon (61) 83 H2
Revel (31) 289 H2
Revel (38) 224 C3
Revel-Tourdan (38) 222 D1
Revelles (80) 17 K2
Revens (30) 253 J6
Reventin-Vaugris (38) 206 A5
Revercourt (28) 56 C5
Revest-des-Brousses (04) 278 A1
Revest-du-Bion (04) 258 C5
le Revest-les-Eaux (83) 300 C3
Revest-les-Roches (06) 281 F1
Revest-Saint-Martin (04) 258 E6
Reviers (14) 32 D3
Revigny (39) 173 G2
Revigny-sur-Ornain (55) 63 K3
Réville (50) 29 G2
Réville-aux-Bois (55) 43 H2
Révillon (02) 40 C3
Revin (08) 22 C1
Revonnas (01) 189 H2
Rexingen (67) 68 E5
Rexpoëde (59) 3 J3
Reygade (19) 216 C6
Reynel (52) 92 C4
Reynès (66) 314 E5
Reyniès (82) 269 G2
Reyrevignes (46) 234 C5
Reyrieux (01) 188 C5
Reyssouze (01) 172 A5
Reyvroz (74) 175 G6
Rezay (18) 166 D2
Rezé (44) 123 G4
Rézentières (15) 218 C4
Rezonville (57) 44 D5

Rezza (2A) 320 D2
Rhèges (10) 90 A1
le Rheu (35) 79 F4
Rhinau (67) 71 D4
Rhodes (57) 67 H4
Rhodon (41) 108 D5
Rhuis (60) 38 C3
Ri (61) 54 B4
Ria-Sirach (66) 314 B3
Riaillé (44) 103 K6
le Rialet (81) 290 C1
Rians (18) 149 J1
Rians (83) 278 B6
Riantec (56) 100 A4
Riaucourt (52) 92 B6
Riaville (55) 44 A5
Ribagnac (24) 231 H3
Ribarrouy (64) 284 E1
Ribaute (11) 309 K1
Ribaute-les-Tavernes (30) 274 D1
le Ribay (53) 81 J3
Ribeaucourt (55) 92 C1
Ribeaucourt (80) 9 J5
Ribeauville (02) 12 D6
Ribeauvillé (68) 96 B2
Ribécourt-Dreslincourt (60) 38 E1
Ribécourt-la-Tour (59) 11 J5
Ribemont (02) 20 B3
Ribemont-sur-Ancre (80) 18 D1
Ribennes (48) 237 H5
Ribérac (24) 213 G3
Ribes (07) 239 F6
Ribeyret (05) 258 B1
Ribiers (05) 259 F3
Ribouisse (11) 289 G6
Riboux (83) 297 G4
la Ricamarie (42) 221 G1
Ricarville (76) 15 F5
Ricarville-du-Val (76) 16 B3
Ricaud (11) 289 G4
Ricaud (65) 285 K6
les Riceys (10) 114 D3
la Richardais (35) 50 D3
Richardménil (54) 66 A6
Richarville (91) 86 B2
la Riche (37) 127 J4
Riche (57) 66 E2
Richebourg (52) 116 A2
Richebourg (62) 6 B5
Richebourg (78) 57 H4
Richecourt (55) 65 G2
Richelieu (37) 145 G3
Richeling (57) 68 C4
Richemont (57) 45 F3
Richemont (76) 16 E3
Richerenches (84) 257 F2
Richeval (57) 67 H5
Richeville (27) 36 C4
Richtolsheim (67) 96 E2
Richwiller (68) 97 B2
Ricourt (32) 285 J2
Ricquebourg (60) 19 F6
Riec-sur-Belon (29) 99 G3
Riedisheim (68) 97 C2
Riedseltz (67) 25 C1
Riedwihr (68) 96 D3
Riel-les-Eaux (21) 115 G3
Riencourt (80) 17 J1
Riencourt-lès-Bapaume (62) 11 F5
Riencourt-lès-Cagnicourt (62) 11 G4
Riervescemont (90) 119 H5
Riespach (68) 97 C5
Rieucazé (31) 305 K1
Rieucros (09) 308 A1
Rieulay (59) 12 A1
Rieumajou (31) 289 F3
Rieumes (31) 287 J3
Rieupeyroux (12) 251 H3
Rieussec (34) 291 F3
Rieutort-de-Randon (48) 237 J5
Rieux (31) 287 K5
Rieux (51) 61 J4
Rieux (56) 102 B5
Rieux (60) 38 B4
Rieux (76) 16 E1
Rieux-de-Pelleport (09) 307 J2
Rieux-en-Cambrésis (59) 12 B4
Rieux-en-Val (11) 309 H1
Rieux-Minervois (11) 290 D5
Riez (04) 278 A3
Rigarda (66) 314 D3
Rigaud (06) 261 G6
Rignac (12) 251 J2
Rignac (46) 234 A3
Rigney (25) 138 B4
Rignieux-le-Franc (01) 189 G5
Rignosot (25) 138 B4
Rignovelle (70) 118 E5
Rigny (70) 137 G3
Rigny-la-Nonneuse (10) 89 G3
Rigny-la-Salle (55) 65 G6
Rigny-le-Ferron (10) 89 G6
Rigny-Saint-Martin (55) 65 G6
Rigny-sur-Arroux (71) 170 B4
Rigny-Ussé (37) 126 E6
Riguepeu (32) 267 F5
Rilhac-Lastours (87) 198 D4
Rilhac-Rancon (87) 181 H6
Rilhac-Treignac (19) 199 K5
Rilhac-Xaintrie (19) 217 F4
Rillans (25) 138 D3
Rillé (37) 126 E4
Rillieux-la-Pape (69) 206 B1
Rilly-la-Montagne (51) 41 F5
Rilly-Sainte-Syre (10) 89 K3
Rilly-sur-Aisne (08) 42 A1

Rilly-sur-Loire (41) 128 C4
Rilly-sur-Vienne (37) 145 J3
Rimaucourt (52) 92 C5
Rimbach-près-Guebwiller (68) 96 A6
Rimbach-près-Masevaux (68) 119 J4
Rimbachzell (68) 96 A6
Rimbez-et-Baudiets (40) 247 F6
Rimboval (62) 4 E6
Rimeize (48) 237 G3
Rimling (57) 69 F3
Rimogne (08) 22 B1
Rimon-et-Savel (26) 241 G4
Rimondeix (23) 183 F2
Rimons (33) 230 D5
Rimont (09) 307 F2
Rimou (35) 51 H6
Rimplas (06) 261 J5
Rimsdorf (67) 68 E5
Ringeldorf (67) 69 J6
Ringendorf (67) 69 J6
Rinxent (62) 2 B1
Riocaud (33) 231 F3
Riolas (31) 287 G4
Riols (34) 291 F2
le Riols (81) 250 E5
Riom (63) 185 F6
Riom-ès-Montagnes (15) 217 K2
Rioms (26) 258 B3
Rion-des-Landes (40) 264 C2
Rions (33) 229 K4
Riorges (42) 186 E4
Riotord (43) 221 H3
Rioux (17) 195 F3
Rioux-Martin (16) 212 D3
Rioz (70) 138 A3
Riquewihr (68) 96 B3
Ris (63) 185 K5
Ris (65) 305 F4
Ris-Orangis (91) 59 F6
Riscle (32) 266 B5
Risoul (05) 227 A4
Ristolas (05) 227 D2
Rittershoffen (67) 25 C3
Ritzing (57) 27 K3
Riupeyrous (64) 284 E3
Rivarennes (36) 165 F3
Rivarennes (37) 127 F6
Rivas (42) 204 E4
Rive-de-Gier (42) 205 J5
Rivecourt (60) 38 D3
Rivedoux-Plage (17) 158 D6
Rivehaute (64) 283 H3
Rivel (11) 308 E3
Riventosa (2B) 321 F1
Rivèrenert (09) 306 E3
Riverie (69) 205 J4
Rivery (80) 18 B2
les Rives (34) 273 F3
Rives (38) 223 J1
Rives (47) 232 A5
Rivesaltes (66) 310 B5
la Rivière (33) 229 K1
Rivière (37) 145 G2
la Rivière (38) 223 J2
la Rivière-de-Corps (10) 90 A5
la Rivière-Drugeon (25) 156 D5
la Rivière-Enverse (74) 192 A3
Rivière-les-Fosses (52) 136 C1
Rivière-Saas-et-Gourby (40) 264 A5
la Rivière-Saint-Sauveur (14) 34 A2
Rivière-sur-Tarn (12) 253 H5
Rivières (16) 197 G2
Rivières (30) 255 J4
Rivières (81) 270 C2
les Rivières-Henruel (51) 63 F6
Rivières-le-Bois (52) 116 E5
Riville (76) 14 E4
Rivolet (69) 188 A5
Rix (39) 156 C6
Rix (58) 133 F4
Rixheim (68) 97 C2
la Rixouse (39) 173 K4
Rizaucourt-Buchey (52) 91 J5
Roaillan (33) 230 A6
Roaix (84) 257 G4
Roanne (42) 187 F4
Roannes-Saint-Mary (15) 235 H2
Robécourt (88) 93 G6
Robecq (62) 5 K4
Robersart (59) 12 E4
Robert-Espagne (55) 63 K4
Robert-Magny-Laneuville-
 à-Rémy (52) 91 J2
Robertot (76) 15 G4
Roberval (60) 38 C4
Robiac-Rochessadoule (30) 255 H3
la Robine-sur-Galabre (04) 259 J4
Robion (84) 276 E3
le Roc (46) 233 H2
le Roc-Saint-André (56) 101 J4
Rocamadour (46) 233 K3
Rocbaron (83) 298 A4
Rocé (41) 108 D5
Roche (38) 206 E4
Roche (42) 204 C4

la Roche-Derrien (22) 48 B3
la Roche-des-Arnauds (05) 242 D5
Roche-en-Brenil (21) 134 C5
Roche-en-Régnier (43) 220 C3
Roche-et-Raucourt (70) 137 G1
la Roche-Guyon (95) 36 C5
la Roche-Molière (42) 205 F6
la Roche-l'Abeille (87) 198 E4
la Roche-le-Peyroux (19) 217 G1
la Roche-lès-Clerval (25) 138 D5
la Roche-lez-Beaupré (25) 138 B5
la Roche-Mabile (61) 82 B2
la Roche-Maurice (29) 46 C5
la Roche-Morey (70) 117 G6
la Roche-Noire (63) 202 E3
la Roche-Posay (86) 146 B6
la Roche-Rigault (86) 145 F1
Roche-Saint-Secret-
 Béconne (26) 257 G1
la Roche-sur-Foron (74) 191 H3
la Roche-sur-Grane (26) 240 D4
la Roche-sur-le-Buis (26) 257 K3
Roche-sur-Linotte-et-
 Sorans-les-Cordiers (70) 138 B3
la Roche-sur-Yon (85) 159 H1
la Roche-Vanneau (21) 135 F3
la Roche-Vineuse (71) 171 J6
Rochebaudin (26) 240 E5
la Rochebeaucourt-et-
 Argentine (24) 197 G5
Rochebrune (05) 243 F6
Rochebrune (26) 257 J2
Rochechinard (26) 223 F5
Rochechouart (87) 198 A1
Rochecolombe (07) 239 H6
Rochecorbon (37) 127 K4
Rochefort (17) 177 F5
Rochefort (73) 207 K4
Rochefort-du-Gard (30) 276 A1
Rochefort-en-Terre (56) 101 K5
Rochefort-en-Valdaine (26) 240 C6
Rochefort-en-Yvelines (78) 86 B1
Rochefort-Montagne (63) 202 A3
Rochefort-Samson (26) 222 E6
Rochefort-sur-Brévon (21) 115 H6
Rochefort-sur-la-Côte (52) 92 B5
Rochefort-sur-Loire (49) 125 F5
Rochefort-sur-Nenon (39) 155 H2
la Rochefoucauld (16) 197 G2
Rochefourchat (26) 241 G5
la Rochegiron (04) 258 D5
Rochegude (26) 256 E4
Rochegude (30) 255 J4
Rochejean (25) 156 E6
la Rochelle (17) 176 D2
la Rochelle (70) 117 G5
la Rochelle-Normande (50) 51 J2
Rochemaure (07) 240 A5
la Rochénard (79) 177 J2
Rochepaule (07) 221 H5
la Rochepot (21) 153 J4
Rocher (07) 239 G5
le Rochereau (86) 162 D1
Roches (23) 182 E1
Roches (41) 109 F5
Roches-Bettaincourt (52) 92 C4
les Roches-de-Condrieu (38) 206 A6
les Roches-Blamont (25) 139 H3
les Roches-l'Évêque (41) 108 A5
Roches-Prémarie-Andillé (86) 163 F4
Roches-sur-Marne (52) 63 K6
Rocheservière (85) 141 J4
Rochessauve (07) 239 K4
Rochesson (88) 119 G1
Rochetaillée (52) 116 B4
Rochetaillée-sur-Saône (69) 206 A1
Rochetoirin (38) 207 G4
Rochetrejoux (85) 142 D6
la Rochette (04) 280 C1
la Rochette (05) 243 F4
la Rochette (07) 239 F1
la Rochette (16) 197 F1
la Rochette (73) 208 D5
la Rochette (77) 87 H2
la Rochette-du-Buis (26) 258 A3
Rocheville (50) 28 D4
Rochonvillers (57) 27 F3
Rochy-Condé (60) 37 H2
Rocles (03) 168 B5
Rocles (07) 239 F5
Rocles (48) 238 B4
Roclincourt (62) 10 E2
Rocourt (88) 117 G1
Rocourt-Saint-Martin (02) 39 K5
Rocquancourt (14) 32 E6
la Rocque (14) 53 G3
Rocquefort (76) 15 G5
Rocquemont (60) 38 D4
Rocquemont (76) 16 B5
Rocquencourt (60) 18 C5
Rocquencourt (78) 58 C4
Rocques (14) 33 K4
Rocquigny (02) 13 H6
Rocquigny (08) 21 J4
Rocquigny (62) 11 G5
Rocroi (08) 22 B1
Rodalbe (57) 68 A5
Rodelinghem (62) 2 D4
Rodelle (12) 252 C1
Rodemack (57) 27 H3
Roderen (68) 119 K4
Rodern (68) 96 C2
Rodès (66) 314 D2
Rodez (12) 252 B3
Rodilhan (30) 275 H3
Rodome (11) 308 D5

la Roë (53) 104 B3
Rœllecourt (62) 10 B2
Rœschwoog (67) 25 D3
Rœulx (59) 12 B2
Rœux (62) 11 F2
Roézé-sur-Sarthe (72) 106 C4
Roffey (89) 113 K4
Roffiac (15) 218 D5
Rogécourt (02) 20 B5
Rogerville (76) 34 A1
Rogéville (54) 65 J3
Roggenhouse (68) 96 D6
Rogliano (2B) 317 D2
Rogna (39) 173 J6
Rognac (13) 296 D5
Rognaix (73) 209 G3
Rognes (13) 277 H5
Rognon (25) 138 C3
Rognonas (13) 276 B2
Rogny (02) 20 E3
Rogny-les-Sept-Écluses (89) 111 K6
Rogues (30) 273 J4
Rogy (80) 18 A4
Rohaire (28) 56 A6
Rohan (56) 77 F6
Rohr (67) 70 D2
Rohrbach-lès-Bitche (57) 69 F3
Rohrwiller (67) 25 B4
Roiffé (86) 144 D2
Roiffieux (07) 221 K3
Roiglise (80) 19 H4
Roilly (21) 134 D4
Roinville (28) 85 J3
Roinville (91) 86 B2
Roinvilliers (91) 86 D4
Roisel (80) 19 J1
les Roises (55) 93 F2
Roisey (42) 221 K1
Roissard (38) 241 K1
Roissy-en-Brie (77) 59 H4
Roissy-en-France (95) 59 G2
Roiville (61) 54 E3
Roizy (08) 41 G2
Rolampont (52) 116 C3
Rolbing (57) 69 G2
Rollainville (88) 93 G3
Rollancourt (62) 9 J1
Rolleboise (78) 57 H1
Rolleville (76) 14 B5
Rollot (80) 18 E6
Rom (79) 179 G1
Romagnat (63) 202 D3
la Romagne (08) 21 K4
Romagne (33) 230 B3
Romagné (35) 80 A3
la Romagne (49) 142 D2
Romagne (86) 179 H1
Romagne-sous-les-Côtes (55) 43 J3
Romagne-sous-Montfaucon (55) 42 E3
Romagnieu (38) 207 J4
Romagny (50) 52 D6
Romagny (68) 139 K1
Romagny-sous-Rougemont (90) 119 J5
Romain (25) 138 D3
Romain (39) 137 H6
Romain (51) 40 C3
Romain (54) 94 C1
Romain-aux-Bois (88) 117 G1
Romain-sur-Meuse (52) 92 E6
Romainville (93) 59 F3
Roman (27) 56 C3
Romanèche-Thorins (71) 188 B2
Romange (39) 155 H1
Romans (01) 188 E3
Romans (79) 161 K6
Romans-sur-Isère (26) 222 D5
Romanswiller (67) 70 C2
Romazières (17) 178 D5
Romazy (35) 79 J1
Rombach-le-Franc (68) 96 B1
Rombas (57) 44 E3
Rombies-et-Marchipont (59) 12 E2
Rombly (62) 5 H4
Romegoux (17) 177 G6
Romelfing (57) 67 J3
Romenay (71) 172 B4
Romeny-sur-Marne (02) 60 D2
Romeries (59) 12 D4
Romery (02) 20 E2
Romery (51) 40 E6
Romescamps (60) 17 G4
Romestaing (47) 247 F2
Romeyer (26) 241 H2
la Romieu (32) 267 H1
Romigny (51) 40 C5
Romiguières (34) 273 F4
Romillé (35) 78 E3
Romilly (41) 108 C3
Romilly-la-Puthenaye (27) 56 A1
Romilly-sur-Aigre (28) 108 E3
Romilly-sur-Andelle (27) 35 K3
Romilly-sur-Seine (10) 89 H2
Romont (88) 94 E3
Romorantin-Lanthenay (41) 129 J5
Rompon (07) 240 B3
Rônai (61) 54 B4
Roncenay (10) 90 A6
le Roncenay-Authenay (27) 56 C3
Roncey (50) 31 F5
Ronchamp (70) 119 F5
Ronchaux (25) 156 A2
Ronchères (02) 40 B5
Ronchères (89) 132 C1
Roncherolles-en-Bray (76) 16 D5
Roncherolles-sur-le-Vivier (76) 35 J1
Ronchin (59) 6 E4

Ronchois (76) 16 E4
Roncourt (57) 44 D4
Roncq (59) 6 E2
la Ronde (17) 160 D6
la Ronde-Haye (50) 30 E3
Rondefontaine (25) 156 D6
Ronel (81) 270 E4
Ronfeugerai (61) 53 H4
Rongères (03) 185 J1
Ronnet (03) 184 B2
Ronno (69) 187 J3
Ronquerolles (95) 37 J5
Ronsenac (16) 197 F5
Ronssoy (80) 19 J1
Rontalon (69) 205 J3
Rontignon (64) 284 D4
Ronvaux (55) 43 K5
Roost-Warendin (59) 11 H1
Roppe (90) 119 J6
Roppenheim (67) 25 D3
Roppentzwiller (68) 97 C5
Roppeviller (57) 69 H2
la Roque-Alric (84) 257 G5
la Roque-Baignard (14) 33 J5
la Roque-d'Anthéron (13) 277 G4
la Roque-Esclapon (83) 280 A4
la Roque-Gageac (24) 232 E2
la Roque-Sainte-Marguerite (12) 253 J5
la Roque-sur-Cèze (30) 256 B4
la Roque-sur-Pernes (84) 276 E1
la Rouaudière (53) 104 A4
Roquebillière (06) 311 A3
Roquebrun (34) 291 J2
Roquebrune (32) 267 F5
Roquebrune (33) 230 D5
Roquebrune-Cap-Martin (06) 281 J3
Roquebrune-sur-Argens (83) 299 F2
la Roquebrussanne (83) 297 J3
Roquecor (82) 248 E3
Roquecourbe (81) 271 F6
Roquecourbe-Minervois (11) 290 E5
Roquedur (30) 273 K2
Roquefère (11) 290 B3
Roquefeuil (11) 308 C5
Roquefixade (09) 307 K3
Roquefort (32) 267 J4
Roquefort (40) 246 B6
Roquefort (47) 248 B5
Roquefort-de-Sault (11) 313 K1
Roquefort-des-Corbières (11) 310 C3
Roquefort-la-Bédoule (13) 296 E4
Roquefort-les-Cascades (09) 307 K3
Roquefort-les-Pins (06) 280 E4
Roquefort-sur-Garonne (31) 287 G6
Roquefort-sur-Soulzon (12) 272 C2
Roquelaure (32) 267 H5
Roquelaure-Saint-Aubin (32) 268 C5
Roquemaure (30) 256 E6
Roquemaure (81) 269 J4
Roquepine (32) 267 G2
Roqueredonde (34) 273 F4
Roques (31) 288 D2
Roques (32) 267 F3
Roquesérière (31) 269 J5
Roquessels (34) 292 A1
Roquesteron (06) 280 E2
Roquestéron-Grasse (06) 280 E2
Roquetaillade (11) 308 E2
la Roquette (27) 36 A4
la Roquette-sur-Siagne (06) 280 D5
la Roquette-sur-Var (06) 281 F2
Roquettes (31) 288 D2
Roquevaire (13) 296 E3
Roquevidal (81) 270 B6
Roquiague (64) 283 H5
la Roquille (33) 231 F3
Rorbach-lès-Dieuze (57) 67 G3
Rorschwihr (68) 96 C3
Rosans (05) 258 B2
Rosay (39) 173 F3
Rosay (76) 16 B4
Rosay (78) 57 J3
Rosay-sur-Lieure (27) 36 B3
Rosazia (2A) 320 C2
Rosbruck (57) 68 B2
Roscanvel (29) 72 C5
Roscoff (29) 47 F2
Rosel (14) 32 D4
Rosenau (68) 97 E3
Rosenwiller (67) 70 C4
Roset-Fluans (25) 155 K1
Rosey (70) 137 K2
Rosey (71) 171 H1
Rosheim (67) 70 C4
la Rosière (70) 119 F3
Rosières (07) 255 J1
Rosières (43) 220 D4
Rosières (60) 38 D5
Rosières (81) 270 E1
Rosières-aux-Salines (54) 66 C6
Rosières-en-Haye (54) 65 J3
Rosières-en-Santerre (80) 18 E3
Rosières-près-Troyes (10) 90 B5
Rosières-sur-Barbèche (25) 139 G5
Rosières-sur-Mance (70) 117 H4
Rosiers-de-Juillac (19) 215 G2
Rosiers-d'Égletons (19) 216 D1
les Rosiers-sur-Loire (49) 125 K5
Rosis (34) 272 D6
Rosnay (36) 164 D2
Rosnay (51) 40 D4
Rosnay (85) 159 J3
Rosnay-l'Hôpital (10) 90 E2
Rosnoën (29) 74 C2
Rosny-sous-Bois (93) 59 F3
Rosny-sur-Seine (78) 57 H2

Rosoy (60) 38 B3
Rosoy-en-Multien (60) 39 F6
Rosoy-le-Vieil (45) 112 A1
Rospez (22) 48 A3
Rospigliani (2B) 321 G1
Rosporden (29) 99 F2
Rosselange (57) 44 E3
Rossfeld (67) 70 E6
Rossillon (01) 207 J1
Rosteig (67) 69 G5
Rostrenen (22) 76 A3
Rosult (59) 7 G6
Rosureux (25) 139 G6
Rotalier (39) 173 F3
Rotangy (60) 17 J6
Rothau (67) 70 A5
Rothbach (67) 69 H5
Rotherens (73) 208 D5
la Rothière (10) 91 F4
Rothois (60) 17 H6
Rothonay (39) 173 G3
les Rotours (61) 54 A4
Rots (14) 32 D4
Rott (67) 25 B1
Rottelsheim (67) 25 A4
Rottier (26) 241 H6
Rou-Marson (49) 126 A6
Rouairoux (81) 290 D2
Rouans (44) 122 D4
Roubaix (59) 6 E3
Roubia (11) 291 F5
Roubion (06) 261 H5
Roucamps (14) 53 G1
Roucourt (59) 11 J2
Roucy (02) 40 D3
Roudouallec (56) 75 G4
Rouécourt (52) 92 A4
Rouède (31) 306 B2
Rouellé (61) 53 F6
Rouelles (52) 116 A5
Rouen (76) 35 H2
Rouessé-Fontaine (72) 82 D4
Rouessé-Vassé (72) 82 A6
Rouet (34) 274 B4
Rouez (72) 82 B6
Rouffach (68) 96 B5
Rouffange (39) 137 G6
Rouffiac (15) 216 E6
Rouffiac (16) 212 E2
Rouffiac (17) 195 H3
Rouffiac (81) 270 D3
Rouffiac-d'Aude (11) 309 F1
Rouffiac-des-Corbières (11) 309 J4
Rouffiac-Tolosan (31) 269 H5
Rouffignac (17) 211 J1
Rouffignac-de-Sigoulès (24) 231 H3
Rouffignac-Saint-Cernin-de-Reilhac (24) 214 D5
Rouffigny (50) 52 A3
Rouffilhac (46) 233 H3
Rouffy (51) 62 B2
Rougé (44) 103 J3
la Rouge (61) 83 J5
Rouge-Perriers (27) 35 F5
Rougefay (62) 9 K3
Rougegoutte (90) 119 H5
Rougemont (21) 134 C1
Rougemont (25) 138 D3
Rougemont-le-Château (90) 119 J5
Rougemontiers (27) 34 E3
Rougemontot (25) 138 C4
Rougeou (41) 129 G5
Rougeries (02) 20 E3
les Rouges-Eaux (88) 95 G4
le Rouget (15) 235 F2
Rougeux (52) 117 F4
Rougiers (83) 297 H3
Rougnac (16) 197 G5
Rougnat (23) 183 K4
Rougon (04) 279 H3
Rouhe (25) 156 B2
Rouhling (57) 68 C2
Rouillac (16) 196 C2
Rouillac (22) 77 K3
Rouillé (86) 162 C5
Rouillon (72) 106 D2
Rouilly (77) 88 D1
Rouilly-Sacey (10) 90 C4
Rouilly-Saint-Loup (10) 90 B5
Roujan (34) 292 B2
Roulans (25) 138 C5
le Roulier (88) 95 F5
Roullée (72) 83 F2
Roullens (11) 290 A6
Roullet-Saint-Estèphe (16) 196 D4
Roullours (14) 52 A3
Roumagne (47) 231 G5
Roumare (76) 35 G1
Roumazières-Loubert (16) 180 A6
Roumégoux (15) 235 F2
Roumégoux (81) 271 F4
Roumengoux (09) 308 B2
Roumens (31) 289 G2
Roumoules (04) 279 F3
Rountzenheim (67) 25 C4
Roupeldange (57) 45 H4
Rouperroux (61) 82 B1
Rouperroux-le-Coquet (72) 83 G5
Roupy (02) 19 J3
la Rouquette (12) 251 F3
Roure (06) 261 H5
le Rouret (06) 280 E4
Rousies (59) 13 H3
Roussac (87) 181 G4
Roussas (26) 256 E1

Roussay (49) 142 D2
Roussayrolles (81) 250 D6
Rousseloy (60) 37 K4
Roussennac (12) 251 J1
Roussent (62) 9 F2
les Rousses (39) 174 B4
Rousses (48) 254 B4
Rousset (05) 243 G6
Rousset (13) 297 F1
le Rousset (71) 171 F3
Rousset-les-Vignes (26) 257 F2
la Roussière (27) 55 H2
Roussieux (26) 258 B2
Roussillon (38) 222 B1
Roussillon (84) 277 F3
Roussillon-en-Morvan (71) 152 D3
Roussines (16) 197 J2
Roussines (36) 165 F5
Rousson (30) 255 H4
Rousson (89) 112 D1
Roussy-le-Village (57) 27 G3
Routelle (25) 156 A1
Routes (76) 15 G4
Routier (11) 308 D1
Routot (27) 34 E2
Rouvenac (11) 308 E3
Rouves (14) 54 D1
Rouvignies (59) 12 C2
la Rouvière (30) 275 G2
Rouville (60) 38 E5
Rouville (76) 14 E5
Rouvillers (60) 38 C2
Rouvray (21) 134 B4
Rouvray (27) 57 F1
Rouvray (89) 113 H4
Rouvray-Catillon (76) 16 D6
Rouvray-Saint-Denis (28) 86 A5
Rouvray-Saint-Florentin (28) 85 H5
Rouvray-Sainte-Croix (45) 109 J2
Rouvrel (80) 18 C3
Rouvres (14) 54 D1
Rouvres (28) 57 G4
Rouvres (77) 59 H1
Rouvres-en-Multien (60) 39 F6
Rouvres-en-Plaine (21) 136 B6
Rouvres-en-Woëvre (55) 44 A3
Rouvres-en-Xaintois (88) 93 K4
Rouvres-la-Chétive (88) 93 G4
Rouvres-les-Bois (36) 147 K3
Rouvres-les-Vignes (10) 91 H5
Rouvres-Saint-Jean (45) 86 D4
Rouvres-sous-Meilly (21) 153 H1
Rouvrois-sur-Meuse (55) 64 E2
Rouvrois-sur-Othain (55) 43 K2
Rouvroy (02) 20 A2
Rouvroy (62) 11 G1
Rouvroy-en-Santerre (80) 18 E3
Rouvroy-les-Merles (60) 18 B5
Rouvroy-Ripont (51) 42 B4
Rouvroy-sur-Audry (08) 22 B3
Rouvroy-sur-Marne (52) 92 B4
Rouvroy-sur-Serre (02) 21 J4
le Roux (07) 238 E4
Rouxeville (50) 31 J3
la Rouxière (14) 124 B3
Rouxmesnil-Bouteilles (76) 15 K2
Rouy (58) 151 H3
Rouy-le-Grand (80) 19 G3
Rouy-le-Petit (80) 19 G3
Rouze (09) 313 J1
Rouziers (15) 235 F3
Rouziers-de-Touraine (37) 127 J3
le Rove (13) 296 B3
Roville-aux-Chênes (88) 94 E3
Roville-devant-Bayon (54) 94 B2
Rovon (38) 223 H3
Roy-Boissy (60) 17 H6
Royan (17) 194 C3
Royas (38) 206 D5
Royat (63) 202 D2
Royaucourt (60) 18 D5
Royaucourt-et-Chailvet (02) 40 A1
Royaumeix (54) 65 H4
Roybon (38) 223 F2
Roye (70) 118 E6
Roye (80) 19 F4
Roye-sur-Matz (60) 19 F6
Royer (71) 171 J2
Royère-de-Vassivière (23) 200 B1
Royères (87) 199 G1
Roynac (26) 240 D4
Royon (62) 4 E6
Royville (76) 15 J3
Roz-Landrieux (35) 51 F4
Roz-sur-Couesnon (35) 51 H4
Rozay-en-Brie (77) 60 A6
le Rozel (50) 28 A4
Rozelieures (54) 94 D2
Rozérieulles (57) 44 E5
Rozerotte (88) 93 K5
Rozès (32) 267 G4
Rozet-Saint-Albin (02) 39 J5
le Rozier (48) 253 H5
Rozier-Côtes-d'Aurec (42) 220 B6
Rozier-en-Donzy (42) 205 F1
Rozières-en-Beauce (45) 109 J3
Rozières-sur-Crise (02) 39 J3
Rozières-sur-Mouzon (88) 93 G6
Roziers-Saint-Georges (87) 199 H3
Rozoy-Bellevalle (02) 60 E3
Rozoy-sur-Serre (02) 21 J4
Ruages (58) 133 H5
Ruan (45) 110 A1
Ruan-sur-Egvonne (41) 108 D2

Ruaudin (72) 106 E3
Rubécourt-et-Lamécourt (08) 23 F4
Rubelles (77) 87 H1
Rubempré (80) 10 B6
Rubercy (14) 31 K1
Rubescourt (80) 18 D5
Rubigny (08) 21 J4
Rubrouck (59) 3 H4
Ruca (22) 50 A4
Ruch (33) 230 C3
Rucqueville (14) 32 C4
Rudeau-Ladosse (24) 197 H5
Rudelle (46) 234 C4
Rue (80) 8 B3
la Rue-Saint-Pierre (60) 37 J2
la Rue-Saint-Pierre (76) 16 B6
Ruederbach (68) 97 B5
Rueil-la-Gadelière (28) 56 B5
Rueil-Malmaison (92) 58 D3
Ruelisheim (68) 97 C1
Ruelle-sur-Touvre (16) 196 E3
les Rues-des-Vignes (59) 11 K5
Ruesnes (59) 12 D3
Rueyres (46) 234 B3
Ruffec (16) 179 G4
Ruffec (36) 164 D3
Ruffey-le-Château (25) 137 H5
Ruffey-lès-Beaune (21) 154 B3
Ruffey-lès-Echirey (21) 136 B4
Ruffey-sur-Seille (39) 173 F1
Ruffiac (47) 247 F2
Ruffiac (56) 102 A2
Ruffieu (01) 190 A4
Ruffieux (73) 190 C6
Rufigné (44) 103 H3
Rugles (27) 55 K4
Rugney (88) 94 B3
Rugny (89) 114 B4
Ruhans (70) 138 B3
Ruillé-en-Champagne (72) 106 B2
Ruillé-Froid-Fonds (53) 105 F3
Ruillé-le-Gravelais (53) 104 D1
Ruillé-sur-Loir (72) 107 H6
Ruisseauville (62) 5 F6
Ruitz (62) 5 H6
Rullac-Saint-Cirq (12) 252 A5
Rully (14) 53 F3
Rully (60) 38 C4
Rully (71) 153 K5
Rumaucourt (62) 11 H3
Rumegies (59) 7 G6
Rumersheim-le-Haut (68) 97 D1
Rumesnil (14) 33 H5
Rumigny (08) 21 J3
Rumigny (80) 18 A3
Rumilly (62) 4 E5
Rumilly (74) 190 D6
Rumilly-en-Cambrésis (59) 11 J5
Rumilly-lès-Vaudes (10) 114 C1
Ruminghem (62) 3 F4
Rumont (55) 64 C3
Rumont (77) 87 F5
Runan (22) 48 C3
Rungis (94) 58 E5
Ruoms (07) 255 H1
Rupéreux (77) 60 D6
Ruppes (88) 93 G2
Rupt (52) 92 B3
Rupt-aux-Nonains (55) 64 A5
Rupt-devant-Saint-Mihiel (55) 64 D3
Rupt-en-Woëvre (55) 43 J6
Rupt-sur-Moselle (88) 119 F3
Rupt-sur-Othain (55) 43 J2
Rupt-sur-Saône (70) 137 J1
Rurange-lès-Thionville (57) 45 F3
Rurey (25) 156 B2
Rusio (2B) 319 G5
Russ (67) 70 B4
Russange (57) 26 E3
le Russey (25) 157 J1
Russy (14) 32 A3
Russy-Bémont (60) 39 F4
Rustenhart (68) 96 D5
Rustiques (11) 290 C5
Rustrel (84) 277 J2
Rustroff (57) 27 J3
Rutali (2B) 319 H2
Ruvigny (10) 90 C5
Ruy (38) 207 F4
Ruyaulcourt (62) 11 H5
Ruynes-en-Margeride (15) 219 G3
Ry (76) 36 A1
Rye (39) 155 G5
Ryes (14) 32 C3

S

Saâcy-sur-Marne (77) 60 C2
Saales (67) 95 K3
Saâne-Saint-Just (76) 15 J3
Saasenheim (67) 96 C3
Sabadel-Latronquière (46) 234 D4
Sabadel-Lauzès (46) 233 K6
Sabaillan (32) 287 F2
Sabalos (65) 285 J4
Sabarros (65) 286 B5
Sabazan (32) 266 C5
Sablé-sur-Sarthe (72) 105 J4
les Sables-d'Olonne (85) 158 C3
Sablet (84) 257 G6
Sablières (07) 238 C6
Sablonceaux (17) 194 D2

Sablonnières (77) 60 D3
Sablons (33) 212 B5
Sablons (38) 222 B2
Sabonnères (31) 287 H2
la Sabotterie (08) 22 C6
Sabran (30) 256 B5
Sabres (40) 245 H5
Saccourville (31) 305 H5
Sacé (53) 81 F6
Sacey (50) 51 J5
Saché (37) 127 H6
Sachin (62) 5 H6
Sachy (08) 23 G4
Sacierges-Saint-Martin (36) 165 F4
Saclas (91) 86 C4
Saclay (91) 58 C5
Saconin-et-Breuil (02) 39 H3
Sacoué (65) 305 H2
le Sacq (27) 56 C3
Sacquenay (21) 136 D2
Sacquenville (27) 35 H6
Sacy (51) 40 E5
Sacy (89) 133 J1
Sacy-le-Grand (60) 38 B3
Sacy-le-Petit (60) 38 C3
Sadeillan (32) 286 A3
Sadillac (24) 231 H5
Sadirac (33) 229 J3
Sadournin (65) 286 B4
Sadroc (19) 215 G3
Saessolsheim (67) 70 D2
Saffais (54) 66 C6
Saffloz (39) 173 J2
Saffré (44) 103 G6
Saffres (21) 135 G5
Sagelat (24) 232 D3
Sagnat (23) 182 B1
Sagnes-et-Goudoulet (07) 239 F3
Sagonne (18) 150 A6
Sagy (71) 172 D3
Sagy (95) 58 A1
Sahorre (66) 314 B4
Sahune (26) 257 J1
Sahurs (76) 35 G3
Sai (61) 54 C5
Saignes (15) 217 H2
Saignes (46) 234 B3
Saigneville (80) 9 F4
Saignon (84) 277 H2
Saiguède (31) 287 J1
Sail-les-Bains (42) 186 C2
Sail-sous-Couzan (42) 204 C2
Sailhan (65) 305 H5
Saillac (19) 215 K5
Saillac (46) 250 D3
Saillagouse (66) 313 H5
Saillans (26) 241 F4
Saillans (33) 212 A6
Saillant (63) 204 B6
Saillat-sur-Vienne (87) 180 C6
Saillenard (71) 172 E1
Sailly (08) 23 H5
Sailly (52) 92 C3
Sailly (71) 171 G4
Sailly (78) 57 K1
Sailly-Achâtel (57) 66 B2
Sailly-au-Bois (62) 10 D5
Sailly-en-Ostrevent (62) 11 G3
Sailly-Flibeaucourt (80) 9 F4
Sailly-Labourse (62) 6 A6
Sailly-Laurette (80) 18 D2
Sailly-le-Sec (80) 18 D1
Sailly-lez-Cambrai (59) 11 J4
Sailly-lez-Lannoy (59) 7 F4
Sailly-Saillisel (80) 11 G6
Sailly-sur-la-Lys (62) 6 B4
Sain-Bel (69) 205 J1
Saincaize-Meauce (58) 150 D5
Sainghin-en-Mélantois (59) 6 E5
Sainghin-en-Weppes (59) 6 C5
Sainneville (76) 14 C6
Sainpuits (89) 132 D3
Sains (35) 51 H4
Sains-du-Nord (59) 13 H5
Sains-en-Amiénois (80) 18 B3
Sains-en-Gohelle (62) 6 A6
Sains-lès-Fressin (62) 4 E6
Sains-lès-Marquion (62) 11 H4
Sains-lès-Pernes (62) 5 H6
Sains-Morainvillers (60) 18 C6
Sains-Richaumont (02) 20 D3
le Saint (56) 75 J5
Saint-Abit (64) 284 D5
Saint-Abraham (56) 101 J3
Saint-Acheul (80) 9 K4
Saint-Adjutory (16) 197 H2
Saint-Adrien (22) 48 C6
Saint-Affrique (12) 272 B2
Saint-Affrique-les-
  -Montagnes (81) 289 K1
Saint-Agathon (22) 48 D5
Saint-Agil (41) 108 B2
Saint-Agnan (02) 61 G1
Saint-Agnan (58) 134 B5
Saint-Agnan (71) 169 H4
Saint-Agnan (81) 269 K5
Saint-Agnan (89) 88 B5
Saint-Agnan-de-Cernières (27) . . . 55 H2
Saint-Agnan-en-Vercors (26) . . . 223 H6
Saint-Agnan-le-Malherbe (14) . . . 32 C4
Saint-Agnan-sur-Erre (61) 83 K4
Saint-Agnan-sur-Sarthe (61) 55 G6
Saint-Agnant (17) 177 F6
Saint-Agnant-de-Versillat (23) . . . 181 K1
Saint-Agnant-près-Crocq (23) . . . 201 F2
Saint-Agne (24) 231 K2

Saint-Agnet (40) 265 J6
Saint-Agnin-sur-Bion (38) 206 E4
Saint-Agoulin (63) 185 F4
Saint-Agrève (07) 221 H6
Saint-Aignan (08) 22 E5
Saint-Aignan (33) 212 A6
Saint-Aignan (41) 129 F6
Saint-Aignan (56) 76 D4
Saint-Aignan (72) 83 F5
Saint-Aignan (82) 268 D1
Saint-Aignan-de-Couptrain (53) . . 81 K2
Saint-Aignan-de-Cramesnil (14) . . 33 F6
Saint-Aignan-des-Gués (45) 110 E5
Saint-Aignan-des-Noyers (18) . . . 167 K1
Saint-Aignan-Grandlieu (44) 123 F5
Saint-Aignan-le-Jaillard (45) 111 F6
Saint-Aignan-sur-Roë (53) 104 B4
Saint-Aignan-sur-Ry (76) 36 A1
Saint-Aigny (36) 164 C2
Saint-Aigulin (17) 212 D4
Saint-Ail (54) 44 D4
Saint-Albain (71) 171 K5
Saint-Alban (01) 189 J3
Saint-Alban (22) 49 J5
Saint-Alban (31) 269 G5
Saint-Alban-Auriolles (07) 255 J1
Saint-Alban-d'Ay (07) 221 K3
Saint-Alban-de-Montbel (73) 208 A4
Saint-Alban-de-Roche (38) 206 E4
Saint-Alban-des-Hurtières (73) . . 209 F5
Saint-Alban-des-Villards (73) . . . 225 F1
Saint-Alban-du-Rhône (38) 206 A6
Saint-Alban-en-Montagne (07) . . . 238 C4
Saint-Alban-les-Eaux (42) 186 D5
Saint-Alban-Leysse (73) 208 C4
Saint-Alban-sur-Limagnole (48) . . 237 H3
Saint-Albin-de-Vaulserre (38) . . . 207 K5
Saint-Alexandre (30) 256 A6
Saint-Algis (02) 20 E2
Saint-Allouestre (56) 101 G2
Saint-Alpinien (23) 183 G5
Saint-Alyre-d'Arlanc (63) 219 K1
Saint-Alyre-ès-Montagne (63) . . . 218 D1
Saint-Amadou (09) 307 K1
Saint-Amancet (81) 289 J2
Saint-Amand (23) 183 G5
Saint-Amand (50) 31 J4
Saint-Amand (62) 10 C4
Saint-Amand-de-Belvès (24) 232 D3
Saint-Amand-de-Coly (24) 215 F5
Saint-Amand-de-Vergt (24) 214 A6
Saint-Amand-des-
  -Hautes-Terres (27) 35 G4
Saint-Amand-en-Puisaye (58) . . . 132 B3
Saint-Amand-Jartoudeix (23) 182 B6
Saint-Amand-le-Petit (87) 200 A2
Saint-Amand-les-Eaux (59) 7 H4
Saint-Amand-Longpré (41) 128 B1
Saint-Amand-Magnazeix (87) 181 J3
Saint-Amand-Montrond (18) 167 G2
Saint-Amand-sur-Fion (51) 63 F4
Saint-Amand-sur-Ornain (55) 64 D6
Saint-Amand-sur-Sèvre (79) 143 F5
Saint-Amandin (15) 218 A2
Saint-Amans (09) 288 C6
Saint-Amans (11) 289 G5
Saint-Amans (48) 237 H4
Saint-Amans-de-Pellagal (82) . . . 249 G4
Saint-Amans-des-Cots (12) 235 K4
Saint-Amans-du-Pech (82) 248 E3
Saint-Amans-Soult (81) 290 C2
Saint-Amans-Valtoret (81) 290 C2
Saint-Amant (16) 212 E1
Saint-Amant-de-Boixe (16) 196 E1
Saint-Amant-de-Bonnieure (16) . . 197 F1
Saint-Amant-de-Nouère (16) 196 C2
Saint-Amant-Roche-Savine (63) . . 203 J4
Saint-Amant-Tallende (63) 202 D3
Saint-Amarin (68) 119 K3
Saint-Ambreuil (71) 171 K2
Saint-Ambroix (18) 148 D5
Saint-Ambroix (30) 255 H4
Saint-Amé (88) 119 F1
Saint-Amour (39) 172 E5
Saint-Amour-Bellevue (71) 188 B1
Saint-Andelain (58) 132 A6
Saint-Andéol (26) 241 G2
Saint-Andéol (38) 223 J6
Saint-Andéol-de-Berg (07) 239 J6
Saint-Andéol-de-
  -Clerguemort (48) 255 F3
Saint-Andéol-de-Fourchades (07) . . 239 G2
Saint-Andéol-de-Vals (07) 239 H4
Saint-Andéol-le-Château (69) . . . 205 K4
Saint-Andeux (21) 134 B4
Saint-Andiol (13) 276 C3
Saint-André (31) 287 F5
Saint-André (32) 287 F1
Saint-André (66) 315 H4
Saint-André (73) 225 K2
Saint-André (81) 271 H2
Saint-André-Capcèze (48) 255 F2
Saint-André-d'Allas (24) 232 E2
Saint-André-d'Apchon (42) 186 D4
Saint-André-de-Bâgé (01) 188 D1
Saint-André-de-Boëge (74) 191 H2
Saint-André-de-Bohon (50) 31 F2
Saint-André-de-Briouze (61) 53 K5
Saint-André-de-Buèges (34) 273 K3
Saint-André-de-Chalencon (43) . . 220 D2
Saint-André-de-Corcy (01) 188 D5
Saint-André-de-Cruzières (07) . . . 255 J3
Saint-André-de-Cubzac (33) 211 J6
Saint-André-de-Double (24) 213 G4
Saint-André-de-la-Marche (49) . . . 142 D2
Saint-André-de-la-Roche (06) . . . 281 G3

Saint-André-de-Lancize (48) 254 E4
Saint-André-de-l'Épine (50) 31 J3
Saint-André-de-l'Eure (27) 56 C3
Saint-André-de-Lidon (17) 195 F4
Saint-André-de-Majencoules (30) . . 273 K1
Saint-André-de-Messei (61) 53 H5
Saint-André-de-Najac (12) 251 G5
Saint-André-de-
  -Roquelongue (11) 310 B1
Saint-André-de-
  -Roquepertuis (30) 256 A4
Saint-André-de-Rosans (05) 258 B2
Saint-André-de-Sangonis (34) . . . 273 H6
Saint-André-de-Seignanx (40) . . . 262 C6
Saint-André-de-Valborgne (30) . . 254 C5
Saint-André-de-Vézines (12) 253 J3
Saint-André-d'Embrun (05) 243 K4
Saint-André-des-Eaux (22) 78 D1
Saint-André-des-Eaux (44) 121 K4
Saint-André-d'Hébertot (14) 34 A3
Saint-André-d'Huiriat (01) 188 D2
Saint-André-d'Olérargues (30) . . . 256 B5
Saint-André-du-Bois (33) 230 B5
Saint-André-en-Barrois (55) 64 B1
Saint-André-en-Bresse (71) 172 B2
Saint-André-en-Morvan (58) 133 J4
Saint-André-en-Royans (38) 223 G4
Saint-André-en-Terre-Plaine (89) . . 134 B3
Saint-André-en-Vivarais (07) 221 H4
Saint-André-et-Appelles (33) 231 F2
Saint-André-Farivillers (60) 18 A6
Saint-André-Goule-d'Oie (85) . . . 142 B5
Saint-André-la-Côte (69) 205 J3
Saint-André-Lachamp (07) 239 F6
Saint-André-le-Bouchoux (01) . . . 188 E3
Saint-André-le-Coq (63) 185 H5
Saint-André-le-Désert (71) 171 G4
Saint-André-le-Gaz (38) 207 H4
Saint-André-le-Puy (42) 205 F3
Saint-André-les-Alpes (04) 279 J1
Saint-André-les-Vergers (10) 90 A5
Saint-André-lez-Lille (59) 6 D4
Saint-André-sur-Cailly (76) 16 B6
Saint-André-sur-Orne (14) 32 E5
Saint-André-sur-Sèvre (79) 143 G6
Saint-André-sur-Vieux-Jonc (01) . . 189 F2
Saint-André-Treize-Voies (85) . . . 141 K4
Saint-Androny (33) 211 G3
Saint-Ange-et-Torçay (28) 56 D6
Saint-Ange-le-Viel (77) 87 K5
Saint-Angeau (16) 197 F1
Saint-Angel (03) 167 J6
Saint-Angel (19) 200 E5
Saint-Angel (63) 184 D5
Saint-Anthème (63) 204 B5
Saint-Anthot (21) 135 G5
Saint-Antoine (15) 235 G3
Saint-Antoine (25) 157 F6
Saint-Antoine (32) 268 A1
Saint-Antoine (33) 211 J5
Saint-Antoine-Cumond (24) 213 F2
Saint-Antoine-d'Auberoche (24) . . 214 C4
Saint-Antoine-de-Breuilh (24) . . . 230 E2
Saint-Antoine-de-Ficalba (47) . . . 248 C3
Saint-Antoine-du-Queyret (33) . . . 230 D3
Saint-Antoine-du-Rocher (37) . . . 127 H3
Saint-Antoine-la-Forêt (76) 14 E6
Saint-Antoine-l'Abbaye (38) 223 F3
Saint-Antoine-sur-l'Isle (33) 212 D5
Saint-Antonin (06) 280 D1
Saint-Antonin (32) 268 A5
Saint-Antonin-de-Lacalm (81) . . . 271 F4
Saint-Antonin-de-Sommaire (27) . . 55 H2
Saint-Antonin-du-Var (83) 298 B1
Saint-Antonin-Noble-Val (82) . . . 250 D5
Saint-Antonin-sur-Bayon (13) . . . 296 E1
Saint-Aoustrille (36) 148 C5
Saint-Août (36) 166 B1
Saint-Apollinaire (05) 243 H5
Saint-Apollinaire (21) 136 B5
Saint-Apollinaire-de-Rias (07) . . . 239 K1
Saint-Appolinaire (69) 187 J5
Saint-Appolinard (38) 223 F3
Saint-Appolinard (42) 221 K1
Saint-Aquilin (24) 213 J3
Saint-Aquilin-de-Corbion (61) 55 H6
Saint-Aquilin-de-Pacy (27) 57 F1
Saint-Araille (31) 287 H1
Saint-Arailles (32) 267 F6
Saint-Arcons-d'Allier (43) 219 J5
Saint-Arcons-de-Barges (43) 238 C2
Saint-Arey (38) 242 B1
Saint-Armel (35) 79 G5
Saint-Armel (56) 121 F1
Saint-Armou (64) 284 D3
Saint-Arnac (66) 309 H5
Saint-Arnoult (14) 33 J3
Saint-Arnoult (41) 108 A6
Saint-Arnoult (60) 17 G5
Saint-Arnoult (76) 15 F6
Saint-Arnoult-des-Bois (28) 84 E2
Saint-Arnoult-en-Yvelines (78) . . . 86 A1
Saint-Arroman (32) 286 C2
Saint-Arroman (65) 305 F2
Saint-Arroumex (82) 268 C1
Saint-Astier (24) 213 J4
Saint-Astier (47) 231 F3
Saint-Auban (06) 280 B2
Saint-Auban-d'Oze (05) 242 C6
Saint-Auban-sur-l'Ouvèze (26) . . . 258 A3
Saint-Aubert (59) 12 C4
Saint-Aubert-sur-Orne (61) 53 K4
Saint-Aubin (02) 39 H1
Saint-Aubin (10) 89 F2
Saint-Aubin (21) 153 J4
Saint-Aubin (36) 148 D6

Saint-Aubin (39) 155 F3
Saint-Aubin (40) 264 E4
Saint-Aubin (47) 248 E1
Saint-Aubin (59) 13 G4
Saint-Aubin (62) 4 B6
Saint-Aubin (91) 58 C5
Saint-Aubin-Celloville (76) 35 J3
Saint-Aubin-Château-Neuf (89) . . 112 D5
Saint-Aubin-d'Appenai (61) 83 F1
Saint-Aubin-d'Arquenay (14) 33 F4
Saint-Aubin-d'Aubigné (35) 79 G2
Saint-Aubin-de-Blaye (33) 211 H2
Saint-Aubin-de-Bonneval (61) 55 G2
Saint-Aubin-de-Branne (33) 230 B2
Saint-Aubin-de-Cadelech (24) . . . 231 H4
Saint-Aubin-de-Courteraie (61) . . . 55 G6
Saint-Aubin-de-Crétot (76) 15 F6
Saint-Aubin-de-Lanquais (24) . . . 231 J3
Saint-Aubin-de-Locquenay (72) . . . 82 C5
Saint-Aubin-de-Luigné (49) 125 F5
Saint-Aubin-de-Médoc (33) 229 F1
Saint-Aubin-de-Nabirat (24) 233 F4
Saint-Aubin-de-Scellon (27) 34 C5
Saint-Aubin-de-Terregatte (50) . . . 52 A6
Saint-Aubin-d'Écrosville (27) 35 G4
Saint-Aubin-des-Bois (14) 52 C3
Saint-Aubin-des-Bois (28) 85 F2
Saint-Aubin-des-Châteaux (44) . . 103 H3
Saint-Aubin-des-Chaumes (58) . . 133 H4
Saint-Aubin-des-Coudrais (72) . . . 83 H6
Saint-Aubin-des-Grois (61) 83 J4
Saint-Aubin-des-Hayes (27) 55 J1
Saint-Aubin-des-Landes (35) 79 K4
Saint-Aubin-des-Ormeaux (85) . . 142 D3
Saint-Aubin-des-Préaux (50) 51 J1
Saint-Aubin-du-Cormier (35) 79 J2
Saint-Aubin-du-Désert (53) 82 A4
Saint-Aubin-du-Pavail (35) 79 J5
Saint-Aubin-du-Perron (50) 30 E3
Saint-Aubin-du-Plain (79) 143 J4
Saint-Aubin-du-Thenney (27) 55 H1
Saint-Aubin-en-Bray (60) 37 F2
Saint-Aubin-en-Charollais (71) . . . 170 D4
Saint-Aubin-Épinay (76) 35 J2
Saint-Aubin-Fosse-Louvain (53) . . . 80 E2
Saint-Aubin-la-Plaine (85) 160 B4
Saint-Aubin-le-Cauf (76) 16 A2
Saint-Aubin-le-Cloud (79) 161 J2
Saint-Aubin-le-Dépeint (37) 127 F1
Saint-Aubin-le-Guichard (27) 55 J1
Saint-Aubin-le-Monial (03) 168 B4
Saint-Aubin-le-Vertueux (27) 55 J1
Saint-Aubin-lès-Elbeuf (76) 35 H4
Saint-Aubin-les-Forges (58) 150 E2
Saint-Aubin-Montenoy (80) 17 J2
Saint-Aubin-Rivière (80) 17 G2
Saint-Aubin-Routot (76) 14 C6
Saint-Aubin-sous-Erquery (60) . . . 38 C3
Saint-Aubin-sur-Aire (55) 64 D5
Saint-Aubin-sur-Gaillon (27) 36 A5
Saint-Aubin-sur-Loire (71) 169 J3
Saint-Aubin-sur-Mer (14) 32 E3
Saint-Aubin-sur-Mer (76) 15 K2
Saint-Aubin-sur-Quillebeuf (27) . . . 34 C1
Saint-Aubin-sur-Scie (76) 15 K2
Saint-Aubin-sur-Yonne (89) 112 E3
Saint-Augustin (17) 194 B3
Saint-Augustin (19) 200 B6
Saint-Augustin (77) 60 B4
Saint-Augustin-des-Bois (49) . . . 124 E3
Saint-Aulaire (19) 215 G3
Saint-Aulais-la-Chapelle (16) . . . 196 C6
Saint-Aulaye (24) 212 E3
Saint-Aunès (34) 274 C6
Saint-Aunix-Lengros (32) 266 C6
Saint-Aupre (38) 207 K6
Saint-Austremoine (43) 219 G4
Saint-Auvent (87) 198 C1
Saint-Avaugourd-des-
  -Landes (85) 159 H3
Saint-Avé (56) 101 F5
Saint-Aventin (31) 305 H5
Saint-Avertin (37) 127 J5
Saint-Avit (16) 212 D3
Saint-Avit (26) 222 D3
Saint-Avit (40) 265 H2
Saint-Avit (41) 108 B1
Saint-Avit (47) 231 F5
Saint-Avit (63) 201 H1
Saint-Avit (81) 289 J2
Saint-Avit-de-Soulège (33) 230 E2
Saint-Avit-de-Tardes (23) 183 H6
Saint-Avit-de-Vialard (24) 232 B1
Saint-Avit-Frandat (32) 267 J1
Saint-Avit-le-Pauvre (23) 183 F5
Saint-Avit-les-Guespières (28) . . . 84 E5
Saint-Avit-Rivière (24) 232 C3
Saint-Avit-Saint-Nazaire (33) . . . 231 F2
Saint-Avit-Sénieur (24) 232 B3
Saint-Avold (57) 68 A3
Saint-Avre (73) 225 G1
Saint-Ay (45) 109 J4
Saint-Aybert (59) 7 K6
Saint-Babel (63) 203 F4
Saint-Baldoph (73) 208 C4
Saint-Bandry (02) 39 H3
Saint-Baraing (39) 155 G3
Saint-Barbant (87) 180 D3
Saint-Bard (23) 183 J6
Saint-Bardoux (26) 222 D4
Saint-Barnabé (22) 77 G5
Saint-Barthélemy (38) 222 E1
Saint-Barthélemy (40) 282 D1
Saint-Barthélemy (50) 52 D5
Saint-Barthélemy (56) 100 D2
Saint-Barthélemy (70) 119 F5

Saint-Barthélemy (77) 60 E4
Saint-Barthélemy-d'Agenais (47) . . 231 G6
Saint-Barthélemy-d'Anjou (49) . . . 125 H3
Saint-Barthélemy-de-
  -Bellegarde (24) 213 F5
Saint-Barthélemy-de-
  -Bussière (24) 198 A4
Saint-Barthélemy-de-
  -Séchilienne (38) 224 B5
Saint-Barthélemy-de-Vals (26) . . 222 C3
Saint-Barthélemy-Grozon (07) . . . 221 K6
Saint-Barthélemy-le-Meil (07) . . . 239 J1
Saint-Barthélemy-le-Plain (07) . . . 222 B5
Saint-Barthélemy-Lestra (42) . . . 205 F2
Saint-Basile (07) 221 K6
Saint-Baslemont (88) 93 K6
Saint-Baudel (18) 148 E6
Saint-Baudelle (53) 81 G4
Saint-Baudille-de-la-Tour (38) . . . 207 F1
Saint-Baudille-et-Pipet (38) 242 B2
Saint-Bauld (37) 146 B1
Saint-Baussant (54) 65 G2
Saint-Bauzeil (09) 307 H1
Saint-Bauzély (30) 275 F2
Saint-Bauzile (07) 240 A4
Saint-Bauzile (48) 254 B1
Saint-Bauzille-de-la-Sylve (34) . . 273 J6
Saint-Bauzille-de-Montmel (34) . . 274 C4
Saint-Bauzille-de-Putois (34) . . . 274 A3
Saint-Bazile (87) 198 A2
Saint-Bazile-de-la-Roche (19) . . . 216 A5
Saint-Bazile-de-Meyssac (19) . . . 216 A5
Saint-Béat (31) 305 J3
Saint-Beaulize (12) 272 E3
Saint-Beauzeil (82) 248 E3
Saint-Beauzély (12) 253 F5
Saint-Beauzile (81) 270 A1
Saint-Beauzire (43) 219 F2
Saint-Beauzire (63) 202 E1
Saint-Bénézet (30) 274 E1
Saint-Bénigne (01) 172 A5
Saint-Benin (59) 12 D5
Saint-Benin-d'Azy (58) 151 G4
Saint-Benin-des-Bois (58) 151 G2
Saint-Benoist-sur-Mer (85) 159 J5
Saint-Benoist-sur-Vanne (10) 89 H5
Saint-Benoît (01) 207 J2
Saint-Benoît (04) 260 E6
Saint-Benoît (11) 308 D2
Saint-Benoît (86) 163 F3
Saint-Benoît-de-Carmaux (81) . . . 270 D1
Saint-Benoît-des-Ombres (27) . . . 34 D4
Saint-Benoît-des-Ondes (35) 50 E3
Saint-Benoît-d'Hébertot (14) 34 A3
Saint-Benoît-du-Sault (36) 165 F5
Saint-Benoit-en-Diois (26) 241 G4
Saint-Benoît-la-Chipotte (88) 95 G3
Saint-Benoît-la-Forêt (37) 145 G1
Saint-Benoît-sur-Loire (45) 110 E5
Saint-Benoît-sur-Seine (10) 90 A4
Saint-Bérain (43) 219 K5
Saint-Berain-sous-
  -Sanvignes (71) 170 D2
Saint-Bérain-sur-Dheune (71) . . . 153 J6
Saint-Bernard (01) 188 B5
Saint-Bernard (21) 154 C1
Saint-Bernard (38) 224 C1
Saint-Bernard (68) 97 B3
Saint-Béron (73) 207 K5
Saint-Berthevin (53) 104 E1
Saint-Berthevin-la-Tannière (53) . . . 80 D3
Saint-Bertrand-de-
  -Comminges (31) 305 H2
Saint-Biez-en-Belin (72) 106 E5
Saint-Bihy (22) 76 E2
Saint-Blaise (06) 281 G2
Saint-Blaise (74) 190 E3
Saint-Blaise-du-Buis (38) 223 J1
Saint-Blaise-la-Roche (67) 70 A6
Saint-Blancard (32) 286 D4
Saint-Blimont (80) 8 D5
Saint-Blin (52) 92 D5
Saint-Boès (64) 283 J1
Saint-Bohaire (41) 128 E1
Saint-Boil (71) 171 H2
Saint-Boingt (54) 94 D2
Saint-Bois (01) 207 J2
Saint-Bomer (28) 84 A6
Saint-Bômer-les-Forges (61) 53 G6
Saint-Bon (51) 61 F6
Saint-Bon-Tarentaise (73) 209 J5
Saint-Bonnet (16) 196 B5
Saint-Bonnet-Avalouze (19) 216 B3
Saint-Bonnet-Briance (87) 199 H3
Saint-Bonnet-de-Bellac (87) 180 E3
Saint-Bonnet-de-Chavagne (38) . . 223 F4
Saint-Bonnet-de-Chirac (48) 237 G6
Saint-Bonnet-de-Condat (15) . . . 218 B2
Saint-Bonnet-de-Cray (71) 187 F2
Saint-Bonnet-de-Four (03) 184 D1
Saint-Bonnet-de-Joux (71) 171 F4
Saint-Bonnet-de-Montauroux (48) . . 238 A2
Saint-Bonnet-de-Mure (69) 206 C3
Saint-Bonnet-de-Rochefort (03) . . 185 F3
Saint-Bonnet-de-
  -Salendrinque (30) 274 B1
Saint-Bonnet-de-Salers (15) 217 H4
Saint-Bonnet-de-Valclérieux (26) . . 222 E3
Saint-Bonnet-de-
  -Vieille-Vigne (71) 170 D4
Saint-Bonnet-des-Bruyères (69) . . 187 J1
Saint-Bonnet-des-Quarts (42) . . . 186 C3
Saint-Bonnet-du-Gard (30) 275 J2
Saint-Bonnet-Elvert (19) 216 C4
Saint-Bonnet-en-Bresse (71) 154 D5
Saint-Bonnet-en-Champsaur (05) . . 242 E3

393

394

Saint-Bonnet-la-Rivière (19) 215 G2
Saint-Bonnet-le-Bourg (63). 203 J6
Saint-Bonnet-le-Chastel (63) 203 J6
Saint-Bonnet-le-Château (42) 204 D6
Saint-Bonnet-le-Courreau (42) 204 B3
Saint-Bonnet-le-Froid (43) 221 H4
Saint-Bonnet-le-Troncy (69) 187 J4
Saint-Bonnet-l'Enfantier (19) 215 J2
Saint-Bonnet-lès-Allier (63). 205 E2
Saint-Bonnet-les-Oules (42) 205 F5
Saint-Bonnet-les-
-Tours-de-Merle (19). 216 D5
Saint-Bonnet-près-Bort (19). 201 G5
Saint-Bonnet-près-Orcival (63). . . . 202 B3
Saint-Bonnet-près-Riom (63) 185 F6
Saint-Bonnet-sur-Gironde (17) 211 G1
Saint-Bonnet-Tronçais (03) 167 J2
Saint-Bonnot (58). 151 F1
Saint-Bouize (18) 131 K6
Saint-Brancher (89) 134 A4
Saint-Branchs (37) 146 B1
Saint-Brandan (22) 77 F2
Saint-Brès (30) 255 H3
Saint-Brès (32) 267 K4
Saint-Brès (34) 274 D5
Saint-Bresson (30) 273 K2
Saint-Bresson (70) 118 E3
Saint-Bressou (46) 234 C4
Saint-Brevin-les-Pins (44) 122 B3
Saint-Briac-sur-Mer (35). 50 C3
Saint-Brice (16) 195 K3
Saint-Brice (33) 230 B4
Saint-Brice (50) 52 A5
Saint-Brice (53) 105 H4
Saint-Brice (61) 81 G1
Saint-Brice (77) 88 D1
Saint-Brice-Courcelles (51). 40 E4
Saint-Brice-de-Landelles (50). 80 B1
Saint-Brice-en-Coglès (35) 51 K6
Saint-Brice-sous-Forêt (95) 58 E2
Saint-Brice-sous-Rânes (61). 54 A5
Saint-Brice-sur-Vienne (87). 180 E6
Saint-Brieuc (22) 49 G6
Saint-Brieuc-de-Mauron (56) 77 K6
Saint-Brieuc-des-Iffs (35) 78 E2
Saint-Bris-des-Bois (17). 195 H2
Saint-Bris-le-Vineux (89). 113 G6
Saint-Brisson (58). 134 B6
Saint-Brisson-sur-Loire (45) 131 H1
Saint-Broing (70) 137 G3
Saint-Broing-les-Moines (21) 115 J6
Saint-Broingt-le-Bois (52). 116 E6
Saint-Broingt-les-Fosses (52). 116 C6
Saint-Broladre (35) 51 G4
Saint-Bueil (38) 207 K5
Saint-Calais (72) 107 K4
Saint-Calais-du-Désert (53) 81 K2
Saint-Calez-en-Saosnois (72). 83 F4
Saint-Cannat (13). 277 G6
Saint-Caprais (03) 167 J4
Saint-Caprais (18) 149 F4
Saint-Caprais (32) 268 A6
Saint-Caprais (43) 232 E5
Saint-Caprais-de-Blaye (33) 211 H2
Saint-Caprais-de-Bordeaux (33) . . 229 J3
Saint-Caprais-de-Lerm (47) 248 C4
Saint-Capraise-de-Lalinde (24) . . . 231 K2
Saint-Capraise-d'Eymet (24). 231 H4
Saint-Caradec (22) 77 F4
Saint-Caradec-Trégomel (56) 76 A6
Saint-Carné (22) 50 C6
Saint-Carreuc (22) 77 G2
Saint-Cassien (24) 232 B4
Saint-Cassien (38) 223 J1
Saint-Cassin (73) 208 B4
Saint-Cast-le-Guildo (22) 50 B3
Saint-Castin (64) 284 D3
Saint-Célerin (72) 107 G1
Saint-Céneré (53) 105 G1
Saint-Céneri-le-Gérei (61). 82 B3
Saint-Céols (07) 149 J1
Saint-Céré (46). 234 C2
Saint-Cergues (74) 191 H1
Saint-Cernin (17) 217 H5
Saint-Cernin (46) 233 J5
Saint-Cernin-de-Labarde (24) 231 J3
Saint-Cernin-de-Larche (19) 215 H5
Saint-Cernin-de-l'Herm (24) 232 D5
Saint-Césaire (17) 195 H2
Saint-Césaire-de-Gauzignan (30) . . 275 F1
Saint-Césaire-sur-Siagne (06) 280 C5
Saint-Cézert (31) 268 E4
Saint-Chabrais (23) 183 G3
Saint-Chaffrey (05) 225 K6
Saint-Chamant (15) 217 H5
Saint-Chamant (19) 216 C4
Saint-Chamarand (46) 233 H4
Saint-Chamas (13) 295 J3
Saint-Chamassy (24) 232 C2
Saint-Chamond (42) 205 H5
Saint-Champ (01). 207 K1
Saint-Chaptes (30) 275 F1
Saint-Charles-de-Percy (14). 53 F2
Saint-Charles-la-Forêt (53) 105 G3
Saint-Chartier (36) 166 B3
Saint-Chef (38) 207 F3
Saint-Chels (46) 234 B6
Saint-Chély-d'Apcher (48) 237 G3
Saint-Chély-d'Aubrac (12) 236 C5
Saint-Chéron (51) 63 F6
Saint-Chéron (91). 86 C1
Saint-Chinian (34). 291 H3
Saint-Christ-Briost (80). 19 G2
Saint-Christaud (31) 287 J6
Saint-Christaud (32) 285 K1
Saint-Christo-en-Jarez (42) 205 H5

Saint-Christol (07) 239 H2
Saint-Christol (34) 274 E5
Saint-Christol (84) 258 B6
Saint-Christol-de-Rodières (30) . . . 256 B3
Saint-Christol-lès-Alès (30). 255 G6
Saint-Christoly-de-Blaye (33) 211 H4
Saint-Christoly-Médoc (33). 210 E1
Saint-Christophe (03) 186 A3
Saint-Christophe (16) 180 D5
Saint-Christophe (17) 177 F2
Saint-Christophe (23) 182 D4
Saint-Christophe (28) 109 F1
Saint-Christophe (69) 187 K1
Saint-Christophe (73) 208 A3
Saint-Christophe (81) 251 G5
Saint-Christophe (86) 145 G5
Saint-Christophe-à-Berry (02). 39 G2
Saint-Christophe-d'Allier (43) 238 A2
Saint-Christophe-de-
-Chaulieu (61). 52 E4
Saint-Christophe-de-Double (33) . . 212 D5
Saint-Christophe-de-Valains (35) . . 79 J1
Saint-Christophe-des-Bardes (33) . . 230 B1
Saint-Christophe-des-Bois (35) . . . 80 A5
Saint-Christophe-Dodinicourt (10) . 90 E3
Saint-Christophe-du-Bois (49) 142 E4
Saint-Christophe-du-Foc (50) 28 B3
Saint-Christophe-du-Jambet (72) . . 82 C5
Saint-Christophe-du-
-Ligneron (85). 141 G5
Saint-Christophe-du-Luat (53) 81 H6
Saint-Christophe-en-Bazelle (36) . . 148 A1
Saint-Christophe-en-
-Boucherie (36). 166 C2
Saint-Christophe-en-Bresse (71) . . 172 A1
Saint-Christophe-en-
-Brionnais (71) 187 F1
Saint-Christophe-en-
-Champagne (72) 106 A3
Saint-Christophe-en-Oisans (38) . . 225 F6
Saint-Christophe-et-le-Laris (26) . . 222 E3
Saint-Christophe-la-
-Couperie (49) 124 A6
Saint-Christophe-le-Chaudry (18). . 167 F3
Saint-Christophe-le-Jajolet (61) . . . 54 C6
Saint-Christophe-sur-Avre (27) . . . 56 A5
Saint-Christophe-sur-Condé (27) . . 34 D4
Saint-Christophe-sur-
-Dolaison (43). 220 B6
Saint-Christophe-sur-Guiers (38) . . 208 A6
Saint-Christophe-sur-le-Nais (37) . . 127 G2
Saint-Christophe-sur-Roc (79) 161 J5
Saint-Christophe-Vallon (12). 251 K1
Saint-Cibard (33) 230 C1
Saint-Cierge-la-Serre (07). 240 A3
Saint-Cierge-sous-le-
-Cheylard (07) 239 H1
Saint-Ciergues (52). 116 C4
Saint-Ciers-Champagne (17) 195 K6
Saint-Ciers-d'Abzac (33) 212 A5
Saint-Ciers-de-Canesse (33) 211 G4
Saint-Ciers-du-Taillon (17) 195 G6
Saint-Ciers-sur-Bonnieure (16) . . . 197 F1
Saint-Ciers-sur-Gironde (33). 211 H2
Saint-Cirgue (81) 271 G2
Saint-Cirgues (43) 219 H4
Saint-Cirgues (46) 234 E4
Saint-Cirgues-de-Jordanne (15) . . 217 J6
Saint-Cirgues-de-Malbert (15) . . . 217 G5
Saint-Cirgues-de-Prades (07) 239 G5
Saint-Cirgues-en-Montagne (07). . . 238 E3
Saint-Cirgues-la-Loutre (19) 216 E5
Saint-Cirgues-sur-Couze (63) 202 D5
Saint-Cirice (82) 248 D6
Saint-Cirq (24) 232 C1
Saint-Cirq (82) 250 B5
Saint-Cirq-Lapopie (46) 250 C5
Saint-Cirq-Madelon (46) 233 G3
Saint-Cirq-Souillaguet (46) 233 H4
Saint-Civran (36) 165 F4
Saint-Clair (07) 222 A2
Saint-Clair (46) 233 H4
Saint-Clair (82) 248 E5
Saint-Clair (86) 144 D5
Saint-Clair-d'Arcey (27) 34 D6
Saint-Clair-de-Halouze (61) 53 D5
Saint-Clair-de-la-Tour (38) 207 H4
Saint-Clair-du-Rhône (38). 206 A4
Saint-Clair-sur-Epte (95). 36 D5
Saint-Clair-sur-Galaure (38) 222 E2
Saint-Clair-sur-l'Elle (50) 31 H2
Saint-Clair-sur-les-Monts (76). . . . 15 G5
Saint-Clar (32) 267 K3
Saint-Clar-de-Rivière (31) 287 K2
Saint-Claud (16) 179 K6
Saint-Claude (39) 173 K5
Saint-Claude-de-Diray (41). 129 F2
Saint-Clément (02) 21 H3
Saint-Clément (03) 186 B4
Saint-Clément (07) 221 G6
Saint-Clément (15) 217 K6
Saint-Clément (19) 216 A2
Saint-Clément (30) 274 D3
Saint-Clément (54) 94 E1
Saint-Clément (89) 88 D6
Saint-Clément-à-Arnes (08) 41 J3
Saint-Clément-de-la-Place (49) . . . 124 C2
Saint-Clément-de-Régnat (63) 185 H5
Saint-Clément-de-Rivière (34) 274 D5
Saint-Clément-de-Valorgue (63) . . 204 B5
Saint-Clément-de-Vers (69) 187 J2
Saint-Clément-des-Baleines (17) . . 158 B5
Saint-Clément-des-Levées (49) . . . 126 A5
Saint-Clément-les-Places (69) 205 G2
Saint-Clément-Rancoudray (50) . . . 52 E5
Saint-Clément-sur-Durance (05) . . . 243 K4

Saint-Clément-sur-Guye (71) 171 G3
Saint-Clément-sur-Valsonne (69) . . 187 J6
Saint-Clémentin (79). 143 J4
Saint-Clet (22) 48 D4
Saint-Cloud (92) 58 D4
Saint-Cloud-en-Dunois (28) 109 G2
Saint-Colomb-de-Lauzun (47) 231 H5
Saint-Colomban (44) 141 J3
Saint-Colomban-des-Villards (73) . . 225 F1
Saint-Côme (33) 246 D1
Saint-Côme-de-Fresné (14) 32 C3
Saint-Côme-d'Olt (12) 236 B6
Saint-Côme-du-Mont (50) 29 F6
Saint-Côme-et-Maruéjols (30) 275 F3
Saint-Congard (56) 101 K4
Saint-Connan (22) 76 D1
Saint-Connec (22) 76 E4
Saint-Constant (15) 235 F4
Saint-Contest (14) 32 D4
Saint-Corneille (72) 107 F2
Saint-Cornier-des-Landes (61) 53 F5
Saint-Cosme (68) 119 K5
Saint-Cosme-en-Vairais (72) 83 G5
Saint-Couat-d'Aude (11). 290 E6
Saint-Couat-du-Razès (11). 308 D2
Saint-Coulitz (29) 74 D3
Saint-Coulomb (35) 50 E3
Saint-Coutant (16) 179 K5
Saint-Coutant (79) 178 E2
Saint-Coutant-le-Grand (17) 177 H5
Saint-Créac (32) 268 A2
Saint-Créac (65) 304 B1
Saint-Crépin (05) 243 K3
Saint-Crépin (17) 177 H4
Saint-Crépin-aux-Bois (60). 39 F1
Saint-Crépin-d'Auberoche (24). . . . 214 C4
Saint-Crépin-de-Richemont (24). . . 197 J6
Saint-Crépin-et-Carlucet (24) 215 F6
Saint-Crépin-Ibouvillers (60). 37 G3
Saint-Crespin (76) 15 K3
Saint-Crespin-sur-Moine (49) 142 C2
Saint-Cricq (32) 268 C5
Saint-Cricq-Chalosse (40) 264 E5
Saint-Cricq-du-Gave (40) 283 G1
Saint-Cricq-Villeneuve (40). 265 J2
Saint-Cybardeaux (16) 196 C2
Saint-Cybranet (24) 232 E3
Saint-Cyprien (19) 215 G3
Saint-Cyprien (24) 232 D2
Saint-Cyprien (42) 204 E5
Saint-Cyprien (46) 249 J3
Saint-Cyprien (66) 315 H3
Saint-Cyprien-sur-Dourdou (12) . . 235 H6
Saint-Cyr (07) 222 A2
Saint-Cyr (50) 28 E4
Saint-Cyr (71) 171 K2
Saint-Cyr (86) 163 G1
Saint-Cyr (87) 198 C2
Saint-Cyr-au-Mont-d'Or (69). 206 A1
Saint-Cyr-de-Favières (42) 187 F5
Saint-Cyr-de-Salerne (27) 34 D5
Saint-Cyr-de-Valorges (42) 187 H6
Saint-Cyr-des-Gâts (85) 160 D3
Saint-Cyr-du-Bailleul (50) 80 E1
Saint-Cyr-du-Doret (17) 177 G1
Saint-Cyr-du-Gault (41) 128 B2
Saint-Cyr-du-Ronceray (14) 55 F1
Saint-Cyr-en-Arthies (95) 57 J1
Saint-Cyr-en-Bourg (49) 144 C1
Saint-Cyr-en-Pail (53) 82 A3
Saint-Cyr-en-Talmondais (85) 159 J4
Saint-Cyr-en-Val (45) 110 B5
Saint-Cyr-la-Campagne (27) 35 H4
Saint-Cyr-la-Lande (79) 144 C3
Saint-Cyr-la-Rivière (91) 86 C4
Saint-Cyr-la-Roche (19) 215 H3
Saint-Cyr-la-Rosière (61) 83 J4
Saint-Cyr-le-Chatoux (69). 187 K4
Saint-Cyr-le-Gravelais (53) 104 C5
Saint-Cyr-l'École (78) 58 B4
Saint-Cyr-les-Champagnes (24) . . . 215 G1
Saint-Cyr-les-Colons (89) 113 H6
Saint-Cyr-les-Vignes (42) 205 F3
Saint-Cyr-Montmalin (39) 155 J4
Saint-Cyr-sous-Dourdan (91) 86 B1
Saint-Cyr-sur-le-Rhône (69) 206 B5
Saint-Cyr-sur-Loire (37) 127 J4
Saint-Cyr-sur-Menthon (01) 188 D1
Saint-Cyr-sur-Mer (83) 297 G5
Saint-Cyr-sur-Morin (77) 60 C3
Saint-Cyran-du-Jambot (36). 146 E3
Saint-Dalmas-le-Selvage (06). 261 F2
Saint-Daunès (46) 249 H3
Saint-Denis (11) 289 K4
Saint-Denis (30) 255 G6
Saint-Denis (89) 88 D5
Saint-Denis (93) 58 E2
Saint-Denis-Catus (46). 233 G6
Saint-Denis-Combarnazat (63) 185 H5
Saint-Denis-d'Aclon (76) 15 J2
Saint-Denis-d'Anjou (53) 105 H5
Saint-Denis-d'Augerons (27). 55 G2
Saint-Denis-d'Authou (28) 84 B4
Saint-Denis-de-Cabanne (42) 187 G4
Saint-Denis-de-Gastines (53) 80 E4
Saint-Denis-de-Jouhet (36) 166 A4
Saint-Denis-de-l'Hôtel (45) 110 C4
Saint-Denis-de-Mailloc (14) 34 A6
Saint-Denis-de-Méré (14) 53 H3
Saint-Denis-de-Palin (18) 149 H5
Saint-Denis-de-Pile (33) 212 B6
Saint-Denis-de-Vaux (71) 153 J6
Saint-Denis-de-Villenette (61). . . . 81 H2
Saint-Denis-des-Coudrais (72) 83 G6
Saint-Denis-des-Monts (27) 35 H4
Saint-Denis-des-Murs (87) 199 H2

Saint-Denis-des-Puits (28) 84 D3
Saint-Denis-d'Oléron (17). 176 B4
Saint-Denis-d'Orques (72) 105 K2
Saint-Denis-du-Béhélan (27) 56 B3
Saint-Denis-du-Maine (53) 105 H3
Saint-Denis-du-Payré (85) 159 K5
Saint-Denis-du-Pin (17) 177 K5
Saint-Denis-en-Bugey (01) 189 H5
Saint-Denis-en-Margeride (48) . . . 237 J3
Saint-Denis-en-Val (45) 110 A4
Saint-Denis-la-Chevasse (85) 142 A5
Saint-Denis-le-Ferment (27) 36 D3
Saint-Denis-le-Gast (50) 31 F5
Saint-Denis-le-Thiboult (76) 36 A2
Saint-Denis-le-Vêtu (50) 30 E5
Saint-Denis-lès-Bourg (01) 189 G2
Saint-Denis-lès-Martel (46) 233 K1
Saint-Denis-lès-Ponts (28) 108 E2
Saint-Denis-lès-Rebais (77) 60 C4
Saint-Denis-Maisoncelles (14) 31 K5
Saint-Denis-sur-Coise (42) 205 G4
Saint-Denis-sur-Huisne (61) 83 H2
Saint-Denis-sur-Loire (41). 129 F2
Saint-Denis-sur-Ouanne (89) 112 C5
Saint-Denis-sur-Sarthon (61) 82 B2
Saint-Denis-sur-Scie (76) 15 K4
Saint-Deniscourt (60) 17 G5
Saint-Denœux (62) 4 D6
Saint-Denoual (22) 49 K6
Saint-Derrien (29) 46 D4
Saint-Désert (71) 171 H1
Saint-Désir (14) 33 K5
Saint-Désirat (07) 222 B2
Saint-Désiré (03) 167 F4
Saint-Dézéry (30) 275 F1
Saint-Didier (21) 134 C5
Saint-Didier (35) 79 K4
Saint-Didier (39) 173 F1
Saint-Didier (58) 133 G5
Saint-Didier (84) 276 E1
Saint-Didier-au-Mont-d'Or (69) . . . 206 A1
Saint-Didier-d'Allier (43) 220 A6
Saint-Didier-d'Aussiat (01) 172 B6
Saint-Didier-de-Bizonnes (38) 207 F5
Saint-Didier-de-Formans (01) 188 C5
Saint-Didier-de-la-Tour (38) 207 H4
Saint-Didier-des-Bois (27) 35 H4
Saint-Didier-en-Bresse (71) 154 C5
Saint-Didier-en-Brionnais (71). . . . 170 C6
Saint-Didier-en-Donjon (03) 169 K6
Saint-Didier-en-Velay (43) 221 G2
Saint-Didier-la-Forêt (03) 185 H2
Saint-Didier-sous-Aubenas (07) . . . 239 H5
Saint-Didier-sous-Écouves (61) . . . 82 C1
Saint-Didier-sur-Arroux (71) 152 D6
Saint-Didier-sur-Beaujeu (69) 187 K3
Saint-Didier-sur-Chalaronne (01). . 188 C2
Saint-Didier-sur-Doulon (43) 219 J2
Saint-Didier-sur-Rochefort (42). . . . 204 A2
Saint-Dié-des-Vosges (88) 95 J4
Saint-Dier-d'Auvergne (63) 203 H3
Saint-Diéry (63) 202 C5
Saint-Dionizy (30) 275 F4
Saint-Disdier (05) 242 C3
Saint-Divy (29) 46 B6
Saint-Dizant-du-Bois (17) 195 G6
Saint-Dizant-du-Gua (17) 195 F6
Saint-Dizier (52) 63 J6
Saint-Dizier-en-Diois (26) 241 J4
Saint-Dizier-la-Tour (23) 183 G3
Saint-Dizier-les-Domaines (23) . . . 182 E1
Saint-Dizier-l'Évêque (90) 139 J2
Saint-Dizier-Leyrenne (23) 182 B4
Saint-Dolay (56) 102 B5
Saint-Domet (23) 183 H4
Saint-Domineuc (35) 78 E1
Saint-Donan (22) 49 F6
Saint-Donat (63) 201 K6
Saint-Donat-sur-l'Herbasse (26) . . 222 D4
Saint-Dos (64) 283 G2
Saint-Doulchard (18) 149 G4
Saint-Drézéry (34) 274 D5
Saint-Dyé-sur-Loire (41) 129 G1
Saint-Ebremond-de-
-Bonfossé (50) 31 G4
Saint-Edmond (71) 187 G2
Saint-Égrève (38) 224 A2
Saint-Elier (27) 56 B2
Saint-Éliph (28). 84 C3
Saint-Élix (32) 286 E2
Saint-Élix-le-Château (31) 287 J5
Saint-Élix-Séglan (31). 287 F6
Saint-Élix-Theux (32) 286 B3
Saint-Ellier-du-Maine (53) 80 C3
Saint-Ellier-les-Bois (61) 82 B2
Saint-Éloi (01). 189 F5
Saint-Éloi (23). 182 C4
Saint-Éloi (58). 150 E4
Saint-Éloi-de-Fourques (27) 35 H4
Saint-Eloy (29) 74 D1
Saint-Éloy-d'Allier (03) 166 E4
Saint-Éloy-de-Gy (18). 149 G2
Saint-Éloy-la-Glacière (63) 203 J5
Saint-Éloy-les-Mines (63) 184 D5
Saint-Éloy-les-Tuileries (19) 199 F6
Saint-Éman (28) 84 D4
Saint-Émiland (71) 153 G5
Saint-Émilion (33). 230 B1
Saint-Ennemond (03) 169 F2
Saint-Épain (37) 145 J3
Saint-Epvre (89) 66 C1
Saint-Erblon (35) 79 G5
Saint-Erblon (53) 104 B5
Saint-Erme-Outre-et-
-Ramecourt (02) 40 D1

Saint-Escobille (91) 86 B3
Saint-Esteben (64) 282 E3
Saint-Estèphe (24) 197 K4
Saint-Estèphe (33) 211 F2
Saint-Estève (66) 315 G2
Saint-Estève-Janson (13) 277 H5
Saint-Étienne (42). 205 G6
Saint-Étienne-à-Arnes (08) 41 K3
Saint-Étienne-au-Mont (62) 4 A3
Saint-Étienne-au-Temple (51) 62 D1
Saint-Étienne-aux-Clos (19) 201 H5
Saint-Étienne-Cantalès (15) 235 F1
Saint-Étienne-d'Albagnan (34) . . . 291 G1
Saint-Étienne-de-Baïgorry (64) . . . 282 C5
Saint-Étienne-de-Boulogne (07) . . 239 J4
Saint-Étienne-de-Brillouet (85) . . . 160 C3
Saint-Étienne-de-Carlat (15) 235 J1
Saint-Étienne-de-Chigny (37) 127 G5
Saint-Étienne-de-Chomeil (15) . . . 217 K2
Saint-Étienne-de-Crossey (38) 207 J6
Saint-Étienne-de-Cuines (73) 225 G1
Saint-Étienne-de-Fontbellon (07) . . 239 H5
Saint-Étienne-de-Fougères (47) . . . 248 B2
Saint-Étienne-de-Fursac (23) 181 K3
Saint-Étienne-de-Gourgas (34) . . . 273 G4
Saint-Étienne-de-Lisse (33) 230 C1
Saint-Étienne-de-l'Olm (30) 255 H6
Saint-Étienne-de-Lugdarès (07) . . . 238 D4
Saint-Étienne-de-Maurs (15). 235 F4
Saint-Étienne-de-Montluc (44) . . . 122 E3
Saint-Étienne-de-Puycorbier (24) . . 213 G5
Saint-Étienne-de-
-Saint-Geoirs (38). 223 G1
Saint-Étienne-de-Serre (07) 239 J2
Saint-Étienne-de-Tinée (06) 261 F3
Saint-Étienne-de-Tulmont (82) . . . 269 H1
Saint-Étienne-de-Valoux (07) 222 B3
Saint-Étienne-de-Vicq (03) 185 K3
Saint-Étienne-de-Villeréal (47) . . . 232 A5
Saint-Étienne-des-Champs (63) . . . 201 J1
Saint-Étienne-des-Guérets (41) . . . 128 C2
Saint-Étienne-des-Oullières (69) . . 188 A4
Saint-Étienne-des-Sorts (30) 256 D4
Saint-Étienne-d'Orthe (40) 262 E6
Saint-Étienne-du-Bois (01) 189 G1
Saint-Étienne-du-Bois (85) 141 H5
Saint-Étienne-du-Grès (13). 276 A4
Saint-Étienne-du-
-Gué-de-l'Isle (22) 77 G5
Saint-Étienne-du-Rouvray (76) . . . 35 H3
Saint-Étienne-du-Valdonnez (48) . . 254 B1
Saint-Étienne-du-Vauvray (27) . . . 35 J4
Saint-Étienne-du-Vigan (43) 238 B3
Saint-Étienne-en-Bresse (71) 172 B1
Saint-Étienne-en-Coglès (35) 51 K6
Saint-Étienne-en-Dévoluy (05) . . . 242 D3
Saint-Étienne-Estréchoux (34) 272 D5
Saint-Étienne-la-Cigogne (79). . . . 177 K3
Saint-Étienne-la-Geneste (19) 201 F6
Saint-Étienne-la-Thillaye (14) 33 J3
Saint-Étienne-la-Varenne (69) 188 A4
Saint-Étienne-l'Allier (27) 34 C4
Saint-Étienne-Lardeyrol (43) 220 D5
Saint-Étienne-le-Laus (05) 243 F6
Saint-Étienne-le-Molard (42). 204 D2
Saint-Étienne-les-Orgues (04). . . . 258 E6
Saint-Étienne-lès-
-Remiremont (88) 119 F1
Saint-Étienne-Roilaye (60) 39 F3
Saint-Étienne-sous-Bailleul (27) . . 36 A6
Saint-Étienne-sous-Barbuise (10) . . 90 B2
Saint-Étienne-sur-Blesle (43) 218 C2
Saint-Étienne-sur-
-Chalaronne (01). 188 C2
Saint-Étienne-sur-
-Reyssouze (01) 172 B5
Saint-Étienne-sur-Suippe (51). . . . 41 F2
Saint-Étienne-sur-Usson (63) 203 H3
Saint-Étienne-Vallée-
-Française (48) 254 E5
Saint-Eugène (02). 61 F1
Saint-Eugène (17). 195 K5
Saint-Eugène (71). 170 C1
Saint-Eulien (51) 63 J5
Saint-Euphraise-et-Clairizet (51). . . 40 D5
Saint-Euphrône (21) 134 C3
Saint-Eusèbe (71) 171 F1
Saint-Eusèbe (74) 190 D5
Saint-Eusèbe-en-
-Champsaur (05) 242 E3
Saint-Eustache (74) 208 D1
Saint-Eustache-la-Forêt (76). 14 D6
Saint-Eutrope (16) 196 D6
Saint-Eutrope-de-Born (47) 231 K5
Saint-Évarzec (29) 98 D2
Saint-Évroult-de-Montfort (61) . . . 55 F6
Saint-Evroult-Notre-Dame-
-du-Bois (61) 55 G6
Saint-Exupéry (33) 230 B5
Saint-Exupéry-les-Roches (19) . . . 201 G5
Saint-Fargeau (89) 112 B4
Saint-Fargeau-Ponthierry (77). . . . 87 G2
Saint-Fargeol (03). 184 A3
Saint-Faust (64) 284 C4
Saint-Félicien (07) 221 K5
Saint-Féliu-d'Amont (66) 315 F2
Saint-Féliu-d'Avall (66) 315 F2
Saint-Félix (03) 185 K2
Saint-Félix (16) 212 D1
Saint-Félix (17) 177 J3
Saint-Félix (46) 234 E5
Saint-Félix (60) 37 J3
Saint-Félix (74) 208 C1
Saint-Félix-de-Bourdeilles (24) . . . 197 J6
Saint-Félix-de-Foncaude (33) 230 C4

Saint-Félix-de-l'Héras (34) 273 F3
Saint-Félix-de-Lodez (34) 273 H5
Saint-Félix-de-Lunel (12) 235 J6
Saint-FéIix-de-Pallières (30) 274 C1
Saint-Félix-de-Reillac-et-
 Mortemart (24) 214 C6
Saint-Félix-d'Auroure (43) 221 F1
Saint-Félix-de-Rieutord (09) 307 J2
Saint-Félix-de-Sorgues (12) 272 C3
Saint-Félix-de-Tournegat (09) . . . 307 K1
Saint-Félix-de-Villadeix (24) 231 K1
Saint-Félix-Lauragais (31) 289 G2
Saint-Fergeux (08) 21 J6
Saint-Ferjeux (70) 138 C4
Saint-Ferme (33) 230 D4
Saint-Ferréol (74) 209 F1
Saint-Ferréol-d'Auroure (43) . . . 221 F1
Saint-Ferréol-de-Comminges (31) . 286 E4
Saint-Ferréol-des-Côtes (63) . . . 203 K5
Saint-Ferréol-Trente-Pas (26) . . . 257 J1
Saint-Ferriol (11) 308 E4
Saint-Fiacre (22) 48 D6
Saint-Fiacre (77) 60 A3
Saint-Fiacre-sur-Maine (44) 123 H5
Saint-Fiel (23) 182 D2
Saint-Firmin (05) 242 D2
Saint-Firmin (54) 94 A4
Saint-Firmin (58) 151 G3
Saint-Firmin (71) 153 G6
Saint-Firmin-des-Bois (45) 111 K3
Saint-Firmin-des-Prés (41) 108 C5
Saint-Firmin-sur-Loire (45) 131 J2
Saint-Flavy (10) 89 H3
Saint-Florent (2B) 319 G1
Saint-Florent (45) 131 F1
Saint-Florent-des-Bois (85) 159 J2
Saint-Florent-le-Vieil (49) 124 C4
Saint-Florent-sur-Auzonnet (30) . . 255 H4
Saint-Florent-sur-Cher (18) 149 F4
Saint-Florentin (36) 148 B3
Saint-Florentin (89) 113 H3
Saint-Floret (63) 202 D5
Saint-Floris (62) 5 K4
Saint-Flour (15) 218 E5
Saint-Flour (63) 203 H3
Saint-Flour-de-Mercoire (48) . . . 238 B4
Saint-Flovier (37) 146 D4
Saint-Floxel (50) 29 F4
Saint-Folquin (62) 3 F2
Saint-Fons (69) 206 B2
Saint-Forgeot (71) 153 F4
Saint-Forget (78) 58 B5
Saint-Forgeux (69) 205 G1
Saint-Forgeux-Lespinasse (42) . . 186 D3
Saint-Fort (53) 105 F5
Saint-Fort-sur-Gironde (17) 195 F5
Saint-Fort-sur-le-Né (16) 195 K4
Saint-Fortunat-sur-Eyrieux (07) . . 240 A2
Saint-Fraigne (16) 178 E5
Saint-Fraimbault (61) 81 F2
Saint-Fraimbault-de-Prières (53) . . 81 G4
Saint-Frajou (31) 287 F4
Saint-Franc (73) 207 K5
Saint-Franchy (58) 151 G2
Saint-François-de-Sales (73) . . . 208 C2
Saint-François-Lacroix (57) 27 K4
Saint-François-Longchamp (73) . . 209 F6
Saint-Frégant (29) 46 B4
Saint-Fréjoux (19) 201 G5
Saint-Frézal-d'Albuges (48) 238 B6
Saint-Frézal-de-Ventalon (48) . . . 254 C1
Saint-Frichoux (11) 290 D5
Saint-Frion (23) 200 E1
Saint-Fromond (50) 31 H2
Saint-Front (16) 179 H6
Saint-Front (43) 220 E6
Saint-Front-d'Alemps (24) 214 B2
Saint-Front-de-Pradoux (24) . . . 213 G5
Saint-Front-la-Rivière (24) 197 K6
Saint-Front-sur-Lémance (47) . . . 232 C5
Saint-Front-sur-Nizonne (24) . . . 197 J5
Saint-Froult (17) 176 E5
Saint-Fulgent (85) 142 B5
Saint-Fulgent-des-Ormes (61) . . . 83 G4
Saint-Fuscien (80) 18 B3
Saint-Gabriel-Brécy (14) 32 C3
Saint-Gal (48) 237 H4
Saint-Gal-sur-Sioule (63) 184 E3
Saint-Galmier (42) 205 F4
Saint-Gand (70) 137 J2
Saint-Ganton (35) 102 E4
Saint-Gatien-des-Bois (14) 33 K3
Saint-Gaudens (31) 305 K1
Saint-Gaudent (86) 179 H3
Saint-Gaudéric (11) 308 C1
Saint-Gaultier (36) 165 F3
Saint-Gauzens (81) 270 B4
Saint-Gein (40) 265 J3
Saint-Gelais (79) 161 H5
Saint-Gelven (22) 76 C3
Saint-Gély-du-Fesc (34) 274 B5
Saint-Génard (79) 178 D2
Saint-Gence (87) 181 F6
Saint-Généroux (79) 144 C5
Saint-Genès-Champanelle (63) . . 202 C3
Saint-Genès-Champespe (63) . . . 218 A1
Saint-Genès-de-Blaye (33) 211 G3
Saint-Genès-de-Castillon (33) . . . 230 C1
Saint-Genès-de-Fronsac (33) . . . 211 K5
Saint-Genès-de-Lombaud (33) . . . 229 K3
Saint-Genès-du-Retz (63) 185 G4
Saint-Genès-la-Tourette (63) . . . 203 H5
Saint-Genest (03) 184 A2
Saint-Genest (88) 94 E3
Saint-Genest-d'Ambière (86) . . . 145 G6
Saint-Genest-de-Beauzon (07) . . . 255 H1
Saint-Genest-de-Contest (81) . . . 270 E4

Saint-Genest-Lachamp (07) 239 H2
Saint-Genest-Lerpt (42) 205 F6
Saint-Genest-Malifaux (42) 221 H1
Saint-Genest-sur-Roselle (87) . . . 199 G3
Saint-Geneys-près-
 Saint-Paulien (43) 220 B4
Saint-Gengoulph (02) 39 H6
Saint-Gengoux-de-Scissé (71) . . . 171 J4
Saint-Gengoux-le-National (71) . . 171 J5
Saint-Geniès (24) 215 F6
Saint-Geniès-Bellevue (31) 269 H5
Saint-Geniès-de-Comolas (30) . . . 256 D6
Saint-Geniès-de-Fontedit (34) . . . 291 K2
Saint-Geniès-de-Malgoirès (30) . . 275 D4
Saint-Geniès-de-Varensal (34) . . . 272 C5
Saint-Geniès-des-Mourgues (34) . . 274 D5
Saint-Geniez (04) 259 G3
Saint-Geniez-d'Olt (12) 253 F1
Saint-Geniez-ô-Merle (19) 216 D5
Saint-Genis (05) 258 E2
Saint-Genis-de-Saintonge (17) . . . 195 G5
Saint-Génis-des-Fontaines (66) . . 315 H4
Saint-Genis-d'Hiersac (16) 196 C2
Saint-Genis-du-Bois (33) 230 B4
Saint-Genis-l'Argentière (69) . . . 205 H2
Saint-Genis-Laval (69) 206 A3
Saint-Genis-les-Ollières (69) . . . 205 K2
Saint-Genis-Pouilly (01) 190 E1
Saint-Genis-sur-Menthon (01) . . . 188 E1
Saint-Genix-sur-Guiers (73) 207 J4
Saint-Genou (36) 147 G5
Saint-Genouph (37) 127 H5
Saint-Geoire-en-Valdaine (38) . . . 207 J5
Saint-Geoirs (38) 223 J1
Saint-Georges (15) 218 E6
Saint-Georges (16) 179 H5
Saint-Georges (32) 268 B5
Saint-Georges (47) 248 E1
Saint-Georges (57) 67 H5
Saint-Georges (62) 9 J2
Saint-Georges (82) 250 C4
Saint-Georges-Antignac (17) . . . 195 H5
Saint-Georges-Armont (25). 139 F4
Saint-Georges-Blancaneix (24) . . . 231 G1
Saint-Georges-Buttavent (53) . . . 81 F4
Saint-Georges-d'Annebecq (61) . . 53 K6
Saint-Georges-d'Aunay (14) 53 G1
Saint-Georges-d'Aurac (43) 219 J4
Saint-Georges-de-Baroille (42) . . . 204 D1
Saint-Georges-de-Bohon (50) . . . 31 F1
Saint-Georges-de-Chesné (35) . . . 80 A4
Saint-Georges-de-Commiers (38) . . 224 A5
Saint-Georges-de-Didonne (17) . . 194 C3
Saint-Georges-de-Gréhaigne (35) . . 51 H4
Saint-Georges-de-la-Couée (72) . . 107 H5
Saint-Georges-de-la-Rivière (50) . . 28 B6
Saint-Georges-de-Lévéjac (48) . . . 253 J3
Saint-Georges-de-Livoye (50) . . . 52 B4
Saint-Georges-de-
 Longuepierre (17) 178 B4
Saint-Georges-de-Luzençon (12) . . 253 F6
Saint-Georges-de-Mons (63) . . . 184 C6
Saint-Georges-de-Montaigu (85) . . 142 A4
Saint-Georges-de-Montclard (24) . . 231 K1
Saint-Georges-de-Noisné (79) . . . 161 K4
Saint-Georges-de-
 Pointindoux (85) 159 G2
Saint-Georges-de-Poisieux (18) . . 167 G2
Saint-Georges-de-
 Reintembault (35) 80 A1
Saint-Georges-de-Reneins (69) . . . 188 B4
Saint-Georges-de-Rex (79) 177 J1
Saint-Georges-de-Rouelley (50) . . 53 F6
Saint-Georges-d'Elle (50) 31 J3
Saint-Georges-des-Agoûts (17) . . 211 G1
Saint-Georges-des-Coteaux (17) . . 195 F2
Saint-Georges-des-Gardes (49) . . 143 G1
Saint-Georges-des-
 Groseillers (61) 53 H4
Saint-Georges-des-Hurtières (73) . . 209 F5
Saint-Georges-des-
 Sept-Voies (49) 125 J5
Saint-Georges-d'Espéranche (38) . . 206 D4
Saint-Georges-d'Oléron (17) . . . 176 B4
Saint-Georges-d'Orques (34) . . . 274 B6
Saint-Georges-du-Bois (17) 177 H3
Saint-Georges-du-Bois (49) 125 K3
Saint-Georges-du-Bois (72) 106 D3
Saint-Georges-du-Mesnil (27) . . . 34 C4
Saint-Georges-du-Rosay (72) . . . 83 G6
Saint-Georges-du-Vièvre (27) . . . 34 D4
Saint-Georges-en-Auge (14) 54 D1
Saint-Georges-en-Couzan (42) . . . 204 B3
Saint-Georges-Haute-Ville (42) . . . 204 D5
Saint-Georges-la-Pouge (23) . . . 182 E5
Saint-Georges-Lagricol (43) 220 C2
Saint-Georges-le-Fléchard (53) . . . 105 H2
Saint-Georges-le-Gaultier (72) . . . 82 B4
Saint-Georges-lès-
 Baillargeaux (86) 163 F2
Saint-Georges-les-Bains (07) . . . 240 B2
Saint-Georges-les-Landes (87) . . . 164 E6
Saint-Georges-Montcocq (50) . . . 31 H3
Saint-Georges-Motel (27) 57 F4
Saint-Georges-Nigremont (23) . . . 201 F1
Saint-Georges-sur-Allier (63) . . . 202 E3
Saint-Georges-sur-Arnon (36) . . . 148 D4
Saint-Georges-sur-Baulche (89) . . 113 F5
Saint-Georges-sur-Cher (41) . . . 128 C5
Saint-Georges-sur-Erve (53) . . . 81 K6
Saint-Georges-sur-Eure (28) . . . 85 F3
Saint-Georges-sur-Fontaine (76) . . 16 A4
Saint-Georges-sur-la-Prée (18) . . 148 C1
Saint-Georges-sur-Layon (49) . . . 143 K4
Saint-Georges-sur-l'Aa (59) 3 F2
Saint-Georges-sur-Loire (49) . . . 124 E4

Saint-Georges-sur-Moulon (18) . . 149 G1
Saint-Georges-sur-Renon (01) . . . 188 E3
Saint-Geours-d'Auribat (40) 264 C1
Saint-Geours-de-Maremne (40) . . 262 D4
Saint-Gérand (56) 76 E5
Saint-Gérand-de-Vaux (03) 169 K5
Saint-Gérand-le-Puy (03) 185 K2
Saint-Géraud (47) 230 C1
Saint-Géraud-de-Corps (24) 213 F6
Saint-Géréon (44) 124 A4
Saint-Germain (07) 239 H6
Saint-Germain (10) 90 A5
Saint-Germain (54) 94 C2
Saint-Germain (70) 118 E5
Saint-Germain (86) 164 A3
Saint-Germain-au-Mont-d'Or (69). . 188 D4
Saint-Germain-Beaupré (23) 182 A1
Saint-Germain-Chassenay (58) . . . 169 F1
Saint-Germain-d'Anxure (53) . . . 81 F5
Saint-Germain-d'Arcé (72) 126 E1
Saint-Germain-de-Belvès (24) . . . 232 D3
Saint-Germain-de-Calberte (48) . . 254 E4
Saint-Germain-de-
 Clairefeuille (61) 54 E5
Saint-Germain-de-Confolens (16) . . 180 B4
Saint-Germain-de-Coulamer (53) . . 82 A5
Saint-Germain-de-Fresney (27). . . 56 E2
Saint-Germain-de-Grave (33) . . . 230 A5
Saint-Germain-de-Joux (01) 190 B2
Saint-Germain-de-la-Coudre (61) . . 83 H5
Saint-Germain-de-la-Grange (78) . . 58 A4
Saint-Germain-de-la-Rivière (33) . . 211 K6
Saint-Germain-de-Livet (14) 33 K6
Saint-Germain-de-
 Longue-Chaume (79) 161 J1
Saint-Germain-de-Lusignan (17). . . 195 H6
Saint-Germain-de-
 Marencennes (17) 177 C3
Saint-Germain-de-Martigny (61) . . 83 G1
Saint-Germain-de-Modéon (21) . . . 134 B5
Saint-Germain-de-Montbron (16) . . 197 G4
Saint-Germain-de-
 Montgommery (14) 54 E2
Saint-Germain-de-Pasquier (27) . . 35 G4
Saint-Germain-de-Prinçay (85) . . . 160 C1
Saint-Germain-de-Salles (03) . . . 185 G3
Saint-Germain-de-Tallevende-
 la-Lande-Vaumont (14) 52 E4
Saint-Germain-de-Tournebut (50) . . 28 E4
Saint-Germain-de-Varreville (50) . . 29 G5
Saint-Germain-de-Vibrac (17). . . . 195 K6
Saint-Germain-d'Ectot (14) 32 B5
Saint-Germain-d'Elle (50) 31 J3
Saint-Germain-des-Angles (27) . . 35 J4
Saint-Germain-des-Bois (18) . . . 149 H5
Saint-Germain-des-Bois (58) . . . 133 F5
Saint-Germain-des-Champs (89) . . 133 K4
Saint-Germain-des-Essourts (76) . . 16 B6
Saint-Germain-des-Fossés (03) . . 185 J2
Saint-Germain-des-Grois (61) . . . 84 A3
Saint-Germain-des-Prés (24) . . . 214 D2
Saint-Germain-des-Prés (45) . . . 111 K3
Saint-Germain-des-Prés (49) . . . 124 D2
Saint-Germain-des-Prés (81) . . . 289 J1
Saint-Germain-des-Vaux (50) . . . 28 A1
Saint-Germain-d'Esteuil (33) . . . 210 E2
Saint-Germain-d'Étables (76) . . . 16 A2
Saint-Germain-du-Bel-Air (46) . . . 233 H5
Saint-Germain-du-Bois (71) 172 C1
Saint-Germain-du-Corbéis (61). . . 82 C3
Saint-Germain-du-Crioult (14) . . . 53 G3
Saint-Germain-du-Pert (14) 29 H6
Saint-Germain-du-Pinel (35) . . . 104 B2
Saint-Germain-du-Plain (71) . . . 172 A1
Saint-Germain-du-Puch (33) . . . 229 K2
Saint-Germain-du-Puy (18) 149 H3
Saint-Germain-du-Salembre (24) . . 213 H4
Saint-Germain-du-Seudre (17) . . . 195 F5
Saint-Germain-du-Teil (48) 253 H1
Saint-Germain-en-Brionnais (71) . . 170 D6
Saint-Germain-en-Coglès (35) . . . 80 A3
Saint-Germain-en-Laye (78) 58 C3
Saint-Germain-en-Montagne (39) . . 156 B6
Saint-Germain-et-Mons (24) 231 J2
Saint-Germain-la-
 Blanche-Herbe (14) 32 D5
Saint-Germain-la-Campagne (27). . 55 G1
Saint-Germain-la-Chambotte (73) . . 208 B1
Saint-Germain-la-Montagne (42) . . 187 H2
Saint-Germain-la-Poterie (60) . . . 37 G2
Saint-Germain-la-Ville (51) 62 E3
Saint-Germain-l'Aiguiller (85) . . . 160 D1
Saint-Germain-Langot (14) 53 K2
Saint-Germain-Laprade (43) 220 D5
Saint-Germain-Laval (42) 204 C1
Saint-Germain-Laval (77) 88 A3
Saint-Germain-Lavolps (19) 200 E4
Saint-Germain-Laxis (77) 87 H1
Saint-Germain-le-Châtelet (90) . . 119 J5
Saint-Germain-le-Fouilloux (53) . . 80 E6
Saint-Germain-le-Gaillard (28) . . 84 E3
Saint-Germain-le-Gaillard (50) . . 28 B4
Saint-Germain-le-Guillaume (53) . . 80 E5
Saint-Germain-le-Rocheux (21) . . 115 G6
Saint-Germain-le-Vasson (14) . . . 53 K1
Saint-Germain-le-Vieux (61) 55 F6
Saint-Germain-Lembron (63) . . . 202 E6
Saint-Germain-lès-Arlay (39) . . . 155 H6
Saint-Germain-lès-Arpajon (91) . . 86 D1
Saint-Germain-lès-Belles (87) . . . 199 H4
Saint-Germain-lès-Buxy (71) . . . 171 J1
Saint-Germain-lès-Corbeil (91) . . 59 F6
Saint-Germain-lès-Paroisses (01) . . 207 J1
Saint-Germain-lès-Senailly (21) . . 134 D2
Saint-Germain-les-Vergnes (19) . . 215 K2

Saint-Germain-Lespinasse (42). . . 186 D3
Saint-Germain-l'Herm (63) 203 H6
Saint-Germain-près-Herment (63). . 201 H3
Saint-Germain-Source-Seine (21). . 135 H3
Saint-Germain-sous-Cailly (76). . . 16 A6
Saint-Germain-sous-Doue (77). . . 60 C3
Saint-Germain-sur-Avre (27) 56 E4
Saint-Germain-sur-Ay (50) 30 C1
Saint-Germain-sur-Bresle (80) . . . 17 F3
Saint-Germain-sur-Eaulne (76) . . . 16 D3
Saint-Germain-sur-Ecole (77) . . . 87 G2
Saint-Germain-sur-Ille (35) 79 G2
Saint-Germain-sur-l'Arbresle (69) . . 205 J1
Saint-Germain-sur-Meuse (55) . . . 65 F5
Saint-Germain-sur-Moine (49) . . . 142 C2
Saint-Germain-sur-Morin (77) . . . 59 K3
Saint-Germain-sur-Renon (01) . . . 188 E3
Saint-Germain-sur-Rhône (74) . . . 190 C3
Saint-Germain-sur-Sarthe (72) . . . 82 D5
Saint-Germain-sur-Sèves (50) . . . 30 E2
Saint-Germain-sur-Vienne (37) . . . 144 C1
Saint-Germain-Village (27) 34 C3
Saint-Germainmont (08) 41 G1
Saint-Germé (32) 266 A5
Saint-Germer-de-Fly (60) 36 E2
Saint-Germier (31) 288 C2
Saint-Germier (32) 268 B5
Saint-Germier (79) 162 B4
Saint-Germier (81) 270 E5
Saint-Géron (43) 219 G2
Saint-Gérons (15) 235 F1
Saint-Gervais (30) 256 C4
Saint-Gervais (33) 211 J5
Saint-Gervais (38) 223 J3
Saint-Gervais (85) 140 D4
Saint-Gervais (95) 36 E5
Saint-Gervais-d'Auvergne (63) . . . 184 C4
Saint-Gervais-de-Vic (72) 107 K4
Saint-Gervais-des-Sablons (61) . . 54 D3
Saint-Gervais-du-Perron (61) . . . 82 D1
Saint-Gervais-en-Belin (72) 106 E4
Saint-Gervais-en-Vallière (71) . . . 154 B4
Saint-Gervais-la-Forêt (41) 129 F2
Saint-Gervais-les-Bains (74) 192 B5
Saint-Gervais-les-
 Trois-Clochers (86) 145 H5
Saint-Gervais-sous-
 Meymont (63) 203 J3
Saint-Gervais-sur-Couches (71) . . 153 H4
Saint-Gervais-sur-Mare (34) 272 D6
Saint-Gervais-sur-Roubion (26) . . 240 C5
Saint-Gervasy (30) 275 H3
Saint-Gervazy (63) 219 F1
Saint-Géry (24) 213 G6
Saint-Géry (46) 250 B1
Saint-Geyrac (24) 214 C5
Saint-Gibrien (51) 62 C2
Saint-Gildas (22) 76 E1
Saint-Gildas-de-Rhuys (56) 120 E2
Saint-Gildas-des-Bois (44) 102 C6
Saint-Gilles (30) 275 H5
Saint-Gilles (35) 78 E3
Saint-Gilles (36) 165 G5
Saint-Gilles (50) 31 G3
Saint-Gilles (51) 40 B4
Saint-Gilles (71) 153 J5
Saint-Gilles-Croix-de-Vie (85) . . . 158 D1
Saint-Gilles-de-Crétot (76) 15 F6
Saint-Gilles-de-la-Neuville (76) . . 14 D6
Saint-Gilles-des-Marais (61) 53 F6
Saint-Gilles-du-Mené (22) 77 J3
Saint-Gilles-les-Bois (22) 48 D4
Saint-Gilles-les-Forêts (87) 199 K4
Saint-Gilles-Pligeaux (22) 76 D2
Saint-Gilles-Vieux-Marché (22) . . . 76 E3
Saint-Gineis-en-Coiron (07) 239 J5
Saint-Gingolph (74) 175 J5
Saint-Girod (73) 208 C1
Saint-Girons (09) 306 D3
Saint-Girons (64) 264 D6
Saint-Girons-d'Aiguevives (33) . . . 211 H4
Saint-Gladie-Arrive-Munein (64) . . 283 H3
Saint-Glen (22) 77 J2
Saint-Goazec (29) 75 G4
Saint-Gobain (02) 20 B6
Saint-Gobert (02) 20 E3
Saint-Goin (64) 283 K5
Saint-Gondon (45) 131 G1
Saint-Gondran (35) 78 E2
Saint-Gonlay (35) 78 C4
Saint-Gonnery (56) 77 F5
Saint-Gor (40) 246 C6
Saint-Gorgon (56) 102 A4
Saint-Gorgon (88) 95 F3
Saint-Gorgon-Main (25) 156 E3
Saint-Gouéno (22) 77 H3
Saint-Gourgon (41) 128 B1
Saint-Gourson (16) 179 H5
Saint-Goussaud (23) 182 A4
Saint-Gratien (80) 18 C1
Saint-Gratien (95) 58 D2
Saint-Gratien-Savigny (58) 151 J3
Saint-Gravé (56) 102 A3
Saint-Grégoire (81) 271 F2
Saint-Grégoire-d'Ardennes (17) . . 195 H5
Saint-Grégoire-du-Vièvre (27) . . . 34 D4
Saint-Griède (32) 266 B4
Saint-Groux (16) 179 G6
Saint-Guen (22) 76 E4
Saint-Guilhem-le-Désert (34) . . . 273 J5
Saint-Guillaume (38) 223 K6
Saint-Guinoux (35) 50 E4
Saint-Guiraud (34) 273 H5
Saint-Guyomard (56) 101 H4

Saint-Haon-le-Châtel (42). 186 D4
Saint-Haon-le-Vieux (42) 186 D4
Saint-Héand (42) 205 G5
Saint-HéIen (22) 50 D5
Saint-Hélier (21) 135 G4
Saint-Hellier (76) 16 A4
Saint-Herblain (44) 123 F4
Saint-Herblon (44) 124 B4
Saint-Hérent (63) 202 E6
Saint-Hernin (29) 75 H3
Saint-Hervé (22) 77 F3
Saint-Hilaire (03) 168 B4
Saint-Hilaire (11) 309 G1
Saint-Hilaire (25) 138 C4
Saint-Hilaire (31) 288 A3
Saint-Hilaire (38) 224 C1
Saint-Hilaire (43) 219 H1
Saint-Hilaire (46) 234 E3
Saint-Hilaire (63) 184 A4
Saint-Hilaire (91) 86 D1
Saint-Hilaire-au-Temple (51) . . . 62 D1
Saint-Hilaire-Bonneval (87) 199 G3
Saint-Hilaire-Cottes (62) 5 H5
Saint-Hilaire-Cusson-la-
 Valmitte (42) 220 D1
Saint-Hilaire-de-Beauvoir (34). . . 274 C4
Saint-Hilaire-de-Brens (38) 207 F3
Saint-Hilaire-de-Brethmas (30) . . 255 H6
Saint-Hilaire-de-Briouze (61) . . . 53 K5
Saint-Hilaire-de-Chaléons (44) . . . 122 D5
Saint-Hilaire-de-Clisson (44) . . . 142 A2
Saint-Hilaire-de-Court (18) 148 D1
Saint-Hilaire-de-Gondilly (18) . . . 150 B3
Saint-Hilaire-de-la-Côte (38) . . . 207 F6
Saint-Hilaire-de-la-Noaille (33) . . 230 D5
Saint-Hilaire-de-Lavit (48) 254 E4
Saint-Hilaire-de-Loulay (85) 142 A3
Saint-Hilaire-de-Lusignan (47) . . . 248 A4
Saint-Hilaire-de-Riez (85) 140 E6
Saint-Hilaire-de-Villefranche (17) . . 177 K6
Saint-Hilaire-de-Voust (85) 161 F3
Saint-Hilaire-des-Landes (35) . . . 79 K1
Saint-Hilaire-des-Loges (85) 161 F4
Saint-Hilaire-d'Estissac (24) 213 J6
Saint-Hilaire-d'Ozilhan (30) 275 K1
Saint-Hilaire-du-Bois (17) 195 H6
Saint-Hilaire-du-Bois (33) 230 C4
Saint-Hilaire-du-Harcouët (50) . . . 52 C6
Saint-Hilaire-du-Maine (53) 80 D5
Saint-Hilaire-du-Rosier (38) 223 F4
Saint-Hilaire-en-Lignières (18) . . . 166 D1
Saint-Hilaire-en-Morvan (58) . . . 152 B3
Saint-Hilaire-en-Woëvre (55) . . . 44 B6
Saint-Hilaire-Foissac (19) 216 E2
Saint-Hilaire-Fontaine (58) 169 H1
Saint-Hilaire-la-Croix (63) 184 E5
Saint-Hilaire-la-Forêt (85) 159 G4
Saint-Hilaire-la-Gérard (61) 54 D6
Saint-Hilaire-la-Gravelle (41) . . . 108 D4
Saint-Hilaire-la-Palud (79) 177 H1
Saint-Hilaire-la-Plaine (23) 182 E3
Saint-Hilaire-la-Treille (87) 181 H2
Saint-Hilaire-le-Château (23) . . . 182 D5
Saint-Hilaire-le-Châtel (61) 83 F1
Saint-Hilaire-le-Grand (51) 41 K5
Saint-Hilaire-le-Lierru (72) 107 H1
Saint-Hilaire-le-Petit (51) 41 J4
Saint-Hilaire-le-Vouhis (85) 160 B1
Saint-Hilaire-les-Andrésis (45) . . . 112 B2
Saint-Hilaire-les-Courbes (19) . . . 200 A4
Saint-Hilaire-les-Monges (63) . . . 201 J1
Saint-Hilaire-les-Places (87) 198 E4
Saint-Hilaire-lez-Cambrai (59) . . . 12 C4
Saint-Hilaire-Luc (19) 217 F1
Saint-Hilaire-Petitville (50) 31 G1
Saint-Hilaire-Peyroux (19) 215 K3
Saint-Hilaire-Saint-Mesmin (45) . . 109 K4
Saint-Hilaire-sous-Charlieu (42) . . 187 G3
Saint-Hilaire-sous-Romilly (10) . . 89 G2
Saint-Hilaire-sur-Benaize (36) . . . 164 C3
Saint-Hilaire-sur-Erre (61) 83 K4
Saint-Hilaire-sur-Helpe (59) 13 G4
Saint-Hilaire-sur-Puiseaux (45) . . 111 H4
Saint-Hilaire-sur-Risle (61) 55 H5
Saint-Hilaire-sur-Yerre (28) 108 E2
Saint-Hilaire-Taurieux (19) 216 B5
Saint-Hilarion (78) 57 J6
Saint-Hilliers (77) 60 D6
Saint-Hippolyte (12) 235 K4
Saint-Hippolyte (15) 218 A3
Saint-Hippolyte (17) 177 F5
Saint-Hippolyte (25) 139 H4
Saint-Hippolyte (33) 230 B2
Saint-Hippolyte (37) 146 E3
Saint-Hippolyte (66) 310 C5
Saint-Hippolyte (68) 96 C2
Saint-Hippolyte-de-Caton (30) . . . 255 J6
Saint-Hippolyte-de-Montaigu (30). . 275 J1
Saint-Hippolyte-du-Fort (30). . . . 274 B2
Saint-Hippolyte-le-Graveyron (84) . . 257 H5
Saint-Honoré (38) 224 B6
Saint-Honoré (76) 16 A3
Saint-Honoré-les-Bains (58) 152 A5
Saint-Hostien (43) 220 D5
Saint-Hubert (57) 45 G4
Saint-Huruge (71) 171 G3
Saint-Hymer (14) 33 K4
Saint-Hymetière (39) 173 G5
Saint-Igeaux (22) 76 C3
Saint-Igest (12) 251 G2
Saint-Ignan (31) 286 D6
Saint-Ignat (63) 185 H6
Saint-Igny-de-Roche (71) 187 H2
Saint-Igny-de-Vers (69) 187 J2
Saint-Illide (15) 217 G5
Saint-Illiers-la-Ville (78) 57 G2

395

Saint-Illiers-le-Bois (78) 57 G2
Saint-Ilpize (43) 219 H3
Saint-Imoges (51) 40 E6
Saint-Inglevert (62) 2 B3
Saint-Ismier (38) 224 B2
Saint-Izaire (12) 271 K2
Saint-Jacques (04) 279 H1
Saint-Jacques-d'Aliermont (76) 16 B2
Saint-Jacques-d'Ambur (63) 184 C6
Saint-Jacques-d'Atticieux (07) . . . 221 K1
Saint-Jacques-de-la-Lande (35) . . . 79 F5
Saint-Jacques-de-Néhou (50) 28 C5
Saint-Jacques-de-Thouars (79) . . . 144 C1
Saint-Jacques-des-Arrêts (69) 188 A1
Saint-Jacques-des-Blats (15) 218 A5
Saint-Jacques-des-Guérets (41) . . 107 K5
Saint-Jacques-en-
    -Valgodemard (05) 242 E2
Saint-Jacques-sur-Darnétal (76) . . . 35 J2
Saint-Jacut-de-la-Mer (22) 50 B3
Saint-Jacut-du-Mené (22) 77 J3
Saint-Jacut-les-Pins (56) 102 A3
Saint-Jal (19) 215 K1
Saint-James (50) 51 K5
Saint-Jammes (64) 284 E3
Saint-Jans-Cappel (59) 6 A2
Saint-Jean (31) 269 H5
Saint-Jean-aux-Amognes (58) . . . 151 F4
Saint-Jean-aux-Bois (08) 21 K4
Saint-Jean-aux-Bois (60) 38 E3
Saint-Jean-Bonnefonds (42) 205 G6
Saint-Jean-Brévelay (56) 101 G3
Saint-Jean-Cap-Ferrat (06) 281 H4
Saint-Jean-Chambre (07) 239 J1
Saint-Jean-d'Aigues-Vives (09) . . 308 B3
Saint-Jean-d'Alcapiès (12) 272 C2
Saint-Jean-d'Angély (17) 177 K5
Saint-Jean-d'Angle (17) 194 D1
Saint-Jean-d'Ardières (69) 188 B3
Saint-Jean-d'Arves (73) 225 G2
Saint-Jean-d'Arvey (73) 208 C4
Saint-Jean-d'Assé (72) 82 D6
Saint-Jean-d'Ataux (24) 213 H4
Saint-Jean-d'Aubrigoux (43) 220 B1
Saint-Jean-d'Aulps (74) 192 A1
Saint-Jean-d'Avelanne (38) 207 K5
Saint-Jean-de-Barrou (11) 310 B3
Saint-Jean-de-Bassel (57) 67 H3
Saint-Jean-de-Beauregard (91) . . . 58 C6
Saint-Jean-de-Belleville (73) . . . 209 H5
Saint-Jean-de-Beugné (85) 160 B3
Saint-Jean-de-Blaignac (33) 230 B2
Saint-Jean-de-Bœuf (21) 153 K1
Saint-Jean-de-Boiseau (44) 123 F4
Saint-Jean-de-Bonneval (10) 90 A6
Saint-Jean-de-Bournay (38) 206 D5
Saint-Jean-de-Braye (45) 110 B4
Saint-Jean-de-Buèges (34) 273 K3
Saint-Jean-de-Ceyrargues (30) . . . 255 J6
Saint-Jean-de-Chevelu (73) 208 A2
Saint-Jean-de-Côle (24) 198 B6
Saint-Jean-de-Cornies (34) 274 D3
Saint-Jean-de-Couz (73) 208 A5
Saint-Jean-de-Crieulon (30) 274 D2
Saint-Jean-de-Cuculles (34) 274 B4
Saint-Jean-de-Daye (50) 31 H2
Saint-Jean-de-Duras (47) 231 F4
Saint-Jean-de-Folleville (76) 14 E6
Saint-Jean-de-Fos (34) 273 J5
Saint-Jean-de-Gonville (01) 190 D1
Saint-Jean-de-la-Blaquière (34) . . 273 H5
Saint-Jean-de-la-Croix (49) 125 G4
Saint-Jean-de-la-Forêt (61) 83 J4
Saint-Jean-de-la-Haize (50) 51 K3
Saint-Jean-de-la-Léqueraye (27) . . 34 C4
Saint-Jean-de-la-Motte (72) 106 C6
Saint-Jean-de-la-Neuville (76) . . . 14 D6
Saint-Jean-de-la-Porte (73) 208 D4
Saint-Jean-de-la-Rivière (50) 28 B5
Saint-Jean-de-la-Ruelle (45) 110 A4
Saint-Jean-de-Laur (46) 250 E2
Saint-Jean-de-Lier (40) 264 D3
Saint-Jean-de-Linières (49) 125 F3
Saint-Jean-de-Liversay (17) 177 G1
Saint-Jean-de-Livet (14) 33 K6
Saint-Jean-de-Losne (21) 154 E2
Saint-Jean-de-Luz (64) 263 B1
Saint-Jean-de-Marcel (81) 251 J6
Saint-Jean-de-Marsacq (40) 262 D5
Saint-Jean-de-Maruéjols-et-
    -Avéjan (30) 255 J4
Saint-Jean-de-Maurienne (73) . . . 225 G2
Saint-Jean-de-Minervois (34) . . . 291 G3
Saint-Jean-de-Moirans (38) 223 J1
Saint-Jean-de-Monts (85) 140 D5
Saint-Jean-de-Muzols (07) 222 B6
Saint-Jean-de-Nay (43) 220 A5
Saint-Jean-de-Niost (01) 206 E1
Saint-Jean-de-Paracol (11) 308 D3
Saint-Jean-de-Rebervilliers (28) . . 84 E1
Saint-Jean-de-Rives (81) 270 A4
Saint-Jean-de-Sauves (86) 144 E5
Saint-Jean-de-Savigny (50) 31 J2
Saint-Jean-de-Serres (30) 274 C1
Saint-Jean-de-Sixt (74) 191 J5
Saint-Jean-de-Soudain (38) 207 G4
Saint-Jean-de-Tholome (74) 191 H3
Saint-Jean-de-Thouars (79) 144 B4
Saint-Jean-de-Thurac (47) 248 C5
Saint-Jean-de-Thurigneux (01) . . 188 D3
Saint-Jean-de-Touslas (69) 205 J4
Saint-Jean-de-Trézy (71) 153 H6
Saint-Jean-de-Valériscle (30) . . . 255 H4
Saint-Jean-de-Vals (81) 271 F5
Saint-Jean-de-Vaulx (38) 224 B5
Saint-Jean-de-Vaux (71) 153 J6

Saint-Jean-de-Védas (34) 293 G1
Saint-Jean-de-Verges (09) 307 J2
Saint-Jean-Delnous (12) 271 H1
Saint-Jean-des-Baisants (50) 31 J3
Saint-Jean-des-Bois (61) 53 F5
Saint-Jean-des-Champs (50) 51 J1
Saint-Jean-des-Échelles (72) . . . 107 J1
Saint-Jean-des-Essartiers (14) . . . 31 K4
Saint-Jean-des-Mauvrets (49) . . . 125 H4
Saint-Jean-des-Ollières (63) 203 G4
Saint-Jean-des-Vignes (69) 188 B6
Saint-Jean-d'Estissac (24) 213 J5
Saint-Jean-d'Étreux (39) 172 E5
Saint-Jean-d'Eyraud (24) 213 H6
Saint-Jean-d'Hérans (38) 242 B1
Saint-Jean-d'Heurs (63) 203 G1
Saint-Jean-d'Illac (33) 229 F2
Saint-Jean-d'Ormont (88) 95 J3
Saint-Jean-du-Bois (72) 106 B4
Saint-Jean-du-Bouzet (82) 268 B1
Saint-Jean-du-Bruel (12) 273 G1
Saint-Jean-du-Cardonnay (76) . . . 35 H1
Saint-Jean-du-Castillonnais (09) . . 306 B3
Saint-Jean-du-Corail (50) 52 D6
Saint-Jean-du-Corail-
    -des-Bois (50) 52 B4
Saint-Jean-du-Doigt (29) 47 G3
Saint-Jean-du-Falga (09) 307 J1
Saint-Jean-du-Gard (30) 254 E6
Saint-Jean-du-Pin (30) 255 G5
Saint-Jean-du-Thenney (27) 55 G1
Saint-Jean-en-Royans (26) 223 G5
Saint-Jean-en-Val (63) 203 F5
Saint-Jean-et-Saint-Paul (12) . . . 272 C2
Saint-Jean-Froidmentel (41) 108 D3
Saint-Jean-Kerdaniel (22) 48 D5
Saint-Jean-Kourtzerode (57) 70 A1
Saint-Jean-la-Bussière (69) 187 H5
Saint-Jean-la-Fouillouse (48) . . . 238 A4
Saint-Jean-la-Poterie (56) 102 B4
Saint-Jean-la-Vêtre (42) 204 A2
Saint-Jean-Lachalm (43) 238 A1
Saint-Jean-Lagineste (46) 234 B2
Saint-Jean-Lasseille (66) 315 G3
Saint-Jean-le-Blanc (14) 53 G2
Saint-Jean-le-Blanc (45) 110 A4
Saint-Jean-le-Centenier (07) . . . 239 J5
Saint-Jean-le-Comtal (32) 286 C1
Saint-Jean-le-Thomas (50) 51 J2
Saint-Jean-le-Vieux (01) 189 H4
Saint-Jean-le-Vieux (38) 224 C3
Saint-Jean-le-Vieux (64) 282 E5
Saint-Jean-lès-Buzy (55) 44 B5
Saint-Jean-les-Deux-
    -Jumeaux (77) 60 A2
Saint-Jean-lès-Longuyon (54) . . . 43 J1
Saint-Jean-Lespinasse (46) 234 B2
Saint-Jean-Lherm (31) 269 J5
Saint-Jean-Ligoure (87) 199 F3
Saint-Jean-Mirabel (46) 234 E4
Saint-Jean-Pied-de-Port (64) . . . 282 D5
Saint-Jean-Pierre-Fixte (28) 84 A5
Saint-Jean-Pla-de-Corts (66) . . . 315 F4
Saint-Jean-Poudge (64) 284 E1
Saint-Jean-Poutge (32) 267 F5
Saint-Jean-Rohrbach (57) 68 B4
Saint-Jean-Roure (07) 239 H1
Saint-Jean-Saint-Germain (37) . . 146 D3
Saint-Jean-Saint-Gervais (63) . . 219 G1
Saint-Jean-Saint-Maurice-
    -sur-Loire (42) 186 E5
Saint-Jean-Saint-Nicolas (05) . . . 243 G4
Saint-Jean-Saverne (67) 70 B1
Saint-Jean-Soleymieux (42) 204 C5
Saint-Jean-sur-Couesnon (35) . . . 79 K2
Saint-Jean-sur-Erve (53) 105 J2
Saint-Jean-sur-Mayenne (53) . . . 81 F6
Saint-Jean-sur-Moivre (51) 63 F3
Saint-Jean-sur-Reyssouze (01) . . 172 B5
Saint-Jean-sur-Tourbe (51) 42 B5
Saint-Jean-sur-Veyle (01) 188 D1
Saint-Jean-sur-Vilaine (35) 79 K4
Saint-Jean-Trolimon (29) 98 B3
Saint-Jeannet (04) 278 E1
Saint-Jeannet (06) 281 F3
Saint-Jeanvrin (18) 166 D3
Saint-Jeoire (74) 191 J2
Saint-Jeoire-Prieuré (73) 208 C4
Saint-Jeure-d'Andaure (07) 221 H5
Saint-Jeure-d'Ay (07) 222 A4
Saint-Jeures (43) 221 F5
Saint-Joachim (44) 122 A2
Saint-Jodard (42) 187 F6
Saint-Joire (55) 64 D6
Saint-Jores (50) 30 C1
Saint-Jorioz (74) 191 F6
Saint-Jory (31) 269 G4
Saint-Jory-de-Chalais (24) 198 B5
Saint-Jory-las-Bloux (24) 214 C1
Saint-Joseph (42) 205 J4
Saint-Joseph (50) 28 D3
Saint-Joseph-de-Rivière (38) . . . 207 K6
Saint-Joseph-des-Bancs (07) . . . 239 H3
Saint-Josse (62) 4 B6
Saint-Jouan-de-l'Isle (22) 78 B2
Saint-Jouan-des-Guérets (35) . . . 50 D4
Saint-Jouin (14) 33 H4
Saint-Jouin-Bruneval (76) 14 B5
Saint-Jouin-de-Blavou (61) 83 J3
Saint-Jouin-de-Marnes (79) 144 C3
Saint-Jouin-de-Milly (79) 161 F1
Saint-Jouvent (87) 181 G5
Saint-Juan (25) 138 D5
Saint-Judoce (22) 78 D1
Saint-Juéry (12) 271 K2

Saint-Juéry (48) 236 E2
Saint-Juéry (81) 270 E2
Saint-Juire-Champgillon (85) . . . 160 B3
Saint-Julia (31) 289 G1
Saint-Julia-de-Bec (11) 309 F4
Saint-Julien (21) 136 B4
Saint-Julien (22) 77 F1
Saint-Julien (34) 291 H1
Saint-Julien (39) 173 F5
Saint-Julien (69) 188 A4
Saint-Julien (83) 278 C4
Saint-Julien (88) 117 J2
Saint-Julien-aux-Bois (19) 216 E4
Saint-Julien-Beychevelle (33) . . . 211 F3
Saint-Julien-Boutières (07) 221 G6
Saint-Julien-Chapteuil (43) 220 E5
Saint-Julien-d'Ance (43) 220 C2
Saint-Julien-d'Armagnac (40) . . . 266 A1
Saint-Julien-d'Arpaon (48) 254 C3
Saint-Julien-d'Asse (04) 278 E2
Saint-Julien-de-Bourdeilles (24) . . 213 J1
Saint-Julien-de-Briola (11) 289 G6
Saint-Julien-de-Cassagnas (30) . . 255 H4
Saint-Julien-de-Chédon (41) . . . 128 D5
Saint-Julien-de-Civry (71) 170 D2
Saint-Julien-de-Concelles (44) . . 123 J3
Saint-Julien-de-Coppel (63) 203 F3
Saint-Julien-de-Crempse (24) . . . 231 J1
Saint-Julien-de-Gras-Capou (09) . . 308 B2
Saint-Julien-de-Jonzy (71) 187 F2
Saint-Julien-de-la-Liègue (27) . . . 35 K6
Saint-Julien-de-la-Nef (30) 273 K2
Saint-Julien-de-Lampon (24) . . . 233 G4
Saint-Julien-de-l'Escap (17) . . . 177 K5
Saint-Julien-de-l'Herms (38) . . . 206 D6
Saint-Julien-de-Mailloc (14) 34 A6
Saint-Julien-de-Peyrolas (30) . . . 256 B3
Saint-Julien-de-Raz (38) 223 K1
Saint-Julien-de-Toursac (15) . . . 235 F3
Saint-Julien-de-Vouvantes (44) . . 124 A1
Saint-Julien-des-Chazes (43) . . . 219 K5
Saint-Julien-des-Landes (85) . . . 159 F2
Saint-Julien-des-Points (48) . . . 255 F2
Saint-Julien-d'Eymet (24) 231 H3
Saint-Julien-d'Oddes (42) 204 C1
Saint-Julien-du-Gua (07) 239 H1
Saint-Julien-du-Pinet (43) 220 D4
Saint-Julien-du-Puy (81) 270 D4
Saint-Julien-du-Sault (89) 112 D2
Saint-Julien-du-Serre (07) 239 H4
Saint-Julien-du-Terroux (53) 81 J2
Saint-Julien-du-Tournel (48) . . . 254 C1
Saint-Julien-du-Verdon (04) . . . 279 K1
Saint-Julien-en-Beauchêne (05) . . 242 A4
Saint-Julien-en-Born (40) 244 C6
Saint-Julien-en-Champsaur (05) . . 243 F4
Saint-Julien-en-Genevois (74) . . 190 E2
Saint-Julien-en-Quint (26) 241 G2
Saint-Julien-en-Saint-Alban (07) . . 240 A3
Saint-Julien-en-Vercors (26) . . . 223 H5
Saint-Julien-Gaulène (81) 271 G2
Saint-Julien-la-Geneste (63) . . . 184 B4
Saint-Julien-la-Genête (23) . . . 183 K3
Saint-Julien-la-Vêtre (42) 204 A1
Saint-Julien-Labrousse (07) . . . 239 J1
Saint-Julien-l'Ars (86) 163 G3
Saint-Julien-le-Châtel (23) 183 H3
Saint-Julien-le-Faucon (14) 33 J6
Saint-Julien-le-Pèlerin (19) . . . 216 E6
Saint-Julien-le-Petit (87) 199 K1
Saint-Julien-le-Roux (07) 240 A2
Saint-Julien-le-Vendômois (19) . . 199 F6
Saint-Julien-lès-Gorze (54) 65 H1
Saint-Julien-lès-Metz (57) 45 F5
Saint-Julien-lès-Montbéliard (25) . . 139 G2
Saint-Julien-les-Rosiers (30) . . . 255 H5
Saint-Julien-lès-Russey (25) . . . 139 G6
Saint-Julien-les-Villas (10) 90 B5
Saint-Julien-Maumont (19) 216 A5
Saint-Julien-Molhesabate (43) . . 221 H3
Saint-Julien-Molin-Molette (42) . . 221 K4
Saint-Julien-Mont-Denis (73) . . . 225 H2
Saint-Julien-près-Bort (19) 217 H1
Saint-Julien-Puy-Lavèze (63) . . . 201 K3
Saint-Julien-sous-les-Côtes (55) . . 65 F3
Saint-Julien-sur-Bibost (69) . . . 205 H1
Saint-Julien-sur-Calonne (14) . . . 33 K3
Saint-Julien-sur-Cher (41) 129 J6
Saint-Julien-sur-Dheune (71) . . . 153 H6
Saint-Julien-sur-Garonne (31) . . 287 J5
Saint-Julien-sur-Reyssouze (01) . . 172 C5
Saint-Julien-sur-Sarthe (61) 83 J3
Saint-Julien-sur-Veyle (01) 188 D2
Saint-Julien-Vocance (07) 221 J3
Saint-Junien (87) 180 D6
Saint-Junien-la-Bregère (23) . . . 182 C6
Saint-Junien-les-Combes (87) . . 181 F4
Saint-Jure (57) 66 A2
Saint-Jurs (04) 279 F2
Saint-Just (01) 189 G2
Saint-Just (07) 256 C3
Saint-Just (15) 237 F2
Saint-Just (18) 149 H4
Saint-Just (24) 213 J2
Saint-Just (27) 36 B6
Saint-Just (34) 274 E5
Saint-Just (35) 103 J3
Saint-Just (63) 204 A6
Saint-Just-Chaleyssin (38) 206 C4
Saint-Just-d'Avray (69) 187 J5
Saint-Just-de-Claix (38) 223 G5
Saint-Just-en-Bas (42) 204 B2
Saint-Just-en-Brie (77) 88 B1
Saint-Just-en-Chaussée (60) 38 A1
Saint-Just-en-Chevalet (42) . . . 186 C6
Saint-Just-et-le-Bézu (11) 309 F4

Saint-Just-et-Vacquières (30) . . . 255 J5
Saint-Just-Ibarre (64) 283 F5
Saint-Just-la-Pendue (42) 187 G6
Saint-Just-le-Martel (87) 199 G1
Saint-Just-Luzac (17) 194 C1
Saint-Just-Malmont (43) 221 G1
Saint-Just-près-Brioude (43) . . . 219 G3
Saint-Just-Saint-Rambert (42) . . 204 E5
Saint-Just-Sauvage (51) 89 H1
Saint-Just-sur-Dive (49) 144 C1
Saint-Just-sur-Viaur (12) 251 K5
Saint-Justin (32) 285 J2
Saint-Justin (40) 265 K1
Saint-Juvat (22) 78 D1
Saint-Juvin (08) 42 D3
Saint-Lactencin (36) 147 H5
Saint-Lager (69) 188 B3
Saint-Lager-Bressac (07) 240 A4
Saint-Lamain (39) 155 H6
Saint-Lambert (14) 53 H2
Saint-Lambert (78) 58 B5
Saint-Lambert-du-Lattay (49) . . . 125 F5
Saint-Lambert-et-
    Mont-de-Jeux (08) 42 A1
Saint-Lambert-la-Potherie (49) . . 125 F3
Saint-Lambert-sur-Dive (61) 54 D4
Saint-Langis-lès-Mortagne (61) . . 83 H2
Saint-Lanne (65) 266 B6
Saint-Laon (86) 144 D4
Saint-Lary (09) 306 B3
Saint-Lary (32) 267 H5
Saint-Lary-Boujean (31) 286 E5
Saint-Lary-Soulan (65) 304 E4
Saint-Lattier (38) 223 F4
Saint-Launeuc (22) 77 K4
Saint-Laure (63) 185 H6
Saint-Laurent (08) 22 D3
Saint-Laurent (18) 148 E1
Saint-Laurent (22) 48 C4
Saint-Laurent (31) 287 F4
Saint-Laurent (47) 247 K4
Saint-Laurent (74) 191 H3
Saint-Laurent-Blangy (62) 11 F2
Saint-Laurent-Bretagne (64) . . . 284 E3
Saint-Laurent-Chabreuges (43) . . 219 G2
Saint-Laurent-d'Agny (69) 205 K3
Saint-Laurent-d'Aigouze (30) . . . 275 F6
Saint-Laurent-d'Andenay (71) . . 171 F1
Saint-Laurent-d'Arce (33) 211 J5
Saint-Laurent-de-Belzagot (16) . . 212 E1
Saint-Laurent-de-Brèvedent (76) . . 14 C6
Saint-Laurent-de-Carnols (30) . . 256 B4
Saint-Laurent-de-Cerdans (66) . . 314 E6
Saint-Laurent-de-Céris (16) . . . 179 K5
Saint-Laurent-de-
    -Chamousset (69) 205 G2
Saint-Laurent-de-Cognac (16) . . 195 J3
Saint-Laurent-de-Condel (14) . . . 53 J1
Saint-Laurent-de-Cuves (50) 52 C4
Saint-Laurent-de-Gosse (40) . . . 282 D1
Saint-Laurent-de-Jourdes (86) . . 163 H5
Saint-Laurent-de-la-Barrière (17) . . 177 H4
Saint-Laurent-de-
    -la-Cabrerisse (11) 309 H1
Saint-Laurent-de-la-Plaine (49) . . 124 E5
Saint-Laurent-de-la-Prée (17) . . . 176 E4
Saint-Laurent-de-
    -la-Salanque (66) 310 C5
Saint-Laurent-de-la-Salle (85) . . 160 C3
Saint-Laurent-de-Lévézou (12) . . 253 F4
Saint-Laurent-de-Lin (37) 126 D3
Saint-Laurent-de-Mure (69) 206 C3
Saint-Laurent-de-Muret (48) . . . 237 F5
Saint-Laurent-de-Neste (65) . . . 305 G1
Saint-Laurent-de-Terregatte (50) . . 52 A6
Saint-Laurent-de-Trèves (48) . . . 254 C4
Saint-Laurent-de-Vaux (69) 205 J2
Saint-Laurent-de-Veyrès (48) . . . 236 E3
Saint-Laurent-des-Arbres (30) . . 256 D6
Saint-Laurent-des-Autels (49) . . 124 A5
Saint-Laurent-des-Bâtons (24) . . 214 A6
Saint-Laurent-des-Bois (27) 56 E5
Saint-Laurent-des-Bois (41) . . . 109 F5
Saint-Laurent-des-Combes (16) . . 212 D1
Saint-Laurent-des-Combes (33) . . 230 B1
Saint-Laurent-des-Hommes (24) . . 213 F5
Saint-Laurent-des-Mortiers (53) . . 105 G5
Saint-Laurent-des-Vignes (24) . . 231 H2
Saint-Laurent-d'Oingt (69) 187 K5
Saint-Laurent-d'Olt (12) 253 G1
Saint-Laurent-d'Onay (26) 222 E3
Saint-Laurent-du-Bois (33) 230 B4
Saint-Laurent-du-Cros (05) 242 E4
Saint-Laurent-du-Mont (14) 33 H5
Saint-Laurent-du-Mottay (49) . . 124 C5
Saint-Laurent-du-Pape (07) . . . 240 B2
Saint-Laurent-du-Plan (33) 230 B5
Saint-Laurent-du-Pont (38) . . . 207 K6
Saint-Laurent-du-Tencement (27) . . 55 G1
Saint-Laurent-du-Var (06) 281 G4
Saint-Laurent-du-Verdon (04) . . . 278 E4
Saint-Laurent-en-Beaumont (38) . . 242 C1
Saint-Laurent-en-Brionnais (71) . . 187 G1
Saint-Laurent-en-Caux (76) 15 H4
Saint-Laurent-en-Gâtines (37) . . 127 K2
Saint-Laurent-en-Grandvaux (39) . . 174 A3
Saint-Laurent-en-Royans (26) . . 223 G5
Saint-Laurent-la-Conche (42) . . . 204 E3
Saint-Laurent-la-Gâtine (28) 57 G5
Saint-Laurent-la-Roche (39) . . . 173 F3
Saint-Laurent-la-Vallée (24) . . . 232 E3
Saint-Laurent-la-Vernède (30) . . 256 A5
Saint-Laurent-l'Abbaye (58) . . . 132 A5
Saint-Laurent-le-Minier (30) . . . 273 K2
Saint-Laurent-les-Bains (07) . . . 238 D1

Saint-Laurent-les-Églises (87) . . 181 K5
Saint-Laurent-les-Tours (46) . . . 234 C2
Saint-Laurent-Lolmie (46) 249 H3
Saint-Laurent-Médoc (33) . . . . +210 F4
Saint-Laurent-Nouan (41) 109 H6
Saint-Laurent-Rochefort (42) . . . 204 B2
Saint-Laurent-sous-Coiron (07) . . 239 J5
Saint-Laurent-sur-Gorre (87) . . . 198 C2
Saint-Laurent-sur-Manoire (24) . . 214 B4
Saint-Laurent-sur-Mer (14) 29 K6
Saint-Laurent-sur-Othain (55) . . . 43 J2
Saint-Laurent-sur-Oust (56) . . . 101 K4
Saint-Laurent-sur-Saône (01) . . . 188 C1
Saint-Laurent-sur-Sèvre (85) . . . 142 E4
Saint-Laurs (79) 161 G4
Saint-Léger (06) 261 F6
Saint-Léger (16) 196 D6
Saint-Léger (17) 195 G3
Saint-Léger (47) 247 J3
Saint-Léger (53) 105 H1
Saint-Léger (62) 11 F4
Saint-Léger (73) 209 F5
Saint-Léger (77) 60 D4
Saint-Léger-aux-Bois (60) 39 F1
Saint-Léger-aux-Bois (76) 16 E3
Saint-Léger-Bridereix (23) 182 A1
Saint-Léger-de-Balson (33) 246 A1
Saint-Léger-de-Fougeret (58) . . . 152 B3
Saint-Léger-de-la-Martinière (79) . . 178 D2
Saint-Léger-de-Montbrillais (86) . . 144 D3
Saint-Léger-de-Montbrun (79) . . 144 C4
Saint-Léger-de-Peyre (48) 237 G5
Saint-Léger-de-Rôtes (27) 34 D6
Saint-Léger-des-Aubées (28) . . . 85 J3
Saint-Léger-des-Bois (49) 125 F3
Saint-Léger-des-Prés (35) 51 G6
Saint-Léger-des-Vignes (58) . . . 151 G6
Saint-Léger-du-Bois (71) 153 G3
Saint-Léger-du-Bourg-Denis (76) . . 35 J2
Saint-Léger-du-Gennetey (27) . . . 34 E4
Saint-Léger-du-Malzieu (48) . . . 237 G4
Saint-Léger-du-Ventoux (84) . . . 257 J4
Saint-Léger-Dubosq (14) 33 H4
Saint-Léger-en-Bray (60) 37 G2
Saint-Léger-en-Yvelines (78) . . . 57 J5
Saint-Léger-la-Montagne (87) . . 181 J4
Saint-Léger-le-Guérétois (23) . . . 182 C3
Saint-Léger-le-Petit (18) 150 C2
Saint-Léger-lès-Authie (80) 10 C5
Saint-Léger-lès-Domart (80) 9 J4
Saint-Léger-les-Mélèzes (05) . . . 243 F4
Saint-Léger-les-Paray (71) 170 C4
Saint-Léger-les-Vignes (44) . . . 123 F5
Saint-Léger-Magnazeix (87) . . . 181 H1
Saint-Léger-près-Troyes (10) . . . 90 B5
Saint-Léger-sous-Beuvray (71) . . 152 D5
Saint-Léger-sous-Brienne (10) . . 90 E3
Saint-Léger-sous-Cholet (49) . . . 142 C2
Saint-Léger-sous-
    -la-Bussière (71) 187 K1
Saint-Léger-sous-Margerie (10) . . 90 E4
Saint-Léger-sur-Bresle (80) 17 F2
Saint-Léger-sur-Dheune (71) . . . 153 J5
Saint-Léger-sur-Roanne (42) . . . 186 E4
Saint-Léger-sur-Sarthe (61) 83 F2
Saint-Léger-sur-Vouzance (03) . . 170 A5
Saint-Léger-Triey (21) 136 D5
Saint-Léger-Vauban (89) 134 B4
Saint-Léomer (86) 164 B5
Saint-Léon (03) 169 H5
Saint-Léon (31) 288 D3
Saint-Léon (33) 230 A3
Saint-Léon (47) 247 H3
Saint-Léon-d'Issigeac (24) 231 K4
Saint-Léon-sur-l'Isle (24) 213 J4
Saint-Léon-sur-Vézère (24) . . . 214 E6
Saint-Léonard (32) 267 K3
Saint-Léonard (51) 41 F4
Saint-Léonard (62) 4 B3
Saint-Léonard (76) 14 D4
Saint-Léonard (88) 95 J5
Saint-Léonard-de-Noblat (87) . . 199 H1
Saint-Léonard-des-Bois (72) . . . 82 B4
Saint-Léonard-des-Parcs (61) . . . 55 F6
Saint-Léonard-en-Beauce (41) . . 109 F5
Saint-Léons (12) 253 F4
Saint-Léopardin-d'Augy (03) . . . 168 C2
Saint-Léry (56) 78 A4
Saint-Leu-d'Esserent (60) 38 A5
Saint-Leu-la-Forêt (95) 58 D1
Saint-Lézer (65) 285 H3
Saint-Lézin (49) 124 E6
Saint-Lieux-Lafenasse (81) 270 E4
Saint-Lieux-lès-Lavaur (81) . . . 270 A4
Saint-Lin (79) 161 K4
Saint-Lions (04) 260 A6
Saint-Lizier (09) 306 D2
Saint-Lizier-du-Planté (32) . . . 287 G3
Saint-Lô (50) 31 H3
Saint-Lô-d'Ourville (50) 28 C6
Saint-Lon-les-Mines (40) 264 A5
Saint-Longis (72) 83 F4
Saint-Lormel (22) 50 B4
Saint-Lothain (39) 155 H5
Saint-Loube (32) 287 H3
Saint-Loubert (33) 230 B5
Saint-Loubès (33) 229 J1
Saint-Loubouer (40) 265 H5
Saint-Louet-sur-Seulles (14) . . . 32 B6
Saint-Louet-sur-Vire (50) 31 J3
Saint-Louis (57) 70 A2
Saint-Louis (68) 97 F4
Saint-Louis-de-Montferrand (33) . . 211 H6
Saint-Louis-en-l'Isle (24) 213 G5
Saint-Louis-et-Parahou (11) . . . 309 F4
Saint-Louis-lès-Bitche (57) 69 G4

Saint-Loup (03) 168 E6
Saint-Loup (17) 177 J4
Saint-Loup (23) 183 H3
Saint-Loup (39) 154 E3
Saint-Loup (41) 129 K6
Saint-Loup (50) 52 A5
Saint-Loup (51) 61 J5
Saint-Loup (58) 132 A4
Saint-Loup (69) 187 K6
Saint-Loup (82) 248 D6
Saint-Loup-Cammas (31) 269 H5
Saint-Loup-de-Buffigny (10) . . . 89 G3
Saint-Loup-de-Fribois (14) 33 H6
Saint-Loup-de-Gonois (45) 111 K2
Saint-Loup-de-Naud (77) 88 C2
Saint-Loup-des-Varennes (71) . . 171 K1
Saint-Loup-des-Chaumes (18) . . 149 G6
Saint-Loup-des-Vignes (45) 111 F2
Saint-Loup-d'Ordon (89) 112 C2
Saint-Loup-du-Dorat (53) 105 J4
Saint-Loup-du-Gast (53) 81 G3
Saint-Loup-en-Champagne (08) . 41 G1
Saint-Loup-en-Comminges (31) . . 286 C5
Saint-Loup-Géanges (71) 154 B4
Saint-Loup-Hors (14) 32 B3
Saint-Loup-Lamairé (79) 144 B6
Saint-Loup-Nantouard (70) 137 G4
Saint-Loup-sur-Aujon (52) 116 A4
Saint-Loup-sur-Semouse (70) . . . 118 C3
Saint-Loup-Terrier (08) 22 C6
Saint-Loyer-des-Champs (61) . . . 54 C5
Saint-Lubin-de-Cravant (28) 56 C5
Saint-Lubin-de-la-Haye (28) 57 H4
Saint-Lubin-des-Joncherets (28) . . 56 D4
Saint-Lubin-en-Vergonnois (41) . . 128 D2
Saint-Luc (27) 56 E2
Saint-Lucien (28) 57 H6
Saint-Lumier-en-Champagne (51) . . 63 F4
Saint-Lumier-la-Populeuse (51) . . 63 H5
Saint-Lumine-de-Clisson (44) . . . 142 A2
Saint-Lumine-de-Coutais (44) . . . 141 G2
Saint-Lunaire (35) 50 C3
Saint-Luperce (28) 84 E3
Saint-Lupicin (39) 173 J5
Saint-Lupien (10) 89 H4
Saint-Lyé (10) 90 A4
Saint-Lyé-la-Forêt (45) 110 B2
Saint-Lyphard (44) 121 K3
Saint-Lys (31) 287 J2
Saint-Macaire (33) 230 A5
Saint-Macaire-du-Bois (49) 144 A5
Saint-Macaire-en-Mauges (49) . . 142 D2
Saint-Maclou (27) 34 B3
Saint-Maclou-de-Folleville (76) . . 15 K4
Saint-Maclou-la-Brière (76) 14 E5
Saint-Macoux (86) 179 H3
Saint-Maden (22) 78 C1
Saint-Magne (33) 229 G6
Saint-Magne-de-Castillon (33) . . 230 C2
Saint-Maigner (63) 184 B4
Saint-Maigrin (17) 195 K6
Saint-Maime (04) 278 B2
Saint-Maime-de-Péreyrol (24) . . . 213 K6
Saint-Maixant (33) 183 G5
Saint-Maixant (23) 230 A5
Saint-Maixent (72) 107 J1
Saint-Maixent-de-Beugné (79) . . 161 F4
Saint-Maixent-l'École (79) 161 K5
Saint-Maixent-sur-Vie (85) 141 F6
Saint-Maixme-Hauterive (28) . . . 84 D1
Saint-Malo (35) 50 D3
Saint-Malo-de-Beignon (56) 78 B6
Saint-Malo-de-Guersac (44) 122 B2
Saint-Malo-de-la-Lande (50) 30 D4
Saint-Malo-de-Phily (35) 103 F1
Saint-Malo-des-
  -Trois-Fontaines (56) 101 J1
Saint-Malo-du-Bois (85) 142 E4
Saint-Malo-en-Donziois (58) . . . 132 D6
Saint-Malon-sur-Mel (35) 78 C4
Saint-Mamert (69) 188 A1
Saint-Mamert-du-Gard (30) 275 F3
Saint-Mamet (31) 305 H5
Saint-Mamet-la-Salvetat (15) . . . 235 G2
Saint-Mammès (77) 87 J4
Saint-Mandé (94) 59 F4
Saint-Mandé-sur-Brédoire (17) . . 178 B4
Saint-Mandrier-sur-Mer (83) . . . 300 C5
Saint-Manvieu-Bocage (14) 52 D2
Saint-Manvieu-Norrey (14) 32 D5
Saint-Marc (15) 237 F1
Saint-Marc-à-Frongier (23) 183 F6
Saint-Marc-à-Loubaud (23) 200 C1
Saint-Marc-du-Cor (41) 108 B3
Saint-Marc-Jaumegarde (13) . . . 296 E1
Saint-Marc-la-Lande (79) 161 J4
Saint-Marc-le-Blanc (35) 79 J1
Saint-Marc-sur-Couesnon (35) . . 79 K2
Saint-Marc-sur-Seine (21) 115 G6
Saint-Marcan (35) 51 G4
Saint-Marceau (08) 22 D4
Saint-Marceau (72) 82 D6
Saint-Marcel (01) 188 E5
Saint-Marcel (08) 22 B3
Saint-Marcel (27) 36 B6
Saint-Marcel (36) 165 G3
Saint-Marcel (54) 44 D5
Saint-Marcel (56) 101 J3
Saint-Marcel (70) 117 H4
Saint-Marcel (71) 154 B6
Saint-Marcel (73) 209 H4
Saint-Marcel-Bel-Accueil (38) . . 206 E3
Saint-Marcel-Campes (81) 251 F6
Saint-Marcel-d'Ardèche (07) . . . 256 C3
Saint-Marcel-de-Careiret (30) . . 256 B5
Saint-Marcel-de-Félines (42) . . . 187 G6

Saint-Marcel-du-Périgord (24) . . 232 A1
Saint-Marcel-d'Urfé (42) 186 D6
Saint-Marcel-en-Marcillat (03) . . 184 A3
Saint-Marcel-en-Murat (03) 184 E1
Saint-Marcel-l'Éclairé (69) 187 J6
Saint-Marcel-lès-Annonay (07) . . 221 K2
Saint-Marcel-lès-Sauzet (26) . . . 240 B5
Saint-Marcel-lès-Valence (26) . . . 222 D6
Saint-Marcel-Paulel (31) 269 J6
Saint-Marcel-sur-Aude (11) 291 H5
Saint-Marcelin-de-Cray (71) . . . 171 G3
Saint-Marcellin (38) 223 G4
Saint-Marcellin-en-Forez (42) . . . 204 E5
Saint-Marcellin-lès-Vaison (84) . . 257 H4
Saint-Marcet (31) 286 E5
Saint-Marcory (24) 232 C4
Saint-Marcouf (14) 31 J1
Saint-Marcouf (50) 29 F4
Saint-Mard (02) 40 B2
Saint-Mard (17) 177 H3
Saint-Mard (54) 94 B1
Saint-Mard (77) 59 H1
Saint-Mard (80) 19 F4
Saint-Mard-de-Réno (61) 83 J2
Saint-Mard-de-Vaux (71) 153 J6
Saint-Mard-lès-Rouffy (51) 62 B2
Saint-Mard-sur-Auve (51) 63 G1
Saint-Mard-sur-le-Mont (51) . . . 63 H2
Saint-Mards (76) 15 J3
Saint-Mards-de-Blacarville (27) . . 34 C2
Saint-Mards-de-Fresne (27) 34 C6
Saint-Mards-en-Othe (10) 89 J6
Saint-Marien (23) 166 D5
Saint-Mariens (33) 211 J4
Saint-Mars-de-Coutais (44) 122 E5
Saint-Mars-de-Locquenay (72) . . 107 G3
Saint-Mars-d'Égrenne (61) 81 F1
Saint-Mars-d'Outillé (72) 107 F4
Saint-Mars-du-Désert (44) 123 J2
Saint-Mars-du-Désert (53) 82 A4
Saint-Mars-la-Brière (72) 107 G2
Saint-Mars-la-Jaille (44) 124 A2
Saint-Mars-la-Réorthe (85) 142 E5
Saint-Mars-sous-Ballon (72) . . . 82 E6
Saint-Mars-sur-Colmont (53) . . . 81 F3
Saint-Mars-sur-la-Futaie (53) . . . 80 C2
Saint-Mars-Vieux-Maisons (77) . . 60 D5
Saint-Marsal (66) 314 E4
Saint-Martial (07) 239 G2
Saint-Martial (15) 236 D2
Saint-Martial (16) 212 D1
Saint-Martial (17) 178 A4
Saint-Martial (30) 274 A1
Saint-Martial (33) 230 B4
Saint-Martial-d'Albarède (24) . . . 214 D2
Saint-Martial-d'Artenset (24) . . . 213 F5
Saint-Martial-de-Gimel (19) 216 C3
Saint-Martial-de-Mirambeau (17) . . 211 H1
Saint-Martial-de-Nabirat (24) . . . 233 F3
Saint-Martial-de-Valette (24) . . . 197 J5
Saint-Martial-de-Vitaterne (17) . . 195 J5
Saint-Martial-Entraygues (19) . . . 216 D4
Saint-Martial-le-Mont (23) 183 F4
Saint-Martial-le-Vieux (23) 201 F3
Saint-Martial-sur-Isop (87) 180 D3
Saint-Martial-sur-Né (17) 195 J4
Saint-Martial-Viveyrol (24) 213 G1
Saint-Martin (32) 286 A2
Saint-Martin (54) 67 G6
Saint-Martin (56) 102 A3
Saint-Martin (65) 285 H6
Saint-Martin (66) 309 H5
Saint-Martin (67) 70 B6
Saint-Martin (83) 278 C6
Saint-Martin-au-Bosc (76) 17 F3
Saint-Martin-au-Laërt (62) 5 G2
Saint-Martin-aux-Arbres (76) . . . 15 H5
Saint-Martin-aux-Bois (60) 38 B1
Saint-Martin-aux-Buneaux (76) . . 14 E4
Saint-Martin-aux-Champs (51) . . 62 E4
Saint-Martin-aux-Chartrains (14) . . 33 K3
Saint-Martin-Belle-Roche (71) . . 171 K5
Saint-Martin-Bellevue (74) 191 F5
Saint-Martin-Boulogne (62) 4 B3
Saint-Martin-Cantalès (15) 217 G5
Saint-Martin-Château (23) 200 A1
Saint-Martin-Choquel (62) 4 D3
Saint-Martin-Curton (47) 247 F3
Saint-Martin-d'Abbat (45) 110 D4
Saint-Martin-d'Ablois (51) 61 J1
Saint-Martin-d'Août (26) 222 D3
Saint-Martin-d'Arberoue (64) . . . 282 E3
Saint-Martin-d'Arc (73) 225 H2
Saint-Martin-d'Arcé (49) 126 B2
Saint-Martin-d'Ardèche (07) . . . 256 B3
Saint-Martin-d'Armagnac (32) . . 266 B5
Saint-Martin-d'Arrossa (64) 282 D4
Saint-Martin-d'Ary (17) 212 B3
Saint-Martin-d'Aubigny (50) 31 F2
Saint-Martin-d'Audouville (50) . . 29 F4
Saint-Martin-d'Auxigny (18) . . . 149 G1
Saint-Martin-d'Auxy (71) 171 G1
Saint-Martin-de-Bavel (01) 190 B6
Saint-Martin-de-Beauville (47) . . 248 D4
Saint-Martin-de-Belleville (73) . . 209 H6
Saint-Martin-de-Bernegoue (79) . . 178 B2
Saint-Martin-de-Bienfaite-
  -la-Cressonnière (14) 55 F1
Saint-Martin-de-Blagny (14) . . . 31 J2
Saint-Martin-de-Bonfossé (50) . . 31 G4
Saint-Martin-de-Boscherville (76) . . 35 G2
Saint-Martin-de-Bossenay (10) . . 89 H3
Saint-Martin-de-Boubaux (48) . . 255 F4
Saint-Martin-de-Bréthencourt (78) . . 86 A2
Saint-Martin-de-Brômes (04) . . . 278 D3
Saint-Martin-de-Caralp (09) 307 H3

Saint-Martin-de-Castillon (84) . . . 277 J3
Saint-Martin-de-Cenilly (50) 31 F5
Saint-Martin-de-Clelles (38) 241 K2
Saint-Martin-de-Commune (71) . . 153 H5
Saint-Martin-de-Connée (53) 82 A5
Saint-Martin-de-Coux (17) 212 C4
Saint-Martin-de-Crau (13) 276 B5
Saint-Martin-de-Fontenay (14) . . . 32 E5
Saint-Martin-de-Fraigneau (85) . . 160 E5
Saint-Martin-de-
  -Fressengeas (24) 198 B6
Saint-Martin-de-Fugères (43) . . . 238 C1
Saint-Martin-de-Goyne (32) 267 H1
Saint-Martin-de-Gurson (24) . . . 212 E6
Saint-Martin-de-Hinx (40) 262 D6
Saint-Martin-de-Juillers (17) . . . 178 B5
Saint-Martin-de-Jussac (87) 180 E6
Saint-Martin-de-la-Brasque (84) . . 277 J4
Saint-Martin-de-la-Cluze (38) . . . 224 A6
Saint-Martin-de-la-Lieue (14) . . . 33 K6
Saint-Martin-de-la-Mer (21) 134 C6
Saint-Martin-de-la-Place (49) . . . 126 A5
Saint-Martin-de-la-Porte (73) . . . 225 H2
Saint-Martin-de-Lamps (36) 147 J4
Saint-Martin-de-Landelles (50) . . 80 B1
Saint-Martin-de-Lansuscle (48) . . 254 D4
Saint-Martin-de-l'Arçon (34) . . . 291 H1
Saint-Martin-de-Laye (33) 212 A5
Saint-Martin-de-Lenne (12) 253 F2
Saint-Martin-de-Lerm (33) 230 C4
Saint-Martin-de-Lixy (71) 187 G2
Saint-Martin-de-Londres (34) . . . 274 A4
Saint-Martin-de-Mâcon (79) 144 C3
Saint-Martin-de-Mailloc (14) 34 A6
Saint-Martin-de-Mieux (14) 54 A3
Saint-Martin-de-Nigelles (28) . . . 85 H1
Saint-Martin-de-Queyrières (05) . . 243 K1
Saint-Martin-de-Ré (17) 158 C5
Saint-Martin-de-Ribérac (24) . . . 213 G3
Saint-Martin-de-
  -Saint-Maixent (79) 161 K5
Saint-Martin-de-Salency (71) . . . 171 F4
Saint-Martin-de-Sallen (14) 53 H2
Saint-Martin-de-Sanzay (79) . . . 144 B2
Saint-Martin-de-Seignanx (40) . . 262 B6
Saint-Martin-de-Sescas (33) 230 B5
Saint-Martin-de-Valamas (07) . . . 239 H1
Saint-Martin-de-Valgalgues (30) . . 255 G5
Saint-Martin-de-Varreville (50) . . 29 F4
Saint-Martin-de-Vaulserre (38) . . 207 K5
Saint-Martin-de-Vers (46) 233 J5
Saint-Martin-de-Villeréal (47) . . . 232 B5
Saint-Martin-de-Villereglan (11) . . 308 E1
Saint-Martin-d'Ecublei (61) 55 J4
Saint-Martin-d'Entraunes (06) . . . 260 E4
Saint-Martin-des-Besaces (14) . . . 31 K5
Saint-Martin-des-Bois (41) 107 K6
Saint-Martin-des-Champs (18) . . . 150 B2
Saint-Martin-des-Champs (29) . . . 47 G4
Saint-Martin-des-Champs (50) . . . 51 K3
Saint-Martin-des-Champs (77) . . . 60 D4
Saint-Martin-des-Champs (78) . . . 57 J4
Saint-Martin-des-Champs (89) . . . 132 B1
Saint-Martin-des-Combes (24) . . . 213 K6
Saint-Martin-des-Entrées (14) . . . 32 B3
Saint-Martin-des-Fontaines (85) . . 160 D3
Saint-Martin-des-Lais (03) 169 H2
Saint-Martin-des-Landes (61) 82 B1
Saint-Martin-des-Monts (72) 107 H1
Saint-Martin-des-Noyers (85) . . . 160 A1
Saint-Martin-des-Olmes (63) 204 A5
Saint-Martin-des-Pézerits (61) . . . 55 G6
Saint-Martin-des-Plains (63) 203 F5
Saint-Martin-des-Prés (22) 76 D3
Saint-Martin-des-Puits (11) 309 J2
Saint-Martin-des-Tilleuls (85) . . . 142 D3
Saint-Martin-d'Estréaux (42) . . . 186 C2
Saint-Martin-d'Hardinghem (62) . . 5 F4
Saint-Martin-d'Hères (38) 224 B3
Saint-Martin-d'Heuille (58) 150 E3
Saint-Martin-d'Ollières (63) 203 G6
Saint-Martin-Don (14) 52 D2
Saint-Martin-d'Oney (40) 265 F2
Saint-Martin-d'Ordon (89) 112 C2
Saint-Martin-d'Oydes (09) 288 C6
Saint-Martin-du-Bec (76) 14 B5
Saint-Martin-du-Bois (33) 212 A5
Saint-Martin-du-Bois (49) 104 E6
Saint-Martin-du-Boschet (77) . . . 60 E5
Saint-Martin-du-Clocher (16) . . . 179 G4
Saint-Martin-du-Fouilloux (49) . . 125 F4
Saint-Martin-du-Fouilloux (79) . . 162 A3
Saint-Martin-du-Frêne (01) 189 K3
Saint-Martin-du-Lac (71) 186 E2
Saint-Martin-du-Limet (53) 104 C4
Saint-Martin-du-Manoir (76) . . . 14 B6
Saint-Martin-du-Mesnil-Oury (14) . . 54 D1
Saint-Martin-du-Mont (01) 189 H3
Saint-Martin-du-Mont (21) 135 H4
Saint-Martin-du-Mont (71) 172 D2
Saint-Martin-du-Puy (33) 230 C4
Saint-Martin-du-Puy (58) 133 K5
Saint-Martin-du-Tartre (71) 171 G2
Saint-Martin-du-Tertre (89) 88 D4
Saint-Martin-du-Tertre (95) 37 K6
Saint-Martin-du-Tilleul (27) 34 C6
Saint-Martin-du-Var (06) 281 F2
Saint-Martin-du-
  -Vieux-Bellême (61) 83 H3
Saint-Martin-du-Vivier (76) 35 J1
Saint-Martin-d'Uriage (38) 224 B3
Saint-Martin-en-Bière (77) 87 G3
Saint-Martin-en-Bresse (71) 154 C6
Saint-Martin-en-Campagne (76) . . 16 B1
Saint-Martin-en-Gâtinois (71) . . . 154 C4
Saint-Martin-en-Haut (69) 205 H3

Saint-Martin-en-Vercors (26) . . . 223 H5
Saint-Martin-Gimois (32) 287 F2
Saint-Martin-la-Campagne (27) . . 56 C1
Saint-Martin-la-Garenne (78) . . . 57 J1
Saint-Martin-la-Méanne (19) 216 D4
Saint-Martin-la-Plaine (42) 205 J5
Saint-Martin-la-Patrouille (71) . . 171 G3
Saint-Martin-la-Sauveté (42) 204 B1
Saint-Martin-Labouval (46) 250 D1
Saint-Martin-Lacaussade (33) . . . 211 G4
Saint-Martin-Laguépie (81) 251 F5
Saint-Martin-l'Aiguillon (61) 54 A6
Saint-Martin-Lalande (11) 289 H4
Saint-Martin-l'Ars (86) 180 A2
Saint-Martin-Lars-en-
  -Sainte-Hermine (85) 160 C3
Saint-Martin-le-Beau (37) 128 A5
Saint-Martin-le-Bouillant (50) . . . 52 B4
Saint-Martin-le-Châtel (01) 189 F1
Saint-Martin-le-Colonel (26) 223 G6
Saint-Martin-le-Gaillard (76) 16 C1
Saint-Martin-le-Gréard (50) 28 C3
Saint-Martin-le-Hébert (50) 28 C4
Saint-Martin-le-Mault (87) 164 D6
Saint-Martin-le-Nœud (60) 37 G2
Saint-Martin-le-Pin (24) 197 J5
Saint-Martin-le-Redon (46) 232 D6
Saint-Martin-le-Vieil (11) 289 J4
Saint-Martin-le-Vieux (87) 198 D2
Saint-Martin-le-Vinoux (38) 224 A3
Saint-Martin-les-Eaux (04) 278 B2
Saint-Martin-lès-Langres (52) . . . 116 C4
Saint-Martin-lès-Melle (79) 178 D2
Saint-Martin-lès-Seyne (04) 259 J1
Saint-Martin-Lestra (42) 205 F2
Saint-Martin-l'Heureux (51) 41 J4
Saint-Martin-l'Hortier (76) 16 C4
Saint-Martin-Longueau (60) 38 C3
Saint-Martin-Lys (11) 308 E1
Saint-Martin-Osmonville (76) 16 B5
Saint-Martin-Petit (47) 230 D5
Saint-Martin-Rivière (02) 12 D6
Saint-Martin-Saint-Firmin (27) . . . 34 C4
Saint-Martin-
  -Sainte-Catherine (23) 182 A5
Saint-Martin-Sepert (19) 199 H5
Saint-Martin-sous-Montaigu (71) . . 153 K6
Saint-Martin-sous-Vigouroux (15) . . 236 B1
Saint-Martin-sur-Armançon (89) . . 114 B4
Saint-Martin-sur-Cojeul (62) 11 F3
Saint-Martin-sur-Écaillon (59) . . . 12 D1
Saint-Martin-sur-la-Chambre (73) . . 209 H6
Saint-Martin-sur-Lavezon (07) . . . 240 A4
Saint-Martin-sur-Nohain (58) . . . 132 A5
Saint-Martin-sur-Ocre (45) 131 H1
Saint-Martin-sur-Ocre (89) 112 E6
Saint-Martin-sur-Ouanne (89) . . . 112 B5
Saint-Martin-Terressus (87) 181 J6
Saint-Martin-Valmeroux (15) . . . 217 H4
Saint-Martin-Vésubie (06) 261 K5
Saint-Martinien (03) 183 K1
Saint-Martory (31) 287 G6
Saint-Mary (16) 197 G1
Saint-Mary-le-Plain (15) 218 E4
Saint-Masmes (51) 41 H3
Saint-Mathieu (87) 198 A3
Saint-Mathieu-de-Tréviers (34) . . 274 B4
Saint-Mathurin (85) 159 F3
Saint-Mathurin-sur-Loire (49) . . . 125 J4
Saint-Matré (46) 249 G2
Saint-Maudan (22) 77 F5
Saint-Maudez (22) 50 B5
Saint-Maugan (35) 78 C4
Saint-Maulvis (80) 17 G2
Saint-Maur (18) 166 E3
Saint-Maur (32) 286 A2
Saint-Maur (36) 147 K6
Saint-Maur (39) 173 G2
Saint-Maur (60) 17 H5
Saint-Maur-des-Bois (50) 52 B3
Saint-Maur-des-Fossés (94) 59 F4
Saint-Maur-sur-le-Loir (28) 109 F1
Saint-Maurice (52) 116 D4
Saint-Maurice (58) 151 H2
Saint-Maurice (63) 202 E3
Saint-Maurice (94) 59 F4
Saint-Maurice-aux-Forges (54) . . . 95 G1
Saint-Maurice-aux-
  -Riches-Hommes (89) 89 F4
Saint-Maurice-Colombier (25) . . . 139 F3
Saint-Maurice-Crillat (39) 173 J3
Saint-Maurice-d'Ardèche (07) . . . 239 H6
Saint-Maurice-de-Beynost (01) . . 206 C1
Saint-Maurice-de-Cazevieille (30) . . 275 F1
Saint-Maurice-de-Gourdans (01) . . 206 E1
Saint-Maurice-de-Lestapel (47) . . 231 J5
Saint-Maurice-de-Lignon (43) . . . 220 B3
Saint-Maurice-de-Rémens (01) . . . 189 G5
Saint-Maurice-de-Rotherens (73) . . 207 K3
Saint-Maurice-de-Satonnay (71) . . 171 J5
Saint-Maurice-de-Tavernole (17) . . 195 J5
Saint-Maurice-de-Ventalon (48) . . 254 E3
Saint-Maurice-des-Champs (71) . . 171 H2
Saint-Maurice-des-Lions (16) . . . 180 B5
Saint-Maurice-des-Noues (85) . . . 160 E3
Saint-Maurice-d'Ételan (76) 34 D1
Saint-Maurice-d'Ibie (07) 239 J6
Saint-Maurice-du-Désert (61) 53 J6
Saint-Maurice-en-Chalencon (07) . . 239 H2
Saint-Maurice-en-Cotentin (50) . . 28 C5
Saint-Maurice-en-Gourgois (42) . . 221 F1
Saint-Maurice-en-Quercy (46) . . . 234 C3
Saint-Maurice-en-Rivière (71) . . . 154 C5

Saint-Maurice-en-Trièves (38) . . . 242 A3
Saint-Maurice-
  -en-Valgodemard (05) 242 E2
Saint-Maurice-la-Clouère (86) . . . 163 F6
Saint-Maurice-
  -la-Fougereuse (79) 143 J3
Saint-Maurice-la-Souterraine (23) . . 181 J2
Saint-Maurice-le-Girard (85) 160 E2
Saint-Maurice-le-Vieil (89) 112 E5
Saint-Maurice-les-Brousses (87) . . 198 E3
Saint-Maurice-
  -lès-Charencey (61) 55 K6
Saint-Maurice-
  -lès-Châteauneuf (71) 187 G2
Saint-Maurice-lès-Couches (71) . . 153 H5
Saint-Maurice-l'Exil (38) 205 J6
Saint-Maurice-Montcouronne (91) . . 86 C1
Saint-Maurice-Navacelles (34) . . . 273 J3
Saint-Maurice-près-Crocq (23) . . 201 F1
Saint-Maurice-près-Pionsat (63) . . 184 A4
Saint-Maurice-
  -Saint-Germain (28) 84 C2
Saint-Maurice-sous-
  -les-Côtes (55) 65 F1
Saint-Maurice-sur-Adour (40) . . . 265 H4
Saint-Maurice-sur-Aveyron (45) . . 112 A5
Saint-Maurice-sur-Dargoire (69) . . 205 J4
Saint-Maurice-sur-Eygues (26) . . 257 G3
Saint-Maurice-sur-Fessard (45) . . 111 H3
Saint-Maurice-sur-Huisne (61) . . . 83 J3
Saint-Maurice-sur-Mortagne (88) . . 94 D3
Saint-Maurice-sur-Moselle (88) . . 119 H3
Saint-Maurice-sur-
  -Vingeanne (21) 136 D2
Saint-Maurice-Thizouaille (89) . . 112 E5
Saint-Maurin (47) 248 E4
Saint-Max (54) 66 A5
Saint-Maxent (80) 9 F6
Saint-Maximin (30) 275 H1
Saint-Maximin (38) 208 C6
Saint-Maximin (60) 38 A5
Saint-Maximin-
  -la-Sainte-Baume (83) 297 H2
Saint-Maxire (79) 161 H5
Saint-May (26) 257 K1
Saint-Mayeux (22) 76 D3
Saint-Méard (87) 199 H3
Saint-Méard-de-Drône (24) 213 H3
Saint-Méard-de-Gurçon (24) . . . 230 E1
Saint-Médard (16) 196 B5
Saint-Médard (17) 195 J6
Saint-Médard (31) 306 A1
Saint-Médard (32) 286 B2
Saint-Médard (36) 147 F2
Saint-Médard (46) 233 G6
Saint-Médard (57) 66 E3
Saint-Médard (64) 284 A1
Saint-Médard (79) 178 C2
Saint-Médard-d'Aunis (17) 177 F2
Saint-Médard-de-Guizières (33) . . 212 C5
Saint-Médard-de-Mussidan (24) . . 213 G5
Saint-Médard-de-Presque (46) . . 234 B2
Saint-Médard-d'Excideuil (24) . . 214 D2
Saint-Médard-d'Eyrans (33) 229 H3
Saint-Médard-en-Forez (42) 205 G4
Saint-Médard-en-Jalles (33) 229 F1
Saint-Médard-la-Rochette (23) . . 183 F2
Saint-Médard-Nicourby (46) 234 D3
Saint-Médard-sur-Ille (35) 79 G3
Saint-Méen-le-Grand (35) 78 B3
Saint-Melaine-sur-Aubance (49) . . 125 H4
Saint-Mélany (07) 238 E6
Saint-Méloir-des-Bois (22) 50 B5
Saint-Méloir-des-Ondes (35) 50 E3
Saint-Même-le-Tenu (44) 141 F3
Saint-Même-les-Carrières (16) . . 196 B3
Saint-Memmie (51) 62 D2
Saint-Menge (88) 93 J4
Saint-Menges (08) 23 F3
Saint-Menoux (03) 168 C3
Saint-Merd-de-Lapleau (19) 216 D3
Saint-Merd-la-Breuille (23) 201 G2
Saint-Merd-les-Oussines (19) . . . 200 C4
Saint-Méry (77) 87 J1
Saint-Meslin-du-Bosc (27) 35 F5
Saint-Mesmes (77) 59 H2
Saint-Mesmin (10) 89 K3
Saint-Mesmin (21) 135 G5
Saint-Mesmin (24) 215 F1
Saint-Mesmin (85) 143 G6
Saint-Mexant (19) 215 K2
Saint-Mézard (32) 267 H1
Saint-M'Hervé (35) 80 B6
Saint-M'Hervon (35) 78 C2
Saint-Micaud (71) 171 G2
Saint-Michel (02) 21 H1
Saint-Michel (09) 307 H1
Saint-Michel (16) 196 D3
Saint-Michel (31) 287 H6
Saint-Michel (32) 286 B3
Saint-Michel (34) 273 G2
Saint-Michel (45) 110 E2
Saint-Michel (64) 282 E6
Saint-Michel (82) 268 B1
Saint-Michel-Chef-Chef (44) . . . 122 B4
Saint-Michel-d'Aurance (07) . . . 239 H1
Saint-Michel-de-Bannières (46) . . 216 A6
Saint-Michel-de-Boulogne (07) . . 239 H4
Saint-Michel-de-Castelnau (33) . . 246 E3
Saint-Michel-
  -de-Chabrillanoux (07) 239 K2
Saint-Michel-de-Chaillol (05) . . . 243 F3
Saint-Michel-de-Chavaignes (72) . . 107 H2
Saint-Michel-de-Dèze (48) 255 F4
Saint-Michel-de-Double (24) 213 F5

397

Saint-Michel-de-Feins (53) 105 G5
Saint-Michel-de-Fronsac (33) 230 A1
Saint-Michel-de-la-Pierre (50) 30 E1
Saint-Michel-de-la-Roë (53) 104 B4
Saint-Michel-de-Lanès (11) 289 F4
Saint-Michel-de-Lapujade (33) . . . 230 D5
Saint-Michel-de-Livet (14) 54 D1
Saint-Michel-de-Llotes (66) 314 E2
Saint-Michel-de-Maurienne (73) . . . 225 J2
Saint-Michel-de-Montaigne (24) . . . 230 D2
Saint-Michel-de-Montjoie (50) 52 C4
Saint-Michel-de-Plélan (22) 50 B5
Saint-Michel-de-Rieufret (33) 229 J5
Saint-Michel-de-Saint-Geoirs (38) . 223 G2
Saint-Michel-de-Vax (81) 250 D6
Saint-Michel-de-Veisse (23) 183 F5
Saint-Michel-de-Villadeix (24) 214 A6
Saint-Michel-de-Volangis (18) 149 H2
Saint-Michel-des-Andaines (61) . . . 81 J1
Saint-Michel-d'Euzet (30) 256 B4
Saint-Michel-d'Halescourt (76) 17 C1
Saint-Michel-en-Beaumont (38) . . . 242 C1
Saint-Michel-en-Brenne (36) 146 E6
Saint-Michel-en-Grève (22) 47 J3
Saint-Michel-en-l'Herm (85) 159 K5
Saint-Michel-Escalus (40) 262 D2
Saint-Michel-et-Chanveaux (49) . . . 104 B6
Saint-Michel-Labadié (81) 271 G1
Saint-Michel-le-Cloucq (85) 160 K4
Saint-Michel-les-Portes (38) 241 K1
Saint-Michel-l'Observatoire (04) . . . 278 A2
Saint-Michel-Loubéjou (46) 234 B2
Saint-Michel-Mont-Mercure (85) . . . 142 E5
Saint-Michel-sous-Bois (62) 4 D5
Saint-Michel-sur-Loire (37) 127 F5
Saint-Michel-sur-Meurthe (88) 95 H3
Saint-Michel-sur-Orge (91) 58 E6
Saint-Michel-sur-Rhône (42) 205 K6
Saint-Michel-sur-Savasse (26) 222 E4
Saint-Michel-sur-Ternoise (62) 10 B2
Saint-Michel-Tubœuf (61) 55 J5
Saint-Mihiel (55) 64 E2
Saint-Mitre-les-Remparts (13) 295 J4
Saint-Molf (44) 121 J3
Saint-Momelin (59) 3 G4
Saint-Mont (32) 266 A5
Saint-Montan (07) 256 C1
Saint-Moré (89) 133 J2
Saint-Moreil (23) 199 K1
Saint-Morel (08) 42 B3
Saint-Morillon (33) 229 H4
Saint-Mury-Monteymond (38) 224 C2
Saint-Myon (63) 185 F5
Saint-Nabor (67) 70 C5
Saint-Nabord (88) 118 E1
Saint-Nabord-sur-Aube (10) 90 C2
Saint-Nauphary (82) 269 G2
Saint-Nazaire (30) 256 C4
Saint-Nazaire (44) 122 A3
Saint-Nazaire (66) 315 H2
Saint-Nazaire-d'Aude (11) 291 G5
Saint-Nazaire-de-Ladarez (34) 291 J2
Saint-Nazaire-de-Pézan (34) 274 E6
Saint-Nazaire-de-Valentane (82) . . . 249 F4
Saint-Nazaire-des-Gardies (30) . . . 274 D1
Saint-Nazaire-en-Royans (26) 223 F5
Saint-Nazaire-le-Désert (26) 241 G5
Saint-Nazaire-les-Eymes (38) 224 B2
Saint-Nazaire-sur-Charente (17) . . . 176 E5
Saint-Nectaire (63) 202 C4
Saint-Nexans (24) 231 J2
Saint-Nic (29) 74 B3
Saint-Nicodème (22) 76 A2
Saint-Nicolas (62) 10 E2
Saint-Nicolas-aux-Bois (02) 20 B6
Saint-Nicolas-d'Aliermont (76) 16 B2
Saint-Nicolas-d'Attez (27) 56 B4
Saint-Nicolas-de-Bliquetuit (76) . . . 34 E1
Saint-Nicolas-de-Bourgueil (37) . . . 126 D6
Saint-Nicolas-de-la-Balerme (47) . . 248 D5
Saint-Nicolas-de-la-Grave (82) . . . 249 F6
Saint-Nicolas-de-la-Haie (76) 15 F6
Saint-Nicolas-de-la-Taille (76) 34 C1
Saint-Nicolas-de-Macherin (38) . . . 207 J6
Saint-Nicolas-de-Pierrepont (50) . . . 28 D6
Saint-Nicolas-de-Port (54) 66 B5
Saint-Nicolas-de-Redon (44) 102 C4
Saint-Nicolas-de-Sommaire (61) . . . 55 J4
Saint-Nicolas-des-Biefs (03) 186 C4
Saint-Nicolas-des-Bois (50) 52 B4
Saint-Nicolas-des-Bois (61) 82 C2
Saint-Nicolas-des-Laitiers (61) 55 G3
Saint-Nicolas-des-Motets (37) 128 C2
Saint-Nicolas-du-Bosc (27) 35 F5
Saint-Nicolas-du-Pélem (22) 76 C2
Saint-Nicolas-du-Tertre (56) 102 A2
Saint-Nicolas-la-Chapelle (10) 89 F2
Saint-Nicolas-la-Chapelle (73) 191 K6
Saint-Nicolas-lès-Cîteaux (21) 154 C2
Saint-Nizier-d'Azergues (69) 187 J4
Saint-Nizier-de-Fornas (42) 220 E1
Saint-Nizier-du-Moucherotte (38) . . 223 K3
Saint-Nizier-le-Bouchoux (01) 172 C4
Saint-Nizier-le-Désert (01) 189 F4
Saint-Nizier-sous-Charlieu (42) . . . 187 F3
Saint-Nizier-sur-Arroux (71) 152 D6
Saint-Nolff (56) 101 G5
Saint-Nom-la-Bretèche (78) 58 B3
Saint-Offenge-Dessous (73) 208 C2
Saint-Offenge-Dessus (73) 208 C2
Saint-Omer (14) 53 J2
Saint-Omer (62) 5 G3
Saint-Omer-Capelle (62) 3 F3
Saint-Omer-en-Chaussée (60) 17 J6
Saint-Ondras (38) 207 H5
Saint-Onen-la-Chapelle (35) 78 B3

Saint-Oradoux-de-Chirouze (23) . . . 201 F2
Saint-Oradoux-près-Crocq (23) . . . 201 G1
Saint-Orens (32) 268 B5
Saint-Orens-de-Gameville (31) . . . 288 C1
Saint-Orens-Pouy-Petit (32) 267 G2
Saint-Ost (32) 286 B3
Saint-Ouen (17) 178 D6
Saint-Ouen (41) 108 C5
Saint-Ouen (80) 9 A4
Saint-Ouen (93) 58 E3
Saint-Ouen-d'Attez (27) 56 B4
Saint-Ouen-d'Aunis (17) 176 E1
Saint-Ouen-de-la-Cour (61) 83 H3
Saint-Ouen-de-Mimbré (72) 82 C4
Saint-Ouen-de-Pontcheuil (27) 35 G4
Saint-Ouen-de-Sécherouvre (61) . . . 83 G1
Saint-Ouen-de-Thouberville (27) . . . 35 F3
Saint-Ouen-des-Alleux (35) 79 J1
Saint-Ouen-des-Besaces (14) 31 K4
Saint-Ouen-des-Champs (27) 34 C2
Saint-Ouën-des-Toits (53) 80 D6
Saint-Ouën-des-Vallons (53) 81 G6
Saint-Ouen-Domprot (51) 62 D6
Saint-Ouen-du-Breuil (76) 15 J5
Saint-Ouen-du-Mesnil-Oger (14) . . . 33 G5
Saint-Ouen-du-Tilleul (27) 35 G4
Saint-Ouen-en-Belin (72) 106 C5
Saint-Ouen-en-Brie (77) 87 K1
Saint-Ouen-en-Champagne (72) . . . 106 A3
Saint-Ouen-la-Rouërie (35) 51 J5
Saint-Ouen-l'Aumône (95) 58 C1
Saint-Ouen-le-Brisoult (61) 81 K2
Saint-Ouen-le-Houx (14) 54 E2
Saint-Ouen-le-Mauger (76) 15 J3
Saint-Ouen-le-Pin (14) 33 J5
Saint-Ouen-lès-Parey (88) 93 G5
Saint-Ouen-les-Vignes (37) 128 B4
Saint-Ouen-Marchefroy (28) 57 G3
Saint-Ouen-sous-Bailly (76) 16 B2
Saint-Ouen-sur-Gartempe (87) 181 F3
Saint-Ouen-sur-Iton (61) 55 J5
Saint-Ouen-sur-Loire (58) 151 F5
Saint-Ouen-sur-Maire (61) 54 A5
Saint-Ouen-sur-Morin (77) 60 C3
Saint-Oulph (10) 89 J2
Saint-Ours (63) 202 B1
Saint-Ours (73) 208 C1
Saint-Outrille (18) 148 B2
Saint-Ovin (50) 52 A5
Saint-Oyen (73) 209 H4
Saint-Pabu (29) 72 C2
Saint-Paër (76) 35 F1
Saint-Pair (14) 33 F5
Saint-Pair-sur-Mer (50) 51 H1
Saint-Pal-de-Chalencon (43) 220 C1
Saint-Pal-de-Mons (43) 221 G3
Saint-Pal-de-Senouire (43) 219 K3
Saint-Palais (03) 166 E5
Saint-Palais (18) 149 G1
Saint-Palais (33) 211 H2
Saint-Palais (64) 283 G3
Saint-Palais-de-Négrignac (17) . . . 212 B2
Saint-Palais-de-Phiolin (17) 195 G5
Saint-Palais-du-Né (16) 195 K4
Saint-Palais-sur-Mer (17) 194 B3
Saint-Pancrace (24) 197 K6
Saint-Pancrace (73) 225 G2
Saint-Pancrasse (38) 224 C2
Saint-Pancré (54) 26 B2
Saint-Pandelon (40) 264 B5
Saint-Pantaléon (46) 249 J2
Saint-Pantaléon (84) 277 F2
Saint-Pantaléon-de-Lapleau (19) . . 217 F2
Saint-Pantaléon-de-Larche (19) . . . 215 H4
Saint-Pantaléon-les-Vignes (26) . . . 257 G2
Saint-Pantaly-d'Ans (24) 214 D3
Saint-Pantaly-d'Excideuil (24) 214 D2
Saint-Papoul (11) 289 H4
Saint-Pardon-de-Conques (33) 230 B5
Saint-Pardoult (17) 178 A4
Saint-Pardoux (63) 184 E4
Saint-Pardoux (79) 161 J3
Saint-Pardoux (87) 181 H4
Saint-Pardoux-Corbier (19) 199 G6
Saint-Pardoux-d'Arnet (23) 201 F1
Saint-Pardoux-de-Drône (24) 213 H3
Saint-Pardoux-du-Breuil (47) 247 H1
Saint-Pardoux-et-Vielvic (24) 232 D3
Saint-Pardoux-Isaac (47) 231 G5
Saint-Pardoux-la-Croisille (19) 216 D3
Saint-Pardoux-la-Rivière (24) 197 K5
Saint-Pardoux-le-Neuf (19) 201 F4
Saint-Pardoux-le-Neuf (23) 183 G6
Saint-Pardoux-les-Cards (23) 183 F4
Saint-Pardoux-l'Ortigier (19) 215 J2
Saint-Pardoux-Morterolles (23) . . . 182 C6
Saint-Pargoire (34) 292 D1
Saint-Parize-en-Viry (58) 168 L1
Saint-Parize-le-Châtel (58) 150 E6
Saint-Parres-aux-Tertres (10) 90 B5
Saint-Parres-lès-Vaudes (10) 90 C6
Saint-Parthem (12) 235 J3
Saint-Pastour (47) 248 B1
Saint-Pastous (65) 304 B2
Saint-Paterne (72) 82 D3
Saint-Paterne-Racan (37) 127 G2
Saint-Pathus (77) 59 J1
Saint-Patrice (37) 126 E6
Saint-Patrice-de-Claids (50) 30 E2
Saint-Patrice-du-Désert (61) 81 K1
Saint-Paul (06) 281 F4
Saint-Paul (19) 216 C3
Saint-Paul (33) 211 H4
Saint-Paul (60) 37 G2
Saint-Paul (61) 53 G4

Saint-Paul (65) 305 G1
Saint-Paul (73) 208 A3
Saint-Paul (87) 199 G3
Saint-Paul (88) 93 H4
Saint-Paul-aux-Bois (02) 19 K6
Saint-Paul-Cap-de-Joux (81) 270 C6
Saint-Paul-de-Baïse (32) 267 F4
Saint-Paul-de-Fenouillet (66) 309 H5
Saint-Paul-de-Fourques (27) 35 F4
Saint-Paul-de-Jarrat (09) 307 J3
Saint-Paul-de-Loubressac (46) 250 A3
Saint-Paul-de-Salers (15) 217 J4
Saint-Paul-de-Serre (24) 213 K5
Saint-Paul-de-Tartas (43) 238 C3
Saint-Paul-de-Varax (01) 189 F3
Saint-Paul-de-Varces (38) 223 K4
Saint-Paul-de-Vern (46) 234 C2
Saint-Paul-de-Vézelin (42) 187 F6
Saint-Paul-des-Landes (15) 235 G1
Saint-Paul-d'Espis (82) 249 F5
Saint-Paul-d'Izeaux (38) 223 H1
Saint-Paul-d'Oueil (31) 305 H4
Saint-Paul-du-Bois (49) 143 J2
Saint-Paul-du-Vernay (14) 32 A4
Saint-Paul-d'Uzore (42) 204 D3
Saint-Paul-en-Born (40) 244 D4
Saint-Paul-en-Chablais (74) 175 G5
Saint-Paul-en-Cornillon (42) 221 F1
Saint-Paul-en-Forêt (83) 280 B6
Saint-Paul-en-Gâtine (79) 161 F2
Saint-Paul-en-Jarez (42) 205 J5
Saint-Paul-en-Pareds (85) 142 D5
Saint-Paul-et-Valmalle (34) 273 K6
Saint-Paul-la-Coste (30) 255 F6
Saint-Paul-la-Roche (24) 198 C6
Saint-Paul-le-Froid (48) 237 J3
Saint-Paul-le-Gaultier (72) 82 B4
Saint-Paul-le-Jeune (07) 255 H3
Saint-Paul-lès-Dax (40) 264 B4
Saint-Paul-lès-Durance (13) 278 A5
Saint-Paul-les-Fonts (30) 256 C6
Saint-Paul-lès-Monestier (38) 223 K6
Saint-Paul-lès-Romans (26) 222 E5
Saint-Paul-Lizonne (24) 213 G2
Saint-Paul-Mont-Penit (85) 141 H5
Saint-Paul-sur-Isère (73) 209 G3
Saint-Paul-sur-Save (31) 268 E5
Saint-Paul-sur-Ubaye (04) 227 B5
Saint-Paul-Trois-Châteaux (26) . . . 256 D2
Saint-Paulet (11) 289 G3
Saint-Paulet-de-Caisson (30) 256 C3
Saint-Paulien (43) 220 B4
Saint-Pé-d'Ardet (31) 305 J2
Saint-Pé-de-Bigorre (65) 304 A1
Saint-Pé-de-Léren (64) 283 G1
Saint-Pé-Delbosc (31) 286 E5
Saint-Pé-Saint-Simon (47) 266 D1
Saint-Pée-sur-Nivelle (64) 282 A3
Saint-Pellerin (28) 108 D2
Saint-Pellerin (50) 31 G1
Saint-Péran (35) 78 C5
Saint-Péravy-la-Colombe (45) 109 J3
Saint-Péray (07) 222 C6
Saint-Perdon (40) 265 F2
Saint-Perdoux (24) 231 J3
Saint-Perdoux (46) 234 D4
Saint-Père (35) 50 E4
Saint-Père (58) 132 A4
Saint-Père (89) 133 J4
Saint-Père-en-Retz (44) 122 C4
Saint-Père-sur-Loire (45) 110 E6
Saint-Péreuse (58) 152 A3
Saint-Pern (35) 78 D2
Saint-Perreux (56) 102 B4
Saint-Péver (22) 48 D6
Saint-Pey-d'Armens (33) 230 B2
Saint-Pey-de-Castets (33) 230 C2
Saint-Phal (10) 114 A1
Saint-Philbert-de-Bouaine (85) . . . 141 J3
Saint-Philbert-de-Grand-Lieu (44) . . 141 H2
Saint-Philbert-des-Champs (14) . . . 34 A4
Saint-Philbert-du-Peuple (49) 126 B4
Saint-Philbert-en-Mauges (49) 142 D1
Saint-Philbert-sur-Boissey (27) 34 E4
Saint-Philbert-sur-Orne (61) 53 J3
Saint-Philbert-sur-Risle (27) 34 D3
Saint-Philibert (21) 154 C1
Saint-Philibert (56) 100 D6
Saint-Philippe-d'Aiguille (33) 230 C1
Saint-Philippe-du-Seignal (33) . . . 231 F2
Saint-Piat (28) 85 H2
Saint-Pierre (04) 280 D1
Saint-Pierre (15) 217 H1
Saint-Pierre (31) 269 J6
Saint-Pierre (39) 173 K3
Saint-Pierre (51) 62 C2
Saint-Pierre (67) 70 D6
Saint-Pierre-à-Arnes (08) 41 J3
Saint-Pierre-Aigle (02) 39 H3
Saint-Pierre-Avez (05) 258 E3
Saint-Pierre-Azif (14) 33 H3
Saint-Pierre-Bellevue (23) 182 D6
Saint-Pierre-Bénouville (76) 15 J4
Saint-Pierre-Bois (67) 70 C6
Saint-Pierre-Brouck (59) 3 F3
Saint-Pierre-Canivet (14) 54 A2
Saint-Pierre-Chérignat (23) 182 A5
Saint-Pierre-Colamine (63) 202 C5
Saint-Pierre-d'Albigny (73) 208 D4
Saint-Pierre-d'Allevard (38) 208 D6
Saint-Pierre-d'Alvey (73) 207 K3
Saint-Pierre-d'Amilly (17) 177 H2
Saint-Pierre-d'Argençon (05) 242 A6
Saint-Pierre-d'Arthéglise (50) 28 C5
Saint-Pierre-d'Aubézies (32) 266 D6

Saint-Pierre-d'Aurillac (33) 230 B5
Saint-Pierre-d'Autils (27) 36 B6
Saint-Pierre-de-Bailleul (27) 36 A6
Saint-Pierre-de-Bat (33) 230 A4
Saint-Pierre-de-Belleville (73) 209 F5
Saint-Pierre-de-Bœuf (42) 222 A4
Saint-Pierre-de-Bressieux (38) . . . 223 G2
Saint-Pierre-de-Buzet (47) 247 H4
Saint-Pierre-de-Cernières (27) 55 H2
Saint-Pierre-de-Chandieu (69) . . . 206 C3
Saint-Pierre-de-Chartreuse (38) . . . 224 B1
Saint-Pierre-de-Chérennes (38) . . . 223 G4
Saint-Pierre-de-Chevillé (72) 127 G1
Saint-Pierre-de-Chignac (24) 214 B4
Saint-Pierre-de-Clairac (47) 248 D5
Saint-Pierre-de-Côle (24) 214 B1
Saint-Pierre-de-Colombier (07) . . . 239 G4
Saint-Pierre-de-Cormeilles (27) . . . 34 B4
Saint-Pierre-de-Coutances (50) . . . 30 E4
Saint-Pierre-de-Curtille (73) 208 A1
Saint-Pierre-de-Frugie (24) 198 C4
Saint-Pierre-de-Fursac (23) 181 K3
Saint-Pierre-de-Genebroz (73) . . . 207 K5
Saint-Pierre-de-Jards (36) 148 C3
Saint-Pierre-de-Juillers (17) 178 B5
Saint-Pierre-de-la-Fage (34) 273 H4
Saint-Pierre-de-Lages (31) 288 D1
Saint-Pierre-de-Lamps (36) 147 H4
Saint-Pierre-de-l'Île (17) 178 A4
Saint-Pierre-de-Maillé (86) 164 A2
Saint-Pierre-de-Mailloc (14) 34 A6
Saint-Pierre-de-Manneville (76) . . . 35 G2
Saint-Pierre-de-Méaroz (38) 242 B1
Saint-Pierre-de-Mésage (38) 224 B5
Saint-Pierre-de-Mézoargues (13) . . 275 K3
Saint-Pierre-de-Mons (33) 230 A5
Saint-Pierre-de-Nogaret (48) 253 H1
Saint-Pierre-de-Plesguen (35) 50 E5
Saint-Pierre-de-Rivière (09) 307 H3
Saint-Pierre-de-Salerne (27) 34 D5
Saint-Pierre-de-Semilly (50) 31 J3
Saint-Pierre-de-Soucy (73) 208 D5
Saint-Pierre-de-Trivisy (81) 271 G4
Saint-Pierre-de-Varengeville (76) . . 35 G1
Saint-Pierre-de-Varennes (71) 153 H5
Saint-Pierre-de-Vassols (84) 257 H5
Saint-Pierre-dels-Forcats (66) 313 J4
Saint-Pierre-d'Entremont (38) 208 B6
Saint-Pierre-d'Entremont (61) 53 G4
Saint-Pierre-d'Entremont (73) 208 B6
Saint-Pierre-des-Bois (72) 106 A3
Saint-Pierre-des-Champs (11) 309 J2
Saint-Pierre-des-Corps (37) 127 J4
Saint-Pierre-des-Échaubrognes (79) . . 143 G3
Saint-Pierre-des-Fleurs (27) 35 G4
Saint-Pierre-des-Ifs (14) 33 J6
Saint-Pierre-des-Ifs (27) 34 D4
Saint-Pierre-des-Jonquières (76) . . 16 D2
Saint-Pierre-des-Landes (53) 80 C4
Saint-Pierre-des-Loges (61) 55 G5
Saint-Pierre-des-Nids (53) 82 B3
Saint-Pierre-des-Ormes (72) 83 G4
Saint-Pierre-des-Tripiers (48) 253 J4
Saint-Pierre-d'Exideuil (86) 179 H3
Saint-Pierre-d'Eyraud (24) 231 G2
Saint-Pierre-d'Irube (64) 282 B1
Saint-Pierre-d'Oléron (17) 176 B5
Saint-Pierre-du-Bosguérard (27) . . . 35 F4
Saint-Pierre-du-Bû (14) 54 A3
Saint-Pierre-du-Champ (43) 220 C3
Saint-Pierre-du-Chemin (85) 161 F1
Saint-Pierre-du-Fresne (14) 53 F1
Saint-Pierre-du-Jonquet (14) 33 G5
Saint-Pierre-du-Lorouër (72) 107 G5
Saint-Pierre-du-Mont (14) 29 J6
Saint-Pierre-du-Mont (40) 265 G2
Saint-Pierre-du-Mont (58) 133 F5
Saint-Pierre-du-Palais (17) 212 B4
Saint-Pierre-du-Perray (91) 87 F1
Saint-Pierre-du-Regard (61) 53 H3
Saint-Pierre-du-Val (27) 34 B2
Saint-Pierre-du-Vauvray (27) 35 J4
Saint-Pierre-Église (50) 28 E2
Saint-Pierre-en-Faucigny (74) 191 H3
Saint-Pierre-en-Port (76) 14 E3
Saint-Pierre-en-Val (76) 8 C6
Saint-Pierre-en-Vaux (21) 153 H3
Saint-Pierre-es-Champs (60) 36 D2
Saint-Pierre-Eynac (43) 220 D5
Saint-Pierre-la-Bourlhonne (63) . . . 203 K3
Saint-Pierre-la-Bruyère (61) 83 K4
Saint-Pierre-la-Cour (53) 104 C1
Saint-Pierre-la-Garenne (27) 36 A5
Saint-Pierre-la-Noaille (42) 187 F2
Saint-Pierre-la-Palud (69) 205 J1
Saint-Pierre-la-Rivière (61) 54 E4
Saint-Pierre-la-Vieille (14) 53 H2
Saint-Pierre-Lafeuille (46) 233 H6
Saint-Pierre-Langers (50) 51 J1
Saint-Pierre-Laval (03) 186 C2
Saint-Pierre-Lavis (76) 15 F5
Saint-Pierre-le-Bost (23) 166 E6
Saint-Pierre-le-Chastel (63) 202 B2
Saint-Pierre-le-Moûtier (58) 150 D6
Saint-Pierre-le-Vieux (48) 237 G6
Saint-Pierre-le-Vieux (71) 187 K1
Saint-Pierre-le-Vieux (76) 15 H2
Saint-Pierre-le-Vieux (85) 160 K5
Saint-Pierre-le-Viger (76) 15 H3
Saint-Pierre-lès-Bitry (60) 39 G2
Saint-Pierre-lès-Bois (18) 166 E2
Saint-Pierre-lès-Elbeuf (76) 35 H4
Saint-Pierre-les-Étieux (18) 167 H1

Saint-Pierre-lès-Franqueville (02) 20 E3
Saint-Pierre-lès-Nemours (77) 87 H5
Saint-Pierre-Montlimart (49) 124 C5
Saint-Pierre-Quiberon (56) 120 B1
Saint-Pierre-Roche (63) 202 A3
Saint-Pierre-Saint-Jean (07) 255 H1
Saint-Pierre-sur-Dives (14) 54 C1
Saint-Pierre-sur-Doux (07) 221 H4
Saint-Pierre-sur-Dropt (47) 230 E4
Saint-Pierre-sur-Erve (53) 105 J2
Saint-Pierre-sur-Orthe (53) 82 A5
Saint-Pierre-sur-Vence (08) 22 C4
Saint-Pierre-Tarentaine (14) 53 F2
Saint-Pierre-Toirac (46) 234 C6
Saint-Pierremont (02) 21 F4
Saint-Pierremont (08) 42 D1
Saint-Pierremont (88) 94 E2
Saint-Pierreville (07) 239 G2
Saint-Pierrevillers (55) 26 C4
Saint-Plaisir (03) 168 B3
Saint-Plancard (31) 286 C6
Saint-Planchers (50) 51 J1
Saint-Plantaire (36) 165 J5
Saint-Point (71) 171 H6
Saint-Point-Lac (25) 156 E5
Saint-Pois (53) 52 C1
Saint-Poix (53) 104 C3
Saint-Pol-de-Léon (29) 47 J3
Saint-Pol-sur-Mer (59) 3 H1
Saint-Pol-sur-Ternoise (62) 10 B1
Saint-Polgues (42) 186 E6
Saint-Polycarpe (11) 309 F2
Saint-Pompain (79) 161 F5
Saint-Pompont (24) 232 E4
Saint-Poncy (15) 219 F4
Saint-Pons (04) 260 C1
Saint-Pons (07) 239 K5
Saint-Pons-de-Mauchiens (34) . . . 292 D2
Saint-Pons-de-Thomières (34) 291 F2
Saint-Pons-la-Calm (30) 256 B5
Saint-Pont (03) 185 H3
Saint-Porchaire (17) 194 E1
Saint-Porquier (82) 268 E1
Saint-Pôtan (22) 50 A4
Saint-Pouange (10) 90 A5
Saint-Pourçain-sur-Besbre (03) . . . 169 H5
Saint-Pourçain-sur-Sioule (03) . . . 185 H1
Saint-Prancher (88) 93 J3
Saint-Préjet-Armandon (43) 219 J3
Saint-Préjet-d'Allier (43) 237 K1
Saint-Prest (28) 85 G2
Saint-Preuil (16) 196 A4
Saint-Priest (07) 239 J4
Saint-Priest (23) 183 H4
Saint-Priest (69) 206 B3
Saint-Priest-Bramefant (63) 185 H4
Saint-Priest-d'Andelot (03) 185 G4
Saint-Priest-de-Gimel (19) 216 C2
Saint-Priest-des-Champs (63) 184 C5
Saint-Priest-en-Jarez (42) 205 G5
Saint-Priest-en-Murat (03) 168 A6
Saint-Priest-la-Feuille (23) 181 K2
Saint-Priest-la-Marche (18) 166 C5
Saint-Priest-la-Plaine (23) 182 A3
Saint-Priest-la-Prugne (42) 186 B5
Saint-Priest-la-Roche (42) 187 F6
Saint-Priest-la-Vêtre (42) 204 A1
Saint-Priest-les-Fougères (24) 198 C5
Saint-Priest-Ligoure (87) 199 F3
Saint-Priest-Palus (23) 182 B6
Saint-Priest-sous-Aixe (87) 198 D1
Saint-Priest-Taurion (87) 181 J6
Saint-Prim (38) 206 A6
Saint-Privat (07) 239 H5
Saint-Privat (19) 216 E4
Saint-Privat (34) 273 H4
Saint-Privat-d'Allier (43) 220 A4
Saint-Privat-de-Champclos (30) . . . 255 K3
Saint-Privat-de-Vallongue (48) 254 E3
Saint-Privat-des-Prés (24) 213 F3
Saint-Privat-des-Vieux (30) 255 H5
Saint-Privat-du-Dragon (43) 219 J4
Saint-Privat-du-Fau (48) 237 G1
Saint-Privat-la-Montagne (57) 44 D4
Saint-Privé (71) 171 G4
Saint-Privé (89) 132 A1
Saint-Prix (03) 186 A2
Saint-Prix (07) 239 J1
Saint-Prix (71) 152 C4
Saint-Prix (95) 58 D1
Saint-Prix-lès-Arnay (21) 153 G2
Saint-Projet (46) 233 H3
Saint-Projet (82) 250 D3
Saint-Projet-de-Salers (15) 217 J5
Saint-Projet-Saint-Constant (16) . . . 197 G3
Saint-Prouant (85) 142 D6
Saint-Pryvé-Saint-Mesmin (45) . . . 109 K4
Saint-Puy (32) 267 G3
Saint-Python (59) 12 C4
Saint-Quantin-de-Rançanne (17) . . 195 G5
Saint-Quay-Perros (22) 48 A2
Saint-Quay-Portrieux (22) 49 F4
Saint-Quentin (02) 20 A2
Saint-Quentin-au-Bosc (76) 16 C1
Saint-Quentin-de-Baron (33) 230 A2
Saint-Quentin-de-Blavou (61) 83 G2
Saint-Quentin-de-Caplong (33) . . . 230 E2
Saint-Quentin-de-Chalais (16) 212 C3
Saint-Quentin-des-Isles (27) 55 H1
Saint-Quentin-des-Prés (60) 36 E3
Saint-Quentin-du-Dropt (47) 231 J4
Saint-Quentin-en-Mauges (49) . . . 124 D5
Saint-Quentin-en-Tourmont (80) . . . 8 A2
Saint-Quentin-Fallavier (38) 206 C3
Saint-Quentin-la-Chabanne (23) . . 200 E1

Saint-Quentin-la-Motte-Croix-au-Bailly (80) 8 C5
Saint-Quentin-la-Poterie (30) 256 A6
Saint-Quentin-la-Tour (09) 308 B2
Saint-Quentin-le-Petit (08) 21 H6
Saint-Quentin-le-Verger (51) . . . 61 H6
Saint-Quentin-les-Anges (53) . . . 104 D5
Saint-Quentin-lès-Beaurepaire (49) 126 B1
Saint-Quentin-les-Chardonnets (61) 53 F4
Saint-Quentin-les-Marais (51) . . . 63 G4
Saint-Quentin-sur-Charente (16) . . . 197 K1
Saint-Quentin-sur-Coole (51) . . . 62 D3
Saint-Quentin-sur-Indrois (37) . . . 146 D1
Saint-Quentin-sur-Isère (38) . . . 223 J2
Saint-Quentin-sur-le-Homme (50) . . 52 A5
Saint-Quentin-sur-Nohain (58) . . . 132 B5
Saint-Quentin-sur-Sauxillanges (63) 203 G5
Saint-Quintin-sur-Sioule (63) . . . 185 F4
Saint-Quirc (09) 288 C5
Saint-Quirin (57) 67 J5
Saint-Rabier (24) 214 E4
Saint-Racho (71) 187 H1
Saint-Rambert-d'Albon (26) . . . 222 B2
Saint-Rambert-en-Bugey (01) . . . 189 J3
Saint-Raphaël (24) 214 E2
Saint-Raphaël (83) 299 G2
Saint-Régis-du-Coin (42) . . . 221 H2
Saint-Règle (37) 128 C4
Saint-Remèze (07) 256 B2
Saint-Remimont (54) 94 B1
Saint-Remimont (88) 93 J5
Saint-Rémy (01) 189 F2
Saint-Rémy (12) 251 G2
Saint-Rémy (14) 53 H2
Saint-Rémy (19) 201 F3
Saint-Rémy (21) 134 D1
Saint-Rémy (24) 230 E1
Saint-Remy (70) 118 A4
Saint-Rémy (71) 171 J1
Saint-Rémy (79) 161 G5
Saint-Remy (88) 95 G3
Saint-Rémy-au-Bois (62) 9 G2
Saint-Rémy-aux-Bois (54) 94 C2
Saint-Rémy-Blanzy (02) 39 J4
Saint-Rémy-Boscrocourt (76) 8 C6
Saint-Remy-Chaussée (59) 13 G4
Saint-Rémy-de-Blot (63) 184 D4
Saint-Rémy-de-Chargnat (63) . . . 203 F5
Saint-Rémy-de-Chaudes-Aigues (15) . . . 236 D3
Saint-Rémy-de-Maurienne (73) . . . 209 F6
Saint-Rémy-de-Provence (13) . . . 276 B4
Saint-Rémy-de-Sillé (72) 82 B6
Saint-Rémy-des-Landes (50) . . . 28 C6
Saint-Rémy-des-Monts (72) . . . 83 G4
Saint-Remy-du-Nord (59) 13 G3
Saint-Rémy-du-Plain (35) 79 H1
Saint-Rémy-du-Val (72) 82 E4
Saint-Remy-en-Bouzemont-Saint-Genest-et-Isson (51) . . 63 G6
Saint-Remy-en-l'Eau (60) 38 A1
Saint-Rémy-en-Mauges (49) . . . 124 B5
Saint-Rémy-en-Rollat (03) 185 J3
Saint-Rémy-la-Calonne (55) 43 K6
Saint-Rémy-la-Vanne (77) 60 C4
Saint-Rémy-la-Varenne (49) . . . 125 J4
Saint-Rémy-le-Petit (08) 41 H2
Saint-Rémy-lès-Chevreuse (78) . . 58 C5
Saint-Rémy-l'Honoré (78) 58 A5
Saint-Remy-sous-Barbuise (10) . . . 90 B2
Saint-Remy-sous-Broyes (51) 61 H5
Saint-Rémy-sur-Avre (28) 56 E5
Saint-Rémy-sur-Bussy (51) 42 A6
Saint-Rémy-sur-Creuse (86) . . . 146 A4
Saint-Rémy-sur-Durolle (63) . . . 186 A6
Saint-Renan (29) 72 C4
Saint-Restitut (26) 256 E3
Saint-Révérend (85) 158 E1
Saint-Révérien (58) 151 H1
Saint-Rieul (22) 77 K1
Saint-Rigomer-des-Bois (72) . . . 82 D3
Saint-Rimay (41) 108 B6
Saint-Riquier (80) 9 H4
Saint-Riquier-en-Rivière (76) . . . 16 E4
Saint-Riquier-ès-Plains (76) . . . 15 F3
Saint-Rirand (42) 186 C4
Saint-Rivoal (29) 74 E1
Saint-Robert (19) 215 G3
Saint-Robert (47) 248 C4
Saint-Roch (37) 127 H4
Saint-Roch-sur-Égrenne (61) . . . 81 F1
Saint-Rogatien (17) 176 D2
Saint-Romain (16) 212 E2
Saint-Romain (21) 153 J3
Saint-Romain (63) 204 D4
Saint-Romain (86) 179 J2
Saint-Romain-au-Mont-d'Or (69) . . 206 A1
Saint-Romain-d'Ay (07) 222 A4
Saint-Romain-de-Benet (17) . . . 194 E2
Saint-Romain-de-Colbosc (76) . . . 14 C6
Saint-Romain-de-Jalionas (38) . . 206 E2
Saint-Romain-de-Lerps (07) . . . 222 B6
Saint-Romain-de-Monpazier (24) . . 232 B4
Saint-Romain-de-Popey (69) . . . 205 H1
Saint-Romain-de-Surieu (38) . . . 222 C1
Saint-Romain-d'Urfé (42) 186 C6
Saint-Romain-en-Gal (69) 206 A5
Saint-Romain-en-Gier (69) 205 K4
Saint-Romain-en-Jarez (42) . . . 205 H4
Saint-Romain-en-Viennois (84) . . 257 H3
Saint-Romain-et-Saint-Clément (24) . . . 198 B6
Saint-Romain-la-Motte (42) . . . 186 E4

Saint-Romain-la-Virvée (33) 211 J6
Saint-Romain-Lachalm (43) 221 G2
Saint-Romain-le-Noble (47) 248 D5
Saint-Romain-le-Preux (89) 112 D3
Saint-Romain-le-Puy (42) 204 D4
Saint-Romain-les-Atheux (42) . . . 221 G2
Saint-Romain-sous-Gourdon (71) . . 170 E3
Saint-Romain-sous-Versigny (71) . . 170 C2
Saint-Romain-sur-Cher (41) 129 F5
Saint-Romain-sur-Gironde (17) . . . 194 E5
Saint-Roman (26) 241 H4
Saint-Roman-de-Codières (30) . . . 274 A1
Saint-Roman-de-Malegarde (84) . . 257 F3
Saint-Romans (38) 223 G4
Saint-Romans-des-Champs (79) . . 178 B2
Saint-Romans-lès-Melle (79) . . . 178 D2
Saint-Rome (31) 288 E3
Saint-Rome-de-Cernon (12) 272 C1
Saint-Rome-de-Dolan (48) 253 H4
Saint-Rome-de-Tarn (12) 272 B1
Saint-Romphaire (50) 31 H4
Saint-Rustice (31) 269 F4
Saint-Saëns (76) 16 B5
Saint-Saire (76) 16 D4
Saint-Salvadou (12) 251 G4
Saint-Salvadour (19) 216 B1
Saint-Salvi-de-Carcavès (81) . . . 271 J4
Saint-Salvy (47) 247 K3
Saint-Salvy-de-la-Balme (81) . . . 271 G6
Saint-Samson (14) 33 G5
Saint-Samson (53) 82 A2
Saint-Samson-de-Bonfossé (50) . . 31 G4
Saint-Samson-de-la-Roque (27) . . 34 B2
Saint-Samson-la-Poterie (60) . . . 17 F6
Saint-Samson-sur-Rance (22) . . . 50 D5
Saint-Sandoux (63) 202 D4
Saint-Santin (12) 235 F5
Saint-Santin-Cantalès (15) 217 F6
Saint-Santin-de-Maurs (15) 235 F5
Saint-Sardos (47) 248 A3
Saint-Sardos (82) 268 D2
Saint-Satur (18) 131 K5
Saint-Saturnin (15) 218 B3
Saint-Saturnin (16) 196 D5
Saint-Saturnin (18) 166 D4
Saint-Saturnin (48) 253 H2
Saint-Saturnin (51) 61 K6
Saint-Saturnin (63) 202 D3
Saint-Saturnin (72) 106 D2
Saint-Saturnin-de-Lenne (12) . . . 253 G2
Saint-Saturnin-de-Lucian (34) . . . 273 H5
Saint-Saturnin-du-Bois (17) 177 J3
Saint-Saturnin-du-Limet (53) . . . 104 B4
Saint-Saturnin-lès-Apt (84) 277 H1
Saint-Saturnin-lès-Avignon (84) . . 276 C1
Saint-Saturnin-sur-Loire (49) . . . 125 H4
Saint-Saud-Lacoussière (24) . . . 198 A5
Saint-Sauflieu (80) 18 A3
Saint-Saulge (58) 151 H2
Saint-Saulve (59) 12 D1
Saint-Saury (15) 234 E2
Saint-Sauvant (17) 195 H2
Saint-Sauvant (86) 162 C6
Saint-Sauves-d'Auvergne (63) . . . 201 K4
Saint-Sauveur (05) 243 J5
Saint-Sauveur (21) 136 E4
Saint-Sauveur (24) 231 J2
Saint-Sauveur (29) 46 E6
Saint-Sauveur (31) 269 G4
Saint-Sauveur (33) 210 E3
Saint-Sauveur (38) 223 G4
Saint-Sauveur (54) 67 J6
Saint-Sauveur (60) 38 D3
Saint-Sauveur (70) 118 D4
Saint-Sauveur (80) 18 A1
Saint-Sauveur (86) 145 K6
Saint-Sauveur-Camprieu (30) . . . 254 A6
Saint-Sauveur-d'Aunis (17) 177 G2
Saint-Sauveur-de-Carrouges (61) . . 82 B1
Saint-Sauveur-de-Cruzières (07) . . 255 J3
Saint-Sauveur-de-Flée (49) 104 E5
Saint-Sauveur-de-Ginestoux (48) . . 237 K4
Saint-Sauveur-de-Landemont (49) . . . 123 K3
Saint-Sauveur-de-Meilhan (47) . . 247 F1
Saint-Sauveur-de-Montagut (07) . . 239 K2
Saint-Sauveur-de-Peyre (48) . . . 237 G4
Saint-Sauveur-de-Pierrepont (50) . . 28 C6
Saint-Sauveur-de-Puynormand (33) . . . 212 C6
Saint-Sauveur-d'Émalleville (76) . . . 14 C5
Saint-Sauveur-des-Landes (35) . . 79 K1
Saint-Sauveur-en-Diois (26) . . . 241 F4
Saint-Sauveur-en-Puisaye (89) . . 132 C2
Saint-Sauveur-en-Rue (42) 221 J2
Saint-Sauveur-Gouvernet (26) . . . 257 K2
Saint-Sauveur-la-Pommeraye (50) . . . 51 J1
Saint-Sauveur-la-Sagne (63) . . . 219 K1
Saint-Sauveur-la-Vallée (46) . . . 233 J5
Saint-Sauveur-Lalande (24) 213 F6
Saint-Sauveur-Lendelin (50) 30 E3
Saint-Sauveur-lès-Bray (77) 88 C3
Saint-Sauveur-Marville (28) 84 E1
Saint-Sauveur-sur-École (77) . . . 87 G2
Saint-Sauveur-sur-Tinée (06) . . . 261 H5
Saint-Sauvier (03) 166 E6
Saint-Sauvy (32) 268 A5
Saint-Savin (33) 211 J4
Saint-Savin (38) 207 F3
Saint-Savin (65) 304 A2
Saint-Savin (86) 164 A3
Saint-Savinien (17) 177 H6
Saint-Saviol (86) 179 H3
Saint-Savournin (13) 296 E2

Saint-Sébastien (23) 165 G6
Saint-Sébastien (38) 242 B1
Saint-Sébastien-d'Aigrefeuille (30) . . . 255 G6
Saint-Sébastien-de-Morsent (27) . . 56 C1
Saint-Sébastien-de-Raids (50) . . . 30 E2
Saint-Sébastien-sur-Loire (44) . . . 123 H4
Saint-Secondin (86) 163 G6
Saint-Ségal (29) 74 D3
Saint-Séglin (35) 102 D1
Saint-Seine (58) 169 K1
Saint-Seine-en-Bâche (21) 155 F2
Saint-Seine-l'Abbaye (21) 135 H4
Saint-Seine-sur-Vingeanne (21) . . 136 E2
Saint-Selve (33) 229 H4
Saint-Senier-de-Beuvron (50) . . . 52 A6
Saint-Senier-sous-Avranches (50) . . . 51 K3
Saint-Senoch (37) 146 C3
Saint-Senoux (35) 103 F1
Saint-Sériès (34) 274 E4
Saint-Sernin (07) 239 H5
Saint-Sernin (11) 289 F5
Saint-Sernin (47) 231 F4
Saint-Sernin-du-Bois (71) 153 G6
Saint-Sernin-du-Plain (71) 153 J5
Saint-Sernin-lès-Lavaur (81) . . . 289 H1
Saint-Sernin-sur-Rance (12) . . . 271 J3
Saint-Sérotin (89) 88 C5
Saint-Servais (22) 76 A1
Saint-Servais (29) 46 D5
Saint-Servant (56) 101 J2
Saint-Setiers (19) 200 D3
Saint-Seurin-de-Bourg (33) 211 H5
Saint-Seurin-de-Cadourne (33) . . 211 F2
Saint-Seurin-de-Cursac (33) . . . 211 G3
Saint-Seurin-de-Palenne (17) . . . 195 H3
Saint-Seurin-de-Prats (24) 230 D2
Saint-Seurin-sur-l'Isle (33) 212 D5
Saint-Sève (33) 230 C5
Saint-Sever (40) 265 G4
Saint-Sever-Calvados (14) 52 C3
Saint-Sever-de-Rustan (65) 285 J3
Saint-Sever-de-Saintonge (17) . . 195 H3
Saint-Sever-du-Moustier (12) . . . 271 K4
Saint-Séverin (16) 213 F2
Saint-Séverin-d'Estissac (24) . . . 213 H5
Saint-Séverin-sur-Boutonne (17) . . 178 A3
Saint-Siffret (30) 275 H1
Saint-Sigismond (45) 109 J3
Saint-Sigismond (49) 124 C3
Saint-Sigismond (74) 192 A3
Saint-Sigismond (85) 160 E6
Saint-Sigismond-de-Clermont (17) . . . 195 H6
Saint-Silvain-Bas-le-Roc (23) . . . 183 G1
Saint-Silvain-Bellegarde (23) . . . 183 H5
Saint-Silvain-Montaigut (23) . . . 182 C3
Saint-Silvain-sous-Toulx (23) . . . 183 G2
Saint-Siméon (27) 34 C4
Saint-Siméon (61) 81 F2
Saint-Siméon (77) 60 C4
Saint-Siméon-de-Bressieux (38) . . 223 F1
Saint-Simeux (16) 196 C3
Saint-Simon (02) 19 J4
Saint-Simon (15) 235 J1
Saint-Simon (16) 196 B3
Saint-Simon (46) 234 B4
Saint-Simon-de-Bordes (17) . . . 195 H6
Saint-Simon-de-Pellouaille (17) . . 195 F3
Saint-Sixt (74) 191 H3
Saint-Sixte (42) 204 C2
Saint-Sixte (47) 248 D6
Saint-Solve (19) 215 H2
Saint-Sorlin (69) 205 J4
Saint-Sorlin-d'Arves (73) 225 F2
Saint-Sorlin-de-Conac (17) 211 G1
Saint-Sorlin-de-Morestel (38) . . . 207 H3
Saint-Sorlin-de-Vienne (38) 206 B5
Saint-Sorlin-en-Bugey (01) 189 H6
Saint-Sorlin-en-Valloire (26) . . . 222 C2
Saint-Sornin (03) 168 B5
Saint-Sornin (16) 197 G3
Saint-Sornin (17) 194 C1
Saint-Sornin-la-Marche (87) . . . 180 E2
Saint-Sornin-Lavolps (19) 215 H1
Saint-Sornin-Leulac (87) 181 H2
Saint-Soulan (32) 287 F2
Saint-Souplet (59) 12 D5
Saint-Souplet-sur-Py (51) 41 K4
Saint-Soupplets (77) 59 J1
Saint-Sozy (46) 233 J2
Saint-Stail (88) 95 K3
Saint-Suliac (35) 50 D4
Saint-Sulpice (01) 172 B6
Saint-Sulpice (46) 234 B6
Saint-Sulpice (49) 125 H4
Saint-Sulpice (53) 105 F3
Saint-Sulpice (58) 151 F3
Saint-Sulpice (60) 37 H3
Saint-Sulpice (63) 201 J4
Saint-Sulpice (70) 138 D2
Saint-Sulpice (73) 208 A4
Saint-Sulpice (81) 269 K6
Saint-Sulpice-d'Arnoult (17) . . . 194 E1
Saint-Sulpice-de-Cognac (16) . . . 195 J2
Saint-Sulpice-de-Faleyrens (33) . . 230 B1
Saint-Sulpice-de-Favières (91) . . 86 D2
Saint-Sulpice-de-Grimbouville (27) . . . 34 B2
Saint-Sulpice-de-Guilleragues (33) . . . 230 D5
Saint-Sulpice-de-Mareuil (24) . . . 197 H6
Saint-Sulpice-de-Pommeray (41) . . 128 E2
Saint-Sulpice-de-Pommiers (33) . . 230 B4
Saint-Sulpice-de-Roumagnac (24) . . 213 H3

Saint-Sulpice-de-Royan (17) . . . 194 C3
Saint-Sulpice-de-Ruffec (16) . . . 179 H5
Saint-Sulpice-des-Landes (35) . . . 103 G3
Saint-Sulpice-des-Landes (44) . . . 124 A2
Saint-Sulpice-des-Rivoires (38) . . 207 J5
Saint-Sulpice-et-Cameyrac (33) . . 229 J1
Saint-Sulpice-en-Pareds (85) . . . 160 D2
Saint-Sulpice-la-Forêt (35) 79 H3
Saint-Sulpice-Laurière (87) 181 K4
Saint-Sulpice-le-Dunois (23) . . . 182 C1
Saint-Sulpice-le-Guérétois (23) . . 182 C2
Saint-Sulpice-le-Verdon (85) . . . 141 K4
Saint-Sulpice-les-Bois (19) 200 D3
Saint-Sulpice-les-Champs (23) . . 182 E5
Saint-Sulpice-les-Feuilles (87) . . 181 J1
Saint-Sulpice-sur-Lèze (31) 288 A4
Saint-Sulpice-sur-Risle (61) 55 J4
Saint-Supplet (54) 26 C4
Saint-Sylvain (14) 33 F6
Saint-Sylvain (19) 216 C4
Saint-Sylvain (76) 15 F2
Saint-Sylvain-d'Anjou (49) 125 H3
Saint-Sylvestre (07) 222 B6
Saint-Sylvestre (74) 190 E6
Saint-Sylvestre (87) 181 J5
Saint-Sylvestre-Cappel (59) 3 K5
Saint-Sylvestre-de-Cormeilles (27) . . . 34 B4
Saint-Sylvestre-Pragoulin (63) . . . 185 J5
Saint-Sylvestre-sur-Lot (47) . . . 248 D2
Saint-Symphorien (27) 34 C3
Saint-Symphorien (33) 246 A1
Saint-Symphorien (48) 237 G4
Saint-Symphorien (72) 106 B1
Saint-Symphorien-d'Ancelles (71) . . 188 B2
Saint-Symphorien-de-Lay (42) . . . 187 G5
Saint-Symphorien-de-Mahun (07) . . 221 J4
Saint-Symphorien-de-Marmagne (71) . . . 153 F6
Saint-Symphorien-de-Thénières (12) . . . 236 A4
Saint-Symphorien-des-Bois (71) . . 170 D6
Saint-Symphorien-des-Bruyères (61) . . . 55 H4
Saint-Symphorien-des-Monts (50) . . . 80 D1
Saint-Symphorien-d'Ozon (69) . . . 206 B3
Saint-Symphorien-le-Château (28) . . . 85 J2
Saint-Symphorien-le-Valois (50) . . 30 C5
Saint-Symphorien-sous-Chomérac (07) . . . 240 A3
Saint-Symphorien-sur-Coise (69) . . 205 G3
Saint-Symphorien-sur-Couze (87) . . 181 G4
Saint-Symphorien-sur-Saône (21) . . 154 E2
Saint-Thégonnec (29) 47 F5
Saint-Thélo (22) 77 F4
Saint-Théodorit (30) 274 E2
Saint-Théoffrey (38) 224 B5
Saint-Thibaud-de-Couz (73) 208 A5
Saint-Thibault (10) 90 B6
Saint-Thibault (21) 135 F5
Saint-Thibault (60) 17 G4
Saint-Thibault-des-Vignes (77) . . . 59 H3
Saint-Thibaut (02) 40 B3
Saint-Thibéry (34) 292 C3
Saint-Thiébaud (39) 156 A3
Saint-Thiébault (52) 93 F5
Saint-Thierry (51) 40 E3
Saint-Thois (29) 75 F4
Saint-Thomas (02) 40 D1
Saint-Thomas (31) 287 H2
Saint-Thomas-de-Conac (17) . . . 195 H6
Saint-Thomas-de-Courceriers (53) . . 81 K5
Saint-Thomas-en-Argonne (51) . . 42 D5
Saint-Thomas-en-Royans (26) . . . 223 G5
Saint-Thomas-la-Garde (42) 204 D4
Saint-Thomé (07) 239 K6
Saint-Thonan (29) 46 B5
Saint-Thual (35) 78 E1
Saint-Thurial (35) 78 D5
Saint-Thuriau (56) 76 D2
Saint-Thurien (27) 34 C2
Saint-Thurien (29) 99 H2
Saint-Thurin (42) 204 B1
Saint-Tricat (62) 2 C3
Saint-Trimoël (22) 77 J2
Saint-Trinit (84) 258 B5
Saint-Trivier-de-Courtes (01) . . . 172 B4
Saint-Trivier-sur-Moignans (01) . . 188 D4
Saint-Trojan (33) 211 H4
Saint-Trojan-les-Bains (17) 176 C6
Saint-Tropez (83) 299 F4
Saint-Tugdual (56) 76 A5
Saint-Ulphace (72) 83 K6
Saint-Ulrich (68) 97 A4
Saint-Uniac (35) 78 D3
Saint-Urbain (29) 46 C6
Saint-Urbain (85) 140 D3
Saint-Urbain-Maconcourt (52) . . . 92 D3
Saint-Urcisse (47) 248 D5
Saint-Urcisse (81) 269 J2
Saint-Urcize (15) 236 D4
Saint-Usage (10) 115 G3
Saint-Usage (21) 154 E2
Saint-Usuge (71) 172 D2
Saint-Utin (51) 90 E1
Saint-Uze (26) 222 C3
Saint-Vaast-de-Longmont (60) . . . 38 C3
Saint-Vaast-d'Équiqueville (76) . . 16 B3
Saint-Vaast-Dieppedalle (76) . . . 15 G3
Saint-Vaast-du-Val (76) 15 J4

Saint-Vaast-en-Auge (14) 33 H3
Saint-Vaast-en-Cambrésis (59) . . . 12 C4
Saint-Vaast-la-Chaussée (80) . . . 18 A1
Saint-Vaast-la-Hougue (50) 29 G3
Saint-Vaast-lès-Mello (60) 37 K4
Saint-Vaast-sur-Seulles (14) 32 E5
Saint-Vaize (17) 195 G1
Saint-Valbert (70) 118 C2
Saint-Valentin (36) 148 B4
Saint-Valérien (85) 160 C3
Saint-Valérien (89) 88 B6
Saint-Valery (60) 17 F4
Saint-Valery-en-Caux (76) 15 G2
Saint-Valery-sur-Somme (80) 8 E4
Saint-Vallerin (71) 171 H2
Saint-Vallier (16) 212 C2
Saint-Vallier (26) 222 B3
Saint-Vallier (71) 170 E2
Saint-Vallier (88) 94 C4
Saint-Vallier-de-Thiey (06) 280 C4
Saint-Vallier-sur-Marne (52) 116 D4
Saint-Varent (79) 144 B5
Saint-Vaury (23) 182 C2
Saint-Venant (62) 5 K4
Saint-Vénérand (43) 238 A2
Saint-Vérain (58) 132 B3
Saint-Véran (05) 227 C3
Saint-Vérand (38) 223 G3
Saint-Vérand (69) 187 K6
Saint-Vérand (71) 188 B1
Saint-Vert (43) 219 J1
Saint-Viance (19) 215 H3
Saint-Viâtre (41) 130 A3
Saint-Viaud (44) 122 C3
Saint-Victeur (72) 82 C4
Saint-Victor (03) 167 H6
Saint-Victor (07) 222 A4
Saint-Victor (15) 217 G6
Saint-Victor (24) 213 H2
Saint-Victor-de-Buthon (28) 84 B3
Saint-Victor-de-Cessieu (38) . . . 207 G4
Saint-Victor-de-Chrétienville (27) . . 34 C6
Saint-Victor-de-Malcap (30) 255 J4
Saint-Victor-de-Morestel (38) . . . 207 H2
Saint-Victor-de-Réno (61) 83 J2
Saint-Victor-d'Épine (27) 34 D5
Saint-Victor-des-Oules (30) 256 B6
Saint-Victor-en-Marche (23) 182 C3
Saint-Victor-et-Melvieu (12) 272 B1
Saint-Victor-la-Coste (30) 256 C6
Saint-Victor-la-Rivière (63) 202 B5
Saint-Victor-l'Abbaye (76) 16 A4
Saint-Victor-Malescours (43) . . . 221 G2
Saint-Victor-Montvianeix (63) . . . 186 A6
Saint-Victor-Rouzaud (09) 307 H1
Saint-Victor-sur-Arlanc (43) 220 B2
Saint-Victor-sur-Avre (27) 56 A5
Saint-Victor-sur-Ouche (21) 135 H6
Saint-Victor-sur-Rhins (42) 187 H5
Saint-Victoret (13) 296 B2
Saint-Victour (19) 201 G6
Saint-Victurnien (87) 180 E6
Saint-Vidal (43) 220 B5
Saint-Vigor (27) 35 K6
Saint-Vigor-des-Mézerets (14) . . . 53 G2
Saint-Vigor-des-Monts (50) 52 C2
Saint-Vigor-d'Ymonville (76) 34 B1
Saint-Vigor-le-Grand (14) 32 B3
Saint-Vincent (31) 289 F3
Saint-Vincent (43) 220 C4
Saint-Vincent (63) 202 D5
Saint-Vincent (64) 285 F6
Saint-Vincent (82) 250 A5
Saint-Vincent-Bragny (71) 170 C4
Saint-Vincent-Cramesnil (76) . . . 34 B1
Saint-Vincent-de-Barbeyrargues (34) . . . 274 C5
Saint-Vincent-de-Barrès (07) . . . 240 A4
Saint-Vincent-de-Boisset (42) . . . 187 F5
Saint-Vincent-de-Connezac (24) . . 213 H4
Saint-Vincent-de-Cosse (24) . . . 232 E2
Saint-Vincent-de-Durfort (07) . . . 239 K2
Saint-Vincent-de-Lamontjoie (47) . . 248 A6
Saint-Vincent-de-Mercuze (38) . . . 208 C6
Saint-Vincent-de-Paul (33) 211 J6
Saint-Vincent-de-Paul (40) 264 B4
Saint-Vincent-de-Pertignas (33) . . 230 B2
Saint-Vincent-de-Reins (69) 187 J4
Saint-Vincent-de-Salers (15) . . . 217 J3
Saint-Vincent-de-Tyrosse (40) . . . 262 C5
Saint-Vincent-des-Bois (27) 57 F1
Saint-Vincent-des-Landes (44) . . . 103 H4
Saint-Vincent-des-Prés (71) 171 G4
Saint-Vincent-des-Prés (72) 83 F4
Saint-Vincent-d'Olargues (34) . . . 291 G1
Saint-Vincent-du-Boulay (27) . . . 34 C6
Saint-Vincent-du-Lorouër (72) . . . 107 G5
Saint-Vincent-du-Pendit (46) . . . 234 C2
Saint-Vincent-en-Bresse (71) . . . 172 B2
Saint-Vincent-Jalmoutiers (24) . . . 213 F3
Saint-Vincent-la-Châtre (79) . . . 178 E2
Saint-Vincent-la-Commanderie (26) . . . 222 E6
Saint-Vincent-le-Paluel (24) . . . 233 F2
Saint-Vincent-les-Forts (04) 243 H6
Saint-Vincent-Sterlanges (85) . . . 160 B1
Saint-Vincent-sur-Graon (85) . . . 159 J3
Saint-Vincent-sur-Jabron (04) . . . 258 D4
Saint-Vincent-sur-Jard (85) 159 G5
Saint-Vincent-sur-l'Isle (24) 214 C3
Saint-Vincent-sur-Oust (56) 102 B3
Saint-Vit (25) 155 K1
Saint-Vital (73) 209 F3
Saint-Vite (47) 248 E1

400

Saint-Vitte (18) 167 G4
Saint-Vitte-sur-Briance (87) . . . 199 H4
Saint-Vivien (17) . . . 176 E3
Saint-Vivien (24) . . . 230 E1
Saint-Vivien-de-Blaye (33) . . . 211 H4
Saint-Vivien-de-Médoc (33) . . . 194 C6
Saint-Vivien-de-Monségur (33) . . . 230 E5
Saint-Voir (03) . . . 169 G5
Saint-Vougay (29) . . . 46 D4
Saint-Vrain (51) . . . 63 H5
Saint-Vrain (91) . . . 86 E2
Saint-Vran (22) . . . 77 J4
Saint-Vulbas (01) . . . 207 F1
Saint-Waast (59) . . . 13 F2
Saint-Wandrille-Rançon (76) . . . 15 G6
Saint-Witz (95) . . . 38 B6
Saint-Xandre (17) . . . 176 E2
Saint-Yaguen (40) . . . 264 E2
Saint-Yan (71) . . . 170 B5
Saint-Ybard (19) . . . 199 H6
Saint-Ybars (09) . . . 288 B5
Saint-Yon (91) . . . 86 D1
Saint-Yorre (03) . . . 185 J4
Saint-Yrieix-la-Montagne (23) . . . 182 E6
Saint-Yrieix-la-Perche (87) . . . 198 E5
Saint-Yrieix-le-Déjalat (19) . . . 200 C6
Saint-Yrieix-les-Bois (23) . . . 182 D4
Saint-Yrieix-sous-Aixe (87) . . . 198 D1
Saint-Yrieix-sur-Charente (16) . . . 196 D3
Saint-Ythaire (71) . . . 171 G3
Saint-Yvi (29) . . . 98 E2
Saint-Yvoine (63) . . . 202 E4
Saint-Yzan-de-Soudiac (33) . . . 211 J4
Saint-Yzans-de-Médoc (33) . . . 211 F1
Saint-Zacharie (83) . . . 297 F3
Sainte-Adresse (76) . . . 33 J1
Sainte-Agathe (63) . . . 203 J1
Sainte-Agathe-d'Aliermont (76) . . . 16 C3
Sainte-Agathe-en-Donzy (42) . . . 205 F1
Sainte-Agathe-la-Bouteresse (42) . . . 204 D2
Sainte-Agnès (06) . . . 281 J2
Sainte-Agnès (38) . . . 224 C2
Sainte-Agnès (39) . . . 173 F2
Sainte-Alauzie (46) . . . 249 J3
Sainte-Alvère (24) . . . 232 B1
Sainte-Anastasie (15) . . . 218 D4
Sainte-Anastasie (30) . . . 275 G2
Sainte-Anastasie-sur-Issole (83) . . . 298 A3
Sainte-Anne (25) . . . 156 B4
Sainte-Anne (32) . . . 268 C4
Sainte-Anne (41) . . . 108 C6
Sainte-Anne-d'Auray (56) . . . 100 D4
Sainte-Anne-Saint-Priest (87) . . . 199 K3
Sainte-Anne-sur-Brivet (44) . . . 102 C6
Sainte-Anne-sur-Gervonde (38) . . . 206 E5
Sainte-Anne-sur-Vilaine (35) . . . 102 E3
Sainte-Aulde (77) . . . 60 C2
Sainte-Aurence-Cazaux (32) . . . 286 B3
Sainte-Austreberthe (62) . . . 9 J2
Sainte-Austreberthe (76) . . . 15 J5
Sainte-Barbe (57) . . . 45 G4
Sainte-Barbe (88) . . . 95 F2
Sainte-Barbe-sur-Gaillon (27) . . . 35 K5
Sainte-Bazeille (47) . . . 230 D6
Sainte-Beuve-en-Rivière (76) . . . 16 D3
Sainte-Blandine (38) . . . 207 G4
Sainte-Blandine (79) . . . 178 C1
Sainte-Brigitte (56) . . . 76 C4
Sainte-Camelle (11) . . . 289 F5
Sainte-Catherine (62) . . . 10 E2
Sainte-Catherine (63) . . . 203 H6
Sainte-Catherine (69) . . . 205 H4
Sainte-Catherine-de-Fierbois (37) . . . 145 K2
Sainte-Cécile (36) . . . 147 K1
Sainte-Cécile (50) . . . 52 B3
Sainte-Cécile (71) . . . 171 H5
Sainte-Cécile (85) . . . 142 C6
Sainte-Cécile-d'Andorge (30) . . . 255 F4
Sainte-Cécile-du-Cayrou (81) . . . 270 A1
Sainte-Cécile-les-Vignes (84) . . . 257 F4
Sainte-Céronne-
 -lès-Mortagne (61) . . . 83 H1
Sainte-Cérotte (72) . . . 107 J4
Sainte-Christie (32) . . . 267 J4
Sainte-Christie-d'Armagnac (32) . . . 266 C4
Sainte-Christine (49) . . . 124 D5
Sainte-Christine (63) . . . 184 C4
Sainte-Colombe (05) . . . 258 D3
Sainte-Colombe (16) . . . 197 F1
Sainte-Colombe (17) . . . 212 A4
Sainte-Colombe (21) . . . 134 E4
Sainte-Colombe (25) . . . 156 E4
Sainte-Colombe (33) . . . 230 C1
Sainte-Colombe (35) . . . 103 J1
Sainte-Colombe (40) . . . 265 G5
Sainte-Colombe (46) . . . 234 D4
Sainte-Colombe (50) . . . 28 D5
Sainte-Colombe (69) . . . 206 B5
Sainte-Colombe (76) . . . 15 G3
Sainte-Colombe (77) . . . 88 D2
Sainte-Colombe (89) . . . 134 A2
Sainte-Colombe-de-Duras (47) . . . 230 E4
Sainte-Colombe-de-
 -la-Commanderie (66) . . . 315 F3
Sainte-Colombe-de-Peyre (48) . . . 237 F4
Sainte-Colombe-
 -de-Villeneuve (47) . . . 248 C2
Sainte-Colombe-des-Bois (58) . . . 132 C5
Sainte-Colombe-en-Bruilhois (47) . . . 248 A5
Sainte-Colombe-
 -la-Commanderie (27) . . . 35 G6
Sainte-Colombe-près-
 -Vernon (27) . . . 36 A6
Sainte-Colombe-sur-Gand (42) . . . 187 H6
Sainte-Colombe-sur-Guette (11) . . . 308 E6
Sainte-Colombe-sur-l'Hers (11) . . . 308 C3

Sainte-Colombe-sur-Loing (89) . . . 132 D2
Sainte-Colombe-sur-Seine (21) . . . 115 F4
Sainte-Colome (64) . . . 303 H1
Sainte-Consorce (69) . . . 205 K2
Sainte-Croix (01) . . . 188 E6
Sainte-Croix (02) . . . 40 C1
Sainte-Croix (12) . . . 251 F2
Sainte-Croix (24) . . . 232 B3
Sainte-Croix (26) . . . 241 G3
Sainte-Croix (46) . . . 249 H3
Sainte-Croix (71) . . . 172 D3
Sainte-Croix (81) . . . 270 D2
Sainte-Croix-à-Lauze (04) . . . 277 K2
Sainte-Croix-du-Mont (33) . . . 230 A5
Sainte-Croix-du-Verdon (04) . . . 279 F3
Sainte-Croix-en-Jarez (42) . . . 205 J5
Sainte-Croix-en-Plaine (68) . . . 96 C5
Sainte-Croix-Grand-Tonne (14) . . . 32 C4
Sainte-Croix-Hague (50) . . . 28 B2
Sainte-Croix-sur-Aizier (27) . . . 34 D2
Sainte-Croix-sur-Buchy (76) . . . 16 C6
Sainte-Croix-sur-Mer (14) . . . 32 D3
Sainte-Croix-sur-Orne (61) . . . 53 K4
Sainte-Croix-Vallée-
 -Française (48) . . . 254 D5
Sainte-Croix-Volvestre (09) . . . 306 D1
Sainte-Dode (32) . . . 286 A3
Sainte-Eanne (79) . . . 162 A5
Sainte-Engrâce (64) . . . 302 C2
Sainte-Enimie (48) . . . 254 A2
Sainte-Eugénie-
 -de-Villeneuve (43) . . . 219 K4
Sainte-Eulalie (07) . . . 239 F2
Sainte-Eulalie (11) . . . 289 K5
Sainte-Eulalie (15) . . . 217 G4
Sainte-Eulalie (33) . . . 229 J1
Sainte-Eulalie (48) . . . 237 H3
Sainte-Eulalie-d'Ans (24) . . . 214 D3
Sainte-Eulalie-de-Cernon (12) . . . 272 E4
Sainte-Eulalie-d'Eymet (24) . . . 231 G4
Sainte-Eulalie-d'Olt (12) . . . 253 F1
Sainte-Eulalie-en-Born (40) . . . 244 D3
Sainte-Eulalie-en-Royans (26) . . . 223 G5
Sainte-Euphémie (01) . . . 188 C5
Sainte-Euphémie-sur-
 -Ouvèze (26) . . . 258 A3
Sainte-Eusoye (60) . . . 18 A6
Sainte-Fauste (36) . . . 148 B6
Sainte-Féréole (19) . . . 215 J3
Sainte-Feyre (23) . . . 182 D3
Sainte-Feyre-la-Montagne (23) . . . 183 G6
Sainte-Flaive-des-Loups (85) . . . 159 G2
Sainte-Florence (33) . . . 230 C2
Sainte-Florence (85) . . . 142 C6
Sainte-Florine (43) . . . 219 G1
Sainte-Foi (09) . . . 308 B1
Sainte-Fortunade (19) . . . 216 B3
Sainte-Foy (40) . . . 265 J2
Sainte-Foy (71) . . . 187 F1
Sainte-Foy (76) . . . 16 A3
Sainte-Foy (85) . . . 159 F3
Sainte-Foy-d'Aigrefeuille (31) . . . 288 D1
Sainte-Foy-de-Belvès (24) . . . 232 D3
Sainte-Foy-de-Longas (24) . . . 232 A1
Sainte-Foy-
 -de-Montgommery (14) . . . 54 E2
Sainte-Foy-de-Peyrolières (31) . . . 287 J2
Sainte-Foy-la-Grande (33) . . . 231 F2
Sainte-Foy-la-Longue (33) . . . 230 B5
Sainte-Foy-l'Argentière (69) . . . 205 H3
Sainte-Foy-lès-Lyon (69) . . . 206 A2
Sainte-Foy-Saint-Sulpice (42) . . . 204 D2
Sainte-Foy-Tarentaise (73) . . . 193 B3
Sainte-Gauburge-
 -Sainte-Colombe (61) . . . 55 G5
Sainte-Gemme (17) . . . 194 D1
Sainte-Gemme (32) . . . 268 A4
Sainte-Gemme (33) . . . 230 D5
Sainte-Gemme (36) . . . 147 G6
Sainte-Gemme (51) . . . 40 B5
Sainte-Gemme (79) . . . 144 A5
Sainte-Gemme (81) . . . 251 H6
Sainte-Gemme-en-
 -Sancerrois (18) . . . 131 J5
Sainte-Gemme-la-Plaine (85) . . . 160 B4
Sainte-Gemme-Martaillac (47) . . . 247 G2
Sainte-Gemme-Moronval (28) . . . 57 F5
Sainte-Gemmes (41) . . . 108 E5
Sainte-Gemmes-d'Andigné (49) . . . 104 D6
Sainte-Gemmes-le-Robert (53) . . . 81 J6
Sainte-Gemmes-sur-Loire (49) . . . 125 G4
Sainte-Geneviève (02) . . . 21 H4
Sainte-Geneviève (50) . . . 29 F2
Sainte-Geneviève (54) . . . 65 K2
Sainte-Geneviève (60) . . . 37 J4
Sainte-Geneviève (76) . . . 16 C5
Sainte-Geneviève-des-Bois (45) . . . 111 J5
Sainte-Geneviève-des-Bois (91) . . . 58 E6
Sainte-Geneviève-lès-Gasny (27) . . . 36 C6
Sainte-Geneviève-sur-
 -Argence (12) . . . 236 B3
Sainte-Hélène (33) . . . 210 A4
Sainte-Hélène (48) . . . 237 K6
Sainte-Hélène (56) . . . 100 B4
Sainte-Hélène (71) . . . 171 H1
Sainte-Hélène (88) . . . 95 F4
Sainte-Hélène-Bondeville (76) . . . 14 D3
Sainte-Hélène-du-Lac (73) . . . 208 D5
Sainte-Hélène-sur-Isère (73) . . . 209 F3
Sainte-Hermine (85) . . . 160 B3
Sainte-Honorine-de-Ducy (14) . . . 32 A5

Sainte-Honorine-des-Pertes (14) . . . 32 A2
Sainte-Honorine-du-Fay (14) . . . 32 D6
Sainte-Honorine-
 -la-Chardonne (61) . . . 53 H3
Sainte-Honorine-
 -la-Guillaume (61) . . . 53 J4
Sainte-Innocence (24) . . . 231 H3
Sainte-Jalle (26) . . . 257 J2
Sainte-Jamme-sur-Sarthe (72) . . . 106 D1
Sainte-Julie (01) . . . 189 G6
Sainte-Juliette (82) . . . 249 H3
Sainte-Juliette-sur-Viaur (12) . . . 252 B4
Sainte-Léocadie (66) . . . 313 H5
Sainte-Lheurine (17) . . . 195 J5
Sainte-Livrade (31) . . . 268 D6
Sainte-Livrade-sur-Lot (47) . . . 248 B2
Sainte-Lizaigne (36) . . . 148 D4
Sainte-Luce (38) . . . 242 C1
Sainte-Luce-sur-Loire (44) . . . 123 H3
Sainte-Lucie-de-Tallano (2A) . . . 323 F2
Sainte-Lunaise (18) . . . 149 G5
Sainte-Magnance (89) . . . 134 B4
Sainte-Marguerite (43) . . . 219 K3
Sainte-Marguerite (88) . . . 95 J4
Sainte-Marguerite-
 -de-Carrouges (61) . . . 82 B1
Sainte-Marguerite-de-l'Autel (27) . . . 56 A3
Sainte-Marguerite-de-Viette (14) . . . 54 D1
Sainte-Marguerite-d'Elle (14) . . . 31 J2
Sainte-Marguerite-
 -des-Loges (14) . . . 54 E1
Sainte-Marguerite-en-Ouche (27) . . . 55 J1
Sainte-Marguerite-Lafigère (07) . . . 255 F1
Sainte-Marguerite-sur-
 -Duclair (76) . . . 35 F1
Sainte-Marguerite-sur-
 -Fauville (76) . . . 15 F4
Sainte-Marguerite-sur-Mer (76) . . . 15 J2
Sainte-Marie (05) . . . 258 B1
Sainte-Marie (08) . . . 42 B2
Sainte-Marie (15) . . . 236 C2
Sainte-Marie (25) . . . 139 G2
Sainte-Marie (32) . . . 268 B5
Sainte-Marie (35) . . . 102 C3
Sainte-Marie (58) . . . 151 G2
Sainte-Marie (65) . . . 305 J3
Sainte-Marie (66) . . . 315 J2
Sainte-Marie-à-Py (51) . . . 41 K4
Sainte-Marie-au-Bosc (76) . . . 14 B4
Sainte-Marie-aux-Chênes (57) . . . 44 D4
Sainte-Marie-aux-Mines (68) . . . 96 A2
Sainte-Marie-Cappel (59) . . . 3 J4
Sainte-Marie-d'Alloix (38) . . . 208 C6
Sainte-Marie-d'Alvey (73) . . . 207 K4
Sainte-Marie-de-Chignac (24) . . . 214 B4
Sainte-Marie-de-Cuines (73) . . . 225 G1
Sainte-Marie-de-Gosse (40) . . . 262 D6
Sainte-Marie-de-Ré (17) . . . 158 D6
Sainte-Marie-de-Vatimesnil (27) . . . 36 C4
Sainte-Marie-de-Vaux (87) . . . 198 D1
Sainte-Marie-des-Champs (76) . . . 15 G5
Sainte-Marie-du-Bois (50) . . . 80 E1
Sainte-Marie-du-Bois (53) . . . 81 H2
Sainte-Marie-
 -du-Lac-Nuisement (51) . . . 63 H6
Sainte-Marie-du-Mont (38) . . . 208 C6
Sainte-Marie-du-Mont (50) . . . 29 G6
Sainte-Marie-en-Chanois (70) . . . 118 E4
Sainte-Marie-en-Chaux (70) . . . 118 C4
Sainte-Marie-Kerque (62) . . . 3 F3
Sainte-Marie-la-Blanche (21) . . . 154 B4
Sainte-Marie-la-Robert (61) . . . 54 B6
Sainte-Marie-Lapanouze (19) . . . 201 F6
Sainte-Marie-Laumont (14) . . . 52 E2
Sainte-Marie-Outre-l'Eau (14) . . . 52 D2
Sainte-Marie-sur-Ouche (21) . . . 135 J6
Sainte-Marthe (27) . . . 56 A2
Sainte-Marthe (47) . . . 247 G2
Sainte-Maure (10) . . . 90 A4
Sainte-Maure-de-Peyriac (47) . . . 266 D1
Sainte-Maure-de-Touraine (37) . . . 145 K2
Sainte-Maxime (83) . . . 299 F3
Sainte-Même (17) . . . 178 A6
Sainte-Menehould (51) . . . 42 D6
Sainte-Mère (32) . . . 267 J1
Sainte-Mère-Église (50) . . . 29 F5
Sainte-Mesme (78) . . . 86 A2
Sainte-Mondane (24) . . . 233 G2
Sainte-Montaine (18) . . . 130 E3
Sainte-Nathalène (24) . . . 233 F1
Sainte-Néomaye (79) . . . 161 K6
Sainte-Olive (01) . . . 188 D4
Sainte-Opportune (61) . . . 53 J4
Sainte-Opportune-du-Bois (27) . . . 35 F5
Sainte-Opportune-la-Mare (27) . . . 34 C2
Sainte-Orse (24) . . . 214 E3
Sainte-Osmane (72) . . . 107 H4
Sainte-Ouenne (79) . . . 161 H5
Sainte-Pallaye (89) . . . 133 H1
Sainte-Paule (69) . . . 187 K5
Sainte-Pazanne (44) . . . 122 E5
Sainte-Pexine (85) . . . 160 A3
Sainte-Pience (50) . . . 52 A4
Sainte-Pôle (54) . . . 95 G1
Sainte-Preuve (02) . . . 21 F5
Sainte-Radegonde (12) . . . 252 C3
Sainte-Radegonde (17) . . . 177 G6
Sainte-Radegonde (24) . . . 231 K4
Sainte-Radegonde (32) . . . 267 H3
Sainte-Radegonde (33) . . . 230 D2
Sainte-Radegonde (71) . . . 170 B2
Sainte-Radegonde (79) . . . 144 B4
Sainte-Radégonde (86) . . . 163 J2
Sainte-Radégonde-
 -des-Noyers (85) . . . 160 B5
Sainte-Ramée (17) . . . 195 F6

Sainte-Reine (70) . . . 137 H3
Sainte-Reine (73) . . . 208 D3
Sainte-Reine-de-Bretagne (44) . . . 122 A1
Sainte-Ruffine (57) . . . 44 E5
Sainte-Sabine (21) . . . 153 J1
Sainte-Sabine-Born (24) . . . 232 A4
Sainte-Sabine-sur-Longève (72) . . . 106 D1
Sainte-Savine (10) . . . 90 A5
Sainte-Scolasse-sur-Sarthe (61) . . . 83 G1
Sainte-Segrée (80) . . . 17 H4
Sainte-Sève (29) . . . 47 F5
Sainte-Sévère (16) . . . 196 A2
Sainte-Sévère-sur-Indre (36) . . . 166 C4
Sainte-Sigolène (43) . . . 221 F3
Sainte-Solange (18) . . . 149 J2
Sainte-Soline (79) . . . 179 F1
Sainte-Souline (16) . . . 212 D1
Sainte-Soulle (17) . . . 176 E2
Sainte-Suzanne (09) . . . 288 B5
Sainte-Suzanne (25) . . . 139 H2
Sainte-Suzanne (53) . . . 105 J1
Sainte-Suzanne-sur-Vire (50) . . . 31 H4
Sainte-Terre (33) . . . 230 B2
Sainte-Thérence (03) . . . 184 A2
Sainte-Thorette (18) . . . 148 E3
Sainte-Tréphine (22) . . . 76 C3
Sainte-Trie (24) . . . 215 F2
Sainte-Tulle (04) . . . 278 B3
Sainte-Valière (11) . . . 291 G5
Sainte-Vaubourg (08) . . . 42 A1
Sainte-Verge (79) . . . 144 B3
Sainte-Vertu (89) . . . 113 K6
Saintes (17) . . . 195 G2
Saintes-Maries-de-la-Mer (13) . . . 294 C5
Saintines (60) . . . 38 D3
Saintry-sur-Seine (91) . . . 87 F1
Saints (77) . . . 60 B5
Saints (89) . . . 132 D2
Saints-Geosmes (52) . . . 116 D4
Sainville (28) . . . 86 A3
Saires (86) . . . 145 F5
Saires-la-Verrerie (61) . . . 53 H5
Saissac (11) . . . 289 K4
Saisseval (80) . . . 17 K2
Saisy (71) . . . 153 H4
Saivres (79) . . . 161 K5
le Saix (05) . . . 242 C6
Saïx (81) . . . 289 K1
Saix (86) . . . 144 D2
Saizerais (54) . . . 65 K3
Saizy (58) . . . 133 H5
Sajas (31) . . . 287 H3
Salagnac (24) . . . 215 F2
Salagnon (38) . . . 207 F3
Salaise-sur-Sanne (38) . . . 222 B1
Salans (39) . . . 155 K1
Salasc (34) . . . 273 G6
Salaunes (33) . . . 210 E6
Salavas (07) . . . 255 K2
Salavre (01) . . . 172 E6
Salazac (30) . . . 256 B4
Salbris (41) . . . 130 B4
les Salces (48) . . . 237 F6
Saléchan (65) . . . 305 J3
Saleich (31) . . . 306 B2
Saleignes (17) . . . 178 D4
Saleilles (66) . . . 315 H2
les Salelles (07) . . . 255 G1
les Salelles (48) . . . 253 J1
Salency (60) . . . 19 H6
Salenthal (67) . . . 70 B2
Saléon (05) . . . 258 E2
Salérans (05) . . . 258 D3
Salerm (31) . . . 287 F4
Salernes (83) . . . 279 G6
Salers (15) . . . 217 J2
Sales (74) . . . 190 D6
Salesches (59) . . . 12 D4
la Salette-Fallavaux (38) . . . 242 D1
Salettes (26) . . . 240 D5
Salettes (43) . . . 238 D2
Saleux (80) . . . 18 A2
Salice (2A) . . . 320 D3
Saliceto (2B) . . . 319 G4
Saliès (81) . . . 270 D3
Salies-de-Béarn (64) . . . 283 H2
Salies-du-Salat (31) . . . 306 B1
Salignac (04) . . . 259 G4
Salignac (33) . . . 211 K5
Salignac-de-Mirambeau (17) . . . 211 J1
Salignac-Eyvigues (24) . . . 215 G6
Salignac-sur-Charente (17) . . . 195 J3
Saligney (39) . . . 137 G6
Saligny (85) . . . 141 K5
Saligny (89) . . . 88 E6
Saligny-le-Vif (18) . . . 150 A3
Saligny-sur-Roudon (03) . . . 169 J5
Saligos (65) . . . 304 D3
Salindres (30) . . . 255 H5
Salinelles (30) . . . 274 D4
Salins (15) . . . 217 H4
Salins (77) . . . 88 B3
Salins-les-Bains (39) . . . 156 A4
Salins-les-Thermes (73) . . . 209 H5
Salives (21) . . . 135 K1
Sallagriffon (06) . . . 280 D2
Sallanches (74) . . . 192 A5
Sallaumines (62) . . . 11 F1
la Salle (71) . . . 171 K5
la Salle (88) . . . 95 G3
la Salle-de-Vihiers (49) . . . 143 H1
la Salle-en-Beaumont (38) . . . 242 C1
la Salle-et-Chapelle-Aubry (49) . . . 124 C6
la Salle-les-Alpes (05) . . . 225 K6

la Salle-Prunet (48) . . . 254 C3
Sallebœuf (33) . . . 229 J2
Sallèdes (63) . . . 203 F3
Sallèles-Cabardès (11) . . . 290 C4
Sallèles-d'Aude (11) . . . 291 H5
Sallen (14) . . . 31 K3
Sallenelles (14) . . . 33 F4
Sallenôves (74) . . . 190 E4
Sallertaine (85) . . . 140 E4
Salles (33) . . . 228 E5
les Salles (42) . . . 204 A1
Salles (47) . . . 232 B6
Salles (65) . . . 304 A2
Salles (79) . . . 162 A5
Salles (81) . . . 251 F6
Salles-Adour (65) . . . 285 H6
Salles-Arbuissonnas-en-
 -Beaujolais (69) . . . 188 A4
Salles-Courbatiès (12) . . . 251 G1
Salles-Curan (12) . . . 252 D5
Salles-d'Angles (16) . . . 195 K4
Salles-d'Armagnac (32) . . . 266 B3
Salles-d'Aude (11) . . . 291 K5
Salles-de-Barbezieux (16) . . . 196 B6
Salles-de-Belvès (24) . . . 232 D4
les Salles-de-Castillon (33) . . . 230 D1
les Salles-de-Villefagnan (16) . . . 179 G5
les Salles-du-Gardon (30) . . . 255 G4
Salles-et-Pratviel (31) . . . 305 H4
Salles-la-Source (12) . . . 252 B2
Salles-Lavalette (16) . . . 213 F1
les Salles-Lavauguyon (87) . . . 197 K2
Salles-Mongiscard (64) . . . 283 J1
Salles-sous-Bois (26) . . . 257 F1
Salles-sur-Garonne (31) . . . 287 J5
Salles-sur-l'Hers (11) . . . 289 F4
Salles-sur-Mer (17) . . . 176 E3
les Salles-sur-Verdon (83) . . . 279 F3
Sallespisse (64) . . . 283 K1
Salmagne (55) . . . 64 C4
Salmaise (21) . . . 135 G3
Salmbach (67) . . . 25 D2
Salmiech (12) . . . 252 B5
Salomé (59) . . . 6 C5
Salon (10) . . . 62 A6
Salon (24) . . . 214 B6
Salon-de-Provence (13) . . . 276 E5
Salon-la-Tour (19) . . . 199 H5
Salonnes (57) . . . 66 D3
Salornay-sur-Guye (71) . . . 171 G4
Salouël (80) . . . 18 A2
Salperwick (62) . . . 3 G5
Salsein (09) . . . 306 C3
Salses-le-Château (66) . . . 310 C4
Salsigne (11) . . . 290 B4
Salt-en-Donzy (42) . . . 205 F2
Salvagnac (81) . . . 269 K2
Salvagnac-Cajarc (12) . . . 250 E1
la Salvetat-Belmontet (82) . . . 269 H2
la Salvetat-Lauragais (31) . . . 289 F1
la Salvetat-Peyralès (12) . . . 251 H4
la Salvetat-Saint-Gilles (31) . . . 288 A1
la Salvetat-sur-Agout (34) . . . 271 K6
Salvezines (11) . . . 309 F5
Salviac (46) . . . 233 H4
Salvizinet (42) . . . 205 F2
Salza (11) . . . 309 H3
Salzuit (43) . . . 219 J3
Samadet (40) . . . 265 G5
Saman (31) . . . 286 E5
Samaran (32) . . . 286 C3
Samatan (32) . . . 287 G2
Samazan (47) . . . 247 G1
Sambin (41) . . . 128 C2
Sambourg (89) . . . 114 A5
Saméon (59) . . . 7 G2
Samer (62) . . . 4 C4
Samerey (21) . . . 155 F2
Sames (64) . . . 282 E1
Sammarçolles (86) . . . 144 E3
Sammeron (77) . . . 60 B2
Samoëns (74) . . . 192 B3
Samognat (01) . . . 189 K1
Samogneux (55) . . . 43 H4
Samois-sur-Seine (77) . . . 87 J3
Samonac (33) . . . 211 H5
Samoreau (77) . . . 87 J3
Samouillan (31) . . . 287 G5
Samoussy (02) . . . 20 E6
Sampans (39) . . . 155 G2
Sampigny (55) . . . 64 C5
Sampigny-lès-Maranges (71) . . . 153 J5
Sampolo (2A) . . . 321 F5
Sampzon (07) . . . 255 K1
Samson (25) . . . 156 A2
Samsons-Lion (64) . . . 285 F2
Samuran (65) . . . 305 H2
San-Damiano (2B) . . . 319 J4
San-Gavino-d'Ampugnani (2B) . . . 319 J4
San-Gavino-di-Carbini (2A) . . . 323 G2
San-Gavino-di-Fiumorbo (2B) . . . 321 H4
San-Gavino-di-Tenda (2B) . . . 319 H3
San-Giovanni-di-Moriani (2B) . . . 319 J5
San-Giuliano (2B) . . . 319 J5
San-Lorenzo (2B) . . . 319 G5
San-Martino-di-Lota (2B) . . . 317 D5
San-Nicolao (2B) . . . 319 J5
Sana (31) . . . 287 H5
Sanary-sur-Mer (83) . . . 300 A4
Sancé (71) . . . 171 K6
Sancergues (18) . . . 150 B2
Sancerre (18) . . . 131 K5
Sancey-le-Grand (25) . . . 139 F3
Sancey-le-Long (25) . . . 139 F3
Sancheville (28) . . . 85 H6
Sanchey (88) . . . 94 C5

Sancoins (18) 150 B6
Sancourt (27) 36 D3
Sancourt (59) 11 J3
Sancourt (80) 19 H3
Sancy (54) 26 E4
Sancy (77) 60 A3
Sancy-les-Cheminots (02) 39 K2
Sancy-lès-Provins (77) 60 E5
Sand (67) 70 E6
Sandarville (28) 85 F4
Sandaucourt (88) 93 H4
Sandillon (45) 110 B5
Sandouville (76) 34 A1
Sandrans (01) 188 E4
Sangatte (62) 2 C2
Sanghen (62) 2 D5
Sanguinet (40) 228 C6
Sanilhac (07) 239 G6
Sanilhac-Sagriès (30) 275 H2
Sannat (23) 183 J3
Sannerville (14) 33 F5
Sannes (84) 277 J4
Sannois (95) 58 D2
Sanous (65) 285 G3
Sanry-lès-Vigy (57) 45 G4
Sanry-sur-Nied (57) 45 G6
Sans-Vallois (88) 94 A6
Sansa (66) 313 K3
Sansac-de-Marmiesse (15) 235 G2
Sansac-Veinazès (15) 235 H3
Sansais (79) 177 K1
Sansan (32) 286 D1
Sanssac-l'Église (43) 220 B5
Sanssat (03) 185 J2
Santa-Lucia-di-Mercurio (2B) . . . 319 G5
Santa-Lucia-di-Moriani (2B) 319 K4
Santa-Maria-di-Lota (2B) 317 D4
Santa-Maria-Figaniella (2A) 322 E2
Santa-Maria-Poggio (2B) 319 J5
Santa-Maria-Siché (2A) 320 E6
Santa-Reparata-di-Balagna (2B) . . 318 C2
Santa-Reparata-di-Moriani (2B) . . 319 J5
Sant'Andréa-di-Bozio (2B) 319 H6
Sant'Andréa-di-Cotone (2B) 319 J5
Sant'Andréa-d'Orcino (2A) 320 C4
Santans (39) 155 J3
Sant'Antonino (2B) 318 C2
Santeau (45) 110 C2
Santec (29) 46 E3
Santenay (21) 153 J5
Santenay (41) 128 C2
Santeny (94) 59 G5
Santes (59) 6 C4
Santeuil (28) 85 J4
Santeuil (95) 37 F6
Santigny (89) 134 B2
Santilly (28) 110 A1
Santilly (71) 171 H3
Santo-Pietro-di-Tenda (2B) 319 G2
Santo-Pietro-di-Venaco (2B) 321 F1
Santoche (25) 138 E3
Santosse (21) 153 J3
Santranges (18) 131 J3
Sanvensa (12) 251 G3
Sanvignes-les-Mines (71) 170 D2
Sanxay (86) 162 B4
Sanzay (79) 143 J4
Sanzey (54) 65 H4
Saon (14) 31 K1
Saône (25) 138 B6
Saonnet (14) 31 K1
Saorge (06) 311 D3
Saosnes (72) 82 E4
Saou (26) 240 E4
le Sap (61) 55 F3
le Sap-André (61) 55 G4
Sapignicourt (51) 63 H6
Sapignies (62) 11 H5
Sapogne-et-Feuchères (08) 22 D4
Sapogne-sur-Marche (08) 23 J5
Sapois (39) 156 B6
Sapois (88) 119 G1
Saponay (02) 40 A5
Saponcourt (70) 117 K4
le Sappey (74) 191 F3
le Sappey-en-Chartreuse (38) . . . 224 B2
Saramon (32) 286 E1
Saran (45) 110 A3
Saraz (25) 156 B3
Sarbazan (40) 265 J1
Sarcé (72) 106 E6
Sarceaux (61) 54 C5
Sarcelles (95) 58 E2
Sarcenas (38) 224 B2
Sarcey (52) 116 C2
Sarcey (69) 187 K6
Sarcos (32) 286 D3
Sarcus (60) 17 G4
Sarcy (51) 40 D5
Sardan (30) 274 D2
Sardent (23) 182 D4
Sardieu (38) 223 F1
Sardon (63) 185 G5
Sardy-lès-Épiry (58) 151 K1
Sare (64) 282 A3
Sargé-lès-le-Mans (72) 106 E2
Sargé-sur-Braye (41) 108 A4
Sari-d'Orcino (2A) 320 C3
Sari-Solenzara (2A) 321 J6
Sariac-Magnoac (65) 286 C4
Sarlabous (65) 304 E1
Sarlande (24) 198 D6
Sarlat-la-Canéda (24) 233 F4
Sarliac-sur-l'Isle (24) 214 C3
Sarniguet (65) 285 H4
Sarnois (60) 17 H5

Saron-sur-Aube (51) 89 H1
Sarp (65) 305 H2
Sarpourenx (64) 283 K2
Sarragachies (32) 266 B5
Sarrageois (25) 174 C1
Sarraguzan (32) 286 A3
Sarralbe (57) 68 D4
Sarraltroff (57) 67 J3
Sarran (19) 216 C1
Sarrance (64) 303 F1
Sarrancolin (65) 305 F3
Sarrant (32) 268 B4
Sarras (07) 222 B3
Sarraziet (24) 198 C6
Sarrazac (46) 215 J6
Sarraziet (40) 265 G5
Sarre-Union (67) 68 D5
Sarrebourg (57) 67 J4
Sarrecave (31) 286 D5
Sarreguemines (57) 68 D2
Sarreinsming (57) 68 D3
Sarremezan (31) 286 D5
Sarrewerden (67) 68 D5
Sarrey (52) 116 D2
Sarriac-Bigorre (65) 285 J3
Sarrians (84) 257 G6
Sarrigné (49) 125 J3
Sarrogna (39) 173 G4
Sarrola-Carcopino (2A) 320 C4
Sarron (40) 265 J6
Sarrouilles (65) 285 H5
Sarroux (19) 217 H1
Sarry (51) 62 D2
Sarry (71) 187 F1
Sarry (89) 134 B1
le Sars (62) 10 E5
Sars-et-Rosières (59) 7 G6
Sars-le-Bois (62) 10 B3
Sars-Poteries (59) 13 H4
Sartène (2A) 322 E3
Sartes (88) 93 G5
Sartilly (50) 51 J2
Sarton (62) 10 B5
Sartrouville (78) 58 C2
Sarzay (36) 166 A3
Sarzeau (56) 121 F1
Sasnières (41) 108 B6
Sassangy (71) 171 H1
Sassay (41) 129 F5
Sassegnies (59) 13 F4
Sassenage (38) 224 A4
Sassenay (71) 154 B6
Sassetot-le-Malgardé (76) 15 H3
Sassetot-le-Mauconduit (76) . . . 14 E2
Sasseville (76) 15 F3
Sassey (27) 56 E1
Sassey-sur-Meuse (55) 43 F2
Sassierges-Saint-Germain (36) . . 166 A1
Sassis (65) 304 B4
Sassy (14) 54 B1
Sathonay-Camp (69) 206 B1
Sathonay-Village (69) 206 B1
Satillieu (07) 221 K4
Satolas-et-Bonce (38) 206 D3
Saturargues (34) 274 E5
Saubens (31) 288 A2
Saubion (40) 262 C5
Saubole (64) 285 F4
Saubrigues (40) 262 C5
Saubusse (40) 262 E5
Saucats (33) 229 G4
Saucède (64) 283 K4
la Saucelle (28) 56 C6
Sauchay (76) 16 A1
Sauchy-Cauchy (62) 11 H3
Sauchy-Lestrée (62) 11 H3
Sauclières (12) 273 G2
Saudemont (62) 11 H3
Saudoy (51) 61 H5
Saudron (52) 92 C2
Saudrupt (55) 64 A5
Saugeot (39) 173 J2
Saugnac-et-Cambran (40) 264 B5
Saugnacq-et-Muret (40) 245 H1
Saugon (33) 211 J3
Saugues (43) 237 J1
Sauguis-Saint-Étienne (64) 283 H6
Saugy (18) 148 D4
Saujac (12) 250 E1
Saujon (17) 194 D3
la Saulce (05) 259 G1
Saulce-sur-Rhône (26) 240 B4
Saulces-Champenoises (08) 41 K1
Saulces-Monclin (08) 22 B6
Saulcet (03) 185 G1
Saulchery (02) 60 D2
le Saulchoy (60) 17 K5
Saulchoy (62) 9 G2
Saulchoy-sous-Poix (80) 17 H4
Saulcy (10) 91 H5
le Saulcy (88) 95 J3
Saulcy-sur-Meurthe (88) 95 H3
Saules (25) 156 D1
Saules (71) 171 H3
Saulgé (86) 164 A6
Saulgé-l'Hôpital (49) 125 J5
Saulges (53) 105 J3
Saulgond (16) 180 C5
Sauliac-sur-Célé (46) 234 A4
Saulieu (21) 134 C6
Saulles (52) 116 E6
Saulmory-et-Villefranche (55) . . . 43 F1
Saulnay (36) 147 F5
Saulnes (54) 26 D2
Saulnières (28) 56 E6
Saulnières (35) 103 G1

Saulnot (70) 139 F1
Saulny (57) 44 E5
Saulon-la-Chapelle (21) 154 C1
Saulon-la-Rue (21) 136 A6
Sault (84) 258 A5
Sault-Brénaz (01) 189 J6
Sault-de-Navailles (64) 283 K1
Sault-lès-Rethel (08) 41 J1
Sault-Saint-Remy (08) 41 G2
Saultain (59) 12 D2
Saulty (62) 10 C4
Saulvaux (55) 64 D5
Saulx (70) 118 C6
Saulx-le-Duc (21) 136 A2
Saulx-lès-Champlon (55) 44 A6
Saulx-les-Chartreux (91) 58 D5
Saulx-Marchais (78) 57 K4
Saulxerotte (54) 93 J2
Saulxures (67) 95 K2
Saulxures-lès-Bulgnéville (88) . . . 93 H5
Saulxures-lès-Nancy (54) 66 B5
Saulxures-lès-Vannes (54) 93 H1
Saulxures-sur-Moselotte (88) . . . 119 G2
Saulzais-le-Potier (18) 167 G3
Saulzet (03) 185 G3
Saulzet-le-Froid (63) 202 B4
Saulzoir (59) 12 C3
Saumane (04) 258 D5
Saumane (30) 254 D5
Saumane-de-Vaucluse (84) 276 E2
Sauméjan (47) 247 F4
Saumeray (28) 84 E5
Saumont (47) 247 K5
Saumont-la-Poterie (76) 16 E6
Saumos (33) 210 D6
Saumur (49) 126 B6
Saunay (37) 128 B2
la Saunière (23) 182 D3
Saunières (71) 154 C5
Sauqueville (76) 15 K2
Saurais (79) 162 A2
Saurat (09) 307 H4
Sauret-Besserve (63) 184 C5
Saurier (63) 202 C5
Sausheim (68) 97 C2
Saussan (34) 293 F1
Saussay (28) 57 F3
Saussay (76) 15 J5
Saussay-la-Campagne (27) 36 B3
la Saussaye (27) 35 G4
Saussemesnil (50) 28 E3
Saussenac (81) 271 F1
Saussens (31) 288 E1
Sausset-les-Pins (13) 295 K6
Sausseuzemare-en-Caux (76) . . . 14 C4
Saussey (21) 153 H3
Saussey (50) 30 E4
Saussignac (24) 231 G3
Saussines (34) 274 D4
Saussy (21) 135 K3
Sautel (09) 308 A3
Sauternes (33) 229 K6
Sauteyrargues (34) 274 C3
Sauto (66) 313 J4
Sautron (44) 123 F3
la Sauvagère (61) 53 J6
les Sauvages (69) 187 H6
Sauvagnac (16) 197 J2
Sauvagnas (47) 248 C4
Sauvagnat (63) 201 J2
Sauvagnat-Sainte-Marthe (63) . . 202 E4
Sauvagney (25) 137 J5
Sauvagnon (64) 284 C3
Sauvagny (03) 167 K5
Sauvain (42) 204 B3
Sauvat (15) 217 H2
Sauve (30) 274 C2
la Sauve (33) 229 K3
Sauvelade (64) 283 K3
Sauverny (01) 174 B6
Sauvessanges (63) 220 C1
la Sauvetat (32) 267 H3
la Sauvetat (63) 202 E4
la Sauvetat-de-Savères (47) 248 D4
la Sauvetat-du-Dropt (47) 231 G4
la Sauvetat-sur-Lède (47) 248 C1
Sauveterre (30) 276 B1
Sauveterre (32) 287 F2
Sauveterre (65) 285 H2
Sauveterre (81) 290 D2
Sauveterre (82) 249 J4
Sauveterre-de-Béarn (64) 283 H2
Sauveterre-de-Comminges (31) . . 305 J2
Sauveterre-de-Guyenne (33) . . . 230 C4
Sauveterre-de-Rouergue (12) . . . 251 J4
Sauveterre-la-Lémance (47) 232 D5
Sauveterre-Saint-Denis (47) 248 C5
Sauviac (32) 286 B3
Sauviac (33) 246 D2
Sauvian (34) 292 A4
Sauviat (63) 203 H3
Sauviat-sur-Vige (87) 182 A6
Sauvignac (16) 212 C2
Sauvigney-lès-Gray (70) 137 H3
Sauvigney-lès-Pesmes (70) 137 F5
Sauvigny (55) 93 G2
Sauvigny-le-Beuréal (89) 134 B3
Sauvigny-les-Bois (58) 133 K3
Sauvigny-les-Bois (58) 151 F4
Sauville (08) 22 C6
Sauville (88) 93 G6
Sauvillers-Mongival (80) 18 C4
Sauvimont (32) 287 G2
Sauvoy (55) 65 F6

Saux (46) 249 G2
Saux-et-Pomarède (31) 286 E6
Sauxillanges (63) 203 G5
Sauze (06) 261 F5
le Sauze-du-Lac (05) 243 G6
Sauzé-Vaussais (79) 179 F3
Sauzelles (36) 164 B2
Sauzet (26) 240 B5
Sauzet (30) 275 F2
Sauzet (46) 249 H2
la Sauzière-Saint-Jean (81) 269 J2
Sauzon (56) 120 A3
Savarthès (31) 306 A1
Savas (07) 222 A2
Savas-Mépin (38) 206 D5
Savasse (26) 240 B5
Savenay (44) 122 D2
Savenès (82) 268 E3
Savennes (23) 182 D4
Savennes (63) 201 H4
Savennières (49) 125 F4
Saverdun (09) 288 D5
Savères (31) 287 J3
Saverne (67) 70 B1
Saveuse (80) 18 A2
Savianges (71) 171 G2
Savières (10) 89 K3
Savigna (39) 173 G4
Savignac (12) 251 F3
Savignac (33) 230 B6
Savignac-de-Duras (47) 230 E4
Savignac-de-l'Isle (33) 212 A6
Savignac-de-Miremont (24) 214 C6
Savignac-de-Nontron (24) 197 K5
Savignac-Lédrier (24) 215 F1
Savignac-les-Églises (24) 214 C2
Savignac-les-Ormeaux (09) 313 F1
Savignac-Mona (32) 287 H2
Savignac-sur-Leyze (47) 248 D1
Savignargues (30) 274 E2
Savigné (86) 179 H3
Savigné-l'Évêque (72) 107 F2
Savigné-sous-le-Lude (72) 126 C1
Savigné-sur-Lathan (37) 127 F4
Savigneux (01) 188 C4
Savigneux (42) 204 D4
Savignies (60) 37 F1
Savigny (50) 31 F4
Savigny (52) 117 G6
Savigny (69) 205 H1
Savigny (74) 190 D3
Savigny (88) 94 B3
Savigny-en-Revermont (71) 172 E2
Savigny-en-Sancerre (18) 131 J4
Savigny-en-Septaine (18) 149 J3
Savigny-en-Terre-Plaine (89) 134 B3
Savigny-en-Véron (37) 144 E1
Savigny-le-Sec (21) 136 A4
Savigny-le-Temple (77) 87 G1
Savigny-le-Vieux (50) 80 C1
Savigny-lès-Beaune (21) 154 A3
Savigny-Lévescault (86) 163 G4
Savigny-Poil-Fol (58) 169 K1
Savigny-sous-Faye (86) 145 G5
Savigny-sous-Mâlain (21) 135 H5
Savigny-sur-Aisne (08) 42 B2
Savigny-sur-Ardres (51) 40 C4
Savigny-sur-Braye (41) 107 K4
Savigny-sur-Clairis (89) 112 B2
Savigny-sur-Grosne (71) 171 H3
Savigny-sur-Orge (91) 58 E6
Savigny-sur-Seille (71) 172 B2
Savilly (21) 152 E2
Savines-le-Lac (05) 243 H5
Savins (77) 88 C2
Savoillan (84) 258 A4
Savoisy (21) 114 E6
Savolles (21) 136 C4
Savonnières (37) 127 H5
Savonnières-devant-Bar (55) 64 B4
Savonnières-en-Perthois (55) . . . 64 A6
Savouges (21) 154 C1
Savournon (05) 258 E1
Savoyeux (70) 137 H2
Savy (02) 19 J3
Savy-Berlette (62) 10 D2
Saxel (74) 191 H1
Saxi-Bourdon (58) 151 H3
Saxon-Sion (54) 93 K2
Sayat (63) 202 D1
Saze (30) 276 A2
Sazeray (36) 166 C5
Sazeret (03) 168 A6
Sazilly (37) 145 G2
Sazos (65) 304 B4
Scaër (29) 75 G6
Scata (2B) 319 H4
Sceau-Saint-Angel (24) 197 K5
Sceautres (07) 239 K5
Sceaux (89) 134 A3
Sceaux (92) 58 E4
Sceaux-d'Anjou (49) 125 G3
Sceaux-du-Gâtinais (45) 111 G1
Sceaux-sur-Huisne (72) 107 H1
Scey-Maisières (25) 156 C2
Scey-sur-Saône-et-
    -Saint-Albin (70) 117 K6
Schaeffersheim (67) 70 E5
Schaffhouse-près-Seltz (67) 25 D2
Schaffhouse-sur-Zorn (67) 70 D1
Schalbach (57) 67 K3
Schalkendorf (67) 70 C1
Scharrachbergheim-Irmstett (67) . 70 D3
Scheibenhard (67) 25 D2
Scherlenheim (67) 70 D1
Scherwiller (67) 96 C1

Schillersdorf (67) 69 H5
Schiltigheim (67) 25 A6
Schirmeck (67) 70 A5
Schirrhein (67) 25 B4
Schirrhoffen (67) 25 C4
Schleithal (67) 25 C1
Schlierbach (68) 97 D3
Schmittviller (57) 68 E4
Schneckenbusch (57) 67 J4
Schnersheim (67) 70 D2
Schœnau (67) 71 D5
Schœnbourg (67) 69 F6
Schœneck (57) 68 C1
Schœnenbourg (67) 25 B2
Schopperten (67) 68 D5
Schorbach (57) 69 G3
Schweighouse-sur-Moder (67) . . 69 K6
Schweighouse-Thann (68) 97 A2
Schwenheim (67) 70 C2
Schwerdorff (57) 45 J2
Schweyen (57) 69 G2
Schwindratzheim (67) 70 D1
Schwoben (68) 97 C4
Schwobsheim (67) 96 E2
Sciecq (79) 161 H5
Scientrier (74) 191 H3
Scieurac-et-Flourès (32) 285 J1
Sciez (74) 174 E6
Scillé (79) 161 G3
Scionzier (74) 191 H3
Scolca (2B) 319 H3
Scorbé-Clairvaux (86) 145 H6
Scrignac (29) 47 H6
Script (51) 63 H5
Scy-Chazelles (57) 44 E5
Scye (70) 118 A6
Séailles (32) 266 D4
la Séauve-sur-Semène (43) 221 F2
Sébazac-Concourès (12) 252 B2
Sébécourt (27) 56 A2
Sébeville (50) 29 F5
Seboncourt (02) 20 B1
Sebourg (59) 12 E2
Sébrazac (12) 235 K6
Séby (64) 284 C2
Secenans (70) 139 F2
Séchault (08) 42 B4
Sécheras (07) 222 B4
Sécheval (08) 22 C2
Séchilienne (38) 224 B5
Séchin (25) 138 C4
Seclin (59) 6 D5
Secondigné-sur-Belle (79) 178 B2
Secondigny (79) 161 H3
Secourt (57) 66 B1
Secqueville-en-Bessin (14) 32 C4
Sedan (08) 23 F4
Sédeilhac (31) 286 C6
Séderon (26) 258 B4
Sedze-Maubecq (64) 285 F3
Sedzère (64) 285 F4
Seebach (67) 25 C2
Sées (61) 54 E6
Séez (73) 193 H3
Ségalas (47) 231 J5
Ségalas (65) 285 H3
la Ségalassière (15) 235 F2
Séglien (56) 76 C5
Ségny (01) 174 B6
Segonzac (16) 196 A4
Segonzac (19) 215 F2
Segonzac (24) 213 H3
Ségos (32) 265 K6
Ségoufielle (32) 268 D6
Segré (49) 104 D6
Ségreville (31) 288 E2
Ségrie (72) 82 C6
Ségrie-Fontaine (61) 53 J3
Segrois (21) 154 A1
Ségry (36) 148 D5
la Séguinière (49) 142 E2
Ségur (12) 252 E3
le Ségur (81) 251 G6
Ségur-le-Château (19) 199 F6
Ségur-les-Villas (15) 218 B3
Ségura (09) 307 K2
Séguret (84) 257 G4
Ségus (65) 304 B1
Seich (65) 305 G2
Seichamps (54) 66 B4
Seichebrières (45) 110 D3
Seicheprey (54) 65 G3
Seiches-sur-le-Loir (49) 125 J2
Seignalens (11) 308 C1
Seigné (17) 178 C5
Seignelay (89) 113 G4
Seigneulles (55) 64 B3
Seignosse (40) 262 C4
Seigny (21) 134 E2
Seigy (41) 129 F6
Seilh (31) 269 F5
Seilhac (19) 216 A1
Seilhan (31) 305 H2
Seillac (31) 128 D3
Seillans (83) 280 A5
Seillonnaz (01) 207 H1
Seillons-Source-d'Argens (83) . . . 297 H1
Seine-Port (77) 87 G1
Seingbouse (57) 68 B3
Seissan (32) 286 D2
Seix (09) 306 E4
le Sel-de-Bretagne (35) 103 G1
Selaincourt (54) 93 J1
Selens (02) 39 H1
Sélestat (67) 96 C1
Séligné (79) 178 C3

401

Séligney (39) 155 H4
la Selle-Craonnaise (53) 104 C4
la Selle-en-Coglès (35) 51 J4
la Selle-en-Hermoy (45) 111 K3
la Selle-en-Luitré (35) 80 B4
la Selle-Guerchaise (35) 104 B3
la Selle-la-Forge (61) 53 H4
la Selle-sur-le-Bied (45) 111 K2
Selles (27) 34 C3
Selles (51) 41 H3
Selles (62) 4 D3
Selles (70) 118 A2
Selles-Saint-Denis (41) 130 A5
Selles-sur-Cher (41) 129 G6
Selles-sur-Nahon (36) 147 H4
Sellières (39) 155 H5
Selommes (41) 108 D6
Seloncourt (25) 139 H3
Selongey (21) 136 B2
Selonnet (04) 259 K1
Seltz (67) 25 D3
la Selve (02) 21 G6
la Selve (12) 252 B6
Sem (09) 307 H5
Sémalens (81) 289 J1
Semallé (61) 82 D2
Semarey (21) 135 G6
Sembadel (43) 220 A2
Sembas (47) 248 B3
Semblançay (37) 127 H3
Sembleçay (36) 147 K1
Sembouès (32) 285 J2
Séméac (65) 285 H5
Séméacq-Blachon (64) 285 F2
Sémécourt (57) 44 E4
Sémelay (58) 152 A6
Semens (33) 230 A5
Sementron (89) 132 E1
Sémeries (59) 13 H5
Semerville (41) 109 F3
Semezanges (21) 154 A1
Sémézies-Cachan (32) 286 E2
Semide (08) 42 A3
Semillac (17) 195 G6
Semilly (52) 92 E5
Semmadon (70) 117 J5
Semoine (10) 62 B5
Semond (21) 115 G6
Semondans (25) 139 G2
Semons (38) 206 E6
Semousies (59) 13 H4
Semoussac (17) 195 G6
Semoutiers-Montsaon (52) 116 A2
Semoy (45) 110 A4
Sempesserre (32) 267 J1
Sempigny (60) 19 H6
Sempy (62) 4 D6
Semur-en-Auxois (21) 134 D3
Semur-en-Brionnais (71) 187 F1
Semur-en-Vallon (72) 107 J2
Semussac (17) 194 D4
Semuy (08) 42 B1
le Sen (40) 246 A5
Sénac (65) 285 J3
Senaide (88) 117 H2
Sénaillac-Latronquière (46) 234 D2
Sénaillac-Lauzès (46) 233 K5
Senailly (21) 134 D2
Senan (89) 112 E4
Senantes (28) 57 H6
Senantes (60) 36 E1
Sénarens (31) 287 G4
Senargent-Mignafans (70) 138 E1
Senarpont (80) 17 F2
Sénas (13) 276 E4
Senaud (39) 172 E5
Senaux (81) 271 J4
Sencenac-Puy-de-Fourches (24) . . 213 K2
Senconac (09) 307 K5
Sendets (33) 246 E1
Sendets (64) 284 E4
Séné (56) 101 F6
Sénéchas (30) 255 G3
Sénergues (12) 235 J5
Sénestis (47) 247 H2
Séneujols (43) 220 B6
Senez (04) 279 H1
Sénezergues (15) 235 H4
Sengouagnet (31) 305 K2
Séniergues (46) 233 J4
Senillé (86) 163 H1
Seninghem (62) 4 E3
Senlecques (62) 4 D4
Senlis (60) 38 B5
Senlis (62) 5 F5
Senlis-le-Sec (80) 10 D6
Senlisse (78) 58 B6
Senneçay (18) 149 G4
Sennecey-le-Grand (71) 171 K2
Sennecey-lès-Dijon (21) 136 B5
Sennely (45) 130 C1
Sennevières (37) 146 E2
Senneville-sur-Fécamp (76) 14 D3
Sennevoy-le-Bas (89) 114 D5
Sennevoy-le-Haut (89) 114 D5
Senon (55) 44 A3
Senonches (28) 84 C1
Senoncourt (70) 118 A4
Senoncourt-les-Maujouy (55) 43 H6
Senones (88) 95 J2
Senonges (88) 93 K6
Senonnes (53) 104 A5
Senots (60) 37 G4
Senouillac (81) 270 C2
Sénoville (50) 28 B5
Senozan (71) 171 K5

Sens (89) 88 D6
Sens-Beaujeu (18) 131 H5
Sens-de-Bretagne (35) 79 H1
Sens-sur-Seille (71) 172 D1
Sentein (09) 306 B4
Sentelie (80) 17 J4
Sentenac-de-Sérou (09) 307 G3
Sentenac-d'Oust (09) 306 D4
Sentheim (68) 119 K5
Sentilly (61) 54 B4
la Sentinelle (59) 12 C2
Sentous (65) 286 A5
Senuc (08) 42 C3
Senven-Léhart (22) 76 D1
Sépeaux (89) 112 D3
Sepmeries (59) 12 D3
Sepmes (37) 145 K3
Seppois-le-Bas (68) 97 B5
Seppois-le-Haut (68) 97 B5
Sept-Forges (61) 81 H2
Sept-Frères (14) 52 C3
Sept-Meules (76) 16 C1
Sept-Saulx (51) 41 H5
Sept-Sorts (77) 60 B2
Sept-Vents (14) 31 K4
Septème (38) 206 C4
Septèmes-les-Vallons (13) 296 C3
Septeuil (78) 57 J3
Septfonds (82) 250 B5
Septfontaines (25) 156 D3
Septmoncel (39) 173 K5
Septmonts (02) 39 J3
Septsarges (55) 43 F3
Septvaux (02) 20 B6
Sepvigny (55) 93 F1
Sepvret (79) 178 E1
Sepx (31) 287 F6
Sequedin (59) 6 D4
Sequehart (02) 20 A1
le Sequestre (81) 270 D2
Serain (02) 12 B6
Seraincourt (08) 21 J5
Seraincourt (95) 58 A1
Sérandon (19) 217 G1
Séranon (06) 280 B3
Serans (60) 36 E5
Serans (61) 54 B5
Séranville (54) 94 D2
Séranvillers-Forenville (59) 12 B5
Seraucourt-le-Grand (02) 19 K3
Seraumont (88) 93 F2
Serazereux (28) 85 F1
Serbannes (03) 185 H4
Serbonnes (89) 88 C4
Sercœur (88) 94 E4
Sercus (59) 5 J3
Sercy (71) 171 H3
Serdinya (66) 314 B4
Sère (32) 286 D3
Sère-en-Lavedan (65) 304 A2
Sère-Lanso (65) 304 B1
Sère-Rustaing (65) 285 K5
Serécourt (88) 117 H1
Séreilhac (87) 198 D2
Sérémange-Erzange (57) 44 E3
Sérempuy (32) 268 A3
Sérénac (81) 271 F2
Sérent (56) 101 J3
Sérévillers (60) 18 C5
Serez (27) 57 F2
Sergeac (24) 214 E6
Sergenaux (39) 155 G5
Sergenon (39) 155 G4
Sergines (89) 88 D4
Sergy (01) 190 D1
Sergy (02) 40 B5
Séricourt (62) 10 A3
Sériers (15) 218 K1
Sérifontaine (60) 36 E3
Sérignac (46) 249 G2
Sérignac (82) 268 C2
Sérignac-Péboudou (47) 231 J5
Sérignac-sur-Garonne (47) 248 A4
Sérignan (34) 292 B5
Sérignan-du-Comtat (84) 256 E4
Sérigné (85) 160 D4
Sérigny (61) 83 H4
Sérigny (86) 145 G5
Sérilhac (19) 216 A5
Seringes-et-Nesles (02) 40 A5
Séris (41) 109 G6
Serley (71) 154 E6
Sermages (58) 152 A3
Sermaise (49) 125 K3
Sermaise (91) 86 C2
Sermaises (45) 86 D5
Sermaize (60) 19 G5
Sermaize-les-Bains (51) 63 J4
Sermamagny (90) 119 H5
Sermange (39) 155 J1
Sermentizon (63) 203 H2
Sermérieu (38) 207 G3
Sermersheim (67) 70 D6
Sermesse (71) 154 C5
Sermiers (51) 40 E5
Sermizelles (89) 133 J3
Sermoise (02) 39 K3
Sermoise-sur-Loire (58) 150 E4
Sermoyer (01) 172 A4
Sermur (23) 183 J5
Sernhac (30) 275 J2
Serocourt (88) 117 J1

Séron (65) 285 F4
Serpaize (38) 206 B4
la Serpent (11) 308 E3
Serques (62) 3 F4
Serqueux (52) 117 G2
Serqueux (76) 16 D5
Serquigny (27) 34 E6
Serra-di-Ferro (2A) 322 C2
Serra-di-Fiumorbo (2B) 321 H4
Serra-di-Scopamène (2A) 323 F1
Serralongue (66) 314 D6
Serraval (74) 209 F1
la Serre (12) 271 K3
la Serre-Bussière-Vieille (23) 183 H4
Serres-les-Moulières (39) 137 G6
Serres-les-Sapins (25) 137 K6
Serre-Nerpol (38) 223 F2
Serres (05) 258 D1
Serres (11) 309 F3
Serres (54) 66 D5
Serres-Castet (64) 284 D3
Serres-et-Montguyard (24) 231 H4
Serres-Gaston (40) 265 G5
Serres-Morlaàs (64) 284 C4
Serres-Sainte-Marie (64) 284 B2
Serres-sur-Arget (09) 307 H3
Serreslous-et-Arribans (40) 265 F5
Serrigny (89) 113 K5
Serrigny-en-Bresse (71) 154 D6
Serris (77) 59 J4
Serrouville (54) 26 A4
Serruelles (18) 149 G5
Sers (16) 197 F4
Sers (65) 304 C4
Servais (02) 20 A5
Serval (02) 40 C3
Servance (70) 119 F4
Servanches (24) 212 E4
Servant (63) 184 D3
Servas (01) 189 F3
Servas (30) 255 H5
Servaville-Salmonville (76) 35 K1
Serverette (48) 237 H4
Serves-sur-Rhône (26) 222 B4
Servian (34) 292 B3
Servières (48) 237 H5
Servières-le-Château (19) 216 D4
Serviers-et-Labaume (30) 255 K6
Serviès (81) 270 C6
Serviès-en-Val (11) 309 H1
Servignat (01) 172 B5
Servigney (70) 118 C5
Servigny (50) 30 D3
Servigny-lès-Raville (57) 45 H5
Servigny-lès-Sainte-Barbe (57) . . . 45 G5
Serville (28) 57 G4
Servilly (03) 186 A1
Servin (25) 138 E5
Servins (62) 10 D1
Servon (50) 51 J4
Servon (77) 59 G5
Servon-Melzicourt (51) 42 C4
Servon-sur-Vilaine (35) 79 J4
Servoz (74) 192 B5
Sery (08) 21 K5
Séry (89) 133 H2
Séry-lès-Mézières (02) 20 B3
Séry-Magneval (60) 38 E4
Serzy-et-Prin (51) 40 C4
Sessenheim (67) 25 C2
Sète (34) 293 F3
Setques (62) 5 F3
Seugy (95) 37 K6
Seuil (08) 41 J1
Seuil-d'Argonne (55) 63 K1
Seuillet (03) 185 J2
Seuilly (37) 145 F2
Seur (41) 128 E3
le Seure (17) 195 J1
Seurre (21) 154 D3
Seux (80) 17 K2
Seuzey (55) 64 E1
Sevelinges (42) 187 H3
Sevenans (90) 139 H1
Sévérac (44) 102 C5
Sévérac-le-Château (12) 253 G3
Sévérac-l'Église (12) 252 E2
Seveux (70) 137 H2
Sévignac (22) 78 A1
Sévignacq (64) 284 C2
Sévignacq-Meyracq (64) 284 C6
Sévigny (61) 54 C4
Sévigny-la-Forêt (08) 22 B2
Sévigny-Waleppe (08) 21 H5
Sévis (76) 16 A4
Sevrai (61) 54 B5
Sevran (93) 59 G2
Sèvres (92) 58 D4
Sèvres-Anxaumont (86) 163 G3
Sevrey (71) 171 K1
Sévrier (74) 191 F6
Sévry (18) 150 A2
Sewen (68) 119 J4
Sexcles (19) 216 D5
Sexey-aux-Forges (54) 65 K6
Sexey-les-Bois (54) 65 J4
Sexfontaines (52) 92 A5
Seychalles (63) 203 F2
Seyches (47) 231 F6
Seyne (04) 260 A2

la Seyne-sur-Mer (83) 300 B4
Seynes (30) 255 J5
Seynod (74) 191 F5
Seyre (31) 288 E4
Seyresse (40) 264 B5
Seyssel (01) 190 C5
Seyssel (74) 190 C5
Seysses (31) 288 A2
Seysses-Savès (32) 287 H2
Seyssinet-Pariset (38) 224 A3
Seyssins (38) 224 A3
Seyssuel (38) 206 B4
Seythenex (74) 209 F2
Seytroux (74) 192 A1
Sézanne (51) 61 H5
Siarrouy (65) 285 H4
Siaugues-Sainte-Marie (43) 219 K5
Sibiril (29) 46 E3
Sibiville (62) 10 A2
Siccieu-Saint-Julien-et-
  -Carisieu (38) 207 F2
Sichamps (58) 151 F2
Sickert (68) 119 J4
Sideville (50) 28 C3
Sidiailles (18) 166 E4
Siecq (17) 196 A1
Siegen (67) 25 D2
les Sièges (89) 89 F6
Sierck-les-Bains (57) 27 J3
Sierentz (68) 97 D3
Siersthal (57) 69 G3
Sierville (76) 15 K6
Siest (40) 264 A5
Sieurac (81) 270 D4
Sieuras (09) 288 A6
Siévoz (38) 242 C1
Siewiller (67) 69 F6
Sigale (06) 280 D2
Sigalens (33) 246 E1
Sigean (11) 310 C2
Sigloy (45) 110 D5
Signac (31) 305 J3
Signes (83) 297 H4
Signéville (52) 92 C5
Signy-l'Abbaye (08) 22 A4
Signy-le-Petit (08) 21 J1
Signy-Montlibert (08) 23 J5
Signy-Signets (77) 60 B2
Sigogne (16) 196 B2
Sigolsheim (68) 96 B3
Sigonce (04) 278 C1
Sigottier (05) 258 D1
Sigoulès (24) 231 H3
Sigournais (85) 160 C1
Sigoyer (04) 259 C6
Sigoyer (05) 242 D6
Siguer (09) 307 H5
Sigy (77) 88 C2
Sigy-en-Bray (76) 16 D6
Sigy-le-Châtel (71) 171 G3
Silfiac (56) 76 C4
Silhac (07) 239 K1
Sillans (38) 223 H1
Sillans-la-Cascade (83) 279 F6
Sillars (86) 163 K5
Sillas (33) 246 E2
Sillé-le-Guillaume (72) 82 B6
Sillé-le-Philippe (72) 107 F1
Sillegny (57) 66 A1
Sillery (51) 41 G5
Silley-Amancey (25) 156 D3
Silley-Bléfond (25) 138 C5
Sillingy (74) 190 E5
Silly-en-Gouffern (61) 54 D4
Silly-en-Saulnois (57) 66 B1
Silly-la-Poterie (02) 39 G5
Silly-le-Long (60) 38 D6
Silly-sur-Nied (57) 45 G5
Silly-Tillard (60) 37 H3
Silmont (55) 64 B4
Siltzheim (67) 68 D3
Silvareccio (2B) 319 H4
Silvarouvres (52) 115 H2
Simacourbe (64) 285 F2
Simandre (71) 172 A2
Simandre-sur-Suran (01) 189 J2
Simandres (69) 206 B4
Simard (71) 172 C2
Simencourt (62) 10 D3
Simeyrols (24) 233 G1
Simiane-Collongue (13) 296 D2
Simiane-la-Rotonde (04) 277 J1
Simorre (32) 286 E2
Simplé (53) 104 E4
Sin-le-Noble (59) 11 H2
Sinard (38) 224 A6
Sinceny (02) 19 K6
Sincey-lès-Rouvray (21) 134 B4
Sindères (40) 245 F6
Singles (63) 201 H5
Singleyrac (24) 231 H3
Singly (08) 22 D5
Singrist (67) 70 C2
Sinsat (09) 307 J5
Sinzos (65) 285 J5
Sion (32) 266 C4
Sion-les-Mines (44) 103 G3
Sionne (88) 93 F3
Sionviller (54) 66 D5
Siorac-de-Ribérac (24) 213 G5
Siorac-en-Périgord (24) 232 D2
Siouville-Hague (50) 28 A3
Sirac (32) 268 B5
Siracourt (62) 10 A2
Siradan (65) 305 H3

Siran (15) 234 E1
Siran (34) 290 E4
Sireix (65) 304 A2
Sireuil (16) 196 C5
Sirod (39) 174 A1
Siros (64) 284 B3
Sisco (2B) 317 D3
Sissonne (02) 21 F6
Sissy (02) 20 B3
Sistels (82) 248 D6
Sisteron (04) 259 F4
Sivergues (84) 277 H3
Sivignon (71) 171 F5
Sivry (54) 66 A3
Sivry-Ante (51) 63 H1
Sivry-Courtry (77) 87 J2
Sivry-la-Perche (55) 43 G5
Sivry-sur-Meuse (55) 43 G3
Six-Fours-les-Plages (83) 300 B4
Sixt-Fer-à-Cheval (74) 192 B3
Sixt-sur-Aff (35) 102 C2
Sizun (29) 46 D3
Smarves (86) 163 F4
Smermesnil (76) 16 D2
Soccia (2A) 320 D2
Sochaux (25) 139 H2
Socourt (88) 94 B3
Socx (59) 3 H3
Sode (31) 305 H5
Sœurdres (49) 105 G6
Sognolles-en-Montois (77) 88 C2
Sogny-aux-Moulins (51) 62 D3
Sogny-en-l'Angle (51) 63 H4
Soignolles (14) 54 A1
Soignolles-en-Brie (77) 59 H6
Soindres (78) 57 J2
Soing-Cubry-Charentenay (70) . . . 137 J2
Soings-en-Sologne (41) 129 G4
Soirans (21) 154 E1
Soissons (02) 39 J2
Soissons-sur-Nacey (21) 136 E6
Soisy-Bouy (77) 88 D2
Soisy-sous-Montmorency (95) . . . 58 E2
Soisy-sur-École (91) 87 F2
Soisy-sur-Seine (91) 59 F6
Soize (02) 21 H4
Soizé (28) 84 A6
Soizy-aux-Bois (51) 61 H4
Solaize (69) 206 A3
Solaro (2B) 321 H6
Solbach (67) 70 A5
Soleilhas (04) 280 A2
Solemont (25) 139 G4
Solente (60) 19 G4
le Soler (66) 315 F2
Solérieux (26) 256 E2
Solers (77) 59 H6
Solesmes (59) 12 D4
Solesmes (72) 105 K4
Soleymieu (38) 207 F2
Soleymieux (42) 204 C5
Solférino (40) 245 F5
Solgne (57) 66 B1
Soliers (14) 32 E5
Solignac (87) 199 F2
Solignac-sous-Roche (43) 220 D3
Solignac-sur-Loire (43) 220 C6
Solignat (63) 202 E5
Soligny-la-Trappe (61) 55 H6
Soligny-les-Étangs (10) 89 F3
Sollacaro (2A) 322 D2
Sollières-Sardières (73) 226 B2
Solliès-Pont (83) 300 D3
Solliès-Toucas (83) 300 D3
Solliès-Ville (83) 300 D3
Sologny (71) 171 H6
Solomiac (32) 268 B4
Solre-le-Château (59) 13 J4
Solrinnes (59) 13 J3
Solterre (45) 111 J4
Solutré-Pouilly (71) 188 B1
Somain (59) 12 B2
Sombacour (25) 156 E4
Sombernon (21) 135 H5
Sombrin (62) 10 C3
Sombrun (65) 285 G2
Somloire (49) 143 H3
Sommaing (59) 12 D3
Sommancourt (52) 91 K2
Sommant (71) 152 E3
Sommauthe (08) 42 D1
Somme-Bionne (51) 42 B6
Somme-Suippe (51) 42 A6
Somme-Tourbe (51) 42 B6
Somme-Vesle (51) 63 F2
Somme-Yèvre (51) 63 H2
Sommecaise (89) 112 D5
Sommedieue (55) 43 J6
Sommeilles (55) 63 J2
Sommelans (02) 39 J6
Sommelonne (55) 63 K5
Sommepy-Tahure (51) 42 A4
Sommerance (08) 42 E3
Sommereux (60) 17 J5
Sommeron (02) 21 F1
Sommervieu (14) 32 B3
Sommerviller (54) 66 C5
Sommery (76) 16 D5
Sommesnil (76) 15 F4
Sommesous (51) 62 B5
la Sommette (25) 138 C6
Sommette-Eaucourt (02) 19 J4
Sommeval (10) 89 K6
Sommevoire (52) 91 J3
Sommières (30) 274 E4

Sommières-du-Clain (86) 179 J1
Sompt (79) 178 D3
Sompuis (51) 62 D5
Somsois (51) 90 E1
Son (08) 21 K6
Sonac (46) 234 B4
Sonchamp (78) 86 A1
Soncourt (88) 93 J3
Soncourt-sur-Marne (52) 92 A5
Sondernach (68) 119 K2
Sondersdorf (68) 97 C6
la Sône (38) 223 G4
Songeons (60) 17 G6
Songeson (39) 173 J2
Songieu (01) 190 B5
Songy (51) 62 K4
Sonnac (12) 234 E6
Sonnac (17) 195 K1
Sonnac-sur-l'Hers (11) 308 C2
Sonnay (38) 222 C1
Sonnaz (73) 208 B3
Sonneville (16) 196 B1
Sons-et-Ronchères (02) 20 D3
Sonthonnax-la-Montagne (01) . . . 189 K1
Sonzay (37) 127 G3
Soorts-Hossegor (40) 262 B5
Soppe-le-Bas (68) 119 K5
Soppe-le-Haut (68) 119 K5
Sor (09) 306 C3
Sorans-lès-Breurey (70) 138 A4
Sorbais (02) 21 F2
Sorbets (32) 266 B4
Sorbets (40) 265 J5
Sorbey (55) 43 K2
Sorbey (57) 45 G6
Sorbier (03) 169 H6
Sorbiers (05) 258 C2
Sorbiers (42) 205 G5
Sorbo-Ocagnano (2B) 319 J3
Sorbollano (2A) 323 F1
Sorbon (08) 21 K6
Sorbs (34) 273 G3
Sorcy-Bauthémont (08) 22 B6
Sorcy-Saint-Martin (55) 65 F5
Sorde-l'Abbaye (40) 283 F1
Sore (40) 245 K3
Soréac (65) 285 J4
Sorède (66) 315 H4
Sorel (80) 11 H6
Sorel-en-Vimeu (80) 9 G4
Sorel-Moussel (28) 57 F4
Sorèze (81) 289 J2
Sorgeat (09) 313 F1
Sorges (24) 214 C2
Sorgues (84) 276 C1
Sorigny (37) 127 J6
les Sorinières (44) 123 G5
Sorio (2B) 319 G2
Sormery (89) 113 H1
Sormonne (08) 22 B3
Sornac (19) 200 E3
Sornay (70) 137 G5
Sornay (71) 172 C2
Sornéville (54) 66 C4
Sorquainville (76) 14 K4
Sorrus (62) 4 B6
Sort-en-Chalosse (40) 264 C5
Sortosville (50) 28 E4
Sortosville-en-Beaumont (50) 28 B5
Sos (47) 247 G6
Sospel (06) 281 J1
Sossais (86) 145 G5
Sost (65) 305 H3
Sotta (2A) 323 G4
Sottevast (50) 28 D4
Sotteville (50) 28 B3
Sotteville-lès-Rouen (76) 35 H2
Sotteville-sous-le-Val (76) 35 J3
Sotteville-sur-Mer (76) 15 H2
Soturac (46) 249 F1
Sotzeling (57) 66 E2
Souain-Perthes-lès-Hurlus (51) . . . 41 K5
Soual (81) 289 J1
Souancé-au-Perche (28) 84 A5
Souanyas (66) 314 A4
Souastre (62) 10 D4
Soubès (34) 273 G4
Soubise (17) 176 E5
Soublecause (65) 285 G1
Soubran (17) 211 H1
Soubrebost (23) 182 D5
Soucé (53) 81 G2
Soucelles (49) 125 H2
la Souche (07) 239 F5
Souchez (62) 10 E1
Soucht (57) 69 G4
Soucia (39) 173 J3
Soucieu-en-Jarrest (69) 205 K3
Soucirac (46) 233 J4
Souclin (01) 189 J6
Soucy (02) 39 G3
Soucy (89) 88 D3
Soudaine-Lavinadière (19) 199 K5
Soudan (44) 103 K3
Soudan (79) 162 A5
Soudat (24) 197 J4
Souday (41) 108 A2
Soudé (51) 62 D5
Soudeilles (19) 200 D6
Soudorgues (30) 254 E6
Soudron (51) 62 B3
Soueich (31) 305 K2
Soueix-Rogalle (09) 306 E4
Souel (81) 270 C1
Soues (65) 285 H5
Soues (80) 17 J1

Souesmes (41) 130 C4
Souffelweyersheim (67) 25 A6
Soufflenheim (67) 25 C3
Souffrignac (16) 197 H4
Sougé (36) 147 H4
Sougé (41) 107 J5
Sougé-le-Ganelon (72) 82 C4
Sougéal (35) 51 H5
Sougères-en-Puisaye (89) 132 D2
Sougraigne (11) 309 G4
Sougy (45) 109 K2
Sougy-sur-Loire (58) 151 G6
les Souhesmes-Rampont (55) 43 G6
Souhey (21) 134 E3
le Souich (62) 10 B3
Souilhanels (11) 289 C1
Souilhe (11) 289 G3
Souillac (46) 233 H1
Souillé (72) 106 D1
Souilly (55) 64 C1
Soula (09) 307 K3
Soulac-sur-Mer (33) 194 B5
Soulages (15) 219 G5
Soulages-Bonneval (12) 236 B4
Soulaines-Dhuys (10) 91 H3
Soulaines-sur-Aubance (49) 125 G4
Soulaire-et-Bourg (49) 125 G2
Soulaires (28) 85 H2
Soulan (09) 306 E3
Soulanges (51) 63 F4
Soulangis (18) 149 H1
Soulangy (14) 54 A2
Soulatgé (11) 309 H4
Soulaucourt-sur-Mouzon (52) 93 G5
Soulaures (24) 232 C4
Soulce-Cernay (25) 139 H4
Soulgé-sur-Ouette (53) 105 G1
le Soulié (34) 290 E1
Soulières (51) 61 K3
Soulignac (33) 230 A4
Souligné-Flacé (72) 106 C3
Souligné-sous-Ballon (72) 106 E1
Soulignonne (17) 194 E1
Souligny (10) 90 A6
Soulitré (72) 107 G2
Soullans (85) 140 E5
Soulles (50) 31 G4
Soulom (65) 304 B3
Soulomès (46) 233 J5
Soulosse-sous-Saint-Élophe (88) . . 93 G3
Soultz-Haut-Rhin (68) 96 B6
Soultz-les-Bains (67) 70 D3
Soultz-sous-Forêts (67) 25 B2
Soultzbach-les-Bains (68) 96 A4
Soultzeren (68) 119 K1
Soultzmatt (68) 96 B5
Soulvache (44) 103 H2
Soumaintrain (89) 113 J2
Soumans (23) 183 H1
Soumensac (47) 231 G4
Souméras (17) 211 J2
Soumont (34) 273 G5
Soumont-Saint-Quentin (14) 54 A2
Soumoulou (64) 284 E4
Soupex (11) 289 G3
Soupir (02) 40 B2
Souppes-sur-Loing (77) 87 J6
Souprosse (40) 264 B5
Souraïde (64) 282 B3
Sourans (25) 139 F3
Sourcieux-les-Mines (69) 205 J1
le Sourd (02) 20 E2
Sourdeval (50) 52 D4
Sourdeval-les-Bois (50) 52 A2
Sourdon (80) 18 B4
Sourdun (77) 88 E2
le Sourn (56) 76 D6
Sournia (66) 314 C2
Sourniac (15) 217 G2
Sourribes (04) 259 G4
Sours (28) 85 H3
Soursac (19) 217 F3
Sourzac (24) 213 H5
Sous-Parsat (23) 182 E4
Sousceyrac (46) 234 D2
Sousmoulins (17) 211 K2
Souspierre (26) 240 D6
Soussac (33) 230 D3
Soussans (33) 211 G5
Soussey-sur-Brionne (21) 135 F5
Soustelle (30) 255 G5
Soustons (40) 262 C4
Sousville (38) 224 B6
Souternon (42) 186 E6
la Souterraine (23) 181 K2
Soutiers (79) 161 K3
Souvans (39) 155 H3
Souvignargues (30) 274 E3
Souvigné (16) 179 F5
Souvigné (37) 127 F3
Souvigné (79) 161 K6
Souvigné-sur-Même (72) 83 J5
Souvigné-sur-Sarthe (72) 105 J3
Souvigny (03) 168 D4
Souvigny-de-Touraine (37) 128 C4
Souvigny-en-Sologne (41) 130 C1
Souyeaux (65) 285 J5
Souzay-Champigny (49) 126 B6
Souzy (69) 205 J3
Souzy-la-Briche (91) 86 C2
Soveria (2B) 319 F5
Soyans (26) 240 D4
Soyaux (16) 196 K3
Soye (25) 138 E3
Soye-en-Septaine (18) 149 H3
Soyécourt (80) 19 F2

Soyers (52) 117 G4
Soyons (07) 240 C1
Sparsbach (67) 69 G5
Spay (72) 106 D3
Spechbach-le-Bas (68) 97 B3
Spechbach-le-Haut (68) 97 B3
Speloncato (2B) 318 D3
Spéracèdes (06) 280 C5
Spézet (29) 75 G4
Spicheren (57) 68 C2
Spincourt (55) 44 A3
Sponville (54) 44 C6
Spoy (10) 91 G5
Spoy (21) 136 C3
Spycker (59) 3 G2
Squiffiec (22) 48 C4
Staffelfelden (68) 97 B1
Stains (93) 58 E2
Stainville (55) 64 B5
Staple (59) 5 J3
Stattmatten (67) 25 C4
Stazzona (2B) 319 H5
Steenbecque (59) 5 J3
Steene (59) 3 H2
Steenvoorde (59) 3 K4
Steenwerck (59) 6 B3
Steige (67) 70 A6
Steinbach (68) 97 A1
Steinbourg (67) 70 C1
Steinbrunn-le-Bas (68) 97 C3
Steinbrunn-le-Haut (68) 97 C3
Steinseltz (67) 25 B1
Steinsoultz (68) 97 C3
Stenay (55) 43 F1
Sternenberg (68) 97 A3
Stetten (68) 97 D4
Stigny (89) 114 C5
Still (67) 70 C1
Stiring-Wendel (57) 68 C1
Stonne (08) 23 F6
Storckensohn (68) 119 J3
Stosswihr (68) 119 K1
Stotzheim (67) 70 D6
Strasbourg (67) 71 D1
Strazeele (59) 3 A3
Strenquels (46) 215 K6
Strueth (68) 97 A4
Struth (67) 69 F5
Stuckange (57) 27 H4
Stundwiller (67) 25 C2
Sturzelbronn (57) 69 H2
Stutzheim-Offenheim (67) 70 E2
Suarce (90) 139 K1
Suaux (16) 197 H1
le Subdray (18) 149 F2
Sublaines (37) 128 B6
Subles (14) 32 A4
Subligny (18) 131 J4
Subligny (50) 51 K2
Subligny (89) 88 C2
Suc-et-Sentenac (09) 307 G5
Succieu (38) 207 F5
Sucé-sur-Erdre (44) 123 H2
Sucy-en-Brie (94) 59 G4
Suèvres (41) 129 F1
Sugères (63) 203 G4
Sugny (08) 42 B3
Suhescun (64) 282 E4
Suilly-la-Tour (58) 132 B5
Suin (71) 171 F5
Suippes (51) 41 K5
Suisse (57) 66 E1
Suizy-le-Franc (51) 61 H2
Sulignat (01) 188 D2
Sully (14) 32 A3
Sully (60) 17 G6
Sully (71) 153 G3
Sully-la-Chapelle (45) 110 D3
Sully-sur-Loire (45) 110 E6
Sulniac (56) 101 H5
Sumène (30) 274 A1
Sundhoffen (68) 96 C4
Sundhouse (67) 96 C2
Supt (39) 156 B5
Surat (63) 185 G6
Surba (09) 307 H4
Surbourg (67) 25 B2
Surcamps (80) 9 J5
Surdoux (87) 199 J4
Suré (61) 83 G4
Suresnes (92) 58 D4
Surfonds (72) 107 G3
Surfontaine (02) 20 B4
Surgères (17) 177 H3
Surgy (58) 133 F3
Suriauville (88) 93 H6
Surin (79) 161 H4
Surin (86) 179 J5
Suris (16) 197 H1
Surjoux (01) 190 C4
Surmont (25) 139 F5
Surques (62) 2 D3
Surrain (14) 29 K6
Surtainville (50) 28 B4
Surtauville (27) 35 H5
Survie (61) 54 E3
Surville (14) 33 K3
Surville (27) 35 H5
Surville (50) 30 C1
Survilliers (95) 38 B6
Sury (08) 22 C3
Sury-aux-Bois (45) 110 E3
Sury-en-Vaux (18) 131 J5
Sury-ès-Bois (18) 131 H4
Sury-le-Comtal (42) 204 E5
Sury-près-Léré (18) 131 K3

Surzur (56) 121 G1
Sus (64) 283 J4
Sus-Saint-Léger (62) 10 B3
Susmiou (64) 283 J4
Sussac (87) 199 J3
Sussargues (34) 274 D5
Sussat (03) 185 F3
Sussey (21) 153 F1
Susville (38) 224 B6
Sutrieu (01) 190 A5
Suzan (09) 307 G2
Suzanne (08) 22 C6
Suzanne (80) 19 F1
Suzannecourt (52) 92 B2
Suzay (27) 36 B4
Suze (26) 240 E3
Suze-la-Rousse (26) 256 C3
la Suze-sur-Sarthe (72) 106 C4
Suzette (84) 257 G5
Suzoy (60) 19 G6
Suzy (02) 20 B6
Sy (08) 22 E6
Syam (39) 174 A1
Sylvains-les-Moulins (27) 56 C3
Sylvanès (12) 272 C3
le Syndicat (88) 119 F1

T

Tabaille-Usquain (64) 283 H3
Tabanac (33) 229 J3
la Table (73) 208 E5
le Tablier (85) 159 J3
Tabre (09) 308 B3
la Tâche (16) 179 J6
Tachoires (32) 286 D2
Tacoignières (78) 57 J4
Taconnay (58) 133 F6
Taden (22) 50 D5
Tadousse-Ussau (64) 284 E1
Taglio-Isolaccio (2B) 319 J4
la Tagnière (71) 152 E6
Tagnon (08) 41 H2
Tagolsheim (68) 97 B3
Tagsdorf (68) 97 C4
Tailhac (43) 219 H5
Taillades (84) 276 B3
le Taillan-Médoc (33) 229 G1
Taillancourt (55) 93 G1
Taillant (17) 177 J6
Taillebois (61) 53 J4
Taillebourg (17) 195 G1
Taillebourg (47) 247 H1
Taillecavat (33) 230 E4
Taillecourt (25) 139 H2
la Taillée (85) 160 C5
Taillefontaine (02) 39 F3
Taillepied (50) 28 D6
Taillet (66) 314 C4
Taillette (08) 22 B1
Taillis (35) 80 A5
Tailly (08) 42 E1
Tailly (21) 154 A4
Tailly (80) 17 H1
Tain-l'Hermitage (26) 222 B5
Taingy (89) 132 E2
Taintrux (88) 95 H4
Taisnières-en-Thiérache (59) 13 F4
Taisnières-sur-Hon (59) 13 G2
Taissy (51) 41 F4
Taïx (81) 270 D1
Taizé (71) 171 H4
Taizé (79) 144 C4
Taizé-Aizie (16) 179 H4
Taizy (08) 21 J6
Tajan (65) 286 B6
Talairan (11) 309 K2
Talais (33) 194 C5
Talange (57) 45 F4
Talant (21) 136 A5
Talasani (2B) 319 J4
la Talaudière (42) 205 G5
Talazac (65) 285 H4
Talcy (41) 109 F6
Talcy (89) 134 B2
Talence (33) 229 G2
Talencieux (07) 222 B3
Talensac (35) 78 D4
Talissieu (01) 190 B6
Talizat (15) 218 D4
Tallans (25) 138 C3
Tallard (05) 242 E6
Tallenay (25) 138 A5
Tallende (63) 202 D3
Taller (40) 264 B2
Talloires (74) 191 G6
Tallone (2B) 321 J1
le Tallud (79) 161 J2
Tallud-Sainte-Gemme (85) 160 D1
Talmas (80) 10 A6
Talmont-Saint-Hilaire (85) 159 F4
Talmont-sur-Gironde (17) 194 D4
Talmontiers (60) 36 D2
Talon (58) 133 G5
Talus-Saint-Prix (51) 61 H4
Taluyers (69) 205 K3
Tamerville (50) 28 E4
Tamnay-en-Bazois (58) 151 K3
Tamniès (24) 214 E6
Tanavelle (15) 218 D6
Tanay (21) 136 C3
Tancarville (76) 34 C1

Tancoigné (49) 143 K1
Tancon (71) 187 G2
Tanconville (54) 67 H5
Tancrou (77) 60 B2
Tancua (39) 174 A3
Tangry (62) 5 H6
Taninges (74) 191 K3
Tanis (50) 51 J4
Tanlay (89) 114 B4
Tannay (08) 22 E6
Tannay (58) 133 G5
Tanneron (83) 280 C5
Tannerre-en-Puisaye (89) 112 C6
Tannières (02) 40 A4
Tannois (55) 64 B5
Tanques (61) 54 B5
Tantonville (54) 94 A3
le Tanu (50) 51 K1
Tanus (81) 251 J6
Tanville (61) 82 C1
Tanzac (17) 195 G4
Taponas (69) 188 B3
Taponnat-Fleurignac (16) 197 G2
Tarabel (31) 288 E2
Taradeau (83) 298 D1
Tarare (69) 187 J6
Tarascon (13) 275 K3
Tarascon-sur-Ariège (09) 307 J4
Tarasteix (65) 285 G4
Tarbes (65) 285 H5
Tarcenay (25) 156 C1
Tardes (23) 183 H3
Tardets-Sorholus (64) 283 H6
la Tardière (85) 160 E2
Tardinghen (62) 2 A3
Tarentaise (42) 221 J1
Tarerach (66) 314 C2
Targassonne (66) 313 H4
Target (03) 185 F1
Targon (33) 230 A3
Tarnac (19) 200 C3
Tarnès (33) 211 K6
Tarnos (40) 262 B6
Taron-Sadirac-Viellenave (64) 284 E1
Tarquimpol (57) 67 F3
Tarrano (2B) 319 H5
Tarsac (32) 266 A5
Tarsacq (64) 284 B3
Tarsul (21) 135 K2
Tart-l'Abbaye (21) 154 E1
Tart-le-Bas (21) 154 E1
Tart-le-Haut (21) 154 D1
Tartaras (42) 205 J4
Tartas (40) 264 D3
Tartécourt (70) 117 K4
Tartiers (02) 39 H2
Tartigny (60) 18 B5
Tartonne (04) 260 A5
le Tartre (71) 172 E1
le Tartre-Gaudran (78) 57 H5
Tarzy (08) 21 K2
Tasque (32) 266 C6
Tassé (72) 106 A4
Tassenières (39) 155 G4
Tassillé (72) 106 B2
Tassin-la-Demi-Lune (69) 206 A2
Tasso (2A) 321 F5
Tatinghem (62) 5 G3
le Tâtre (16) 196 A6
Taugon (17) 160 D6
Taulé (29) 47 F4
Taulignan (26) 257 F1
Taulis (66) 314 C4
Taupont (56) 101 J1
Tauriac (33) 211 H5
Tauriac (46) 234 B1
Tauriac (81) 269 J3
Tauriac-de-Camarès (12) 272 D4
Tauriac-de-Naucelle (12) 251 J5
Tauriers (07) 239 G6
Taurignan-Castet (09) 306 D2
Taurignan-Vieux (09) 306 D2
Taurinya (66) 314 C3
Taurize (11) 309 H1
Taussac (12) 235 K2
Taussac-la-Billière (34) 272 D6
Tautavel (66) 310 A5
Tauves (63) 201 J3
Tauxières-Mutry (51) 41 F6
Tauxigny (37) 146 B1
Tavaco (2A) 320 D4
Tavant (37) 145 H2
Tavaux (39) 155 F3
Tavaux-et-Pontséricourt (02) 21 F4
Tavel (30) 276 A1
Tavera (2A) 320 E3
Tavernay (71) 152 D2
Tavernes (83) 278 E6
Taverny (95) 58 D1
Tavers (45) 109 H6
Tavey (70) 139 G1
Taxat-Senat (03) 185 F2
Taxenne (39) 137 G6
Tayac (33) 212 D6
Taybosc (32) 267 K4
Tayrac (12) 251 H4
Tayrac (47) 248 D6
Tazilly (58) 170 A1
le Tech (66) 314 C6
Tèche (38) 223 H3
Técou (81) 270 C3
le Teich (33) 228 C4
Teigny (58) 133 H5
le Teil (07) 240 A6
Teilhède (63) 185 F5
Teilhet (09) 308 A1

403

Teilhet (63) 184 C4
Teillay (35) 103 H2
Teillé (44) 123 K1
Teillé (72) 82 E6
Teillet (81) 271 G3
Teillet-Argenty (03) 183 K2
le Teilleul (50) 80 E1
Teillots (24) 215 F3
Teissières-de-Cornet (15) 217 G6
Teissières-lès-Bouliès (15) 235 J2
Telgruc-sur-Mer (29) 74 B3
Tellancourt (54) 26 B2
Tellecey (21) 136 C5
Tellières-le-Plessis (61) 55 G6
Teloché (72) 106 E4
le Temple (33) 228 D1
le Temple (41) 108 B3
le Temple-de-Bretagne (44) 122 E2
Temple-Laguyon (24) 214 E3
le Temple-sur-Lot (47) 248 A2
Templemars (59) 6 D5
Templeuve (59) 6 E5
Templeux-la-Fosse (80) 19 H1
Templeux-le-Guérard (80) 19 J1
Tenay (01) 189 K5
Tence (43) 221 G4
Tencin (38) 224 C1
Tende (06) 311 D2
Tendon (88) 95 F6
Tendron (18) 150 B4
Tendu (36) 165 H2
Teneur (62) 5 G6
Tennie (72) 106 B1
Tenteling (57) 68 C2
Tercé (86) 163 H4
Tercillat (23) 166 C5
Tercis-les-Bains (40) 264 A5
Terdeghem (59) 3 J4
Tergnier (02) 20 A5
Terjat (03) 184 A2
Termes (08) 42 C3
Termes (11) 309 J2
Termes (48) 237 F3
Termes-d'Armagnac (32) 266 B5
Termignon (73) 226 B1
Terminiers (28) 109 J2
Ternand (69) 187 K5
Ternant (17) 177 J5
Ternant (21) 154 A1
Ternant (58) 169 K1
Ternant-les-Eaux (63) 202 D6
Ternas (62) 10 B2
Ternat (52) 116 B3
Ternay (41) 107 K6
Ternay (69) 206 A4
Ternay (86) 144 C3
les Ternes (15) 218 D6
Ternuay-Melay-et-
   -Saint-Hilaire (70) 119 F4
Terny-Sorny (02) 39 J2
Terramesnil (80) 10 B5
la Terrasse (38) 224 C1
la Terrasse-sur-Dorlay (42) 205 J6
Terrasson-Lavilledieu (24) 215 G4
Terrats (66) 315 F3
Terraube (32) 267 H2
Terre-Clapier (81) 271 F3
Terre-Natale (52) 117 F3
Terrebasse (31) 287 G5
Terrefondrée (21) 115 J6
Terrehault (72) 83 G6
les Terres-de-Chaux (25) 139 G4
la Terrisse (12) 236 B3
Terroles (11) 309 G3
Terron-sur-Aisne (08) 42 B1
Terrou (46) 234 D3
Tersanne (26) 222 D3
Tersannes (87) 181 F1
Terssac (81) 270 D2
le Tertre-Saint-Denis (78) 57 H2
Tertry (80) 19 H2
Terville (57) 27 G4
Tessancourt-sur-Aubette (78) . . . 58 A1
Tessé-Froulay (61) 81 J1
Tessel (14) 32 C5
Tesson (17) 195 G3
Tessonnière (79) 144 B6
la Tessoualle (49) 143 F3
Tessy-sur-Vire (50) 31 H5
la Teste-de-Buch (33) 228 A4
Tétaigne (08) 23 G4
Téteghem (59) 3 J2
Téterchen (57) 45 J3
Téthieu (40) 264 C4
Teting-sur-Nied (57) 45 K6
Teuillac (33) 211 H4
Teulat (81) 269 K6
Teurthéville-Bocage (50) 28 E3
Teurthéville-Hague (50) 28 B3
Teyjat (24) 197 J4
Teyran (34) 274 C5
Teyssières (26) 257 H1
Teyssieu (46) 234 C1
Teyssode (81) 270 C6
Thaas (51) 61 J6
Thaims (17) 194 E3
Thairé (17) 176 E3
Thaix (58) 151 K6
Thal-Drulingen (67) 68 E5
Thal-Marmoutier (67) 70 B2
Thalamy (19) 201 H5
Thann (68) 97 A2
Thannenkirch (68) 96 B3
Thanvillé (67) 96 B1
Thaon (14) 32 D4
Thaon-les-Vosges (88) 94 D4

Tharaux (30) 255 K4
Tharoiseau (89) 133 J4
Tharot (89) 133 J3
Thaumiers (18) 149 K6
Thauron (23) 182 C5
Thauvenay (18) 131 K6
Thèbe (65) 305 H3
Théding (57) 68 C2
Thédirac (46) 233 G5
Thégra (46) 234 A2
Théhillac (56) 102 B5
le Theil (03) 168 C6
le Theil (50) 28 E3
le Theil (61) 83 J5
le Theil-Bocage (14) 53 F5
le Theil-de-Bretagne (35) 103 J1
le Theil-en-Auge (14) 34 A3
le Theil-Nolent (27) 34 C5
Theil-Rabier (16) 179 F4
Theil-sur-Vanne (89) 88 E6
Theillay (41) 130 B6
Theillement (27) 35 F4
Theix (56) 101 G5
Theizé (69) 188 A5
Thel (69) 187 H3
Théligny (72) 83 K6
Thélis-la-Combe (42) 221 J2
Thélod (54) 93 K1
Thelonne (08) 23 F5
Thélus (62) 11 F2
Théméricourt (95) 37 F6
Thémines (46) 234 B3
Théminettes (46) 234 B4
Thénac (17) 195 G3
Thénac (24) 231 G3
Thenailles (02) 21 F3
Thenay (36) 165 F3
Thenay (41) 128 E5
Thenelles (02) 20 B3
Thénésol (73) 209 G2
Theneuil (37) 145 H2
Theneuille (03) 167 K3
Thénezay (79) 162 B1
Thénioux (18) 130 A6
Thenissey (21) 135 G3
Thénisy (77) 88 C2
Thennelières (10) 90 B5
Thennes (80) 18 C3
Thenon (24) 214 D4
Thénorgues (08) 42 D2
Théoule-sur-Mer (06) 280 D6
Therdonne (60) 37 H2
Thérines (60) 17 H5
Thermes-Magnoac (65) 286 D4
Thérondels (12) 236 B2
Thérouanne (62) 5 G4
Thérouldeville (76) 14 E3
Thervay (39) 137 G6
Thésée (41) 128 E5
Thésy (39) 156 B4
Theuley (70) 137 H1
Théus (05) 243 F6
Theuville (28) 85 H4
Theuville (95) 37 G5
Theuville-aux-Maillots (76) 14 E3
Thevet-Saint-Julien (36) 166 C3
Théville (50) 28 E2
Thevray (27) 55 K2
They-sous-Montfort (88) 93 J5
They-sous-Vaudemont (54) 93 K3
Theys (38) 224 D1
Théza (66) 315 H3
Thézac (17) 194 E3
Thézac (47) 249 F2
Thézan-des-Corbières (11) 310 A1
Thézan-lès-Béziers (34) 291 K3
Thèze (04) 259 F2
Thèze (64) 284 D2
Thézey-Saint-Martin (54) 66 B2
Théziers (30) 275 K2
Thézillieu (01) 190 A6
Thézy-Glimont (80) 18 C3
Thiais (94) 58 E5
Thiancourt (90) 139 K2
Thianges (58) 151 H5
Thiant (59) 12 C2
Thiat (87) 180 E1
Thiaucourt-Regniéville (54) 65 H2
Thiaville-sur-Meurthe (54) 95 G2
Thiberville (27) 34 B5
Thibie (51) 62 C2
Thibivillers (60) 37 F4
Thibouville (27) 35 F5
Thicourt (57) 66 D1
Thiébauménil (54) 66 E6
Thiéblemont-Farémont (51) 63 G5
Thiébouhans (25) 139 H5
Thieffrain (10) 90 E6
Thieffrans (70) 138 C2
Thiéfosse (88) 119 G2
Thiel-sur-Acolin (03) 169 G4
Thiembronne (62) 4 E4
Thiénans (70) 138 C3
Thiennes (59) 5 J4
Thiepval (80) 10 E6
Thiergeville (76) 14 E4
Thiernu (02) 20 E3
Thiers (63) 203 H1
Thiers-sur-Thève (60) 38 B5
Thierville (27) 34 E4
Thierville-sur-Meuse (55) 43 H5
Thiéry (06) 261 H6
Thiescourt (60) 19 G6
Thiétreville (76) 14 E4
le Thieulin (28) 84 D3
Thieulloy-la-Ville (80) 17 H4

Thieulloy-l'Abbaye (80) 17 H3
Thieuloy-Saint-Antoine (60) 17 H5
la Thieuloye (62) 10 B1
Thieux (60) 18 B6
Thieux (77) 59 H1
Thiéville (14) 54 C1
Thièvres (62) 10 C5
Thièvres (80) 10 C5
Thiézac (15) 217 K6
Thignonville (45) 86 C5
Thil (01) 206 C1
Thil (10) 91 H4
le Thil (27) 36 C3
Thil (31) 268 D5
Thil (51) 40 E3
Thil (54) 26 E3
Thil-Manneville (76) 15 J2
le Thil-Riberpré (76) 16 E5
Thil-sur-Arroux (71) 152 D6
Thilay (08) 22 D2
le Thillay (95) 59 F2
Thilleux (52) 91 H3
les Thilliers-en-Vexin (27) 36 C4
Thillois (51) 40 E4
Thillombois (55) 64 D2
Thillot (55) 65 F1
le Thillot (88) 119 G3
Thilouze (37) 145 J1
Thimert-Gâtelles (28) 84 E1
Thimonville (57) 66 C1
Thimory (45) 111 G4
Thin-le-Moutier (08) 22 B4
Thiolières (63) 203 K4
Thionne (03) 169 G5
Thionville (57) 27 G4
Thiouville (76) 15 F4
Thiraucourt (88) 93 K4
Thiré (85) 160 C3
Thiron-Gardais (28) 84 B4
This (08) 22 C3
Thise (25) 138 A5
Thivars (28) 85 H3
Thivencelle (59) 7 K6
Thiverny (60) 38 A4
Thiverval-Grignon (78) 58 A3
Thivet (52) 116 C2
Thiviers (24) 198 B6
Thiville (28) 109 F2
Thizay (36) 148 C5
Thizay (37) 144 E1
Thizy (69) 187 H4
Thizy (89) 134 B2
Thoard (04) 259 H4
Thodure (38) 222 E2
Thoigné (72) 82 E5
Thoiras (30) 255 F6
Thoiré-sous-Contensor (72) 82 E4
Thoiré-sur-Dinan (72) 107 G6
Thoires (21) 115 G3
Thoirette (39) 189 K1
Thoiria (39) 173 H3
Thoiry (01) 190 D1
Thoiry (73) 208 C4
Thoiry (78) 57 K3
Thoissey (01) 188 C2
Thoissia (39) 172 E5
Thoisy-la-Berchère (21) 134 D6
Thoisy-le-Désert (21) 134 D6
Thoix (80) 17 J4
Thol-lès-Millières (52) 92 E6
Thollet (86) 164 C5
Thollon-les-Mémises (74) 175 H5
le Tholonet (13) 296 D1
le Tholy (88) 95 G6
Thomer-la-Sôgne (27) 56 D3
Thomery (77) 87 J3
Thomirey (21) 153 H2
Thonac (24) 214 E6
Thônes (74) 191 H5
Thonnance-lès-Joinville (52) . . . 92 B2
Thonnance-les-Moulins (52) 92 C3
Thonne-la-Long (55) 23 K5
Thonne-les-Près (55) 23 K6
Thonnelle (55) 23 K6
Thonon-les-Bains (74) 175 F5
les Thons (88) 117 J2
Thonville (57) 66 D1
le Thor (84) 276 D2
Thorailles (45) 111 K2
Thoraise (25) 156 A1
Thorame-Basse (04) 260 B5
Thorame-Haute (04) 260 C5
Thoras (43) 237 J2
Thoré-la-Rochette (41) 108 B5
Thorée-les-Pins (72) 106 C6
Thorens-Glières (74) 191 G4
Thorey (89) 114 B4
Thorey-en-Plaine (21) 154 D1
Thorey-Lyautey (54) 93 K2
Thorey-sous-Charny (21) 134 E5
Thorey-sur-Ouche (21) 153 J2
Thorigné (79) 178 C1
Thorigné-d'Anjou (49) 125 F1
Thorigné-en-Charnie (53) 105 J2
Thorigné-Fouillard (35) 79 H4
Thorigné-sur-Dué (72) 107 H2
Thorigny (85) 159 K2
Thorigny-sur-le-Mignon (79) . . . 177 K2
Thorigny-sur-Marne (77) 59 H3
Thorigny-sur-Oreuse (89) 88 E5
le Thoronet (83) 298 C2
Thorrenc (07) 222 B3
Thors (10) 91 H4
Thors (17) 195 K1
Thory (80) 18 C4

Thory (89) 133 K2
Thoste (21) 134 C4
le Thou (17) 177 F3
Thou (18) 131 H4
Thou (45) 131 K2
Thouarcé (49) 125 G6
Thouaré-sur-Loire (44) 123 H3
Thouars (79) 144 B4
Thouars-sur-Arize (09) 287 K6
Thouars-sur-Garonne (47) 247 J4
Thouarsais-Bouildroux (85) 160 D2
le Thoult-Trosnay (51) 61 H3
le Thour (08) 21 H6
le Thoureil (49) 125 K4
Thourie (35) 103 H2
Thouron (87) 181 G5
Thourotte (60) 38 E1
Thoury (41) 129 H2
Thoury-Férottes (77) 88 A3
Thoux (32) 268 C5
Thubœuf (53) 81 J2
le Thuel (02) 21 H5
Thuès-Entre-Valls (66) 313 K4
Thueyts (07) 239 F4
Thugny-Trugny (08) 41 J1
la Thuile (73) 208 D4
les Thuiles (04) 260 C1
Thuilley-aux-Groseilles (54) 65 J6
Thuillières (88) 93 K6
Thuir (66) 315 F3
le Thuit (27) 36 A4
le Thuit-Anger (27) 35 G4
Thuit-Hébert (27) 35 F3
le Thuit-Signol (27) 35 G4
le Thuit-Simer (27) 35 G4
Thulay (25) 139 H3
Thumeréville (54) 44 B4
Thumeries (59) 6 D6
Thun-l'Évêque (59) 12 B3
Thun-Saint-Amand (59) 7 H6
Thun-Saint-Martin (59) 12 B3
Thurageau (86) 162 E1
Thuré (86) 145 H6
Thurey (71) 172 C1
Thurey-le-Mont (25) 138 B4
Thurins (69) 205 J3
Thury (21) 153 H3
Thury (89) 132 D2
Thury-en-Valois (60) 39 F5
Thury-Harcourt (14) 53 J1
Thury-sous-Clermont (60) 37 K3
Thusy (74) 190 D5
Thuy (65) 285 K5
Thyez (74) 191 K3
Tibiran-Jaunac (65) 305 H2
Ticheville (61) 55 F3
Tichey (21) 154 E3
Tieffenbach (67) 69 F5
Tiercé (49) 125 H1
Tiercelet (54) 26 E3
le Tiercent (35) 79 J1
Tierceville (14) 32 C3
Tieste-Uragnoux (32) 285 H1
la Tieule (48) 253 H2
Tiffauges (85) 142 C3
Tigeaux (77) 59 K4
Tigery (91) 59 G6
Tignac (09) 308 A6
Tigné (49) 143 K1
Tignécourt (88) 117 J1
Tignes (73) 193 C5
Tignieu-Jameyzieu (38) 206 E2
Tigny-Noyelle (62) 9 F2
Tigy (45) 110 D5
Til-Châtel (21) 136 B3
Tilh (40) 264 D6
Tilhouse (65) 304 E1
Tillac (32) 285 K2
Tillay-le-Péneux (28) 109 J1
Tillé (60) 37 H2
le Tilleul (76) 14 B4
Tillenay (21) 155 F1
Tilleul-Dame-Agnès (27) 56 B1
le Tilleul-Lambert (27) 35 G6
le Tilleul-Othon (27) 35 F6
Tilleux (88) 93 G4
Tillières (49) 142 C1
Tillières-sur-Avre (27) 56 C5
Tilloloy (80) 19 F5
Tillou (79) 178 D3
Tilloy-et-Bellay (51) 63 F1
Tilloy-Floriville (80) 8 E6
Tilloy-lès-Conty (80) 17 K4
Tilloy-lès-Hermaville (62) 10 C2
Tilloy-lès-Mofflaines (62) 11 F3
Tilloy-lez-Cambrai (59) 11 J4
Tilloy-lez-Marchiennes (59) 12 B1
Tilly (27) 36 B5
Tilly (36) 164 D5
Tilly (78) 57 H3
Tilly-Capelle (62) 5 G6
Tilly-la-Campagne (14) 32 E6
Tilly-sur-Meuse (55) 64 D1
Tilly-sur-Seulles (14) 32 B5
Tilques (62) 3 F5
Tincey-et-Pontrebeau (70) 137 H1
Tinchebray (61) 53 F4
Tincourt-Boucly (80) 19 H1
Tincques (62) 10 C2
Tincry (57) 66 C2
Tingry (62) 4 B4
Tinqueux (51) 40 E4
Tinténiac (35) 78 E1
Tintry (71) 153 G4

Tintury (58) 151 J4
Tiranges (43) 220 D2
Tirent-Pontéjac (32) 287 F1
Tirepied (50) 52 A5
Tissey (89) 113 K4
le Titre (80) 9 F4
Tivernon (45) 110 A1
Tiviers (15) 218 E5
Tizac-de-Curton (33) 230 A2
Tizac-de-Lapouyade (33) 212 A5
Tocane-Saint-Apre (24) 213 J3
Tocqueville (27) 34 C3
Tocqueville (50) 29 F2
Tocqueville-en-Caux (76) 15 H3
Tocqueville-les-Murs (76) 14 E5
Tocqueville-sur-Eu (76) 8 E4
Tœufles (80) 9 F5
Toges (08) 42 C2
Togny-aux-Bœufs (51) 62 E3
Tolla (2A) 320 E4
Tollaincourt (88) 117 G1
Tollent (62) 9 H3
Tollevast (50) 28 C3
la Tombe (77) 88 B4
Tombebœuf (47) 231 H5
Tomblaine (54) 66 B5
Tomino (2B) 317 D2
les Tonils (26) 241 F5
Tonnac (81) 250 E6
Tonnay-Boutonne (17) 177 H5
Tonnay-Charente (17) 177 F5
Tonneins (47) 247 J2
Tonnerre (89) 114 A4
Tonneville (50) 28 C2
Tonnoy (54) 94 B1
Tonquédec (22) 48 A3
Torcé (35) 104 A1
Torcé-en-Vallée (72) 107 F1
Torcé-Viviers-en-Charnie (53) . . 105 K1
Torcenay (52) 116 E4
Torchamp (61) 81 F1
Torchefelon (38) 207 G5
Torcheville (57) 68 B5
Torcieu (01) 189 J5
Torcy (62) 4 E6
Torcy (71) 171 F1
Torcy (77) 59 H3
Torcy-en-Valois (02) 39 J6
Torcy-et-Pouligny (21) 134 C3
Torcy-le-Grand (10) 90 B2
Torcy-le-Grand (76) 16 A3
Torcy-le-Petit (10) 90 C2
Torcy-le-Petit (76) 16 A3
Tordères (66) 315 F4
Tordouet (14) 55 F1
Torfou (49) 142 C3
Torfou (91) 86 D2
Torigni-sur-Vire (50) 31 J4
Tornac (30) 274 C1
Tornay (52) 117 F6
le Torp-Mesnil (76) 15 H4
Torpes (25) 156 A1
Torpes (71) 155 F5
le Torpt (27) 34 A4
le Torquesne (14) 33 K4
Torreilles (66) 310 D5
Torsac (16) 196 E4
Torsiac (43) 219 F2
Tortebesse (63) 201 J3
Tortefontaine (62) 9 H2
Tortequesne (62) 11 H3
Torteron (18) 150 C2
Torteval-Quesnay (14) 32 A5
Tortezais (03) 167 K5
Tortisambert (14) 54 D2
Torvilliers (10) 89 K5
Torxé (17) 177 J5
Tosny (27) 36 A5
Tosse (40) 262 C4
Tossiat (01) 189 H3
Tostat (65) 285 H4
Tostes (27) 35 H4
Tôtes (76) 15 K4
Touchay (18) 166 D2
la Touche (26) 240 C6
les Touches (44) 123 K4
les Touches-de-Périgny (17) . . . 178 C6
Toucy (89) 112 D6
Toudon (06) 281 F4
Touët-de-l'Escarène (06) 281 H2
Touët-sur-Var (06) 280 D1
Touffailles (82) 249 F4
Toufflers (59) 7 F4
Touffréville (14) 33 F5
Touffreville (27) 36 B3
Touffreville-la-Cable (76) 15 F6
Touffreville-la-Corbeline (76) . . . 15 G6
Touffreville-sur-Eu (76) 8 B6
Touget (32) 268 C5
Touille (31) 306 B1
Touillon (21) 134 E1
Touillon-et-Loutelet (25) 157 F5
Toujouse (32) 266 A3
Toul (54) 65 H5
Toulaud (07) 240 B1
Toulenne (33) 230 A5
Touligny (08) 22 C4
Toulis-et-Attencourt (02) 20 E4
Toulon (83) 300 C4
Toulon-sur-Allier (03) 168 E4
Toulon-sur-Arroux (71) 170 C2
Toulonjac (12) 251 F2
Toulouges (66) 315 G2
Toulouse (31) 269 G6
Toulouse-le-Château (39) 155 H5

404

Toulouzette (40) 264 E4
Toulx-Sainte-Croix (23) 183 G1
Touques (14) 33 J3
le Touquet-Paris-Plage (62) 4 A5
Touquettes (61) 55 G4
Touquin (77) 60 A5
la Tour (06) 261 J6
la Tour (74) 191 J2
la Tour-Blanche (24) 213 H1
la Tour-d'Aigues (84) 277 J4
la Tour-d'Auvergne (63) 201 K5
Tour-de-Faure (46) 250 C1
la Tour-de-Salvagny (69) 205 K1
la Tour-du-Crieu (09) 307 J1
la Tour-du-Meix (39) 173 H3
le Tour-du-Parc (56) 121 G2
la Tour-du-Pin (38) 207 G4
Tour-en-Bessin (14) 32 A3
la Tour-en-Jarez (42) 205 G5
Tour-en-Sologne (41) 129 G3
la Tour-Saint-Gelin (37) 145 H3
la Tour-sur-Orb (34) 272 E6
Tourailles (41) 128 D1
les Tourailles (61) 53 J4
Tourbes (34) 292 B2
Tourcelles-Chaumont (08) 42 A2
Tourch (29) 75 F6
Tourcoing (59) 6 E3
Tourdun (32) 285 J1
la Tourette (42) 204 D6
la Tourette-Cabardès (11) 290 B3
Tourette-du-Château (06) 281 F1
Tourgéville (14) 33 J3
la Tourlandry (49) 143 G1
Tourlaville (50) 28 D2
Tourliac (47) 232 B4
Tourly (60) 37 F4
Tourmignies (59) 6 E6
Tourmont (39) 155 J5
Tournai-sur-Dive (61) 54 C4
Tournan (32) 286 E3
Tournan-en-Brie (77) 59 J5
Tournans (25) 138 C3
Tournavaux (08) 22 D2
Tournay (65) 285 K6
Tournay-sur-Odon (14) 32 C6
le Tourne (33) 229 J3
Tournebu (14) 53 K2
Tournecoupe (32) 268 A3
Tournedos-Bois-Hubert (27) 35 G6
Tournedos-sur-Seine (27) 35 K4
Tournefeuille (31) 288 K1
Tournefort (06) 281 F1
Tournehem-sur-la-Hem (62) 2 E4
Tournemire (12) 272 D2
Tournemire (15) 217 H5
Tournes (08) 22 C3
le Tourneur (14) 31 K5
Tourneville (27) 35 H6
Tournières (14) 31 J2
Tournissan (11) 309 K1
Tournoisis (45) 109 H3
Tournon (73) 209 F3
Tournon-d'Agenais (47) 249 F2
Tournon-Saint-Martin (36) 164 B1
Tournon-Saint-Pierre (37) 164 B1
Tournon-sur-Rhône (07) 222 B5
Tournous-Darré (65) 286 A4
Tournous-Devant (65) 286 B5
Tournus (71) 171 K3
Tourny (27) 36 C5
Tourouvre (61) 83 J1
Tourouzelle (11) 291 F5
Tourreilles (11) 308 E2
les Tourreilles (31) 305 H1
Tourrenquets (32) 267 J4
Tourrette-Levens (06) 281 G3
les Tourrettes (26) 240 B4
Tourrettes (83) 280 B5
Tourrettes-sur-Loup (06) 280 E4
Tourriers (16) 196 E1
Tours (37) 127 J4
Tours-en-Savoie (73) 209 G3
Tours-en-Vimeu (80) 8 E6
Tours-sur-Marne (51) 62 B1
Tours-sur-Meymont (63) 203 J3
Tourtenay (79) 144 C3
Tourteron (08) 22 C6
Tourtoirac (24) 214 D2
Tourtour (83) 279 G6
Tourtouse (09) 306 D1
Tourtrès (47) 231 H6
Tourtrol (09) 308 A2
Tourves (83) 297 J2
Tourville-en-Auge (14) 33 K3
Tourville-la-Campagne (27) 35 G4
Tourville-la-Chapelle (76) 16 B1
Tourville-la-Rivière (76) 35 H3
Tourville-les-Ifs (76) 14 D4
Tourville-sur-Arques (76) 15 K2
Tourville-sur-Odon (14) 32 D5
Tourville-sur-Pont-Audemer (27) . . 34 C3
Tourville-sur-Sienne (50) 30 D4
Toury (28) 86 A6
Toury-Lurcy (58) 169 F1
Toury-sur-Jour (58) 168 D1
Tourzel-Ronzières (63) 202 D5
Toussaint (76) 14 D4
Toussieu (69) 206 C3
Toussieux (01) 188 C5
Tousson (77) 87 F4
Toussus-le-Noble (78) 58 C1
Toutainville (27) 34 C3
Toutenant (71) 154 D5
Toutencourt (80) 10 C6

Toutens (31) 288 E2
Toutlemonde (49) 143 F3
Toutry (21) 134 B3
Touvérac (16) 212 B1
le Touvet (38) 224 C1
Touville (27) 34 E3
Touvois (44) 141 G4
Touvre (16) 197 F3
Touzac (16) 196 B4
Touzac (46) 249 G1
Tox (2B) 319 G6
Toy-Viam (19) 200 B4
Tracy-Bocage (14) 32 B6
Tracy-le-Mont (60) 39 F1
Tracy-le-Val (60) 39 F1
Tracy-sur-Loire (58) 131 K5
Tracy-sur-Mer (14) 32 B3
Trades (69) 187 K1
Traenheim (67) 70 C3
Tragny (57) 66 C1
Traînel (10) 88 E3
Traînou (45) 110 C3
le Trait (76) 35 F1
Traitiéfontaine (70) 138 A4
Traize (73) 207 K3
Tralaigues (63) 184 A6
Tralonca (2B) 319 F5
Tramain (22) 77 K2
Tramayes (71) 188 A1
Trambly (71) 171 G6
Tramecourt (62) 5 F6
Tramery (51) 40 D4
Tramezaïgues (65) 304 E5
Tramolé (38) 207 F5
Tramont-Émy (54) 93 J3
Tramont-Lassus (54) 93 J3
Tramont-Saint-André (54) 93 J3
Tramoyes (01) 188 D6
Trampot (88) 92 D3
Trancault (10) 89 F4
la Tranche-sur-Mer (85) 159 H5
la Tranclière (01) 189 G3
Trancrainville (28) 85 K5
Trangé (72) 106 D2
le Tranger (36) 147 F4
Trannes (10) 91 F4
Tranqueville-Graux (88) 93 H2
Trans (53) 81 K5
Trans-en-Provence (83) 298 D1
Trans-la-Forêt (35) 51 H5
Trans-sur-Erdre (44) 123 J1
le Translay (80) 17 F1
le Transloy (62) 11 F5
Tranzault (36) 165 K3
Trappes (78) 58 B4
Trassanel (11) 290 C4
Traubach-le-Bas (68) 97 A3
Traubach-le-Haut (68) 97 A3
Trausse (11) 290 C4
Travaillan (84) 257 F4
Travecy (02) 20 A4
Traversères (32) 286 D1
Traves (70) 137 K1
le Travet (81) 271 F4
Trayes (79) 161 H2
Tréal (56) 102 A2
Tréauville (50) 28 B3
Trébabu (29) 46 B2
Treban (03) 168 D5
Tréban (81) 251 K6
Trébas (81) 271 H2
Trébédan (22) 50 B6
Trèbes (11) 290 C5
Trébeurden (22) 47 J2
Trébons (65) 304 D1
Trébons-de-Luchon (31) 305 H5
Trébons-sur-la-Grasse (31) 288 E2
Trébrivan (22) 75 K2
Trébry (22) 77 J2
Tréclun (21) 154 E1
Trécon (51) 62 A3
Trédaniel (22) 77 H2
Trédarzec (22) 48 C2
Trédias (22) 78 B1
Trédion (56) 101 H3
Trédrez-Locquémeau (22) 47 J3
Tréduder (22) 47 J4
Trefcon (02) 19 J2
Treffendel (35) 78 D5
Treffiagat (29) 98 B3
Treffieux (44) 103 H5
Treffléan (56) 101 G5
Treffort (38) 242 A1
Treffort-Cuisiat (01) 189 H1
Treffrin (22) 75 J2
Tréflaouénan (29) 46 D4
Tréflévénez (29) 46 D6
Tréflez (29) 46 C3
Tréfols (51) 61 F4
Tréfumel (22) 78 D1
Trégarantec (29) 46 C4
Trégarvan (29) 74 C2
Trégastel (22) 47 K2
Tréglamus (22) 48 B5
Tréglonou (29) 72 D2
Trégomeur (22) 49 F5
Trégon (22) 50 B4
Trégonneau (22) 48 C4
Trégourez (29) 75 F4
Trégrom (22) 48 A4
Tréguennec (29) 98 A2
Trégueux (22) 49 G6
Tréguidel (22) 48 E5
Tréguier (22) 48 C2
Trégunc (29) 99 F3
Tréhet (41) 107 H6

Tréhorenteuc (56) 78 A5
le Tréhou (29) 74 D1
Treignac (19) 200 A5
Treignat (03) 166 E6
Treigny (89) 132 C3
Treilles (11) 310 C3
Treilles-en-Gâtinais (45) 111 H2
Treillières (44) 123 G2
Treix (52) 92 B6
Treize-Septiers (85) 142 B3
Treize-Vents (85) 143 F4
Tréjouls (82) 249 H4
Trélans (48) 253 G1
Trélazé (49) 125 H3
Trélévern (22) 48 B2
Trelins (42) 204 C2
Trélissac (24) 214 B3
Trélivan (22) 50 C6
Trelly (50) 30 C5
Trélon (59) 13 J5
Trélou-sur-Marne (02) 40 B6
Trémaouézan (29) 46 C5
Trémargat (22) 76 B2
Trémauville (76) 14 E5
la Tremblade (17) 194 B1
Tremblay (35) 51 J6
le Tremblay (49) 104 C6
Tremblay-en-France (93) 59 G2
Tremblay-les-Villages (28) 85 F1
le Tremblay-Omonville (27) 35 G6
le Tremblay-sur-Mauldre (78) . . . 58 A4
Tremblecourt (54) 65 J3
le Tremblois (70) 137 F4
Tremblois-lès-Carignan (08) 23 J4
Tremblois-lès-Rocroi (08) 22 B2
Trémeheuc (35) 51 G6
Trémel (22) 47 J4
Tréméloir (22) 49 F5
Trémentines (49) 143 F2
Tréméoc (29) 98 C2
Tréméreuc (22) 50 D4
Trémery (57) 45 J3
Trémeur (22) 78 B1
Tréméven (22) 48 E4
Tréméven (29) 99 J3
Trémilly (52) 91 H3
Tréminis (38) 242 B3
Trémoins (70) 139 G1
Trémolat (24) 232 B2
Trémons (47) 248 E2
Trémont (49) 143 J1
Trémont (61) 82 E1
Trémont-sur-Saulx (55) 63 K4
Trémonzey (88) 118 B2
Trémorel (22) 78 A3
Trémouille (15) 218 A1
Trémouille-Saint-Loup (63) 201 H6
Trémouilles (12) 252 C4
Trémoulet (09) 288 E6
Trémuson (22) 49 F6
Trenal (39) 173 F2
Trensacq (40) 245 H4
Trentels (47) 248 E1
Tréogan (22) 75 J4
Tréogat (29) 98 B2
Tréon (28) 56 E6
Tréouergat (29) 72 C3
Trépail (51) 41 G6
le Tréport (76) 8 C5
Trépot (25) 156 D1
Tréprel (14) 53 K3
Trept (38) 207 F3
Trésauvaux (55) 43 K6
Tresbœuf (35) 103 H1
Trescault (62) 11 H5
Treschenu-Creyers (26) 241 J3
Trescléoux (05) 258 D2
Trésilley (70) 137 K3
Treslon (51) 40 C4
Tresnay (58) 168 D2
Trespoux-Rassiels (46) 249 K2
Tresques (30) 256 C5
Tressan (34) 292 D1
Tressandans (25) 138 C2
Tressange (57) 27 F4
Tressé (35) 50 E5
Tresserre (66) 315 G4
Tresserve (73) 208 B3
Tresses (33) 229 J2
Tressignaux (22) 48 E4
Tressin (59) 7 F4
Tresson (72) 107 H4
Treteau (03) 169 G6
la Trétoire (77) 60 D3
Trets (13) 297 F2
Treux (80) 18 D1
Treuzy-Levelay (77) 87 J5
Trévé (22) 77 F4
Trévenans (90) 139 H1
Tréveneuc (22) 49 F4
Tréverec (22) 48 D4
Tréverien (35) 78 E1
Trèves (30) 253 K6
Trèves (69) 205 K5
Trévien (81) 251 G6
Trévières (14) 31 K1
Trévignin (73) 208 B2
Trévillach (66) 314 D2
Tréville (11) 289 G3
Trévillers (25) 139 J5
Trévilly (89) 134 B3
Trévol (03) 168 E3
Trévou-Tréguignec (22) 48 B2
Trévoux (01) 188 C5
le Trévoux (29) 99 H3

Trévron (22) 50 C6
Trézelles (03) 186 A1
Trézény (22) 48 B2
Tréziers (11) 308 C2
Trézilidé (29) 46 D4
Trézioux (63) 203 H3
Triac-Lautrait (16) 196 B3
le Triadou (34) 274 B4
Triaize (85) 160 A5
Tribehou (50) 31 G2
Trichey (89) 114 B3
Tricot (60) 18 D6
Trie-Château (60) 36 E4
Trie-la-Ville (60) 36 E4
Trie-sur-Baïse (65) 286 A4
Triel-sur-Seine (78) 58 B2
Triembach-au-Val (67) 70 B6
Trieux (54) 44 C3
Trigance (83) 279 J3
Trignac (44) 122 A2
Trigny (51) 40 D3
Triguères (45) 112 A3
Trilbardou (77) 59 J2
Trilla (66) 314 D1
Trilport (77) 60 A2
Trimbach (67) 25 C2
Trimer (35) 78 E1
la Trimouille (86) 164 C5
Trinay (45) 110 A2
la Trinitat (15) 236 C3
la Trinité (06) 281 H3
la Trinité (27) 56 E2
la Trinité (50) 52 B4
la Trinité (73) 208 D5
la Trinité-de-Réville (27) 55 H1
la Trinité-de-Thouberville (27) . . 35 F3
la Trinité-des-Laitiers (61) 55 G4
la Trinité-du-Mont (76) 14 E6
la Trinité-Porhoët (56) 77 H5
la Trinité-sur-Mer (56) 100 C6
la Trinité-Surzur (56) 101 H6
Triors (26) 222 E4
le Trioulou (15) 235 F4
Tripleville (41) 109 G3
Triqueville (76) 34 C1
Triqueville (27) 34 B3
Trith-Saint-Léger (59) 12 C2
Tritteling-Redlach (57) 45 K5
Trivy (71) 171 F5
Trizac (15) 217 J3
Trizay (17) 177 F6
Trizay-Coutretot-Saint-Serge (28) . . 84 A5
Trizay-lès-Bonneval (28) 84 E6
Troarn (14) 33 F5
Troche (19) 215 H1
Trochères (21) 136 D5
Trocy-en-Multien (77) 60 A1
Troësnes (02) 39 H5
Troguéry (22) 48 C2
Trogues (37) 145 J2
les Trois-Domaines (55) 64 C2
Trois-Fonds (23) 183 G2
Trois-Fontaines-l'Abbaye (51) . . . 63 J5
Trois-Monts (14) 32 D6
Trois-Palis (16) 196 D3
les Trois-Pierres (76) 14 D6
Trois-Puits (51) 41 F5
Trois-Vèvres (58) 151 G5
Trois-Villes (64) 283 H6
Troisfontaines (57) 67 K5
Troisfontaines-la-Ville (52) 91 K1
Troisgots (50) 31 H4
Troissereux (60) 37 G1
Troissy (51) 40 C6
Troisvaux (62) 10 B1
Troisvilles (59) 12 C5
Tromarey (70) 137 G5
Tromborn (57) 45 J3
Troncens (32) 285 J2
la Tronche (38) 224 A3
le Tronchet (35) 51 F5
le Tronchet (72) 82 D6
Tronchoy (89) 113 K4
Tronchy (71) 172 B1
le Troncq (27) 35 G5
Trondes (54) 65 G5
Tronget (03) 168 C5
le Tronquay (14) 32 A4
le Tronquay (27) 36 B2
Tronsanges (58) 150 D2
Tronville (54) 44 C6
Tronville-en-Barrois (55) 64 C5
Troo (41) 107 K5
Trosly-Breuil (60) 39 F2
Trosly-Loire (02) 39 H1
Trouans (10) 62 C6
Troubat (65) 305 H3
Trouhans (21) 154 E1
Trouhaut (21) 135 H4
Trouillas (66) 315 F3
Trouley-Labarthe (65) 285 K4
Troussey (55) 65 G5
Troussencourt (60) 18 A5
Troussey (55) 65 G5
Troussures (60) 37 G2
Trouvans (25) 138 D3
Trouville (76) 15 F6
Trouville-la-Haule (27) 34 D2
Trouville-sur-Mer (14) 33 J2
Trouy (18) 149 G4
Troye-d'Ariège (09) 308 B2
Troyes (10) 90 B4
Troyon (55) 64 D1
la Truchère (71) 172 A4
Truchtersheim (67) 70 D2
Trucy (02) 40 B1

Trucy-l'Orgueilleux (58) 132 E4
Trucy-sur-Yonne (89) 133 H2
le Truel (12) 272 A1
Trugny (21) 154 D4
Truinas (26) 240 E5
Trumilly (60) 38 D4
Trun (61) 54 C3
Trungy (14) 32 B4
Truttemer-le-Grand (14) 52 E4
Truttemer-le-Petit (14) 52 E4
Truyes (37) 128 A6
Tubersent (62) 4 B5
Tuchan (11) 310 A4
Tucquegnieux (54) 44 C3
Tudeils (19) 216 B5
Tudelle (32) 266 E5
Tuffé (72) 107 H1
Tugéras-Saint-Maurice (17) 211 K1
Tugny-et-Pont (02) 19 J3
la Tuilière (42) 186 C5
Tulette (26) 257 F3
Tulle (19) 216 B3
Tullins (38) 223 J2
Tully (80) 8 D5
Tupigny (02) 20 C1
Tupin-et-Semons (69) 206 A5
la Turballe (44) 121 H4
la Turbie (06) 281 J3
Turcey (21) 135 H4
Turckheim (68) 96 B4
Turenne (19) 215 J5
Turgon (16) 179 J5
Turgy (10) 114 A2
Turny (89) 113 H2
Turquant (49) 144 D1
Turquestein-Blancrupt (57) 67 K6
Turqueville (50) 29 F5
Turretot (76) 14 B5
Turriers (04) 259 H1
Tursac (24) 214 D6
Tusson (16) 179 F5
Tuzaguet (65) 305 G1
le Tuzan (33) 245 K1
Tuzie (16) 179 G5

U

Uberach (67) 69 J5
Ubexy (88) 94 B3
Ubraye (04) 280 A1
Ucciani (2A) 320 E3
Ucel (07) 239 H4
Uchacq-et-Parentis (40) 265 G2
Uchaud (30) 275 F4
Uchaux (84) 256 E4
Uchentein (09) 306 C4
Uchizy (71) 171 K4
Uchon (71) 152 E6
Uckange (57) 44 E3
Ueberstrass (68) 97 A5
Uffheim (68) 97 D3
Uffholtz (68) 97 A1
Ugine (73) 209 G1
Uglas (65) 286 B6
Ugnouas (65) 285 H4
Ugny (54) 26 C3
Ugny-le-Gay (02) 19 J5
Ugny-l'Équipée (80) 19 H3
Ugny-sur-Meuse (55) 65 G6
Uhart-Cize (64) 282 D5
Uhart-Mixe (64) 283 G4
Uhlwiller (67) 69 K6
Uhrwiller (67) 69 J5
Ulcot (79) 143 K3
les Ulis (91) 58 C6
Ully-Saint-Georges (60) 37 J4
les Ulmes (49) 144 B1
Umpeau (28) 85 J2
Unac (09) 308 A5
Uncey-le-Franc (21) 135 F5
Unchair (51) 40 C4
Ungersheim (68) 97 B1
Unias (42) 204 E4
Unienville (10) 91 F4
Unieux (42) 221 F1
l'Union (31) 269 H6
Unverre (28) 84 C6
Unzent (09) 288 C6
Upaix (05) 259 F2
Upie (26) 240 D2
Ur (66) 313 G5
Urau (31) 306 B2
Urbalacone (2A) 320 D6
Urbanya (66) 314 A3
Urbeis (67) 96 A1
Urbès (68) 119 J3
Urbise (42) 186 D2
Urçay (03) 167 H3
Urcel (02) 40 A1
Urcerey (90) 139 H1
Urciers (36) 166 C4
Urcuit (64) 282 D1
Urcy (21) 135 J6
Urdens (32) 267 K3
Urdès (40) 284 A2
Urdos (64) 303 F4
Urepel (64) 262 B12
Urgons (40) 265 H5
Urgosse (32) 266 B4
Uriménil (88) 94 D6
Urmatt (67) 70 B4
Urost (64) 285 F4
Urou-et-Crennes (61) 54 C4

Urrugne (64). . . . 263 B2
Urs (09). . . . 307 K5
Urschenheim (68). . . . 96 D4
Urt (64). . . . 282 D1
Urtaca (2B). . . . 319 F2
Urtière (25). . . . 139 J5
Uruffe (54). . . . 93 G1
Urval (24). . . . 232 C2
Urville (10). . . . 91 G6
Urville (14). . . . 53 K1
Urville (50). . . . 28 E5
Urville (88). . . . 93 G5
Urville-Nacqueville (50). . . . 28 B2
Urvillers (02). . . . 20 A3
Ury (77). . . . 87 G4
Urzy (58). . . . 150 E3
Us (95). . . . 37 F6
Usclades-et-Rieutord (07). . . . 239 F3
Usclas-d'Hérault (34). . . . 292 C2
Usclas-du-Bosc (34). . . . 273 G5
Usinens (74). . . . 190 C4
Ussac (19). . . . 215 J3
Ussat (09). . . . 307 J5
Usseau (79). . . . 177 K2
Usseau (86). . . . 145 J5
Ussel (15). . . . 218 C5
Ussel (19). . . . 201 F5
Ussel (46). . . . 233 J5
Ussel-d'Allier (03). . . . 185 G2
Usson (63). . . . 203 F5
Usson-du-Poitou (86). . . . 180 A1
Usson-en-Forez (42). . . . 220 C1
Ussy (14). . . . 53 K2
Ussy-sur-Marne (77). . . . 60 B2
Ustaritz (64). . . . 282 B2
Ustou (09). . . . 306 E5
Utelle (06). . . . 281 G1
Uttenheim (67). . . . 70 E5
Uttenhoffen (67). . . . 69 K5
Uttwiller (67). . . . 69 H6
Uvernet-Fours (04). . . . 260 C1
Uxeau (71). . . . 170 B2
Uxegney (88). . . . 94 C5
Uxelles (39). . . . 173 J2
Uxem (59). . . . 3 J1
Uz (65). . . . 304 A3
Uza (40). . . . 244 C6
Uzan (64). . . . 284 B2
Uzay-le-Venon (18). . . . 149 H6
Uzech (46). . . . 233 H5
Uzein (64). . . . 284 C3
Uzel (22). . . . 77 F3
Uzelle (25). . . . 138 D3
Uzemain (88). . . . 118 C1
Uzer (07). . . . 239 G6
Uzer (65). . . . 304 D1
Uzerche (19). . . . 199 J6
Uzès (30). . . . 275 H1
Uzeste (33). . . . 246 C1
Uzos (64). . . . 284 D4

V

Vaas (72). . . . 126 E1
Vabre (81). . . . 271 G5
Vabre-Tizac (12). . . . 251 H4
Vabres (15). . . . 219 F5
Vabres (30). . . . 274 C1
Vabres-l'Abbaye (12). . . . 272 B2
Vacherauville (55). . . . 43 H4
Vachères (04). . . . 277 K2
Vachères-en-Quint (26). . . . 241 G2
Vacheresse (74). . . . 175 H5
la Vacheresse-et-la-Rouillie (88). . . . 93 H6
la Vacherie (27). . . . 35 J6
Vacognes-Neuilly (14). . . . 32 C6
la Vacquerie (14). . . . 31 K4
la Vacquerie-et-Saint-Martin-de-Castries (34). . . . 273 H4
Vacquerie-le-Boucq (62). . . . 9 K3
Vacqueriette-Erquières (62). . . . 9 J2
Vacqueville (54). . . . 95 G1
Vacqueyras (84). . . . 257 G5
Vacquières (34). . . . 274 C3
Vacquiers (31). . . . 269 H4
Vadans (39). . . . 155 J4
Vadans (70). . . . 137 F5
Vadelaincourt (55). . . . 43 G6
Vadenay (51). . . . 41 J4
Vadencourt (02). . . . 20 C1
Vadencourt (80). . . . 10 C6
Vadonville (55). . . . 64 E4
Vagnas (07). . . . 255 K2
Vagney (88). . . . 119 G2
Vahl-Ebersing (57). . . . 68 A3
Vahl-lès-Bénestroff (57). . . . 68 B5
Vahl-lès-Faulquemont (57). . . . 45 K6
Vaiges (53). . . . 105 H2
Vailhan (34). . . . 292 B1
Vailhauquès (34). . . . 274 A5
Vailhourles (12). . . . 250 E3
Vaillac (46). . . . 233 J4
Vaillant (52). . . . 116 B6
Vailly (10). . . . 90 B4
Vailly (74). . . . 175 G6
Vailly-sur-Aisne (02). . . . 40 A2
Vailly-sur-Sauldre (18). . . . 131 H4
Vains (50). . . . 51 K3
Vairé (85). . . . 158 E2
Vaire-Arcier (25). . . . 138 B5
Vaire-le-Petit (25). . . . 138 B5
Vaire-sous-Corbie (80). . . . 18 D2
Vaires-sur-Marne (77). . . . 59 H3

Vaison-la-Romaine (84). . . . 257 G4
Vaïssac (82). . . . 269 J1
Vaite (70). . . . 137 G1
la Vaivre (70). . . . 118 C3
Vaivre-et-Montoille (70). . . . 138 A1
le Val (83). . . . 297 K2
le Val-d'Ajol (88). . . . 118 E4
Val-d'Auzon (10). . . . 90 D3
le Val-David (27). . . . 56 E2
Val-de-Bride (57). . . . 67 F3
Val-de-Chalvagne (04). . . . 280 C1
Val-de-Fier (74). . . . 190 D5
le Val-de-Gouhenans (70). . . . 138 E1
le Val-de-Guéblange (57). . . . 68 C4
Val-de-la-Haye (76). . . . 35 G2
Val-de-Mercy (89). . . . 133 G1
Val-de-Meuse (52). . . . 116 E2
Val-de-Reuil (27). . . . 35 J4
Val-de-Roulans (25). . . . 138 C4
Val-de-Saâne (76). . . . 15 J4
Val-de-Vesle (51). . . . 41 G5
Val-de-Vière (51). . . . 63 G4
Val-d'Épy (39). . . . 172 E5
Val-des-Marais (51). . . . 61 K3
Val-des-Prés (05). . . . 226 A6
le Val-d'Esnoms (52). . . . 116 C6
Val-d'Isère (73). . . . 193 C5
Val-d'Izé (35). . . . 79 K3
Val-d'Ornain (55). . . . 64 A4
Val-et-Châtillon (54). . . . 67 H6
Val-Maravel (26). . . . 241 K5
le Val-Saint-Éloi (70). . . . 118 B5
le Val-Saint-Germain (91). . . . 86 B1
le Val-Saint-Père (50). . . . 51 K3
Val-Suzon (21). . . . 135 J4
Valady (12). . . . 251 K1
Valailles (27). . . . 34 D6
Valaire (41). . . . 128 E4
Valanjou (49). . . . 125 G6
Valaurie (26). . . . 256 E1
Valavoire (04). . . . 259 H3
Valay (70). . . . 137 G5
Valbeleix (63). . . . 202 C5
Valbelle (04). . . . 259 F4
Valbois (55). . . . 65 F2
Valbonnais (38). . . . 242 C1
Valbonne (06). . . . 280 E5
Valcabrère (31). . . . 305 H2
Valcanville (50). . . . 29 F2
Valcebollère (66). . . . 313 H6
Valcivières (63). . . . 204 A4
Valcourt (52). . . . 63 J6
Valdahon (25). . . . 156 E1
Valdampierre (60). . . . 37 G4
Valdeblore (06). . . . 261 J5
le Valdécie (50). . . . 28 C5
Valderiès (81). . . . 270 E1
Valderoure (06). . . . 280 B3
Valdieu-Lutran (68). . . . 119 K6
Valdivienne (86). . . . 163 H4
Valdoie (90). . . . 119 H6
Valdrôme (26). . . . 241 K6
Valdurenque (81). . . . 290 A1
Valeille (42). . . . 205 F3
Valeilles (82). . . . 248 E2
Valeins (01). . . . 188 C3
Valempoulières (39). . . . 156 A5
Valençay (36). . . . 147 J2
Valence (16). . . . 179 H6
Valence (26). . . . 240 C1
Valence (82). . . . 248 E6
Valence-d'Albigeois (81). . . . 271 G1
Valence-en-Brie (77). . . . 87 K3
Valence-sur-Baïse (32). . . . 267 F3
Valenciennes (59). . . . 12 D2
Valencin (38). . . . 206 C4
Valencogne (38). . . . 207 H5
Valennes (72). . . . 107 K3
Valensole (04). . . . 278 D3
Valentigney (25). . . . 139 H3
Valentine (31). . . . 305 J1
Valenton (94). . . . 59 F5
Valergues (34). . . . 274 D5
Valernes (04). . . . 259 G3
Valescourt (60). . . . 38 A1
Valette (15). . . . 217 K3
la Valette (38). . . . 224 C4
la Valette-du-Var (83). . . . 300 C4
Valeuil (24). . . . 213 K2
Valeyrac (33). . . . 194 D3
Valezan (73). . . . 209 K3
Valff (67). . . . 70 D5
Valfin-sur-Valouse (39). . . . 173 F5
Valflaunès (34). . . . 274 B4
Valfleury (42). . . . 205 H5
Valframbert (61). . . . 82 D2
Valfroicourt (88). . . . 94 A5
Valgorge (07). . . . 238 E5
Valhey (54). . . . 66 D5
Valhuon (62). . . . 10 B1
Valiergues (19). . . . 201 F6
Valignat (03). . . . 185 F3
Valigny (03). . . . 167 K2
Valines (80). . . . 8 E5
Valjouffrey (38). . . . 242 D1
Valjouze (15). . . . 218 D4
la Valla-en-Gier (42). . . . 205 H6
la Valla-sur-Rochefort (42). . . . 204 B2
Vallabrègues (30). . . . 275 K3
Vallabrix (30). . . . 256 B6
Vallan (89). . . . 113 H4
Vallangoujard (95). . . . 37 H6
Vallans (79). . . . 177 K2
Vallant-Saint-Georges (10). . . . 89 K2
Vallauris (06). . . . 280 E5
Valle-d'Alesani (2B). . . . 319 J5

Valle-di-Campoloro (2B). . . . 319 J5
Valle-di-Mezzana (2A). . . . 320 C4
Valle-di-Rostino (2B). . . . 319 G4
Valle-d'Orezza (2B). . . . 319 H5
Vallecalle (2B). . . . 319 H2
la Vallée (17). . . . 177 G6
la Vallée-au-Blé (02). . . . 20 E2
la Vallée-Mulâtre (02). . . . 12 D6
Vallègue (31). . . . 289 F3
Valleiry (74). . . . 190 D3
Vallenay (18). . . . 167 F1
Vallentigny (10). . . . 91 F3
Vallerange (57). . . . 68 A5
Vallérargues (30). . . . 255 K5
Valleraugue (30). . . . 254 C6
Vallères (37). . . . 127 G5
Valleret (52). . . . 91 K2
Vallereuil (24). . . . 213 J5
Vallerois-le-Bois (70). . . . 138 C2
Vallerois-Lorioz (70). . . . 138 B2
Valleroy (25). . . . 138 B4
Valleroy (52). . . . 117 G6
Valleroy (54). . . . 44 C4
Valleroy-aux-Saules (88). . . . 94 A5
Valleroy-le-Sec (88). . . . 93 K5
Vallery (89). . . . 88 B5
Vallesvilles (31). . . . 288 D1
Vallet (44). . . . 142 B1
Valletot (27). . . . 34 D3
Vallica (2B). . . . 318 E3
Vallière (23). . . . 182 E6
Vallières (10). . . . 114 A3
Vallières (74). . . . 190 D5
Vallières-les-Grandes (41). . . . 128 D4
Valliguières (30). . . . 275 J1
Valliquerville (76). . . . 15 F5
Valloire (73). . . . 225 H3
Vallois (54). . . . 94 E2
les Vallois (88). . . . 94 A6
Vallon-en-Sully (03). . . . 167 H4
Vallon-Pont-d'Arc (07). . . . 256 A2
Vallon-sur-Gée (72). . . . 106 B3
Vallorcine (74). . . . 192 D3
Vallouise (05). . . . 243 J1
Valmanya (66). . . . 314 D4
Valmascle (34). . . . 273 F6
Valmeinier (73). . . . 225 J3
Valmestroff (57). . . . 27 H4
Valmigère (11). . . . 309 G3
Valmondois (95). . . . 37 H6
Valmont (57). . . . 68 A3
Valmont (76). . . . 14 E4
Valmunster (57). . . . 45 J3
Valmy (51). . . . 42 C6
Valognes (50). . . . 28 E4
Valojoulx (24). . . . 214 E6
Valonne (25). . . . 139 G4
Valoreille (25). . . . 139 G5
Valouse (26). . . . 257 J1
Valprionde (46). . . . 249 G3
Valprivas (43). . . . 220 D2
Valpuiseaux (91). . . . 86 E3
Valras-Plage (34). . . . 292 B5
Valréas (84). . . . 257 G2
Valros (34). . . . 292 B3
Valroufié (46). . . . 233 H6
Vals (09). . . . 308 A1
Vals-des-Tilles (52). . . . 116 A6
Vals-le-Chastel (43). . . . 219 J2
Vals-les-Bains (07). . . . 239 H4
Vals-près-le-Puy (43). . . . 220 C5
Valsemé (14). . . . 33 J4
Valserres (04). . . . 243 F6
Valsonne (69). . . . 187 J5
le Valtin (88). . . . 95 J6
Valuéjols (15). . . . 218 C5
Valvignères (07). . . . 239 K6
Valz-sous-Châteauneuf (63). . . . 203 G6
Valzergues (12). . . . 251 H1
Vanault-le-Châtel (51). . . . 63 G3
Vanault-les-Dames (51). . . . 63 H3
Vançais (79). . . . 179 F1
Vancé (72). . . . 107 J5
la Vancelle (67). . . . 96 B1
Vanclans (25). . . . 157 F2
Vandeins (01). . . . 188 E2
Vandelainville (54). . . . 65 J1
Vandelans (70). . . . 138 B4
Vandeléville (54). . . . 93 J2
Vandélicourt (60). . . . 38 D1
Vandenesse (58). . . . 151 K5
Vandenesse-en-Auxois (21). . . . 153 H1
Vandeuil (51). . . . 40 D4
Vandières (51). . . . 40 C6
Vandières (54). . . . 65 J1
Vandœuvre-lès-Nancy (54). . . . 66 A5
Vandoncourt (25). . . . 139 J3
Vandré (17). . . . 177 H4
Vandrimare (27). . . . 36 A3
Vandy (08). . . . 42 B2
Vanlay (10). . . . 114 A2
Vannaire (21). . . . 115 F6
Vanne (70). . . . 137 H1
le Vanneau-Irleau (79). . . . 177 J1
Vannecourt (57). . . . 66 D2
Vannecrocq (27). . . . 34 B3
Vannes-le-Châtel (54). . . . 93 G1
Vannes-sur-Cosson (45). . . . 110 D3
Vannoz (39). . . . 156 B6
Vanosc (07). . . . 221 J3
les Vans (07). . . . 255 H2
Vantoux (57). . . . 45 F5
Vantoux-et-Longevelle (70). . . . 137 J3
Vanves (92). . . . 58 E4
Vanvey (21). . . . 115 H4

Vanvillé (77). . . . 88 B1
Vanxains (24). . . . 213 G3
Vany (57). . . . 45 F5
Vanzac (17). . . . 212 A1
Vanzay (79). . . . 179 F2
Vanzy (74). . . . 190 D4
Vaour (81). . . . 250 D6
Varacieux (38). . . . 223 G3
Varades (44). . . . 124 C4
Varages (83). . . . 278 D6
Varaignes (24). . . . 197 H4
Varaire (46). . . . 250 C3
Varaize (17). . . . 178 A5
Varambon (01). . . . 189 H4
Varanges (21). . . . 136 C6
Varangéville (54). . . . 66 B5
Varaville (14). . . . 33 G4
Varces-Allières-et-Risset (38). . . . 224 A4
Vareilles (23). . . . 181 K1
Vareilles (71). . . . 187 G5
Vareilles (89). . . . 89 F6
Varen (82). . . . 250 E5
Varengeville-sur-Mer (76). . . . 15 J2
Varenguebec (50). . . . 28 D6
la Varenne (49). . . . 123 J3
Varenne-l'Arconce (71). . . . 170 C6
Varenne-Saint-Germain (71). . . . 170 B5
Varennes (24). . . . 231 K2
Varennes (31). . . . 288 E2
Varennes (37). . . . 146 C3
Varennes (80). . . . 10 C6
Varennes (82). . . . 269 H3
Varennes (86). . . . 162 D1
Varennes (89). . . . 113 J4
Varennes-Changy (45). . . . 111 H4
Varennes-en-Argonne (55). . . . 42 E4
Varennes-Jarcy (91). . . . 59 G6
Varennes-le-Grand (71). . . . 171 K1
Varennes-lès-Mâcon (71). . . . 188 C1
Varennes-lès-Narcy (58). . . . 150 D1
Varennes-Saint-Honorat (43). . . . 219 K4
Varennes-Saint-Sauveur (71). . . . 172 D2
Varennes-sous-Dun (71). . . . 187 H1
Varennes-sur-Allier (03). . . . 185 J1
Varennes-sur-Fouzon (36). . . . 147 J1
Varennes-sur-Loire (49). . . . 126 C6
Varennes-sur-Morge (63). . . . 185 G6
Varennes-sur-Seine (77). . . . 87 K4
Varennes-sur-Tèche (03). . . . 186 A1
Varennes-sur-Usson (63). . . . 203 F5
Varennes-Vauzelles (58). . . . 150 D4
Varès (47). . . . 247 J1
Varesnes (60). . . . 19 H6
Varessia (39). . . . 173 G3
Varetz (19). . . . 215 H3
Varilhes (09). . . . 307 J2
Varinfroy (60). . . . 39 G6
Variscourt (02). . . . 40 E2
Varize (28). . . . 109 G1
Varize (57). . . . 45 H5
Varmonzey (88). . . . 94 B4
Varnéville (55). . . . 65 F3
Varneville-Bretteville (76). . . . 15 K5
Varogne (70). . . . 118 B5
Varois-et-Chaignot (21). . . . 136 B5
Varouville (50). . . . 29 F2
Varrains (49). . . . 144 C1
Varreddes (77). . . . 59 K2
Vars (05). . . . 227 A4
Vars (16). . . . 196 D2
Vars (70). . . . 137 F2
Vars-sur-Roseix (19). . . . 215 G3
Varsberg (57). . . . 45 K4
Varzay (17). . . . 195 F2
Varzy (58). . . . 132 E5
Vascœuil (27). . . . 36 A2
Vasles (79). . . . 162 B3
Vasperviller (57). . . . 67 J5
Vassel (63). . . . 203 F2
Vasselay (18). . . . 149 G2
Vasselin (38). . . . 207 G3
Vassens (02). . . . 39 G1
Vasseny (02). . . . 40 A3
Vassieux-en-Vercors (26). . . . 241 H1
Vassimont-et-Chapelaine (51). . . . 62 B4
Vassincourt (55). . . . 63 K4
Vassogne (02). . . . 40 C2
Vassonville (76). . . . 15 K4
Vassy (14). . . . 53 G3
Vassy (89). . . . 134 C2
le Vast (50). . . . 29 F2
Vasteville (50). . . . 28 B3
les Vastres (43). . . . 221 F6
Vatan (36). . . . 148 B3
Vathiménil (54). . . . 94 E1
Vatierville (76). . . . 16 D3
Vatilieu (38). . . . 223 H2
Vatimont (57). . . . 66 D1
Vatry (51). . . . 62 C4
Vattetot-sous-Beaumont (76). . . . 14 D5
Vattetot-sur-Mer (76). . . . 14 C4
Vatteville (27). . . . 35 K4
Vatteville-la-Rue (76). . . . 34 E1
Vaubadon (14). . . . 31 K2
Vauban (71). . . . 187 G1
Vaubecourt (55). . . . 64 A2
Vaubexy (88). . . . 94 B4
Vaucelles (14). . . . 32 A3
Vaucelles-et-Beffecourt (02). . . . 20 C6
Vauchamps (25). . . . 138 C5
Vauchamps (51). . . . 61 G3
Vauchassis (10). . . . 89 K5
Vauchelles (60). . . . 19 G6
Vauchelles-lès-Authie (80). . . . 10 C5
Vauchelles-lès-Domart (80). . . . 9 J6
Vauchelles-lès-Quesnoy (80). . . . 9 G5

Vauchignon (21). . . . 153 J3
Vauchonvilliers (10). . . . 91 F5
Vauchoux (70). . . . 117 K6
Vauchrétien (49). . . . 125 H5
Vauciennes (51). . . . 61 J1
Vauciennes (60). . . . 39 F4
Vauclaix (58). . . . 152 A1
Vauclerc (51). . . . 63 G5
Vaucluse (25). . . . 139 G5
Vauclusotte (25). . . . 139 G5
Vaucogne (10). . . . 90 D2
Vauconcourt-Nervezain (70). . . . 117 H6
Vaucouleurs (55). . . . 65 F6
Vaucourt (54). . . . 67 F5
Vaucourtois (77). . . . 60 A3
Vaucresson (92). . . . 58 C4
Vaudancourt (60). . . . 36 E4
Vaudebarrier (71). . . . 170 E5
Vaudelnay (49). . . . 144 B2
Vaudeloges (14). . . . 54 C2
Vaudemange (51). . . . 41 G6
Vaudémont (54). . . . 93 K2
Vaudes (10). . . . 90 C4
Vaudesincourt (51). . . . 41 J4
Vaudesson (02). . . . 40 A1
Vaudeurs (89). . . . 113 F1
Vaudevant (07). . . . 221 K4
Vaudeville (54). . . . 94 B2
Vaudéville (88). . . . 94 E5
Vaudéville-le-Haut (55). . . . 93 F2
Vaudherland (95). . . . 59 F2
Vaudigny (54). . . . 94 B2
le Vaudioux (39). . . . 173 K1
Vaudoncourt (55). . . . 44 A3
Vaudoncourt (88). . . . 93 H5
le Vaudoué (77). . . . 87 G4
Vaudoy-en-Brie (77). . . . 60 B5
Vaudreching (57). . . . 45 J3
Vaudrecourt (52). . . . 93 F5
Vaudrémont (52). . . . 115 J1
le Vaudreuil (27). . . . 35 J4
Vaudreuille (31). . . . 289 H3
Vaudreville (50). . . . 29 F4
Vaudrey (39). . . . 155 H3
Vaudricourt (62). . . . 5 K6
Vaudricourt (80). . . . 8 D3
Vaudrimesnil (50). . . . 30 E3
Vaudringhem (62). . . . 4 E2
Vaudrivillers (25). . . . 138 D5
Vaudry (14). . . . 52 E3
Vaufrey (25). . . . 139 J4
Vaugines (84). . . . 277 H4
Vaugneray (69). . . . 205 J2
Vaugrigneuse (91). . . . 86 C1
Vauhallan (91). . . . 58 D5
Vaujany (38). . . . 224 E3
Vaujours (93). . . . 59 G2
Vaulandry (49). . . . 126 B2
le Vaulmier (15). . . . 217 J4
Vaulnaveys-le-Bas (38). . . . 224 B4
Vaulnaveys-le-Haut (38). . . . 224 B4
Vaulry (87). . . . 181 F4
Vault-de-Lugny (89). . . . 133 J3
Vaulx (62). . . . 9 J3
Vaulx (74). . . . 190 E5
Vaulx-en-Velin (69). . . . 206 B1
Vaulx-Milieu (38). . . . 206 E4
Vaulx-Vraucourt (62). . . . 11 G4
le Vaumain (60). . . . 37 F3
Vaumas (03). . . . 169 H5
Vaumeilh (04). . . . 259 F3
Vaumoise (60). . . . 39 F4
Vaumort (89). . . . 112 E1
Vaunac (24). . . . 214 B1
Vaunaveys-la-Rochette (26). . . . 240 D3
Vaunoise (61). . . . 83 G4
la Vaupalière (76). . . . 35 G1
Vaupillon (28). . . . 84 B3
Vaupoisson (10). . . . 90 C2
Vauquois (55). . . . 42 E4
Vauréal (95). . . . 58 B1
Vaureilles (12). . . . 251 H1
le Vauroux (60). . . . 37 F3
Vausseroux (79). . . . 162 A3
Vautebis (79). . . . 162 A4
Vauthiermont (90). . . . 119 K5
Vautorte (53). . . . 80 E4
Vauvenargues (13). . . . 277 K6
Vauvert (30). . . . 275 G5
Vauville (14). . . . 33 J3
Vauville (50). . . . 28 A2
Vauvillers (70). . . . 118 A3
Vauvillers (80). . . . 18 E2
Vaux (03). . . . 167 H5
Vaux (31). . . . 289 F2
Vaux (57). . . . 44 E5
Vaux (86). . . . 179 H1
Vaux-Andigny (02). . . . 12 D6
Vaux-Champagne (08). . . . 41 K2
Vaux-devant-Damloup (55). . . . 43 H4
Vaux-en-Amiénois (80). . . . 18 A1
Vaux-en-Beaujolais (69). . . . 188 A4
Vaux-en-Bugey (01). . . . 189 H5
Vaux-en-Dieulet (08). . . . 42 E1
Vaux-en-Pré (71). . . . 171 G2
Vaux-en-Vermandois (02). . . . 19 J3
Vaux-et-Chantegrue (25). . . . 156 E5
Vaux-Lavalette (16). . . . 196 E6
Vaux-le-Moncelot (70). . . . 137 J3
Vaux-le-Pénil (77). . . . 87 H2
Vaux-lès-Mouron (08). . . . 42 C3
Vaux-lès-Mouzon (08). . . . 23 G5
Vaux-lès-Palameix (55). . . . 64 E1
Vaux-lès-Prés (25). . . . 137 J6
Vaux-lès-Rubigny (08). . . . 21 J4
Vaux-lès-Saint-Claude (39). . . . 173 J5

Vaux-Marquenneville (80) . . . 17 G1
Vaux-Montreuil (08) . . . 22 B6
Vaux-Rouillac (16) . . . 196 B2
Vaux-Saules (21) . . . 135 J3
Vaux-sous-Aubigny (52) . . . 136 C1
Vaux-sur-Aure (14) . . . 32 B3
Vaux-sur-Blaise (52) . . . 91 K2
Vaux-sur-Eure (27) . . . 57 F1
Vaux-sur-Lunain (77) . . . 88 A6
Vaux-sur-Mer (17) . . . 194 C3
Vaux-sur-Poligny (39) . . . 155 J5
Vaux-sur-Saint-Urbain (52) . . . 92 B3
Vaux-sur-Seine (78) . . . 58 B1
Vaux-sur-Seulles (14) . . . 32 B4
Vaux-sur-Somme (80) . . . 18 D1
Vaux-sur-Vienne (86) . . . 145 J5
Vaux-Villaine (08) . . . 22 B3
Vauxaillon (02) . . . 39 K1
Vauxbons (52) . . . 116 B4
Vauxbuin (02) . . . 39 J3
Vauxcéré (02) . . . 40 B3
Vauxrenard (69) . . . 188 A2
Vauxrezis (02) . . . 39 J2
Vauxtin (02) . . . 40 B3
Vavincourt (55) . . . 64 B3
Vavray-le-Grand (51) . . . 63 G4
Vavray-le-Petit (51) . . . 63 G4
Vaxainville (54) . . . 95 G1
Vaxoncourt (88) . . . 94 D4
Vaxy (57) . . . 66 D2
Vay (44) . . . 103 F5
Vaychis (09) . . . 308 A6
Vaylats (46) . . . 250 C3
Vayrac (46) . . . 234 A1
Vayres (33) . . . 229 K1
Vayres (87) . . . 198 A2
Vayres-sur-Essonne (91) . . . 86 C3
Vazeilles-Limandre (43) . . . 220 A4
Vazeilles-près-Sauges (43) . . . 237 K1
Vazerac (82) . . . 249 J5
Veauce (03) . . . 184 E3
Veauche (42) . . . 205 F4
Veauchette (42) . . . 205 F4
Veaugues (18) . . . 131 J6
Veaunes (26) . . . 222 C5
Veauville-lès-Baons (76) . . . 15 G5
Veauville-lès-Quelles (76) . . . 15 G4
Vèbre (09) . . . 307 K5
Vebret (15) . . . 217 J2
Vebron (48) . . . 254 B4
Veckersviller (57) . . . 67 K2
Veckring (57) . . . 27 J4
Vecoux (88) . . . 119 F2
Vecquemont (80) . . . 18 C2
Vecqueville (52) . . . 92 B2
Vedène (84) . . . 276 C1
Védrines-Saint-Loup (15) . . . 219 G5
Végennes (19) . . . 216 A6
Vého (54) . . . 67 F6
Veigné (37) . . . 127 J4
Veigy-Foncenex (74) . . . 174 D6
Veilhes (81) . . . 270 A6
Veilleins (41) . . . 129 H4
Veilly (21) . . . 153 H2
Veix (19) . . . 200 A5
Velaine-en-Haye (54) . . . 65 J5
Velaine-sous-Amance (54) . . . 66 B4
Velaines (55) . . . 64 C5
Velanne (38) . . . 207 J5
Velars-sur-Ouche (21) . . . 135 K5
Velaux (13) . . . 296 B1
Velennes (60) . . . 37 H1
Velennes (80) . . . 17 J3
Velesmes-Echevanne (70) . . . 137 G4
Velesmes-Essarts (25) . . . 156 A1
Velet (70) . . . 137 F4
Vélieux (34) . . . 291 F3
Vélines (24) . . . 230 E2
Vélizy-Villacoublay (78) . . . 58 D4
Velle-le-Châtel (70) . . . 138 A1
Velle-sur-Moselle (54) . . . 94 B1
Vellèches (86) . . . 145 J4
Vellechevreux-et-
  Courbenans (70) . . . 138 E2
Velleclaire (70) . . . 137 J3
Vellefaux (70) . . . 138 B2
Vellefrey-et-Vellefrange (70) . . . 137 H3
Vellefrie (70) . . . 118 B6
Velleguindry-et-Levrecey (70) . . . 138 A2
Velleminfroy (70) . . . 118 C6
Vellemoz (70) . . . 137 H3
Velleron (84) . . . 276 D1
Vellerot-lès-Belvoir (25) . . . 139 F4
Vellerot-lès-Vercel (25) . . . 138 E6
Velles (36) . . . 165 H2
Velles (52) . . . 117 G4
Vellescot (90) . . . 139 K1
Vellevans (25) . . . 138 E5
Vellexon-Queutrey-et-
  Vaudey (70) . . . 137 H2
Velloreille-lès-Choye (70) . . . 137 H4
Velluire (85) . . . 160 D5
Velogny (21) . . . 134 E4
Velone-Orneto (2B) . . . 319 J4
Velorcey (70) . . . 118 B5
Velosnes (55) . . . 26 A2
Velotte-et-Tatignécourt (88) . . . 94 A4
Vélu (62) . . . 11 G5
Velving (57) . . . 45 J3
Vélye (51) . . . 62 E2
Velzic (15) . . . 217 J6
Vémars (95) . . . 59 G1
Venables (27) . . . 35 K5
Venansault (85) . . . 159 H1
Venanson (06) . . . 261 K5

Venarey-les-Laumes (21) . . . 134 E2
Venarsal (19) . . . 215 K3
Venas (03) . . . 167 A5
Venasque (84) . . . 276 E1
Vence (06) . . . 281 F3
Vendargues (34) . . . 274 C5
Vendat (03) . . . 185 H3
Vendays-Montalivet (33) . . . 210 C1
Vendegies-au-Bois (59) . . . 12 D4
Vendegies-sur-Écaillon (59) . . . 12 D3
Vendel (35) . . . 79 K2
la Vendelée (50) . . . 30 E3
Vendelles (02) . . . 19 J2
Vendémian (34) . . . 292 D1
Vendenesse-lès-Charolles (71) . . . 170 E5
Vendenesse-sur-Arroux (71) . . . 170 B3
Vendenheim (67) . . . 25 A6
Vendes (14) . . . 32 C5
Vendeuil (02) . . . 20 A4
Vendeuil-Caply (60) . . . 18 A5
Vendeuvre (14) . . . 54 B1
Vendeuvre-du-Poitou (86) . . . 162 E1
Vendeuvre-sur-Barse (10) . . . 90 E5
Vendeville (59) . . . 6 C5
Vendhuile (02) . . . 11 J6
Vendières (02) . . . 60 E3
Vendin-le-Vieil (62) . . . 6 C6
Vendin-lès-Béthune (62) . . . 5 K5
Vendine (31) . . . 289 F1
Vendœuvres (36) . . . 147 G6
Vendoire (24) . . . 197 F6
Vendôme (41) . . . 108 C5
Vendranges (42) . . . 187 F5
Vendrennes (85) . . . 142 C5
Vendres (34) . . . 292 A5
Vendresse (08) . . . 22 D5
Vendresse-Beaulne (02) . . . 40 B2
Vendrest (77) . . . 60 B1
la Vendue-Mignot (10) . . . 90 B6
Vénéjan (30) . . . 256 C4
Venelles (13) . . . 277 J6
Vénérand (17) . . . 195 H1
Venère (70) . . . 137 G4
Vénérieu (38) . . . 207 F3
Vénérolles (02) . . . 12 E6
Venerque (31) . . . 288 B3
Vénès (81) . . . 270 E5
Venesmes (18) . . . 149 F6
Vénestanville (76) . . . 15 H3
Venette (60) . . . 38 D2
Veneux-les-Sablons (77) . . . 87 J4
Veney (54) . . . 95 G2
Vengeons (50) . . . 52 D4
Venise (25) . . . 138 A4
Venisey (70) . . . 117 K4
Vénissieux (69) . . . 206 B3
Venizel (02) . . . 39 K3
Venizy (89) . . . 113 H2
Vennans (25) . . . 138 C5
Vennecy (45) . . . 110 B3
Vennes (25) . . . 157 G1
Vennezey (54) . . . 94 D2
Venon (27) . . . 35 H5
Venon (38) . . . 224 B3
Vénosc (38) . . . 224 E5
Venouse (89) . . . 113 H4
Venoy (89) . . . 113 G5
Vensac (33) . . . 194 C6
Vensat (63) . . . 185 G4
Ventabren (13) . . . 296 B1
Ventavon (05) . . . 259 F2
Ventelay (51) . . . 40 D3
Ventenac (09) . . . 307 K2
Ventenac-Cabardès (11) . . . 290 A5
Ventenac-en-Minervois (11) . . . 291 G5
Venterol (04) . . . 259 H1
Venterol (26) . . . 257 H2
les Ventes (27) . . . 56 C2
les Ventes-de-Bourse (61) . . . 82 E2
Ventes-Saint-Rémy (76) . . . 16 B4
Venteuges (43) . . . 219 J6
Venteuil (51) . . . 40 D6
Venthon (73) . . . 209 G2
Ventiseri (2B) . . . 321 H4
Ventouse (16) . . . 179 H6
Ventron (88) . . . 119 H2
la Ventrouze (61) . . . 55 J6
Venzolasca (2B) . . . 319 J3
Ver (50) . . . 30 E6
Ver-lès-Chartres (28) . . . 85 G4
Ver-sur-Launette (60) . . . 38 C6
Ver-sur-Mer (14) . . . 32 C3
Vérac (33) . . . 211 K6
Véranne (42) . . . 221 K1
Vérargues (34) . . . 274 C5
Véraza (11) . . . 309 F3
Verberie (60) . . . 38 C3
Verbiesles (52) . . . 116 B1
Vercel-Villedieu-le-Camp (25) . . . 138 D6
Verchain-Maugré (59) . . . 12 C3
Verchaix (74) . . . 192 A3
Vercheny (26) . . . 241 G3
les Verchers-sur-Layon (49) . . . 144 A1
Verchin (62) . . . 5 H6
Verchocq (62) . . . 4 E5
Vercia (39) . . . 173 F3
Verclause (26) . . . 258 A2
Vercoiran (26) . . . 257 K3
Vercourt (80) . . . 9 F2
Verdaches (04) . . . 259 K3
Verdalle (81) . . . 289 K2
Verdelais (33) . . . 230 A3
Verdelot (77) . . . 60 E3
Verdenal (54) . . . 67 G6
Verderel-lès-Sauqueuse (60) . . . 37 H1
Verderonne (60) . . . 38 B3

Verdes (41) . . . 109 F3
Verdèse (2B) . . . 319 H4
Verdets (64) . . . 284 A5
le Verdier (81) . . . 270 B1
la Verdière (83) . . . 278 D5
Verdigny (18) . . . 131 J5
Verdille (16) . . . 178 D6
Verdilly (02) . . . 39 K6
Verdon (24) . . . 231 K2
Verdon (51) . . . 61 G2
le Verdon-sur-Mer (33) . . . 194 C4
Verdonnet (21) . . . 114 D6
Verdun (09) . . . 307 K5
Verdun (55) . . . 43 H5
Verdun-en-Lauragais (11) . . . 289 J4
Verdun-sur-Garonne (82) . . . 268 C3
Verdun-sur-le-Doubs (71) . . . 154 C5
Vereaux (18) . . . 150 B5
Verel-de-Montbel (73) . . . 207 K4
Verel-Pragondran (73) . . . 208 B3
Véretz (37) . . . 127 K5
Vereux (70) . . . 137 G2
Verfeil (31) . . . 269 J6
Verfeil (82) . . . 250 E5
Verfeuil (30) . . . 256 A5
Vergaville (57) . . . 67 F3
Vergéal (35) . . . 104 A2
la Vergenne (70) . . . 138 E1
le Verger (35) . . . 78 D4
Vergeroux (17) . . . 177 F5
Verges (39) . . . 173 H2
Vergetot (76) . . . 14 C5
Vergezac (43) . . . 220 A5
Vergèze (30) . . . 275 F4
Vergheas (63) . . . 184 A4
Vergies (80) . . . 17 G1
Vergigny (89) . . . 113 H3
Vergisson (71) . . . 188 B1
la Vergne (17) . . . 177 K5
Vergné (17) . . . 177 K3
Vergoignan (32) . . . 265 K4
Vergoncey (50) . . . 51 K4
Vergongheon (43) . . . 219 G1
Vergonnes (49) . . . 104 B5
Vergons (04) . . . 279 K1
Vergranne (25) . . . 138 D3
Vergt (24) . . . 214 A5
Vergt-de-Biron (24) . . . 232 B5
le Verguier (02) . . . 19 J1
Véria (39) . . . 173 F4
Vérignon (83) . . . 279 G5
Vérigny (28) . . . 84 E2
Vérin (42) . . . 205 K6
Vérines (17) . . . 177 F2
Vérissey (71) . . . 172 C1
Verjon (01) . . . 172 E6
Verjux (71) . . . 154 B5
Verlans (70) . . . 139 G1
Verlin (89) . . . 112 D2
Verlincthun (62) . . . 4 B4
Verlinghem (59) . . . 6 D3
Verlus (32) . . . 265 K6
Vermand (02) . . . 19 J2
Vermandovillers (80) . . . 19 F2
Vermelles (62) . . . 6 B6
Vermenton (89) . . . 133 H1
le Vermont (88) . . . 95 J2
Vern-d'Anjou (49) . . . 124 E1
Vern-sur-Seiche (35) . . . 79 G5
Vernais (18) . . . 167 J1
Vernaison (69) . . . 206 A3
Vernajoul (09) . . . 307 J3
Vernancourt (51) . . . 63 H3
Vernantes (49) . . . 126 C4
Vernantois (39) . . . 173 G2
la Vernarède (30) . . . 255 G3
Vernas (38) . . . 207 F1
Vernassal (43) . . . 220 A4
Vernaux (09) . . . 307 K5
Vernay (69) . . . 187 K3
la Vernaz (74) . . . 175 G6
Verne (25) . . . 138 D4
Vernègues (13) . . . 277 F5
Verneiges (23) . . . 183 H2
le Verneil (73) . . . 208 E5
Verneil-le-Chétif (72) . . . 106 E6
Verneix (03) . . . 167 H6
la Vernelle (36) . . . 129 G6
le Vernet (03) . . . 185 J3
le Vernet (04) . . . 260 A3
le Vernet (09) . . . 288 D6
Vernet (31) . . . 288 B3
le Vernet (43) . . . 220 A5
Vernet-la-Varenne (63) . . . 203 G6
Vernet-les-Bains (66) . . . 314 B4
le Vernet-Sainte-Marguerite (63) . . . 202 D5
Verneugheol (63) . . . 201 H2
Verneuil (16) . . . 197 K2
Verneuil (18) . . . 149 J6
Verneuil (51) . . . 40 B6
Verneuil (58) . . . 151 H5
Verneuil-en-Bourbonnais (03) . . . 168 D6
Verneuil-en-Halatte (60) . . . 38 B4
Verneuil-Grand (55) . . . 23 K6
Verneuil-le-Château (37) . . . 145 H3
Verneuil-l'Étang (77) . . . 59 J6
Verneuil-Moustiers (87) . . . 164 C6
Verneuil-Petit (55) . . . 23 K6
Verneuil-sous-Coucy (02) . . . 20 A4
Verneuil-sur-Avre (27) . . . 56 B5
Verneuil-sur-Igneraie (36) . . . 166 B2
Verneuil-sur-Indre (37) . . . 146 D3
Verneuil-sur-Seine (78) . . . 58 B2
Verneuil-sur-Serre (02) . . . 20 D5
Verneuil-sur-Vienne (87) . . . 198 D1

Verneusses (27) . . . 55 G3
Vernéville (57) . . . 44 D5
Vernie (72) . . . 82 C6
Vernierfontaine (25) . . . 156 E2
Vernines (63) . . . 202 B3
Verniolle (09) . . . 307 J1
Vernioz (38) . . . 206 B6
Vernix (50) . . . 52 B4
Vernoil (49) . . . 126 C4
le Vernois (39) . . . 173 G1
Vernois-lès-Belvoir (25) . . . 139 F4
Vernois-lès-Vesvres (21) . . . 136 B1
Vernois-sur-Mance (70) . . . 117 H4
Vernols (15) . . . 218 C3
Vernon (07) . . . 239 F6
Vernon (27) . . . 36 B6
Vernon (86) . . . 163 G5
Vernonvilliers (10) . . . 91 G4
Vernosc-lès-Annonay (07) . . . 222 A3
Vernot (21) . . . 135 K3
la Vernotte (70) . . . 137 J2
Vernou-en-Sologne (41) . . . 129 J3
Vernou-la-Celle-sur-Seine (77) . . . 87 K4
Vernou-sur-Brenne (37) . . . 128 A4
Vernouillet (28) . . . 57 F5
Vernouillet (78) . . . 58 B2
Vernoux (01) . . . 172 C4
Vernoux-en-Gâtine (79) . . . 161 G2
Vernoux-en-Vivarais (07) . . . 239 K1
Vernoux-sur-Boutonne (79) . . . 178 C2
le Vernoy (25) . . . 139 G1
Vernoy (89) . . . 112 C1
Vernusse (03) . . . 184 E1
Verny (57) . . . 66 A1
Vero (2A) . . . 320 D3
Véron (89) . . . 112 D1
Véronne (26) . . . 241 F3
Véronnes (21) . . . 136 C2
Verosvres (71) . . . 171 F5
Verpel (08) . . . 42 D2
la Verpillière (38) . . . 206 D3
Verpillières (80) . . . 19 F5
Verpillières-sur-Ource (10) . . . 115 F2
Verquières (13) . . . 276 C3
Verquin (62) . . . 6 A6
Verrens-Arvey (73) . . . 209 F3
Verreries-de-Moussans (34) . . . 290 E3
Verrey-sous-Drée (21) . . . 135 H5
Verrey-sous-Salmaise (21) . . . 135 G4
Verricourt (10) . . . 90 D3
Verrie (49) . . . 126 A6
la Verrie (85) . . . 142 D4
la Verrière (78) . . . 58 B5
Verrières (08) . . . 42 C1
Verrières (10) . . . 90 B5
Verrières (12) . . . 253 G4
Verrières (16) . . . 195 K4
Verrières (51) . . . 42 D6
Verrières (61) . . . 83 K3
Verrières (63) . . . 202 C4
Verrières (86) . . . 163 H5
Verrières-de-Joux (25) . . . 157 G4
Verrières-du-Grosbois (25) . . . 138 C6
Verrières-en-Forez (42) . . . 204 C4
Verrières-le-Buisson (91) . . . 58 D5
Verrue (86) . . . 144 E5
Verruyes (79) . . . 161 J4
Vers (46) . . . 250 B1
Vers (71) . . . 171 K3
Vers (74) . . . 190 E3
Vers-en-Montagne (39) . . . 156 K5
Vers-Pont-du-Gard (30) . . . 275 J1
Vers-sous-Sellières (39) . . . 155 H5
Vers-sur-Méouge (26) . . . 258 C4
Vers-sur-Selles (80) . . . 18 A2
Versailles (78) . . . 58 C4
Versailleux (01) . . . 189 F5
Versainville (14) . . . 54 B2
la Versanne (42) . . . 221 J2
Versaugues (71) . . . 170 B6
Verseilles-le-Bas (52) . . . 116 C5
Verseilles-le-Haut (52) . . . 116 C5
Versigny (02) . . . 20 B5
Versigny (60) . . . 38 D5
Versols-et-Lapeyre (12) . . . 272 C5
Verson (14) . . . 32 D5
Versonnex (01) . . . 174 B6
Versonnex (74) . . . 190 D5
le Versoud (38) . . . 224 C3
Vert (40) . . . 245 K5
Vert (78) . . . 57 J2
le Vert (79) . . . 178 B3
Vert-en-Drouais (28) . . . 56 E5
Vert-le-Grand (91) . . . 86 E1
Vert-le-Petit (91) . . . 86 E1
Vert-Saint-Denis (77) . . . 87 H1
Vert-Toulon (51) . . . 61 K3
Vertain (59) . . . 12 D3
Vertaizon (63) . . . 203 F2
Vertamboz (39) . . . 173 H2
Vertault (21) . . . 114 D4
Verteillac (24) . . . 213 G1
Verteuil-d'Agenais (47) . . . 247 K1
Verteuil-sur-Charente (16) . . . 179 H3
Verthemex (73) . . . 208 A3
Vertheuil (33) . . . 210 E2
Vertolaye (63) . . . 203 K3
Verton (62) . . . 8 E1
Vertou (44) . . . 123 H5
Vertrieu (38) . . . 189 H6
Vertus (51) . . . 62 A3
Vervant (16) . . . 196 D1
Vervant (17) . . . 178 A5
Vervezelle (88) . . . 95 G5
Vervins (02) . . . 21 F2
Véry (55) . . . 42 E4

Verzé (71) . . . 171 J6
Verzeille (11) . . . 309 F1
Verzenay (51) . . . 41 G5
Verzy (51) . . . 41 G5
Vesaignes-sous-Lafauche (52) . . . 92 D4
Vesaignes-sur-Marne (52) . . . 116 C2
Vesancy (01) . . . 174 B5
Vesc (26) . . . 241 F6
Vescemont (90) . . . 119 H5
Vescheim (57) . . . 69 F6
Vescles (39) . . . 173 G5
Vescours (01) . . . 172 B4
Vescovato (2B) . . . 319 J3
Vesdun (18) . . . 167 F4
Vésigneul-sur-Marne (51) . . . 62 E3
Vésines (01) . . . 171 K6
le Vésinet (78) . . . 58 C3
Vesles-et-Caumont (02) . . . 20 E5
Veslud (02) . . . 20 E6
Vesly (27) . . . 36 D4
Vesly (50) . . . 30 D1
Vesoul (70) . . . 138 B1
la Vespière (14) . . . 55 G1
Vesseaux (07) . . . 239 H4
Vessey (50) . . . 51 J5
Vestric-et-Candiac (30) . . . 275 F4
Vesvres (21) . . . 135 F4
Vesvres-sous-Chalancey (52) . . . 116 B6
Vétheuil (95) . . . 57 J1
Vétraz-Monthoux (74) . . . 191 G2
Vétrigne (90) . . . 119 J6
Veuil (36) . . . 147 J2
Veuilly-la-Poterie (02) . . . 39 H6
Veules-les-Roses (76) . . . 15 H2
Veulettes-sur-Mer (76) . . . 15 F2
le Veurdre (03) . . . 168 B1
Veurey-Voroize (38) . . . 223 K2
la Veuve (51) . . . 62 D1
Veuves (41) . . . 128 C4
Veuvey-sur-Ouche (21) . . . 153 J1
Veuxhaulles-sur-Aube (21) . . . 115 H3
Vevy (39) . . . 173 H2
Vexaincourt (88) . . . 95 J1
le Vey (14) . . . 53 J2
Veynes (05) . . . 242 C5
Veyrac (87) . . . 181 F6
Veyras (07) . . . 239 J3
Veyre-Monton (63) . . . 202 E3
Veyreau (12) . . . 253 J5
Veyrier-du-Lac (74) . . . 191 F6
Veyrières (15) . . . 217 G2
Veyrières (19) . . . 201 G6
Veyrignac (24) . . . 233 G2
Veyrines-de-Domme (24) . . . 232 E3
Veyrines-de-Vergt (24) . . . 214 A6
Veyrins-Thuellin (38) . . . 207 H3
les Veys (50) . . . 29 G6
Veyssilieu (38) . . . 206 E3
Vez (60) . . . 39 F4
Vézac (15) . . . 235 J2
Vézac (24) . . . 232 E2
Vézannes (89) . . . 113 J4
Vézaponin (02) . . . 39 H2
Vèze (15) . . . 218 D3
la Vèze (25) . . . 138 A6
Vézelay (89) . . . 133 H4
Vézelise (54) . . . 93 K2
Vézelois (90) . . . 139 J1
Vezels-Roussy (15) . . . 235 J3
Vézénobres (30) . . . 255 H6
Vézeronce-Curtin (38) . . . 207 G3
Vezet (70) . . . 137 J2
Vézézoux (43) . . . 219 G1
le Vézier (51) . . . 60 E4
Vézières (86) . . . 144 E2
Vézillon (27) . . . 36 A4
Vézilly (02) . . . 40 C5
Vezin-le-Coquet (35) . . . 79 F4
Vézinnes (89) . . . 113 K4
Vezins (49) . . . 143 G2
Vézins-de-Lévézou (12) . . . 253 F4
Vezot (72) . . . 83 F4
Vezzani (2B) . . . 321 G2
Viabon (28) . . . 85 J2
Viala-du-Pas-de-Jaux (12) . . . 272 D2
Viala-du-Tarn (12) . . . 252 E6
Vialas (48) . . . 254 E3
Vialer (64) . . . 285 F1
Viam (19) . . . 200 B4
Viane (81) . . . 271 J5
Vianges (21) . . . 153 F2
Vianne (47) . . . 247 J4
Viâpres-le-Petit (10) . . . 90 A1
Viarmes (95) . . . 37 K6
Vias (34) . . . 292 C4
Viazac (46) . . . 234 E5
le Vibal (12) . . . 252 D3
Vibersviller (57) . . . 68 C5
Vibeuf (76) . . . 15 H4
Vibrac (16) . . . 196 C3
Vibrac (17) . . . 211 K1
Vibraye (72) . . . 107 K2
Vic-de-Chassenay (21) . . . 134 D3
Vic-des-Prés (21) . . . 153 J2
Vic-en-Bigorre (65) . . . 285 H3
Vic-Fezensac (32) . . . 267 F4
Vic-la-Gardiole (34) . . . 293 G2
Vic-le-Comte (63) . . . 202 E4
Vic-le-Fesq (30) . . . 274 E3
Vic-sous-Thil (21) . . . 134 D5
Vic-sur-Aisne (02) . . . 39 G2
Vic-sur-Cère (15) . . . 217 K6
Vic-sur-Seille (57) . . . 66 D3
Vicdessos (09) . . . 307 H5
le Vicel (50) . . . 29 F2
Vichel (63) . . . 202 E6

Vichel-Nanteuil (02) 39 J5
Vichères (28) 84 B5
Vicherey (88) 93 J3
Vichy (03) 185 J3
Vico (2A) 320 C2
la Vicogne (80) 10 A4
la Vicomté-sur-Rance (22) 50 D5
Vicq (03) 185 F3
Vicq (52) 117 F3
Vicq (59) 12 D1
Vicq (78) 57 K4
Vicq-d'Auribat (40) 264 D3
Vicq-Exemplet (36) 166 C3
Vicq-sur-Breuilh (87) 199 G4
Vicq-sur-Gartempe (86) 164 A1
Vicq-sur-Nahon (36) 147 J3
Vicques (14) 54 B2
Victot-Pontfol (14) 33 H5
Vidai (61) 83 F2
Vidaillac (46) 250 D3
Vidaillat (23) 182 D5
Vidauban (83) 298 D2
Videcosville (50) 29 F3
Videix (87) 197 K2
Videlles (91) 87 F3
Vidou (65) 286 A4
Vidouville (50) 31 K3
Vidouze (65) 285 G2
Viefvillers (60) 17 K5
le Vieil-Baugé (49) 126 A3
le Vieil-Dampierre (51) 63 J1
le Vieil-Évreux (27) 56 E1
Vieil-Hesdin (62) 9 J2
Vieil-Moutier (62) 4 D3
Vieille-Brioude (43) 219 H3
Vieille-Chapelle (62) 6 A4
Vieille-Église (62) 2 B1
Vieille-Église-en-Yvelines (78) 58 A6
la Vieille-Loye (39) 155 H3
la Vieille-Lyre (27) 55 K2
Vieille-Toulouse (31) 288 B2
Vieilles-Maisons-sur-Joudry (45) . . . 111 F4
Vieillespesse (15) 218 E4
Vieillevie (15) 235 H5
Vieillevigne (31) 288 E4
Vieillevigne (44) 141 K3
Vieilley (25) 138 A5
Vieilmoulin (21) 135 G5
Viel-Arcy (02) 40 B2
Viel-Saint-Remy (08) 22 B5
Viella (32) 266 A6
Viella (65) 304 B4
Vielle-Adour (65) 285 H6
Vielle-Aure (65) 305 F4
Vielle-Louron (65) 305 F4
Vielle-Saint-Girons (40) 262 D1
Vielle-Soubiran (40) 246 D6
Vielle-Tursan (40) 265 H5
Viellenave-d'Arthez (64) 284 B3
Viellenave-de-Navarrenx (64) 283 J3
Viellesègure (64) 283 K3
Vielmanay (58) 132 C6
Vielmur-sur-Agout (81) 270 D6
Vielprat (43) 238 D2
Viels-Maisons (02) 60 E3
Vielverge (21) 136 E6
Vienne (38) 206 B5
Vienne-en-Arthies (95) 57 J1
Vienne-en-Bessin (14) 32 C3
Vienne-en-Val (45) 110 C5
Vienne-la-Ville (51) 42 D5
Vienne-le-Château (51) 42 D5
Viens (84) 277 K2
Vienville (88) 95 H5
Vier-Bordes (65) 304 B2
Viersat (23) 183 J1
Vierville (28) 86 A4
Vierville (50) 29 G6
Vierville-sur-Mer (14) 29 K6
Vierzon (18) 148 D1
Vierzy (02) 39 J4
Viesly (59) 12 C4
Viessoix (14) 53 F3
Viéthorey (25) 138 D3
Vieu (01) 190 B6
Vieu-d'Izenave (01) 189 K3
Vieure (03) 168 A4
Vieussan (34) 291 H1
Vieuvicq (28) 84 D5
Vieuvy (53) 80 E2
Vieux (14) 32 D6
Vieux (81) 270 B1
Vieux-Berquin (59) 6 A3
Vieux-Boucau-les-Bains (40) 262 B3
Vieux-Bourg (14) 34 A3
le Vieux-Bourg (22) 76 E1
le Vieux-Cérier (16) 179 K5
Vieux-Champagne (77) 88 C1
Vieux-Charmont (25) 139 H2
Vieux-Château (21) 134 B3
Vieux-Condé (59) 7 J4
Vieux-Ferrette (68) 97 C5
Vieux-Fumé (14) 33 G6
Vieux-lès-Asfeld (08) 41 F1
Vieux-Lixheim (57) 67 K3
Vieux-Manoir (76) 16 B6
le Vieux-Marché (22) 47 K4
Vieux-Mareuil (24) 197 H6
Vieux-Mesnil (59) 13 G3
Vieux-Moulin (60) 38 E2
Vieux-Moulin (88) 95 J2
Vieux-Pont (61) 54 B6
Vieux-Pont-en-Auge (14) 54 D1
Vieux-Port (27) 34 D2
Vieux-Reng (59) 13 H2

Vieux-Rouen-sur-Bresle (76) 17 F3
la Vieux-Rue (76) 35 K1
Vieux-Ruffec (16) 179 J5
Vieux-Thann (68) 97 A2
Vieux-Viel (35) 51 H5
Vieux-Villez (27) 35 K5
Vieux-Vy-sur-Couesnon (35) 79 J1
Vieuzos (65) 286 B5
Viévigne (21) 136 C4
Viéville (52) 92 B5
Viéville-en-Haye (54) 65 H2
Viévy (21) 153 G3
Vievy-le-Rayé (41) 108 E4
Vif (38) 224 A5
Viffort (02) 60 E2
le Vigan (30) 273 J1
le Vigan (46) 233 H3
le Vigean (15) 217 G3
le Vigeant (86) 180 B2
le Vigen (87) 199 F2
Vigeois (19) 215 J1
Viger (65) 304 B1
Vigeville (23) 183 F3
Viggianello (2A) 322 E4
Viglain (45) 110 E6
Vignacourt (80) 9 K5
Vignale (2B) 319 H3
Vignats (14) 54 B3
le Vignau (40) 265 J4
Vignaux (31) 268 D5
les Vigneaux (05) 243 J1
Vignec (65) 304 E4
Vignely (77) 59 J2
Vignemont (60) 38 D1
les Vignes (48) 253 J4
Vignes (64) 284 C1
Vignes (89) 134 B3
Vignes-la-Côte (52) 92 C5
Vigneul-sous-Montmédy (55) 23 J3
Vigneulles (54) 66 C6
Vigneulles-lès-Hattonchâtel (55) 65 F1
Vigneux-de-Bretagne (44) 123 F2
Vigneux-Hocquet (02) 21 G4
Vigneux-sur-Seine (91) 59 F5
Vignevieille (11) 309 H2
Vignieu (38) 207 G3
Vignoc (35) 79 F2
Vignol (58) 133 H5
Vignoles (21) 154 A3
Vignolles (16) 196 B5
Vignols (19) 215 H2
Vignonet (33) 230 B2
Vignory (52) 92 A5
Vignot (55) 65 F4
Vignoux-sous-les-Aix (18) 149 H1
Vignoux-sur-Barangeon (18) 148 E1
Vigny (57) 66 B1
Vigny (95) 37 F6
Vigoulant (36) 166 C5
Vigoulet-Auzil (31) 288 C2
Vigoux (36) 165 G4
Vigueron (82) 268 C3
Vigy (57) 45 G4
Vihiers (49) 143 J2
Vijon (36) 166 C5
Vilcey-sur-Trey (54) 65 J2
Vildé-Guingalan (22) 50 C5
le Vilhain (03) 167 K4
Vilhonneur (16) 197 G3
Villabé (91) 87 F1
Villabon (18) 149 K3
Villac (24) 215 F4
Villacerf (10) 90 A3
Villacourt (54) 94 C2
Villadin (10) 89 H4
Villafans (70) 138 E1
Village-Neuf (68) 97 E4
Villaines-en-Duesmois (21) 135 F1
Villaines-la-Carelle (72) 83 F3
Villaines-la-Gonais (72) 107 H1
Villaines-la-Juhel (53) 81 K4
Villaines-les-Prévôtes (21) 134 D2
Villaines-les-Rochers (37) 145 J1
Villaines-sous-Bois (95) 37 K6
Villaines-sous-Lucé (72) 107 G4
Villaines-sous-Malicorne (72) 106 B5
Villainville (76) 14 C5
Villalet (27) 56 C2
Villalier (11) 290 B5
Villamblain (45) 109 G3
Villamblard (24) 213 J5
Villamée (35) 80 A2
Villampuy (28) 109 G2
Villandraut (33) 246 D1
Villandry (37) 127 G5
Villanière (11) 290 B4
Villanova (2A) 320 A5
Villapourçon (58) 152 B4
Villar-d'Arêne (05) 225 G3
Villar-en-Val (11) 309 H1
Villar-Loubière (05) 243 F2
Villar-Saint-Anselme (11) 309 F2
Villar-Saint-Pancrace (05) 243 K1
Villard (23) 182 B1
Villard (74) 191 J1
Villard-Bonnot (38) 224 C2
Villard-de-Lans (38) 223 J4
Villard-d'Héry (73) 208 D4
Villard-Léger (73) 208 D4
Villard-Notre-Dame (38) 224 D5
Villard-Reculas (38) 224 D4
Villard-Reymond (38) 224 D5
Villard-Saint-Christophe (38) 224 B6
Villard-Saint-Sauveur (39) 173 K5
Villard-Sallet (73) 208 D5

Villard-sur-Bienne (39) 173 K4
Villard-sur-Doron (73) 209 H2
Villardebelle (11) 309 G2
Villardonnel (11) 290 A4
Villards-d'Héria (39) 173 H5
les Villards-sur-Thônes (74) 191 H5
Villarembert (73) 225 G2
Villargent (70) 138 E2
Villargoix (21) 134 D6
Villargondran (73) 225 G2
Villariès (31) 269 H4
Villarlurin (73) 209 H5
Villarodin-Bourget (73) 226 A2
Villaroger (73) 193 B3
Villaroux (73) 208 D5
Villars (24) 198 A6
Villars (28) 85 G5
Villars (42) 205 F6
le Villars (71) 172 A4
Villars (84) 277 H2
Villars-Colmars (04) 260 C4
Villars-en-Azois (52) 115 H2
Villars-en-Pons (17) 195 G4
Villars-et-Villenotte (21) 134 E3
Villars-Fontaine (21) 154 A2
Villars-le-Pautel (70) 117 J3
Villars-le-Sec (90) 139 K3
Villars-lès-Blamont (25) 139 J4
Villars-les-Bois (17) 195 J1
Villars-les-Dombes (01) 188 E4
Villars-Saint-Georges (25) 155 K2
Villars-Santenoge (52) 115 K5
Villars-sous-Dampjoux (25) 139 G4
Villars-sous-Écot (25) 139 G3
Villars-sur-Var (06) 280 E1
Villarzel-Cabardès (11) 290 C5
Villarzel-du-Razès (11) 308 E1
Villasavary (11) 289 H5
Villate (31) 288 B2
Villaudric (31) 269 G3
Villautou (11) 289 F6
Villavard (41) 108 A6
Villaz (74) 191 F5
Ville (60) 19 G6
Villé (67) 70 B6
Ville-au-Montois (54) 26 D4
Ville-au-Val (54) 65 K3
la Ville-aux-Bois (10) 91 G3
la Ville-aux-Bois-lès-Dizy (02) 21 G5
la Ville-aux-Bois-
   lès-Pontavert (02) 40 D2
la Ville-aux-Clercs (41) 108 C4
la Ville-aux-Dames (37) 127 K4
Ville-d'Avray (92) 58 D4
Ville-devant-Belrain (55) 64 C3
Ville-devant-Chaumont (55) 43 J3
Ville-di-Paraso (2B) 318 D3
Ville-di-Pietrabugno (2B) 317 D5
la Ville-Dieu-du-Temple (82) 268 E1
Ville-Dommange (51) 40 E5
la Ville-du-Bois (91) 58 D6
Ville-du-Pont (25) 157 G3
Ville-en-Blaisois (52) 91 K3
Ville-en-Sallaz (74) 191 J2
Ville-en-Selve (51) 41 F6
Ville-en-Tardenois (51) 40 D5
Ville-en-Vermois (54) 66 B6
Ville-en-Woëvre (55) 44 A5
la Ville-ès-Nonais (35) 50 E4
Ville-Houdlémont (54) 26 B2
Ville-la-Grand (74) 191 G1
Ville-Langy (58) 151 H4
Ville-le-Marclet (80) 9 J4
Ville-Saint-Jacques (77) 87 K4
Ville-Savoye (02) 40 B4
Ville-sous-Anjou (38) 222 B1
Ville-sous-la-Ferté (10) 115 H1
la Ville-sous-Orbais (51) 61 G2
Ville-sur-Ancre (80) 18 D1
Ville-sur-Arce (10) 114 E1
Ville-sur-Cousances (55) 43 F6
Ville-sur-Illon (88) 94 B5
Ville-sur-Jarnioux (69) 188 A5
Ville-sur-Lumes (08) 22 D3
Ville-sur-Retourne (08) 41 J2
Ville-sur-Saulx (55) 64 A5
Ville-sur-Terre (10) 91 H4
Ville-sur-Tourbe (51) 42 C5
Ville-sur-Yron (54) 44 C5
Villeau (28) 85 H5
Villebadin (61) 54 D4
Villebarou (41) 128 E2
Villebaudon (50) 31 G5
Villebazy (11) 309 F2
Villebéon (77) 88 A6
Villebernier (49) 126 B6
Villeberny (21) 135 G4
Villebichot (21) 154 C2
Villeblevin (89) 88 B4
Villebois (01) 189 J6
Villebois-Lavalette (16) 197 F5
Villebois-les-Pins (26) 258 C2
Villebon (28) 84 D3
Villebon-sur-Yvette (91) 58 D5
Villebougis (89) 88 C6
Villebourg (37) 127 H1
Villebout (41) 108 D3
Villebramar (47) 231 H6
Villebret (03) 184 B2
Villebrumier (82) 269 G2
Villecelin (18) 148 E6
Villecerf (77) 87 K4
Villecey-sur-Mad (54) 65 J1
Villechantria (39) 173 F5
Villechauve (41) 128 B1
Villechenève (69) 205 G1

Villechétif (10) 90 B4
Villechétive (89) 113 F1
Villechien (50) 52 D6
Villecien (89) 112 D3
Villécloye (55) 23 K6
Villecomtal (12) 235 J6
Villecomtal-sur-Arros (32) 285 J3
Villecomte (21) 136 A3
Villeconin (91) 86 C2
Villecourt (80) 19 H3
Villecresnes (94) 59 G5
Villecroze (83) 279 G6
Villedaigne (11) 291 G5
Villedieu (15) 218 D6
la Villedieu (17) 178 B4
Villedieu (21) 114 C4
la Villedieu (23) 200 B2
les Villedieu (25) 156 E6
Villedieu (48) 237 F4
Villedieu (84) 257 G3
la Villedieu-du-Clain (86) 163 F5
la Villedieu-en-Fontenette (70) 118 B5
Villedieu-la-Blouère (49) 142 D1
Villedieu-le-Château (41) 107 J3
Villedieu-lès-Bailleul (61) 54 C4
Villedieu-les-Poêles (50) 52 B3
Villedieu-sur-Indre (36) 147 J6
Villedômain (37) 147 F3
Villedômer (37) 128 A3
Villedoux (17) 176 E1
Villedubert (11) 290 C5
Villefagnan (16) 179 F4
Villefargeau (89) 113 F5
Villefavard (85) 181 G3
Villeferry (21) 135 F4
Villefloure (11) 309 G1
Villefollet (79) 178 C3
Villefontaine (38) 206 D4
Villefort (11) 308 C3
Villefort (48) 255 F1
Villefranche (32) 286 E3
Villefranche (89) 112 C3
Villefranche-d'Albigeois (81) 271 F3
Villefranche-d'Allier (03) 167 K6
Villefranche-de-Conflent (66) 314 B3
Villefranche-de-Lauragais (31) 288 E3
Villefranche-de-Lonchat (24) 212 D6
Villefranche-de-Panat (12) 252 C6
Villefranche-de-Rouergue (12) 251 F3
Villefranche-du-Périgord (24) 232 D5
Villefranche-du-Queyran (47) 247 H3
Villefranche-le-Château (26) 258 C4
Villefranche-sur-Cher (41) 129 J6
Villefranche-sur-Mer (06) 281 H4
Villefranche-sur-Saône (69) 188 B5
Villefrancœur (41) 128 D1
Villefrancon (70) 137 H4
Villefranque (64) 282 B2
Villefranque (65) 285 G2
Villegailhenc (11) 290 B5
Villegats (16) 179 G5
Villegats (27) 57 G2
Villegaudin (71) 154 D6
Villegenon (18) 131 G4
Villegly (11) 290 C5
Villegongis (36) 147 J5
Villegouge (33) 212 A6
Villegouin (36) 147 G4
Villegusien-le-Lac (52) 116 D6
Villeherviers (41) 129 K5
Villejésus (16) 179 F6
Villejoubert (16) 196 E1
Villejuif (94) 58 E4
Villejust (91) 58 D6
Villelaure (84) 277 H4
Villeloin-Coulangé (37) 147 F2
Villelongue (65) 304 B3
Villelongue-d'Aude (11) 308 D2
Villelongue-de-la-Salanque (66) . . . 315 H1
Villelongue-dels-Monts (66) 315 G4
Villeloup (10) 89 J4
Villemade (82) 249 J6
Villemagne (11) 289 J4
Villemagne-l'Argentière (34) 272 E6
Villemain (79) 178 D4
Villemandeur (45) 111 H3
Villemanoche (89) 88 C5
Villemardy (41) 108 D6
Villemaréchal (77) 87 K5
Villemareuil (77) 60 A2
Villematier (31) 269 H3
Villemaur-sur-Vanne (10) 89 H5
Villembits (65) 286 A4
Villembray (60) 37 F1
Villemer (77) 87 J5
Villemer (89) 113 F4
Villemereuil (10) 90 B6
Villemeux-sur-Eure (28) 57 G6
Villemoirieu (38) 206 E2
Villemoiron-en-Othe (10) 89 J6
Villemoisan (49) 124 D3
Villemoisson-sur-Orge (91) 58 E6
Villemolaque (66) 315 G3
Villemomble (93) 59 G3
Villemontais (42) 186 D5
Villemontoire (02) 39 J4
Villemorien (10) 114 D1
Villemorin (17) 178 B4
Villemort (86) 164 B4
Villemotier (01) 172 E6
Villemoustaussou (11) 290 B5
Villemoutiers (45) 111 G3
Villemoyenne (10) 90 C6
Villemur (65) 286 C5
Villemur-sur-Tarn (31) 269 H3
Villemurlin (45) 130 E1

Villemus (04) 278 A2
Villenauxe-la-Grande (10) 89 F1
Villenauxe-la-Petite (77) 88 D3
Villenave (40) 264 D1
Villenave-de-Rions (33) 229 K4
Villenave-d'Ornon (33) 229 H3
Villenave-près-Béarn (65) 285 F3
Villenave-près-Marsac (65) 285 H4
Villenavotte (89) 88 C5
Villeneuve (01) 188 C4
Villeneuve (04) 278 C2
Villeneuve (09) 306 C3
Villeneuve (12) 251 F2
la Villeneuve (23) 183 J3
Villeneuve (33) 211 G4
Villeneuve (63) 202 E6
Villeneuve (71) 154 D4
la Villeneuve-au-Châtelot (10) 89 G1
Villeneuve-au-Chemin (10) 113 J1
la Villeneuve-au-Chêne (10) 90 D5
la Villeneuve-Bellenoye-et-
   -la-Maize (70) 118 C6
Villeneuve-d'Allier (43) 219 H3
Villeneuve-d'Amont (25) 156 C4
Villeneuve-d'Ascq (59) 6 E4
Villeneuve-d'Aval (39) 155 K4
Villeneuve-de-Berg (07) 239 J5
Villeneuve-de-Duras (47) 231 F3
Villeneuve-de-la-Raho (66) 315 H3
Villeneuve-de-Marc (38) 206 D5
Villeneuve-de-Marsan (40) 265 J2
Villeneuve-de-Rivière (31) 305 J1
Villeneuve-d'Entraunes (06) 260 E4
Villeneuve-d'Olmes (09) 308 A4
Villeneuve-du-Latou (09) 288 B6
Villeneuve-du-Paréage (09) 288 D6
la Villeneuve-en-Chevrie (78) 57 G1
Villeneuve-en-Montagne (71) 171 G1
Villeneuve-Frouville (41) 108 E5
Villeneuve-la-Comptal (11) 289 G5
Villeneuve-la-Comtesse (17) 177 K3
Villeneuve-la-Dondagre (89) 112 C1
Villeneuve-la-Garenne (92) 58 E2
Villeneuve-la-Guyard (89) 88 B4
Villeneuve-la-Lionne (51) 60 E4
Villeneuve-la-Rivière (66) 315 F2
Villeneuve-l'Archevêque (89) 89 F5
Villeneuve-le-Comte (77) 59 J4
Villeneuve-le-Roi (94) 59 F5
Villeneuve-Lécussan (31) 286 C6
Villeneuve-lès-Avignon (30) 276 B1
Villeneuve-lès-Béziers (34) 292 A4
Villeneuve-lès-Bordes (77) 88 B2
Villeneuve-lès-Bouloc (31) 269 G4
Villeneuve-les-Cerfs (63) 185 H5
la Villeneuve-lès-Charleville (51) . . . 61 H4
Villeneuve-lès-Charnod (39) 173 F6
la Villeneuve-les-Convers (21) 135 F2
Villeneuve-les-Corbières (11) 310 A3
Villeneuve-les-Genêts (89) 112 B6
Villeneuve-lès-Lavaur (81) 270 A6
Villeneuve-lès-Maguelone (34) 293 G1
Villeneuve-lès-Montréal (11) 289 G6
Villeneuve-les-Sablons (60) 37 G4
Villeneuve-Loubet (06) 281 F4
Villeneuve-Minervois (11) 290 C4
Villeneuve-Renneville-
   Chevigny (51) 62 A2
Villeneuve-Saint-Denis (77) 59 J4
Villeneuve-Saint-Georges (94) 59 F5
Villeneuve-Saint-Germain (02) 39 J3
Villeneuve-Saint-Nicolas (28) 85 H5
Villeneuve-Saint-Salves (89) 113 G4
Villeneuve-Saint-Vistre-et-
   -Villevotte (51) 61 H6
Villeneuve-sous-Charigny (21) 134 E4
Villeneuve-sous-Dammartin (77) . . . 59 H1
Villeneuve-sous-Pymont (39) 173 G1
la Villeneuve-sous-Thury (60) 39 G5
Villeneuve-sur-Allier (03) 168 D2
Villeneuve-sur-Auvers (91) 86 D2
Villeneuve-sur-Bellot (77) 60 D3
Villeneuve-sur-Cher (18) 148 E3
Villeneuve-sur-Conie (45) 109 H2
Villeneuve-sur-Fère (02) 40 A5
Villeneuve-sur-Lot (47) 248 C2
Villeneuve-sur-Verberie (60) 38 C4
Villeneuve-sur-Vère (81) 270 C1
Villeneuve-sur-Yonne (89) 112 D2
Villeneuve-Tolosane (31) 288 A2
Villeneuvette (34) 273 G6
Villennes-sur-Seine (78) 58 B2
Villenouvelle (31) 288 E3
Villenoy (77) 59 K2
Villentrois (36) 147 H1
Villeny (41) 129 J2
Villepail (53) 81 K3
Villeparisis (77) 59 G2
Villeparois (70) 118 B6
Villeperdrix (26) 257 J1
Villeperdue (37) 145 K1
Villeperrot (89) 88 C5
Villepinte (11) 289 J5
Villepinte (93) 59 G2
Villeporcher (41) 128 B1
Villepot (44) 103 K3
Villepreux (78) 58 B4
Villequier (76) 34 E1
Villequier-Aumont (02) 19 K5
Villequiers (18) 150 A3
Viller (57) 66 E1
Villerable (41) 108 C6
Villerbon (41) 129 F1
Villeréal (47) 232 A5
Villereau (45) 110 B2
Villereau (59) 12 E3

Villerest (42) 186 E5
Villeret (02) 19 J1
Villeret (10) 91 F2
Villereversure (01) 189 H2
Villermain (41) 109 G4
Villeromain (41) 108 D6
Villeron (95) 59 G1
Villerouge-Termenès (11) 309 J2
Villeroy (77) 59 J2
Villeroy (80) 17 F1
Villeroy (89) 88 C6
Villeroy-sur-Méholle (55) 64 E6
Villers (42) 187 G3
Villers (88) 94 A4
Villers-Agron-Aiguizy (02) 40 C5
Villers-Allerand (51) 41 F5
Villers-au-Bois (62) 10 D2
Villers-au-Flos (62) 11 G5
Villers-au-Tertre (59) 11 J2
Villers-aux-Bois (51) 61 K2
Villers-aux-Érables (80) 18 D3
Villers-aux-Nœuds (51) 40 E5
Villers-aux-Vents (55) 63 K3
Villers-Bocage (14) 32 B6
Villers-Bocage (80) 10 A6
Villers-Bouton (70) 137 K3
Villers-Bretonneux (80) 18 D2
Villers-Brûlin (62) 10 C2
Villers-Buzon (25) 137 J6
Villers-Campsart (80) 17 G2
Villers-Canivet (14) 54 A2
Villers-Carbonnel (80) 19 G2
Villers-Cernay (08) 23 G4
Villers-Châtel (62) 10 D1
Villers-Chemin-et-
  -Mont-lès-Étrelles (70) 137 J3
Villers-Chief (25) 138 E6
Villers-Cotterêts (02) 39 G4
Villers-devant-Dun (55) 43 F2
Villers-devant-le-Thour (08) . . . 41 F1
Villers-devant-Mouzon (08) . . . 23 G5
Villers-Écalles (76) 15 J4
Villers-en-Argonne (51) 63 J1
Villers-en-Arthies (95) 36 D6
Villers-en-Cauchies (59) 12 C3
Villers-en-Haye (54) 65 J3
Villers-en-Ouche (61) 55 G3
Villers-en-Prayères (02) 40 B2
Villers-en-Vexin (27) 36 C4
Villers-Farlay (39) 155 K3
Villers-Faucon (80) 19 J1
Villers-Franqueux (51) 40 E3
Villers-Grélot (25) 138 C4
Villers-Guislain (59) 11 J6
Villers-Hélon (02) 39 H4
Villers-la-Chèvre (54) 26 C2
Villers-la-Combe (25) 138 E6
Villers-la-Faye (21) 154 A2
Villers-la-Montagne (54) 26 D3
Villers-la-Ville (70) 138 E2
Villers-le-Château (51) 62 C2
Villers-le-Lac (25) 157 H2
Villers-le-Rond (54) 43 J1
Villers-le-Sec (02) 20 C3
Villers-le-Sec (51) 63 H4
Villers-le-Sec (55) 64 C6
Villers-le-Sec (70) 138 B1
Villers-le-Tilleul (08) 22 D5
Villers-le-Tourneur (08) 22 B5
Villers-les-Bois (39) 155 H4
Villers-lès-Cagnicourt (62) 11 G3
Villers-lès-Guise (02) 20 D1
Villers-lès-Luxeuil (70) 118 C5
Villers-lès-Mangiennes (55) . . . 43 J2
Villers-lès-Moivrons (54) 66 B3
Villers-lès-Nancy (54) 66 A5
Villers-les-Ormes (36) 147 K5
Villers-les-Pots (21) 155 F1
Villers-lès-Roye (80) 18 E4
Villers-l'Hôpital (62) 9 K3
Villers-Marmery (51) 41 H5
Villers-Outréaux (59) 12 B6
Villers-Pater (70) 138 B3
Villers-Patras (21) 115 F3
Villers-Plouich (59) 11 J5
Villers-Pol (59) 12 C3
Villers-Robert (39) 155 G4
Villers-Rotin (21) 155 F1
Villers-Saint-Barthélemy (60) . . 37 F2
Villers-Saint-Christophe (02) . . 19 J3
Villers-Saint-Frambourg (60) . . 38 C4
Villers-Saint-Genest (60) 38 E6
Villers-Saint-Martin (25) 138 D4
Villers-Saint-Paul (60) 38 A4
Villers-Saint-Sépulcre (60) 37 J3
Villers-Semeuse (08) 22 D3
Villers-Sir-Simon (62) 10 C2
Villers-Sire-Nicole (59) 13 H2
Villers-sous-Ailly (80) 9 H5
Villers-sous-Chalamont (25) . . 156 C4
Villers-sous-Châtillon (51) 40 D6
Villers-sous-Foucarmont (76) . . 16 E2
Villers-sous-Montrond (25) . . . 156 C1
Villers-sous-Pareid (55) 44 B5
Villers-sous-Prény (54) 65 J2
Villers-sous-Saint-Leu (60) 37 K5
Villers-Stoncourt (57) 66 H5
Villers-sur-Auchy (60) 36 E1
Villers-sur-Authie (80) 9 F2
Villers-sur-Bar (08) 22 E4
Villers-sur-Bonnières (60) 17 H6
Villers-sur-Coudun (60) 38 D1
Villers-sur-Fère (02) 40 A5
Villers-sur-le-Mont (08) 22 C4
Villers-sur-le-Roule (27) 36 A5
Villers-sur-Mer (14) 33 H3

Villers-sur-Meuse (55) 64 D1
Villers-sur-Nied (57) 66 D2
Villers-sur-Port (70) 118 A6
Villers-sur-Saulnot (70) 139 F2
Villers-sur-Trie (60) 36 E3
Villers-Tournelle (80) 18 C5
Villers-Vaudey (70) 117 H6
Villers-Vermont (60) 17 F6
Villers-Vicomte (60) 18 A5
Villerserine (39) 155 J5
Villersexel (70) 138 D2
Villerupt (54) 26 E3
Villerville (14) 33 J2
Villery (10) 90 A6
Villes (01) 190 C3
Villes-sur-Auzon (84) 257 A6
Villeselve (60) 19 J4
Villeseneux (51) 62 B3
Villesèque (46) 249 J2
Villesèque-des-Corbières (11) . 310 B2
Villesèquelande (11) 289 K5
Villesiscle (11) 289 J5
Villespassans (34) 291 G3
Villespy (11) 289 J4
Villetaneuse (93) 58 E2
la Villetelle (23) 183 H6
Villethierry (89) 88 B5
Villeton (47) 247 H2
Villetoureix (24) 213 G2
Villetritouls (11) 309 H1
Villetrun (41) 108 D5
la Villette (14) 53 H2
Villette (54) 43 K1
Villette (78) 57 J2
Villette-d'Anthon (38) 206 D1
Villette-de-Vienne (38) 206 B4
Villette-lès-Arbois (39) 155 K4
Villette-lès-Dole (39) 155 G3
Villette-sur-Ain (01) 189 G5
Villette-sur-Aube (10) 90 B2
Villettes (27) 35 H5
les Villettes (43) 221 F3
Villeurbanne (69) 206 B2
Villevallier (89) 112 D2
Villevaudé (77) 59 H3
Villevenard (51) 61 J4
Villevêque (49) 125 H2
Villeveyrac (34) 292 E2
Villevieille (30) 274 E4
Villevieux (39) 173 F1
Villevocance (07) 221 K3
Villevoques (45) 111 H4
Villexanton (41) 109 F6
Villexavier (17) 211 J1
le Villey (39) 155 G5
Villey-le-Sec (54) 65 J5
Villey-Saint-Étienne (54) 65 J4
Villey-sur-Tille (21) 136 B2
Villez-sous-Bailleul (27) 36 A4
Villez-sur-le-Neubourg (27) . . . 35 F5
Villié-Morgon (69) 188 B3
Villiers (36) 146 E5
Villiers (86) 162 D2
Villiers-Adam (95) 58 D1
Villiers-au-Bouin (37) 126 E2
Villiers-aux-Corneilles (51) 89 H1
Villiers-Charlemagne (53) 105 F3
Villiers-Couture (17) 178 D5
Villiers-en-Bière (77) 87 G2
Villiers-en-Bois (79) 178 A3
Villiers-en-Désœuvre (27) 57 G2
Villiers-en-Lieu (52) 63 J5
Villiers-en-Morvan (21) 152 E2
Villiers-en-Plaine (79) 161 G5
Villiers-Fossard (50) 31 H3
Villiers-Herbisse (10) 62 B6
Villiers-le-Bâcle (91) 58 C5
Villiers-le-Bel (95) 58 E1
Villiers-le-Bois (10) 114 C3
Villiers-le-Duc (21) 115 H5
Villiers-le-Mahieu (78) 57 J3
Villiers-le-Morhier (28) 57 H6
Villiers-le-Pré (50) 51 K5
Villiers-le-Roux (16) 179 F4
Villiers-le-Sec (14) 32 C3
Villiers-le-Sec (52) 116 A1
Villiers-le-Sec (58) 132 E5
Villiers-le-Sec (95) 58 E1
Villiers-lès-Aprey (52) 116 C5
Villiers-les-Hauts (89) 114 B6
Villiers-Louis (89) 88 E6
Villiers-Saint-Benoît (89) 112 C5
Villiers-Saint-Denis (02) 60 D2
Villiers-Saint-Fréderic (78) 58 A4
Villiers-Saint-Georges (77) 60 E6
Villiers-Saint-Orien (28) 109 G1
Villiers-sous-Grez (77) 87 H4
Villiers-sous-Mortagne (61) . . . 83 H2
Villiers-sous-Praslin (10) 114 C2
Villiers-sur-Chizé (79) 178 B3
Villiers-sur-Loir (41) 108 B5
Villiers-sur-Morin (77) 59 K3
Villiers-sur-Orge (91) 58 E6
Villiers-sur-Seine (77) 88 E3
Villiers-sur-Suize (52) 116 B3
Villiers-sur-Tholon (89) 112 E4
Villiers-sur-Yonne (58) 133 G4
Villiers-Vineux (89) 113 J4
Villiersfaux (41) 108 B6
Villieu-Loyes-Mollon (01) 189 G5
Villing (57) 45 K3
Villognon (16) 179 F6
Villon (89) 114 C4
Villoncourt (88) 94 E4

Villons-les-Buissons (14) 32 D4
Villorceau (45) 109 H5
Villosanges (63) 184 B6
Villotran (60) 37 G3
Villotte (88) 117 H1
Villotte-devant-Louppy (55) . . . 64 A3
Villotte-Saint-Seine (21) 135 H4
Villotte-sur-Aire (55) 64 C3
Villotte-sur-Ource (21) 115 G4
Villouxel (88) 93 F4
Villuis (77) 88 E3
Villy (08) 23 H5
Villy (89) 113 H4
Villy-Bocage (14) 32 B6
Villy-en-Auxois (21) 135 G4
Villy-en-Trodes (10) 90 D6
Villy-le-Bois (10) 90 B6
Villy-le-Bouveret (74) 191 F4
Villy-le-Maréchal (10) 90 B6
Villy-le-Moutier (21) 154 B3
Villy-le-Pelloux (74) 191 F4
Villy-lez-Falaise (14) 54 B3
Villy-sur-Yères (76) 16 D1
Vilory (70) 118 B5
Vilosnes-Haraumont (55) 43 G3
Vilsberg (57) 70 A1
Vimarcé (53) 82 A6
Vimenet (12) 253 F2
Viménil (88) 95 F5
Vimines (73) 208 B4
Vimont (14) 33 F5
Vimory (45) 111 H3
Vimoutiers (61) 54 E2
Vimpelles (77) 88 C3
Vimy (62) 11 F2
Vinantes (77) 59 J1
Vinassan (11) 291 J6
Vinax (17) 178 C4
Vinay (38) 223 H3
Vinay (51) 61 J1
Vinça (66) 314 D3
Vincelles (39) 173 F3
Vincelles (51) 40 B6
Vincelles (71) 172 D2
Vincelles (89) 113 G6
Vincelottes (89) 113 G6
Vincennes (94) 59 F4
Vincent (39) 155 G6
Vincey (88) 94 C3
Vincly (62) 5 F5
Vincy-Manœuvre (77) 39 H4
Vincy-Reuil-et-Magny (02) 21 H4
Vindecy (71) 170 B6
Vindefontaine (50) 28 E6
Vindelle (16) 196 D2
Vindey (51) 61 J1
Vindrac-Alayrac (81) 250 E6
Vinets (10) 90 C2
Vineuil (36) 147 K5
Vineuil (41) 129 F2
Vineuil-Saint-Firmin (60) 38 B5
la Vineuse (71) 171 G4
Vinezac (07) 239 G6
Vingrau (66) 310 A4
Vingt-Hanaps (61) 82 D2
Vinnemerville (76) 14 E3
Vinneuf (89) 88 C4
Vinon (18) 131 K6
Vinon-sur-Verdon (83) 278 B4
Vins-sur-Caramy (83) 298 A4
Vinsobres (26) 257 G2
le Vintrou (81) 290 C2
Vinzelles (63) 185 J6
Vinzelles (71) 188 B1
Vinzier (74) 175 G5
Vinzieux (07) 222 A2
Viocourt (88) 93 H4
Viodos-Abense-de-Bas (64) . . 283 H5
Violaines (62) 6 B5
Violay (42) 205 F1
Violès (84) 257 F5
Violot (52) 116 E2
Viols-en-Laval (34) 274 A4
Viols-le-Fort (34) 274 A4
Vioménil (88) 118 B1
Vion (07) 222 B4
Vion (72) 105 K5
Vions (73) 208 A1
Vionville (57) 44 D5
Viozan (32) 286 B3
Viplaix (03) 168 B3
Vira (09) 308 A2
Vira (66) 309 G5
Virac (81) 270 D1
Virandeville (50) 28 B3
Virargues (15) 218 C4
Virazeil (47) 231 F6
Vire (14) 52 E3
Viré (71) 171 K5
Viré-en-Champagne (72) 105 K3
Vireaux (89) 114 A5
Virecourt (54) 94 C2
Virelade (33) 229 J4
Vireux-Molhain (08) 24 C2
Vireux-Wallerand (08) 24 C2
Virey (50) 52 B6
Virey-le-Grand (71) 154 A5
Virey-sous-Bar (10) 114 D1
Virginy (51) 42 C5
Viriat (01) 189 G1
Viricelles (42) 205 H1
Virieu (38) 207 H5
Virieu-le-Grand (01) 190 A6
Virieu-le-Petit (01) 190 B5
Virigneux (42) 205 F3

Virignin (01) 207 K2
Viriville (38) 223 F2
Virlet (63) 184 B3
Virming (57) 68 A5
Viroflay (78) 58 C4
Virollet (17) 195 F4
Vironchaux (80) 9 G3
Vironvay (27) 35 J3
Virsac (33) 211 J5
Virson (17) 177 F3
Virville (76) 14 C5
Viry (39) 173 J6
Viry (71) 170 E4
Viry (89) 190 E3
Viry-Châtillon (91) 58 E6
Viry-Noureuil (02) 19 K5
Vis-en-Artois (62) 11 G3
Visan (84) 257 F3
Viscomtat (63) 203 K1
Viscos (65) 304 B3
Viserny (21) 134 D2
Visker (65) 285 H6
Vismes (80) 8 E6
Visoncourt (70) 118 C5
Vissac-Auteyrac (43) 219 K4
Vissec (30) 273 H1
Visseiche (35) 79 K6
Viterbe (81) 270 B5
Viterne (54) 65 K6
Vitot (27) 35 G5
Vitrac (15) 235 G3
Vitrac (24) 233 F2
Vitrac (63) 184 D5
Vitrac-en-Viadène (12) 236 B3
Vitrac-Saint-Vincent (16) 197 H2
Vitrac-sur-Montane (19) 216 C1
Vitrai-sous-Laigle (61) 55 J5
Vitray (03) 167 H3
Vitray-en-Beauce (28) 85 H5
Vitré (35) 80 A6
Vitré (79) 178 D1
Vitreux (39) 137 G6
Vitrey (54) 93 K2
Vitrey-sur-Mance (70) 117 H4
Vitrimont (54) 66 D6
Vitrolles (05) 259 F1
Vitrolles (13) 296 B2
Vitrolles-en-Lubéron (84) 277 K3
Vitry-aux-Loges (45) 110 D3
Vitry-en-Artois (62) 11 G2
Vitry-en-Charollais (71) 170 B5
Vitry-en-Montagne (52) 116 A4
Vitry-en-Perthois (51) 63 F4
Vitry-la-Ville (51) 62 E3
Vitry-Laché (58) 151 H1
Vitry-le-Croisé (10) 91 F6
Vitry-le-François (51) 63 F5
Vitry-lès-Cluny (71) 171 G4
Vitry-lès-Nogent (52) 116 D2
Vitry-sur-Loire (71) 169 J2
Vitry-sur-Orne (57) 44 E3
Vitry-sur-Seine (94) 58 E4
Vittarville (55) 43 H2
Vitteaux (21) 135 F4
Vittefleur (76) 15 F3
Vittel (88) 93 J5
Vittersbourg (57) 68 C5
Vittoncourt (57) 45 H6
Vittonville (54) 65 K1
Vitz-sur-Authie (80) 9 J3
Viuz-en-Sallaz (74) 191 H2
Viuz-la-Chiésaz (74) 208 C1
Vivaise (02) 20 C5
Vivans (42) 186 D2
Vivario (2B) 321 F2
Viven (64) 284 D2
Viverols (63) 204 B6
Vivès (66) 315 F4
Vivey (52) 116 A6
le Vivier (66) 309 H5
Vivier-au-Court (08) 22 E3
le Vivier-sur-Mer (35) 51 F4
Vivières (02) 39 G4
Viviers (07) 256 D1
Viviers (57) 66 C2
Viviers (89) 113 K5
Viviers-du-Lac (73) 208 B4
Viviers-le-Gras (88) 93 J6
Viviers-lès-Lavaur (81) 270 A6
Viviers-lès-Montagnes (81) . . 289 K1
Viviers-lès-Offroicourt (88) . . . 93 K4
Viviers-sur-Artaut (10) 114 E1
Viviers-sur-Chiers (54) 43 K1
Viviès (09) 308 A2
Viviez (12) 235 F6
Viville (16) 196 B5
Vivoin (72) 82 D5
Vivonne (86) 162 E5
Vivy (49) 126 B5
Vix (21) 115 F4
Vix (85) 160 D5
Vizille (38) 224 B4
Vizos (65) 304 B3
Vizzavona (2B) 321 F2
Vocance (07) 221 K3
Vodable (63) 202 D5
Vœgtlinshoffen (68) 96 B5
Vœlfling-lès-Bouzonville (57) . . 45 J3
Vœllerdingen (67) 69 K2
Vœuil-et-Giget (16) 196 E4
Vogelgrun (68) 96 E5
Voglans (73) 208 B3
Vogüé (07) 239 H6
Voharies (02) 20 E3
Void-Vacon (55) 65 F5
Voigny (10) 91 H5
Voilemont (51) 63 H1

Voillans (25) 138 D4
Voillecomte (52) 91 J2
Voimhaut (57) 45 H6
Voinémont (54) 94 A1
Voingt (63) 201 H2
Voinsles (77) 60 A5
Voipreux (51) 62 A3
Voires (25) 156 C2
Voiron (38) 223 K1
Voiscreville (27) 34 E4
Voise (28) 85 J3
Voisenon (77) 87 H1
Voisey (52) 117 H3
Voisines (52) 116 B4
Voisines (89) 88 E5
Voisins-le-Bretonneux (78) . . . 58 B5
Voissant (38) 207 K5
Voissay (17) 177 J5
Voiteur (39) 155 H6
la Voivre (70) 118 E4
la Voivre (88) 95 H3
les Voivres (88) 118 C1
Voivres-lès-le-Mans (72) 106 C3
Volckerinckhove (59) 3 H4
Volesvres (71) 170 C4
Volgelsheim (68) 96 E5
Volgré (89) 112 D4
Volksberg (67) 69 F4
Vollore-Montagne (63) 203 J2
Vollore-Ville (63) 203 J2
Volmerange-lès-Boulay (57) . . 45 H4
Volmerange-les-Mines (57) . . . 27 F3
Volmunster (57) 69 G2
Volnay (21) 153 K3
Volnay (72) 107 G3
Volon (70) 137 G1
Volonne (04) 259 G5
Volpajola (2B) 319 H3
Volstroff (57) 45 F3
Volvent (26) 241 H5
Volvic (63) 202 C1
Volx (04) 278 C2
Vomécourt (88) 94 E4
Vomécourt-sur-Madon (88) . . . 94 A3
Voncourt (52) 117 G6
Voncq (08) 42 B1
Vonges (21) 136 E5
Vongnes (01) 207 K1
Vonnas (01) 188 E2
Voray-sur-l'Ognon (70) 137 K5
Voreppe (38) 223 K2
Vorey (43) 220 C3
Vorges (02) 40 B1
Vorges-les-Pins (25) 156 A1
Vorly (18) 149 H4
Vornay (18) 149 J4
Vosbles (39) 173 G6
Vosne-Romanée (21) 154 B1
Vosnon (73) 113 J1
Vou (37) 146 B3
Vouarces (51) 89 J1
Voudenay (21) 153 F2
Voué (10) 90 B3
Vouécourt (52) 92 B5
Vougécourt (70) 117 K3
Vougeot (21) 154 B1
Vougrey (10) 114 C1
Vougy (42) 187 F3
Vougy (74) 191 J3
Vouharte (16) 196 D1
Vouhé (17) 177 G2
Vouhé (79) 161 K3
Vouhenans (70) 118 E6
Vouillé (79) 161 J6
Vouillé (86) 162 D2
Vouillé-les-Marais (85) 160 C5
Vouillers (51) 63 H5
Vouillon (36) 148 C6
Vouilly (14) 31 H1
Voujeaucourt (25) 139 H2
Voulaines-les-Templiers (21) . 115 H5
Voulangis (77) 59 K3
Voulême (86) 179 H3
Voulgézac (16) 196 D5
Voulon (86) 162 E6
Voulpaix (02) 20 E2
la Voulte-sur-Rhône (07) 240 B2
Voultegon (79) 143 J4
Voulton (77) 60 D6
Voulx (77) 88 A5
Vouneuil-sous-Biard (86) 162 E3
Vouneuil-sur-Vienne (86) 163 H1
Vourey (38) 223 J1
Vourles (69) 206 A3
Voussac (03) 185 F1
Voutenay-sur-Cure (89) 133 J2
Voutezac (19) 215 H2
Vouthon (16) 197 H3
Vouthon-Bas (55) 93 F2
Vouthon-Haut (55) 93 F2
Voutré (53) 81 K6
Vouvant (85) 160 E3
Vouvray (37) 127 K4
Vouvray-sur-Huisne (72) 107 H1
Vouvray-sur-Loir (72) 107 G6
Vouxey (88) 93 H3
Vouzailles (86) 162 C1
Vouzan (16) 197 G4
Vouzeron (18) 130 D6
Vouziers (08) 42 B2
Vouzon (41) 130 B1
Vouzy (51) 62 B2
Voves (28) 85 H5
Vovray-en-Bornes (74) 191 F3
Voyenne (02) 20 E4
Voyennes (80) 19 H3

Voyer (57). 67 J5
la Vraie-Croix (56). 101 H5
Vraignes-en-Vermandois (80) 19 H2
Vraignes-lès-Hornoy (80) 17 H3
Vraincourt (52) 92 B5
Vraiville (27) 35 H4
Vraux (51). 62 C1
Vrécourt (88) 93 G6
Vred (59) 11 J1
Vregille (70) 137 J5
Vregny (02). 39 K2
Vrély (80) 18 E3
le Vrétot (50). 28 C4
Vrianges (39) 155 H1
Vrigne-aux-Bois (08). 22 E3
Vrigne-Meuse (08) 22 E4
Vrigny (45) 110 D2
Vrigny (51) 40 E4
Vrigny (61) 54 C5
Vritz (44). 124 B2
Vrizy (08) 42 B2
Vrocourt (60) 37 F1
Vroil (51). 63 J3
Vron (80) 9 F2
Vroncourt (54) 93 K2
Vroncourt-la-Côte (52) 92 E6
Vroville (88) 94 A4
Vry (57) 45 G4
Vue (44) 122 D4
Vuillafans (25). 156 D2
Vuillecin (25). 156 E4
Vuillery (02) 39 K2
Vulaines (10). 89 G5
Vulaines-lès-Provins (77) 88 C1
Vulaines-sur-Seine (77). 87 J3
Vulbens (74). 190 D3
Vulmont (57). 66 B2
Vulvoz (39) 173 J6
Vy-le-Ferroux (70). 137 K1
Vy-lès-Filain (70). 138 B2
Vy-lès-Lure (70) 118 D6
Vy-lès-Rupt (70) 137 J1
Vyans-le-Val (70) 139 G2
Vyt-lès-Belvoir (25). 139 F4

W

Waben (62). 8 E1
Wacquemoulin (60). 38 C1
Wacquinghen (62) 2 B4
Wadelincourt (08) 23 F4
Wagnon (08). 22 A5
Wahagnies (59) 6 D6
Wahlbach (68) 97 C4
Wahlenheim (67). 70 E1
Wail (62) 9 J2
Wailly (62) 10 E3
Wailly-Beaucamp (62) 9 F1
Walbach (68) 96 B4
Walbourg (67) 25 A3
la Walck (67) 69 J5
Waldersbach (67) 70 A5
Waldhambach (67) 69 F5
Waldhouse (57) 69 H2
Waldighofen (68) 97 C5
Waldolwisheim (67) 70 C1
Waldweistroff (57). 27 K4
Waldwisse (57). 45 J1
Walheim (68) 97 B4
Walincourt-Selvigny (59). 12 B5
Wallers (59) 12 C1
Wallers-Trélon (59) 13 K5
Wallon-Cappel (59). 5 J3
Walschbronn (57). 69 H2
Walscheid (57) 67 K5

Waltembourg (57) 70 A1
Waltenheim (68) 97 D3
Waltenheim-sur-Zorn (67) 70 E1
Waly (55) 64 A1
Wambaix (59) 12 B5
Wambercourt (62). 9 H1
Wambez (60) 36 E1
Wambrechies (59) 6 C5
Wamin (62) 9 J1
Wanchy-Capval (76). 16 C2
Wancourt (62). 11 F3
Wandignies-Hamage (59) 12 B1
Wangen (67). 70 C3
Wangenbourg-Engenthal (67) 70 B3
Wannehain (59) 7 F5
Wanquetin (62). 10 D3
la Wantzenau (67). 25 B6
Warcq (08) 22 C3
Warcq (55) 44 A4
Wardrecques (62) 5 H3
Wargemoulin-Hurlus (51) 42 B5
Wargnies (80) 10 A6
Wargnies-le-Grand (59) 12 E2
Wargnies-le-Petit (59) 12 E2
Warhem (59). 3 J2
Warlaing (59) 12 B1
Warlencourt-Eaucourt (62) 11 F3
Warlincourt-lès-Pas (62) 10 C4
Warloy-Baillon (80) 10 C6
Warluis (60) 37 H2
Warlus (62) 10 D3
Warlus (80) 17 H1
Warluzel (62) 10 D3
Warmeriville (51). 41 G3
Warnécourt (08) 22 C4
Warneton (59) 6 C3
Warsy (80) 18 K4
Warvillers (80) 18 E3
Wasigny (08) 21 K5
Wasnes-au-Bac (59). 12 A3
Wasquehal (59) 6 E3
Wasselonne (67) 70 C2
Wasserbourg (68) 96 A5
Wassigny (02) 12 D6
Wassy (52) 91 J2
le Wast (62) 4 C3
Watigny (02) 21 J2
Watronville (55) 43 K5
Watten (59) 3 G4
Wattignies (59) 6 D5
Wattignies-la-Victoire (59). 13 H4
Wattrelos (59) 7 F3
Wattwiller (68) 97 A1
Wavignies (60) 18 B6
Waville (54). 65 J1
Wavrans-sur-l'Aa (62) 5 F3
Wavrans-sur-Ternoise (62) 10 A1
Wavrechain-sous-Denain (59). . . . 12 C2
Wavrechain-sous-Faulx (59) 12 B3
Wavrille (55) 43 H3
Wavrin (59). 6 C5
Waziers (59) 11 H1
Weckolsheim (68) 96 D5
Wegscheid (68) 119 J4
Weinbourg (67) 69 H5
Weislingen (67). 69 F5
Weitbruch (67) 25 A4
Weiterswiller (67) 69 G6
Welles-Pérennes (60) 18 C5
Wemaers-Cappel (59). 3 H4
Wentzwiller (68) 97 D5
Werentzhouse (68) 97 C5
Wervicq-Sud (59) 6 D2
West-Cappel (59) 3 J3
Westhalten (68) 96 B5
Westhoffen (67) 70 C3
Westhouse (67) 70 E5
Westhouse-Marmoutier (67) 70 C2

Westrehem (62) 5 H5
Wettolsheim (68) 96 B4
Weyer (67) 70 K2
Weyersheim (67). 25 B5
Wickerschwihr (68). 96 C3
Wickersheim-Wilshausen (67). . . . 69 J6
Wicquinghem (62) 4 D5
Wicres (59). 6 C5
Widehem (62). 4 B5
Widensolen (68) 96 D4
Wiège-Faty (02) 20 D2
Wiencourt-l'Équipée (80) 18 D2
Wierre-au-Bois (62) 4 C4
Wierre-Effroy (62) 2 B5
Wiesviller (57). 68 E3
Wignehies (59) 13 H6
Wignicourt (08) 22 C6
Wihr-au-Val (68) 96 A4
Wildenstein (68) 119 J2
Wildersbach (67) 70 A5
Willeman (62) 9 K2
Willems (59) 7 F4
Willencourt (62) 9 J3
Willer (68) 97 C4
Willer-sur-Thur (68). 119 K3
Willeroncourt (55) 64 C5
Willerval (62). 11 F2
Willerwald (57) 68 D4
Willgottheim (67) 70 D2
Williers (08) 23 J4
Willies (59) 13 J5
Wilwisheim (67) 70 D1
Wimereux (62) 2 A5
Wimille (62) 4 B2
Wimmenau (67) 69 G5
Wimy (02). 21 G1
Windstein (67) 69 K4
Wingen (67) 25 A1
Wingen-sur-Moder (67) 69 G5
Wingersheim (67) 70 E1
Wingles (62) 6 C6
Winkel (68) 97 B6
Winnezeele (59) 3 J4
Wintersbourg (57) 67 K3
Wintershouse (67) 69 K6
Wintzenbach (67) 25 D2
Wintzenheim (67) 96 B4
Wintzenheim-Kochersberg (67). . . 70 D2
Wirwignes (62) 4 C3
Wiry-au-Mont (80) 17 G1
Wisches (67) 70 A5
Wisembach (88) 95 K4
Wiseppe (55) 43 H1
Wismes (62) 4 E4
Wisques (62) 5 G3
Wissant (62) 2 B3
Wissembourg (67) 25 C1
Wissignicourt (02). 39 K1
Wissous (91) 58 E5
Witry-lès-Reims (51). 41 F1
Wittelsheim (68) 97 B2
Wittenheim (68) 97 C1
Witternesse (62) 5 H4
Witternheim (67). 96 H4
Wittersdorf (68) 97 B4
Wittersheim (67) 70 K6
Wittes (62) 5 H4
Wittisheim (67) 96 E1
Wittring (57) 68 E3
Wiwersheim (67). 70 E2
Wizernes (62) 5 G3
Woël (55) 44 B6
Wœlfling-lès-Sarreguemines (57) . . 68 E3
Wœrth (67). 25 A2
Woignarue (80). 8 D5
Woimbey (55) 64 D1
Woincourt (80) 8 D5
Woippy (57) 44 E5

Woirel (80) 17 G1
Wolfersdorf (68) 97 A4
Wolfgantzen (68) 96 D4
Wolfisheim (67) 70 E3
Wolfskirchen (67) 67 J2
Wolschheim (67). 70 C2
Wolschwiller (68) 97 D6
Wolxheim (67) 70 D3
Wormhout (59) 3 J3
Woustviller (57). 68 D3
Wuenheim (68) 97 B1
Wuisse (57) 66 E2
Wulverdinghe (59) 3 G4
Wy-dit-Joli-Village (95) 36 E6
Wylder (59). 3 J3

X

Xaffévillers (88) 94 E2
Xaintrailles (47) 247 H4
Xaintray (79) 161 H4
Xambes (16) 196 D1
Xammes (54) 65 H1
Xamontarupt (88) 95 F6
Xanrey (57). 66 E4
Xanton-Chassenon (85) 160 E4
Xaronval (88) 94 A3
Xermaménil (54) 94 D1
Xertigny (88). 118 D1
Xeuilley (54) 65 K6
Xirocourt (54) 94 A2
Xivray-et-Marvoisin (55) 65 G3
Xivry-Circourt (54) 26 D4
Xocourt (57) 66 C2
Xonrupt-Longemer (88) 95 H6
Xonville (54) 44 C6
Xouaxange (57) 67 J4
Xousse (54) 67 F5
Xures (54). 67 F4

Y

Y (80) 19 H3
Yainville (76) 35 F2
Yaucourt-Bussus (80) 9 H5
Ychoux (40) 245 F2
Ydes (15) 217 H2
Yèbles (77) 59 J6
Yébleron (76) 14 E5
Yèbres (28). 84 D6
Yenne (73) 207 K2
Yermenonville (28) 85 H1
Yerres (91) 59 F5
Yerville (76). 15 H5
Yèvre-la-Ville (45) 110 E1
Yèvres (28). 84 D6
Yèvres-le-Petit (10). 90 E2
Yffiniac (22) 49 H6
Ygos-Saint-Saturnin (40) 264 E1
Ygrande (03) 168 A4
Ymare (76) 35 J3
Ymeray (28) 85 J2
Ymonville (28) 85 J5
Yolet (15) 235 J1
Yoncq (08) 23 F6
Yonval (80) 9 F5
Youx (63) 184 C3
Yport (76) 14 C4
Ypreville-Biville (76) 14 E4
Yquebeuf (76). 16 B5
Yquelon (50) 30 D6
Yronde-et-Buron (63) 202 E4
Yrouerre (89) 113 K5

Yssac-la-Tourette (63) 185 E2
Yssandon (19) 215 G3
Yssingeaux (43) 220 E4
Ytrac (15) 235 G1
Ytres (62) 11 G5
Yutz (57) 27 G4
Yvecrique (76) 15 H4
Yvernaumont (08) 22 C4
Yversay (86) 162 E2
Yves (17) 176 E4
les Yveteaux (61) 53 K5
Yvetot (76) 15 H4
Yvetot-Bocage (50) 28 D4
Yvias (22) 48 D3
Yviers (16) 212 D1
Yvignac-la-Tour (22) 78 D3
Yville-sur-Seine (76) 35 F2
Yvoire (74) 174 D5
Yvoy-le-Marron (41) 129 K2
Yvrac (33). 229 J1
Yvrac-et-Malleyrand (16) 197 H2
Yvrandes (61) 53 F5
Yvré-le-Pôlin (72) 106 D5
Yvré-l'Évêque (72) 106 E2
Yvrench (80). 9 H4
Yvrencheux (80) 9 H4
Yzengremer (80). 8 D5
Yzernay (49). 143 G3
Yzeron (69). 205 J3
Yzeure (03). 168 E3
Yzeures-sur-Creuse (37). 146 B6
Yzeux (80) 17 K1
Yzosse (40) 264 B4

Z

Zaessingue (68) 97 C4
Zalana (2B). 319 H6
Zarbeling (57) 67 F2
Zegerscappel (59) 3 H3
Zehnacker (67). 70 C2
Zeinheim (67) 70 C2
Zellenberg (68) 96 B3
Zellwiller (67) 70 D5
Zermezeele (59) 3 J4
Zérubia (2A) 323 F1
Zetting (57). 68 E3
Zévaco (2A). 320 H1
Zicavo (2A) 321 F5
Zigliara (2A) 320 E6
Zilia (2B). 318 D3
Zilling (57) 70 A1
Zillisheim (68) 97 B3
Zimmerbach (68) 96 B4
Zimmersheim (68) 97 C3
Zimming (57) 45 J5
Zincourt (88). 94 D4
Zinswiller (67) 69 J5
Zittersheim (67) 69 G5
Zœbersdorf (67) 69 H6
Zommange (57) 67 G2
Zonza (2A) 323 G1
Zoteux (62). 4 D4
Zouafques (62) 2 E4
Zouftgen (57) 27 G3
Zoza (2A) 323 F2
Zuani (2B) 319 H6
Zudausques (62) 5 F3
Zutkerque (62) 2 E4
Zuydcoote (59). 3 J1
Zuytpeene (59) 3 H4

Distances et temps de parcours (F)
Afstanden en reistijden (NL)
Entfernungen und Reisezeiten (D)
Distances and journey times (GB)
Distancias y tiempos de recorrido (E)
Distanze e tempi di percorrenza (I)

temps de parcours en heures et en minutes reistijden Reisezeiten journey times tiempos de recorrido tempi di percorrenza

(Table of journey times and distances between French cities, arranged as a triangular matrix. Diagonal city labels, reading from top-left: PARIS, Amiens, Angers, Angoulême, Annecy, Avignon, Bayonne, Besançon, Bordeaux, Boulogne-sur-Mer, Briançon, Bourges, Brest, Caen, Calais, Cannes, Cherbourg-O'ville, Clermont-Ferrand, Dieppe, Dijon, Dunkerque, Fontainebleau, Grenoble, le Havre, Lille, Limoges, le Mans, la Rochelle, Lyon, Marseille, Metz, Montpellier, Mulhouse, Nancy, Nantes, Nice, Orléans, Pau, Perpignan, Poitiers, Reims, Rennes, Rouen, St-Brieuc, St-Malo, Strasbourg, Toulouse, Tours, Valence, Vannes.)

distances en kilomètres afstanden Entfernungen distances distancias distanze